The Essential AMERICA

The Essential

W • W • NORTON & COMPANY
NEW YORK • LONDON

AMERICA

George B. Tindall

David E. Shi

Thomas Lee Pearcy

For Bruce and Blair
For Jason and Jessica
For Shauna

Printed in the United States of America
First Edition

Editor: Steve Forman
Associate Managing Editor—College Books: Jane Carter
Director of Manufacturing—College: Roy Tedoff
Manuscript Editor: Kate Lovelady
Project Editor: Nan Sinauer
Book Designer: Rubina Yeh
Photograph Editor: Kate Nash
Editorial Assistant: Lory Frenkel
Cartographer: Cartographics

The text of this book is composed in Melior, with the display set in Eurostile.
Composition by The PRD Group.
Manufacturing by R. R. Donnelley & Sons Company.

Library of Congress Cataloging-in-Publication Data:

Tindall, George Brown.
The essential America / George B. Tindall, David E. Shi [and] Thomas Lee Pearcy.
p. cm.
ISBN 0-393-97699-8 (pbk.)
Includes bibliographical references and index.
1. United States—History. I. Shi, David E. II. Pearcy, Thomas L., 1960– III. Title.

E178.T56 2000

00-053698

ISBN 0-393-97699-8 (pbk.)

W. W. Norton & Company, Inc., 500 Fifth Avenue, New York, N.Y. 10110
www.wwnorton.com
W. W. Norton & Company Ltd., 10 Coptic Street, London WC1A 1PU

2 3 4 5 6 7 8 9 0

CONTENTS

ESSENTIAL THEMES

CRITICAL QUESTIONS

- How did the political bases of independence evolve over the colonial period?
- How did the colonists build thriving economies from their subsistence beginnings?
- How did the distinctive social groups in early America interact?
- How did the European settlers respond to their encounters with the peoples and places of America?
- What was America's position in the Atlantic world during the colonial period?

ESSENTIAL THEMES

CRITICAL QUESTIONS

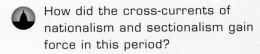

- How did the cross-currents of nationalism and sectionalism gain force in this period?
- How did the Federalists and Republicans address the issues of economic development in the new nation?
- How did issues of race and class enter into debates over the shape of the new nation?
- How did Americans develop a more independent culture in the early national period?
- How did the new nation seek to enhance its international status?

PART 3 | An Expansive Nation (follows p. 158)

ESSENTIAL THEMES

CRITICAL QUESTIONS

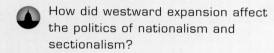

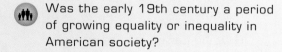

- How did westward expansion affect the politics of nationalism and sectionalism?
- How did the Industrial Revolution affect regional economic distinctions?
- Was the early 19th century a period of growing equality or inequality in American society?
- How did the twin themes of Enlightenment reason and revivalist faith find expression in this period?
- What were the international implications of America's westward expansion in this period?

PART 4 | A House Divided and Rebuilt (follows p. 226)

ESSENTIAL THEMES

CRITICAL QUESTIONS

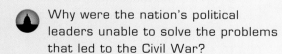

- Why were the nation's political leaders unable to solve the problems that led to the Civil War?
- Did the northern economy give Union forces a decisive advantage in the war?

- What were the social effects of the Civil War in the North and the South?
- Had the North and South come to embrace irreconcilable values at the time of the Civil War?
- What were the most important international implications of the Civil War?

ESSENTIAL THEMES

CRITICAL QUESTIONS

- How did the economic growth of the post–Civil War period influence the politics of protest and reform?
- Why did the economy grow so dramatically in the period after the Civil War?
- What were the most important effects of the shift from a rural to an urban society?

- What were the cultural effects of the growth of cities in the late nineteenth century?
- How was America's global position changing as its economy developed?

ESSENTIAL THEMES

CRITICAL QUESTIONS

- How did the scope of government change in the Progressive and New Deal periods?
- How did the American economy crash and then revive in the 1930s and 1940s?
- What were the effects of the two world wars on American society?
- How did modernism find expression in American culture?
- How did the United States become a global leader in this period?

ESSENTIAL THEMES

CRITICAL QUESTIONS

How did the "rights revolution" develop and what was its significance?

- How did America move from a smokestack economy to a high-tech economy?
- What effects did the baby-boom generation have on society in the last half of the twentieth century?
- How did the counterculture emerge through the 1960s and 1970s?
- How did the cold war develop after World War II and how did it end?

MAPS

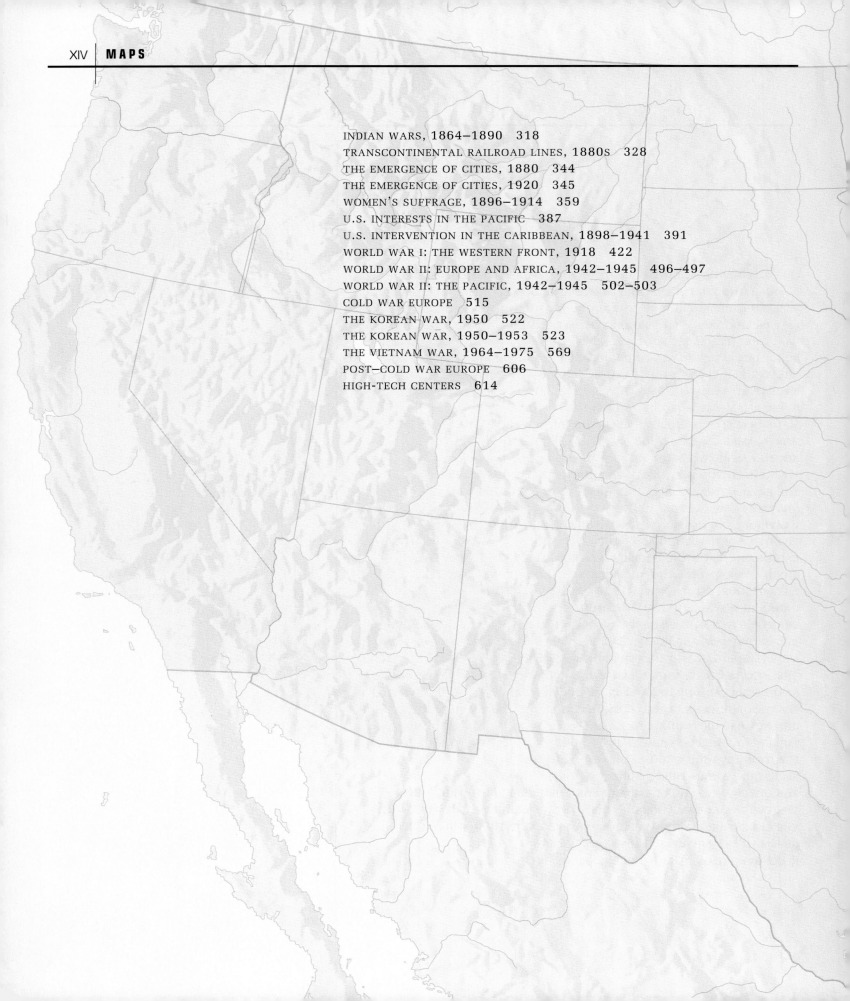

PREFACE

Most observers agree that we are living through a digital revolution. There is less agreement, however, about the impact this revolution will have on our habits of reading and learning. Some confidently predict that printed books will be outmoded in the twenty-first century, completely replaced by digital technologies. At the other end of the spectrum, there are those who express alarm at our willingness to embrace new digital technologies at the expense of the book. Such critics warn that we are sacrificing the opportunity for thinking deeply in our rush to gain access to information.

To a surprising degree, the warring champions of the pixel and the page share the assumption that these technologies represent fundamentally opposed forces that cannot coexist in our high-tech future. We beg to differ. The printed book and the new multimedia technologies can complement each other very well.

This assumption undergirds the publication before you: The printed *Essential America* and the electronic *Essential America* were conceived together and developed in tandem. Printed book and E-book, each makes the most of its distinctive medium to convey the basics of American history to beginning students and arouse in them the desire to know more.

The aim of *The Essential America* is to furnish students with the fundamental elements of American history. To do so, we have compressed the brief version of *America* by at least one-third, omitting some supporting detail, examples, and quotations while maintaining the book's broad coverage, accuracy, and, we hope, appeal. As you can see, the look of *The Essential America* represents a major departure. With its four-color design, large trim size, and clear double-column page, this version of *America* allows us to enrich the essentials with many color illustrations, a new full-color map program, and some new pedagogical features.

The new educational tools aim to help students grasp the essentials while never losing sight of the larger themes running through the book. The seven parts of the book open with multipage spreads that identify and outline five basic themes: political, economic, social, cultural, and global. Each theme is stated by way of a general question that applies to that part of the book. We hope these thematic questions suggest to students the larger developments at work over longer periods of time. The questions can guide students' reading or serve as essay topics. Each theme is also outlined at the start of each part so that students can readily follow its development through the relevant chapters. Finally, each theme is highlighted by an icon that appears "lit" (in color) at the top of each page that addresses that theme. Students can use these icons to follow a thematic thread through the book or to keep themselves oriented thematically as they read chapters. Our aim is to give students thematic guidance throughout the text.

In the electronic *Essential America*, we hope to have realized some of the potential that the new digital technologies hold for teaching and learning. The E-book delivers the full text, maps, and illustrations of the printed text enhanced with multimedia materials for review and enrichment. It employs a technology that achieves a smooth integration of text and multimedia elements. It has an attractive on-screen design, readable type, and intuitive navigation devices. The E-book also furnishes students with a suite of study tools, from highlighters and sticky notes to custom searches and a personal notebook for assembling multimedia materials. For a preview of the electronic *Essential America*, visit the Web site at www.wwnorton.com/eamerica.

To offer a more complete integration of pixel and page, we have also created *The Essential America* On-line Tutor, which students can access at no charge, whether they are using the printed or the electronic *Essential America*. The On-line Tutor features review and research materials developed specifically for *The Essential America*. Its on-line quizzes test the students' grasp of the text; the on-line topic for each chapter encourages further research, since documents, still images, audio, and video materials are accessible through the site.

Just as the pencil has survived the typewriter, we are confident that printed books will survive in our digital world. Through this distinctive attempt to harness the considerable powers of both print and digital technologies, we hope we are advancing the efforts of all to teach and learn American history ever more effectively.

This new version of *America* features an outstanding ancillary package that supplements the text. *For the Record: A Documentary History of America*, by David E. Shi and Holly A. Mayer (Duquesne University), is a rich resource with over 300 primary-source readings from diaries, journals, newspaper articles, speeches, government documents, and novels. It also has four special chapters on interpreting illustrations and photographs as historical documents. The Study Guide, by Charles Eagles (University of Mississippi), is another valuable resource. It contains chapter outlines, learning objectives, timelines, vocabulary exercises, short-answer questions, and essay questions, as well as source readings for each chapter. Norton Presentation Maker is a CD-ROM slide and text resource that includes all the images from the text as well as four-color maps, 1,000 additional images from Library of Congress archives, and 30 audio clips from significant historical speeches. Finally, the Instructor's Manual and Test Bank, by Jonathan Lee (San Antonio College), includes a test bank of short-answer and essay questions as well as detailed chapter outlines, lecture suggestions, and bibliographies that include the addresses of useful Web sites.

This version of *America* benefited from the insights and suggestions of many people. The following scholars have provided close readings at various stages: Lucy Barber (University of California at Davis), Michael Barnhart (State University of New York at Stony Brook), Saul Cornell (Ohio State University), Charles Eagles (University of Mississippi), Timothy Gilfoyle (Loyola University), Tera Hunter (Carnegie-Mellon University), Walter Johnson (New York University), Peter Kolchin (University of Delaware), Christopher Morris (University of Texas at Arlington), Arwen Mohun (University of Delaware), David Parker (Kennesaw State University), Thomas Sugrue (University of Pennsylvania), and Marilyn Westerkamp (University of California at Santa Cruz). Once again, we thank our friends at W. W. Norton & Company, especially Steve Forman, Jon Durbin, Steve Hoge, Kate Lovelady, Kate Nash, Lory Frenkel, Matthew Arnold, Rubina Yeh, and Nan Sinauer for their care and attention along the way.

—George B. Tindall
—David E. Shi
—Thomas L. Pearcy

PART 1
A New World

Long before Christopher Columbus accidentally discovered the New World in his effort to find a passage to Asia, the tribal peoples he mislabeled "Indians" had occupied and shaped the lands of the Western Hemisphere. By the end of the fifteenth century, when Columbus began his voyage west, there were millions of Native Americans living in the "New World." Over the centuries, they had developed stable, diverse, and often highly sophisticated societies, some rooted in agriculture, others in trade or imperial conquest.

The Native American cultures were, of course, profoundly affected by the arrival of peoples from Europe and Africa. The Indians were exploited, enslaved, displaced, and exterminated. Yet this conventional tale of conquest oversimplifies the complex process by which Indians, Europeans, and Africans interacted. The Indians were more than passive victims; they were also trading partners and rivals of the transatlantic newcomers. They became enemies and allies, neighbors and advisors, converts and spouses. As such they fully participated in the creation of the new society known as America.

The Europeans who risked their lives to settle in the New World were themselves quite diverse. Young and old, men and women, they came from Spain, Portugal, France, Great Britain, the Netherlands, Italy, and the various German states. A variety of motives inspired them to undertake the transatlantic voyage. Some were adventurers and fortune seekers, eager to find gold and spices. Others were fervent Christians determined to create kingdoms of God in the New World. Still others were convicts, debtors, indentured servants, or political or religious exiles. Many were simply seeking higher wages and greater economic opportunity. A settler in Pennsylvania noted that "poor people (both men and women) of all kinds can here get three times the wages for their labour than they can in England or Wales."

Yet such enticements were not sufficient to attract enough workers to keep up with the rapidly expanding colonial economies. The Europeans began to force Indians to work for them, but there were never enough of them to meet the unceasing demand. Moreover, Indian slaves often escaped or were so rebellious that several colonies banned their use. The Massachusetts legislature did so because Indians were of such "a malicious, surly and revengeful spirit; rude and insolent in their behavior, and very ungovernable."

Beginning early in the seventeenth century, more and more colonists turned to the African slave trade for their labor needs. This development would transform American society in unexpected ways. Few Europeans during the colonial era saw the contradiction between the New World's promise of individual freedom and the expanding institution of race slavery. Nor did they reckon with the problems associated with introducing into the new society a race of peoples they considered alien and unassimilable.

The intermingling of peoples, cultures, and plants and animals from the three continents of Africa, Europe, and North America gave colonial American society its distinctive vitality and variety. In turn, the diversity of the environment and climate led to the creation of quite different economies and patterns of living in the various regions of North America. As the original settlements grew into prosperous and populous colonies, the transplanted Europeans had to fashion social institutions and political systems to manage growth and control tensions.

At the same time, imperial rivalries among the Spanish, French, English, and Dutch produced numerous intrigues and costly wars. The monarchs of Europe had a difficult time trying to manage and exploit this fluid and often volatile colonial society. Many of the colonists brought with them to the New World a feisty independence that resisted government interference in their affairs. A British official in North Carolina reported that the colonists who settled in the Piedmont region were "without any Law or Order. Impudence is so very high, as to be past bearing." As long as the reins of imperial control were loosely applied, the two parties maintained an uneasy partnership. But as the British authorities tightened their control during the mid–eighteenth century, they met resistance, which escalated into revolt, and culminated in revolution.

ESSENTIAL THEMES

CRITICAL QUESTIONS

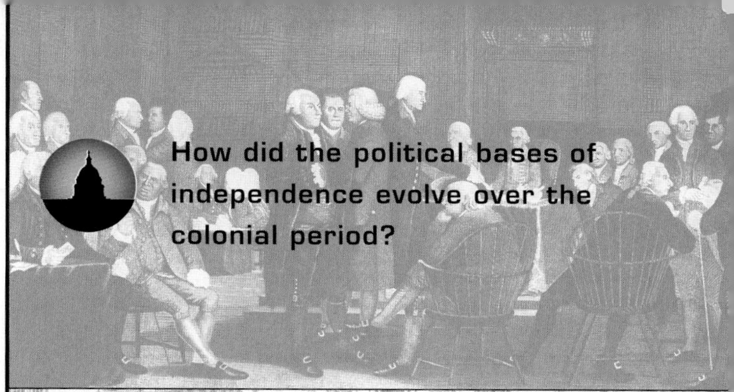
How did the political bases of independence evolve over the colonial period?

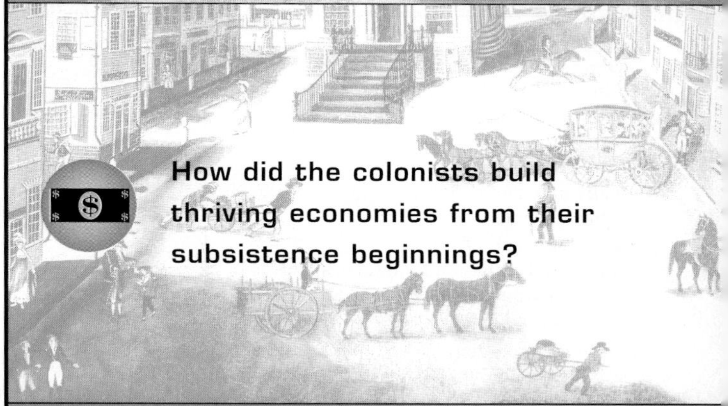
How did the colonists build thriving economies from their subsistence beginnings?

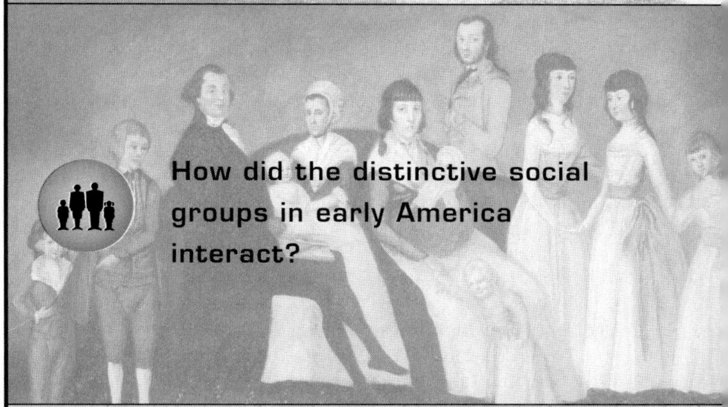
How did the distinctive social groups in early America interact?

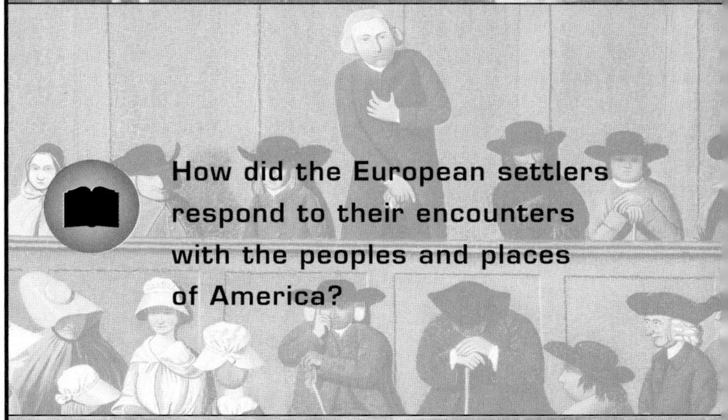
How did the European settlers respond to their encounters with the peoples and places of America?

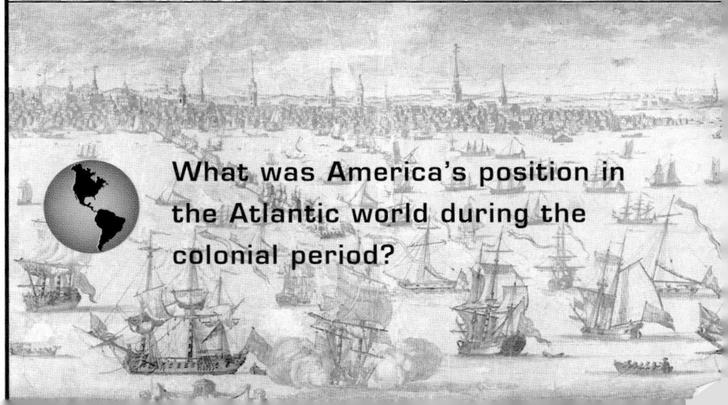
What was America's position in the Atlantic world during the colonial period?

How did the political bases of independence evolve over the colonial period?

CHAPTER 1

Discovery and Settlement

Native-American empires and the extension of European hegemony in the "New World"

- **Zenith of Mayan civilization (300–900 A.D.)**
- Collapse of Mayan civilization (approximately A.D. 900)
- **Aztecs found capital city of Tenochitlàn**
- **Conquest of Aztecs by Cortés (1521)**
- **The Spanish empire in America**
- **English exploration and settlements**
- Jamestown (1607)
- Plymouth and the Mayflower Compact (1620)
- John Winthrop and Massachusetts Bay Colony (1630)
  - The Massachusetts Charter
- Roger Williams and Rhode Island (1636)
- Connecticut (1637)
  - "Fundamental Orders of Connecticut" (1639)
- **The Restoration colonies**
- **Other European settlements in the Americas**
- French Québec (1608)
- Spanish St. Augustine, Fla. (1565), and Santa Fe, N.M. (1610)

CHAPTER 2

Colonial Ways of Life

Diversity and authority

- **An emerging social and political order**
- Slavery in the South
- New England trade
- Diversity in the middle colonies
- The cities

CHAPTER 3

The Imperial Perspective

Precursors to self-government

- **English administration of the colonies**
- The Glorious Revolution in America
- An emerging colonial system
- **The habit of self-government**
- **Judiciaries**
- **Governors**
- **Colonial assemblies**
- House of Burgesses (Virginia)
- House of Delegates (Maryland)
- House of Representatives (Massachusetts)
- **War and self-rule**

CHAPTER 4

From Empire to Independence

The culmination of political tensions between England and America

- **Royal Proclamation of 1763**
- **George Grenville, first lord of the Treasury**
- Sugar Act (1764)
- Currency Act of 1764
- Stamp Act (1765)
- Quartering Act (1765)
- **Charles Townshend, chancellor of the Exchequer**
- Townshend Acts (1767)
- Revenue Act of 1767
- Board of Customs Commissioners established in Boston (1767)
- **Lord North, chancellor of the Exchequer**
- Tea Act of 1773
- Boston Port Act, seeking remuneration for Boston Tea Party (1774)
- A new Quartering Act (1774)
- Massachusetts Governing Act (1774)
- Conciliatory Resolution (1775)
- **Colonial responses to British political intransigence**
- Virginia House of Burgesses responds to Stamp Act (1765)
- Declaration of Rights and Grievances of the Colonies (1765)
- **First Continental Congress assembles in Philadelphia (1774)**
- Suffolk Resolves declare null and void 1774 Intolerable Acts
- Declaration of American Rights adopted
- **Continental Association of 1774 promotes boycott of all British goods**
- **Revolutionary War begins April 18–19 at Lexington and Concord, Massachusetts (1775)**
- **Continental Congress assumes role of government**
- **Second Continental Congress convenes in Philadelphia in May (1775)**
- **Declaration of Independence issued July 4, 1776**

CHAPTER 1

Discovery and Settlement

Economic motives for exploration and empire •

Regional distinctions in early English colonies •

The Virginia Company
John Rolfe and Virginia tobacco
Competition for land triggered by tobacco
The Southern colonies
Trading furs with the Carolina Native Americans
Tobacco and the emergence of an export economy in the South
Slave labor in the emerging economy
New England
Lumber as an economic staple in the North
The sea and shipbuilding in the northern economy
Trade in the middle colonies
Fur trading on the western frontier
The Iroquois League
Economic success of the English colonies
Women as a workforce

CHAPTER 2

Colonial Ways of Life

• Integration into the North Atlantic trade Network

Southern crops and access to British markets
Plantation economics and the increasing demand for slaves
Northern lumber and abundant fishing grounds fueled trade
Northern lack of staples: comparatively sparse agriculture and pastoral resources
The "Triangular Trade" network
Agriculture and trade in the middle colonies
Urban economies

CHAPTER 3

The Imperial Perspective

Challenges to British mercantilism •

Dutch shipping competes with British merchants
French trading posts dot waterways and reach the heartland
The Great Lakes, Des Moines, Terre Haute
British efforts to protect their colonial markets
The Navigation Acts (1651, 1660, 1663, 1673)

CHAPTER 4

From Empire to Independence

• Economic tensions between crown, colonists

British efforts to raise revenues in the colonies
Colonists issue paper money (early 1760s)
Townshend Acts heighten colonial resistance (1767)
Colonists impose embargo on British manufacturers (1765)
Tea Act (1773)
Colonists boycott all British goods (1774)

How did the distinctive social groups in early America interact?

CHAPTER 1
Discovery and Settlement

New World social structures

- **Indian society**
- **Hierarchies in Spanish America**
- **Social structure in the Chesapeake**
- **Religion and gender in New England**
- Anne Hutchinson's trial (1637) and banishment (1638)
- **Indian-white relations in the colonies**

CHAPTER 2
Colonial Ways of Life

Demography, gender, and race

- **The origins of slavery**
- Ethnic diversity of African slaves
- Adapting to slavery
- **Social relations in New England**
- Cohesive forces
- Diversity and social strains
- The Salem witch trials (1692)
- **Social relations in the middle colonies**
- Class
- Ethnic mix
- **Cities**
- The social order
- The urban web
- **Education and society**
- Founding of first colleges
- **The Great Awakening as a social movement**
- Revivalism and clerical authority

CHAPTER 3
The Imperial Perspective

Heightened tensions in the colonies

- **The Glorious Revolution in America**
- Social effects
- **Claims of white settlers on Indian lands**
- King Philip's War (1675–1676)
- Bacon's Rebellion (1676)
- **Social effects of the colonial wars**

CHAPTER 4
From Empire to Independence

Surging American nationalism

- **Sons of Liberty and popular discontent**
- **Social strains on the frontier**
- **The mob as a political force**
- **Committees of Correspondence (1772–1773)**
- **Boston Tea Party (1773)**

Resistance on the frontier

- **Ethan Allen and the Green Mountain Boys (late 1770s)**
- **The Paxton Boys of Pennsylvania**
- **The Regulators of North Carolina and the Battle of Alamance (1771)**
- **Daniel Boone and settlers create the Wilderness Road (1774)**

CHAPTER 1

Discovery and Settlement

The "New World"

Pre-Columbian Indian civilizations
Maya, Inca, Aztec—the "classic" civilizations
Smaller North American indigenous nations
Earliest European contacts with Native Americans
Encounter at Hispaniola
Enslavement and transport to Europe
The great biological exchange and the ecological consequences of contact
Europeans adopt New World plants, clothing, words
Devastating effects of European diseases
Spanish America
Conquests by Hernando Cortés, Francisco Pizarro
Christianity in the New World: the spiritual conquest
Patterns of life in Spanish America: European culture
French explorations
Québec
Beyond discovery and exploration: a permanent English presence
The Chesapeake
- Relations with Indians in Virginia and Maryland

New England
- The Pilgrims
- William Bradford

Puritan culture
- The first Thanksgiving (1621)
- John Winthrop's "city upon a hill"

Relations with Native Americans
- The Powhatan Confederation
- John Smith and Pocahontas
- Pequot War of 1637 (Massachusetts)
- Yamasee War (1715–1717)

Dutch New York
Quaker culture in Pennsylvania

CHAPTER 2

Colonial Ways of Life

The genesis of "American" culture

British folkways
Conflicting views regarding the land: communal resource vs. privately-owned commodity
African roots and black culture
Kinship ties
Agricultural techniques
Religion
Lifestyles
Southern plantations
- Tidewater gentry
- Religion

New England townships
- Dwellings and daily life
- Enterprise
- Religion

The American Enlightenment
The Great Awakening

CHAPTER 3

The Imperial Perspective

Cultures at War

British wars with the Native Americans
British wars with France

CHAPTER 4

From Empire to Independence

American nationalism and the Revolutionary War

Newspapers incite colonists against Grenville's measures (1765)
Colonists boycott British goods (1765)
John Dickinson's *Letters of a Pennsylvania Farmer* criticizes Townshend Acts (1767)
Thomas Paine's *Common Sense* (1776)

What was America's position in the Atlantic world during the colonial period?

CHAPTER 1

Discovery and Settlement

European exploration and settlement
- Columbus's first voyage to the New World (1492)
- Portugese arrive in Brazil (1500)
- Ponce de Léon explores Florida coast (1513)
- Spaniards conquer Aztec capital (1519–1521)
- Jacques Cartier explores the St. Lawrence River (1542)
- Sir Walter Raleigh sails for North America (1548)

Cromwell governs England as Lord Protector (1653–1658)

Restoration in England (1660)

CHAPTER 2

Colonial Ways of Life

Continuing migrations

Waves of British colonists
- Puritans to Massachusetts, 1629–1641
- Wealthier persons from southern England to Virginia
- Quakers from England's north midlands to West Jersey, Pennsylvania, and Delaware
- Celtic-Britons and Scotch-Irish to the Appalachian Mountains, 1717–1775

Indentured servants

CHAPTER 3

The Imperial Perspective

Developments in Europe affect the British colonies in America
- English Civil War and Restoration
- LaSalle traverses Mississippi River to the Gulf of Mexico (1682)
- The Glorious Revolution (1688–1689)
- King William's War (1689–1697)
- The War of the Spanish Succession (1702–1713)
- Spanish America in decline
- The French and Indian War (1754–1763)
- Peace of Paris (1763)

British supremacy in North America

CHAPTER 4

From Empire to Independence

Legacy of Seven Years War
- The Revolutionary controversy and Britain's global interest

CHAPTER

1

Discovery and Settlement

This chapter focuses on

- The reasons for the founding of the different colonies.
- The ways in which Europeans and Native Americans adapted to each other's presence.
- The factors making for England's success in colonizing North America.

THE *ESSENTIAL AMERICA* ON-LINE TUTOR

www.wwnorton.com/eamerica/ch1

- **Topic: The great biological exchange**
  www.wwnorton.com/eamerica/ch1/topic.htm

  The European "discovery" of America brought different worlds into contact. Explore the great biological exchange and its significance through woodcuts and other images, contemporary accounts by Native Americans and European settlers, maps, and historical analyses. What were the consequences of this exchange?

- **Chapter review: On-line quiz and chapter summary**
  www.wwnorton.com/eamerica/ch1/review.htm

- **Chapter resources: Multimedia index**
  www.wwnorton.com/eamerica/ch1/media.htm

The Western Hemisphere was originally an uninhabited frontier. But like all frontiers, it served as a powerful magnet for dreamers and adventurers. Until recent years, archeologists and anthropologists believed that the first people to settle in the Western Hemisphere were northeastern Asians. Some 11,500 years ago, according to the traditional interpretation, Asian immigrants entered the New World from Siberia to what is now Alaska. New archaeological discoveries, however, have raised questions about the conventional view of America's human origins. Skeletal remains found in Brazil, Nebraska, Washington, and Minnesota resemble South Asians or Europeans—not northeastern Asians. And such evidence also suggests that people were in the Western Hemisphere more than 12,000 years ago.

Pre-Columbian Indian Civilizations

Whatever their place of origin and time of arrival, the first Americans spread across North and South America, establishing new communities and cultures. In the high altitudes of Mexico and Peru, the Mayas, Aztecs, Incas, and others built great empires supported by large-scale agriculture and a far-flung commerce.

The Mayas, Aztecs, and Incas

By about 2000–1500 B.C., the nomadic Indian tradition began to give way in what is today Central America to more permanent farming settlements. The more settled life in turn fostered more complex cultures through the cultivation of religion, crafts, art, science, civic administration—and organized warfare. A stratified social structure also developed. From about A.D. 300–900, this Middle American region reached its cultural peak, with great religious centers, gigantic pyramids and temples, and ceremonial courts, all supported by the surrounding villages.

This page from the Codex Mendoza, a European-style picture book painted by a native artist for the first Viceroy of New Spain, depicts Aztec officers at the time of conquest. Note the tall emblems worn on the officers' backs, which identified rank to troops being led into battle.

The Mayas, living in present-day Yucatán, Guatemala, Belize, and western Honduras and El Salvador, were a warlike people who ruled a loosely controlled empire. They built dozens of pyramids, devised a complex writing system based on hieroglyphs, and developed enough mathematics and astronomy to devise a calendar more accurate than the one used by Columbus.

Then, about A.D. 900, for reasons unknown, Mayan culture abruptly collapsed, and the religious centers were abandoned. The Mayas were succeeded by the Toltecs, who conquered most of the region in the tenth century. But around A.D. 1200, the Toltecs too mysteriously withdrew.

The equally warlike Aztecs, who arrived from the northwest, founded the city of Tenochtitlán (now Mexico City) in 1325 and gradually extended their control over central Mexico. When the Spaniards invaded in 1519, the Aztec Empire under Montezuma II ruled over 5 million people. Their economy depended on agriculture, and their religious practices included human sacrifices to the sun god. Farther south, Incas by the fifteenth century controlled an

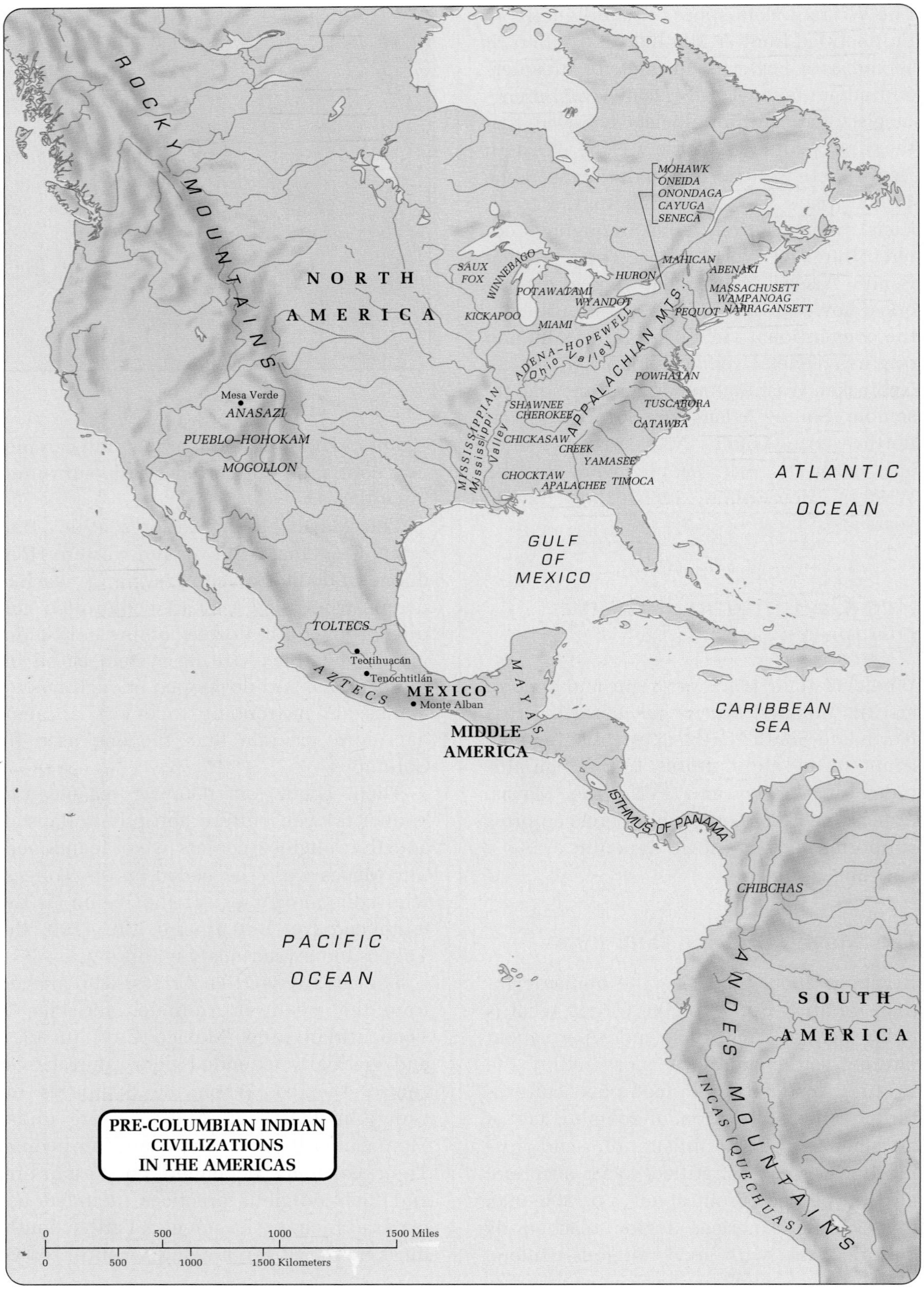
PRE-COLUMBIAN INDIAN CIVILIZATIONS IN THE AMERICAS
ROCKY MOUNTAINS
NORTH AMERICA
MOHAWK
ONEIDA
ONONDAGA
CAYUGA
SENECA
MAHICAN
ABENAKI
MASSACHUSETT
WAMPANOAG
NARRAGANSETT
PEQUOT
HURON
SAUX
FOX
WINNEBAGO
POTAWATAMI
WYANDOT
KICKAPOO
MIAMI
ADENA-HOPEWELL
Ohio Valley
APPALACHIAN MTS
POWHATAN
TUSCARORA
CATAWBA
SHAWNEE
CHEROKEE
CHICKASAW
CREEK
YAMASEE
CHOCKTAW
APALACHEE
TIMOCA
MISSISSIPPIAN
Mississippi Valley
Mesa Verde
ANASAZI
PUEBLO-HOHOKAM
MOGOLLON
ATLANTIC OCEAN
GULF OF MEXICO
TOLTECS
Teotihuacán
Tenochtitlán
AZTECS
MEXICO
Monte Alban
MAYAS
MIDDLE AMERICA
CARIBBEAN SEA
ISTHMUS OF PANAMA
CHIBCHAS
PACIFIC OCEAN
ANDES MOUNTAINS
SOUTH AMERICA
INCAS (QUECHUAS)
0 500 1000 1500 Miles
0 500 1000 1500 Kilometers

empire that stretched a thousand miles along the Andes Mountains from Ecuador to Chile, connected by an elaborate system of roads and organized under an autocratic government that dominated community life.

Indian Cultures of North America

The North American tribes tended to be smaller, more scattered, and less settled than the Mayas or Aztecs. Most of them migrated with the seasons in search of food—fish, deer, rabbits, maize (corn), nuts, berries—and temperate locales. They built few permanent structures and tended to own land communally.

Indian societies of the sixteenth century were ill-equipped to resist the dynamic European cultures invading their world. The Indians of Mexico, for example, had copper and bronze but no iron. They had domesticated dogs, turkeys, and llamas, but horses were unknown until the Spaniards arrived. When fighting erupted, arrows and tomahawks were seldom a match for guns. And the new diseases contracted from European invaders proved to be catastrophic for the Native American peoples.

Yet the Indians resisted European invaders for centuries. They displayed an amazing capacity for adapting to changing circumstances, incorporating European technology and weaponry, forging new alliances, changing their own community structures, and converting whites to their way of life. Many Spanish, English, and French settlers voluntarily joined Indian society or chose to stay after being captured.

First Contacts

The European discovery of the New World coincided with the extension of European power and culture around the world. Such expansion derived from the revival of learning and the rise of an inquiring spirit; the explosive growth of trade, towns, and modern corporations; the decline of feudalism and the rise of nations; the religious zeal generated by the Protestant Reformation and the Catholic Counter-Reformation; and on the darker side, some old sins—greed, conquest, racism, and slavery.

By the fifteenth century, these forces had combined to focus European eyes on new lands to conquer or settle and on new peoples to convert, civilize, or exploit. Europeans were especially attracted by the lure of Asia, a near-mythical land of spices, silks, jewels, and millions of "heathens" to be Christianized.

The Voyages of Columbus

The Orient's storied wealth caught the expansive vision of Christopher Columbus, a gold-loving adventurer. Born in 1451, the son of an Italian weaver, Columbus hatched a scheme to reach Asia by sailing west. He turned to Spain for backing, and after years of disappointment and disgrace, he finally won the support of Ferdinand and Isabella, the Spanish monarchs.

On August 2, 1492, Columbus set off across the Atlantic with a squadron of three small ships and eighty-seven men. Early on October 12, 1492, a lookout called out, "*Tierra! Tierra!* [Land! Land!]" It was an island in the Bahamas that Columbus named San Salvador (Blessed Savior). Assuming that he was near the Indies, he called the islanders "Indios," Indians. He described them as naked people, "very well made, of very handsome bodies and very good faces." The Indians paddled out in dugout logs, which they called *canoa,* and offered gifts of parrots and javelins to the strangers.

At the moment, however, Columbus was more interested in gold than gifts. He continued to explore the Bahamian Cays down to Cuba, a place name that suggested Cipangua (Japan), and then eastward to the island he named Española (or Hispaniola), where he first found significant amounts of gold jewelry.

On the night before Christmas in 1492, the *Santa María* ran aground off Hispaniola, and Columbus, still believing he had reached Asia, decided to return home. He left about forty men behind and seized a dozen natives to present as gifts to Spain's royal couple. After Columbus reached Spain, the news of his discovery spread rapidly throughout Europe, and Ferdinand and Isabella instructed him to prepare for a second voyage.

Columbus made three more voyages to the New World. In each instance, he grew more greedy for gold and more brutal in his treatment of the people he called Indians. His savagery eventually led to his arrest and return to Spain in chains. To the end, Columbus insisted that he had discovered parts of Asia.

Ironically, the New World was named not for its discoverer but for another Italian, Amerigo Vespucci. Vespucci was a Florentine merchant and navigator who helped outfit Columbus for the transatlantic crossing. Later, Vespucci himself made several voyages to the New World. In 1507 a young geographer named Martin Waldseemuller published a book in which he mistakenly credited Vespucci with having reached South America before Columbus. For that reason, Waldseemuller suggested that the new continent be named "America" in his honor.

Actually, Vespucci's first voyage began in 1499, and there is no firm evidence that he, any more than Columbus, ever believed he had discovered anything other than a part of East Asia. Waldseemuller's idea stuck, however, and the name for the New World took hold.

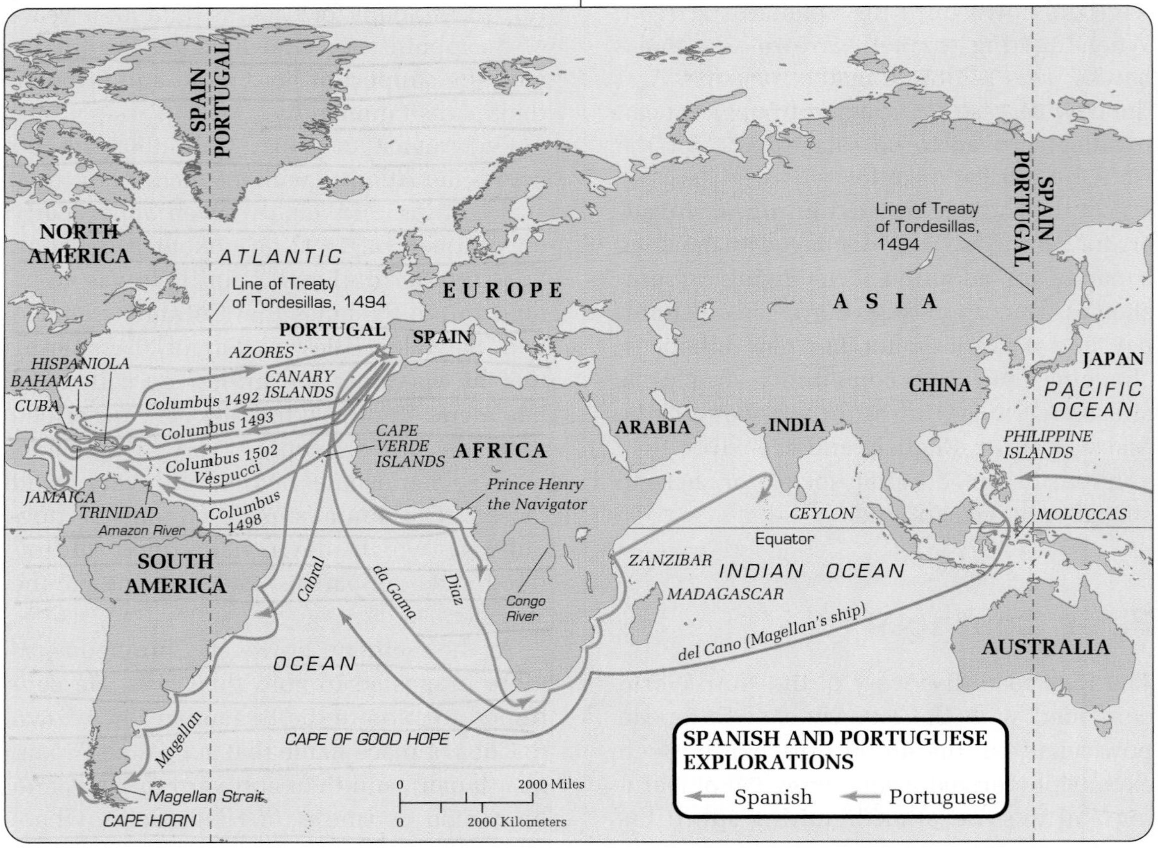

The Great Biological Exchange

European contact with the New World produced more than a diffusion of human cultures. If anything, the plants and animals of the two worlds were more different than the people and their ways of life. Europeans, for instance, had never seen creatures such as the iguana, flying squirrel, catfish, rattlesnake, or anything quite like several other species native to America: bison, cougars, armadillos, opossums, sloths, anacondas, electric eels, vampire bats, toucans, condors, or hummingbirds. Nor did the Native Americans know of horses, cattle, pigs, sheep, goats, and (maybe) chickens, which soon arrived from Europe in abundance.

The transfer of plant life worked a revolution in the diets of both hemispheres. Before 1492 three main staples of the modern diet were unknown in the Old World: maize (corn), potatoes (sweet and white), and many kinds of beans (snap, kidney, lima, and others). Other New World food plants were peanuts, squash, peppers, tomatoes, pumpkins, pineapples, papayas, avocados, cacao (the source of chocolate), and chicle (for chewing gum). Europeans in turn introduced rice, wheat, barley, oats, wine grapes, melons, coffee, olives, bananas, "Kentucky" bluegrass, daisies, and dandelions.

The beauty of the ecological exchange between old and new worlds was that the food plants were more complementary than competitive. They grew in different soils and climates, or in different seasons. Indian corn, it turned out, could flourish almost anywhere, and it spread quickly throughout the world. Before the end of the 1500s, American maize and sweet potatoes were staple crops in China. The green revolution exported from the Americas thus helped nourish a worldwide population explosion probably greater than any since the invention of agriculture.

Europeans also adopted many Native American devices, such as snowshoes, hammocks, kayaks, dogsleds, toboggans, and parkas. The rubber ball and the game of lacrosse had Indian origins. Indian words entered the European vocabulary: succotash, tobacco, moose, skunk, opossum, woodchuck, chipmunk, tomahawk, hickory, pecan, raccoon, and hundreds of others. There were still other New World contributions: tobacco and a number of other drugs, including coca (for cocaine and novocaine), curare (a muscle relaxant), and cinchona bark (for quinine).

Unfortunately, the Europeans in exchange presented the Indians with illnesses they could not handle. Even minor diseases such as measles killed Indians who had never encountered them and had built no immunity to them. Major infections such as smallpox and typhus killed all the more speedily. The first contacts with some of Columbus's sailors devastated whole Indian communities. The epidemics spread rapidly into the interior, and some tribes lost 90 to 95 percent of their population within the first century of European colonization. In central Mexico alone, some 8 million people, perhaps a third of the entire population, died of disease within a decade after the Spaniards arrived.

Exploration and Conquest of the New World

Excited by Columbus's discoveries, professional explorers, mostly Italians, probed the shorelines of America during the early sixteenth century in the vain search for a passage to China. In the process they greatly increased European knowledge of the New World. Yet during the sixteenth century the New World remained a Spanish preserve, except for Brazil, which was a Portuguese colony. After establishing colonies on Hispaniola and at Santo Domingo, which became the capital of the West Indies, the Spaniards proceeded eastward to Puerto Rico (1508) and westward to Cuba (1511–

1514). Their motives were explicit. Said one soldier: "We came here to serve God and the king, and also to get rich."

A Clash of Cultures

The great adventure of mainland conquest began in 1519, when Spaniard Hernando Cortés and 600 men landed on the site of Vera Cruz, Mexico, which he founded. Cortés then set about a daring conquest of the Aztec Empire. The 200-mile march from Vera Cruz through difficult mountain passes to the magnificent Aztec capital of Tenochtitlán, and the subjugation of the Aztecs, were two of the most remarkable—and tragic—feats in human history.

After a year of fighting, in 1521 Cortés and his officers replaced the former Aztec overlords as rulers over the Indian empire. In doing so, they set the style for other conquistadors (Spanish soldiers) to follow. Within twenty years, conquistadors had established an empire for Spain that was far larger than Rome's had ever been. Between 1522 and 1528, various lieutenants of Cortés conquered the remnants of Indian culture in Yucatán and Guatemala. Then in 1531 Francisco Pizarro led a band of soldiers down the Pacific coast from Panama toward Peru, where they subdued the Inca Empire. From Peru, conquistadors extended Spanish authority through Chile, and to the north, in present-day Colombia.

Unarmed Aztecs are killed by Cortés's men during a religious festival in the month of Toxcatl.

Spanish America

The Spanish conquistadors transferred to America a system known as the *encomienda,* whereby favored officers became privileged landowners (*encomenderos*) who controlled Indian villages. The *encomenderos* protected the villages and supported missionary priests. In turn, they required tribute from the villagers in the form of goods and labor. Spanish America therefore developed from the start a society of extremes: affluent European conquistadors and native peoples who were held in poverty.

Yet by the mid-1500s Indians were nearly extinct in the West Indies, killed more by European diseases than by Spanish exploitation. To take their place, the colonizers as early as 1503 began to import slaves from Africa. They eventually would transport over 9 million people across the Atlantic in bondage. In all of Spain's New World empire, the Indian population dropped from about 50 million at the outset to 4 million in the seventeenth century, and slowly rose again to 7.5 million. Whites, who totaled no more than 100,000 in the mid–sixteenth century, numbered over 3 million by the end of the colonial period.

For most of the colonial period, much of what is now the United States belonged to Spain, and Spanish culture has left a lasting imprint upon American ways of life. Spain's colonial presence lasted more than three centuries, much longer than either England's or France's, and its possessions were much more far-reaching. New Spain was centered in Mexico, but its frontiers extended from the Florida Keys to Alaska and included areas not currently thought of as formerly Spanish, such as the Deep South (Memphis was founded as San Fernando, Vicksburg as Nogales) and the lower Midwest. Hispanic influences in art, architecture, literature, music, law, and cuisine survive today.

Although Spain's influence was strongest from Mexico southward, the "Spanish borderlands" of the southern United States from Florida to California preserve many reminders of the Spanish presence. The earliest known exploration of Florida was made in 1513 by Juan Ponce de León, then governor of Puerto Rico. He sought the mythic fountain of youth but instead found alligators, swamps, and abundant wildlife. Meanwhile, other Spanish explorers skirted the Gulf coast from Florida to Vera Cruz, scouted the Atlantic coast from Cuba to Newfoundland, established a town at St. Augustine, Florida, and a mission at Santa Fe, New Mexico.

Spain established provinces in North America not so much as commercial enterprises but as defensive buffers protecting its more lucrative trading empire in Mexico and South America. The Spaniards were concerned about French traders infiltrating from Louisiana, English settlers crossing into Florida, and Russian seal hunters wandering down the California coast. Yet the Spanish settlements in what is today the United States never flourished. The Spaniards failed to realize that a prosperous and

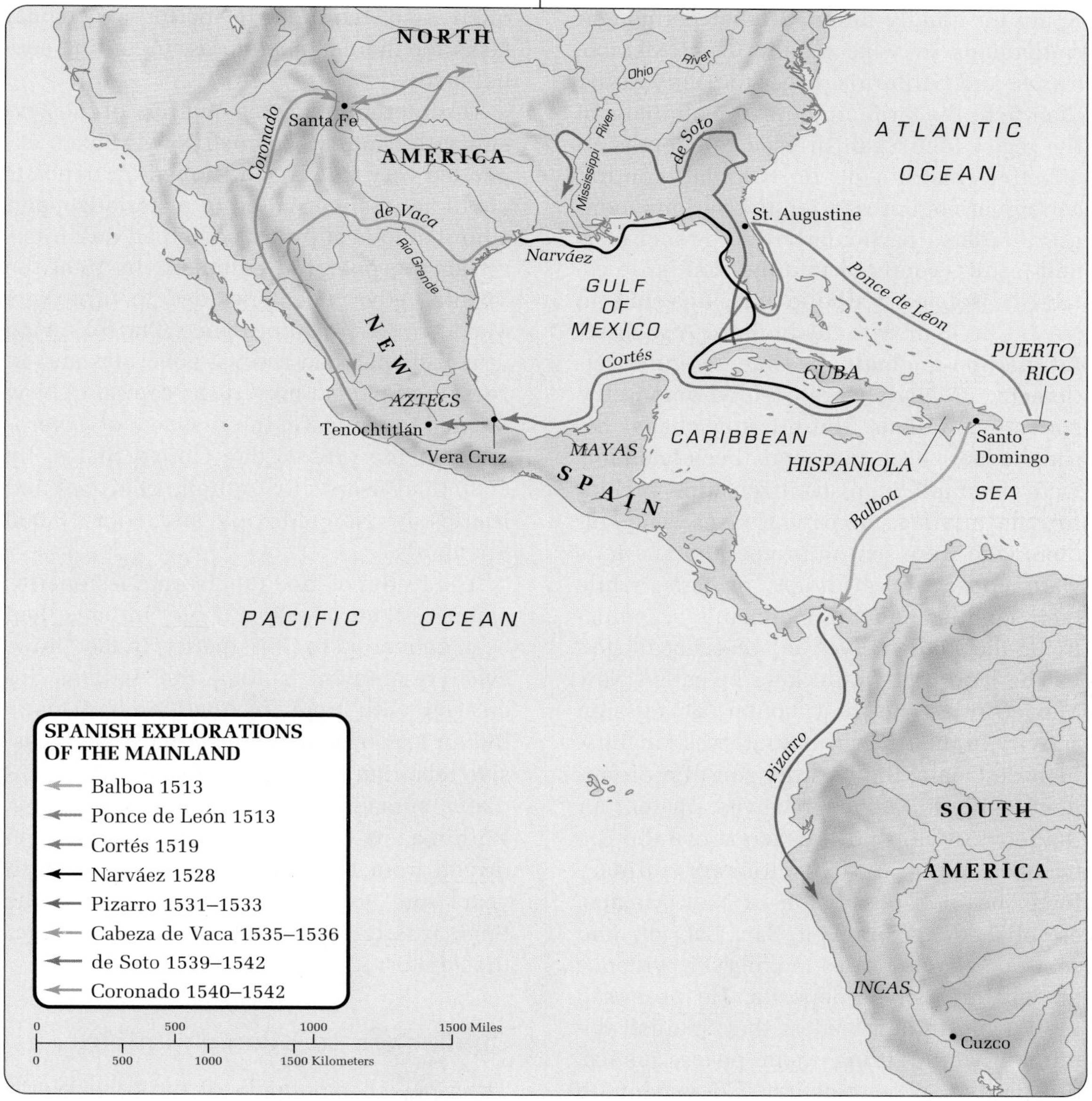

enduring colonial empire depended on self-sustaining economic development. England and France surpassed Spain in the development of an American presence because Spain failed to embrace what the other imperial powers decided early on: that developing a thriving Indian trade in goods was more important than the conversion of "heathens" and the vain search for gold and silver.

The Spanish Southwest

Spain eventually founded other permanent settlements in what is now New Mexico, Texas, and California. Eager to pacify rather than fight the far more numerous Indians of the region, the Spanish used religion as an effective instrument of colonial control. Missionaries representing the various monastic orders, particularly the Franciscans and Jesuits, ventured into the frontier to establish isolated Catholic missions and to teach Christianity to the Indians. A successful mission gradually became a secular settlement: its lands were divided among the converted Indians, the mission chapel became a parish church, and the inhabitants were given full Spanish citizenship—including the privilege of paying taxes. The soldiers who were sent to protect the missions were housed in *presidios,* or forts, while their families and the merchants accompanying the soldiers lived in adjacent villages.

The land that would later be called New Mexico was the first center of mission activity in the American Southwest. In 1598 Juan de Oñate, the wealthy son of a prominent family in Mexico, received a patent for the territory north of Mexico above the Rio Grande. With an expeditionary military force, he took possession of New Mexico, established a capital at San Gabriel, and sent out search parties looking for evidence of gold and silver deposits. He promised the Pueblo Indian leaders that Spanish dominion would bring them peace, justice, prosperity, and protection. Conversion to Catholicism offered even greater benefits: "an eternal life of great bliss" instead of "cruel and everlasting torment."

Some Indians welcomed the missionaries as "powerful witches" capable of easing their burdens. Others tried to use the Spanish as allies against rival Indian tribes. Still others saw no alternative but to submit. The Spanish priests smashed, burned, or confiscated the objects deemed sacred by the Indians and suppressed spiritual rituals and ceremonial dances. The Indians living in Spanish New Mexico were required to pay tribute to their *encomenderos.* Indians were often also required to perform personal tasks for the *encomenderos,* including sexual favors.

During the first three-quarters of the seventeenth century, Spanish New Mexico expanded very slowly. The hoped-for deposits of gold and silver failed to materialize, and a limited food supply also helped dull interest among potential colonists. In 1608 the Spanish government decided to turn New Mexico into a royal province. The following year it dispatched a royal governor, and in 1610 the Spanish moved the capital of New Mexico to Santa Fe, the first seat of government in the present-day United States. By 1630 there were fifty Catholic churches and friaries in New Mexico and some 3,000 Spaniards.

The leader of the Franciscan missionaries claimed that 86,000 Pueblo Indians had been converted to Christianity. In fact, however, resentment among the Indians increased with time. In 1680 a charismatic Indian leader named Popé organized a massive rebellion that involved some 17,000 Indians spread across hundreds of miles. Within a few weeks, the Spaniards had been driven from New Mexico. It took fourteen years and four military assaults for the Spaniards to reestablish their control over the territory.

Challenges to Spanish Empire

The Spanish monopoly of the New World colonies remained intact throughout the sixteenth century, but not without challenge from national rivals lusting for New World booty. The French were the first to pose a serious threat. In 1524 the French king sent an Italian named Giovanni da Verrazano in search of a passage to Asia. Sighting land (probably at Cape Fear, North Carolina), Verrazano ranged along the coast as far north as Maine, but it was not until a decade later that the French made their first colonization effort. On three voyages, Jacques Cartier explored the Gulf of St. Lawrence and ventured up the St. Lawrence River as far as present-day Montréal. Near Québec he established a short-lived colony in 1542.

Thereafter, however, French interest in Canada waned, as the French were preoccupied with the religious civil wars wracking their country. Not until the early seventeenth century, when the bold explorer Samuel de Champlain established new settlements in Acadia (Nova Scotia) and at Québec, did French colonization in America begin in earnest. Enterprising French traders negotiated with Indians for their fur pelts, and French Jesuit missionaries cultivated their souls. Unlike many Spanish missionaries, the French Jesuits were not determined to strip their converts of all vestiges of Indian culture. Instead they displayed considerable respect for Native American values.

Acquiring furs and converts took the French southward as well. In 1673 Louis Jolliet and Père Jacques Marquette, a Jesuit priest, took the first expedition down the Mississippi River, but fearing an encounter with the Spaniards, they turned back before reaching the Gulf of Mexico. Nine years later, Robert Cavalier, sieur de La Salle, ventured all the way to the Gulf of Mexico. There, near the river's delta, the French in the early eighteenth century would establish a settlement called New Orleans. The French thereby came to control not only Canada but also the major inland waterway in North America. It was a deceptive control, however, because the French monarchy never emphasized permanent settlement. Instead it viewed the region almost solely as a source for trade, and French America remained only sparsely populated.

From the mid-1500s, greater threats to Spanish power in the New World arose from the growing strength of the Dutch and English. The prosperous provinces of the Netherlands, which had passed by inheritance to the Spanish king, and which had become largely Protestant, rebelled against Spanish rule in 1567. A protracted, bloody struggle for independence was interrupted by a twelve-year truce, but Spain did not accept the independence of the Dutch republic until 1648.

Almost from the beginning of the revolt, Dutch privateers plundered Spanish ships. While Queen Elizabeth of England steered a tortuous course to avoid open war with Catholic Spain, she encouraged both Dutch and English sea captains to attack the Spanish. Sporadic British piracy against the Spanish continued until 1587, when Queen Elizabeth had her Catholic cousin, Mary, Queen of Scots, beheaded for her involvement in an unsuccessful coup. In revenge, Spain's Philip II decided to crush Protestant England and began to gather his ill-fated Armada. The ambitious enterprise quickly became a case of incompetence and mismanagement accompanied by bad luck. The heavy Spanish galleons fell victim to the smaller, faster English vessels commanded by Sir Francis Drake and others. Defeat of the Armada convinced the English that the Spanish navy was no longer invincible and cleared the way for English colonization of the Americas.

Early English Explorations

English colonization in North America began in 1584 when Sir Walter Raleigh, eager "to seek new worlds for gold, for praise, for glory," sent an expedition to explore prospects for founding a colony in America. Sailing by way of the West Indies, they came to the Outer Banks of North Carolina

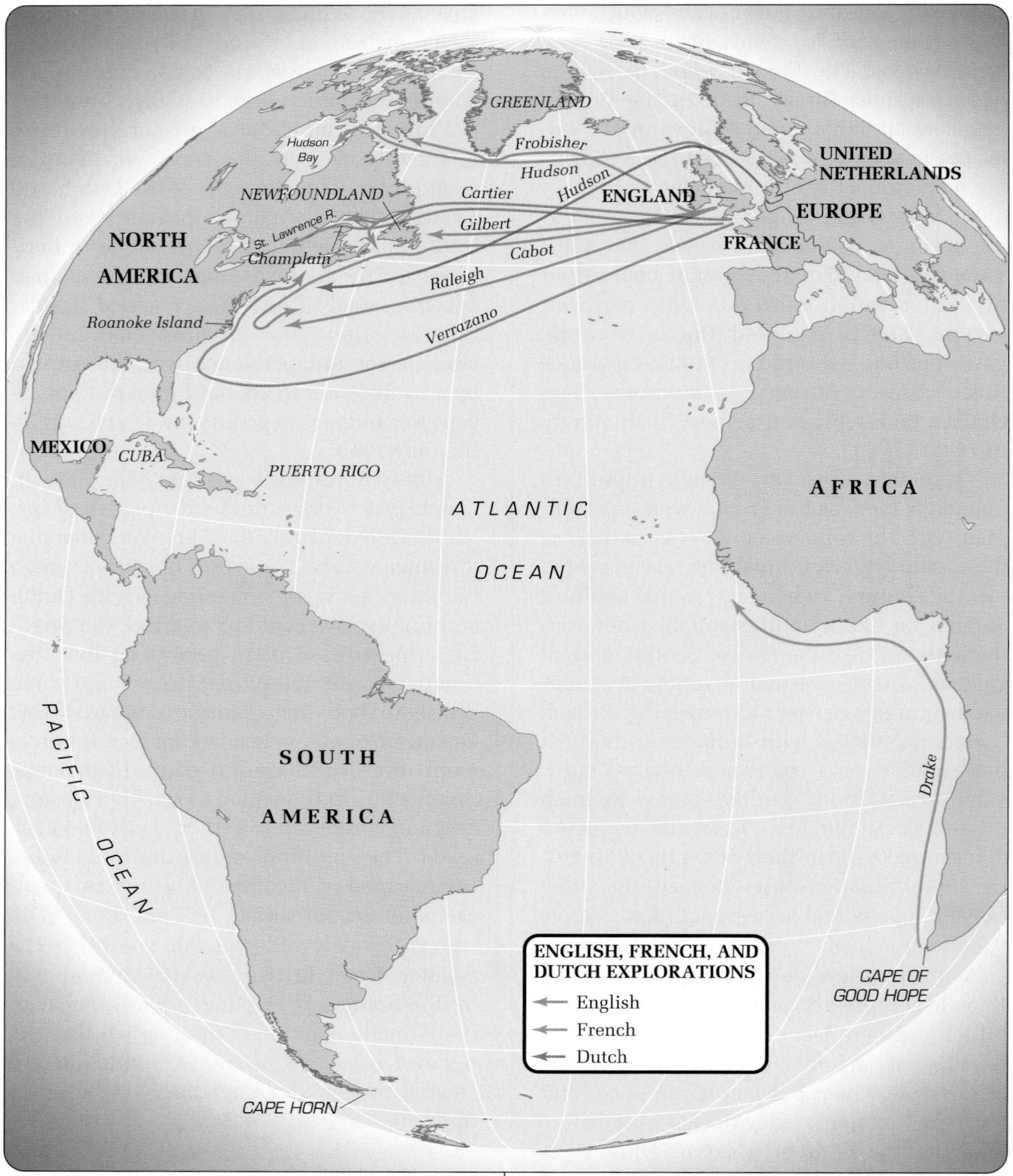

and discovered Roanoke Island, where the soil seemed fruitful and the natives friendly. Three years later, 117 settlers arrived, including women and children, under the leadership of Governor John White. After a month in Roanoke, White returned to England to get supplies, leaving behind the other colonists, including his daughter, Eleanor, her husband, and her baby, Virginia Dare, the first English child born in the New World. White, however, was long delayed because of the war with Spain.

When he finally returned in 1590, he found the village of "Ralegh" abandoned and pillaged, possibly by hostile Indians or by Spaniards. No trace of the "lost colonists" was ever found. When Queen Elizabeth died in 1603, there were no English settlers in North America.

Settling the Chesapeake

With the death of Queen Elizabeth, the Tudor line ended and the throne fell to her cousin James VI of Scotland, the son of the ill-fated Mary, Queen of Scots. The first of the Stuarts, he ruled England as James I. The Stuart dynasty spanned most of the seventeenth century, a turbulent time of religious and political tensions, civil war, and foreign intrigues. During these eventful years in English history, all but one of the thirteen North American colonies and several more in the Caribbean were founded. They were quite diverse in geography, motives, and composition.

In 1606, having made peace with Spain, thereby freeing up resources and men for colonization, James I chartered the Virginia Company with two divisions, the First Colony of London and the Second Colony of Plymouth. The stockholders expected a potential return from gold and products such as wine, citrus fruits, olive oil, pitch, tar, potash, and other forest products needed for naval use. Many also still hoped to discover a passage to India. Few if any investors foresaw what the first English colony would become: a bountiful source of tobacco.

From the outset, the pattern of English colonization diverged significantly from the Spanish emphasis on conquest and conversion. The English settled along the Atlantic seaboard, where the native populations were relatively weak. There was no Aztec or Inca Empire to conquer and rule. The colonists thus had to establish their own communities within a largely wilderness setting and among a more diverse array of Indian tribes.

Virginia

The London group of the Virginia Company planted the first permanent colony in Virginia, named after Elizabeth I, the "Virgin Queen." On May 6, 1607, three ships loaded with about 100 men reached Chesapeake Bay after four storm-tossed months at sea. They chose a river with a northwest bend—in hope of a passage to Asia—and settled about 40 miles inland to hide from marauding Spaniards.

The river they called the James, and the colony Jamestown. After building a fort, thatched huts, a storehouse, and a church, the colonists began planting, but most were either townsmen unfamiliar with farming or "gentlemen" adventurers who scorned manual labor. They had come to find gold, not to establish a farm settlement. Supplies from England were undependable, and only firm leadership and their trade with the Indians, who taught the colonists to grow maize, enabled them to survive.

The Indians of the region were loosely organized. Wahunsonacock, called Powhatan by the English after the name of his tribe, was the chief of some thirty Algonquian-speaking tribes in eastern Virginia. The Indians making up the so-called Powhatan Confederacy were largely an agricultural people who lived along rivers in fortified towns and resided in framed houses sheathed with bark. Despite occasional clashes with the colonists, the Indians of Virginia initially adopted a stance of nervous assistance and watchful waiting. Powhatan apparently hoped to develop a lucrative trade and military alliance with the newcomers; he realized too late that the English intended to expropriate his lands and subjugate his people.

The colonists, as it happened, had more than a match for Powhatan in Captain John Smith, a soldier of fortune with rare powers of leadership and self-promotion. The Virginia Company appointed Smith a member of the resident council to manage the new colony in America. With the colonists on the verge of starvation, he imposed strict discipline and forced all to labor, declaring that "he that will not work shall not eat." Smith also bargained with the Indians and mapped the Chesapeake region. Through his efforts, Jamestown survived the first two winters, but in 1609 Smith suffered a gunpowder burn and sailed back to England. The colony lapsed into anarchy and suffered the "starving time" of the winter of 1609–1610, during which most of the colonists, weakened by hunger, fell prey to disease. A relief party found only about sixty settlers still alive in 1610. All poultry and livestock (including horses) had been eaten, and one man reportedly had dined on his wife.

For the next seven years, the colony limped along until it gradually found a reason for being: tobacco. In 1612 John Rolfe had begun to experiment with the harsh-tasting Virginia tobacco, and by 1616 a smoother-tasting variety had become an export staple. Meanwhile Rolfe had made another contribution to stability by marrying Pocahontas, the daughter of Powhatan. Their marriage helped to ease deteriorating relations between the Indians and English settlers, who continued to try to take the Indians' crops, either through extortion or plundering. Distinguished Virginians still boast of their descent from the Indian "princess," who died of smallpox in London in 1620.

In 1618 officials in London initiated a series of reforms intended to shore up their struggling American colony. They first inaugurated a new "headright" policy. Anyone who bought a share in the company, or who could transport himself to Virginia, could have fifty acres, and fifty more for any servants he might send or bring. The following year the company promised that the settlers should have the "rights of Englishmen," including a representative assembly. On July 30, 1619, the first General Assembly of Virginia met in the Jamestown church. It was an eventful year in two other respects. During 1619, a ship arrived with ninety "young maidens," to be sold to likely husbands of their own choice for the cost of transportation (about 125 pounds of tobacco). And a Dutch vessel dropped off "20 Negars," the first blacks in English America.

Yet despite its successes, Jamestown again fell upon evil days. The profitable tobacco trade intensified the settlers' lust for Indian lands because they had already been cleared and were ready to be planted. In 1622 the Indians tried to repel the land-grabbing English. They killed some 350 colonists, including John Rolfe.

The English thereafter sought to wipe out the Indian presence along their frontier. In 1623 Captain William Tucker and a band of soldiers met with Indian leaders to negotiate a settlement. After signing a treaty, Tucker invited the Indians to drink a toast to celebrate their truce. Unwittingly, the Indians drank the proffered wine, only to realize too late that it had been poisoned. Two hundred Indians died from the doctored brew. The soldiers then burned Indian villages and plundered their corn, killed another fifty and "brought home part of their heads." This process of "continual incursions" into Indian territory spanned the decade.

Yet the English foothold in Virginia remained tenuous. Some 14,000 people had migrated to the colony since 1607, but the population in 1624 stood at a precarious 1,132. The king appointed a commission to investigate the running of the struggling colony by the Virginia Company, and on the commission's recommendation a court dissolved the company. In 1624 Virginia became a royal colony.

Maryland

In 1634, ten years after Virginia became a royal colony, a neighboring settlement named Maryland appeared on the northern shores of Chesapeake Bay. It was the first so-called proprietary colony, granted not to a joint-stock company but to an individual, Lord Baltimore. Sir George Calvert, the first Lord Baltimore, had announced in 1625 his conversion to Catholicism and sought the colony as a refuge for English Catholics, who were subjected to discrimination at home.

His son, Cecilius Calvert, the second Lord Baltimore, actually founded the colony in 1634 at St. Mary's near the mouth of the Potomac River. Calvert brought along Catholic gentlemen as landholders, but a majority of the servants were Protestants. The charter gave Calvert power to make laws with the consent of the freemen (all property holders). The first legislative assembly met in 1635 and later divided into two houses, with the governor and council sitting separately. The charter also empowered the proprietor to grant huge manorial estates, and Maryland had some sixty before 1676. But the Lords Baltimore soon found that to draw large numbers of settlers they had to offer small farms. The colony was meant to rely on mixed farming, but its fortunes, like those of Virginia, soon came to depend on tobacco.

Settling New England

Plymouth

Meanwhile, far to the north of the Chesapeake, quite different colonies were taking shape. The Pilgrims who established Plymouth Colony were bent not on finding gold or making a fortune but on building a Christian commonwealth. They belonged to the most uncompromising sect of Puritans, the Separatists, who had severed all ties with the Church of England. Persecuted by James I and Anglican officials, they fled to Holland in 1607. The Calvinistic Dutch, who shared their belief in predestination and a rigid moral code, granted them asylum and toleration, but restricted them mainly to unskilled laboring jobs. After ten years in Holland, the Pilgrims had wearied of such discrimination, and they decided to found a colony in the New World.

In 1620, 101 men, women, and children, led by William Bradford, crammed into the *Mayflower* for the transatlantic voyage. Only half of the voyagers were Pilgrim "Saints"—people recognized as having been elected by God for salvation; the rest were non-Pilgrim "Strangers"—ordinary settlers, hired hands, and indentured servants. The leaders undertook the voyage, as Bradford asserted, "for the glorie of God, and advancements of the Christian faith and honour of our king & countrie."

A stormy voyage led them to Cape Cod, far north of Virginia. They called their settlement Plymouth. Forty-one of the Pilgrims entered into a formal agreement to abide by laws made by leaders of their own choosing—the Mayflower Compact of November 21, 1620. Later used as a model by other New England settlers, the compact helped establish the distinctive American tradition of consensual government.

The Pilgrims built and occupied their dwellings amid the winter snows, and nearly half of them died of exposure and disease. In the spring of 1621, the colonists met a Wampanoag Indian named Squanto, who showed them how to grow maize. By autumn the Pilgrims had a bumper crop of corn, a flourishing fur trade, and a supply of lumber for shipment. To celebrate, they held a harvest feast with the Wampanoags, an annual ritual that later would be dubbed Thanksgiving.

Massachusetts Bay

Plymouth Colony's population never rose above 7,000, and after ten years it was overshadowed by its larger neighbor, the Massachusetts Bay Colony. It, too, was intended to be a holy commonwealth made up of religious folk bound together in the harmonious worship of God. Like the Pilgrims, the Puritans who colonized Massachusetts Bay

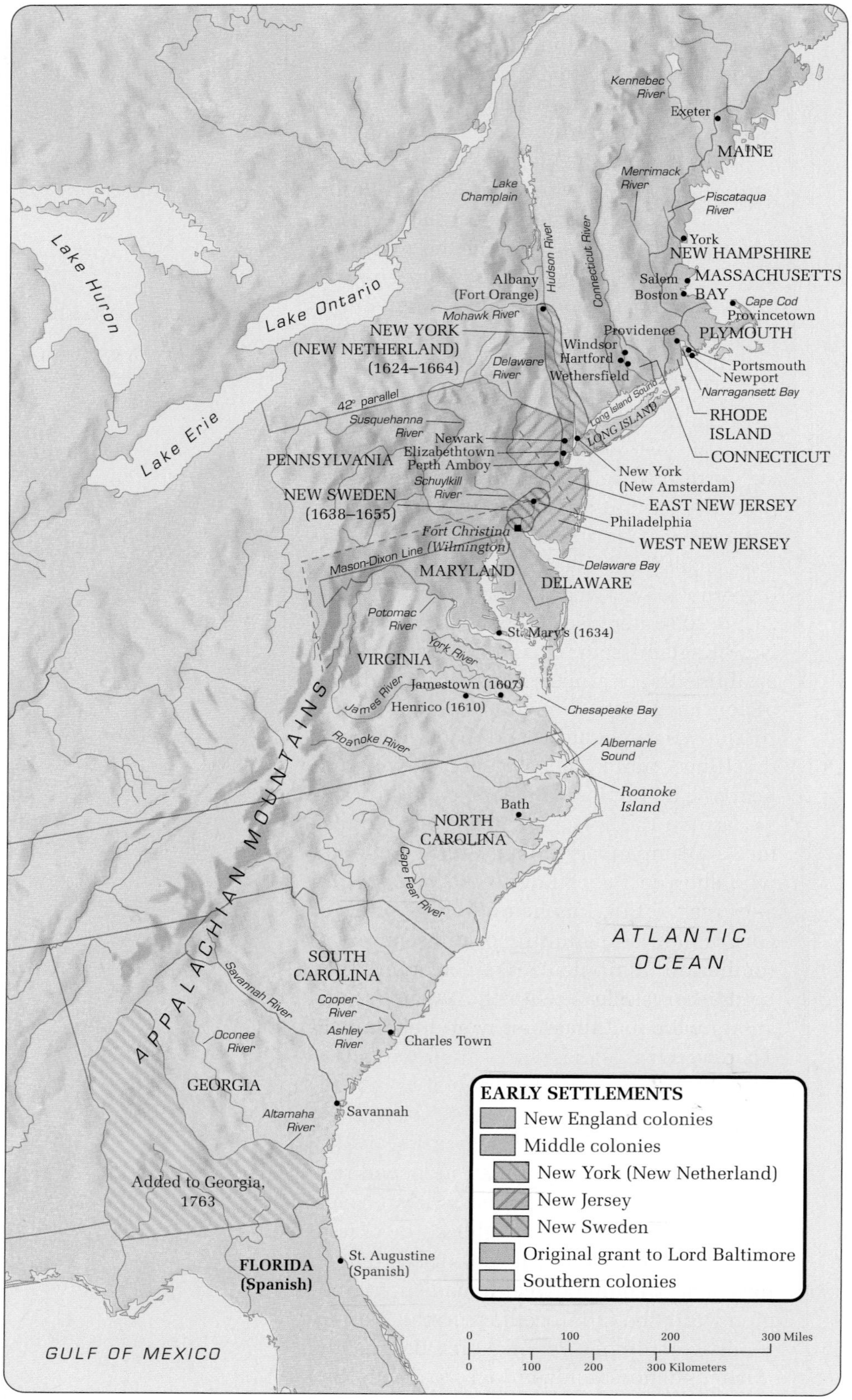

were primarily Congregationalists who wanted self-governing churches whose members would be limited to "visible saints," those who could demonstrate their receipt of the gift of God's grace. Unlike the Plymouth Separatists, however, the Puritans who settled Massachusetts hoped that the Church of England could be reformed. Thus they were called Non-Separating Congregationalists, or Nonconformists.

In 1629 a group of Puritans and merchants convinced King Charles I to grant their newly formed Massachusetts Bay Company an area north of Plymouth Colony for settlement. Leaders of the company at first looked upon it mainly as a business venture, but a majority faction led by John Winthrop, a respected lawyer, resolved to use the colony as a refuge for persecuted Puritans.

In 1630 the *Arbella,* with Governor John Winthrop and the charter aboard, embarked with six other ships for Massachusetts. In a speech entitled "A Model of Christian Charity," delivered on board, Winthrop told his fellow Puritans "we must consider that we shall be a city upon a hill"—an exemplary beacon showing all people what a truly godly community could be. By the end of 1630, seventeen more ships bearing an additional 1,000 colonists joined Winthrop's band of colonists. As settlers—Puritan and non-Puritan—poured into the region, Boston became the chief city and capital. The next several years witnessed the Great Migration, in which 80,000 people left their homeland, including some 40,000 to 50,000 English settlers who went to the New World, fleeing persecution and economic depression at home.

Winthrop was a courageous leader who shrewdly took advantage of a fateful omission in the charter for the

Massachusetts Bay Company: the usual proviso that the company maintain its home office in England. Winthrop's group took its charter with them, thereby transferring the entire government of the colony to Massachusetts Bay, where they hoped to ensure Puritan control.

The transfer of the Massachusetts charter, whereby an English trading company evolved into a provincial government, was a unique venture in colonization. Under this royal charter, power rested with the General Court, which elected the governor and his assistants and which consisted of shareholders, called freemen (those who had the "freedom of the company").

At first the freemen had no power except to choose legislators known as assistants, who in turn elected the governor and deputy governor. The procedure violated provisions of the charter, but Winthrop kept the document hidden, and few knew of its exact provisions. Controversy simmered until 1634, when each town sent two delegates to Boston to confer on matters coming before the General Court. There they demanded to see the charter, which Winthrop reluctantly produced, and they read that the power to pass laws and levy taxes rested in the General Court. Winthrop argued that the body of freemen had grown too large, but when it met, the General Court responded by turning itself into a representative body with two or three deputies to represent each town. They also chose a new governor, and Winthrop did not resume the office until three years later. A final stage in the evolution of the government, a two-house legislature, came in 1644, with the deputies and assistants sitting apart and all decisions requiring a majority in each house.

Thus over a period of fourteen years, the Massachusetts Bay Company, a trading corporation, evolved into the governing body of a commonwealth. Membership in a Puritan church replaced the purchase of stock as a means of becoming a freeman, which was to say a voter. The General Court, like Parliament, became a representative body of two houses, with the House of Assistants corresponding roughly to the House of Lords, and the House of Deputies to the House of Commons.

Rhode Island

More by accident than design, Massachusetts became the staging area for the rest of New England, as new colonies grew out of religious quarrels within the fold. Puritanism created a volatile mixture: on the one hand, the search for God's will could lead to a rigid orthodoxy; on the other hand, it could lead troubled consciences to diverse, radical, or even bizarre convictions.

Young Roger Williams, who arrived in 1631, was among the first to cause problems, precisely because he was the purest of Puritans, a Separatist troubled by the failure of the Massachusetts Nonconformists to repudiate the Church of England entirely. Williams's belief that a true church must have no relations with the English government, the Anglican establishment, or with the unregenerate led him to the conclusion that no true church was possible, unless perhaps consisting of himself and his wife—and he may have had doubts about her.

The purity of the church that Williams espoused required complete separation of church and state and freedom from coercion in matters of faith. "Forced worship," he declared, "stinks in God's nostrils." Such views were too advanced even for the radical church of Salem, which finally removed him. In 1635 a provoked General Court banished him to England. Aided by Narragansett Indian friends, however, Williams and a few followers fled into the wilderness, and they eventually were taken in by the Narragansetts. In the spring of 1636 Williams bought some land from the Indians and established the town of Providence at the head of Narragansett Bay, the first permanent settlement in Rhode Island, and the first in America to legislate freedom of religion.

Governor John Winthrop, who envisioned the Massachusetts Bay Colony as "a city upon a hill."

Anne Hutchinson quarreled with the Puritan leaders for different reasons. Strong-willed and articulate, she worked as a healer and midwife and hosted meetings in her Boston home to discuss sermons. Soon, however, those discussions turned into forums for Hutchinson to provide her own commentaries on religious matters. She claimed to have had direct revelations from the Holy Spirit that convinced her that only two or three Puritan ministers actually preached the appropriate "covenant of grace." The others, she charged, were deluded and were promoting a "covenant of works" that led people to believe that good conduct would ensure their salvation.

Hutchinson's beliefs were provocative for several reasons. Puritan theology affirmed the Calvinist doctrine that people could be saved only by God's grace rather than through their own willful actions. But Puritanism in practice also insisted that ministers were necessary to interpret God's will for the people so as to "prepare" them for the possibility of their being selected for salvation. In challenging the very legitimacy of the ministerial community as well as the hard-earned assurances of salvation enjoyed by current church members, Hutchinson was undermining the stability of an already fragile social system and theological order. What made the situation worse in such a male-dominated society, of course, was that a *woman* had the audacity to make such charges and assertions.

A pregnant Hutchinson was hauled before the General Court in 1637, and for two days she verbally sparred on equal terms with the presiding magistrates and testifying ministers. As the intense trial continued, Hutchinson was eventually lured into convicting herself by claiming direct divine inspiration. Banished in 1638 as "a woman not fit for our society," she settled with her family and a few followers on an island near what is now Portsmouth, Rhode Island. The arduous journey had taken a toll, however. Hutchinson grew sick and her baby was stillborn. Hutchinson's spirits never recovered. After her husband's death in 1643, she moved to Long Island, then under Dutch jurisdiction, and the following year she and five of her children were massacred during an Indian attack.

Thus the colony of Rhode Island, the smallest in America, grew up in Narragansett Bay as a refuge for dissenters who believed that the state had no right to coerce religious belief. In 1640 they formed a confederation and in 1643 secured their first charter. Roger Williams lived until 1683, an active and beloved citizen of the commonwealth he founded in a society that, during his lifetime at least, lived up to his principles of religious freedom and a government based on the consent of the people.

Connecticut, New Hampshire, and Maine

Connecticut had a more orthodox beginning than did Rhode Island. It was founded by groups of Massachusetts Puritans seeking better lands and access to the fur trade farther west. In 1636 three entire church congregations trekked westward by the "Great Road," and moved to the Connecticut River towns of Wethersfield, Windsor, and Hartford.

Led by Thomas Hooker, they organized the self-governing colony of Connecticut in 1637 as a response to the danger of attack from the Pequot Indians, who lived east of the river. In 1639 the Connecticut General Court adopted the "Fundamental Orders of Connecticut," a series of laws providing for a government like that of Massachusetts. Voting in the Connecticut colony, however, was not limited to church members.

To the north of Massachusetts, most of what is now New Hampshire and Maine was granted in 1622 by the Council for New England to Sir Ferdinando Gorges and Captain John Mason and their associates. In 1629 Mason and Gorges divided their territory at the Piscataqua River, Mason taking the southern part, which he named New Hampshire, and Gorges taking the northern part, which became the province of Maine. In the 1630s, Puritan immigrants began filtering in, and in 1638 the Reverend John Wheelwright, one of Anne Hutchinson's group, founded Exeter. Maine consisted of a few scattered and small settlements, mostly fishing stations.

Indians in New England

The settlers who poured into New England found not a "virgin land" of uninhabited wilderness but a developed region populated by over 100,000 Indians. The Native Americans coped with the newcomers and changing circumstances in different ways. Some resisted, others sought accommodation, and still others grew dependent on European culture. In some areas, Indians survived and even flourished in concert with European settlers over long periods of time. In other areas, land-hungry Europeans quickly displaced or decimated the native populations. The interactions of the two cultures involved misunderstandings, the mutual need for trade and adaptation, and sporadic outbreaks of epidemics and warfare.

In general, the English colonists adopted a different strategy for dealing with the Native Americans than that of the French and the Dutch. Merchants from France and the Netherlands were preoccupied with exploiting the fur trade. To do so, they established permanent trading outposts among the Indians. This nurtured amicable relations with the far more numerous Indians in the region. In contrast, the English colonists were more interested in fish and farms. They were quite willing to manipulate and exploit Indians rather than deal with them on an equal footing. Their goal was subordination rather than reciprocity.

In Maine the Abenakis were mainly hunters and gatherers dependent upon the natural offerings of the land and waters. The men did the hunting and fishing, women the gathering and cooking. Women were also responsible for setting up and breaking camp and raising the children. The Algonquian tribes of southern New England—the Massachusetts, Nausets, Narragansetts, Pequots, and Wampanoags—were more horticultural. While the men still hunted, fished, or traded surplus grain, women planted crops.

Although often portrayed as a monolithic group, the various Indian tribes of New England often fought among themselves, usually over disputed land. Had they been able to forge a solid alliance, they would have been better able to resist the encroachments of white settlers. As it was, they not only were fragmented but also vulnerable to the infectious diseases carried on board the ships transporting European settlers to the New World. Epidemics of smallpox devastated the coastal Indian population. Between 1610 and 1675, the Abenakis declined from 12,000 to 3,000, and the southern New England tribes from 65,000 to 10,000.

Those Indians who survived the epidemics and refused to yield their lands were often dislodged by force. In 1636 white settlers in Massachusetts accused a Pequot of murdering a colonist. Joined by Connecticut colonists, they retaliated by setting fire to a Pequot village. As the Indians fled their burning huts, the Puritans shot and killed them—men, women, and children. In less than an hour, all but seven escapees were dead.

Sassacus, the Pequot chief, then organized the survivors and attacked the whites. During the Pequot War of 1637, the colonists and their Narragansett allies massacred hundreds of Pequots. Most of the survivors were sold into slavery in Bermuda. Under the terms of the Treaty of Hartford (1638), the Pequot nation was dissolved.

After the Pequot War, the prosperous fur trade contributed to peaceful relations between whites and the remaining Indians, but the relentless growth of the colony and the decline of the animal population began to reduce the eastern tribes to relative poverty. The colonial government repeatedly encroached upon the Indian settlements, forcing them to acknowledge English laws and customs. Colonial leaders argued that the Indians should be deprived of their land because they were not using it as efficiently as the English would.

The era of fairly peaceful coexistence that began with the Treaty of Hartford came to an end during the last quarter of the seventeenth century. In 1675 Philip (Metacom), chief of the Wampanoags, forged an alliance among the remaining tribes of southern New England—the Narragansetts, Mohegans, and Wampanoags. Provoked by the hanging of three Indians for murder, Metacom's forces attacked English settlements. What came to be known as King Philip's War lasted through 1676. In the end, Metacom and over 3,000 Indians were killed. With them died organized resistance to white expansion.

Renewed Settlement

Before 1640, English settlers in New England and around Chesapeake Bay had established two great beachheads on the Atlantic coast, separated by the Dutch colony of New Netherland. After 1640, however, the power struggle back in England between king and Parliament, which erupted into civil war in 1642 between those who backed Parliament and those who supported the king, distracted attention from colonization. As a result, British migration dwindled to a trickle for more than twenty years. During the time of the English Civil War and Oliver Cromwell's Puritan dictatorship, the struggling colonies were left pretty much alone.

The Restoration of King Charles II in England in 1660 involved scarcely any changes in colonial governments, since little had occurred there under Cromwell. Renewed emigration rapidly expanded the populations of Virginia and Maryland. Fears of reprisals against Puritan New England by the reestablishment of the Anglican Church as the official church of England proved unfounded, at least for the time being. Massachusetts gained reconfirmation of its charter in 1662, and Connecticut and Rhode Island received the first royal charters in 1662 and 1663. All three retained their status as self-governing corporations.

The Restoration of the king also rekindled enthusiasm for colonial expansion. Within twelve years, the English had conquered New Netherland, had settled Carolina, and had nearly filled out the shape of the colonies. In the middle region formerly claimed by the Dutch, four new colonies sprang into being: New York, New Jersey, Pennsylvania, and Delaware. Without exception, the new colonies were proprietary, awarded by the king to "proprietors," men who had remained loyal during the civil war.

Settling the Carolinas

Carolina from the start comprised two widely separated areas of settlement. The northernmost part, long called Albemarle, remained a remote scattering of settlers along the shores of Albemarle Sound, isolated from Virginia by the Dismal Swamp and lacking easy access for oceangoing vessels. Albemarle had no governor until 1664, no assembly until 1665, and not even a town until a group of French Huguenots (Protestants) founded the village of Bath in 1704.

The eight Lords Proprietors to whom the king gave Carolina neglected Albemarle from the outset and focused on more promising sites to the south. Eager to find settlers who had already been seasoned in the colonies, they looked first to Barbados. The rise of large-scale sugar production in Barbados had persuaded small planters to try their luck elsewhere. Sir Anthony Ashley-Cooper finally spurred the enterprise by convincing his fellow proprietors to take on more of the financial burden of settlement. In 1669 three ships left London with about 100 settlers recruited in England; they sailed first to Barbados to pick up more settlers and then north to Bermuda. The expedition finally landed in America at a place several miles up the Ashley River. There Charles Town (later known as Charleston) remained from 1670 to 1680, when it was moved downstream to Oyster Point.

The government rested on one of the most curious documents of colonial history, the "Fundamental Constitutions of Carolina," drawn up by Lord Ashley-Cooper with the help of his secretary, the philosopher John Locke. Its cumbersome form of government and its provisions for an almost feudal social system and an elaborate nobility had little effect in the colony except to encourage a practice of large land grants, but from the beginning smaller "headrights" were given to immigrants who paid their own way. The provision that had greatest effect was a grant of religious toleration, designed to encourage immigration, which gave South Carolina a distinctive degree of indulgence (extending even to Jews and heathens) and ethnic pluralism.

Ambitious English planters from Barbados dominated the colony and soon organized a major trade in Indian slaves, whom the Westo Indians obligingly drove to the coast for shipment to the Caribbean. The first major export other than furs and slaves was cattle, and a true staple crop was not developed until the introduction of rice in the 1690s.

South Carolina became a separate royal colony in 1719. North Carolina remained under the proprietors' rule for ten more years, when they surrendered their governing rights to the crown.

The Southern Indians

The major Indian tribes in Florida, the Carolinas, Georgia, and what is today Alabama and Mississippi—the Apalachee, Timucua, Catawba, Cherokee, Chickasaw, Choctaw, Creek, and Tuscarora—combined farming with hunting and fishing to produce a thriving culture. They clustered in matrilineal clans (in which authority and property descended through the maternal line). The women raised beans, potatoes, and especially corn. The men hunted, traded, and made war.

Beginning in the late seventeenth century, the Creeks developed a flourishing trade with the British settlers, exchanging deerskins for manufactured goods—hoes, copper kettles, knives, beads, blankets, and clothing. During this same time, English merchants—mostly illiterate adventurers—began traveling southward from Virginia into the Piedmont region of Carolina, where they did business with the Catawbas. By 1690 traders from Charleston, South Carolina, made their way up the Savannah River to arrange deals with the Cherokees, Creeks, and Chickasaws. Between 1699 and 1715, Carolina exported an average of 54,000 deerskins per year. The voracious demand for the soft skins almost exterminated the deer population.

Trading with the English exposed the Indians to contagious diseases and also entwined them in a dependent relationship that would prove disastrous to their traditional way of life. Eager to receive more manufactured goods, weapons, and ammunition, the Indians were easily manipulated by English entrepreneurs and government officials. The English traders began providing the Indians with firearms and rum as incentives to capture rival tribesmen to be sold as slaves.

The continuing Indian trade led to repeated troubles. In 1715, Creeks, Choctaws, and members of smaller tribes organized a massive revolt against English control. This so-called Yamasee War began when Indians killed several English traders. The English colonists won out by playing the Indians against one another, convincing the Cherokees to join their side. When the Creek leaders visited the Cherokees in an effort to gain

(*Left*) Carolina Indians fishing, by John White, one of the earliest English settlers in America. Two methods of fishing are depicted here—nets and spears for daylight, and by firelight for night. (*Right*) Secotan dance, watercolor by John White.

their support, the Cherokees killed them, an incident that engendered hatred between the two tribes for years thereafter. The Yamasee War ended in 1717, when the Creeks signed a peace treaty, but infighting among the Indians continued.

New Netherland Becomes New York

Meanwhile, to the west of New England, the English resolved to pluck out that old thorn in their side—New Netherland. The Dutch colony was older than New England and had been planted when the two Protestant powers of England and the Netherlands enjoyed friendly relations in opposition to Catholic Spain. The Dutch East India Company (organized in 1602) had hired an English captain, Henry Hudson, to seek the elusive passage to China. In 1609 Hudson had discovered Delaware Bay and had explored the river named for him to a point probably beyond Albany, where he and a group of Mohawks made merry with brandy. From that contact stemmed a lasting trade between the Dutch and Iroquois nations. In 1614 the Dutch established fur-trading posts on Manhattan Island and upriver at Fort Orange (later Albany). Ten years later, a newly organized West India Company began permanent settlements. In 1626 Governor Peter Minuit purchased Manhattan from the Indians, and the new village of New Amsterdam became the capital of New Netherland.

Like the French, the Dutch were interested mainly in the fur trade and less in agricultural settlements. In 1629, however, the Dutch West India Company (organized in 1621) provided that any stockholder might obtain a large estate (a patroonship) if he peopled it with fifty adults within four years. The patroon supplied cattle, tools, and buildings. His tenants, in turn, paid him rent, used his gristmill (a mill for grinding grain), gave him first option to buy their surplus crops, and submitted to a court he established. It amounted to transplanting the feudal manor into the New World. Volunteers for serfdom were hard to find, however, when there was land to be had elsewhere, and most settlers took advantage of the company's provision that one could have as farms all the lands one could improve.

The colony's government was under the almost absolute control of a governor sent out by the Dutch West India Company. The governors were mostly stubborn autocrats, either corrupt or inept, especially at Indian relations. They depended on a small professional garrison for defense, and the inhabitants (including a number of English settlers on Long Island) showed almost total indifference in 1664 when Governor Peter Stuyvesant called them to arms against a threatening British fleet. Almost defenseless, old soldier Stuyvesant blustered about on his wooden leg, but he finally surrendered to the English without firing a shot.

The plan of conquest had been hatched by Charles II's brother, James, the duke of York, later King James II. When James and his advisers counseled that New Netherland could easily be conquered, Charles II granted the region to his brother. The English transformed New Amsterdam into New York and Fort Orange into Albany, and they held the country thereafter, except for a brief Dutch reoccupation in 1673–1674. Nonetheless, the Dutch left a permanent imprint on the land and the language. While the Dutch vernacular faded away, places like Wall Street (the original wall provided protection against Indians) and Broadway (Breede Wegh) remained, along with family names like Rensselaer, Roosevelt, and Van Buren. The Dutch presence lingered in the Dutch Reformed church; in words like *boss, cookie, crib, snoop, stoop, and spook;* and in the legendary Santa Claus and Rip Van Winkle.

The Iroquois League

One of the most significant effects of European settlement in North America during the seventeenth century was the intensification of warfare between Indian peoples. The same combination of forces that weakened the Indian population of New England and the Carolinas befell the tribes around New York City and the lower Hudson Valley. Dissension among the Indians and susceptibility to infectious disease left them vulnerable to exploitation by whites and by other Indians.

In the interior of New York, however, a different situation arose. There the Iroquois (an Algonquian term signifying "snake" or "terrifying man") nation would eventually forge an alliance so strong that the outnumbered Dutch and, later, English traders were forced to work with the federation of five tribes that spoke related languages—the Mohawk, Oneida, Onondaga, Cayuga, and Seneca (a sixth tribe, the Tuscaroras, joined them from Carolina in 1712).

By the early 1600s, some fifty sachems (chiefs) governed the 12,000 members of the Iroquois League. The well-organized Iroquois tribes lived in rectangular "long houses" sheathed in bark. Although a patriarchal society, the Iroquois granted considerable powers to women, who controlled the nominations for the tribal councils and could remove ineffective leaders.

When the Iroquois began to deplete the local game supply during the 1640s, they used firearms furnished by their Dutch trading partners to seize the Canadian hunting grounds of the neighboring Hurons and Eries. During the so-called Beaver Wars, the Iroquois defeated the western tribes and thereafter hunted the region's beavers to extinction. Other Indian nations such as the Fox, Sauk, and Kickapoo fled in terror at the approach of the Iroquois.

During the second half of the seventeenth century, the relentless search for furs and captives led Iroquois war parties to range far and wide across eastern North America. They gained control over a huge area from the St. Lawrence River to Tennessee and from Maine to Michigan. These wars helped reorient the political relationships in the eastern half of the continent, especially in the area from the Ohio Valley northward across the Great Lakes basin. Besieged by the Iroquois League, the western tribes forged defensive alliances with the French.

In the 1690s the French and their Indian allies gained the advantage over the Iroquois. They destroyed their crops and villages, infected them with smallpox, and re-

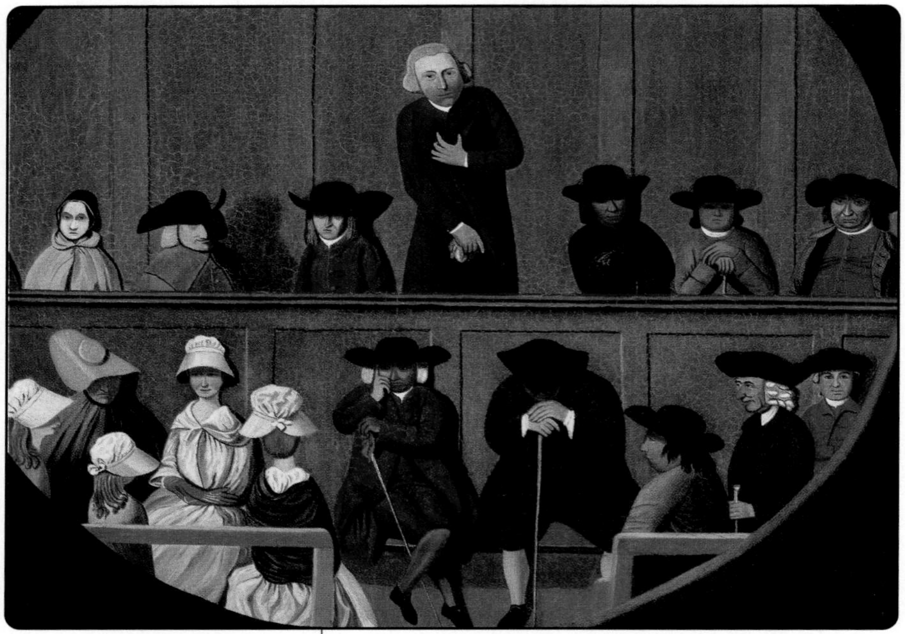

A Quaker meeting. The presence of women is evidence of Quaker views on the equality of the sexes.

duced the male population by more than a third. Facing extermination, the Iroquois made peace with the French in 1701. They had tired of serving the English as a "Pack of Hounds" to harass the French. During the first half of the eighteenth century, the Iroquois maintained a shrewd neutrality between the two rival European powers that enabled them to play off the British against the French, all the while creating a thriving fur trade for themselves.

New Jersey

Shortly after the conquest of New York, still in 1664, the duke of York granted his lands between the Hudson and the Delaware Rivers to Sir George Carteret and Lord John Berkeley and named the territory for Carteret's native island of Jersey. In East New Jersey, peopled at first by perhaps 200 Dutch who had crossed the Hudson, new settlements gradually arose: disaffected Puritans from New Haven founded Newark, and a group of Scots founded Perth Amboy. In the west, which faced the Delaware, a scattering of Swedes, Finns, and Dutch remained, soon to be overwhelmed by swarms of English Quakers. In 1702 East and West Jersey were united as a royal colony.

Pennsylvania and Delaware

The Quaker sect, as the Society of Friends was called in ridicule (because they told their followers to "tremble at the word of the Lord"), became the most influential of many radical groups that sprang from the turbulence of the English Civil War. Founded by George Fox about 1647, the Quakers carried further than any other group the doctrine of individual spiritual inspiration and interpretation—the "inner light," they called it. They discarded all formal sacraments and formal ministry, refused deference to persons of rank, used the familiar "thee" and "thou" in addressing everyone, declined to take oaths because that was contrary to Scripture, and embraced simple living and pacifism. Quakers experienced intense persecution—often in their zeal they seemed to invite it—but never inflicted it on others. Their toleration extended to complete religious freedom for all and the equality of the sexes, including the full participation of women in religious affairs.

In 1673 George Fox returned to England from a visit to America with the vision of a Quaker commonwealth in the New World and enticed others with his idea. The entrance of Quakers into New Jersey encouraged other Friends to migrate, especially to the Delaware River side. Soon, across the river arose the Quaker Commonwealth, the colony of Pennsylvania.

William Penn, the colony's founder, was born in 1644 and raised as a proper gentleman, but in 1667 he converted to Quakerism. In 1681 King Charles II awarded Penn a huge tract of land in America, and Penn named it, at the king's insistence, for his father: Pennsylvania (literally Penn's Woods). Penn vigorously recruited settlers to his new colony, and religious dissenters from England and the Continent—Quakers,

Mennonites, Amish, Moravians, Baptists—flocked to the region. Indian relations were good from the beginning because of the Quakers' friendliness and Penn's careful policy of purchasing land titles from the Indians.

Pennsylvania's government resembled that of other proprietary colonies, except that the councilors as well as the assembly were elected by the freemen (taxpayers and property owners) and the governor had no veto—although Penn as proprietor did. Penn hoped to show that a government could run in accordance with Quaker principles, that it could maintain peace and order without oaths or wars, that religion could flourish without an established church and with absolute freedom of conscience.

In 1682 the duke of York also granted Penn the area of Delaware, another part of the Dutch territory. At first Delaware became part of Pennsylvania, but after 1701 the settlers were granted the right to choose their own assembly. From then until the American Revolution, Delaware had a separate assembly but the same governor as Pennsylvania.

Georgia

Georgia was the last of the British continental colonies to be established, half a century after Pennsylvania. In 1732 George II gave the land between the Savannah and Altamaha Rivers to the twenty-one trustees of Georgia. In two respects Georgia was unique among the colonies: it was set up both as a philanthropic experiment and a military buffer against Spanish Florida. General James E. Oglethorpe, who accompanied the first colonists as resident trustee, represented both concerns: as a soldier who organized the colony's defenses, and as a philanthropist who championed prison reform and sought a colonial refuge for the poor and religiously persecuted.

In 1733 Oglethorpe and a band of 120 colonists founded Savannah near the mouth of the Savannah River. Soon thereafter they were joined by Protestant refugees from central Europe, who made the colony for a time more German than English. The addition of Scottish Highlanders, Portuguese Jews, Welsh, and others gave the early colony a cosmopolitan character much like that of Charleston, South Carolina.

As a buffer against Spanish Florida the colony succeeded, but as a philanthropic experiment it failed. Efforts to develop silk and wine production floundered. Landholdings were limited to 500 acres, rum was prohibited, and the importation of slaves forbidden, partly to leave room for servants brought on charity, partly to ensure security. But the utopian rules soon collapsed. The regulations against rum and slavery were widely disregarded and finally abandoned. By 1759 all restrictions on landholding were removed.

In 1753 the trustees' charter expired and the province reverted to the crown. As a royal colony, Georgia acquired for the first time an effective government. The province developed slowly over the next decade but grew rapidly in population and wealth after 1763. Instead of wine and silk, Georgians exported rice, indigo, lumber, naval stores, beef, and pork, and they carried on a lively trade with the West Indies. The colony finally had become a commercial success.

Thriving Colonies

After a late start and with little design, the English outstripped both the French and the Spanish in the New World. The lack of plan marked the genius of English colonization, for it gave free rein to a variety of human impulses. The centralized control imposed by the monarchs of Spain and France got their colonies off the mark more quickly but eventually brought their downfall because it hobbled innovation and responsiveness to new circumstances. The British preferred private investment with a minimum of royal control. In the English colonies, poor immigrants had a much greater chance of getting at least a small parcel of land, and a degree of self-government made the English colonies more responsive to new challenges—if sometimes stalled by controversy.

Moreover, the compact model of English settlement contrasted sharply with the pattern of Spain's far-flung conquests or France's far-reaching trade routes to the interior by way of the St. Lawrence and Mississippi Rivers. Geography reinforced Eng-

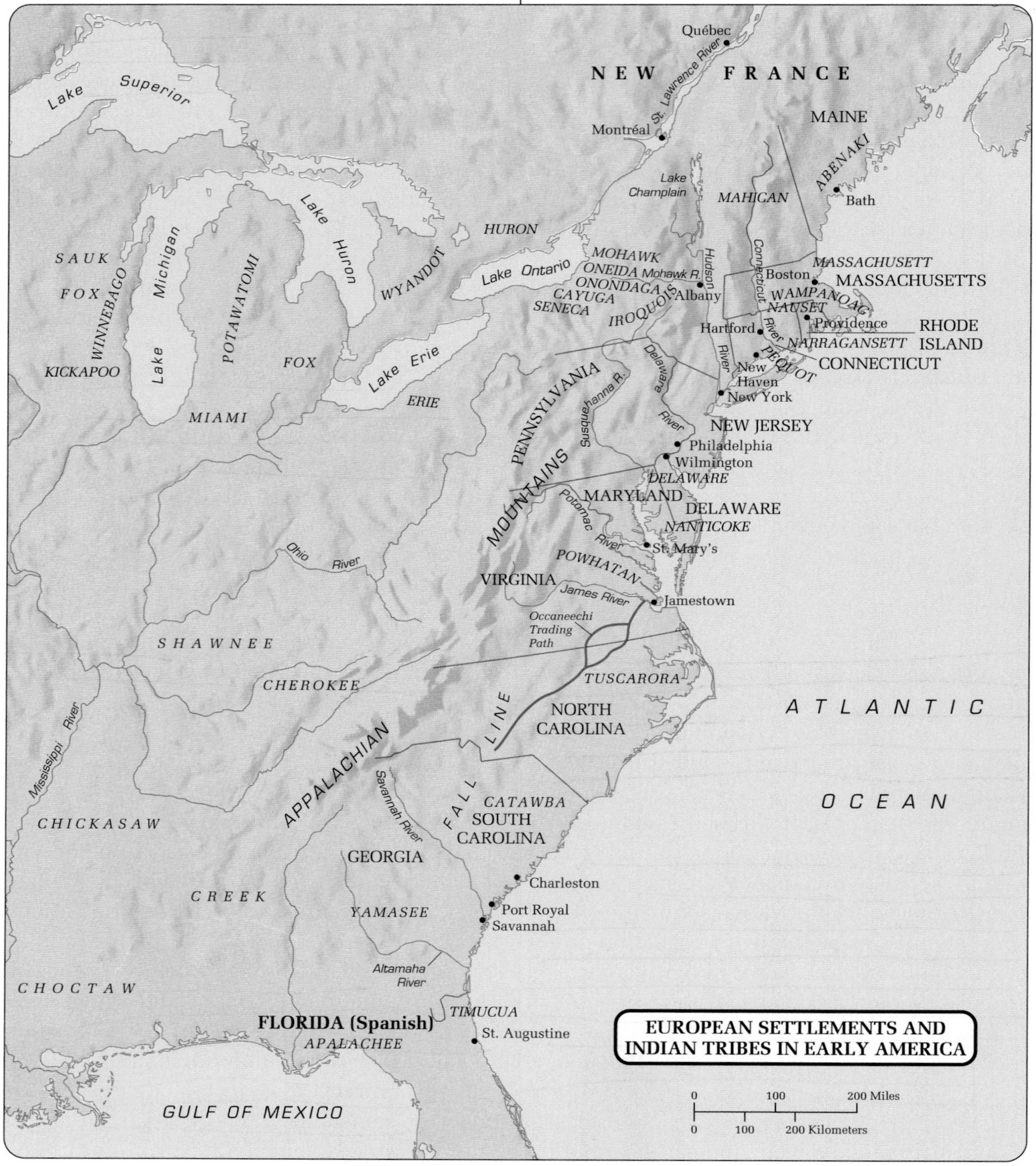

land's bent for concentrated occupation and settlement of its colonies. The rivers and bays indenting the coasts served as veins of communication along which colonies first sprang up, but no great river offered a highway to the far interior. About a hundred miles back in Georgia and the Carolinas, and nearer the coast to the north, the "fall line" of the rivers presented rocky rapids that marked the head of navigation and the end of the coastal plain. About a hundred miles beyond that, and farther back in Pennsylvania, stretched the rolling expanse of the Piedmont, literally the foothills. The final backdrop of English America was the Appalachian Mountain range running from New England to Georgia. For 150 years, the western outreach of settlement stopped at the slopes of the mountains. To the east lay the wide expanse of ocean, which served as a highway for the transit of European culture to America, but also as a barrier beyond which Old World values and folkways took to new paths in a new environment.

CHAPTER

2

Colonial Ways of Life

This chapter focuses on

- The social and economic differences among the southern, middle, and New England colonies.
- How various groups of people of different genders, races, and classes fit into colonial society.
- The impact of the Enlightenment and the Great Awakening on the American colonies.

THE *ESSENTIAL AMERICA* ON-LINE TUTOR

www.wwnorton.com/eamerica/ch2

- **Topic: The trans-Atlantic slave trade**
  www.wwnorton.com/eamerica/ch2/topic.htm

  The trans-Atlantic slave trade brought millions of Africans to the Americas. Examine the trans-Atlantic slave trade and its implications using slave narratives, historical analyses, maps, and art. How did slavery affect its victims?

- **Chapter review: On-line quiz and chapter summary**
  www.wwnorton.com/eamerica/ch2/review.htm

- **Chapter resources: Multimedia index**
  www.wwnorton.com/eamerica/ch2/media.htm

Those who colonized America during the seventeenth and eighteenth centuries were part of a massive social migration occurring throughout Europe and Africa. People were migrating from farms to villages, from villages to cities, and from homelands to colonies. They moved for different reasons. Most were responding to powerful social and economic forces: rapid population growth, the rise of commercial agriculture, and the early stages of the industrial revolution. Others sought political security or religious freedom. Moreover, Africans were moved to new lands against their will.

The Shape of Early America

Most of the migrants to America were young (over half were under twenty-five), and most were male. Almost half were indentured servants or slaves, and during the eighteenth century, England transported some 50,000 convicts to the North American colonies. About a third of the settlers journeyed with their families, but most arrived alone. A very few were wealthy, but many more were impoverished. Most immigrants were of the "middling sort," neither very rich nor very poor.

British Folkways

The vast majority of early settlers came from Great Britain. Four mass migrations from distinct regions of Britain occurred during the seventeenth and eighteenth centuries. The first involved some 20,000 Puritans who settled in Massachusetts between 1629 and 1641; most of these settlers hailed from the East Anglian counties east of London. A generation later, a smaller group of wealthy royalist cavaliers and their indentured servants migrated from southern England to Virginia. These English aristocrats, mostly Anglicans, were already accustomed to severe social inequalities and so had few qualms about the introduction of African slavery.

The third migratory wave brought some 23,000 Quakers from the north midlands of England to the Delaware Valley colonies of West Jersey, Pennsylvania, and Delaware. They imported with them a social system stressing spiritual equality, suspicion of class distinctions and powerful elites, and commitment to plain living and high thinking. The fourth and largest surge of colonization occurred between 1717 and 1775. It included hundreds of thousands of Celtic Britons and Scotch-Irish from northern Ireland, the Scottish Lowlands, and the northern counties of England; these were mostly coarse, feisty, clannish folk who settled in the rugged backcountry along the Appalachian Mountains.

Although most British settlers spoke a common language and shared the Protestant faith, they were in fact diverse people who carried with them—and retained—sharply different cultural attitudes and customs from their home regions. They spoke distinct dialects, ate different foods, built their houses in contrasting architectural styles, engaged in disparate games and forms of recreation, and organized their societies differently.

Seaboard Ecology

The ecology of America was shaped both by Native Americans and by European settlers. For thousands of years, Indian hunting practices produced what one scholar has called the "greatest known loss of wild species" in American history. In addition, the Indians burned woods and undergrowth to provide cropland, to ease travel through hardwood forests, and to nourish the grasses, berries, and other forage for the animals they hunted. This "slash and burn" agriculture halted the normal forest succession and, especially in the Southeast, created large stands of longleaf pines, still the most common source of timber in the region.

Whereas the Native Americans tended to be migratory, considering land and animals as communal resources to be shared and consumed only as necessary, many European colonizers viewed natural resources as privately owned commodities. Settlers quickly set about evicting Indians, clearing, fencing, improving, and selling land, growing cash crops, and trapping game for commercial use.

In time, a more dense population of humans and their domestic animals created a landscape of fields, meadows, fences, barns, and houses. Such innovations radically altered the ecology of the New World environment. Cleared and grazed land is warmer and drier, more subject to flooding and erosion. Foraging cattle, sheep, horses, and pigs gradually changed the distribution of trees, shrubs, and grasses. Indians, far from being passive observers, contributed to the process of environmental change by trading furs for metal or glass trinkets. This decimated the populations of large mammals that had earlier been central to Indian culture—and to the ecological balance. By 1750 such unintended consequences had transformed the physical environment from what it had been in 1600. New England, for example, by then had become a commercial success but an agricultural wasteland.

Birthrates and Death Rates

America's plentiful land beckoned immigrants and induced them to replenish the earth with large families. Where labor was scarce, children could lend a hand, and once grown, they could find new land for themselves if need be. Colonists tended, as a result, to marry and start new families at an earlier age than their European counterparts.

The initial scarcity of women in the colonies had significant social effects. Whereas in England the average age of women at marriage was twenty-five to twenty-six, in America it dropped to twenty or twenty-one. Men also married younger in the colonies than in the Old World. The birthrate rose accordingly, since those who married earlier had time for about two additional pregnancies during the childbearing years. Later a gradual reversion to a more even sex ratio brought the average age at marriage back toward the European norm. Even so, given the better economic prospects in the colonies, a greater proportion of American women married, and the birthrate remained much higher than in Europe.

Equally important in explaining rapid population growth in the New World was its much lower death rate, at least in the New England colonies (in the South, death rates remained higher due to malaria, dysentary, and other diseases). After the difficult first years of settlement, infants generally had a better chance to reach maturity, and adults had a better chance to reach old age than their counterparts in England and Europe. This greater longevity resulted less from a more temperate climate than from the character of the settlements themselves. Since the land was more bountiful, famine seldom occurred after a settlement's first year. Though the winters were more severe than in England, firewood was plentiful. Being younger on the whole—the average

"A little commonwealth." This eighteenth-century American family shows the "stairstep" pattern of child-bearing, in which children were born at approximately two-year intervals.

age in the colonies in 1790 was sixteen!—Americans were less susceptible to disease than were Europeans in the Old World. More widely scattered, they were also less exposed to disease. This began to change, of course, as cities grew and trade and travel increased. By the mid–eighteenth century, the colonies were beginning to experience levels of contagion much like those in Europe.

Women in the Colonies

Colonists brought to America deeply rooted convictions concerning the inferiority of women. God and nature, it was widely assumed, had stained women with original sin and made these "weaker vessels" smaller in stature, feebler in mind, and prone to both excited emotions and psychological dependency. Women were expected to be meek and model housewives. Their role in life was clear: to obey and serve their husbands, nurture their children, and maintain their households. Both social custom and legal codes ensured that women remained deferential and powerless. They could not vote, preach, hold office, attend public schools or colleges, bring lawsuits, make contracts, or own property except under extraordinary conditions.

In the eighteenth century, "women's work" typically involved activities in the house, garden, and yard. Farm women usually rose at four in the morning and prepared breakfast by five-thirty. They then fed and watered the livestock, awakened the children, churned butter, tended the garden, prepared lunch, played with the children, worked the garden again, cooked dinner, milked the cows, readied the children for bed, and cleaned the kitchen before retiring about nine.

Despite the conventional mission of women to serve in the domestic sphere, the scarcity of labor in the colonies opened new social opportunities. Quite a few women, either by necessity or choice, assumed gainful occupations outside the home. In the towns, women commonly served as tavern hostesses and shopkeepers, but some women also worked as doctors, printers, upholsterers, painters, silversmiths, and shipwrights. These women often, but not always, were widows who carried on their husbands' trades. Some women in the South managed plantations.

The acute shortage of women in the early years of colonial settlement made them more highly valued than in Europe, and the Puritan emphasis on well-ordered family life led to laws protecting wives from physical abuse and allowing for divorces. In addition, colonial laws gave wives greater control over property that they contributed to a marriage or that was left after a husband's death. But the traditional notion of female subordination and domesticity remained firmly entrenched in the New World.

Society and Economy in the Southern Colonies

Crops and Land

The southern colonies had one unique economic advantage—the climate, which enabled them to grow exotic staples (market crops) prized by the mother country. Tobacco smoking had become the rage among Europeans during the seventeenth century, and Virginia planters took full advantage of the situation. As one of them stressed, "all our riches for the present do consist in tobacco." Tobacco, however, was only one of many cash crops in the southern colonies. After 1690 rice became the staple in South Carolina. The southern woods also provided harvests of lumber and naval stores (tar, pitch, and turpentine).

In 1614 each of the Virginia Company's colonists received three acres, and this marked the beginning of a "headright" policy that provided every settler in the colony with a plot of land. In 1618 the Virginia Company increased land grants, giving 100 acres each to those already in the colonies, and 50 acres each to new settlers or to anyone paying the passage of immigrants (for example, indentured servants) to Virginia. Lord Baltimore adopted the same practice in Maryland, and successive proprietors in the other southern and middle colonies offered variations on the plan.

Indentured Servants and Slaves

The plantation economy depended upon manual labor, and voluntary indentured servitude accounted for probably half the white settlers in all the colonies outside New England. The name derived from the indenture, or contract, by which a person would agree to work for a fixed number of years in return for transportation to the New World.

Although many migrants saw the opportunity to go to the New World as a chance to better themselves, not all went voluntarily. One servant recalled how he and others were "stolen in Ireland" by English soldiers. On occasion, orphans were bound off to the New World, and from time to time the mother country sent convicts into colonial servitude. Once the indenture had run its course, usually after four to seven years, the servant claimed the "freedom dues" set by law—some money, tools, clothing, food—and often took up land-owning.

Slavery, long a dying institution in Europe, evolved in the Chesapeake Bay colonies after 1619, when a Dutch vessel dropped off twenty Africans in Jamestown. Some of the first were treated as indentured servants, with a limited term. Those who worked out their term of indenture gained freedom and a fifty-acre parcel of land. They themselves sometimes acquired slaves and white indentured servants. But gradually, with rationalizations based on color difference or heathenism, the practice of perpetual black slavery became the custom and the law of the land.

An idyllic view of a Tidewater plantation. Note the easy access to ocean-going vessels.

As colonists developed staple crops for commercial markets, the demand for slaves grew, and as readily available lands diminished, Virginians were less eager to bring in indentured servants who would lay claim to land at the end of their service. Though British North America brought less than 5 percent of the total slave imports to the Western Hemisphere during the more than three centuries of that traffic—400,000 out of some 9,500,000—it offered slaves better chances for survival, if few for human fulfillment. The natural increase of black immigrants in America approximated that of whites, and by the end of the colonial period, over 20 percent of the American population was black. In South Carolina blacks were in the majority.

African Roots and Black Culture

Slaves are so often lumped together as a social group that their great ethnic diversity is overlooked. They came from lands as remote from each other as the Congo and Senegal, the west coast of Africa, and the area around the hump in between, and they

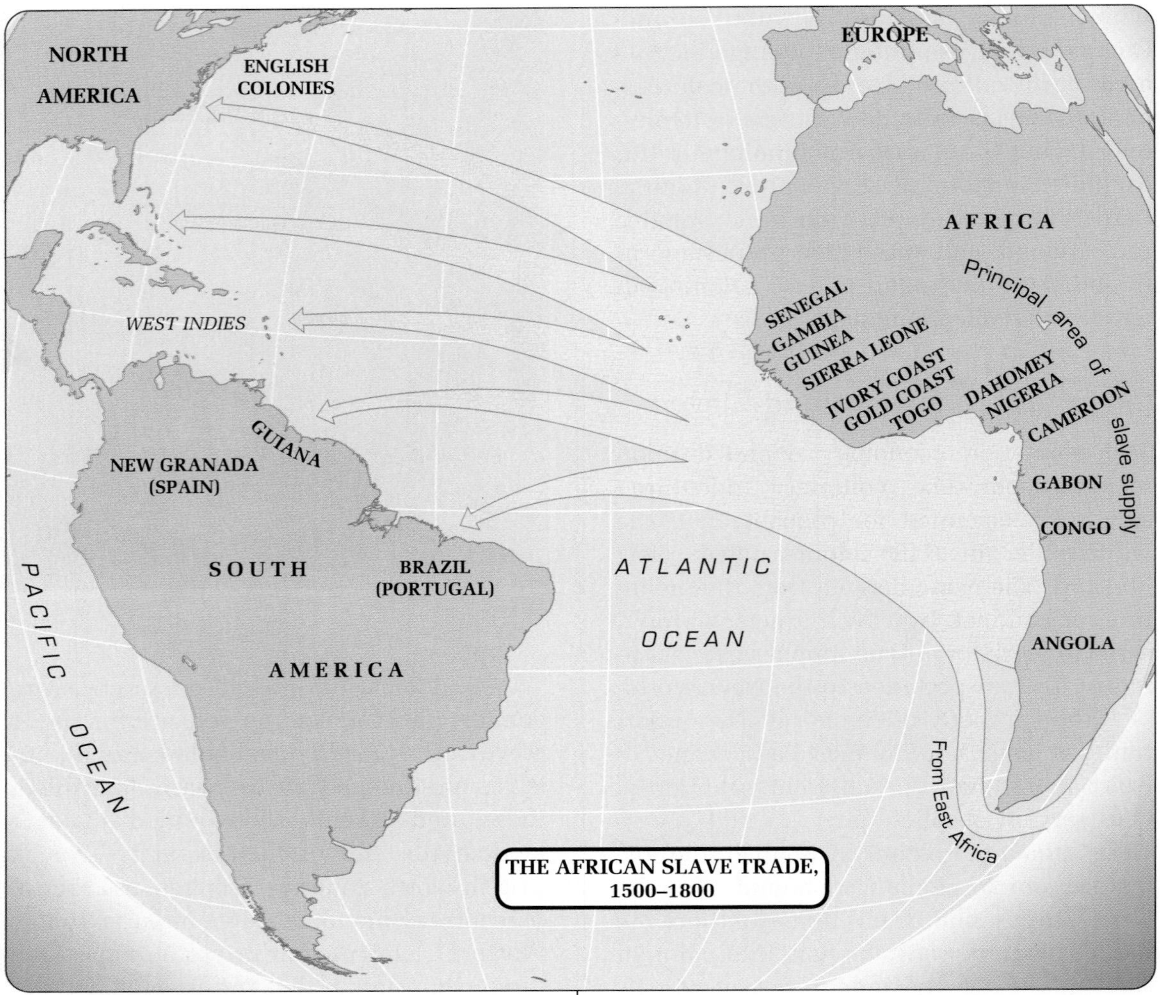

spoke Mandingo, Ibo, Kongo, and countless other languages. For all of their differences, however, the many peoples of Africa did share similar kinship and political systems. African societies were often matrilineal; property and political status descended through the mother rather than the father. Priests and the nobility lorded over the masses of farmers and craftspeople. Below the masses were the slaves, typically war captives, criminals, or debtors.

Most of the slaves who arrived in English North America during the seventeenth century did not come directly from Africa. Instead, they had first been taken from Africa to the sugar-producing colonies in Brazil and the Caribbean. Many had Spanish or Portuguese surnames, spoke a European language, and had been exposed to Christianity. Once in America, they often worked alongside white identured servants. A surprising number of the early slaves were able to earn money on the side and buy their freedom. Thus, seventeenth-century slaves had a more fluid and independent existence than their successors.

During the eighteenth century, with the rapid development of a plantation economy in the Chesapeake region and the low country of South Carolina, the demand for slaves grew so quickly that a much higher proportion came directly from the African interior—Angola, Biafra, and Senegambia. Planters wanted field hands, so most of these newer slaves were young males who had had no exposure to European culture or languages, a factor that discouraged relations between the races in America. As plantation slave culture evolved during the eighteenth century, discipline was more harshly enforced.

Some of the slaves rebelled against their masters, resisting work orders, sabotaging crops and tools, or running away to the frontier. In a few cases, slaves organized rebellions that were ruthlessly suppressed. After capturing slaves who participated in the Stono uprising in South Carolina in 1739, enraged planters "Cutt off their heads and set them up at every Mile Post."

Outnumbered and unarmed, most slaves resigned themselves to the overwhelming authority of their owners. Yet in the process of being forced into lives of bondage, blacks from diverse homelands forged a new identity as African Americans, while at the same time leaving entwined in the fabric of American culture many strands of African heritage.

On one level, slaves used songs, stories, and sermons to distract them from their toil; on another level, these modes of expression conveyed coded protests against masters or overseers. Slave religion, a unique blend of African and Christian beliefs, was frequently practiced in secret. Its fundamental theme was deliverance: God, they believed, would eventually free them from slavery and open up the gates to the promised land. The planters, however, sought to strip slave religion of its liberationist hopes. They insisted that being "born again" had no effect upon their workers' status as slaves. In 1667 the Virginia legislature declared that "the conferring of baptism does not alter the condition of the person as to his bondage or freedom."

The Gentry

By the early eighteenth century, Virginia and South Carolina were being led by a social elite known as the Tidewater gentry. The new aristocracy tried to replicate the life of the English country gentleman, indulging in the pleasures of hunting, fishing, riding, and gambling on horse races, cards, and dice. In their zest for the good life, the planters purchased the latest London luxury goods, buying on credit extended for future years' crops. Indebtedness to London merchants remained a chronic southern problem lasting far beyond the colonial period.

The survival of African culture among American slaves is evident in this late-eighteenth-century painting of a South Carolina plantation. The musical instruments, pottery, and clothing are of African origin, probably Yoruba.

Religion

Although Americans during the seventeenth century took religion more seriously than at any time since, the proportion of church members to residents in the southern colonies was less than one in fifteen. The tone of religious belief and practice in the Chesapeake colonies was quite different from that in Puritan New England or Quaker Pennsylvania. Anglicanism predominated in the region, and it proved especially popular among the large landholders. As in England, colonial Anglicans were more conservative, rational, and formal in their forms of worship than their Puritan, Quaker, or

Baptist counterparts. Anglicans tended to stress collective rituals over personal religious experience. Through most of the seventeenth century, the Church of England was "established" (tax supported) only in Virginia and Maryland, but by the early eighteenth century it had become the established church throughout the South.

In the colonial environment, the Anglican church evolved into something quite unlike the state church of England. The scattered population and the absence of bishops in America made centralized control difficult. In practice therefore, if not in theory, the Anglican churches became as independent of any hierarchy as the Puritan congregations of New England. Standards were often lax, and the Anglican clergy around the Chesapeake became notorious for its "sporting parsons," addicted to fox-hunting, gambling, drunkenness, and worse. Their congregations showed little toleration for being chastised from the pulpit. One minister lamented that the powerful planters removed any preacher who "had the courage and resolution to preach against any Vices taken into favor by the leading Men of his Parish."

Society and Economy in New England

Townships

By contrast to the seaboard planters who transformed the English manor into the southern plantation, the Puritans transformed the English village into the New England town, although there were many varieties. Land policy in New England had a stronger social and religious purpose than elsewhere. The headright system of the Chesapeake never took root in New England. There were cases of large individual land grants, but the standard practice was one of township grants to organized groups of settlers, often gathered already into a congregation.

Dwellings and Daily Life

The first colonists in New England arrived to find what one called a "hideous and desolate wilderness, full of wild beasts & wild men." Forced first to live in caves, tents, or "English wigwams," they soon built simple, small frame houses clad with hand-split clapboards. The roofs were steeply pitched to reduce the buildup of snow and were covered with thatched grasses or reeds.

By the end of the seventeenth century, most New England homes were plain but sturdy dwellings centered on a fireplace. Some had glass windows brought from England. The interior walls were often plastered and whitewashed, but the exterior boards were rarely painted. The interiors were dark, illuminated only by candles or oil lamps, both of which were expensive; most people usually went to sleep soon after sunset.

Family life revolved around the main room on the ground floor, called the "hall." Here meals would be cooked within a large fireplace. Pots would be suspended on an iron rod over the fire, and food would be served at a table made of rough-hewn planks called "the board." The father was sometimes referred to as the "chair man" because he sat in the only chair. The rest of the family usually stood to eat or sat on stools or benches.

Below the main floor of a New England house was a cellar for storing food and other supplies for the long winters. Above the hall was a loft where older children might sleep on bedrolls.

Enterprise

New England farmers and their families led hard lives. Simply clearing the glacier-scoured soil of rocks might require sixty days of strenuous labor per acre. The growing season was short, and the harsh climate precluded any profitable cash crops such as tobacco. With virgin forests ready for conversion into masts, lumber, and ships, and

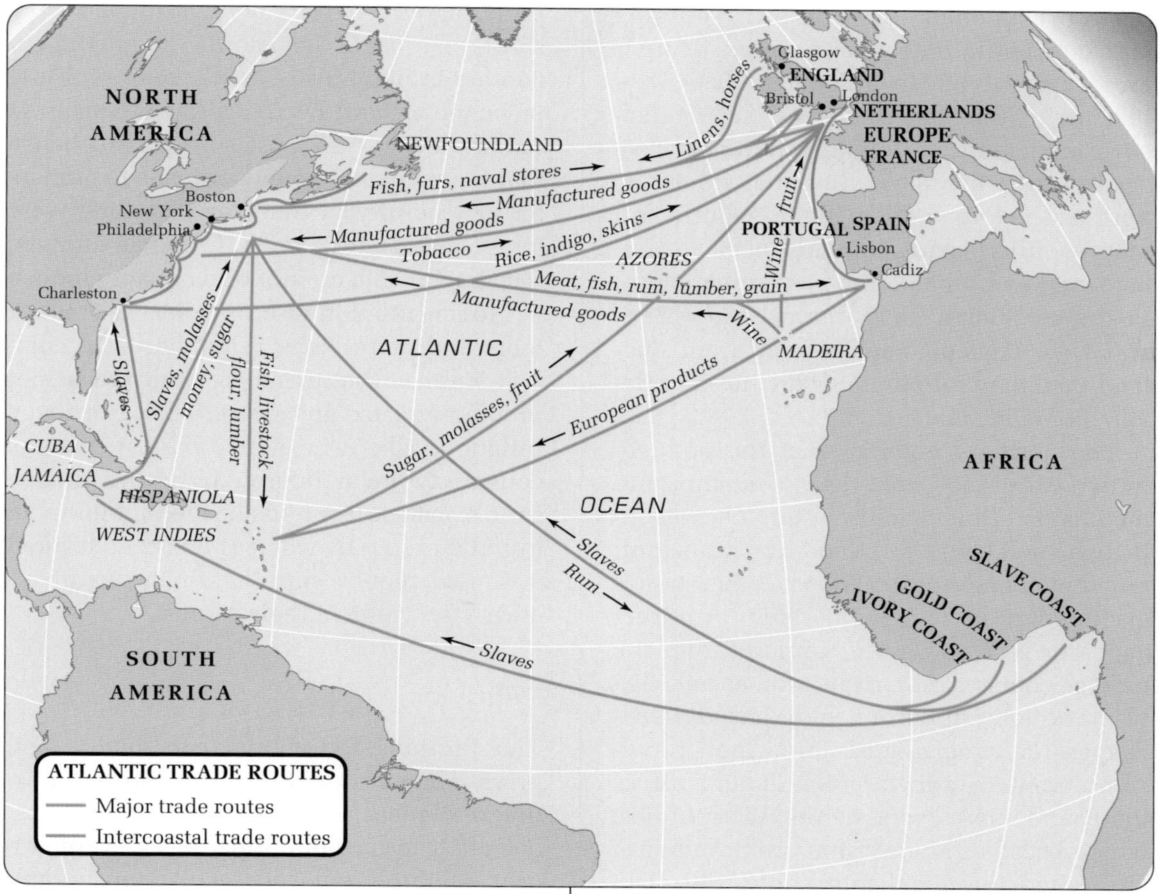

abundant fishing grounds that stretched northward to Newfoundland, New Englanders turned to the sea for their livelihood, and the region became America's most important maritime center. Whales, too, abounded in New England waters and supplied oil for lighting and lubrication.

New England's fisheries, unlike its farms, provided profitable exports to Europe, while lesser grades of fish went to the West Indies as food for slaves. Fisheries encouraged the development of shipbuilding, and experience at seafaring spurred commerce. This in turn led to wider contacts in the Atlantic world and a degree of materialism and cosmopolitanism that clashed with the Puritan credo of plain living and high thinking.

Trade

By the end of the seventeenth century, America had become part of a great North Atlantic commercial network, trading not only with the British Isles and the British West Indies, but also—and often illegally—with Spain, France, Portugal, Holland, and their colonies. Since they lacked the means to produce goods themselves, the colonists had to import manufactured items from Britain and Europe. Their central economic problem was to find the means of paying for these imports.

The mechanism of trade in New England and the middle colonies differed from that in the South in two respects: the northern colonies were at a disadvantage in their lack of staples to exchange for English goods, but the abundance of their own shipping and mercantile enterprise worked in their favor. After 1660, in order to protect English agriculture and fisheries, the English government raised prohibitive duties (taxes) against certain major imports from the northern colonies—fish, flour, wheat, and meat—while leaving the door open to timber, furs, and whale oil. As a consequence, in the early eighteenth century New York and New England bought more from England than they sold there, incurring an unfavorable trade balance.

The northern colonies met the problem in two ways: they used their own ships and merchants, thus avoiding the charges to British merchants for trade and transport; and they found other markets for the staples excluded from England, thus acquiring goods or gold to pay for imports from the mother country. American lumber and fish went to southern Europe for money or in exchange for wine; lumber, rum, and provisions went to Newfoundland; and all of these and more went to the West Indies, which became the most important outlet of all. American merchants could sell fish, flour, corn, pork, beef, and horses to West Indian planters who specialized in sugarcane. In return they got money, sugar, molasses, rum, indigo, and other products, much of which went eventually to England. This gave rise to the famous "triangular trade" (more a descriptive convenience than a rigid pattern) in which New Englanders shipped rum to the west coast of Africa and bartered for slaves, took the slaves to the West Indies, and returned home with various commodities, including molasses, from which they manufactured rum. In another version, they shipped provisions to the West Indies, carried sugar and molasses to England, and returned with manufactured goods from Europe.

The unfavorable balance of trade left the colonies with a chronic shortage of hard money, which drifted away to pay for imports. Various expedients met the currency shortage. Most of the colonies at one time or another issued bills of credit, on promise of payment in hard currency later (hence the dollar "bill"), and most set up land banks that issued paper money for loans to farmers on the security of their lands, which were mortgaged to the banks. Colonial farmers, recognizing that an inflation of paper money led to an inflation of crop prices, asked for more and more paper. Thus began in colonial politics what was to become a recurrent problem in later times, the issue of currency inflation. Wherever the issue arose, debtors commonly favored growth in the money supply, which would make it easier for them to settle accounts, whereas creditors favored a limited money supply, which would increase the value of their capital.

Religion

The Puritans for many years had a bad press. The picture of the dour Puritan, hostile to all pleasures, rings false. Puritans, especially those of the upper class, wore colorful clothing, enjoyed secular music, and drank rum, though a person found incapacitated by reason of strong drink was subject to arrest, and repeat "drunkards" were forced to wear the letter "D" in public.

Moderation in all things except piety was the Puritan guideline. This was true for sexual activity as well. Contrary to prevailing images of the Puritans as prudes, they readily recognized natural human desires. One minister emphasized that "the Use of the Marriage Bed" is "founded in man's Nature." Churches occasionally expelled members for failing to satisfy their partner's sexual needs. Sexual activity outside the bounds of marriage was strictly forbidden, but, like most prohibitions, the rule seemed to provoke transgression. New England court records bulge with cases of adultery and fornication. In part the abundance of sexual offenses reflected the disproportionate number of men in the colonies. Many were unable to find a wife and were therefore tempted to satisfy their sexual desires outside of marriage.

The Puritans who settled Massachusetts, unlike the Separatists of Plymouth, proposed only to form a purified version of the Anglican church. They believed that they could remain loyal to the Church of England, the unity of church and state, and the principle of compulsory uniformity. But their remoteness from England led them very quickly to a congregational form of church government identical to that of the Pilgrim Separatists.

In the Puritan theology, God had voluntarily entered into a covenant, or contract, with people through which his creatures could secure salvation. By analogy, therefore, an assembly of true Christians could enter into a church covenant, a voluntary union for the common worship of God. From this it was a fairly short step to the idea of a voluntary union for purposes of government.

The covenant theory contained certain kernels of democracy in both church and state. Democracy, however, was no part of Puritan political thought, which like so much else in Puritan belief began with original sin. Innate human depravity made governments necessary. The Puritan was dedicated to seeking not the will of the people but the will of God. The ultimate source of authority resided in the Bible, but the Bible had to be interpreted by those trained to the purpose.

While Puritan New England has often been called a theocracy, the church in theory was entirely separated from the state—except that town residents were taxed for its support. And if not all inhabitants were church members, they were to be present for church services. Life in the small rural townships was intimate and essentially cooperative. Studies of Andover, Dedham, and Plymouth, Massachusetts, among other towns, suggest that, at least in the seventeenth century, family ties grew stronger and village life more cohesive than in the homeland.

Diversity and Social Strains

Such harmony, however, was frequently short-lived. Increasing diversity and powerful disruptive forces combined to erode the consensual society envisioned by the founding settlers. Despite long-enduring myths, New England towns were not always pious, harmonious, static, and self-sufficient rural utopias populated by praying Puritans. Many communities were founded as centers of fishing, trade, and commerce rather than farming, religion, and morality, and the animating concerns of residents in such towns tended to be more entrepreneurial than spiritual.

Sectarian disputes and religious indifference often developed. The emphasis on a direct accountability to God, which lay at the base of all Protestant theology, led believers to challenge authority in the name of private conscience. Massachusetts repressed such heresy in the 1630s, but it resurfaced during the 1650s among Quakers and Baptists, and in 1659–1660 the colony hanged four Quakers who persisted in returning after they were expelled. The hangings caused such revulsion—and an investigation by the crown—that they were not repeated, although heretics continued to face harassment and persecution.

More damaging to the Puritan utopia was the increasing pluralism and worldliness of New England, which placed growing strains on church discipline. More and more children of the "visible saints" found themselves unable to testify that they had received the gift of God's grace. In 1662 an assembly of ministers at Boston accepted the "Half-Way Covenant," whereby baptized children of church members could be admitted to a "half-way" membership. Their own children could be baptized, but such "half-way" members could neither vote nor take communion. A further blow to Puritan convention and control came with the Massachusetts royal charter of 1691, which required toleration of dissenters and based the right to vote on property rather than on church membership.

New England Witchcraft

The strains accompanying Massachusetts's transition from Puritan utopia to royal colony reached a bizarre climax in the witchcraft hysteria at Salem Village (now the town of Danvers) in 1692. Belief in witchcraft pervaded European and New England society in the seventeenth century. Prior to the dramatic episode in Salem, almost 300 New Englanders (mostly lower-class, middle-aged, marginal women—spinsters or widows) had been accused as witches, and more than thirty had been hanged.

Still, the Salem outbreak exceeded all precedents in its scope and intensity. The episode began when a few teenage girls became entranced listeners to voodoo stories told by Tituba, a West Indian slave. The girls began acting strangely—shouting, barking, groveling, and twitching for no apparent reason. The town doctor concluded that they had been bewitched, and the girls pointed to Tituba and two older white women as the culprits. Town dwellers panicked as word spread that the devil was in their midst. At a hearing before the magistrates, the "afflicted" girls rolled on the floor in convulsive fits as the three women were questioned by the magistrates. The crazed girls accused dozens of residents, including several of the most respected members of the community. Within a few months, the Salem jail overflowed with townspeople—men, women, and children—accused of practicing witchcraft. Before the hysteria ran its course ten months later, nineteen people (including some men) had been hanged, one man—stubborn Giles Corey, who refused to plead either guilty or not guilty—pressed to death by heavy stones, and more than 100 others jailed.

When the afflicted girls accused Samuel Willard, the distinguished pastor of Boston's First Church and president of Harvard College, the stunned magistrates had seen enough. Shortly thereafter, the governor intervened when his own wife was accused of serving the devil. He disbanded the special court and ordered the remaining suspects released. A year after it had begun, the fratricidal event was finally over. Nearly everybody responsible for the Salem executions later recanted, and nothing quite like it happened in the colonies again.

What explains the witchcraft hysteria at Salem? Some have argued that it may have represented nothing more than a contagious exercise in adolescent imagination intended to enliven the dreary routine of everyday life. Yet it was adults who pressed the formal charges against the accused and provided most of the testimony. This has led some scholars to speculate that long-festering local feuds and property disputes may have triggered the prosecutions.

More recently, historians have focused on the fact that almost all of the accused witches were women who had in some way defied the traditional roles assigned to females. Some had engaged in business transactions outside the home, others did not attend church; some were curmudgeons. Most of them were middle-aged or older, beyond child-bearing age, and without sons or brothers. They thus stood to inherit property and live as independent women. The notion of autonomous spinsters flew in the face of prevailing social conventions.

Society and Economy in the Middle Colonies

An Economic Mix

Both geographically and culturally the middle colonies stood between New England

and the South, blending their own influences with elements derived from the older regions on either side. In so doing, they more completely reflected the diversity of colonial life and more fully foreshadowed the pluralism of the later American nation than the regions on either side. Their crops were those of New England but more bountiful, owing to better land and a longer growing season, and they developed surpluses of foodstuffs for export to the plantations of the South and the West Indies: wheat, barley, and livestock. Three great rivers—the Hudson, Delaware, and Susquehanna—and their tributaries gave the middle colonies easy access to their backcountry and to the fur trade of the interior, where New York and Pennsylvania long enjoyed friendly relations with the Indians. As a consequence, the region's commerce rivaled that of New England, and Philadelphia in time supplanted Boston as the largest city in the colonies.

Land policies followed the headright system of the South. In New York the early royal governors carried forward, in practice if not in name, the Dutch device of the patroonship, granting to influential favorites vast estates on Long Island and up the Hudson and Mohawk Valleys. These estates most nearly approached the Old World manor. They were self-contained domains farmed by tenants who paid fees to use the landlords' mills, warehouses, smokehouses, and wharves. But with free land elsewhere, New York's population languished, and the new waves of immigrants sought the promised land of Pennsylvania.

An Ethnic Mix

In the makeup of their population, the middle colonies stood apart from both the mostly English Puritan settlements and the biracial plantation colonies to the south. In New York and New Jersey, for instance, Dutch culture and language lingered for some time, along with the Dutch Reformed Church. Up and down the Delaware River, the few Swedes and Finns, the first settlers, were overwhelmed by the influx of English and Welsh Quakers, followed in turn by the Germans and Scotch-Irish.

The Germans came mainly from the Rhineland. William Penn's brochures on the bounties of Pennsylvania had circulated in German translation, and his promise of religious freedom brought an excited response from persecuted sects, especially the Mennonites, whose beliefs resembled those of the Quakers. They were but the vanguard of a swelling migration in the eighteenth century that included Lutherans, Reformed Calvinists, Moravians, Dunkers, and others, a large proportion of whom paid their way as indentured servants or "redemptioners," as they were commonly called. West of Philadelphia these thrifty farmers and artisans created a belt of settlement in which the "Pennsylvania Dutch" (a corruption of "Deutsch," meaning German) predominated.

The Scotch-Irish began to arrive later and moved still farther out in the backcountry. "Scotch-Irish" is an enduring misnomer for Ulster Scots, Presbyterians transplanted from Scotland to confiscated lands in northern Ireland to give that country a more Protestant tone. The Ulster Scots suffered economic disaster and Anglican persecution. They fled mainly to Pennsylvania and the fertile valleys stretching southwestward into Virginia and Carolina. Unlike the more communal and pastoral Germans, they tended to settle in the backcountry—wilderness areas, usually the western portions of the colonies, where they cleared the land, built isolated log cabins, and lived by hunting and scratch farming. The Scotch-Irish were virulently anti-English and suspicious of all governments. From such rugged, hardheaded, and hardfisted people would come many powerful leaders, such as John Calhoun, Andrew Jackson, Sam Houston, and Woodrow Wilson.

The Germans and Scotch-Irish became the most numerous of the non-English

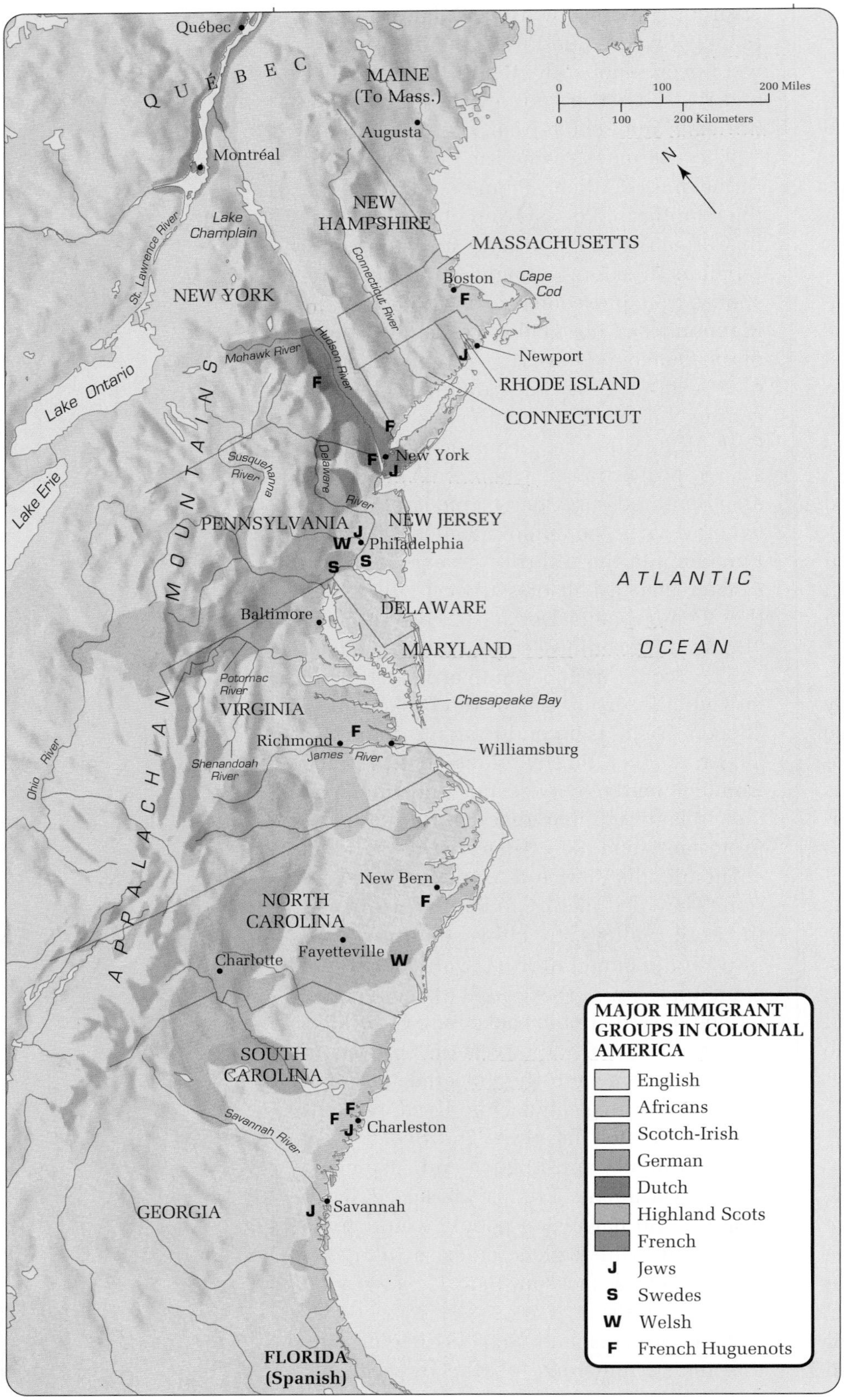

groups in the colonies, but others also enriched the diversity of population in New York and the Quaker colonies: French Huguenots, Irish, Welsh, Swiss, Jews, and others. By 1790 barely half the populace could trace their origins to England.

Colonial Cities

Since commerce was their chief reason for being, colonial cities hugged the coastline or, like Philadelphia, sprang up on rivers where oceangoing vessels could reach them. Never having more than 10 percent of the colonial population, they exerted a disproportionate influence in commerce, politics, and culture. By the end of the colonial period, Philadelphia had some 30,000 people and was the largest city in the colonies, second only to London in the British Empire; New York, with about 25,000, ranked second; Boston numbered 16,000; Charleston, 12,000; and Newport, 11,000.

The Social and Political Order

Merchants formed the upper crust of urban society, and below them resided a middle class of craftspeople, retailers, innkeepers, and artisans who met a variety of needs. Almost two-thirds of adult male workers were artisans, people who made their living at handicrafts. At the bottom of the pecking order were sailors and unskilled workers. Such class stratification in the cities became more pronounced during the eighteenth century and after.

Problems created by urban growth are nothing new. Colonial cities had traffic that required not only paved streets and lighting but regulations to protect children and animals in the streets from reckless riders. Other regulations restrained citizens from tossing their garbage into the streets. Devastating fires led to building codes, restrictions on burning rubbish, and the organization of fire companies. Crime and violence made necessary more police protection. And in cities the poor became more visible than in the countryside. Colonists brought with them the English principle of public responsibility for the needy. The number of Boston's poor receiving public assistance rose from 500 in 1700 to 4,000 in 1736; New York's rose from 250 in 1698 to 5,000 in the 1770s. Most of the aid went to "outdoor" relief in the form of money, food, clothing, and fuel, but almshouses also appeared in colonial cities.

The Urban Web

Transit within and between early American cities was difficult. The first roads were likely to be Indian trails, which themselves often followed the tracks of bison through the forests. The trails widened with travel, then were made roads by order of provincial and local authorities. Land travel at first was by horse or by foot. The first stagecoach line for the public opened in 1732. From the main ports, good roads might reach thirty or forty miles inland, but all were dirt roads subject to washouts and mudholes. There was not a single hard-surfaced road during the entire colonial period, aside from city streets.

Roadside taverns were an important adjunct of colonial travel, since movement by night was too risky. By the end of the seventeenth century, there were more taverns in America than any other business. Like private clubs today, colonial taverns and inns were places to drink, relax, read the newspaper, play cards or billiards, gossip about people or politics, learn news from travelers, or conduct business. Local ordinances regulated and licensed the taverns, setting their prices and usually prohibiting them from serving liquor to blacks, Indians, servants, or apprentices.

Postal service through the seventeenth century was almost nonexistent—people entrusted letters to travelers or sea captains. Under a parliamentary law of 1710, the postmaster of London named a deputy in charge of the colonies and a postal system eventually extended the length of the Atlantic seaboard. Benjamin Franklin, who served as deputy postmaster from 1753 to 1774, speeded up the service with shorter routes and night-traveling post riders, and he increased the volume by inaugurating lower rates.

More reliable deliveries gave rise to newspapers in the eighteenth century. Before 1745, twenty-two newspapers had been started, seven in New England, ten in the middle colonies, and five in the South. An important landmark in the progress of freedom of the press was John Peter Zenger's trial for seditious libel for publishing criticisms of New York's governor in his newspaper, the *New York Weekly Journal.* Zenger was imprisoned for ten months and brought to trial in 1735. The established rule in English common law held that one might be punished for criticism that fostered "an ill opinion of the government." The jury's function was only to determine whether the defendant had published the opinion. Zenger's lawyer startled the court with his claim that the editor had published the truth—which the judge ruled an unacceptable defense. The jury, however, agreed with the assertion and held the editor not guilty. The libel law remained standing as before, but editors thereafter were emboldened to criticize officials more freely.

The Enlightenment

In the world of ideas a new fashion dazzled minds: the Enlightenment. During the seventeenth century, Europe experienced a scientific revolution in which the prevailing notion of an earth-centered universe was overthrown by the new sun-centered system of Polish astronomer Nicolaus Copernicus. The revolution climaxed in 1687 when England's Sir Isaac Newton set forth his theory of gravitation. Newton disclosed a mechanistic universe moving in accordance with natural laws that could be grasped by human reason and explained by mathematics.

By analogy from Newton's view of the world as a machine, one could reason that natural laws governed all things—the orbits of the planets and also the orbits of human relations: politics, economics, and society. People reasoned, for instance, that the natural law of supply and demand governed economics and that natural rights to life, liberty, and property determined the limits and functions of government.

The way to improve both society and human nature was by the application and improvement of Reason—which was the highest Virtue (Enlightenment thinkers often capitalized both words).

The American Enlightenment

However interpreted, such ideas profoundly affected the climate of thought in the eighteenth century. As a Connecticut minister recognized in 1788, "The present age is an enlightened one." Anybody who pretended to a degree of learning revealed a curiosity about natural philosophy, and some carried it to considerable depth.

Benjamin Franklin epitomized the Enlightenment more than any other single person. Born in Boston in 1706, Franklin left home at the age of seventeen and relocated to Philadelphia. There he owned a print shop, where he edited and published the *Pennsylvania Gazette* and *Poor Richard's Almanac*. Before he retired from business at the age of forty-two, Franklin, among other achievements, had founded a library, set up a fire company, helped start the academy that became the University of Pennsylvania, and organized a debating club that grew into the American Philosophical Society.

After his early retirement, Franklin devoted himself to public affairs and the sciences. His speculations and inventions extended widely to the fields of medicine, meteorology, geology, astronomy, physics, and music.

Benjamin Franklin. By the time he retired from business at the age of forty-two, Franklin had, among other things, owned a print shop, edited and published a newspaper, established a fire company, and invented the lightning rod and Franklin stove.

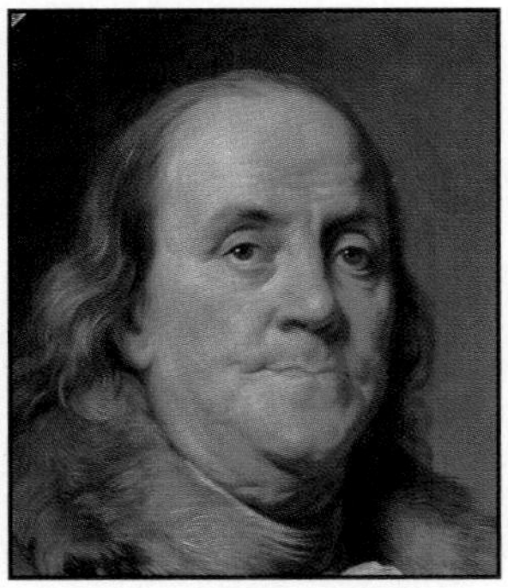

Education in the Colonies

The Age of Enlightenment prized education. And in the American colonies people promoted schooling for a variety of reasons. The Puritan emphasis on Scripture reading, which all Protestants shared to some degree, implied an obligation to ensure literacy. In 1647 Massachusetts Bay required every town of fifty or more families to set up a grammar school (a Latin school that could prepare a student for college). Although the act was widely evaded, it set an example that the rest of New England emulated.

In Pennsylvania, the Quakers financed a number of private schools teaching practical as well as academic subjects. In the southern colonies, efforts to establish schools were hampered by the more scattered populations, and in parts of the backcountry by indifference and neglect. Some of the wealthiest planters and merchants of the Tidewater sent their children to England or hired tutors, who in some cases would also serve the children of neighbors. In some places, wealthy patrons or the people collectively managed to raise some kind of support for secondary academies.

The Great Awakening

The new currents of learning and the Enlightenment prompted many people to drift away from orthodox religion. Many of the best educated were attracted to deism (which denied that God interfered with the laws and working of the universe) and to skepticism (which questioned accepted assumptions and religious beliefs). Meanwhile, out along the fringes of settlement there grew up a great backwater of the unchurched, people who had no minister to preach or administer sacraments or perform marriages. By the 1730s, the sense of falling away from religious orthodoxy prompted a widespread revival of faith, the Great Awakening, a wave of evangelism that within a few years swept the colonies from one end to the other.

Edwards and Whitefield

In 1734–1735 a remarkable spiritual revival occurred in the congregation of Jonathan Edwards, a Congregationalist minister in Northampton, in western Massachusetts. One of America's most brilliant philosophers and theologians, Edwards took charge of the Congregational church in Northampton in 1726 and found the congregation's spirituality at low ebb. He was convinced that Christians had become too preoccupied with making and spending money and that religion had become too intellectual and in the process had lost its emotional force. His vivid descriptions of the torments of hell and the delights of heaven helped rekindle spiritual fervor among his congregants.

The true catalyst of the Great Awakening, however, was a twenty-seven-year-old English minister, George Whitefield, whose reputation as a spellbinding evangelist preceded him to the colonies. Congregations were lifeless, he claimed, "because dead men preach to them." To restore the fires of religious fervor to American congregations, Whitefield reawakened the notion of individual salvation. In the autumn of 1739 he made a triumphal procession from Georgia to New England, drawing great crowds and releasing "Gales of Heavenly Wind" that dispersed sparks throughout the colonies.

Young and magnetic, possessed of a golden voice and a squinting left eye, Whitefield enthralled audiences with his unparalleled eloquence. The English revivalist stressed the need for individuals to experience a sudden and emotional moment of conversion and salvation—and the dangers of an unconverted ministry that had not experienced such rebirth. By the end of his sermon, one listener reported, the entire congregation was "in utmost Confusion, some crying out, some laughing, and Bliss still roaring to them to come to Christ, as they answered, *I will, I will, I'm coming, I'm coming.*"

Piety and Reason

Whatever their motive or method, the revivalists succeeded in awakening the piety of many Americans. Between 1740 and 1742, some 25,000 to 50,000 New Englanders, out of a total population of 300,000, joined churches. The Great Awakening spawned a proliferation of new religious groups and sects that helped undermine the notion of state-supported churches. Everywhere the revivals brought splits, especially in the more Calvinistic churches. Traditional clergymen found their position undermined as church members chose sides and either dismissed their ministers or deserted them. Many of the revivalists, or "New Lights," went over to the Baptists, and others flocked to Presbyterian or, later, Methodist groups, which in turn divided and subdivided into new sects.

By the middle of the eighteenth century, New England Puritanism had finally fragmented. The precarious balance in which the founders had held the elements of piety and reason was shattered, and Baptists, Presbyterians, Anglicans, and other denominations began establishing footholds in formerly Congregationalist Puritan communities. Yet the revival frenzy scored its most lasting victories along the chaotic frontiers of the middle and southern colonies. In contrast, in the more sedate churches of Boston, rational religion ultimately got the upper hand in a reaction against the excesses of revival emotion. The rationality of the Enlightenment crept more and more into the sermons of Boston ministers, and they embarked on the road to Unitarianism and Universalism.

In reaction to taunts that the "born-again" revivalist ministers lacked learning, the Great Awakening gave rise to denominational colleges. The three colleges already in existence had originated earlier from religious motives: Harvard, founded in 1636, because the Puritans dreaded "to leave an illiterate ministry to the church when our present ministers shall lie in the dust"; the College of William and Mary, in 1693, to strengthen the Anglican ministry; and Yale College, in 1701, to serve the Puritans of Connecticut, who felt that Harvard was drifting from the strictest orthodoxy. Over the next hundred and fifty years, scores of other denominational colleges and academies were founded across the country.

The Great Awakening, like the Enlightenment, set in motion powerful currents that still flow in American life. It implanted permanently in American culture evangelical principles and the appeal of revivalism. The movement weakened the status of the established clergy and encouraged believers to exercise their own judgment, and it thereby weakened habits of deference generally. The proliferation of denominations heightened the need for toleration of dissent. In some respects, the Great Awakening, characterized by piety and emotion, and the Enlightenment, dominated by reason and rationality, led by different roads to similar ends. Both emphasized the power and right of individual choice and popular resistance to established authority, and both aroused millennial hopes that America would become the promised land in which people might approach the perfection of piety or reason, if not of both. Such hopes had both social and political, as well as religious, implications. As the eighteenth century advanced, fewer and fewer people were willing to defer to the ruling social and political elite, and many such rebellious, if pious, folk would be transformed into revolutionaries.

CHAPTER 3

The Imperial Perspective

This chapter focuses on

- England's changing policies in the political and economic administration of the colonies.
- How colonial governments were structured.
- The relations between English colonists and their neighbors in North America: the French and the Indians.

THE *ESSENTIAL AMERICA* ON-LINE TUTOR

www.wwnorton.com/eamerica/ch3

- **Topic: The French and Indian War**
  www.wwnorton.com/eamerica/ch2/topic.htm

  The French and Indian War ended French domination of northern North America while altering relations between the British crown and its thirteen colonies. Study the French and Indian War using a variety of historical analyses, maps, primary documents, and period cartoons. What was at issue in the French and Indian War, and how did it affect the colonists?

- **Chapter review: On-line quiz and chapter summary**
  www.wwnorton.com/eamerica/ch3/review.htm

- **Chapter Resources: Multimedia index**
  www.wwnorton.com/eamerica/ch3/media.htm

For the better part of the seventeenth century, England remained too distracted by the struggle between Parliament and the Stuart kings to perfect either a systematic colonial policy or effective agencies of imperial control. After the Restoration of the Stuart dynasty in 1660, the British government slowly developed a new plan of colonial administration. By the end of the century, however, it still lacked coherence and efficiency, leaving Americans accustomed to rather loose colonial reins.

English Administration of the Colonies

Throughout the colonial period, the British king was the source of legal authority in America, and land titles derived ultimately from royal grants. After the Restoration, the king tried to reassert his control over the colonies, but administration by the mother country continued to be inefficient, lax, and often inconsistent. For instance, the British government granted home rule to the settlements along the Atlantic coast and then sought to keep them from exercising it. It regarded English colonists as citizens, but it refused to grant them the privileges of citizenship. It insisted that the settlers contribute to the expense of maintaining the colonies, but it refused to allow them a voice in the shaping of administrative policies. Such inconsistencies bred festering tensions. By the mid–eighteenth century, when the British tried to impose on their American colonies the kind of controls that were reaping huge profits in India, it was too late. British Americans had developed a far more powerful sense of their rights than any other colonial people, and they were determined to assert and defend those rights.

The Mercantile System

Like all the other major European powers of the seventeenth and eighteenth centuries, England adopted the mercantile system, or mercantilism, which assumed that the total of the world's gold and silver remained essentially fixed, with only a nation's share in that wealth subject to change. Thus a nation could gain wealth only at the expense of another country—by seizing its gold and silver and dominating its trade. To get and keep gold and silver, the government had to direct all economic activities, limiting foreign imports and preserving a favorable balance of trade. This required the government to encourage manufacturing, through subsidies and monopolies if need be, to develop and protect its own shipping, and to make use of colonies as sources of raw materials and markets for its finished goods.

During the English Civil War, colonial trade had fallen largely to Dutch shipping. To win back this trade, Oliver Cromwell, in 1651, convinced Parliament to adopt a Navigation Act requiring that all goods imported into England or the colonies must arrive on English ships, and that the majority of each crew must be English.

The Navigation Act of 1660 added a new twist to Cromwell's act of 1651. Ships' crews now had to be three-quarters English, and certain articles not produced by the mother country were to be shipped from the colonies only to England or other English colonies. The list of "enumerated goods" included tobacco, cotton, indigo dye, and sugar. Later, rice, naval stores, masts, copper, and furs were added. Not only did England (and its colonies) become the sole outlet for these colonial exports, but three years later the Navigation Act of 1663 sought to make England the funnel through which all colonial imports had to be routed. The act was sometimes called the Staple Act because it made England the staple market (or trade center) for goods sent to the colonies. Virtually all ships carrying goods from Europe to America had to dock in England, be offloaded, and pay a duty before proceeding. A third major act rounded out the trade system. The Navigation Act of 1673 (some-

This view of eighteenth-century Boston shows the importance of shipping and its regulation in the colonies, especially in Massachusetts Bay.

times called the Plantation Duty Act) required that every ship loading enumerated articles in the colonies had to pay a duty or tax on the item.

Enforcing the Navigation Acts

The Navigation Acts supplied a convenient rationale for a colonial system to serve the economic needs of the mother country. Their enforcement in far-flung colonies, however, was another matter. In 1675 King Charles II designated certain of his advisers as Lords of Trade, a name reflecting the overall importance of economic factors. The Lords of Trade were to make the colonies abide by the mercantile system and to make them more profitable to the crown. To these ends, they named colonial governors, wrote or reviewed the governors' instructions, and handled all reports and correspondence dealing with colonial affairs.

Between 1673 and 1679, British collectors of customs duties arrived in all the colonies, and with them appeared the first seeds of colonial resentment. New England's expanding commercial interests counseled prudence and accommodation, but the Puritan leaders harbored a persistent distrust of Stuart intentions. Consequently, the Massachusetts Bay Colony not only ignored royal wishes; it tolerated violations of the Navigation Acts. This led the Lords of Trade to begin legal proceedings against the colonial charter, and in 1684, the Lords of Trade won a court decision annulling the Massachusetts charter.

The Dominion of New England

The Massachusetts Bay government was placed in the hands of a special royal commission. Then in 1685 Charles II died and was succeeded by his brother, the duke of York, as James II, the first Catholic sovereign since Queen Mary. James II asserted his prerogatives more forcefully than his brother. The new king readily approved a proposal to create a Dominion of New England and to place under its jurisdiction all colonies south through New Jersey.

The Dominion was to have a government named by royal authority, a governor and council that would rule without any colonial assembly. The royal governor, Sir Edmund Andros, appeared in Boston in 1686 to establish his rule, which he soon extended over Connecticut and RhodeIsland, and in 1688 over New York and East and West Jersey. Andros was honest, efficient, and loyal to the crown, but tactless in circumstances that called for the utmost diplomacy—the uprooting of long-established institutions in the face of popular hostility.

Andros levied taxes without consent of the Massachusetts General Court, and when residents protested against such taxation without representation, he imprisoned or fined a number of them. Andros suppressed town governments, enforced the trade laws, and clamped down on smuggling. Most ominous of all, he and his lieutenants took over one of Boston's Puritan churches for Anglican worship.

But the Dominion of New England was scarcely established before word arrived from Britain of the Glorious Revolution of 1688–1689. James II, like Andros in New England, had aroused resentment in England by his arbitrary measures and, what was more, by openly parading his Catholic faith. In 1688, parliamentary leaders, their patience exhausted, invited James's Protestant daughter Mary and her husband, the Dutch leader William of Orange, to assume the throne as joint monarchs. James II, his support dwindling, fled to France.

The Glorious Revolution in America

When news reached Boston that William and Mary had landed in England, Boston staged its own Glorious Revolution, as bloodless as that in England. Andros and his councilors were arrested, and Massachusetts reverted to its former government, as did the other colonies that had been absorbed into the Dominion. All were permitted to retain their former status except Massachusetts and Plymouth, which, after some delay, were united under a new charter in 1691 as the royal colony of Massachusetts Bay.

The Glorious Revolution had significant long-term effects on American history. The Bill of Rights and Toleration Act, passed in England in 1689, limited the powers of rulers and affirmed freedom of worship for Christians. These acts influenced attitudes and the course of events in the colonies. The overthrow of James II also set a precedent for revolution against the monarch. In defense of that action, the English philosopher John Locke published his *Two Treatises on Government* (1690), which had an enormous impact on political thought in the colonies. Locke's contract theory of government argued that people were endowed with natural rights to life, liberty, and property. When rulers violated these rights, the people had the right—in extreme cases—to overthrow the monarch and change their government.

An Emerging Colonial System

William and Mary oversaw a refinement of the Navigation Acts and the administrative system for regulating the American colonies. The Navigation Act of 1696 required colonial governors to enforce the Navigation Acts, allowed customs officials to use "writs of assistance" (general search warrants that did not have to specify the place to be searched), and ordered that accused violators be tried in admiralty courts, because colonial juries habitually refused to convict their peers. Admiralty cases were decided by judges whom the governors appointed.

Also in 1696, William III created a Board of Trade to take the place of the Lords of Trade. Colonial officials were required to report to the board, which continued to make policy through the remainder of the colonial period. Intended to ensure that the colonies served the mother country's economy, the board oversaw the enforcement of the Navigation Acts and recommended ways to limit manufacturing in the colonies and to encourage their production of raw materials.

From 1696 to 1725 the Board of Trade subjected the colonies to a more efficient royal control. After 1725, however, its energies and activities waned. This was during the reign of the Hanoverian monarchs, George I (1714–1727) and George II (1727–1760), German princes who became English kings by virtue of their descent from James I. At the same time, the cabinet (a kind of executive committee in the Privy Council) emerged as the central agency of administration in England. Robert Walpole, as first minister (1721–1742), deliberately followed a lenient policy toward the colonies, a policy that the philosopher Edmund Burke later called "a wise and salutary neglect."

The Habit of Self-Government

Government within the colonies, like colonial policy, evolved essentially without plan. In broad outline, the governor, council, and assembly in each colony corresponded to the king, lords, and commons of the mother country. However, over the years certain anomalies appeared as colonial governments diverged from trends in England. On the one hand, the governors retained powers and prerogatives that the king had lost in the course of the seventeenth century. On the other hand, the assemblies acquired powers, particularly with respect to appointments, that Parliament had yet to gain.

Powers of the Governors

The crown never vetoed acts of Parliament after 1707, but the colonial governors still held an absolute veto over the assemblies, and the crown could disallow (in effect, veto) colonial legislation on advice of the Board of Trade. With respect to the assembly, the governor still had the power to determine when and where it would meet, to prorogue (adjourn or recess) sessions, and to dissolve the assembly for new elections or to postpone elections indefinitely. In contrast, in the mother country, the crown had pledged to summon Parliament every three years and call elections at least every seven, and could not prorogue sessions.

With respect to the judiciary, in all but the charter colonies, the governor still held the prerogative of creating courts and of naming and dismissing judges, powers explicitly denied the king in England. Over time, however, the colonial assemblies generally made good their claim that courts should be created only by legislative authority, although the crown repeatedly disallowed acts to grant judges life tenure in order to make them more independent.

As chief executive, the colonial governor could appoint and remove officials, command the militia and naval forces, grant pardons, and, as his commission often put it, "execute everything which doth and of right ought to belong to the governor"—which might cover a multitude of powers. Yet as the eighteenth century unfolded, colonial assemblies nibbled away at the governors' power of appointment; at the same time, the authorities in England increasingly drew the control of colonial patronage into their own hands.

Powers of the Assemblies

Unlike the governor and council, appointed by either king or proprietor, the colonial assembly was elected. Whether called the House of Burgesses (Virginia), or Delegates (Maryland), or Representatives (Massachusetts), or simply "assembly," the lower houses were chosen by popular vote in counties or towns or, in South Carolina, parishes. Religious tests for voting were abandoned during the seventeenth century, and the chief restriction left was a property qualification, based on the notion that only men who held a "stake in society" could vote responsibly. Yet the property qualifications generally set low hurdles in the way of potential voters. A greater proportion of the population could vote in the colonies than anywhere else in the world of the eighteenth century. Women, Indians, and blacks were excluded.

By the early eighteenth century, the assemblies, like Parliament, held two important strands of power. First, they held the power of the purse string in their right to vote on taxes and expenditures. Second, they held the power to initiate legislation and not merely, as in the early history of some colonies, the right to act on proposals from the governor and council. Governors were held on a tight leash by the assembly's control of political salaries.

Throughout the eighteenth century, the assemblies expanded their power and influence, sometimes in conflict with the governors and sometimes in harmony with them. Often in the course of routine business, the assemblies passed laws and set precedents, the collective significance of which neither they nor the imperial authorities fully recognized. Once established, however, these laws and practices became fixed principles, parts of the "constitution" of the colonies. Self-government in the colonies became first a habit, then a "right."

Troubled Neighbors

Relations between the colonists and Indians were at times cooperative and at times viciously hostile. Indian-white relations transformed the human and ecological landscape of colonial North America, stirred up colonial politics, and disrupted or destroyed the fabric of Indian culture. Relations between European settlers and North American Indians were themselves agitated by the fluctuating balance of power in Europe. The French and the English each sought to use Indians to their advantage in fighting one another for control of New World territory.

Displacing the Indians

The English invasion of North America would have been a different story, maybe a shorter and simpler one, had the English encountered greater Indian resistance. Instead, they encountered scattered and mutually hostile tribes whom they subjected to a policy of divide and conquer. Whether tempted by trade goods or the promise of alliances, or intimidated by a show of force, most of the Native Americans let matters drift until the English were too entrenched to be pushed back into the sea.

In the mid-1670s, both New England and Virginia went through a time of troubles: in New England an Indian war, and in Virginia a civil war masquerading as an Indian war. For a long time in New England, the Indian fur trade had contributed to peaceful relations, but the growth of settlement and the decline of the animal population were reducing the eastern tribes to relative poverty. Colonial governments encroached on the Indians repeatedly, forcing Indians to acknowledge English laws and customs, including Puritan codes of behavior, and to permit English arbitration of disputes. On occasion, colonial justice imposed fines, whippings, and worse. At the same time, Puritan missionaries reached out to the tribes. By 1675 several thousand converts had settled in special "praying Indian" towns.

The spark that set New England ablaze was struck by the murder of Sassamon, a "praying Indian" who had attended Harvard, later strayed from the faith while serving King Philip of the Wampanoag tribe, and then returned to the Christian fold. When Plymouth tried and executed three Wampanoags for the murder of Sassamon, King Philip's tribesmen attacked.

war was caused by the murder of a "praying Indian"

Thus began "King Philip's War," which the land-hungry leaders of Connecticut and Massachusetts quickly enlarged by assaulting the peaceful Narragansetts at their chief refuge in Rhode Island—a massacre the Rhode Island authorities were helpless to prevent. During 1675, Indian attacks ravaged the interior of Massachusetts and Plymouth, and sporadic fighting continued through 1676. Finally, depleted supplies and the casualty toll wore down Indian resistance. Philip's wife and son were captured and sold into slavery, and Philip himself was tracked down and killed. Sporadic fighting continued until 1678 in New Hampshire and Maine. Indians who survived the slaughter had to submit to colonial authority and accept confinement to ever-dwindling plots of land.

Bacon's Rebellion

The news from New England heightened tensions among settlers in the interior of Virginia and contributed to the tangled events thereafter known as Bacon's Rebellion. Depressed tobacco prices, rising taxes, and crowds of freed servants lusting for Indian lands provided the fuel for the rebellion. The discontent turned to violence in 1675 when a petty squabble between a frontier planter and local Indians on the Potomac River led to a series of killings. Soon a force of Virginia and Maryland militiamen laid siege to the Susquehannocks and murdered in cold blood five chieftains who came out for a parley. The enraged Indian survivors took their revenge on frontier settlements. Scattered attacks continued on down to the James River, where Nathaniel Bacon's overseer was killed.

In 1676 Bacon defied Governor William Berkeley's authority by assuming command of a group of frontier vigilantes. The twenty-nine-year-old Bacon had a talent for trouble and an enthusiasm for punitive expeditions against peaceful Indians. After threatening to kill the governor and the assembly if they tried to intervene, Bacon began preparing for a total war against all Indians. To prevent any governmental interference, he ordered the governor arrested, thus pitting his followers (who were largely servants, small farmers, and even slaves) against the wealthy planters and political leaders of Virginia. Berkeley's forces resisted—but only feebly—and Bacon's men burned Jamestown in 1676. But Bacon could not savor the victory long; he fell ill and died of swamp fever a month later.

Governor Berkeley quickly regained control and subdued the leaderless rebels. A royal commission made treaties of pacification with the remaining Indians, but the fighting had opened new lands to the colonists and confirmed the power of an inner group of established landholders who sat on the Virginia council.

Spanish America in Decline

At the start of the eighteenth century, the Spanish ruled over a huge colonial empire spanning North America. Yet their settlements in the borderlands north of Mexico were a colossal failure when compared to the colonies of the other European powers.

The Spanish failed to create thriving North American colonies for several reasons. Perhaps the most obvious was that the region lacked the gold and silver as well as the large native populations that attracted Spain to Mexico and Peru. In addition, the Spanish were distracted by their need to control the perennial unrest in Mexico among the natives and *mestizos* (people of mixed Indian and European ancestry). Moreover, those Spaniards who led the colonization effort in the borderlands were so preoccupied with military and religious exploitation that they never developed viable settlements with self-sustaining economies. Instead they concentrated on building missions and forts and looking—in vain—for gold. Whereas the French and the English built their Indian policies around trading relationships (including firearms), Spain emphasized conversion to Catholicism and stubbornly adhered to an outdated mercantilism that forbade manufacturing within the colonies and strictly limited trade with the natives.

New France and Louisiana

Permanent French settlement in the New World began soon after the Jamestown landing, far away at Port Royal, Acadia (later Nova Scotia). In 1608, the French explorer Samuel de Champlain founded a settlement at Québec, and from there pushed his explorations into the Great Lakes as far as Lake Huron, and southward to the lake that still bears his name. There, in 1609, he joined a band of Huron and Ottawa allies in a fateful encounter, fired his gun into the ranks of their Iroquois foes, and thereby kindled a hatred that pursued New France to the end. Thenceforth the Iroquois stood as a buffer against any French designs to invade New York and Pennsylvania.

From the Great Lakes, French explorers moved southward. In 1673 Louis Joliet and Père Jacques Marquette ventured into Lake Michigan and then journeyed down the Mississippi. In 1682, the daring explorer La Salle went down the Mississippi River all the way to the Gulf of Mexico and named the area Louisiana after King Louis XIV. Actual settlement of the Louisiana region occurred later, when the French built several fortified towns, the most important of which was New Orleans, founded in 1718.

The French thus enjoyed access to the great water routes that led to the heartland of the continent. In the Illinois region, scattered settlers began farming the fertile soil, and courageous priests established missions at places such as Terre Haute ("high land") and Des Moines ("some monks"). In the dense woods around the Great Lakes, rugged French Canadians became adept trappers and traders. Unlike their English counterparts, many of these hardy *coureurs de bois* (runners of the woods) shed their Old World culture and adopted Indian ways of dress and living. Some of them married Indian women.

Yet French involvement in North America never approached that of the British. In part this was because the French-held areas were less inviting than the English seaboard settlements. Few French settlers were willing to challenge the interior's rugged terrain, fierce winters, and hostile Indians. In addition, the French government impeded colonization by refusing to allow French Protestants (Huguenots) to migrate. New France was to remain Roman Catholic. It also remained largely a wilderness, home to a mobile population of traders, trappers, missionaries—and, mainly, Indians. In 1750, when the English colonists numbered about 1.5 million, the French population was no more than 80,000.

An Iroquois warrior in an eighteenth-century French engraving.

In some ways, however, the French had the edge on the British. Their relatively small numbers forced the French to develop cooperative relationships with the Indians. Unlike the English settlers, the French established trading outposts (to trade European goods for fur) rather than farms, mostly along the St. Lawrence River, on lands not claimed by Indians. Thus they did not have to confront initial hostility. In addition, the French served as effective mediators between rival Great Lakes tribes. This diplomatic role gave them much more local authority and influence than their English counterparts, who disdained such mediation. The heavily outnumbered and disproportionately male French settlers sought to integrate themselves with Indian culture rather than to displace it. They also encouraged the Indians to embrace Catholicism and hate the English. This fraternal bond between the French and the Indians proved to be a source of strength in the wars with the English. French governors could mobilize for action without any worry about quarreling assemblies or ethnic and religious diversity. New France was thus able to survive until 1760, despite the lopsided disparity in numbers between the colonies of the two powers.

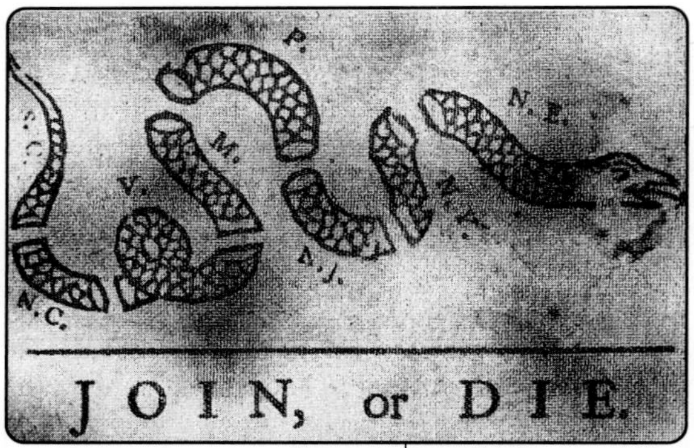

Benjamin Franklin's symbol of the need to unite the colonies against the French in 1754 would become popular again twenty years later, when the colonies faced a different threat.

The Colonial Wars

For most of the seventeenth century, the French and British Empires developed in relative isolation from each other; for most of that century, the homelands remained at peace. After the Restoration, the British and French monarchs cooperated. The Glorious Revolution of 1688, however, abruptly reversed English diplomacy. William III, the new British king from the Dutch Republic, had fought a running conflict against French ambitions in the Netherlands. His ascent to the throne brought England into a Grand Alliance against the French in the War of the League of Augsburg, known in the colonies simply as King William's War (1689–1697). This was the first of four great European and intercolonial wars over the next sixty-four years.

The other three major European wars were: the War of the Spanish Succession (known in the colonies as Queen Anne's War, 1702–1713), the War of the Austrian Succession (known in the colonies as King George's War, 1744–1748), and the Seven Years' War (known in the colonies as the French and Indian War, which lasted nine years in America, 1754–1763). In all except the last, the battles in America were but a sideshow to greater battles in Europe. The alliances shifted from one fight to the next, but Britain and France were pitted against each other every time.

So for much of the century, after the great Indian conflicts of 1676, the colonies were embroiled in wars and rumors of wars. The effect on much of the population was devastating. It is estimated that 900 Boston men (about 2.5 percent of the eligible males) died in the fighting. One result of such carnage was that Boston's population stagnated through the eighteenth century while the population of Philadelphia and New York continued to grow, and Boston had to struggle to support a large population of widows and orphans. Eventually, the economic impact of the four wars left increasing numbers of poor people in New England, and many of them would participate in the popular unrest leading to the Revolutionary movement. Moreover, frequent conflict with France led the English government to incur an enormous debt, establish a huge navy and standing army, and excite a fervent nationalism. These changes would ultimately lead to a reshaping of the relationship between the mother country and its American colonies.

The French and Indian War

Of the four major wars involving the European powers and their New World colonies, the climactic conflict between Britain and France in North America was the French and Indian War. It began in 1754 after enterprising Virginians crossed the Appalachians into the upper Ohio Valley in order to trade with Indians and survey 200,000 acres granted them by King George. This infuriated the French, who saw such activity as a threat to their holdings, and they set about building a string of forts in the disputed area.

When news of the forts reached Williamsburg, the governor sent an emissary to warn off the French. An ambitious young officer in the Virginia militia, Major George Washington, volunteered for the mission. With a few companions, he made his way to Fort LeBoeuf and returned with a polite but firm French refusal to give way. The Virginia governor then sent a small force to erect a fort at the strategic fork where the Allegheny and Monongahela Rivers meet to form the great Ohio. No sooner was it started than a larger French force appeared, ousted the Virginians, and proceeded to build Fort Duquesne on the same strategic site.

Meanwhile, George Washington had been organizing a force of volunteers, and in the spring of 1754 he set out with an advance guard and a few Indian allies. Their clash with a French detachment marked the first bloodshed of a long—and finally decisive—war that reached far beyond America. Washington fell back with his prisoners and hastily constructed a stockade, Fort Necessity, which soon fell under siege by a larger French force. On July 4, 1754, Washington surrendered and was permitted to withdraw with his survivors.

In London the government decided to force a showdown with the French in America, but things went badly at first. In 1755 the British fleet failed to halt the landing of French reinforcements in Canada, but it scored one success in Nova Scotia with the capture of a fort. The British buttressed their hold on the area by expelling most of its French population. Some 5,000 to 7,000 Acadians scattered through the colonies from Maine to Georgia refused to take an oath of allegiance to the British crown. Impoverished and homeless, many of them desperately found their way to French Louisiana, where they became the "Cajuns" (a corruption of "Acadians") whose descendants still preserve elements of the French language along the remote bayous and in many urban centers.

A World War

For two years, war raged along the American Canadian frontier without becoming the cause of war in Europe. In 1756, however, the colonial war merged with what became the Seven Years' War in Europe. There

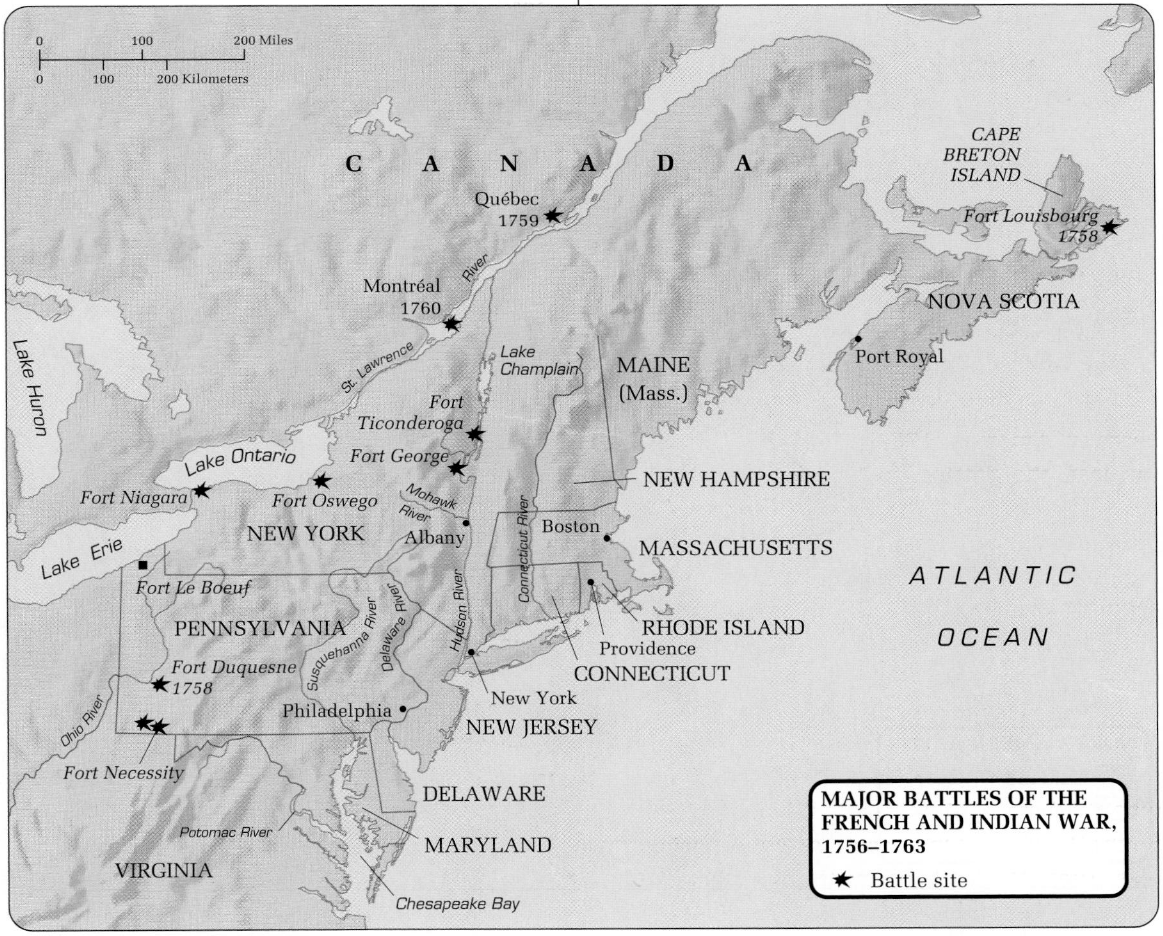

Austria allied with its old enemy, France, to oppose Prussia and its new ally, Britain. British sea power soon began to cut off French reinforcements and supplies to the New World—and the trading goods with which they bought Indian allies. In 1758 the British captured several key French forts. The following year, the decisive battle occurred at Québec.

Commanding the British expedition up the St. Lawrence was General James Wolfe. For two months Wolfe probed the defenses of Québec, seemingly impregnable on its fortified heights. Finally Wolfe's troops found a path up the cliffs behind Québec. During the night of September 12–13, they scrambled up the sheer walls and emerged on the Plains of Abraham, athwart the main roads to the city. There, in a battle more like conventional European warfare than a frontier skirmish, the British forces allowed the French to advance within close range and

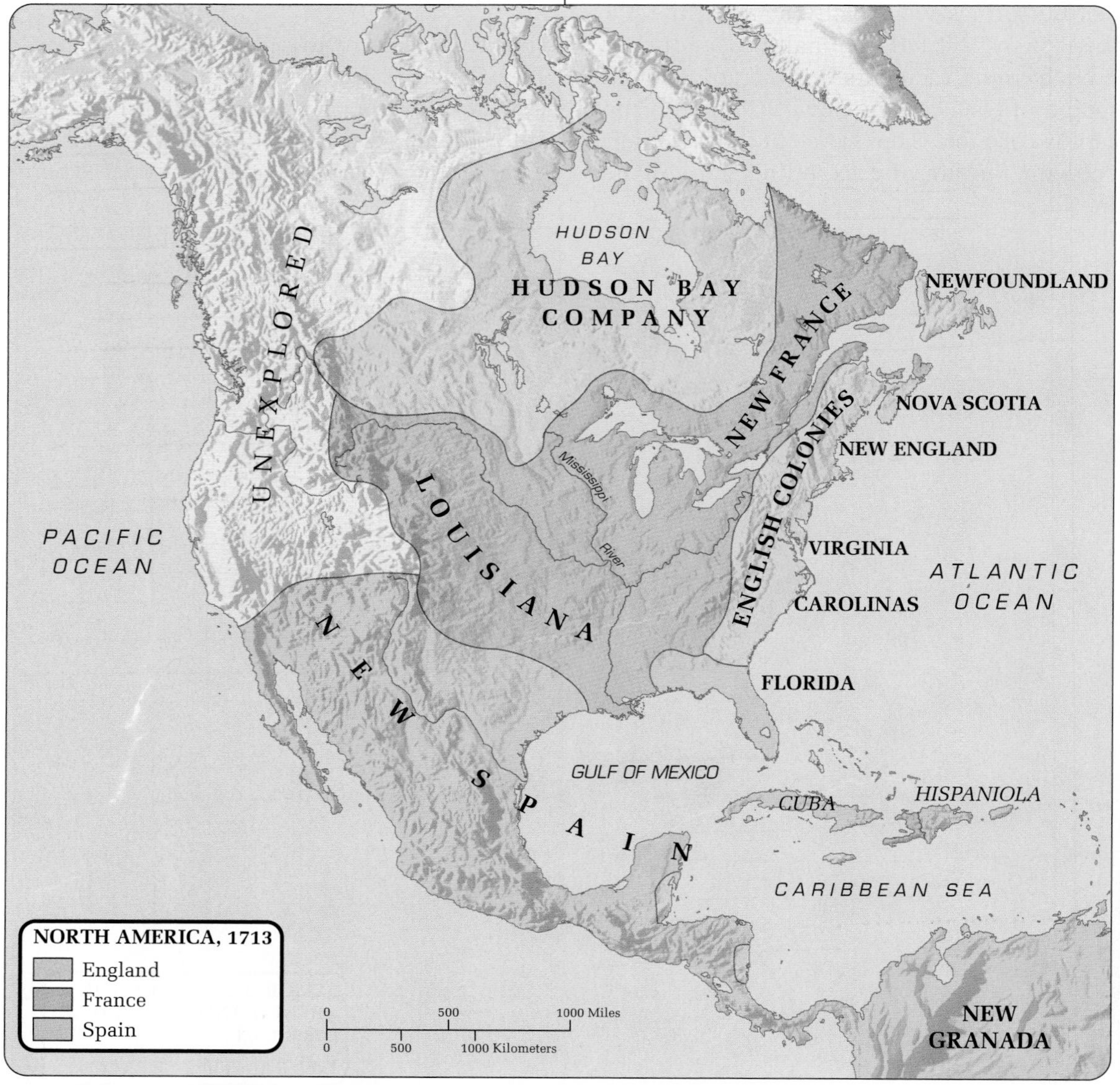

then fired two devastating volleys that ended French power in North America for all time.

The war dragged on until 1763, but the rest was a process of mopping up. In the South, where little significant action had occurred, the Cherokee nation flared into belated hostility, but a force of British regulars and provincials broke Cherokee resistance in 1761. In the North, just as peace was signed, an Ottawa chief, Pontiac, attempted to unify all the Indians of the frontier and launched a series of attacks that were not finally suppressed until the end of 1764, after the backwoods had been ablaze for ten years.

The Peace of Paris

The war culminated in the Peace of Paris of 1763. It ended French power in North America. Britain took all of France's possessions east of the Mississippi River (except

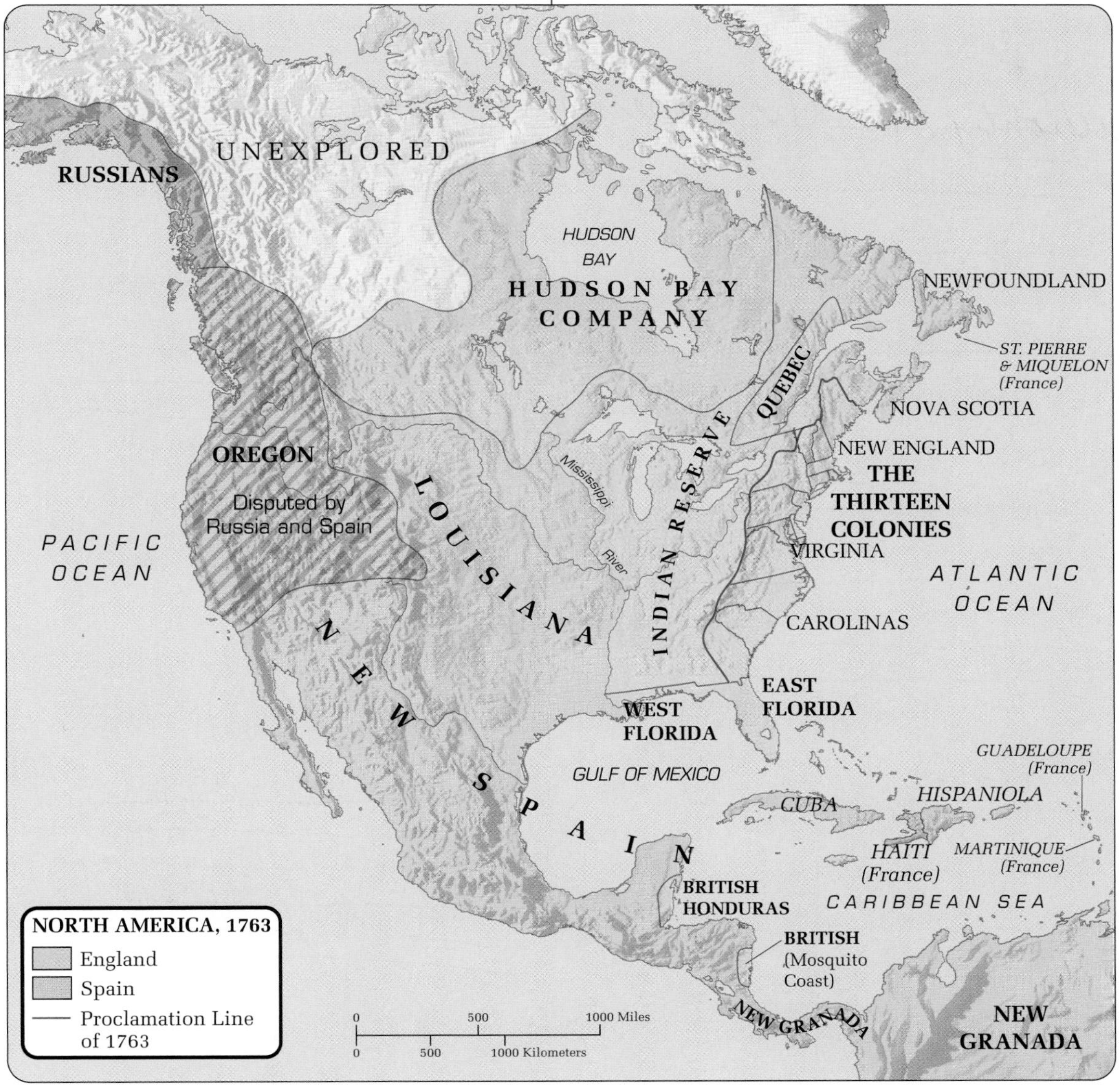

New Orleans), several islands in the West Indies, and all of Spanish Florida. In compensation for the loss of Florida, Spain received Louisiana (New Orleans and all French land west of the Mississippi River) from France. Spain would hold title to Louisiana for nearly four decades, but it would never succeed in erasing the region's French roots. The French-born settlers always outnumbered the Spanish.

The loss of Louisiana left France with no territory on the continent of North America. British power reigned supreme over North America east of the Mississippi. But a fatal irony would pursue the British victory. In gaining Canada, the British government put in motion a train of events that would end twenty years later with the loss of all the rest of British North America. France, humiliated in 1763, thirsted for revenge.

Legal authority over the American colonies

CHAPTER

4

From Empire to Independence

This chapter focuses on

- The changes in British colonial policy after 1763.
- How the Whig ideology shaped the colonial response to changes in British policy.
- The role of Revolutionary leaders, including Samuel Adams, John Dickinson, Thomas Paine, and Thomas Jefferson.

THE *ESSENTIAL AMERICA* ON-LINE TUTOR

www.wwnorton.com/eamerica/ch4

- **Topic: The Declaration of Independence**
  www.wwnorton.com/eamerica/ch2/topic.htm

  The Declaration of Independence is one of the most significant documents in American history, and in light of its influence abroad, in world history. Research the Declaration using primary sources, first-person accounts, historical analyses, and paintings. What basic ideas did the colonists espouse in the Declaration of Independence?

- **Chapter review: On-line quiz and chapter summary**
  www.wwnorton.com/eamerica/ch4/review.htm

- **Chapter resources: Multimedia index**
  www.wwnorton.com/eamerica/ch4/media.htm

Seldom if ever since the days of Queen Elizabeth had England thrilled with such pride as in the closing years of the Great War for Empire. The victories of 1759 had delivered Canada and India to British control. In 1760 the young, vigorous George III ascended to the throne. Three years later, the Peace of Paris confirmed the possession of a great new British empire. The end of the French imperial domain in North America unleashed development of the sprawling region between the Appalachian Mountains and the Mississippi River and from the Gulf of Mexico to Hudson Bay.

The American colonists shared in the euphoria of victory, but the moment of celebration served to mask festering resentments and new problems. Underneath the pride in the growing British Empire was a maturing sense of American nationalism. For over a generation, the colonists had essentially been allowed to govern themselves and were beginning to think and speak of themselves more as Americans than as English or British.

The Heritage of War

In the aftermath of victory, the British ministry faced new problems. How should it manage the defense and governance of the new possessions it had acquired from France and Spain? What should be done with the western American lands? How were the British to pay an unprecedented debt built up during the war and bear the new burdens of greater colonial administration and more far-flung defense? And—the thorniest problem of all, as it turned out—what role should the colonies play in all this? The problems were of a magnitude and complexity to challenge men of the greatest statesmanship and vision, but those qualities were rare among the ministers of George III. The king himself, while a conscientious and deeply religious man, was obstinate and unimaginative, and overly dependent on his advisers and ministers.

In the British politics of the day, Whigs predominated. "Whig" had been the name given to those who had opposed James II, led the Glorious Revolution of 1688, and secured the Protestant Hanoverian succession in 1714. The Whigs were the champions of individual liberty and parliamentary supremacy, but with the passage of time Whiggism had drifted into complacency, and leadership settled upon an aristocratic elite of the Whig gentry. Throughout the 1760s, the king turned first to one and then to another prime minister, and the government grew more and more unstable just as the new problems of empire required forceful solutions. Colonial policy remained marginal to the chief concerns of British politics. The result was first inconsistency and vacillation, followed by stubborn inflexibility.

Western Lands

No sooner was peace arranged in 1763 than events rapidly thrust the problem of America's new western lands upon the British government. The Indians of the Ohio region, unable to believe that their French friends were helpless and fearing the incursion of English settlers, grew restless and receptive to the warnings of Pontiac, chief of the Ottawa. In 1763, the western tribes joined Pontiac's attempt to reopen frontier warfare, and within a few months wiped out every British post in the Ohio region except Fort Detroit and Fort Pitt.

To secure peace on the frontier, the ministers in London postponed further settlement of the western lands. The immediate need was to stop Pontiac's warriors and pacify the Indians. The king signed the Royal Proclamation of 1763, which drew an imaginary line along the crest of the Appalachians beyond which settlers were forbidden to go. It also established the new British colonies of Quebec and East and West Florida.

But Pontiac did not agree to peace until 1766, and Britain's Proclamation Line did not remain intact for long. During the turbulent decade that followed, hardy pioneers pushed over the Appalachian ridges. By 1770 the town of Pittsburgh had twenty log houses. Four years later, Daniel Boone and a party of settlers cut the Wilderness Road through the Cumberland Gap in southwestern Virginia to the Kentucky River.

Grenville's Colonial Policy

As the Proclamation of 1763 was being drafted, a new ministry in London began to grapple with the problems of imperial finances. The new chief minister, George Grenville, first lord of the Treasury, was much like the king: industrious, honest, meticulous, and unaware of the complexities of colonial relations. Grenville assumed the need for British redcoats to defend the frontier, although the colonies had been left mostly to their own devices before 1754. He also wanted to keep a large army in America to avoid a rapid demobilization that would force many influential officers to retire and thereby provoke political criticism at home. But on top of an already staggering debt, he faced sharply rising costs for American defense.

Customs and Currency

Because there was a heavy tax burden at home and a much lighter one in the colonies, Grenville reasoned that the Americans must share the cost of their own defense. He also learned that the American customs service was amazingly inefficient. Evasion and corruption were rampant. Grenville thus issued stern orders to colonial officials and dipatched the navy to patrol the coasts for smugglers. Parliament agreed to set up a new maritime or vice-admiralty court in Halifax with jurisdiction over all the colonies. Decisions would be made by judges appointed by the crown rather than by juries of colonists sympathetic to smugglers. The old habits of salutary neglect in the enforcement of the Navigation Acts were coming to an end, causing no little annoyance to American shippers.

The old Molasses Act of 1733 had set a sixpence-per-gallon duty on molasses in order to prevent trade with the French sugar islands. New England merchants evaded this duty, smuggling in French molasses to make rum. Recognizing that the duty, if enforced, would ruin the business of the rum distillers, Grenville put through the Sugar Act (1764), which cut the duty in half. This, he believed, would reduce the temptation to smuggle or to bribe customs officers. In addition, the Sugar Act levied new duties on imports into the colonies of foreign textiles, wines, coffee, indigo, and sugar. The act, Grenville estimated, would bring in enough revenue to help defray "the necessary expenses of defending, protecting, and securing" the colonies. For the first time, Parliament had adopted customs duties designed to raise revenues in the colonies rather than just to regulate trade.

Another measure in Grenville's new colonial program that had an important impact on the colonies was the Currency Act of 1764. The colonies faced a chronic shortage of hard money, which kept going out to pay debts in England. To meet the shortage, they issued their own paper money. British creditors, however, feared receiving payment in such a depreciated currency. To alleviate their fears, Parliament in 1751 had forbidden the New England colonies to make their currency legal tender. Now Grenville extended the prohibition to all the colonies. The value of existing paper money soon plummeted, since nobody was obligated to accept it in payment of debts, even within the colonies. The deflationary impact of the Currency Act, combined with new duties and stricter enforcement, delivered a severe shock to a colonial economy already suffering a postwar slump.

The Stamp Act

Grenville's new design entailed two more key provisions. Because the Sugar Act would defray only part of the cost of maintaining the 10,000 British troops to be stationed along the western frontier, he proposed another measure to raise money in America, a stamp tax. Enacted on February 13, 1765, the Stamp Act created revenue stamps that were to be attached to printed matter and legal documents of all kinds: newspapers, pamphlets, almanacs, bonds, leases, deeds, licenses, insurance policies, ship clearances, college diplomas, even dice and playing cards. The requirement would go into effect on November 1, 1765.

In March 1765 Grenville put through the final measure of his new program, the Quartering Act. It required the colonies to supply British troops with provisions and to provide them barracks or submit to their use of inns and vacant buildings. It applied to all colonies, but affected mainly New York, headquarters of the British forces.

The Ideological Response

The cumulative effect of Grenville's measures raised colonial suspicions to a fever pitch. Unwittingly, the king's chief minister had stirred up a storm of protest and set in motion a profound reassessment of America's relation to England. Grenville had loosed upon the colonies the very engines of tyranny from which Parliament had rescued England in the seventeenth century. A standing army encouraged despots, and now several thousand British soldiers remained in the colonies. Among fundamental English rights were trial by jury and the presumption of innocence, but the new vice-admiralty courts excluded juries and put the burden of proof on the defendant. Most important, the English had the right to be taxed only by their elected representatives. Parliament claimed that privilege in England, and the colonial assemblies had long exercised it in America. Now, with the Stamp Act, Parliament was usurping the assemblies' power of the purse strings.

Protest in the Colonies

The Stamp Act became the chief target of colonial protest. It affected the most articulate elements in the community: merchants, planters, lawyers, printer-editors—all strategically placed to influence public opinion. In a flood of colonial pamphlets, speeches, and resolutions, debate on the Stamp Tax turned mainly on the point expressed in a slogan familiar to all Americans: "no taxation without representation."

Through the spring and summer of 1765, popular resentment against Grenville boiled over into mass meetings, parades, bonfires, and other demonstrations. To be sure, only a minority engaged in such public protests. They included farmers, laborers, dock workers, and seamen. But lawyers, editors, and merchants took the lead or lent support. Calling themselves Sons of Liberty, they met underneath "Liberty Trees"—in Boston a great elm, in Charleston a live oak.

The widespread protests encouraged colonial unity, as Americans discovered that they had more in common with each other than with London. In May 1765, the Virginia House of Burgesses struck the first blow against the Stamp Act in the Virginia Resolves, a series of resolutions inspired by young Patrick Henry. Virginians, the burgesses declared, were entitled to all English rights, and the English could be taxed only by their own representatives. Virginians, moreover, had always been governed by laws passed with their own consent. Newspapers spread the resolutions throughout the colonies, along with even more radical statements that were kept out of the final version, and other assemblies hastened to

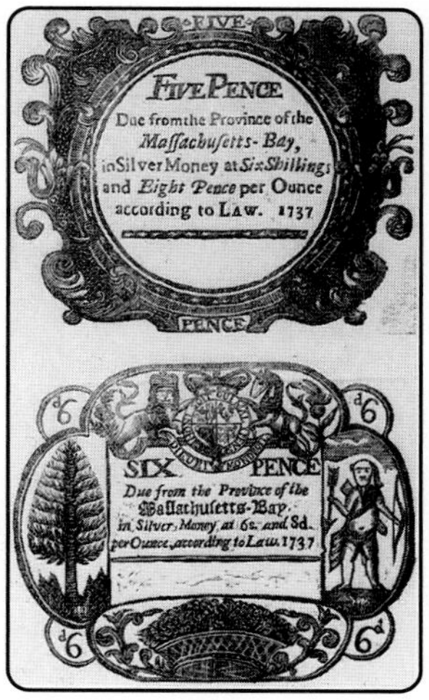

Two examples of British stamps.

copy Virginia's example. In June 1765, the Massachusetts House of Representatives invited the various assemblies to send delegates to confer in New York on appeals for relief from the king and Parliament.

Nine colonial assemblies responded, and on October 7 the Stamp Act Congress of twenty-seven delegates convened and issued expressions of colonial sentiment: a Declaration of the Rights and Grievances of the Colonies, a petition to the king for relief, and a petition to Parliament for repeal of the Stamp Act. The delegates argued that Parliament might have powers to legislate for the regulation of colonial trade, but it had no right to levy taxes, which were a gift granted by the people through their representatives.

By November 1, its effective date, the Stamp Act was a dead letter. Business went on without the stamps. Newspapers appeared with the skull and crossbones where the stamp belonged. Colonial rebels were beginning to sense their power. After passage of the Sugar Act, a movement had begun to boycott British goods. Now colonists adopted nonimportation agreements to exert pressure on British merchants. Americans knew they had become a major market for British products. By shutting off imports they could exercise real leverage.

Repeal of the Stamp Act

Colonial resistance had scarcely begun before Grenville's ministry was turned out of office, dismissed not because of the turmoil in America but because of tensions with the king over the distribution of lucrative government offices. In July 1765 the king installed a new minister, the marquis of Rockingham, leader of the "Rockingham Whigs," who sympathized with the colonists' views. Rockingham resolved to end the quarrel with America by repealing the Stamp Act. When Parliament assembled early in 1766, Parliamentary leader William Pitt demanded that the Stamp Act be repealed "absolutely, totally, and immediately," but he urged that Britain's authority over the colonies "be asserted in as strong terms as possible," except on the point of taxation. In March 1766 Parliament passed the repeal, but at the same time it passed the Declaratory Act, which asserted the full power of Parliament to make laws binding the colonies "in all cases whatsoever." It was a cunning evasion that made no concession with regard to taxes but made no mention of them either. Amid the rejoicing and relief on both sides of the Atlantic there were no omens that the quarrel would be reopened within a year.

Fanning the Flames

Meanwhile, the king continued to have his ministers play musical chairs. Rockingham fell because he lost the confidence of the king, and his own administration suffered a paralyzing fragmentation. The king invited William Pitt to form a ministry that included the major factions of Parliament. Soon thereafter, however, Pitt slipped over the fine line between genius and madness, and he resigned in 1768. For a time in 1767 the guiding force in the ministry was Charles Townshend, chancellor of the Exchequer, whose "abilities were superior to those of all men," according to Horace Walpole, "and his judgment below that of any man." Townshend took advantage of Pitt's absence to reopen the question of colonial taxation and seized upon the notion that "external" taxes on exports and imports were tolerable to the colonies—not that he believed it for a moment.

The Townshend Acts

In May and June 1767 Townshend put his plan through the House of Commons, and in September he died, leaving a bitter legacy: the Townshend Acts. Their first objective was to bring the New York assembly to its senses. That body had defied the Quartering Act and refused to provide beds or supplies for the king's troops. Parliament, at Townshend's behest, suspended all acts of the New York assembly until it yielded. New York finally caved in, inadvertently confirming the British suspicion that too much indulgence had encouraged colonial bad manners. Townshend followed up with the Revenue Act of 1767, which levied duties ("external taxes") on colonial imports of glass, lead, paints, paper, and tea. Next, he set up a Board of Customs Commissioners at Boston, the colonial headquarters of smuggling. Finally, he reorganized the vice-admiralty courts, providing four in the continental colonies—at Halifax, Boston, Philadelphia, and Charleston.

The Townshend duties did increase government revenues, but the intangible costs were greater. The duties taxed goods exported from England, indirectly hurting British manufacturers, and they had to be collected in colonial ports, increasing collection costs. More important, the new taxes accelerated colonial resistance. The Revenue Act of 1767 posed a more severe threat to colonial assemblies than Grenville's taxes, for Townshend proposed to apply the revenues to pay the salaries of governors and other officers and thereby release them from financial dependence on the assemblies.

Dickinson's *Letters*

The Townshend Acts provoked the colonists to boycott British goods and to develop their own manufactures. Once again the colonial press spewed out expressions of protest, most notably the essays of John Dickinson, a Philadelphia lawyer. Late in 1767 his twelve *Letters of a Pennsylvania Farmer* (as he chose to style himself) began to appear in the *Pennsylvania Chronicle*, from which they were copied in other papers and in pamphlet form. He argued that Parliament might regulate commerce and collect duties incidental to that purpose, but it had no right to levy taxes for revenue, whether they were internal or external taxes. Dickinson used moderate language throughout. The colonists, he declared, should "speak at the same time the language of affliction and veneration" toward the mother country.

Samuel Adams and the Sons of Liberty

But the affliction grew and the veneration waned. British ministers could neither conciliate moderates like Dickinson nor cope with firebrands like Boston's Samuel Adams, who was now emerging as the supreme genius of revolutionary agitation. Adams insisted that Parliament had no right to legislate for the colonies, that Massachusetts must return to the spirit of its Puritan founders and defend itself froma new conspiracy against its liberties. Adams whipped up the Sons of Liberty, writing incendiary newspaper articles and letters and organizing protests in the Boston pubs, town meetings, and the provincial assembly. The royal governor called him "the most dangerous man in Massachusetts." Early in 1768 Adams and Boston lawyer James Otis formulated another Massachusetts circular letter, which the assembly dispatched to the other colonies. The letter restated the illegality of parliamentary taxation, warned that the new duties would be used to pay colonial officials, and invited the other colonies to join in a boycott of British goods.

The Boston Massacre

In Boston roving gangs enforced the boycott of goods from England, intimidating Tory merchants and their customers. This led the governor to appeal for military support, and two British regiments sailed from Halifax. The presence of soldiers in Boston had always been a source of provocation, but now tensions boiled over. On March 5, 1770, in the square before the customs house, a mob

Paul Revere's partisan engraving of the Boston Massacre.

of toughs began heaving taunts, snowballs, and oyster shells at the British sentry, whose call for help brought reinforcements. Then somebody rang the town firebell, drawing a larger crowd to the scene. At its head, or so the story goes, was Crispus Attucks, a runaway mulatto slave. The riotous crowd began striking at the British troops with sticks and knocked one soldier down. He rose to his feet and fired into the crowd. Others fired too, and when the smoke cleared, five people lay dead or dying and eight more were wounded.

The cause of colonial resistance now had its first martyrs, and the first to die was Crispus Attucks. Governor Thomas Hutchinson moved the soldiers out of town to avoid another incident. The troops involved in the shooting were indicted for murder but were defended by John Adams, who portrayed them as the victims of circumstance, provoked, he said, by a "motley rabble of saucy boys, negroes and mulattoes, Irish teagues and outlandish Jack tars." All were acquitted except two, who were convicted of manslaughter and branded on their thumbs.

The Boston Massacre sent shock waves through the colonies. The incident, remembered one Bostonian, "created a resentment which emboldened the timid" and "determined the wavering." But late in April 1770 news arrived that Parliament had repealed all the Townshend duties save one. The cabinet, by a vote of five to four, had advised keeping the tea tax as a token of parliamentary authority. Colonial diehards insisted that pressure should be kept on British merchants until Parliament gave in altogether, but the nonimportation movement soon faded. Parliament, after all, had given up the substance of the taxes, with one exception, and much of the colonists' tea was smuggled in from Holland anyway.

For two years thereafter, discontent simmered down, and suspicions began to fade on both sides of the ocean. The Stamp Act was gone, as were all the Townshend duties, except that on tea. Yet most of the hated innovations remained in effect: the Sugar Act, the Currency Act, the Quartering Act, the vice-admiralty courts, the Board of Customs Commissioners. The redcoats had left Boston, but they remained nearby, and the British navy still patrolled the coast. Each remained a source of irritation and the cause of occasional incidents. Colonial patriots were primed to resist new tyrannies.

Discontent on the Frontier

Many colonists showed no interest in the disputes over British regulatory policies raging along the seaboard. Parts of the backcountry had stirred with quarrels that had nothing to do with the Stamp and Townshend Acts. Rival land claims to the east of Lake Champlain pitted New York against New Hampshire, and the Green Mountain Boys led by Ethan Allen against both. Eventually the residents of the area would simply create their own state of Vermont in 1777, although it was not recognized as a member of the Union until 1791.

In Pennsylvania a group of frontier ruffians took the law into their own hands. Outraged at the lack of frontier protection provided by the Quaker-influenced assembly during Pontiac's rebellion, a group called the "Paxton Boys" took revenge by massacring peaceful Conestoga Indians in Lancaster County, then threatened the so-called Moravian Indians, a group of Moravian converts near Bethlehem. When the Moravian Indians took refuge in Philadelphia, some 1,500 Paxton Boys marched on the capital, where Benjamin Franklin talked them into returning home by promising that more protection would be forthcoming.

Farther south, South Carolina frontier folk voiced similar complaints about the lack of settled government and the need for protection against horse thieves, cattle rustlers, and Indians. They organized societies called "Regulators" to administer vigilante justice in the region and refused to pay taxes until they gained effective government. In 1769 the assembly finally set up six new circuit courts in the region and revised the taxes, but it still did not respond to the backcountry's demand for representation in the legislature.

In North Carolina the protest was less over the lack of government than over the abuses and extortion inflicted by government appointees from the eastern part of the colony. Farmers felt especially oppressed at the government's refusal either to issue paper money or to accept produce in payment of taxes, and in 1766 they organized to resist. Efforts of these Regulators to stop seizures of property and other court proceedings led to more disorders and a new law that made the rioters guilty of treason. In the spring of 1771 the royal governor and 1,200 militiamen defeated some 2,000 ill-organized Regulators in the Battle of Alamance. The pitched battle illustrated the growing tensions between backcountry settlers and the wealthy planters in the eastern part of the colony, tensions that would erupt again during and after the Revolution.

These internal disputes and revolts within the colonies illustrate the fractious diversity of opinion and outlook evident among Americans on the eve of the Revolution. Colonists were of many minds about many things, including British rule. The disputatious frontier in colonial America also helped convince British authorities that the colonies were inherently unstable and that they required even firmer oversight, even to the extent of using military force to ensure civil stability.

A Worsening Crisis

Two events in June 1772 shattered the period of calm in the quarrels with the mother country. Near Providence, Rhode Island, a British schooner, the *Gaspee,* patrolling for smugglers, accidentally ran aground. Under cover of darkness a crowd from the town boarded the ship, removed the crew, and set fire to the vessel. Four days after the burning, Massachusetts' governor, Thomas Hutchinson, told the provincial assembly that his salary thenceforth would come out of the customs revenues. Superior Court judges would be paid from the same source and would thereby no longer be dependent on the assembly for their income. The assembly feared that this portended "a despotic administration of government."

To keep the pot simmering, in November 1772 Sam Adams convinced the Boston Town Meeting to form a Committee of Correspondence, which issued a statement of rights and grievances and invited other towns to do the same. Committees of Correspondence sprang up in Massachusetts and other colonies. In March 1773 the Virginia assembly proposed the formation of such committees on an intercolonial basis, and a network of the committees spread across the colonies, mobilizing public opinion and fanning colonial resentments.

The Boston Tea Party

Lord North, who had replaced Townshend as chancellor of the Exchequer, soon brought colonial resentment from a simmer to a boil. In May 1773 he contrived a scheme to bail out the foundering East India Company. The company had in its British warehouses some 17 million pounds of unsold tea. Under the Tea Act of 1773, the government would refund the British duty of twelvepence per pound on all tea shipped to the colonies and collect only the existing threepence duty payable at the colonial port. By this arrangement, colonists could get tea more cheaply than the English could, for less even than the black market Dutch tea. North, however, miscalculated in assuming that price alone would govern colonial reaction. And he erred even worse by permitting the East India Company to serve retailers directly through its own agents or consignees, bypassing the colonial wholesalers who had handled it before. Once that kind of monopoly was established, colonial merchants began to wonder, how soon would the precedent apply to other commodities?

The Committees of Correspondence, backed by colonial merchants, alerted people to the new danger. The government, they reported, was trying to purchase their loyalty and passivity with cheap tea. Before the end of the year, large shipments of tea went out to major colonial ports. In Boston, Governor Hutchinson and Sam Adams engaged in a test of will. The tea ships' captains, alarmed by the radical opposition, proposed to turn back, but Hutchinson refused permission until the tea was landed and the duty paid. On December 16, 1773, a group of colonial Patriots disguised themselves as Mohawk Indians, boarded the three ships, and threw the 342 chests of tea overboard—cheered on by a crowd along the shore.

Americans Throwing the Cargoes of the Tea Ships into the River, at Boston (1773).

British authorities were now convinced that the very existence of the empire was at stake. "The colonists must either submit or triumph," George III wrote to Lord North, and North hastened to make the king's judgment a self-fulfilling prophecy.

The Coercive Acts

In April 1774 Parliament enacted harsh measures designed by North to discipline Boston. The Boston Port Act closed the port from June 1, 1774, until the lost tea was paid for. A new Quartering Act directed local authorities to provide lodging for British soldiers, in private homes if necessary. The Massachusetts Government Act made the colony's council and law-enforcement officers all appointive, rather than elected; sheriffs would select jurors; no town meeting could be held without the governor's consent, except for the annual election of town officers.

Designed to isolate Boston and make an example of the colony, the actions instead cemented colonial unity and emboldened resistance. If these "Intolerable Acts," as the colonists labeled the Coercive Acts, were not resisted, they would eventually be applied to the other colonies.

Colonists throughout America rallied to the cause of besieged Boston, taking up collections and sending provisions. When the Virginia assembly met in May 1774, a young member of the Committee of Correspondence, Thomas Jefferson, proposed to set aside June 1, the effective date of the Boston Port Act, as a day of fasting and prayer in Virginia. The irate colonial governor thereupon dissolved the assembly, whose members retired to a nearby tavern and drew up a resolution for a "Continental Congress" to make representations on behalf of all the colonies. Similar calls were coming from Providence, New York, Philadelphia, and elsewhere, and in June the Massachusetts assembly suggested a September meeting in Philadelphia. Shortly before George Washington left to represent Virginia at the meeting, he wrote to a friend that "the crisis is arrived when we must assert our rights, or submit to every imposition, that can be heaped upon us, till custom and use shall make us as tame and abject slaves, as the blacks we rule over with such arbitrary sway."

The Continental Congress

On September 5, 1774, the First Continental Congress assembled in Philadelphia. The fifty-five delegates represented twelve continental colonies, all but Georgia, Quebec, Nova Scotia, and the Floridas. The Congress endorsed the radical Suffolk Resolves, resolutions that declared the Intolerable Acts null and void, urged Massachusetts to arm for defense, and called for economic sanctions against British commerce. The Congress also adopted a Declaration of American Rights, which denied Parliament's authority with respect to internal colonial affairs. In addition, the Congress sent the king a petition for relief and issued addresses to the people of Great Britain and the colonies.

Finally, the Congress adopted the Continental Association of 1774, which recommended that every county, town, and city form committees to enforce a boycott on all British goods. These committees would become the organizational and communications network for the Revolutionary movement, connecting every locality to the leadership. The Continental Association also included provisions for the nonimportation of British goods and the nonexportation of American goods to Britain.

British critics of the American actions reminded the colonists that Parliament had absolute sovereignty. Power could not be shared. Parliament could not relinquish its claim to authority in part without abandoning it altogether. So Parliament declared Massachusetts in rebellion, forbade the New England colonies to trade with any nation outside the empire, and excluded New Englanders from the North Atlantic fisheries. Lord North's Conciliatory Resolution, adopted February 27, 1775, was as far as they would go. Under its terms, Parliament would levy taxes only to regulate trade and would grant to each colony the duties collected within its boundaries, provided the colonies would contribute voluntarily to a quota for defense of the empire. It was a formula not for peace but for new quarrels.

Forging Fetters for the Americans. A cartoon attacking British parliamentary measures of 1775–1776.

Shifting Authority

Events were already moving beyond conciliation. All through late 1774 and early 1775, the Patriot defenders of American rights were seizing the initiative. The uncertain and unorganized Loyalists (also called Tories) were put on the defensive. The Continental Congress urged each colony to mobilize its militia. Royal and proprietary officials were losing control as provincial congresses assumed authority and colonial militias organized and gathered arms and gunpowder. Still, British military officers remained smugly confident. Major John Pitcairn wrote home from Boston in March: "I am satisfied that one active campaign, a smart action, and burning two or three of their towns, will set everything to rights."

Lexington and Concord

Pitcairn soon had his chance. On April 14, 1775, General Thomas Gage, the new royal governor of Massachusetts, received orders to suppress the "open rebellion." Gage decided to seize Sam Adams and John Hancock in Lexington and to destroy the militia's supply depot at Concord, about twenty miles away from his Boston headquarters. On the night of April 18, Lieutenant-Colonel Francis Smith and Major Pitcairn gathered 700 men on Boston Common and set out to Concord by way of Lexington. But local Patriots got wind of the plan, and Boston's Committee of Safety sent silversmith Paul Revere and tanner William Dawes by separate routes on their famous ride to spread the alarm. Revere reached Lexington about midnight and alerted Hancock and Adams. Joined by Dawes and Dr. Samuel Prescott, who had been visiting in Lexington, he rode on toward Concord. A British patrol intercepted the trio, but Prescott slipped through with the warning.

The Retreat. An American cartoon showing the retreat of British forces at Lexington and Concord, April 1775.

At dawn on April 19, the British advance guard found Captain John Parker and about seventy Minute Men lined up on the dewy Lexington village green. Parker apparently intended only a silent protest, but Pitcairn rode onto the green, swung his sword, and brusquely yelled, "Disperse, you damned rebels! You dogs, run!" The Americans already had begun backing away when someone fired a single pistol shot, whereupon the British soldiers loosed a volley into the Minute Men and then charged them with bayonets, leaving eight dead and ten wounded.

The British officers hastily reformed their men and proceeded to Concord. There the Americans had already carried off most of their valuable supplies, but the British destroyed what they could. In the meantime, enraged Patriots were swarming over the countryside, eager to wreak vengeance on the hated British troops. At Concord's North Bridge, the growing American forces inflicted fourteen casualties on a British platoon, and about noon the exhausted redcoats began marching back to Boston.

By then, however, the road back had turned into a gauntlet of death as the embattled colonists from "every Middlesex village and farm" sniped at the redcoats from behind stone walls, trees, barns, and farmhouses, all the way back to Charlestown peninsula. By nightfall the British survivors were safe under the protection of the fleet and army at Boston, having suffered over 250 killed or wounded; the Americans had lost nearly a hundred. A British general reported to London that the rebels, though untrained, had earned his respect: "Whoever looks upon them as an irregular mob will find himself much mistaken."

The Spreading Conflict

The war had started. When the Second Continental Congress convened at Philadelphia on May 10, 1775, British-held Boston was under siege by the Massachusetts militia.

On the very day that Congress met, a force of Green Mountain Boys under Ethan Allen of Vermont and Massachusetts volunteers under Benedict Arnold of Connecticut captured strategic Fort Ticonderoga in New York. In a prodigious feat of daring energy, the Americans then managed to transport sixty captured British cannon down rivers and over ridges to support the siege of Boston.

The Continental Congress, with no legal authority and no resources, met amid reports of spreading warfare and had little choice but to assume the role of Revolutionary government. The Congress accepted a request that it "adopt" the motley army gathered around Boston, and on June 15 it named George Washington commander-in-chief. He accepted on the condition that he receive no pay.

On June 17, the very day that Washington was commissioned, the colonial rebels and British troops engaged in their first major fight, the Battle of Bunker Hill. While the Congress deliberated, both American and British forces in and around Boston had increased in strength. Militiamen from Rhode Island, Connecticut, and New Hampshire joined in the siege. British reinforcements included three major-generals—Sir William Howe, Sir Henry Clinton, and John Burgoyne. On the day before the battle, Americans began to fortify the high ground of Charlestown peninsula, overlooking Boston. Breed's Hill was the battle location, nearer to Boston than Bunker Hill, the site first chosen (and the source of the battle's erroneous name).

The rebels were spoiling for a fight. As Joseph Warren, a dapper Boston physician, put it, "The British say we won't fight; by heavens, I hope I shall die up to my knees in blood!" He soon got his wish. With civilians looking on from rooftops and church steeples, Gage ordered a conventional frontal assault in the blistering heat, with 2,200 British troops moving in tight formation through tall grass. The Americans watched from behind hastily built earthworks as the waves of brightly uniformed British troops advanced up the hill. Ordered not to fire until they could "see the whites of their eyes," the militiamen waited until the attackers came within fifteen to twenty paces, then loosed a shattering volley. Through the cloud of oily smoke, the Americans could see fallen bodies "as thick as sheep in a fold." The militiamen cheered as they watched the greatest soldiers in the world retreating in panic.

Within a half hour, however, the British had re-formed and attacked again. Another sheet of flame and lead greeted them, and the vaunted redcoats retreated a second time. Still, the proud British generals were determined not to be humiliated by such ragtag rustics. On the third attempt, when the colonials began to run out of gunpowder and were forced to throw stones, a bayonet charge ousted them. The British took the high ground, but at the cost of 1,054 casualties. Colonial losses were about 400. "A dear bought victory," recorded General Clinton; "another such would have ruined us."

The Battle of Bunker Hill had two profound effects. First, the high number of British casualties made the English generals more cautious in subsequent encounters with the Continental Army. Second, Congress recommended after the battle that all able-bodied men enlist in the militia. This tended to divide the male population into Patriot and Loyalist camps. A middle ground was no longer tenable.

While Boston remained under siege, the Continental Congress sought a possible compromise. On July 5 and 6, 1775, the delegates issued two major documents: an appeal to the king, thereafter known as the Olive Branch Petition, and a Declaration of the Causes and Necessity of Taking Up Arms. The Olive Branch Petition, written by John Dickinson, professed continued loyalty to George III and begged him to restrain further hostilities pending a reconciliation. The Declaration, also largely Dickinson's work, rejected independence but affirmed the colonists' purpose to fight for their rights rather than submit to slavery. Such efforts failed to impress the outraged king. On August 22 he declared the colonists "as open and avowed enemies."

As the fighting spread north into Canada and south into Virginia and the Carolinas, the Continental Congress assumed the functions of government. It appointed commissioners to negotiate peace treaties with Indian tribes, organized a Post Office Department with Benjamin Franklin as postmaster-general, and authorized formation of a navy and a marine corps. A committee began to explore the possibility of gaining foreign military alliances. Still, the delegates continued to hold back from the seeming abyss of formal independence. Yet through late 1775 and early 1776, word came of one British action after another that proclaimed rebellion and war. In December 1775 Parliament declared the colonies closed to all commerce, and the king began hiring German soldiers. Eventually almost 30,000 Germans served, about 17,000 of them from the region of Hesse-Kassel, and "Hessian" became the epithet applied to them all.

When Washington arrived outside of Boston to take charge of the American forces after the Battle of Bunker Hill, the military situation was stalemated, and so it remained through the winter, until early March 1776. At that time, American forces occupied Dorchester Heights to the south of Boston, bringing the city under threat of bombardment with cannon and mortars. General William Howe, who had replaced Gage as British commander, retreated with his forces by water to Halifax, Nova Scotia. The last British troops, along with fearful American Loyalists, embarked from Boston on March 17, 1776. By that time, British power had collapsed nearly everywhere, and the British faced not the suppression of a rebellion but the reconquest of a continent.

Common Sense

In early 1776 Thomas Paine's pamphlet *Common Sense* was published anonymously in Philadelphia, transforming the revolutionary controversy. Born of Quaker parents, Paine had distinguished himself in England chiefly as a drifter, a failure in marriage and business. At age thirty-seven, he sailed for America with the purpose of setting up a school for young ladies. When that did not work out, he moved into the political controversy as a freelance writer and, with *Common Sense*, proved himself the consummate revolutionary rhetorician. Until his pamphlet appeared, the squabble had been mainly with Parliament, but Paine directly attacked allegiance to the monarchy, the last frayed connection to Britain. The common sense of the matter, to Paine, was that King George III and his advisers bore the responsibility for the malevolence toward the colonies. Americans should consult their own interests, abandon George III, and declare their independence: "The blood of the slain, the weeping voice of nature cries, 'TIS TIME TO PART."

Independence

Within three months, more than 100,000 copies of Paine's pamphlet were in circulation, an enormous number for the time. One by one the provincial governments authorized their delegates in the Continental Congress to take the final step. On June 7, 1776, Richard Henry Lee of Virginia moved "that these United Colonies are, and of right ought to be, free and independent states." Sam Adams immediately endorsed the idea, but others balked. South Carolina and Pennsylvania initially opposed severing ties with England. After feverish lobbying by radical Patriots, however, the dissenters changed their minds, and the resolution passed on July 2. The more memorable date, however, became July 4, 1776, when Congress adopted the Declaration of Independence.

Jefferson's Declaration

Although Jefferson is often called the "author" of the Declaration of Independence, he is more accurately termed its draftsman. In June 1776 the Continental Congress appointed a committee of five men—Jefferson, Benjamin Franklin, John Adams, Robert Livingston of New York, and Roger Sherman of Connecticut—to explain the reasons for colonial discontent and to provide a rationale for independence. The group asked Adams and Jefferson to produce a first draft, whereupon Adams deferred to Jefferson because of the thirty-three-year-old Virginian's reputation as an eloquent writer.

During two days in mid-June 1776, Jefferson wrote the first statement of American grievances and principles. Jefferson drew primarily upon two sources: his own draft preamble to the Virginia Constitution written a few weeks earlier, and George Mason's draft of Virginia's Declaration of Rights, which appeared in Philadelphia newspapers in mid-June. It was Mason's text that stimulated many of Jefferson's most famous phrases.

The Continental Congress made eighty-six changes in Jefferson's declaration, including shortening its overall length by one-fourth. Jefferson said his colleagues had "mangled" the document. But overall the legislative editing improved the declaration, making it more concise, accurate, and coherent—and, as a result, more powerful.

The Declaration of Independence constitutes an eloquent restatement of John Locke's contract theory of government—the theory, in Jefferson's words, that governments derive "their just Powers from the consent of the people," who are entitled to "alter or abolish" those that deny their "unalienable rights" to "life, Liberty, and the pursuit of Happiness." The appeal was no longer simply to "the rights of Englishmen" but to the broader "laws of Nature and Nature's God." The document set forth "a history of repeated injuries and usurpations, all having in direct object the establishment of an absolute Tyranny over these States." The "Representatives of the United States of America," therefore, declared the thirteen "United Colonies" to be "Free and Independent States."

The Continental Congress votes for independence, July 2, 1776.

"We Always Had Governed Ourselves"

So it had come to this, thirteen years after Britain had won domination of North America. Historians have advanced numerous explanations as to what caused the Revolutionary controversy: "unfair" trade regulation, the restrictions on British settlement of western lands, the tax controversy, the debts to British merchants, the lack of representation in Parliament, ideologies of Whiggery and the Enlightenment, the abrupt shift from a mercantile to an "imperial" policy after 1763.

Each of these factors contributed something to collective colonial grievances that rose to a climax in a gigantic failure of British statesmanship. A conflict between British sovereignty and American rights had come to a point of confrontation that adroit statesmanship might have avoided, sidestepped, or outflanked. Irresolution and vacillation in the British ministry finally gave way to the stubborn determination to force an issue long permitted to drift. The colonists saw these developments as the conspiracy of a corrupted oligarchy—and finally, they decided, of a despotic king—to impose an "absolute Tyranny."

Perhaps the last word on how the Revolution came about should belong to an obscure participant, Levi Preston, a Minute Man from Danvers, Massachusetts. Asked sixty-seven years after Lexington and Concord about British oppressions, he responded, as his young interviewer reported later: " 'What were they? Oppressions? I didn't feel them.' " When asked about the hated Stamp Act, he claimed that he " 'never saw one of those stamps,' " and was " 'certain I never paid a penny for one of them.' " Nor had he ever heard of John Locke or his theories. " 'We read only the Bible, the Catechism, Watts's Psalms and Hymns, and the Almanack.' " When his exasperated interviewer asked why, then, did he support the Revolution, Preston replied: " 'Young man, what we meant in going for those redcoats was this: we always had governed ourselves, and we always meant to. They didn't mean we should.' "

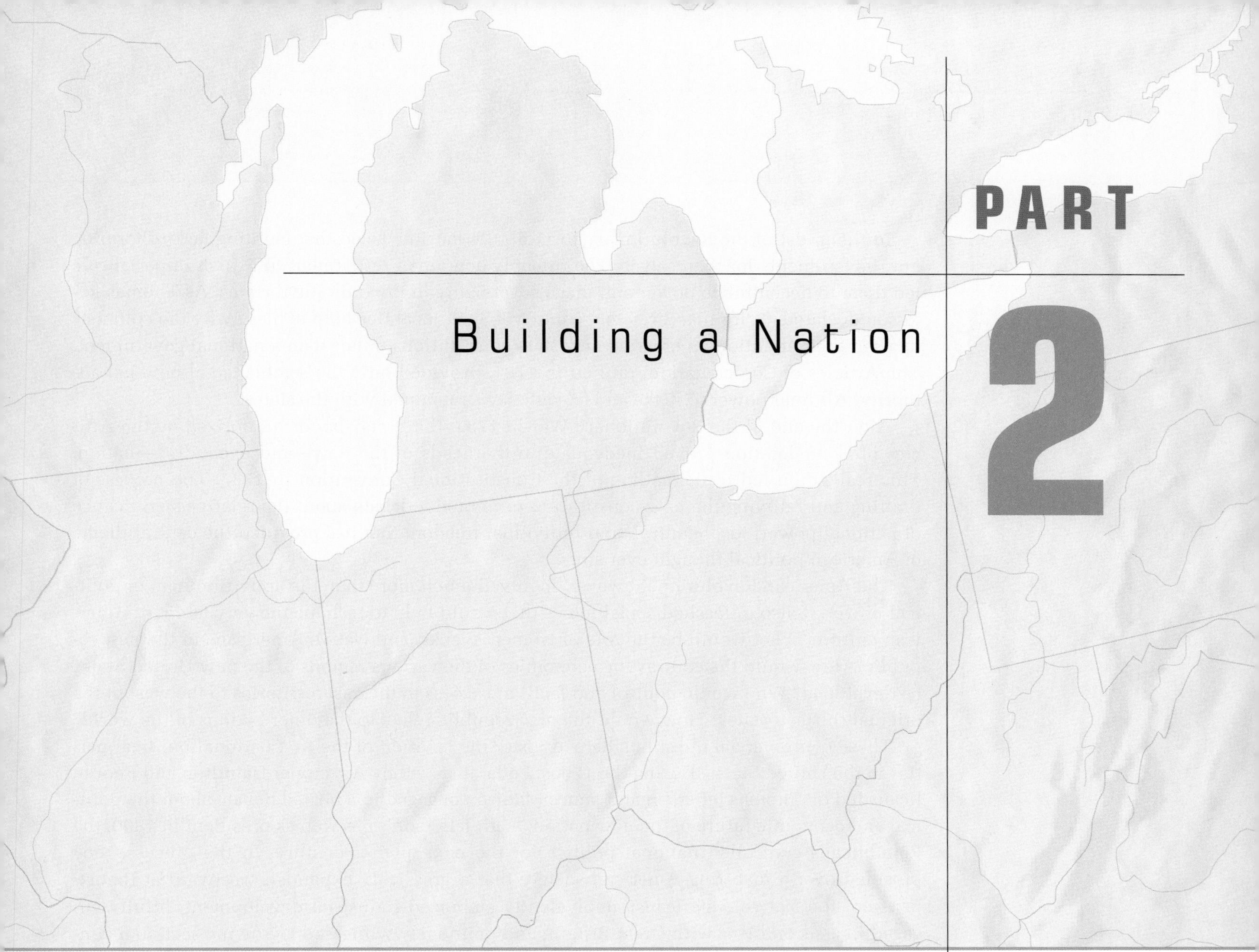

PART 2

Building a Nation

The signing of the Declaration of Independence generated great excitement among the rebellious colonists. Yet it was one thing for Patriot leaders to declare American independence from British authority; it was quite another to win it on the battlefield. Barely a third of the colonists actively supported the revolution, the new nation was politically fragile, and George Washington found himself in command of a poorly supplied, untested army.

Yet the Revolutionary movement would persevere and prevail. The skill and fortitude of Washington and his lieutenants enabled the Americans to exploit their geographic advantages. Equally important was the intervention of the French on behalf of the Revolutionary cause. The Franco-American alliance proved to be decisive. After eight years of sporadic fighting and heavy human and financial losses, the British gave up the fight and their American colonies.

In the midst of the Revolutionary turmoil, the Patriots faced the daunting task of forming new governments for themselves. Their deeply engrained resentment of British imperial rule led them to decentralize power and place sovereignty in the individual states. As Thomas Jefferson declared, "Virginia, Sir, is my country." Such local ties help explain why the colonists focused their attention on creating new state constitutions rather than a national government. The Articles of Confederation, ratified in 1781, provided only the semblance of national authority. All final power to make and execute laws remained with the states.

After the end of the Revolutionary War in 1783, the flimsy bonds authorized by the Articles of Confederation proved inadequate to the needs of the new—and expanding—nation. This realization led to the calling of the Constitutional Convention in 1787. The process of drafting and ratifying the new constitution prompted a debate about the relative significance of national power, local control, and individual freedom that has provided the central theme of American political thought ever since.

The American Revolution, however, involved much more than the apportionment of political power. It also unleashed social forces that would help to reshape the very fabric of American culture. What would be the role of women, blacks, and Native Americans in the new republic? How would the contrasting economies of the various regions of the new United States be developed? Who would control and facilitate access to the vast territories to the west of the original thirteen states? How would the new republic relate to the other nations of the world?

These controversial questions helped foster the creation of the first national political parties in the United States. During the 1790s, Federalists led by Alexander Hamilton and Republicans led by Thomas Jefferson and James Madison engaged in a heated debate about the political and economic future of the new nation. With Jefferson's election as president in 1800, the Republicans controlled national politics for the next quarter century. In the process, they presided over a maturing American society that aggressively expanded westward at the expense of the Native Americans, ambivalently embraced industrial development, fitfully engaged in a second war with Great Britain, and ominously witnessed a growing sectional controversy over slavery.

ESSENTIAL THEMES

CRITICAL QUESTIONS

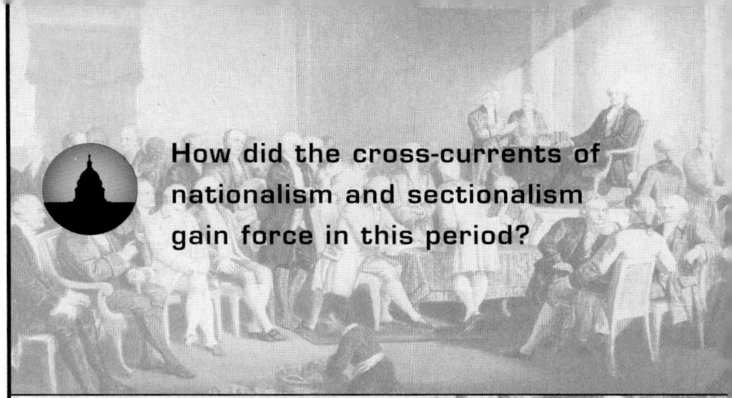

How did the cross-currents of nationalism and sectionalism gain force in this period?

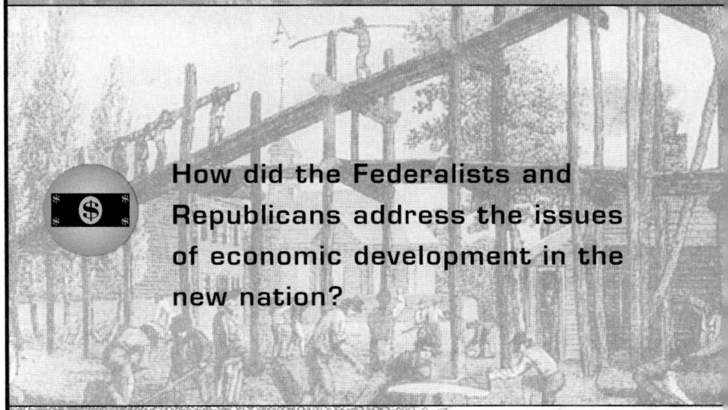

How did the Federalists and Republicans address the issues of economic development in the new nation?

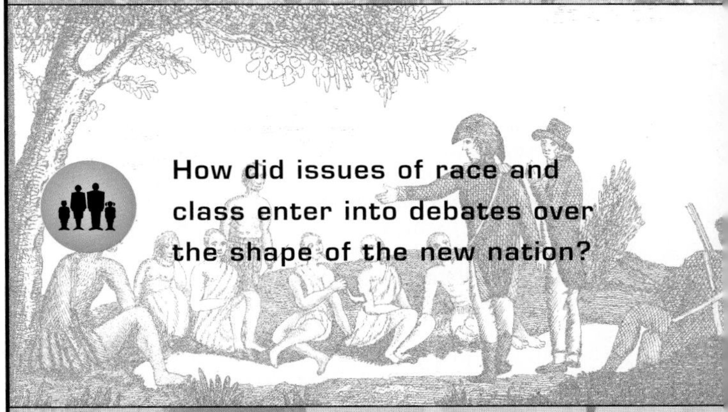

How did issues of race and class enter into debates over the shape of the new nation?

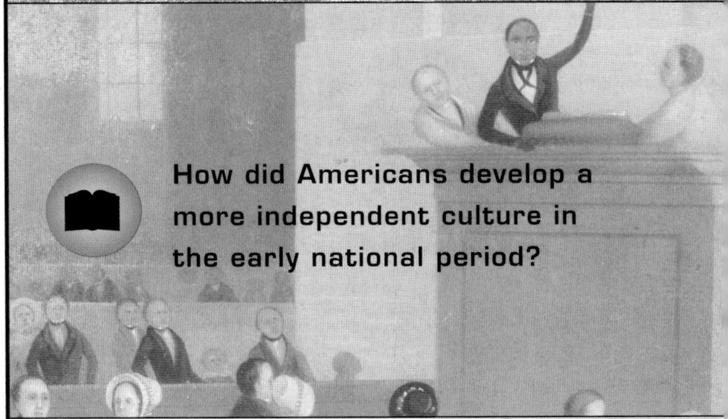

How did Americans develop a more independent culture in the early national period?

How did the new nation seek to enhance its international status?

How did the cross-currents of nationalism and sectionalism gain force in this period?

CHAPTER 5

The American Revolution

Independence

Critical junctures in the Revolutionary War
Trenton and Princeton (1776–1777)
Saratoga (1777)
Valley Forge (1778)
Yorktown (1781)
British peace overtures following Saratoga
Transition to a republic
Articles of Confederation establish weak central government (1781)
New state constitutions (1776–1787)

CHAPTER 6

Shaping a Federal Union

Western lands, states' rights, and the constitution

Northwest Ordinance regulates population and government of western lands (1787)
The Constitutional Convention (1787)
The Virginia and New Jersey Plans
The Great Compromise
The Federalist: Hamilton, Madison, and Jay (1787–1788)
Confederation Congress yields to constitutional rule (October 1788)

CHAPTER 7

The Federalists: Washington and Adams

Federalist rule

Washington elected first president of the United States (March 1789)
John Jay becomes first chief justice of the Supreme Court (1789)
Alexander Hamilton named first secretary of the treasury (1789)
The Bill of Rights protects individual liberties (1791)
Land policy and the frontier policy (1796)
John Adams wins nation's first partisan election (1796)
Congress creates Department of the Navy (1798)
Jefferson wins presidency in 1800

CHAPTER 8

Republicanism: Jefferson and Madison

An orderly transfer of power in 1800

Thomas Jefferson as president (1800–1804)
Republican simplicity and the "Revolution of 1800"
Marbury v. *Madison* (1803) defines relationship between court, executive branch
The Louisiana Purchase (1803)
Divisions in the Republican party
John Randolph and the *Tertium Quid* (1806)
The Burr Conspiracy
Jefferson and the politics of war

CHAPTER 9

Nationalism and Sectionalism

Nationalism and sectionalism

Judicial nationalism: Chief Justice John Marshall
Dartmouth College v. *Woodward* (1819)
McCulloch v. *Maryland* (1819)
Gibbons v. *Ogden* (1824)
Expansion and sectional tension: the Missouri Compromise (1820)
John Quincy Adams becomes president (1824)
The 1828 election

CHAPTER 5

The American Revolution

Economic dimensions of the revolutionary war

- **Destruction and confiscation of property**
- **Inflation and war profiteering**

CHAPTER 6

Shaping a Federal Union

Confederation finance

- **Acute economic contraction between 1770 and 1790**
- **Robert Morris establishes Bank of North America (1781)**
- **Currency crisis, mounting debt**
- **Tariffs and foreign trade**
- **Shays's Rebellion (1787) and the debt problem**
- **Economic interests and the Constitution**

CHAPTER 7

The Federalists: Washington and Adams

Conflicting economic ideologies of Federalists and Republicans

- **Hamilton promulgates a strong central government that favors capitalist development**
- Establishment of a national bank, national mint (1790–1791)
- Protective tarrifs to raise revenue and assist nascent American industry (1790s)
- Treasury begins retiring Revolutionary War debt, attracting foreign investment (1790s)
- **Jefferson and Madison favor a decentralized, agricultural republic**

CHAPTER 8

Republicanism: Jefferson and Madison

Republican finance

- **Republicans repeal whiskey tax (1802) and other Federalist excises**
- **Government finances depend on tariff revenues and sale of western lands**
- **Economic effects of war in Europe**
- **Lewis and Clark and the fur trade (1804–1806)**
- **Economic causes of the War of 1812**

CHAPTER 9

Nationalism and Sectionalism

Economic effects of the War of 1812

- **President Madison promotes economic balance and a "national" economy**
- Tarriff of 1816 protects American manufacturing
- Canals and new roads improve transportation
- Second Bank of the United States established (1816)
- **Early industrialization**
- **The Panic of 1819**
- **Tariff of 1824 and sectional interests**
- **The Marshall Court and the economy (1819)**

How did issues of race and class enter into debates over the shape of the new nation?

CHAPTER 5

The American Revolution

Revolution and society

Social effects of the Revolution
Social realignment and the erosion of social deference
The status of women
The paradox of slavery
Religious pluralism
Virginia's Declaration of Rights (1776) and Statute of Religious Freedom (1786)
Emergence of national church bodies
Indian-white relations
Revolution weakens tribes along frontier, clearing way for later settlement
The home front during the war
Tories vs. Loyalists
Demands for social equality by working classes

CHAPTER 6

Shaping a Federal Union

The ongoing struggle for equality

The Confederation
Northwest Ordinance prohibits slavery, guarantees religious freedom in Northwest (1787)
Social unrest under the Confederation
The Constitution (1787)
Race: the Three-Fifths Compromise and racial inequality
Gender: women continue to lack basic constitutional rights
Indian nations forced to yield their lands to American expansion (1780s)
Congress funds public schools on the western frontier (1785)

CHAPTER 7

The Federalists: Washington and Adams

The new nation

The first census (1790)
In 1790, 750,000 African Americans and 150,000 Native Americans living in the United States
Unrest on the frontier
The Whiskey Rebellion (1794)
Cherokees, Chickasaws, Choctaws, Creeks, and Seminoles reject American authority (1790s)
Federalist-Antifederalist debate between centralized capitalism and decentralized agrarianism
Alien and Sedition Acts and the politics of nationality (1798)

CHAPTER 8

Republicanism: Jefferson and Madison

Jeffersonian America

Worsening white-Indian relations during the War of 1812
Tecumseh (Shawnee), William Henry Harrison, and the Battle of Tippecanoe (1811)
Tecumseh's death at the Battle of the Thames (1813)
Creeks cede two-thirds of their lands to the United States (1814)
Jefferson outlaws foreign slave trade effective January 1, 1808
Nearly 300,000 slaves smuggled into southern states 1808–1861

CHAPTER 9

Nationalism and Sectionalism

Race and the national agenda

Jackson pursues Seminoles into Florida; Jackson takes Seminole lands for the United States (1817–1818)
The Missouri Compromise (1819)
Rapid territorial expansion

CHAPTER 5

The American Revolution

The ideology of republicanism

- **Emergence of an American culture**
- **America's "mission" and the sense of common nationality**
- **American painting**
- **Education**
- State-supported public education
- Chartering of state universities

CHAPTER 6

Shaping a Federal Union

Literature and art in the confederation

- ***The Federalist* and the foundations of American political thought**
- **Thomas Pritchard Rossiter and Charles Willson Peale**

CHAPTER 7

The Federalists: Washington and Adams

Life and values in early America

- **Thomas Jefferson's enlightened world**
- Monticello, the Virginia Capitol, and the University of Virginia
- **Life on the American frontier**
- Daniel Boone and the Wilderness Road (1770)
- Corn-based foods and "likker"
- **Westward migration**

CHAPTER 8

Republicanism: Jefferson and Madison

American identity in the first years of nationhood

- **The Louisiana Purchase**
- **Exploring the trans-Mississippi wilderness: Lewis and Clark (1804–1806)**
- **The War of 1812—the "Second War of Independence"**

CHAPTER 9

Nationalism and Sectionalism

Culture and the expansion of territorial boundaries

- **Slavery and the "cotton culture" expand into Missouri and Arkansas**
- **French and Spanish culture in Florida and the Southwest**

How did the new nation seek to enhance its international status?

CHAPTER 5

The American Revolution

A world war: England fights the four powers

- **American diplomacy**
- **France enters the war on the side of the Americans (1778)**
- **Spain joins France against England (1779)**
- **England declares war on Holland (1780)**
- **Peace of Paris (1783)**

CHAPTER 6

Shaping a Federal Union

American diplomacy following the war

- **British forts along the Canadian border**
- **American trade**
- **The United States and Spain negotiate boundaries, navigation of Mississippi (1780s)**
- **Spanish governor of Louisiana incites Creeks, Choctaws, Chicasaws, and other tribes against the United States (1780s)**

CHAPTER 7

The Federalists: Washington and Adams

Events in Europe affecting the United States

- **The French Revolution and the Terror (1789–1794)**
- **Britain, Spain, and Holland go to war with France (1793)**
- **President Washington declares U.S. neutrality in British-French hostilities (1793)**
- Free American navigation of the Mississippi River
- **Jay's Treaty aims to soothe U.S.–British relations (1794)**
- **Pinckney's Treaty (1795)**
- **The XYZ Affair and war with France (1797–1800)**
- Congress renounces 1778 alliance with France
- Napoleon's dictatorship sets stage for Louisiana Purchase

CHAPTER 8

Republicanism: Jefferson and Madison

Ongoing relations with Europe

- **Jefferson's abhorrence of "entangling alliances"**
- **The Louisiana Purchase (1803)**
- **Spaniards remain in Florida**
- **The "paper blockade" (1806)**
- **Napoleon's Continental System (1806–1807)**
- Jefferson's Embargo Act and "peaceable coercion" (1807)
- The Non-Intercourse Act (1809)
- Macon's Bill Number 2 (1810)
- **The War of 1812**
- Trade issues
- Land issues
- Anti-British sentiment
- British burn Washington, D.C. (1814)
- Treaty of Ghent ends war (1814)

CHAPTER 9

Nationalism and Sectionalism

New nationalism and improving relations with Britain

- **Andrew Jackson attacks Spanish strongholds in Florida (1817–1818)**
- **Spain cedes Florida with Transcontinental Treaty (1819)**
- **Russia cedes Pacific Northwest (1824)**
- **The Monroe Doctrine (1823)**
- Origins
- Significance

CHAPTER

5

The American Revolution

This chapter focuses on

- American and British military strategies and the Revolutionary War's major turning points.
- The effect of the war on the home front.
- The American Revolution considered as a "social revolution" in matters of social equality, slavery, the rights of women, and religious freedom.
- The beginnings of a distinctive American culture.

THE *ESSENTIAL AMERICA* ON-LINE TUTOR

www.wwnorton.com/eamerica/ch5

- **Topic: The paintings of Charles Willson Peale**
  www.wwnorton.com/eamerica/ch5/topic.htm

  The paintings of Charles Willson Peale helped shape the American memory of the Revolution and its advocates. Explore Peale's work and its significance using paintings, historical analyses, and personal correspondence. What does Peale's work contribute to our understanding of the Revolution?

- **Chapter review: On-line quiz and chapter summary**
  www.wwnorton.com/eamerica/ch5/review.htm

- **Chapter resources: Multimedia index**
  www.wwnorton.com/eamerica/ch5/media.htm

The Americans lost most of the battles in the Revolutionary War, but they eventually forced the British to sue for peace and grant the colonists their independence. The surprising result was due to the tenacity of the Patriots, the importance of the French alliance, and the peculiar difficulties facing the British as they tried to conduct a demanding military campaign thousands of miles from home.

Like all major military events, the Revolution had unexpected consequences. It not only secured American independence, generated a new sense of nationalism, and created a unique system of self-governance; it also began a process of societal definition and change that has yet to run its course. The turmoil of the Revolution upset traditional class and social relationships and helped transform the lives of people who have long been relegated to the periphery of historical concern—blacks, women, and Indians. In important ways, then, the Revolution was much more than simply a war for independence. It was an engine for political experimentation and social change.

1776: Washington's Narrow Escape

On July 2, 1776, the day that Congress voted independence, British redcoats landed on Staten Island, off the coast of New York City. They were the vanguard of a gigantic effort to reconquer America and the first elements of an enormous force that gathered around New York Harbor over the next month. By mid-August, General William Howe, with the support of a fleet under his older brother, had some 32,000 men at his disposal, including 9,000 German Hessians—the biggest single force ever mustered by the British in the eighteenth century. To counter the British, Washington transferred most of his men from Boston, but he could muster only about 19,000 Continental soldiers and militiamen. Such a force could not defend New York, but Congress wanted it held. This forced Washington to expose his men to entrapments from which they escaped more by luck and Howe's caution than by the American commander's skill. Washington was still learning the art of generalship, and the New York campaign taught him some costly lessons.

George Washington at Princeton, detail of a painting by Charles Willson Peale.

Fighting in New York and New Jersey

By invading and occupying New York, the British sought to sever New England from the rest of the rebellious colonies. In late August 1776, Howe inflicted heavy losses and forced Washington to evacuate Long Island and withdraw to Manhattan. Had Howe moved quickly, he could have trapped Washington's army in lower Manhattan. But the main American force of 6,000 men withdrew northward to mainland New York, crossed the Hudson River, and then retreated slowly across New Jersey and the Delaware River into Pennsylvania.

In the retreating army marched a volunteer from England, Thomas Paine. Having opened an eventful year with his inspiring pamphlet *Common Sense*, he now composed *The American Crisis*, in which he exhorted Americans to fight on with the immortal line "These are the times that try men's souls." The eloquent pamphlet, ordered read in the Revolutionary army camps, helped restore shaken morale.

General Howe, comfortably based in New York (which the British held throughout the war), settled down with his army to wait out the winter. But Washington was not yet ready to hibernate; instead he seized the initiative. On Christmas night 1776, he slipped across the icy Delaware River with 2,400 men. Near dawn at Trenton, New Jersey, the Americans surprised a garrison of 1,500 Hessians. The daring raid was a total rout from which only 500 royal soldiers escaped death or capture. Washington's men suffered only six casualties. At nearby Princeton, on January 3, the Americans repelled three regiments of redcoats before taking refuge in winter quarters at Morristown, in the hills of northern New Jersey. The campaigns of 1776 had ended, after repeated American defeats, with two minor but uplifting victories. Howe had missed his great chance to bring the rebellion to a speedy end.

American Society at War

Divided Loyalties

The Revolution seemed to have been a fight between the Americans and the British, but the War for Independence was also a civil war that divided families and communities. After the outbreak of war, opinion concerning the Revolution divided in three ways: Patriots or Whigs (as the revolutionaries called themselves), Tories (as Patriots called the Loyalists, recalling the die-hard royalists in England), and an indifferent middle group swayed by the better organized and more energetic radicals.

American Tories were concentrated mainly in the seaport cities, but they came from all walks of life. Almost all governors, judges, and other royal officials were loyal to Britain; most Anglican ministers also preferred the mother country; colonial merchants might be tugged one way or the other, depending on how much they had benefited or suffered from mercantilist regulation; the great planters were swayed one way by dependence on British bounties, another by their debts to British merchants. In the backcountry of New York and the Carolinas, many humble folk rallied to the crown. Whereas planter aristocrats tended to be Whig, as in North Carolina, backcountry farmers (many of them recently Regulators) leaned toward the Tories. When Patriots took control of an area, Loyalists in the region faced a difficult choice: either accompany the British and leave behind their property or stay and face the wrath of the Patriots.

"One of those ubiquitous American frontiersmen-turned-soldier," second from right. Sketches of the American militia by a French soldier at Yorktown.

Militia and Army

Since the end of the French and Indian War, the colonies had required all adult males between the ages of fifteen and sixty to enroll in their local militia company, to attend monthly drills, and to turn out on short notice for emergencies. The Patriot militia kept springing to life whenever the redcoats appeared nearby, and all adult white males, with few exceptions, were obligated under state law to serve when called.

In the backcountry, the militia engaged in a brutal warfare that defied prevailing rules of combat. Dressed in hunting shirts and armed with muskets with long, grooved barrels, they preferred to ambush their opponents or engage them in hand-to-hand combat rather than fight in traditional formations. They also tended to kill unnecessarily and to torture prisoners. To repel an attack, the militia somehow materialized; the danger past, it evaporated, for there were chores to do at home. They "come in, you cannot tell how," George Washington said in exasperation, "go, you cannot tell when, and act you cannot tell where, consume your provisions, exhaust your stores, and leave you at last at a critical moment."

The Continental Army was on the whole better trained and motivated than the militias. While many American troops were attracted by bounties of land or cash, and some deserted, most harbored a genuine patriotic fervor and a thirst for adventure that enabled them to survive the horrors of combat and camp life. Unlike the full-time professional soldiers in the British army, Washington's army, which fluctuated in size from 5,000 to 20,000, was populated mostly by citizen-soldiers, poor native-born Americans or immigrants who had been indentured servants or convicts.

Behind the Lines

Civilians saw their lives profoundly altered by the Revolutionary War. British forces occupied the major cities (Boston, New York, Philadelphia, Savannah, Charleston). They also confiscated crops and livestock.

Some civilians took selfish advantage of the war. The inflationary spiral generated by a scarcity of consumer goods and the supplies needed for the military effort created new opportunities for quick profits and graft. Throughout the war years, George Washington complained that "speculation, peculation, and an insatiable thirst for riches seems to have got the better of every other of Men."

The poor suffered most amid the war's disruptions and skyrocketing prices. A bushel of wheat that sold for less than a dollar in 1777 brought $80 two years later. Many consumers appealed to authorities to institute price controls so they could afford basic necessities. Others took more direct action. In Boston a throng of women paraded a merchant accused of hoarding through the streets while "a large concourse of men stood amazed." No longer willing to defer quietly to gouging merchants and retailers, the working classes grabbed the opportunity afforded by the Revolution to claim new economic and political rights.

To Revolutionary leaders such as John Adams, the "democratical" demands for political and social equality put forward by the laboring classes were as odious as British regulatory measures. The specter of unlearned mechanics and laborers exercising political power horrified him. The American people, he and others insisted, must accept social inequality as a fact of human existence and defer to the leadership of their betters.

1777: Setbacks for the British

Indecision, overconfidence, and poor communications plagued British military planning for the campaigns of 1777. The profoundly confident General "Gentleman Johnny" Burgoyne sought to bisect the colonies. His men would advance southward from Canada to the Hudson River while another force moved eastward down the Mohawk Valley. Howe had proposed a similar plan, combined with an attack on New England. Had he stuck to it, he might have cut the colonies in two and delivered them a disheartening blow. But he changed his mind and decided to move against the Patriot capital, Philadelphia, expecting that the Pennsylvania Tories would then rally to the crown and secure the colony.

Washington, sensing Howe's purpose, withdrew most of his men from New Jersey to meet the new threat. At Brandywine Creek, south of Philadelphia, Howe pushed Washington's forces back on September 11,

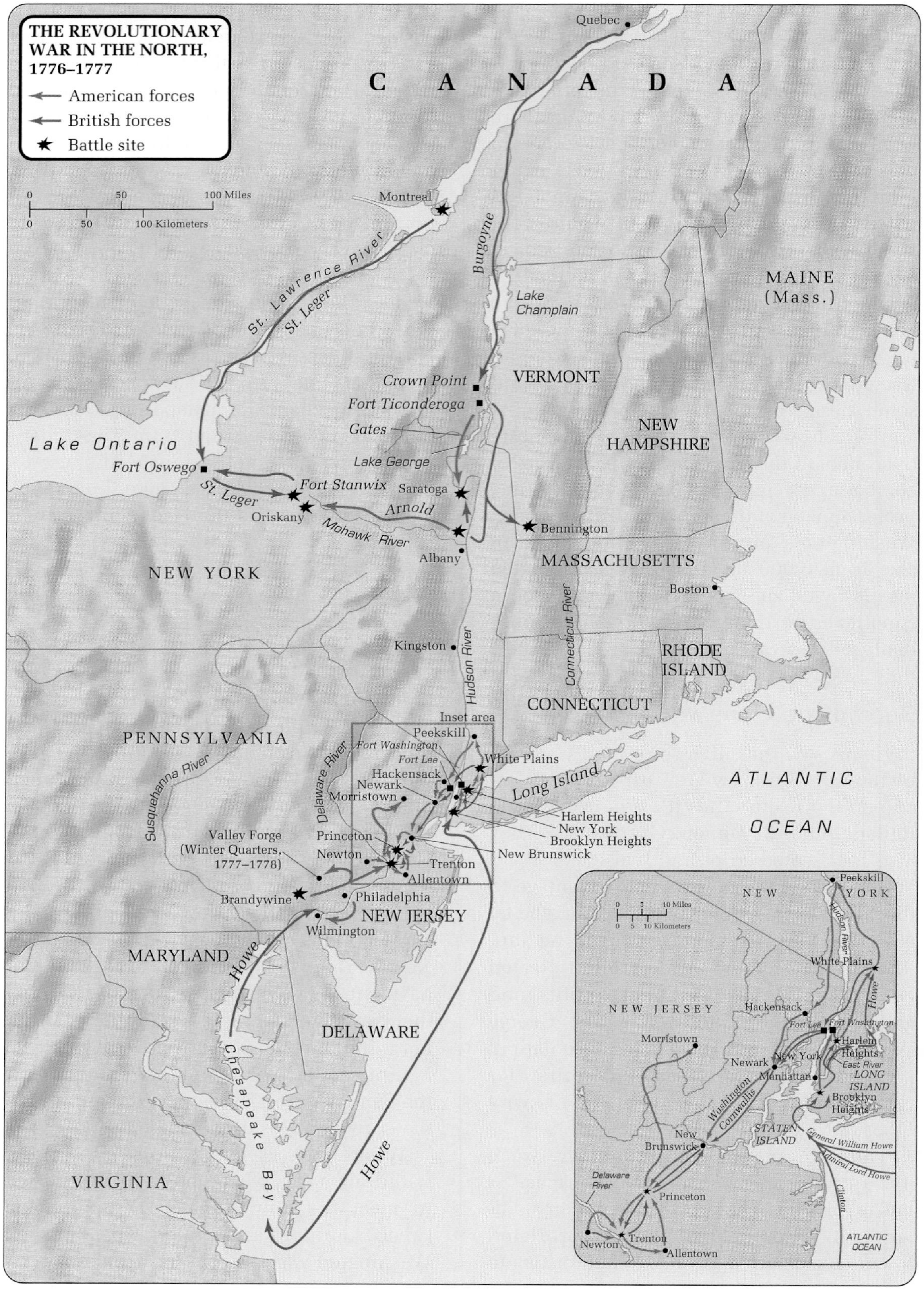
THE REVOLUTIONARY WAR IN THE NORTH, 1776–1777
American forces
British forces
Battle site
0 50 100 Miles
0 50 100 Kilometers
CANADA
Quebec
Montreal
St. Lawrence River
St. Leger
Burgoyne
Lake Champlain
MAINE (Mass.)
Crown Point
Fort Ticonderoga
VERMONT
Gates
NEW HAMPSHIRE
Lake Ontario
Lake George
Fort Oswego
Fort Stanwix
Saratoga
Oriskany
Arnold
Mohawk River
Bennington
Albany
MASSACHUSETTS
NEW YORK
Boston
Connecticut River
Kingston
Hudson River
RHODE ISLAND
CONNECTICUT
Inset area
Peekskill
PENNSYLVANIA
Fort Washington
Fort Lee
White Plains
Hackensack
Newark
Morristown
Long Island
ATLANTIC OCEAN
Delaware River
Susquehanna River
Harlem Heights
New York
Brooklyn Heights
New Brunswick
Valley Forge (Winter Quarters, 1777–1778)
Princeton
Newton
Trenton
Allentown
Brandywine
Philadelphia
NEW JERSEY
Wilmington
MARYLAND
Howe
DELAWARE
Chesapeake Bay
VIRGINIA
NEW YORK
0 5 10 Miles
0 5 10 Kilometers
Hudson River
NEW JERSEY
Washington
Cornwallis
Manhattan
East River
LONG ISLAND
STATEN ISLAND
General William Howe
Admiral Lord Howe
Clinton
ATLANTIC OCEAN

and fifteen days later British troops occupied Philadelphia. Washington retired into winter quarters at Valley Forge while Howe and his men remained for the winter in the relative comfort of Philadelphia, twenty miles away. Howe's plan had succeeded, up to a point. He had taken Philadelphia, but the Tories there proved fewer than he expected. Meanwhile, Burgoyne was stumbling into disaster in the north.

Saratoga

Burgoyne moved southward toward Lake Champlain in 1777 with about 7,000 men, his mistress, and a baggage train that included some thirty carts filled with his personal trappings and a large supply of champagne. A powerful force on paper, the expedition was in fact much too cumbersome to be effective in the dense forests and rugged terrain of upstate New York. Burgoyne sent part of his army down the St. Lawrence River with Lieutenant-Colonel Barry St. Leger and a force of Iroquois allies. This combined group headed east toward Albany. When they met the more mobile Americans, the British suffered two serious reversals.

At Oriskany, New York, on August 6, 1777, a band of militia thwarted an ambush by Tories and Indians and gained time for General Benedict Arnold to bring a thousand Continentals to the relief of Fort Stanwix, which had been under siege by St. Leger. The Indians, convinced they faced a force greater than they actually did, deserted, and the Mohawk Valley was secured for the Patriot forces. To the east, at Bennington, Vermont, on August 16, New England militia repulsed a British foraging party. American reinforcements continued to gather, and after two sharp clashes, Burgoyne pulled back to Saratoga, where American forces under General Horatio Gates surrounded him. On October 17, 1777, Burgoyne, resplendent in his scarlet, gold, and white uniform, surrendered to the plain, blue-coated Gates. Most of Burgoyne's soldiers were imprisoned in Virginia, but "Gentleman Johnny" himself was permitted to go home, where he received an icy reception. The victory at Saratoga proved critically important to the American cause.

Alliance with France

On December 2, 1777, news of the American triumph at Saratoga reached London; two days later it reached Paris, where it was celebrated almost as if it were a French victory. Its impact on the French made the Battle of Saratoga a decisive turning point of the war. In 1776 the French had taken their first step toward aiding the colonists by sending fourteen ships with military supplies to America; most of the Continental Army's gunpowder in the first years of the war came from this source. Besides arms, artillery, and ammunition, the French had also secretly sent clothing, shoes, and other supplies to help the Americans. After Saratoga, the French saw their chance to strike a sharper blow at their hated enemy and entered into serious negotiations with the Americans.

On February 6, 1778, France and America signed two treaties: a Treaty of Amity and Commerce, in which France recognized the United States and offered trade concessions, including important privileges to American shipping, and a Treaty of Alliance. Under the latter, both agreed, first, that if France entered the war, both countries would fight until American independence was won; second, that neither would conclude a "truce or peace" without the consent of the other; and third, that each guaranteed the other's possessions in America "from the present time and forever against all other powers." France further bound itself to seek neither Canada nor other British possessions on the mainland of North America.

By June 1778, British vessels had fired on French ships, and the two nations were at war. In 1779, after extracting promises from the French to help it regain territories taken by the British in the previous war, including Gibraltar, Spain entered the war as an ally of France, but not of the United States. The following year, Britain declared war on the Dutch, who persisted in a profitable trade with the French and Americans. Thus, the American Revolution sparked another world war, and the fighting now spread to the Mediterranean, Africa, India, the West Indies, and the high seas.

1778: Both Sides Regroup

Revolutionary Army at Valley Forge

For Washington's army, bivouacked at Valley Forge, near Philadelphia, the winter of 1777–1778 was a season of suffering far worse than the previous winter at Morristown. The American force, encamped in crowded, lice-infested log huts, endured cold, hunger, and disease. Many died and others deserted or resigned their commissions. Much of the suffering and lack of rations was because the local farmers refused to sell their cattle, bread, and meat to Washington's army for paper money, preferring to send their produce to Philadelphia for British gold and silver.

Desperate for relief, Washington ordered foraging expeditions. His troops confiscated horses, cattle, and livestock in exchange for "receipts" to be honored by the Continental Congress. By March, the once-gaunt troops at Valley Forge saw their strength restored. Their improved health enabled Washington to begin a training program designed to bring unity and order to his motley forces. By the end of March, the ragtag soldiers were beginning to resemble a professional army. Moreover, as winter drew to an end, the army's morale gained strength from congressional promises of extra pay and bonuses after the war.

British Peace Overtures and Withdrawal

After the defeat at Saratoga, Lord North, the British prime minister, knew that winning the war was unlikely, but the king refused to let him either resign or make peace. On March 16, 1778, the House of Commons adopted a program that in effect granted all the American demands prior to independence. Parliament repealed the Townshend tea duty, the Massachusetts Government Act, and the Prohibitory Act, which had closed the colonies to commerce. It then dispatched a peace commission to negotiate an end to the war, but its members did not reach Philadelphia until after Congress had ratified the French treaties. The Congress refused to begin any negotiations until independence was recognized or British forces withdrawn, neither of which the commissioners could promise.

Unbeknownst to the British commissioners, the crown had already authorized the evacuation of British troops from Philadelphia, a withdrawal that further weakened what little bargaining power the commissioners had. After Saratoga, General Howe resigned his command and Sir Henry Clinton replaced him. Clinton pulled his troops out of Philadelphia and sent them to New York by sea and land. His orders were to abandon New York, if necessary, but to keep Newport, Rhode Island, taking a defensive stance except in the South, where the British government believed Tory sentiment in the backcountry needed only a visible British presence for its release. The pro-British sentiment turned out once again, as in other theaters of war, to be weaker than it seemed.

As General Clinton's forces withdrew eastward toward New York, Washington pursued them across New Jersey. On June 28, 1778, he engaged the British in an indecisive battle at Monmouth Court House. Clinton's forces then slipped away into New York while Washington took up a position at White Plains, north of the city. From that time on, the northern theater, scene of the major campaigns and battles in the first years of the war, settled into a long stalemate, interrupted by minor and mostly inconclusive engagements.

Actions on the Frontier

The one major American success of 1778 occurred far from the New Jersey battlefields. Out to the west, at Forts Niagara and Detroit, the British under Colonel William Hamilton had incited frontier Tories and Indians to raid western settlements and had offered to pay for American scalps. To end such attacks, young George Rogers Clark took 175 frontiersmen and a flotilla of flatboats down the Ohio River in early 1778. They marched through the woods and on the evening of July 4 surprised the British at Kaskaskia. At the end of the year, Clark marched his men (almost half French volunteers) through icy rivers and flooded prairies and captured an astonished British garrison at Vincennes.

Meanwhile, Tories and Iroquois Indians in western Pennsylvania continued to terrorize frontier settlements through the summer of 1778. Led by the charismatic Mohawk Joseph Brant, the Iroquois killed hundreds of militiamen along the Pennsylvania frontier. In response, Washington dispatched 4,000 men under General John Sullivan to the area. At Newton (now Elmira) the American force defeated the only serious opposition on August 29, 1779. The American troops burned about forty Seneca and Cayuga villages together with their orchards and food stores. The destruction broke the power of the Iroquois federation for all time.

In the Kentucky territory, Daniel Boone and his small band of settlers risked constant attack from the Shawnees and their British and Tory allies. During the Revolution, they survived frequent ambushes, at least seven skirmishes, and three pitched battles. Despite such ferocious fighting and dangerous circumstances, the white settlers refused to leave Kentucky.

By thus weakening the major Indian tribes along the frontier, the American Revolution, among its other results, cleared the way for rapid settlement of the trans-Appalachian West after the war ended.

The War in the South

At the end of 1778, the focus of British military action shifted suddenly to the South. The whole region from Virginia southward had been free from major action since 1776. Now the British would test King George's belief that a sleeping Tory power in the South needed only the presence of a few redcoats to awaken it. The war in the Carolinas eventually involved not only opposing British and American armies, but also guerrilla-style civil conflicts between local Loyalists and local Patriots.

The Carolinas

In November 1778, British forces took Savannah, Georgia. The British then headed for Charleston, South Carolina, plundering plantation houses along the way. Outside Charleston, the British encamped and awaited additional naval and land forces from New York and New Jersey. After their arrival with General Clinton and General Charles Cornwallis in February 1780, the British launched a massive assault against the Patriot defenders, and on May 12 American general Benjamin Lincoln surrendered the city and its 5,500 defenders. This was the single greatest American loss of the war.

At this point, against Washington's advice, Congress turned to Horatio Gates, the victor of Saratoga, and sent him south to take command of the Revolutionary troops there. Meanwhile, General Clinton sailed back to New York, leaving General Corn-

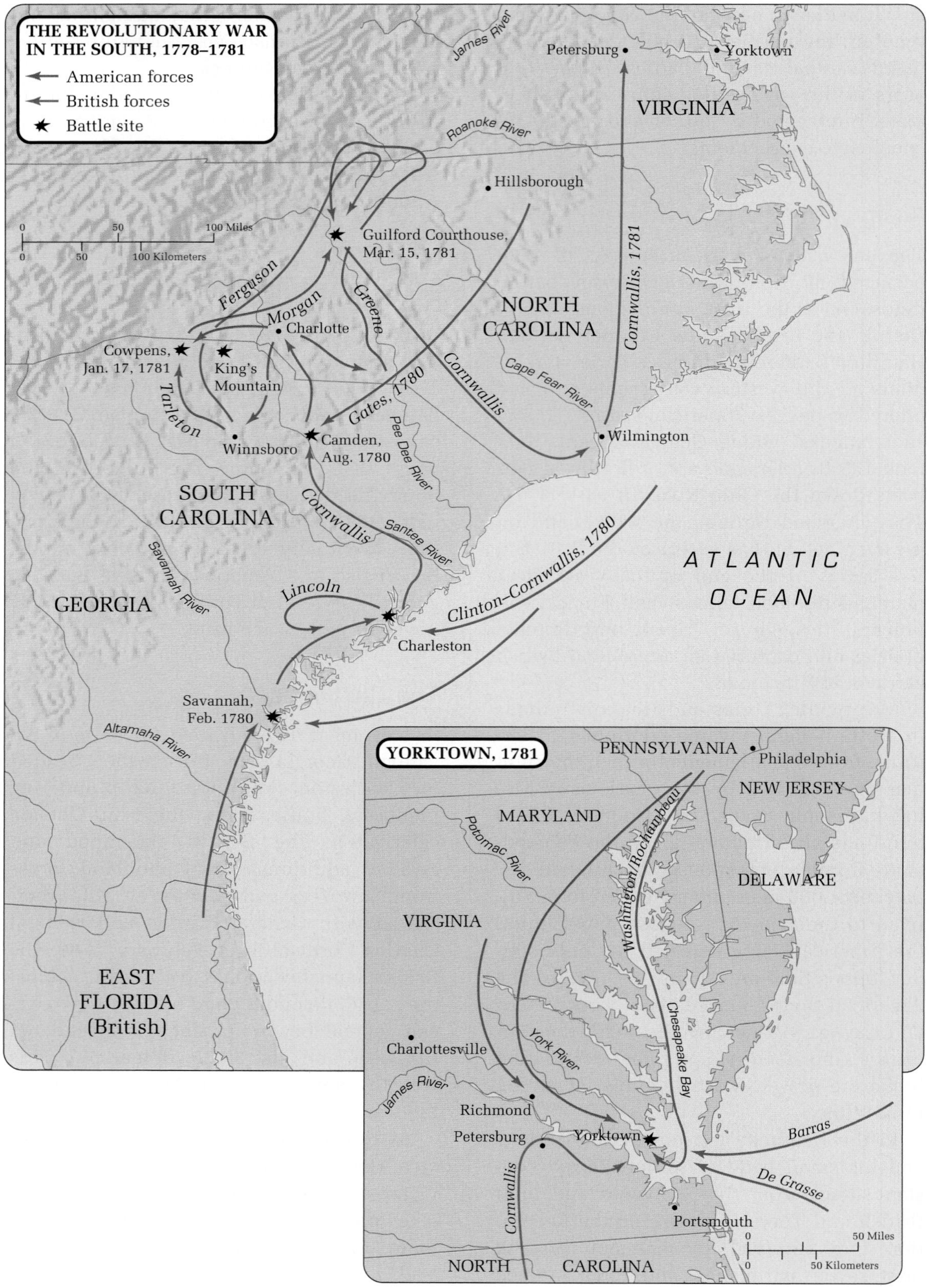
THE REVOLUTIONARY WAR IN THE SOUTH, 1778–1781
American forces
British forces
Battle site
0 50 100 Miles
0 50 100 Kilometers
James River
Petersburg
Yorktown
VIRGINIA
Roanoke River
Hillsborough
Guilford Courthouse, Mar. 15, 1781
Cornwallis, 1781
Ferguson
Morgan
Greene
NORTH CAROLINA
Charlotte
Cowpens, Jan. 17, 1781
King's Mountain
Tarleton
Gates, 1780
Cornwallis
Cape Fear River
Winnsboro
Camden, Aug. 1780
Pee Dee River
Wilmington
SOUTH CAROLINA
Cornwallis
Santee River
ATLANTIC OCEAN
Savannah River
Clinton–Cornwallis, 1780
GEORGIA
Lincoln
Charleston
Savannah, Feb. 1780
Altamaha River
EAST FLORIDA (British)
YORKTOWN, 1781
PENNSYLVANIA
Philadelphia
NEW JERSEY
MARYLAND
Potomac River
Washington/Rochambeau
DELAWARE
VIRGINIA
Chesapeake Bay
York River
Charlottesville
James River
Richmond
Petersburg
Yorktown
Barras
De Grasse
Cornwallis
Portsmouth
0 50 Miles
0 50 Kilometers
NORTH CAROLINA

wallis in charge of the British troops in the South. Cornwallis's troops clashed with Gates's forces outside Camden in August 1780, and the American army was routed by the British. The Patriots retreated all the way to Hillsborough, North Carolina, 160 miles away.

Cornwallis had South Carolina just about under British control, but his cavalry leaders, Banastre Tarleton and Patrick Ferguson, who mobilized Tory militiamen, overreached themselves in their effort to subdue the Whigs. "Tarleton's Quarter" became bywords for savagery, because "Bloody Tarleton" ordered rebels killed after they surrendered. Ferguson sealed his own doom when he threatened to march over the mountains and hang the revolutionary leaders there. Instead the feisty "overmountain men" went after Ferguson. Allied with other backcountry Whigs, they caught him and his Tories on Kings Mountain along the border between North and South Carolina. There, on October 7, 1780, they routed his force. Kings Mountain was the turning point of the war in the South. By proving that the British were not invincible, it emboldened small farmers to join guerrilla bands under partisan leaders like Francis Marion, "the Swamp Fox," and Thomas Sumter, "the Gamecock."

While the "overmountain men" were closing in on Ferguson, Congress had chosen a new commander for the southern theater, General Nathanael Greene, the "fighting Quaker" of Rhode Island. Greene shrewdly lured Cornwallis and his troops into chasing the Americans across the Carolinas, thus taxing British energies and supplies. Splitting his army, Greene sent out about 700 men under General Daniel Morgan toward Cornwallis's headquarters in Winnsboro in western Carolina. With his force of militia and Continental soldiers, Morgan faced off with Tarleton's 1,000 men at Cowpens, a cow-grazing area in northern South Carolina, on January 17, 1781. The Americans routed the British. Morgan and his men then linked up with Greene's main force, and the combined army offered battle near Guilford Courthouse on March 15, 1781. After inflicting heavy losses, Greene prudently withdrew. Cornwallis was left in possession of the field, but at a cost of nearly 100 men killed and more than 400 wounded. In London, when the word arrived, a parliamentary leader moaned, "Another such victory and we are undone."

Cornwallis marched off toward the coast at Wilmington to lick his wounds and take on new supplies. Greene then resolved to go back into South Carolina in the hope of drawing Cornwallis after him or forcing the British to give up the state. There he joined forces with the guerrillas already on the scene, and in a series of brilliant actions he kept losing battles while winning the war: "We fight, get beat, rise, and fight again," he said. By September 1781, he had narrowed British control in the Deep South to Charleston and Savannah, although for more than a year longer Whigs and Tories slashed at each other "with savage fury" in the backcountry, where there was "nothing but murder and devastation in every quarter," Greene said.

Meanwhile, Cornwallis had headed north away from Greene, reasoning that Virginia must be eliminated as a source of reinforcement before the Carolinas could be subdued. In 1781 Cornwallis met up with Benedict Arnold, now a *British* general. From July until September 1780, he had been American commander at West Point. Overweening in ambition, lacking in moral scruples, and a reckless spender, he had nursed a grudge over an official reprimand for his extravagances as commander of reoccupied Philadelphia. Arnold plotted to sell out the West Point garrison to the British. The American seizure of the British go-between, Major John André, ended Arnold's plot. Forewarned that his plan had been discovered, Arnold joined the British in New York, and the Americans hanged André as a spy.

Yorktown

Cornwallis arrived at Yorktown, Virginia, with an army of 7,200, far more than the small American force they faced. There appeared to be little reason to worry about a siege, since Washington's main land force seemed preoccupied with attacking New York and the British navy controlled American waters.

To be sure, there was a small American navy, but it was no match for the British fleet. Most celebrated were the exploits of Captain John Paul Jones, who sailed east across the Atlantic in 1778 and on September 23, 1779, won a desperate battle off England's coast with a British frigate, which he captured and occupied before his own ship sank. This was the occasion for his stirring and oft-repeated response to a British demand for surrender: "I have not yet begun to fight."

Such heroics, however, were little more than nuisances to the British. But at a critical point, thanks to the French navy, the British lost control of the Chesapeake waters off Virginia. Indeed, it is impossible to imagine an American victory in the Revolution without the assistance of the French. As long as the British navy maintained supremacy at sea, the Americans could not hope to force a settlement to their advantage. For three years, Washington had waited to get some military benefit from the French alliance. In July 1780 the French had finally landed a force of about 6,000 at Newport, but the French army under the comte de Rochambeau sat there for a year, blockaded by the British fleet.

Surrender of Lord Cornwallis. John Trumbull completed his painting of the pivotal British surrender at Yorktown in 1794.

Then, in 1781, the elements for combined action suddenly fell into place. As Cornwallis moved into Virginia in May, Washington persuaded Rochambeau to join forces for an attack on New York. The two armies linked up in July, but before they could strike at New York, word came from the West Indies that Admiral De Grasse was bound for Chesapeake Bay with his entire French fleet and some 3,000 soldiers. Washington and his troops secretly slipped out of New York and met up with the French in Philadelphia. The combined American-French forces immediately set out toward Yorktown. Meanwhile, the French fleet finally evaded the British barricade at Newport and sailed south toward Chesapeake Bay.

On August 30, De Grasse's fleet reached Yorktown, where his troops joined the American force already watching Cornwallis. On September 6, De Grasse forced the British to give up the effort to relieve Cornwallis, whose fate was quickly sealed. De Grasse then sent ships up the Chesapeake to ferry to Williamsburg Washington's 16,000 American and French forces, double the size of Cornwallis's army.

The siege began on September 28. On October 14, two major outposts guarding the left of the British line fell to French and American attackers, the latter led by Washington's aide Alexander Hamilton. A British counterattack failed to retake them. Later that night, a squall forced Cornwallis to abandon a desperate plan to escape with his troops across the York River. On October 17, 1781, four years to the day after Saratoga, a red-coated drummer boy climbed atop the British parapet and began beating the call for a truce. Cornwallis sued for peace, and on October 19 the British force marched out, their flags furled, to the tune of "The World Turned Upside Down." Cornwallis himself claimed to be too "ill" to appear.

Negotiations

Whatever lingering hopes of victory the British may have harbored vanished at Yorktown. "Oh God, it is all over," Lord North groaned at news of the surrender. On February 27, 1782, the House of Commons voted against continuing the war, and on March 5 it authorized the crown to make peace. On March 20, Lord North resigned. The new ministry included old friends of the Americans headed by the duke of Rockingham, who had brought about repeal of the Stamp Act. The new colonial minister, Lord Shelburne, became chief minister after Rockingham's death in September and directed the Paris negotiations with American commissioners appointed by the Continental Congress.

The American peace commissioners in Paris were John Adams; John Jay, minister to Spain; Benjamin Franklin; Henry Laurens from South Carolina; and Franklin's nephew, William Temple Franklin. Their difficult task was immediately complicated by commitments France had made to Spain. The United States and Spain were both allied with France, but not with each other. America was bound by its alliance to fight on until the French made peace, and the French had pledged to help the Spanish recover Gibraltar from England. Unable to deliver Gibraltar, or so the tough-minded Jay reasoned, the French might try to bargain off American land west of the Appalachians in its place. Fearful that the French were angling for a separate peace with the British, Jay persuaded Franklin to play the same game. Ignoring their instructions to consult fully with the French, they agreed to further talks with the British. On November 30, 1782, the talks produced a preliminary treaty with Great Britain. If it violated the spirit of the alliance, it did not violate the strict letter of the treaty with France, for the French minister was notified the day before it was signed, and final agreement still depended on a Franco-British settlement.

The Peace of Paris

Early in 1783, France and Spain gave up on acquiring Gibraltar and reached an armistice with Britain. The Peace of Paris was finally signed on September 3, 1783. In accord with the bargain already struck, Great Britain recognized the independence of the United States and agreed to a Mississippi River boundary to the west. Both the northern and southern borders left ambiguities that would require further definition. Florida, as it turned out, passed back to Spain. The British further granted Americans the "liberty" of fishing off Newfoundland and in the Gulf of St. Lawrence, and the right to dry their catches on the unsettled coasts of Canada. On the matter of pre–Revolutionary War debts, the best the British could get was a promise that British merchants should "meet with no legal impediment" in seeking to collect them. And on the tender point of Loyalists whose property had been confiscated, the negotiators agreed that Congress would "earnestly recommend" to the states the restoration of confiscated property. Each of the last two points was little more than a face-saving gesture for the British.

The Political Revolution

Republican Ideology

The Revolutionary War served as the catalyst for a prolonged debate about what new

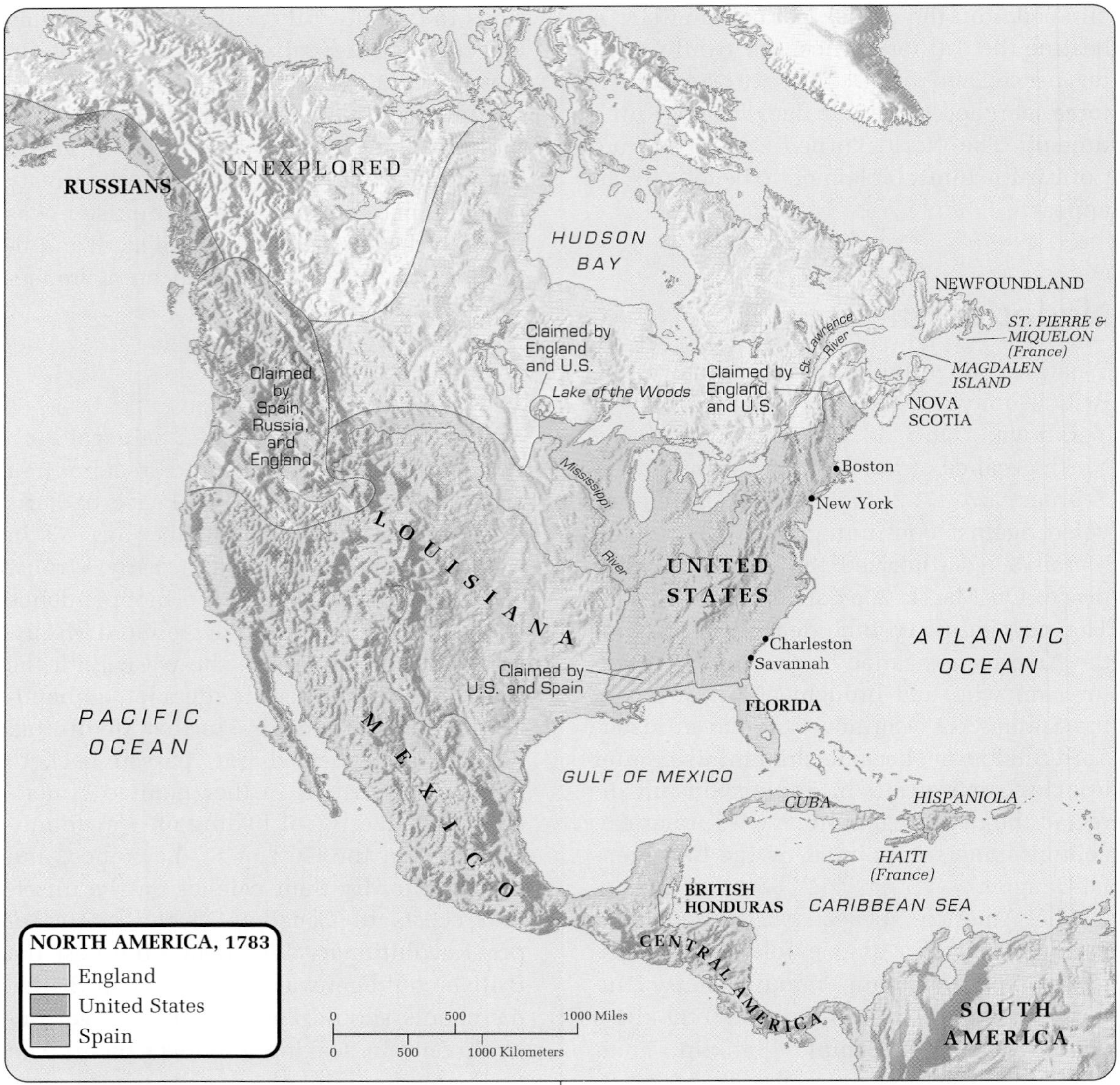

forms of government would best serve an independent republic. Americans knew that they must develop new political assumptions and institutions. They had no monarchy or aristocracy. Yet how could sovereignty reside in the common people? How could Americans ensure the survival of a republican form of government, long assumed to be the most fragile? The war thus provoked a spate of state constitution-making that remains unique in history.

Such ideas as the contract theory of government, the sovereignty of the people, the separation of powers, and natural rights found their way quickly, almost automatically, into the new frames of government that were devised while the fight went on—amid other urgent business.

The very idea of republican government—a balanced polity animated by civic virtue—was a far more radical departure in that day than it would seem to later generations. The new American republic, people assumed, would endure only as long as the majority of the people were virtuous and willingly placed the good of society above the self-interest of individuals. Herein lay the hope and the fragility of the American experiment in popular government: even as leaders enthusiastically fashioned new state constitutions, they feared that their experiments in republicanism would fail because of a lack of civic virtue.

New State Constitutions

Most political experimentation between 1776 and 1787 occurred at the state level. Innovations devised in the state constitutional conventions created the core principle of the American political system: representative government defined in written constitutions in which the people are sovereign and delegate limited authority to the government. In addition, the states initiated bills of rights to protect individuals and fashioned procedures for constitutional conventions that have also remained an essential part of the American political system.

At the onset of the fighting, every colony experienced the departure of governors and other British officials. Loyalists were usually expelled from the assemblies, which then assumed power as provincial "congresses" or "conventions." But they were acting as revolutionary bodies without any legal basis for the exercise of authority. In two of the states this presented little difficulty. Connecticut and Rhode Island, which had been virtually little republics as corporate colonies, simply purged their charters of any reference to colonial ties. Massachusetts followed their example until 1780.

In the other states, the prevailing notions of social contract and popular sovereignty led to written constitutions that specified the framework and powers of government. Constitution-making began even before independence. In May 1776, Congress advised the colonies to set up new governments "under the authority of the people."

The first state constitutions varied mainly in detail. They formed governments much like the colonial administrations, with elected governors and senates instead of appointed governors and councils. Generally they embodied, sometimes explicitly, a separation of powers as a safeguard against abuses. Most of them also included a bill of rights that protected the time-honored rights of petition, freedom of speech, trial by jury, freedom from self-incrimination, and the like. Most state constitutions tended to limit the powers of governors and increase the powers of the legislatures, which had led the people in their quarrels with the colonial governors. Pennsylvania went so far as to eliminate the governor and upper house of the legislature altogether. It had a twelve-man executive council and operated until 1790 with a unicameral legislature limited only by a house of "censors," who reviewed its work every five years.

The Articles of Confederation

The central government, like the state governments, grew out of an extralegal revolutionary body. The Continental Congress exercised governmental powers without any constitutional sanction before 1781. Plans for a permanent frame of government were started very early, however, when on July 12, 1776, a committee headed by John Dickinson produced a draft constitution, the "Articles of Confederation and Perpetual Union." For more than a year Congress debated the articles in between more urgent matters and finally adopted them in November 1777, subject to ratification by all the states.

The central government created by the Articles of Confederation was intentionally weak. The Congress was not a legislature, nor a sovereign entity unto itself, but a collective substitute for the monarch. In essence, it was to be a plural executive rather than a parliamentary body.

For all the weaknesses of the central government proposed by the Articles of Confederation, it represented the most appropriate structure for the new nation. After all, the Revolution on the battlefields had yet to be won, and the statesmen did not have the luxury of engaging in prolonged and perhaps divisive debates over the distribution of power that proposals for other systems would have provoked. There would be time later for modifications.

The Social Revolution

Americans formed a consensus on the general frame of government—the forms grew naturally out of the experience and the ideas of the colonial period. On other issues raised by the Revolution, however, there was sharp disagreement. What did the Revolution mean to those workers, servants, farmers, and freed slaves who participated in the Stamp Act demonstrations, supported the boycotts, idolized Tom Paine, and fought with Washington and Greene?

Many laboring folk hoped that the Revolution would remove, not reinforce, the traditional political and social advantages exercised by colonial elites. The more conservative Patriots would have been content to replace royal officials with the rich, the well-born, and the able, and let it go at that. But more radical elements, in the apt phrase of one historian, raised the question not only of home rule, but of who shall rule at home.

Equality and Its Limits

This spirit of equality weakened old habits of deference. Participation in the army or militia stirred to action people who had taken little interest in politics. The large number of new political opportunities afforded by the creation of new state governments thus led more ordinary citizens into participation than ever before. The social base of the new legislatures was much broader than that of the old assemblies.

Men fighting for their liberty found it difficult to justify denying other white men the rights of suffrage and representation. The property qualifications for voting, which already admitted an overwhelming majority of white males, were lowered still further in some states. In Pennsylvania, Delaware, North Carolina, Georgia, and Vermont, any male taxpayer could vote, although officeholders had to meet higher property requirements. In the state legislatures, older representatives, some of whom had been Loyalists, were often replaced by newcomers with less property and little education. Some states concentrated much power in a legislature chosen by a wide suffrage, but not even Pennsylvania, which adopted the most radical state constitution, went quite so far as universal male suffrage. Others, like New York and Maryland, took a more conservative stance and instituted stiff property requirements for voting.

The Paradox of Slavery

The Revolutionary generation of leaders was the first to confront the issue of slavery and to consider abolishing it. The principles of liberty and equality so crucial to the rebellion had clear implications for America's enslaved blacks. Jefferson's draft of the Declaration of Independence had indicted the king for having violated the "most sacred rights of life and liberty of a distant people" by encouraging the slave trade in the colonies, but he deleted the clause to satisfy leaders from South Carolina and Georgia.

Black soldiers or sailors were present at most of the major battles, from Lexington to Yorktown; most were on the Loyalist side. Slaves who served in the cause of independence got their freedom and in some cases land bounties. But the British army, which freed probably tens of thousands of slaves during the war, was a greater instrument of emancipation than the American forces. Most of the newly freed blacks found their way to Canada or to British colonies in the Caribbean.

In the northern states, which had fewer slaves than the southern, the doctrines of liberty led swiftly to emancipation for all either during the fighting or shortly afterward. South of Pennsylvania the potential consequences of emancipation were so staggering—South Carolina had a black majority—that whites refused to extend the principle of liberty to their slaves. Although some southern slaveholders like Washington, Jefferson, Patrick Henry, and others were troubled, most could not bring themselves to free their own slaves.

Slaves, especially in the upper South, also earned freedom through their own actions during the Revolutionary era, frequently by running away. They often gravitated to the growing number of African-American communities in the North. Because of emancipation laws in the northern states, and with the formation of free black neighborhoods in the North and in several southern cities, runaways found refuge and the opportunities for new lives. It is estimated that 55,000 slaves fled to freedom during the Revolution.

The Status of Women

The logic of liberty applied to the status of women as much as to that of slaves. Women had remained essentially confined to the domestic sphere during the eighteenth century. They could not vote or preach or hold office. Few had access to formal education. Although in some colonies women could own property and execute contracts, in other colonies they could not legally own even their own clothes, and they had no legal rights over their children. Divorces were extremely difficult to obtain.

The Revolutionary ferment offered women new opportunities and new roles. They plowed fields and melted down pots and pans to make shot. Women also assisted the armies in various ways, such as handling supplies and serving as spies or couriers. Wives sometimes followed their husbands to camp, where they nursed the wounded and sick, cooked and washed for the able, and frequently buried the dead. On occasion, women took their places in the firing line.

Yet the legal status of women did not benefit dramatically from the equalitarian doctrine fostered by the Revolution. Most women retained the narrow domestic outlook that had long been imposed on them. A few free-spirited reformers, however, argued that only educated and independent mothers could raise children fit for republican citizenship. Some demanded equal treatment. In an essay entitled "On the Equality of the Sexes," written in 1779 and published in 1790, Judith Sargent Murray of Gloucester, Massachusetts, stressed the importance of mutuality in marriage: "Mutual esteem, mutual friendship, mutual confidence, begirt about by mutual forbearance." Murray and others insisted that women were perfectly capable of excelling outside the domestic sphere.

Freedom of Religion

The Revolution also set in motion a transition from the toleration of religious dissent to a complete freedom of religion in the separation of church and state. The Anglican church, established as the official religion in five colonies and parts of two others, was especially vulnerable because of its association with the crown and because dissenters outnumbered Anglicans in most states except Virginia. All but Virginia removed tax support for the church before the fighting was over. In 1776, the Virginia Declaration of Rights (a bill of rights) guar-

The Congregational church developed a national body in the early nineteenth century; Lemuel Haynes, depicted here, was its first black preacher.

anteed the free exercise of religion, and in 1786 the Virginia Statute of Religious Freedom (written by Thomas Jefferson) declared that "no man shall be compelled to frequent or support any religious worship, place or ministry whatsoever," and "that all men shall be free to profess and by argument to maintain, their opinions in matters of religion." These statutes and the Revolutionary ideology that spawned them helped shape the course that religion would take in the new United States: pluralistic and voluntary rather than monolithic and state supported.

In churches as well as in government, the Revolution set off a period of constitution-making, as some of the first national church bodies emerged. In 1784 the Methodists, who at first were an offshoot of the Anglicans, organized a general conference at Baltimore. The Anglican church, rechristened Episcopal, gathered in a series of meetings which by 1789 had united the various dioceses in a federal union; in 1789 the Presbyterians also held their first general assembly in Philadelphia. The following year, 1790, the Catholic church had its first bishop in the United States when John Carroll was named bishop of Baltimore. Other churches would follow in the process of organizing on a national basis.

Emergence of an American Culture

The Revolution generated among some Americans a sense of common nationality. As early as the Stamp Act Congress of 1765, Christopher Gadsden, leader of the Charleston radicals, had said: "There ought to be no New England man, no New Yorker, known on the Continent; but all of us Americans." In the first Continental Congress Patrick Henry asserted that such a sense of national identity had come to pass: "The distinctions between Virginians, Pennsylvanians, New Yorkers, and New Englanders are no more. I am not a Virginian but an American." Henry claimed too much. Before long he and others would reassert state loyalties, but for now an American spirit was in the air.

Art in the New Nation

The Revolution provided the first generation of native artists with inspirational subjects. It also filled them with high expectations that individual freedom would release creative energies and vitalize both commerce and the arts.

Ironically, the best American painters of the time spent all or most of the Revolution in England, studying with Benjamin West of Pennsylvania and John Singleton Copley of Massachusetts, both of whom had set up shop in London before the outbreak of hostilities. Even John Trumbull, who had served in the siege of Boston and the Saratoga campaign, somehow managed a visit to London during the war. Later he highlighted patriotic themes in numerous canvases celebrating scenes from the Revolution. Similarly, Charles Willson Peale, who fought at Trenton and Princeton and survived the winter at Valley Forge, produced a virtual portrait gallery of Revolutionary War figures. Over twenty-three years he painted George Washington seven times from life and produced in all sixty portraits of the general.

Education

The most lasting cultural effect of postwar nationalism may well have been its mark on education. The colonies had founded a total of nine colleges, but after the Revolution eight more sprang up in the 1780s and six more in the 1790s. Several of the state constitutions provided for state universities. Georgia's was the first chartered, in 1785, but the University of North Carolina (chartered in 1789) was the first to open, in 1795.

Even more important, the Revolution provided the initial impetus for state-supported public school systems. Many of the founders believed that the survival of the new nation depended upon instilling in the public an appreciation for the fragility of republican government and its utter dependence on private and civic virtue. They viewed public schools as the best agencies for such moral and civic development. Yet schemes for most public schools came to naught. Wealthy critics opposed spending tax money on schools that would mingle their sons "in a vulgar and suspicious communion" with the masses.

Mission

In a special sense, American nationalism embodied an idea of divine mission. Many people, at least since the time of the Pilgrims, had thought America to be singled out by God for a special identity, a special mission. This sense of mission was neither limited to New England nor rooted solely in Calvinism. From the democratic rhetoric of Jefferson, to the pragmatism of Washington, to heady toasts bellowed in South Carolina taverns, patriots everywhere articulated a special American leadership role in human history. The mission was now a call to lead the way toward liberty and equality. Meanwhile, however, Americans had to address more immediate problems created by their new nationhood. Benjamin Rush, the Philadelphia patriot, doctor, and scientist, issued a prophetic statement in 1787: "The American war is over: but this is far from being the case with the American Revolution. On the contrary, but the first act of the great drama is closed."

CHAPTER 6

Shaping a Federal Union

This chapter focuses on

- The achievements and weaknesses of the Confederation government.
- The issues involved in writing the Constitution.
- The debate over ratifying the Constitution.

THE *ESSENTIAL AMERICA* ON-LINE TUTOR

www.wwnorton.com/eamerica/ch6

- **Topic: The Constitutional Convention**
  www.wwnorton.com/eamerica/ch6/topic.htm

  The Constitutional Convention of 1787 was a remarkable moment of political creation, notable for its achievements and its shortcomings. Explore the convention through paintings, primary source materials, historical analyses, personal correspondence, and biographical sketches. How did such a diverse group successfully arrive at conclusions that have endured for more than two centuries?

- **Chapter review: On-line quiz and chapter summary**
  www.wwnorton.com/eamerica/ch6/review.htm

- **Chapter resources: Multimedia index**
  www.wwnorton.com/eamerica/ch6/media.htm

In an address to fellow graduates at the Harvard commencement in 1787, young John Quincy Adams lamented "this critical period" when the country was struggling to establish itself as a new nation. Historians thereafter used his phrase to designate the years when the United States operated under the Articles of Confederation, 1781 to 1787. Fear of government power dominated the period, and such concerns ensured that the new Confederation would not threaten state sovereignty. Yet while there were weaknesses of the Confederation, there were also major achievements during the so-called critical period. Moreover, lessons learned under the Confederation would prompt the formulation of a new Constitution intended to balance central and local authority.

The Confederation

The Congress of the Confederation had little authority. It could only request money from the states; it could make treaties with foreign countries but could not enforce them; it could borrow money but lacked the means to ensure repayment. The Congress was virtually helpless to cope with the postwar problems of diplomacy and economic depression, problems that would have challenged the resources of a much stronger government. It was not easy to find men of stature to serve in such a body, and often hard to gather a quorum of those who did. Yet, in spite of its handicaps, the Confederation Congress somehow managed to keep afloat and to lay important foundations for the future. It concluded the Peace of Paris in 1783, created the first executive departments, and formulated principles of land distribution and territorial government that guided expansion all the way to the Pacific coast.

The Articles of Confederation

When the Articles of Confederation took effect in 1781, they did little more than make legal the status quo. Congress had a multitude of responsibilities but little authority to carry them out. It had full power over foreign affairs and questions of war and peace; it could decide disputes between the states; it had authority over coinage, postal service, and Indian affairs, and responsibility for the government of the western territories. But it had no courts and no power to enforce its resolutions and ordinances upon either states or individuals. The Confederation had neither an executive nor a judicial branch; there was no administrative head of government (only the president of the Congress, chosen annually) and no federal courts. It also had no power to levy taxes but had to rely on requisitions, which state legislatures could ignore at their will.

The states, after their colonial battles with Parliament, were in no mood for a strong central government. The Congress in fact had less power than the colonists had once accepted in Parliament, since it could not regulate interstate and foreign commerce. For certain important acts, moreover, a "special majority" was required. Nine states had to approve measures dealing with war, privateering, treaties, coinage, finances, or the army and navy. Unanimous approval by the states was needed to levy tariffs (often called "duties") on imports. Amendments to the Articles of Confederation also required unanimous ratification by the states.

Throughout most of the War for Independence, the Congress had remained distrustful of executive power. It had assigned administrative duties to its committees and thereby imposed a painful burden on conscientious members. At one time or another John Adams, for instance, had served on some eighty committees. In 1781, however, anticipating ratification of the Articles of Confederation, Congress began to set up three departments: Foreign Affairs, Finance, and War. Each was to have a single head responsible to Congress. Given time and stability, Congress and the department heads might have evolved into something like the parliamentary cabinet system. As it turned out, these agencies were the forerunners of the government departments to be established under the Constitution.

Finance

Since there was neither president nor prime minister, but only the presiding officer of Congress and its secretary, the closest thing to an executive head of the Confederation was Robert Morris, who was superintendent of finance in the final years of the war. Morris wanted to make both himself and the Confederation more powerful. He envisioned a coherent program of taxation and debt management to make the government financially stable.

As the foundation of his plan, Morris secured in 1781 a congressional charter for the Bank of North America, which would hold government deposits, lend money to the government, and issue bank notes that would provide a stable currency for the country at large. But his program depended ultimately on a secure source of revenue for the Confederation government, and it proved impossible to win the unanimous approval of the states for the necessary amendments to the Articles of Confederation. Local interests and the fear of a central authority hobbled action. As a consequence, the Confederation never put its finances in order. The Continental currency quickly proved worthless, and each year Congress ran a deficit on its operating expenses.

Land Policy

The one source from which Congress might hope to draw an independent income was the sale of western lands, but throughout the Confederation period that income remained more a fleeting promise than an accomplished fact. The Confederation nevertheless dealt more effectively with the western lands than with anything else. There Congress had direct authority, at least on paper. Thinly populated by Indians, French settlers, and a growing number of American squatters, the region north of the Ohio River had long been the site of overlapping claims by colonies and speculators. By 1786 all states had abandoned their claims in the area except for a 120-mile strip along Lake Erie, which Connecticut held until 1800 as its "Western Reserve."

As early as 1779, Congress had decided not to treat the western lands as colonies but as equal states. Between 1784 and 1787, policies for western development emerged in three major ordinances of the Confederation Congress. These documents, which rank among its greatest achievements, set precedents that the United States would follow in its future expansion. Thomas Jefferson wanted to grant self-government to western territories at an early stage, when settlers would meet and choose their own officials. Under Jefferson's Ordinance of 1784, when a territory's population equaled that of the smallest existing state, it would achieve full statehood.

In the Land Ordinance of 1785, the delegates outlined a plan of surveys and sales that eventually stamped a rectangular pattern on much of the nation's surface. Wherever Indian titles had been extinguished, the Northwest was to be surveyed into townships six miles square along east-west and north-south lines. Each township in turn was to be divided into thirty-six lots (or sections), each one mile square (or 640 acres). The 640-acre sections were to be auctioned for no less than $1 per acre, or $640 total. Such terms favored land speculators, of course, since few common folk had that much money or were able to work that much land. In later years, new land laws would make smaller lots available at lower prices. In each township, Congress reserved the income from the sixteenth section for the support of schools—a significant departure at a time when public schools were rare.

Robert Morris, the most influential figure in the Confederation government, in a portrait by Charles Willson Peale.

Spurred by the plans for land sales and settlement, Congress drafted a more specific form of territorial government to replace Jefferson's Ordinance of 1784. The new plan backed off from the commitment to early self-government. Because of the trouble that might be expected from squatters who were clamoring for free land, the Northwest Ordinance of 1787 required a period of colonial tutelage. At first the territory fell subject to a governor, a secretary, and three judges, all chosen by Congress. When any territory in the Northwest region had 5,000 free male adults, it could choose an assembly, and Congress would name a governing council from names proposed by the assembly. The governor would have a veto and so would Congress.

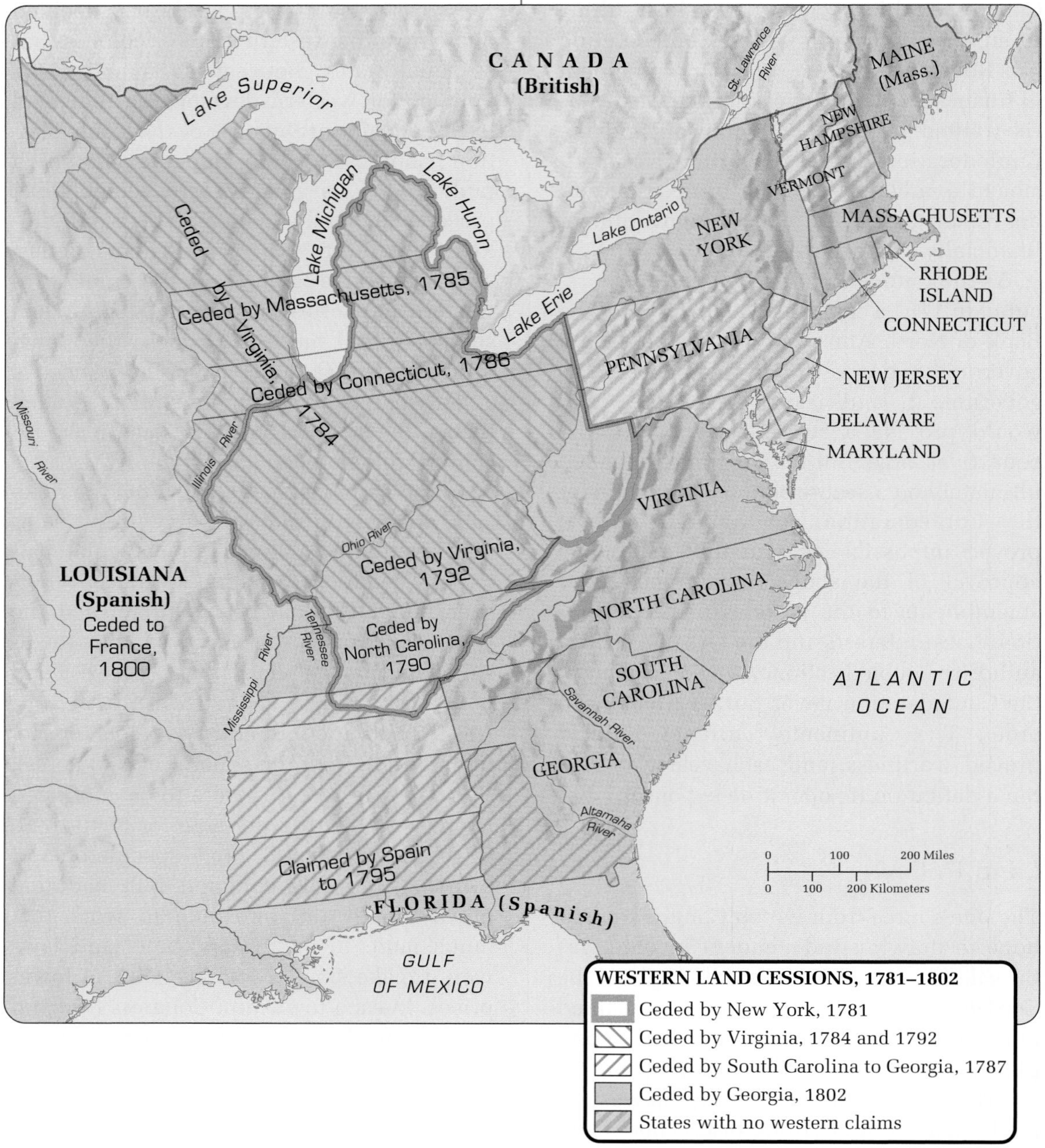

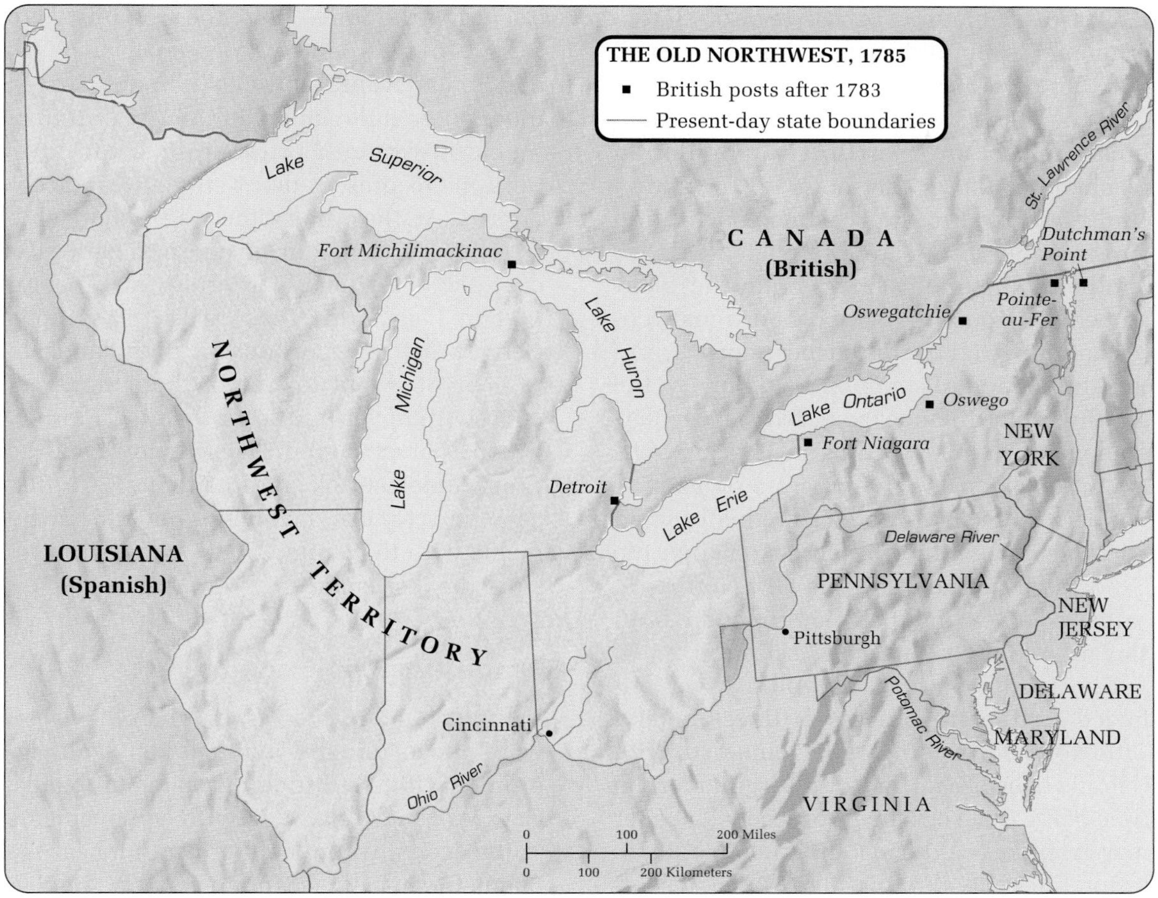
THE OLD NORTHWEST, 1785
British posts after 1783
Present-day state boundaries
Lake Superior
Fort Michilimackinac
CANADA
(British)
St. Lawrence River
Dutchman's Point
Pointe-au-Fer
Oswegatchie
Lake Huron
Lake Michigan
NORTHWEST TERRITORY
Lake Ontario
Oswego
Fort Niagara
NEW YORK
Detroit
Lake Erie
LOUISIANA
(Spanish)
Delaware River
PENNSYLVANIA
Pittsburgh
NEW JERSEY
DELAWARE
MARYLAND
Potomac River
Cincinnati
Ohio River
VIRGINIA
0
100
200 Miles
0
100
200 Kilometers

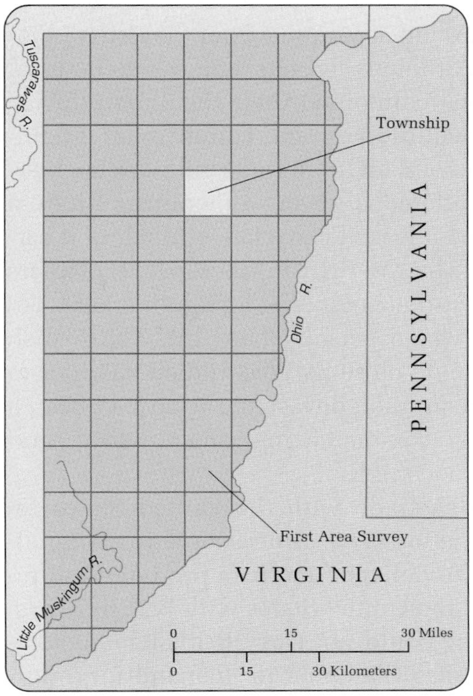
Tuscarawas R.
Township
PENNSYLVANIA
Ohio R.
First Area Survey
VIRGINIA
Little Muskingum R.
0
15
30 Miles
0
15
30 Kilometers

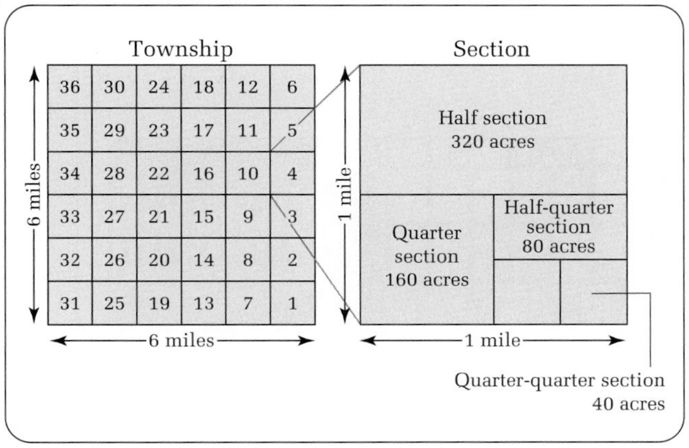
Township
36 30 24 18 12 6
35 29 23 17 11 5
34 28 22 16 10 4
33 27 21 15 9 3
32 26 20 14 8 2
31 25 19 13 7 1
6 miles
6 miles
Section
Half section
320 acres
Quarter section
160 acres
Half-quarter section
80 acres
1 mile
1 mile
Quarter-quarter section
40 acres

The resemblance of these territorial governments to the old royal colonies is clear, but there were two significant differences. For one, the Ordinance anticipated statehood when any territory's population reached 60,000. At that point, a convention could be called to draft a state constitution and to apply to Congress for statehood. For another, it included a bill of rights that guaranteed religious freedom, proportional representation, trial by jury, habeas corpus, and the application of common law. Finally, the Northwest Ordinance excluded slavery permanently from the Northwest. This proved a fateful decision. As the progress of emancipation in the existing states gradually freed all slaves above the Mason-Dixon line, the Ohio River boundary of the Old Northwest extended the line between freedom and slavery all the way to the Mississippi.

The lands south of the Ohio River followed a different process of development. Title to the western lands remained with Georgia, North Carolina, and Virginia for the time being, but settlement proceeded at a far more rapid pace during and after the Revolution, despite the Indians' fierce resentment. Substantial population centers grew up in Kentucky and Tennessee.

Merchants' Counting House. Americans involved in overseas trade, such as the merchants depicted here, were sharply affected by the dislocations of war.

During the mid-1780s, the Iroquois were forced to cede land in western New York and Pennsylvania, and the Cherokees forced to give up all claims in South Carolina, much of western North Carolina, and large portions of present-day Kentucky and Tennessee. At the same time, the major Ohio tribes lost their claim to most of Ohio, except for a segment bordering the western part of Lake Erie. The Creeks, pressed by Georgia to cede portions of their lands in 1784–1785, went to war in the summer of 1786 with covert aid from Spanish Florida. When Spanish support lapsed, however, the Creek chief struck a bargain in 1791 that gave the Creeks favorable trade arrangements with the United States but did not restore the lost lands.

Trade and the Economy

In its economic life, as in planning westward expansion, the young nation dealt vigorously with the difficult wartime problems. Congress had little to do with achievements in the economy, but neither could it bear the blame for an acute economic contraction between 1770 and 1790, the result primarily of the war and separation from the British Empire. Although farmers enmeshed in local markets maintained their livelihood during the Revolutionary era, commercial agriculture dependent upon trade with foreign markets suffered a severe downturn. Virginia suffered a loss of slave labor, much of it carried off by the British. Chesapeake planters also lost their lucrative foreign markets. Tobacco was especially hard hit. The British decision to close its West Indian colonies to American trade devastated what had been a thriving commerce in timber, wheat, and other foodstuffs.

British trade with the United States resumed after 1783. American ships were allowed to deliver American products and return to the United States with British goods, but they could not carry British goods anywhere else. The pent-up demand for familiar goods created a vigorous market in America for imports, fueled by British credits and the hard money that had come into the new nation from foreign aid, the expenditures of foreign armies, and wartime trade and privateering. The result was a quick cycle of postwar boom and bust, a buying spree followed by a money shortage and economic troubles that lasted several years.

In colonial days the chronic trade deficit with Britain had been offset by the influx of coins from trade with the West Indies. Now American ships found themselves legally excluded from the British West Indies. But the islands still demanded wheat, fish, lumber, and other products from the mainland, and American shippers had not lost their talent for smuggling. By 1787, Americans were also trading with the Dutch, Swedes, Prussians, Moroccans, and Chinese, and American seaports were flourishing more than ever. By 1790, American commerce and exports had far outrun the trade of the colonies. American merchants had more ships than before the war. Farm exports were twice what they had been. Although most of the exports were the products of American forests, fields, and fisheries, during and after the war more workers had turned to small-scale manufacturing—shoes, textiles, soap—mainly for domestic markets.

Diplomacy

The achievements of the flourishing young nation are more visible in hindsight than they were at the time. Until 1787, the shortcomings and failures of the Confederation government remained far more apparent—and the advocates of a stronger central government were extremely vocal on the subject. In diplomacy, there remained the nagging problems of relations with Great Britain and Spain, both of which kept military posts on American soil and conspired with Indians and white settlers in the West. The British, despite the peace treaty of 1783, held on to a string of forts along the Canadian border. From these they kept a hand in the fur trade and a degree of influence with the Indian tribes.

Another major irritant was the confiscation of Loyalist property. The peace treaty had obligated Congress to stop confiscations, to guarantee immunity to Loyalists for twelve months during which they could return and wind up their affairs, and to recommend that the states return confiscated property. Persecutions, even lynchings, of Loyalists still occurred until after the end of the war. Some Loyalists returned unmolested, however, and once again took up their lives in their former homes. By the end of 1787, moreover, all the states had rescinded laws discriminating against former Tories.

With Spain, the chief issues were the southern boundary and the right to navigate the Mississippi. According to the preliminary treaty with Britain, the United States claimed as its traditional boundary a line running eastward from the mouth of the Yazoo River. The American treaty with Britain had also specified the right to navigate the Mississippi River to its mouth, but the river was entirely within Spanish Louisiana in its lower reaches. The right to navigation assumed importance because of the growing settlements in Kentucky and Tennessee, but in 1784 Louisiana's Spanish governor closed the river to American commerce. He also began to intrigue with the Creeks, Choctaws, Chickasaws, and other Indians of the Southwest against the American settlers and with the settlers themselves against the United States. The issue of American access to the lower Mississippi remained unsettled for nearly another decade.

The Confederation's Problems

Of greatest concern to most Americans were protection for infant American industries and the currency shortage. Mechanics (skilled workers who made, used, or repaired tools and machines) and artisans (skilled workers who made products) were developing exports ranging from crude iron nails to the fine silver bowls of Paul Revere. They were frustrated by British policies excluding them from British markets, and in retaliation they sought from the states tariffs (taxes on imports) on foreign goods that competed with theirs. The country would be on its way to economic independence, they argued, if only the money that flowed into the country were invested in domestic manufactures instead of being paid out for foreign goods. Nearly all the states gave some preference to American goods, but the lack of consistency in their laws put them at cross purposes, and so urban mechanics along with merchants were drawn into the movement demanding a stronger central government in the interest of uniform regulation of trade.

The shortage of cash and other economic difficulties generated demands for paper currency as legal tender, for postponement of tax and debt payments, and for laws to "stay" the foreclosure of mortgages. Farmers who had profited during the war found themselves squeezed by depressed crop prices and mounting debts while merchants sorted out and opened up new trade routes. Creditors demanded hard money, but it was in short supply—and paper money was both scarce and virtually worthless after the depreciation of the Continental currency. The result was an outcry among debtor groups for relief, and around 1785 the demand for new paper money became the most divisive issue in state politics. In 1785–1786 seven states (Pennsylvania, New York, New Jersey, South Carolina, Rhode Island, Georgia, and North Carolina) issued paper money. In spite of the cries of calamity at the time, the money served positively as a means of credit to hard-pressed farmers through state loans on farm mortgages. It was also used to fund state debts and to pay off the claims of veterans.

Led by Daniel Shays, a band of disgruntled farmers attacked the federal arsenal at Springfield, Massachusetts, in January 1787, but were repulsed by the militia.

Shays's Rebellion

Many Americans—especially bankers and merchants—hated such inflationary policies. Developments in Massachusetts provided the final proof (some said) that the country was poised on the brink of anarchy: Shays's Rebellion. After 1780, Massachusetts had remained in the grip of a rigidly conservative regime. Ever higher poll and land taxes were levied to pay off a large war debt, held mainly by wealthy creditors in Boston. The taxes fell most heavily upon beleaguered farmers and the working poor in general.

When the legislature adjourned in 1786 without providing either paper money or any other relief from taxes and debts, three western counties erupted into spontaneous revolt. Armed bands closed the courts and prevented foreclosures, and a ragtag "army" of some 1,200 disgruntled farmers led by Captain Daniel Shays, a destitute farmer and "brave and good" war veteran, advanced upon the federal arsenal at Springfield in 1787. Shays and his followers sought a more flexible monetary policy, laws allowing them to use corn and wheat as money, and the right to postpone paying taxes until the depression lifted.

A small militia force scattered Shays's men with a single volley that left four dead. The rebels nevertheless had a victory of sorts. The new state legislature included members sympathetic to the agricultural crisis. They omitted direct taxes the following year, lowered court fees, and exempted clothing, household goods, and tools from the debt process. But a more important consequence was the impetus the rebellion gave to conservatism and nationalism.

Rumors, at times deliberately inflated, greatly exaggerated the extent of Shays's rebellion. The uprising seemed to provide an ominous example of possible greater turmoil, and panic set in among the republic's elite. New York's Gouverneur Morris was typically blunt: "The mob begin to think and reason. Poor reptiles! They bask in the sun and ere noon they will bite, depend upon it. The gentry begin to fear this."

Calls for a Stronger Government

Shays's Rebellion convinced many political leaders that the Articles of Confederation were incapable of providing an effective basis for the new republican government. Self-interest frequently led bankers, merchants, and mechanics to promote a stronger central government. At the same time, many public-spirited men saw it as the only alternative to anarchy. Gradually people were losing the ingrained fear of central authority as they saw evidence that tyranny might come from other quarters, including the common people themselves.

By the mid-1780s, in fact, several prominent political spokesmen had become convinced that the new state governments were being run by uneducated entrepreneurs pursuing selfish economic and petty political interests. Men of humble origins and parochial points of view were allegedly displacing the "wise and virtuous" from seats of power. Such inexperienced and frequently uncouth lawmakers were passing an avalanche of legislation merely to serve particular interest groups and constituents rather than the general welfare. They were printing excessive amounts of paper money and passing "stay" laws (laws that granted stays, or postponements of debt payments) preventing judicial action against debtors.

Such developments led many of the Revolutionary leaders to revise their assessment of American character. "We have, probably," concluded George Washington in 1786, "had too good an opinion of human nature in forming our confederation." The following year James Madison reported to Jefferson that America was displaying "symptoms . . . truly alarming, which have tainted the faith of most orthodox republicans." People were stretching the meaning of liberty far beyond what he and others had envisioned. He found a "spirit of *locality*" rampant in the state legislatures that was destroying the "aggregate interests of the community." Even worse, he saw people taking the law and other people's property into their own hands. Such developments led Madison and others to revise their assumptions about the degree of republican virtue in the American people. At any given time, they decided, only a distinct minority could be relied upon to set aside their private interests in favor of the common good. Madison and these so-called Federalists concluded that the new republic must now depend for its success on the constant virtue of the few rather than the public-spiritedness of the many. For these reasons and others, nationalists demanded revisions to the Articles of Confederation.

Adopting the Constitution

After stalling for several months, Congress, in 1787, passed a resolution endorsing a convention "for the sole and express purpose of revising the Articles of Confederation." By then five states had already named

James Madison was only thirty-six when he assumed a major role in the drafting of the Constitution. This miniature is by Charles Willson Peale (c. 1783).

delegates; before the meeting, six more states had acted. Rhode Island kept aloof throughout, leading critics to label it "Rogue Island."

The Constitutional Convention

Twenty-nine delegates began work in Philadelphia on May 25. Altogether seventy-three men were elected by the state legislatures, fifty-five attended at one time or another, and after four months, thirty-nine signed the Constitution they had drafted.

The document's durability and flexibility testify to the remarkable quality of the men who made it. The delegates were surprisingly young—forty-two was the average age. Only two were small farmers. Most were planters, merchants, lawyers, judges, bankers—many of them widely read in history, law, and political philosophy, yet at the same time practical men of experience, tested in the fires of the Revolution. Twenty-one had fought in the conflict, seven had been state governors, most of them had served in the Continental Congress, and eight had signed the Declaration of Independence.

The delegates spent four sweltering months fighting flies, the humidity, and each other. They worked with a sense of urgency, five to six hours a day, six days a week, hammering out the compromises embedded in the Constitution. On certain fundamentals they generally agreed: that government derived its just powers from the consent of the people, but that society must be protected from the tyranny of the majority; that the people at large must have a voice in their government, but that checks and balances must be provided to keep any one group from dominating; that a stronger central authority was essential, but that all power was subject to abuse. Even the best of people were naturally selfish, they believed, and therefore government could not be founded upon a trust in goodwill and virtue. Yet by carefully checking power with countervailing power, the Founding Fathers hoped to devise institutions that could somehow constrain individual sinfulness and channel individual self-interest on behalf of the public good.

The Virginia and New Jersey Plans

James Madison was the key figure at the convention. He arrived in Philadelphia with trunks of books and a head full of ideas, and he set about drafting the proposals that came to be called the "Virginia Plan," presented on May 29. This plan called for separate legislative, executive, and judicial branches, and a truly national government whose laws would be binding upon individual citizens as well as upon states. Congress would be divided into two houses, a lower house to be chosen by popular vote and an upper house to be chosen by the lower house from nominees of the state legislatures. Congress could disallow state laws under the plan and would itself define the extent of its and the states' authority.

On June 15 William Paterson submitted the "New Jersey Plan," which kept the existing equal representation of states in a unicameral Congress but gave the Congress power to levy taxes, regulate commerce, and name a plural executive (with no veto) and a Supreme Court. The different plans presented the convention with two major issues: whether to amend the Articles of Confederation or draft an entirely new document, and whether to apportion congressional representation by population or by states.

On the first point, the Convention voted to work toward a national government as envisioned by the Virginians. Experience had persuaded the delegates that an effective central government, as distinguished from a confederation, needed the power to levy taxes, to regulate commerce, to raise an army and navy, and to make laws binding upon individual citizens. The lessons of the

1780s suggested to them, moreover, that in the interest of order and uniformity the states must be denied certain powers: to issue money, to void contracts, to make treaties or wage war, and to levy tariffs.

But other issues provoked furious disagreements. The first clash in the Convention involved the issue of representation, and it was solved by the "Great Compromise," sometimes called the "Connecticut Compromise," offered by Roger Sherman. In the House of Representatives, apportionment would be by population, which pleased the more populous states; in the Senate, there would be equal representation of each state (although votes would be by individuals and not by states), which protected state power.

An equally contentious struggle ensued between northern and southern delegates over slavery, an omen of future sectional controversies. Few if any of the framers even considered the possibility of abolishing slavery in those states—mostly southern—where it was still legal. The interest of southern delegates, with slaves so numerous in their states, dictated that slaves be counted as part of the population in determining the number of representatives. Northerners were willing to have slaves counted in deciding each state's share of direct taxes but not for purposes of representation. The delegates, with little dissent, agreed in a compromise to count three-fifths of the slaves as a basis for apportioning both representatives and direct taxes.

A more sensitive issue involved an effort to prevent the new central government from stopping the transatlantic slave trade. Eventually a compromise emerged whereby the delegates established a time limit after which the slave trade would be prohibited. Congress could not prohibit the traffic until 1808, but it could levy a tax of $10 a head on all slaves imported. In drafting both provisions, a sense of delicacy—and hypocrisy—dictated the use of euphemisms. The Constitution thus spoke of "free persons" and "all other persons," of persons "held to Service of Labor." The odious word "slavery" did not appear in the Constitution until the Thirteenth Amendment (1865) abolished the "peculiar institution" by name.

If the delegates found the slavery issue distracting, they considered irrelevant any discussion of the legal or political role of women under the new Constitution. There was never any formal discussion of women's rights at the Convention. The new nationalism still defined politics and government as outside the realm of female endeavor.

The Separation of Powers

Some delegates displayed a thumping disdain for any democratizing of the political system. Alexander Hamilton called the people "a great beast," and Elbridge Gerry asserted that most of the nation's problems "flow from an excess of democracy." These elitist views were incorporated into the Constitution's mixed legislative system, which allowed direct popular choice of just one chamber of the Congress. The lower house was designed to be closest to the voters, who elected it every two years. The House of Representatives would be, according to Virginia's George Mason, "the grand repository of the democratic principle of the Government." Its members should "sympathize with their constituents, should think as they think, and feel as they feel; and for these purposes should even be residents among them." The upper house, or Senate, was elected by state legislatures rather than directly by the voters. Staggered six-year terms prevented the choice of a majority in any given year, and thereby further isolated senators from the passing fancies of public passion.

The decision that a single person be made the chief executive caused the delegates "considerable pause," according to Madison. George Mason protested that this would create a "fetus of monarchy." Indeed, although subject to election every four years, the

Signing the Constitution, September 17, 1787. Thomas Pritchard Rossiter's painting shows George Washington presiding over what Thomas Jefferson called "an assembly of demigods."

chief executive would wield powers that would exceed those of the British king. This was the sharpest departure from the recent experience in state government, in which the office of governor had commonly been diluted because of the memory of struggles with the colonial executives. The president could veto acts of Congress, subject to being overridden by a two-thirds vote in each house, was commander-in-chief of the armed forces, and was responsible for the execution of the laws. The chief executive could make treaties with the advice and consent of two-thirds of the Senate and appoint diplomats, judges, and other officers with the consent of a Senate majority.

But the president's powers were limited in certain key areas. The chief executive could neither declare war nor make peace; those powers were reserved for Congress. Unlike the British king, moreover, the president could be removed. The House could impeach (indict) the chief executive—and other civil officers—on charges of treason, bribery, or "other high crimes and misdemeanors"; the president could then be removed by the Senate with a two-thirds vote to convict.

The third branch of government, the judiciary, caused surprisingly little debate. Both the Virginia and New Jersey Plans had called for a Supreme Court, which the Constitution established, providing specifically for a chief justice of the United States and leaving up to Congress the number of other justices. Article VI declared the federal constitution, federal laws, and treaties to be the "supreme law of the land," state laws or constitutions to the contrary notwithstanding.

While the Constitution extended vast new powers to the national government, the delegates' mistrust of unchecked power is apparent in repeated examples of countervailing forces: the separation of the three branches of government, the president's veto, the congressional power of impeachment and removal, the Senate's power over treaties and appointments, the courts' implied right of judicial review. In addition, the new form of government specifically forbade Congress to pass ex post facto laws (laws adopted after the fact to make past deeds criminal). It also reserved to the states large areas of sovereignty—a reservation soon made explicit by the Tenth Amendment. By dividing sovereignty between the people and the government, the framers of the Constitution provided a distinctive contribution to political theory. That is, by vesting ultimate authority in the people, they divided sovereignty *within* the government. This constituted a dramatic break with the colonial tradition. The British had always insisted that the sovereignty of the king-in-Parliament was indivisible.

The Fight for Ratification

The final article of the Constitution provided that it would become effective upon ratification by nine states (not quite the three-fourths majority required for amendment). The Congress submitted the Convention's work to the states on September 28, 1787. In the ensuing political debate, advocates of the new Constitution, who might properly have been called Nationalists because they preferred a strong central government, assumed the more reassuring name of Federalists. Opponents, who favored a more decentralized federal system, became Antifederalists.

The Federalists were not only better prepared but better organized, and on the whole they represented the more articulate elements in the community. The Federalists were usually clustered in or near cities and tended to be more cosmopolitan, urbane, and well educated. Antifederalists tended to be small farmers and frontiersmen who saw little to gain from the promotion of interstate commerce and much to lose from prohibitions on paper money and "stay" laws. Many of them also feared that an expansive land policy was likely to favor speculators.

Historians have long debated what motivated the advocates of the new Constitution. Some, like Charles A. Beard, have argued that the Philadelphia Convention was made up of men who held large amounts of depreciated government securities and otherwise stood to gain from the power and stability of the new central government. But most of the delegates had no compelling economic interests at stake. Many prominent nationalists had no western lands or bonds. Some opponents of the Constitution, on the contrary, held large blocks of bonds and securities. Economic interests certainly figured in the process of constitution-making, but they functioned in a complex interplay of state, sectional, group, and individual interests that turned largely on how well people had fared under the Confederation.

The Federalist

Among the supreme legacies of the debate over the Constitution was a collection of essays called *The Federalist,* originally published in New York newspapers between 1787 and 1788. Initiated by Alexander Hamilton, the eighty-five articles published under the name "Publius" included about thirty by James Madison, nearly fifty by Hamilton, and five by John Jay. Written in support of ratification, the essays defended the principle of a supreme national authority but at the same time sought to reassure doubters that there was little reason to fear tyranny by the new government.

In perhaps the most famous single essay, Number Ten, Madison argued that the country's very size and diversity would make it impossible for any single faction to form a majority that could dominate the government. This contradicted prevailing notions of republican government. Republics, the conventional wisdom of the times insisted, could work only in small, homogeneous countries like Switzerland and the Netherlands. In larger countries, republican government would descend into anarchy and tyranny through the influence of factions. Quite the contrary, Madison argued. A republic with a balanced federal government could survive in a large and diverse country better than in a smaller country. "Extend the sphere," he wrote, "and you take in a greater variety of parties and interests; you make it less probable that a majority of the whole will have a common motive to invade the rights of other citizens."

The Federalists insisted that the new union would contribute to prosperity, in part to link their movement with the economic recovery already under way. The Antifederalists, however, highlighted the dangers of power. They noted the absence in the proposed Constitution of a bill of rights protecting individuals and states, and they found the ratification process highly irregular, which it was—indeed, illegal under the Articles of Confederation. The two groups disagreed, however, more over means than ends. Both sides for the most part agreed that a stronger national authority was needed, and that it required an independent income to function properly. Both were convinced that the people must erect safeguards against tyranny, even the tyranny of the majority. Once the new government had become an accomplished fact, few diehards were left who wanted to undo the work of the Philadelphia Convention.

The Decision of the States

Ratification of the new federal Constitution gained momentum throughout 1787, and New Hampshire was the ninth to ratify, on June 21, 1788. The Confederation Congress then began to draft plans for an orderly transfer of power. On September 13, 1788, it selected New York City as the seat of the new government and fixed the date for elections. On October 10, 1788, the Confederation Congress transacted its last business and passed into history. "Our constitution is in actual operation," the elderly Ben Franklin wrote to a friend; "everything appears to promise that it will last; but in this world nothing is certain but death and taxes." George Washington was even more uncertain about the future under the new plan of government. He had told a fellow delegate as the convention adjourned: "I do not expect the Constitution to last for more than twenty years."

"A More Perfect Union"

The Constitution has lasted much longer, of course, and in the process it has provided a model of republican government whose features have been repeatedly borrowed by other nations through the years. Yet what makes the American Constitution so distinctive is not its specific provisions but its remarkable harmony with the particular "genius of the people" it governs. The Constitution has been neither a static abstraction nor a "machine that would go of itself," as the poet James Russell Lowell would later assert. Instead it has provided a flexible system of government that presidents, legislators, judges, and the people have modified to accord with a fallible human nature and changing social, economic, and political circumstances. In this sense, the Founding Fathers not only created "a more perfect Union" in 1787; they engineered a form of government whose resilience has enabled later generations to continue to perfect their republican experiment. But the framers of the Constitution failed in one significant respect. In skirting the issue of slavery so as to cement the new union, they unknowingly allowed tensions over what southerners came to call their "peculiar institution" to reach the point at which there would be no political solution—only civil war.

CHAPTER

7

The Federalists: Washington and Adams

This chapter focuses on

- The early operation of the new government.
- Alexander Hamilton's Federalist program.
- The beginnings of the first party system (Federalists and Republicans).
- The elements of Federalist foreign policy.

THE *ESSENTIAL AMERICA* ON-LINE TUTOR

www.wwnorton.com/eamerica/ch7

- **Topic: Pierre L'Enfant and the federal city**
  www.wwnorton.com/eamerica/ch7/topic.htm

  In 1791 French architect Pierre L'Enfant drew up plans for the nation's new capitol—plans that included fifteen major public squares connected by broad, tree-lined avenues. Explore L'Enfant's design of Washington, D.C., using his drawings, historical analyses, personal correspondence, and maps. How did L'Enfant's design differ from the more traditional gridiron pattern used elsewhere in the young nation?

- **Chapter review: On-line quiz and chapter summary**
  www.wwnorton.com/eamerica/ch7/review.htm

- **Chapter resources: Multimedia index**
  www.wwnorton.com/eamerica/ch7/media.htm

The adoption of the new Constitution set in motion the creation of a new central government to deal more effectively with the problems of the vast new nation. The election of the first president, the writing of a bill of rights, and numerous domestic and foreign crises faced the fledgling nation.

A New Nation

The framers of the Constitution sought to create a new federal government capable of administering a rapidly expanding territory and population. In 1789 the United States and the western territories covered an area from the Atlantic Ocean to the Mississippi River and included almost 4 million people. The United States was predominantly a rural society. Eighty percent of households were involved in agricultural production. Only a few cities had more than 5,000 people. The first national census, taken in 1790, reported that there were 750,000 African Americans, almost one-fifth of the population. Most of them lived in the five southernmost states. Less than 10 percent of blacks lived outside the South. Most African Americans, of course, were slaves, but there were many free blacks as a result of the Revolutionary turmoil. In fact, the proportion of free blacks to slaves was never higher than in 1790.

The 1790 census did not include the many Indians still living east of the Mississippi River. Most Americans still viewed the Native Americans as those peoples whom the Declaration of Independence dismissed as "merciless Indian savages." It is estimated that there were over eighty tribes numbering perhaps as many as 150,000 persons in 1790. In the South, the five most powerful tribes—the Cherokees, Chickasaws, Choctaws, Creeks, and Seminoles—numbered between 50,000 and 100,000. They steadfastly refused to recognize American authority and used Spanish-supplied weapons to thwart white settlement.

Only about 125,000 whites and blacks lived west of the Appalachian Mountains in 1790. But that was soon to change. The great theme of nineteenth-century American history would be the ceaseless stream of migrants flowing westward from the Atlantic seaboard. By foot, horse, boat, and wagon, pioneers and adventurers headed west. Rapid population growth, cheap land, and new economic opportunities fueled western development. Although immigrants contributed significantly to the rising numbers, the extraordinary growth rate resulted primarily from natural increase. The average white woman gave birth to eight children, and the white population doubled approximately once every twenty-two years. This made for a very young population on average. In 1790 almost half of all white Americans were under sixteen.

A New Government

The men who drafted the Constitution knew that many questions were left unanswered, and they feared that putting the new form of government into practice would pose unexpected challenges. The new Congress of the United States opened with a whimper rather than a bang. On March 4, 1789, the appointed date of its first session in bustling New York City, only eight senators and thirteen representatives took their seats. A month passed before both chambers gathered a quorum. Only then could the temporary presiding officer of the Senate count the ballots and certify the foregone conclusion that George Washington, with sixty-nine votes, was the unanimous choice of the electoral college for president. John Adams, with thirty-four votes, the second-highest number, became vice-president.

Washington was a reluctant president. He greeted the news with "a heart filled with distress," yet he felt compelled to serve because he had been "summoned by my country." A self-made man with little formal education, Washington had a remarkable capacity for moderation and mediation that helped keep the infant republic from disintegrating.

Governmental Structure

Washington inherited but the shadow of a federal government: a foreign office with John Jay at its head and two clerks; a Treasury Board with little or no treasury; a 300-pound secretary of war, Henry Knox, with a lightweight army of 672 officers and men, and no navy at all; a heavy federal debt and almost no federal revenue.

During the summer of 1789, Congress created executive departments corresponding in each case to those already formed under the Confederation. To head the Department of State, Washington named Thomas Jefferson, recently back from his mission to France. Leadership of the Department of the Treasury went to Washington's wartime aide Alexander Hamilton, who had since become a prominent lawyer in New York. Tall, graceful Edmund Randolph, former governor of Virginia and owner of a plantation worked by 200 slaves, assumed the new position of attorney-general.

In 1789 Washington named New Yorker John Jay as the first chief justice of the Supreme Court, and he served until 1795. Born in New York City in 1745, Jay graduated from King's College (now Columbia University). His distinction as a lawyer led New York to send him as its representative to the First and Second Continental Congresses. After serving as president of the Continental Congress in 1779, Jay became the American minister in Spain. While in Europe, he helped John Adams and Benjamin Franklin negotiate the Treaty of Paris in 1783. After the Revolution, Jay served as secretary of foreign affairs. He then joined Madison and Hamilton as coauthor of *The Federalist* and became one of the most effective champions of the Constitution.

The Bill of Rights

In the new House of Representatives, James Madison made a bill of rights one of the first items of business. The lack of protection for individual rights had been one of the Antifederalists' major objections to the Constitution. During the ratification debate, Madison and other Federalists had argued that the Constitution needed no enumeration of specific "rights" because, as Madison said, "everything not granted is reserved." Madison and other Federalists also worried that specifying such rights might imply the existence of a parallel set of powers never meant to be delegated to the central government.

But public anxiety about individual rights persisted, so in May 1789 Madison reluctantly drew the first eight amendments from the Virginia Declaration of Rights, which George Mason had written in 1776. These provided safeguards for certain fundamental individual rights: freedom of religion, press, speech, and assembly; the right to keep and bear firearms; the right to refuse to house soldiers in private homes; protection from unreasonable searches and seizures; the right to refuse to testify against oneself; the right to a speedy public trial before an impartial jury and to have legal counsel present; and protection against cruel and unusual punishment. The states voted separately on each proposed amendment, and the Bill of Rights became effective December 15, 1791.

Hamilton's Vision of America

Revenue was the new federal government's most critical need, and Congress quickly enacted a tariff on imports intended to raise revenue and protect America's new manufacturers from foreign competition. Yet tariffs resulted in higher prices on imported goods bought by Americans, most of whom were tied to the farm economy. This raised a basic and perennial question: should these rural consumers be forced to subsidize the nation's infant manufacturing sector?

The import tariff launched the effort to get the country on a sound financial basis. In finance, with all its broad implications for policy in general, it was thirty-four-year-old Alexander Hamilton who seized the initiative. The first secretary of the treasury was the protégé of the president. Born out of wedlock on a Caribbean island, Hamilton found his way at seventeen to New York, attended King's College, and entered the Revolutionary army, where he became a favorite of George Washington. After the Revolution, he studied law, established a legal practice in New York, and served as collector of revenues and member of the Confederation Congress. An early convert to nationalism, he played a crucial part in promoting the Constitutional Convention and defending its work in *The Federalist*.

The new government needed all of Hamilton's ambition and brilliance. In a series of classic reports submitted to Congress in 1790 and 1791, he outlined his program for government finances and the economic development of the United States.

Establishing the Public Credit

The First Report on the Public Credit made two key recommendations: first, funding of the federal debt at face value, which meant that those citizens holding government securities could exchange them for new interest-bearing bonds of the same face value; and second, the federal government's assumption of state debts from the Revolution to the amount of $21 million. The funding scheme was controversial because many farmers and soldiers in need of immediate money had sold their securities for a fraction of their value to speculators. Spokesmen for these Americans argued that they should be reimbursed for their losses; otherwise, the speculators would gain a windfall. Hamilton sternly resisted. The speculators, he argued, had "paid what the commodity was worth in the market, and took the risks."

Payment of the national debt, Hamilton felt, would be not only a point of national honor and sound finance, ensuring the country's credit for the future; it would also be an occasion to assert a federal taxing power and thus instill respect for the authority of the national government. It was on this point, however, that Madison, who had been Hamilton's close ally in the movement for a stronger government, broke with him. Madison did not question that the debt should be paid, but he was troubled that speculators and "stock-jobbers" would become the chief beneficiaries. Also disturbing to the Virginian was that northerners held most of the debt. Madison's opposition touched off a vigorous debate that deadlocked the whole question of debt funding and assumption through much of 1790.

The stalemate finally ended when Hamilton, Jefferson, and Madison reached an understanding. In return for northern votes in favor of locating the permanent national capital on the Potomac River on the Virginia border, Madison pledged to seek enough southern votes to pass the debt assumption bill, with the further arrangement that those states with smaller debts would get in effect outright grants from the federal government to equalize the difference. These arrangements secured enough votes to carry Hamilton's funding and assumption plans. The national capital would be moved from New York to Philadelphia for ten years, after which it would be located in a new federal city on the Potomac River, the site to be chosen by the president. In August 1790 Congress finally passed the legislation for Hamilton's plan.

A National Bank

Through this vast program of funding and assumption, Hamilton had called up from nowhere, as if by magic, a great sum of cap-

Alexander Hamilton, secretary of the treasury from 1789 to 1795.

ital for the new federal government. Having established the public credit, Hamilton moved on to a related measure essential to his vision of national greatness. He called for a national bank, which by issuance of bank notes (paper money) might provide a uniform currency as well as a source of capital for the developing economy. Government bonds held by the bank would back up the currency. The national bank, chartered by Congress, would remain under governmental surveillance, but private investors would supply four-fifths of the $10 million capital and name twenty of the twenty-five directors; the government would purchase the other fifth of the capital and name five directors. Government bonds would be received in payment for three-fourths of the stock in the bank, and the other fourth would be payable in gold and silver.

Once again Madison rose to lead the opposition, arguing that he could find no basis in the Constitution for such a bank. That was enough to raise in President Washington's mind serious doubts as to the constitutionality of the measure, which Congress passed over Madison's objections. Before signing the bill into law, therefore, the president sought the advice of his cabinet and found an equal division of opinion. This resulted in the first great debate on constitutional interpretation. Should there be a strict or a broad construction of the document? Were the powers of Congress only those explicitly stated in the Constitution or were others implied? The argument turned chiefly on Article I, Section 8, which authorized Congress to "make all laws which shall be necessary and proper for carrying into execution the foregoing Powers."

Such language left room for disagreement and led to a confrontation between Jefferson and Hamilton. Jefferson pointed to the Tenth Amendment, which reserved to the states and the people powers not delegated to Congress. A bank might be a convenient aid to Congress in collecting taxes and regulating the currency, but it was not, as Article I, Section 8, specified, *necessary*. Hamilton insisted that the power to charter corporations was included in the sovereignty of any government, whether or not expressly stated. The president accepted Hamilton's argument and signed the bill. By doing so, in Jefferson's words, he opened up "a boundless field of power," which in coming years would lead to a further broadening of implied powers with the approval of the Supreme Court.

Encouraging Manufactures

Hamilton's imagination and his ambitions for the new country were not yet exhausted. At the end of 1790, he submitted a Second Report on Public Credit, which included a proposal for an excise tax on alcoholic beverages to aid in raising revenue to cover the nation's debts. Six weeks later, the secretary proposed a national mint, which was established in 1792. And finally, on December 5, 1791, as the culmination of his basic reports, in his Report on Manufactures he proposed an extensive program of government aid to the development of manufacturing enterprises.

In the Report on Manufactures, Hamilton argued for the active encouragement of manufacturing to provide productive uses for the new capital he had created by his funding, assumption, and banking schemes. To secure his ends, Hamilton advocated protective tariffs, "which in some cases might be put so high as to keep out foreign products altogether; restraints on the export of raw materials; bounties and premiums to encourage certain industries; inducements to inventions and discoveries; and finally, the encouragement of internal improvements in transportation, the development of roads, canals, and navigable streams."

Some of Hamilton's tariff proposals were enacted in 1792. Otherwise the program was filed away—but not forgotten. It provided an arsenal of arguments for the manufacturing sector in years to come. Hamilton denied that his scheme favored the northern states. If, as seemed likely, the northern and middle states should become the chief sites for manufacturing, he claimed, they would create robust markets for agricultural products, some of which the southern states were peculiarly qualified to produce. The nation as a whole would benefit, he argued, as commerce between North and South increased, supplanting the trade across the Atlantic.

Hamilton's Achievement

Largely because of the skillful Hamilton, the Treasury Department began retiring the Revolutionary War debt, enhanced the value of a "Continental" dollar, secured the government's credit, and attracted foreign investment capital. Prosperity, so elusive in the 1780s, began to flourish once again during the 1790s, although President Washington cautioned against attributing "to the Government what is due only to the goodness of Providence."

Hamilton professed a truly nationalist outlook, and he focused his energies on the rising power of commercial capitalism. Tying the government closely to the rich and the well-born, Hamilton believed, promoted the government's financial stability and guarded the public order against the potential turbulence that had always haunted him.

But many Americans then and since have interpreted such views as elitist and self-serving. To be sure, Hamilton never understood the people of the small villages and farms, the people of the frontier. They were foreign to his world, despite his own humble beginnings. And they, along with the planters of the South, would be at best only indirect beneficiaries of his programs. There were, in short, vast numbers of people who saw little gain from the Hamiltonian program and thus were drawn into opposition. Indeed, Jefferson claimed that he and Hamilton were "pitted against each other every day in the cabinet like two fighting-cocks."

The Republican Alternative

The split over the Hamiltonian program planted the seeds of the first national political parties. Hamilton emerged as the embodiment of the party known as the Federalists; Madison and Jefferson assumed the leadership of those who took the name Republicans and thereby implied that the Federalists really aimed at a monarchy. Yet parties were slow in developing, or at least in being acknowledged as legitimate. All the political philosophers of the age deplored the spirit of party, or faction.

Neither side in the disagreement over national policy deliberately set out to create parties. But there were important differences of both philosophy and self-interest that simply would not dissolve, and the strongly partisan newspapers of the day ensured that such differences were repeatedly accented for the reading public.

The crux of the debate centered on the relative power of the federal government and the states. At the outset, Madison assumed leadership of Hamilton's opponents in the Congress, and he argued that Hamilton was trampling upon states' rights in forging a consolidated central government. After the compromise on the funding of state debts, Jefferson joined Madison in ever more resolute opposition to Hamilton's policies. They opposed his move to place an excise tax on whiskey, which would especially burden the trans-Appalachian farmers, whose grain was the source of the whiskey; and they opposed his proposal for a national bank and his Report on Manufactures. As these differences developed, the personal hostility between Jefferson and

Thomas Jefferson.

Hamilton festered, much to the distress of President Washington. In the process, Jefferson, the secretary of state, emerged as the leader of the opposition to Hamilton's policies within the administration, while Madison continued to direct the opposition in Congress.

Jefferson's Agrarian View

Thomas Jefferson, twelve years Hamilton's senior, was in most respects his opposite. Displaying little of Hamilton's ordered intensity, Jefferson instead conveyed an aristocratic carelessness and a breadth of cultivated interests that ranged perhaps more widely in science, the arts, and the humanities than those of any contemporary, even Franklin. Jefferson read or spoke seven languages. He was an architect of some distinction (Monticello, the Virginia Capitol, and the University of Virginia are monuments to his talent), a man who understood mathematics and engineering, an inventor, an agronomist.

Philosophically, Hamilton and Jefferson had contrasting visions of the character of the Union, and their opposite views defined certain fundamental issues of American life that still echo two centuries later. Hamilton foresaw a diversified capitalistic economy, agriculture balanced by commerce and industry, and was thus the better prophet. Jefferson feared the growth of crowded cities divided into a capitalistic aristocracy on the one hand and a deprived working class on the other. Hamilton feared anarchy and loved order; Jefferson feared tyranny and loved liberty.

Whereas Hamilton wanted a strong central government run by a wealthy elite promoting capitalistic enterprise, Jefferson desired a decentralized agrarian republic. Jefferson's ideal republic was to remain one in which small farmers predominated: "Those who labor in the earth," he wrote, "are the chosen people of God." Jefferson feared that the unlimited expansion of commerce and industry would produce a class of propertyless wage laborers who were dependent on others for their livelihood and therefore subject to political manipulation and economic exploitation.

Crises Foreign and Domestic

As the disputes between Jefferson and Hamilton intensified, Washington proved ever more adept at holding things together with his unmatched prestige. In 1792 he won unanimous reelection. No sooner had his second term begun than problems of foreign relations leapt to center stage, brought there by the consequences of the French Revolution, which had begun during the first months of Washington's presidency. Americans supported the popular revolt against the French monarchy, up to a point. By the spring of 1792, though, the experiment in liberty, equality, and fraternity had turned into a monster that plunged France into war with Austria and Prussia and began devouring its own children along with its enemies in the Terror of 1793–1794.

After the execution of King Louis XVI in 1793, Great Britain joined with the monarchies of Spain and Holland in a war against the French Republic. For the next twenty-two years, Britain and France were at war, with only a brief respite, until the final defeat of the French forces under Napoleon in 1815.

Americans wanted no part of the war. They were determined to maintain their lucrative trade with both sides of the European conflict. Of course, the combatants resented and resisted America's profitable neutrality. For their part, Hamilton and Jefferson found in the neutrality policy one issue on which they could agree. Where they differed was in how best to implement the policy. On April 22, 1793, President Washington issued a neutrality proclamation that simply declared the United States "friendly and impartial toward the belligerent powers."

Citizen Genêt

At the same time, Washington accepted Jefferson's argument that the United States should recognize the new revolutionary French government (becoming the first country to do so) and receive its new ambassador, Edmond Charles Genêt. Early in 1793, Genêt landed at Charleston, South Carolina, and made his way northward to Philadelphia. Along the way, he brazenly engaged in un-neutral activities. He outfitted privateers for use against the British royal navy and intrigued with frontiersmen and land speculators to attack Spanish Florida and Louisiana in retaliation for Spain's opposition to the French Revolution.

Genêt quickly became an embarrassment even to his Republican friends. "His conduct has been that of a madman," Madison charged. The cabinet finally agreed unanimously that he had to go, and Washington demanded his recall. Genêt's foolishness and the growing excesses of the French radicals were fast cooling American support for their revolution. The French made it hard even for Republicans to retain sympathy for the French Revolution, but Jefferson and others swallowed hard and made excuses. Nor did the British make it easy for Federalists to rally to their side. Near the end of 1793, they announced Orders in Council, which allowed them to seize the cargoes of American ships with provisions for or produce from French islands in the Caribbean. Despite the offenses by both sides, the French and British causes polarized American opinion and the two parties.

Jay's Treaty

Early in 1794, Republican leaders in Congress were gaining support for commercial retaliation to bring the British to their senses, when the British gave President Washington a timely opening for a settlement. They repealed the Orders under which American ships were being seized, and on April 16, 1794, Washington named Chief Justice John Jay as a special envoy to Great Britain. Jay left with instructions to settle all major issues: to get the British soldiers out of their posts along the northwestern frontier and to win reparations for the losses of American shippers, compensation for slaves carried away in 1783, and a commercial treaty that would legalize American commerce with the British West Indies.

The pro-British Jay, however, had little leverage with which to wring concessions from the British, and after seven months of negotiations he won only two pledges: the British promised to evacuate the northwestern military posts by 1796 and to pay damages for the seizures of American ships and cargoes in 1793–1794. In exchange for these concessions, Jay agreed to the British definition of neutral rights. He accepted the principles that naval stores, food, and military supplies headed to enemy ports on neutral ships were contraband, and that trade with enemy colonies prohibited in peacetime could not be opened in wartime (the "Rule of 1756"). Britain also gained most-favored-nation treatment in American commerce and a promise that French privateers would not be outfitted in American ports. Finally, Jay conceded that the British need not compensate Americans for the slaves who had escaped during the Revolutionary War, and he promised that the long-standing American debts to British merchants would be paid by the American government. Perhaps most important, he failed to gain unrestricted access for American shippers to the British West Indies.

Public outrage greeted the terms of Jay's Treaty. Even Federalist shippers, ready for settlement on almost any terms, criticized Jay's failure to open fully the British West Indies to American commerce. But much of the outcry came from disappointed Republican partisans who sought an escalation of conflict with hated England. Jay remarked that he could travel across the country by the light of his burning effigies. Yet the Senate debated the treaty in secret, and in the end moderation prevailed. Without a single vote to spare, Jay's Treaty won the necessary two-thirds majority on June 24, 1795.

The Frontier Stirs

Other events also had an important bearing on Jay's Treaty, adding force to the importance of its settlement of the Canadian frontier. While Jay was haggling in London, frontier conflict with Indians escalated, with American troops suffering two defeats. At last, Washington named General Wayne, known as "Mad Anthony," to head an expedition into the Northwest Territory. In the fall of 1793, Wayne marched into Indian country with some 2,600 men.

On August 4, 1794, Indians representing eight tribes, and reinforced by some Canadian militia, attacked Wayne's force at the Battle of Fallen Timbers. The Americans repulsed them with heavy Indian losses, after which American detachments destroyed their fields and villages. Dispersed and decimated, the Indians finally agreed to the Treaty of Greenville, signed in 1795. In the treaty, at the cost of a $10,000 annuity, the United States bought from twelve tribes the rights to the southeastern quarter of the Northwest Territory (now Ohio and Indiana) and enclaves at the sites of Vincennes, Detroit, and Chicago.

The Whiskey Rebellion

Wayne's forces were still mopping up after the Battle of Fallen Timbers when the administration decided on another show of strength in the backcountry against the so-called Whiskey Rebellion. Hamilton's excise tax on liquor, levied in 1791, had angered frontier farmers because it taxed their staple crop. Their grain was more easily transported to market in concentrated liquid form than in bulk. A pack horse, for example, could carry two bushels of unprocessed rye, but it could carry two barrels of whiskey representing twenty-four bushels of rye. Frontiersmen considered the tax another part of Hamilton's scheme to pick the pockets of the poor to enrich privileged speculators. All through the backcountry, from Georgia to Pennsylvania and beyond, the liquor tax provoked resistance and evasion.

In the summer of 1794, the rumblings of discontent broke into open rebellion in Pennsylvania's four western counties, where vigilantes, mostly of Scottish or Irish descent, terrorized federal revenue agents. On August 7, 1794, President Washington issued a proclamation ordering the rebels to disperse and go home, and calling out militiamen from Virginia, Maryland, Pennsylvania, and New Jersey. Getting no response from the "Whiskey Boys," he issued a proclamation for suppression of the rebellion.

Under the command of Virginia's governor, General Henry (Light-Horse Harry) Lee, 13,000 men, a force larger than any Washington had ever commanded in the Revolution, marched out from Harrisburg across the Alleghenies, itching to smite the insurgents. But the rebels vaporized like corn mash when heated. By dint of great effort and much marching, the troops finally rounded up twenty barefoot, ragged prisoners, whom they paraded down Market Street in Philadelphia and clapped into prison.

The government had made its point in defense of the rule of law and federal authority. The use of force, however, led many who sympathized with the frontiersmen to become Republicans, who scored heavily in the next Pennsylvania elections.

Pinckney's Treaty

While these stirring events were transpiring in Pennsylvania, Spain was suffering setbacks to its schemes to consolidate control over Florida and the Louisiana territory. Spain had refused to recognize the legitimacy of America's southern boundary established by the Treaty of Paris in 1783, and its agents thereafter sought to thwart American expansion southward. Spanish intrigues among the Indians were keeping up the same turmoil the British had fomented along the Ohio.

But for reasons growing out of the shifting balance of power in Europe, Spain decided in the mid-1790s to end its designs on America. This change of heart resulted in Pinckney's Treaty (1795), by which the U.S. minister, Thomas Pinckney, won acceptance of an American boundary at the thirty-first parallel; free navigation of the Mississippi River; the right to deposit goods at New Orleans without having to pay customs duties for a period of three years (with promise of renewal); a commission to settle American claims against Spain; and a promise on each side to refrain from inciting Indian attacks on the other.

Land Settlement

Now that Jay and Pinckney had settled matters with Britain and Spain, and General Wayne in the Northwest had ended organized Indian resistance, settlers flocked to the West. New lands, ceded by the Indians in the Treaty of Greenville, revealed Congress once again divided on land policy. There were two basic viewpoints on the matter: one that the public domain should serve mainly as a source of revenue; the other that it was more important to accommodate settlers with low prices, even free land, and get the country settled. Policy would evolve from the first toward the second viewpoint, but for the time being the government's need for revenue took priority.

Land Policy

Opinions on land policy, like other issues, separated Federalists from Republicans. Federalists involved in speculation might prefer lower land prices, but the more influential Federalists like Hamilton and Jay preferred to build the population of the eastern states first, lest the East lose political influence and a labor force important to the future growth of manufactures. Men of their persuasion favored high land prices to enrich the Treasury, and the sale of relatively large parcels of land to speculators rather than small tracts to actual settlers. Jefferson and Madison were reluctantly prepared to go along with such a land policy for the sake of reducing the national debt, but Jefferson yearned for a plan by which the lands could be more readily settled.

The Federalist land policy prevailed in the Land Act of 1796, which retained the 640-acre minimum size mandated by the Northwest Ordinance of 1787 while doubling the price per acre to $2 and requiring that the full amount be paid within a year. This was well beyond the means of most settlers and even many speculators. As a result, by 1800, government land offices had sold fewer than 50,000 acres. Continuing demands for cheaper land led to the Land Act of 1800, which reduced the minimum sale to 320 acres and spread the payments over four years. Thus with a down payment of $160 one could get a farm. The Land Act of 1804 further reduced the minimum parcel to 160 acres, which became the traditional homestead, and the price per acre went down to $1.64.

The Wilderness Trail

The lure of western lands led thousands of settlers to follow Daniel Boone into the territory known as Kentucky or "Kaintuck"—from the Cherokee name Ken-ta-ke ("great meadow"). In the late eighteenth century, Kentucky was a farmer's fantasy and a hunter's paradise, with its fertile soils and abundant forests teeming with buffalo, deer, and wild turkeys.

In 1773 Boone led the first group of settlers through the Appalachian Mountains at

Daniel Boone Escorting Settlers through the Cumberland Gap by George Caleb Bingham.

Cumberland Gap in southwestern Virginia. Two years later, Boone and thirty woodsmen used axes to create what became known as the Wilderness Road, a passage that more than 300,000 settlers would use over the next twenty-five years.

A steady stream of settlers, mostly Scotch-Irish folk from Pennsylvania, Virginia, and North Carolina, poured into Kentucky during the last quarter of the eighteenth century. The backcountry settlers came on foot or on horseback, often leading a mule or cow that carried their few tools and possessions. On a good day they might cover fifteen miles.

On their new farms, corn was the preferred crop because it kept well and had so many uses. Ears were roasted and eaten on the cob, and kernels were ground into meal for making mush, hominy grits, hoecake, and "johnnycake" (a dry biscuit suitable for travelers that was originally called journeycake). Pigs and cows provided pork and milk, butter and cheese. Many of the frontier families also built crude stills to manufacture a potent whiskey known as "corn likker."

Transfer of Power

By 1796 President Washington had decided that two terms in office were enough. Tired of the political quarrels and the venom of the partisan press, he was ready to retire to Mount Vernon. He left behind a formidable record of achievement: the organization of a national government with demonstrated power, establishment of the national credit, the settlement of territory previously held by Britain and Spain, stabilization of the northwestern frontier, and the admission of three new states: Vermont (1791), Kentucky (1792), and Tennessee (1796).

Washington's Farewell

Washington's farewell address focused on domestic policy and particularly on the need for unity among Americans in backing their new government. He decried the "baneful effects" of sectionalism and partisanship, while acknowledging that parties were "useful checks upon the administration of the government, and serve to keep alive the spirit of liberty."

In foreign relations, Washington asserted, America should show "good faith and justice toward all nations" and avoid either "an habitual hatred or an habitual fondness" for other countries. The United States should also "steer clear of permanent alliances with any portion of the foreign world." Later spokesmen for such an isolationist policy would distort Washington's position by claiming that he had opposed any "entangling alliances." On the contrary, Washington was not preaching isolationism; he was instead warning against any further permanent arrangements like the one with France, still technically in effect. Washington recognized that "we may safely trust to temporary alliances for extraordinary emergencies." Washington's warning against permanent foreign entanglements thereafter served as a fundamental principle in American foreign policy until the early twentieth century.

The Election of 1796

With Washington out of the race, the United States in 1796 held its first partisan election for president. The logical choice of the Federalists would have been Washington's protégé Hamilton, the chief architect of their programs. But Hamilton's policies had left scars and made enemies. Nor did he suffer fools gladly, a common affliction of Federalist leaders, including the man on whom the choice fell. In Philadelphia a caucus of Federalist congressmen chose John Adams as heir apparent, with Thomas Pinckney of South Carolina, fresh from his triumph in Spain, as nominee for vice-president. As expected, the Republicans drafted Jefferson and added geographical balance to the ticket with Aaron Burr of New York.

The rising strength of the Republicans, largely due to the smoldering resentment toward Jay's Treaty, very nearly swept Jefferson into office, and perhaps would have but for the public appeals of the French ambassador for Jefferson's election—an action that backfired. The Federalists won a majority among the electors, but Alexander Hamilton hatched an impulsive scheme that very nearly threw the election away after all. Thomas Pinckney, Hamilton thought, would be easier to influence than the strong-minded Adams. He therefore sought to have South Carolina Federalists withhold a few votes from Adams and bring Pinckney in first. The Carolinians cooperated, but New Englanders got wind of the scheme and dropped Pinckney. The upshot of Hamilton's intrigue was to cut Pinckney out of both offices and elect Jefferson as vice-president with sixty-eight votes, second to Adams's seventy-one.

The Adams Years

John Adams.

Adams had behind him a distinguished career as a Massachusetts lawyer; as a leader in the Revolutionary movement and the Continental Congress; as a diplomat in France, Holland, and Britain; and as vice-president. His political philosophy fell somewhere between Jefferson's and Hamilton's. He shared neither the one's faith in the common people nor the other's fondness for an aristocracy of "paper wealth." He favored the classic republican balance of aristocratic, democratic, and monarchical elements in government. A man of powerful intellect, forthright convictions, and uncontrollable vanity, Adams was haunted by the feeling that he was never properly appreciated—and he may have been right. On the overriding issue of his administration, war and peace, he kept his head when others about him were losing theirs—probably at the cost of his reelection.

War with France

Adams inherited from Washington his divided cabinet—there was as yet no precedent for changing personnel at the start of each new administration. Adams also inherited a menacing quarrel with France, a byproduct of Jay's Treaty. When Jay accepted the British position that food supplies and naval stores—as well as war matériel—bound for enemy ports were contraband subject to seizure, the French reasoned that American cargoes in the British trade were subject to the same interpretation. The French loosed their corsairs with even more devastating effect than the British had in 1793–1794. By the time of Adams's inauguration in 1797, the French had plundered some 300 American ships and had broken diplomatic relations with the United States.

Adams immediately acted to restore relations in the face of an outcry for war from the "High Federalists." Hamilton, however, agreed with Adams on this point and approved his last-ditch effort for a settlement. In 1797 Charles C. Pinckney (brother of Thomas) sailed for Paris with John Marshall (a Virginia Federalist) and Elbridge Gerry (a Massachusetts Republican) for further negotiations. After long, nagging delays, the three commissioners were accosted by three French counterparts (whom Adams labeled X, Y, and Z in his report to Congress). The three French diplomats delicately let it be known that negotiations could begin only if there were a loan to France of $12 million, a bribe of $250,000 to the five directors then heading the government, and suitable apologies for remarks recently made in Adams's message to Congress.

Such bribes were common eighteenth-century diplomatic practice—Washington himself had bribed a Creek chieftain, as well as ransomed American sailors from Algerian pirates at a cost of $100,000 each—but Talleyrand's price was high merely for a promise to negotiate. The answer, according to the commissioners' report, was "no, no, not a sixpence." When the XYZ Affair was reported in Congress and the public press, this was translated into the more stirring slogan "Millions for defense but not one cent for tribute." Expressions of hostility toward France rose in a crescendo—even the most partisan Republicans were hard put to make any more excuses—and many of them joined a chorus for war. An undeclared naval war in fact raged from 1798 to 1800, but Adams resisted a formal declaration of war. Congress, however, authorized the capture of armed French ships, suspended commerce with France, and renounced the alliance of 1778, which was already defunct.

A cartoon indicating the anti-French feeling generated by the XYZ Affair. The three American ministers at left reject the "Paris Monster's" demand for money.

Adams used the French crisis to strengthen American defenses. An American navy had ceased to exist at the end of the Revolution, but after Algerian pirates began to prey on American merchant vessels in the Mediterranean, Congress, in 1794, authorized the arming of six ships. Three of these—the *Constitution*, the *United States*, and the *Constellation*—were eventually completed in 1797. In 1798 Congress created a Department of the Navy, and by the end of 1799 the number of naval ships had increased to thirty-three. By then American ships had captured eight French vessels and provided secure passage for American commerce.

By the fall of 1798, even before the naval war was fully under way, the French began to make peace overtures. Adams named three peace commissioners, who arrived in Paris to find themselves confronting a new government under First Consul Napoleon Bonaparte. They sought two objectives: $20 million to pay for the American ships seized by the French, and the formal cancellation of the 1778 Treaty of Alliance. By the Convention of 1800, ratified in 1801, the French agreed only to terminate the alliance and the quasi-war.

The War at Home

The real purpose of the French crisis all along, the more ardent Republicans suspected, was to create an excuse to put down domestic political opposition. The Alien and Sedition Acts of 1798 lent credence to their suspicions. These four measures, passed amid the wave of patriotic war fever, limited freedom of speech and the press and the liberty of aliens. Three of the four acts reflected native hostility to foreigners, especially the French and Irish, a large number of whom had become active Republicans and were suspected of revolutionary intent.

The Naturalization Act changed the residence requirement for citizenship from five to fourteen years. The Alien Act empowered the president to deport "dangerous" aliens at his discretion. The Alien Enemy Act authorized the president in time of declared war to expel or imprison enemy aliens at will. Finally, the Sedition Act defined as a high misdemeanor any conspiracy against legal measures of the government, including interference with federal officers and insurrection or riot. What is more, the law forbade writing, publishing, or speaking anything of "a false, scandalous and malicious" nature against the government or any of its officers.

The purpose of such laws was transparently partisan, designed to punish Republicans. Of the ten convictions under the act, all were directed at Republicans. To offset the Alien and Sedition Acts, Jefferson and Madison promoted what came to be known as the Kentucky and Virginia Resolutions. These passed the legislatures of the two states in late 1798. The resolutions, much alike in their arguments, denounced the Alien and Sedition Acts as unconstitutional and advanced the state-compact theory. Since the Constitution arose as a compact among the states, the resolutions argued, it followed logically that the states retained the right to say when Congress had exceeded its powers. The states could "interpose" their judgment on acts of Congress and "nullify" them if necessary.

These doctrines of interposition and nullification, revised and edited by later theorists, were destined to be used for causes unforeseen by the authors of the Kentucky and Virginia Resolutions. At the time, it seems, both Jefferson and Madison intended the resolutions to serve chiefly as propaganda, the opening guns in the political campaign of 1800. Neither Kentucky nor Virginia took steps to nullify or interpose its authority against enforcement of the Alien and Sedition Acts. Instead, both called upon the other states to help them win a repeal in Congress.

Republican Victory

As the presidential election of 1800 approached, many grievances were mounting against Federalist policies: taxation to support an unneeded army, the Alien and Sedition Acts, the hostilities aroused by Hamilton's programs, the suppression of the Whiskey Rebellion, and Jay's Treaty. When Adams decided for peace in 1800, he probably doomed his one chance for reelection. Only a wave of patriotic war fever with a united party behind him could have gained him victory at the polls. His decision gained him much goodwill among the people at large, but it left the Hamiltonians unreconciled and his party divided.

In 1800 the Federalists summoned enough unity to name Adams and Charles C. Pinckney as their candidates. But the Hamiltonians continued to snipe at the president and his policies, and soon after his renomination Adams removed two of them from his cabinet. Hamilton struck back with a pamphlet questioning Adams's fitness to be president, citing his "disgusting egotism." Intended for private distribution among Federalist leaders, the pamphlet reached the hands of Aaron Burr, who put it in general circulation.

Jefferson and Burr, as the Republican candidates, once again represented the alliance of Virginia and New York. Jefferson, perhaps even more than Adams, became the target of abuse. Unscrupulous opponents labeled him an atheist and a supporter of the excesses of the French Revolution. Jefferson refused to answer the attacks and directed the campaign by mail from his home at Monticello. He was portrayed as the farmers' friend, the champion of states' rights, frugal government, liberty, and peace.

Adams proved more popular than his party, whose candidates generally fared worse than the president, but the Republicans edged him out by seventy-three electoral votes to sixty-five. Still, the result was not final, for Jefferson and Burr had tied with seventy-three votes each, and the choice of the president was thrown into the House of Representatives, where Federalist diehards tried vainly to give the election to Burr. This was too much for Hamilton, who opposed Jefferson but held a much lower opinion of Burr. Eventually the deadlock was broken when a confidant of Jefferson assured a Federalist congressman from Delaware that Jefferson would refrain from wholesale removals of Federalists and would uphold the new fiscal system. The representative resolved to vote for Jefferson, and several other Federalists agreed simply to cast blank ballots, permitting Jefferson to win without any of them actually having to vote for him.

Before the Federalists relinquished power to the Jeffersonian Republicans on March 4, 1801, Congress passed the Judiciary Act of 1801. Intended to ensure Federalist control of the judicial system, this act provided that the next vacancy on the Supreme Court should not be filled, created sixteen Circuit Courts with a new judge for each, and increased the number of attorneys, clerks, and marshals. Before he left office, Adams named John Marshall to the vacant office of Chief Justice and appointed Federalists to all the new positions, including forty-two justices of the peace for the new District of Columbia. The Federalists, defeated and destined never to regain national power, had in the words of Jefferson "retired into the judiciary as a stronghold."

CHAPTER

8

Republicanism: Jefferson and Madison

This chapter focuses on

- The domestic policies of the Republicans in power.
- Political divisions in the early republic.
- The causes and effects of the War of 1812.

THE *ESSENTIAL AMERICA* ON-LINE TUTOR

www.wwnorton.com/eamerica/ch8

- **Topic: The Lewis and Clark expedition**
  www.wwnorton.com/eamerica/ch8/topic.htm

  In 1804 the "Corp of Discovery" led by Merriwether Lewis and William Clark set out on a scientific and commercial exploration of the vast trans-Mississippi West. Employing images, maps, journal entries, and historical analyses, consider the significance of the Lewis and Clark expedition. How did their experiences and findings affect the popular perception of the American West?

- **Chapter review: On-line quiz and chapter summary**
  www.wwnorton.com/eamerica/ch8/review.htm

- **Chapter resources: Multimedia index**
  www.wwnorton.com/eamerica/ch8/media.htm

On March 4, 1801, the soft-spoken, brilliant, and charming Thomas Jefferson became the first president to be inaugurated in the new federal city, Washington, District of Columbia. Tall and thin, with ill-fitting clothes, chiseled features, red hair, and a ruddy complexion, the new president walked two blocks to the unfinished Capitol, entered the Senate chamber, took the oath from the recently appointed Chief Justice John Marshall, and returned to his boardinghouse for dinner.

Jefferson in Office

The deliberate display of republican simplicity at Jefferson's inauguration set the style of his administration. He took pains to avoid the monarchical trappings of his Federalist predecessors. Jefferson, a widower, discarded the coach and six in which Washington and Adams had traveled to state occasions and rode about the city on horseback. He also continued to attire himself in plain clothes. But Jefferson had by no means ceased to be the Virginia gentleman, nor had he abandoned elegant manners or the good life. The cuisine of his French chef and the wines for his frequent dinners strained his budget to the point that he had to borrow money.

Jefferson liked to think of his election as the "Revolution of 1800." He placed in policy-making positions men of his own party, and he was the first president to pursue the role of party leader, cultivating congressional support at his dinner parties and otherwise. In the cabinet the leading figures were Secretary of State James Madison, a longtime neighbor and political ally, and Swiss-born Secretary of the Treasury Albert Gallatin, a Pennsylvania Republican. In an effort to cultivate Federalist New England, Jefferson chose men from that region for the positions of attorney-general, secretary of war, and postmaster-general.

In lesser offices, however, Jefferson resisted the wholesale removal of Federalists, preferring to wait until vacancies appeared. But pressure from Republicans often forced him to yield and remove Federalists, trying as best he could to assign some other than partisan causes for the removals. In one area, however, he managed to remove the offices rather than the appointees. In 1802 Congress repealed the Judiciary Act of 1801, and so abolished the circuit judgeships and other offices to which Adams had made his "midnight appointments." A new judiciary act restored to six the number of Supreme Court justices and set up six circuit courts, each headed by a justice.

Marbury v. *Madison*

Adams's "midnight appointments" as he left office sparked the important case of *Marbury* v. *Madison* (1803), the first in which the Supreme Court asserted its right to declare an act of Congress unconstitutional. The case involved the appointment of William Marbury as justice of the peace in the District of Columbia. Marbury's official letter of appointment, or commission, signed by President Adams two days before he left office, remained undelivered when Madison became secretary of state, and Jefferson directed him to withhold it. Marbury then sued for a court order (a writ of mandamus) directing Madison to deliver his commission.

John Marshall, Jefferson's distant Virginia cousin with staunch Federalist views, wrote the Court's opinion. He held that Marbury deserved his commission, but he then denied that the Court had jurisdiction in the case. Marshall and the court ruled that Section 13 of the Judiciary Act of 1789, which gave the Court original jurisdiction in mandamus proceedings, was unconstitutional because the Constitution specified that the Court should have original jurisdiction only in cases involving ambassadors or states.

A painting of the president's house during Jefferson's term in office. Jefferson called it "big enough for two emperors, one pope, and the grand lama in the bargain."

The Court, therefore, could issue no order in the case. With one bold stroke, Marshall thus had chastised the Jeffersonians while avoiding an awkward confrontation with an administration that might have defied his order. At the same time, he established the precedent that the Court could declare a federal law invalid on the grounds that it violated provisions of the Constitution.

Domestic Reforms

Jefferson's first term was a succession of triumphs in both domestic and foreign affairs. He did not set out to discard Hamilton's economic program. Under Treasury Secretary Gallatin's tutoring, he learned to accept the national bank as an essential convenience. It was too late, of course, to undo Hamilton's funding and debt assumption operations, but none too soon, in the opinion of both Jefferson and Gallatin, to begin retiring the resultant federal debt. In 1802 Jefferson won the repeal of the whiskey tax, much to the relief of backwoods distillers, drinkers, and grain farmers.

Without the revenue from excise taxes, frugality was all the more necessary to a government dependent for income on tariffs and the sale of western lands. Happily for the federal Treasury, both flourished. The European war brought a continually increasing traffic to American shipping and revenues to the Treasury. At the same time, settlers flocked to the western lands, which were coming more and more within their reach. The admission of Ohio in 1803 increased the number of states to seventeen.

By the "wise and frugal government" promised in the inaugural, Jefferson and Gallatin reasoned, the United States could live within its income, like a prudent farmer. The basic formula was simple: cut back expenses on the military. A standing army threatened a free society anyway. It therefore should be kept to a minimum, with defense left to the militia. The navy, which the Federalists had already reduced after the quasi-war with France, ought to be reduced further. Coastal defense, Jefferson argued, should rely on fortifications and a "mosquito fleet" of small gunboats.

In 1807 Jefferson crowned his reforms by signing an act that outlawed the foreign slave trade as of January 1, 1808, the earliest date possible under the Constitution. South Carolina was the only state that still permitted the trade, but for years to come an illegal traffic in African slaves would continue. Perhaps 300,000 slaves were smuggled into southern states between 1808 and 1861.

The Barbary Pirates

Issues of foreign relations intruded on Jefferson early in his term, when events in the Mediterranean gave him second thoughts about the need for a navy. On the Barbary Coast of North Africa, the rulers of Morocco, Algiers, Tunis, and Tripoli (now part of Libya) had for years practiced piracy and extortion. After the Revolution, American shipping in the Mediterranean became fair game, no longer protected by British payments of tribute. The new American government paid protection money too, first to Morocco in 1786, then to the others in the 1790s. In 1801, however, the pasha of Tripoli upped his demands and declared war on the United States. Jefferson thereupon sent warships to blockade Tripoli.

A wearisome war dragged on until 1805, punctuated in 1804 by the notable exploit of Lieutenant Stephen Decatur, who slipped into Tripoli Harbor by night and set fire to the frigate *Philadelphia*, which had been captured (along with its crew) after it ran aground. In 1805 the pasha settled for $60,000 ransom and released the *Philadelphia*'s crew (mostly British subjects), whom he had held hostage for more than a year. It was still tribute, but less than the $300,000 the pasha had demanded, and much less than the cost of the war.

The Louisiana Purchase

Meanwhile, events elsewhere had conspired to produce the greatest single achievement of the Jefferson administration. The Louisiana Purchase of 1803 more than doubled the territory of the United States by acquiring the entire Mississippi Valley west of the river itself. Soon after taking power in France in 1799, Napoleon Bonaparte forced the Spanish to return the territory to France and expressed his intention of creating a North American empire. When word of the deal reached Washington in 1801, Jefferson hastened Robert R. Livingston, the new minister to France, on his way to Paris. Napoleon in control of the Mississippi outlet could only mean serious trouble.

Livingston and the French engaged in a series of frustrating negotiations that dragged out into 1803. In April Napoleon's minister, Talleyrand, suddenly asked if the United States would like to buy the whole of Louisiana. Livingston snapped up the offer. Napoleon had apparently decided simply to cut his losses in the New World, turn a quick profit, please the Americans, and go back to reshaping the map of Europe.

By the treaty of cession, dated April 30, 1803, the United States paid about $15 million for the huge territory. In defining the boundaries of Louisiana, the treaty's vague language could be stretched to provide a tenuous claim on Texas and a much stronger claim on West Florida, from Baton Rouge on the Mississippi River past Mobile to the Perdido River on the east. When Livingston asked about the boundaries, Talleyrand responded: "I can give you no direction. You have made a noble bargain for yourselves, and I suppose you will make the most of it."

The turn of events had indeed presented Jefferson with a noble bargain, a great new "empire of liberty," but also with a constitutional dilemma. Nowhere did the Constitution mention the purchase of territory. Jefferson at first thought to resolve the matter by amendment, but his advisers argued against delay lest Napoleon change his mind. The power to purchase territory, they reasoned, resided in the power to make treaties. Jefferson relented, trusting, he said, "that the good sense of our country will correct the evil of loose construction when it shall produce ill effects." New England Federalists boggled at the prospect of new western states that would probably strengthen the Jeffersonian party, and in a reversal that foreshadowed many future reversals on constitutional issues, Federalists found themselves arguing strict construction of the Constitution while Republicans brushed aside such scruples.

The Senate ratified the treaty by an overwhelming vote of 26 to 6, and on December 20, 1803, American representatives took formal possession of Louisiana. The Spanish kept West Florida, but within a decade it would be ripe for the plucking. American settlers in 1810 staged a rebellion in Baton Rouge and proclaimed the Republic of West Florida, which was quickly annexed and occupied by the United States as far eastward as the Pearl River. In 1812 the state of Louisiana absorbed the region. The following year, with Spain itself a battlefield for French and British forces, American troops took over the rest of West Florida, now the Gulf coast of Mississippi and Alabama.

Exploring The Continent

An amateur scientist long before he was president, Jefferson asked Congress in 1803 for money to send an expedition to explore the far Northwest, beyond the Mississippi River, in what was still foreign territory. Jefferson was keenly interested in mapping the trans-Mississippi wilderness and collecting scientific information, as well as promoting trade with the Indians of the interior. Congress approved the project, and Jefferson assigned as commanders twenty-nine-year-old Meriwether Lewis, the president's private secretary, and another Vir-

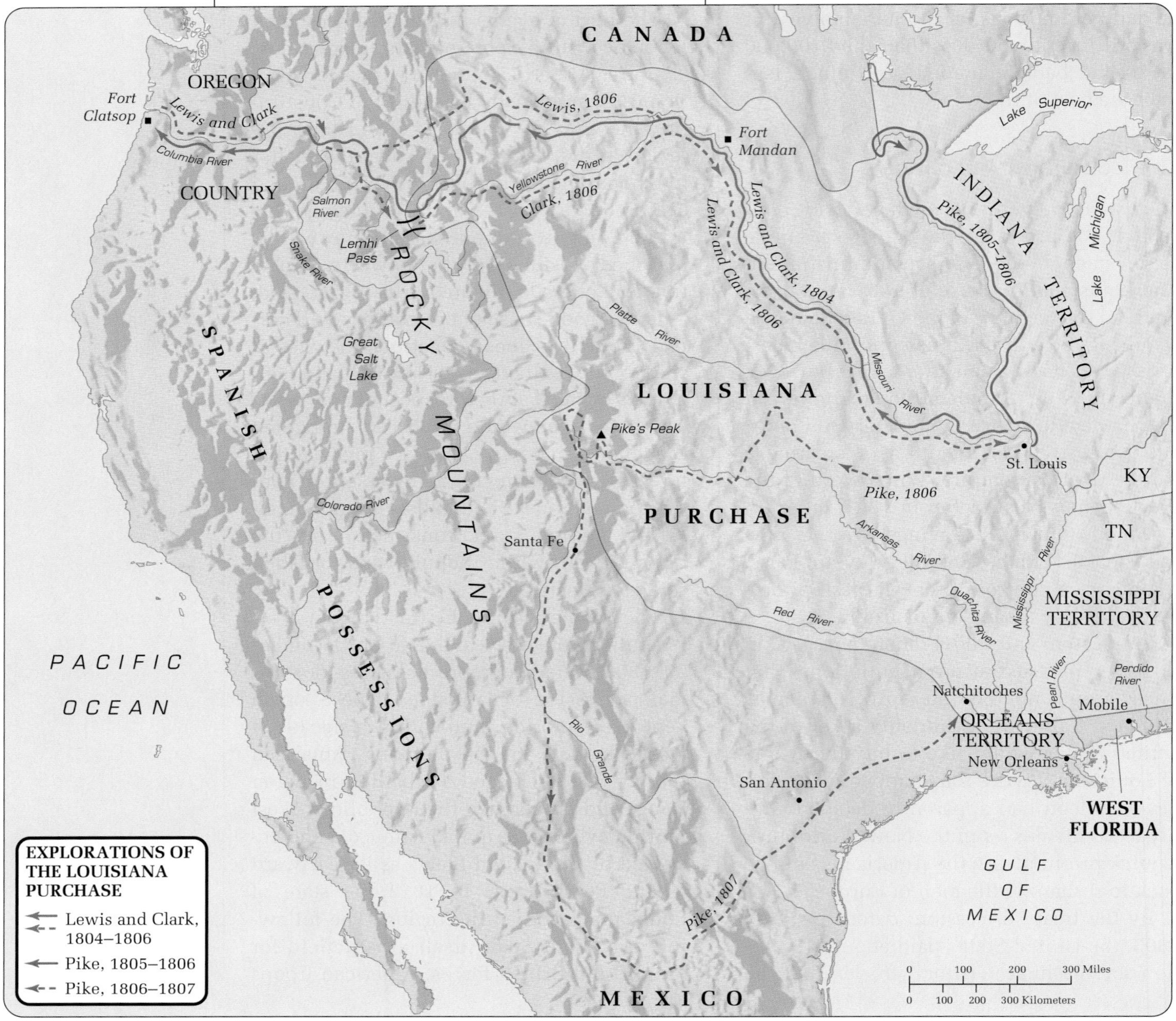

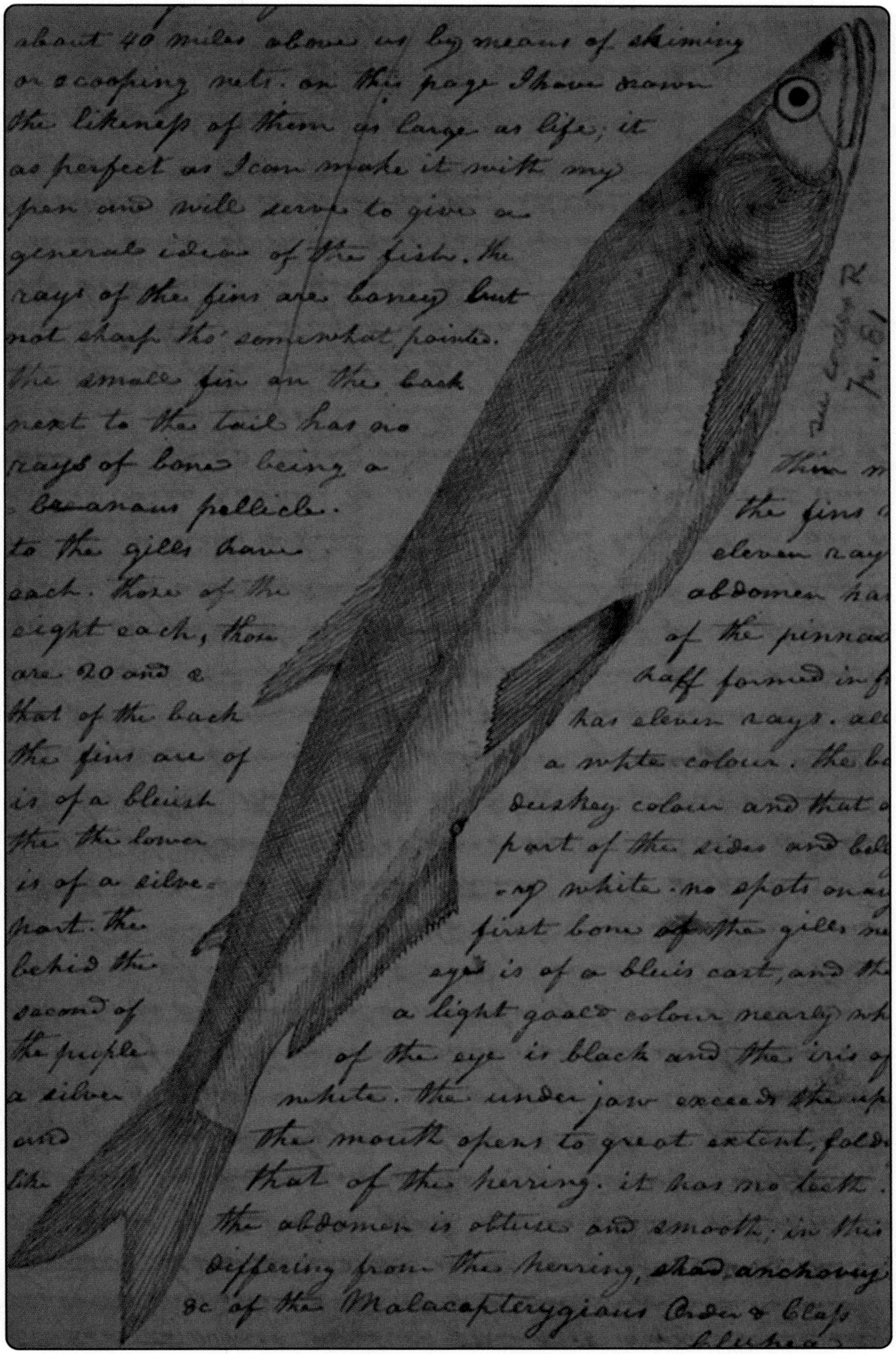

Documented in an illustration from William Clark's diary, the eulachon, or candlefish, was one of many new species encountered on the expedition.

ginian, William Clark, the much younger brother of the Revolutionary hero George Rogers Clark.

In 1804 the "Corps of Discovery," numbering nearly fifty, set out from St. Louis to ascend the Missouri River. Six months later, near the Mandan Sioux villages in what is now North Dakota, they built a fort for the winter. In the spring they added to the main party a French guide and his remarkable Shoshone wife, Sacajawea ("Canoe Launcher"), who proved an enormous help as interpreter among the Indians of the region, and they set out once again upstream. At the head of the Missouri River, they took the north fork, thenceforth the Jefferson River, crossed the Continental Divide, braved attacks by grizzly bears, and in dugout canoes descended the Snake and Columbia Rivers to the Pacific. The following spring, they split into two parties, with Lewis heading back east by almost the same route, and Clark going by way of the Yellowstone River. They reunited at the juncture of the Missouri and Yellowstone Rivers, returning together to St. Louis in 1806, having been gone nearly two and a half years. Their reports of friendly Indians and abundant pelts attracted many traders and trappers to the region.

The Jeffersonians in Power

Jefferson's policies, including the Louisiana Purchase, brought him almost solid support in the South and West. Even New Englanders were moving to his side. By 1809 even John Quincy Adams, the son of the second president, would become a Republican. Diehard Federalists read the handwriting on the wall. The acquisition of a vast new empire in the West would reduce New England to insignificance in political affairs, and along with it the Federalist cause. Under the leadership of Senator Timothy Pickering, a group of bitter Massachusetts Federalists called the Essex Junto considered seceding from the Union, an idea that would simmer in New England for another decade.

Randolph and the Tertium Quid

The presidential campaign of 1804 began when a Republican congressional caucus renominated Jefferson. Opposed by the Federalist Charles C. Pinckney, Jefferson won 162 of 176 electoral votes.

Freed from a strong opposition—Federalists made up only a quarter of the new Congress—the Republican majority began to lose its cohesion. John Randolph, a Jeffersonian mainstay in the first term, became the most conspicuous of the dissidents. Randolph became the crusty spokesman for a shifting group of "Old Republicans," whose adherence to party principles had rendered them more Jeffersonian than Jefferson himself. Their philosopher was John Taylor, a Virginia planter-pamphleteer whose theories reflected the continuing fear that the national government was growing in power and scope at the expense of individual liberty and states' rights.

Randolph broke with Jefferson in 1806, when the president sought an appropriation of $2 million for a thinly disguised bribe to win French influence in persuading Spain to give up the Floridas. "I found I might co-operate or be an honest man—I have therefore opposed and will oppose them," Randolph pledged. Thereafter he resisted Jefferson's initiatives almost out of reflex. Randolph and his colleagues were sometimes called "Quids," or the Tertium Quid (the "third something"), and their dissents gave rise to talk of a third party, neither Republican nor Federalist. But Quids never coalesced into a party.

The Burr Conspiracy

If feisty John Randolph was sincerely committed to principle, opportunistic Aaron Burr was sincerely committed to himself.

Sheer brilliance and shrewdness carried the New Yorker to the vice-presidency, and he might have become heir apparent to Jefferson, but for his taste for intrigue. He ended his political career once and for all when he killed Alexander Hamilton in a duel. Indicted in New York and New Jersey for murder and heavily in debt, Burr fled first to Spanish-held Florida. Once the furor subsided, he boldly returned to Washington to preside over the Senate. As long as he stayed out of New York and New Jersey, he was safe.

But Burr focused his attention less on the Senate than on a cockeyed scheme to carve out a personal empire for himself in the West. The so-called Burr Conspiracy originated when Burr met with General James Wilkinson, an old friend with a tainted Revolutionary War record who was a spy for the Spanish and had a penchant for easy money, a taste for rum, and an eye for intrigue. Just what he and Burr were up to probably will never be known. The most likely explanation is that they sought to organize a secession of Louisiana and set up an independent republic. Wilkinson developed cold feet, however, and sent a letter to Jefferson warning of "a deep, dark, wicked and wide-spread conspiracy." Traveling south to recruit adventurers, Burr was apprehended in disguise and taken to Richmond, Virginia, for trial.

Charged with treason, Burr was brought for trial before Chief Justice John Marshall. Events then revealed both Marshall and Jefferson at their partisan worst. Jefferson, determined to get a conviction at any cost, published relevant affidavits in advance and promised pardons to conspirators who helped to convict Burr. The Federalist Marshall in turn was so indiscreet as to attend a dinner given by the defense counsel at which Burr himself was present.

The case established two major constitutional precedents. First, on the grounds of executive privilege, Jefferson ignored a subpoena requiring him to appear in court with certain papers. He believed that the independence of the executive branch would be compromised if the president were subject to a court writ. The second major precedent was the rigid definition of treason. On this issue, John Marshall adopted the strictest of constructions. Treason under the Constitution, he concluded, consisted of "levying war against the United States or adhering to their enemies" and required "two witnesses to the same overt act" for conviction. Since the prosecution failed to produce two such witnesses, the jury found him not guilty. To avoid further legal entanglements, Burr left the country for France. He returned in 1812 to practice law in New York and died at age eighty.

War in Europe

Burr was more an annoyance than a threat to Jefferson. The more intractable problems of his second term involved the renewal of the European war in 1803, which helped resolve the problem of Louisiana but put more strains on Jefferson's desire to avoid "entangling alliances" and the quarrels of Europe. In 1805 Napoleon's defeat of Russian and Austrian forces gave him control of western Europe. The same year, the British defeat of the French and Spanish fleets in the Battle of Trafalgar secured Britain's control of the seas. Napoleon was dominant on land, the British dominant on the water, neither able to strike a decisive blow at the other, and neither restrained by an appreciation of neutral rights or international law.

Harassment by Britain and France

For two years after the renewal of hostilities in Europe, American shippers took over trade with the French and Spanish West Indies. But in the case of the *Essex* (1805), a British court ruled that the practice of shipping French and Spanish goods through

Preparation for War to Defend Commerce. In 1806 and 1807 American shipping was caught in the crossfire of war between Britain and France.

American ports while on their way elsewhere did not neutralize enemy goods. Such a practice violated the British rule of 1756, under which trade closed in time of peace remained closed in time of war. Goods shipped in violation of the rule, the British held, could be seized at any point under the doctrine of continuous voyage. After 1807, British interference with American shipping increased, not just to keep supplies from Napoleon's continent but also to hobble competition with British merchant ships.

In 1806, the British ministry set up a paper blockade of Europe. Vessels headed for continental ports had to get licenses and accept British inspection or be liable to seizure. It was a "paper blockade" because even the powerful British navy was not large enough to monitor every European port. Napoleon retaliated with his "Continental System," proclaimed in the Berlin Decree of 1806 and the Milan Decree of 1807. In the first, he declared his own paper blockade of the British Isles; in the second, he ruled that neutral ships that complied with British regulations were subject to seizure when they reached continental ports. The situation presented American shippers with a dilemma. If they complied with the demands of one side, they were subject to seizure by the other.

The risks were daunting, but the prospects for profits were so great that shippers ran the risk. Seamen faced a more dangerous risk: a renewal of the practice of impressment. The use of press gangs to kidnap men in British (and colonial) ports was a longstanding method of recruitment for the British navy. The seizure of British subjects from American vessels became a new source of recruits, justified on the principle that British subjects remained British subjects for life: "Once an Englishman, always an Englishman."

In the summer of 1807, a British frigate, the *Leopard*, accosted an American naval vessel, the *Chesapeake*, just outside territorial waters off Norfolk. After the *Chesapeake's* captain refused to allow his ship to be searched, the *Leopard* opened fire, killing three and wounding eighteen. The *Chesapeake*, caught unready for battle, was forced to surrender. A British search party seized four men, one of whom was later hanged for desertion from the British navy. Soon after the *Chesapeake* limped back into Norfolk, a Washington newspaper editorialized: "We have never, on any occasion, witnessed such a thirst for revenge. . . ." Public wrath was so aroused that Jefferson could have had war on the spot. But like Adams before him, he resisted the war fever and suffered politically as a result. One Federalist called Jefferson a "dish of skim milk curdling at the head of our nation."

The Embargo

Jefferson resolved to channel public indignation into an effort at "peaceable coercion." In December 1807, in response to his request, Congress passed the Embargo Act, which stopped all export of American goods and prohibited American ships from leaving for foreign ports. It also effectively ended imports, since it was unprofitable for foreign ships to return from America empty. The constitutional basis of the embargo was the power to regulate commerce, which in this case Republicans interpreted broadly as the power to prohibit commerce.

Jefferson's embargo, however, failed from the beginning, for the public was unwilling to make the necessary sacrifices. Trade remained profitable despite the risks, and violating the embargo was almost laughably easy. Neither France nor Great Britain was significantly hurt by Jefferson's policy.

But Jefferson's presidency was seriously injured. The embargo revived the languishing Federalist party in New England, which renewed the charge that Jefferson was in league with the French. Jefferson finally accepted failure and on March 1, 1809, he repealed the embargo shortly before he relinquished the "splendid misery" of the presidency. In the election of 1808, the presidency passed to another Virginian, Secretary of State James Madison.

The Drift to War

Madison was entangled in foreign affairs from the beginning of his presidency. Still insisting on neutral rights and freedom of the seas, he pursued Jefferson's policy of "peaceful coercion" by different but equally ineffective means. In place of the embargo, Congress had substituted the Non-Intercourse Act, which reopened trade with all countries except France and Great Britain and authorized the president to reopen trade with whichever warring nation gave up its restrictions. Nonintercourse proved as ineffective as the embargo. In the vain search for an alternative, in 1810, Congress reversed its ground and adopted a measure introduced by Nathaniel Macon of North Carolina. Macon's Bill Number 2 reopened trade with the warring powers but provided that, if either dropped its restrictions, nonintercourse would be restored with the other.

Napoleon's foreign minister, the duc de Cadore, informed the American minister in Paris that he had withdrawn the Berlin and Milan Decrees, but the carefully worded Cadore letter had strings attached: revocation of the decrees depended on the British revoking their paper blockade. The strings were plain to see, but either Madison misunderstood or, more likely, went along in hope of putting pressure on the British. In response to the Cadore letter, he restored nonintercourse with the British. London refused to give in, but Madison clung to his policy despite Napoleon's continued seizure of American ships.

The seemingly hopeless effort did finally work. With more time, patience, or a transatlantic cable, Madison's policy would have been vindicated without resort to war. On June 16, 1812, the British foreign minister, facing economic crisis, revoked its blockade. Britain preferred not to risk war with the United States on top of its war with Napoleon. But it was too late. On June 1 Madison had asked for war, and on June 18, 1812, the Congress concurred, unaware of the British repeal.

The War of 1812

Causes

The main cause of the war—the demand for neutral rights—seems clear enough. Neutral rights dominated Madison's war message and provided the salient reason for mounting public hostility toward the British. Yet the geographical distribution of the congressional vote for war raised a troubling question. Most votes for war came from the farm regions that stretched from Pennsylvania southward and westward. The maritime

Tecumseh, the Shawnee leader who tried to unite the tribes in defense of their lands. He was killed in 1813 at the Battle of the Thames.

states of New York and New England, the region that bore the brunt of British attacks on American trade, voted against the declaration of war. One explanation for this seeming anomaly is simple enough. The farming regions suffered damage to their markets for grain, cotton, and tobacco, while New England shippers made profits in spite of British restrictions.

Other plausible explanations for the sectional vote, however, include frontier Indian attacks that were blamed on the British, western land hunger, and the desire for territory in British Canada and Spanish Florida. The constant pressure to open new lands repeatedly forced or persuaded Indians to sign treaties they did not always understand, causing stronger resentment among tribes that were losing more and more of their lands. It was an old story, dating from the Jamestown settlement, but one that took a new turn with the rise of a powerful Shawnee leader, Tecumseh.

Tecumseh recognized the consequences of Indian disunity and set out to form a confederation of tribes to defend hunting grounds. He insisted that no land cession was valid without the consent of all tribes, since they held the land in common. By 1811 Tecumseh had matured his plans and headed south from the Indiana Territory to win the Creeks, Cherokees, Choctaws, and Chickasaws to his cause.

General William Henry Harrison, governor of the Indian Territory, learned of Tecumseh's plans, met with him twice, and pronounced him "one of those uncommon geniuses who spring up occasionally to produce revolutions and overturn the established order of things." In the fall of 1811, Harrison decided that Tecumseh must be stopped. He gathered a thousand troops near Tecumseh's capital on the Tippecanoe River. The Indians took the bait and attacked Harrison's encampment. The Shawnees lost the Battle of Tippecanoe, although about a quarter of Harrison's men died or were wounded in the battle. Harrison then burned the Shawnee town and destroyed all its supplies. Tecumseh's dreams of an Indian confederacy went up in smoke, and he fled to British protection in Canada.

The Battle of Tippecanoe reinforced suspicions that the British were inciting the Indians. To eliminate the Indian menace, frontier settlers reasoned, they needed to remove its foreign support. Conquest of Canada, they decided, would end British influence among the Indians and open a new empire for land-hungry Americans. East Florida, still under the Spanish flag, also posed a threat, since Spain was either too weak or unwilling to prevent sporadic Indian attacks across the frontier. Moreover, the British were suspected of smuggling through Florida and intriguing with the Indians on the southwest border.

Such concerns helped generate a war fever within the frontier states. In the Congress that assembled in 1811, a number of young members from southern and western districts began to clamor for war in defense of "national honor." Among them were Henry Clay of Kentucky, who became Speaker of the House; Richard M. Johnson, also of Kentucky; and John C. Calhoun of South Carolina. John Randolph of Roanoke christened these "new boys" the "War Hawks." After they entered the House, Randolph said, "We have heard but one word—like the whip-poor-will, but one eternal monotonous tone—Canada! Canada! Canada!"

Preparations

As it turned out, the War Hawks would get neither Canada nor Florida. For in 1812 James Madison had led into war a country that was ill prepared both financially and militarily. The year before, despite urgent pleas from Treasury Secretary Gallatin, Congress had let the twenty-year charter of the Bank of the United States expire. A combination of strict-constructionist Republicans and Anglophobes, who feared the large British interest in the Bank, caused its demise. Meanwhile, trade had collapsed and tariff revenues had declined. Loans were needed for about two-thirds of the war costs, but northeastern opponents of the war were reluctant to lend money.

The military situation was almost as bad. War had been likely for nearly a decade, but Republican budgetary constraints had prevented preparations. When the war began, the army numbered only 6,700 men, ill-trained, poorly equipped, and led by aging officers. The navy, on the other hand, was in comparatively good shape, with able officers and trained men whose seamanship had been tested in the fighting against France and Tripoli. Its ships were well outfitted and seaworthy—all sixteen of them. In the first year of the war, the navy produced the only American victories in isolated duels with British vessels, but their effect was mainly an occasional lift to morale. Within a year, the British had blockaded the coast, except for New England, where they hoped to cultivate antiwar feeling, and most of the little American fleet was bottled up in port.

The War in the North

The only place where the United States could effectively strike at the British was Canada. The administration opted for a three-pronged drive against Canada: along the Lake Champlain route toward Montreal, with General Henry Dearborn in command; along the Niagara River, with forces under General Stephen Van Rensselaer; and into Upper Canada (north of Lake Erie and Lake Ontario) from Detroit, with General William Hull and some 2,000 men. In Detroit, the sickly and senile Hull procrastinated, while his position worsened and the news arrived that an American fort isolated at the head of Lake Huron had surrendered. The British commander cleverly played upon Hull's worst fears. Gathering what redcoats he could to parade in view of Detroit's defenders, he announced that thousands of Indian allies were at the rear and that once fighting began he would be unable to control them. Fearing massacre, Hull, without consulting his officers and without a shot being fired, surrendered his entire force.

Along the Niagara front, General Van Rensselaer was more aggressive. An advance party of 600 Americans crossed the Niagara River and worked its way up the bluffs on the Canadian side to occupy Queenstown Heights. The stage was set for a major victory, but the New York militia refused to reinforce Van Rensselaer's men, claiming that their military service did not obligate them to leave the country. They complacently remained on the New York side and watched their outnumbered countrymen fall to a superior force across the river.

On the third front, the old invasion route via Lake Champlain, the incompetent General Dearborn led his army north from Plattsburgh toward Montreal. He marched them up to the border, where the local militia once again stood on its alleged constitutional rights and refused to cross, and then marched them back to Plattsburgh.

Madison's navy secretary now pushed vigorously for American control of inland waters. At Presque Isle (Erie), Pennsylvania, twenty-eight-year-old Commodore Oliver H. Perry, already a fourteen-year veteran who had seen action against Tripoli, was busy building ships from green timbers. By the end of the summer, Perry set out in search of the British, whom he found at Lake Erie's Put-in-Bay on September 10, 1813.

Two British warships used their superior weapons to pummel the *Lawrence*, Perry's flagship, at long distance. After four hours of intense shelling, none of the *Lawrence*'s guns was left working and most of the crew were dead or wounded. The British ex-

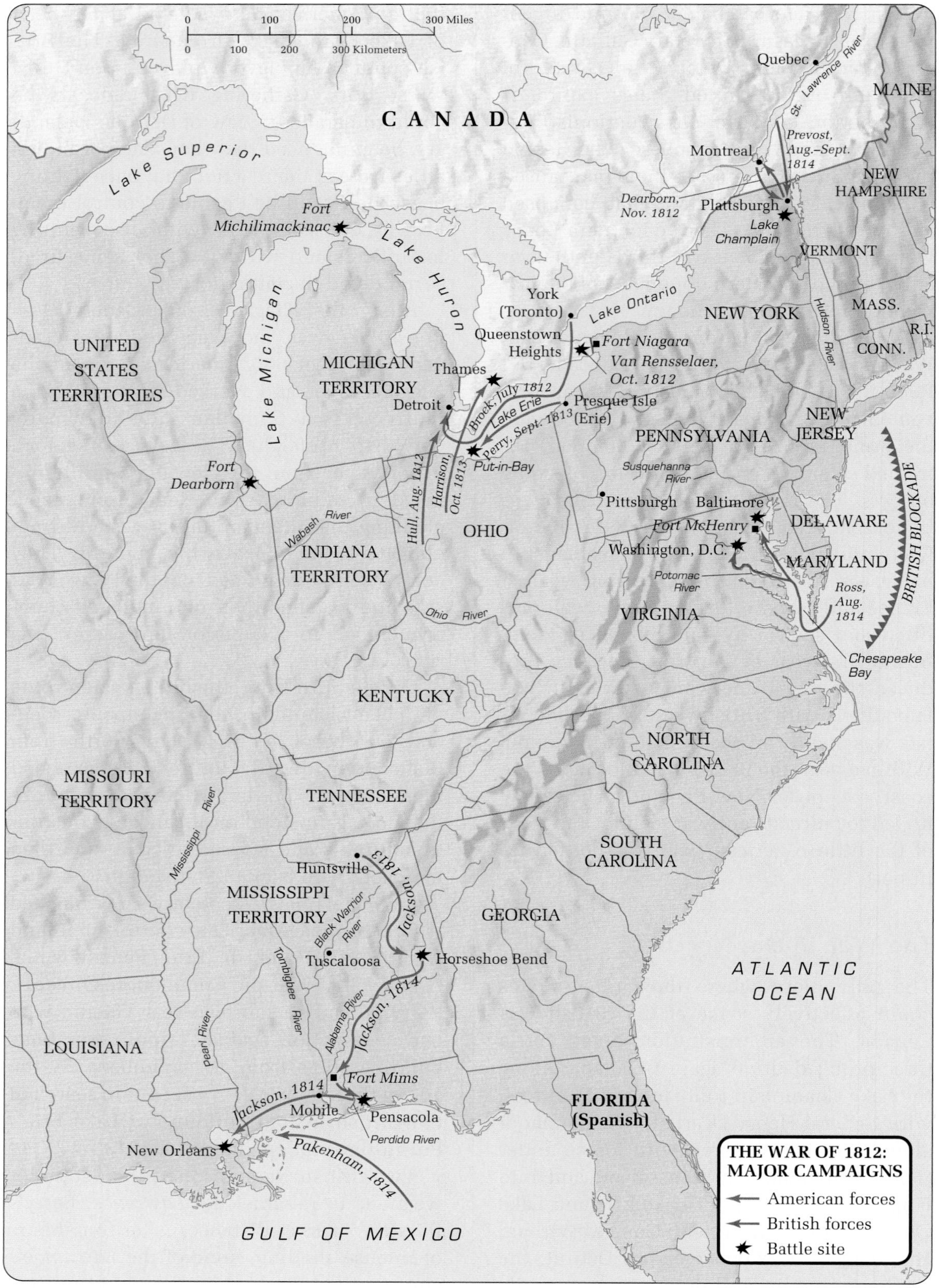
0 100 200 300 Miles
0 100 200 300 Kilometers
CANADA
Quebec
St. Lawrence River
MAINE
Lake Superior
Montreal
Prevost, Aug.–Sept. 1814
NEW HAMPSHIRE
Dearborn, Nov. 1812
Plattsburgh
Lake Champlain
VERMONT
Fort Michilimackinac
Lake Huron
Lake Michigan
York (Toronto)
Lake Ontario
NEW YORK
Hudson River
MASS.
R.I.
CONN.
Queenstown Heights
Fort Niagara
Van Rensselaer, Oct. 1812
UNITED STATES TERRITORIES
MICHIGAN TERRITORY
Thames
Brock, July 1812
Detroit
Lake Erie
Presque Isle (Erie)
Perry, Sept. 1813
Put-in-Bay
PENNSYLVANIA
NEW JERSEY
Fort Dearborn
Hull, Aug. 1812
Harrison, Oct. 1813
Susquehanna River
Pittsburgh
Baltimore
Fort McHenry
DELAWARE
BRITISH BLOCKADE
Wabash River
OHIO
INDIANA TERRITORY
Washington, D.C.
MARYLAND
Potomac River
Ross, Aug. 1814
Ohio River
VIRGINIA
Chesapeake Bay
KENTUCKY
NORTH CAROLINA
MISSOURI TERRITORY
TENNESSEE
Mississippi River
SOUTH CAROLINA
Huntsville
Jackson, 1813
MISSISSIPPI TERRITORY
Black Warrior River
GEORGIA
Tuscaloosa
Horseshoe Bend
Tombigbee River
Alabama River
Jackson, 1814
ATLANTIC OCEAN
Pearl River
LOUISIANA
Fort Mims
Jackson, 1814
Mobile
Pensacola
Perdido River
FLORIDA (Spanish)
New Orleans
Pakenham, 1814
GULF OF MEXICO
THE WAR OF 1812: MAJOR CAMPAIGNS
American forces
British forces
Battle site

pected the Americans to turn tail, but Perry refused to quit. He himself rowed to another vessel, carried the battle to the enemy, and finally accepted surrender of the entire British squadron. Hatless, begrimed, and bloodied, Perry sent General William Henry Harrison the long-awaited message: "We have met the enemy and they are ours."

More good news followed. At the Battle of the Thames (October 5), in Canadian territory east of Detroit, General William Henry Harrison eliminated British power in Upper Canada and released the Northwest from any further threat. In the course of the battle, Tecumseh was killed, and his persistent dream of Indian unity died with him.

The War in the South

In the Southwest, too, the war flared up in 1813. On August 30 the Creeks attacked Fort Mims, on the Alabama River above Mobile, killing almost half the people in the fort. The news found Andrew Jackson home in bed in Nashville, recovering from a street brawl with Thomas Hart Benton, later a senator from Missouri. As major-general of the Tennessee militia, a recovered Jackson summoned about 2,000 volunteers and set out on a campaign that crushed Creek resistance. The decisive battle occurred on March 27, 1814, at the Horseshoe Bend of the Tallapoosa River, in the heart of the upper Creek country. In the Treaty of Fort Jackson, the Indians ceded two-thirds of their lands to the United States, including part of Georgia and most of Alabama.

British Strategy

Four days after the Battle of Horseshoe Bend, Napoleon's empire collapsed. Now free to deal with America, the British developed a threefold plan of operations for 1814. They would launch a two-pronged invasion of America via Niagara and Lake Champlain to increase the clamor for peace in the Northeast; extend the naval blockade to New England, subjecting coastal towns to raids; and seize New Orleans to cut the Mississippi River, lifeline of the West.

The main British effort focused on the invasion via Lake Champlain. A land assault might have taken Plattsburgh and forced American troops out of their protected positions nearby. But England's army, led by General George Prevost, bogged down while its navy engaged an American naval squadron, led by Commodore Thomas Macdonough, in a deadly battle on Lake Champlain. The battle ended in September 1814 with the entire British flotilla either destroyed or captured.

Fighting in the Chesapeake

Meanwhile, American forces suffered the most humiliating experience of the war, the capture and burning of Washington, D.C. With attention focused on the Canadian front, the Chesapeake Bay offered the British a number of inviting targets, including Baltimore, then the fourth-largest city in America. On the evening of August 24, 1814, the British marched unopposed into Washington. They burned the White House, the Capitol, and most other government buildings.

The attack on Baltimore was a different story. Some 13,000 American soldiers, chiefly militia, fortified the heights behind the city. About 1,000 men held Fort McHenry, on an island in the harbor. When the British finally came into sight of the city, they halted in the face of American defenses. All through the following night the British fleet bombarded Fort McHenry to no avail, and the invaders abandoned the attack on the city. Francis Scott Key, a Washington lawyer, watched the siege from a vessel in the harbor. The sight of the flag still in place at dawn inspired him to draft the verses of "The Star-Spangled Banner." Later revised and set to the tune of an English drinking song, it eventually became the national anthem.

Andrew Jackson's defeat of the British at the Battle of New Orleans, January 1815.

The Battle of New Orleans

The British failure at Baltimore followed by three days their failure on Lake Champlain, and their offensive against New Orleans had yet to run its course. Along the Gulf coast, General Andrew Jackson had been busy shoring up the defenses of Mobile and New Orleans. In late 1814, without authorization, he invaded Spanish Florida and took Pensacola, ending British intrigues there. Back in Louisiana by the end of November, he began to erect defenses on the approaches to New Orleans. But the British fleet, with some 8,000 troops under General Sir Edward Pakenham, cautiously took up positions on a level plain near the Mississippi just south of New Orleans.

Pakenham's painfully careful approach—he waited until all his artillery was available—gave Jackson time to build earthworks bolstered by cotton bales. It was an almost invulnerable position, but Pakenham, contemptuous of Jackson's motley array of frontier militiamen, Creole aristocrats, free blacks, and pirates, ordered a frontal assault at dawn on January 8, 1815. His redcoats emerged out of the morning fog and ran into a murderous hail of enemy fire. Before the British withdrew, about 2,000 had been killed or wounded, including Pakenham himself.

The Battle of New Orleans occurred after a peace treaty had already been signed. But this is not to say that it was an anticlimax or that it had no effect on the outcome of the war. The treaty was yet to be ratified and the British might have exploited to advantage the possession of New Orleans had they won it. The battle assured ratification of the treaty as it stood, and both governments acted quickly.

The Treaty of Ghent and the Hartford Convention

Peace efforts had begun in 1812, even before hostilities commenced, but negotiations bogged down after the fighting started. The British were stalling, awaiting news of smashing victories to strengthen their hand. Word of the American victory on Lake Champlain weakened the British resolve. Their will to fight was further eroded by a continuing power struggle in Europe, by the eagerness of British merchants to renew trade with America, and by the war weariness of a tax-burdened public. The British finally decided that the war was not worth the cost. Envoys from both sides eventually agreed to end the fighting, return prisoners, restore previous boundaries, and to settle nothing else. The Treaty of Ghent was signed on Christmas Eve, 1814.

While the diplomats converged on a peace settlement, an entirely different kind of meeting took place in Hartford, Connecticut. The Hartford Convention represented the climax of New England's disaffection with "Mr. Madison's War." New England had managed to keep aloof from the war and extract a profit from illegal trading and privateering. After the fall of Napoleon, however, the British extended their blockade to New England, occupied part of Maine, and conducted several raids along the coast. Even Boston seemed threatened. Instead of rallying to the American flag, however, Federalists in the Massachusetts legislature voted to convene a meeting of New England states to plan independent action.

On December 15, the Hartford Convention assembled with delegates chosen by the legislatures of Massachusetts, Rhode Island, and Connecticut, two delegates from Vermont and one from New Hampshire: twenty-two in all. They proposed seven constitutional amendments designed to limit Republican influence, including the requirement of a two-thirds vote to declare war or admit new states, a prohibition on embargoes lasting more than sixty days, a one-term limit for the presidency, and a ban on successive presidents from the same state.

Their call for a later convention in Boston carried the unmistakable threat of secession if the demands were ignored. Yet the threat quickly evaporated. When messengers from Hartford reached Washington, they found the battered capital celebrating the good news from Ghent and New Orleans. The consequence was a fatal blow to the Federalist party, which never recovered from the stigma of disloyalty and narrow provincialism stamped on it by the Hartford Convention.

The War's Aftermath

For all the ineptitude with which the War of 1812 was fought, it generated intense patriotic feeling. Despite the standoff with which it ended at Ghent, the American public felt victorious, thanks to Andrew Jackson and his men at New Orleans as well as to the heroic exploits of American frigates in their duels with British ships. Remembered too were the vivid words of the dying Captain James Lawrence on the *Chesapeake*: "Don't give up the ship." Under Republican leadership, the nation had survived a "Second War of Independence" against the greatest military power on earth and emerged with new symbols of nationhood and a new gallery of heroes.

We Owe Allegiance to No Crown. The War of 1812 generated a new feeling of nationalism.

The war revealed America's need for a more efficient system of internal transportation—roads, bridges, canals. Even more important, the conflict launched the United States toward economic independence, as the interruption of trade encouraged the birth of American manufactures. This was a profound development, for the emergence of an American factory system would generate far-reaching social effects as well as economic growth. After forty years of independence, it dawned on the world that the new republic might not simply survive but might flourish.

As if to underline the point, Congress authorized a quick, decisive blow at the Barbary pirates. During the War of 1812, they had renewed plundering American ships. On March 3, 1815, little more than two weeks after the Senate ratified the Treaty of Ghent, Congress authorized a naval expedition against the Mediterranean pirates. On May 10, Captain Stephen Decatur sailed from New York with ten vessels. He first seized two Algerian ships and then sailed boldly into the harbor of Algiers. On June

30, 1815, the pirates' leaders agreed to cease molesting American ships and to return all American prisoners. Decatur then forced similar concessions from Tunis and Tripoli. Piracy against American vessels was over.

One of the strangest results of the War of 1812 was a reversal of roles by the Republicans and Federalists. Out of the wartime experience the Republicans had learned some lessons in nationalism. The necessities of war had "Federalized" Madison, or "re-Federalized" the father of the Constitution. Perhaps, he reasoned, a peacetime army and navy would not be so bad after all. He also had come to see the value of a national bank and of higher tariffs to protect infant American industries from foreign competition. But while Madison was embracing such nationalistic measures, the Federalists were borrowing the Jeffersonian theory of states' rights and strict construction. It was yet another reversal of roles in constitutional interpretation. It would not be the last.

CHAPTER

9

Nationalism and Sectionalism

This chapter focuses on

- The elements of the "Era of Good Feelings."
- How economic policies, diplomacy, and judicial decisions reflected the nationalism of these years.
- The various issues that promoted sectionalism.
- The fate of the Republican party after the collapse of the Federalists.

THE *ESSENTIAL AMERICA* ON-LINE TUTOR

www.wwnorton.com/eamerica/ch9

- **Topic: The Monroe Doctrine**
  www.wwnorton.com/eamerica/ch9/topic.htm

  The Monroe Doctrine (1823) became one of the keynotes of American foreign policy. Relying on government documents, maps, historical analyses, and personal correspondence, explore the significance of the Monroe Doctrine. What was the purpose of Monroe's declaration, and how did the international community receive it?

- **Chapter review: On-line quiz and chapter summary**
  www.wwnorton.com/eamerica/ch9/review.htm

- **Chapter resources: Multimedia index**
  www.wwnorton.com/eamerica/ch9/media.htm

Amid the jubilation after the War of 1812 Americans began to transform their young republic into a sprawling nation. Hundreds of thousands of people began to stream westward at the same time that what had been a largely local economy was maturing into a national market. The dispersion of plantation slavery and the cotton culture from the Atlantic coast into the Old Southwest—Georgia, Alabama, Mississippi, Louisiana, and Texas—disrupted family ties and changed social life. In the North and West, meanwhile, a dynamic middle class began to emerge and grow within towns and cities. Such dramatic changes prompted strident political debates over economic policies, transportation improvements, and the extension of slavery into the new territories. In the process, the nation began to divide into three powerful regional blocs—North, South, and West—whose shifting coalitions shaped the political landscape until the Civil War.

Economic Nationalism

After the War of 1812, the idea spread that the country needed a more balanced and "national" economy of farming, commerce, and manufacturing, as well as a more muscular military. President Madison, in his first annual message to Congress after the war, recommended several steps toward these ends: better fortifications, a standing federal army and a strong navy, a new national bank, effective protection of the new infant industries, a system of canals and roads for commercial and military use, and to top it off, a great national university, to be located in Washington, D.C. "The Republicans have out-Federalized Federalism," one observer remarked.

The Bank of the United States

The trinity of what came to be called economic nationalism—proposals for a second national bank, protective tariffs, and internal improvements—inspired the greatest controversies of the time. After the national bank's charter expired in 1811, the country had fallen into a financial muddle. State-chartered banks mushroomed with little or no control, and their bank notes (paper money) flooded the channels of commerce with money of uncertain value. Because hard money had been so scarce during the war, many state banks had suspended specie (gold or silver) payments in redemption of their notes, thereby further depressing their value. And this was the money on which Americans depended.

To remedy this situation, in 1816 Congress created a new Bank of the United States (B.U.S.), which would be located in Philadelphia. Modeled after Hamilton's bank, its charter again ran for twenty years, the government owned a fifth of the stock and named five of the twenty-five directors, and it served as the depository for government funds. Its bank notes were accepted in payments to the government. In return for its privileges, the Bank had to keep the government's funds without charge, lend the government $5 million on demand, and pay the government a cash bonus of $1.5 million.

The bitter debate about the Bank set the pattern of regional alignment for most other economic issues. Western senators predicted that the currency-short western towns would be at the mercy of such a centralized eastern bank.

The debate over the national bank featured the great triumvirate of John C. Calhoun of South Carolina, Henry Clay of Kentucky, and Daniel Webster of New Hampshire, later of Massachusetts. Calhoun, as an economic nationalist and leading War Hawk who helped maneuver the United States into war with Great Britain in 1812, introduced the measure and pushed it through, justifying its constitutionality by citing the congressional power to regulate the currency. Clay, who had earlier opposed Hamilton's bank, now asserted that new circumstances had made the Bank indispensable. Webster, however, led the opposition of the New Englanders who did not want Philadelphia to displace Boston as the nation's banking center. Later, after he moved from New Hampshire to Massachusetts, Webster would return to Congress as the champion of a much stronger national power, while events would carry Calhoun in the other direction.

A Protective Tariff

Peace in 1815 brought a sudden renewal of cheap British imports and provoked a movement for the protection of young American industries from foreign competition. The self-interest of the manufacturers, who as yet had little political impact, was reinforced by a patriotic desire for economic independence from Britain.

The Tariff of 1816, the first intended more for the protection of industry against foreign competition than for revenue, easily passed Congress. The South and New England both split their votes, with New England registering a majority of its votes for the tariff and the South directing a majority of its votes against the bill, while the Middle States and Old Northwest cast only five negative votes altogether. Led by Calhoun, the minority of southerners who voted for the tariff had hoped that the South might itself become a manufacturing center. Although in 1810 the southern states had almost as many manufacturers as New England, within a few years New England moved ahead of the South, and Calhoun turned against tariff protection. The tariff then became a sectional issue, with manufacturers and food growers favoring higher tariffs, while export-crop planters and shipping interests favored lower duties.

Internal Improvements

The third major economic issue of the time involved the government-financed road construction and the development of water transportation. The federal government had entered the field of internal improvements under Jefferson. In 1803, when Ohio became a state, Congress decreed that 5 percent of the proceeds from state land sales would go to building a National Road from the Atlantic coast into Ohio and beyond as the territory developed. Construction of the National Road began in 1811.

Originally called the Cumberland Road, it was the first federally financed interstate road network. By 1818, the road ran from Cumberland, Maryland, to Wheeling on the Ohio River; by 1838 the road extended all the way to Vandalia, Illinois. By reducing transportation costs and opening up new markets, the National Road and privately financed turnpikes helped accelerate the commercialization of agriculture.

In 1817 Calhoun put through the House a bill to place in a fund for internal improvements the $1.5 million bonus the Bank of the United States had paid for its charter, as well as all future dividends on the government's bank stock. Opposition centered in New England and the South, regions that expected to gain least from transportation improvements. Support came largely from the West, which urgently needed good roads. Madison, bothered by its constitutionality, vetoed the bill. For another hundred years, internal improvements remained, with few exceptions, the responsibility of states and private enterprise.

Nonetheless, despite disagreements about funding, improved transportation and communications (mass newspapers, express mail service, the telegraph) during the second quarter of the nineteenth century helped create a national market for goods and services. No longer limited to local or regional markets, farmers and manufacturers rapidly expanded production. Banks offered easy access to capital, and enterprising Americans rushed to take advantage of unprecedented entrepreneurial opportunities. Commercial agriculture and the factory system began to displace subsistence farming and household production. Mills and factories sprouted across the countryside. New technologies greatly increased productivity and in the process changed the rhythms of work and the relationships between laborers and employers. These first stirrings of an industrial revolution spawned a sustained economic expansion that would transform American society and politics.

The Union Manufactories of Maryland in Patapsco Falls, Baltimore County, c. 1815. A textile mill begun during the embargo of 1807; by 1825 the Union Manufactories would employ over 600 people.

"Good Feelings"

James Monroe

As President James Madison approached the end of a turbulent tenure he, like Jefferson, turned to a fellow Virginian, another secretary of state, as his successor: James Monroe. Monroe never displayed the depth in scholarship or political theory of his Republican predecessors, but what he lacked in intellect he made up in dedication to public service. Monroe served in the Virginia assembly, as governor, in the Confederation Congress and United States Senate, and as U.S. minister to France, England, and Spain. Under Madison he had been secretary of state and twice had doubled as secretary of war. In the 1816 presidential election he overwhelmed his Federalist opponent, Rufus King of New York. Tall, rawboned Monroe, with his powdered wig, cocked hat, and knee breeches, was the last of the Revolutionary generation to serve in the White House.

Firmly grounded in traditional Republican principles of states' rights and a limited role for the national government, Monroe was never able to keep up with the onrush of the "new nationalism," which advocated federal economic policies, such as a central national bank and a tariff on imports. In his veto of the Cumberland Road Bill (1822), he denied the authority of Congress to collect tolls for its repair and maintenance. Rather he urged a constitutional amendment, as had Jefferson and Madison, to remove all doubt about federal authority in the field of internal improvements.

Whatever his limitations, Monroe surrounded himself with some of the ablest young Republican leaders: John Quincy Adams became secretary of state, William Crawford of Georgia continued as secretary of the treasury, and John C. Calhoun headed the War Department. The new administration took power with America at peace and the economy flourishing. The period became known as the "Era of Good Feelings." Like many a maxim, it conveys just enough truth to be sadly misleading. The collapse of the Federalist party did not mean that the Republicans grew more unified. They continued to suffer from rancorous internal tensions. Moreover, the social order began to show signs of increasing stratification as the nation experienced dramatic economic growth and rapid westward migration. Finally, a resurgence of sectionalism erupted just as the postwar prosperity collapsed in the Panic of 1819.

For a time, however, general harmony in national politics reigned, and even when troubles arose, little of the blame fell on Monroe. In 1820 he was reelected without opposition, as the Federalists were too weak to put up a candidate. Monroe won all the electoral votes except for three abstentions and one vote from New Hampshire for John Quincy Adams.

Improving Relations with Britain

Adding to the prevailing contentment after the war was a growing rapprochement with England. American shippers resumed trade with Britain in 1815. The Treaty of Ghent had left unsettled a number of minor disputes, but thereafter, two important compacts—the Rush-Bagot Agreement of 1817 and the Convention of 1818—removed several potential causes of irritation. In the first, resulting from an exchange of notes between Acting Secretary of State Richard Rush and British minister Charles Bagot, the threat of naval competition on the Great Lakes vanished with an arrangement to limit forces there. Although the exchange made no reference to the land boundary between the United States and Canada, its spirit gave rise to the tradition of an unfortified border, the longest in the world.

The Convention of 1818 covered three major points. The northern limit of the Louisiana Purchase was settled by extending the national boundary along the Forty-ninth Parallel west from Lake of the Woods to the crest of the Rocky Mountains. West of that point the Oregon country would be open to joint U.S.-British occupation. The right of Americans to fish off Newfoundland and Labrador, granted in 1783, was acknowledged once again.

Extension of Boundaries

A whole sequence of developments came into focus in 1819, one of the more fateful years in American history. Controversial efforts to expand American territory, a sharp financial panic, a tense debate over the extension of slavery, and several landmark Supreme Court cases combined to bring an unsettling end to the "Era of Good Feelings."

The aggressive new nationalism reached a climax with the acquisition of Florida. Spanish sovereignty over Florida was more a technicality than an actuality. The thinly populated province had been a thorn in the side of the United States during the recent war, a center of British intrigue, a military haven for Creek refugees who were beginning to take the name Seminole ("runaway" or "separatist"), and a harbor for runaway slaves and criminals.

Spain, once the dominant power of the Americas, was now a nation in rapid decline, suffering from both internal and colonial revolt, and unable to enforce its obligations under the Pinckney Treaty of 1795 to pacify the frontiers. In 1817 Secretary of War Calhoun authorized a military campaign against the Seminoles in Florida and summoned General Andrew Jackson from Nashville to take command.

Jackson's orders allowed him only to pursue the offenders into Spanish territory, not to attack any Spanish post, but the general was not a man to bother with technicalities. Jackson pushed eastward through Florida, reinforced by Tennessee volunteers and friendly Creeks, taking a Spanish post and skirmishing with the Seminoles. Jackson hanged two of their leaders without a trial. The Florida panhandle was in American hands by the end of May 1818.

News of Jackson's exploits aroused anger in Madrid and concern in Washington. Spain demanded the return of its territory, reparations, and the punishment of Jackson. Monroe's cabinet at first prepared to disavow Jackson's action, especially his direct attack on Spanish posts. Calhoun, as secretary of war, wanted to discipline Jackson for disregarding orders—a stand that later caused bad blood between the two men—but privately confessed a certain pleasure at the outcome. In any case, a man as popular as Jackson was almost invulnerable. And he had one important friend in Washington, Secretary of State John Quincy Adams, who realized that Jackson had strengthened his hand in negotiations already under way with the Spanish minister. American forces withdrew from Florida, but negotiations resumed with the knowledge that the United States could retake Florida at any time.

With Florida's fate a foregone conclusion, Adams cast his eye on a larger purpose, a final definition of the western boundary of the Louisiana Purchase and—his boldest stroke—extension of a boundary to the Pacific coast. In lengthy negotiations, Adams gradually gave ground on claims to Texas, but he stuck to his demand for a transcontinental boundary line. Agreement finally came early in 1819. With the Transcontinental Treaty, Spain ceded all of Florida to the United States in return for American assumption of private claims against Spain up to $5 million. The western boundary of the Louisiana Purchase would run along the Sabine River and then in stair-step fashion up to the Red River, along the Red, and up to the Arkansas River. From the source of the Arkansas it would go north to the Forty-second Parallel and thence west to the Pacific coast. Florida became a territory, and its first governor was briefly Andrew Jackson. In 1845 Florida finally achieved statehood.

Crises and Compromises

The Panic of 1819

Adams's Transcontinental Treaty was a triumph of foreign policy and the climactic event of America's postwar nationalism. Even before it was signed in early 1819, however, two thunderclaps signaled the end of the brief "Era of Good Feelings" and gave warning of stormy weather ahead: the financial Panic of 1819 and the controversy over statehood for Missouri. The panic resulted from a sudden collapse of cotton prices in the English market, as British textile mills turned away from American sources to cheaper East Indian cotton. The price collapse set off a decline in the demand for other American goods and suddenly revealed the fragility of the prosperity that had begun after the War of 1812.

Since 1815, much of the economic boom had been built on a shaky foundation. Businessmen, bankers, farmers, and land speculators had caused a volatile expansion of credit. Even the directors of the Second Bank of the United States engaged in the same reckless extension of loans that state banks had pursued. In 1819, Langdon Cheves, former congressman from South Carolina, assumed control of the Bank and established sounder policies.

Cheves rescued the B.U.S. from near-ruin, but only by putting heavy pressure on the state banks. They in turn put pressure on their debtors, who found it harder to renew old loans or get new ones. The Cheves policies were the result rather than the cause of the Panic, but hard-pressed debtors found it all the more difficult to meet their obligations. Hard times lasted about three years, and in the popular mind the Bank deserved much of the blame. The Panic passed, but resentment of the national bank lingered, and it never fully regained the confidence of the South and the West.

The Missouri Compromise

Just as the Panic was breaking over the country, another cloud appeared on the horizon, the onset of a sectional controversy over slavery. By 1819, the country had an equal number of slave and free states, eleven of each. The line between them was defined by the southern and western boundaries of Pennsylvania and the Ohio River. Although slavery lingered in some places north of the line, it was on the way to extinction there. Beyond the Mississippi River, however, no move had been made to extend the dividing line across the Louisiana Purchase territory, where slavery had existed from the days when France and Spain had colonized the area. At the time, the Missouri Territory embraced all of the Louisiana Purchase except the state of Louisiana (1812) and the Arkansas Territory (1819). In the westward rush of population, the old French town of St. Louis became the funnel through which settlers pushed on beyond the Mississippi. These were largely settlers from the South who brought their slaves with them.

In early 1819, the House of Representatives debated legislation enabling Missouri to draft a state constitution, its population having passed the minimum of 60,000. Representative James Tallmadge, Jr., a New York congressman, introduced a resolution prohibiting the further introduction of slaves into Missouri, which already had some 10,000 slaves, and providing freedom at age twenty-five to those born after the territory's admission as a state. After brief but fiery exchanges, the House passed the Tallmadge amendment on an almost strictly sectional vote, and the Senate rejected it by a similar tally, but with several northerners joining the opposition. With population at the time growing faster in the North, a political balance between the free and slave states could be held only in the Senate. In the House, slave states had 81 votes while free states had 105; a balance was unlikely to be restored in the House.

Maine's application for statehood made it easier to arrive at an agreement. Since colonial times Maine had been the northern province of Massachusetts. The Senate linked its request for separate statehood with Missouri's and voted to admit Maine as a free state and Missouri as a slave state, thus maintaining the balance between free and slave states in the Senate. An Illinois senator further extended the compromise by an amendment to exclude slavery from the rest of the Louisiana Purchase north of 36°30′, Missouri's southern border. Slavery thus would continue in the Arkansas Territory and in Missouri, and be excluded from the remainder of the area. On August 10, 1821, President Monroe proclaimed the admission of Missouri as the twenty-fourth state. For the time, the controversy was settled. "But this momentous question," the aging Thomas Jefferson wrote to a friend, "like a firebell in the night awakened and filled me with terror. I considered it at once as the knell of the Union."

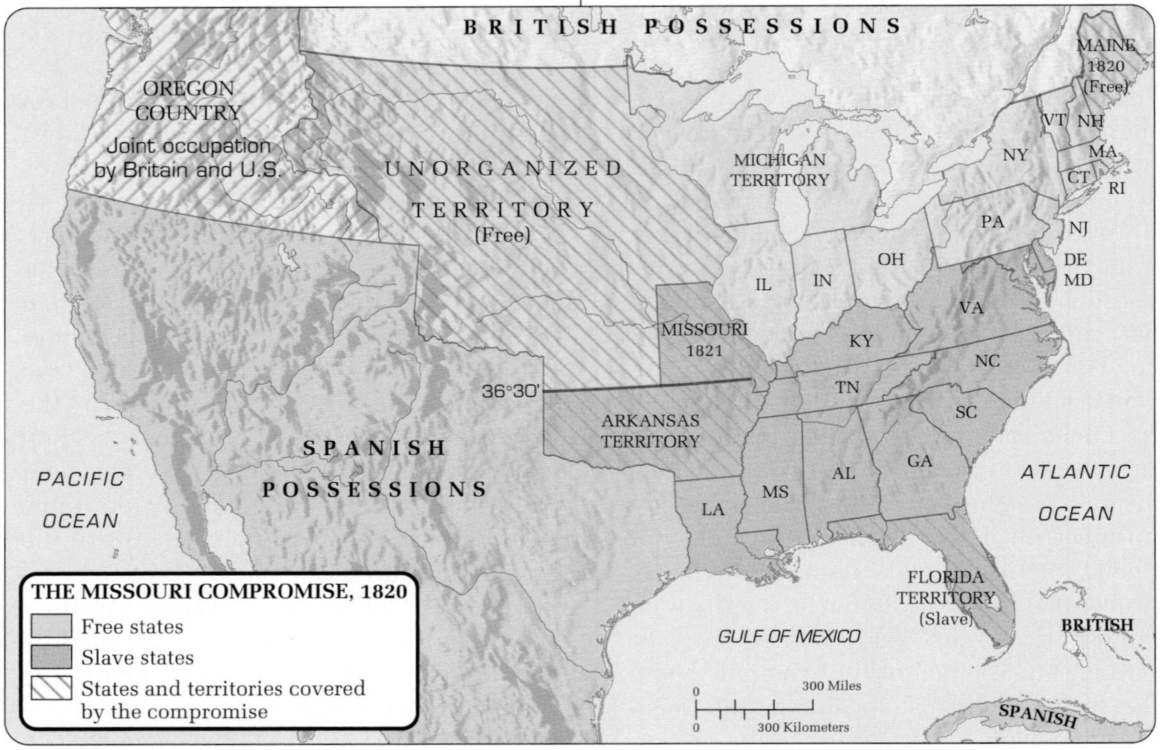

Judicial Nationalism

John Marshall

During the early nineteenth century, many of the nation's leading attorneys and judges were nationalists. They believed that an expanding nation needed a central government with enough power and responsibility to override local interests. And they argued that an independent judiciary system should have the authority to settle disputes between the states and the federal government. The leader among these judicial nationalists was John Marshall. A Virginia lawyer who served as secretary of state for John Adams, Marshall established the power of the Supreme Court by his force of mind and determination. During Marshall's early years on the Court (altogether he served thirty-four years), he affirmed the principle of judicial review of legislative acts. In *Marbury* v. *Madison* (1803) and *Fletcher* v. *Peck* (1810), the Marshall Court first struck down a federal law and then a state law as unconstitutional.

Expanding Power of Federal Government

In the fateful year 1819, Marshall and the Court made two decisions of major importance in checking the power of the states and expanding the power of the federal government: *Dartmouth College* v. *Woodward*, and *McCulloch* v. *Maryland*.

The Dartmouth College case involved an attempt by the New Hampshire legislature to alter a charter granted the college by King George III in 1769, under which the governing body of trustees became a self-perpetuating board. In 1816 the state's Republican legislature, irritated by this residue of monarchical rule as well as by the fact that Federalists dominated the board of trustees, placed Dartmouth under the control of a new board named by the governor. The original trustees sued and lost in the state courts, but with Daniel Webster as their counsel, they gained a hearing before the Supreme Court. The charter, declared Marshall in speaking for the Court, was a valid contract that the legislature had violated, an action expressly forbidden by the Constitution. This decision implied a new and enlarged definition of *contract* that seemed to put private corporations beyond the reach of the states that chartered them. "If business is to prosper," Marshall explained, "men must have the assurance that contracts will be enforced."

Marshall's single most important interpretation of the constitutional system appeared in *McCulloch* v. *Maryland* (1819). In the unanimous decision, the Court upheld the "implied powers" of Congress to charter the Bank of the United States and denied the state of Maryland's attempt to tax the Bank. In a lengthy opinion, Marshall rejected Maryland's argument that the federal government was the creature of sovereign states. Instead, he insisted, it arose directly from the people acting through the conventions that ratified the Constitution ("We, the people of the United States, . . . do ordain and establish . . ."). While sovereignty was divided between the states and the national government, the latter, "though limited in its powers, is supreme within its sphere of action."

Maryland's effort to tax the Bank conflicted with the supreme law of the land. One great principle that "entirely pervades the Constitution," Marshall wrote, was "that the Constitution and the laws made in pursuance thereof are supreme: that they control the Constitution and laws of the respective states, and cannot be controlled by them." The state tax therefore was unconstitutional, for "the power to tax involves the power to destroy"—which was precisely what the legislatures of Maryland and several other states had in mind with respect to the Bank.

Marshall's last great decision, *Gibbons* v. *Ogden* (1824), established national supremacy in regulating interstate commerce,

Chief Justice John Marshall, pillar of judicial nationalism.

and it thereby dealt another blow to proponents of states' rights. In 1808 the New York legislature granted Aaron Ogden the exclusive ferry rights across the Hudson River between New York and New Jersey. A competitor, Thomas Gibbons, protested the state's right to grant such a monopoly. On behalf of a unanimous Court, Marshall ruled that the state's action conflicted with the federal Coasting Act under which Gibbons operated. Congressional power to regulate commerce among the states, the Court said, "like all others vested in Congress, is complete in itself, may be exercised to its utmost extent, and acknowledges no limitations other than are prescribed in the Constitution." In striking down the monopoly created by the state, the nationalist Marshall had opened the way to extensive interstate development of steamboat navigation and, soon afterward, steam railroads. Such judicial nationalism provided an important support for economic expansion.

Nationalist Diplomacy

The Pacific Northwest

In foreign affairs, too, nationalism continued to be an effective force. Within two years after final approval of John Quincy Adams's Transcontinental Treaty, the secretary of state was able to draw another important transcontinental line. In 1819 Spain had abandoned its claim to the Oregon country above the Forty-second Parallel. Russia, however, had claims along the Pacific coast as well, including trading outposts from Alaska as far south as California. In 1823 Secretary of State Adams contested "the right of Russia to any territorial establishment on this continent." The American government, he informed the Russian minister, assumed the principle "that the American continents are no longer subjects for any new European colonial establishments." The upshot of his protest was a treaty signed in 1824 whereby Russia accepted the line of 54°40′ as the southern boundary of its claim. The Oregon Territory, to the south of the line, remained subject to joint occupation by the United States and Great Britain under their agreement of 1818.

The Monroe Doctrine

Adams's disapproval of further colonization also had clear implications for Latin America. One consequence of the Napoleonic Wars and French occupation of Spain and Portugal had been a series of wars of liberation in Latin America. Within little more than a decade after the flag of rebellion was first raised in 1811, Spain had lost almost its entire empire in the Americas. All that was left were the islands of Cuba, Puerto Rico, and Santo Domingo.

In 1823 rumors began to circulate that France might try to help Spain regain its American empire. Monroe and Secretary of War Calhoun were alarmed at the possibility. British foreign minister George Canning was also worried about French and Spanish intentions, and he urged Anglo-American protection of Latin America.

Adams recommended to Monroe and the cabinet that the United States adopt its own unilateral policy against the restoration of Spain's colonies. "It would be more candid," Adams said, "as well as more dignified, to avow our principles explicitly to Russia and France, than to come in as a cockboat in the wake of the British man-of-war." Adams knew that to protect Britain's trade with the area, the British navy would stop any action by a European power in Latin America. The British wanted the United States to agree not to acquire any more Spanish territory, including Cuba, Texas, or California, but Adams preferred to avoid such a commitment.

Monroe incorporated the substance of Adams's views in his annual message to Congress in 1823. The Monroe Doctrine, as it was later called, comprised four major points: (1) that "the American continents . . . are henceforth not to be considered as subjects for future colonization by any European powers"; (2) the political system of European powers was different from that of the United States, which would "consider any attempt on their part to extend their system to any portion of this hemisphere as dangerous to our peace and safety"; (3) the United States would not interfere with existing European colonies; and (4) the United States would keep out of the internal affairs of European nations and their wars.

At the time, the statement drew little attention either in the United States or abroad. Over the years, however, the Monroe Doctrine, not even so called until 1852, became one of the cherished principles of American foreign policy.

One-Party Politics

Almost from the start of Monroe's second term the jockeying for the presidential succession in 1824 had begun. Three members of Monroe's cabinet were active candidates: Secretary of War John Calhoun, Secretary of the Treasury William Crawford, and Secretary of State John Quincy Adams. Henry Clay, longtime Speaker of the House, also thirsted after the office. And on the fringes of the Washington scene a new force appeared in the person of Andrew Jackson, the scourge of the British, Spaniards, and Seminoles, who was elected a senator from Tennessee in 1823. All were Republicans, for again no Federalist stood a chance, but they were competing in a new political world, complicated by the crosscurrents of nationalism and sectionalism. With only one party there was in effect no party, for there existed no generally accepted method for choosing a "regular" candidate.

The "Corrupt Bargain"

The outcome of the election of 1824 turned more on personalities and sectional allegiance than on issues. Adams, the only northern candidate, carried New England, the former bastion of the Federalist party, and won most of New York's electoral votes. Clay took Kentucky, Ohio, and Missouri, while Crawford carried Virginia, Georgia, and Delaware. Jackson swept the Southeast, plus Illinois and Indiana, and with Calhoun's support the Carolinas, Pennsylvania, Maryland, and New Jersey.

The result was inconclusive in both the electoral vote and the popular vote. In the electoral college, Jackson had 99, Adams 84, Crawford 41, and Clay 37; in the popular vote, the proportion ran about the same. Whatever might have been said about the outcome, it was a defeat for Clay's program: New England and New York opposed him on internal improvements, the South and Southwest on the protective tariff. Sectionalism had defeated the national program, yet the advocate of the American System now assumed the role of president-maker, since the election was thrown into the House of Representatives, where Speaker Clay's influence was decisive. Clay had little trouble in choosing, since he regarded Jackson as unfit for the office. "I cannot believe," he muttered, "that killing 2,500 Englishmen at New Orleans qualifies for the various, difficult and complicated duties of the Chief Magistracy." He eventually threw his support to Adams. The final vote in the House, which was by state, carried Adams to victory with thirteen votes to Jackson's seven and Crawford's four.

It was a costly victory, for it united Adams's foes and crippled his administration before it got under way. There is no evidence that Adams entered into any bargain with Clay to win his support, but the charge was widely believed after Adams made Clay his secretary of state, the office from which three successive presidents had risen. A campaign to elect Jackson next time was launched almost immediately after the 1824 decision. "The people have been cheated," Jackson growled. The Crawford people, in-

Henry Clay.

cluding Martin Van Buren, the "Little Magician" of New York politics, soon moved into the Jackson camp.

John Quincy Adams's Presidency

John Quincy Adams was one of the ablest men, hardest workers, and finest intellects ever to enter the White House, but he lacked the common touch and the politician's gift for maneuver. A stubborn man, he suffered from chronic bouts of depression that provoked in him a grim self-righteousness and self-pity, qualities that did not endear him to fellow politicians.

Adams's first annual message to Congress provided a grandiose blueprint for national development, set forth in such a blunt way that it became a political disaster. In the boldness and magnitude of its conception, the Adams plan outdid those of both Hamilton and Clay. The central government, the president asserted, should promote internal improvements, set up a national university, finance scientific explorations, and create a new Department of the Interior.

Adams's federalist presidential message hastened the emergence of a new party system. The minority who cast their lot with Adams and Clay were turning into National-Republicans; the opposition, the growing party of Jacksonians, were the Democratic-Republicans, who would eventually drop the name Republican and become Democrats.

John Quincy Adams, a president of great intellect but without the common touch.

Adams's headstrong plunge into nationalism and his refusal to play the game of politics condemned his administration to utter frustration. Congress ignored his domestic proposals, and in foreign affairs the triumphs he had scored as secretary of state had no sequels. The climactic effort to discredit Adams came on the tariff issue. The Panic of 1819 had provoked calls for a higher tariff in 1820, but the effort failed by one vote in the Senate. In 1824 the advocates of protection renewed the effort, with greater success. The Tariff of 1824 favored the Middle Atlantic and New England manufacturers with higher duties on woolens, cotton, iron, and other finished goods. Clay's Kentucky won a tariff on hemp, a fiber used for making rope. A tariff on raw wool brought the wool-growing interests to the support of the measure. Additional revenues were provided by duties on sugar, molasses, coffee, and salt.

Three years later, Jackson's supporters sought to advance their candidate through an awkward scheme hatched by John Calhoun. The plan was to propose such outrageously high tariffs on raw materials that the eastern manufacturers would join the commercial interests there, and, with the votes of the agricultural South and Southwest, combine to defeat the measure. In the process, Jackson men in the Northeast could take credit for supporting the tariff, and Jackson men, wherever it fitted their interests, could take credit for opposing it—while Jackson himself remained in the background. Virginia's John Randolph saw through the ruse. The bill, he asserted, "referred to manufactures of no sort of kind, but the manufacture of a President of the United States."

The complicated scheme did help elect Jackson in 1828, but in the process Calhoun became a victim of his own shenanigans. His high tariff bill, to his chagrin, passed, thanks to the growing strength of manufacturing interests in New England and to several crucial amendments that exempted certain raw materials. Daniel Webster, now a senator from Massachusetts, explained that he was ready to deny all he had said before against the tariff because New England had built up her manufactures on the understanding that the protective tariff was a settled policy.

When the bill passed on May 11, 1828, it was Calhoun's turn to explain his newfound opposition to the gospel of protection, and nothing so well illustrates the flexibility of constitutional principles as the switch in positions by Webster and Calhoun. Back in South Carolina, Calhoun prepared the *South Carolina Exposition and Protest* (1828), which asserted the right of a state to nullify an act of Congress that it found unconstitutional.

Jackson Sweeps In

Thus far the stage was set for the election of 1828, which might more truly be called a political revolution than that of 1800. But if the issues of the day had anything to do with the election, they were hardly visible in the campaign, in which politicians on both sides reached depths of scurrilousness that had not been plumbed since 1800.

Jackson was denounced as a hot-tempered, ignorant barbarian, whose fame rested on his reputation as a killer. In addition, Jackson's enemies dredged up the old story that he had lived in adultery with his wife, Rachel, before they had been legally married. In fact they had been married for two years in the mistaken belief that her divorce from a former husband was final. As soon as the official divorce had come through, Jackson and Rachel had been remarried. But such distinctions escaped his opponents. Anxiety over this humiliation and her probable reception in Washington may have contributed to an illness from which Rachel died before her husband took office, a tragedy for which Jackson could never forgive his enemies. Jackson blamed Clay and Adams for not restraining their supporters from having made such scurrilous charges against his family.

The Jacksonians, however, were not averse to mudslinging. They got in their licks against Adams, condemning him as a man corrupted by foreigners in the courts of Europe. They called him a gambler and a spendthrift for having bought a billiard table and a chess set for the White House, and a puritanical hypocrite for despising the common people and warning Congress to ignore the will of its constituents. Adams had finally reached the presidency, the Jacksonians claimed, by a "corrupt bargain" with Henry Clay.

In the campaign of 1828, Jackson held most of the advantages. As a military hero, he stirred the patriotism of voters. As a son of the West, he was almost unbeatable there. As a planter and slaveholder, he had the trust of southern planters. Debtors and local bankers who hated the national bank turned to Jackson. In addition, his vagueness on the issues protected him from attack by various interest groups. Not least of all, Jackson benefited from a spirit of democracy in which the common folk were no longer satisfied to look to elites for leadership, as they had done in the past.

Since the Revolution, and especially after 1800, more people were voting as states expanded the suffrage from only those with property to taxpaying white males, and even in some states, to universal male suffrage. After 1815 the new states of the West entered the Union with either white manhood suffrage or a low taxpaying requirement, and older states such as Connecticut (1818), Massachusetts (1821), and New York (1821) abolished their property requirements for voting. As more people voted and participated in political activities, the ideal of social equality took on more importance in the political culture.

Jackson embodied this new, more democratic political world. A tall, sinewy frontiersman born in South Carolina, he had scrambled his way up by will and tenacity.

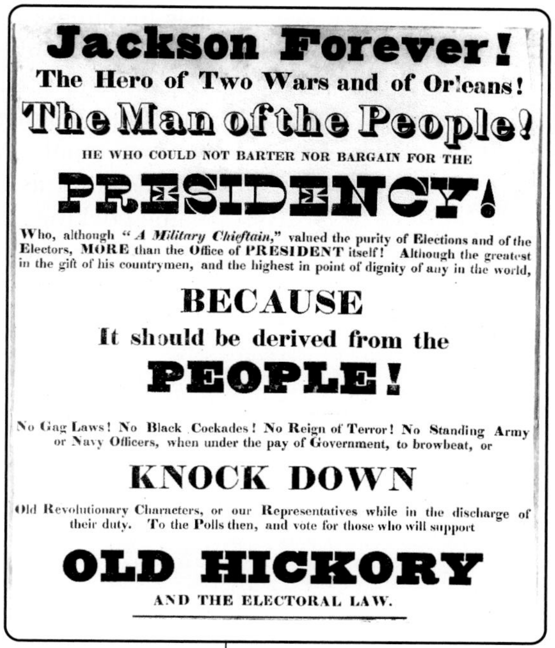
Jackson Forever!
The Hero of Two Wars and of Orleans!
The Man of the People!
HE WHO COULD NOT BARTER NOR BARGAIN FOR THE
PRESIDENCY!
Who, although "*A Military Chieftain,*" valued the purity of Elections and of the Electors, MORE than the Office of PRESIDENT itself! Although the greatest in the gift of his countrymen, and the highest in point of dignity of any in the world,
BECAUSE
It should be derived from the
PEOPLE!
No Gag Laws! No Black Cockades! No Reign of Terror! No Standing Army or Navy Officers, when under the pay of Government, to browbeat, or
KNOCK DOWN
Old Revolutionary Characters, or our Representatives while in the discharge of their duty. To the Polls then, and vote for those who will support
OLD HICKORY
AND THE ELECTORAL LAW.

This 1828 handbill identifies Jackson, "The Man of the People," with the democratic impulse of the time.

His toughness inspired his soldiers to nickname him "Old Hickory." As a fighter, horse trader, land speculator, and frontier lawyer, Jackson symbolized the rugged new western temperament. A fellow law student described him as a "most roaring, rollicking, game-cocking, horse-racing, card-playing, mischievous fellow."

The 1828 returns revealed that Jackson had won by a comfortable margin. The electoral vote was 178 to 83. Adams won all of New England, except for one of Maine's nine electoral votes, and a scattering of votes in New York and Maryland. All the rest belonged to Jackson. A new, convulsive era in American politics was about to begin.

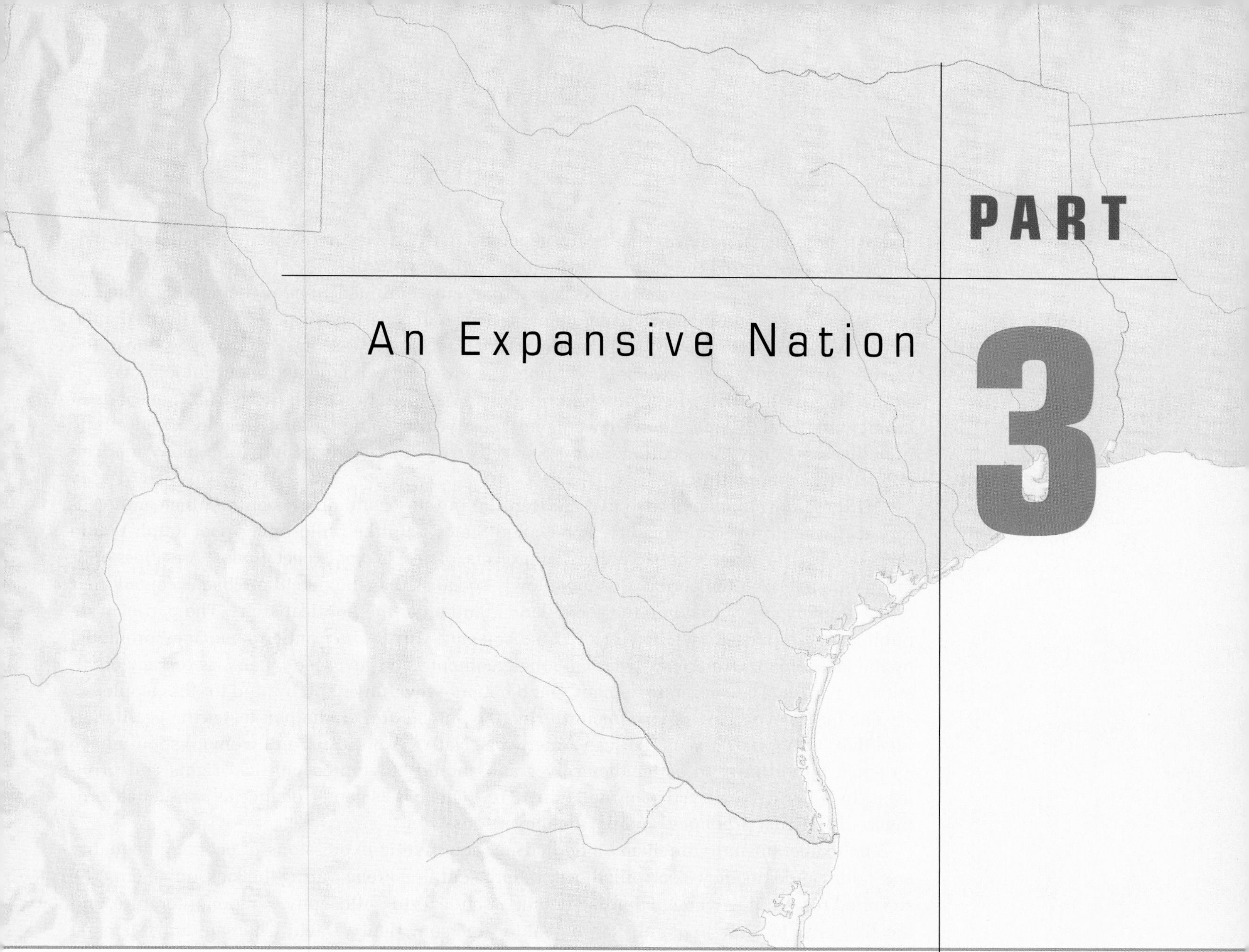

PART 3

An Expansive Nation

The election of Andrew Jackson signaled a new era in American history. By 1828 the United States was no longer an infant nation hugging the Atlantic coast. The maturing republic now included twenty-four states and almost 13 million people. Many Americans were on the move during the early nineteenth century. They formed a relentless migatory stream that spilled over the Appalachian Mountains, spanned the Mississippi River, and in the 1840s reached the Pacific Ocean. Wagons, canals, flatboats, steamboats, and eventually railroads transported the settlers westward.

The feverish expansion of the United States into new western territories brought Americans into conflict with Native Americans, Mexicans, and the British. Only a few Americans, however, expressed moral reservations about displacing others. Most believed it was the "manifest destiny" of the United States to spread across the entire continent—at whatever cost and at whomever's expense. Americans generally felt that they enjoyed the blessing of Providence in consolidating the entire continent under their control.

While most Americans during the Jacksonian era continued to earn their living from the soil, textile mills and manufacturing plants began to dot the landscape and transform the nature of work and the pace of life. By mid-century the United States was emerging as one of the world's major industrial powers. In addition, the lure of cheap land and plentiful jobs, as well as the promise of political equality and religious freedom, attracted hundreds of thousands of immigrants from Europe. These newcomers, mostly from Germany and Ireland, faced ethnic prejudices, religious persecution, and language barriers that made assimilation into American culture all the more difficult.

All these developments gave to American life in the second quarter of the nineteenth century its dynamic and fluid quality. The United States, said the philosopher-poet Ralph Waldo Emerson, was "a country of beginnings, of projects, of designs, of expectations." A restless optimism characterized the period. People of lowly social status who heretofore had accepted their lot in life now strove to climb the social ladder and enter the political arena. The patrician republicanism espoused by Jefferson and Madison gave way to the frontier democracy promoted by the Jacksonians. Americans were no longer content to be governed by an aristrocracy of talent and wealth. They began to demand—and obtain—government of, by, and for the people.

The fertile economic environment during the antebellum era helped foster the egalitarian idea that individuals (except African Americans, Native Americans, and women) should have an equal opportunity to better themselves and should be granted political rights and privileges. In America, observed a journalist in 1844, "One has as good a chance as another according to his talents, prudence, and personal exertions."

The exuberant individualism embodied in such mythic expressions of economic equality and political democracy also spilled over into the cultural arena during the Jacksonian era. The so-called romantic movement applied democratic ideals to philosophy, religion, literature, and the fine arts. In New England, Ralph Waldo Emerson, Henry David Thoreau, and Margaret Fuller joined other transcendentalists in espousing a radical individualism. Other reformers were motivated more by a sense of spiritual mission that democratic individualism. In striving to enhance personal morality and the general welfare, mostly middle-class reformers sought to create public-supported schools, abolish slavery, promote temperance in the use of alcoholic beverages, and improve the lot of the disabled, insane, and imprisoned. Their efforts helped address some of the problems created by the frenetic pace of economic growth and territorial expansion. But the reformers made little headway against slavery. It would take a brutal civil war to dislodge America's "peculiar institution."

ESSENTIAL THEMES

CRITICAL QUESTIONS

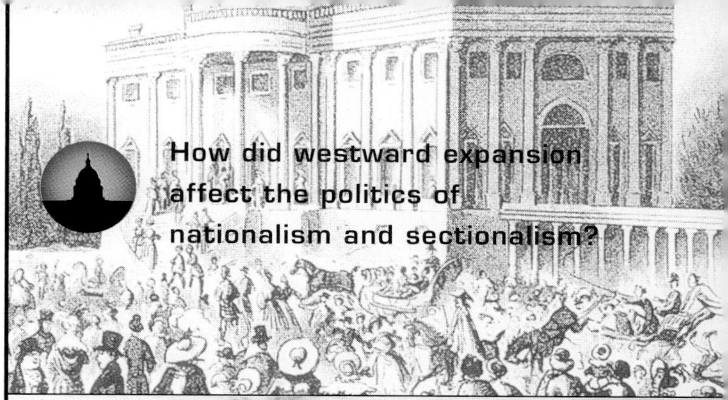

How did westward expansion affect the politics of nationalism and sectionalism?

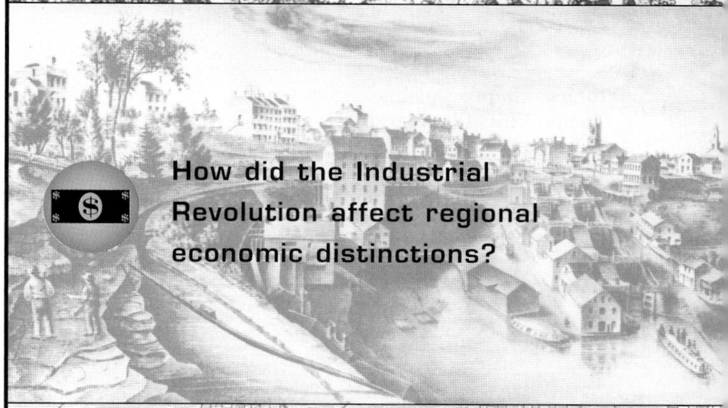

How did the Industrial Revolution affect regional economic distinctions?

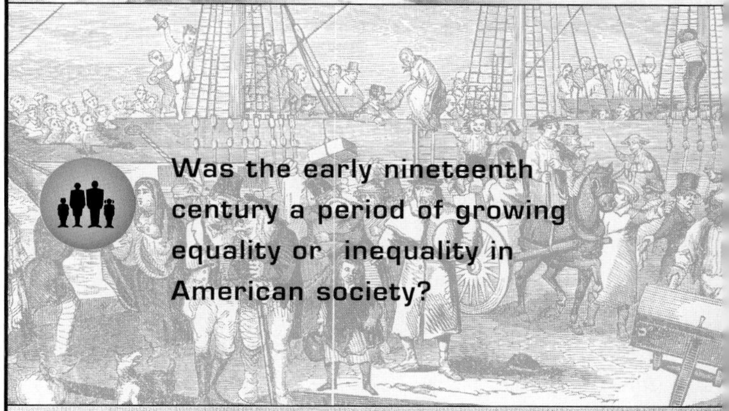

Was the early nineteenth century a period of growing equality or inequality in American society?

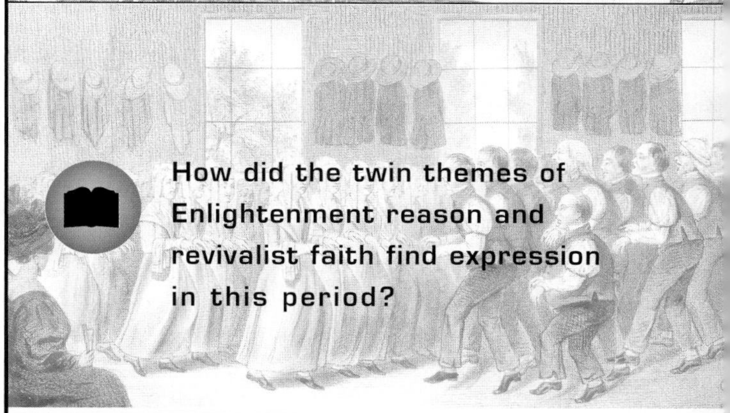

How did the twin themes of Enlightenment reason and revivalist faith find expression in this period?

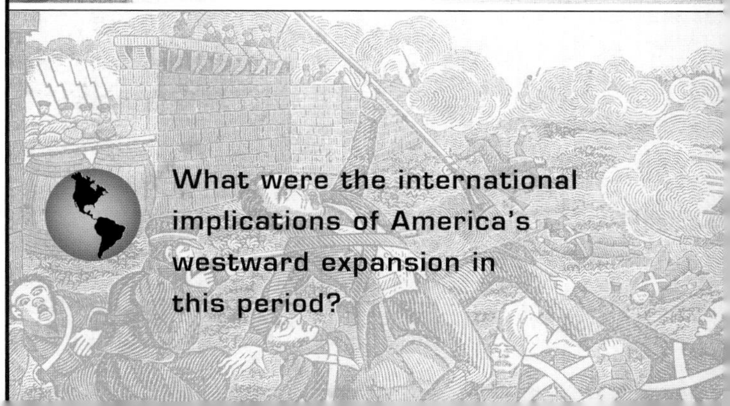

What were the international implications of America's westward expansion in this period?

CHAPTER 10

The Jacksonian Impulse

Jacksonian politics

- **Expansion of the franchise among white males**
- Development of political party activity
- Voter participation
- The Jackson administration
- **Nullification and sectional tensions**
- The tariffs of 1828 and 1832
- John C. Calhoun's *South Carolina Exposition and Protest* (1828)
- The Webster-Hayne debate (1830)
- South Carolina's nullification ordinance (1832)
- Clay's compromise and the Force Bill (1833)
- **Indian policy**
- **The Bank of the United States controversy**
- **The new party system**
- The Whigs

CHAPTER 11

The Dynamics of Growth

Government and the economy

- **Internal improvements**
- **The politics of immigration**
- **Labor politics**
- ***Commonwealth* v. *Hunt* (1842) legalizes trade unions**

CHAPTER 12

An American Renaissance: Religion, Romanticism, and Reform

The politics of reform

- **Education and citizenship**
- Horace Mann
- Female seminaries
- **American Temperance Union formed (1833)**
- **Prison reform**
- **State-run asylums**
- Dorthea Dix
- **The civil rights of women: Seneca Falls (1848)**

CHAPTER 13

Manifest Destiny

National politics in the 1840s

- **The Indian wars: the clash between white interests and Native Americans**
- **The Ft. Laramie Treaty and the beginnings of the reservation system (1851)**
- **The Annexation of Texas (1836)**
- The Alamo (1836)
- Sam Houston
- **Polk's presidency (1845–1849)**
- **The Mexican War**

CHAPTER 10
The Jacksonian Impulse
Jackson and the economy

- **The development of the market economy**
- **Industrialization and regional specialization**
- **The spread of wage labor**
- **Jackson and the Bank of the United States**
- **Sectionalism and the tariff question: the South Carolina nullification ordinance (1832)**
- **Distribution of the federal surplus to the states**
- **The Panic of 1837**

CHAPTER 11
The Dynamics of Growth
The Industrial Revolution in America

- **The cotton gin (1793)**
- **The cotton economy and slavery**
- **The transportation revolution**
  - Turnpikes
  - Canals and steamboats
  - Railroads
- **Government and the economy**
- **Technology and the growth of industry**
  - The "Lowell System"
  - The McCormick reaper (1840s)
  - Goodyear rubber (1844)
  - Morse's telegraph
- **Industry and the cities**
- **Immigrant labor**
- **Organized labor**

CHAPTER 12
An American Renaissance: Religion, Romanticism, and Reform
American culture in the new industrial landscape

- **Literature: introduction of cheap penny newspapers**
- **Movements and social and economic change**
- **Reform: in response to factory system**
  - **Owens founds New Harmony (1825)**

CHAPTER 13
Manifest Destiny
Economic motives for westward migration

- **Pioneers seek to exploit the natural resources of the new western lands**

Was the early nineteenth century a period of growing equality or inequality in American society?

CHAPTER 10

The Jacksonian Impulse

- Jacksonian democracy
  - **Politics and the changing social order**
  - **Politics and gender**
  - **Politics and race**
    - Racism in Northern cities
    - Antiblack riots in Philadelphia (1834)
    - Pennsylvania disenfranchises blacks (1838); other states follow suit
    - Antiblack riots occur in many northern cities (1830s–1850s)
  - **Congress approves the Indian Removal Act (1830)**
  - ***Cherokee Nation* v. *Georgia* (1831)**
  - **Trail of Tears (late 1830s)**
  - **Indian wars devastate Native-American populations**
  - **Growth of America's urban population**

CHAPTER 11

The Dynamics of Growth

- Inequality in Jacksonian America
  - **Workers begin organizing: National Trades' Union (1834)**
  - **Increasing social stratification**
  - **Irish immigration**
  - **German immigration**
  - **Nativist backlash to immigrant labor**
    - Anti-Catholic violence
  - **Labor organizations grow**
  - **The growth of cities and urban poverty**

CHAPTER 12

An American Renaissance: Religion, Romanticism, and Reform

- Early social reform
  - **Spread of public education and university training**
  - **Rise of urban middle class**
  - **Temperance movement**
  - **Women's rights movement**
    - Seneca Falls Convention organized by Lucretia Mott and Elizabeth Cady Stanton (1848)
    - Declaration of Sentiments, fashioned after the Declaration of Independence
  - **Utopian communities**

CHAPTER 13

Manifest Destiny

- The social order on the western frontier
  - **Western Indians**
  - **The Spanish West**
  - **California**
  - **Movements westward**

CHAPTER 10

The Jacksonian Impulse

- Political culture
  - **"Log Cabin and Hard Cider" presidential campaign (1839-1840)**
  - **Jacksonian democracy**
  - Cultural expressions of partisanship

CHAPTER 11

The Dynamics of Growth

- The Culture of Industry
  - **Lowell and the values of industry**
  - **Literary lectures**
  - Ralph Waldo Emerson
  - Henry Ward Beecher
  - **Popular entertainment**
  - Blood sports
  - Theaters and minstrel shows

CHAPTER 12

An American Renaissance: Religion, Romanticism, and Reform

- The American Renaissance
  - **Romanticism**
  - **The flowering of American literature**
  - **Newspapers and the popular press**
  - **Public education**
  - **Unitiarianism and Universalism**
  - **The Second Great Awakening**
  - Charles Grandison Finney and the Burned-Over District
  - Joseph Smith establishes Mormon church (1830)
  - Brigham Young leads exodus of Mormons westward
  - **Transcendentalism**
  - **The women's movement**
  - **Utopian communities**
  - Shakers
  - Brook Farm
  - Oneida Community (1840s–1850s)

CHAPTER 13

Manifest Destiny

- The Multicultural Southwest
  - **The Indians of the West**
  - **The Spanish West**
  - **Mountain men of the fur trade**
  - The arduous Oregon Trail

What were the international implications of America's westward expansion in this period?

CHAPTER 10

The Jacksonian Impulse

Jacksonian America and events abroad

- **The tariff issue and international prices**
- **Influx of foreign silver triggers inflation, financial situation (mid-1830s)**
- **The world economy and the Panic of 1837**

CHAPTER 11

The Dynamics of Growth

America's industrial development and the world economy

- **The cotton South**
- **Textile manufactures**
- Irish labor migrates to America (1840s–1850s)
- German professionals migrate to America (1840s–1850s)

CHAPTER 12

An American Renaissance: Religion, Romanticism, and Reform

America's cultural independence

- **Romanticism and American culture**
- **An indigenous culture**

CHAPTER 13

Manifest Destiny

American pioneers encroach on Indian lands and Mexican territory as they move westward

- **Mexico welcomes American settlers as a means of stabilizing the Mexican–U.S. border (1823)**
- **Manifest Destiny**
- **Annexation of Texas from Mexico (1843)**
- Santa Anna's costly victory at the Alamo (1836)
- Sam Houston and the independence of Texas (1836)
- **Oregon: "Fifty-four forty or fight" and relations with Britain**
- **Texas gains statehood (1845)**
- **Polk asks Congress for permission to end joint occupation of Oregon with Britain (1845)**
- **Annexation of California (1847)**
- **Treaty of Guadalupe Hidalgo completes continental United States (1848)**

Britain and America clash over the suppression of the slave trade

- **Webster-Ashburton Treaty (1842)**

CHAPTER

10

The Jacksonian Impulse

This chapter focuses on

- The social and political context of the Jackson/Van Buren administrations.
- Andrew Jackson's attitudes and actions concerning the tariff (and nullification), Indian policy, and the Bank of the United States.
- The rise of a new party system (Democrats and Whigs).

THE *ESSENTIAL AMERICA* ON-LINE TUTOR

www.wwnorton.com/eamerica/ch10

- **Topic: The Trail of Tears**
  www.wwnorton.com/eamerica/ch10/topic.htm

  The "Trail of Tears" was forged by thousands of Cherokees, Choctaws, Chickasaws, Creeks, and Seminoles during their forced removal from tribal lands in the Southeast to reservations west of Arkansas. Utilizing tribal records, maps, historical analyses, and Native art, study the plight of these nations as they made their trek westward to new lands.

- **Chapter review: On-line quiz and chapter summary**
  www.wwnorton.com/eamerica/ch10/review.htm

- **Chapter resources: Multimedia index**
  www.wwnorton.com/eamerica/ch10/media.htm

The election of Andrew Jackson coincided with a distinctive new era in American politics, economic development, and social change. Jackson was the first president not to come from a prominent colonial family. As a self-made soldier-politician-land speculator from the backcountry, he symbolized a transformation in the nation's social structure and political temper.

Profound economic and social forces were reshaping the young United States. In 1828 there were twenty-four states and almost 13 million people, many of them recent arrivals from Germany and Ireland. Surging foreign demand for cotton and other goods helped fuel a transportation revolution and an economic boom. Textile mills and shoe factories sprouted like mushrooms across the New England countryside, their spinning looms fed by cotton grown in the newly cultivated lands of Alabama and Mississippi.

Cities increasingly became the centers of the nation's commerce, industry, finance, and political activity. The urban population grew twice as fast as the rural population during the second quarter of the nineteenth century. A more urban society and a more diversified and speculative economy created more instability as people took greater risks to make money. A more stratified social order also emerged, as some people acquired great wealth while most others worked for wages.

An agrarian economy that earlier had produced crops and goods for household use or for local exchange expanded into a market-oriented economy engaged in national and international commerce. New canals and roads opened up eastern markets to western farmers in the Ohio Valley. The new economic order brought with it regional specialization and increasing division of labor. As more land was put into cultivation and commercial farmers came to rely on banks for credit to buy land and seed, they were subject to greater risks and the volatility of the market. In the midst of periodic financial panics and sharp business depressions, farmers unable to pay their debts lost their farms to "corrupt" banks that they believed had engaged in reckless speculative ventures and had benefited from government favoritism.

For many people, the transition to cash-crop agriculture and capitalist manufacturing was painful and unsettling. A traditional economy of independent artisans and subsistence farmers was giving way to a new system of centralized workshops, mills, and factories based on wage labor. Chartered corporations and commercial banks began to dominate local economies. The onset of the factory system and urban commerce called into question the assumption of Thomas Jefferson and others that a republic could survive only if most of its citizens were independent, self-reliant property owners, neither too rich to dominate other people nor too poor to become dependent and subservient.

A New Political Culture

At the same time that the urban population was increasing and more people were engaging in wage labor, many states, especially those on the frontier, were reducing or eliminating the property requirement for voting. The easing of voting restrictions reflected the feeling that a more democratic ballot would help combat the rising influence of commercial and manufacturing interests. Four times as many people voted in the 1828 presidential election as had voted in the 1824 election.

The mass-based Democratic party that ushered Jackson into the White House reflected the emergence of a new political culture during the 1820s. Up to that time, well-organized national political parties had been virtually nonexistent. The Jacksonian era witnessed the crystallization of formal parties (the Democratic party and the Whig party), which took particular stands on issues and held formal nominating conventions for selecting presidential and vice-presidential candidates.

This era also ushered in a new style of politicking that featured fierce polemics, expensive and well-organized campaigns, tightly controlled local party "machines," and intense partisan loyalties. Politics during the Jacksonian era was a vibrant public phenomenon that involved mass marches, spontaneous chanting, vigorous debates, and high voter turnout. The local party machines used a partisan network of employers and landlords to help party members find jobs and housing; in return, they could expect their members to vote without question for the candidates designated by the machine.

The Democratic party that arose during this time was an unstable coalition of northern industrial workers (many of them Irish and German immigrants) and small farm owners, landless farm laborers, and aspiring entrepreneurs from all sections of the country. Their shared concern was the preservation of a "just" and "virtuous" society in which most people were small property holders jealous of their freedom from monopolists or corrupt politicians. Democrats therefore opposed tariffs and the national bank, and any other efforts to centralize governmental power. At the same time, frontier folk settling in the new states of the Old Northwest (Ohio, Indiana, Illinois) and the Old Southwest (Alabama, Mississippi, Louisiana) were no longer willing to defer to traditional political and social elites.

Yet to call the Jacksonian era the "age of the common man," as many historians have done, is misleading. While political participation increased during the Jacksonian era, most of the common folk remained *common* folk. The period never produced true economic and social equality. Power and privilege, for the most part, remained in the hands of an "uncommon" elite. Moreover, many Jacksonians in power proved to be as opportunistic and manipulative as the "corrupt" politicians they displaced. And, for all of their egalitarian rhetoric, Jacksonian Democrats never embraced the principle of economic equality. "True republicanism," one commentator declared, "requires that every man . . . shall be free to become as unequal as he can." But in the afterglow of Jackson's election victory, few observers troubled with such distinctions. It was time to celebrate the commoner's ascension to the presidency.

George Caleb Bingham's *Verdict of the People* depicts the increasingly democratic politics of the early to middle nineteenth century.

Jackson Takes Office

Inauguration

On Inauguration Day, March 4, 1829, the new president, a sixty-two-year-old widower, said that he favored retirement of the national debt, a proper regard for states' rights, a "just" policy toward Indians, and rotation in federal office holders, which he pronounced "a leading principle in the republican creed"—a principle his enemies would dub the "spoils system."

After his speech, Jackson mounted his horse and rode off to the White House, where he hosted a reception for all who chose to come. A huge crowd pushed into the White House, surged through the rooms, leaped onto the furniture—all in an effort to shake the president's hand or at least get a glimpse of him. To Supreme Court Justice Joseph Story, "the reign of 'King Mob' seemed triumphant."

Appointments and Political Rivalries

Jackson believed that government workers who stayed too long in office became corrupted. So he set about replacing Adams's appointees with his own supporters. But his use of the "spoils system" has been exaggerated. During his first year in office, Jackson replaced only about 9 percent of the appointed officials in the federal government, and during his entire term fewer than 20 percent.

Jackson's administration was from the outset a house divided between the partisans of Secretary of State Martin Van Buren of New York and Vice-President John C. Calhoun of South Carolina. Much of the political history of the next few years would turn upon the rivalry between the two, as each man jockeyed for position as Jackson's heir apparent. Van Buren held most of the advantages, foremost among them his skill at timing and tactics. Jackson, new to political administration, leaned heavily on him for advice and for help in soothing the ruffled feathers of rejected office seekers.

But Calhoun could not be taken lightly. He, too, expected to be Jackson's successor. A man of towering intellect, he possessed a demonic sense of duty. Since returning from Washington to his plantation in South Carolina in 1825, Calhoun had nurtured his crops and his ardent love for his native region. Now, as vice-president, he was determined to defend southern interests against the advance of northern industrialism and abolitionism.

The Eaton Affair

In his battle for political power with Calhoun, Van Buren had luck as well as political skill on his side. Fate had quickly handed him a trump card: the succulent scandal of the Peggy Eaton affair. Peggy Eaton was a vivacious Irish widow whose husband supposedly had committed suicide upon learning of her affair with Tennessee senator John Eaton. Her marriage to Eaton, three months before he entered Jackson's cabinet as secretary of war, had scarcely made a virtuous woman of her in the eyes of the proper ladies of Washington. Floride Calhoun, the vice-president's wife, especially objected to Peggy Eaton's lowly origins and unsavory past. She pointedly snubbed her, and other cabinet wives followed suit.

Peggy's plight reminded Jackson of the gossip that had pursued his wife, Rachel, and he pronounced Peggy "chaste as a virgin." But the cabinet members were unable to cure their wives of what Van Buren dubbed "the Eaton Malaria." Van Buren, however, was a widower, and therefore free to lavish on poor Peggy all the attention that Jackson thought was her due. Mrs. Eaton herself finally wilted under the chill and withdrew from society. The outraged Jackson came to link Calhoun with what he called a conspiracy against her and drew even closer to Van Buren.

Internal Improvements

During the chilly winter of 1829–1830, Van Buren delivered some additional blows to Calhoun. It was easy to bring Jackson into opposition to internal improvements and thus to federal programs with which Calhoun had long been identified. In 1830 the Maysville Road Bill, passed by Congress, offered Jackson a happy chance for a dual thrust at both Calhoun and Henry Clay. The bill authorized the government to buy stock in a road from Maysville to Clay's home-

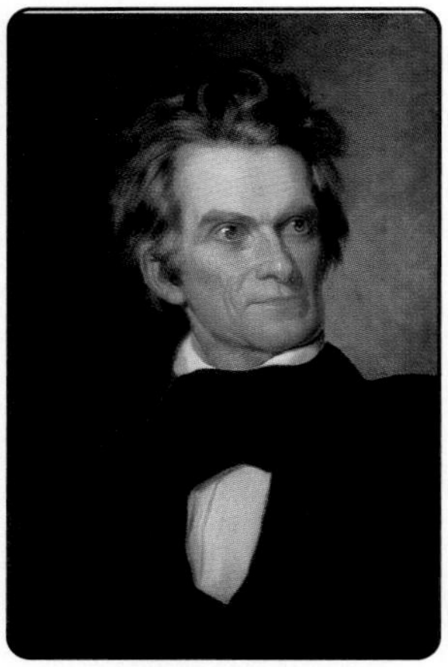
John C. Calhoun (detail).

town of Lexington. The road lay entirely within the state of Kentucky, and though part of a larger scheme to link up with the National Road via Cincinnati, it could be viewed as a purely local undertaking. On that ground, Jackson vetoed the bill, prompting widespread popular acclaim. Yet while Jackson continued to oppose federal aid to local projects, he supported projects such as the National Road, as well as road building in the territories, and rivers and harbors bills, the "pork barrels" of federal funds from which every congressman tried to pluck a morsel for his district. Even so, Jackson's attitude toward the Maysville Road set an important precedent, on the eve of the railroad age, for limiting federal initiative in internal improvements. Railroads would be built altogether by state and private capital at least until 1850.

Nullification

Calhoun's Theory

Calhoun was now in midpassage from his early phase as an economic nationalist to his later phase as a states'-rights sectionalist—and open to thrusts on both flanks. Conditions in his home state had brought on this change. Suffering from agricultural depression, South Carolina lost almost 70,000 people to emigration during the 1820s, and it would lose nearly twice that number in the 1830s. Most South Carolinians blamed the protective tariff, which tended to raise the prices of manufactured goods. Insofar as tariffs discouraged the sale of foreign goods in the United States, they reduced the ability of British and French traders to acquire the American money with which to buy American cotton. This worsened already existing problems of low cotton prices and exhausted lands. The South Carolinians' malaise was compounded by the increasing criticism of slavery. Hardly had the country emerged from the Missouri controversy when the city of Charleston was thrown into panic by the thwarted Denmark Vesey slave insurrection of 1822.

The unexpected passage of the Tariff of 1828, called the Tariff of Abominations by its critics because of its high taxes on imports, left Calhoun no choice but to join the opposition or give up his home base. Calhoun's *South Carolina Exposition and Protest* (1828), written in opposition to that tariff, contained a finespun theory of nullification, whereby a state could impose state authority and in effect repeal a federal law. This theory stopped just short of justifying secession from the Union. The unsigned statement accompanied resolutions of the South Carolina legislature protesting the tariff. Calhoun, however, had not entirely abandoned his earlier nationalism. He wanted to preserve the Union by protecting the minority rights that the agricultural and slaveholding South claimed. The fine balance he struck between states' rights and central authority was actually not far removed from Jackson's own philosophy, but growing tension between the two men would complicate the issue. The flinty Jackson, in addition, was determined to draw the line at any defiance of federal law.

The Webster-Hayne Debate

South Carolina had proclaimed its dislike for the tariff, but it had postponed any action against its enforcement, awaiting with hope the election of 1828 in which Calhoun was the Jacksonian candidate for vice-president. The state anticipated a new tariff policy from the Jackson administration. There the issue stood until 1830, when the great Webster-Hayne debate sharpened the lines between states' rights and the Union. The immediate occasion for the debate, however, was the question of lands owned by the federal government.

Late in 1829 a Connecticut senator, fearing the continued drain of able-bodied folk from New England, sought to restrict land sales in the West. When his resolution came before the Senate in 1830, Missouri's Thomas Hart Benton, who for years had been calling for lower land prices, denounced it as a sectional attack designed to impede the settlement of the West so that the East might maintain its supply of cheap factory labor.

Robert Y. Hayne of South Carolina took Benton's side. Hayne saw in the public-lands issue a chance to strengthen the alliance of South and West reflected in the vote for Jackson. The government, said Hayne, endangered the Union by imposing a hardship upon one section to the benefit of another. The use of public lands as a source of revenue to the central government would create "a fund for corruption—fatal to the sovereignty and independence of the states."

At this point Daniel Webster of Massachusetts, widely recognized as the nation's foremost orator and lawyer, rose to offer a dramatic defense of the East. With the gallery hushed, he began by denying that the East had ever sought to restrict development of the West. He then lured Hayne into defending states' rights and upholding the doctrine of nullification.

Hayne took the bait. Young, handsome, and himself an accomplished speaker, Hayne launched into a defense of Calhoun's *South Carolina Exposition*, arguing that the union was a compact of the states, and therefore the states remained free to judge when the national government had overstepped the bounds of its constitutional authority. The right of state "interposition," whereby a state could interpose its authority over a federal law in order to thwart an unjust federal statute, was as "full and complete as it was before the Constitution was formed."

In rebuttal to the state-compact theory, Webster defined a nationalistic view of the Constitution. From the beginning, he asserted, true sovereignty resided in the people as a whole, for whom both federal and state governments acted as agents in their respective spheres. If a single state could nullify a law of the general government, then the Union would be a "rope of sand," a practical absurdity. A state could neither nullify a federal law nor secede from the Union. The practical outcome of nullification would be a confrontation leading to civil war.

Those sitting in the Senate galleries and much of the country at large thrilled to Webster's eloquence. His closing statement has become justly famous: "Liberty and Union, now and forever, one and inseparable." In the practical world of coalition politics, Webster also had the better of the argument, for the Union and majority rule meant more to westerners, including Jackson, than the abstractions of state sovereignty and nullification. As for the public lands, the disputed resolution was soon defeated anyway.

The Rift with Calhoun

As yet, however, the enigmatic Jackson had not spoken out on the issue. Like Calhoun, he was a slaveholder, albeit a westerner, and he might be expected to sympathize with South Carolina, his native state. Soon all doubt was removed, at least on the point of nullification. On April 13, 1830, the Jefferson Day Dinner, honoring the birthday of the former president, was held in Washington. Jackson and Van Buren agreed that the president should offer a toast that would indicate his opposition to nullification. When his turn came, Jackson rose, raised his glass, pointedly stared at Calhoun, and announced: "Our Union—it must be preserved!" Calhoun tried quickly to retrieve the situation with a toast to "The Union, next to our liberty most dear!" But Jackson had set off a bombshell that exploded the plans of the states'-righters.

Nearly a month afterward, the final nail was driven into the coffin of Calhoun's presidential ambitions. On May 12, 1830, Jackson saw a letter confirming reports that in 1818 Calhoun, as secretary of war, had proposed to discipline Jackson for his reckless behavior during the Florida invasion. This discovery provoked a tense correspondence between President Jackson and Calhoun and ended with a curt note from the president cutting it off. "Understanding you now," Jackson wrote, "no further communication with you on this subject is necessary."

The growing rift prompted Jackson to remove all Calhoun partisans from the cabinet. He then named Van Buren as minister to London, pending Senate approval. In the fall of 1831 Jackson announced his readiness for one more term, with the idea of returning Van Buren from London in time for the New Yorker to succeed him as president in 1836. But in 1832, when the Senate reconvened, Van Buren's enemies opposed his appointment as minister and gave Calhoun, as vice-president, a chance to reject the nomination by a tie-breaking vote. "It will kill him [Van Buren], sir, kill him dead," Calhoun told Senator Thomas Hart Benton. Benton disagreed: "You have broken a minister, and elected a Vice-President." So, it turned out, he had. Calhoun's vote against Van Buren aroused popular sympathy for the New Yorker, who would soon be nominated to succeed Calhoun as vice-president.

His own presidential hopes blasted, Calhoun eagerly became the public leader of the nullificationists. These South Carolinians believed that tariff rates remained too high. By the end of 1831, Jackson was calling for further reductions of tariffs to take the wind out of the nullificationists' sails, and the tariff of 1832 did cut revenues another $5 million, but mainly on unprotected items. Average tariff rates were about 25 percent, but rates on cottons, woolens, and iron remained around 50 percent.

The South Carolina Ordinance

In the South Carolina state elections of 1832, the advocates of nullification took the initiative in organization and agitation. A special legislative session called for the election of a state convention, which overwhelmingly adopted a nullification ordinance repudiating the tariff acts of 1828 and 1832 as unconstitutional and forbidding collection of the duties in the state after February 1, 1833. The legislature also chose Robert Hayne as governor and elected Calhoun to succeed him as senator. Calhoun promptly resigned as vice-president to defend nullification on the Senate floor.

In the crisis, South Carolina found itself standing alone. The Georgia legislature dismissed nullification as "rash and revolutionary." Alabama pronounced it "unsound in theory and dangerous in practice." Mississippi stood "firmly resolved" against nullification. Jackson's response was measured and firm, but not rash—at least not in public. In private he threatened to hang Calhoun and all other traitors—and later expressed regret that he had failed to hang at least Calhoun. In his annual message on December 4, 1832, Jackson announced his firm intention to enforce the tariff, but once again he urged Congress to lower the rates. On December 10 he followed up with his Nullification Proclamation, which characterized nullification as an "impractical absurdity." Jackson appealed to the people of his native state not to follow false leaders: "The laws of the United States must be executed. . . . Those who told you that you might peaceably prevent their execution, deceived you. . . . Their object is disunion. But be not deceived by names. Disunion by armed force is treason."

Clay's Compromise

Jackson sent General Winfield Scott to Charleston Harbor with reinforcements of federal soldiers. The nullifiers mobilized the state militia while their local opponents, called Unionists, organized a volunteer force. In 1833 the president requested from

Congress a "Force Bill" authorizing him to use the army to compel compliance with federal law in South Carolina. At the same time, he endorsed a bill in Congress that would have lowered tariff duties to a maximum of 20 percent within two years.

When the Force Bill was introduced, Calhoun immediately rose in opposition, denying that either he or his state favored disunion. He did not want the South to leave the Union; he wanted the region to regain its political dominance of the Union. Passage of the bill eventually came to depend on the support of Henry Clay, who finally yielded to those urging him to save the day. On February 12, 1833, he introduced a plan to reduce the tariff gradually until 1842, by which time no rate would be more than 20 percent.

On March 1, 1833, the compromise tariff and the Force Bill passed Congress, and the next day Jackson signed both. The South Carolina convention then met and rescinded its nullification ordinance. Both sides were able to claim victory. The president had upheld the supremacy of the Union, and South Carolina had secured a reduction of the tariff. Calhoun, worn out by the controversy, returned to his plantation. "The struggle, so far from being over," he ominously wrote, "is not more than fairly commenced."

Racial Prejudice in the Jacksonian Era

The Jacksonian era is filled with contradictions. Many of the same social factors and economic forces that promoted the democratization of the political process during the 1820s also led Democrats, North and South, to justify white supremacy, slavery, and the subjugation of Indians and women.

What explains such contradictory behavior? By asserting the racial inferiority of Indians and blacks, white wage earners could, in a tortured sense, enhance their own self-esteem and justify their own economic interests. In addition, many northern workers feared for their own jobs if runaway slaves continued to stream northward or if all the slaves in the South were freed.

Attitudes toward Blacks

Roger B. Taney, the man Andrew Jackson appointed as the nation's attorney-general, declared in 1831 that blacks were a "separate and degraded people" and therefore could be discriminated against by local and state governments. Free blacks in most northern states during the Jacksonian era were denied basic civil rights and forced to live and operate under segregated conditions. In 1829 government officials in Cincinnati, Ohio, a haven for runaway slaves, ordered all blacks out of the city within thirty days. A mob of whites decided to hurry them on, and they destroyed most of the black neighborhoods in the city.

Such antiblack riots were common in northern cities. Whites who participated in an 1834 riot against blacks in Philadelphia explained that they were simply defending themselves against the efforts of blacks and abolitionists "to break down the distinctive barrier between the colors [so] that the poor whites may gradually sink into the degraded condition of the Negroes—that, like them, they may be slaves and tools" of economic elites. Four years later, in 1838, the state of Pennsylvania officially disenfranchised blacks. By 1860, almost every state, old and new, had disenfranchised free blacks while easing voting qualifications for white males.

The Democratic coalition that elected Jackson thus depended for its survival on a widely shared "white racism" and the ability to avoid potentially divisive discussions of slavery. In the South, the majority of farmers who supported the slaveholding Jackson and identified with the Democrats did not own slaves, but they still embraced theories of racial superiority.

Indian Policy

The attitude of Jackson and many of his followers toward the Indians was the typically western one—that they were barbaric impediments to white social progress and territorial expansion. By the time of his election in 1828, Jackson was convinced that a "just, humane, liberal policy toward Indians" dictated moving them onto the plains west of the Mississippi River, an area fit mainly for horned toads and rattlesnakes. Congress agreed, and in 1830 it approved the Indian Removal Act.

Although sometimes the tribes rebelled, there was, on the whole, remarkably little resistance. In Illinois and Wisconsin Territory an armed clash known as the Black Hawk War sprang up in 1832, when the Sauk and Fox under Chief Black Hawk sought to reoccupy some lands they had abandoned in the previous year. The Illinois militia mobilized to expel them, chased them into Wisconsin Territory, and massacred women and children as they tried to escape across the Mississippi.

Sioux Encamped on the Upper Missouri, Dressing Buffalo Meat and Robes (1832), by George Catlin. Catlin's romantic paintings of Indian life appeared just as the tribes of the Southeast were rooted up and moved west.

In the South two proud Indian nations, the Seminoles and Cherokees, also put up a stubborn resistance. The Seminoles were in fact a group of different tribes that had gravitated to Florida in the eighteenth century. They fought a protracted guerrilla war in the Everglades from 1835 to 1842, but most of the vigor went out of their resistance after 1837, when their leader, Osceola, was seized by treachery under a flag of truce, imprisoned, and left to die. After 1842 only a few hundred Seminoles remained, hiding out in the swamps. Most of the rest had been banished to the West.

The Trail of Tears

The Cherokees had by the end of the eighteenth century fallen back into the mountains of northern Georgia and western North Carolina, onto land guaranteed to them in 1791 by treaty with the United States. In 1827 the Cherokees, relying on their treaty rights, adopted a constitution in which they said pointedly that they were not subject to any other state or nation. The next year Georgia responded with a law stipulating that after June 1, 1830, the authority of state law would extend over the Cherokees living within the boundaries of the state.

The discovery of gold in 1829 whetted the whites' appetite for Cherokee lands and brought bands of rough prospectors into the country. The Cherokees sought relief in the Supreme Court, but in *Cherokee Nation* v. *Georgia* (1831) John Marshall ruled that the Court lacked jurisdiction because the Cherokees were a "domestic dependent nation" rather than a foreign state in the meaning of the Constitution. Marshall added, however, that the Cherokees had "an unquestionable right" to their lands until they wished to cede them to the United States.

In 1830 a Georgia law had required whites in the Cherokee territory to get licenses authorizing their residence there, and to take an oath of allegiance to the state of Georgia. Two New England missionaries

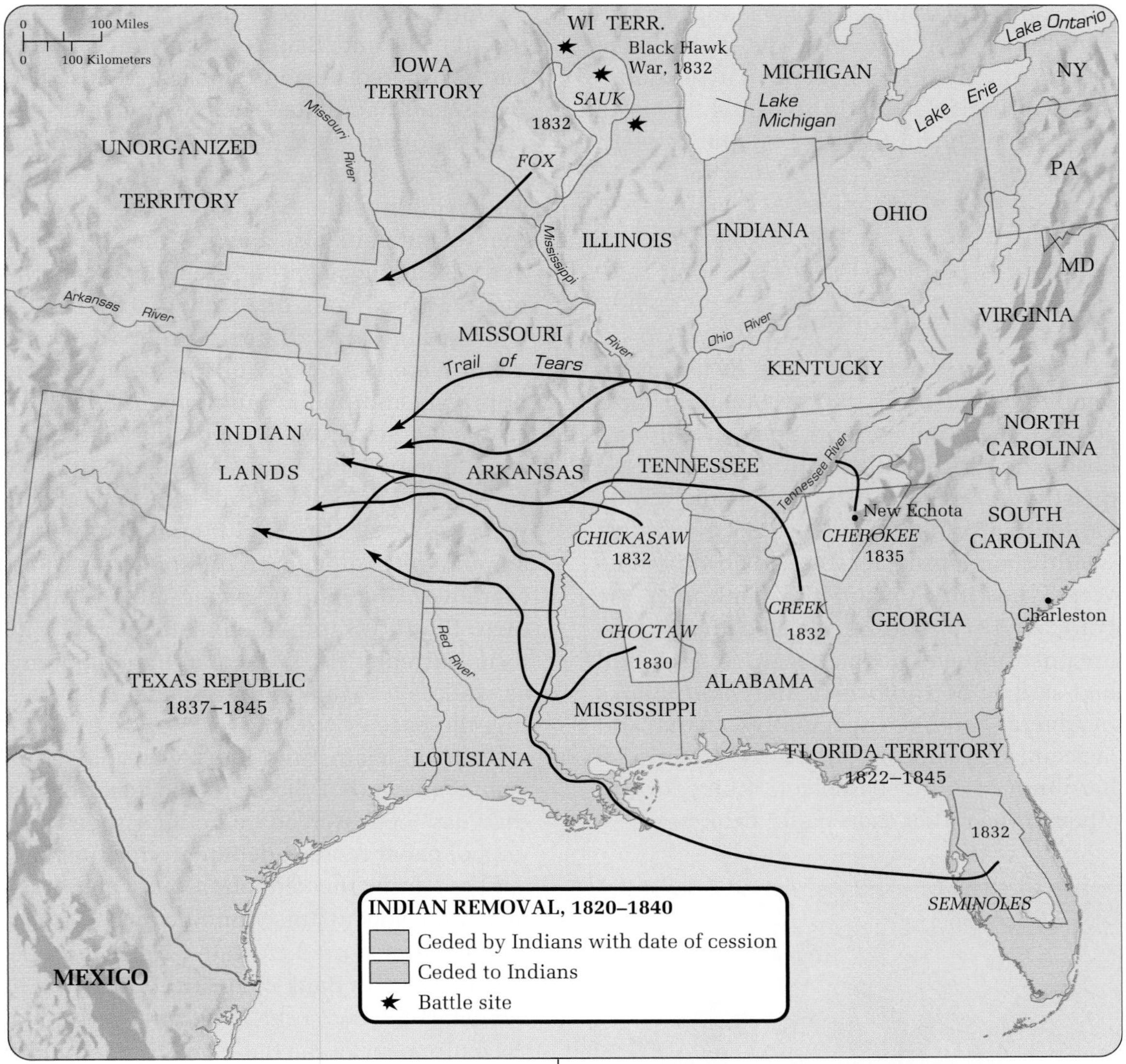

among the Indians refused and were sentenced to four years at hard labor. On appeal, their case reached the Supreme Court as *Worcester* v. *Georgia* (1832), and the court held that the Cherokee nation was "a distinct political community" within which Georgia law had no force. The Georgia law was therefore unconstitutional. Now Georgia faced down the Supreme Court with the tacit consent of the president. Jackson is supposed to have said privately: "Marshall has made his decision, now let him enforce it!" In the circumstances, there was nothing for the Cherokees to do but give in and sign a treaty, which they did in 1835. They gave up their lands in the Southeast in exchange for lands in the Indian Territory west of Arkansas, $5 million from the federal government, and expenses for transportation.

By 1838 some 12,000 Cherokees had departed on the thousand-mile "Trail of Tears" westward, following the Choctaws, Chickasaws, Creeks, and Seminoles. It was a grueling journey marked by the cruelty and neglect of soldiers and private contractors, and scorn and pilferage by whites along the way. Four thousand Cherokees did not survive the trip. A few never left their homeland. They held out in their native mountains and acquired title to lands in North Carolina; thenceforth they were the "Eastern Band" of Cherokees.

The Bank Controversy

The Bank's Opponents

The overriding national issue in the presidential campaign of 1832 was neither Jackson's Indian policy nor South Carolina's obsession with nullification. It was the question of rechartering the Bank of the United States (B.U.S), whose legal mandate would soon lapse. Jackson had absorbed the West's hostility toward the Bank after the Panic of 1819, and he insisted that it was unconstitutional no matter what Marshall had said in *McCulloch* v. *Maryland.* Banks in general had fed a speculative mania, and Jackson, suspicious of all banks, preferred a hard-money policy based solely on gold and silver coins rather than paper bank notes.

Jackson battling the hydra-headed Bank of the United States.

Under the management of Nicholas Biddle, the Second Bank of the United States had prospered during the early 1830s. The Bank had facilitated business expansion and supplied a stable currency by forcing state banks to keep a specie (gold or silver) reserve on hand to back up their paper currency. The Bank also acted as the collecting and disbursing agent for the federal government, which held one-fifth of the Bank's $35 million capital stock. From the start, many were suspicious of this combination of private and public functions. As the government's revenues soared, the Bank became the most powerful lending institution in the country, a central bank, in effect, whose huge size enabled it to determine the amount of available credit for the nation. Moreover, by issuing paper money of its own, the B.U.S. provided a stable and uniform currency for the expanding economy as well as a regulating mechanism controlling the pace of growth.

Arrayed against the Bank were powerful enemies: some of the state and local banks that had been forced to reduce their volume of paper money, debtor groups that had suffered from the reduction, and businessmen and speculators "on the make" who wanted easier credit. States'-rights groups questioned the Bank's constitutionality. Financiers on New York's Wall Street resented the supremacy of the Bank on Philadelphia's Chestnut Street. Many westerners and workingmen, like Andrew Jackson, felt that the Bank was a powerful monopoly controlled by the wealthy few and that this was irreconcilable with a democracy.

The Recharter Effort

Henry Clay, already the presidential candidate of the National-Republicans, proposed to make the Bank the central issue of the 1832 presidential election. Friends of the Bank held a majority in Congress, and Jackson would risk loss of support in the election if he vetoed renewal. But they failed to grasp the depth of popular prejudice against the Bank. They succeeded mainly in handing over to Jackson a charged issue on the eve of the election. "The Bank," Jackson told Martin Van Buren in May 1832, "is trying to kill me. But I will kill it."

Both houses passed the recharter bill by comfortable margins, but without the two-thirds majority needed to override a presidential veto. On July 10, 1832, Jackson vetoed the bill, sending it back to Congress with a ringing denunciation of monopoly and special privilege. An effort to overrule the veto failed in the Senate, where the vote of twenty-two to nineteen for the Bank fell far short of the needed two-thirds majority. The stage was set for a nationwide financial crisis.

Campaign Innovations

The 1832 presidential campaign included a third political party for the first time. The Anti-Masonic party was, like the Bank, the object of strong emotions then sweeping the new democracy. The group had grown out of popular hostility toward the Masonic order, a fraternal organization whose members were suspected of having kidnapped and murdered a New Yorker for revealing the "secrets" of his lodge. Opposition to a secret fraternal order was hardly the foundation on which to build a lasting national political organization, but the Anti-Masonic party had three important "firsts" to its credit: in addition to being the first third party, it was the first party to hold a national nominating convention and the first to announce a platform, all of which it accomplished in 1831 when it nominated William Wirt of Maryland for president.

The major parties followed its example by holding national conventions of their own. In 1831 National-Republican party delegates assembled in Baltimore to nominate Henry Clay for president. Jackson endorsed the idea of a nominating convention for the Democratic party to demonstrate popular support for its candidates. To that purpose, the convention adopted the two-thirds rule for nomination (which prevailed until 1936), and then named Martin Van Buren as Jackson's running mate. The Democrats, unlike the other two parties, adopted no formal platform at their first convention, and they relied substantially on hoopla and the president's personal popularity to carry the election.

The outcome was an overwhelming endorsement of Jackson in the electoral college by 219 votes to 49 for Clay, and a less overwhelming but solid victory in the popular vote, 688,000 to 530,000. William Wirt carried only Vermont. South Carolina, preparing for nullification and unable to stomach either Jackson or Clay, delivered its eleven votes to the governor of Virginia.

Removal of Government Deposits

Jackson viewed the election as a mandate to proceed further against the B.U.S., and he now resolved to remove all government deposits and distribute them to state banks. When Secretary of the Treasury Louis McLane opposed removal of the government deposits and suggested a new and modified version of the Bank, Jackson shook up his cabinet. He kicked McLane upstairs to head the State Department and replaced him with William J. Duane of Philadelphia. Yet Duane saw no merit in removing deposits from the central bank for deposit in countless state banks. So Jackson summarily dismissed Duane and moved Attorney-General Roger Taney to the Treasury, where the new secretary gladly complied with the president's wishes, which corresponded to his own views.

By the end of 1833, there were twenty-three state banks that had the benefit of governmental deposits, "pet banks" as they came to be called. Transferring the government's deposits was a highly questionable action under the law, and the Senate voted to censure Jackson for his actions. Nicholas Biddle refused to surrender. He ordered that

King Andrew the First. This opposition cartoon shows King Andrew Jackson trampling on the Constitution, internal improvements, and the Bank of the United States.

the B.U.S. curtail loans throughout the nation and demand the immediate redemption of state bank notes in specie as fast as possible. He sought to bring the economy to a halt, create a sharp depression, and reveal to the nation the importance of maintaining the Bank. By 1834 the tightness of credit was creating widespread complaints of business distress.

The financial contraction resulting from the bank war quickly gave way, however, to a speculative binge encouraged by the deposit of government funds in the pet state banks. With the restraint of the B.U.S. removed, the state banks unleashed their wildcat tendencies, issuing bank notes without keeping sufficient gold reserves on hand. (The term "wildcat," used in this sense, originated in Michigan, where one of the fly-by-night banks featured a panther, or wildcat, on its worthless notes.) New banks mushroomed, blissfully printing bank notes to lend to speculators. Sales of public lands rose from 4 million acres in 1834 to 15 million in 1835 and to 20 million in 1836. At the same time, the states plunged heavily into debt to finance the building of roads and canals, inspired by the success of New York's Erie Canal in opening up the entire state's economy to the markets of the Eastern Seaboard and Europe. By 1837 total state indebtedness had soared to $170 million, a very large sum for that time.

Fiscal Measures

Still the federal revenues continued to mount as the widespread speculation in public lands continued, and this set off an intense debate over how to deal with the growing federal surplus. Many westerners proposed simply to lower the price of land; southerners preferred to lower the tariff—but such action would now upset the compromise achieved in the Tariff of 1833. Finally, in 1836, the Distribution Act was passed. This was a compromise that allowed the government to distribute most of the surplus as loans to the states in proportion to each state's representation in Congress.

About a month after passage of this Distribution Act, Jackson's treasury secretary issued the Specie Circular of July 11, 1836. With that document, the president belatedly applied his hard-money convictions to the sale of public lands. According to his order, the government after August 15 would accept only gold and silver in payment for lands. Doing so would supposedly "repress frauds," withhold support "from monopoly of the public lands in the hands of speculators and capitalists," and discourage the "ruinous extension" of bank notes and credit.

Both the Distribution Act and the Specie Circular put many state banks in a precarious plight. The distribution reduced their deposits, or at least threw things into disarray by shifting them from bank to bank, and the increased demand for specie put an added strain on the supply of gold and silver. The distribution of the federal surplus to the state governments entailed the removal of large deposits from state banks. In turn, the state banks had to call in many of their loans in order to accumulate enough money to make the transfer of federal funds to the state governments. This disrupted the already chaotic state banking community.

Boom and Bust

But the boom and bust of the 1830s had causes larger even than Andrew Jackson, causes that were beyond his control. The inflation of mid-decade was rooted not solely in a sudden expansion of bank notes, as it seemed at the time, but also in an increase of gold and silver flowing in from England and France, and especially from Mexico, for investment and for the purchase of American cotton and other products.

Contrary to appearances, the specie reserves in American banks actually kept pace with the increase of bank notes, despite reckless behavior by some banks. But by 1836 a tighter economy caused a decline in British investments abroad and in British demand for American cotton, just when the new western lands were creating a rapid increase in cotton supply. Fortunately for Jackson, the Panic of 1837 did not break until he was out of the White House and safely back at his plantation near Nashville. His successor would serve as the scapegoat.

Van Buren and the New Party System

The Whig Coalition

By 1834, Jackson's opponents began to pull together a new coalition of diverse elements united chiefly by their hostility to the president. The imperious demeanor of that champion of democracy had given rise to the name of "King Andrew I." His followers therefore were "Tories," supporters of the king, and his opponents "Whigs," a name that linked them to the patriots of the American Revolution. This diverse coalition clustered around its center, the National-Republican party of John Quincy Adams, Clay, and Webster. Into the combination streamed remnants of the Anti-Masons and Democrats who, for one reason or another, were alienated by Jackson's stands on the Bank, Indian removal, hard money, or internal improvements.

The core Whigs were the supporters of Henry Clay and his "American System" of industrial development, high tariffs, and internal improvements. In the South the Whigs enjoyed the support of the urban banking and commercial interests, as well as their planter associates, owners of most of the slaves in the region. In the West, farmers who valued internal improvements joined the Whig ranks. Most states'-rights supporters eventually dropped away, and by the early 1840s the Whigs were becoming the party of economic nationalism, even in the South. Unlike the Democrats, who attracted Catholic immigrants from Germany and Ireland, Whig voters tended to be native-born and British-American Protestants—Presbyterians, Baptists, and Congregationalists—who were active in promoting social reforms such as abolitionism and temperance.

The Election of 1836

By the presidential election of 1836, a new two-party system was emerging out of the Jackson and anti-Jackson forces, a system that would remain in fairly even balance for twenty years. In 1835, the Democrats held their second national convention and nominated Jackson's handpicked successor, Vice-President Martin Van Buren. The Whig coalition, united chiefly in its opposition to Jackson, adopted a strategy of multiple candidacies, hoping to throw the election into the House of Representatives.

The result was a free-for-all reminiscent of 1824, except that this time one candidate stood apart from the rest. It was Van Buren against the field. In the popular vote, Van Buren outdistanced the entire Whig field, with 765,000 votes to 740,000 votes for the Whigs.

Martin Van Buren, the eighth president, was the first of Dutch ancestry. Son of a tavernkeeper in Kinderhook, New York, he had been schooled in a local academy, read law, and entered politics. Although he kept up a limited legal practice, he had been primarily a professional politician, so skilled in the arts of organization and manipulation that he was dubbed the "Little Magician." After a brief tenure as governor of New York, Van Buren resigned to join Jackson's cabinet and, because of Jackson's support, became minister to London and then vice-president.

Martin Van Buren, the "Little Magician."

The Panic of 1837

Van Buren inherited Jackson's favor and a good part of his following, but he also inherited a financial panic. An already precarious economy was tipped over into crisis by depression in England, which resulted in a drop in the price of cotton from 17½ cents to 13½ cents a pound, and caused English banks and investors to contract their activities in the New World and to refuse extensions of loans. This was a particularly hard blow, since much of America's economic expansion depended on European—and mainly English—capital. As creditors hastened to foreclose, the inflationary spiral went into reverse. States curtailed ambitious plans for roads and canals and in many cases felt impelled to repudiate their debts. In the crunch, many of the wildcat banks succumbed.

By the fall of 1837, a third of the workforce was jobless. Those still fortunate enough to have jobs saw their wages cut by 30 to 50 percent within two years. At the same time, prices for food and clothing skyrocketed. There was no government aid, only that provided by churches and voluntary societies.

Van Buren's advisers and supporters were inclined to blame speculators and bankers for the hard times. At the same time, they expected the evildoers to get what they deserved in a healthy shakeout that would bring the economy back to stability. Van Buren did not believe that he or the government had any responsibility to rescue hard-pressed farmers or businessmen, or to provide public welfare. But he did feel obliged to keep the government itself in a healthy financial situation. To that end, he called a special session of Congress in 1837, which quickly voted to postpone indefinitely the distribution of the federal surplus because of a probable upcoming deficit, and also approved an issue of Treasury notes to cover immediate expenses.

An Independent Treasury

Van Buren proposed that the government cease risking its deposits in shaky banks and set up an Independent Treasury. Under this plan, the government would keep its funds in its own vaults and do business entirely in hard money. Van Buren's Independent Treasury Act encountered stiff opposition from a combination of Whigs and conservative Democrats who feared deflation, and it took the president several years of maneuvering to get what he wanted. Van Buren gained western support for the plan by backing a more liberal federal land policy. Congress finally passed the Independent Treasury Act on July 4, 1840. Although the Whigs repealed it in 1841, it would be restored in 1846.

The protracted struggle over the Treasury was only one of several issues that kept Washington preoccupied through the Van Buren years. Petitions asking Congress to abolish slavery and the slave trade in the District of Columbia provoked tumultuous debate, especially in the House of Representatives. A dispute over the Maine boundary kept British-American animosity at a simmer. But basic to the spreading malaise of the time was the depressed condition of the economy, which lasted through Van Buren's entire term. Fairly or not, the administration became the target of growing discontent. The president won renomination easily enough, but the general election was another matter.

The "Log Cabin and Hard Cider" Campaign

The Whigs got an early start on their 1840 campaign when they met at Harrisburg, Pennsylvania, on December 4, 1839, to choose a candidate. The delegates turned to William Henry Harrison, victor at the battle of Tippecanoe against the Shawnees in 1811, governor of the Indiana territory, and briefly a congressman and a senator from

Ohio. To rally their states'-rights wing, the Whigs chose for vice-president John Tyler of Virginia, Clay's close friend.

The Whigs had no platform. That would have risked dividing a coalition united chiefly by opposition to the Democrats. But they had a slogan, "Tippecanoe and Tyler too," that went trippingly on the tongue. And they soon had a rousing campaign theme, which a Democratic paper unwittingly supplied them when it declared sardonically "that upon condition of his receiving a pension of $2,000 and a barrel of cider, General Harrison would no doubt consent to withdraw his pretensions, and spend his days in a log cabin on the banks of the Ohio." The Whigs seized upon the cider and log cabin symbols to depict Harrison as a simple man sprung from the people. Actually, he sprang from one of the first families of Virginia, was a college graduate, and lived in a commodious Ohio farmhouse.

The campaign produced the largest turnout of any election up to that time. To the general public, Van Buren had come to symbolize the economic slump as well as aristocratic snobbery. "Van! Van! Is a Used-up Man!" went one of the Whig campaign slogans, and down he went by the thumping margin of 234 electoral votes to 60.

Assessing the Jackson Years

The Jacksonian impulse had permanently altered American politics. Long-standing ambivalence about political parties had been purged in the fires of political conflict, and mass political parties had arrived to stay. They were now widely justified as a positive good. By 1840 both parties were tightly organized down to the precinct level, and the proportion of adult white males who voted in the presidential election nearly tripled, from 27 percent in 1824 to 78 percent in 1840. That much is beyond dispute, but the phenomenon of Jackson, the great symbol for an age, has inspired conflicts of interpretation as spirited as those among his supporters and opponents at the time. Was he the leader of a vast democratic movement that welled up in the West and mobilized a farmer-laborer alliance to sweep the "Monster" bank into the dustbin of history? Or was he essentially a frontier tycoon, an opportunist for whom the ideal of democracy provided effective political rhetoric?

Whatever else Jackson and his supporters had in mind, they followed an ideal of republican virtue, of returning to the Jeffersonian vision of the Old Republic in which government would leave people largely to their own devices. In the Jacksonian view, the alliance of government and business invited special favors and provided an eternal source of corruption. The central bank epitomized such evil. Good governmental policy, at the national level in particular, refrained from granting special privileges and let free competition regulate the economy.

In the bustling world of the nineteenth century, however, the idea of a return to agrarian simplicity represented a futile exercise in nostalgia. Instead, Jackson's laissez-faire policies actually opened the way for a host of aspiring entrepreneurs eager to replace the established economic elite with a new order of free enterprise capitalism. And in fact there was no great conflict in the Jacksonian mentality between the farmer or planter who delved in the soil and the independent speculator and entrepreneur who won his way by other means. Jackson himself was all these things. The ultimate irony would be that Jackson's laissez-faire rationale for republican simplicity eventually became the justification for the growth of unregulated centers of economic power far greater than any ever wielded by the Bank of the United States.

CHAPTER 11

The Dynamics of Growth

This chapter focuses on

- The expansion of agriculture, industry, and transportation.
- Patterns of immigration at mid-century.
- The emergence of labor unions.

THE *ESSENTIAL AMERICA* ON-LINE TUTOR

www.wwnorton.com/eamerica/ch11

- **Topic: Industrialization, urbanization, and immigration**
  www.wwnorton.com/eamerica/ch11/topic.htm

  One of the great waves of immigration to America occurred in the 1840s and 1850s, bringing millions of Northern Europeans to the United States. Explore the significance of this immigration utilizing personal accounts, maps, paintings, contemporary newspaper accounts, and historical analyses. How did this wave of immigration affect the United States?

- **Chapter review: On-line quiz and chapter summary**
  www.wwnorton.com/eamerica/ch11/review.htm

- **Chapter resources: Multimedia index**
  www.wwnorton.com/eamerica/ch11/media.htm

The Jacksonian-era political debate between democratic and elitist elements was rooted in a profound transformation of American social and economic life. Between 1815 and 1850, the United States expanded all the way to the Pacific coast. An industrial revolution in the Northeast began to reshape the contours of the economy and propel an unrelenting process of urbanization. In the West an agricultural empire began to emerge based upon the foundation of corn, wheat, and cattle. In the South cotton became king, and its profits came to depend on an expanding institution of slavery. At the same time, innovations in transportation—horse-drawn wagons, canals, steamboats, and railroads—knit together a national market. These economic developments in turn generated changes in every other area of American life, from politics to the legal system, from the family to social values.

Agriculture and the National Economy

The first stage of industrialization brought with it an expansive commercial and urban outlook that by the end of the century would supplant the agrarian philosophy espoused by Thomas Jefferson and many others. "We are greatly, I was about to say fearfully, growing," John C. Calhoun told his congressional colleagues in 1816, and many other statesmen shared his ambivalent outlook. Would the Republic retain its virtue and cohesion amid the turmoil of commercial development?

Cotton

A major source of economic opportunity in the South after 1815 was provided by the cultivation of cotton, the profitable new staple crop that was spreading from South Carolina and Georgia into the new lands of Mississippi and Alabama. For many years, cotton had remained rare and expensive because of the need for hand labor to separate the lint from the tenacious green seeds. But that problem was solved in 1793 when Eli Whitney devised a machine for removing the sticky seeds. The cotton gin enabled a person to separate cotton fifty times faster than could be done by hand.

By inventing the cotton gin, Whitney had unwittingly begun a revolution. Cotton production soared during the first half of the nineteenth century, and planters found a new and profitable use for slavery. Planters and their slaves migrated westward into Kentucky, Tennessee, Alabama, Mississippi, Louisiana, and Texas, and the cotton culture became a way of life that tied together the Old Southwest and the coastal Southeast.

After Napoleon's defeat in 1815, European demand for cotton skyrocketed. From 1815 to 1819, American cotton exports averaged 39 percent of the value of all exports, and from the mid-1830s to 1860 they accounted for more than half the total. For the national economy as a whole during the first half of the century, cotton precipitated a phenomenal expansion. The South supplied the North both raw materials and markets for manufactures. Income from the North's role in handling the cotton trade then provided surpluses for capital investment.

Farming the West

The westward flow of planters and their slaves to Alabama and Mississippi during these flush times mirrored another migration through the Ohio Valley and the Great Lakes region, where the Indians had been steadily pushed westward. By 1860, more than half the nation's population resided west of the Appalachian Mountains, and the restless movement had long since spilled across the Mississippi River and touched the shores of the Pacific.

North of the expanding cotton belt in the Gulf states, the fertile woodland soils, riverside bottom lands, and black loam of the prairies drew farmers from the rocky land of

New England and the exhausted soils of the Southeast. The development of effective iron plows greatly eased the grueling job of breaking the soil. In 1819 a New York farmer developed an improved iron plow with parts that could be replaced separately without buying a whole new plow. Demand for plows grew so fast that the manufacturer could not supply the need. Further improvements would follow, including John Deere's steel plow (1837), which was better suited for breaking up the rock-hard soil of the Great Plains.

A new federal land law of 1820 reduced the minimum price per acre and the minimum plot from 160 to 80 acres. The settler could now buy a homestead for as little as $100, and over the years the proliferation of state banks made it possible to continue buying on credit. Even that was not enough for westerners who began a long—and eventually victorious—agitation for further relaxation of the land laws. They favored *preemption*, the right of squatters to purchase land at the minimum price, and *graduation*, the progressive reduction of the price on lands that did not sell.

Congress eventually responded with two new laws. Under the Preemption Act of 1830, squatters could stake out claims ahead of the land surveys and later get 160 acres at the minimum price of $1.25 per acre. In effect, the law recognized a practice enforced more often than not by frontier vigilantes. Under the Graduation Act of 1854, prices of unsold government lands were to go down in stages until the lands could sell for 12½¢ per acre after thirty years.

Transportation and the National Economy

New Roads

Transportation improvements helped spur the development of a national market. In 1795 the Wilderness Road, which followed the trail blazed by Daniel Boone twenty years before, was opened to wagon and stagecoach traffic, thereby easing the route through the Cumberland Gap in Kentucky. In the Deep South there were no such major highways. South Carolinians and Georgians

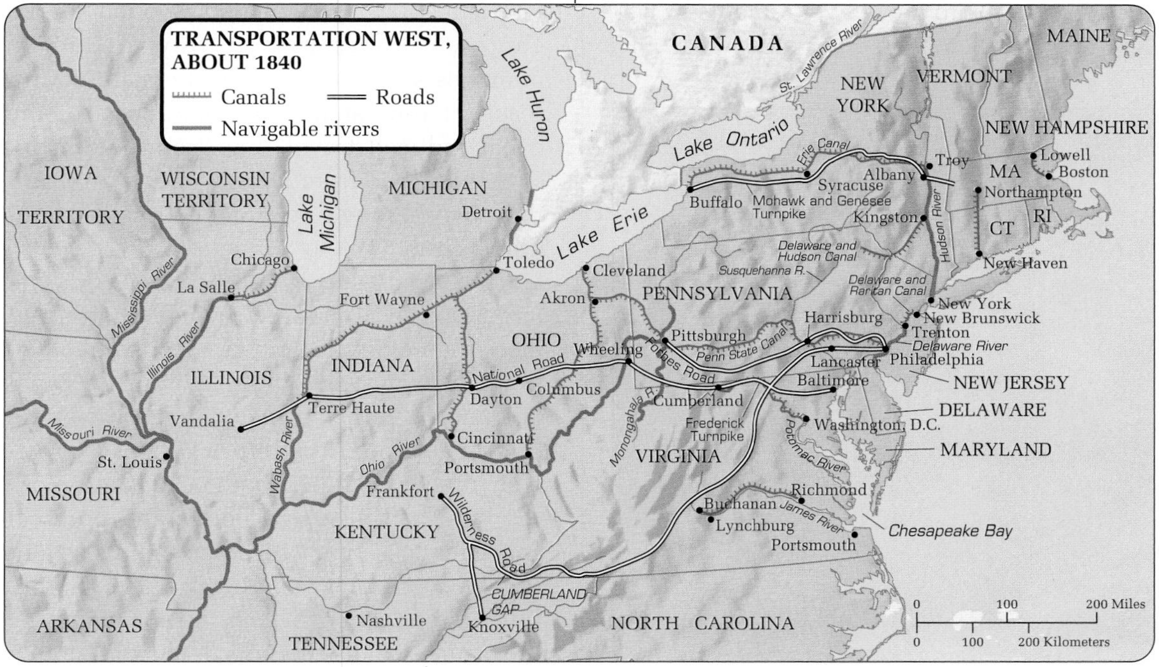

pushed westward on whatever trails or rutted roads had appeared.

To the northeast, public demand for paved roads packed with crushed stones gathered momentum after completion of the Philadelphia-Lancaster Turnpike in 1794 (the term derives from a pole or pike at the tollgate, turned to admit the traffic). By 1821 there were some 4,000 miles of turnpikes, mainly connecting eastern cities, but western traffic could move along the Frederick Turnpike to Cumberland and thence along the National Road to Wheeling on the Ohio River in 1818, then to Columbus, Ohio, in the Northwest Territory, and to Vandalia, Illinois, by about mid-century.

Water Transport

Once turnpike travelers had reached the Ohio River, they could float westward in comparative comfort on flatboats. In the early 1820s some 3,000 flatboats went down the Ohio River every year, and for many years thereafter the flatboat remained the chief means for conveying heavy traffic downstream.

By the early 1820s, the turnpike boom was giving way to new developments in water transportation: the river steamboat and the canal barge, which carried bulk commodities far more cheaply than did Conestoga wagons on the National Road. The first commercially successful steamboat appeared when Robert Fulton and Robert R. Livingston sent the *Clermont* up the Hudson River to Albany in 1807.

By 1836, 361 steamboats navigated the far reaches of the Mississippi Valley, up rivers such as the Wabash, the Monongahela, the Cumberland, the Tennessee, the Missouri, and the Arkansas. By bringing cheaper and faster two-way traffic to the Mississippi Valley, the steamboats helped create a continental market and an agricultural empire that became the new breadbasket of America. Along with the new farmers came promoters, speculators, and retailers. Villages at strategic trading points along the streams evolved into centers of commerce and urban life. The port of New Orleans grew in the 1830s and 1840s to lead all others in exports.

But by then the Erie Canal was drawing eastward much of the trade that once went down to the Gulf. In 1817 the New York legislature had endorsed Governor De Witt Clinton's dream of a canal connecting the Hudson River with Lake Erie. Eight years later, in 1825, the canal was open for its entire 350 miles from Albany to Buffalo; branches soon put most of the state within reach of the canal. The completion of the canal reduced travel time from New York City to Buffalo from twenty days to six, and the cost of moving a ton of freight plummeted from $100 to $5.

The speedy success of the New York system inspired a mania for canals that lasted more than a decade and created about 3,000 miles of waterways by 1837. But no canal ever matched the spectacular success of the Erie. It rendered the entire Great Lakes region an economic tributary to New York City and had major economic and political consequences tying together the West and East while further isolating the Deep South. With the addition of new canals spanning Ohio and Indiana from north to south, much

Lockport, New York. Eighty-three locks were required for the Erie Canal to cross the rise in elevation in western New York, including five at Lockport.

of the upper Ohio Valley was also drawn within New York's economic sphere.

Railroads

In 1825, the year the Erie Canal was completed, the world's first commercial steam railway began operations in England, and soon the port cities of Baltimore, Charleston, and Boston were alive with schemes to penetrate the hinterlands by rail. By 1840, American railroads, with a total of 3,328 miles, had outdistanced the canals by just two miles. Over the next twenty years,

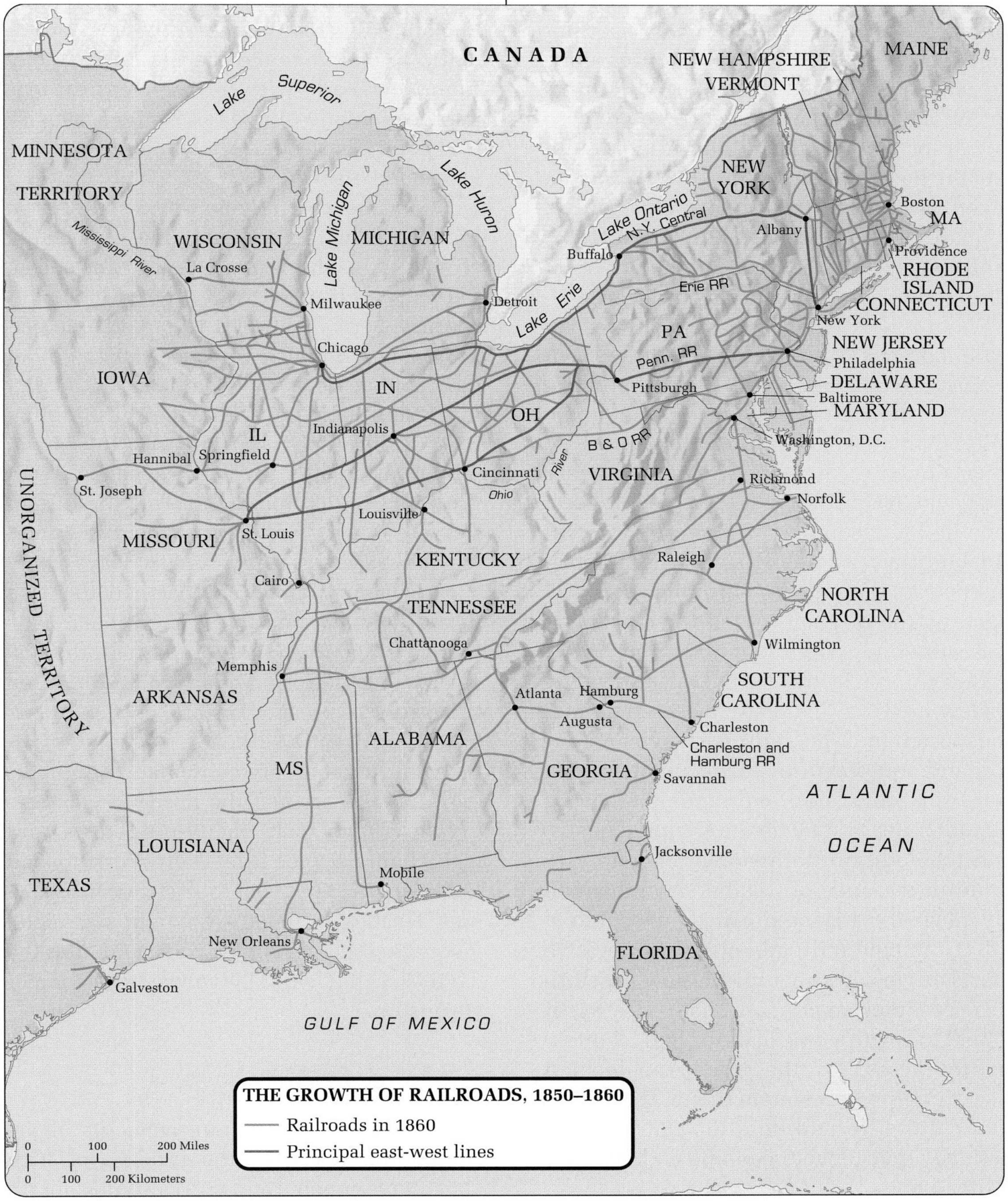

THE GROWTH OF RAILROADS, 1850–1860

though, railroads grew nearly tenfold to cover 30,626 miles; more than two-thirds of this total was built in the 1850s. But it was not until the eve of the Civil War that railroads surpassed canals in total haulage: in 1859 they carried a little over 2 billion tons compared to 1.6 billion on canals.

Travel on the early railroads tested the courage of passengers. Wood was used for fuel, and the sparks often caused fires along the way or damaged passengers' clothing. Invention of the "spark arrester" and the use of coal for fuel alleviated but did not eliminate the hazard. Different track widths often forced passengers to change trains until a standard gauge became national in 1882. Land travel, whether by stagecoach or train, was a jerky, bumpy, wearying ordeal.

Water travel, where available, offered far more comfort, but railroads gained supremacy over other forms of transport because of their economy, speed, and reliability. Early trains averaged ten miles an hour, doubling the speed of stagecoaches and canal boats. Railroads provided indirect benefits by encouraging frontier settlement and boosting farming. During the antebellum period, the reduced shipping costs provided by the railroads aided the expansion of farming more than manufacturing, since manufacturers in the Northeast, especially in New England, had better access to water transportation. The railroads' demand for iron and equipment of various kinds, however, did provide an enormous market for the industries that made these capital goods. And the ability of railroads to operate year round in all kinds of weather gave them an advantage in carrying finished goods, too.

But the epic railroad boom had negative effects as well. By opening up new possibilities for quick and often shady profits, it helped to corrupt political life, and by opening up access to the trans-Appalachian West, it helped accelerate the decline of Indian culture. In addition, the railroad dramatically quickened the tempo and mobility of life.

Ocean Transport

For oceangoing traffic, the start of service on regular schedules was the most important change of the early 1800s. In the first week of 1818, ships of the New York–based Black Ball Line inaugurated a weekly transatlantic service between New York and Liverpool, England. By 1845 some fifty-two transatlantic lines ran square-riggers on schedule from New York, with three regular sailings per week. Many others ran in the coastwise trade, to Charleston, Savannah, New Orleans, and elsewhere.

The same year, 1845, witnessed a great innovation with the launching of the first clipper ship, the *Rainbow*. Built for speed, the sleek clippers were the nineteenth-century equivalent of the supersonic jetliner. They doubled the speed of the older merchant vessels. Long and lean, with taller masts and more sails, they cut dashing figures during their brief but colorful career, which lasted less than two decades. What provoked the clipper boom was the lure of Chinese tea, a drink long coveted in America but in scarce supply. The tea leaves were a perishable commodity that had to reach market quickly, and the new clippers made this possible. Even more important, the discovery of California gold in 1848 lured thousands of prospectors and entrepreneurs from the Atlantic seaboard. These new settlers generated an urgent demand for goods, and the clippers met the need. In 1854 the *Flying Cloud* took eighty-nine days and eight hours to get from New York to San Francisco, a speed that took steamships several decades to equal. But clippers, while fast, lacked ample cargo space, and after the Civil War they would give way to the larger steamship.

The Role of Government

The massive internal improvements of the antebellum era were the product of both state government and private initiatives, sometimes undertaken jointly and sometimes separately. After the Panic of 1837, however, the states left railroad development mainly to private corporations, the source of most investment capital. Still, several southern and western states built their own lines, and most states granted generous tax concessions to private developers.

The federal government helped, too, despite the constitutional scruples of some against direct involvement in internal improvements. The government bought stock in turnpike and canal companies and, after the success of the Erie Canal, extended land grants to several western states for the support of canal projects. Congress provided for railroad surveys by government engineers, granted tracts of land, and reduced the tariff duties on iron used in railroad construction.

The Growth of Industry

While the South and West developed the agricultural basis for a national economy, the Northeast was laying the foundation for an industrial revolution. Technology in the form of the cotton gin, the grain harvester, and improvements in transportation quickened agricultural development and to some extent decided its direction. But technology altered the economic landscape even more profoundly by giving rise to the textile factory system.

The beginnings of an American textile industry were slow and faltering until Jefferson's embargo in 1807 and the War of 1812 restricted imports and encouraged New England merchant capitalists to switch their resources into manufacturing. New England had one distinct advantage in that its ample rivers were near the coast, where water transportation was readily available. By 1815, New England textile mills numbered in the hundreds. The foundations of textile manufacture were laid, and they spurred the growth of garment trades and a machine-tool industry to build and service the mills.

Technology in America

Meanwhile, American ingenuity was adding other bases for industrial growth. In 1804 Oliver Evans developed a high-pressure steam engine adapted to a variety of uses in ships and factories. Thirty years later, in 1834, Cyrus Hall McCormick of Virginia invented a primitive grain reaper, a development as significant to the agricultural economy of the Old Northwest as the cotton gin was to the South.

With a hand-operated sickle a farmer could harvest half an acre of wheat a day; with a McCormick reaper two people could work twelve acres a day. McCormick's success attracted other manufacturers and inventors, and soon there were mechanical threshers to separate the grains of wheat from the straw. As the volume of agricultural products soared, prices dropped, income rose, and the standard of living for many farm families in the Old Northwest improved.

A spate of inventions in the 1840s generated profound changes in American life. In 1844 Charles Goodyear patented a process for vulcanizing rubber, which made it stronger and more elastic and in the process created the fabric for rainproof coats. In the same year the first intercity telegraph message was transmitted from Baltimore to Washington on the device Samuel F. Morse had invented back in 1832. The telegraph was slow to catch on at first, but seventeen years after that demonstration, with the completion of connections to San Francisco, an entire continent had been wired for instant communication. In 1846 Elias Howe invented the sewing machine, soon improved by Allen B. Wilson and Isaac Merritt Singer.

It is hard to exaggerate the importance of science and technology in changing the ways people lived by mid-century. To cite but a few examples: improved transportation and a spreading market economy combined with innovations in canning and refrigeration to provide people a more healthful and varied diet. Fruit and vegetables, heretofore available only during harvest season, could be shipped during much of the year. Scientific breeding of cattle helped make meat and milk more abundant.

Technological advances also helped improve living conditions: houses were larger, better heated, and better illuminated. Although working-class residences had few creature comforts, the affluent were able to afford indoor plumbing, central heating, gas lighting, bathtubs, iceboxes, and sewing machines. Even the lower classes were able to afford new coal-burning, cast-iron cooking stoves that facilitated more varied meals and improved heating. The first sewer systems began to help rid city streets of human and animal waste, while underground water lines enabled fire companies to use hydrants rather than bucket brigades.

The Lowell System

Before the 1850s, the factory system still had not become widespread. Handicraft and domestic production remained common, and as late as 1860 the United States was still preponderantly rural and agricultural. But modern industrialism made significant inroads, especially in New England. At Lowell, Massachusetts, along the Merrimack River, the Merrimack Manufacturing Company in 1822 developed a new plant similar to one in Waltham, Massachusetts, in which spinning and weaving by power machinery had been brought under one roof for the first time in 1813. The town of Lowell grew dramatically, and it soon provided the model for other mill towns in Massachusetts, New Hampshire, and Maine.

The chief features of the "Lowell System" were a large capital investment, the concentration of all production processes in one plant under unified management, and specialization in a relatively coarse cloth requiring minimum skill by the workers. Lowell's founders insisted that they could design model factory centers that would enhance rather than corrupt the social fabric. The drab, crowded, and wretched life of English mill villages would be avoided by locating American mills in the countryside and then establishing an ambitious program of paternal supervision for the workers. The operatives were mostly young women from New England farm families who were increasingly without gainful employment and faced diminishing prospects for finding husbands. With so many men migrating westward, New England had been left with a surplus of women. Moreover, much of the household production previously carried out by daughters had given way to "store-bought" goods. Many women workers were also drawn to the mills by the chance to escape the routine of farm life and to earn money to help the family or improve their own circumstances.

Initially visitors to Lowell praised the well-designed mills. The laborers appeared "healthy and happy." The women workers lived in dormitories staffed by matronly supervisors, church attendance was manda-

Women workers carding, drawing, and roving cotton cloth in a textile mill, 1834.

tory, and temperance regulations and curfews were rigidly enforced. Despite the thirteen-hour days and six-day workweek, one woman operative described Lowell's community life as approaching "almost Arcadian simplicity." But Lowell soon lost its innocence as it experienced mushrooming growth. By 1840, Lowell had thirty-two mills and factories in operation, and the blissful rural town had become a bustling, grimy, bleak industrial city.

Other factory centers began sprouting up across New England, displacing forests and farms and engulfing villages, filling the air with smoke, noise, and stench. Between 1820 and 1840, the number of Americans engaged in manufactures increased eightfold, and the number of city dwellers more than doubled.

During the 1830s, as prices and wages dropped, relations between workers and managers rapidly deteriorated. A new generation of owners and foremen stressed efficiency and profit margins over community values. The machines and their operatives were worked at a faster pace, and workers organized strikes to protest deteriorating conditions. Visitors now noted the growing similarity between Lowell and the dismal factory towns of England immortalized in Charles Dickens's writings.

Industry and Cities

In 1855 a journalist exclaimed that "the great phenomenon of the Age is the growth of cities." Using the census definition of "urban" as places with 8,000 inhabitants or more, the proportion of urban population grew from 3 percent in 1790 to 16 percent in 1860. Because of their strategic locations and their importance as centers of trade and transportation, the Atlantic seaports of New York, Philadelphia, Baltimore, and Boston were the four largest U.S. cities throughout the pre–Civil War period. New York outpaced all its competitors and the nation as a whole in its population growth. By 1860, it was the first American city to boast a population of more than a million, largely because of its superior harbor and its unique access to commerce afforded by the Erie Canal.

Pittsburgh, at the head of the Ohio River, was already a center of iron production by 1800, and Cincinnati, at the mouth of the Little Miami, soon surpassed all other centers of meat packing, with pork a specialty. Louisville, because it stood at the falls of the Ohio River, became an important trade center. On the Great Lakes, the leading cities also benefited from easy access to water transportation: Buffalo, Cleveland, Detroit, Chicago, and Milwaukee. Chicago was especially well located to become a hub of both water and rail transportation on into the trans-Mississippi West. During the 1830s, St. Louis tripled in size, mainly because most of the trans-Mississippi grain and fur trade was funneled down the Missouri River.

The Popular Culture

During the colonial era, working Americans had little time for play or amusement. Their priority was simply survival. Yet over time they fashioned engaging forms of recreation and entertainment. In rural areas people participated in barn raisings and cornhusking parties, shooting matches and foot races, while on the seacoast people sailed and fished. In colonial cities, people attended balls, sleigh rides, picnics, and played "parlor games" at home—billiards, cards, and chess.

By the early nineteenth century, however, a more urban society could indulge in new forms of recreation. As more people moved into cities in the first half of the nineteenth century, they began to create a distinctive urban culture. Laborers and shopkeepers sought new forms of leisure and entertainment as pleasant diversions from their long workdays.

Bare Knuckles. Blood sports emerged as a popular entertainment in the cities for men of all social classes.

Urban Recreation

In working-class neighborhoods at mid-century, young men formed volunteer fire companies and fraternal societies whose primary activities were drinking and gambling. The more affluent and educated people viewed leisure time as an opportunity for self-improvement and attended lectures by prominent figures such as philosopher Ralph Waldo Emerson and minister Henry Ward Beecher. Circuses began touring the country. Foot races, horse races, and boat races began attracting thousands of spectators.

So-called blood sports were also a popular form of amusement. Cockfighting and dogfighting at saloons attracted excited crowds and frenzied betting. Prizefighting (also known as boxing) eventually displaced the animal contests. Imported from Britain, boxing surged into prominence at mid-century, and then, as now, proved popular with all social classes. Contestants fought with bare knuckles, and the results were brutal. A match ended only when a contestant could not continue. One such bout in 1842 lasted 119 rounds and ended when one fighter died in his corner. Such matches prompted clergymen to condemn prizefighting, and several cities outlawed the practice, only to see it reappear as an underground activity.

The Performing Arts

The most popular form of indoor entertainment was theatrical. During the first half of the nineteenth century, the theater played the popular role that movie houses would provide in the first half of the twentieth century. People of all social classes flocked to opera houses and theaters to watch a wide spectrum of performances: Shakespeare's tragedies, "blood and thunder" melodramas, comedies, minstrel shows, operas, magic shows, acrobatic troupes, and local pageants.

The audiences were predominantly young and middle-aged men. "Respectable" women were deterred from attending because of the boisterous atmosphere and the prevailing "cult of domesticity" that kept women in the home. People went to the theater not simply to watch the performances but also to socialize, to see and be seen, to talk business and gossip. Patrons were participants as well as spectators. Audiences cheered the heroes and heroines and hissed the villains. They often joined the actors in reciting famous passages or yelled out the punch lines for familiar jokes. If an actor did not meet expectations, audiences would hurl epithets, nuts, eggs, fruit, shoes, or chairs.

By mid-century, the arbiters of taste dealt with the problem of cultural rowdiness by creating separate theaters for the genteel elite and for laboring folk. As historian Lawrence Levine has remarked, the theaters and opera houses "no longer functioned as an expressive form that embodied all classes within a shared public space." Theaters grew darker, quieter, and more secure; audiences grew more affluent and passive.

Minstrel Shows

The 1830s witnessed the emergence of the first uniquely American form of mass entertainment: the blackface minstrel show featuring white performers made up as blacks.

"Minstrelsy" drew upon African-American subjects and reinforced prevailing racial stereotypes. It featured banjo and fiddle music, "shuffle" dances, and low-brow humor. Between the 1830s and 1870s, the minstrel shows were immensely popular throughout the nation, especially among northern working-class ethnics and southern whites, who were eager to flaunt their presumed superiority to blacks. The shows expanded to include entire troupes of performers who would tour the country, often using riverboats as their means of transportation, giving performances that included jokes, sentimental songs, dances, comedy routines, and skits.

Although antebellum minstrel shows usually portrayed slaves as blissfully contented and caricatured free blacks in the North as superstitious buffoons who preferred slavery to freedom, minstrelsy represented more than an expression of virulent racism and white exploitation of black culture; it also provided a medium for the expression of authentic African-American art forms.

Immigration

Throughout the nineteenth century, land remained plentiful and relatively cheap, while labor was scarce and relatively expensive. A decline in the birthrate coinciding with the onset of industry and urbanization reinforced this condition. The United States in the nineteenth century remained a strong magnet to immigrants, offering them chances to take up farms in the country or jobs in the cities. Glowing reports from early arrivals who made good also reinforced romantic views of American economic opportunity and political and religious freedom.

During the forty years from the outbreak of the Revolution until the end of the War of 1812, immigration had slowed to a trickle. The wars of the French Revolution and Napoleon restricted travel from Europe until 1815. Within a few years, however, passenger ships had begun to cross the north Atlantic. The years from 1845 to 1854 saw the greatest proportionate influx of immigrants in American history, 2.4 million, or about 14.5 percent of the total population in 1845.

Most European immigrants entered the United States through the Port of New York. Ships would discharge passengers at wharves, and the newcomers would have to fend for themselves in their alien environment. Thieves, thugs, and con men preyed upon the new arrivals. The infectious diseases that many of the immigrants brought with them also aroused popular concern. In 1855 the problems associated with the immigrants' arrival in America provoked the New York State legislature to lease Castle Garden, at the southern tip of Manhattan, for use as an immigration receiving center. Inside the depot, clerks would record the names, nationalities, and destinations of the new arrivals, physicians would give them a cursory physical exam, and labor bureau representatives would assist them in seeking jobs.

The Irish

In 1860 America's population was 31 million, with more than one of every eight foreign born. The largest groups among the immigrants were 1.6 million Irish, 1.2 million Germans, and 588,000 British (mostly English). The Irish had a long-standing reason for migrating from their country: resentment of British rule, British landlords, British Protestantism, and British taxes. But what caused so many Irish to flee their homeland in the nineteenth century was the onset of a prolonged depression that brought immense social hardship. The most densely populated country in Europe, Ireland was so ravaged by the economic collapse that in rural areas the average age at death declined to nineteen. By the 1830s, the number of Irish migrants to America was growing quickly, and after an epidemic of potato rot in 1845 brought a famine to rural Ireland that killed upward of a million peasants, the flow of Irish immigrants to Canada and the United States rose to a flood.

By 1850, the Irish constituted 43 percent of the foreign-born population in the United States. Unlike the German immigrants, who were predominantly male, the Irish newcomers were more evenly apportioned by sex; in fact a slight majority of them were women, most of them single young adults.

Many Irish men hired on with construction gangs building the canals and railways—about 3,000 set to work on the Erie Canal as early as 1818. Others worked in iron foundries, steel mills, warehouses, and shipyards. Many Irish women found jobs as domestic servants, laundresses, or textile mill workers in New England. In 1845, the Irish constituted only 8 percent of the workforce in the Lowell mills; by 1860, they made up 50 percent.

Landing from an Immigrant Ship. In 1847, nearly 214,000 Irish emigrated to the United States and Canada, 30 percent of whom died on board ship.

Few immigrants during the Jacksonian era found their way into the South, where land was expensive and industries scarce. The widespread use of slaves also left few opportunities in the region for manual laborers. Too poor to move inland, most of the destitute Irish congregated in the eastern cities, in or near their port of entry. By the 1850s, the Irish made up over half the populations of Boston and of New York City, and they were almost as prominent in Philadelphia. They clustered in murky slums and around Catholic churches, both of which became familiar features of the urban scene. Irish newcomers crowded into filthy, poorly ventilated buildings plagued by high rates of crime, infectious disease, prostitution, alcoholism, and infant mortality. The archbishop of New York City at mid-century described the Irish as "the poorest and most wretched population that can be found in the world."

But many enterprising Irish immigrants seized opportunities in their new environment to forge remarkable success stories. Twenty years after arriving in New York, Alexander T. Stewart became the owner of America's largest department store and thereafter accumulated vast real estate holdings in Manhattan. Michael Cudahy, who began work in a Milwaukee meat-packing business at age fourteen, became head of the Cudahy Packing Company and developed the process for the summer curing of meats under refrigeration. Dublin-born Victor Herbert emerged as one of America's most revered composers, and Irish dancers and playwrights came to dominate the American stage. Irishmen were equally successful in the boxing arena.

These accomplishments did little to quell the intense anti-Irish sentiments prevalent in nineteenth-century America. Irish immigrants confronted demeaning stereotypes and violent anti-Catholic prejudices. It was commonly assumed that the Irish were ignorant, filthy, clannish folk incapable of assimilation. "No Irish Need Apply" signs sprouted in every eastern city. But the Irish could be equally contemptuous of other groups, such as free blacks who competed with them for low-status jobs. In 1850 the *New York Tribune* expressed consternation at the fact that the Irish, having themselves escaped from "a galling, degrading bondage" in their homeland, typically voted against any proposal for equal rights for the Negro. For their part, many blacks viewed the Irish with equal disdain.

The Irish, after becoming naturalized citizens, formed powerful blocs of voters and found their way into American politics more quickly than any other immigrant group. Drawn mainly to the party of Andrew Jackson, they set a crucial pattern of identification with the Democrats that other ethnic groups by and large followed.

Although property requirements initially kept most Irish Americans from voting, a New York State law extended the franchise in 1821, and five years later the state removed the property qualification altogether. The following year masses of Irish voters made the difference in the election between Jackson and John Quincy Adams. Although women, blacks, and Indians still could not vote, the Irish newcomers were able to use the franchise to exert a remarkable political influence.

Perhaps the greatest collective achievement of the Irish immigrants was stimulating the growth of the Catholic Church in the United States. Years of persecution had instilled in Irish Catholics a fierce loyalty to the doctrines of the church, leading one Irish American to proclaim that religion "overrides all other sovereigns, and has the supreme authority over all the affairs of the world." Such passionate attachment to Catholicism generated both community cohesion among Irish Americans and fear among American Protestants.

The Germans, Scandinavians, and Chinese

During the eighteenth century, Germans had responded to William Penn's offer of free religious expression and cheap, fertile land by coming in large numbers to America. As a consequence, when a new wave of German migration formed in the 1830s, there were still large German enclaves in Pennsylvania and Ohio.

The new German migration took on a markedly different cast. It peaked in 1854, just a few years after the crest of Irish arrivals, when 215,000 Germans disembarked at American ports. These immigrants included a large number of learned, cultured professional people—doctors, lawyers, teachers, engineers—some of them refugees from the failed German revolutions of 1830 and 1848. The Germans brought with them a variety of religious preferences. A third of the new arrivals were Catholic, most were Protestants (usually Lutherans), and a significant number were Jewish, free-thinking atheists, or agnostics.

Unlike the Irish, the Germans included many independent farmers, skilled workers, and shopkeepers who arrived with enough money to get themselves established in skilled labor or on the land. They also migrated in families and groups rather than as individuals, and this clannish quality helped them sustain elements of German language and culture in their New World environment.

Among those who prospered in America were Ferdinand Schmacher, who began peddling oatmeal in glass jars in Ohio and eventually formed the Quaker Oats Company; Heinrich Steinweg, a piano maker from Lower Saxony, who in America changed his name to Steinway and became famous for the quality of his pianos; and Levi Strauss, a Jewish tailor who followed the gold rushers to California and began making long-wearing denim work pants that later were dubbed blue jeans or Levi's.

Two other groups that began to arrive in some number during the 1840s and 1850s were but the vanguard of greater numbers to come later. Annual arrivals from Scandinavia, most of them religious dissenters, did not exceed 1,000 until 1843, but by 1860 a total of 72,600 Scandinavians lived in America. The Norwegians and Swedes gravitated usually in family groups to Wisconsin and Minnesota, where the climate and woodlands reminded them of home.

By the 1850s, the sudden development of California after the discovery of gold attracted Chinese, who, like the Irish in the East, did the heavy work of construction. Infinitesimal in numbers until 1854, the Chinese in America numbered 35,500 by 1860. The migrants were mostly married, illiterate men desperate for work. Single women did not travel abroad, and married women usually stayed behind to raise the children. During the mid–nineteenth century, a laborer in southern China might earn five dollars a month; in California, he could work for a railroad or a mine and make six times as much. After three or four years of such work, an immigrant could return to China with his savings and become a "big, very big gentleman."

Nativism

For many native-born Americans, these waves of strangers posed a threat of unknown languages, mysterious customs, and, perhaps worst, feared religions. The flood of Irish and German Catholics aroused Protestant hostility to "popery." A militant Protestantism growing out of the early nineteenth-century revivals heated up the climate of suspicion. There were fears of political radicalism among the Germans and of voting blocs among the Irish, but above all hovered the menace of unfamiliar religious practices. Catholic authoritarianism was widely perceived as a threat to hard-won American liberties, religious and political.

By the 1830s, nativism was conspicuously on the rise. In 1834 a series of anti-Catholic sermons by the leading New England minister of the era, revivalist and later abolitionist Lyman Beecher, aroused feelings to the extent that a mob attacked and burned a convent in Charlestown, Massachusetts. In 1844 armed clashes between Protestants and Catholics in Philadelphia ended with about twenty killed and one hundred injured. Sporadically, the nativist spirit took organized form in groups that proved their patriotism by hating foreigners and Catholics.

In 1854 delegates from thirteen states gathered to form the American political party, which had the trappings of a secret fraternal order. Members pledged never to vote for any foreign-born or Catholic candidate. When asked about the organization, they were to say "I know nothing," and in popular parlance the American party thus became the Know-Nothing party. In state and local campaigns during 1854, the Know-Nothings carried one election after another. They swept the Massachusetts legislature, winning all but two seats in the lower house. That fall they elected more than forty congressmen. For a while the Know-Nothings threatened to control New England, New York, and Maryland and showed strength elsewhere, but the movement subsided when slavery became the focal issue of the 1850s.

The Know-Nothings demanded the exclusion of immigrants and Catholics from public office and the extension of the period for naturalization from five to twenty-one years, but the party never gathered the political strength to effect such legislation. Nor did Congress act during the period to restrict immigration in any way.

Immigrant Labor

By meeting the need for cheap, unskilled labor, immigrants made a twofold contribution to economic growth: they moved into jobs vacated or bypassed by those who went into the factories, and they themselves made up a pool of labor from which in time factory workers were drawn.

In New England the large numbers of Irish workers, accustomed to hard treatment and willing to work for what natives considered low wages, spelled the end of the "Lowell girls." By 1860, immigrants made up more than half the labor force in New England mills. Even so, their pay was generally higher than that of the women and children who worked to supplement family incomes. The flood of immigration never rose fast enough to stop the long-term rise in wages. Factory labor thus continued to draw people from the countryside. Work in the cities offered higher real wages than work on the farm. Labor costs encouraged factory owners to seek ever more efficient machines in order to increase production without hiring more workers. In addition, the owners' desire to control the upward pressure on wage rates accelerated the emphasis on mass production.

By stressing high production and low prices, owners made it easier for workers to buy the items they made. Artisans who emphasized quality and craftsmanship found it hard to meet such competitive conditions. Many artisans in fact found that their skills were going out of style. Some took work as craftsmen in factories, while others went into small-scale manufacturing or shopkeeping, and some bought homesteads to practice their crafts in the West.

Organized Labor

As early as the colonial period, craftsmen had formed fraternal and mutual-benefit societies, much like the medieval guilds, through which they regulated a system for training apprentices. These organizations continued to flourish well into the national period. After the Revolution, however, organizations of journeymen carpenters, masons, shipfitters, tailors, printers, and cordwainers (as shoemakers were called) became concerned with wages, hours, and working conditions and began to back up their demands with devices such as the strike and the closed shop (in which only union members could work). These organizations were local, often largely social in purpose, and frequently lasted only for the duration of the dispute with the employer. During the 1820s and 1830s, few workers belonged to unions. Increasingly, however, a growing fear that they were losing status led artisans of the major cities into intense activity in labor politics and unions.

Early Unions

Early efforts to form labor unions faced serious legal obstacles. Unions were prosecuted as unlawful conspiracies. In 1806, for instance, Philadelphia shoemakers were found guilty of a "combination to raise their wages." The decision broke the union. Such precedents were used for many years to hamstring labor organizations until the Massachusetts Supreme Court made a landmark ruling in the case of *Commonwealth* v. *Hunt* (1842). The court ruled that forming a trade union was not in itself illegal, nor was a demand that employers hire only members of the union.

Until the 1820s, labor organizations took the form of local trade unions, confined to one city and one craft. During the ten years from 1827 to 1837, organization on a larger scale began to take hold. In 1834 the National Trades' Union was set up to federate the city societies. At the same time, national craft unions were established by the shoemakers, printers, combmakers, carpenters, and hand-loom weavers, but all the national groups and most of the local ones vanished in the economic collapse of 1837.

Labor Politics

With the widespread removal of property qualifications for voting, labor politics flourished briefly in the 1830s. Working Men's parties appeared in New York, Boston, Philadelphia, and about fifteen states. These labor parties faded quickly for a variety of reasons: the inexperience of labor politicians that left the parties prey to manipulation by political professionals; the fact that some of their issues were also espoused by the major parties; and their vulnerability to attack on grounds of radicalism. In addition, they often splintered into warring factions, which limited their effectiveness.

Once the labor parties had faded, many of their supporters found their way into a radical wing of the Jacksonian Democrats, which became the Equal Rights party. In 1835 party members acquired the name "Locofocos" when their opponents from New York City's regular Democratic organization, Tammany Hall, turned off the gas lights at one of their meetings, and the Equal Rights supporters produced candles, lighting them with the new friction matches known as Locofocos. The Locofocos soon faded as a separate group but endured as a radical faction within the Democratic party.

Though the labor parties elected few candidates, they did draw notice to their demands, many of which attracted the support of middle-class reformers. Above all they called for free government-funded education and the abolition of imprisonment for debt, causes that won widespread popular support. The labor parties and unions also actively promoted the ten-hour workday. In 1836 President Andrew Jackson established the ten-hour workday at the Philadelphia Navy Yard in response to a strike, and in 1840 President Martin Van Buren extended the limit to all government offices and projects. In private jobs the ten-hour workday became increasingly common, although by no means universal, before 1860.

The Revival of Unions

After the Panic of 1837, the nascent labor movement went into decline, but it began to revive with improved business conditions in the early 1840s. Still, the unions of the time remained local, weak, and given to sporadic activity. Often they came and went with a single strike. The greatest labor dispute before the Civil War came on February 22, 1860, when shoemakers at Lynn and Natick, Massachusetts, walked out for higher wages. Before the strike ended, it had spread throughout New England, involving perhaps twenty-five towns and 20,000 workers. It stood out also because it was a strike the workers won. Most of the employers agreed to wage increases, and some also agreed to recognize the union as a bargaining agent.

This reflected the growing tendency of workers to view their unions as permanent. Workers sought union recognition and regular collective bargaining agreements. They also shared a rising sense of solidarity. In 1852 the National Typographical Union revived the effort to organize skilled crafts on a national scale. Others followed, and by 1860 about twenty such organizations had appeared, although none was strong enough as yet to do much more than hold national conventions and pass resolutions.

Jacksonian Inequality

During the years before the Civil War, the United States had begun to develop a distinctive working class, and the gap between rich and poor visibly widened. In 1828 the top 1 percent of New York's families (owning $34,000 or more) held 40 percent of the wealth, and the top 4 percent held 76 percent. Similar circumstances prevailed in Philadelphia, Boston, and other cities.

A supreme irony of the times was that the so-called age of the common man, the age of Jacksonian Democracy, seems actually to have been an age of increasing social stratification. Years before, in the late eighteenth century, slavery aside, American society probably approached equality more closely than any other population of its size anywhere else in the world. During the last half of the 1700s, social mobility was higher than either before or since. By the time popular egalitarianism caught up with reality,

reality was moving back toward greater inequality.

Why this happened is difficult to say, except that the boundless wealth of the untapped frontier narrowed as the land was occupied and claims on various opportunities were staked out. Such developments took place in New England towns even before the end of the seventeenth century. But despite growing social distinctions, it seems likely that the majority of the white population of America, at least, was better off than the general run of European peoples. New frontiers, both geographical and technological, raised the level of material well-being for all.

CHAPTER 12

An American Renaissance: Religion, Romanticism, and Reform

This chapter focuses on

- The rise of new religious movements.
- The development of a distinctive American literary culture.
- The variety of social reform movements.

THE *ESSENTIAL AMERICA* ON-LINE TUTOR

www.wwnorton.com/eamerica/ch12

- **Topic: The Seneca Falls Convention**
  www.wwnorton.com/eamerica/ch12/topic.htm

  The Seneca Falls Convention of 1848 helped launch the Women's Rights movement in the United States and began the long struggle for women's suffrage. Using photographs, newspaper articles, personal accounts, speech texts, and historical analyses, examine the convention and its significance for the women's movement. How did the convention affect the women's movement?

- **Chapter review: On-line quiz and chapter summary**
  www.wwnorton.com/eamerica/ch12/review.htm

- **Chapter resources: Media index**
  www.wwnorton.com/eamerica/ch12/media.htm

The American novelist Nathaniel Hawthorne once lamented "the difficulty of writing a romance about a country where there is no shadow, no antiquity, no mystery, no picturesque and gloomy wrong." Unlike nations of the Old World, rooted in shadow and mystery, entwined in historic cultures and traditions, the United States was an infant nation swaddled in the commonsense ideas of the Enlightenment. Those ideas, most vividly set forth in Jefferson's Declaration of Independence, had in turn a universal application that would influence religion, literature, and various social reform movements.

Rational Religion

American thought and culture in the early nineteenth century remained rooted in Puritan piety and Enlightenment rationalism. The United States, it was widely believed, had a mission to stand as an example to the world, for the religious fervor quickened in the Great Awakening had reinforced the idea of providential national destiny. In turn, the sense of high calling infused the national character with an element of perfectionism—and an element of impatience when reality fell short of expectations. The combination of religious belief and social idealism brought major reforms and advances in human rights. It also brought disappointments that could fester into cynicism and alienation.

Deism

The currents of the Enlightenment and the Great Awakening, now mingling, now parting, flowed on into the nineteenth century and in different ways eroded the remnants of Calvinist orthodoxy. As time passed, the image of a just but stern God promising predestined hellfire and damnation gave way to a more optimistic religious outlook. Enlightenment rationalism increasingly stressed inherent human goodness rather than depravity, and it encouraged a belief in social progress and the promise of individual perfectibility.

Many leaders of the Revolutionary War era, such as Thomas Jefferson and Benjamin Franklin, became deists, even while nominally attached to churches. Deism, which arose in eighteenth-century Europe, carried the logic of Sir Isaac Newton's image of the world as a smoothly operating machine to its logical conclusion. The God of the deist had planned the universe, built it, set it in motion, and then left it to its own devices. By the use of reason, people might grasp the natural laws governing the universe. Orthodox Christians could hardly distinguish such a doctrine from atheism, but Enlightenment rationalism soon began to make deep inroads into American Protestantism.

Unitarianism and Universalism

By the end of the eighteenth century, many New Englanders were embracing Unitarianism, a belief emphasizing the oneness and benevolence of God, the inherent goodness of humankind, and the primacy of the individual's reason and conscience over established religious creeds and Scriptural literalism. Humans were not inherently depraved, Unitarianism stressed; people were capable of doing tremendous good and all were eligible for salvation. Boston's revered Unitarian minister William Ellery Channing emerged as the chief spokesman for the liberal religious position. "I am surer that my rational nature is from God," he said, "than that any book is an expression of his will."

A parallel movement, called Universalism, attracted people of more humble means. Universalists stressed the salvation of all men and women, not just the predestined elect of the Calvinist doctrine. God, they taught, was too merciful to condemn anyone to eternal punishment; eventually all souls would come into harmony with God. "Thus, the Unitarians and Universalists were in fundamental agreement," wrote one historian of religion, "the Universalists holding that God was too good to damn man; the Unitarians insisting that man was too good to be damned."

The Second Great Awakening

Around 1800, fears that secularism was taking root sparked a revival of religious orthodoxy that grew into the Second Great Awakening. The new wave of evangelical fervor fed upon the spreading notion of social equality. Methodists and Baptists, neither of whom featured an educated clergy, sought to democratize religious practices and congregational structures. Such "populist" tendencies were reinforced by the growing popularity of the concept of "free will." Salvation was available to everyone.

Frontier Revivals

In its frontier phase, the Second Great Awakening, like the first, generated great excitement and strange manifestations. It gave birth, moreover, to a new ritual, the camp meeting, in which the fires of faith were repeatedly rekindled. Missionaries found ready audiences among lonely frontier folk hungry for spiritual meaning and a sense of community. In the backwoods and in small rural hamlets, the traveling revival was as welcome an event as the traveling circus.

The Baptists embraced a simplicity of doctrine and organization that appealed especially to the common people of the frontier. Their theology was grounded in the authority of the Bible and the recognition of a person's innate depravity. But they replaced the Calvinist notion of predestination with the concept of universal redemption and highlighted the ritual of adult baptism. They also stressed the equality of all men and women before God, regardless of wealth, social standing, or educational training.

Methodist Camp Meeting, 1837. Religious revivals at times so infused people with religious fervor that they went into trances or jerked and twitched.

The Methodists, who shared with the Baptists an emphasis on salvation by free will, established the most effective recruiting method of all: the circuit rider who sought out people in the most remote areas with the message of salvation as a gift free for the taking. The system began with Francis Asbury, a tireless British-born revivalist who scoured the trans-Appalachian frontier for lost souls, preaching some 25,000 sermons while defying hostile Indians and suffering through harsh winters. Asbury's mobile evangelism perfectly suited the frontier environment and the new democratic age. By the 1840s the Methodists had grown into the largest Protestant denomination in the country.

The revivals spread quickly through the West and into more settled regions back East. Camp meetings were held typically in late summer or fall, when farm work slackened. People converged from far and wide, camping in wagons, tents, or crude shacks. Blacks, whether slave or free, were allowed to set up their own adjacent camp revivals, often separated from the white camp by a plank partition. On the final meeting day of the week, the wall would be taken down, enabling both groups to join in a song festival and a "marching ceremony." The largest camp meetings tended to be ecumenical affairs, with Baptist, Methodist, and Presbyterian ministers working as a team.

The crowds often numbered in the thousands, and the unrestrained atmosphere made for chaos. If a particular hymn or sermon excited someone, they would cry, shout, dance, or repeat the phrase. Infusions of the spirit provoked some participants into cataleptic trances; others contracted the "jerks," laughed the "holy laugh," babbled in unknown tongues, or got down on all fours and barked like dogs to "tree the Devil."

But dwelling on the bizarre aspects of the camp meetings distorts a social institution that offered a meaningful outlet to isolated rural folk. Camp meetings also brought a more settled community life through the churches they spawned, and they helped spread a more democratic faith among the frontier people.

Finney and the "Burned-Over District"

Regions swept by such revival fevers have been compared to forests devastated by fire. In 1830–1831 alone, the number of churches in New England grew by one-third. Lyman Beecher called the Great Awakening of 1831 "the greatest work of God, and the greatest revival of religion, that the world has ever seen." Western New York from Lake Ontario to the Adirondacks and including Rochester experienced such intense levels of evangelical activity that it was labeled the "Burned-Over District."

The most successful evangelist in the region was a lawyer named Charles Grandison Finney, whose own religious awakening occurred one evening in 1821, when a "mighty baptism of the Holy Ghost overwhelmed him." The next day he announced a new profession as a revivalist. In 1823 Finney was ordained, and during the next decade he became the greatest single exemplar of evangelical Protestantism, and the inventor of professional revivalism.

Finney wrestled with an age-old question that had plagued Protestantism: what role can the individual play in earning salvation? Orthodox Calvinists had long argued that people could neither earn nor choose salvation on their own accord. Grace was a gift of God, a predetermined decision incapable of human understanding or control. In contrast, Finney insisted that people could control their own salvation. Finney transformed revivals into collective conversion experiences in which spectacular public events displaced private communion and the unregenerate were brought into intense contact with praying Christians.

Untrained in theology, Finney read the Bible and worked out his own theology of free will. His gospel also combined faith and good works; one led to the other. "All sin consists in selfishness," he declared, "and all holiness or virtue, in disinterested benevolence." Regeneration therefore produced "a change from selfishness to benevolence, from having a supreme regard to one's own interest to an absorbing and controlling choice of the happiness and glory of God's Kingdom."

In 1835 Finney became a professor of theology at the new Oberlin College, founded by pious New Englanders in Ohio's Western Reserve. Later he served as its president. From the start, Oberlin radiated a spirit of social reform predicated on faith; it was the first college in America to admit women and blacks, and it was a hotbed of antislavery activity. Finney himself, however, held that people must be reformed from within, and he cautioned against relying primarily on political action for moral ends.

The Mormons

In addition to providing the scene of revivals, the Burned-Over District gave rise to several new religious departures, of which the most important was the Church of Jesus Christ of Latter-day Saints, or the Mormons. The founder of the Mormon church, Joseph Smith, Jr., grew up in the village of Palmyra, New York. In 1820 young Smith (then fourteen) had a vision of "two Personages, whose brightness and glory defy all description." They identified themselves as the Savior and God the Father and cautioned him that all existing religious beliefs were false. About three years later, Smith claimed, an angel named Moroni led him to a hill near his father's farm in upstate New York, where he found the Book of Mormon, a lost section of the Bible. It told the story of ancient Hebrews who had inhabited the New World and to whom Jesus had made an appearance.

On the basis of this revelation, Smith began forming his own church in 1830, and after a few years he was gathering converts by the thousands. Mostly poor New England farmers, these religious seekers found in Mormonism the promise of a pure kingdom of Christ in America and an alternative to the social turmoil and the degrading materialism of the era. Mormons rejected the notion of original sin staining the human race. They instead professed an optimistic creed stressing human goodness and the virtues of common folk.

In their search for a refuge from persecution, the Mormons moved from New York to Ohio, then to several places in Missouri, and finally in 1839 to Nauvoo, Illinois, where they settled for some five years. Nauvoo became a bustling city, and Joseph Smith, "the Prophet," became the community's leading entrepreneur. At Nauvoo he codified the theocratic church organization and instituted the practice of "plural marriage." In 1844 a crisis arose when dissidents accused Smith of justifying polygamy. The upshot was a schism in the church, a gathering movement among non-Mormons in the neighboring counties to attack Nauvoo, and the arrest of Smith and his brother Hyrum. On June 27, 1844, an anti-Mormon mob stormed the feebly defended Nauvoo jail and shot both Joseph and Hyrum Smith.

In Brigham Young, the remarkable successor to Joseph Smith, the Mormons found a leader who was strong-minded, intelligent, and decisive. He was also prolific, eventually marrying sixteen women and fathering fifty-seven children. After the murder of Smith, Young patched up an unsure peace with the neighbors by promising to leave Illinois. Before the year was out, Young had chosen a new destination near the Great Salt Lake in Utah, guarded by mountains to the east and north, deserts to the west and south, yet itself fed by mountain streams of melted snow.

Brigham Young trusted God, but he made careful preparations. As a result, the epic Mormon trek was better organized and less arduous than most of the overland migrations of the time. By the fall of 1846, all 15,000 of the migrants had reached winter quarters on the Missouri River, where they paused until the first bands set out the next spring for the Promised Land. The first arrivals at Salt Lake in July 1847 found only "a broad and barren plain hemmed in by mountains . . . the paradise of the lizard, the cricket and the rattlesnake." But by the end of 1848, the Mormons had developed an efficient irrigation system and over the next decade, by cooperative labor, they brought about a spectacular greening of the desert. They organized at first their own State of Deseret (meaning "land of the honey bee," according to Young), but their independence was short-lived. Congress incorporated the Utah Territory, including the Mormons' Salt Lake settlement, into the United States in 1849. Nevertheless, with Brigham Young named the territorial governor, the new arrangement afforded the Mormons almost the same control. By 1869, some 80,000 Mormons had settled in Utah. Today there are 9 million Mormons, and it is the fastest growing religion in the world.

Romanticism in America

The revival of emotional piety and the founding of new religions during the early 1800s represented a widespread tendency in the Western world to accentuate the stirrings of the spirit over the dry logic of reason. Another great victory of heart over head was the romantic movement in thought, literature, and the arts. By the 1780s, a revolt was brewing in Europe against the well-ordered world of Enlightenment thinkers. Were there not, many wondered, more things in this world than reason and logic could box up and explain: moods, impressions, feelings; mysterious, unknown, and half-seen things?

Transcendentalism

The most intense expression of such romantic ideas in America was the transcendentalist movement of New England, which drew its name from its emphasis on transcending (or rising above) the limits of reason. American transcendentalism was largely inspired by European thinkers such as Immanuel Kant and Samuel Taylor Coleridge, but it was rooted in New England Puritanism, to which it owed a pervasive moral idealism. It also had a close affinity with the Quaker doctrine of the inner light. The inner light, a gift from God's grace, was transformed by transcendentalists into an emphasis on intuition, a faculty of the mind.

Heart of the Andes (1859), by Frederick E. Church. Church, a prominent Hudson River School painter, captured the spirit of the transcendentalist movement in the arts, which emphasized the inspiring beauty of nature.

In 1836 an informal discussion group named the Transcendental Club began to meet in Boston and Concord. It drew at different times clergymen such as Theodore Parker and George Ripley; philosophical writers such as Henry David Thoreau, Bronson Alcott, and Orestes Brownson; and learned women like Margaret Fuller and Elizabeth and Sophia Peabody. Fuller edited the group's quarterly review, *The Dial* (1840–1844), before the duty fell to Ralph Waldo Emerson, soon to become the acknowledged high priest of transcendentalism.

Emerson and Thoreau

More than any other person, Emerson spread the transcendentalist gospel. Sprung from a line of New England ministers, he set out to be a Unitarian parson, then quit the "cold and cheerless" denomination before he was thirty because of growing doubts about its vitality. After travel to Europe, where he met England's great literary romantics, Emerson settled in Concord to take up the life of an essayist, poet, and popular speaker on the lecture circuit, preaching the good news of optimism, self-reliance, and the individual's unlimited potential. He was determined to *transcend* the limitations of inherited conventions and of rationalism in order to penetrate the inner recesses of the self. As he once suggested, transcendentalism meant belief in a realm "a little beyond" the rational world.

Emerson's young friend and Concord neighbor, Henry David Thoreau, practiced the introspective self-reliance that Emerson preached. Thoreau displayed an uncompromising integrity, outdoor vigor, and tart individuality that Emerson found captivating. Short and sinewy, Thoreau was an acknowledged master of the woodland arts and a probing thinker.

He was also a thoroughgoing individualist. "If a man does not keep pace with his companion," Thoreau wrote, "perhaps it is because he hears a different drummer." After graduating from Harvard, Thoreau settled down in Concord to eke out a living as a part-time surveyor and pencil-maker. But he yearned to be a writer and a philosophical naturalist, and he made almost daily escapes to the woods and fields to drink in the beauties of nature and reflect upon the mysteries of life. The scramble for wealth among his neighbors disgusted rather than tempted him. "The mass of men," he wrote, "lead lives of quiet desperation."

Determined himself to practice "plain living and high thinking," Thoreau embarked on an experiment in self-reliant simplicity. On July 4, 1845, he took to the woods to live in a cabin he had built on Emerson's land beside Walden Pond. He wanted to free himself from the complexities and hypocrisies of modern life and devote his time to reflection and writing. "I went to the woods because I wished to live deliberately," he wrote in *Walden, or Life in the Woods* (1854), ". . . and not, when I came to die, discover that I had not lived."

While Thoreau was at Walden Pond, the Mexican War erupted. He saw the conflict as a corrupt attempt to advance the cause of slavery. So he refused to pay his state poll tax as a gesture of opposition, for which he was put in jail (for only one night; an aunt paid the tax). Out of the incident grew the classic essay "Civil Disobedience" (1849), which would later influence the passive-resistance movements of Mahatma Gandhi in India and Martin Luther King, Jr., in the American South. "If the law is of such a nature that it requires you to be an agent of unjustice to another," Thoreau wrote, "then, I say, break the law. Let your life be a counter friction to stop the machine."

The influence of Thoreau's ideas more than a century after his death shows the impact a contemplative individual can have on the larger world of action. Thoreau and the transcendentalists shied away from organized reform or political activities. They prized their individual freedom and distrusted all institutions—even those promoting causes they deemed worthy. As principled individualists, they primarily supplied the force of an animating idea: people must follow their consciences. In doing so, they inspired reform movements and were the quickening force for a generation of writers who produced the first classic age of American literature.

The Flowering of American Literature

Ever since gaining independence, the United States had suffered from a cultural inferiority complex. The Old World continued to set the standards in philosophy, literature, and the fine arts. As a British critic sneered in 1819, the "Americans have no national literature." That may have been true, but during the Jacksonian era and after, American culture began to flower.

Dickinson

The poet Emily Dickinson lived as a recluse in Amherst, Massachusetts. Only two of her almost 1,800 poems had been published (anonymously) before her death in 1886, and the full corpus of her work remained unknown for years thereafter. Yet she possessed an imaginative power and inventive genius superior to her more famous male peers. Born in Amherst in 1830, she received a first-rate education and then attended the new Mount Holyoke Female Seminary. Neither she nor her sister married, and they both lived out their lives in their parents' home.

Dickinson's intense isolation led her to write about elemental themes: life, death, fear, loneliness, nature, and, above all, God, a "Force illegible," a "distant, stately lover."

Ralph Waldo Emerson, author of *Nature,* America's "intellectual Declaration of Independence."

Henry David Thoreau, author of the American classics *Walden* and "Civil Disobedience."

Hawthorne

Nathaniel Hawthorne, the best of the New England group of fiction writers, never shared the sunny optimism of his transcendentalist neighbors or their perfectionist belief in reform. He was haunted by the knowledge of evil bequeathed to him by his Puritan forebears—one of whom had been a judge at the Salem witchcraft trials. After graduating from Bowdoin College in Maine, he worked in obscurity in Salem, gradually began to sell a few stories, and finally earned some degree of fame with his collection of *Twice-Told Tales* (1837). In these, as in most of his later work, he presented powerful moral allegories. His central themes explored evil and its consequences: pride and selfishness, secret guilt, selfish egotism, the impossibility of rooting sin out of the human soul. His greatest novel, *The Scarlet Letter* (1850), explicitly pondered such burdens, focusing on the guilt felt by a woman and a minister who had committed adultery.

Poe

Edgar Allan Poe, born in Boston and reared in Virginia, was a literary genius, and many Europeans considered him the most important American writer of the time. As a poet, he strove to craft verses that would display the classic virtues of restraint, discipline, and unity. "The Raven" is a masterful example of his preoccupation with form as well as his interest in probing the dark recesses of the human soul. The tormented, hard-drinking, quarrelsome Poe was also a master of Gothic horror in the short story and the inventor of the detective story. He judged prose by its ability to provoke emotional tension, and since he considered fear to be the most powerful emotion, he focused his efforts on making the grotesque and supernatural seem disturbingly real to his readers. Anyone who has read the "Tell-Tale Heart" or "The Pit and the Pendulum" can testify to his success.

Melville

Although today considered one of America's greatest novelists, Herman Melville during his later years saw his literary reputation evaporate. Born in New York in 1819, at age twenty he shipped out as a seaman. He wound up in the South Seas and jumped ship with a companion. After a month spent with a friendly tribe in the valley of the Typees, he signed onto an Australian whaler, jumped ship again in Tahiti, was jailed for mutiny, and obtained his release by signing on as a harpooner. After landing in Hawaii, he finally returned to Boston as a seaman aboard a navy frigate. An embroidered account of his exotic adventures, in *Typee* (1846), became an instant popular success, which he repeated in *Omoo* (1847), based on his stay in Tahiti.

Melville then produced a masterpiece in *Moby-Dick* (1851), a novel rich in action as well as symbolism. Unhappily, neither the larger reading public nor many of the critics at the time appreciated the novel, and after the Civil War, Melville's career wound down into futility.

Whitman

The most provocative American writer during the antebellum period was Walt Whitman, a remarkably vibrant personality who disdained inherited social conventions and artistic traditions. There was something elemental in Whitman's character, something bountiful and generous and compelling—even his faults and inconsistencies were ample. Born on a Long Island farm, he moved with his family to Brooklyn, and from the age of twelve worked mainly as a handyman and journalist, frequently taking the ferry across the river to booming, bustling Manhattan. The city fascinated him, and he gorged himself on the urban spectacle—shipyards, crowds, factories, shop windows.

From such material, Whitman drew his editorial opinions and poetic inspiration, but he remained relatively obscure until the first edition of *Leaves of Grass* (1855) caught the eye and aroused the ire of readers. Emerson found it "the most extraordinary piece of wit and wisdom that America has yet contributed," but more conventional critics shuddered at Whitman's explicit homosexual references and groused at his indifference to rhyme and meter as well as his buoyant egotism. The jaunty Whitman, however, refused to conform to genteel notions of art, and he spent most of his career working on his gargantuan collection of poems, *Leaves of Grass*, enlarging and reshaping it in successive editions. He identified the growth of the book with the growth of the country, which he celebrated in all its variety.

The Popular Press

The flowering of American literature came at a time of massive expansion of newspaper circulation. In 1847 Richard Hoe of New York invented the Hoe Rotary Press, which printed 20,000 sheets an hour. It expedited production of cheap "penny" newspapers as well as magazines and books. The availability of newspapers costing only a penny each transformed daily reading into a form of popular entertainment. Circulation soared in every city. As readership grew, the content of newspapers expanded beyond political news and commentary to include social gossip, sports, and sensational crime and accident reports. The *New York Sun*, the first successful penny daily, and others like it often ignored the important news of the day in favor of scandals and sensations, true or false.

Education

Literacy in Jacksonian America was surprisingly widespread, given the condition of public education. In 1840, according to census data, some 78 percent of the total population and 91 percent of the white population could read and write. Since the colonial period, in fact, Americans had enjoyed the highest literacy rate in the Western world.

War News from Mexico (1848), by Richard Caton Woodville. The immediacy of telegraphic news combined with the invention of the Hoe Rotary Press increased the circulation and popularity of newspapers.

Early Public Schools

By the 1830s, the demand for state-supported public schools was rising fast. Reformers argued that popular government depended upon a literate and informed electorate. Workers also wanted free schools to give their children an equal chance at economic and social success. Education, it was also argued, would be a means of social reform by improving manners and lessening crime and poverty.

Horace Mann of Massachusetts stood out in the early drive for statewide school systems. He shepherded through the legislature in 1837 a bill that created a state board of education, which he then served as secretary. Mann went on to sponsor many reforms in Massachusetts, including the first state-supported training for teachers, a state association of teachers, and a minimum school year of six months.

While the North made great strides in public education by 1850, the educational pattern in the South continued to reflect the region's aristocratic pretensions and rural isolation: the South had a higher percentage of college students than any other region, but a lower percentage of public school students. And the South had some 500,000 white illiterates, more than half the total number in the country.

Higher Education

The post-Revolutionary proliferation of colleges continued after 1800 with the spread of small church schools and state universities. Of the seventy-eight colleges and universities in 1840, thirty-five had been founded after 1830, almost all as church-supported schools. Federal policy abetted the spread of universities into the West. When Congress granted statehood to Ohio in 1803, it set aside two townships for the support of a state university and kept up that policy in other new states.

American colleges and universities during the nineteenth century were tiny when compared to today's institutions of higher learning. Most enrolled a hundred students or less, and the largest rarely had more than 600. Virtually all of these students were men. Elementary education for girls was generally accepted, but training beyond that level was not. Progress began with the academies, some of which taught boys and girls alike. Good "female seminaries" like those founded by Emma Willard at Troy, New York (1824), and Mary Lyon at Mount Holyoke, Massachusetts (1836), prepared the way for women's colleges.

The work in female seminaries usually differed from the courses in men's schools, giving more attention to the social amenities and such "embellishments" as music and art. Vassar, opened at Poughkeepsie, New York, in 1865, is usually credited with being the first women's college to give priority to conventional academic subjects and standards. In general, the West gave the greatest impetus to coeducation, with state universities in the lead. But once admitted, women students remained in a subordinate status. At Oberlin College in Ohio, for instance, women were expected to clean male students' rooms and were not allowed to speak in class or recite at graduation exercises. Coeducation did not mean equality.

The George Barrell Emerson School, Boston, c. 1850. Although higher education for women initially met with some resistance, female seminaries like this one were started in the 1820s and 1830s and taught women mathematics, physics, and history, as well as music, art, and the social amenities.

Some Movements for Reform

The urge to eradicate evil from nineteenth-century America had its roots in the American sense of mission, which in turn drew upon rising faith in the perfectibility of humankind. The revival fever of the Second Great Awakening helped generate a widespread belief that people could eradicate many of the evils afflicting society. Transcendentalism, the spirit of which infected even those unfamiliar with its philosophical roots, offered a romantic faith in the individual and the belief that human intuition led to right thinking.

Such a perfectionist bent found outlet in diverse reform movements and activities during the Jacksonian era. Few areas of life escaped the concerns of the reformers: dueling, crime and punishment, the hours and conditions of work, poverty, vice, care of the handicapped, pacifism, temperance, women's rights, the abolition of slavery.

While a perfectionist impulse helped excite the reform movements of the Jacksonian era, social and economic changes helped supply the reformers themselves, most of whom were women. The rise of an urban middle class offered affluent women greater time to devote to social concerns. Material prosperity enabled them to hire maids and cooks, which in turn freed them from household chores. Many of them joined various charitable organizations, most of which were led by men. Some reformers proposed legislative remedies for social ills; others stressed personal conversion or private philanthropy. Whatever the method or approach, social reformers mobilized in great numbers during the second quarter of the nineteenth century.

Temperance

The crusade against alcohol abuse was perhaps the most widespread of all the reform movements. The temperance movement rested on a number of arguments. First and foremost was the religious demand that "soldiers of the cross" lead blameless lives. Others stressed the social and economic costs of drunk workers. The dynamic new economy, with factories and railroads moving on strict schedules, made tippling by the labor force a far greater problem than it had been in a simple agrarian economy. Humanitarians emphasized the relations between drinking and poverty. Much of the movement's propaganda focused on the sufferings of innocent mothers and children.

In 1826 a group of Boston ministers organized the American Society for the Promotion of Temperance. The society pursued its objectives through lecturers, press campaigns, an essay contest, and the formation of local and state societies. A favorite device was to ask those who took the pledge to put by their signatures a T for Total Abstinence. With that a new word entered the language: "teetotaler."

In 1833 the society called a national convention in Philadelphia, where the American Temperance Union was formed. The convention, however, revealed internal tensions: Was the goal moderation or total abstinence, and if the latter, abstinence merely from liquor or also from wine, cider, and beer? Should the movement work by persuasion or by legislation? Like nearly every reform movement of the day, temperance had a wing of perfectionists who rejected all compromises, and in 1836, they called for abstinence from all alcoholic beverages—which caused moderates to abstain from the reform movement instead. Still, between 1830 and 1860, the temperance agitation drastically reduced Americans' per-capita consumption of alcohol.

Prisons and Asylums

The Jacksonian-age belief that people are innately good and capable of improvement brought major changes in the treatment of prisoners, the handicapped, and dependent children. In the colonial period, prisons were usually places for brief confinement before punishment, which was either death or some kind of pain or humiliation: whipping, mutilation, confinement in stocks, branding, and the like. A new attitude began to emerge after the Revolution, and gradually the idea of the penitentiary developed. It would be a place where the guilty experienced penitence and underwent rehabilitation, not just punishment.

An early model of the new system, widely copied, was the Auburn Penitentiary, commissioned by New York in 1816. The prisoners at Auburn had separate cells and gathered for meals and group labor. Discipline was severe. The men were marched out in lockstep and never put face to face or allowed to talk. But prisoners were at least reasonably secure from abuse by other prisoners. The system, its advocates argued, had a beneficial effect on the prisoners and saved money, since the workshops supplied prison needs and produced goods for sale at a profit. By 1840, there were twelve prisons of the Auburn type in the United States.

The reform impulse also found an outlet in the care of the insane. The Pennsylvania Hospital (1752), one of the first in the country, had a provision in its charter that it should care for "lunaticks," but before 1800 few hospitals provided care for the mentally ill. There were in fact few hospitals of any kind. The insane were usually confined at home with hired keepers or in jails and almshouses. After 1815, however, public asylums that housed the disturbed separately from criminals began to appear.

The most important figure in arousing the public conscience to the plight of these unfortunates was Dorothea Lynde Dix. A Boston schoolteacher, she was called upon to instruct a Sunday-school class at the East Cambridge House of Correction in 1841. She found there a roomful of insane persons completely neglected, fed slop, and left without heat on a cold March day. In a report to the state legislature in 1843, Dix told of persons confined "in *cages, closets, cellars, stalls, pens! Chained, naked, beaten with rods, and lashed into obedience!*" She won the support of leading reformers as well as a large state appropriation for improving the treatment of the insane. From Massachusetts, she carried her campaign throughout the country and abroad. By 1860, she had convinced twenty states to adopt similar programs to improve the conditions in prisons and asylums.

Elizabeth Cady Stanton (left) and Susan B. Anthony (right).

Women's Rights

The official status of women during the antebellum period remained much as it had been in the colonial era. Legally, a woman was unable to vote, and, after marriage, she was denied legal control of her property and even of her children. A wife could not make a will, sign a contract, or bring suit in court without her husband's permission. Her legal status was thus like that of a minor, a slave, or a free black. Gradually, however, more and more women began to complain about their status.

In 1848 two prominent moral reformers and advocates of women's rights, Lucretia Mott, a Philadelphia Quaker, and Elizabeth Cady Stanton, a graduate of Troy Seminary who refused to be merely "a household drudge," decided to call a convention to discuss "the social, civil, and religious condition and rights of women." The hastily organized Seneca Falls Convention, the first of its kind, issued on July 19, 1848, the Declaration of Sentiments, mainly the work of Stanton, who also was the wife of a prominent abolitionist and mother of seven. In a clever paraphrase of Jefferson's Declaration of Independence, the document proclaimed the self-evident truth that "all men and women are created equal," and the attendant resolutions said that all laws placing women "in a position inferior to that of men, are contrary to the great precept of nature, and therefore of no force or authority." Such language was too strong for most of the thousand delegates, and only about a third of them signed the document. Yet the Seneca Falls gathering represented an important first step in the evolving campaign for women's rights.

From 1850 until the Civil War, the women's rights leaders held annual conventions and carried on a program of organizing, lecturing, and petitioning. Susan B. Anthony, an ardent Quaker already active in temperance and antislavery groups, joined the crusade in the 1850s. Unlike Stanton and Mott, Anthony was unmarried and therefore able to devote most of her attention to the women's crusade. As one observer put it, Stanton "forged the thunderbolts and Miss Anthony hurled them."

The primary objective of the women's movement was the right to vote. While women did not win voting rights until the twentieth century, there were some legal gains before the Civil War. The state of Mississippi, seldom regarded as a hotbed of reform, was the first to grant married women control over their property in 1839; by the 1860s eleven more states had such laws.

Still, the only jobs open to educated women in any numbers were nursing and teaching. Yet if women could be teachers, Susan Anthony asked, why not lawyers or doctors or ministers or intellectuals? Why not indeed, replied a small band of hardy women who carved out professional careers. Harriet Hunt of Boston was a teacher who, after nursing her sister through a serious illness, set up shop in 1835 as a self-taught physician and persisted in medical practice although twice rejected by Harvard Medical School. Voted into Geneva Medical College in western New York as a joke, Elizabeth Blackwell of Ohio had the last laugh when she finished at the head of her class in 1849. She founded the New York Infirmary for Women and Children and later had a long career as a professor of gynecology in the London School of Medicine for Women.

An intellectual prodigy among women of the time—the derisory term was "bluestocking"—was Margaret Fuller, who edited *The Dial* for two years and became literary editor and critic for Horace Greeley's *New York Tribune*. From 1839 to 1844, she conducted "conversations" with the cultivated ladies of Boston. From this classroom-salon emerged her pathbreaking book, *Woman in the Nineteenth Century* (1845), a plea for the removal of all intellectual and economic disadvantages. Minds and souls were neither masculine nor feminine, she argued. Genius had no sex.

Utopian Communities

The pervasive climate of reform during the Jacksonian era and after also provoked a quest for utopia. Over a hundred utopian communities sprang up between 1800 and 1900. Among the most durable were the Shakers, officially the United Society of Believers in Christ's Second Appearing, founded by Ann Lee Stanley (Mother Ann), who reached New York State with eight followers in 1774. Believing religious fervor a sign of inspiration from the Holy Ghost, they had strange fits in which they saw visions and prophesied. These manifestations later evolved into a ritual dance—hence the name Shakers. Mother Ann claimed that she was the female incarnation of God, as Jesus had been the male. She preached celibacy to prepare Shakers for the perfection that was promised them after death.

The Shakers were one of the most durable utopian communities; their services were characterized by a ritual dance of religious fervor

Mother Ann died in 1784, but the movement found new leaders, and by 1830, about twenty groups were flourishing. In Shaker communities all property was held in common, and strict celibacy was practiced. Men and women not only slept separately but also worked and ate separately. Governance of the colonies was concentrated in the hands of select elders chosen by the ministry. The superbly managed Shaker farms were among the leading sources of garden seed and medicinal herbs, and many of their manufactures, including clothing, household items, and especially furniture, were prized for their simple beauty.

John Humphrey Noyes, founder of the Oneida Community, was the son of a Vermont congressman. After discovering true religion at one of Charles G. Finney's revivals, he entered the ministry but was forced out when he concluded that with true conversion came perfection and a complete release from sin. In 1836 he gathered a group of a dozen or so "Perfectionists" around his home in Putney, Vermont. Ten years later Noyes announced a new doctrine of "complex marriage," which meant that every man in the community was married to every woman and vice versa. To outsiders such theology smacked of "free love," and Noyes was arrested. He fled to New York and in 1848 established the Oneida Community, which numbered more than 200 by 1851.

The communal group shared alike in the food, clothing, and shelter produced by their hard work. They eked out a living with farming and logging until the mid-1850s, when the inventor of a new steel trap joined the community. Oneida traps were soon known as the best money could buy. The community then branched out into sewing silk, canning fruits, and making silver tableware. Oneida also carefully regulated its social life. Women enjoyed the same rights as men, and children were raised by the community as a whole, placed in a common nursery, supplied with toys and affection, and allowed to sleep until they awoke themselves.

For well over a generation the passionate community prospered. In 1879, however, it faced a crisis when Noyes fled to Canada to avoid prosecution for adultery. The members then abandoned complex marriage, and in 1881 they decided to convert into a joint-stock company, the Oneida Community, Ltd., which remains today a thriving flatware company.

In contrast to these religious communities, Robert Owen's New Harmony was based on a secular principle. A British capitalist who worried about the social effects of the factory system, Owen bought the town of Harmony, Indiana, and promptly christened it New Harmony. In 1825 about 900 colonists gathered in New Harmony and established a cooperative community. Separate residences were to be built for the married, unmarried, and children. A complete school system, including nursery and university, was to be built along with a library, lecture halls, laboratories, and gymnasium. There were frequent lectures and social gatherings with music and dancing.

But New Harmony soon fell into discord. Leaders complained of "grumbling, carping, and murmuring" members, and others who had the "disease of laziness." In 1827 Owen returned from a visit to England to find New Harmony insolvent. The following year he dissolved the project and sold or leased the lands on good terms, in many cases to the settlers.

Brook Farm was the most celebrated of all the utopian communities, because it had the support of Ralph Waldo Emerson and countless other well-known literary figures of New England. George Ripley, a Unitarian minister and transcendentalist, conceived of Brook Farm as a kind of early-day "think tank," combining high thinking and plain living. The residents would work together in the mornings so that they could spend the afternoons engaged in intellectual and cultural activities.

Brook Farm and most of the utopian communities were short-lived. While such experiments had little effect on the larger society, they did express the deeply ingrained desire for perfectionism inherent in the American character, a desire that would continue to spawn noble, if frequently naive, experiments thereafter.

Among all the targets of reformers' idealism, however, one great evil would finally take precedence over the others—human bondage. The paradox of American slavery coupled with American freedom, of "the world's fairest hope linked with man's foulest crime," in Herman Melville's words, would inspire the climactic crusade of the age, abolitionism, one that would ultimately move to the center of the political stage and sweep the nation into an epic—and tragic—struggle.

CHAPTER

13

Manifest Destiny

This chapter focuses on

- National politics in the 1840s.
- The factors leading to westward migrations and the conditions faced by western settlers.
- The causes, course, and consequences of the Mexican War.

THE *ESSENTIAL AMERICA* ON-LINE TUTOR

www.wwnorton.com/eamerica/ch13

- **Topic: The Oregon Trail**
  www.wwnorton.com/eamerica/ch13/topic.htm

  In the decades following the Lewis and Clark expedition, hundreds of thousands of Americans migrated westward over the Oregon (Overland) Trail. Utilizing maps, sketches, photographs, and historical analyses, investigate the significance of the pioneer experience. What drove these pioneers to brave the wild American West?

- **Chapter review: On-line quiz and chapter summary**
  www.wwnorton.com/eamerica/ch13/review.htm

- **Chapter resources: Multimedia index**
  www.wwnorton.com/eamerica/ch13/media.htm

During the 1840s, the westering impulse, the quest for a better chance and more living room, continued to excite the American imagination. People frustrated by the growing congestion and rising cost of living along the Atlantic seaboard saw in the West a bountiful source of personal freedom, economic opportunity, social democracy—and adventure.

Economic depressions in 1837 and 1841 intensified the appeal of starting anew out West. Texas, Oregon, and Utah were the favored destinations until the discovery of gold in California in 1848 sparked a stampede that threatened to depopulate New England of its young men.

Most of these settlers and adventurers sought to exploit the many economic opportunities afforded by the new lands. Trappers and farmers, miners and merchants, hunters, ranchers, teachers, servants, and prostitutes, among others, headed west seeking their fortunes. Others sought religious freedom or new converts to Christianity. Whatever the reason, they formed an unceasing migratory stream flowing across the Great Plains and the Rocky Mountains. The Indian and Mexican inhabitants of the region soon found themselves swept aside by successive waves of American settlers.

The Tyler Years

When William Henry Harrison took office in 1841, elected like Jackson mainly on the strength of his military record and his lack of a public stand on major issues, the Whig leaders expected him to be a tool in the hands of Daniel Webster and Henry Clay. Webster became secretary of state, and while Clay preferred to stay in the Senate, his friends filled the cabinet. Harrison served the shortest term of any president—after the longest inaugural address. At the inauguration, held on a rainy winter day, he caught cold. The pleadings of office seekers in the following month filled his days and sapped his strength. On April 4, 1841, exactly one month after the inauguration, Harrison died of pneumonia at age sixty-eight.

John Tyler, the first vice-president to succeed on the death of a president, served practically all of Harrison's term. At age fifty-one, the Virginia slaveholder was the youngest president to date. He already had a long career behind him as legislator, governor, congressman, and senator, and his positions on all the important issues had been forcefully stated and were widely known. Although a Whig, he favored a strict construction of the Constitution and was a stubborn defender of states' rights. When someone asked if he were a "nationalist," Tyler retorted that he had "no such word in my political vocabulary." He ardently opposed Clay's American System of protective tariffs, a national bank, and internal improvements at national expense. He had broken with the Democratic party over Andrew Jackson's denial of a state's right to nullify a federal law and Jackson's imperious use of executive authority. Thus Tyler, the states'-rights Whig, had been chosen to "balance" the ticket by the party leaders in 1840; no one expected that he would actually wield power.

Domestic Affairs

When Congress met in special session in 1841, Henry Clay introduced a series of resolutions designed to supply the platform that the Whig party had evaded in the previous election. The chief points were repeal of the Independent Treasury, establishment of a Third Bank of the United States, distribution to the states of proceeds from federal land sales, and a higher tariff. "Tyler dares not resist me. I will drive him before me," Clay predicted.

Tyler, it turned out, was not easily driven. Although he agreed to the repeal of the Independent Treasury and signed a higher tariff bill in 1842, Tyler vetoed Clay's bill for a new national bank. This provoked his entire cabinet, with the exception of Webster, to resign. Tyler replaced the defectors with anti-Jackson Democrats like himself who had become Whigs. The stubborn Tyler became a president without a party. Irate congressional Whigs expelled him, and Democrats viewed him as an untrustworthy "renegade." Clay's leadership of the Whig party was now established beyond question.

Foreign Affairs

In foreign relations, meanwhile, developments of immense significance were taking place. A major issue between Britain and the United States involved the suppression of the African slave trade, which both countries had outlawed in 1808. In 1841 the British prime minister asserted the right to patrol off the coast of Africa and search vessels flying the American flag to see if they carried slaves. But the American government remembered the impressments and seizures during the Napoleonic Wars and refused to accept such intrusions.

Anglo-American relations were further strained by disputes over boundary lines. The vagueness of the treaty of 1783 ending the American Revolution had led to chronic border disputes between Maine and Canada. In 1842 the British sent Lord Ashburton to Washington to discuss the matter. The negotiations settled the Maine boundary as well as other border disputes by accepting the existing line between the Connecticut and St. Lawrence Rivers, and by compromising on the line between Lake Superior and Lake of the Woods. The Webster-Ashburton Treaty (1842) also provided for joint patrols off Africa to suppress the slave trade.

The Western Frontier

In the 1840s, what stirred the blood of the American people was the mounting evidence that more and more pioneers were hurdling the barriers of the "Great American Desert" and the Rocky Mountains, reaching out toward the Pacific coast. In 1845 an eastern magazine editor labeled this bumptious spirit of expansion. "Our manifest destiny," he wrote, "is to overspread the continent allotted by Providence for the free development of our yearly multiplying millions." At its best, this much-trumpeted notion of "Manifest Destiny" offered a moral justification for American expansion, a prescription for what an enlarged United States could and should be. At its worst, it was a cluster of flimsy rationalizations for naked greed and imperial ambition. Whatever the case, hundreds of thousands of people began streaming into the Far West during the 1840s and after.

As they crossed the Mississippi River and made their way westward, American pioneers entered not only a new environment but a new culture as well. The Great Plains and the Far West were already occupied by Indians and Mexicans, peoples who had lived in the region for centuries and had established their own distinctive customs and ways of life. Now they were joined by Americans of diverse ethnic origin and religious persuasion. It made for a volatile mix.

Western Indians

Over 325,000 Indians inhabited the Southwest, the Great Plains, California, and the Pacific Northwest in 1840. These Native Americans were divided into more than 200 different tribes, each with its own language, religion, economic base, kinship practices, and system of governance. Some were primarily farmers; others were nomadic hunters who preyed upon game animals as well as other Indians.

Some twenty-three tribes resided in the Great Plains, a vast grassland stretching from the Mississippi River west to the Rocky Mountains and from Canada to Mexico. Plains Indians such as the Arapaho, Blackfoot, Cheyenne, Kiowa, and Sioux were horse-borne nomads; they moved across the grasslands with the buffalo herds, carrying their teepees with them.

Several quite different Indian tribes lived to the south and west of the Plains Indians. In the arid region including what is today Arizona, New Mexico, and southern Utah were the peaceful Pueblo tribes—Acoma, Hopi, Laguna, Taos, Zia, Zuni. They were sophisticated farmers who lived in adobe villages along rivers that they used to irrigate their crops of corn, beans, and squash. The word *pueblo* comes from the Spanish term for "village." Their rivals were the Apache and Navajo, warlike hunters who roamed the countryside in small bands and preyed upon the Pueblos. They, in turn, were periodically harassed by their powerful enemies, the Comanches.

To the north, in the Great Basin between the Rocky Mountains and the Sierra Nevada range, tribes such as the Paiutes and Gosiutes struggled to survive in the harsh, arid region of what is today Nevada, Utah, and eastern California. They traveled in family groups and subsisted on berries, pine nuts, insects, and rodents. West of the mountains, along the California coast, the Indians lived in small villages. They gathered wild plants and acorns and fished in the rivers and bays. More than 100,000 Indians lived in coastal California in the 1840s.

The Indian tribes living along the northwest Pacific coast—the Nisqually, Spokane, Yakima, Chinook, Klamath, and Nez Percé (pierced noses)—enjoyed the most abundant natural resources and the most temperate climate. The ocean and rivers provided whales, seals, salmon, and crabs. The lush forests just east of the coast harbored game, berries, and nuts. And the majestic stands of fir, redwood, and cedar offered wood for cooking and shelter.

All of the Indian tribes eventually felt the unrelenting pressure of white expansion. Because Indian life on the Plains depended on the buffalo, the influx of white settlers posed a direct threat to their cultural survival. Tribal chiefs appealed to Washington for help, but the federal government turned a deaf ear. It continued to build a string of frontier forts to protect the advancing settlers, and it sought to use treaties to gain control of new lands. When officials of the Indian Bureau could not coerce, cajole, or confuse Indian leaders into selling title to their tribal lands, fighting ensued. And after the discovery of gold in California in 1848, the tidal wave of white expansion flowed all the way to the West Coast.

Buffalo Lancing in the Snow Drifts, c. 1860s. This painting by George Catlin shows the Sioux hunting buffalo.

The Spanish West and Mexican Revolution

As American settlers moved westward, they also encountered Spanish-speaking peoples. Many whites were as contemptuous of Hispanics as they were of Indians. Most Americans in the Southwest viewed Mexicans as ignorant, indolent, and conniving. The vast majority of the Spanish-speaking people in what is today called the American Southwest resided in New Mexico. Most of these people were *mestizos* (of mixed Indian and Spanish blood), and they were usually ranch hands or small farmers and herders.

The Spanish had been less successful in colonizing Arizona and Texas than they had been in New Mexico and Florida. The Yuma and Apache Indians in Arizona and the Comanches and Apaches in Texas thwarted efforts to establish Catholic missions. In eastern Texas during the first half of the eighteenth century, French traders from Louisiana undermined the authority and influence of the Spanish missions. The French supplied the Indians with guns, ammunition, and promises of protection. Several of the Texas missions were abandoned and reestablished near San Antonio in 1731. By 1750 the Pawnees, Wichitas, Comanches, and Apaches were using Spanish horses and French rifles to raid Spanish settlements in Texas. By 1790, the Hispanic population in Texas numbered only 2,510 while in New Mexico it exceeded 20,000.

In 1807 French forces occupied Spain and imprisoned the king. This created both consternation and confusion throughout Spain's colonial possessions, including Mexico. Miguel Hidalgo y Costilla, a *creole* (European born in the New World) Mexican priest, organized a revolt of Indians and *mestizos* against Spanish rule in Mexico.

The poorly organized uprising failed miserably. In 1811 Spanish troops captured Hidalgo and executed him. Other Mexicans, however, continued to yearn for independence. In 1820, Mexican *creoles* again tried to liberate themselves from Spanish authority. By then, the Spanish forces in Mexico had lost much of their cohesion and dedication. Facing a growing revolt, the last Spanish officials withdrew from Mexico in 1821, and it became an independent nation.

Mexican independence unleashed tremors throughout the Southwest. In New Mexico and Arizona, American fur traders streamed into the region and developed a lucrative commerce in beaver pelts. Soon thereafter, wagon trains carrying American settlers began to make their way from Missouri westward along the Santa Fe Trail. In California, American entrepreneurs flooded into the now-Mexican province and soon became a powerful force for change; by 1848 Americans made up half of the non-Indian population. In Texas, American adventurers decided to promote their own independence from a newly independent—and chaotic—Mexican government. Suddenly, it seemed, the Southwest was a new frontier ripe for American exploitation and settlement.

American Settlement of Oregon City (1846), by James Warre. Oregon's fertile soil and temperate climate drew 5,000 settlers by 1845.

The Rockies and Oregon Country

In the Northwest, the western frontier consisted of the Nebraska, Washington, and Oregon Territories. Fur traders were especially drawn to the Missouri River with its many tributaries. The heyday of the mountain fur trade began in 1822 when a Missouri businessman sent his first trading party to the upper Missouri River. But by 1840, the great days of the western fur trade were already over. The streams no longer teemed with beavers.

Beyond the mountains, the Oregon country stretched from the Forty-second Parallel north to 54° 40′. Between these parallels, Spain and Russia had given up their claims, leaving Great Britain and the United States as the only claimants. Under the Convention of 1818, the two countries had agreed to "joint occupation." Until the 1830s, however, joint occupation had been a legal technicality, because few Americans were in the area.

Word of Oregon's fertile soil, temperate climate, and magnificent forests gradually spread, largely through the efforts of Methodist missionaries recently settled there. This enticed adventurous Americans, and by the late 1830s, a trickle of emigrants began flowing along the Oregon (Overland) Trail. Soon "Oregon Fever" spread like a contagion. By 1845 there were about 5,000 settlers in the Willamette Valley of Oregon.

California

California also attracted new settlers and entrepreneurs. For all of its rich natural resources, California remained thinly populated by Indians and mission friars well into the nineteenth century. It was a simple, almost feudal, agrarian society, without schools, industry, or defenses. In 1821, when Mexico wrested its independence from Spain, Californians took comfort in the fact that Mexico City was so far away that it would exercise little effective control over its farthest state. During the next two decades, Californians, including many recent American arrivals, staged ten revolts against the governors dispatched to lord over them.

Yet Mexican rule did produce a dramatic change in California history. In 1824, Mexico passed a colonization act that granted hundreds of huge "rancho" estates to Mexican settlers. With free labor extracted from Indians, who were treated like slaves, these *rancheros* lived a life of self-indulgent luxury and ease, gambling, horse-racing, bull-baiting, and dancing. They soon cast covetous eyes on the vast estates controlled by the Franciscan missions, and in 1833–1834 they convinced the Mexican government to confiscate the California missions, exile the Franciscan friars, release the Indians from church control, and make the mission lands available to new settlement. Within a few years, some 700 huge new rancho grants of 4,500 to 50,000 acres were issued along the coast from San Diego to San Francisco. Organized like feudal estates, these California ranches resembled southern cotton plantations, but the death rate for Indian workers was twice as high as that of slaves in the Deep South.

California's rich natural resources could not long remain a secret, and by the late 1820s, American ships began to enter the "hide and tallow" trade. The *rancheros* produced cowhide and beef tallow in large quantity, and both products enjoyed a brisk demand, cowhides mainly for shoes and the tallow chiefly for candles.

Moving West

Most of the western pioneers during the second quarter of the nineteenth century were American-born whites from the upper South and Midwest. A few free blacks joined in the migration. Between 1841 and 1867, some 350,000 men, women, and children made the arduous trek to California or Oregon, while hundreds of thousands of others settled along the way in Colorado, Texas, Arkansas, and other areas.

The Santa Fe Trail

After gaining its independence in 1821, the new government of Mexico was much more interested in trade with Americans than Spain had been. In Spanish-controlled Santa Fe, in fact, all commerce with the United States had been banned. After 1821, however, trade flouished. Hundreds of enterpreneurs made the thousand-mile trek from St. Louis to Santa Fe, forging a route that became known as the Santa Fe Trail.

The Santa Fe traders pioneered more than a new trail. They showed that heavy wagons could cross the plains and the mountains, and they developed the tech-

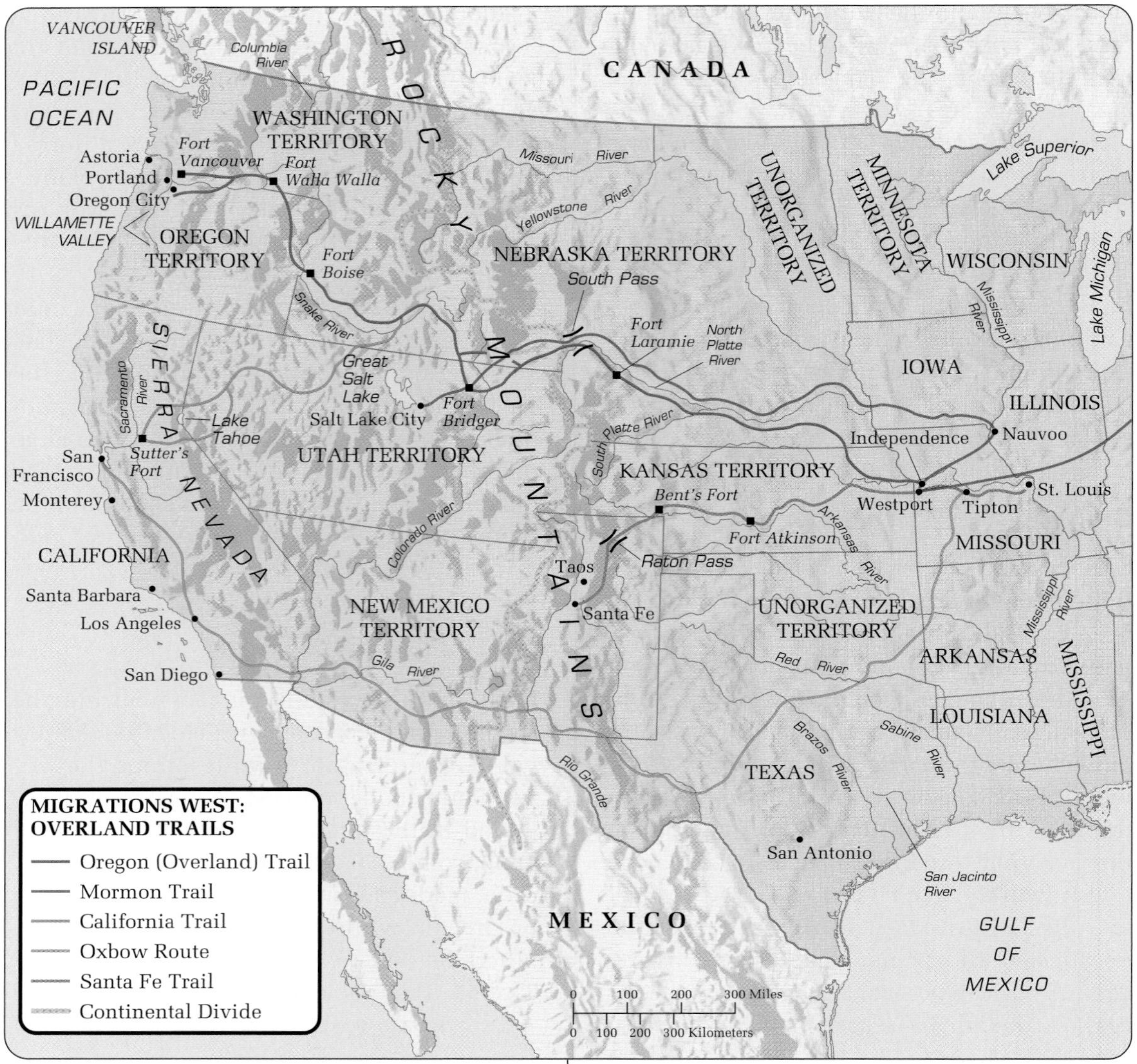

nique of organized caravans for common protection. Such techniques would also be used by those heading west to California and Oregon.

The Overland Trail

As on the Santa Fe Trail, people bound for Oregon and California traveled in wagon caravans. But on the Overland Trail (also known as the Oregon Trail), most of the people were settlers rather than traders. They usually traveled in family groups and came from all over the United States. The wagon trains followed the trail west from Independence, Missouri, along the North Platte River into what is now Wyoming, through South Pass down to Fort Bridger, then down the Snake River to the Columbia River, and along the Columbia to their goal in the fertile Willamette Valley. They usually left Missouri in late spring, completing the 2,000-mile trek in six months. Traveling in ox-drawn, canvas-covered wagons nicknamed "prairie schooners," they traversed rugged mountains at the rate of about fifteen miles per day. By 1845, about 5,000 people were making the arduous journey annually. The discovery of gold in California in 1848 brought some 30,000 pioneers along the Oregon Trail in 1849. By 1850, the peak year of travel along the trail, the number had risen to 55,000.

The journey west was incredibly difficult. Few who embarked on their western quest were adequately prepared for the ordeals they were to face. Cholera claimed many lives. On average there was one grave every eighty yards along the trail between the Missouri River and the Willamette Valley. Some 20,000 pioneers died in all.

The trail's never-ending routine of necessary chores and grinding physical labor took its toll on once-buoyant spirits. This was especially true for women, whose labors went on day and night. One woman settler complained that, unlike the men, who smoked and talked together after supper while the women cleaned, prepared the next day's food, and tended children, "*we have no time for sociability.*"

Hard labor understandably provoked tensions within families and powerful yearnings for home. Many a tired pioneer could identify with the following comment in a girl's journal: "Poor Ma said only this morning, 'Oh, I wish we had never started.' She looks so sorrowful and dejected." Some turned back, but most continued on. And once in Oregon or California they set about establishing stable communities. Noted one settler:

> Friday, October 27—Arrived at Oregon City at the falls of the Willamette.
> Saturday, October 28—Went to work.

The Indians and the Wagon Trains

Contrary to popular myth, the Indians rarely attacked wagon trains. Less than 4 percent of the fatalities associated with the Overland Trail experience resulted from Indian raids. More often, the Indians either allowed the settlers to pass through their tribal lands unmolested or demanded payment. Many wagon trains never encountered a single Indian, and others received generous aid from Indians who served as guides, advisers, or traders. The Indians, one woman pioneer noted, "proved better than represented." To be sure, as the number of pioneers increased dramatically during the 1850s, tensions between overlanders and Indians increased, but never to the degree portrayed in Western novels and films.

The Old Scout's Tale (1853), by William Tylee Ranney. Few settlers traveling in wagon trains were prepared for the hardships of life on the trail.

In 1851 U.S. officials invited the Indian tribes from the northern Plains to a conference held in a grassy valley along the North Platte River, near Ft. Laramie in what is now southeastern Wyoming. Almost 10,000 Indians—men, women, and children—attended the treaty council.

After nearly three weeks of heated discussions and after bestowing on the chiefs a mountain of gifts, federal negotiators and tribal leaders agreed to what became known as the Ft. Laramie Treaty. The American government promised to provide an annual cash payment to the Indians as compensation for the damages caused by wagon trains traversing their hunting grounds. In exchange, the Indians agreed to stop harassing white caravans, to allow federal forts to be built, and to confine themselves to a specified area "of limited extent and well-defined boundaries." Specifically, the Indians were restricted to lands north and south of a corridor through which passed the Overland Trail.

As the first comprehensive treaty with the Plains Indians, this agreement foreshadowed the "reservation" concept of Indian management. Several tribes, however, refused to accept the treaty provisions. The most powerful tribe, the Lakota Sioux, reluctantly signed the agreement but thereafter failed to abide by its restrictions.

The Pathfinder: John Frémont

Despite the hardships and dangers of the overland crossing, the Far West remained an irresistible attraction. The premier press agent for California, and the Far West generally, was John Charles Frémont, "the Pathfinder." Born in Savannah, Georgia, and raised in the South, Frémont became the consummate explorer and romantic adventurer.

Frémont was commissioned a second lieutenant in the United States Topographical Corps in 1838. In 1842 he mapped the Oregon Trail beyond South Pass—and met Christopher "Kit" Carson, one of the most knowledgeable of the mountain men. Carson became Frémont's frequent associate and the most famous frontiersman after Daniel Boone. In 1843–1844 Frémont, typically clad in deerskin shirt, blue army trousers, and moccasins, moved on to Oregon, then made a heroic sweep down the eastern slopes of the Sierras, headed southward through the central valley of California, bypassed the mountains in the south, and returned via the Great Salt Lake. His reports on both expeditions, published together in 1845, gained a wide circulation and helped excite the interest of easterners.

Meanwhile, rumors flourished that the British and French were scheming to grab California, though neither government had such intentions. Political conditions in Mexico left the remote territory in near anarchy much of the time, as governors came and went in rapid succession. Amid the chaos, a substantial number of Californians reasoned that they would be better off if they cut ties to Mexico altogether. Some favored an independent state, perhaps under French or British protection. A larger group admired the balance of central and local authority in the United States and felt their interests might best be served by American annexation. By the time the Americans were ready to light the spark of rebellion in California, there was little will in Mexico to resist.

Annexing Texas

American Settlements

America's lust for land was most clearly at work in the most accessible of all the Mexican borderlands, Texas. More Americans resided there than in all the other coveted regions combined. During the 1820s, Texas was rapidly turning into an American province, for Mexico in 1823 began welcoming American settlers into the region as a means of stabilizing the border.

Foremost among the promoters of Anglo-American settlement in Texas was Stephen F. Austin, a Missouri resident who gained from Mexico a huge land grant originally given to his father by Spanish authorities. By 1824 more than 2,000 hardy souls had settled on Austin's lands. Most of the newcomers were southern farmers drawn to rich new cotton lands selling for only a few cents an acre. By 1830 the coastal region of eastern Texas had approximately 20,000 white settlers and 1,000 black slaves brought in to work the cotton. The newcomers quickly outnumbered the 5,000 Mexicans in the area, and they showed little interest in Catholicism or other aspects of Mexican culture.

The Mexican government grew alarmed at the flood of strangers threatening to engulf the province, and it forbade further immigration. But illegal American immigrants crossed the long border just as illegal Mexican immigrants would later cross over in the other direction. By 1835 the American population had mushroomed to around 30,000, about ten times the number of Mexicans in Texas. Friction mounted in 1832 and 1833 as Americans organized conventions to demand greater representation and power from the Mexican government. Instead of granting the request, General Santa Anna, who had seized power in Mexico, dissolved the national congress late in 1834, abolished the federal system, and became dictator. Texans rose in rebellion, summoned a convention, and pledged to fight for the old Mexican constitution. On March 2, 1836, as Santa Anna approached with an army of conquest, the Texans declared their independence.

Independence from Mexico

The Mexican army delivered its first blow at San Antonio, where it assaulted a small garrison of Texans and American volunteers holed up in an abandoned mission, the Alamo. Among the most celebrated of the volunteers was Davy Crockett, the Tennessee frontiersman who had fought Indians under Andrew Jackson and then served as a congressman.

On February 23, 1836, Santa Anna demanded that the Alamo's defenders surrender, only to be answered with a cannon shot. The 5,000 Mexicans then launched a series of frontal assaults. For twelve days they were repulsed, with fearful losses. Then, on March 6, Santa Anna's men attacked from every side. As the defenders ran low on ammunition, the Mexicans broke through the battered north wall.

Davy Crockett and the other frontiersmen used their muskets as clubs, but they were slain. Santa Anna ordered the wounded Americans put to death and their bodies burned with the rest. The only survivors were sixteen women, children, and servants.

Fall of the Alamo. The Americans' twelve-day stand at the Alamo came to an end on March 6, 1836.

It was a complete victory, but a costly one. The defenders of the Alamo gave their lives at the cost of 1,544 Mexicans, and their heroic stand inspired the rest of Texas to fanatical resistance. While Santa Anna dictated a "glorious" victory declaration, his aide wrote in his diary: "One more such 'glorious victory' and we are finished."

The commander-in-chief of the gathering Texas forces was Sam Houston, a flamboyant Tennessee frontiersman who had joined the army in 1813, fighting alongside Andrew Jackson in the Creek wars. He later served two terms in Congress and in 1827 was elected governor of Tennessee. Two years later, Houston married Eliza Allen, a young woman only half his age. For unexplained reasons, however, the marriage was dissolved almost immediately. The scandal shook the state—and Houston. Rumors of infidelity (unfounded) and alcoholism (legitimate) swirled around him, and in 1829 he resigned as governor and moved to the Indian Territory (now Oklahoma), where he lived for six years with the Cherokees. He took a Cherokee wife and adopted Cherokee citizenship. He also drank so heavily that he became widely known among the Cherokees as the "big drunk." In 1835 Houston moved to Texas and soon thereafter he was named commanding general of the revolutionary army.

Sam Houston.

After the Mexican victory at the Alamo, Houston beat a strategic retreat eastward, gathering reinforcements as he went, including volunteers from the United States. Just west of the San Jacinto River, he finally paused near the site of the city that later bore his name, and on April 21, 1836, he surprised a Mexican encampment there. The 800 Texans and American volunteers charged, yelling "Remember the Alamo," and overwhelmed the Mexican force within fifteen minutes. They killed 630 while losing only 9, and they took Santa Anna prisoner. The Mexican dictator bought his freedom by signing a treaty recognizing Texan independence. The Mexican Congress repudiated the treaty, but the war was at an end.

The Move for Annexation

Residents of the Lone Star Republic then drafted a constitution, made Sam Houston their first president, and voted almost unanimously for annexation to the United States as soon as the opportunity arose. Houston's old friend Andrew Jackson was still the American president, but even Old Hickory could be discreet when delicacy demanded it. The addition of a new slave state threatened to cause a serious sectional quarrel that might endanger Van Buren's election. Worse than that, it raised the specter of war with Mexico. Consequently, Jackson and his successor, Van Buren, shied away from the issue of annexation.

Rebuffed in Washington, Texans turned their thoughts to creating a separate country. Under President Mirabeau Bonaparte Lamar, elected in 1838, they began to talk of expanding to the Pacific as a new nation that would rival the United States. France and Britain extended official recognition to the new nation of Texas and began to develop trade relations. Texas supplied them with an independent source of cotton, new markets, and promised also to become an obstacle to American expansion. The British, who had abolished slavery in their empire in 1833, hoped Texans might embrace abolition in exchange for British protection against any Mexican effort to reassert its sovereignty over Texas.

Many Texans, however, had never abandoned their hopes of annexation to the United States. Reports of growing British influence created anxieties in the United States government and among southern slaveholders, who became the chief advocates of annexation. The United States began secret negotiations with Texas in 1843, and in April John C. Calhoun, the new secretary of state, completed a treaty that went to the Senate for ratification.

Calhoun chose this moment also to send the British minister a letter instructing him on the blessings of slavery and stating that annexation of Texas was needed to foil the British abolitionists. Publication of the note fostered the claim that annexation was planned less in the national interest than to promote the expansion of slavery. It was so worded, one editor wrote Jackson, as to "drive off every northern man from the support of the measure." Sectional division, plus fear of a war with Mexico, contributed to the Senate's overwhelming rejection of the treaty. Solid Whig opposition contributed more than anything else to its defeat.

Polk's Presidency

The Election of 1844

Prudent leaders in both political parties had hoped to keep the divisive issue of Texas out of the 1844 campaign. Clay and Van Buren, the leading candidates, both wrote letters opposing annexation because it would risk civil war. Whig party leaders showed no qualms about Clay's stance. The convention nominated him unanimously, and the Whig platform omitted any reference to Texas.

The Democratic convention was a different story. Van Buren's southern supporters, including Jackson, abandoned him because of his opposition to Texas annexation. With the convention deadlocked, expansionist forces nominated James K. Polk of Tennessee. The party platform took an unequivocal stand favoring territorial expansion. To win support in the North and West as well as the South, it called for "the re-occupation of Oregon and the re-annexation of Texas."

The combination of southern and western expansionism constituted a winning strategy that was so popular that Clay began to hedge his statement on Texas. While he still believed the integrity of the Union to be the chief consideration, he had "no personal objection to the annexation of Texas" if it could be achieved "without dishonor, without war, with the common consent of the Union, and upon just and fair terms." His explanation seemed clear enough, but prudence was no match for spread-eagle oratory and the emotional pull of Manifest Destiny. Clay's stand turned more votes to the Liberty party, an antislavery party begun by a group of abolitionists in 1840. In the western counties of New York, the Liberty party drew enough votes away from the Whigs to give the state to Polk. Had he carried New York, Clay would have won the election by seven electoral votes. Polk won a narrow plurality of 38,000 popular votes nationwide but a clear majority of the electoral college, 170 to 105. At forty-nine Polk was the youngest president up to that time.

Polk and His Program

Born near Charlotte, North Carolina, James K. Polk moved to Tennessee as a young man. After studying mathematics and classics at the University of North Carolina, he became a successful lawyer and planter, entered politics early, served fourteen years in Congress (four as Speaker of the House) and two as governor of Tennessee. Young Hickory, as his partisans liked to call him, had none of Jackson's charisma, but he shared Jackson's strong prejudices and his stubborn determination. Single-mindedly committed to the tasks at hand, Polk was a poor diplomat but a formidable leader.

In domestic affairs, Polk adhered to the principles of Jackson, but he and the new Jacksonians subtly reflected the growing influence of the slaveholding South within the party. Abolitionism, Polk warned, could bring the dissolution of the Union, but his proslavery stance further fragmented public opinion. Antislavery northerners had already begun to drift away from the pro-southern Democratic party.

Polk's major objectives were reduction of the tariff, reestablishment of the Independent Treasury, settlement of the Oregon question, and the acquisition of California. He got them all. The Walker Tariff of 1846, in keeping with Democratic tradition, lowered duties, and in the same year, Polk persuaded Congress to restore the Independent Treasury, which the Whigs had eliminated. Twice Polk vetoed internal improvement bills, leading critics to charge that he was determined to further the regional goals of the South at the expense of the national interest.

Polk's chief concern remained geographic expansion. He privately vowed to acquire California and New Mexico as well, preferably by purchase. The acquisition of Texas was already under way before Polk took office. President Tyler, taking Polk's election as a mandate to act, had asked Congress to accomplish annexation by joint resolution, which required only a simple majority in each house and avoided the two-thirds Senate vote needed to ratify a treaty. Congress had read the election returns too, and after a bitter debate over slavery, the resolution passed by votes of 27 to 25 in the Senate and 120 to 98 in the House. Tyler signed the resolution on March 1, 1845, offering to admit Texas to statehood. Texas voters ratified the action in October, and the new state formally entered the Union on December 29, 1845.

Oregon

Meanwhile, the Oregon issue heated up as expansionists insisted that Polk abandon previous offers to settle on the Forty-ninth Parallel and stand by the platform pledge to take all of Oregon from Great Britain. Some expansionists were prepared to risk war. "Fifty-four forty or fight," they insisted. "All of Oregon or none." In his inaugural address, Polk claimed that the American title to Oregon was "clear and unquestionable," but privately he favored a prudent compromise. The British, however, refused his offer to extend the boundary along the Forty-ninth Parallel. Polk then withdrew the offer and renewed his claim to all of Oregon. In the annual message to Congress at the end of 1845, he asked for permission to give Britain a year's notice that joint occupation would be ended. After a long and bitter debate, Congress adopted the resolution.

Fortunately for Polk, the British government had no enthusiasm for war over that remote wilderness at the cost of profitable trade relations with the United States. In June 1846, the British government submitted a draft treaty to extend the border along the Forty-ninth Parallel and through the main channel south of Vancouver Island. On June 18, the Senate ratified the treaty.

The Mexican War

The Outbreak of War

On March 6, 1845, two days after Polk took office, the Mexican ambassador broke off relations and left for home to protest the annexation of Texas. Polk ordered American troops under General Zachary Taylor to take up positions along the Rio Grande River in the new state of Texas. Polk wanted to goad the Mexicans into a conflict in order to secure Texas and obtain California and New Mexico. As Ulysses S. Grant, then a young officer serving under Taylor, later admitted, "We were sent to provoke a fight, but it was essential that Mexico commence it."

Polk resolved that he could achieve his purposes only by force, and he won the cabinet's approval of a war message to Congress. That very evening, May 9, the news arrived that Mexicans had attacked American soldiers north of the Rio Grande. Eleven Americans were killed, five wounded, and the remainder taken prisoner. Polk's provocative scheme had worked.

In his war message, Polk seized the high ground, declaring that the use of force was a response to aggression, a recognition that war had been forced upon the United States. "The cup of forbearance had been exhausted" before the incident; now, he said, Mexico "has invaded our territory, and shed American blood upon the American soil." The House and Senate quickly passed the war resolution, and Polk signed the declaration of war on May 13, 1846.

Opposition to the War

In the Mississippi Valley, where expansion fever ran high, the war was immensely popular. Likewise in New York, novelist Herman Melville reported that "people here are all in a state of delirium." Whig opinion, however, ranged from lukewarm to hostile. John Quincy Adams, who voted against participation, called it "a most unrighteous war." An obscure one-term congressman from Illinois named Abraham Lincoln, upon taking his seat in 1847, began introducing "spot resolutions," calling on President Polk to name the spot where American blood had been shed on American soil, implying that the troops may in fact have been in Mexico when fired upon. Once again, as in 1812, New England was a hotbed of opposition, largely in the belief that this war was the work of southern slaveholders. Some New Englanders were ready to separate from the slave states, and the Massachusetts legislature pronounced the conflict a war of conquest.

Preparing for Battle

Both the United States and Mexico approached the war ill prepared. The American military was especially small and inexperienced. At the outset of war, the regular army numbered barely over 7,000, in contrast to the Mexican force of 32,000. Many of the Mexicans, however, were pressed into service or recruited from prisons and thus made less than enthusiastic fighters. Before the war ended, the American force grew to 104,000, of whom about 31,000 were regular army troops and marines. The rest were six- and twelve-month volunteers.

Among the volunteers were sons of Henry Clay and Daniel Webster, but most came from coarser backgrounds. Volunteer militia companies, often filled with frontier toughs, made up as raunchy a crew as ever graced the American military—lacking uniforms, standard equipment, and discipline. Repeatedly, despite the best efforts of the commanding generals, these undisciplined forces engaged in plunder, rape, and murder. Nevertheless, these rough-and-tumble Americans consistently defeated larger Mexican forces, which had their own problems with training, discipline, and munitions.

The United States entered the war without even a tentative plan of action, and politics complicated devising one. What Polk wanted, Thomas Hart Benton wrote later, was "a small war, just large enough to require a treaty of peace, and not large enough to make military reputations, dangerous for the presidency." Winfield Scott, general-in-chief of the army, was both a Whig and politically ambitious. Polk nevertheless named him to take charge of the Rio Grande front, but when Scott quarreled with Polk's secretary of war, the exasperated president withdrew the appointment.

There now seemed a better choice. General Zachary Taylor's men had scored two victories over Mexican forces north of the Rio Grande, and on May 18, 1846, they crossed the Rio Grande and occupied Matamoros, which a demoralized and bloodied Mexican army had abandoned. These quick victories brought Taylor instant popularity, and the president responded willingly to the demand that he be made overall commander for the conquest of Mexico. "Old Rough and Ready" Taylor had achieved Polk's main objective, the conquest of Mexico's northern provinces. Taylor became an immediate folk hero to his troops and to Americans back home, so much so that Polk began to see him as a political threat.

Annexation of California

Polk had long coveted the valuable Mexican territory along the Pacific coast and had first tried buying it, but to no avail. He then sought to engineer a Texas-style revolt against Mexican rule among the thousand or so American settlers in California. To that purpose, near the end of 1845, John C. Frémont brought out a band of sixty frontiersmen, including Kit Carson, ostensibly on another exploration of California and Oregon. In 1846 Frémont and his men moved into the Sacramento Valley. Americans in the area fell upon Sonoma on June 14, proclaimed the independent "Republic of California," and hoisted the hastily designed Bear Flag, a California grizzly bear and star painted on white cloth—a version of which became the state flag.

By the end of June, Frémont had endorsed the Bear Flag Republic and set out for Monterey. Before he arrived, the commander of the Pacific Fleet, having heard of the outbreak of hostilities, sent men ashore to raise the American flag and proclaim California a part of the United States. The Republic of California had lasted less than a month, and most Californians of whatever origin welcomed a change that promised order instead of the confusion of the unruly Bear Flaggers. Sporadic clashes with Mexicans continued until 1847, when they finally capitulated. Meanwhile, Colonel

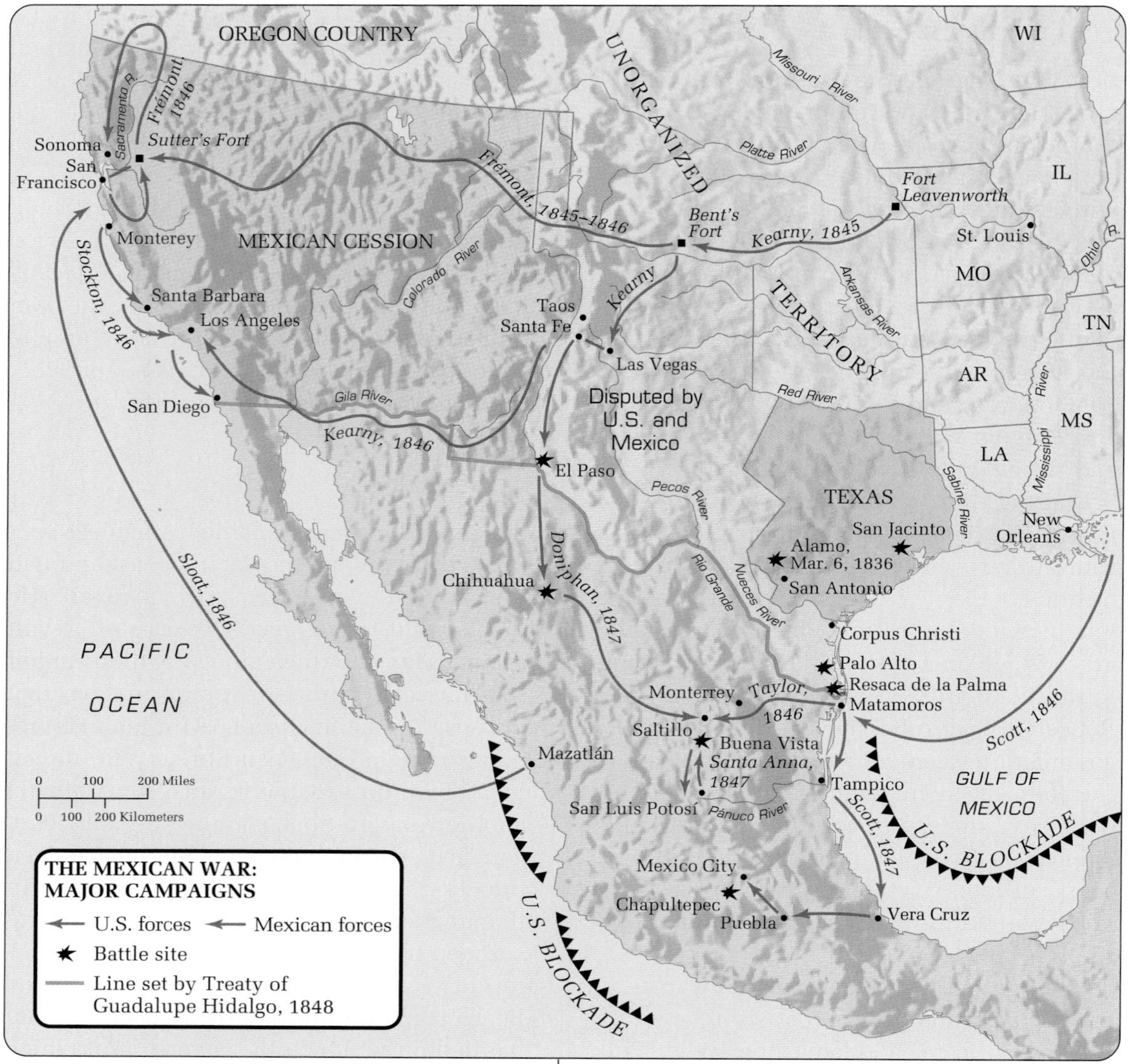

Stephen Kearny and 300 soldiers, having earlier captured Santa Fe, ousted the Mexican forces from southern California and occupied Los Angeles.

Taylor's Battles

Both California and New Mexico had been taken from the Mexicans before General Zachary Taylor fought his first major battle in northern Mexico. Having waited for more men and munitions, Taylor finally headed southward in September 1846 toward the heart of Mexico. His first goal was the fortified city of Monterrey, which he took after a five-day siege.

Having never seen the Mexican desert, Polk wrongly assumed that Taylor's men could live off the country and need not depend on resupply. Polk therefore misunderstood the general's reluctance to strike out across several hundred miles of barren land north of Mexico City. On another point the president was simply duped. The old dictator Santa Anna, forced out in 1844, got word to Polk from his exile in Cuba that in return for the right considerations he could bring about a settlement of the war. Polk in turn assured the Mexican leader that Washington would pay well for any territory taken through such a settlement. In 1846, after another overturn in the Mexican government, American forces allowed Santa Anna to return to his homeland. Soon he was again in command of the Mexican army and then was named president once more. But instead of carrying out his pledge to Polk to negotiate an end to the war, Santa Anna prepared to fight Taylor's army. Polk's secret deal had put the ablest Mexican general back in command of the enemy army.

In October 1846, Polk and his cabinet ordered American troops to move against Mexico City from the south by way of Vera Cruz, which left Taylor's forces idle. Polk would have preferred a Democratic general to lead the new offensive, but for want of a better choice, he named Winfield Scott to the field command. Taylor, miffed at his reduction to a minor role and harboring a "violent disregard" for Scott's abilities, disobeyed orders and took the offensive himself.

Near the hacienda of Buena Vista, Santa Anna's large but ill-trained army met Taylor's untested volunteers. The Mexican general invited the vastly outnumbered Americans to surrender. "Tell him to go to hell," Taylor replied. In the hard-fought Battle of Buena Vista (February 22–23, 1847), Taylor saw his son-in-law, Colonel Jefferson Davis, the future president of the Confederacy, lead a regiment that broke up a Mexican cavalry charge. Neither side could claim victory on the strength of the outcome, but Taylor was convinced that only his lack of trained regular troops prevented him from striking a decisive blow.

Scott's Triumph

Meanwhile, the long-planned southern assault on the enemy capital had begun on March 9, 1847, when Scott's army landed on the beaches south of Vera Cruz. It was the first major amphibious operation by American military forces, and it was carried out without loss. The Mexican commander at Vera Cruz surrendered on March 27 after a week-long siege. Scott and some 14,000 soldiers then retraced the 260-mile route to Mexico City taken by Cortés more than 300 years earlier.

Scott directed a brilliant flanking operation around the lakes and marshes guarding the eastern approaches to Mexico City, then another around the Mexican defenses at San Antonio. On September 13, 1847, American forces entered Mexico City.

Battle of Buena Vista (1847), by Carl Nebel. The last major action on the northern front, neither side could claim victory in this battle.

The Treaty of Guadalupe Hidalgo

After the fall of the capital, Santa Anna resigned and a month later fled the country. By the treaty of Guadalupe Hidalgo, signed on February 2, 1848, Mexico gave up all claims to Texas above the Rio Grande and ceded California and New Mexico to the United States. In return the United States agreed to pay Mexico $15 million and assume the claims of American citizens against Mexico up to a total of $3¼ million.

The seventeen-month-long war had cost the United States 1,721 killed, 4,102 wounded, and far more—11,155—dead of disease, mostly dysentery and chronic diarrhea. It remains the deadliest war in American military history in terms of the percentage of combatants killed. Out of every 1,000 American soldiers in Mexico, some 110 died. The next highest death rate would be in the Civil War, with 65 out of every 1,000 participants.

The military and naval expenditures had been $98 million. For this price, and payments made under the treaty, the United States acquired more than 500,000 square miles of territory (more than a million counting Texas), including the great Pacific harbors of San Diego, Monterey, and San Francisco. Except for a small addition by the Gadsden Purchase in 1853, these annexations rounded out the continental United States.

The War's Legacies

Several important "firsts" are associated with the Mexican War: the first successful American offensive war, the first major amphibious operation, and the nation's first war covered by correspondents. It was also the first significant combat experience for a group of junior officers who would later serve as leading generals during the Civil War: Ulysses S. Grant, Robert E. Lee, Thomas "Stonewall" Jackson, George B. McClellan, George Pickett, George Meade, and others.

Initially, the victory in Mexico provoked a surge of national pride. American triumphs "must elevate the *true* self-respect of the American people," Walt Whitman exclaimed. Others were not so sure. Ralph Waldo Emerson rejected war "as a means of achieving America's destiny," but he then accepted such annexations of new territory by force with the explanation that "most of the great results of history are brought about by discreditable means."

As the years passed, the Mexican War was increasingly seen as a war of selfish conquest. But for a brief season, the glory of victory did add luster to the names of Zachary Taylor and Winfield Scott. Despite Polk's best efforts, he had manufactured the next, and last, two Whig candidates for president. One of them, Taylor, would replace him in the White House, with the storm of sectional conflict already on the horizon.

PART 4

A House Divided and Rebuilt

Of all the regions of the United States during the first half of the nineteenth century, the South was the most distinctive. Southern society remained fundamentally rural and agricultural long after the rest of the nation embraced the urban industrial revolution. Likewise, the southern elite's tenacious effort to preserve and expand the institution of slavery muted social reform impulses in the South and ignited a prolonged political controversy that would end in civil war.

The relentless settlement of the western territories set in motion a feverish competition between North and South for political influence in the burgeoning West. Would the new states in the West be "slave" or "free"? The issue of allowing slavery into the new territories involved more than humanitarian concern for the plight of enslaved blacks. By the 1840s, North and South had developed quite different economic interests. The North wanted high tariffs on imported products to "protect" its infant industries from foreign competition. Southerners, on the other hand, favored free trade because they wanted to import British goods in exchange for the cotton they provided British textile mills.

A series of ingenious political compromises glossed over the fundamental differences between the sections during the first half of the nineteenth century. But abolitionists refused to give up their crusade against slavery. Moreover, a new generation of national political leaders emerged in the 1850s, men from both North and South who were less willing to seek political compromises. The continuing debate over allowing slavery into the new western territories kept sectional tensions at a fever pitch. By the time Abraham Lincoln was elected in 1860, many Americans had decided that the nation could not survive half-slave and half-free; something had to give.

In a desperate effort to preserve the institution of slavery, eleven southern states seceded from the Union and created a separate Confederate nation. This, in turn, prompted northerners such as Lincoln to support a civil war to preserve the Union. No one realized in 1861 how prolonged and costly the war between the states would become. Over 630,000 soldiers and sailors died of wounds or disease. The colossal carnage caused even the most seasoned observers to blanch in disbelief. As President Lincoln confessed in his second inaugural address, no one expected the war to become so "fundamental and astonishing."

Nor did people envision how sweeping the war's effects would be on the future of the nation. The northern victory in 1865 restored the Union and in the process helped to accelerate America's transformation into a modern nation-state. National power and a national consciousness began to displace the sectional emphases of the antebellum era. A Republican-led Congress pushed through legislation to foster industrial and commercial development and western expansion. In the process, the United States began to leave behind the Jeffersonian dream of a decentralized agrarian republic.

The Civil War also ended slavery. Yet the actual status of the 4 million freed blacks remained precarious. How would they fare in a society built upon slavery? In 1865 the daughter of a Georgia planter expressed her concern about such issues when she wrote in her diary that "there are sad changes in store for both races. I wonder the Yankees do not shudder to behold their work" ahead in trying to "reconstruct" the defeated South.

The former slaves found themselves legally free, but most were without property, homes, education, or training. Although the Fourteenth Amendment (1867) set forth guarantees for the civil rights of African Americans and the Fifteen Amendment (1870) provided that black males could vote, local white authorities found shrewd—and often violent—ways to circumvent these new laws.

The restoration of the former Confederate states to the Union did not come easily. Much bitterness and resistance remained among the vanquished. Although Confederate leaders were initially disenfranchised, they continued to exercise considerable authority in political and economic matters. Indeed, in 1877, when the last federal troops were removed from the occupied South, former Confederates declared themselves "redeemed" from the stain of occupation. By the end of the nineteenth century, most states of the former Confederacy had devised a complex system of legal discrimination based on race that re-created many aspects of slavery.

ESSENTIAL THEMES

CRITICAL QUESTIONS

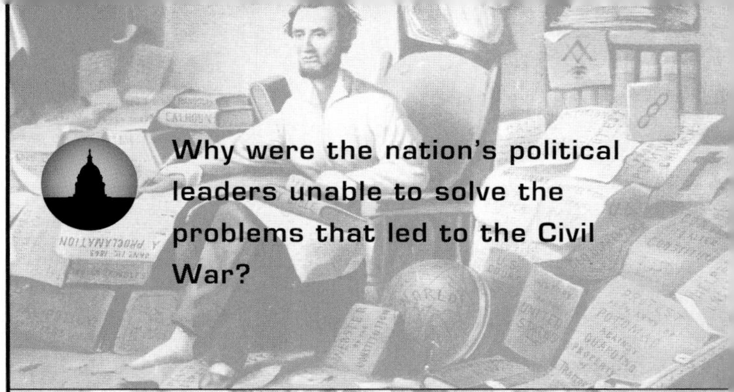

Why were the nation's political leaders unable to solve the problems that led to the Civil War?

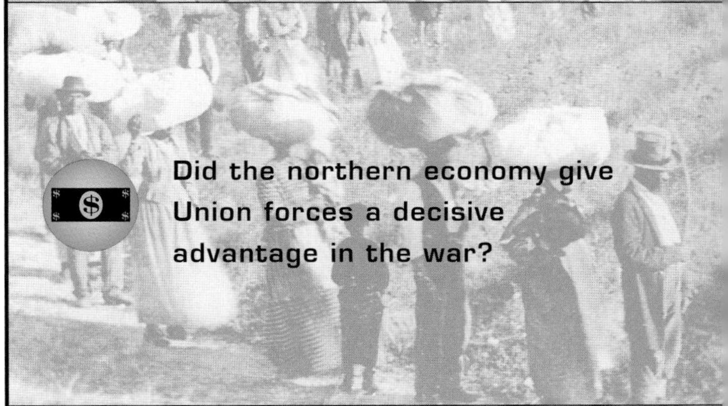

Did the northern economy give Union forces a decisive advantage in the war?

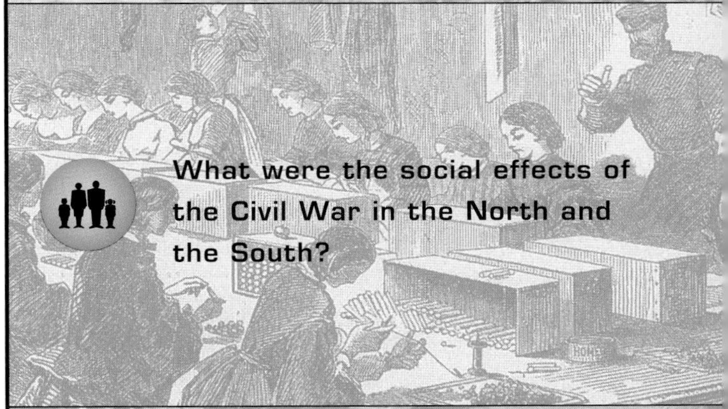

What were the social effects of the Civil War in the North and the South?

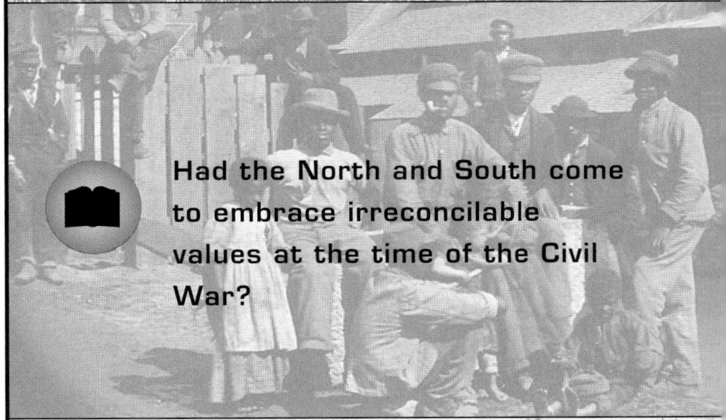

Had the North and South come to embrace irreconcilable values at the time of the Civil War?

What were the most important international implications of the Civil War?

Why were the nation's political leaders unable to solve the problems that led to the Civil War?

CHAPTER 14

The Old South: An American Tragedy

The politics of the slave South

Politics in the white South
Honor and politics
The southern frontier
Antislavery in Congress
The abolitionist movement
Abolitionists petition Congress to end slavery
Black abolitionists: Frederick Douglass and Sojourner Truth

CHAPTER 15

The Crisis of Union

Politicizing slavery: the failure of compromise

The Wilmot Proviso (1846)
Popular sovereignty
The Free Soilers
Compromise of 1850
The Fugitive Slave Act
Emergence of Republican party (1854)
Kansas-Nebraska Act (1854)
"Bleeding" Kansas
"Bully" Brooks
***Dred Scott* v. *Sandford* (1857)**
Lincoln-Douglas debates (1858)
John Brown's raid
Abraham Lincoln elected president (1860)

CHAPTER 16

The War of the Union

The Civil War

Secession (1860–1861)
The outbreak of war
The war's early course
Government during the war
Union politics and civil liberties
Confederate politics
Actions in the Western Theater
McClellan's peninsular campaign
Lincoln issues Emancipation Proclamation (January 1, 1863)
The faltering Confederacy
The Confederacy's defeat
General Lee surrenders, April 9, 1865

CHAPTER 17

Reconstruction: North and South

The battle over Reconstruction

The Radical Republican plan
The Freedmen's Bureau
Andrew Johnson's Reconstruction plan
Johnson's impeachment and trial (1868)
A second revolution: The Thirteenth, Fourteenth, and Fifteenth Amendments
Reconstructing the South
Blacks in southern politics (late 1860s)
Carpetbaggers and scalawags
White terror as a political tool
Conservative resurgence in the South
Ulysses S. Grant elected president (1868)
Scandals and reform
Compromise of 1877

CHAPTER 14

The Old South: An American Tragedy

The economy of the Old South

- **King Cotton**
- **Agricultural diversity**
- **Industry and trade**
- **Slave labor**
- **The economic argument over slavery**

CHAPTER 15

The Crisis of Union

The economic dimension of sectionalism

- **The expansion of slavery**
- **The free labor interest**
- **The gold rush (1849)**
- **Reduced European demand for American grain**
- **The panic of 1857**
- 1860 Republican platform: free homesteads and a transcontinental railroad

CHAPTER 16

The War of the Union

Economic resources North and South

- **The organization of resources**
- **Union finances during the war**
- **Confederate finances during the war**

CHAPTER 17

Reconstruction: North and South

Economic development in the North

- **Northern route for transcontinental railroad**
- **The Morrill Tariff**
- **Morrill Land Grant Act (1862)**
- **Homestead Act (1862)**
- **Devastation in the South**
- Loss of infrastructure
- Damage to agriculture
- Loss of slave labor
- **Government debt in the Grant years**
- **The currency question**

What were the social effects of the Civil War in the North and the South?

CHAPTER 14

The Old South: An American Tragedy

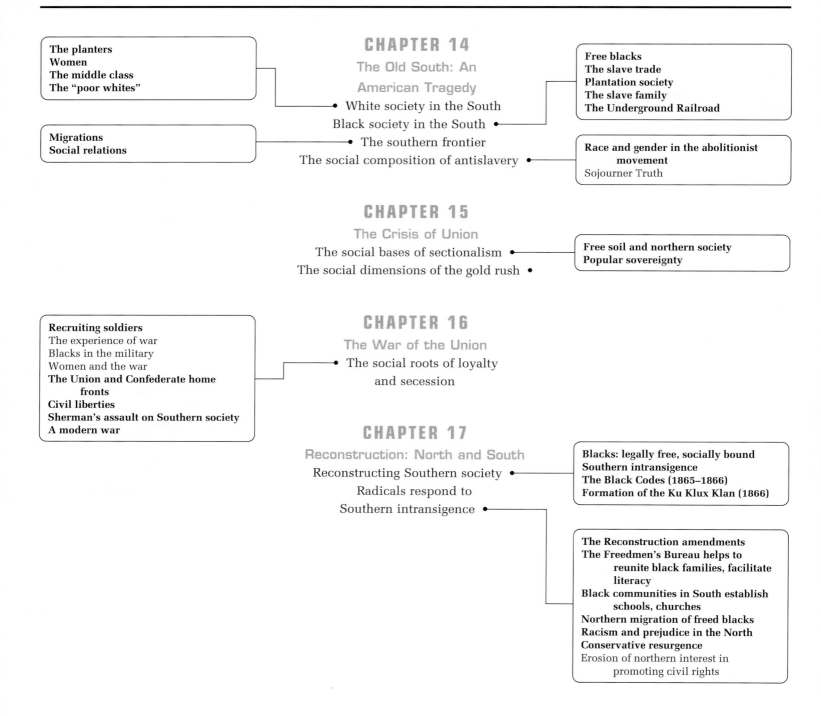

- White society in the South
  - **The planters**
  - **Women**
  - **The middle class**
  - **The "poor whites"**
- Black society in the South
  - **Free blacks**
  - **The slave trade**
  - **Plantation society**
  - **The slave family**
  - **The Underground Railroad**
- The southern frontier
  - **Migrations**
  - **Social relations**
- The social composition of antislavery
  - **Race and gender in the abolitionist movement**
  - Sojourner Truth

CHAPTER 15

The Crisis of Union

- The social bases of sectionalism
  - **Free soil and northern society**
  - **Popular sovereignty**
- The social dimensions of the gold rush

CHAPTER 16

The War of the Union

- The social roots of loyalty and secession
  - **Recruiting soldiers**
  - The experience of war
  - Blacks in the military
  - Women and the war
  - **The Union and Confederate home fronts**
  - **Civil liberties**
  - **Sherman's assault on Southern society**
  - **A modern war**

CHAPTER 17

Reconstruction: North and South

- Reconstructing Southern society
  - **Blacks: legally free, socially bound**
  - **Southern intransigence**
  - **The Black Codes (1865–1866)**
  - **Formation of the Ku Klux Klan (1866)**
- Radicals respond to Southern intransigence
  - **The Reconstruction amendments**
  - **The Freedmen's Bureau helps to reunite black families, facilitate literacy**
  - **Black communities in South establish schools, churches**
  - **Northern migration of freed blacks**
  - **Racism and prejudice in the North**
  - **Conservative resurgence**
  - Erosion of northern interest in promoting civil rights

CHAPTER 14

The Old South: An American Tragedy

- The Old South
  - **The slave community**
  - Language, folklore, and religion among slaves
  - **"Free persons of color"**
  - ***Narrative of the Life of Frederick Douglass* (1845)**
  - **The plantation culture**
  - **The culture of the Southern frontier**

CHAPTER 15

The Crisis of Union

- A culture of extremes
  - **Sectionalism and compromise**
  - **Sectionalism and violence**
  - **The impact of *Uncle Tom's Cabin***
  - **The impact of John Brown's raid**
  - **California's mining camps: a multicultural moment**

CHAPTER 16

The War of the Union

- A culture divides
  - **The justifications for secession**
  - **A clash of cultures**
  - **The impact of emancipation**

CHAPTER 17

Reconstruction: North and South

- Recovering a Nation
  - **The impact of war**
  - **The impact of defeat on the South**
  - **Anarchy and guerilla war on southern frontier (late 1860s)**

What were the most important international implications of the Civil War?

The slave trade
American Colonization Society
Approximately 15,000 blacks migrate to West Africa (Liberia) to escape American slavery
Antislavery as an international movement
Waning of British textile industry (1860)

CHAPTER 14

The Old South: An American Tragedy

The Southern economy and foreign trade

CHAPTER 15

The Crisis of Union

American expansionism and the sectional crisis

Cuba and the expansion of slavery
Diplomacy in the Pacific
Commodore Matthew Perry visits Tokyo (1853)
Harris Convention opens five Japanese ports to American trade (1858)
The international dimension of the gold rush

CHAPTER 16

The War of the Union

The Emancipation Proclamation and alliances abroad
Civil War diplomacy: foreign funding and supply

European trade interests and alliances in the Civil War

CHAPTER 17

Reconstruction: North and South

A new nation: the aftermath of the Civil War

Centralizing political power
Developing the national economy
Harnessing the nation's resources

CHAPTER

14

The Old South: An American Tragedy

This chapter focuses on

- Industry and agriculture in the Old South.
- Southern society, black and white.
- The antislavery movement and southern reactions to it.

THE *ESSENTIAL AMERICA* ON-LINE TUTOR

www.wwnorton.com/eamerica/ch14

- **Topic: The Underground Railroad**
  www.wwnorton.com/eamerica/ch14/topic.htm

  Thousands of black Americans escaped enslavement in the South by following the Underground Railroad to freedom. Explore the Underground Railroad using maps, photographs, drawings, and historical analyses. Who were the principle organizers of the railroad, and how did they insure the safety of those seeking freedom?

- **Chapter review: On-line quiz and chapter summary**
  www.wwnorton.com/eamerica/ch14/review.htm

- **Chapter resources: Multimedia index**
  www.wwnorton.com/eamerica/ch14/media.htm

The South is a region wrapped in enduring myths and stereotypes. The South portrayed in Hollywood films such as *Gone With the Wind* was a stable agrarian society led by paternalistic white planters who lived in white-columned mansions and represented a "natural" aristocracy of virtue and talent within their communities. They were supposedly kind to their slaves and devoted to the rural values of independence and chivalric honor celebrated by Thomas Jefferson.

By contrast, the darker myth about the Old South emerged from abolitionist pamphlets and Harriet Beecher Stowe's best-selling novel *Uncle Tom's Cabin*. These exposés of southern culture portrayed the planters as arrogant autocrats who raped slave women, brutalized slave workers, and lorded over their communities with haughty disdain for the rights and needs of others.

Such contrasting myths died hard, in large part because they are each rooted in reality. Nonetheless, efforts to get at what really set the Old South apart from the rest of the nation generally turn on two lines of thought: the impact of environment (geography and climate) and the effects of human decisions and actions. The South's warm, humid weather fostered the growing of commercial crops, and thus led to the plantation system and slavery. These developments in turn brought sectional conflict and civil war.

Distinctive Features of the Old South

While geography was a key determinant of southern life, explanations that involve human action are more persuasive. In the 1830s, many observers located the origins of southern distinctiveness in the institution of racial slavery. The resolve of whites to maintain such a system muted class conflict. Yet the biracial character of the population influenced other aspects of life. In shaping patterns of speech and folklore, of music and literature, black southerners immeasurably influenced and enriched the region's culture.

The South differed from other sections of the country in that it drew few European immigrants after the Revolution. One reason was that the main shipping lines went to northern ports; another, that immigrants balked at the prospect of competing with slave labor. After the Missouri Controversy of 1819–1821, the South became more and more a self-consciously minority region, its population growth lagging behind that of other sections, its "peculiar institution" of slavery more and more an isolated and odious anachronism.

The South also differed in its hypermasculine culture. Southern men displayed a penchant for fighting, for guns, and for the military. The preponderance of farming also remained a distinctive southern characteristic, whether pictured as the Jeffersonian yeoman living by the sweat of his brow or the lordly planter dispatching his slave gangs. But in the end, what made the South so distinctive was the widespread assumption that it *was* distinctive.

Agricultural Diversity

The focus on King Cotton and other cash crops such as rice and sugar cane has obscured the degree to which the South fed itself from its own fields. Corn grew everywhere, but it went less into the market than into local consumption, as feed and fodder, as hoecake and grits. On many farms and plantations, the rhythms of the growing season permitted the labor force to alternate attention between the commercial staples and the food crops. Livestock added to the diversity of the farm economy.

Yet the picture was hardly one of unbroken prosperity. The South's staple crops (cotton, sugarcane, tobacco) quickly exhausted the soil, and open-row crops such as tobacco, cotton, and corn left the bare ground in between subject to erosion. By 1860, much of eastern Virginia had aban-

Planting sweet potatoes on the Hopkinson plantation, Edisto Island, South Carolina, April 1862.

doned tobacco and in some places had turned to growing wheat for the northern market. The older farming lands had trouble competing with the newer soils farther west, but soon western lands too began to lose their nutrients. So the Southeast and then the Old Southwest faced a growing sense of economic crisis as the nineteenth century advanced.

By 1840, many thoughtful southerners reasoned that by staking everything on agriculture the region had wasted opportunities in manufacturing and trade. After the War of 1812, as cotton growing swept everything before it, the South became increasingly dependent on northern manufacturing and commerce. Cotton and tobacco were exported mainly in northern vessels. Southerners also relied on connections in the North for imported goods. The South became, economically if not formally, a kind of colonial dependency of the North.

White Society in the South

If an understanding of the Old South must begin with a knowledge of potent social myths, it must end with a sense of tragedy. White southerners had won short-term economic gains at the cost of both lagging social development and moral isolation in the eyes of the world. The concentration on land and slaves, as well as the paucity of cities and immigrants, deprived the South of dynamic bases of economic and social innovation. The slaveholding South hitched its wagon to the European demand for cotton. The only perceived threat to "King Cotton" was the growing antislavery sentiment in the North. The unperceived threat was an imminent slackening of the world cotton market. The heyday of expansion in British textiles ended by 1860, but by then the Deep South was locked into cotton production for generations to come.

The Planters

During the first half of the nineteenth century, wealth in the South was increasingly concentrated in the hands of the planter elite. Although great plantations were relatively few in number, they set the tone of economic and social life in the South. What distinguished the plantation from the farm, in addition to its size, was the use of a large slave labor force, managed by overseers. A clear-cut distinction between management and labor set the planter apart from the small slaveholder, who often worked side by side with slaves at the same tasks.

If, to be called a planter, one had to own twenty slaves, only 1 out of every 30 whites in the South in 1860 was a planter. Fewer than 11,000 planters, however, owned fifty or more slaves, and the owners of over one hundred slaves numbered 2,292. The census listed only 11 planters with five hundred slaves and just 1 with as many as one thousand slaves. Yet this privileged elite tended to think of its class interest as synonymous with the interest of the entire South.

The planter group, less than 4 percent of the adult white males in the South, owned more than half the slaves and produced most of the cotton and tobacco and all of the sugar and rice. In a white population numbering just over 8 million in 1860, the total number of slaveholders was only 383,637. But assuming that each family numbered five people, the whites with some proprietary interest in slavery came to 1.9 million, or roughly one-fourth of the South's white population. While the preponderance of southern whites belonged to the small-farmer class, the presumptions of the planters were seldom challenged. In part, such deference reflected the desire of many small farmers to become planters themselves. Over time, however, land and slave prices soared, thereby narrowing prospects for upward social mobility. Between 1830 and 1860, the Cotton Belt witnessed a growing concentration of wealth in the hands of a slaveholding elite.

White women reinforced the plantation slave system. The plantation "mistress" supervised the domestic household in the same way her husband took care of the business: overseeing food, linens, housecleaning, the care of the sick, and a hundred other details. While plantation wives also enjoyed entertaining and being entertained, they owed their genteel circumstances to the domestic services provided by slaves.

White women living within a slave-owning culture confronted a double standard in terms of moral and sexual behavior. While they were expected to be models of Christian piety and sexual discretion, their husbands, brothers, and sons enjoyed greater latitude. Many white planters and their sons viewed slave women not only as sources of labor but also as sources of sexual satisfaction.

The Middle Class

Overseers on the largest plantations generally came from the middle class of small farmers or skilled workers (artisans), or were younger sons of planters. Most wanted to become slaveholders themselves, and sometimes they rose to that status, but others were constantly on the move in search of better positions. Occasionally there were black overseers, but the highest management position to which a slave could aspire was usually that of "driver" or leader, placed in charge of a small group of slaves.

The most numerous white southerners were the yeoman farm families, who lived in modest two-room cabins. They raised a few hogs and chickens, grew some corn and cotton, and traded with neighbors more than with stores. Women and children worked in the fields during harvest time, but most of their days were spent attending to domestic chores. Many of these "middling" farmers owned a handful of slaves, but most owned none.

Small farmers in the South were typically mobile folk, willing to pull up stakes and move west or southwest in pursuit of better land. They tended to be fiercely independent, easily provoked, and suspicious of government authority, and they overwhelmingly identified with the party of Andrew Jackson and the spiritual fervor of evangelical Protestantism. Even though only a minority of the middle-class farmers owned slaves, most of them supported the slave system. They feared that the slaves, if freed, would compete with them for land, and they also enjoyed the "superior" status that racially based slavery afforded them. Such sentiments pervaded the border states as well as the Deep South. Kentucky, for example, held a popular referendum on the issue of slavery in 1849, and the voters, most of whom owned no slaves, resoundingly endorsed the slave system.

Honor and Violence in the Old South

From colonial times, most southern white males prided themselves on adhering to a moral code centered on a prickly sense of honor. The dominant ethical code for the southern white elite included a combative sensitivity to slights, loyalty to family, locality, state, and region, deference to elders and social "betters," and an almost theatrical hospitality. It manifested itself in a fierce defense of female purity and a propensity to magnify personal insults into capital offenses.

Southern white women were the object of masculine chivalry and the subjects of male rule. The mythic southern "lady" was placed on a pedestal celebrating domestic devotion. While men cultivated and defended their *honor*, women paraded and protected their *virtue*. The southern lady presided over the morals and manners of the household—while submitting to patriarchal authority. She subordinated her own individuality in order to serve her husband and children. A southern lady, according to the prevailing standard, was to remain sexually pure, spiritually pious, and domestically submissive—all while she managed the household.

Southern men were preoccupied with an often reckless manliness. As a northern traveler observed, "the central trait of the 'chivalrous southerner' is an intense respect for virility." The duel constituted the ultimate public expression of personal honor and manly courage. Although not confined to the South, dueling was much more common there than in the rest of the young nation, a fact that gave rise to the observation that southerners will be polite until they are angry enough to kill you.

Many of the most prominent southern leaders engaged in duels—congressmen, senators, governors, editors, and planters. The roster of participants included Andrew Jackson, Henry Clay, Sam Houston, and Jefferson Davis. A dueling society, southerners assumed in the early nineteenth century, was a more polite—and honorable—society.

So many duels and deaths occurred in the South that "anti-dueling societies" emerged to lobby against the social ritual. Most states outlawed the practice, but to little avail. As a grand jury in Savannah, Georgia, noted in 1819, "the frequent violations of the law to prevent dueling have made the practice fashionable and almost meritorious among its chivalrous advocates." Judges were reluctant to punish their fellow "gentlemen" for upholding their honor. It was not until after the Civil War that dueling fell into widespread disgrace and began a rapid decline. Humorist Mark Twain deserves the last word: "I thoroughly disapprove of duels. If a man should challenge me, I would take him kindly and forgivingly by the hand and lead him to a quiet place and kill him."

Black Society in the South

Slavery was one of the fastest growing elements of American life during the first half of the nineteenth century. In 1790 there had been less than 700,000 slaves in the United States. By 1830 there were more than 2 million, and by 1860 there were almost 4 million. Although they all suffered the injustices of white racism, African Americans had diverse experiences in the United States, depending upon their geographic location and the nature of their working and living conditions.

"Free Persons of Color"

Not all blacks were slaves. In the Old South, "free persons of color" occupied an uncertain status, balanced somewhere between slavery and freedom, subject to legal restrictions not imposed on whites. Over the years, some slaves were able to purchase their freedom, while some gained freedom as a reward for service in American wars. Others were simply freed by concerned masters.

By 1830, there were 319,000 free blacks in the United States, about 150,000 of whom lived in the South. The free persons of color included a large number of mulattoes, people of mixed white and black ancestry, some of whom built substantial fortunes and even became slaveholders. In Louisiana a mulatto bought an estate with ninety-one slaves for $250,000.

But black slaveholders were a tiny minority. The 1830 census revealed that only

3,775 free blacks owned 12,760 slaves. Although most of these black slave owners were in the South, some also lived in Rhode Island, Connecticut, Illinois, New Jersey, New York, and the border states. Some blacks owned slaves for humanitarian purposes. One minister, for instance, bought slaves and then enabled them to purchase their freedom from him on easy terms. Most often, black slaveholders were free blacks who bought their own family members with the express purpose of later freeing them. But some blacks engaged in slavery for purely selfish rather than humanitarian reasons. Like their white counterparts, they participated in slave auctions and advertised for the return of runaways.

Free blacks were often skilled artisans (blacksmiths, carpenters, cobblers), farmers, or common laborers. The increase in their numbers slowed as legislatures put more and more restrictions on the right to free slaves, but by 1860 there were 262,000 free blacks in the slave states, a little over half the national total of 488,000. They were most numerous in the upper South and tended to congregate in urban areas.

Free blacks were victims of widespread discrimination. All southern states required them to carry identification passes. Whites often fraudulently claimed that a free black was in fact one of their runaway slaves, and if the African American did not have an official certificate of freedom, he could be enslaved. In many other ways, free blacks were not truly "free." Most southern states prohibited them from voting. Blacks were not allowed to testify in court against whites, and they could not hold church services without the presence of a white minister.

The Trade in Slaves

When the African slave trade was outlawed in 1808, it only added to the value of those slaves already present. The rise in slave value often brought better treatment. "Massa was purty good," one ex-slave recalled later. "He treated us jus' 'bout like you would a good mule." Some owners hired wage laborers, often Irish immigrants, for ditching and other dangerous work rather than risk the lives of the more valuable slaves.

The end of the foreign slave trade gave rise to a flourishing domestic trade, with slaves being moved mainly from the used-up lands of the Southeast into the booming new country of the Old Southwest. Many slaves moved south and west with their owners, but there also developed an organized business with brokers, slave pens, and auctioneers. The worst aspect of the slave trade was its breakup of families.

Plantation Slavery

More than half of all slaves in 1860 worked on plantations, and most of those were fieldhands. The preferred jobs were those of household servants and skilled workers, including blacksmiths, carpenters, and coopers. Fieldhands worked long hours from dawn to dusk and were usually housed in one- or two-room wooden shacks with dirt floors, some without windows. Based on detailed records from eleven plantations in the lower South, scholars have calculated that more than half of all slave babies died in the first year of life, a mortality rate more than twice that of white infants.

The difference between a good owner and a bad one, according to one ex-slave, was the difference between one who did not "whip too much" and one who "whipped till he bloodied you and blistered you." A slave's ultimate recourse was rebellion or flight, but most recognized the futility of such measures, with whites wielding the

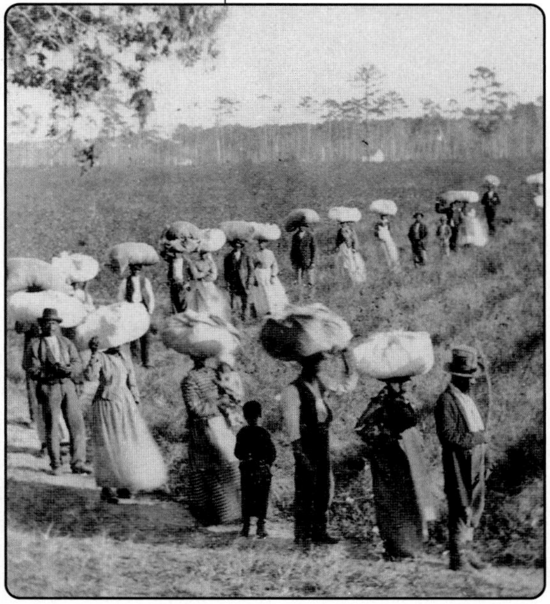

African Americans return from laboring in the South Carolina cotton fields.

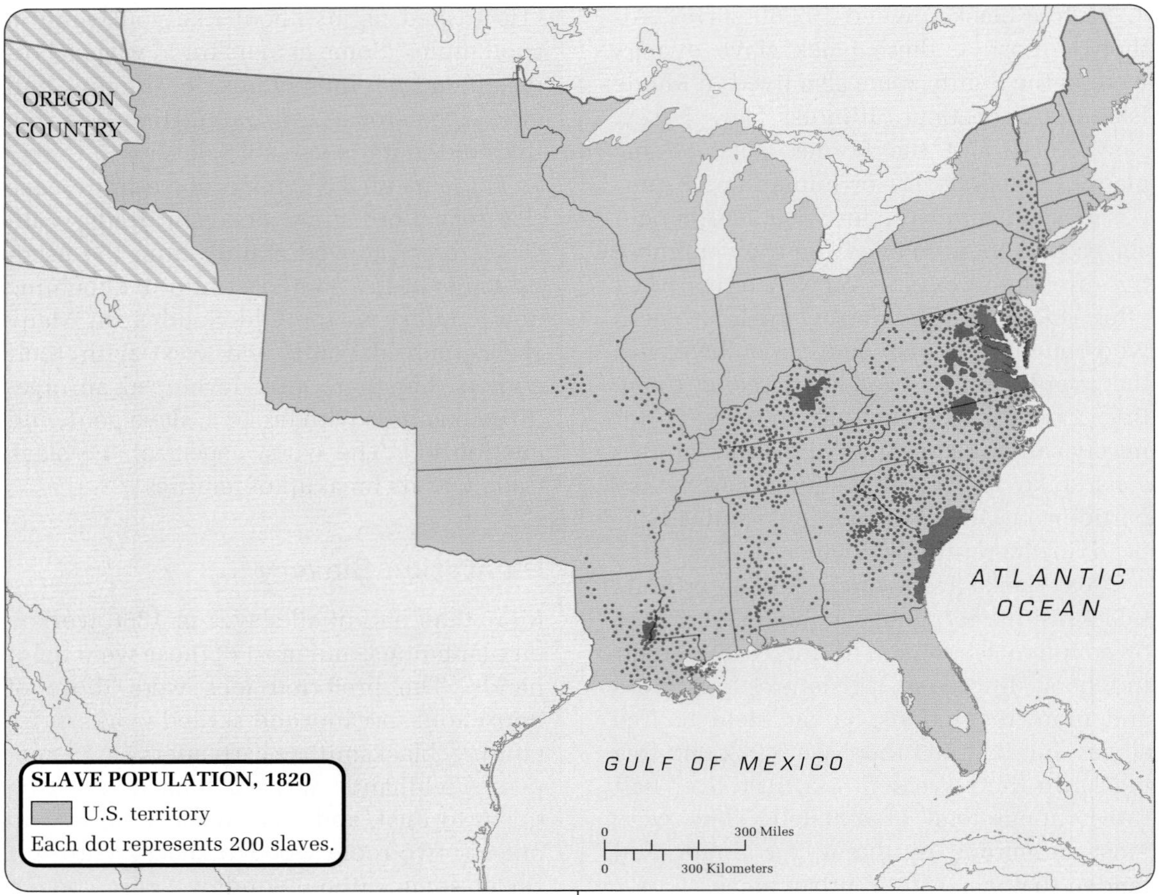

power and weapons. In the nineteenth century only three slave insurrections drew much notice, and two of those were betrayed before they got under way.

Only the Nat Turner insurrection of 1831 in rural Virginia got beyond the planning stage. Turner, a black overseer, was also a religious exhorter who professed a divine mission in leading the rebellion. The revolt began when a small group killed Turner's master's family and set off down the road repeating the process at other farmhouses, where other slaves joined in. Before it ended, at least fifty-five whites had been killed. Eventually trials resulted in seventeen hangings and seven deportations. The Virginia militia, for its part, killed large numbers of slaves indiscriminately in the process of putting down the rebels.

Forging the Slave Community

The slave experience could be as varied as people are. Slaves were victims, but to stop with so obvious a perception would be to miss an important story of endurance and achievement. If ever there was a melting pot in American history, the most effective may have been that in which Africans from a variety of ethnic, linguistic, and tribal origins fused into a new community and a new culture as African Americans.

Among the most important manifestations of slave culture was its religion, a mixture of African and Christian elements. Most Africans brought with them a concept of a Creator, or Supreme God, whom they could recognize in Jehovah, and lesser gods whom they might identify with Christ, the Holy

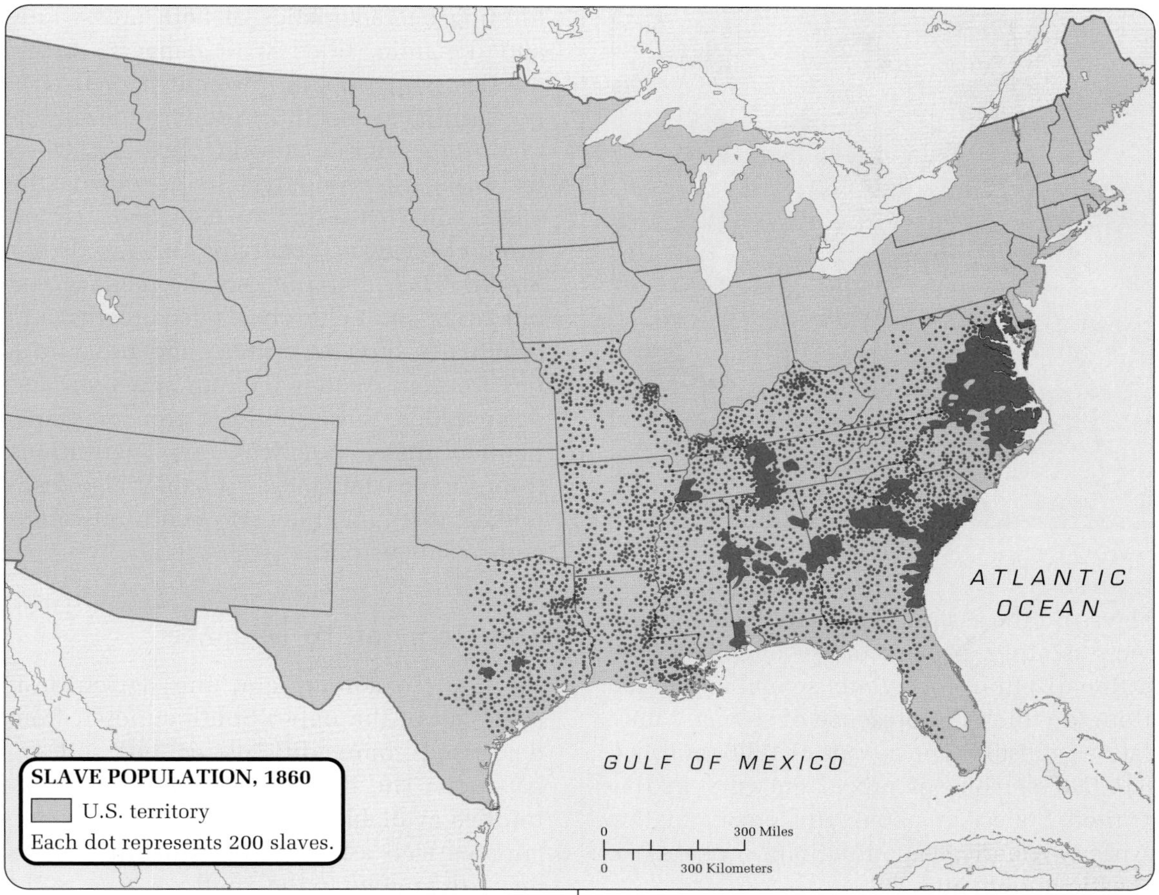

Ghost, and the saints, thereby reconciling their earlier beliefs with the new Christian religion. Alongside the church, they also retained African beliefs in spirits, magic spells and herbs, and conjuring (the practice of healing and warding off evil spirits). Belief in magic is a common human response to conditions of danger or helplessness.

Slaves, however, found greater comfort in the church. There they could find both balm for the soul and release for their emotions, and they brought with them from Africa a demonstrative spirituality. Some owners openly encouraged religious meetings among their slaves, but those who were denied the open use of "praise houses" held "bush meetings" in secret. The preachers and exhorters who sprang up in the slave world commonly won the acceptance of the owners, if only because efforts to get rid of them proved futile. The peculiar cadences of their exhortations, chants, and spirituals have produced music of great rhythmic complexity, forms of dance and body language, and folk tales.

The Slave Family

Slave marriages had no legal status, but slave owners generally accepted marriage as a stabilizing influence on the plantation. Most slave children were socialized into their culture through the nuclear family, which afforded some degree of independence from white influence. Slaves were not always allowed to realize this norm. In some cases, the matter of family arrangements was ignored or left entirely up to the

Lynchburg Negro Dance, 1853. Slaves successfully maintained some aspects of their African culture, incorporating it into their religion, music, and dance.

slaves on the assumption that black females were simply promiscuous—a convenient rationalization for white sexual exploitation, to which the presence of so many mulattoes attested. The census of 1860 reported 412,000 persons of mixed ancestry in the United States, or about 10 percent of the African-American population, probably a drastic undercount.

The Culture of the Southern Frontier

Despite enduring myths to the contrary, there was substantial social and cultural diversity within the South during the three decades before the Civil War. The antebellum southern frontier, for example, was a quite different region from the more settled areas in the states along the Atlantic seaboard. Of all the many frontiers that have combined to produce a distinctive American culture, the Old Southwest is perhaps the least well known. It included the states and territories west of Georgia—Alabama, Mississippi, Louisiana, Texas, and Arkansas—as well as the frontier areas in Tennessee, Kentucky, and Florida.

Largely unsettled until the 1820s, this region bridged the South and the West, exhibiting characteristics of both areas. Raw and dynamic, filled with dangers, uncertainties, and opportunities, it served as a powerful magnet, luring thousands of settlers from Virginia and the Carolinas when the seaboard economy faltered during the 1820s and 1830s. By the 1830s, most cotton production was occurring in the lower South. The migrating southerners carved out farms, built churches, raised towns, and eventually brought culture and order to a raw frontier. As they took up new lives and occupations, these southern pioneers transplanted many practices and institutions from the coastal states. But they also fashioned a distinctly new set of cultural values and social customs.

The Decision to Migrate

By the Jacksonian era, the agricultural economy of the upper South suffered from depressed commodity prices and soil exhaustion. The dwindling economic opportunities available in the Carolinas and Virginia as well as restrictive kinship ties led many to migrate to the Southwest.

Like their northern counterparts, restless sons of the southern planter and professional elite wanted to make it on their own, to be "self-made men," economically self-reliant and socially independent. To them, speculative profit-seeking was more enticing than family stability. A North Carolinian expected to "rise and soar like an eagle" in the Southwest because he would be freed from the strictures of his family circle, which he perceived as holding him back.

Women were underrepresented among migrants to the Old Southwest. Most dreaded the thought of taking up life on a disease-ridden, violent, and primitive frontier. The new region did not offer them independence or adventure. They would remain part of a patriarchal culture in either area. And their never-ending routine of domestic tasks would only increase in the frontier environment. In general, women regretted more than men the loss of kinship ties that migration would entail. To them a stable family life was more important than the prospect of material gain.

Slaves had many of the same reservations about moving west. Almost a million captive African Americans joined in the migration to the Southwest during the antebellum era, most of them making the journey in the 1830s. Like white women, they feared the harsh working conditions and torpid heat and humidity of the Southwest. They also were despondent at the breaking of their family ties.

Journey and Settlement

Most of the migrants to the Southwest headed for the fertile lands of Alabama, Mississippi, and central Tennessee. The typical trek was about 500 miles long. Along rough roads and trails, the pioneers averaged about fifteen miles per day, occasionally staying overnight in taverns, more often camping in the open amid panthers, bears, and wolves. At times the route was clogged with people. Slaves traveled on foot, tied or chained together. Many drowned while fording rivers.

Once in the Southwest, the pioneers bought land that had been appropriated from the Indians. Parcels of 640 acres sold for as little as two dollars an acre. Land in Alabama's black belt (named for the color of the soil) brought higher prices. As cotton prices soared in the 1830s, aspiring planters bought as much land and as many slaves as possible. As a result, the average size of farms and plantations in the Southwest was larger than that in the Carolinas and Virginia.

But the Old Southwest was much more unhealthy than the Carolina Piedmont. The hot climate, contaminated water, and poor sanitation combined to unleash an epidemic of diseases on the new settlers and their slaves. Malaria was especially common. Life in tents and rude log cabins made many newcomers yearn for the material comforts they had left behind. Many decided to return home or move farther west.

Antislavery Movements

Early Opposition to Slavery

Scattered criticism of slavery developed in the North and the South in the decades after the Revolution, but the emancipation movement accelerated with the formation of the American Colonization Society in 1817. The society proposed to resettle freed slaves in Africa. Its supporters included prominent figures such as James Madison, James Monroe, Henry Clay, John Marshall, and Daniel Webster. Some backed it as an antislavery group, while others saw it as a way to bolster slavery by getting rid of potentially troublesome free blacks. Many in the free black community denounced it from the start. A group of free blacks in Philadelphia, for example, stressed in 1817 that they had "no wish to separate from our present homes for any purpose whatever." America, they insisted, was now their native land.

Nevertheless, in 1821 agents of the society acquired from local chieftains in West Africa a parcel of land that became the nucleus of a new country. In 1822 the first freed slaves arrived there, and twenty-five years later the society relinquished control to the independent republic of Liberia. But given its uncertain purpose, the coloniza-

Several generations of a family raised in slavery. Plantation of J. J. Smith, Beaufort, South Carolina, 1862.

William Lloyd Garrison.

tion movement received only meager support from either antislavery or proslavery elements. By 1860, only about 15,000 blacks had migrated to Africa, approximately 12,000 with the help of the Colonization Society. The number was infinitesimal compared to the number of slave births in the United States.

From Gradualism to Abolitionism

Meanwhile, in the early 1830s the antislavery movement took a new departure. In 1831 William Lloyd Garrison began publication in Boston of a new antislavery newspaper, *The Liberator*. In 1832 Garrison and his followers set up the New England Anti-Slavery Society. A year later two wealthy New York merchants, Arthur and Lewis Tappan, founded a similar group in their state. They then helped start a national organization called the American Anti-Slavery Society, with Garrison and others. They hoped to build on the publicity gained by the British antislavery movement, which in 1833 had induced Parliament to end slavery, with compensation to slaveholders, throughout the British Empire. The American Anti-Slavery Society called for immediate emancipation and argued that blacks should "share an equality with the whites, of civil and religious privileges." The group issued a barrage of propaganda for its cause, including periodicals, tracts, agents, lecturers, organizers, and fund-raisers.

The Movement Splits

As the antislavery movement spread, debates over tactics intensified. The Garrisonians, mainly New Englanders, were radicals who felt that American society had been corrupted from top to bottom. Garrison embraced every important reform movement of the day: antislavery, temperance, pacifism, and women's rights. Deeply affected by the perfectionism of the times, he refused to compromise principle for expediency, to sacrifice one reform for another. Abolition was not enough. He opposed colonization of freed slaves and stood for equal rights. He broke with the organized church, which to his mind was in league with slavery. The federal government was all the more so. The Constitution, he said, was "a covenant with death and an agreement with hell." Garrison therefore refused to vote. He was, however, prepared to collaborate with those who did or with those who disagreed with him on other matters.

Other reformers saw American society as fundamentally sound and concentrated their attention on purging it of slavery. Most of these abolitionists were evangelical Christians, and they promoted pragmatic political organization as the best instrument of reform. Garrison struck them as an impractical fanatic.

A showdown came in 1840 on the issue of women's rights. Women had joined the abolition movement from the start, but quietly and largely in groups without men. The activities of the Grimké sisters brought the issue of women's rights to center stage. Sarah and Angelina Grimké, daughters of a prominent slave-owning family in South Carolina, had broken with their parents and moved north to embrace Quakerism, antislavery, and feminism. They set out speaking to women in New England and slowly widened their audiences to include both men and women.

Such unseemly behavior inspired male leaders to chastise the Grimké sisters and other women activists for engaging in "unfeminine" activity. Angelina Grimké stoutly rejected such conventional arguments. "It is a woman's right," she insisted, "to have a voice in all laws and regulations by which she is to be governed, whether in church or in state."

This debate over the role of women in the antislavery movement crackled and simmered until it finally exploded in 1840. At the American Anti-Slavery Society's annual meeting, the Garrisonians insisted on the right of women to participate equally in the organization, and they carried their point. They did not commit the group to women's rights in any other way, however. Contrary opinion ranged from outright antifeminism to simple fear of scattering shots over too many reforms. The New Yorkers broke away to form the American and Foreign Anti-Slavery Society.

Black Antislavery Activity

White male antislavery activists also balked at granting full recognition to black abolitionists of either sex. Often blindly patronizing, white leaders expected free blacks to take a back seat in the movement. Blacks became exasperated at whites' tendency to value purity over results, to strike a moral posture at the expense of action. Despite the invitation to form separate black groups, black leaders were active in the white societies from the beginning. Three attended the organizational meeting of the American Anti-Slavery Society in 1833, and some became outstanding agents for the movement, notably the former slaves who could speak from firsthand experience.

Among the black abolitionists, one of the most effective was Sojourner Truth. Born in New York State in 1797, the daughter of slaves owned by a Dutch-American family, she was given the name Isabella. She renamed herself in 1843 after experiencing a mystical conversation with God, who told her "to travel up and down the land" preaching the sins of slavery. She did just that, crisscrossing the country during the 1840s and 1850s, exhorting audiences to support abolitionism and women's rights. Having been a slave until she fled to freedom in 1827, Sojourner Truth was able to speak with added conviction and knowledge about the evils of the "peculiar institution" and the inequality of women. As she reportedly told a gathering of the Ohio Women's Rights Convention in 1851, "I have plowed, and planted, and gathered into barns, and no man could head me—and ar'n't I a woman? I have borne thirteen children, and seen 'em mos' all sold off into slavery, and when I cried out with a mother's grief, none but Jesus heard—and ar'n't I a woman?" Through such compelling testimony, Sojourner Truth demonstrated the powerful intersection of abolitionism and women's rights agitation, and in the process she tapped the distinctive energies that women brought to reformist causes.

An equally gifted black abolitionist was Frederick Douglass of Maryland. Blessed with an imposing frame and a simple eloquence, he became the best-known black man in America. "I appear before the immense assembly this evening as a thief and a robber," he told a Massachusetts group in 1842. "I stole this head, these limbs, this body from my master, and ran off with them." Fearful of capture after publishing his *Narrative of the Life of Frederick Douglass* (1845), he left for an extended lecture tour of the British Isles and returned two years later with enough money to purchase his freedom. He then started an abolitionist newspaper for blacks, the *North Star*, in Rochester, New York.

Douglass's *Narrative* was the best known among several thousand such accounts. Escapees often made it out on their own—Douglass borrowed a pass from a free black seaman—but many were aided by the Underground Railroad, which grew in legend into a vast system to conceal runaways and spirit them to freedom, often over the Canadian border. Actually, there seems to have been more spontaneity than system about the matter, and blacks contributed more than was credited in the legend.

Sojourner Truth (*top*) and Frederick Douglass (*bottom*) were both leading abolitionists.

Reactions to Antislavery

In the 1830s abolitionism took a political turn, focusing at first on Congress. One shrewd strategy was to deluge Congress with petitions calling for the abolition of slavery in the nation's capital, the District of Columbia. Most such petitions were presented by former president John Quincy Adams, elected to the House from Massachusetts in 1830. In 1836, however, the House adopted a rule to lay abolition petitions automatically on the table, in effect ignoring them. Adams, "Old Man Eloquent," stubbornly fought this "gag rule" as a violation of the First Amendment and hounded its supporters until the gag rule was finally repealed in 1844.

Meanwhile, in 1840, the year of the schism in the antislavery movement, a small group of abolitionists called a convention in Albany, New York, and launched the Liberty party, with James G. Birney, one-time slaveholder from Alabama and Kentucky, as its candidate for president. In the 1840 election, Birney polled only 7,000 votes, but in 1844 his total rose to 60,000, and from that time forth an antislavery party contested every national election until Abraham Lincoln won the presidency in 1860.

The Defense of Slavery

Birney was but one among a number of southerners propelled north during the 1830s by the South's growing hostility to emancipationist ideas. Antislavery in the upper South had its last stand in 1831–1832, when the Virginia legislature debated a plan of gradual emancipation and colonization, then rejected it by a vote of 73 to 58. Thereafter, southern partisans worked out an elaborate intellectual defense of slavery, presenting it as a positive good.

The evangelical Christian churches, which had widely condemned slavery at one time, gradually turned proslavery, at least in the South. Ministers of all denominations joined in the argument. Had not Saint Paul advised servants to obey their masters and told a fugitive servant to return to his master? And had not Jesus remained silent on the subject, at least so far as the Gospels reported his words? In 1843–1844 disputes over slavery split two great denominations along sectional lines and led to the formation of the proslavery Southern Baptist Convention and Methodist Episcopal Church, South. Presbyterians, the only other major denomination to split, did not divide until the Civil War.

A more fundamental feature of the proslavery argument stressed the intrinsic inferiority of blacks. Other arguments took a more "practical" view of slavery. Not only was slavery profitable, ran one line of argument, it was a matter of social necessity. Jefferson, for instance, in his *Notes on Virginia* (1785), had argued that emancipated slaves and whites could not live together without risk of race war growing out of the recollection of past injustices. What is more, it seemed clear that blacks could not be expected to work if freed. They were too shiftless and improvident, it was believed.

In his books *Sociology for the South; or, The Failure of a Free Society* (1854) and *Cannibals All! or, Slaves Without Masters* (1857), George Fitzhugh of Virginia argued that slavery provided security for the black workers in sickness and old age, whereas workers in the North were exploited for profit and then cast aside. People were not born equal, he insisted. Fitzhugh argued for an organic, hierarchical society, much like the family, in which each had a place with both rights and obligations.

Within one generation, such ideas had triumphed in the white South over the post-Revolutionary apology for slavery as an evil bequeathed by the forefathers. Opponents of the orthodox faith in slavery as a positive good were either silenced or exiled. Freedom of thought in the Old South had become a victim of the nation's growing obsession with slavery.

CHAPTER

15

The Crisis of Union

This chapter focuses on

- The politicization of slavery.
- How the Compromise of 1850 and the Kansas-Nebraska Act reflected sectional tensions.
- The rise of a new party system: Republicans and Democrats.
- The specific events that led to the secession of the southern states.

THE *ESSENTIAL AMERICA* ON-LINE TUTOR

www.wwnorton.com/eamerica/ch15

- **Topic: John Brown's raid on the federal arsenal at Harper's Ferry**
  www.wwnorton.com/eamerica/ch15/topic.htm

  In October of 1859 John Brown shocked many Americans when he led a raid on the Federal arsenal at Harper's Ferry, Virginia. Examine Brown's raid on Harper's Ferry using photographs, newspaper accounts, comments by Brown's contemporaries, and historical analyses. What significance did Brown's actions have for black Americans, and how did the white population view his raid?

- **Chapter review: On-line quiz and chapter summary**
  www.wwnorton.com/eamerica/ch15/review.htm

- **Chapter resources: Multimedia index**
  www.wwnorton.com/eamerica/ch15/media.htm

Wars have a way of corrupting ideals and breeding new wars, often in unforeseen ways. For example, America's victory over Mexico and acquisition of territory gave rise to quarrels over the newly acquired lands. These quarrels set in motion a series of political disputes that would culminate in a crisis of union.

Slavery in the Territories

The Wilmot Proviso

The Mexican War was less than three months old when the seeds of a new conflict began to sprout. On August 8, 1846, a freshman Democrat from Pennsylvania, David Wilmot, stood up in the House of Representatives to discuss President Polk's request for $2 million to expedite negotiations with Mexico. Wilmot favored territorial expansion, even the annexation of Texas as a slave state. But he proposed that in lands acquired from Mexico, "neither slavery nor involuntary servitude shall ever exist in any part of said territory."

Within ten minutes an otherwise obscure congressman had immortalized his name. The Wilmot Proviso politicized slavery once and for all. Since the Missouri Controversy of 1819–1821, the issue of slavery in new territories had been lurking in the wings, kept there most of the time by politicians who feared its disruptive force. But for the two decades following Wilmot's proposal the question would never be far from center stage.

The House adopted the Wilmot Proviso, but the Senate balked. When Congress reconvened in December 1846, Polk prevailed on Wilmot to withhold his amendment, but by then others were ready to take up the cause. When a New York congressman revived the proviso, he signaled a revolt by the Van Burenites in concert with the antislavery forces of the North. Once again the House approved the amendment; again the Senate refused. The House finally gave up, but in one form or another Wilmot's idea kept being revived. Abraham Lincoln recalled that during one term as congressman, 1847–1849, he voted for it "as good as forty times."

South Carolina Senator John C. Calhoun meanwhile devised a thesis to counter the proviso, and he set it before the Senate in four resolutions on February 19, 1847. The Calhoun Resolutions, which never came to a vote, argued that since the territories were the common possession of the states, Congress had no right to prevent citizens from taking slaves into them. To do so would violate the Fifth Amendment, which forbade Congress to deprive any person of life, liberty, or property without due process of law, and slaves were property. By this clever stroke of logic, Calhoun took the basic guarantee of liberty, the Bill of Rights, and turned it into a basic guarantee of slavery. The irony was not lost on his critics, but the point became established southern dogma—echoed by his colleagues and formally endorsed by the Virginia legislature.

Senator Thomas Hart Benton of Missouri, himself a slaveholder but also a Jacksonian nationalist, found in Calhoun's resolutions a set of abstractions "leading to no result." Wilmot and Calhoun between them, he said, had fashioned a pair of shears. Neither blade alone would cut very well, but joined together they could sever the ties of union.

Popular Sovereignty

Many others, like Benton, refused to be polarized, seeking to bypass the brewing conflict. President Polk was among the first to suggest extending the Missouri Compromise dividing free and slave territory at latitude 36°30′ all the way to the Pacific. Senator Lewis Cass of Michigan, an ardent Whig expansionist, suggested that the citizens of a territory "regulate their own internal concerns" like the citizens of a state. Such an approach would combine the merits of expediency and democracy. It would take the issue out of the national arena and put it in the hands of those directly affected.

Popular sovereignty, or squatter sovereignty, as the idea was also called, had much to commend it. Without directly challenging the slaveholders' access to the new lands, it promised to open them quickly to non-slaveholding farmers who would almost surely dominate the territories. With this tacit understanding, the idea of letting the territories decide for themselves the slavery issue prospered in Cass's Old Northwest, where Stephen A. Douglas of Illinois and other prominent Democrats soon endorsed it.

When the Mexican War ended in 1848, the question of bondage in the new territories was no longer hypothetical—unless one reasoned, as many did, that their arid climate excluded plantation crops and therefore excluded slavery. For Calhoun that was beside the point, since the right to carry slaves into the territories was inviolate. In fact, there is little reason in retrospect to credit the argument that slavery had reached its natural limits of expansion. Slavery had been adapted to occupations other than plantation agriculture. On irrigated lands, cotton later became a staple crop of the Southwest.

Nobody doubted that Oregon would become free soil, but it too was drawn into the growing controversy. Oregon's territorial status, pending since 1846, was delayed because its provisional government had excluded slavery. To concede that provision would imply an authority drawn from the powers of Congress, since a territory was created by Congress. After much wrangling, Oregon was allowed to organize without slavery. Polk signed the bill on the principle that Oregon was north of $36°30'$.

Polk had promised to serve only one term, and having reached his major goals, he refused to run again in 1848. At the Democratic convention, Lewis Cass, the author of squatter sovereignty, won nomination, but the platform simply denied the power of Congress to interfere with slavery in the states and criticized all efforts to bring the question before Congress. The Whigs devised an even more artful shift. Once again, as in 1840, they passed over Henry Clay, their party leader, for a general, Zachary Taylor, whose popularity had grown since the Battle of Buena Vista. A legal resident of Louisiana and owner of more than a hundred slaves, he was an apolitical figure who had never voted in a national election. Once again, as in 1840, the party adopted no platform at all.

The Free-Soil Coalition

But the antislavery impulse was not easily squelched. Wilmot had raised a standard to which a broad coalition could rally. People who shied away from the abolitionism of William Lloyd Garrison could readily endorse the exclusion of slavery from all the new territories. By doing so, moreover, they could strike a blow for liberty whether or not they cared about slavery itself, or about the slaves. Many simply wanted free soil for white farmers, and to keep the unwelcome blacks far away in the South, where they belonged. Free soil in the new territories, therefore, rather than abolition in the South itself, became the rallying point—and also the name of a new party.

Three major groups entered the free-soil coalition: rebellious northern Democrats, antislavery Whigs, and members of the antislavery Liberty party. Disaffection among the Democrats centered in New York, where the Van Burenites seized on the free-soil issue as a moral imperative. Free-soil principles among the Whigs centered in Massachusetts, where a group of "Conscience" Whigs battled the "Cotton" Whigs. Conscience Whigs rejected the slaveholding nominee of their party, Zachary Taylor.

In 1848 these groups—Van Buren Democrats, Conscience Whigs, and Liberty party followers—organized the Free Soil party in a convention at Buffalo. Its presidential nomination went to Martin Van Buren. The Free Soil party platform pledged to abolish slavery, and it entered the campaign with the catchy slogan of "free soil, free speech, free labor, and free men."

Its impact on the election was mixed. The Free Soilers split the Democratic vote enough to throw New York to Zachary Taylor, and the Whig vote enough to give Ohio to Lewis Cass, but Van Buren's total of 291,000 votes was far below the popular totals of 1,361,000 for Taylor and 1,222,000 for Cass. Taylor won with 163 to 127 electoral votes, and both major parties retained a national following.

The California Gold Rush

Meanwhile, a new dimension had been introduced into the question of the territories. On January 24, 1848, gold was discovered in the California territory, and the rush was on. During 1849 more than 80,000 persons reached California, with 55,000 going overland and the rest by sea.

Unlike the land-hungry pioneers who traversed the overland trails, the miners were mostly unmarried young men representing a wide spectrum of ethnic and cultural backgrounds. Few miners were interested in permanent settlement. They wanted to strike it rich quickly and return home. The mining camps in California valleys, canyons, and along creek beds thus sprang up like mushrooms and disappeared almost as rapidly.

The mining shantytowns were disorderly and often lawless communities where leisure time revolved around saloons and gambling halls. One newcomer reported that "in the short space of twenty-four days, we have had murders, fearful accidents, bloody deaths, a mob, whippings, a hanging, an attempt at suicide, and a fatal duel." Within six months of arriving in California in 1849, one in every five of the gold seekers was dead. The gold fields and mining towns were so dangerous that insurance companies refused to provide coverage. Everyone carried weapons—usually pistols or bowie knives. Suicides were common, and disease was rampant. Cholera and scurvy plagued every camp.

Women were as rare in the mining camps as liquor was abundant. In 1850 less than 8 percent of California's total population was female, and even fewer women risked life in the camps. Those who did could demand quite a premium for their work as cooks, laundresses, entertainers, and prostitutes.

In the camps, the white miners often looked with disdain upon the Hispanics and Chinese who were most often employed as wage laborers to help in the panning process, separating gold from sand and gravel. But the miners focused their contempt on the Indians. In the mining culture it was not a crime to kill Indians or work them to death. American miners tried several times to outlaw foreigners in the mining country but had to settle for a tax on foreign miners that was applied to Mexicans in express violation of the treaty ending the Mexican War.

California Statehood

As civic leaders emerged within the burgeoning California population, they grew increasingly frustrated by the inability of military authorities to maintain law and order. In this context the new president, Zachary Taylor, thought he saw an ideal opportunity to use California statehood as a lever to end the stalemate in Congress caused by the slavery issue.

Born in Virginia and raised in Kentucky, Zachary Taylor had acquired a home in Louisiana and a

Gold Miners, c. 1850. Daguerreotype of miners panning for gold at their claim.

plantation in Mississippi. Southern Whigs had rallied to his support, expecting him to uphold the cause of slavery. Instead they had found a southern man with Union principles. Slavery should be upheld where it existed, Taylor felt, but he had little patience with abstract theories about slavery in territories where it probably could not exist. Why not make the California and New Mexico territories, acquired from Mexico, into states immediately, Taylor reasoned, and bypass the whole issue?

But the Californians, in need of organized government, were already ahead of him. By December 1849, without consulting Congress, California organized a "free-state government," which meant slavery was not permitted. New Mexico responded more slowly, but by 1850 Americans there had adopted another free-state constitution. In Taylor's annual message on December 4, 1849, he endorsed immediate statehood for California and enjoined Congress to avoid injecting slavery into the issue.

The Compromise of 1850

The spotlight fell on the Senate, where the Compromise of 1850, one of the great dramas of American politics, was enacted by a stellar cast: the great triumvirate of Henry Clay, John Calhoun, and Daniel Webster, with support from William H. Seward, Stephen A. Douglas, Jefferson Davis, and Thomas Hart Benton. Seventy-three-year-old Clay once again took the role of the "Great Compromiser," which he had played in the Missouri and nullification controversies.

The Great Debate

In January 1850 Clay presented a package of eight resolutions designed to solve all the disputed issues. He proposed to (1) admit California as a free state, (2) organize the remainder of the Southwest without restriction as to slavery, (3) deny Texas its extreme claim to a Rio Grande boundary up to its source, (4) compensate Texas for this by assuming the Texas debt, (5) uphold slavery in the District of Columbia, but (6) abolish the slave trade across its boundaries, (7) adopt a more effective fugitive slave act, and (8) deny congressional authority to interfere with the interstate slave trade. His proposals, in substance, became the Compromise of 1850, but only after a prolonged debate, the most celebrated in the annals of Congress—and the final great debate for Calhoun, Clay, and Webster.

On February 5–6 Clay summoned all his eloquence in defending the settlement. In the interest of "peace, concord and harmony" he called for an end to "passion, passion—party, party—and intemperance." Otherwise, continued sectional bickering would lead to a "furious, bloody, implacable, exterminating" civil war. To avoid such a catastrophe, he stressed, California should be admitted on the terms that its own people had approved. The debate continued sporadically through February, with Sam Houston rising to support Clay's compromise, Jefferson Davis defending the slavery cause on every point, and none endorsing President Taylor's straightforward plan.

Taylor believed that slavery in the South could best be protected if southerners avoided injecting the issue into the dispute over new territories. Unlike Calhoun, he did not believe the new western territories were suitable for slave-based agriculture. Because in his mind the issue of bringing slaves into the territories was moot, he continued to urge the Congress to admit California and New Mexico without reference to slavery. But few others embraced such a simple solution.

Then on March 4, Calhoun, desperately ill with tuberculosis, from which he would die in a few weeks, dramatically left his sickbed to sit in the Senate chamber. A colleague read his defiant remarks. "I have, Senators, believed from the first that the agitation of the subject of slavery would, if not prevented by some timely and effective measure, end in disunion," wrote Calhoun. Neither Clay's compromise nor Taylor's efforts, he declared, would serve the Union. The South needed simply an acceptance of its rights: equality of treatment in the territories, the return of fugitive slaves, and some guarantee of "an equilibrium between the sections."

Three days later Calhoun returned to hear Daniel Webster. The supreme orator in an age of superb oratory, he chose as his central theme the preservation of the Union: "I wish to speak today, not as a Massachusetts man, not as a Northern man, but as an American . . . I speak today for the preservation of the Union." The extent of slavery was already determined, he insisted, by the Northwest Ordinance, by the Missouri Compromise, and in the new lands by the law of nature. Both sections, to be sure, had legitimate grievances: on the one hand, the excesses of "infernal fanatics and abolitionists" in the North; and on the other hand, southern efforts to expand slavery. But instead of threatening secession, he declared, let people "enjoy the fresh air of liberty and union."

The March 7 speech was a classic gesture of conciliation, and Webster had knowingly brought down a storm upon his head. New England abolitionists labeled him a traitor for not aggressively supporting the free-soil cause and for endorsing the new fugitive slave law. On March 11 William H. Seward, freshman Whig senator from New York, gave the antislavery reply to Webster. Compromise with slavery, he argued, was "radically wrong and essentially vicious." There was "a higher law than the Constitution" that demanded the abolition of slavery.

In mid-April a select Committee of Thirteen bundled Clay's suggestions into one comprehensive bill. Taylor continued to oppose Clay's compromise, and their feud threatened to split the Whig party wide open. Another crisis loomed when word came that a convention in New Mexico was applying for statehood, with Taylor's support, and with boundaries that conflicted with the Texas claim to the east bank of the Rio Grande.

Toward a Compromise

On July 4, 1850, friends of the Union staged a grand rally at the base of the unfinished Washington Monument. President Taylor attended the ceremonies in the hot sun. Back at the White House he quenched his thirst with iced water and milk, ate some cherries or cucumbers, and contracted cholera morbus (gastroenteritis). Five days later he was dead. The outcome of the sectional quarrel, had he lived, probably would have been different, whether for better or worse one cannot know.

Taylor's sudden death, however, strengthened the chances of compromise. The soldier in the White House was followed by a politician, Millard Fillmore. The son of a poor farmer in upper New York, Fillmore had made his own way as a lawyer and then as a candidate in the rough-and-tumble world of New York politics. Experience had taught him caution, which some saw as indecision, but he had made up his mind to support Clay's compromise and had so informed Taylor. It was a strange switch. Taylor, the Louisiana slaveholder, who had nevertheless stoutly opposed the expansion of slavery, was ready to make war on his native region if it pressed the issue; Fillmore, whom southerners thought was antislavery, was ready to make peace.

At this point, young Senator Stephen A. Douglas of Illinois, a rising star of the Democratic party, rescued Clay's faltering compromise. His strategy was in fact the same one that Clay had used to pass the Missouri Compromise thirty years before. Reasoning that nearly everybody objected to one or another provision of Clay's proposal, Douglas broke it up into six (later five) separate measures. Few members were pre-

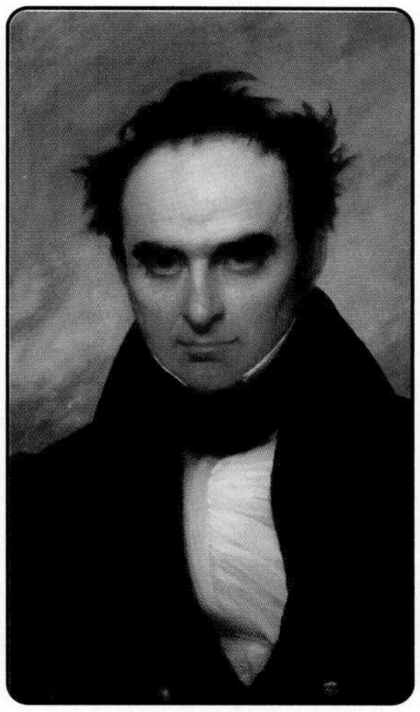

Daniel Webster in an 1835 portrait by Francis Alexander.

pared to vote for all of them, but from different elements Douglas hoped to mobilize a majority for each.

It worked. In September 1850, Fillmore signed the last of the five measures into law. The Union had muddled through, and the settlement went down in history as the Compromise of 1850. For the time, it defused an explosive situation and settled each of the major points at issue.

First, California entered the Union as a free state, ending forever the old balance of free and slave states. Second, the Texas and New Mexico Act made New Mexico a territory and set the Texas boundary at its present location. In return for giving up its claims east of the Rio Grande, Texas was paid $10 million. Third, the Utah Act set up another territory. The territorial act in each case omitted reference to slavery except to give the territorial legislature authority over "all rightful subjects of legislation" with provision for appeal to federal courts. For the sake of agreement, the deliberate ambiguity of the statement was its merit. Northern congressmen could assume that territorial legislatures might act to exclude slavery on the unstated principle of popular sovereignty. Southern congressmen assumed that they could not do so.

Fourth, a new Fugitive Slave Act put the matter of retrieving runaways wholly under federal jurisdiction and stacked the cards in favor of slave-catchers. Fifth, as a gesture to antislavery forces, the slave trade, but not slavery itself, was abolished in the District of Columbia.

Millard Fillmore pronounced the five measures making up the Compromise of 1850 "a final settlement." Still, doubts lingered that either North or South could be reconciled to the measures permanently. In the South, the disputes of 1846–1850 had transformed the abstract doctrine of secession into a movement animated by such "fire-eaters" as Robert Barnwell Rhett of South Carolina, William L. Yancey of Alabama, and Edmund Ruffin of Virginia. In

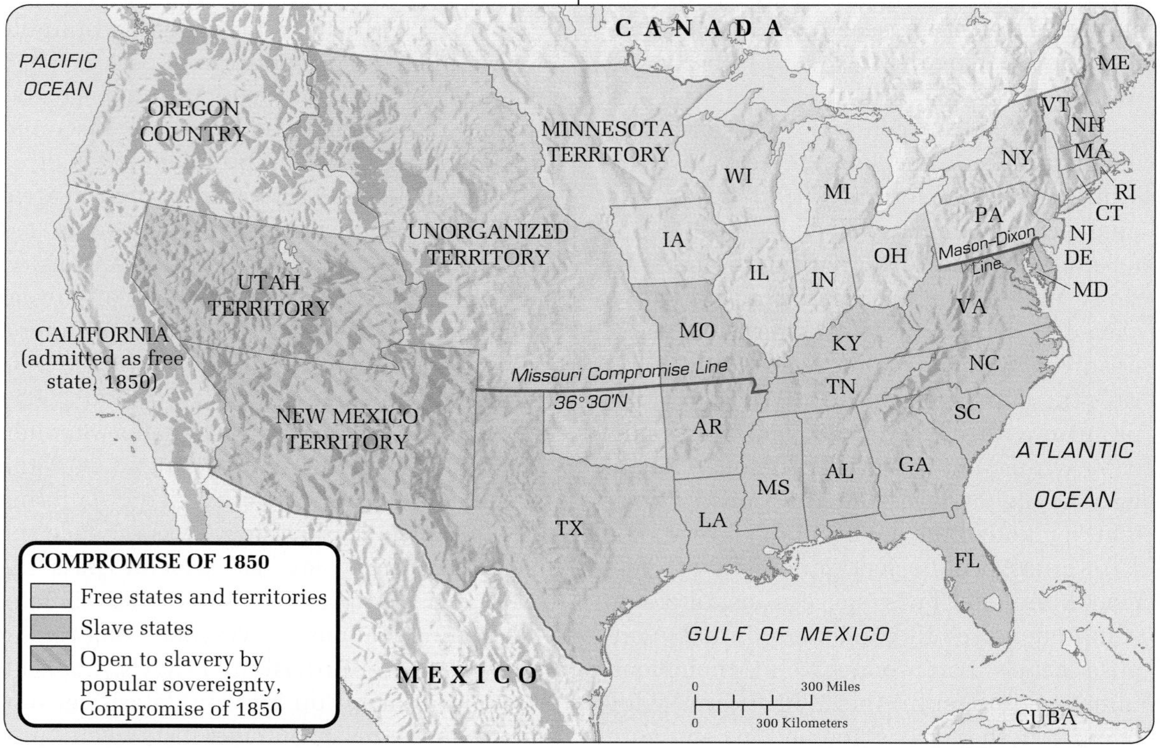

their view slavery must expand into the territories or it would wither and die—and southern culture would die along with it. They refused to view the matter as settled, and they would do all in their power to see it returned to the center stage of political debate.

The Fugitive Slave Act

Northern abolitionists were equally determined to keep slavery's evils in the forefront of public concerns. Southern intransigence in demanding the Fugitive Slave Act had presented abolitionists an emotional new focus for agitation. The law offered a strong temptation to kidnap free blacks by denying alleged fugitives a jury trial and by providing a fee of $10 for each fugitive delivered to federal authorities. In addition, federal marshals could require citizens to help in its enforcement; violators could be imprisoned for up to six months and fined $1,000. Within a month of the law's enactment, claims were filed in New York, Philadelphia, Harrisburg, Detroit, and other cities. Trouble followed. In Detroit the authorities used military force to stop the rescue of an alleged fugitive by an outraged mob.

There were relatively few such incidents, however. In the first six years of the Fugitive Slave Act, only three runaways were forcibly rescued from the slave-catchers. On the other hand, probably fewer than 200 were returned to bondage during the same years. More than that were rescued by stealth, often through the Underground Railroad. Still, the Fugitive Slave Act had the tremendous effect of widening and deepening the antislavery impulse in the North.

Uncle Tom's Cabin

Antislavery forces found their most persuasive appeal not in opposition to the Fugitive Slave Act but in the fictional drama of Harriet Beecher Stowe's *Uncle Tom's Cabin* (1852). The novel was filled with unlikely saints and sinners, stereotypes and melodramatic escapades, and was a smashing commercial success. Slavery, seen through Stowe's eyes, subjected its victims either to callous brutality or, at the hands of indulgent masters, to the indignity of extravagant ineptitude and bankruptcy. Stowe poignantly portrayed the evils of the interstate slave trade, especially the breaking up of slave families, and she highlighted the horrors of the Fugitive Slave Act. It took time for the novel to work its effect on public opinion, however. The country was enjoying a surge of prosperity, and the course of the presidential campaign in 1852 reflected a common desire to lay sectional quarrels to rest.

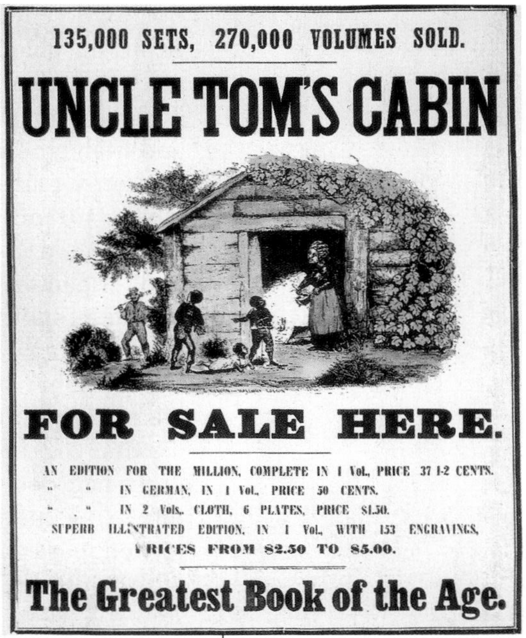

"The Greatest Book of the Age." *Uncle Tom's Cabin,* as this advertisement indicates, was a tremendous commercial success.

The Election of 1852

As their nominee for president, the Democrats turned to Franklin Pierce of New Hampshire, a personable veteran of the Mexican War with little political experience. The platform pledged the Democrats to "abide by and adhere to a faithful execution of the acts known as the Compromise measures. . . ." Pierce rallied both the southern rights' men and the Van Burenite Democrats. The Free Soilers, as a consequence, mustered only half as many votes as they had totaled in 1848.

The Whigs repudiated the lackluster Fillmore, who had faithfully supported the Compromise, and tried to exploit martial glory by choosing Winfield Scott, the hero of Mexico City, a native of Virginia backed mainly by northern Whigs. The convention dutifully endorsed the Compromise of 1850, but with some opposition from the North. Scott, an able field commander but politically inept, had gained a reputation for antislavery and nativism, alienating German and Irish ethnic voters. In the end, Scott carried only four states. The popular vote was closer: 1.6 million to 1.4 million.

Pierce, a former congressman, senator, and brigadier in Mexico, was, like Polk, touted as another "Young Hickory." But the youngest president turned out to be made of more pliable stuff, unable to dominate the warring factions of his party. By the end of his first year in office, the leaders of his own party had decided he was a failure. By trying to be all things to all people, Pierce looked more and more like a "Northern man with Southern principles."

Foreign Adventures

Cuba

Foreign diversions now distracted attention from domestic quarrels. Cuba, one of Spain's earliest possessions in the New World, had long been an object of American desire, especially to southerners determined to expand slavery into new areas. In 1854 the Pierce administration instructed Pierre Soulé, the American minister in Madrid, to offer $130 million for Cuba, which Spain spurned. Soulé then joined the American ministers to France and Britain in drafting the Ostend Manifesto. It declared that if Spain, "actuated by stubborn pride and a false sense of honor refused to sell," then the United States must ask itself, "does Cuba, in the possession of Spain, seriously endanger our internal peace and existence of our cherished Union?" If so, "we shall be justified in wresting it from Spain." Publication of the supposedly confidential dispatch left the administration no choice but to disavow what northern opinion widely regarded as a "slaveholders' plot" to acquire Cuba.

Diplomatic Gains in the Pacific

In the Pacific, American diplomacy scored some important achievements. In 1844 China signed an agreement with the United States that opened four ports, including Shanghai, to American trade. A later treaty opened eleven more ports and granted Americans the right to travel and trade throughout China. China quickly became a special concern of American Protestant missionaries as well. About fifty were already there by 1855, and for nearly a century, China remained far and away the most active mission field for American evangelism.

Japan meanwhile had remained for two centuries closed to American trade. Moreover, American whalers wrecked on the shores of Japan had been forbidden to leave the country. Mainly in their interest President Fillmore entrusted a special Japanese expedition to Commodore Matthew Perry, who arrived in Tokyo in 1853. Perry attempted to impress—and intimidate—the Japanese with American military and technological superiority. Negotiations followed, and Japan eventually agreed to an American consulate, promised good treatment to castaways, and permitted visits in certain ports for supplies and repairs. Broad commercial relations began after the first envoy, Townsend Harris, negotiated the Harris Convention of 1858, which opened five Japanese ports to American trade. Japan continued to ban emigration to the United States but found the law increasingly difficult to enforce, and by the 1880s the Japanese government abandoned its efforts to prevent Japanese from seeking work abroad.

The Kansas-Nebraska Crisis

American commercial interests in Asia were in part responsible for the growing interest in constructing a transcontinental railroad line linking the eastern seaboard with the

Pacific coast. Other powerful motives were at work as well. Railroad developers and land speculators also promoted this transportation link, as did slaveholders who were eager to expand the area open to slavery. During the 1850s, the idea of building a transcontinental railroad, though a great national goal, spawned sectional rivalries in still another quarter and reopened the slavery issue.

Douglas's Proposal

In 1852 and 1853 Congress debated several likely routes for the rail line. For various reasons, including terrain, climate, and sectional interest, Secretary of War Jefferson Davis favored a southern route and encouraged what became known as the Gadsden Purchase, a barren stretch of land in present New Mexico and Arizona. In 1853, at a cost of $10 million, the United States acquired the area from Mexico as a likely route for a Pacific railroad.

But midwestern spokesmen had other ideas concerning the path of the transcontinental railroad. Since 1845, Illinois senator Stephen A. Douglas and others had offered bills for a new territory in the lands west of Missouri and Iowa, bearing the Indian name Nebraska. In 1854, Douglas put forward yet another Nebraska bill, which included the entire unorganized portion of the Louisiana Purchase to the Canadian border. At this point, fateful connections began to transform his proposal from a railroad bill to a proslavery bill. Douglas needed the support of southerners, and to win that support he needed to make some concession on slavery in the new territories. This he did by writing the principle of "popular sovereignty" into the bill, allowing territories to decide the issue themselves.

It was a clever dodge, since the Missouri Compromise would still exclude slaves until the territorial government had made a decision, preventing slaveholders from getting established before a popular vote decided the issue. Southerners quickly spotted the problem for them, however, and Douglas as quickly made two more concessions. He supported an amendment for repeal of the Missouri Compromise insofar as it excluded slavery north of 36°30′, and he then agreed to organize two territories: Kansas, west of Missouri; and Nebraska, west of Iowa and Minnesota.

Douglas's motives remain unclear. Railroads were surely foremost in his mind, but he also hoped that popular sovereignty would defuse the slavery issue and open the Great Plains. But he had blundered, thus damaging his presidential chances and setting the country on the road to civil war. He had failed to appreciate the depth of antislavery feelings. Douglas himself preferred that the territories become free. Their climate and geography excluded plantation agriculture, he reasoned, and he could not comprehend how people could get so wrought up over abstract rights. Yet he had in fact opened the possibility that slavery might gain a foothold in Kansas.

Douglas's move to repeal the Missouri Compromise was less than a week old before six antislavery congressmen published a protest called the "Appeal of the Independent Democrats." Their moral indignation quickly spread among those who opposed Douglas. Across the North, editorials, sermons, speeches, and petitions denounced Douglas's bill as a conspiracy to extend slavery. But Douglas had the votes and, once committed, he forced the issue with tireless energy. President Pierce impulsively added his support, and the bill passed in May 1854 by 37 to 14 in the Senate and 113 to 100 in the House.

Very well, many in the North reasoned, if the Missouri Compromise was not a sacred pledge, then neither was the Fugitive Slave Act. On June 2, 1854, Boston witnessed the most dramatic demonstration against the act. After several attempts had failed to rescue a fugitive named Anthony Burns from being returned south, soldiers dispatched

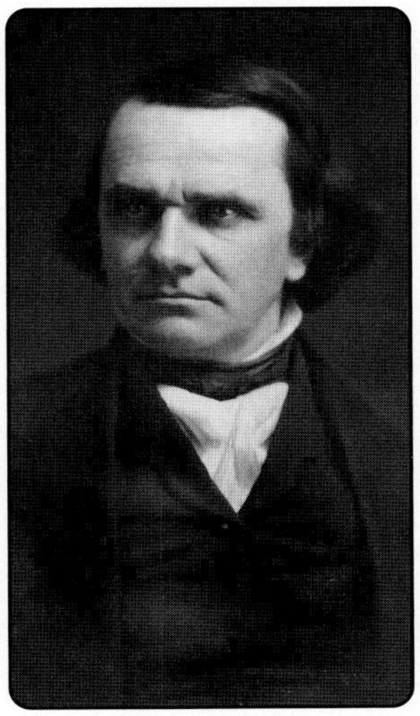

Stephen A. Douglas.

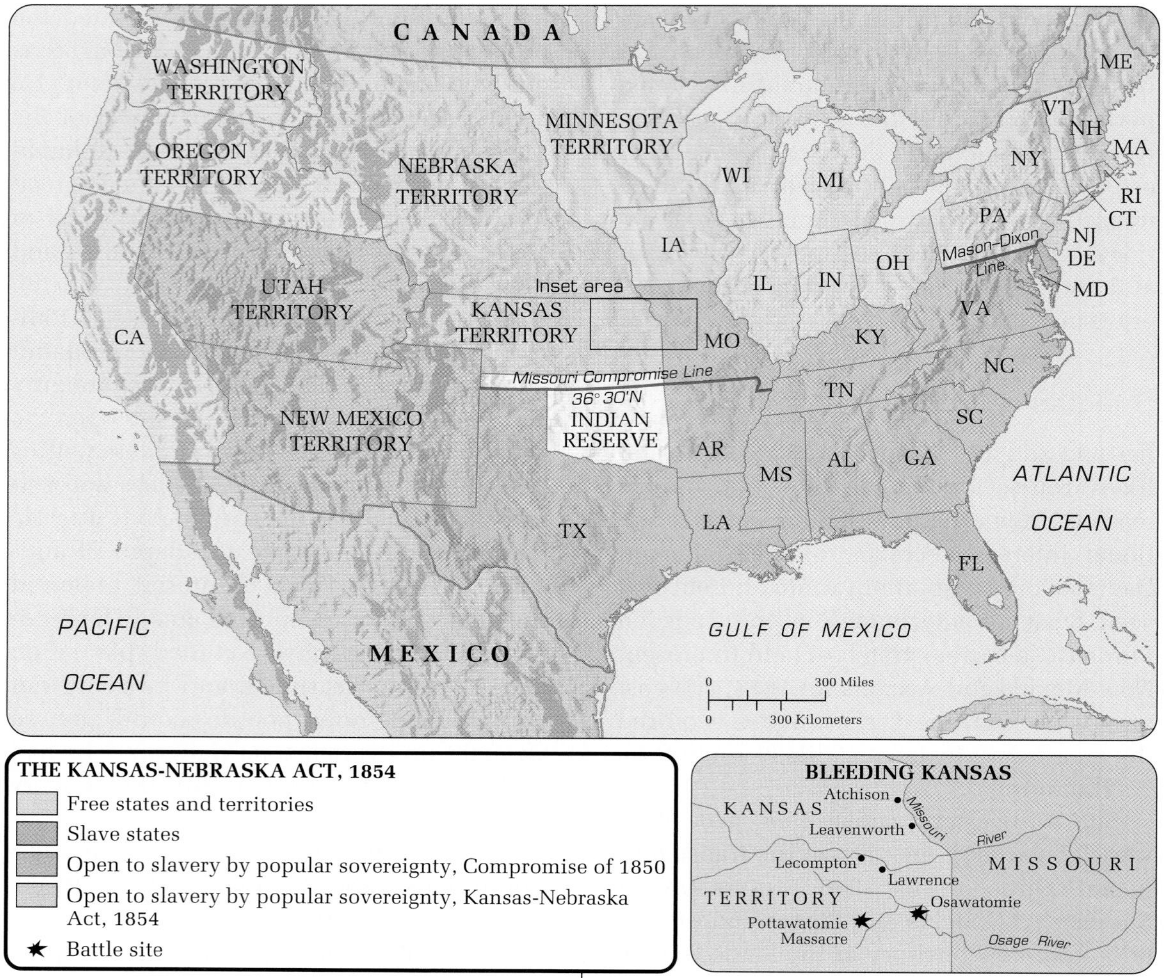

by President Pierce marched him to a waiting ship through streets lined with people shouting "Kidnappers!" Burns was the last fugitive slave to be returned from Boston and was himself soon freed through purchase by Boston's black community. New Englanders blamed Pierce for this sorry episode.

The Emergence of the Republican Party

In 1854 what John C. Calhoun had called the cords holding the Union together were fraying. The national church organizations of Baptists and Methodists, for instance, had split over slavery by 1845. The national political parties, which had created mutual interests transcending sectional issues, were beginning to unravel under the strain. The Democrats managed to postpone disruption for yet a while, but their congressional delegation lost heavily in the North, enhancing the influence of the southern wing.

The strain of the Kansas-Nebraska Act, however, soon destroyed the Whig party. Southern Whigs now tended to abstain from voting, while Northern Whigs moved toward two new parties. One was the new American (Know-Nothing) party, which had raised the banner of native Americanism and the hope of serving the patriotic cause of Union. Even more Northern Whigs joined with independent Democrats and Free Soilers in spontaneous antislavery coalitions with an array of confusing names, including "anti-Nebraska," "Fusion," and "People's party." These coalitions finally converged in 1854 on the name "Republican," evoking the memory of Thomas Jefferson.

"Bleeding" Kansas

After passage of the Kansas-Nebraska Act, attention swung to the plains of Kansas, where opposing elements gathered to stage what would turn out to be a dress rehearsal for civil war. All agreed that Nebraska would be free, but Kansas soon exposed the potential for mischief in Douglas's concept of popular sovereignty. The people of Kansas were "perfectly free to form and regulate their domestic institutions in their own way, subject only to the Constitution." That in itself invited conflicting interpretations, but the law failed to specify the time of decision about slavery, adding to each side's sense of urgency about getting control of the territory.

The settlement of Kansas therefore differed from the usual pioneering efforts. Groups sprang up North and South to hurry right-minded settlers westward. In fact, however, few New Englanders migrated to Kansas. Most of the settlers were from Missouri and surrounding states. Although few of them owned slaves, they were not sympathetic to militant abolitionism. Racism was prevalent even among non-slaveholding whites. Many of the Kansas settlers wanted to keep all blacks, slave or free, out of the territory. By 1860, there were only 627 African Americans in the territory.

When Kansas's first territorial governor arrived in 1854, he ordered a census and scheduled an election for a territorial legislature in 1855. On election day, several thousand "Border Ruffians" crossed over from Missouri, illegally cast proslavery votes, and pledged to kill every "God-damned abolitionist in the Territory." The governor denounced the vote as a fraud, but he did nothing to alter the results, for fear of being killed himself. The new legislature expelled the few antislavery members, adopted a drastic slave code, and made it a capital offense to aid a fugitive slave.

Free-state advocates rejected this "bogus" government and quickly formed their own. In 1855 a constitutional convention, the product of an election of dubious legality, met in Topeka, drafted a state constitution excluding both slavery and free blacks from Kansas, and applied for admission to the Union. By 1856 a free-state "governor" and "legislature" were functioning in Topeka. Thus the territory had two illegal governments competing for recognition and control, and both sides began to arm. On May 21, 1856, 700 proslavery thugs entered the free-state town of Lawrence and smashed newspaper presses, set fire to the free-state governor's home, stole property, and destroyed the Free State Hotel.

The "sack of Lawrence" left just one casualty, but the incident aroused a fanatical Kansas Free Soiler named John Brown, who had a history of mental instability. On May 24, two days after the sack of Lawrence, Brown, the father of twenty children, set out

Kansas Free State Battery. The establishment of two illegal governments in Kansas led to fighting in 1856.

with four of his sons and three other men toward Pottawatomie Creek, site of a proslavery settlement, where they dragged five men from their houses and hacked them to death in front of their screaming wives and children, ostensibly as revenge for the deaths of free-state men.

The Pottawatomie Massacre (May 24–25, 1856) set off a guerrilla war in the territory that lasted through the fall. On August 30, Missouri ruffians raided the free-state settlement at Osawatomie. They looted the houses, burned them to the ground, and shot John Brown's son Frederick through the heart. The elder Brown, who barely escaped, swore to his surviving sons and followers that he would "die fighting for this cause." Altogether, by the end of 1856, Kansas lost about 200 killed and $2 million in property destroyed during the territorial civil war.

Violence in the Senate

Violence in Kansas spilled over into Congress itself. On May 20, 1856, Senator Charles Sumner of Massachusetts delivered an inflammatory speech in which he described the proslavery forces' treatment of Kansas as "the rape of a virgin territory." Sumner then called Senator Andrew P. Butler of South Carolina a liar and implied that he kept a slave mistress.

Sumner's rudeness might well have backfired had it not been for Butler's nephew Preston S. Brooks, a fiery-tempered South Carolina congressman. Brooks confronted Sumner at his Senate desk on May 22. He accused him of slander and began beating him about the head with a cane while stunned senators, including Douglas, looked on. Sumner, struggling to rise, wrenched the desk from the floor and collapsed.

Brooks had satisfied his rage, but in the process he had created a martyr for the antislavery cause. For two and a half years Sumner's empty seat was a solemn reminder of the violence done to him. Some thought the senator was feigning injury, others that he really was physically disabled. In fact, although his injuries were bad enough, including two gashes to the skull, he seems to have suffered psychosomatic shock that left him incapable of functioning. When the House censured Brooks, he resigned, but he was triumphantly reelected. His southern admirers presented him with new canes.

Sectional Politics

Within the span of five days in May of 1856, "Bleeding Kansas," "Bleeding Sumner," and "Bully Brooks" had set the tone for another presidential year. The major parties could no longer evade the slavery issue. Already it had split the American party wide open. Southern delegates, with help from New York, killed a resolution to restore the Missouri Compromise, and they nominated Millard Fillmore for president. Later, what was left of the Whig party endorsed him as well.

At its first national convention, the new Republican party followed the Whig tradition by seeking out a military hero, John C. Frémont, the "Pathfinder" and leader in the conquest of California. The Republican platform owed much to the Whigs too. It favored a transcontinental railroad and, in general, more internal improvements. It condemned the repeal of the Missouri Compromise and the Democratic policy of expansion. The campaign slogan echoed that of the Free Soilers: "Free soil, free speech, and Frémont." It was the first time a major party platform had taken a stand against slavery.

The Democrats rejected Pierce, the hapless victim of so much turmoil. They also spurned Douglas because of the damage done by his Kansas-Nebraska Act. The party therefore turned to James Buchanan of Pennsylvania, who had long sought the nomination. The Democratic platform endorsed the Kansas-Nebraska Act and urged Congress not to interfere with slavery in either states or territories. The party reached out to its newly acquired Irish and German Catholic voters by condemning nativism and endorsing religious liberty.

The campaign of 1856 resolved itself into two sectional campaigns. The "Black Republicans," as the new party was called by proslavery forces, had few southern supporters and only a handful in the border states, where fears of disunion held many Whigs in line. Buchanan thus went into the campaign as the candidate of the only remaining national party. Frémont swept the northernmost states with 114 electoral votes, but Buchanan added five free states to his southern majority for a total of 174.

Few presidents before Buchanan had a broader experience in politics and diplomacy. He had been in Congress, had served as minister to Russia and Britain, and had been Polk's secretary of state in between. His long quest for the presidency had been built on a southern alliance, and his political debts reinforced his belief that saving the Union depended on concessions to the South. Republicans charged that he lacked the backbone to stand up to the southerners who dominated the Democratic majorities in Congress. To them his choice of four slave-state and only three free-state men for his cabinet seemed a bad omen.

The Deepening Sectional Crisis

During Buchanan's first six months in office, he encountered three crises in succession: the Supreme Court's Dred Scott decision, new troubles in Kansas, and a widespread business panic.

The Dred Scott Case

On March 6, 1857, two days after the inauguration, the Supreme Court rendered a decision in the long-pending case of *Dred Scott* v. *Sandford*. Dred Scott, born a slave in Virginia about 1800, had been taken to St. Louis in 1830 and sold to an army surgeon, who took him as a body servant to Illinois, then to the Wisconsin Territory (later Minnesota), where slavery was prohibited, and finally returned him to St. Louis in 1842. While in the Wisconsin Territory, Scott met and married Harriet Robinson, and they eventually had two daughters.

After his master's death in 1843, Scott tried unsuccessfully to buy his freedom. In 1846, Harriet Scott convinced her husband to file suit in Missouri courts claiming that residence in Illinois and Wisconsin Territory had made them free. A jury decided in their favor, reaffirming the widespread notion that "once free, forever free." But the state supreme court ruled against the Scotts, arguing that a slave state did not have to honor freedom granted to slaves by free states. When the case rose on appeal to the Supreme Court, the country anxiously awaited its opinion on the issue of whether freedom once granted could be lost by returning to a slave state.

Each of the eight justices filed a separate opinion, except one who concurred with Chief Justice Roger B. Taney. By different lines of reasoning, seven justices ruled that Scott reverted to slave status upon his return to Missouri. The aging Taney ruled that Scott lacked standing in court because he lacked citizenship. At the time the Constitution was adopted, Taney added, blacks "had for more than a century been regarded as . . . so far inferior, that they had no rights which the white man was bound to respect."

To clarify the definition of Scott's status, Taney moved to a second major question. He argued that the Missouri Compromise, by ruling that certain new territories were to exclude slaves, had deprived citizens of property in slaves, an action "not warranted by the Constitution." The Supreme Court had declared an act of Congress unconstitutional for the first time since *Marbury* v. *Madison* (1803). Congress had repealed the Missouri Compromise in the Kansas-

Nebraska Act three years earlier, but the Dred Scott decision now challenged the concept of popular sovereignty. If Congress itself could not exclude slavery from a territory, as Taney argued, then presumably neither could a territorial government created by act of Congress.

Proslavery elements, of course, greeted the court's opinion with glee. Many northerners denounced Taney's ruling. Little wonder that Republicans protested: the Court had declared their free-soil program unconstitutional. It had also reinforced the suspicion that the slavocracy was hatching a conspiracy. Were not all but one of the justices who joined Taney southerners? And had not Buchanan chatted with the chief justice at the inauguration and then urged the people to accept the early decision as a final settlement, "Whatever this may be?"

And what of Dred Scott himself? Ironically, his owner, now a widow, married a prominent Massachusetts abolitionist, who saw to it that the slave and his family were freed in 1857. A year later Scott died of tuberculosis.

The Lecompton Constitution

Out in Kansas, meanwhile, the struggle continued through 1857. The contested politics in the territory now resulted in an antislavery legislature and a proslavery constitutional convention. The convention, meeting at Lecompton, drew up a constitution under which Kansas would become a slave state. A referendum on the document was set for December 21, 1857, with rules and officials chosen by the convention.

Although Kansas had only about 200 slaves at the time, free-state men boycotted the election, claiming that it was rigged. At this point President Buchanan took a fateful step. Influenced by southern advisers and politically dependent upon southern congressmen, he decided to support the action of the proslavery Lecompton Convention. The election went according to form: 6,226 votes for the constitution with slavery, 569 for the constitution without slavery. Meanwhile, the acting governor had convened the antislavery legislature, which called for another election to vote the Lecompton Constitution up or down. Most of the proslavery settlers boycotted this election, and the result on January 4, 1858, was overwhelming: 10,226 against the constitution, 138 for the constitution with slavery, 24 for the constitution without slavery.

The combined results suggested a clear majority against slavery, but Buchanan stuck to his support of the Lecompton Constitution, driving another wedge into the Democratic party. Senator Douglas, up for reelection in Illinois, broke dramatically with the president in a tense confrontation, but Buchanan persisted in trying to drive Lecompton "naked" through the Congress. In the Senate, administration forces held firm, and in 1858 Lecompton was passed. In the House, enough anti-Lecompton Democrats combined to put through an amendment for a new and carefully supervised popular vote in Kansas. Enough senators went along to pass the House bill. Southerners were confident that a new vote in Kansas would favor slavery, because to reject slavery the voters would have to reject the constitution, which would postpone statehood until the population reached 90,000. On August 2, 1858, Kansas voters nevertheless rejected Lecompton by 11,300 to 1,788. With that vote, Kansas, now firmly in the hands of its antislavery legislature, largely ended its role in the sectional controversy.

The Panic of 1857

The third crisis of Buchanan's first half year in office, a financial panic, broke in August 1857. It was brought on by a reduction in Europe's demand for American grain, a surge in manufacturing production that outran the growth of markets, and the continued weakness and confusion of the state bank-note system. Failure of the Ohio Life Insurance and Trust Company precipitated the panic, which brought on a depression from which the country did not emerge until 1859.

The panic further highlighted sectional differences. Northern businessmen tended to blame the depression on the Democratic Tariff of 1857, which had put rates at their lowest level since 1816. The agricultural South weathered the crisis better than the North. Cotton prices fell, but slowly, and world markets for cotton quickly recovered. The result was an exalted notion of King Cotton's importance to the world, and apparent confirmation of the growing argument that the southern system was superior to the free-labor system of the North.

Douglas versus Lincoln

Amid the recriminations over Dred Scott, Kansas, and the depression, the center could not hold. The Lecompton battle put severe strains on the most substantial cord of Union that was left, the Democratic party. To many, Douglas seemed the best hope, one of the few remaining Democratic leaders with support in both sections. But now Douglas was being whipsawed between the extremes. Kansas-Nebraska had cast him in the role of "doughface," a southern sympathizer. His opposition to Lecompton, the fraudulent fruit of popular sovereignty, however, had alienated him from Buchanan's southern junta. But for all his flexibility and opportunism, Douglas had convinced himself that popular sovereignty was a point of principle, a bulwark of democracy and local self-government. In 1858 he faced reelection to the Senate against the opposition of both "Buchanan Democrats" and Republicans. The year 1860 would give him a chance for the presidency, but first he had to secure his home base in Illinois.

To oppose him, Illinois Republicans named Abraham Lincoln of Springfield, the former Whig state legislator and one-term congressman. Born in a Kentucky log cabin in 1809, raised on frontier farms in Indiana and Illinois, the young Lincoln had the wit and will to rise above his coarse beginnings. Striking out on his own, he managed a general store in New Salem, Illinois, learned surveying, served in the Black Hawk War (1832), won election to the legislature in 1834 at the age of twenty-five, read law, and was admitted to the bar in 1836.

Abraham Lincoln.

As a Whig regular, Lincoln stayed in the state legislature until 1842, and in 1846 he won a term in Congress. After a single term he retired from active politics to cultivate his law practice in Springfield.

In 1854 the Kansas-Nebraska debate drew Lincoln back into the political arena. In 1856 he joined the Republicans, getting over 100 votes for their vice-presidential nomination. By 1858 he was the obvious Republican choice to oppose Douglas himself for the Senate, and Douglas knew he was up against a formidable foe. Lincoln resorted to the classic ploy of the underdog: he challenged the favorite to a debate. The legendary Lincoln-Douglas debates took place that summer and fall.

The two men presented a striking contrast. Lincoln was well over six feet tall, sinewy, and craggy-featured, with a long neck and deep-set, brooding eyes. Unassuming in manner, he conveyed an air of simplicity, sincerity, and common sense. Douglas was short, rotund, bulb-nosed, stern, and cocky, attired in the finest custom-tailored suits and possessed of supreme self-confidence. A man of considerable abilities and even greater ambition, he strutted to the platform with the pugnacious air of a predestined champion.

At the time and since, much attention focused on the second debate, at Freeport, where Lincoln asked Douglas how he could reconcile popular sovereignty with the Dred Scott ruling that citizens had the right to

John Brown.

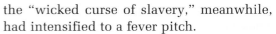

carry slaves into any territory. Douglas's answer, thenceforth known as the Freeport Doctrine, was to state the obvious. Whatever the Supreme Court might say about slavery, it could not exist anywhere unless supported by local police regulations. Thus, if settlers did not want slavery, they simply should refuse to adopt a local code protecting it.

Douglas then tried to set some traps of his own. He accused Lincoln of advocating racial equality. Lincoln countered with a statement affirming white supremacy. There was, he asserted, a "physical difference between the white and black races," and it would "forever forbid the two races living together on terms of social and political equality." But Lincoln insisted that blacks did have an "equal" right to their freedom and the fruits of their labor. He favored the containment of slavery where it existed so that "the public mind shall rest in the belief that it is in the course of ultimate extinction." But the basic difference between the two men, Lincoln insisted, lay in Douglas's professed indifference to the moral question of slavery.

If Lincoln had the better of the argument, at least in the long view, Douglas had the better of the election, which he won on a vote by the Illinois legislature. Across the nation, the elections recorded one loss after another for Buchanan Democrats. The administration had lost control of the House.

John Brown's Raid

The gradual return of prosperity in 1859 offered hope that the political storms of the 1850s might yet pass. But the sectional issue still haunted the public mind, and like lightning on the horizon, it warned that a storm was still brewing. In 1859 John Brown once again surfaced, this time in the East. Since the Pottawatomie Massacre in 1856, he had led a furtive existence, engaging in fund-raising, recruiting, and occasional bushwhacking. His commitment to abolish the "wicked curse of slavery," meanwhile, had intensified to a fever pitch.

On October 16, 1859, Brown launched his supreme gesture. From a Maryland farm he crossed the Potomac with about twenty men, including five blacks, and occupied the federal arsenal in Harper's Ferry, Virginia (now West Virginia). He apparently intended to arm the Maryland slaves he assumed would flock to his cause, set up a black stronghold in the mountains of western Virginia, and provide a nucleus of support for slave insurrections across the South.

What Brown actually did was to take the arsenal by surprise, seize a few hostages, and hole up in the fire-engine house. There he and his band were quickly surrounded by militiamen and town residents. The next morning Brown sent his son Watson and another supporter out under a white flag, but the enraged crowd shot them both. Intermittent shooting then broke out, and another Brown son was mortally wounded.

That night Lieutenant-Colonel Robert E. Lee, U.S. Cavalry, arrived with his aide, Lieutenant J. E. B. Stuart, and a force of marines. The following morning, on October 18, Stuart and his troops broke down the barricaded doors and captured Brown and his men. Brown was quickly tried for treason, convicted, and sentenced to be hanged. When Brown, still unflinching, met his end, northern sympathizers held solemn observances. "That new saint," Ralph Waldo Emerson predicted, ". . . will make the gallows glorious as the Cross." William Lloyd Garrison, the lifelong pacifist, now wished "success to every slave insurrection at the South and in every slave country." By far the gravest effect of Brown's raid was to leave proslavery southerners in no mood to distinguish between John Brown and the Republican party. All through the fall and winter of 1859–1860, rumors of conspiracy and insurrection swept the region. Every northern visitor, commercial traveler, or schoolteacher came under suspicion, and many were driven out.

The Center Comes Apart

The Democrats Divide

Amid emotional hysteria, the nation approached a presidential election destined to be the most fateful in its history. The Democrats met in Charleston, South Carolina, for their 1860 convention. Douglas's supporters reaffirmed the platform of 1856, which simply promised congressional noninterference with slavery. Southern firebrands, however, now demanded a federal code protecting slavery in the territories. Buchanan supporters, hoping to stop Douglas, encouraged the strategy. The platform debate reached a heady climax when the Alabama extremist William L. Yancey informed the northern Democrats that they had erred by failing to defend slavery as a positive good. An Ohio senator offered a blunt reply: "Gentlemen of the South," he declared, "you mistake us—you mistake us. We will not do it."

When the southern planks lost, Alabama's delegation walked out of the convention, followed by delegates from Georgia, South Carolina, Arkansas, and Delaware. The convention then decided to leave the overwrought atmosphere of Charleston and reassemble in Baltimore on June 18. The Baltimore convention finally nominated Douglas on the 1856 platform. The Charleston seceders met first in Richmond, then in Baltimore, where they adopted the slave-code platform defeated in Charleston and named Vice-President John C. Breckinridge of Kentucky for president. Another cord of union had snapped: the last remaining national party.

Lincoln's Election

The Republicans meanwhile gathered in Chicago. There everything suddenly came together for "Honest Abe" Lincoln, "the Railsplitter," the uncommon common man. Lincoln had suddenly emerged in the national view during his senatorial campaign two years before and had since taken a stance designed to make him available for the nomination. He was strong enough on the containment of slavery to satisfy the abolitionists, yet moderate enough to seem less threatening than they were.

Lincoln won the Republican nomination on the third ballot. The party platform foreshadowed future policy better than most. It denounced John Brown's raid as "among the gravest of crimes" and affirmed that each state should "order and control its own domestic institutions." The party repeated its resistance to the extension of slavery and, in an effort to gain broader support, endorsed a higher protective tariff for manufacturers, free homesteads for farmers, a more liberal naturalization law, and internal improvements, including a transcontinental railroad. With this platform, Republicans made a strong appeal to eastern businessmen, western farmers, and the large immigrant population.

Both major conventions revealed that opinion tended to become more radical in the upper North and Deep South. Attitude seemed to follow latitude. In the border states a sense of moderation aroused the die-hard Whigs there to make one more try at reconciliation. Meeting in Baltimore a week before the Republicans met in Chicago, they reorganized into the Constitutional Union party and named John Bell of Tennessee for president. Their platform simply called for the preservation of the Constitution and the Union.

Of the four candidates, not one was able to command a national following, and the campaign resolved into a choice between Lincoln and Douglas in the North, Breckinridge and Bell in the South. One consequence of these separate campaigns was that each section gained a false impression of the other. The South never learned to distinguish Lincoln from the radicals; the North failed to gauge the force of southern intransigence—and in this Lincoln was among the worst. He stubbornly refused to offer the South assurances or to explain his position on slavery, which he insisted was a matter of public record.

The one man who tried to break through the veil that was falling between the sections was Douglas, who tried to mount a national campaign. Only forty-seven, but already weakened by excessive drink, ill health, and disappointments, he wore himself out in one final glorious campaign. Throughout the South, he carried appeals on behalf of the Union. "I do not believe that every Breckinridge man is a disunionist," he said, "but I do believe that every disunionist is a Breckinridge man."

By midnight of November 6, however, Lincoln's victory was clear. In the final count he had about 39 percent of the total popular vote, but a clear majority with 180 votes in the electoral college. He carried all eighteen free states by a wide margin. Among all the candidates, only Douglas had electoral votes from both slave and free states, but his total of 12 was but a pitiful remnant of Democratic Unionism. He ran last. Bell took Virginia, Kentucky, and Tennessee, and Breckinridge swept the other slave states to come in second with 72 electoral votes.

Secession of the Deep South

Soon after the election, the South Carolina legislature, which had assembled to choose the state's electors, set a special election for December 6 to choose delegates to a convention. In Charleston on December 20, 1860, the convention unanimously voted an Ordinance of Secession, declaring the state's ratification of the Constitution repealed and the union with other states dissolved. By February 1, 1861, Mississippi, Florida, Alabama, Georgia, Louisiana, and Texas had also seceded from the Union. On February 4, a convention of those seven states met in Montgomery, Alabama, and on February 7 it adopted a provisional constitution for the Confederate States of America. Two days later, the delegates elected Jefferson Davis as its president. He was inaugurated February 18, with Alexander Stephens of Georgia as vice-president.

In all seven states of the southernmost tier, a solid majority had voted for secessionist convention delegates, but their combined vote would not have been a

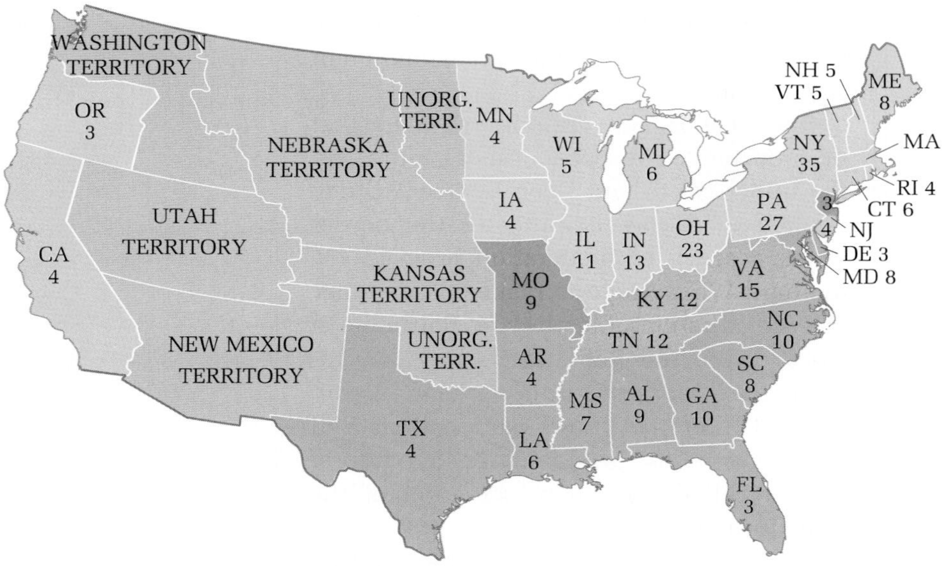

ELECTION OF 1860	Electoral vote	Popular vote
Abraham Lincoln (Republican)	**180**	**1,866,000**
Stephen A. Douglas (Democrat, Northern)	12	1,383,000
John C. Breckinridge (Democrat, Southern)	72	848,000
John Bell (Constitutional Union)	39	593,000

majority of the presidential vote in November. What happened, it seemed, was what often happens in revolutionary situations: a determined minority acted quickly in an emotionally charged climate and carried its program against a confused and indecisive opposition. Trying to decide if a majority of southern whites actually favored secession probably is beside the point—a majority was vulnerable to the decisive action of the secessionists.

Southern Unionists lamented this situation, noting that the "fire-eaters" rather than true statesmen were in control. "Webster and Clay are gone," mourned one Louisianan, "and God has given us over to fools and mad men." Others predicted that secession, instead of conserving traditional southern society, would in fact accelerate its demise.

Buchanan's Waiting Game

History is full of might-have-beens. A bold stroke, even a bold statement, by the lame-duck president at this point might have defused the crisis, but there was no Jacksonian will in Buchanan. Besides, a bold stroke might simply have hastened the conflict. No bold stroke came from Lincoln either, nor would he consult with the administration during the long months before his inauguration on March 4, 1861. He inclined all too strongly to the belief that secession was just another bluff.

Seeking compromise, in his annual message on December 3, 1860, Buchanan argued that secession was illegal, but that he lacked authority to coerce a state. "Seldom have we known so strong an argument come to so lame and impotent a conclusion," the *Cincinnati Enquirer* editorialized. There was, however, a hidden weapon in the president's reaffirmation of a duty to "take care that the laws be faithfully executed" insofar as he was able. If the president could enforce the law upon all citizens, he would have no need to "coerce" a state. Indeed, Buchanan's position became the policy of the Lincoln administration, which fought a war on the theory that individuals but not states as such were in rebellion.

Buchanan held firmly to his resolve. On the day after Christmas, the small federal garrison at Charleston's Fort Moultrie had been moved into the nearly completed Fort Sumter by Major Robert Anderson, a Kentucky Unionist. Anderson's move struck South Carolina authorities as provocative. Commissioners of the newly "independent" state demanded withdrawal of all federal forces, but they had overplayed their hand. Buchanan's cabinet, with only one southerner left, insisted it would be a gross violation of duty, perhaps grounds for impeachment, for the president to yield. His backbone thus stiffened, he sharply rejected the South Carolina ultimatum to withdraw. He decided instead to hunker down and ride out the remaining weeks of his term, hoping against hope that one of several compromise efforts would yet prove fruitful.

Last Efforts at Compromise

Forlorn efforts at compromise continued in Congress until the dawn of Lincoln's inauguration day. On December 18, Senator John J. Crittenden of Kentucky had proposed a series of resolutions that recognized slavery in the territories south of 36°30′ and guaranteed to maintain it where it already existed. The fight for a compromise was carried to the floor of each house, and Crittenden's resolutions were subjected to intensive but inconclusive debate during January and February.

Meanwhile, a peace conference met in a Washington hotel in February 1861. Twenty-one states sent delegates and former president John Tyler presided, but the convention's proposal, substantially the same as the Crittenden Compromise, failed to win the support of either house of Congress. The only compromise proposal that met with any success was an amendment guaranteeing slavery where it existed. Many Republicans, including Lincoln, were prepared to go that far to save the Union, but they were unwilling to repudiate their stand against slavery in the territories. As it happened, after passing the House, the amendment passed the Senate without a vote to spare, by 24 to 12, on the dawn of inauguration day. It would have become the Thirteenth Amendment, with the first use of the word "slavery" in the Constitution, but the states never ratified it. When a Thirteenth Amendment was ratified in 1865, it did not guarantee slavery—it abolished slavery.

CHAPTER

16

The War of the Union

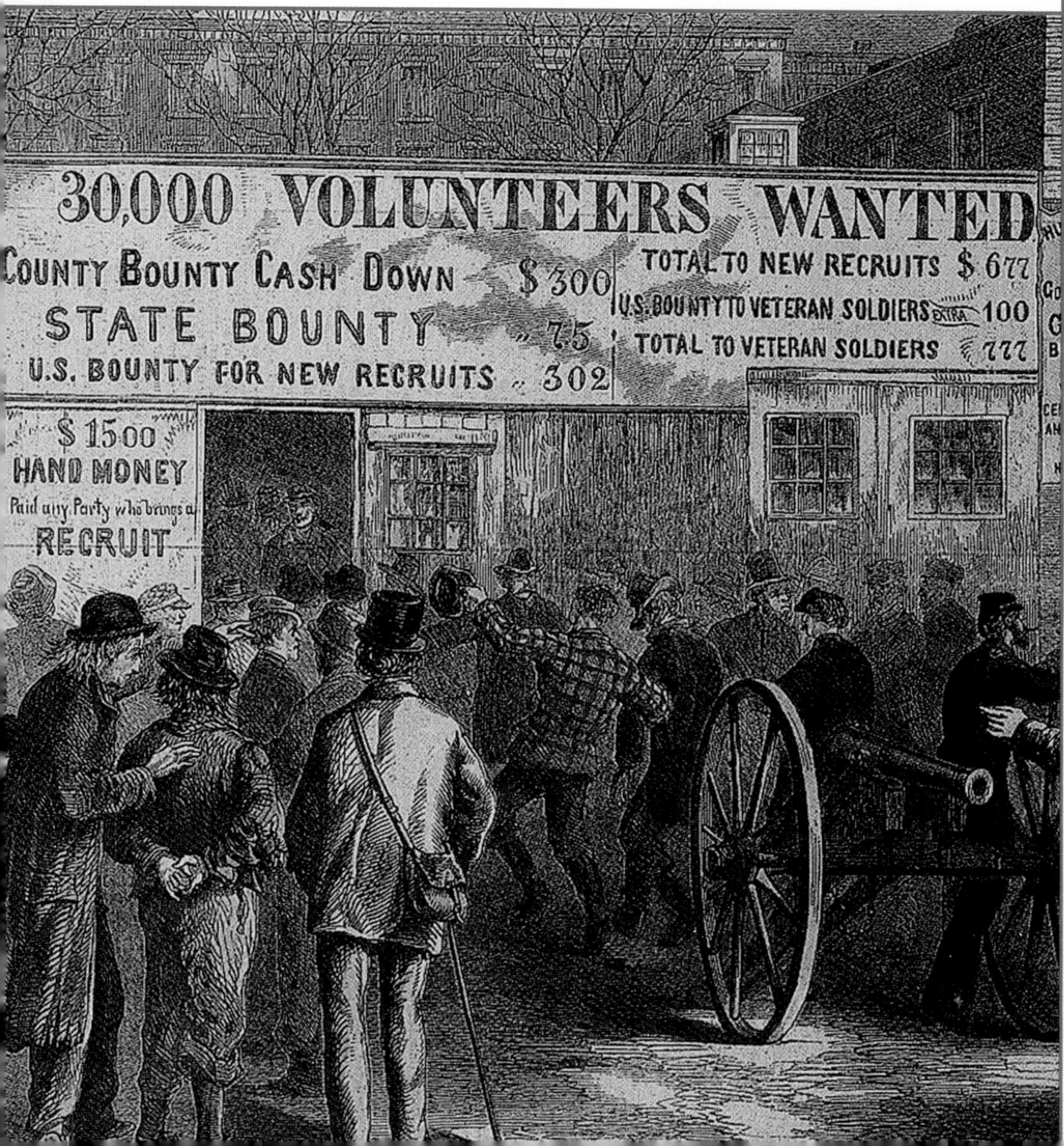

This chapter focuses on

- The main course and major strategies of the Civil War.
- How the war affected the home front, North and South.
- The reasons for, and results of, Lincoln's Emancipation Proclamation.

THE *ESSENTIAL AMERICA* ON-LINE TUTOR

www.wwnorton.com/eamerica/ch16

- **Topic: The Battle of Gettysburg**
  www.wwnorton.com/eamerica/ch16/topic.htm

  In July of 1863 Union troops confronted Confederate soldiers at Gettysburg in an attempt to prevent Southern forces from advancing further into Union territory. Using maps, personal accounts, photographs, and historical analyses, explore the Battle of Gettysburg. Who won at Gettysburg, and how did that victory affect the course of the war?

- **Chapter review: On-line quiz and chapter summary**
  www.wwnorton.com/eamerica/ch16/review.htm

- **Chapter resources: Multimedia index**
  www.wwnorton.com/eamerica/ch16/media.htm

The Civil War has become shrouded in an ever-thickening mist of gallant images and larger-than-life mythology. As a result, the Union triumph has acquired the mantle of inevitability. Was not the North destined to win? The Confederacy's fight for independence, on the other hand, has taken on the aura of a romantic lost cause, doomed from the start by the region's sparse industrial development, smaller pool of able-bodied men, paucity of capital resources and warships, and spotty transportation network.

But in 1861 the military situation was by no means so clear-cut. For all of the South's obvious disadvantages, it initially enjoyed a captive labor force, superior officers, the prospects of foreign assistance, and the benefits of fighting a defensive campaign on familiar territory. Jefferson Davis and other Confederate leaders were genuinely confident that their cause would prevail on the battlefields. It is important to remember that this epochal event was endowed from the start not with inevitability but with uncertainty, and its outcome was decided as much by human decisions and human willpower as by physical resources.

End of the Waiting Game

In early 1861, as Abraham Lincoln prepared to take office and the possibility of civil war captured the attention of a divided nation, no one imagined that a conflict of horrendous scope and intensity awaited them. On both sides, people believed that the fighting would be over quickly and that their daily lives would go on as usual.

Lincoln and Secession

In his inaugural address on March 4, 1861, Lincoln reassured southerners that he had no intention of interfering with "slavery in the States where it exists." But secession was another matter. He insisted that the "Union of these States is perpetual," and he promised to "hold, occupy, and possess" areas belonging to the federal government.

But the momentum of secession took control of events. The day after Lincoln's inauguration, word arrived from Charleston that time was running out for the federal garrison at Fort Sumter. The fort had enough supplies for only a month. On April 4, 1861, Lincoln decided to resupply Ft. Sumter. The Confederate government demanded that Ft. Sumter surrender. The federal commander refused, and just before dawn on April 12, Confederate batteries began shelling the fort. After thirty-three hours, the federal troops surrendered.

The guns of Charleston signaled the end of the tense waiting game. On April 15, Lincoln issued a proclamation calling upon the loyal states to supply 75,000 militiamen to put down the rebellion. Volunteers in both the North and the South soon crowded recruiting stations for both sides, and huge new armies began to form. On April 19, Lincoln proclaimed a blockade of southern ports, which, as the Supreme Court later ruled, confirmed the existence of a state of war.

Taking Sides

Lincoln's call to arms led four upper South states to join the Confederacy—Virginia, Arkansas, Tennessee, and North Carolina. Each had areas (mainly in the mountains) where both slaves and secessionists were scarce and where Union sentiment ran strong. In fact, Unionists in western Virginia, bolstered by a Union army from Ohio under General George B. McClellan, formed a new state. In 1863 Congress admitted West Virginia with a state constitution that provided for emancipation of the few slaves there.

Of the other slave states, Delaware remained firmly in the Union, but Maryland, Kentucky, and Missouri went through bitter struggles for control. The secession of Maryland would have encircled Washington,

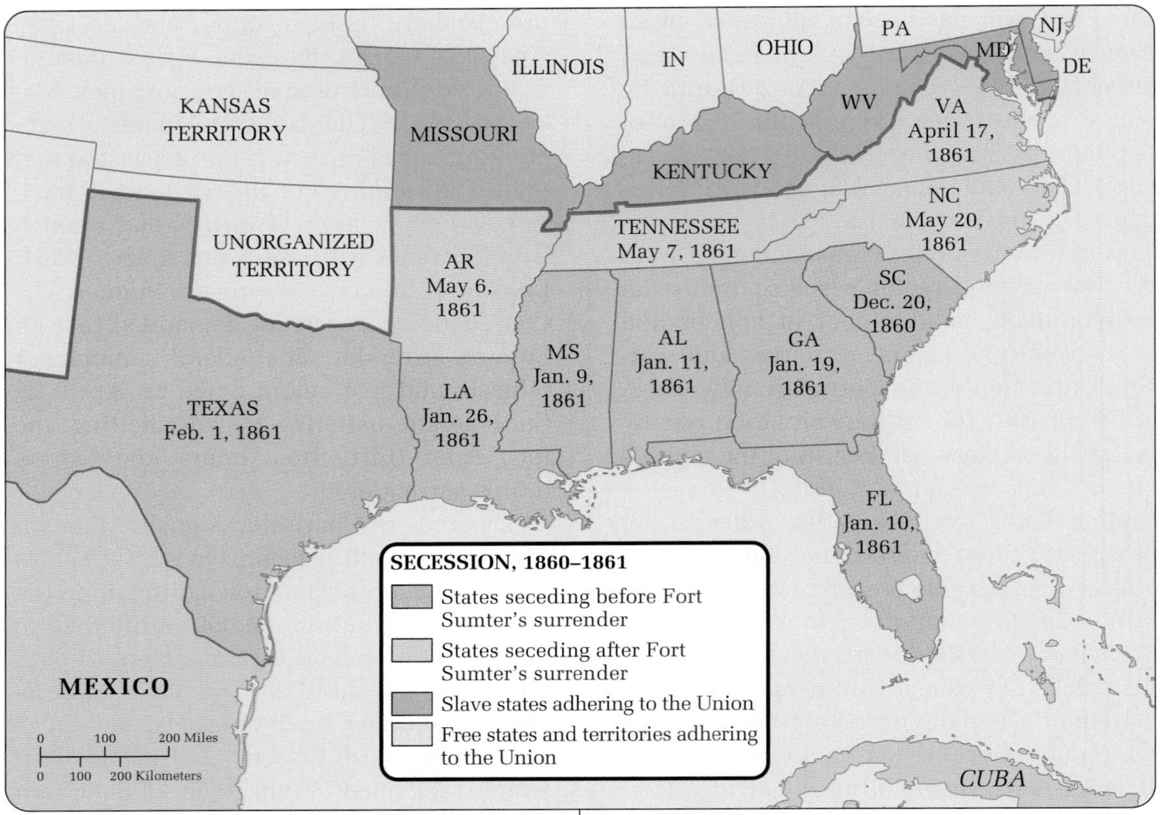

D.C., with Confederate states. To hold the state, Lincoln took drastic measures: he suspended the writ of habeas corpus (under which judges could require arresting officers to produce their prisoners and justify their arrest) and jailed pro-Confederate leaders. The fall elections ended the threat of Maryland's secession by returning a solidly Unionist majority in the state.

The Kentucky legislature proclaimed its "neutrality" in the conflict, but that only lasted until September 3, 1861, when a Confederate force captured several towns. General Ulysses S. Grant then moved troops into Paducah. Thereafter, Kentucky for the most part remained with the Union. It joined the Confederacy, some have said, only after the war.

In Missouri, Unionists had a numerical advantage, but secessionist sympathies were strong, and a Confederate militia began to gather near St. Louis. Unionist forces broke the back of Confederate resistance in Missouri at the battle of Pea Ridge (March 6–8, 1862), just over the state line in Arkansas. Nevertheless, border warfare continued in Missouri, pitting against each other rival bands of gunslingers who kept up their feuding and banditry for years after the war ended.

Robert E. Lee epitomized the agonizing choice facing many border-state residents. Son of "Lighthorse Harry" Lee, a Revolutionary War hero, and married to a descendant of Martha Washington, Lee had graduated second in his class from West Point, had fought with distinction during the Mexican War, and had served in the United States Army for thirty years. Now a colonel and master of Arlington, an elegant estate facing Washington across the Potomac, he was summoned by Lincoln's seventy-five-year-old general-in-chief, Winfield Scott, another Virginian, and offered command of the new Federal forces. After a sleepless night pacing the floor, he told Scott he could not go against his "country," meaning Virginia. Lee resigned his commission, retired to his estate, and soon answered a call to command the Virginia—later the Confederate—military forces.

In contrast, many southerners made great sacrifices to remain loyal to the Union. Some left their native region once the fighting began. Others who remained in the South found ways to support the Union. In every Confederate state except South Carolina, whole regiments were organized to fight for the Union, and at least 100,000 men from the southern states fought against the Confederacy. Of course, some of these southern "Tories" changed sides out of expediency rather than loyalty. Confederate soldiers who had been captured occasionally chose to switch sides and serve on the Indian frontier rather than remain in prison. Others, however, never embraced the Confederate cause. Many of the southern Unionists were Irish or German immigrants who had no love for slavery or the planter elite.

Northern and Southern Advantages

A balance sheet of the sections in 1860 shows that the Union held twenty-three states, including four border slave states, while the Confederacy had eleven, claiming also Missouri and Kentucky. Ignoring conflicts of allegiance within various states, which might roughly cancel each other out, the population count was about 22 million in the Union to 9 million in the Confederacy, and about 3.5 million of the latter were slaves. To help redress the imbalance, the Confederacy mobilized 80 percent or more of its military-age white males, and a third of them would die during the prolonged war.

An even greater advantage for the North was its industry. The states that joined the Confederacy produced just 7.4 percent of the nation's manufactures on the eve of the war, and little of this was in heavy industry. The Union states, in addition to making most of the country's shoes, textiles, and iron products, turned out 97 percent of the firearms and 96 percent of the railroad equipment. They had most of the trained mechanics, most of the shipping and mercantile firms, and the bulk of the banking and financial resources.

Even in farm production the northern states overshadowed the rural South, for most of the North's population was still rooted in the soil. As the progress of the war upset southern agricultural output, northern farms managed to increase theirs, despite the loss of workers to the army. The Confederacy produced enough food to meet minimal needs, but the disruption of transport caused shortages that led to inflation.

The North's advantage in transport weighed heavily as the war went on. The Union had more wagons, horses, and ships than the Confederacy, and an impressive edge in railroads: about 20,000 miles to the South's 10,000. The actual discrepancy was even greater, for southern railroads were mainly short lines built to different gauges (widths), and they had few replacements for train cars that broke down or wore out.

However, the South did have the advantage of geography: the Confederates could fight a defensive war on their own territory. In addition, the South initially had more experienced military leaders.

Bull Run

Caught up in the frothy excitement of military preparation, both sides predicted an easy and quick victory.

Nowhere was this naive optimism more clearly displayed than at the first battle at Bull Run (Manassas).* An impatient public

* The Federals most often named battles for natural features; the Confederates, for nearby towns, thus Bull Run (Manassas), Antietam (Sharpsburg), Stone's River (Murfreesboro), and the like.

pressured both armies to strike quickly and decisively. The battle-hungry Confederate general P. G. T. Beauregard hurried his forces in Virginia to Manassas Junction, about twenty-five miles west of Washington. Lincoln decided that General Irvin McDowell's hastily assembled army of some 30,000 might overrun the outnumbered Confederates and quickly march on to Richmond, the Confederate capital.

It was a dry summer day on July 21, 1861, when McDowell's raw recruits encountered Beauregard's army dug in behind a little stream called Bull Run. The two generals, who had been classmates at West Point, adopted similar plans—each would try to turn the other's left flank. The Federals almost achieved their purpose early in the afternoon, but Confederate reinforcements poured in to check the Union offensive. Amid the fury, a South Carolina general rallied his men by pointing to Thomas Jackson's brigade of Virginians: "Look at Jackson standing there like a damned stone wall." It was true, and Jackson was called "Stonewall" thereafter.

Their attack blunted, the exhausted Union troops eventually broke, and their confused and frantic retreat turned into a panic as fleeing soldiers and civilian spectators clogged the Washington road. Lincoln read a gloomy dispatch from the front: "The day is lost. Save Washington and the remnants of this army. The routed troops will not re-form." But the Confederates were almost as disorganized and exhausted by the battle as the Yankees were, and they failed to give chase.

The Battle of Bull Run was a sobering experience for both sides. Much of the new war's romance—the splendid uniforms, bright flags, fervent songs—gave way to the agonizing realization that this would be a long, mean, and costly struggle. *Harper's Weekly* bluntly warned: "From the fearful day at Bull Run dates war. Not polite war . . . but war that breaks hearts and blights homes."

The War's Early Course

The Battle of Bull Run demonstrated that the war would not be decided with one sudden stroke. Union general Winfield Scott had predicted as much, and now Lincoln fell back upon the three-pronged "Anaconda strategy" that Scott had long before proposed. It called first for the Army of the Potomac to defend Washington and exert constant pressure on the Confederate capital at Richmond. At the same time, the navy would blockade the southern coast and dry up the Confederacy's access to foreign goods and weapons. The final component of the plan would divide the Confederacy by sending navy gunboats and transports to invade the South along the main water routes: the Mississippi, Tennessee, and Cumberland Rivers.

The Confederate strategy was simpler. If the Union forces could be stalemated, Davis and others hoped, then the British or French might be convinced to join their cause, or perhaps public sentiment in the North would force Lincoln to seek a negotiated settlement. So at the same time that armies were forming in the South, Confederate diplomats were seeking assistance in London and Paris, and Confederate sympathizers in the North were urging an end to the Union's war effort.

Naval Actions

After the Battle of Bull Run and for the rest of 1861 and early 1862, the most important military actions involved naval warfare and a blockade of southern ports. The Union navy grew from 90 ships at the start of the war to 650 vessels of all types. It never completely sealed off the South, but it raised to desperate levels the hazards of blockade running.

The one great threat to the Union navy proved to be short-lived. The Confederates in Norfolk had fashioned an ironclad ship from an abandoned Union steam frigate, the *Merrimack*. Rechristened the *Virginia*, it ventured out on March 8, 1862, and wrought havoc among the Union ships at the entrance to Chesapeake Bay. But as luck would have it, a new Union ironclad, the *Monitor*, arrived from New York in time to engage the *Virginia* the next day. They fought to a draw, and the *Virginia* returned to port, where the

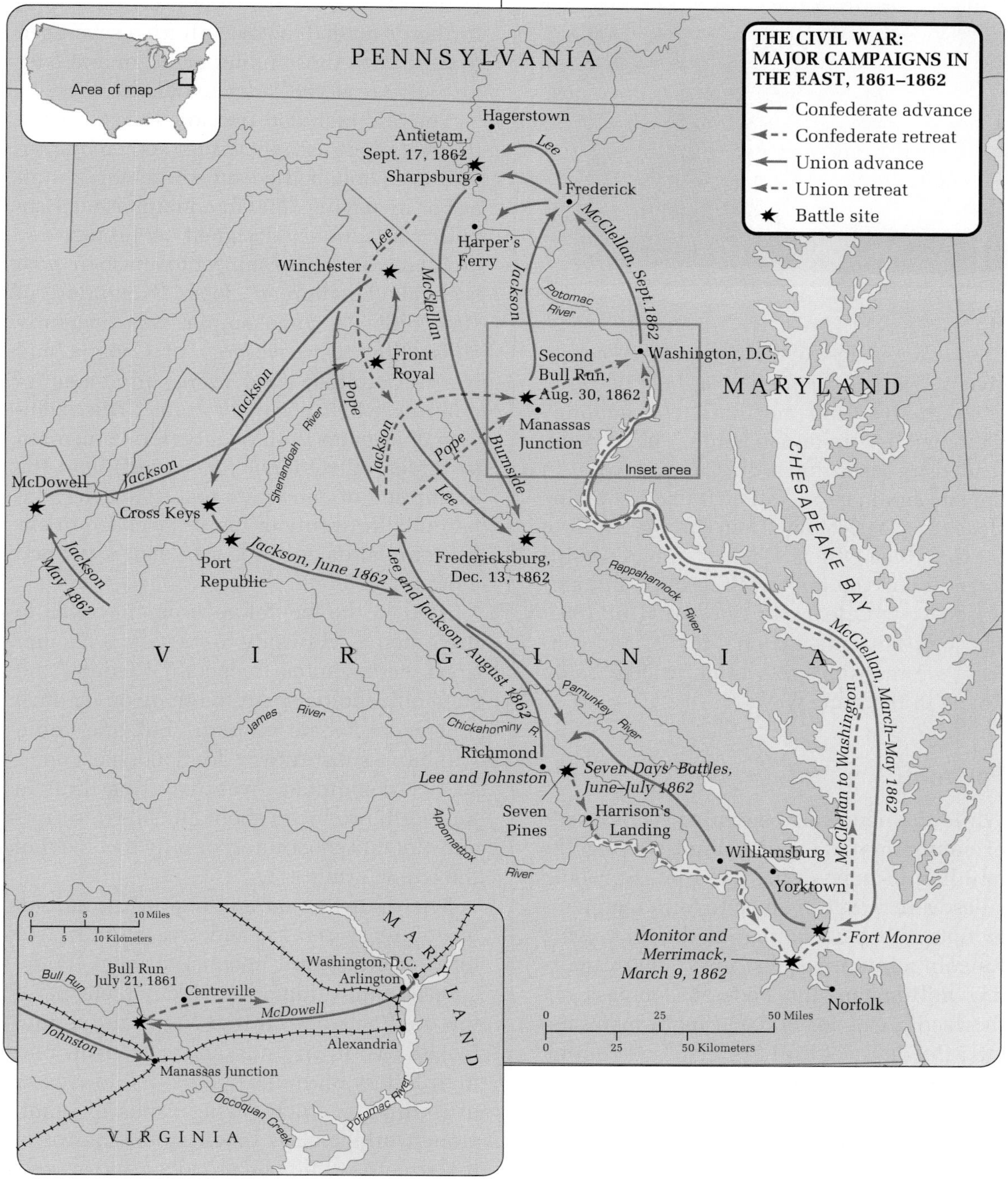

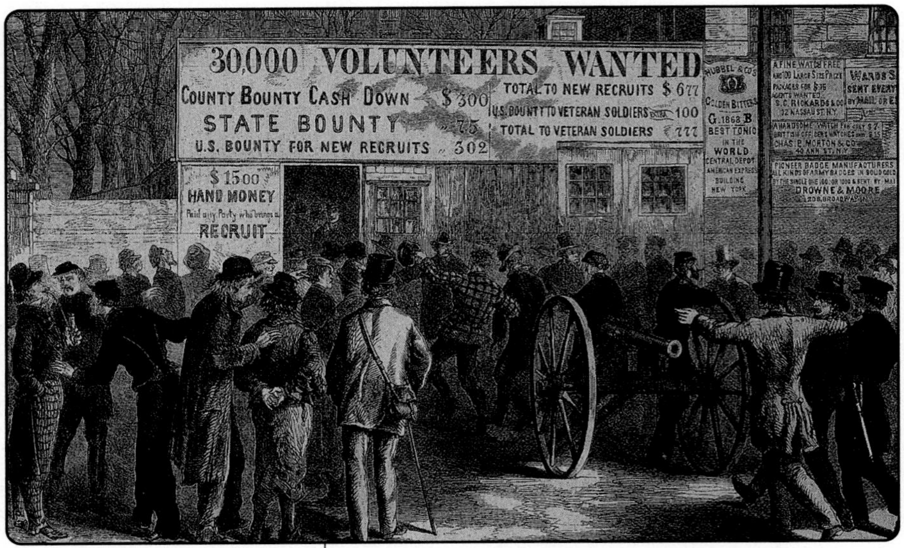

Enlisting Union soldiers. Neither side was prepared for the magnitude of the nation's first "modern" war.

Confederates destroyed it when they had to give up Norfolk soon afterward.

Gradually, the northern "Anaconda" tightened its grip on the South. The navy extended its bases down the Carolina coast in the late summer and fall of 1862, first laying siege to Charleston. Then in the Gulf of Mexico, Flag Officer David Farragut's ships forced open the lower Mississippi and surprised New Orleans in the spring of 1862. The city surrendered on May 1, and Farragut's forces then moved on to take Baton Rouge in the same way.

Forming Armies

While the navy was beginning its blockade of southern ports and commissioning the building of new ships, the armies on both sides were recruiting men to form regiments to fight the land battles of the war. After Lincoln's initial request for 75,000 ninety-day militiamen, the Federal Congress authorized a call for 500,000 more men, and after the Battle of Bull Run it added another 500,000. By the end of 1861, the first half million had enlisted in the Union Army.

In the Confederacy, the first mass enlistment put a great strain on limited means. After first trying to recruit volunteers, the Confederates turned to conscription. On April 16, 1862, all white male citizens, eighteen to thirty-five, were declared members of the army for three years, and those already in service were required to serve out three years. In 1862 the upper age was raised to forty-five, and in 1864 the age limits were further extended to cover all from seventeen to fifty, with those under eighteen and over forty-five reserved for state defense.

The law included two loopholes. First, a draftee might escape service either by providing an able-bodied substitute not of draft age or by paying $500 in commutation. Second, exemptions, designed to protect key civilian work, were subject to abuse by men seeking "bombproof" jobs. Exemption of state officials, for example, was flagrantly abused by the governors of Georgia and North Carolina, who were in charge of defining which jobs were vital. The exclusion of teachers with twenty pupils inspired a sudden educational renaissance, and the exemption of one white man for each plantation with twenty or more slaves led to bitter complaints about "a rich man's war and a poor man's fight."

In 1863 the federal government began to draft men aged twenty to forty-five. Exemptions were granted to specified federal and state officeholders and to others on medical or compassionate grounds, but one could still buy a substitute or, for $300, have one's service commuted. Eventually the draft in the North produced about 46,000 conscripts and 118,000 substitutes, or only 6 percent of the Union armies.

The draft flouted an American tradition of voluntary service and was widely held to be arbitrary and unconstitutional. Widespread opposition limited enforcement of the draft acts both in the North and South. In New York City, the announcement of a draft lottery on July 11, 1863, led to a week of rioting in which roving bands of immigrant working-class toughs took control of the streets. Although provoked by opposition to the draft, the riots exposed emerging racial and ethnic tensions. The mobs assaulted conscription offices, factories, docks, and the homes of prominent Republicans. But they directed their wrath most furiously at blacks. In their tortured reasoning, they blamed blacks for causing the war and for threatening to take their own unskilled jobs. The violence ran completely out of control; 120 people died, and an estimated $2 million in property was destroyed before soldiers brought from Gettysburg restored order.

The West and the Civil War

During the Civil War, western settlement continued. New discoveries of gold and silver along the eastern slopes of the Sierra Nevadas and in Montana and Colorado lured thousands of prospectors and their suppliers. Dakota, Colorado, and Nevada gained territorial status in 1861, Idaho and Arizona in 1863, and Montana in 1864. Silver-rich Nevada gained its statehood in 1864.

With the firing on Fort Sumter, many of the regular army units assigned to frontier outposts in the West moved east to meet the Confederate threat. In Texas, the Indian Territory (Oklahoma), and southern New Mexico, Union soldiers left altogether. Elsewhere they left behind skeleton units to man the forts. Despite the lessened federal presence, Texas was the only western state to join the Confederacy. For the most part, the federal government maintained its control of the other western territories during the war.

Many Indian tribes found themselves caught up in the Civil War. Indian regiments fought on both sides, and in the Indian Country they fought against each other. Many Oklahoma Indians owned African-American slaves and felt a natural bond with southern whites. Oklahoma's proximity to Texas also influenced the Choctaws and Chickasaws to support the Confederacy. The Cherokees, Creeks, and Seminoles were more divided in their loyalties.

Actions in the Western Theater

After the Battle of Bull Run, little happened in the Eastern Theater (east of the Appalachians) before May 1862. The Western Theater (from the mountains to the Mississippi), on the other hand, flared up with several clashes and an important penetration of the Confederate states. In western Kentucky, Confederate general Albert Sidney Johnston had perhaps 40,000 men stretched over some 150 miles. Early in 1862 Union general Ulysses S. Grant attacked the weak center of Johnston's overextended lines. Moving out of Paducah, Kentucky, with a gunboat flotilla, Grant's army swung southward up the Tennessee River toward Fort Henry. After a pounding from the Union gunboats, the fort fell on February 6. Grant then moved overland to attack Fort Donelson, and on February 16 his army captured its 12,000 men. Grant's blunt demand of "immediate and unconditional surrender" and his quick success sent a thrill through the dispirited North.

Ulysses S. "Unconditional Surrender" Grant had not only opened a water route to Nashville but had thrust his forces between the two strongholds of the western Confederates. Johnston therefore had to give up his foothold in Kentucky and abandon Nashville to General Don Carlos Buell's Army of the Ohio. The disheveled Grant, who had graduated from West Point in the lower half of his class and had resigned from the army in disgrace for drunkenness in 1854, was now a national hero. But not for long.

Shiloh

After defeats in Kentucky and Tennessee, General Johnston regrouped the Confederate forces in Corinth, Mississippi, in hopes of retaking control of the Mississippi Valley. As Grant prepared to assault Corinth, he made a costly mistake. He clumsily placed his troops on a rolling plateau between two creeks flowing into the Tennessee River and

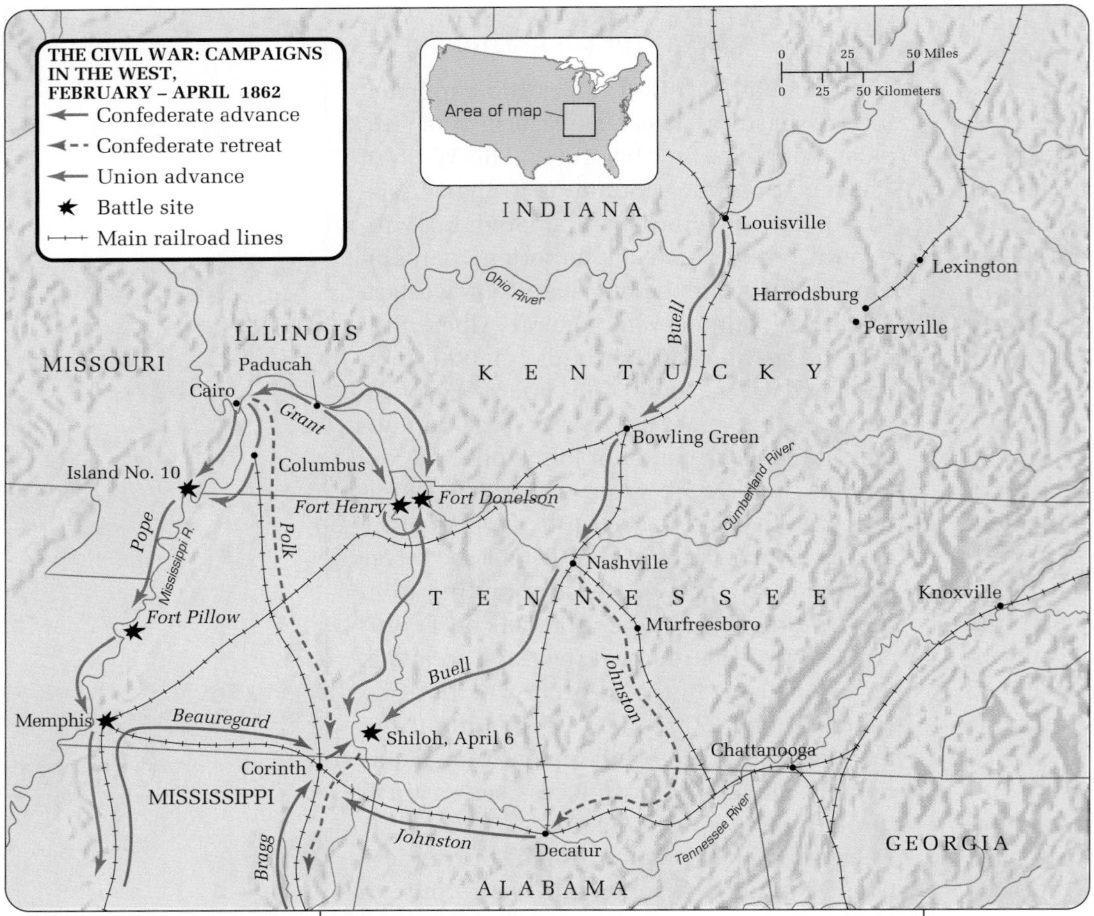

failed to set up defensive trenches. Johnston shrewdly recognized Grant's oversight, and on the morning of April 6, his forces attacked the vulnerable Federals.

The Confederates struck suddenly at Shiloh, a log church in the center of the Union camp. There they found most of Grant's troops still sleeping or eating breakfast. Some died in their bedrolls. After a day of bloody carnage and confusion, Grant's men were pinned against the river. They may well have been annihilated had the Confederate commander, General Johnston, not been mortally wounded at the peak of the battle. His second in command called off the attack. Under the cover of gunboats and artillery at nearby Pittsburg Landing, Grant and the brilliant general from Ohio, William Tecumseh Sherman, rallied their troops. Reinforcements arrived that night during a torrential rainstorm, and the next day Grant took the offensive. The Confederates glumly withdrew to Corinth, leaving the Union army too battered to pursue.

Shiloh, a Hebrew word meaning "place of peace," was the costliest battle in American history up to that point, although worse was yet to come. "The scenes on this field," Sherman sadly noted, "would have cured anybody of war." Combined casualties of nearly 20,000 exceeded the total dead and wounded of the Revolution, the War of 1812, and the Mexican War. After Shiloh, the Confederates and Federals realized there would not be a quick end to the war. Moreover, after this battle, the Union lost for a while the leadership of its finest general. Grant had blundered badly. Some critics charged that he had been drinking and called upon Lincoln to replace him. But the president, faced with the dithering of his other generals (especially George McClellan in the Eastern Theater), declined: "I can't spare this man; he fights." Grant's superior, General Henry Halleck, however, was not as forgiving. He relieved Grant of his command for several months, and as a result the Union thrust southward ground to a halt. For the remainder of 1862 the chief action in the Western Theater was a series of inconclusive maneuvers and a few sharp engagements.

McClellan's Peninsular Campaign

The Eastern Theater remained fairly quiet for nine months after Bull Run. After the Union defeat, Lincoln had replaced McDowell with the brilliant, if theatrical and hesitant, General George B. McClellan. As head of the Army of the Potomac, he instituted a rigid training regimen, determined that his men would be ready for their next battle. On the surface, McClellan exuded confidence. Yet for all of his organizational ability and dramatic flair, his innate caution would prove crippling. His foremost concern was to avoid defeat rather than inflict it on the enemy.

Time passed, and McClellan kept building his forces to meet the superior numbers he always claimed were facing him. Lincoln initially gave McClellan his complete support, yet after nine months of such prolonged preparation, the president and much of the public had grown understandably impatient. An exasperated Lincoln, convinced that his general "has got the slows," ordered McClellan to begin forward movement by February 22, 1862. McClellan brashly predicted: "I will be in Richmond in ten days."

In mid-March 1862, McClellan's army finally embarked, and before the end of May his advance units sighted the church steeples in Richmond. Thousands of Richmond residents fled the city in panic. President Davis sent his own family to a safe haven west of the city. But McClellan failed to capitalize on his situation. On May 31 Confederate general Joseph E. Johnston struck at Union forces isolated by floodwaters on the south bank of the Chickahominy River. In the battle of Seven Pines (Fair Oaks), only the arrival of reinforcements prevented a disastrous Union defeat. Both sides took heavy casualties, and Johnston was severely wounded.

At this point, the fifty-five-year-old Robert E. Lee assumed command of the Army of Northern Virginia, changing the course of the war. Lee was a reticent Christian gentleman in private, but a slashing, daring leader in uniform. Unlike Johnston, he enjoyed Davis's trust and assembled a galaxy of superb field commanders led by Stonewall Jackson, the fearless, pious mathematics professor from the Virginia Military Institute.

Once in command, Lee quickly decided to hit the Union forces north of the Chickahominy River on June 26, 1862, leaving only a token force in Richmond. But heavy losses prevented the Confederates from sustaining their momentum. Lee launched a final desperate attack at Malvern Hill (July 1), where the Confederates were riddled by artillery. This week of intense fighting, lumped together as the Seven Days' Battles, failed to dislodge the Union forces.

Second Bull Run

McClellan evacuated the peninsula and joined forces with the bombastic John Pope for a new assault against Richmond from the north. As McClellan's Army of the Potomac pulled out, Lee moved northward to strike Pope before the Union forces could be joined. Dividing his forces, he sent Stonewall Jackson's famous "foot cavalry" on a sweep around Pope's right flank to attack his supply lines and the federal depot at Manassas Junction.

At Second Bull Run (or Second Manassas), fought on almost the same site as the earlier battle, the Confederates thoroughly confused Pope. On August 30, 1862, General James Longstreet's corps of 30,000 Confederates, screaming the Rebel yell "like demons emerging from the earth," drove the Union forces from the field. One New York regiment lost 124 of its 490 men, the highest percentage of deaths in any battle of the war. In the next few days, the whipped Union forces pulled back into fortifications around Washington, where McClellan once again took command and reorganized. The disgraced Pope was dispatched to Minnesota to fight in the Indian wars.

Antietam

Still on the offensive, Lee determined to move the battlefield out of the South and perhaps thereby gain foreign recognition of the Confederacy. In September 1862 he led his troops into western Maryland and headed for Pennsylvania. As luck would have it, however, his bold strategy was uncovered when a Union soldier picked up a bundle of cigars and discovered a secret order from Lee wrapped around them. The paper revealed that Lee had again divided his army, sending Jackson off to take Harper's Ferry.

McClellan, instead of leaping at his unexpected opportunity, delayed for sixteen crucial hours, still worried—as always—about enemy strength. Lee was thereby able to reassemble most of his tired army behind Antietam Creek.

On September 17, 1862, McClellan's forces attacked, and the furious Battle of Antietam (Sharpsburg) began. Still outnumbered more than two to one, the Confederates forced a standoff in the bloodiest single day of the Civil War, a day participants thought would never end.

In the late afternoon McClellan backed off, letting Lee slip away across the Potomac. Lincoln fumed at McClellan's failure to follow up and gain a truly decisive victory. He fired off the following tart message to the general: "I have just read your dispatch about sore-tongued and fatigued horses. Will you pardon me for asking what the horses of your army have done . . . that fatigues anything?" Later the president sent his commander a one-sentence letter: "If you don't want to use the army, I should like to borrow it for a while." Failing to receive a satisfactory answer, Lincoln then removed McClellan and assigned him to recruiting duty in New Jersey. Never again would he command troops.

Fredericksburg

Lee's failed invasion had dashed the Confederacy's hopes of foreign recognition. A Rebel victory might have convinced England and France to assist the Confederacy. But however disappointing the Confederates were after Lee's failed offensive, the war was far from over. In his search for a fighting general, Lincoln now turned to Ambrose E. Burnside, a modest figure whose main achievement to that time had been to grow his famous whiskers ("sideburns").

On December 13, 1862, Burnside sent his men across the icy Rappahannock River to face Lee's forces, well entrenched behind a stone wall and on high ground just west of Fredericksburg, Virginia. Blessed with a clear field of fire, Confederate artillery and muskets chewed up the valorous Union ranks as they crossed a mile of open land west of the town.

Six times the courageous but suicidal Union assaults melted under the murderous fire coming from protected Confederate positions above and below them. The scene was both awful and awe-inspiring, prompting Lee to remark: "It is well that war is so terrible—we should grow too fond of it."

After seeing his men suffer more than 12,000 casualties, twice as many as the Confederates, Burnside wept as he gave the order to withdraw, and his battered forces limped back across the river. A northern reporter aptly summarized the battle: "It can hardly be in human nature for men to show more valor, or generals to manifest less judgment."

Thus the year 1862 ended with forces in the East deadlocked and the Federal advance in the West stalled since midyear. Union morale reached a low ebb. Northern Democrats were calling for a negotiated peace, while the so-called Radical Republicans were pushing Lincoln to prosecute the war even more forcefully. Several questioned the president's competence.

In the midst of such second-guessing and carping, the deeper currents of the war were in fact turning in favor of the Union: in a lengthening war, its superior resources began to tell on the morale of the Confederacy. In both the Eastern and Western Theaters, the Confederate counterattack had been

Two views of the Emancipation Proclamation. The Union view (*left*) shows a thoughtful Lincoln composing the proclamation with the Constitution and the Holy Bible in his lap. The Confederate view (*right*) shows a demented Lincoln with his foot on the Constitution using an inkwell held by the devil.

repulsed. And while the armies clashed, Lincoln by a stroke of a pen changed the conflict from a war for the Union into a revolutionary struggle for abolition. On January 1, 1863, he signed the Emancipation Proclamation.

Emancipation

The Emancipation Proclamation was the product of long and painful deliberation, as opinion was divided even in the North as to whether the slaves should all be freed. While most abolitionists favored both complete emancipation and social integration of the races, many antislavery activists only wanted to prohibit slavery from new territories and states, and they were willing to allow slavery to continue in the South.

Lincoln had always insisted that the purpose of the conflict was to restore the Union, and that he did not have the authority to free the slaves. Yet the prolonged war forced the issue. Slaves began to turn up in Union army camps, and generals did not know whether to declare them free or not. Some put these "contrabands" to work building fortifications; others liberated those who belonged to Confederate owners, thus risking upsetting border-state slaveholders. Lincoln himself edged toward emancipation.

As the war ground on, Lincoln eventually decided that complete emancipation was required for several reasons: slave labor bolstered the Confederate cause; sagging morale in the North needed the lift of a transcendent moral ideal; and public opinion was swinging that way as the war continued. Proclaiming a war on slavery, moreover, would end forever any chance that France or Britain would support the Confederacy.

The time to act came after Antietam. It was a dubious victory, but it did force Lee's withdrawal from the North. On September 22, 1862, Lincoln issued a preliminary Emancipation Proclamation to warn that on January 1, 1863, all slaves in Confederate states or areas still under active rebellion would be "thenceforward and forever free."

The proclamation, with few exceptions, freed only those slaves still under Confederate control, as cynics noted then and later. But critics missed a point that slaves readily grasped. "In a document proclaiming liberty," wrote a black historian, "the unfree never bother to read the fine print."

Lincoln's Emancipation Proclamation

reaffirmed the policy that blacks could enroll in the Union armed services and sparked efforts to organize new all-black units. The War Department authorized general recruitment of blacks all over the country, which transformed a war to preserve the Union into a revolution to overthrow the social, economic, and racial status quo in the South. The first challenge for black troops, however, was to overcome embedded racial fears of northern whites and to get an opportunity to prove themselves in battle. Finally, by mid-1863, black soldiers were involved in significant combat both in the Eastern and Western Theaters. Lincoln reported that several of his commanders believed that "the use of colored troops constitutes the heaviest blow yet dealt to the rebels."

Altogether, between 180,000 and 200,000 black men served in the Union army, providing around 10 percent of its total. Some 38,000 gave their lives. Blacks accounted for about a fourth of all enlistments in the navy, and of these, almost 3,000 died.

As the war entered its final months, freedom emerged more fully as a legal reality. The Thirteenth Amendment, which abolished slavery everywhere, was ratified by three-fourths of the states and became part of the Constitution on December 18, 1865, thus removing any lingering doubts about the legality of emancipation. By then, in fact, slavery remained only in the border states of Kentucky and Delaware.

Clara Barton was one of 200,000 women serving the Union Army as nurses or other health-related volunteers.

Women and the War

While breaking the bonds of slavery, the Civil War also loosened traditional restraints on female activity. Women on both sides played prominent roles in the conflict, and in the process many saw their outlook and status transformed. Initially the call to arms revived heroic images of female self-sacrifice and domestic skills. Women in the North and South sewed uniforms, composed uplifting poetry and songs, and raised money and supplies. Thousands of northern women worked with the United States Sanitary Commission, which organized medical relief and other services for soldiers. Others supported the freedmen's-aid movement to help ex-slaves.

In the North alone, some 20,000 women served as nurses or other health-related volunteers. The two most famous nurses were Dorothea Dix and Clara Barton, both untiring volunteers in service to the wounded and dying. Dix, the veteran reformer of the nation's insane asylums, became the Union Army's first Superintendent of Women Nurses. Barton was a former schoolteacher who worked as a nurse in the Civil War. Instead of accepting an assignment to a general hospital, she followed the troops on her own, working in makeshift field hospitals. At Antietam, she came so close to the fighting that, as she worked on a wounded soldier, a Confederate bullet ripped through the sleeve of her dress and killed the man. Barton challenged both male doctors' control of battlefield medicine and male bureaucrats' efforts to restrict the nurses' sphere of operations.

The war experience of women helped generate greater confidence in their abilities. The departure of hundreds of thousands of men for the battlefields forced women to assume the public and private roles the men left behind. A resident of Lexington, Virginia, reported in 1862 that there were "no men left" in town by mid-1862. Women in both the North and South suddenly found themselves in charge of households, farms, and businesses. They became farmers or plantation managers, clerks, munitions plant workers, and schoolteachers. In North Carolina in 1860, for example, only 7 percent of teachers were women. By the end of the Civil War, a majority of the state's teachers were women. Some 400 women disguised themselves as men and fought in the war; dozens worked as spies; others traveled with the armies, cooking meals, writing letters, and assisting with amputations.

Government during the War

Striking the shackles from 4 million slaves and loosening the restraints on female activity constituted a monumental social and economic revolution. But an even broader revolution developed as political power shifted from South to North after secession. Before the war, southern congressmen had been able to frustrate the legislative initiatives of both Free Soilers and Whigs. But once the secessionists abandoned Congress to the Republicans, a dramatic change occurred. A new protective tariff, a transcontinental railroad to run through Omaha to Sacramento, a homestead act that granted free farms of 160 acres to settlers who occupied the land for five years—all acts that had been stalled by sectional controversy—were adopted before the end of 1862. That year also saw the passage of the Morrill Land Grant Act, which provided federal aid to state colleges of "agricultural and mechanic arts." The National Banking Act, which created a uniform system of banking and bank-note currency, followed in 1863 and helped the Union address a critical problem: how to finance the war.

Union Finances

Congress had three options for solving the problem of financing the war: raising taxes, printing paper money, and borrowing. The higher taxes came chiefly in the form of the Morrill Tariff and excise taxes, which fell on manufacturers and nearly every profession. An income tax rounded out the revenue measures.

But tax revenues trickled in so slowly that Congress in 1862 ordered the printing of paper money. Eventually $450 million in "greenbacks" were printed, enough to pay the bills but not unleash the kind of runaway inflation that burdened the Confederacy after Jefferson Davis allowed the unlimited issue of paper money.

Women workers filling cartridges with gunpowder at the Federal arsenal in Watertown, Massachusetts.

Still, paper money and taxes provided only about two-thirds of the money to finance the war. The rest came chiefly from the sale of bonds. A Philadelphia banker named Jay Cooke mobilized a network of agents and propaganda for the sale of government war bonds. It worked well, and over $2 billion was raised in the process.

All wars provide opportunities for quick profits, and the Civil War was no different. Many American entrepreneurs reaped quick riches from war contracts. Several cut corners in the process, providing shoddy goods, paying bribes and kickbacks, or in some cases, not delivering supplies at all. Not all wartime fortunes, however, were made dishonestly. Their long-run importance was in promoting the capital accumulation that fueled the phenomenal postwar expansion of the national economy.

Confederate Finances

Confederate finances were a disaster from the start. Tariffs were tried, but imports were low and therefore raised little revenue. In 1863 the Confederate Congress passed a measure that taxed nearly everything. A 10 percent tax on all agricultural products, however, did more to outrage farmers and planters than to supply the army. Enforcement was so lax and evasion so easy that the taxes produced only negligible income.

The last resort, printing paper money, was in fact resorted to early. Beginning in 1861, the new Confederate government began an extended inflationary binge. Altogether the Confederacy turned out more than $1 billion in paper money, forcing prices up geometrically. By 1864, a turkey sold in a Richmond market for $100, flour went for $425 a barrel, and bacon for $10 a pound. Those living on fixed incomes were caught in a merciless inflationary squeeze.

Confederate Diplomacy

No sooner had the war begun than the Confederate government focused on gaining help from foreign governments in the form of supplies, formal recognition, or perhaps even armed intervention. The first Confederate emissaries to England and France took hope when the British foreign minister received them informally after their arrival in London in 1861. In Paris, French leader Napoleon III even promised them that he would recognize the Confederacy if England would lead the way. But when the agents returned to London, the government refused to see them, partly because of Union pressures and partly out of British self-interest.

Confederate negotiators were far more successful at getting supplies than gaining formal recognition. The most spectacular feat was the procurement of raiding ships. Although British law prohibited the sale of warships to belligerents, a southern agent was able to have the ships built and then, on trial runs, to escape and be outfitted with guns. In all, eighteen such ships were activated and saw action in the Atlantic, Pacific, and Indian Oceans, where they sank hundreds of Yankee ships and sparked terror in the rest.

Union Politics and Civil Liberties

On the home fronts during the Civil War, there was no moratorium on partisan politics, North or South. Within his own party, Lincoln faced a Radical wing composed mainly of prewar abolitionists. Led by House members such as Thaddeus Stevens and George Julian, and senators such as Charles Sumner, Benjamin Wade, and Zachariah Chandler, the so-called Radical Republicans formed a Joint Committee on the Conduct of the War, which increasingly pressured Lincoln to emancipate the slaves, confiscate southern plantations, and prosecute the war more vigorously. The majority of Republicans, however, supported the president, and the party was virtually united on economic matters.

The Democratic party suffered the loss of its southern wing as well as the death of its leader, Stephen A. Douglas, in June 1861. By and large, northern Democrats supported a war for the "Union as it was" before 1860, giving reluctant support to war policies but opposing wartime constraints on civil liberties and the new economic legislation. "War Democrats" such as Senator Andrew Johnson from Tennessee and Secretary of War Edwin Stanton fully supported Lincoln's policies, however, while a Peace Wing of the Democratic party preferred a negotiated end to the fighting, even at the risk of the Union. An extreme fringe among the Peace Democrats even flirted with outright disloyalty. The "Copperheads," as they were called, were strongest in Ohio, Indiana, and Illinois, states with many transplanted southerners, some of whom were pro-Confederate.

Such open sympathy for the enemy provoked Lincoln to crack down hard. Early in the war, he assumed certain emergency powers such as the suspension of the writ of habeas corpus (which entitled people who had been jailed to demand that a court hear their case). Lincoln also asserted his right to invoke martial law. When critics charged that such measures violated the Constitution, Lincoln's congressional supporters pushed through the Habeas Corpus Act of 1863, which authorized the suspension of the writ. Some 14,000 arrests of Confederate sympathizers resulted.

At their 1864 national convention, the Democrats called for an immediate armistice to stop the war and named General McClellan as their candidate, but he distanced himself from the peace platform by declaring that the two sides must agree on reunion before the fighting should stop. Radical Republicans, who still regarded Lincoln as being too soft on the traitorous southerners, tried to thwart his renomination, but Lincoln outmaneuvered them at every turn. In a shrewd move, he named as his vice-presidential running mate Andrew Johnson, a War Democrat from Tennessee, and called their ticket the "National Union" so as to minimize partisanship. As the war ground on through 1864, with General Grant's forces taking heavy losses in Virginia, Lincoln fully expected to lose the election, but key military victories in August and September turned the tide. McClellan carried only New Jersey, Delaware, and Kentucky.

Confederate Politics

Unlike Lincoln, Jefferson Davis never had to contest a presidential election. Both he and his vice-president, Alexander Stephens, were elected for a six-year term. But discontent flourished in the South as events went from bad to worse. Food was in short supply, and prices had skyrocketed by the spring of 1863. A bread riot in Richmond in 1863 ended only when Davis himself persuaded the mob (mostly women) to disperse.

Davis, like Lincoln, also had to contend with dissenters. Especially troublesome were those committed to states' rights who had supported secession but steadfastly opposed the centralizing tendencies of the government in Richmond. Georgia and North Carolina were strongholds of such sentiment. They challenged, among other things, the legality of conscription, taxes on farm produce, and above all, the suspension of habeas corpus. Vice-President Stephens himself carried on a running battle with Davis, accusing the president of trying to establish a "military despotism."

Such internal bickering did not alone cause the Confederacy's defeat, but it certainly contributed to it. Whereas Lincoln was the consummate pragmatist, Davis was a brittle dogmatist with a waspish temper. His fundamental insecurity made him indecisive, but once he made a decision, nothing could change his mind. Such a personality was ill suited to the chief executive of an infant nation.

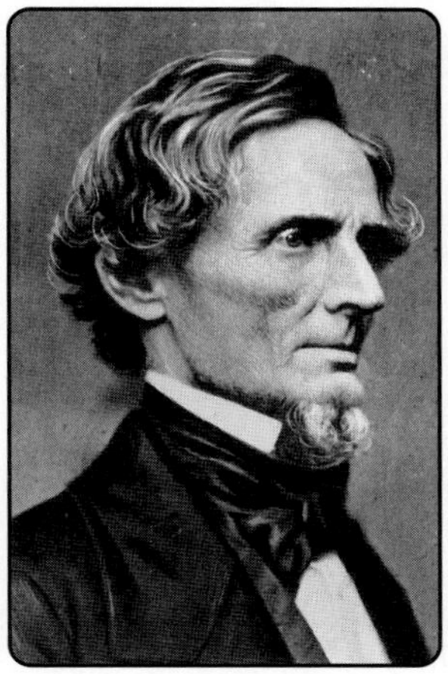

Jefferson Davis.

The Faltering Confederacy

In 1863 the hinges of fate began to close the door on the brief career of the Confederacy. After the Union disaster at Fredericksburg, Lincoln's frustrating search for a capable general turned to one of Burnside's disgruntled lieutenants, Joseph E. Hooker, a hard-drinking character whose pugnacity had earned him the nickname "Fighting Joe." But he was no more able to deliver the goods than Burnside. Hooker failed his test at Chancellorsville in May 1863.

Chancellorsville

With a force of perhaps 130,000 men, the largest Union army yet gathered, and a brilliant plan, Hooker suffered a loss of control at the critical juncture during the Battle of Chancellorsville. Lee, with perhaps half that number of troops, staged what became a textbook classic of daring and maneuver. Hooker's plan was to leave his base, opposite Fredericksburg, on a sweeping movement upstream across the Rappahannock and Rapidan Rivers, and flank Lee's position. A large diversionary force was to cross the Rappahannock below the town. Initially all went well, but Lee sniffed out the ruse. He moved his main force to meet Hooker and dispatched Stuart's cavalry to disrupt the Union lines of communications. Hooker suddenly lost sight of his opponents and was caught by surprise when rebel skirmishers fired on his advance columns. He then ordered his troops to pull back to the Chancellorsville crossroads. "I just lost faith in Joe Hooker," Hooker himself later admitted, and Lee quickly took advantage of his opponent's failure of nerve. He divided his army again, sending Jackson with more than half the men on a long march to hit the enemy's exposed right flank.

On May 2, Jackson surprised Hooker's right flank at the edge of a densely wooded area called the Wilderness. The Confederates slammed into the Union lines with such furor that the defenders panicked and ran. The thick undergrowth made troop movements more chaotic than usual, and the fighting died out in confusion as darkness fell. The next day was Lee's, however, as his troops forced Hooker's army to recross the Rappahannock. It was the peak of Lee's career, but Chancellorsville was his last significant victory, and his costliest: the South suffered more than 12,000 casualties, including 1,600 killed, among them Stonewall Jackson, mistakenly shot by his own men in the confused fighting. "I have lost my right arm," lamented Lee.

Vicksburg

While Lee held the Federals at bay in the East, Grant, his command now restored, had been groping his way down the Mississippi River toward Vicksburg in western Mississippi. Grant knew that if he could capture Vicksburg, the Union forces could gain control of the Mississippi River and thereby split the Confederacy in two. Located on a bluff 200 feet above the river, Vicksburg had withstood repeated naval attacks. For months Grant tried to discover a way to penetrate the city's heavily fortified defenses. His army crossed to Louisiana, took a roundabout route to Jackson, Mississippi, where it routed the Confederates, and headed back to Vicksburg. The Federals pinned down 30,000 Confederates in Vicksburg, and Grant resolved to starve them out.

Gettysburg

The plight of besieged Vicksburg put the Confederate high command in a quandary. Lee proposed a diversion. If he could win a great victory on northern soil, he reasoned, he might do more than just relieve the pressure on Vicksburg; he might bring an end to the war. In June 1863 he moved his forces into the Shenandoah Valley and headed north across Maryland. Neither side chose Gettysburg, Pennsylvania, as the site for the climactic battle, but a Confederate foraging party entered the town in search of shoes and encountered units of Union cavalry. The main forces then quickly converged there.

On July 1, a hot, steamy day, the Confederates pushed the Federals out of the town, but into stronger positions on high ground to the south. The new Union commander, George G. Meade, hastened reinforcements to the new lines along the heights. On July 2, Lee, hampered by a lack of information, ordered assaults at both the extreme left and the extreme right flanks of Meade's army. The Confederates fought fiercely, but the Federals, who outnumbered their attackers almost two to one, fought just as bravely—and the assaults were repulsed.

The next day Lee staked everything on one final attack on the Union center at Cemetery Ridge. His plan, however, suffered from a fatal problem: his generals were not unified in their support of it. As a result, General James Longstreet, who remained skeptical of a frontal assault, did not position his forces to assist General George Pick-

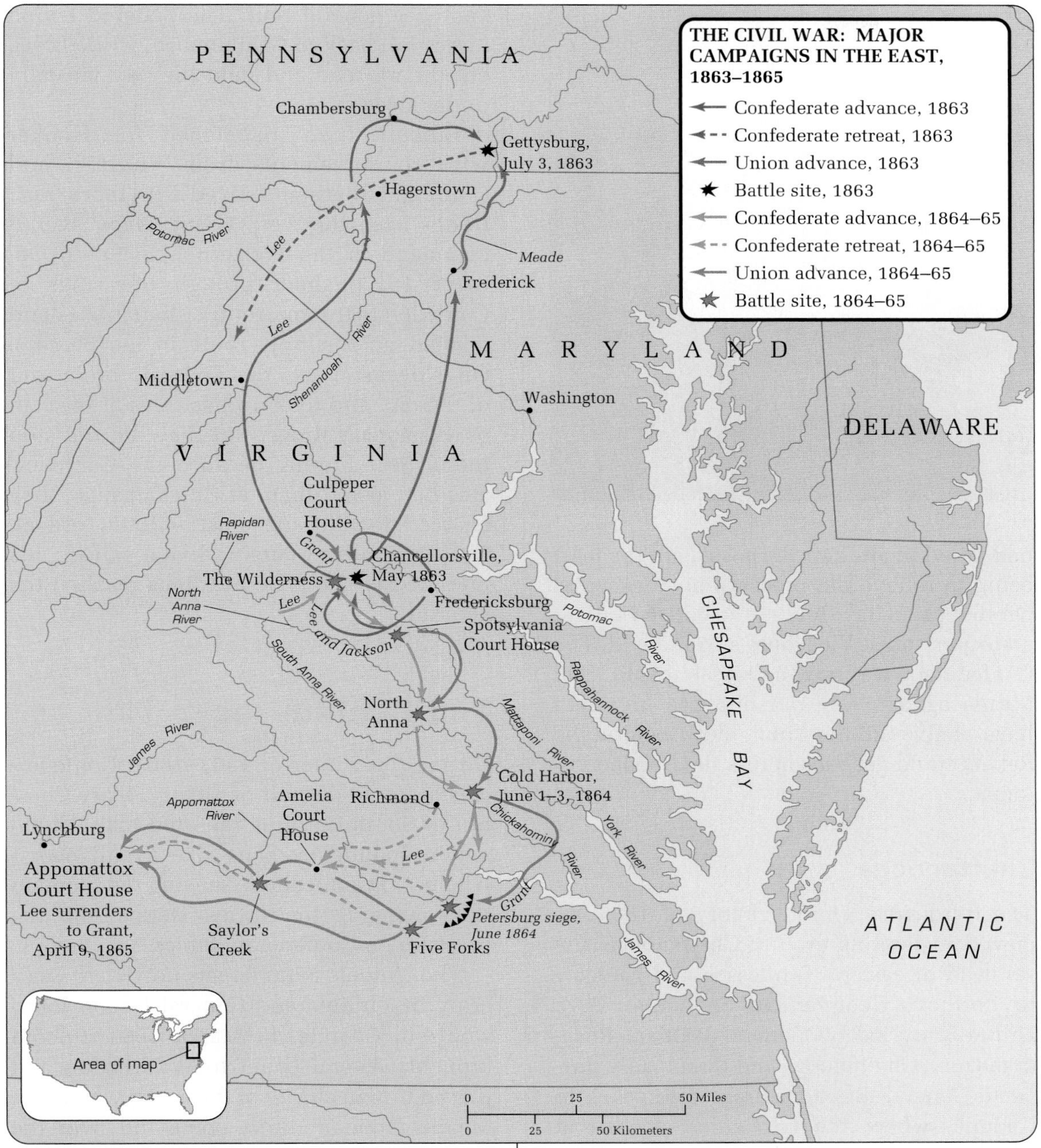

ett's division, which Lee had ordered to take Cemetery Ridge.

About 2 P.M. Pickett's 15,000 troops emerged from the woods west of Cemetery Ridge and began their advance across rising open ground commanded by Union artillery. It was as hopeless as Burnside's assault at Fredericksburg. Those who avoided the shelling by Federal cannons were devastated by a wall of musket fire. Of the 14,000 attackers, barely half returned, leading Lee to mutter: "All this has been my fault."

With nothing left to do but retreat, Lee's mangled army began to slog south in a driving rain. They left about a third of their number behind on the ground. They also

Harvest of Death.
T. H. O'Sullivan's grim photograph of the dead at Gettysburg.

had failed in all their purposes, not the least being to relieve the pressure on Vicksburg. On that same day, July 4, the entire Confederate garrison at Vicksburg surrendered. The Confederacy was now irrevocably split. Had Meade aggressively pursued Lee he might have delivered the final blow before the Rebels could get back across the flooded Potomac.

Chattanooga

The third great Union victory of 1863 occurred in fighting around Chattanooga, the railhead of eastern Tennessee and gateway to northern Georgia. On September 9, a Union army led by General William Rosecrans took Chattanooga and then rashly pursued General Braxton Bragg's forces into Georgia, where the two sides clashed at Chickamauga (an old Cherokee word meaning "river of death"). The battle (September 19–20) had the makings of a Union disaster, because it was one of the few times when the Confederates had a numerical advantage (about 70,000 to 56,000). On the second day, Bragg smashed the Federal right, and only the stubborn stand on the left under Virginia Unionist George H. Thomas (thenceforth known as the "Rock of Chickamauga") prevented a general rout. The battered Union forces fell back to Chattanooga, while Bragg cut the railroad and held the city virtually under siege.

Lincoln then dispatched Joe Hooker with reinforcements from Virginia, and Grant and Sherman arrived with more fresh troops from the west. Grant, given overall command of the Western Theater on October 16, pushed through the rings of Confederate troops around Chattanooga and opened up a supply route in the process. On November 24, the Federals broke out of the city and took up positions at the foot of Missionary Ridge. But they did not stop there. Still fuming because the Confederates had jeered them at Chickamauga, they charged toward the crest without orders. Despite Bragg's "cursing like a sailor," his men fled as the Federal troops reached the summit.

The Confederacy's Defeat

During the winter of 1863–1864, Confederates began to despair of victory. Mary Chesnut of South Carolina reported that "gloom and despondency hang like a pall everywhere." Union leaders, sensing the momentum swinging their way, stepped up the pressure on Confederate forces.

The Union's main targets now were Lee's army in Virginia and General Joseph Johnston's in Georgia. In March 1864 Lincoln brought General Grant to Washington and placed him in charge of the entire war effort. Meade retained direct command over the Army of the Potomac; operations in the West were entrusted to Grant's longtime lieutenant, William T. Sherman. As Sherman later wrote, Grant "was to go for Lee, and I was to go for Joe Johnston." Grant brought with him a new strategy against Lee. Whereas his predecessors had all hoped for the climactic single battle, he adopted a war of attrition. He would keep the pressure on the Confederates, grinding down their numbers and sapping their will to fight. Victory, he had decided, would come to the side "which never counted its dead." Grant ordered his commanders to wage total war, confiscating or destroying any and all civilian property of military use. It was a brutal, costly, but ultimately effective plan.

Grant's Pursuit of Lee

In May 1864 the Army of the Potomac, numbering about 115,000 to Lee's 64,000, moved south across the Rappahannock into the Wilderness, where Hooker had earlier come to grief in the Battle of Chancellorsville. In the Battle of the Wilderness (May 5–6), the armies fought blindly through the tangled brush and vines. Grant's men suffered heavier casualties than Lee's, but the Confederates were running out of replacements. Always before, Lee's adversaries had retreated to lick their wounds, but Grant slid off to the left and continued his relentless advance southward, now toward Spotsylvania Court House.

There the armies settled down for five days of carnage, May 8–12. Along the Chickahominy River, the two sides clashed again at Cold Harbor (June 1–3). In twenty minutes, 7,000 attacking Federals were killed or wounded. Battered and again repulsed, Grant soon had his men moving again, headed for Petersburg, the junction of railroads into Richmond from the south. "I shall take no backward steps," he declared.

Lee's army dug in around the town while Grant laid siege. For nine months the two forces faced each other down while Grant kept trying to break the railroad arteries that were Lee's lifeline. Grant's men were generously supplied by vessels moving up the James River, while Lee's forces, beset by hunger, cold, and desertion, wasted away in their muddy trenches. Petersburg had become Lee's prison, while disasters piled up for the Confederacy elsewhere.

Sherman's March

While Grant was chasing Lee in Virginia, the battle-hardened Sherman was doggedly pursuing Joe Johnston's army through north Georgia toward Atlanta. Tightly strung, profane, and plagued by fits of depression, Sherman was one of the few generals to appreciate the concept of total war. Whereas Sherman loved a toe-to-toe fight, Johnston preferred retreat and evasion, determined not to risk a single life until the perfect conditions for fighting were obtained.

An impatient President Davis finally exploded at Johnston's retreat and replaced him with the towering, blond-bearded Texan John B. Hood, who did not know the meaning of retreat or evasion. As Lee once noted, he was "all lion, none of the fox." During late July 1864, Hood's army struck three times from his base at Atlanta, each time fighting desperately but meeting a bloody rebuff. Sherman then circled the city and cut off the rail lines, forcing Hood to evacuate on September 1.

Sherman now resolved to make all of "Georgia howl," as his army embarked on its devastating march southeast through central Georgia. His intention was to "whip the rebels, to humble their pride . . . and

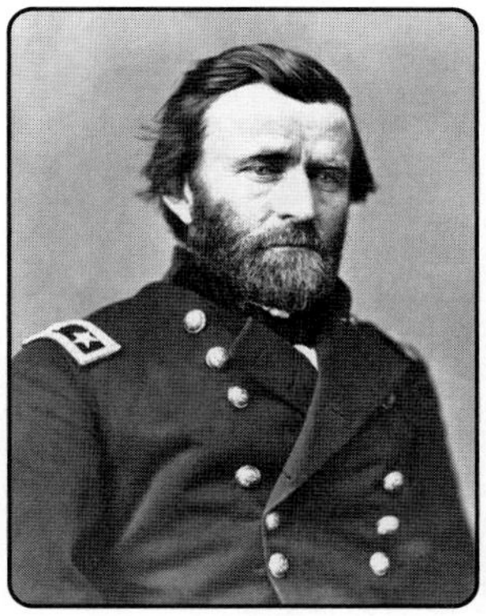

General Ulysses S. Grant.

The tattered colors of the 56th and 36th Massachusetts regiments, marching through Virginia, 1864.

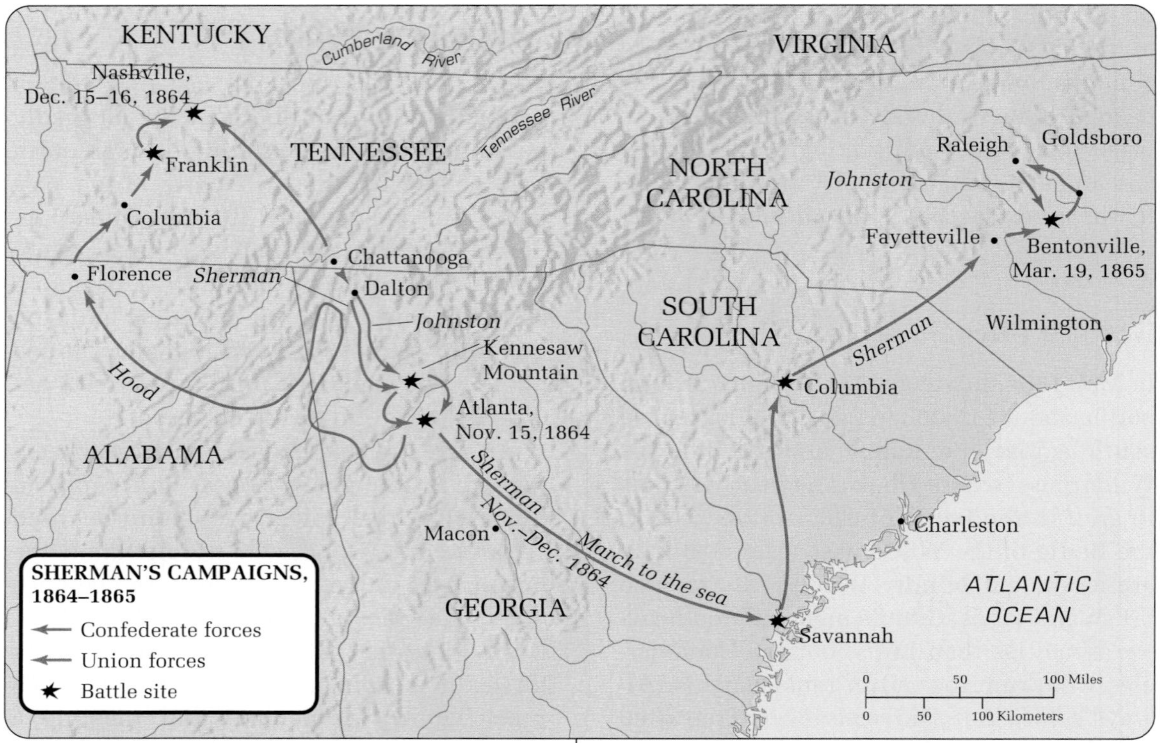

make them fear and dread us." Hood went in the other direction, cutting through northern Alabama and into Tennessee in the hope of luring Sherman away from the undefended Deep South. But Sherman refused to take the bait, although he did dispatch 30,000 men to keep watch on Hood and his troops.

William T. Sherman.

They did more than observe, however. In the Battle of Franklin (November 30), Hood sent his army across two miles of open Tennessee ground. Six waves of Confederate soldiers crashed against the Union lines but never broke through. "It is impossible to exaggerate the fierce energy with which the Confederate soldiers . . . threw themselves against the works," recalled a Union colonel. They fought "with what seemed the very madness of despair." One dead general had been hit by forty-nine bullets. A month later, on December 27, Hood suffered another devastating defeat at Nashville that effectively ended Confederate activity in Tennessee.

During all this, Sherman and the main Union force were marching triumphantly through Georgia, pioneering the modern practice of total war against the enemy's resources and will to resist. "War is war," Sherman bluntly declared, "not a popularity contest." On November 15, 1864, his men burned much of Atlanta. When, after a month, Sherman's army approached Savannah, it had cut a swath of desolation 250 miles long.

On December 21 Sherman rode into Savannah, and three days later he offered the city as a Christmas gift to Lincoln. Sherman paused only long enough to resupply his forces, who then moved on across the river into that "hell-hole of secession," South Carolina. There his men wrought even greater destruction. More than a dozen towns were torched, including the state capital of Columbia, captured on February 17, 1865. That same day, the Confederates defending Charleston abandoned the city and headed north to join an army Joe Johnston was desperately trying to form.

Appomattox

During this final season of the Confederacy, Grant kept pushing, probing, and battering the Petersburg defenses. News of Sherman's devastating sweep through Dixie only added to the Confederacy's gloom. Under siege for almost ten months, Lee decided to sneak away and try to join Johnston's forces in North Carolina. In Richmond President Davis, exhausted but still defiant, gathered what papers and treasure he could carry and escaped by train. Torching everything of military and industrial value in Richmond, the Confederate army left the city, and the Union army entered, accompanied by Abraham Lincoln himself. Jefferson Davis would be captured in Georgia on May 10 by Union cavalry, but by then the Confederacy was already dead.

As Richmond lay burning, Lee pulled his shrunken army out of the trenches around Petersburg with Grant's men in hot pursuit. Lee soon found his escape route cut by Philip Sheridan's cavalry. While the Confederates fought desperately to hold their lines, their hunger, weariness, and the loss of so many men by death or desertion enabled the Union soldiers to break through and cut the rail lines that would have carried Lee and his men to the Carolinas. Lee decided it was senseless to waste any more lives.

On April 9 (Palm Sunday), 1865, Lee donned a crisp dress uniform and met the mud-spattered Grant in the parlor of the McLean home at Appomattox to tender his surrender. Grant, at Lee's request, let the Confederate officers keep their sidearms and permitted soldiers to keep their own horses and mules. Three days later, the Confederate troops formed ranks for the last time as they prepared for the formal surrender. As the ceremony unfolded, there was not a sound—no trumpets or drums, no cheers or jeers, simply "an awed stillness . . . as if it were the passing of the dead." On April 18, Johnston surrendered his forces to Sherman near Durham, North Carolina.

Robert E. Lee. Mathew Brady took this photograph in Richmond eleven days after Lee's surrender at Appomattox.

A Modern War

The Civil War was in many respects the first modern war. Its scope was unprecedented. One out of every twelve adult American males served in the war, and few families were unaffected by the event. Over 630,000 combatants died in the conflict, 50 percent more than in World War II. Because battlefield surgeons were constantly overworked and frequently lacked equipment, supplies, and knowledge, almost any stomach or head wound proved fatal, and gangrene was rampant. Fifty thousand of the survivors returned home with one or more limbs amputated. Disease, however, was the greatest threat to soldiers, killing twice as many as were lost in battle.

The Civil War was a total war, fought not solely by professional armies but by and against whole societies. Farms became battlefields, cities were transformed into armed encampments, and homes were commandeered for field hospitals.

The Civil War was also modern in that much of the killing was distant, impersonal, and mechanical. The opposing forces used an array of new weapons and instruments of war: artillery with "rifled" or grooved barrels for greater accuracy, repeating rifles, ironclad ships, and observation balloons.

Men were killed without even knowing who had fired the shot that felled them.

The debate over why the North won and the South lost the Civil War will probably never end, but as in other modern wars, firepower and manpower were essential factors. Lee's own explanation of the Confederate defeat retains an enduring legitimacy: "After four years of arduous service marked by unsurpassed courage and fortitude, the Army of Northern Virginia has been compelled to yield to overwhelming numbers and resources."

CHAPTER

17

Reconstruction: North and South

This chapter focuses on

- The different approaches to Reconstruction.
- Congressional efforts to reshape southern society.
- The role of African Americans in the early postwar years.
- National politics in the 1870s.

THE *ESSENTIAL AMERICA* ON-LINE TUTOR

www.wwnorton.com/eamerica/ch17

- **Topic: The Radical Reconstruction plan**
  www.wwnorton.com/eamerica/ch17/topic.htm

  Following the conclusion of the Civil War in April 1865, the nation underwent twelve tumultuous years of Reconstruction. Relying on historical analyses, government documents, hand bills, photographs, and maps, study the significance of Reconstruction. How did Radical Republicans believe Reconstruction ought to proceed?

- **Chapter review: On-line quiz and chapter summary**
  www.wwnorton.com/eamerica/ch17/review.htm

- **Chapter resources: Multimedia index**
  www.wwnorton.com/eamerica/ch17/media.htm

In the spring of 1865 the wearying war was over. At the frightful cost of 630,000 lives and the destruction of the southern economy and much of its landscape, American nationalism emerged triumphant, and some 4 million slaves emerged free. But peace had come only on the battlefields. Now the North faced the imposing task of "reconstructing" a ravaged and resentful South.

The War's Aftermath

In the war's aftermath, important questions faced the victors in the North: Should the Confederate leaders be tried for treason? How should new governments be formed? How and at whose expense was the South's economy to be rebuilt? What was to be done with the freed slaves? Were they to be given land? social equality? education? voting rights? Such complex questions required sober reflection and careful planning, but policy makers did not have the luxury of time or the benefits of consensus.

Economic Development in the North

To some Americans the Civil War had been more truly a social revolution than the War of Independence, for it reduced the once-dominant power of the planter elite in national politics and elevated that of the northern "captains of industry." Government became more friendly to businessmen and unfriendly to those who would probe into their activities. The wartime Republican Congress had delivered on the major platform promises of 1860, which had cemented the allegiance of northeastern businessmen and western farmers.

In the absence of southern members, Congress during the war had seized the opportunity to expand national power. In this regard, it passed the Morrill Tariff, which doubled the average level of import duties. The National Banking Act created a uniform system of banking and bank-note currency and helped to finance the war. Congress also passed legislation to construct the first transcontinental railroad along a north-central route from Omaha to Sacramento. In the Homestead Act of 1862, moreover, Congress voted free farms of 160 acres to settlers who occupied the land for five years before gaining title. The Morrill Land Grant Act of the same year conveyed to each state 30,000 acres of public land per member of Congress from the state, the proceeds from the sale of which went to create colleges of "agriculture and mechanic arts." Such measures helped stimulate the North's economy in the years after the Civil War.

Devastation in the South

The postwar South, where most of the fighting had occurred, offered a sharp contrast to the victorious North. Along the path of General William T. Sherman's army, one observer reported in 1866, the countryside "looked for many miles like a broad black streak of ruin and desolation." The border states of Missouri and Kentucky had experienced a guerrilla war that lapsed into postwar anarchy. Marauding bands of bushwhackers such as the notorious James boys, Frank and Jesse, turned into outlaws.

Throughout the South, property values had collapsed. Confederate war bonds and money were worthless; railroads were damaged or destroyed. Cotton that had escaped destruction was seized as Confederate property or in forfeit of federal taxes. Emancipation of the slaves wiped out perhaps $4 billion of human capital and left the labor system in disarray. The great age of expansion in the cotton market was over. Not until 1879 would the cotton crop again equal the record harvest of 1860; tobacco production did not regain its prewar level until 1880, the sugar crop of Louisiana not until 1893.

According to a former Confederate general, recently freed blacks had "nothing but freedom."

A Transformed South

The defeat of the Confederacy transformed much of southern society. The freeing of slaves, the destruction of property, and the free-fall in land values left many among the former planter elite destitute and homeless. Genteel southerners accustomed to relying on slaves for their every need were unprepared for the tasks at hand. Those who still had some money often recruited former slaves to work as domestic servants. Now, however, they had to pay for the services. "It seems humiliating to be compelled to bargain and haggle with our servants about wages," wrote one exasperated woman.

After the Civil War, many former Confederates were so embittered by defeat and so resistant to the idea of living under northern rule that they abandoned their native region rather than submit to "Yankee rule." Some migrated to Canada, Europe, Mexico, South America, and Asia. Others preferred the western territories and states. Still others moved north, settling in northern and midwestern cities on the assumption that their educational and economic opportunities would be better among the victors.

Legally Free, Socially Bound

In the former Confederate states, the newly freed slaves suffered as well. According to Frederick Douglass, the black abolitionist, the former slave remained dependent: "He had neither money, property, nor friends. He was free from the old plantation, but he had nothing but the dusty road under his feet. . . . He was turned loose, naked, hungry, and destitute to the open sky."

A few northerners argued that what the ex-slaves needed most was their own land. There was talk of giving each freed slave "forty acres and a mule" to provide them with an economic foundation. But even dedicated abolitionists shrank from endorsing measures of land reform that might have given the freed slaves self-support and independence. Citizenship and legal rights were one thing, wholesale confiscation of property owned by whites andland redistribution quite another. Instead of land or material help, the freed slaves more often got advice and moral platitudes.

The Freedmen's Bureau

On March 3, 1865, Congress set up within the War Department the Bureau of Refugees, Freedmen, and Abandoned Lands, to provide "such issues of provisions, clothing, and fuel" as might be needed to relieve "destitute and suffering refugees and freedmen and their wives and children." The Freedmen's Bureau would also take over abandoned or confiscated land, but the amount of such land was limited. Agents of the Freedmen's Bureau were entrusted with negotiating labor contracts (something new for both blacks and planters), providing medical care, and setting up schools.

White intransigence and racial prejudice, however, thwarted the efforts of Freedmen's Bureau agents to protect and assist the former slaves. Congress was not willing to strengthen the powers of the Freedmen's Bureau to deal with such problems. Beyond temporary relief measures, no program of Reconstruction ever incorporated much more than constitutional and legal rights for freedmen. These rights were important in themselves, of course, but the extent to which even these should go was very uncertain, to be settled more by the course of events than by any clear-cut commitment to equality.

The Battle over Reconstruction

The problem of reconstructing the South involved creating new governments in the defeated states. As Federal forces advanced into the Confederacy, Lincoln in 1862 named military governors for Tennessee, Arkansas, and Louisiana. By the end of the following year, he had formulated a plan for regular civilian governments in those states and any others that might be liberated from Confederate rule.

Lincoln's Plan and Congress's Response

Acting under his pardon power, President Lincoln issued late in 1863 a Proclamation of Amnesty and Reconstruction, under which any Rebel state could form a Union government whenever a number of citizens equal to 10 percent of those who had voted in 1860 took an oath of allegiance to the Constitution and to the Union and received a presidential pardon. Participants also had to swear support for laws and proclamations dealing with emancipation. Excluded from the pardon, however, were certain groups: civil, diplomatic, and high military officers of the Confederacy; judges, congressmen, and military officers of the United States who had left their federal posts to aid the rebellion; and those accused of failure to treat captured black soldiers and their officers as prisoners of war.

Under Lincoln's plan, loyal governments appeared in Tennessee, Arkansas, and Louisiana, but Congress refused to recognize them. In the absence of any specific provisions for Reconstruction in the Constitution, politicians disagreed as to where authority properly rested. Lincoln claimed the right to direct Reconstruction under the presidential pardon power, and also under the Constitutional obligation to guarantee each state a republican form of government.

A few conservative and most moderate Republicans supported Lincoln's program of immediate restoration. A small but influential group known as Radical Republicans, however, demanded a sweeping transformation of southern society that would include making the freed slaves full-fledged citizens. The Radicals hoped to reconstruct southern society so as to mirror the North's emphasis on small-scale capitalism. This meant thwarting the efforts of the old planter class to reestablish a caste system and keep the freed blacks in a state of peonage.

Glimpses at the Freedmen. The Freedmen's Union Industrial School in Richmond, Virginia, was set up by the War Department in 1865.

The Radicals maintained that Congress, not the president, should supervise the Reconstruction program. To this end, they helped pass in 1864 the Wade-Davis Bill, sponsored by Senator Benjamin Wade of Ohio and Representative Winter Davis of Maryland. In contrast to Lincoln's 10 percent plan, the Wade-Davis Bill required that a *majority* of white male citizens declare their allegiance. Only those who swore an "ironclad" oath that they had always remained loyal to the Union could vote or serve in the state constitutional conventions. The conventions, moreover, would have to abolish slavery, deny political rights to high-ranking civil and military officers of the Confederacy, and repudiate Confederate war debts. Passed during the closing days of the 1864 session, the Wade-Davis Bill went unsigned by Lincoln, and this "pocket veto" provoked the bill's sponsors to issue the

Wade-Davis Manifesto, a blistering statement that accused the president of usurping power and attempting to use readmitted states to ensure his reelection.

Lincoln issued his final statement on Reconstruction in his last public address, on April 11, 1865. Speaking from the White House balcony, he dismissed the theoretical question of whether the Confederate states had technically remained in the Union as "good for nothing at all—a mere pernicious abstraction." These states were simply "out of their proper practical relation with the Union," and the object was to get them "into their proper practical relation" as quickly as possible. Lincoln wanted "no persecution, no bloody work," no dramatic restructuring of southern social and economic life.

That evening Lincoln went to Ford's Theater and his rendezvous with death. Shot in the head by John Wilkes Booth, a crazed actor and Confederate zealot, the president died the next morning. Pursued into Virginia, Booth was trapped and shot in a burning barn. Three collaborators were tried and hanged.

Johnson's Plan

Lincoln's death elevated to the White House Vice-President Andrew Johnson of Tennessee, a man whose state remained in legal limbo and whose party affiliation was unclear. He was a War Democrat who had been put on the Union ticket with the Republican Lincoln in 1864 as a gesture of bipartisan unity.

Andrew Johnson (detail).

Of humble origins like Lincoln, Johnson had moved as a youth from his birthplace in Raleigh, North Carolina, to Greenville, Tennessee, where he became proprietor of a tailor shop. Over the years he grew prosperous, acquiring several slaves in the process. A bitter critic of the "swaggering" planter aristocracy "who are too lazy and proud to work," Johnson was a fervent populist who promoted free land for the poor, defended slavery, and promoted white supremacy. A notoriously stubborn man, he became a self-righteous, hot-tempered orator who enjoyed strong drink and employed abusive language to belittle his opponents. His fiery speeches and firm principles helped him win election as mayor, congressman, governor, and senator.

Like many other whites in mountainous eastern Tennessee, Johnson ardently believed in the Union. In 1861 he was the only southern senator from a Confederate state to vote against secession, leading critics to denounce him as a "traitor" to the region. Yet his devotion to the Union did not include opposition to slavery. He hated the Confederacy because he hated the planter elite. "Damn the Negroes," Johnson bellowed to a friend during the war, "I am fighting those traitorous aristocrats, their masters."

Some of the Radicals at first thought Johnson, unlike Lincoln, was one of them, but his loyalty to the Union sprang from a strict adherence to the Constitution. The Confederate states, Johnson believed, should be brought back into their proper relation to the Union because the states and the Union were indestructible. In 1865 Johnson declared that "there is no such thing as Reconstruction. Those states have not gone out of the Union. Therefore Reconstruction is unnecessary."

Johnson's plan to restore the Union thus closely resembled Lincoln's. A new Proclamation of Amnesty (May 29, 1865) added to the list of those Lincoln had excluded from pardon everybody with taxable property worth more than $20,000. These wealthy planters and merchants were the people Johnson believed had led the South into secession. But those in the excluded groups might make special applications for presidential pardon, and before the year was out Johnson had issued some 13,000 pardons.

In each of the Rebel states not already organized by Lincoln, Johnson named a Unionist provisional governor with authority to call a convention of men elected by loyal voters. Lincoln's 10 percent requirement was omitted. Johnson called upon the conventions to invalidate the secession ordinances, repudiate all debts incurred to aid the Confederacy, and ratify the Thirteenth Amendment, which ended slavery. Like Lincoln, Johnson endorsed limited voting rights for blacks. He reminded the provisional governor of Mississippi, for example, that the state conventions might "with perfect safety" extend suffrage to those blacks with education or with military service so as to "disarm the adversary"—the adversary being "radicals who are wild upon Negro franchise [voting]."

Southern Intransigence

When Congress met in December 1865, for the first time since the end of the war, it faced the fact that new state governments were functioning in the South, according to Johnson's requirements, and they were remarkably like the old. Among the new members presenting themselves to Congress were Georgia's Alexander H. Stephens, late vice-president of the Confederacy, four Confederate generals, eight colonels, six cabinet members, and a host of lesser Rebel officials. The Congress forthwith defied Johnson by denying seats to all members from the eleven former Confederate states. It was too much to expect, after four bloody years, that Unionists would welcome ex-Confederates back like prodigal sons.

Furthermore, the new southern legislatures, in passing repressive "Black Codes" restricting the freedom of blacks, baldly revealed that they intended to preserve the trappings of slavery as nearly as possible. As one southerner stressed, the "ex-slave was not a free man; he was a free Negro."

The details of the Black Codes varied from state to state, but some provisions were common. On the one hand, existing black marriages were recognized (although interracial marriages were prohibited), and testimony by blacks was accepted in legal cases involving them—in six states in all cases. Blacks could own property. They could sue and be sued in the courts. On the other hand, blacks in Mississippi could not own farm lands, and in South Carolina they could not own city lots. Unlike whites, blacks were required to enter into annual labor contracts, with provision for punishment in case of violation. Dependent children were subject to compulsory apprenticeship and corporal punishment by masters. Vagrant blacks were punished with severe fines, and, if unable to pay, they were forced to work in the fields for whites who paid the courts for such cheap labor. To many people, it seemed that slavery was being revived in another guise.

The Radicals

Faced with such evidence of southern intransigence, moderate Republicans drifted more and more toward the Radical camp. The new Congress set up a Joint Committee on Reconstruction, with nine members from the House and six from the Senate, to gather evidence and submit proposals. As a parade of witnesses testified to the Rebels' impenitence, initiative on the committee fell to determined Radicals: Benjamin Wade of Ohio, George W. Julian of Indiana, Henry Wilson of Massachusetts—and most conspicuously of all, Thaddeus Stevens of Pennsylvania and Charles Sumner of Massachusetts.

Stevens, a crusty bachelor with a chiseled face and brooding eyes, was the domineering floor leader in the House. Driven by a genuine, if at times fanatical, idealism, he insisted that the "whole fabric of southern society *must* be changed." Sumner, Stevens's counterpart in the Senate, agreed. He strove to see the South *reconstructed* rather than simply restored. This put him at odds with Johnson. After visiting the White House, Sumner found the president "harsh, petulant, and unreasonable." He was especially disheartened by Johnson's "prejudice, ignorance, and perversity" regarding the treatment of blacks. Sumner and other Radicals resolved to take matters into their own hands. The southern plantations, seedbeds of aristocratic pretension and secession, he declared, "must be broken up, and the freedmen must have the pieces."

Most of these Radical Republicans had long been connected with the antislavery cause, and they approached the question of black rights with a sincere humanitarian impulse. Few, however, could escape the bitterness bred by the long and bloody war or remain unaware of the partisan advantage that would come to the Republican party from "Negro suffrage." But they reasoned that their party, after all, could best guarantee the fruits of victory and that granting suffrage could best secure black rights.

The growing conflict of opinion over Reconstruction policy brought about an inversion in constitutional reasoning. Secessionists—and Johnson—were now arguing that their states had in fact remained in the Union, and some Radicals were contriving arguments that they had left the Union after all. Most congressmen embraced the "forfeited rights theory," which held that the southern states continued to exist, but by the acts of secession and war had forfeited "all civil and political rights under the Constitution." And Congress was the proper authority to determine conditions under which such rights might be restored.

Johnson's Battle with Congress

A long year of political battling remained, however, before this idea triumphed. By the end of 1865, Radical views had gained only a slight majority in Congress, insufficient to override presidential vetoes. But the critical year 1866 saw the gradual waning of Johnson's power and influence, much of this self-induced. Johnson first challenged Congress in February, when he vetoed a bill to extend the life of the Freedmen's Bureau. Since it was no longer valid as a war measure, Johnson believed it violated the Constitution. For the moment, Johnson's prestige remained sufficiently intact that the Senate upheld his veto.

Three days after the veto, however, Johnson undermined his already weakening prestige by launching an intemperate assault on Radical leaders during an impromptu speech on George Washington's Birthday. From that point forward, moderate Republicans backed away from the president, and Radical Republicans went on the offensive.

In mid-March 1866, Congress passed the Civil Rights Act. A direct response to the Black Codes, this bill declared that "all persons born in the United States . . . excluding Indians not taxed," were citizens entitled to "full and equal benefit of all laws." The grant of citizenship to native-born blacks, Johnson claimed, went beyond anything formerly held to be within the scope of federal power. It would, moreover, "foment discord among the races." He vetoed the measure, but this time, in April 1866, Congress overrode the presidential veto. Then in July it enacted a revised Freedmen's Bureau Bill, again overturning a veto. From that point on, Johnson's public and political support steadily eroded.

The Fourteenth Amendment

To remove all doubt about the validity of the new Civil Rights Act, the Joint Committee recommended a new constitutional amendment, which passed Congress in 1866 and was ratified by the states in 1868. The Fourteenth Amendment, however, went far beyond the Civil Rights Act, and it would have significant effects long thereafter. The first section asserted four principles: it reaffirmed state and federal citizenship for all persons—regardless of race—born or naturalized in the United States, and it forbade any *state* to abridge the "privileges and immunities" of citizens; to deprive any *person* of life, liberty, or property without "due process of law"; or to deny any person "the equal protection of the laws."

The last three of these clauses have been the subject of lawsuits resulting in applications not foreseen at the time. The "due-process clause" has come to mean that state as well as federal power is subject to the Bill of Rights, and it has been used to protect corporations, as legal "persons," from "unreasonable" regulation by the states. Other provisions of the amendment had less far-reaching effects. One section specified that the debt of the United States "shall not be questioned," but it declared "illegal and void" all debts contracted in aid of the rebellion.

Johnson's home state was among the first to ratify the Fourteenth Amendment. In Tennessee, which had harbored probably more Unionists than any other Confederate state, the government had fallen under Radical control. But the rest of the South steadfastly resisted the Radical challenge to Johnson's program. In 1866 bloody race riots in Memphis and New Orleans added fuel to the flames. Both incidents sparked massacres of blacks by local police and white mobs. The rioting, Radicals argued, was the natural fruit of Johnson's foolish policy.

Reconstructing the South

The Triumph of Congressional Reconstruction

As 1866 drew to an end, the upcoming congressional elections promised to be a referendum on the growing split between Johnson and the Radicals. Johnson embarked on a speaking tour of the Midwest, a "swing around the circle," which provoked undignified shouting contests between the president and his audiences. Johnson's tour backfired; when the election returns came in, the Republicans had well over a two-thirds majority in each house, a comfortable margin with which to override any presidential vetoes.

The Congress actually enacted a new program even before new members took office. On March 2, 1867, two days before the old Congress expired, it passed three basic laws of congressional Reconstruction over Johnson's vetoes: the Military Reconstruction Act, the Command of the Army Act, and the Tenure of Office Act.

The first of the three acts prescribed conditions under which new southern state governments should be formed. The other two sought to block obstruction by the president. The Command of the Army Act required that all orders from the president as commander-in-chief go through the general of the army, Ulysses S. Grant. The Radicals trusted Grant, who was already leaning their way. The Tenure of Office Act required the consent of the Senate for the president to remove any officeholder whose appointment the Senate had to confirm in the first place. In large measure, it was intended to retain Secretary of War Edwin M. Stanton, the one Radical sympathizer in Johnson's cabinet. But an ambiguity crept into the wording of the act. Cabinet officers, it said, should serve during the term of the president who appointed them—and Lincoln had appointed Stanton, although, to be sure, Johnson was serving out Lincoln's term.

The Military Reconstruction Act, often hailed or denounced as the triumphant victory of "Radical" Reconstruction, actually fell short of a thoroughgoing transformation. Originally intended by the Radical Republicans to give military commanders in the South ultimate control over law enforcement and to leave open indefinitely the terms of future restoration, it was diluted by moderate Republicans, until it boiled down to little more than a requirement that southern states accept black suffrage and ratify the Fourteenth Amendment.

Tennessee, which had already ratified the Fourteenth Amendment, was exempted from the act. The other ten southern states were divided into five military districts, and the commanding officer of each was authorized to keep order and protect the "rights of persons and property." The Johnson governments remained intact for the time being, but new constitutions were to be framed "in conformity with the Constitution of the United States," in conventions elected by male citizens twenty-one and older "of whatever race, color, or previous condition." Each state constitution had to provide the same universal male suffrage. Then, once the constitution was ratified by a majority of voters and accepted by Congress, and once the state legislature had ratified the Fourteenth Amendment, and once the amendment became part of the Constitution, any given state would be entitled to representation in Congress. Persons excluded from officeholding by the proposed amendment were also excluded from participation in the process. Before the end of 1867, new elections had been held in all the states but Texas.

Having clipped the president's wings, the Republican Congress moved a year later to safeguard its program from possible interference by the Supreme Court. On March 27, 1868, Congress simply removed the power of the Supreme Court to review cases arising under the Military Reconstruction Act, which Congress clearly had the constitutional right to do under its power to define the Court's appellate jurisdiction. The Court accepted this curtailment of its authority on the same day it affirmed the notion of an "indestructible Union" in *Texas* v. *White* (1868). In that case, it also acknowledged the right of Congress to reframe state governments, thus endorsing the Radical point of view.

The Impeachment and Trial of Johnson (1868)

By 1868, Radical Republicans were convinced that Johnson had to be removed from office. Johnson had continued to pardon former Confederates and transferred several of the district military commanders who had displayed Radical sympathies. Johnson was revealing himself to be a man of limited ability and narrow vision. He lacked Lincoln's resilience and pragmatism.

The Republicans unsuccessfully tried to impeach Johnson early in 1867, alleging a variety of flimsy charges, none of which represented an indictable crime. But Johnson himself provided the occasion for impeachment when he deliberately violated the Tenure of Office Act in order to test its constitutionality. Secretary of War Edwin Stanton had become a thorn in the president's side, refusing to resign despite his disagreements with Johnson's Reconstruction policy. On August 12, 1867, during a congressional recess, Johnson suspended Stanton and named General Grant in his place. When the Senate refused to confirm Johnson's action, however, Grant returned the office to Stanton.

The Radicals now saw their chance to remove the president, and they were quite explicit about their political purposes. As Charles Sumner declared, "Impeachment is a political proceeding before a political body with a political purpose." The debate in the House was clamorous and vicious. One congressman denounced the president as "an ungrateful, despicable, besotted traitorous man—an incubus." On February 24, 1868, the House passed eleven articles of impeachment by a party-line vote of 126 to 47.

Of the eleven articles of impeachment, eight focused on the charge that Johnson had unlawfully removed Stanton and had failed to give the Senate the name of a successor. Article 9 accused the president of issuing orders in violation of the Command of the Army Act. The last two articles in effect charged him with criticizing Congress by "inflammatory and scandalous harangues." Article 11 also accused Johnson of "unlawfully devising and contriving" to violate the

Reconstruction Acts, contrary to his obligation to execute the laws. At the very least, it stated, Johnson had tried to obstruct Congress's will while observing the letter of the law.

The Senate trial began on March 5, 1868, and continued until May 26, with Chief Justice Salmon P. Chase presiding. It was a great spectacle before a packed gallery. However, as the weeks passed, the trial grew tedious. Senators slept during the proceedings, spectators passed out in the unventilated room, and poor acoustics prompted repeated cries of "We can't hear." Debate eventually focused on Stanton's removal, the most substantive impeachment charge. Johnson's lawyers argued that Lincoln, not Johnson, had appointed Stanton, so the Tenure of Office Act did not apply to him. At the same time, they claimed (correctly, as it turned out) that the law was unconstitutional.

When the five-week trial ended and the voting began in May 1868, seven moderate Republicans and all twelve Democrats voted to acquit. The final tally was 35 to 19 for conviction, one vote short of the two-thirds needed for removal from office. The renegade Republicans offered two primary reasons for their controversial votes: they feared damage to the separation of powers among the branches of government if Johnson were removed, and they were assured by Johnson's attorneys that he would stop obstructing congressional policy in the South.

Although the Senate failed to remove Johnson, the trial crippled his already weak presidency. During the remaining ten months of his term, he initiated no other clashes with Congress. In 1868 Johnson sought the Democratic presidential nomination but lost to New York governor Horatio Seymour, who then lost to Republican Ulysses Grant in the general election. A bitter Johnson refused to attend Grant's inauguration. His final act as president was to issue a pardon to former Confederate president Jefferson Davis.

The Senate transformed into a court of impeachment for the trial of Andrew Johnson.

Impeachment of Johnson was in the end a great political mistake, for the failure to remove the president damaged Radical morale and support. Nevertheless, the Radical cause did gain something. To blunt the opposition, Johnson agreed not to obstruct the process of Reconstruction, and thereafter Radical Reconstruction began in earnest.

Radical Republican Rule in the South

In June 1868 Congress agreed that seven states had met its conditions for readmission, all but Virginia, Mississippi, and Texas. Congress rescinded Georgia's admission, however, when the state legislature expelled twenty-eight black members and seated some former Confederate leaders. The military commander of Georgia then forced the legislature to reseat the black members and remove the Confederates, and the state was compelled to ratify the Fifteenth Amendment before being readmitted in July 1870. Virginia, Mississippi, and Texas had returned earlier in 1870, under the added requirement that they too ratify the Fifteenth Amendment. This amendment, ratified in 1870, forbade the states to deny any citizen the right to vote on grounds of race, color, or previous condition of servitude.

Long before the new governments were established, partisan Republican groups began to spring up in the South, promoted by the Union League, an organization founded in 1862 to rally support for the federal government. Its representatives enrolled blacks and loyal whites as members, initiated them into the secrets and rituals of the order, and instructed them "in their rights and duties." These Union Leagues became a powerful source of Republican political strength in the South and as a result drew the ire of unreconstructed whites.

The Reconstructed South

The Freed Slaves

To focus solely on what white Republicans did to reconstruct the defeated South creates the false impression that the freed slaves were simply pawns in the hands of others. In fact, however, southern blacks were active agents in affecting the course of Reconstruction activities. Although many of them found themselves liberated but destitute after the fighting ended, and often widely separated from family members, the mere promise of freedom raised their hopes about achieving a biracial democracy, equal justice, and economic opportunity.

Participation in the Union army or navy gave many freedmen a training ground in leadership. Black military veterans would form the core of the first generation of African-American political leaders in the postwar South. Military service provided many former slaves with the first opportunities to learn to read and write. Army life also alerted them to alternative social choices and to new opportunities for advancement and respectability.

Former slaves established independent black churches after the war, churches that would serve as the foundation of African-American community life. Blacks preferred Baptist churches over other denominations, in part because of their decentralized structure that allowed each congregation to worship in its own way. By 1890, there were over 1.3 million black Baptists in the South, nearly three times as many as any other black denomination.

As for making a living, the freed slaves had little money or technical training and were thus faced with the prospect of becoming wage laborers to support themselves. To avoid this and to retain as much autonomy as possible over their productive energies and those of their children on both a daily and seasonal basis, many former slaves chose to become sharecroppers. This meant that they were tenant farmers who gained access to separate plots of land owned by whites in exchange for a share of their crop. In payment for the use of the land and cabin, and sometimes even for use of the tools, seed, and fertilizer needed to farm the land, they gave between one-half and two-thirds of the harvested crops to the white landowners. This gave them higher status than they would have had as wage laborers; it gave them the freedom to set their own hours and work as much or as little as they pleased; and it enabled mothers and wives to devote more of their time to domestic needs while still contributing to family income.

Blacks in Southern Politics

The new role of blacks in politics caused the most controversy, then and afterward. Several hundred black delegates participated in the statewide political conventions. Most had been selected by local political meetings or by churches, fraternal societies,

Union Leagues, and black federal army units, although a few simply appointed themselves.

By 1867, former slaves began to gain political influence and to vote in large numbers, and this revealed emerging tensions within the black community. Some southern blacks resented the presence of northern brethren who moved south after the war, while others complained that few ex-slaves were represented in leadership positions. Northern blacks and the southern free black elite, most of whom were urban dwellers, tended to oppose efforts to confiscate and redistribute land to the rural freedmen, and many insisted that political equality did not mean social equality. In general, however, unity rather than dissension prevailed, and blacks focused on common concerns such as full equality under the law.

Brought suddenly into politics in times that tried the most skilled of statesmen, many blacks served with distinction during so-called Radical Reconstruction. Nonetheless, the derisive label "black Reconstruction" used by later critics exaggerates black political influence, which was limited mainly to voting, and overlooks the large numbers of white Republicans, especially in the mountain areas of the upper South. Only one of the new state conventions, South Carolina's, had a black majority, 76 to 41. Louisiana's was evenly divided racially, and in only two other conventions were more than 20 percent of the members black: Florida's, with 40 percent, and Virginia's, with 24 percent.

In the new state governments, any black participation was a novelty. Although some 600 blacks served as state legislators, no black was elected governor and few served as judges. In Louisiana, however, Pinckney B. S. Pinchback, a northern black and former Union soldier, won the office of lieutenant-governor and served as acting governor when the white governor was indicted for corruption. Several blacks were elected lieutenant-governors, state treasurers, or secretaries of state. There were two black senators in Congress, Hiram Revels and Blanche K. Bruce, both from Mississippi, and fourteen black members of the House during Reconstruction. Among these were some of the ablest congressmen of the time.

A freedman casts his vote in 1867. Although the Fifteenth Amendment was not passed until 1870, former slaves had been registering and voting in state elections since 1867.

Carpetbaggers and Scalawags

The top positions in southern state governments went for the most part to white Republicans, whom the opposition soon labeled "carpetbaggers" and "scalawags," depending on their place of birth. Northern opportunists who allegedly came south with all their belongings in carpetbags to reap political spoils were more often than not Union veterans who had arrived as early as 1865 or 1866, drawn south by the hope of economic opportunity. Others were lawyers, businessmen, editors, teachers, social workers, or preachers who came on missionary endeavors.

The "scalawags," or southern white Republicans, were even more reviled and misrepresented. Most "scalawags" had opposed secession, forming a Unionist majority in many mountain counties as far south as Georgia and Alabama, and especially in the hills of eastern Tennessee. Though many were indeed crass opportunists who indulged in corruption at the public's expense, several were quite distinguished figures. They included former Confederate general James A. Longstreet, who decided after Appomattox that the Old South must change its ways. To that end, he became a successful cotton broker in New Orleans, joined the Republican party, and supported the Radical Reconstruction program.

The Radical Republican Record

Former Confederates resented carpetbaggers and scalawags, and they also objected to the new state constitutions, primarily because of their provisions for black suffrage and civil rights. Nonetheless, most of the state constitutions remained in effect for some years after the end of Radical control, and later constitutions incorporated many of their features. Conspicuous among Radical innovations were steps toward greater democracy such as requiring universal manhood suffrage, reapportioning legislatures more nearly according to population, and making more state offices elective.

Given the hostile circumstances in which the Radical governments arose and operated, their achievements were remarkable. In most of the South, they established the first state school systems. Some 600,000 black pupils were in schools by 1877. State governments under the Radicals also gave more attention to orphanages, asylums, and institutions for the disabled of both races. Public roads, bridges, and buildings were repaired or rebuilt. Blacks achieved new rights and opportunities that would never again be taken away, at least in principle: equality before the law, and the right to own property, carry on business, enter professions, attend schools, and learn to read and write.

Yet several of these Republican regimes also practiced systematic corruption. Public money and public credit were often voted to privately owned corporations, notably railroads, under conditions that invited influence peddling. Bids for contracts were accepted at absurd prices, and some public officials took their cut. Taxes and public debt rose in every state. Still, corruption was not invented by the Radical regimes, nor did it die with them. In Mississippi, the Republican governments of Reconstruction were quite honest compared to their Democratic successors.

(*Left*) This Thomas Nast cartoon accuses the Ku Klux Klan and the White League of promoting conditions "worse than slavery" for southern blacks after the Civil War. (*Right*) Alabama Klansmen, 1868.

White Terror

The case of Mississippi suggests that whites were hostile to Republican regimes less because of their corruption than because of their inclusion of blacks. Most white southerners remained unreconstructed, so conditioned by slavery that they were unable to conceive of blacks as citizens or even free agents. In some places, hostility to the new regimes took the form of white terror. Efforts to oust Republican rule focused largely on violence.

The prototype of terrorist groups was the Ku Klux Klan (KKK), first organized in 1866 by some young men of Pulaski, Tennessee, as a social club with the costumes, secret ritual, and mumbo-jumbo common to fraternal groups. At first a group of pranksters, they soon began to intimidate blacks and white Republicans, and the KKK spread rapidly across the South in answer to the Republican party's Union League. Klansmen rode about the countryside hiding under masks

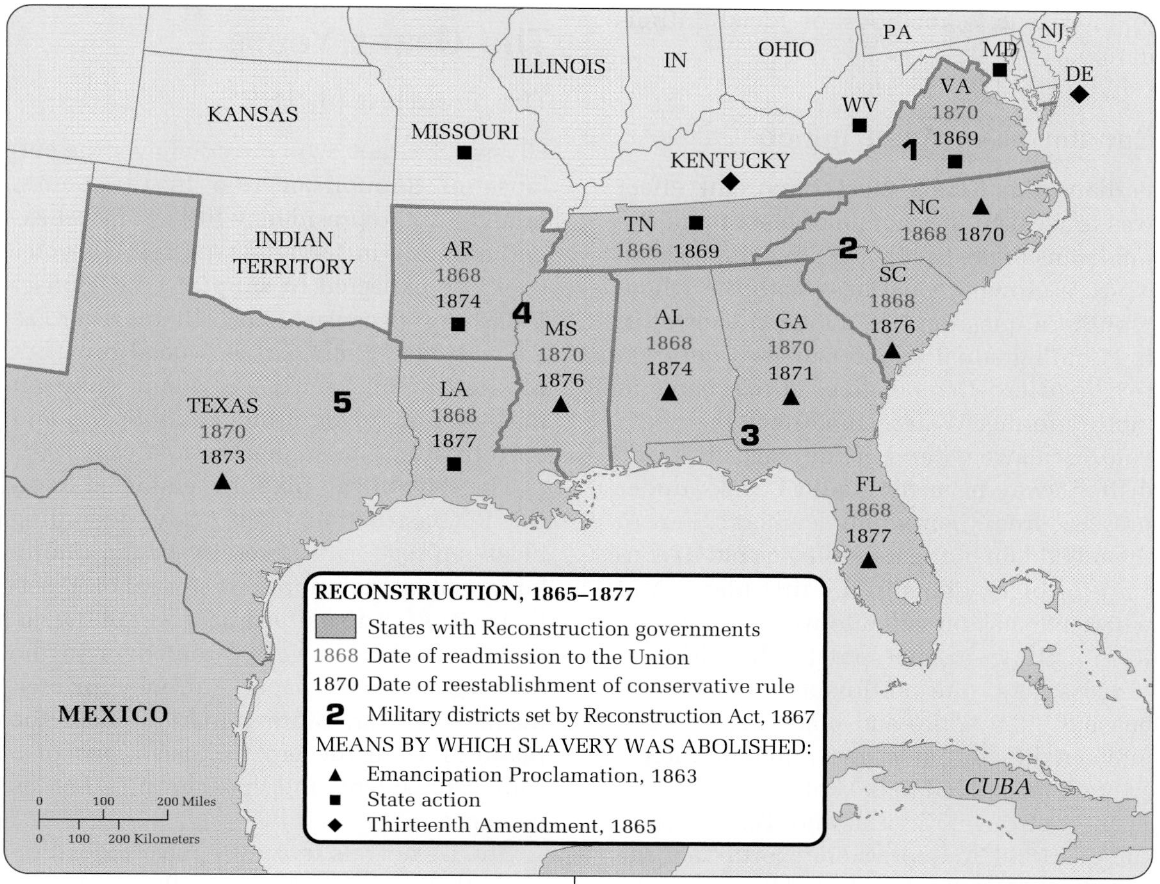

and robes, spreading horrendous rumors, harassing blacks, and wreaking violence and destruction.

In Mississippi, Klansmen mutilated a black Republican leader in front of his family. Three white "scalawag" Republicans were murdered in Georgia in 1870. That same year, an armed mob of whites disrupted a Republican political rally in Alabama, killing four blacks and wounding fifty-four. In South Carolina the Klan was especially active. Virtually the entire white male population of York County joined the Klan, and they were responsible for eleven murders and hundreds of whippings. In 1871 some 500 masked men laid siege to the Union County jail and eventually lynched eight black prisoners. Although most Klansmen were poor farmers and tradesmen, middle-class whites—planters, merchants, bankers, lawyers, doctors, even ministers—also joined the group and participated in its brutalities.

Congress responded to such racial terrorism with three Enforcement Acts (1870–1871) to protect black voters. The first of these measures levied penalties on persons who interfered with any citizen's right to vote. A second placed the election of congressmen under surveillance by federal election supervisors and marshals. The third (the Ku Klux Klan Act) outlawed the characteristic activities of the Klan—forming conspiracies, wearing disguises, resisting officers, and intimidating officials. The program of federal enforcement broke the back of the Klan, whose activities declined steadily as recalcitrant southerners resorted to more subtle methods of racial intimidation.

Conservative Resurgence

Perhaps the Klan's most important effect was to weaken the morale of blacks and Republicans in the South and strengthen in the North a growing weariness with the whole "southern question." Republican control in the South gradually loosened as "Conservative" parties—Democrats used that name to mollify former Whigs—mobilized the white vote. Scalawags, and many carpetbaggers, drifted away from the Radical ranks under pressure from their white neighbors. Few of them had joined the Republicans out of concern for black rights in the first place. And where persuasion failed to work, Democrats were willing to manipulate the electoral process. As one enthusiastic Democrat boasted, "the white and black Republicans may outvote us, but we can outcount them."

Such factors led to the collapse of Republican control in Virginia and Tennessee as early as 1869, in Georgia and North Carolina in 1870. Reconstruction lasted longest in the Deep South states with the heaviest black population, where whites abandoned Klan hoods for barefaced intimidation in paramilitary groups like the Mississippi Rifle Club and the South Carolina Red Shirts. By 1876, Radical regimes survived only in Louisiana, South Carolina, and Florida, but these all collapsed after the elections of that year.

The erosion of northern interest in promoting civil rights in the postwar South reflected both weariness with Reconstruction as well as interest in other activities. Western expansion, Indian wars, economic development, and political debates over the tariff and currency distracted attention from southern outrages. In addition, a business panic that occurred in 1873 led to a sharp depression and created both social problems and new racial tensions in the North and the South.

The Grant Years

The Election of 1868

Ulysses S. Grant, who presided over the collapse of Republican rule in the South, brought to the presidency little political experience. But in 1868 the rank-and-file voter could be expected to support "the Lion of Vicksburg" because of his brilliant record as a war leader. Both parties wooed him, but his falling-out with President Johnson pushed him toward the Republicans and built trust in him among the Radicals.

The Republican platform endorsed Radical Reconstruction, cautiously defending black suffrage as a necessity in the South, but a matter each northern state should settle for itself. It also urged payment of the nation's war debt in gold rather than in the new "greenback" paper currency printed during the war. More important than the platform were the great expectations of a soldier-president and his slogan: "Let us have peace."

The Democrats took an opposite position on both Reconstruction and the debt. The Republican Congress, the platform charged, had "subjected ten states, in the time of profound peace, to military despotism and Negro supremacy." As to the public debt, the party endorsed Representative George H. Pendleton's "Ohio idea" that, since most bonds had been bought with depreciated greenbacks, they should be paid off in greenbacks unless they specified payment in gold. With no conspicuously available candidate in sight, the convention turned to Horatio Seymour, war governor of New York and chairman of the convention. The Democrats made a closer race than expected, attesting to the strength of traditional party loyalties. While Grant swept the electoral college by 214 to 80, his popular majority was only 307,000 out of a total of over 5.7 million votes. More than 500,000 black voters accounted for Grant's margin of victory.

Grant had proven himself a great leader in the war, but in the White House he seemed blind to the political forces and influence peddlers around him. Although personally honest, he was dazzled by men of wealth and unaccountably loyal to greedy subordinates who betrayed his trust. In the formulation of policy he passively followed the lead of Congress. This approach endeared him at first to party leaders, but it left him at last ineffective and caused others to grow disillusioned with his leadership.

The Government Debt

Financial issues dominated the political agenda during Grant's presidency. After the war, the Treasury had assumed that the $432 million worth of greenbacks issued during the conflict would be retired from circulation and that the nation would revert to a "hard-money" currency—gold coins. Congress in 1866 granted the Treasury discretion to redeem the paper money gradually. Many agrarian and debtor groups resisted this contraction of the money supply, believing that it would mean lower crop prices and harder-to-pay debts. In 1868 "soft money" supporters in Congress halted the retirement of greenbacks, leaving $356 million outstanding. There matters stood when Grant took office.

The "sound" or "hard" money advocates, mostly bankers, merchants, and other creditors, claimed that Grant's election was a mandate to save the country from the Democrats' "Ohio idea" of using greenbacks to repay government bonds. Quite influential in Republican circles, the "sound-money" advocates also had the benefit of a deeply ingrained popular assumption that hard money was morally preferable to paper currency. Grant agreed, and in his inaugural address he endorsed payment of the national debt in gold as a point of national honor.

Scandals

Within less than a year of his election, Grant fell into a cesspool of scandal. In the summer of 1869 two young railroad entrepreneurs, Jay Gould and Jim Fisk, connived with the president's brother-in-law to corner the gold market. Gould concocted an argument that the government should refrain from selling gold on the market because the resulting rise in gold prices would raise temporarily depressed farm prices. Grant apparently smelled a rat from the start, but he was seen in public with the speculators. As the rumor spread on Wall Street, gold prices rose sharply. Finally, on "Black Friday," September 24, 1869, Grant ordered the Treasury to sell a large quantity of gold, and the bubble burst. Fisk got out by repudiating his agreements and hiring thugs to intimidate his creditors.

The plot to corner the gold market was only the first of several scandals that rocked the Grant administration. In 1872 the public first learned about the financial buccaneering of the Crédit Mobilier, a construction company that had milked the Union Pacific Railroad for exorbitant fees to line the pockets of insiders who controlled both firms. Rank-and-file Union Pacific shareholders were left holding the bag. This chicanery

The People's Handwriting on the Wall. An 1872 engraving comments on the corruption engulfing Grant.

had transpired before Grant's election in 1868, but it now touched a number of prominent Republican congressmen who had been given shares of Crédit Mobilier stock in exchange for favorable votes. Of thirteen congressmen involved, only two were censured.

Even more odious disclosures followed, and some involved the president's cabinet. Grant's secretary of war, it turned out, had accepted bribes from merchants who traded with Indians at army posts in the West. He was impeached, but he resigned in time to elude trial. Postoffice contracts, it was revealed, went to carriers who offered the highest kickbacks to government officials. In St. Louis a "Whiskey Ring" bribed tax collectors to bilk the government of millions in revenue. Grant's private secretary was enmeshed in that scheme, taking large sums of money and other valuables in return for inside information. There is no evidence that Grant himself participated in any of the fraud, but his poor choice of associates earned him widespread censure.

Reform and the Election of 1872

Long before Grant's first term ended, Republicans broke ranks with the president. Their alienation was a reaction against the Radical Reconstruction measures and the incompetence and corruption in the administration. The so-called Liberal Republicans favored free trade, gold to redeem greenbacks, a stable currency, the restoration of the rights of former Confederates, and civil service reform. Open revolt broke out first in Missouri, where Carl Schurz, a German immigrant and war hero, led a group of Liberal Republicans that, with Democratic help, elected a governor in 1870 and sent Schurz to the Senate.

In 1872 the Liberal Republicans held a clamorous national convention that produced a compromise platform condemning the Republican party's "vindictive" southern policy and favoring civil service reform, but which remained silent on the protective tariff.

The delegates stampeded toward an anomalous presidential candidate: Horace Greeley, editor of the *New York Tribune*, traditionally a strong protectionist and enthusiastic reformer. During his long journalistic career, Greeley had promoted vegetarianism, brown bread, free-thinking, socialism, and spiritualism. His image as a visionary eccentric was complemented by his open hostility to Democrats, whose support the Liberals needed. The Democrats swallowed their reservations and gave their nomination to Greeley as the only hope of beating Grant and the Radical Republicans. Greeley's promise to end Radical Reconstruction and restore "self government" to the South won over Democrats who otherwise despised the man and his beliefs.

The 1872 election result surprised no one. Republican regulars duly endorsed Radical Reconstruction and the protective tariff. Grant still had seven carpetbag states in his pocket, generous support from business and banking interests, and the stalwart support of the Radicals. Above all he still evoked the glory of Vicksburg and Appomattox. Greeley, despite an exhausting tour of the country—still unusual for a presidential candidate—carried only six southern and border states and none in the North. Devastated by his crushing defeat and the simultaneous death of his wife, Greeley entered a mental sanitarium and died three weeks later.

Panic and Redemption

A paralyzing economic panic followed closely upon the public scandals besetting the Grant administration. Contraction of the money supply brought about by the Treasury's postwar withdrawal of greenbacks and the reckless overexpansion of the railroads helped precipitate a financial crisis.

During 1873 some twenty-five strapped railroads defaulted on their interest payments. Caught short, the prominent investment firm of Jay Cooke and Company went bankrupt on September 18, 1873. A financial panic in Vienna forced many financiers to unload American stocks and bonds. The ensuing stampede of selling forced the stock market to close for ten days. The Panic of 1873 set off a depression that lasted for six years. It was the longest and most severe that Americans had yet suffered, marked by widespread bankruptcies, chronic unemployment, and a drastic slowdown in railroad building.

The hard times and corruption hurt Republicans in the midterm elections of 1874, allowing the Democrats to win control of the House of Representatives and gain seats in the Senate. The new Democratic House immediately launched inquiries into the Grant scandals and unearthed further evidence of corruption in high places. The panic meanwhile focused attention once more on greenback currency. Since greenbacks were valued less than gold, most people spent greenbacks first and held their gold or used it to settle foreign accounts, which drained much gold out of the country. To relieve this deflationary spiral and stimulate business, therefore, the Treasury reissued $26 million in greenbacks previously withdrawn.

For a time, the advocates of paper money were riding high. But Grant vetoed an attempt to issue more greenbacks in 1874, and in his annual message he called for their gradual withdrawal and the resumption of payments of gold for greenbacks. Congress obliged the president by passing the Resumption Act of 1875. The resumption of paying gold to customers who turned in their greenbacks began on January 1, 1879, after the Treasury had built a gold reserve for that purpose and reduced the value of greenbacks in circulation. This act infuriated those promoting an inflationary monetary policy and provoked the formation of the National Greenback party. The much debated "money question" would remain one of the most divisive issues in American politics until the end of the century.

The Compromise of 1877

Grant yearned to run for president again in 1876, but the recent scandals precluded any challenge to the tradition of presidents serving no more than two terms. James G. Blaine of Maine, former Speaker of the House, emerged as the Republican front-runner, but he too bore the taint of scandal. Letters in the possession of James Mulligan of Boston linked Blaine to some dubious railroad dealings. Newspapers soon published these "Mulligan Letters," and Blaine's candidacy was dealt a body blow.

The Republican convention therefore eliminated Blaine and several other hopefuls in favor of Ohio's favorite son, Rutherford B. Hayes. Three times governor of Ohio and an advocate of hard money, Hayes had a sterling character and had been a civil service reformer. But his chief virtue, as Henry Adams put it, was "that he is obnoxious to no one."

The Democratic convention was abnormally harmonious from the start. The nomination went on the second ballot to Samuel J. Tilden, corporation lawyer and reform governor of New York, who had directed a campaign to overthrow first the corrupt Tweed Ring that controlled New York City politics and then the Canal Ring in Albany that had bilked New York State of millions.

The campaign generated no burning issues, and early election returns pointed to a Tilden victory. Tilden had a 300,000 edge in the popular vote and had 184 electoral votes, just one short of a majority. Hayes had 165 electoral votes, but Republicans also claimed 19 disputed electoral votes from Florida, Louisiana, and South Carolina. The Democrats laid a counterclaim to 1 of Oregon's 3 votes. The Republicans had clearly carried Oregon, but the outcome in the South was less certain, and given the fraud and intimidation perpetrated on both sides, nobody will ever know the truth of the matter. In all three of the disputed southern states, rival canvassing boards sent in different returns. The Constitution offered no guidance in this unprecedented situation.

The impasse dragged on for months, and there was even talk of public violence. Finally, on January 29, 1877, Congress set up a special Electoral Commission. It had fifteen members, five each from the House, the Senate, and the Supreme Court. The decision on each disputed state went by a vote of 8 to 7 along party lines, in favor of Hayes. After much bluster and threat of filibuster by Democrats, the House voted on March 2 to declare Hayes elected by an electoral vote of 185 to 184.

Critical to this outcome was the defection of southern Democrats who had made several informal agreements with the Republicans. On February 26, 1877, a secret bargain was struck at the Wormley House, a Washington hotel, between prominent Ohio Republicans (including James A. Garfield) and powerful southern Democrats. The Republicans promised that, if elected, Hayes would withdraw federal troops from Louisiana and South Carolina, letting the Republican governments there collapse. In return, the Democrats pledged to withdraw their opposition to Hayes, and to accept in good faith the Thirteenth, Fourteenth, and Fifteenth Amendments.

Southern Democrats could now justify deserting Tilden. This so-called Compromise of 1877 brought a final "redemption" from the "Radicals" and a return to "home rule" in the South, which actually meant rule by native white Democrats. Other, more informal promises bolstered the secret agreement. Hayes's friends pledged more support for Mississippi River levees and other internal improvements, including a federal subsidy for a transcontinental railroad along a southern route. Southerners extracted a further promise that Hayes would name a white southerner as postmaster-general, the cabinet position with the most patronage jobs at hand. In return, southerners would let Republicans make James Garfield Speaker of the new House. Such a deal illustrates the relative weakness of the presidency compared to Congress during the period.

The End of Reconstruction

In 1877 Hayes withdrew federal troops from the state houses in Louisiana and South Carolina, and the Republican governments there soon collapsed—along with much of Hayes's claim to legitimacy. Hayes chose a Tennessean as postmaster-general. But after southern Democrats failed to permit the choice of Garfield as Speaker, Hayes expressed doubt about any further subsidy for southern railroad building, and none was voted. Most of the other Wormley House promises were either renounced or forgotten.

As to southern promises regarding the civil rights of blacks, only a few Democratic leaders remembered them for long. Over the next three decades, those rights crumbled under the pressure of white rule in the South and the force of Supreme Court decisions narrowing the application of the Fourteenth and Fifteenth Amendments. Radical Reconstruction never offered more than an uncertain commitment to racial equality before the law. Yet it left an enduring legacy, the Thirteenth, Fourteenth, and Fifteenth Amendments—not dead but dormant, waiting to be revived. If Reconstruction did not provide social equality or substantial economic opportunities for blacks, it did create the opportunity for future transformation.

PART 5

Growing Pains

The northern victory in 1865 restored the Union and in the process helped to accelerate America's transformation into a modern nation-state. A distinctly national consciousness began to displace the sectional emphases of the antebellum era. During and after the Civil War, the Republican-led Congress pushed through legislation to foster industrial and commercial development and western expansion. In the process, the United States abandoned the Jeffersonian dream of a decentralized agrarian republic and began to forge a dynamic new industrial outlook generated by an increasingly national market.

After 1865, many Americans turned their attention to the unfinished business of settling a continent and completing an urban-industrial revolution begun before the war. Huge new national corporations based upon mass production and mass marketing began to dominate the economic order. As the prominent sociologist William Graham Sumner remarked, the process of industrial development "controls us all because we are all in it. It creates the conditions of our own existence, sets the limits of our social activity, and regulates the bonds of our social relations."

The industrial revolution was not only an urban phenomenon; it transformed rural life as well. Those who resisted the new emphasis on large-scale, highly mechanized commercial agriculture and ranching were brusquely pushed aside. Farm folk, as one New Englander stressed, "must understand farming as a business; if they do not it will go hard with them." The friction between new market forces and traditional folkways generated political revolts and social unrest during the last quarter of the nineteenth century. Fault lines appeared throughout the social order, and they unleashed tremors that exerted what one writer called "a seismic shock, a cyclonic violence" upon the body politic.

The clash between tradition and modernity came to a climax during the decade of the 1890s, one of the most strife-ridden in American history. A deep economic depression, agrarian unrest, and labor violence provoked the possibility of a class war. This turbulent situation transformed the presidential election campaign of 1896 into a clash between two rival visions of America's future. The Republican candidate, William McKinley, campaigned on behalf of modern urban-industrial values. By contrast, William Jennings Bryan, the nominee of both the Democratic and Populist parties, was an eloquent defender of America's agrarian values. McKinley's victory proved to be a watershed in American political and social history. By 1900, the United States would emerge as one of the world's greatest industrial powers, and it would thereafter assume a new leadership role in world affairs. At the same time, it witnessed widening disparities between rich and poor, powerful and powerless.

ESSENTIAL THEMES

CRITICAL QUESTIONS

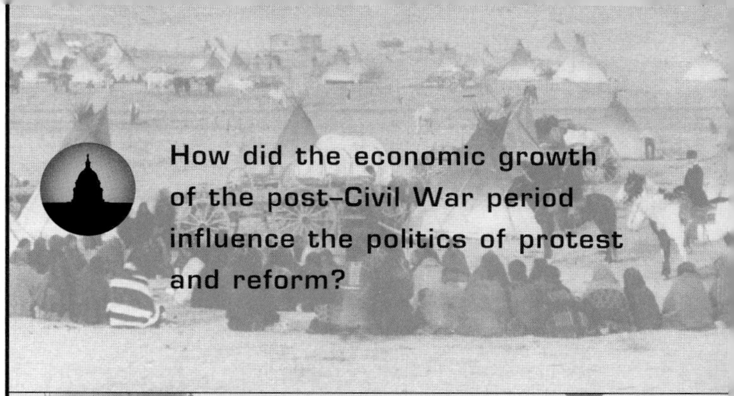

How did the economic growth of the post–Civil War period influence the politics of protest and reform?

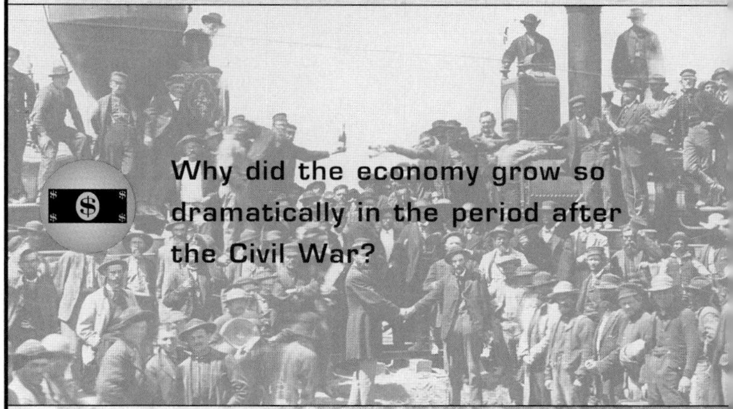

Why did the economy grow so dramatically in the period after the Civil War?

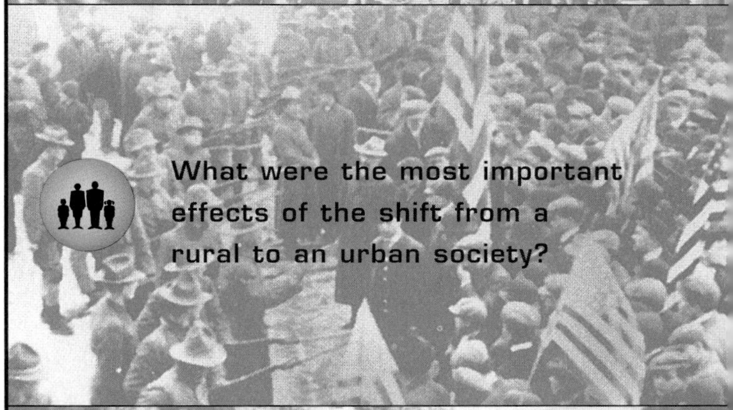

What were the most important effects of the shift from a rural to an urban society?

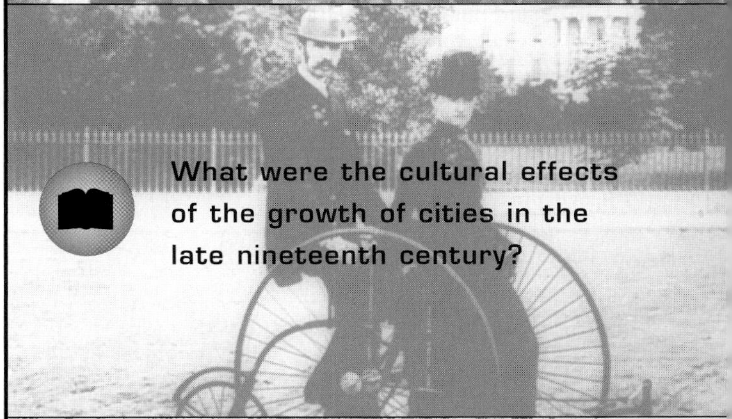

What were the cultural effects of the growth of cities in the late nineteenth century?

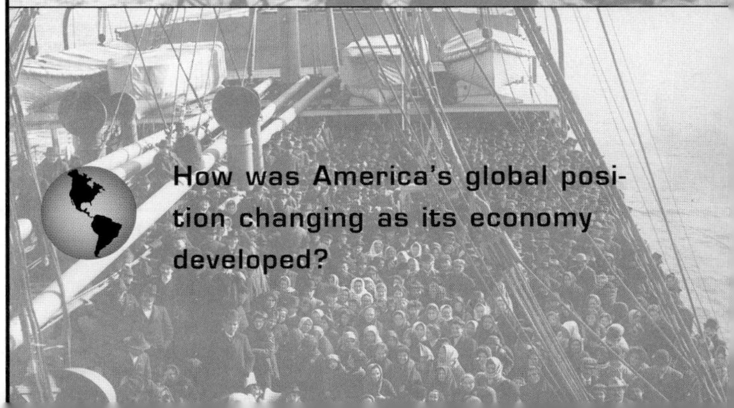

How was America's global position changing as its economy developed?

How did the economic growth of the post–Civil War period influence the politics of protest and reform?

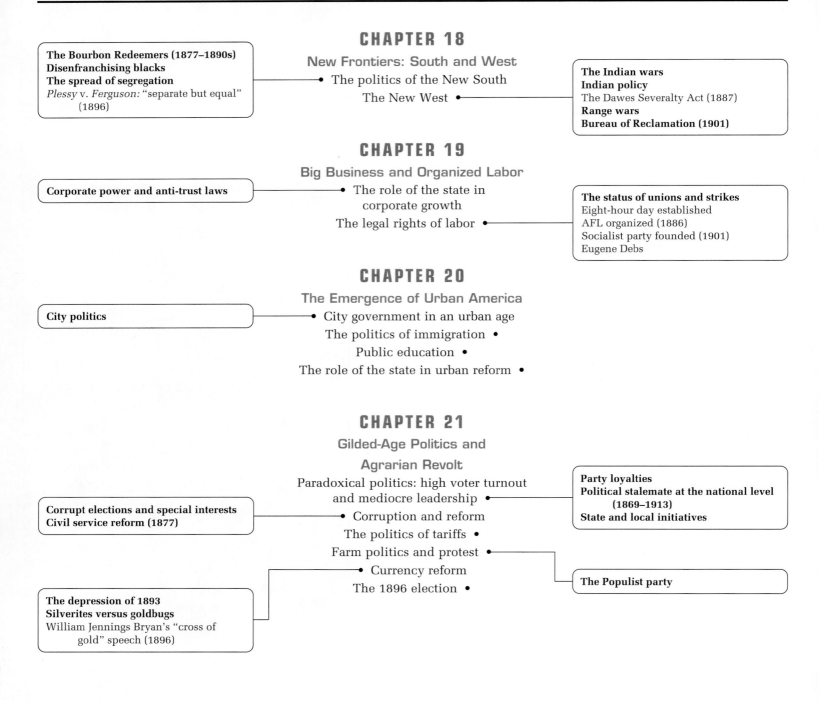

CHAPTER 18

New Frontiers: South and West

- The politics of the New South
  - **The Bourbon Redeemers (1877–1890s)**
  - **Disenfranchising blacks**
  - **The spread of segregation**
  - *Plessy* v. *Ferguson:* "separate but equal" (1896)
- The New West
  - **The Indian wars**
  - **Indian policy**
  - The Dawes Severalty Act (1887)
  - **Range wars**
  - **Bureau of Reclamation (1901)**

CHAPTER 19

Big Business and Organized Labor

- The role of the state in corporate growth
  - **Corporate power and anti-trust laws**
- The legal rights of labor
  - **The status of unions and strikes**
  - Eight-hour day established
  - AFL organized (1886)
  - Socialist party founded (1901)
  - Eugene Debs

CHAPTER 20

The Emergence of Urban America

- City government in an urban age
  - **City politics**
- The politics of immigration
- Public education
- The role of the state in urban reform

CHAPTER 21

Gilded-Age Politics and Agrarian Revolt

- Paradoxical politics: high voter turnout and mediocre leadership
  - **Party loyalties**
  - **Political stalemate at the national level (1869–1913)**
  - **State and local initiatives**
- Corruption and reform
  - **Corrupt elections and special interests**
  - **Civil service reform (1877)**
- The politics of tariffs
- Farm politics and protest
  - **The Populist party**
- Currency reform
  - **The depression of 1893**
  - **Silverites versus goldbugs**
  - William Jennings Bryan's "cross of gold" speech (1896)
- The 1896 election

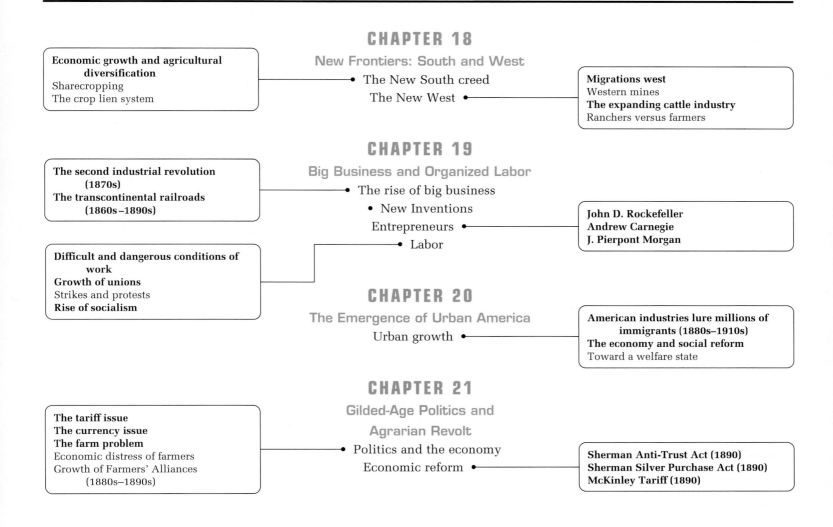

CHAPTER 18

New Frontiers: South and West

- The New South creed
  - **Economic growth and agricultural diversification**
  - Sharecropping
  - The crop lien system
- The New West
  - **Migrations west**
  - Western mines
  - **The expanding cattle industry**
  - Ranchers versus farmers

CHAPTER 19

Big Business and Organized Labor

- The rise of big business
  - **The second industrial revolution (1870s)**
  - **The transcontinental railroads (1860s–1890s)**
- New Inventions
- Entrepreneurs
  - **John D. Rockefeller**
  - **Andrew Carnegie**
  - **J. Pierpont Morgan**
- Labor
  - **Difficult and dangerous conditions of work**
  - **Growth of unions**
  - Strikes and protests
  - **Rise of socialism**

CHAPTER 20

The Emergence of Urban America

- Urban growth
  - **American industries lure millions of immigrants (1880s–1910s)**
  - **The economy and social reform**
  - Toward a welfare state

CHAPTER 21

Gilded-Age Politics and Agrarian Revolt

- Politics and the economy
  - **The tariff issue**
  - **The currency issue**
  - **The farm problem**
  - Economic distress of farmers
  - Growth of Farmers' Alliances (1880s–1890s)
- Economic reform
  - **Sherman Anti-Trust Act (1890)**
  - **Sherman Silver Purchase Act (1890)**
  - **McKinley Tariff (1890)**

What were the most important effects of the shift from a rural to an urban society?

CHAPTER 18
New Frontiers: South and West

- Social change in the New South
  - **Bourbon rule and the black South (1877–1890s)**
  - **The spread of segregation**
  - Booker T. Washington and accommodation
  - W. E. B. Du Bois and "ceaseless agitation"
- Social change in the New West
  - **African Americans migrate west**
  - **Immigrants move west**
  - **Displacing the Indians**
  - **Pioneer women**
  - **The frontier and social democracy**

CHAPTER 19
Big Business and Organized Labor

- Industrial combination and the social order
  - **New industries, new workforce**
  - **Chinese railroad workers**
  - **Rising wages**
  - **Poor working and living conditions**
  - **Labor discontent**
  - **The Molly Maguires**
- Union organizing
  - **The railroad strike of 1877**
  - **The "Sand Lot" incident**
  - **The Knights of Labor (1869–1893)**
  - **The Haymarket Square affair (1886)**
  - **The American Federation of Labor (AFL)**
  - **The Homestead Steel Strike of 1892**
  - **The Pullman Strike of 1894**
- Socialism and the unions
  - **"Big Bill" Haywood and the Wobblies**

CHAPTER 20
The Emergence of Urban America

- Metropolitan America
  - **Growth of cities**
  - The lure of the city
  - Housing
  - Public services
  - Mass transit
- The new immigration
  - **Eastern and southern european immigrants**
  - Ellis Island
  - Settling in America
  - **Nativist reaction**
- Public entertainments
- The spread of public education
  - **Education of women**
- Social Darwinism and the new society
  - **Reform Darwinist response**
- Religious reform: the Social Gospel
- Urban reform
  - **The settlement house movement**
  - **Women's employment and suffrage**
  - Susan B. Anthony and Elizabeth Cady Stanton
  - **Toward a general welfare state**

CHAPTER 21
Gilded-Age Politics and Agrarian Revolt

- The social functions of political parties
- State and local reform
- Problems on the farm
  - **The Granger movement founded (1867)**
  - **Farmers' Alliances**
  - **Farm politics**
  - **The Populist party**
- Effects of the 1893 depression
- Rural versus urban America in the 1896 election

CHAPTER 18

New Frontiers: South and West

- The New South
  - **Henry Grady's New South Creed**
  - **The spread of segregation**
  - **Washington and Du Bois**
- The New West
  - **Exodusters (1870s–1880s)**
  - **European immigrants**
  - **Cattle and cowboys**
  - **Barbed wire and the end of the open range**
  - **The violent West**
  - Frederick Jackson Turner: "The frontier has gone." (1893)

CHAPTER 19

Big Business and Organized Labor

- The second industrial revolution and material culture
  - **Rise of consumerism**
  - Sears and Roebuck catalog
  - **Increasing inequality**
  - Industrial wealth
  - Aggrieved labor

CHAPTER 20

The Emergence of Urban America

- Urban culture
  - **The new immigration**
  - **Popular culture**
  - Wild West shows (1880s–1917)
  - Vaudeville
  - Outdoor recreation
  - Spectator sports
- The rise of professionalism
- Realism
  - **Social Darwinism**
  - **Reform Darwinism**
  - **Pragmatism**
  - Samuel Clemens, *The Adventures of Huckleberry Finn* (1884)
- Literary Naturalism
  - **Stephen Crane's *The Red Badge of Courage* (1895)**
- Social criticism
  - **Henry Lloyd, *Wealth Against Commonwealth* (1894)**
- Religious reform
- Social reform

CHAPTER 21

Gilded-Age Politics and Agrarian Revolt

- Gilded-Age corruption
- Farm life and agrarian protest
- Rural versus metropolitan interests

How was America's global position changing as its economy developed?

CHAPTER 18

New Frontiers: South and West

- The New South vision and the world economy
- Peopling the West
  - Immigrants from Mexico, Europe, Asia, and Canada
  - Multicultural mining communities

CHAPTER 19

Big Business and Organized Labor

- Foreign investment and American industrial growth
- International dimensions of the labor movement
  - Immigrants and the unions
  - The effects of European labor movements
  - Socialism and the unions
  - The Wobblies

CHAPTER 20

The Emergence of Urban America

- The new immigration
  - Eastern and southern European origins
  - Conditions at home
  - Ethnic identity in America
- Immigration restrictions
  - Chinese Exclusion Act (1882)
- Higher education and the German model
  - The influence of Darwinian thought
- International roots of religious reform

CHAPTER 21

Gilded-Age Politics and Agrarian Revolt

- International dimensions of tariff policy
- International dimensions of urrency policy
- World markets and the American farm
- British banking and the depression of 1893

CHAPTER

18

New Frontiers: South and West

This chapter focuses on

- The economic and political policies of the states in the post-Reconstruction South.
- Race relations in the New South.
- The farmers', miners', and cowboys' frontiers.
- Late-nineteenth-century Indian policy.

THE *ESSENTIAL AMERICA* ON-LINE TUTOR

www.wwnorton.com/eamerica/ch18

- **Topic: Booker T. Washington and W. E. B. Du Bois**
  www.wwnorton.com/eamerica/ch18/topic.htm

  In the final decades of the nineteenth century, black Americans debated their role in American society. Over the course of this debate, two leaders emerged—Booker T. Washington and W. E. B. Du Bois—who promulgated fundamentally different resolutions. Consider the significance of the debate between Washington and Du Bois using photographs, historical analyses, and their own writings. Over what issues did Du Bois take issue with Washington?

- **Chapter review: On-line quiz and chapter summary**
  www.wwnorton.com/eamerica/ch18/review.htm

- **Chapter resources: Multimedia index**
  www.wwnorton.com/eamerica/ch18/media.htm

After the Civil War, the West and the South provided enticing opportunities for pioneers and entrepreneurs alike. Before 1860, most people had viewed the region between the Mississippi River and California as a barren landscape suitable only for Indians and animals. Half of the state of Texas, for instance, was still not settled at the end of the Civil War. After 1865, however, the federal government encouraged western settlement and economic development. The construction of transcontinental railroads, the military conquest of the Indians, and a liberal land distribution policy combined to lure thousands of pioneers and expectant capitalists westward. As a result of the mass migration to the West, fourteen new states were created out of America's western territories during the century after the Civil War.

Although the first great wave of railroad building occurred in the 1850s, the most spectacular growth took place during the quarter century after the Civil War. From about 35,000 miles of track in 1865, the network grew to nearly 200,000 miles by 1897. The transcontinental rail lines led the way, and they helped populate the plains and the Far West. Of course, the expense of such massive railroad development was enormous, and the long-term corporate debt required to finance construction would become a major cause of the Panic of 1893 and the ensuing depression.

Meanwhile, southern rail lines were rebuilt and supplemented with new branch lines. The defeated South offered capitalists fertile ground for investment and industrial development. Proponents of a "New South" after 1865 argued that the region must abandon its single-minded preoccupation with agriculture and pursue industrial and commercial development. As a result, the South as well as the West experienced dramatic social and economic changes during the last third of the nineteenth century. By 1900, these new "frontiers" had been transformed in ways that few could have predicted.

The New South

A Fresh Vision

After the Civil War, many southerners looked back wistfully to the plantation life that had characterized their region before the firing on Fort Sumter. A few prominent leaders, however, insisted that the postwar South must liberate itself from such nostalgia and create a new society of small farms, thriving industries, and bustling cities. The major prophet of this "New South" was Henry W. Grady, the thirty-six-year-old editor of the *Atlanta Constitution.* During the 1880s, Grady declared that the Old South of slavery and agriculture must give way to a New South of diverse industries and racial harmony.

It was a compelling vision, and other advocates of this New South Creed soon emerged. In the aftermath of the Civil War, these men, and their Yankee patrons, preached the gospel of industrial development with evangelical fervor. The Confederacy, they reasoned, had lost because it relied too much on King Cotton. From that central belief flowed certain implications: that a more diversified and efficient agriculture would be a foundation for economic growth, that more widespread education, especially vocational training, would promote material success. By the late 1870s, with Reconstruction over and the Panic of 1873 forgotten, a mood of economic progress permeated the speeches of the day.

Economic Growth

The chief accomplishment of the New South movement was an expansion of the area's textile production, which began in the 1880s and overtook its older New England competitors by the 1920s. From 1880 to 1900, the number of cotton mills in the South grew from 161 to 400, and the number of mill workers (among whom women and children outnumbered the men) increased fivefold.

Tobacco growth also increased significantly, entering a new era with the development of two new varieties of the weed: burley, which first appeared in southern Ohio, and bright leaf, which was grown on otherwise infertile soils and cured by a charcoal process invented by a slave in 1839.

Crucial to the rise of the tobacco industry was Washington Duke's family, who had a farm near Durham, North Carolina. By 1872 the Dukes had a factory producing 125,000 pounds of tobacco annually. Son Buck Duke poured large sums into advertising, undersold competitors in their own markets, and cornered the supply of ingredients. Eventually his competitors were ready to take the hint that they join forces, and in 1890 Duke brought most of them into the American Tobacco Company, which controlled nine-tenths of the nation's cigarette production. In 1911 the Supreme Court ruled that the company was in violation of the antitrust laws and ordered it broken up, but by then Duke had found new worlds to conquer in hydroelectric power and aluminum.

Systematic use of other natural resources helped revitalize the area along the Appalachian Mountain chain from West Virginia to Alabama. Coal production in the South (including West Virginia) grew from 5 million tons in 1875 to 49 million tons by 1900. At the southern end of the mountains, Birmingham, Alabama, sprang up during the 1870s as a major steel-producing center and soon named itself the "Pittsburgh of the South."

Industrial growth created a need for wood-framed housing, and after 1870 lumbering became a thriving industry in the South. By the turn of the century, it had surpassed textiles in value. Tree cutting seemed to know no bounds, despite the resulting ecological devastation. In time the industry would be saved only by the warm climate, which fostered quick renewal of forests, and the rise of scientific forestry.

Two forces that would impel an even greater industrial revolution were already on the southern horizon at the turn of the century: petroleum in the Southwest and hydroelectric power in the Southeast. In 1901 the Spindletop oil gusher in Texas brought a huge bonanza. Electrical power proved equally profitable, and local power plants dotted the South by the 1890s. Richmond, Virginia, boasted the nation's first electric streetcar system in 1888, and Columbia, South Carolina, boasted the first electrically powered cotton mill in 1894. The greatest advance would begin in 1905 when Buck Duke's Southern Power Company set out to electrify entire river valleys in the Carolinas.

Agriculture, Old and New

Although there was some industrial growth, most of the South remained agrarian at the turn of the century. King Cotton survived the Civil War and expanded over new acreage even as its export markets leveled off. Louisiana cane sugar, probably the most war-devastated of all crops, also flourished again by the 1890s.

Most southern farmers were not flourishing, however. A prolonged deflation in crop prices affected the entire western world during the last third of the nineteenth century. Sagging prices made it more difficult than ever to own land. Sharecropping and tenancy grew increasingly prevalent. By 1890, most southern farms were worked by people who did not own the land. High tenancy rates in the Deep South belied the rosy rhetoric of New South prophets: South Carolina, 61 percent; Georgia, 60 percent; Alabama, 58 percent; Mississippi, 62 percent; and Louisiana, 58 percent.

How did the system work? Sharecroppers, who had nothing to offer the landowner but their labor, tilled the land in return for supplies and a share of the crop, generally about half. Tenant farmers, hardly better off, might have their own mule, a plow, and credit with the country store. They were entitled to claim a larger share, commonly three-fourths of the cash crop and two-thirds of the subsistence crop, which was mainly corn. The system was horribly inefficient, for the tenant lacked incentive to care for the land, and the owner had little chance to supervise the work.

The crop lien system was equally flawed. At best, it supplied credit where cash was scarce. It worked this way: country merchants furnished supplies in return for liens (or mortgages) on farmers' crops. To a few tenants and small farmers who seized the chance, such credit offered a way out of dependency, but to most it offered only a hopeless cycle of perennial debt. The merchant, who assumed great risks, generally charged interest that ranged, according to one journalist, "from 24 percent to grand larceny." The merchant, like the planter (often the same man), required his farmer clients to grow a cash crop that could be readily sold at harvest time. Thus, for all the New South promoters' ballyhoo about diversification, the routines of tenancy and sharecropping were geared to a staple crop, usually cotton. The resulting stagnation of rural life held millions, white and black, in bondage to privation and ignorance.

The Bourbon Redeemers

After Reconstruction ended in 1877, a planter-merchant elite, collectively known as Redeemers or Bourbons, dominated southern politics. The supporters of these postwar leaders referred to them as "Redeemers" because they supposedly "redeemed," or saved, the South from Yankee domination as well as from the limitations of a purely rural economy. The Redeemers included a rising class of entrepreneurs who were eager to promote a more diversified economy based on industrial development and railroad expansion.

The opponents of the "Redeemers" labeled them "Bourbons" in an effort to depict them not as virtuous progressives but as self-serving reactionaries. Like the French royal family that, Napoleon said, forgot nothing and learned nothing in the ordeal of revolution, Bourbons of the postwar South were said to have forgotten nothing and learned nothing in the ordeal of the Civil War.

The term "Bourbon" came to signify the leaders of the Democratic party, whether they were real reactionaries or, more commonly, champions of an industrial New South who embraced a new order of economic development.

These Bourbons of the New South were members of the rural elite and upstart capitalists who perfected a political alliance with northeastern conservatives and an economic alliance with northeastern capitalists. They generally pursued a government policy of laissez-faire, except for the lavish tax exemptions and other favors they offered to their business supporters. They avoided political initiatives, making the transition from Republican rule to Bourbon rule less abrupt than is often assumed. The Bourbons' favorable disposition toward the railroads was not unlike that of the Radicals. And despite their reputation for honesty, Bourbon office holders were occasionally caught with their fingers in the till.

The Bourbons focused on cutting back the size and cost of government. This spelled austerity for public services, including the school systems started during Reconstruction. In 1871 the southern Atlantic states were spending $10.27 per pupil; by 1880 the figure was down to $6.00, and in 1890 it stood at only $7.63. Illiteracy rates at the time ran at about 12 percent of the white population and 50 percent of the black population.

The Bourbons' urge to economize led them to adopt the degrading system of leasing convicts for labor. The destruction of prisons during the Civil War and the poverty of state treasuries afterward combined with the demand for cheap labor on the railroads, in the mines, and in lumber camps to make convict labor a way for southern states to avoid expenses and generate revenue. The burden of detaining criminals grew after the war because freed slaves, who had been subject to the discipline of masters, were now subject to the criminal law. Convict leasing, in the absence of state supervision, allowed inefficiency, neglect, and disregard for human life to proliferate.

The Bourbons scaled down not only state expenditures but also the public debt, and by a simple means—they repudiated a vast amount of debt that had been issued by the Radical state regimes. The corruption and extravagance of Radical rule were commonly advanced as justification for the process, but repudiation did not stop with Reconstruction debts. Altogether nine states repudiated more than half of what they owed to bondholders and various other creditors.

These scrimping Bourbon regimes did respond to the demand for public commissions to regulate the rates charged by railroads for commercial transport. They also established boards of agriculture and public health, agricultural experiment stations, agricultural and mechanical colleges, teacher-training schools and women's colleges, even state colleges for African Americans. Nor can any simplistic interpretation encompass the variety of Bourbon Democratic leaders. The Democratic party was then a mongrel coalition that threw Old Whigs, Unionists, secessionists, businessmen, small farmers, hillbillies, planters, and even some Republicans together in alliance against the Reconstruction Radicals. Democrats therefore, even those who bore the Bourbon or Redeemer label, often marched to different drummers, and the Bourbon regimes never achieved complete unity in philosophy or government. Nor were they always exemplars of honest government and economic prudence.

Perhaps the ultimate paradox of the Bourbons' rule was that these paragons of white supremacy tolerated a lingering black voice in politics and showed no haste about raising legal barriers of racial separation. Blacks sat in the state legislature of South Carolina until 1900, of Georgia until 1908, and of Virginia until 1890; some of these black representatives were Democrats. The South sent black congressmen to Washington in every election until 1900 except one, though they always represented gerrymandered districts into which most of the black voters had been thrown. Under the Bourbons, the disenfranchisement of black voters remained inconsistent, a local matter brought about mainly by fraud and intimidation, although it occurred often enough to ensure white control of the southern states.

A like flexibility applied in other areas of race relations. The color line was drawn less strictly than it would be in the twentieth-century South. In some places, to be sure, racial segregation appeared before the end of Reconstruction, especially in schools, churches, hotels and rooming houses, and in private social relations. In other public places such as trains, depots, theaters, and soda fountains, however, segregation was more sporadic.

Disenfranchising Blacks

During the 1890s, the attitudes of patrician benevolence that permitted moderation in racial attitudes eroded swiftly. One reason was political. The rise of populism, a farm-based protest movement that culminated in the creation of a third political party in the 1890s, divided the white vote to such an extent that in some places the black vote became the determining factor in local elections. Some populists courted black votes. In response, the Bourbons revived the race issue, insisting that the black vote be eliminated completely from southern elections. Some farm leaders hoped that disenfranchisement of blacks would make it possible for whites to divide politically without raising the specter of "Negro domination."

But since the Fifteenth Amendment made it illegal to disenfranchise blacks as such, racists accomplished their purpose indirectly with devices such as poll taxes (or head taxes) and literacy tests. Some opposed such devices because they also kept poor whites from voting, and they created loopholes through which illiterate whites could slip.

Mississippi led the way to near-total disenfranchisement of blacks. The state called a constitutional convention in 1890 to change the suffrage provisions of the old Radical constitution of 1868. The resulting Mississippi plan set the pattern that seven more states would follow over the next twenty years. First, a residence requirement—two years in the state, one year in the election district—struck at those black tenant farmers who were in the habit of moving yearly in search of better land and terms of lease. Second, voters were disqualified if convicted of certain crimes, many of them petty. Third, all taxes, including a poll tax, had to be paid by February 1 of each election year, which left plenty of time for white officials to lose the receipt before the fall vote. This proviso fell most heavily on the poor, most of whom were black. Fourth and finally, all voters had to be literate. The alternative, designed as a loophole for whites otherwise disqualified, was an "understanding" clause. The voter, if unable to read the Constitution, could qualify by "understanding" it—to the satisfaction of the registrar. Fraud was thus institutionalized by "legal" disenfranchisement.

In other states, variations on the Mississippi plan added a few flourishes. In 1898 Louisiana invented the "grandfather clause," which allowed illiterates to qualify if their fathers or grandfathers had been eligible to vote on January 1, 1867, when blacks were still excluded. By 1910 Georgia, North Carolina, Virginia, Alabama, and Oklahoma had adopted the grandfather clause. Every southern state, moreover, adopted a statewide Democratic primary which became the only meaningful election outside isolated areas of Republican strength. With minor exceptions, the Democratic primaries excluded black voters altogether. The effectiveness of these measures can be seen in a few sample figures: Louisiana in 1896 had 130,000 black voters registered, and in 1900, only 5,320. Alabama in 1900 had 121,159 literate black males over twenty-one, according to the census; only 3,742 were registered to vote.

Segregation Spreads

What came to be called "Jim Crow" segregation accompanied efforts to restrict black voting. The term "Jim Crow" derived from a popular blackface minstrel-show character. From 1875 to 1883, any racial segregation violated a federal Civil Rights Act, which forbade discrimination in places of public accommodation. But in 1883 the Supreme Court ruled on seven *Civil Rights Cases* involving discrimination against blacks by

African-American women sweeping. In the postwar South, most jobs offered to African Americans were in domestic service and agriculture.

Booker T. Washington.

W. E. B. Du Bois.

corporations or individuals. The Court held, with only one dissent, that the force of federal law could not extend to individual action. The Fourteenth Amendment, which provided that "no State" could deny citizens the equal protection of the laws, stood as a prohibition only against state, not individual, action.

This left as an open question the validity of state laws *requiring* racially separate public facilities under the rubric of "separate but equal." In 1888 Mississippi required railway passengers, under penalty of law, to occupy the car set aside for their race. When Louisiana followed suit in 1890, the law was challenged in the case of *Plessy* v. *Ferguson,* which the Supreme Court decided in 1896.

The test case originated in New Orleans when Homer Plessy, an octoroon (a person of one-eighth black ancestry), refused to leave a white railroad car when asked to do so. He was convicted, and the case rose on appeal to the Supreme Court. The Court ruled that segregation laws "have been generally, if not universally recognized as within the competency of state legislatures in the exercise of their police power." Soon the principle of statutory racial segregation extended into every area of southern life, including street railways, hotels, restaurants, hospitals, recreations, sports, and employment.

Violence accompanied the so-called Jim Crow laws that mandated segregated facilities. From 1890 to 1899, lynchings in the United States averaged 187 per year, 82 percent of which occurred in the South; from 1900 to 1909, they averaged 93 per year, of which 92 percent occurred in the South. Whites constituted 32 percent of the victims during the first period, only 11 percent in the latter. A young Episcopal priest in Montgomery remarked that extremists had proceeded "from an undiscriminating attack upon the Negro's ballot to a like attack upon his schools, his labor, his life."

Washington and Du Bois

A few brave souls, black and white, spoke out against racist efforts, but by and large blacks had to accommodate as best they could. The chief spokesman for this accommodationist philosophy was Booker T. Washington, the black prophet of the New South Creed. Born in Virginia of a slave mother and a white father, Washington had fought extreme adversity to get an education at Hampton Institute, one of the postwar missionary schools. In 1881, he helped create Tuskegee Institute, in Alabama, a leading college for blacks.

Washington argued that blacks should not antagonize whites by demanding social or political equality; instead they should concentrate on establishing an economic base for their advancement. In his famous 1895 speech labeled the "Atlanta Compromise," Washington advised fellow blacks to stress their opportunities rather than their grievances: "Cast down your bucket where you are—cast it down in making friends . . . of the people of all races by whom we are surrounded. Cast it down in agriculture, mechanics, in commerce, in domestic service, and in the professions." He conspicuously omitted any reference to politics and implied an endorsement of segregation: "In all things that are purely social we can be as separate as the five fingers, yet one as the hand in all things essential to mutual progress."

Some people bitterly criticized Washington for sacrificing broad education and civil rights for the creation of economic opportunities for blacks. W. E. B. Du Bois led blacks in this criticism of Washington. A native of Great Barrington, Massachusetts, the son of free blacks, Du Bois first experienced southern racism as an undergraduate at Fisk University in Nashville. Later he earned a Ph.D. in history from Harvard and afterward attended the University of Berlin. In addition to an active career in racial protest, he left a distinguished record as a teacher and scholar.

Not long after he began his teaching career at Atlanta University in 1897, Du Bois began to assault Washington's accommodationist philosophy and promote his own program of "ceaseless agitation." Washington, Du Bois argued, preached "a gospel of Work and Money to such an extent" that it overshadowed "the higher aims of life." The education of blacks, he maintained, should not be merely vocational but should nurture leaders willing to challenge segregation and discrimination through social protest and political action.

A Not-So-New South

By 1900 the South remained a predominantly agrarian and relatively poor region. Despite the hopes and rhetoric of "New South" boosters, the former Confederacy had made little progress toward improved race relations or a diversified economy. In fact, its proportion of manufacturing production in 1900 was smaller than it had been in 1860. Likewise, the region's per capita income when compared to national figures was lower than it had been in 1860.

The New West

For vast reaches of western America, the great epics of the Civil War and Reconstruction were remote events hardly touching the lives of Indians, Mexicans, Asians, and the trappers, miners, cowboys, traders, and Mormons scattered through the plains and mountains. There the march of westward settlement and exploitation continued its inexorable course. On one level, the settlement of the West beyond the Mississippi constituted a colorful drama of determined pioneers overcoming all obstacles to secure their visions of freedom and opportunity amid the region's awesome and arid vastness. On another level, however, the colonization of the Far West involved shortsighted greed and irresponsible behavior, a story of reckless exploitation that nearly exterminated the culture of Native Americans, scarred the land, and decimated its wildlife. Both images of the process of western settlement are accurate in some respects; neither tells the complete story.

In the second tier of trans-Mississippi states—Iowa, Kansas, Nebraska—and in western Minnesota, farmers began spreading out onto the Great Plains after the Civil War. From California the miners' frontier stretched east through the mountains as scattered enclaves sprang up at one new strike after another. From Texas the nomadic cowboys migrated northward into the plains and across the Rockies into the Great Basin.

As settlement moved west, the environment gradually altered. The scarcity of water and timber in the Great Plains rendered obsolete the axe, the log cabin, the rail fence, and the usual methods of tilling the soil. For a long time, the region had been called the Great American Desert, a barrier to cross on the way to the Pacific, unfit for human habitation. But that pattern changed in the last half of the nineteenth century as a result of new finds of gold, silver, and other minerals, completion of transcontinental railroads, the rise of the range-cattle industry, and the dawning realization that the arid region need not be a sterile desert. With the use of what water was available, techniques of "dry farming" and irrigation could make the land fruitful after all.

The Migratory Stream

During the second half of the nineteenth century, a growing stream of migrants flowed into the largely Indian and Hispanic West. Millions of Anglo Americans, African Americans, Mexicans, and European and Chinese immigrants transformed the patterns of western society and culture. Most of the settlers were relatively prosperous white, native-born farming families. Because of the expense of transportation, land,

An American family on their way west.

and supplies, the very poor could not afford to relocate. Three-quarters of the western migrants were men.

The largest number of foreign immigrants who settled in the West came from northern Europe and Canada. In the northern plains, Germans, Scandinavians, and Irish were especially numerous. Not surprisingly, these foreign settlers tended to cluster together according to ethnic and kinship ties.

After the collapse of Radical Republican rule in the South, thousands of blacks began migrating west from Kentucky, Tennessee, Louisiana, Arkansas, Mississippi, and Texas. Some 6,000 southern blacks arrived in Kansas in 1879 alone, and as many as 20,000 may have come the following year. They came to be known as Exodusters, making their exodus out of the South in search of a haven from racism and poverty.

The black exodus to Kansas and Oklahoma Territory died out by the early 1880s. Many southern blacks were prevented from leaving the South, which needed their labor, through threats and intimidation. And many of the black settlers were unprepared for the quite different living and working conditions on the plains. Their homesteads were not large enough to be self-sufficient, and most of the black farmers were forced to supplement their income by hiring themselves out to white ranchers in the area. Drought, grasshoppers, prairie fires, and dust storms led to crop failures. Many of the black pioneers soon abandoned their land and moved to the few cities in the state. Nonetheless, by 1890, some 520,000 blacks lived west of the Mississippi River. As many as 25 percent of the cowboys who participated in the Texas cattle drives were African Americans.

In 1866 Congress passed legislation establishing two "colored" cavalry units and dispatched them to the western frontier. Nicknamed "Buffalo Soldiers" by the Indians, the soldiers were mostly Civil War veterans from Louisiana and Kentucky. They built and maintained forts, mapped vast areas of the Southwest, strung hundreds of miles of telegraph lines, protected railroad construction crews, subdued hostile Indians, and captured outlaws and rustlers. For this they were paid $13 a month. Eighteen of the "Buffalo Soldiers" won Congressional Medals of Honor for their service in the West.

Mining the West

Miners were also ethnically diverse. Every race and nationality was represented in the mining communities. The California miners of 1849 (the "Forty-niners") set the typical pattern in which the disorderly rush of prospectors was quickly followed by the arrival of the camp followers, a motley array of saloonkeepers, prostitutes, card sharps, hustlers, and assorted desperadoes out to mine the miners. An era of lawlessness eventually gave way to vigilante rule and, finally, to a stable community and more subtle forms of exploitation.

The drama of the 1849 gold rush was reenacted time and again in the following three decades. Though the California fever had passed by 1851, and no big strikes were made for seven years, new finds in Colorado and Nevada revived hopes for riches. While nearly 100,000 early rushers were crowding around Pike's Peak in Colorado in 1859, miners discovered the Comstock Lode at Gold Hill, Nevada.

The growing demand for orderly government in the West led to the hasty creation of new territories, and eventually the admission of a host of new states. In 1861 Nevada became a territory, and in 1864 the state of Nevada was admitted in time to give its three electoral votes to Lincoln. After Colorado was admitted in 1876, however, no new states entered for over a decade because Democrats in Congress were reluctant to create states out of territories that were heavily Republican. After the sweeping Republican victory of 1888, however, Congress admitted the Dakotas, Montana, and Washington in 1889, and Idaho and Wyoming in 1890, completing a tier of states from coast to coast. Utah entered in 1896 (after the Mormons abandoned the practice of polygamy), Oklahoma in 1907, and in 1912 Arizona and New Mexico rounded out the forty-eight continental states.

The Indian Wars

Perhaps 250,000 Indians in the Great Plains and mountain regions lived mainly off the buffalo herds that provided food and, from their hides, clothing and shelter. In 1851 the chiefs of the principal Plains tribes had gathered at Fort Laramie in Wyoming Territory, where they had agreed to accept new tribal borders and to leave the emigrants unmolested on their trails. Fighting resumed, however, as the emigrants began to encroach upon Indian lands rather than merely passing through them. From 1850 to 1860, for example, 150,000 whites moved into Sioux territory in violation of treaty agreements.

From the early 1860s until the late 1870s, the frontier raged with Indian wars, and intermittent outbreaks continued through the 1880s. In Colorado Territory, where Cheyenne and Arapaho chiefs were forced to accept a treaty reducing their lands, Indians began sporadic raids on trains and mining camps. In 1864 Colonel J. M. Chivington's poorly trained militia fell upon an Indian camp along Sand Creek and slaughtered 150 to 200 Indians—men, women, and children.

With other scattered battles erupting, a congressional committee began to gather evidence in 1865 on the grisly Indian wars and massacres. Its 1867 *Report on the Condition of the Indian Tribes* led Congress to establish an Indian Peace Commission charged with removing the causes of Indian wars in general. Congress decided this was best accomplished at the expense of the Indians, by persuading them to take up life on out-of-the-way reservations. This solution continued the persistent encroachment on Indian hunting grounds.

In 1867 a conference at Medicine Creek Lodge, Kansas, ended with the Kiowa, Comanche, Arapaho, and Cheyenne reluctantly accepting lands in western Oklahoma. The following spring, the Sioux agreed to settle within the Black Hills reservation in Dakota Territory. But Indian resistance in the southern plains continued until the Red River War of 1874–1875. Soldiers led by General Philip Sheridan, the hard-charging Civil War cavalryman, scattered the Indians and finally forced them to terms in the spring of 1875.

By then trouble was brewing once again in the north. In 1874, Lieutenant-Colonel

An 1851 treaty allowed settlers to pass safely through Indian lands, but they soon encroached on Indian territory, which led to fighting.

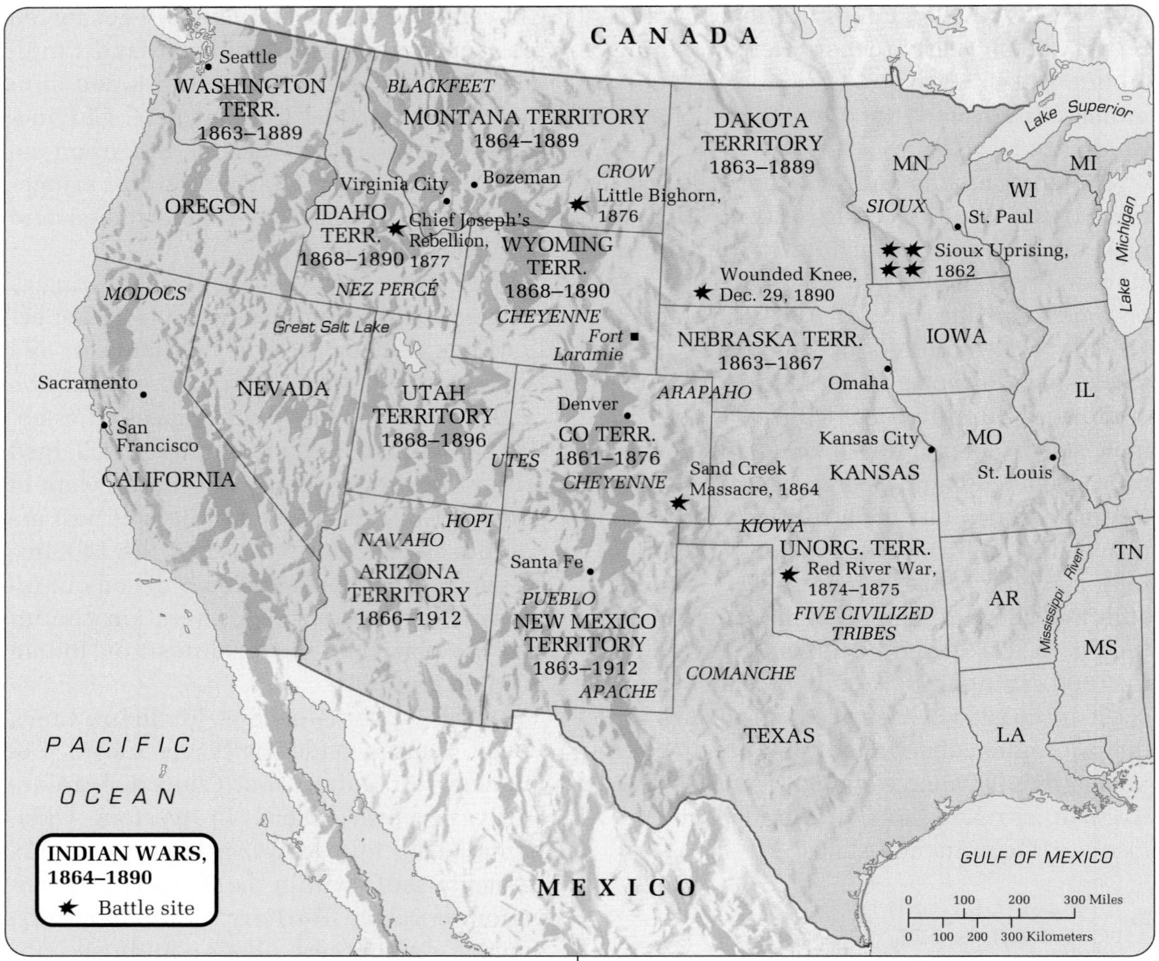

George A. Custer led an exploring expedition into the Black Hills, accompanied by gold seekers. Miners were soon filtering into the Sioux hunting grounds despite promises that the army would keep them out. The army had done little to protect the Indian lands, but when ordered to move against wandering bands of Sioux hunting on the range according to their treaty rights, the army moved vigorously.

What became the Great Sioux War was the largest military event since the end of the Civil War. It lasted fifteen months and entailed some fifteen battles in a vast area of present-day Wyoming, Montana, South Dakota, and Nebraska. After several indecisive encounters, Custer found the main encampment of Sioux and their northern Cheyenne allies on the Little Bighorn River. Separated from the main body of his men, Custer and 210 soldiers were surrounded by 2,500 warriors and annihilated.

The army regained the offensive, and the Sioux were forced to give up their hunting grounds and the gold fields in return for payments. Relocated to reservations situated on the least valuable lands in the region, the Indians soon found themselves struggling to subsist under harsh conditions. Many of them died of starvation or disease.

In the Rockies and westward the same story of hopeless resistance was repeated. In Idaho the peaceful Nez Percés finally refused to surrender lands along the Salmon River. Chief Joseph tried to avoid war, but when some unruly braves started a fight, he directed a masterful campaign against overwhelming odds, one of the most spectacular feats in the history of Indian warfare. After a 1,500-mile retreat through mountains and plains, he was finally caught thirty miles short of the Canadian border, and exiled to Oklahoma. A generation of Indian wars virtually ended in 1886 with the capture of Geronimo, a chief of the Chiricahua Apaches, who had fought encroachments in the Southwest for fifteen years.

There would be one tragic epilogue, however. In 1890 an effort by white authorities to arrest Chief Sitting Bull of the Sioux led to his death. Shortly afterward, on December 29, 1908, a bloodbath occurred at Wounded Knee, South Dakota. Nervous soldiers fired into a group of Indians who had come to surrender. Nearly 200 Indians and 25 soldiers died in the "Battle of Wounded Knee." The Indian wars had ended with characteristic brutality.

Over the long run, the collapse of Indian resistance resulted as much from the killing off of the buffalo herds on which they subsisted as from warfare. White hunters felled buffaloes for sport, sometimes firing from train windows merely for the pleasure of seeing the large animals die. In the 1870s, a systematic slaughter of the buffalo served the demand of fashionable easterners for buffalo robes and overcoats. By the mid-1880s, the herds were near extinction.

Indian Policy

Many easterners who were far removed from frontier dangers decried the slaughter and mistreatment of Indians. The Dawes Severalty Act of 1887 proposed to introduce the Indians to individual land ownership and agriculture. The Dawes Act permitted the president to divide the lands of any tribe and grant 160 acres to each head of family and lesser amounts to others. To protect an Indian's property, the government held it in trust for twenty-five years, after which the owner won full title and became a citizen. In 1901 citizenship was extended to the Five Civilized Tribes of Oklahoma, and in 1924 to all Indians.

But the more it changed, the more Indian policy remained the same. Although well-intended, the Dawes Act broke up reservations and often led to the loss of Indian lands to whites. Between 1887 and 1934, Indians lost an estimated 86 million of their 130 million acres. Most of what remained was unsuited for agriculture.

Cattle and Cowboys

While the West was being taken from the Indians, cattle entered the grasslands where the buffalo had roamed. Much of the romance of the open-range cattle industry derived from its Mexican roots. The Texas longhorns and the cowboys' horses derived from stock brought over by the Spaniards, and many of the industry's trappings had been worked out in Mexico first: the cowboy's saddle, chaps (*chaparejos*) to protect the legs, spurs, and lariat.

For many years, wild cattle competed with the buffalo in the Spanish borderlands.

The Battle of Little Bighorn in a pictograph by an Oglala Sioux, Amos Bad Heart Bull, 1876

Issue Day. Native Americans confined to the Pine Ridge Reservation in South Dakota could no longer hunt for themselves and had to wait for government-issued food rations.

Natural selection and contact with "Anglo" scrub cattle produced the Texas longhorns: lean and rangy, they were noted more for speed and endurance than for providing a choice steak. They had little value, moreover, because the largest markets for beef were too far away. At the end of the Civil War, perhaps as many as 5 million longhorns roamed the grasslands of Texas, still neglected—but not for long. In the upper Mississippi Valley, where herds had been depleted by the war, cattle were in great demand, and the Texas cattle could be had just for the effort of rounding them up.

The cattle drives after the Civil War took on a scale far greater than before. New opportunities arose as railroads pushed farther west, where cattle could be driven through relatively vacant lands. Joseph G. McCoy, an Illinois livestock dealer, realized the possibilities and encouraged railroad executives to run a line from the prairies to Chicago, the meat-packing center. The Kansas-Pacific Railroad liked McCoy's vision, and with its help he made Abilene, Kansas, the western terminus of a new line. In 1867, the first shipment of Texas cattle went to Chicago. As the railroads moved west, so did the cowtowns. These included Ellsworth, Wichita, Caldwell, and Dodge City, all in Kansas; and farther north Ogallala, Nebraska; Cheyenne, Wyoming; and Miles City, Montana.

During the twenty years after the Civil War, some 40,000 cowboys roamed the Great Plains. They were young—the average age was twenty-four—and from diverse backgrounds. Thirty percent were either Mexican or African American, and hundreds were Indians. Many others were Civil War veterans from North and South who now rode side by side, and a number had come from Europe. The life of a cowboy, for the most part, was rarely as exciting as motion pictures and television shows have depicted. Being a ranchhand involved grueling, dirty, wage labor interspersed with drudgery and boredom.

The secret to higher profits for the cattle industry was to devise a way to slaughter the cattle in the Midwest and ship the dressed carcasses east and west. That required refrigeration to keep the meat from spoiling. In 1869 G. H. Hammond, a Chicago meat packer, shipped the first refrigerated beef in an air-cooled rail car from Chicago to Boston. Eight years later, Gustavus Swift developed a more efficient system of mechanical refrigeration, an innovation that earned him a fortune and provided a major stimulus to the growth of the cattle industry.

The flush times of the cowtowns soon passed. The long cattle drives played out because they were economically unsound. The dangers of the trail, the wear and tear on men and cattle, the charges levied on drives that crossed Indian territory, and the advance of farms across the trails combined to persuade cattlemen that they could best function near the railroads. As railroads spread out into Texas and the plains, the cattle business spread with them as far as Montana and on into Canada.

In the absence of laws governing the open range, cattlemen at first worked out their own arrangements when rights and uses conflicted. As cattle wandered onto others' property, cowboys would "ride the line" to keep them off the adjoining ranch. In the spring, they would "round up" the mixed herds and sort out ownership by identifying the distinctive mark "branded" into the cattle. All this changed in 1873, when Joseph Glidden, an Illinois farmer, invented the first effective barbed wire, which ranchers thereafter used to fence off their claims at relatively low cost.

Range Wars

The growth of the cattle industry placed a premium upon land. Conflicting claims over land and water rights ignited violent disputes between ranchers and farmers. Ranchers often tried to drive off neighboring farmers, and farmers in turn tried to sabotage the cattle barons, cutting their fences and spooking their herds. There also developed a perennial tension over grassland use between large and small cattle ranchers. The large ranchers fenced in huge tracts of public lands, leaving the smaller ranchers with too little pasture. To survive, the smaller ranchers cut the fences. In central Texas this practice sparked the Fence-Cutters' War of 1883–1884. Several ranchers were killed and dozens wounded before the state ended the conflict by passing legislation outlawing fence cutting.

Farmers and the Land

Among the legendary figures of the West, farmers projected an unromantic image in contrast to the cowboys, cavalry, and Indians. After 1860, on paper at least, the federal land laws offered favorable terms to the farmer. Under the Homestead Act of 1862, a farmer could either realize the old dream of free land simply by staking out a claim and living on it for five years, or by buying the land at $1.25 an acre after six months.

The unchangeable fact of aridity, rather than land laws, however, shaped institutions in the New West. Where farming was impossible, the ranchers simply established dominance by control of the water, regardless of the laws. Belated legislative efforts to develop irrigable lands finally achieved a major success when the Newlands Reclamation Act (aptly named after Senator Francis G. Newlands of Nevada) of 1901 set up the Bureau of Reclamation. The proceeds of public land sales in sixteen states created a fund for irrigation projects, and the Reclamation Bureau set about building major dams throughout the West.

The lands of the New West, as on previous frontiers, passed to their ultimate owners more often from private hands than directly from the government. Many of the 274 million acres claimed under the Homestead Act passed quickly to cattle ranchers or speculators, and thence to settlers. The land-grant railroads got some 200 million acres of the public domain in the twenty years from 1851 to 1871, and sold much of this land to build population centers and traffic along the lines. The New West of ranchers and farmers was in fact largely the product of the railroads.

The first arrivals on the sod house frontier faced a grim struggle against danger, adversity, and monotony. Though land was relatively cheap, horses, livestock, wagons, wells, fencing, seed, and fertilizer were not. Freight rates and interest rates on loans seemed criminally high. As in the South, declining crop prices produced chronic indebtedness that led strapped western farmers to embrace virtually any plan to inflate the money supply. The virgin land itself, although fertile, resisted planting; the heavy sod broke many a plow. Since wood was almost nonexistent on the prairies, pioneer families used buffalo chips (dried dung) for fuel.

As time passed and farmers were able to lay aside some money from their labor, farm families could leave their dugouts or sod houses and build frame houses with lumber carried by the railroads arriving from

Husband and wife in front of their sod house near West Union in Custer County, Nebraska, 1886.

Chicago. New machinery also helped open fresh opportunities for farmers. In 1868 James Oliver of Indiana made a successful chilled-iron plow. With further improvements his "sodbuster" was ready for mass production by 1878, easing the task of breaking the shallow but tough grass roots of the Plains. Improvements and new inventions lightened the burden of labor but added to the capital outlay of the farmer.

Pioneer Women

The West remained a largely male society throughout the nineteenth century. In Texas, for example, the ratio of men to women in 1890 was 110 to 1. Women settlers continued to face traditional legal barriers and social prejudice. A wife could not sell property without her husband's approval. In Texas women could not sue except for divorce, nor could they serve on juries, act as lawyers, or witness a will.

But the fight for survival in the trans-Mississippi West often made husbands and wives more equal partners than their eastern counterparts. Prairie life also allowed women more independence than could be had by those living domestic lives back East. Explained one Kansas woman: "The outstanding fact is that the environment was such as to bring out and develop the dominant qualities of individual character. Kansas women of that day learned at an early age to depend on themselves—to do whatever work there was to be done, and to face danger when it must be faced, as calmly as they were able."

A Violent Culture

Although often exaggerated in films and television shows, the western frontier during the second half of the nineteenth century was indeed a violent place. Guns, rifles, and knives were prevalent, and people readily used them to resolve disputes. The need to protect one's family or homestead in the face of threats helped nourish what came to be called the Code of the West. It stressed the need for a man to stand and fight when threatened or wronged, and this spawned a reckless preoccupation with individual honor.

"The Frontier Has Gone"

American life reached an important juncture in the last decade of the nineteenth century. After the 1890 population count, the superintendent of the census noted that he could no longer locate a continuous frontier line beyond which population thinned out to fewer than two persons per square mile. This misleading fact inspired the historian Frederick Jackson Turner to develop his influential frontier thesis, first outlined in his paper "The Significance of the Frontier in American History," delivered to the American Historical Association in 1893. "The existence of an area of free land," Turner wrote, "its continuous recession, and the advance of American settlement westward, explain American development." But, Turner ominously concluded, "the frontier has gone and with its going has closed the first period of American history."

Turner's "frontier thesis" guided several generations of scholars and students in their understanding of the distinctive characteristics of American history. His view of the frontier as the westward-moving source of America's democratic politics, open society, unfettered economy, and rugged individualism, far removed from the corruptions of urban life, gripped the popular imagination as well. But it left much out of the story. Turner's description of the frontier experience exaggerated the homogenizing effect of the physical environment and virtually ignored the roles of woman, blacks, Indians, Mormons, Hispanics, and Asians in shaping the diverse human geography of the western United States. Turner also implied that the West would be fundamentally different after 1890 because the frontier experience was essentially over. But settlement did not end in 1890; nor did the qualities associated with the frontier. In many respects the trans-Mississippi West has retained the qualities associated with the rush for land, gold, timber, and water rights during the post–Civil War decades.

CHAPTER

19

Big Business and Organized Labor

This chapter focuses on

- Factors that fueled the growth of the post–Civil War economy.
- The methods and achievements of major entrepreneurs.
- The rise of large labor unions.

THE *ESSENTIAL AMERICA* ON-LINE TUTOR

www.wwnorton.com/eamerica/ch19

- **Topic: Andrew Carnegie's "Gospel of Wealth"**
  www.wwnorton.com/eamerica/ch19/topic.htm

  In the early twentieth century, philanthropist Andrew Carnegie gave away hundreds of millions of dollars in an effort to help America's poor learn to read and improve themselves. Using a sound recording, photographs, and Carnegie's own writings, explore the causes and significance of his philanthropy. Were Carnegie's efforts purely altruistic, or did they epitomize an underlying belief in Social Darwinism?

- **Chapter review: On-line quiz and chapter summary**
  www.wwnorton.com/eamerica/ch19/review.htm

- **Chapter resources: Multimedia index**
  www.wwnorton.com/eamerica/ch19/media.htm

America became an industrial and agricultural giant in the late nineteenth century. Between 1869 and 1899, the nation's population nearly trebled, farm production more than doubled, and the value of manufactures grew sixfold. Within three generations after the Civil War, a predominantly rural republic became a highly structured, increasingly centralized, urban-industrial society buffeted by the demands of mass production, mass consumption, and time-clock efficiency. Bigness became the prevailing standard of corporate life, and social tensions worsened with the rising scale of business enterprise and the growing congestion of urban life.

The Rise of Big Business

The industrial revolution created huge corporations that came to dominate the economy—as well as political and social life—during the late nineteenth century. The older economy dependent upon small business and craftspeople could not satisfy the rapidly growing national market. Entrepreneurs who recognized this development focused their attention on developing systems of mass production and distribution. To do so, they took advantage of many technological innovations and generous government support. As the scale of these businesses grew, the owners sought to integrate all the processes of production and distribution into single companies, thus producing even larger firms. Others joined forces with their competitors through "pools" or "trusts" in an effort to dominate entire industries. This process of industrial combination and concentration provoked widespread dissent and the emergence of an organized labor movement.

The Second Industrial Revolution

Americans living during the second half of the nineteenth century experienced what economic historians have termed the second industrial revolution. The first industrial revolution began in Britain during the late eighteenth century. It was propelled by the convergence of three new technologies—the coal-powered steam engine; textile machines for spinning thread and weaving cloth; and blast furnaces to produce iron.

The second industrial revolution began in the mid–nineteenth century and was centered in the United States and Germany. It involved three major interrelated developments. The first of these was the creation of an interconnected *national* transportation and communication network that in turn facilitated the emergence of a national and even international market for American goods and services. Contributing to this economic revolution were the completion of the national telegraph and railroad system, the development of steamships, and the laying of the undersea telegraph cable spanning the Atlantic Ocean and connecting the United States with Europe.

During the 1880s, a second major breakthrough—the use of electric power—accelerated the pace of change. Electricity created dramatic advances in the capacity and efficiency of industrial machinery. It also spurred urban growth through the addition of electric trolleys and subways, and it greatly enhanced the production of steel and chemicals.

The third major aspect of the second industrial revolution was the systematic application of scientific research to industrial processes. Laboratories sprouted across the country, and scientists and engineers worked at finding new ways to improve industrial processes. Researchers, for example, discovered how to refine kerosene and gasoline from crude oil. They also developed improved techniques for refining steel from iron. Such innovations accelerated production, created new products—telephones, typewriters, adding machines, sewing machines, cameras, elevators, and farm machinery—and lowered consumer prices. These advances in turn expanded the scope of industrial organizations. Capital-intensive industries such as steel and oil, and processed food and tobacco, took advantage of new technologies to gain economies of scale that emphasized maximum production and national as well as international marketing and distribution.

Building the Transcontinental Railroads

Railroads were the first big business, the first magnet for the great financial markets, and the first industry to develop a large-scale management bureaucracy. The railroads opened the West, connected raw materials to factories and markets, and in so doing created a national market for the nation's goods and produce. At the same time, they were themselves gigantic markets for iron, steel, lumber, and other capital goods.

The renewal of railroad building after the Civil War filled out the railway network east of the Mississippi, but the most spectacular exploits were the transcontinental lines built across the plains and mountains. Before the Civil War, sectional differences over routes delayed the start of a transcontinental line. Secession finally permitted passage of the Pacific Railway Bill, which Lincoln signed into law in 1862. The act authorized a line along a north-central route, to be built jointly by the Union Pacific Railroad westward from Omaha and the Central Pacific Railroad eastward from Sacramento.

The Union Pacific pushed across the plains at a rapid pace. The work crews, mostly ex-soldiers and Irish immigrants, had to cope with bad roads, water shortages, brutal weather, and Indian attacks. The Central Pacific construction crews were mainly Chinese workers lured first by the California gold rush and then by railroad jobs. Thousands of Chinese men migrated to America, raising their numbers in the United States from 7,500 in 1850 to 105,000 in 1880. By 1867, the Central Pacific Railroad's 12,000 Chinese laborers represented 90 percent of its workforce.

Fifty-seven miles east of Sacramento the Central Pacific construction crews encountered the towering Sierras, but they were eventually able to cut through to the more level country in Nevada. The Union Pacific had built 1,086 miles to the Central Pacific's 689 when the race ended on the salt plains of Utah near Ogden, at Promontory. There, on May 10, 1869, Leland Stanford, governor of California and one of the organizers of the Central Pacific Railroad, drove a gold spike that symbolized the completion of the first transcontinental railroad. Several more were to follow.

Financing the Railroads

The railroads were built by private companies that raised money for construction primarily by selling bonds to American and foreign investors. Many states also subsidized the building of railroads within their own borders. In 1850, Stephen Douglas managed to secure from Congress a federal

The celebration after the last spike was driven at Promontory, Utah, on May 10, 1869, completing the first transcontinental railroad.

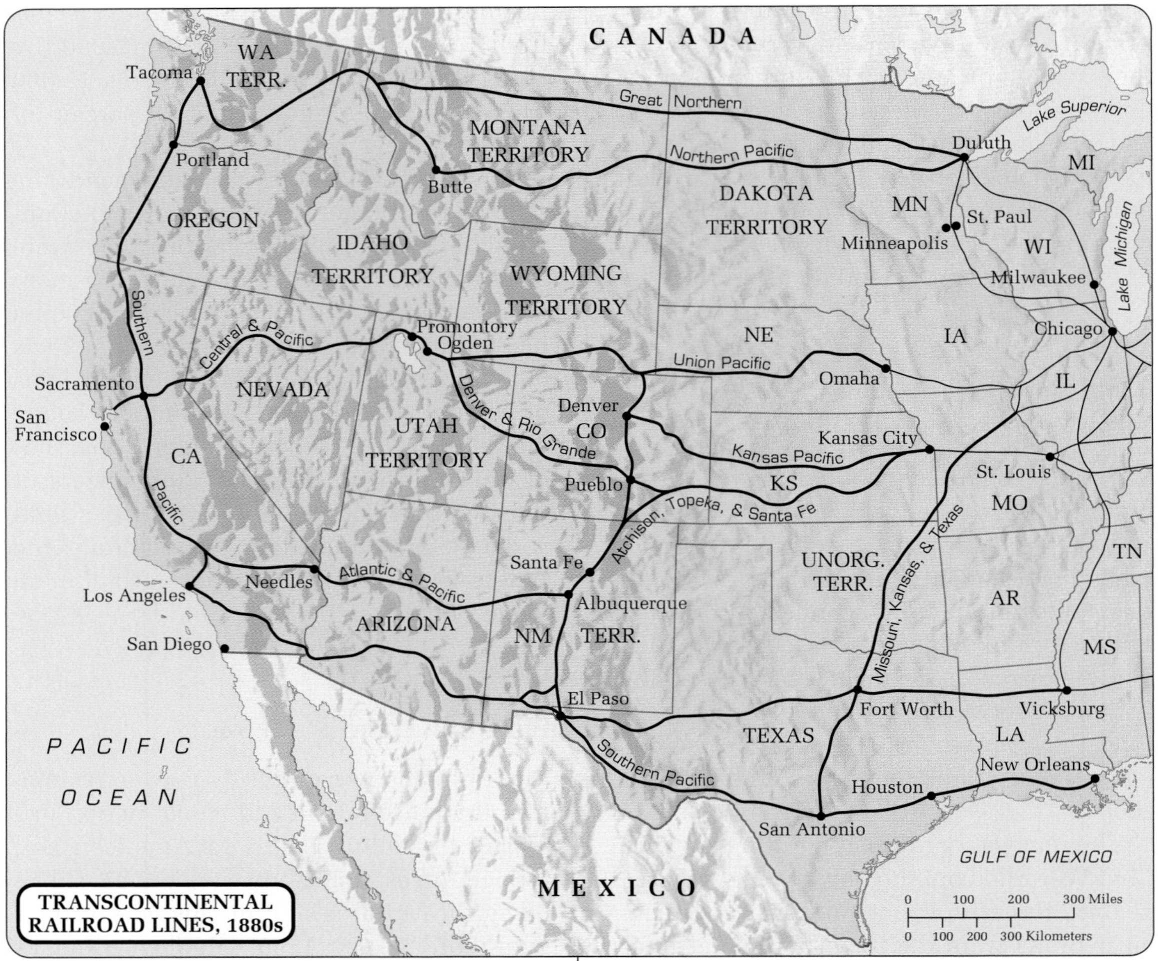

TRANSCONTINENTAL RAILROAD LINES, 1880s

grant of public lands to subsidize two north-south railroads connecting Chicago and Mobile, Alabama. Over the next twenty years, transcontinentals received generous government aid in the form of federal land grants, as well as loans and tax breaks from federal, state, and local governments.

In the long run, the federal government recovered much if not all of its investment in transcontinentals. As farms, ranches, and towns sprouted around the rail lines, the value of the alternate sections of government land on both sides of the tracks skyrocketed. The railroads also benefited the public by hauling government freight, military personnel and equipment, and the mails at half fare or at no charge. Moreover, by helping to accelerate the creation of a national market, the railroads spurred economic growth and thereby increased government revenues.

The vast sums of money used to finance the building of the transcontinental lines, however, also generated shameless profiteering through construction companies controlled by insiders who overcharged the railroad companies. Few railroad fortunes were built in those freewheeling times by purely ethical methods, but most railroad entrepreneurs at least took some interest in the welfare of their companies, if not always in that of the public.

Cornelius Vanderbilt, called "Commodore" by virtue of his early exploits in steamboating, stands out among the railroad barons. Already rich before the Civil War, he decided to give up the hazards of wartime shipping and move his money into land transport. His great achievement was consolidating separate trunk lines into a single powerful rail network led by the New York Central. After the Commodore's death in 1877, his son William Henry extended the Vanderbilt lines to include more than 13,000 miles in the Northeast. Similar buyouts occurred nationwide. About two-thirds of the nation's railroad mileage fell under the control of only seven major groups by 1900.

Manufacturing and Inventions

The story of manufacturing after the Civil War shows much the same pattern of expansion and merger in both old and new industries. The Patent Office, which had recorded only 276 inventions during its first decade of existence, the 1790s, registered 234,956 in the decade of the 1890s. The list of innovations after the Civil War can be extended indefinitely: farm implements, steam turbines, gas distribution and electrical devices, the typewriter (1867), vacuum cleaner (1869), and countless others. Before 1900, the internal combustion engine and the motion picture were laying foundations for new industries of the twentieth century.

These technological advances altered the lives of ordinary people far more than politics or intellectual developments. In no field was this truer than in the applications of electricity to communications and power. Few if any inventions of the times could rival the importance of the telephone, which Alexander Graham Bell patented in 1876.

In the rise of electrical industries, the name of Thomas Alva Edison stands above those of other inventors. Edison invented the phonograph in 1877, and the first successful incandescent light bulb in 1879. At his laboratories in Menlo Park, New Jersey, he created or perfected hundreds of new devices and processes, including the storage battery, dictaphone, mimeograph, dynamo, electric transmission, and the motion picture. In the process, Edison and his assistants demonstrated the significance of "research and development" activities to American business.

In 1882, with the backing of financier J. P. Morgan, the Edison Electric Illuminating Company began to supply current to eighty-five customers in New York City, beginning the great electric utility industry. A number of companies making light bulbs merged into the Edison General Electric Company in 1888.

The use of direct current limited Edison's lighting system to a radius of about two miles. To get more distance required an alternating current, which could be transmitted at high voltage and then stepped down by transformers. George Westinghouse, inventor of the air brake for trains, developed the first alternating-current system in 1886 and manufactured the equipment through the Westinghouse Electric Company. Edison considered the new method too dangerous, but the Westinghouse system won the "Battle of the Currents," and the Edison companies had to switch over. After the invention of the alternating-current motor in 1888, Westinghouse acquired and improved the motor, which started a revolution. Capable now of using electricity as a power source, factories no longer had to cluster around waterfalls and coal supplies.

Entrepreneurs

Edison and Westinghouse were rare examples of inventors with the luck and foresight to get rich from the industries they created. Most of the architects of industrial growth—the great captains of industry—were not inventors but pure entrepreneurs, men skilled mainly in organizing and promoting industry. Three post–Civil War business titans stand out for their achievements and for their greed, guile, and enterprise: John D. Rockefeller, Andrew Carnegie, and J. Pier-

John D. Rockefeller, whose Standard Oil Company dominated the oil business.

pont Morgan. Each of them in different ways replaced the small-scale economy of the early republic with vast new industries that forever altered the size and scope of the nation's business. Two other entrepreneurs, Richard Sears and Alvah Roebuck, perfected a new way of retailing and distributing the goods produced by the large-scale manufacturers in the new economy.

Rockefeller and the Oil Trust

Born in New York State, the son of a con man and a devout Baptist mother, Rockefeller moved as a youth to Cleveland. Soon thereafter, his father abandoned his family. Raised by his mother, John Rockefeller developed a passion for systematic organization and self-discipline. He was obsessed with precision and tidiness. And early on, he decided to bring order and rationality to the chaotic oil industry.

Cleveland's railroad and ship connections made it a strategic location for servicing the oil fields of western Pennsylvania. In economic importance the Pennsylvania oil rush of the 1860s far outweighed the California gold rush of just ten years earlier. Well before the end of the Civil War, drilling derricks checkered the area around Titusville, Pennsylvania, where the first oil well was struck, and refineries sprang up in Pittsburgh and Cleveland.

While other young men were going off to fight the Civil War, young Rockefeller moved aggressively into the oil business. In 1862 he and a partner started a refinery business. The firm expanded, and in 1870 Rockefeller incorporated his various interests as the Standard Oil Company of Ohio.

In 1872 Rockefeller created the South Improvement Company, which he made the marketing agent for a large percentage of his oil shipments. By controlling this traffic, he gained clout with the railroads, which gave him large rebates (or secret refunds) on the standard freight rates in order to keep his high-volume business. In some cases, they even gave him information on competitors' shipments. Rockefeller then approached his Cleveland competitors and pressured them to sell out. Most of them complied. Those who resisted were forced out. By 1879, Standard Oil had come to control 90 to 95 percent of the oil refined throughout the country.

Much of Rockefeller's success reflected his determination to "pay nobody a profit." Instead of depending on the products or services of other firms, known as "middlemen," Standard Oil Company undertook to make its own barrels, cans, and whatever else it needed. Economists label this "vertical integration." The company kept large amounts of cash reserves to make it independent of banks in case of a crisis. Rockefeller also set out to control his transportation needs. With Standard owning most of the pipelines leading to railroads, as well as the tank cars and the oil-storage facilities, it was able to dissuade the railroads from servicing eastern competitors. Those rivals who insisted on holding out then faced a giant marketing organization capable of driving them to the wall with price wars.

Eventually, in order to consolidate scattered business interests under more efficient control, Rockefeller and his advisers resorted to the legal device of the "trust." In 1882 all of the thirty-seven stockholders in various Standard Oil enterprises conveyed their stock to nine trustees, getting "trust certificates" in return. The nine trustees were thus empowered to give central direction to all the Standard companies.

The trust device, widely copied in the 1880s, proved legally vulnerable to prosecution under state laws against monopoly or restraint of trade, and in 1892 the Supreme Court of Ohio ordered the Standard Oil Trust dissolved. Gradually, Rockefeller took to the idea of the holding company, a company that controlled other companies by holding all or at least a majority of their stock. He was convinced that big business was a natural result of capitalism at work.

"It is too late," he declared in 1899, "to argue about the advantages of industrial combinations. They are a necessity."

Rockefeller not only made a fortune, he also gave much of it away, mainly to education and medicine. Rockefeller became the world's leading philanthropist. He donated more than $500 million during his ninety-eight-year life. "I have always regarded it as a religious duty," Rockefeller said late in life, "to get all I could honorably and to give all I could."

Carnegie and the Steel Industry

Andrew Carnegie, like Rockefeller, experienced an untypical rise from poverty to riches. Born in Scotland, he migrated with his family to Allegheny, Pennsylvania, in 1848. At fourteen he was getting $2.50 per week as a telegraph messenger. Quick-witted, he worked hard, and in 1853 he became personal secretary and telegrapher to the district superintendent of the Pennsylvania Railroad. When the superintendent became the president of the line, Carnegie took his place, and the pace of his career accelerated. During the Civil War, Carnegie went to Washington, where he developed a military telegraph system and personally helped evacuate the wounded from Bull Run.

Carnegie kept on moving—from telegraphy to railroading to bridge building, then to iron and steel-making, and investments. In his *Autobiography*, he recalled his growing determination to allow "nothing to interfere for a moment with my business career." He kept his pledge. In 1872 he met Sir Henry Bessemer, the British inventor of a new process of steel-making. The process dazzled Carnegie, and he returned to America a converted prophet of steel, exclaiming to a friend: "The day of iron has passed!"

Steel was the miracle material of the post–Civil War era not because it was new but because it suddenly was cheap. Until the mid–nineteenth century, the only way to make steel was from wrought iron—itself expensive—and in small quantities. Then in 1856 Bessemer invented what became known as the Bessemer converter, a process by which steel could be produced directly and quickly from pig iron by using forced air to heat the metal. As the volume of steel rose, its price dropped and its uses increased. In 1860 the United States produced only 13,000 tons of steel. By 1880 production had reached 1,400,000 tons.

Carnegie was never a technical expert on steel. Instead he was a promoter, salesman, and organizer with a gift for finding and using men of expert ability. Fiercely competitive and obsessed with efficiency and innovation, he always insisted on up-to-date machinery and equipment, and he used times of recession to expand more cheaply. During business depressions, when construction costs were low and competitors were forced to the wall, Carnegie used his surplus capital to buy them out and expand. He also preached to his employees a philosophy of constant innovation in order to reduce operating costs.

In much of this, Carnegie was a typical businessman of the time, if abler and luckier than most. But he stands out from the lot as

Andrew Carnegie, apostle of "The Gospel of Wealth."

Factory workers were often subjected to hazardous working conditions.

J. Pierpont Morgan. This is the famous portrait by the photographer Edward Steichen, done in 1903.

a thinker who publicized a philosophy for big business. In "The Gospel of Wealth," published in 1889, he argued that the emergence of super wealthy businessmen testified to the superiority of the free enterprise system. The law of competition was "best for the race, because it insures the survival of the fittest in every department." But Carnegie also believed that the wealthy had a moral obligation to exercise philanthropy. "The man who dies rich dies disgraced." Carnegie insisted that the wealthy should provide means for people to help themselves by supporting universities, libraries, hospitals, parks, halls for meetings and concerts, swimming baths, and church buildings—in that order. To his credit, Carnegie devoted his wealth to many such benefactions and to the cause of world peace. He spent some $60 million on public libraries and another $60 million on higher education.

J. P. Morgan, the Financier

J. Pierpont Morgan was born to wealth in Hartford, Connecticut, and increased it enormously. As an investment banker, he bought corporate stocks and bonds wholesale and then sold them at a profit. Since the investment business depended on the general good health of client companies, investment bankers became involved in the operation of their clients' firms, demanding places on boards of directors and helping to shape their fiscal dealings. By these means, bankers could influence company policies, often emphasizing fiscal matters to the detriment of technical innovation.

Morgan realized that railroads were the key to the times, and he acquired and reorganized one rail line after another. After the Panic of 1893, when hard times gutted the net worth of many railroads, Morgan took over many of them, and by the 1890s, he alone controlled one-sixth of America's railway system.

Morgan's crowning triumph was his purchase of the steel industry. In 1901 he bought out Carnegie's huge steel and iron holdings. After closing the deal, Morgan told the steel king, "Mr. Carnegie, I want to congratulate you on being the richest man in the world." Like Rockefeller, Morgan scorned competition as wasteful, and, in rapid succession, he acquired competing steel mills. The new United States Steel Corporation, a holding company for these varied interests, was a marvel of the new century, the first billion-dollar corporation, the climactic event in that age of corporate consolidation.

Sears, Roebuck, and Company, catalog cover, 1897. Sears' extensive mail-order service and discounted prices allowed its many products to reach people in both cities and backcountry.

Sears and Roebuck

American inventors helped manufacturers after the Civil War produce a vast number of new products, but problems of distribution remained acute. The most important challenge was how to extend the reach of modern commerce to the millions of people who lived on isolated farms and in small towns. In the aftermath of the Civil War, a traveling salesman from Chicago named Aaron Montgomery Ward decided that he could reach more people by mail than on foot and in the process could eliminate the "middlemen" whose services increased the retail price of goods. Beginning in the early 1870s, the Montgomery Ward Company began selling goods at a 40 percent discount through mail-order catalogs.

By the end of the century, a new retailer came to dominate the mail-order industry: Sears, Roebuck and Company, founded by two young midwestern entrepreneurs, Richard Sears and Alvah Roebuck, who began offering a cornucopia of goods by mail in the early 1890s. With the advent of free rural mail delivery in 1898 and the widespread distribution of Sears catalogs, families on farms and in small towns and villages could purchase by mail the products that heretofore were either prohibitively expensive or available only to city dwellers. By the turn of the century, 6 million catalogs were distributed each year, and the catalog had become the single most widely read book in the nation except for the Bible.

Labor Conditions and Organization

Social Trends

Accompanying the spread of these industrial giants was a rising standard of living for most people. If the rich were still getting richer, a lot of other people were at least becoming better off. The continuing demand for workers meanwhile was filled by new groups entering the workforce at the bottom: immigrants above all, but also growing numbers of women and children. Because of a long-term decline in prices and the cost of living, real wages and earnings in manufacturing went up about 50 percent between 1860 and 1890, and another 37 percent from 1890 to 1914.

By present-day standards, however, working conditions then were dreary indeed. At the turn of the century, the average hourly wage in manufacturing was 21.6¢ and average annual earnings were $490. The average workweek was fifty-nine hours, which amounted to nearly six ten-hour workdays, but that was only an average. Most steelworkers put in a twelve-hour workday, and as late as the 1920s, a great many worked a seven-day, or eighty-four-hour, workweek.

Moreover, although wages were steadily rising, working and living conditions remained precarious. In 1913, for instance, there were some 25,000 factory fatalities and some 700,000 injuries that required at least four weeks' disability—more than half the number of American casualties in World War I.

Disorganized Protest

After the Civil War, labor activists sought to organize for shorter workdays and better working conditions. Yet among workers recently removed from an agrarian world, the idea of permanent unions was slow to take hold. Immigrant workers represented diverse and frequently antagonistic cultures and spoke different languages. Many, if not most, saw their jobs as transient, the first rung on the ladder to success. They hoped to move on to a homestead, or to return with their earnings to the old farms of their European homelands. With or without unions, though, workers often staged impromptu strikes protesting long working hours and wage cuts. Such action often led to violence, and three incidents of the 1870s colored much of the public's view of labor unions thereafter.

The decade's early years saw a reign of terror in the eastern Pennsylvania coal fields, attributed to an Irish group called the Molly Maguires. Taking their name from an Irish patriot who had directed violent resistance against the British, the group was incited by the dangerous working conditions in the mines and the owners' brutal efforts to suppress union activity. The Molly Maguires aimed to right perceived wrongs against Irish workers through intimidation, beatings, and killings. Their terrorism reached its peak in 1874–1875. At trials in 1876, twenty-four of the Molly Maguires were convicted, and the next year twenty of them were hanged. The trials also resulted in a wage reduction in the mines.

The Railroad Strike of 1877

Far more significant, because more widespread, was the Great Railroad Strike of 1877, the first major interstate strike. After the Panic of 1873 and the ensuing depression, the major rail lines in the East had cut wages. In 1877 they made another 10 percent cut, which provoked most of the railroad workers at Martinsburg, West Virginia, to walk off the job and block the tracks. Without organized direction, however, their picketing groups degenerated into a mob that burned and plundered railroad property.

Walkouts and sympathy demonstrations spread spontaneously from Maryland to San Francisco. The strike engulfed hundreds of cities and towns, leaving in its wake over a hundred people killed and millions of dollars in property destroyed. Federal troops finally quelled the violence. For many people, the strike raised the specter of a worker-based social revolution. As a Pittsburgh newspaper warned, "This may be the beginning of a great civil war in this country between labor and capital." Equally disturbing to those in positions of corporate and political power was the presence of many women among the protesters. From the point of view of organized labor, however, the Great Railroad Strike demonstrated potential strength and the need for tighter organization. As the labor leader Samuel Gompers later recalled, "The railroad strike of 1877, was the tocsin that sounded a ringing message of hope for us all."

The "Sand Lot" Incident

In California the railroad strike indirectly gave rise to a political movement. At San Francisco's "Sand Lot," a meeting to express sympathy for the strikers ended with attacks on some passing Chinese. Within a few days, sporadic anti-Chinese riots led to a mob attack on Chinatown. Depression had hit the West Coast especially hard, and the Chinese were handy scapegoats for frustrations.

Soon an Irish immigrant, Dennis Kearney, organized the "Workingmen's Party of California." Its platform called for the end of further Chinese immigration. A gifted agitator, himself only recently naturalized, Kearney warned supporters of the dangers of the "foreign peril" and assaulted the rich for exploiting the poor. In 1878 his new party won a hefty number of seats in a state constitutional convention, but it accomplished little. Kearney lacked the gift for building a durable movement, but as his party went to pieces, his anti-Chinese theme became a national issue. In 1882 Congress voted to prohibit Chinese immigration for ten years.

Toward Permanent Unions

Meanwhile, efforts to build a union movement had begun to bear fruit. Earlier attempts, in the 1830s and 1840s, had been dominated by reformers with schemes that ranged from free homesteads to utopian socialism. But the 1850s witnessed the beginning of "job-conscious" unions in certain skilled trades. By 1860 there were about twenty such unions, and during the Civil War, because of the demand for labor, these so-called craft unions grew in strength and numbers.

There was no overall federation of these groups until 1866, when the first National Labor Union (NLU) convened in Baltimore. The NLU was composed of delegates from labor and reform groups more interested in political and social change than in bargaining with employers. The groups espoused ideas such as the eight-hour workday, workers' cooperatives, paper money, and equal rights for women and blacks. But the organization lost momentum after the death of its president in 1869, and by 1872 it had entirely collapsed.

The National Labor Union, however, was not a total failure. It was influential in persuading Congress to enact an eight-hour workday for federal employees and to repeal the 1864 Contract Labor Law, which allowed employers to bind immigrant laborers (contract laborers) by paying for their passage from Europe. That such immigrants were willing to work for low wages made them unpopular with American workers.

The Knights of Labor

Before the National Labor Union collapsed, another labor group of national standing had emerged, the Noble and Holy Order of the Knights of Labor. The name evoked the aura of medieval guilds. The founder of the Knights of Labor, Uriah S. Stephens, a Philadelphia tailor, was involved with several secret orders, including the Masons. Secrecy, he felt, along with a semireligious ritual, would protect members against retaliation by bosses and at the same time create a sense of solidarity.

The Knights of Labor, started in 1869,

grew slowly, but during the years of depression after 1873, as other unions collapsed, it spread more rapidly. In 1878 its first General Assembly established a national organization. Its preamble and platform endorsed producers' and consumers' cooperatives, hoping to replace the wage-labor system with worker-owned factories. The Knights also called for free homesteads, bureaus of labor statistics, elimination of convict-labor competition, the eight-hour workday, and the acceptance of greenbacks as currency in order to enlarge the money supply and ease credit. One plank in the platform, far ahead of the times, called for equal pay for equal work by both men and women.

Throughout their existence the Knights preferred boycotts to strikes as a way to put pressure on employers. They also had a liberal membership policy, welcoming all who had ever worked for wages, except lawyers, doctors, bankers, and those who sold liquor. Theoretically it was one big union of all workers, skilled and unskilled, regardless of race, color, creed, or sex.

Stephens was elected as the first Grand Master Workman to head the organization. In 1879 he gave way to Terence V. Powderly, the thirty-year-old mayor of Scranton, Pennsylvania. In many ways Powderly was unsuited to the new job. He was temperamentally opposed to strikes, and when they did occur, he did not always back up the locals. Yet the Knights ironically owed their greatest growth to strikes that occurred under his leadership.

In the mid-1880s membership in the Knights grew rapidly. In 1884 a successful strike against wage cuts in the Union Pacific shops at Denver led many railroad workers to form new local chapters. Then, in 1885, the Knights scored a startling victory over Jay Gould, one of the most notorious railroad titans. Late the previous year and early in 1885 Gould had cut wages on several of his railroads. A spontaneous strike on these lines in 1885 spread to Gould's Missouri-Pacific, and as organizers from the Knights of Labor moved in, Gould restored the wage cuts. Such successes allowed the Knights to grow rapidly from about 100,000 members to more than 700,000 in 1886.

But the Knights peaked that year and then went into rapid decline. Jay Gould in 1886 provoked another strike by firing a foreman in the Texas-Pacific shops. When the Knights struck, Gould refused arbitration and hired Pinkerton agents to harass strikers and keep the trains running. The Knights had to call off the strike. The organization was further damaged by an incident in Chicago's Haymarket Square that very night, with which the Knights had little to do but which provoked widespread revulsion against labor groups in general.

The Haymarket Affair

On May 3, 1886, Chicago's International Harvester agricultural equipment plant witnessed an unfortunate clash between strikers and policemen in which one striker was killed. Leaders of a minuscule anarchist movement in Chicago scheduled an open meeting the following night at Haymarket Square to protest the killing. The anarchists believed that government, any government, was in itself an abusive device used by the rich and powerful to oppress and exploit the working poor. Many of them believed that the transition to a stateless society could be hurried along by promoting revolutionary action among the masses. Under a light drizzle people listened to long speeches promoting socialism and anarchism. The crowd was beginning to break up when a group of policemen arrived and called upon the activists to disperse. At that point someone threw a bomb at the police, killing one and wounding others. The police fired into the crowd, killing four demonstrators. Six policemen were also killed.

In a trial marked by prejudice and hysteria, seven anarchist leaders were sentenced to death, despite the lack of any evidence linking them to the bomb-thrower, whose identity was never established. Of the seven, two were reprieved and later pardoned, one committed suicide in prison, and four were hanged.

Despite his best efforts, Powderly could never dissociate in the public mind the Knights from the anarchists. He clung to leadership until 1893, but after that the union evaporated. A number of problems accounted for the Knights' decline: a leadership devoted more to reform than to pragmatic organization, and a preoccupation with politics rather than hard-nosed negotiations with management.

The Knights nevertheless attained some lasting achievements, among them the creation of the Federal Bureau of Labor Statistics and the Foran Act of 1885, which penalized employers who imported contract laborers from abroad. The Knights also spread the idea of unionism and initiated a new type of union organization: the industrial union, an industry-wide union of both the skilled and unskilled.

Gompers and the AFL

The craft unions opposed the industrial unionism of the Knights. They organized workers who shared special skills, such as typographers or cigarmakers. Leaders feared that joining with the unskilled would mean a loss of their separate craft identities and a loss of the bargaining power held by skilled workers. In the summer of 1886, delegates from craft unions met at Columbus, Ohio, and organized the American Federation of Labor (AFL). It differed from the Knights in that it was a federation of national craft organizations, each of which retained a large degree of autonomy and exercised greater leverage against management.

Samuel Gompers of the Cigarmakers Union served as president of the AFL from its start until his death in 1924. The Cigarmakers tended to be the intellectuals of the labor movement; to relieve the tedium of their task, they hired young men to read aloud as they worked, and debated such weighty topics as socialism and Darwinism. But Gompers and other leaders of the union focused on concrete economic gains, avoiding involvement with utopian ideas or politics.

Gompers hired organizers to spread unionism and worked as a diplomat to prevent overlapping unions and to settle jurisdictional disputes. The federation represented workers in matters of national legislation and acted as a sounding board for their cause. On occasion it exercised its power to request dues from members for the support of strikes. Gompers advocated using the strike to achieve labor's objectives. His preference, though, was to achieve these objectives through agreements with management that included provisos for union recognition in the form of closed shops (which could hire only union members) or union-preference shops (which could hire others only if no union members were available).

The AFL at first grew slowly, but by 1890 it had already surpassed the Knights of Labor in membership. By the turn of the century, it claimed 500,000 members in affiliated unions; in 1914, on the eve of World War I, it had 2 million; and in 1920, it reached a peak of 4 million. But even then the AFL embraced less than 15 percent of the nonagricultural workers. Organized labor's strongholds were in transportation and the building trades. Most of the larger manufacturing industries, including textiles, tobacco, and packinghouses, remained unorganized.

The Homestead Strike

Two violent labor incidents in the 1890s scarred the emerging industrial union movement and set it back for forty years to come—the Homestead Steel Strike of 1892 and the Pullman Strike of 1894. The Amalgamated Association of Iron and Steel Workers, founded in 1876, had by 1891 a membership of more than 24,000 and was probably the largest craft union at that time.

But it excluded the unskilled and had failed to organize the larger steel plants. The Homestead Works at Pittsburgh was an important exception. There the union had enjoyed friendly relations with the Carnegie company until H. C. Frick became its president in 1889.

In 1892 the union contract came up for renewal. As negotiations dragged on, the company announced it would deal with workers as individuals unless an agreement was reached by June 29. A strike, or more properly a lockout of unionists, began on that date. Even before the negotiations ended, Frick had begun barricading the plant and hired as plant guards 300 Pinkerton detectives whose specialty was union-busting. On the morning of July 6, 1892, when the Pinkertons floated up the Monongahela River on barges, union workers were waiting behind iron breastworks on shore. A battle erupted in which nine workers and seven Pinkertons died. In the end, the Pinkertons surrendered and marched away, to the taunts of crowds. Six days later, 8,000 state militiamen appeared at the plant to protect the strikebreakers hired to restore production. The strike dragged on until November, but by then the union was dead at Homestead. Its cause was not helped when an anarchist shot and wounded Frick. Much of the local sympathy for the strikers evaporated.

The Pullman Strike

Two years later, in 1894, the Pullman Strike of 1894 became the most notable walkout in American history. It paralyzed the economies of twenty-seven states and territories making up the western half of the nation. It grew out of a dispute at the "model" town of Pullman, Illinois, just outside Chicago, which housed workers of the Pullman Palace Car Company in neat brick homes nestled on grassy lots along shaded streets. The town's idyllic appearance, however, was deceptive. Employees were required to live there, pay rents and utility costs higher than in nearby towns, and buy their goods from company stores. With the onset of the depression in 1893, George Pullman laid off 3,000 of 5,800 employees and cut wages 25 to 40 percent, but not his rents and other charges. When Pullman fired three members of a grievance committee, a strike began on May 11, 1894.

During this tense period, the Pullman workers had been joining the American Railway Union, founded the previous year by Eugene V. Debs. The tall, gangly Debs was a charismatic man who led by example and by the electric force of his convictions. A child of working-class immigrants, he quit school in 1869 at age fourteen to go to work for an Indiana railroad. There he soon "learned of the hardships of the rail in snow, sleet, and hail, of the . . . uncertainty of employment, scant wages and altogether trying lot of the workingman, so that from my very boyhood I was made to feel the wrongs of labor." He eagerly accepted an invitation to start a local of the railroad brotherhood, a craft union of skilled workers.

Still, it was not until the Haymarket bombing that Debs decided that there was an inevitable conflict between labor and management. By the early 1890s, he had become a tireless spokesman for labor radicalism, and he launched a crusade to organize *all* railway workers—skilled and unskilled—into the American Railway Union. Debs's earnest appeal generated a tremendous response, and soon he was in charge of a powerful new labor organization. He quickly turned his attention to the Pullman controversy.

After Pullman refused Debs's plea for arbitration, the union workers in June 1894 stopped handling Pullman cars. By the end of July, the strike had tied up most of the railroads in the Midwest. The rail owners then brought strikebreakers from Canada and elsewhere, instructing them to connect mail cars to Pullman cars so that interference with Pullman cars also meant inter-

Eugene V. Debs, founder of the American Railway Union and later candidate for president as head of the Socialist Party of America.

ference with the federal mail. Attorney-General Richard Olney, a former railroad attorney, swore in 3,400 special deputies to keep the trains running. When clashes occurred, some strikers ignored Debs's plea for an orderly boycott and repeated the violent scenes of the 1877 strike.

Finally, on July 3, 1894, President Grover Cleveland answered an appeal from the railroads to send federal troops into the Chicago area, where the strike was centered. As strikers clashed with troops and burned hundreds of cars, the federal district court granted an injunction forbidding any interference with the mails or any combination to restrain interstate commerce. On July 13 the union called off the strike, and on the same day the district court cited Debs for violating the injunction and sentenced him to six months in jail. The Supreme Court upheld the decree in the case of *In re Debs* (1895) on broad grounds of national sovereignty: "The strong arm of the national government may be put forth to brush away all obstructions to the freedom of interstate commerce or the transportation of the mails." Debs served his jail term, during which time he read deeply in socialist literature, and he emerged to devote the rest of his life to that cause.

Socialism and the Unions

The major American unions, for the most part, never allied themselves with the socialists, as many European labor movements did. The socialist movement gained little notice in the United States before the rise of Daniel DeLeon in the 1890s as the dominant figure in the Socialist Labor party. A native of the Dutch West Indies, DeLeon proposed to organize industrial unions with a socialist purpose, and to build a political party that would abolish government once it gained power.

Yet Debs was more successful than DeLeon at building a socialist movement in America. To many, DeLeon seemed doctrinaire and inflexible. Debs, however, built his new party by following a method now traditional in the United States: he formed a coalition that embraced viewpoints ranging from moderate reform to doctrinaire Marxism. In 1897 Debs organized the Social Democratic party from the remnants of the American Railway Union. In 1901 his followers joined a number of secessionists from DeLeon's party to set up the Socialist Party of America. In 1904 Debs polled over 400,000 votes as the party's candidate for president and more than doubled that to almost 900,000 votes in 1912, or 6 percent of the popular vote.

By 1912 the Socialist party seemed well on the way to becoming a permanent fixture in American politics. Thirty-three cities had socialist mayors. The Socialist party sponsored five English-language daily newspapers, eight foreign-language dailies, and a number of weeklies and monthlies. Its support was not confined to urban workers and intellectuals. In the Southwest the party built a sizable grassroots following among farmers. But the party reached its peak in 1912. During World War I, it was wracked by disagreements over America's participation in the war, and it fragmented. The Great Depression of the 1930s served only to interrupt, not halt, its decline.

The Wobblies

During the years of Socialist party growth, there emerged a parallel effort to revive industrial unionism, led by the Industrial Workers of the World (IWW), dubbed the Wobblies. The chief base for this group was the Western Federation of Miners, organized at Butte, Montana, in 1893. Over the next decade, the Western Federation was the storm center of violent confrontation with unyielding bosses who mobilized private armies against it in Colorado, Idaho, and elsewhere. A radical manifesto issued from the founding convention of the IWW in 1905 declared that there was an "irrepressible conflict between the capitalist class and the working class."

Like the Knights of Labor, the IWW was designed to be "One Big Union," including all workers, skilled or unskilled. Its roots were in the mining and lumber camps of the West, where unstable conditions of employment created a large number of nomadic workers, to whom neither the AFL's pragmatic approach nor the socialists' political appeal held much attraction. The revolutionary goal of the Wobblies was the destruction of the government and its replacement by one big union. How it would govern remained vague.

William D. "Big Bill" Haywood emerged as the leader of the IWW and managed to hold the fractious group together. Well over six feet tall, Haywood commanded the attention and respect of his listeners. He despised the AFL and its conservative labor philosophy. Haywood promoted the concept of one all-inclusive union whose credo would be the promotion of a socialism "with its working clothes on."

Haywood and the Wobblies reached out to the fringe elements that had the least power and influence, chiefly the migratory workers of the West and the ethnic groups of the East. They engaged in spectacular battles with corporate America but scored few victories. The largest was a textile strike at Lawrence, Massachusetts, in 1912; the strikers won wage raises, overtime pay, and other benefits. But the next year a strike of silk workers at Paterson, New Jersey, ended in disaster, and the IWW entered a rapid decline.

The fading of the movement was accelerated by the hysterical opposition it engendered. Branded as a collection of anarchists, bums, and criminals, the IWW was effectively destroyed during World War I, when most of its leaders were jailed for their militant opposition to the war. Nonetheless, the Wobblies left behind a rich folklore of nomadic working folk and a gallery of heroic agitators such as Elizabeth Gurley Flynn, a dark-haired Irish girl who at age eighteen, ardent and pregnant, chained herself to a lamppost to impede her arrest during a strike.

Textile workers strike, Lawrence, Massachusetts, 1912. The IWW of this Lawrence mill engaged in a violent strike for increased wages, overtime pay, and other benefits.

A Nation Transformed

By the end of the nineteenth century, the ever-accelerating industrial revolution had transformed the nature of work and social life, generated a new urban consciousness and culture, and provoked rising class tensions. With each passing year, more and more people jettisoned traditional rural folkways in favor of new urban environs, a more secular outlook, and enticing new economic and social opportunities.

The recurring theme of American life after the Civil War was an acute sense of accelerated social and intellectual change. Of course, the pressure of history, the pneumatic push of extraordinary new social developments and ideas, never rests. Yet the velocity and scope of change at mid-century and after seemed especially bewildering.

To many, the United States seemed to have lost much of its stability and cohesion as a result of urban-industrial development and western expansion. It had become a loose aggregate of competing individuals, divided from one another by economic differences and ethnic, racial, and class prejudices. How to restore a sense of community and cohesion would become the collective challenge of all Americans.

CHAPTER

20

The Emergence of Urban America

This chapter focuses on

- Immigration and the growth of the modern city.
- The rise of powerful reform movements.
- The impact of Darwinian thought on the social sciences.
- Literary and philosophical trends of the late nineteenth century.

THE *ESSENTIAL AMERICA* ON-LINE TUTOR

www.wwnorton.com/eamerica/ch20

- **Topic: Baseball's early years**
  www.wwnorton.com/eamerica/ch20/topic.htm

  In the mid–nineteenth century, baseball became America's national pastime. Using baseball cards, photographs, personal accounts, and historical analyses, explore how and why baseball became the hobby of millions of Americans. How did baseball evolve from a street game to a professional sport with such sweeping popular appeal?

- **Chapter review: On-line quiz and chapter summary**
  www.wwnorton.com/eamerica/ch20/review.htm

- **Chapter resources: Multimedia index**
  www.wwnorton.com/eamerica/ch20/media.htm

During the second half of the nineteenth century, the United States experienced an urban revolution unparalleled in world history. As factories, mines, and mills sprouted across the landscape, cities developed around them. Between 1860 and 1910, the urban population grew from 6 million to 44 million. The United States was rapidly losing its rural flavor. By 1920, more than half of the population would be living in urban areas.

The rise of big cities during the nineteenth century created a distinctive urban culture. People from different ethnic and religious backgrounds poured into the high-rise apartment buildings and ramshackle tenements springing up in every major city. They came in search of jobs, wealth, and new opportunities. Rising wages and dazzling consumer goods in the new downtown department stores improved the material standard of living for millions—while widening the gap between the poor and affluent.

The rise of metropolitan America created an array of social problems. Rapid urban development produced widespread poverty and political corruption. It also generated filth and disease, substandard housing, and unsafe working conditions in factories, mines, mills, and slaughterhouses. People needed basic services like access to education, transportation, sewers, fresh water, inoculations against disease, and factory inspections to prevent unsafe working conditions. Eventually, broadened access to public education and to public health services would improve literacy and lower infant mortality rates (although the death rate for adult black males would remain quite high). Breakthroughs in medical science would bring cures for tuberculosis, typhoid, and diphtheria—although these infectious diseases would remain the century's leading killers. But in the meantime, the problems of how to feed, clothe, shelter, and educate the new city dwellers taxed the imagination—and the patience of many Americans.

America's Move to Town

The urban-industrial revolution greatly increased the national wealth and transformed the pace and tenor of American life. City dwellers, while differing significantly among themselves, became distinctively and recognizably urban in demeanor and outlook.

Explosive Urban Growth

The frontier provided a social safety valve, the historian Frederick Jackson Turner said in his influential thesis on American development. Its cheap lands had eased the population pressures mounting in the cities. Yet during the second half of the nineteenth century, when Turner developed his "frontier thesis," the flow of population toward the city was greater than toward the West.

Much of the westward migration in fact was itself an urban movement, as new towns sprouted near the mining digs or at the railheads. The Pacific coast boasted a greater urban proportion of the population in the West than anywhere else; its major concentrations were first around San Francisco Bay and then in Los Angeles, which became a boom town after the arrival of the Southern Pacific and Santa Fe Railroads in the 1880s. Seattle also grew quickly, first as the terminus of three transcontinental railroad lines, and by the end of the century as the staging area for the Yukon gold rush. The South, too, produced new cities: Durham, North Carolina, and Birmingham, Alabama, which were centers of tobacco and iron manufactures, and Houston, Texas, which handled cotton and cattle, and later, oil.

The cities expanded both vertically and horizontally to absorb their surging populations. In either case, technological innovations played an important role: steam heating and radiators, elevators, streetcars, and, before the end of the century, the first automobiles. In the 1870s heating innovations, such as steam circulating through pipes and radiators, contributed to the building of multiple-apartment dwellings, since landlords no longer had the expense of providing fireplaces and fuel to heat every room. In 1889 the Otis Elevator Company installed the first electric elevator, which made possible taller buildings. Before the Civil War, few structures had gone higher than three or four stories. During the 1880s, engineers developed cast-iron and steel-frame construction, which was stronger than brick and therefore facilitated the development of taller apartment and office buildings.

Before the 1890s, the chief power sources of urban transport were either animals or steam. Horse- and mule-drawn streetcars had appeared in antebellum cities, but they were slow and cumbersome, and cleaning up horse manure from the streets added to their cost. In 1873 San Francisco became the first city to use cars pulled by steam-driven cables. Some cities used steam-powered commuter trains or elevated tracks, but by the 1890s electric trolleys were preferred. Mass transportation received an added boost when subway systems began to function in Boston, New York, and Philadelphia. Moreover, advances in bridge building through the use of steel and the perfection of the steel-cable suspension bridge also extended the reach of mass transportation.

The spread of mass transit made it possible for large numbers of people to become commuters, and a growing middle class (laborers often could not afford even the nickel fare) retreated to quieter, tree-lined "streetcar suburbs." The emergence of suburbs began to segregate people according to their economic standing. The more affluent moved outside the city, leaving the working folk, many of whom were immigrants, behind. The poorer districts in the city became more congested and crime-ridden as the population grew, fueled by waves of newcomers from abroad.

Allure and Problems of the City

The wonder of the cities—their glittering new electric lights, their streetcars, telephones, vaudeville shows and other amusements, newspapers and magazines, and a thousand other attractions—cast a magnetic lure on rural youth. Thousands left their farms and villages for the cities in search of opportunity and personal freedom.

Yet, those who moved to the city often traded one set of problems for another. Workers in the big cities often had no choice but to live in crowded apartments, most of which were poorly designed. Some city blocks housed almost 4,000 people.

Shoehorned into such cramped quarters, families had no privacy, free space, or sunshine; children had few places to play except in the city streets; infectious diseases and noxious odors were rampant. Not surprisingly, the mortality rate for the urban poor was much higher than that of the general population. In one poor Chicago district at the end of the century, three babies of every five died before their first birthday.

City Politics

The sheer size of the cities helped create a new form of politics. Urban governments were now expected to provide services such as transit, paving, water, sewers, street lighting and cleaning, and fire and police protection. To coordinate such city-wide services, urban political machines emerged. The political bosses who led such machines engaged in patronage favors and graft, buying and selling

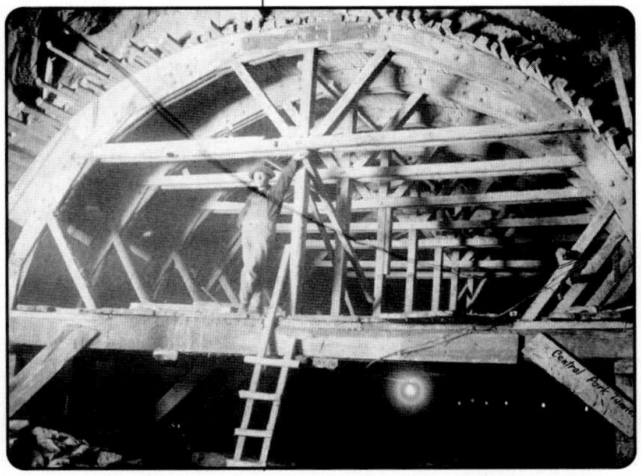

Central Park Tunnel, 1903. The subway system helped abate the street-level congestion that plagued cities at the turn of the century.

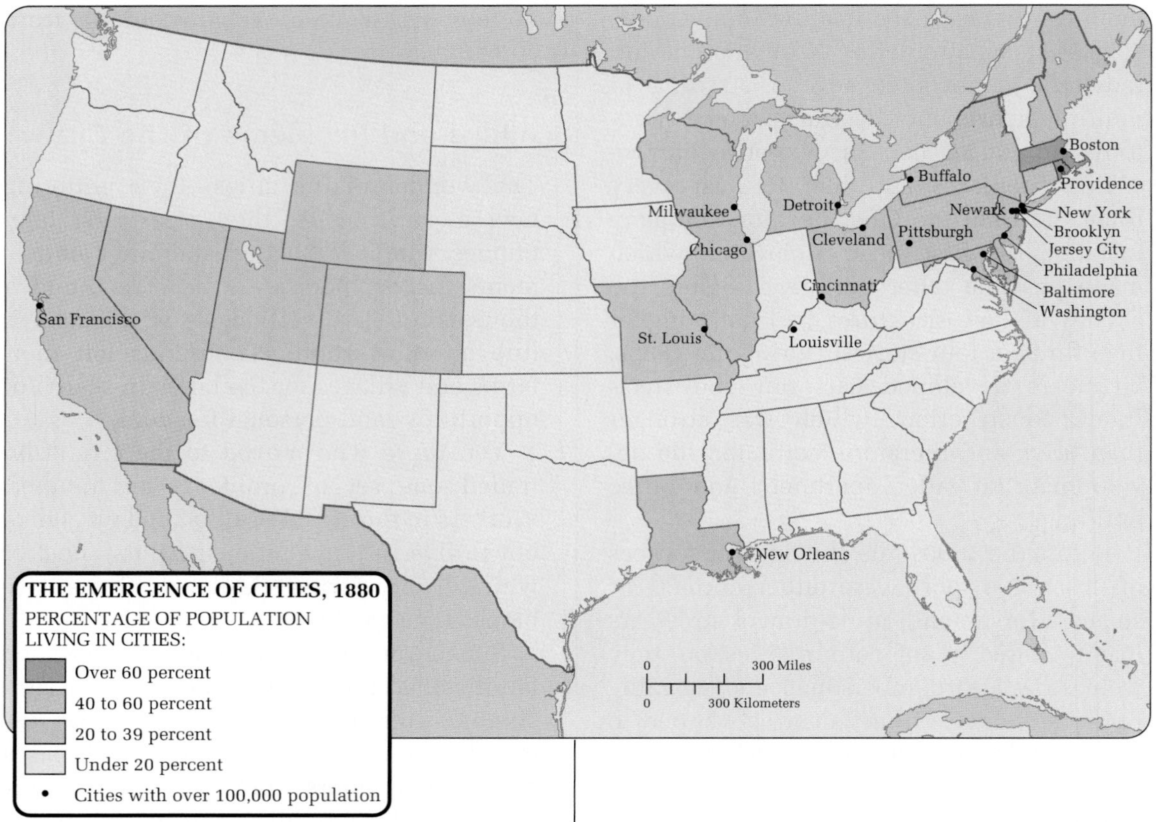

votes, taking kickbacks and payoff money, but they also provided needed services. They distributed food, coal, and money to the poor; found jobs for those who were out of work; sponsored English-language classes for immigrants; organized sports teams, social clubs, and neighborhood gatherings; fixed problems at city hall; and generally helped newcomers adjust to their new life.

The New Immigration

The industrial revolution brought waves of new immigrants from every part of the globe. By the end of the century, nearly 30 percent of the residents of major cities were foreign-born. These newcomers provided much-needed labor, but their arrival also provoked ugly racial and ethnic tensions.

America's Pull

European immigrants increasingly moved from the great agricultural areas of eastern and southern Europe directly to the foremost cities of America. They wanted to live with others of like language, customs, and religion, and they lacked the funds to go west and settle on farms. During the peak decade of immigration, 1900–1910, 41 percent of the urban newcomers arrived from abroad.

American industries, seeking cheap immigrant labor, sent recruiters abroad. Railroads, eager to sell land and build up the traffic on their lines, distributed tempting propaganda in a medley of languages. Many of the western and southern states set up official bureaus and agents to attract immigrants. Under the Contract Labor Law of 1864, the federal government itself encouraged immigration by allowing companies to

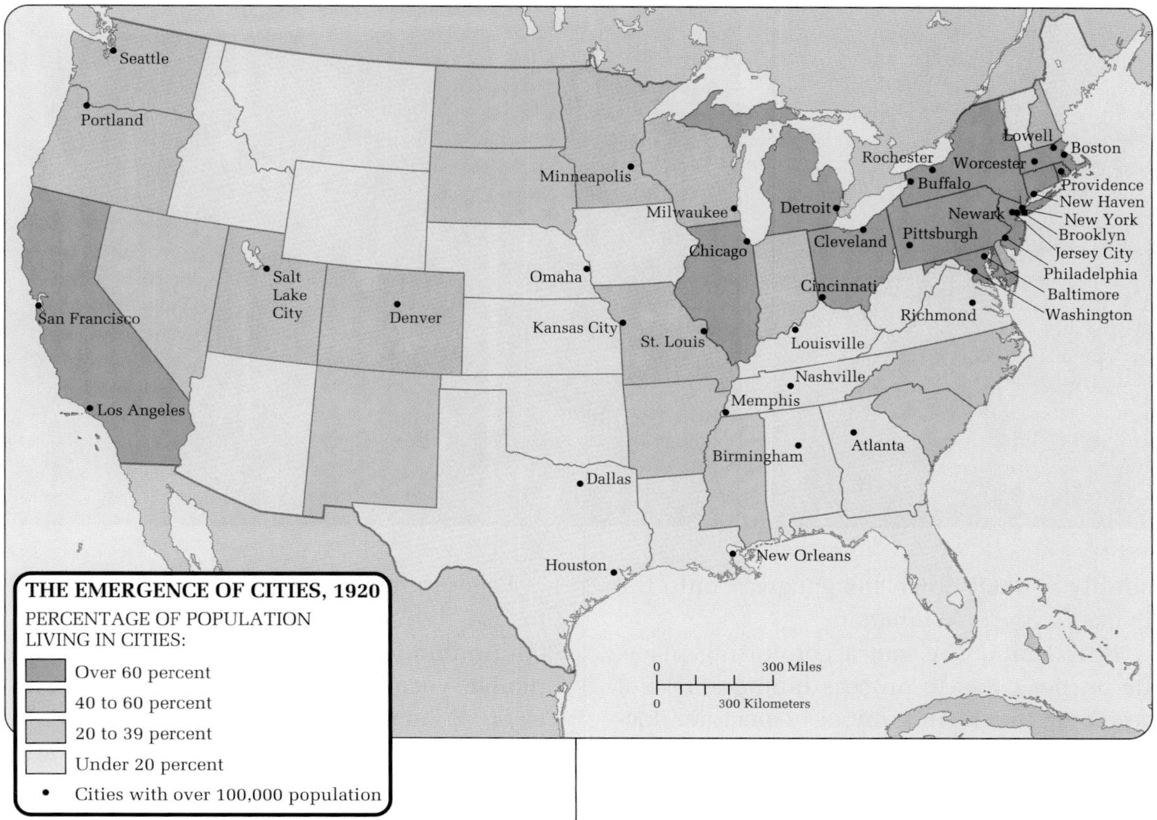

pay for the immigrants' passage and then recoup the money from their wages. The law was repealed in 1868, but not until 1885 did the government forbid companies to import contract labor.

After the Civil War, the tide of immigration rose from just under 3 million in the 1870s to more than 5 million in the 1880s, then fell to a little over 3.5 million in the depression decade of the 1890s, and rose to its high-water mark of 8.8 million in the first decade of the new century.

A New Wave

Before 1880 immigrants were mainly of Germanic and Celtic origin, hailing from northern and western Europe. During the 1870s, however, the proportion of Latin, Slavic, and Jewish people from southern and eastern Europe rose sharply. After 1890, these groups made up a majority of the newcomers, and by the first decade of the new century they formed 70 percent of the immigrants to the United States. Among these new immigrants were Italians, Hungarians, Czechs, Slovaks, Poles, Serbs, Croats, Russians, Romanians, and Greeks.

Ellis Island

In 1892 Ellis Island, the new receiving center 1,300 feet from the Statue of Liberty, opened its doors. In 1907, the reception center's busiest year, more than a million new arrivals passed through the cavernous Great Hall. These were the immigrants who traveled crammed into the steerage compartments of ship hulls. Those immigrants who could afford first- and second-class cabins did not have to visit Ellis Island; they were examined on board ship, and most of them

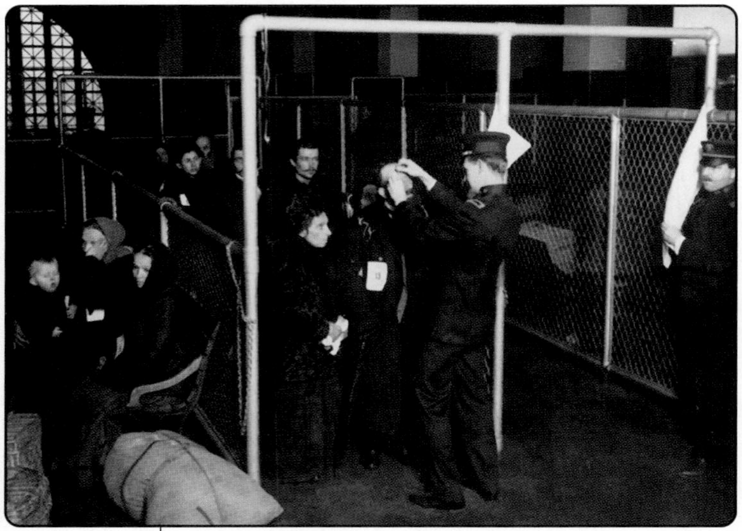

(*Left*) In 1907 Ellis Island received more than a million new arrivals. Many immigrants made the journey to the Port of New York from Eastern Europe. (*Right*) A health inspector checks immigrants on Ellis Island, 1909. Before being granted entry, each immigrant was examined for contagious diseases, including trachoma, an eye disease that could lead to blindness.

simply walked down the gangway onto the docks in lower Manhattan.

Ellis Island was not a comforting place. Its purpose was to process immigrants, not welcome them. An army of inspectors, doctors, nurses, and public officials questioned, examined, and documented the newcomers. Although some who were sick or lame were detained for days or weeks, the vast majority of immigrants received stamps of approval. Only 2 percent of the newcomers were denied entry altogether, usually because they were criminals, strikebreakers, anarchists, or carriers of some "loathsome or dangerous contagious disease." These luckless folk were then returned to their places of origin, with the steamship companies picking up the tab. Between 1892 and 1954, 70 percent of all European immigrants circulated through Ellis Island.

Making Their Way

Once on American soil, immigrants were greeted by representatives of the many immigrant aid societies or by agents offering the men jobs in mines, mills, and sweatshops. Since most knew little if any English and nothing about American employment practices, the immigrants were easy subjects for exploitation.

Eager to retain a sense of community and to use the skills they brought with them, ethnic immigrants tended to cluster in particular vocations. Poles, Hungarians, Slovaks, Bohemians, and Italians flocked to coal mines, just as the Irish, Cornish, and Welsh had done at mid-century; Slavs and Poles comfortable with muscle work gravitated to the steel mills; Greeks preferred working in textile mills; Russian and Polish Jews peopled the sewing trades and pushcart markets of New York. The vast majority of female immigrants found work as domestic servants or in textile mills or urban "sweatshops." A few determined peasants made their way west and were able to find work on farms or even a parcel of land for themselves.

Most of the immigrants, however, settled in the teeming cities. As strangers in a new land, they gravitated to neighborhoods populated by their own kind. These immigrant enclaves—nicknamed Little Italy, Little Hungary, Chinatown, and so on—enabled new arrivals to practice their religions and native customs, converse in their native tongue, and fill an aching loneliness. But there was a price for such community solidarity. When the "new immigrants" moved into an area, older residents typically moved out, taking with them whatever social prestige and political influence they had achieved. The quality of living quickly deteriorated as housing and sanitation codes then went unenforced.

The Nativist Response

Many Americans saw the new immigration as a threat, and a surge of nativism resurfaced during the late nineteenth century, mainly in anti-Catholic and anti-Semitic sentiments. But more than religious prejudice underlay hostility toward the latest newcomers. Cultural differences confirmed in the minds of nativists the assumption that the Anglo-Saxon peoples of the old immigration were superior to the Slavic and Latin peoples of the new immigration. Many of the new immigrants were illiterate, and more appeared so because they could not speak English. Some resorted to crime in order to survive in the new land, and political and social radicals turned up among these immigrant groups in sufficient numbers to encourage nativists to blame labor disputes on alien agitators.

Nativism led to a movement to restrict immigration. In 1891 Representative Henry Cabot Lodge of Massachusetts tried to exclude illiterates—a measure that would have affected much of the new immigration. Several times during the next twenty-five years Congress passed bills restricting immigration, but they were vetoed by Presidents Cleveland, Taft, and Wilson. In 1917, however, Congress overrode Wilson's veto.

Advocates of immigration restriction did succeed in excluding the Chinese, who were victims of everything the new European immigrants suffered and color prejudice as well. By 1880 there were some 75,000 Chinese in California, about one-ninth of the state's population. Many white workers resented the Chinese for accepting lower wages, and efforts to restrict their entry into the United States intensified during the 1870s.

In 1882 President Chester Arthur signed a bill authorizing a ten-year suspension of Chinese immigration. The Chinese Exclusion Act was periodically renewed before being extended indefinitely in 1902. Not until 1943 were such barriers to Chinese immigration finally removed.

The West Coast counterpart to Ellis Island was the Immigration Station on rugged Angel Island, six miles offshore from San Francisco. Opened in 1910, it served as a processing center for tens of thousands of Asian immigrants, most of them Chinese. Although the Chinese Exclusion Act had sharply reduced the flow of Chinese immigrants, it did not stop the influx completely. Those arrivals who could claim a Chinese-American parent were allowed to enter, as were certain officials, teachers, merchants, and students. The powerful prejudice the Chinese immigrants encountered helps explain why over 30 percent of the arrivals at Angel Island were denied entry.

Popular Culture

As more people moved to large towns and cities, new patterns of recreation and leisure emerged. Whereas people in rural areas were tied into the rituals of the harvest season and lived with or near their extended families, most middle-class urban whites were mobile and lived in nuclear families (made up of only parents and children). Their affluence enabled them to enjoy greater leisure time and rising discretionary income. Middle- and upper-class urban families spent much of their free time together at home, usually in the parlor, singing around the piano, reading novels, or playing cards, dominoes, chess, and checkers.

In the congested metropolitan areas, politics became as much a form of public entertainment as it was a process of providing civic representation and public services. People flocked to hear visiting candidates give speeches. Huge crowds regularly at-

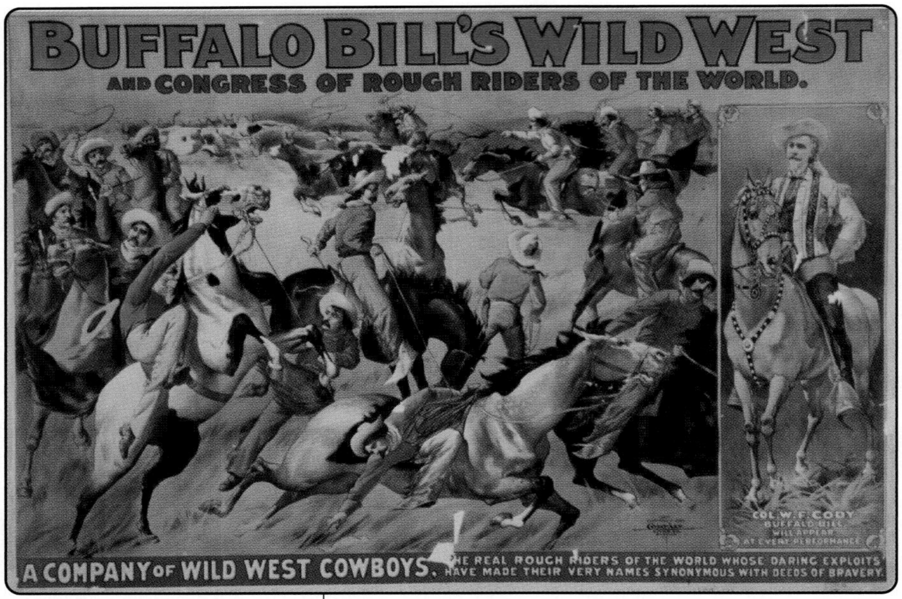

Buffalo Bill's Wild West. Although the shows included genuine cowboys and authentic Indians, they romanticized the American West.

tended political rallies, and membership in a political party was akin to belonging to a social club. In addition, labor unions also included activities that were more social than economic in nature, and members often visited the union hall as much to socialize as to discuss working conditions. The sheer numbers of people in cities also helped generate a market for new forms of mass entertainment such as traveling Wild West shows, vaudeville shows, and spectator sports.

Wild West Shows

One of the touring extravaganzas that enjoyed incredible popularity during the last quarter of the nineteenth century was "Buffalo Bill's Wild West" traveling show. William "Buffalo Bill" Cody was a rugged frontiersman and sharpshooter who served as a Union scout during the Civil War. After the war, he became a renowned buffalo hunter, providing meat for the crews building railroads. His hunting ability earned him the nickname Buffalo Bill. From 1868 to 1872, Cody served as a scout for army troops and was awarded the Congressional Medal of Honor.

Cody took advantage of his celebrity status to organize a stage show that included live elk and buffalo, hundreds of horses, genuine cowboys, authentic Indians, rope tricks, shooting exhibitions, cowgirl Annie Oakley, and Cody himself as the star attraction. One advertisement promised "a horde of warpainted Arapahoes, Cheyenne, and Sioux Indians." The Indians were always portrayed as the aggressors, and the whites as the victims. These images set in motion the mythic depiction of the West that later became the staple of television and movie Westerns. When Buffalo Bill died in 1917, his shows died with him, but he bequeathed to Americans a new form of entertainment that has since taken deep root: the rodeo.

Vaudeville

During the late nineteenth century, rising family incomes and innovations in urban transportation—cable cars, subways, electric streetcars and streetlights—enabled more people to take advantage of urban cultural life. Attendance at theaters, operas, dance halls, and symphony concerts soared. The most popular—and diverse—form of theatrical entertainment in the late nineteenth century was known as vaudeville. The term derives from a French word meaning a play accompanied by music.

Vaudeville "variety" shows featured comedians, musicians, blackface minstrels, farcical plays, animal acts, gymnasts, dancers, mimes, and magicians. Because variety shows were held in seedy beer halls populated by drunks and prostitutes and because the entertainers often included vulgar material, they quickly developed a bad reputation. To encourage families to attend, promoters of variety shows built elegant new theaters, banned alcoholic beverages, upgraded the performers, hired policemen and bouncers to handle "rowdies," and began to use the more elegant French word "vaudeville" to describe the genre.

Vaudeville houses sprouted like mushrooms in cities across the United States in the 1870s and 1880s. They quickly became popular gathering places for all social classes and types—men, women, and children. To commemorate the opening of a palatial new Boston theater in 1894, an actress read a dedicatory poem in which she announced that "All are equals here." The vaudeville house was the people's theater; it knew "no favorites, no class" in its efforts "ever to please—and never to offend."

Outdoor Recreation

The congestion and diseases associated with urban life led many people to participate in forms of outdoor recreation intended to restore their vitality and improve their health. City parks, although originally intended as places where people could walk and commune with nature, soon offered more vigorous forms of exercise and recreation—for men and women.

Croquet and tennis courts were among the first additions to city parks because they took up little space and required little maintenance. Croquet was born in the British Isles in the mid–nineteenth century and soon migrated to most other English-speaking countries. Because croquet could be played by both sexes, it combined the virtues of sport with the opportunities of courtship. Croquet as a public sport suffered a setback in the 1890s, however, when Boston clergymen lambasted the drinking, gambling, and licentious behavior associated with it on the Boston Common, where croquet matches were held.

Lawn tennis was invented by an Englishman in 1873 and arrived in the United States a year later. By 1885 New York's Central Park had thirty tennis courts. Lawn tennis was originally viewed as a leisurely sport best suited for women. The Harvard student newspaper declared in 1878 that the sport was "well enough for a lazy or *weak* man, but men who have rowed or taken part in a nobler sport should blush to be seen playing Lawn Tennis."

Even more popular than croquet or tennis was cycling or "wheeling." In the 1870s, bicycles began to be manufactured in the United States, and by the end of the century a "bicycle craze" had swept the country. The first bicycles were called "high-wheelers" or "boneshakers" because the front wheel was huge, as much as five feet high, while the rear wheel was tiny, no more than a foot in diameter. The high-wheelers were hard to ride, uncomfortable, and dangerous, as they had no brakes. During the 1880s, an Englishman named J. K. Starley produced the first "safety bicycle." These bicycles had wheels of equal size and axles with ball bearings, which made them easier and safer to ride than high-wheelers. By 1890, bicycles had air-filled rubber tires and brakes. Millions of middle-class Americans (who could afford the new invention) discovered a new mobility and freedom through the bicycle, which, unlike horses, went where they were pointed, did not need to be fed, and did not leave droppings in the road.

Marshall W. "Major" Taylor (1878–1932), African-American cyclist, held seven world records in sprint cycling in the late 1890s.

Bicycles were especially popular with women who chafed at the restricting conventions of Victorianism. The new vehicles offered exercise, freedom, and access to the countryside. Critics feared that the bicycle mania was encouraging young women to grow independent and shun conventional domestic responsibilities. Some guardians of morality believed that cycling was also sexually provocative. In 1899 the Reverend W. W. Reynolds expressed outrage because a

Tandem tricycle. In spite of the danger and discomfort of early bicycles, wheeling became a popular form of recreation and mode of transportation.

"large number of female bicyclists wear shorter dresses than the laws of morality and decency permit, thereby inviting the improper conversations and remarks of the depraved and immoral." He found cycling "detrimental to the advancement of morality."

The working poor in the cities could not afford to acquire a bicycle or join a croquet club. Nor did they have as much free time as the affluent. They toiled long hours, six days a week, and at the end of their long days they eagerly sought recreation and fellowship on street corners or on the front stoops of their apartment buildings. Organ grinders and musicians would perform on the sidewalks among the food vendors. Those with a few extra dollars to spend frequented the saloons and dance halls available in each city. In 1900 New York City alone had 10,000 saloons featuring five-cent beer and free lunch. In the late nineteenth century, saloons often doubled as gymnasiums. Back rooms often housed handball courts, pool tables, bowling alleys, and dart boards.

Many ethnic groups, especially the Germans and the Irish, formed male singing, drinking, or gymnastic clubs. Working folk also attended bare-knuckle boxing matches or baseball games, and on Sundays they would gather for picnics. By the end of the century, large-scale amusement parks such as New York's Luna Park on Coney Island provided inexpensive entertainment for the entire family. Yet many inner-city youth could not afford the trolley fare to visit a suburban amusement park, so the crowded streets and dangerous alleys became their playgrounds.

Spectator Sports

In the last quarter of the nineteenth century, horse racing and prizefighting remained popular, but team sports also began to attract legions of fans. New spectator sports such as college football and basketball and professional baseball gained mass popularity, reflecting the growing urbanization of American life. People could gather easily for sporting events in the large cities. And news of the games could be conveyed quickly by newspapers and specialized sporting magazines relying upon telegraph reports. Saloons also posted the scores. Athletic rivalries between distant cities were made possible by the network of railroads spanning the continent and facilitating team travel. Spectator sports became urban extravaganzas, unifying the diverse ethnic groups in the large cities and attracting people with the leisure time and ready cash to spend (or bet) on watching others perform.

Football emerged as a modified form of soccer and rugby. The College of New Jersey (Princeton) and Rutgers played the first college football game in 1869. The teams at first used twenty-five players at a time, and players literally kicked the ball along the ground. By 1880, the number of players had been reduced to eleven, and they carried the ball rather than kicking it. The players wore no protective padding or headgear, and the games often resembled organized fights. In fact, advocates of football portrayed it as a "blood sport" that provided a modern substitute for the frontier experience.

Early games featured unregulated mayhem, with slugging and kicking commonplace. Scores of players died from injuries. In 1905 alone, 18 players were killed and 150 seriously injured. Gambling on college football games was also widespread.

Football became so controversial that President Theodore Roosevelt intervened in 1905. He had long promoted strenuous exercise and "rough, manly sports" for young men leading sedentary lives in cities. With the closing of the frontier, he feared that boys growing up in urban centers would become weak and anemic. Roosevelt championed football as a means of instilling in young men the virtues of "pluck, endurance, and physical address," yet he appealed to coaches, professors, and alumni to "come to a gentlemen's agreement not to have mucker play." His appeal did little good, and the roughness and foul play continued. As a result, Columbia University and the Massachusetts Institute of Technology abolished football. Stanford and the University of California replaced it with rugby. In a further effort to curb injuries and abuses, the National Collegiate Athletics Association (NCAA) was founded in 1910.

Basketball was invented in 1891 when Dr. James Naismith, a physical education instructor, nailed two peach baskets to the walls of the YMCA training school in Springfield, Massachusetts. Naismith wanted to create an indoor winter game that could be played between the fall football and spring baseball seasons. Basketball quickly grew in popularity among both boys and girls. Vassar and Smith Colleges added the sport in 1892. In 1893, Vanderbilt became the first college to field a men's team.

Baseball laid claim to being America's national pastime at mid-century. Contrary to popular opinion, Abner Doubleday did not invent the game. Instead, Alexander Cartwright, a New York bank clerk and sportsman, was the father of organized baseball. In 1845 he gathered a group of merchants, stockbrokers, and physicians to form the Knickerbocker Base Ball Club of New York.

The first professional baseball team was the Cincinnati Red Stockings, which made its appearance in 1869. Seven years later, seven other teams joined the Red Stockings in creating the National League. Reporters began to cover the games, and sports sections appeared in every newspaper. In 1901 the American League was organized, and two years later the first World Series was held.

Baseball became the most democratic sport in America. People from all social classes (mostly men) attended the games, and ethnic immigrants were among the most faithful fans. The *St. Louis Post-Dispatch* reported in 1883 that "a glance at the audience on any fine day at the ball park will reveal . . . telegraph operators, printers who work at night, travelling men [salesmen] . . . men of leisure . . . men of capital, bank clerks who get away [from work] at 3 P.M., real estate men . . . barkeepers . . . hotel clerks, actors and employees of the theater, policemen and firemen on their day off . . . butchers and bakers." Cheering for a city baseball team gave rootless people a common loyalty and a sense of belonging.

Only white players were allowed in the major leagues. African Americans played on "minor league" teams or in all-black "Negro leagues." In 1867 the National Association of Base Ball Players excluded black clubs from membership. And the National League followed suit when it was organized nine years later. In 1887 black players were banned from minor league teams as well.

The excitement of rooting for the home team united all classes as they watched the athletes who graced the playing field.

By the end of the nineteenth century, sports of all kinds had become a major cultural phenomenon in the United States. A writer in *Harper's Weekly* announced in 1895 that "ball matches, football games, tennis tournaments, bicycle races, [and] regattas, have become part of our national life." They "are watched with eagerness and discussed with enthusiasm and understanding by all manner of people, from the day-laborer to the millionaire."

Education and the Professions

The determination to "Americanize" immigrant children prompted efforts to expand public schools after the Civil War. In 1870 there were 7 million pupils enrolled; by 1920 the number had tripled. Despite such progress, educational leaders had to struggle against a pattern of political appointments, corruption, and incompetence in the public schools.

The spread of secondary schools accounted for much of the increased enrollment in public schools. In antebellum America, private academies had prepared those who intended to enter college. At the beginning of the Civil War, there were only about 100 public high schools in the whole country, but their number grew rapidly to about 800 in 1880 and to 6,000 at the turn of the century.

Higher Education

American colleges sought to instill discipline and morality. They featured a curriculum heavy on mathematics and the classics (and in church schools, theology), along with ethics and rhetoric. History, modern languages and literature, and some science courses were tolerated, although laboratory work was usually limited to a professor's demonstration in class.

The demand for higher learning drove the college student population up from 52,000 in 1870 to 157,000 in 1890 and to 600,000 in 1920. During the same years, the number of institutions rose from 563 to about 1,000. To accommodate the diverse needs of these growing numbers, colleges moved away from rigidly prescribed courses toward an elective system. The new approach allowed students to favor their strong points and colleges to expand their scope. But critics complained that the elective system was intellectually less rigorous.

Women's access to higher education improved markedly in this period. Before the Civil War, a few colleges had already gone coeducational, and state universities in the West were commonly open to women from the start. But colleges in the South and East fell in line very slowly. Vassar (1865) was the first women's college to teach by the same standards as the best of the men's colleges. In 1875 two more excellent women's schools appeared in Massachusetts: Wellesley and Smith, the latter being the first to set the same admission requirements as men's colleges. Thereafter the older women's colleges rushed to upgrade their standards in the same way.

The dominant new trend in American higher education after the Civil War was the rise of the graduate school. Heretofore, most professors had a knowledge more broad than deep. Few engaged in research, nor were they expected to advance the frontiers of knowledge. Gradually, however, more and more American scholars studied at German universities, where training was more systematic and focused. After the Civil War, the German system became the basis for the modern American graduate university. By the 1890s, the Ph.D. was fast becoming the ticket of admission to the guild of professors.

The Rise of Professionalism

The Ph.D. revolution was but one aspect of a growing emphasis on professionalism, with its imposition of uniform standards, licensing of practitioners, and accreditation of professional schools. The number of professional schools grew rapidly in fields such as theology, law, medicine, dentistry, pharmacy, and veterinary medicine.

Along with advanced schooling went a movement for licensing practitioners in certain fields. During the second half of the nineteenth century, the first state licensing laws were enacted for dentistry, pharmacy, veterinary medicine, accounting, and architecture. Such licensing benefited the public by certifying competence in a given field, but it also benefited members of the profession by controlling the number of practitioners and thereby limiting competition.

Realism in Thought, Culture, and Literature

Just as popular culture was transformed as a result of the urban-industrial revolution, so, too, did intellectual life adapt to its incessant demands. Before the Civil War, various forms of idealism dominated American thought. Although quite diverse in motive and method, idealists shared a basic conviction that fundamental truths rested in the unseen world of ideas and spirit or in the distant past rather than in the tangible world of fact and contemporary experience. The most prominent writers, artists, and philosophers were more concerned with romantic or biblical themes than with common aspects of "real" life.

At mid-century and after, however, a more "realistic" sensibility began to challenge this idealistic tradition. The realistic movement matured into a full-fledged cultural force during the second half of the nineteenth century. More and more thinkers and artists focused their attention on the emerging realities of scientific research and technology, factories and railroads, cities and immigrants, wage labor and social tensions.

The rise of realism resulted from a transformed social, intellectual, and moral landscape. The horrors of the Civil War led many people to adopt a less romantic outlook. Another factor contributing to the rise of realism was the growing impact of the modern scientific method. The prestige of empirical science increased enormously during the second half of the nineteenth century as researchers explored electromagnetic induction, the conservation of matter, the laws of thermodynamics, and the relationship between heat and energy. Breakthroughs in chemistry led to new understandings of the formation of compounds and the nature of reactions. Fossil discoveries opened up new horizons in geology and paleontology, and greatly improved microscopes enabled zoologists to decipher cell structures.

Darwinism and Social Darwinism

Every field of thought in the post–Civil War years felt the impact of Charles Darwin's *On the Origin of Species* (1859). It argued that existing species, including humanity itself, had evolved through a long process of "natural selection" from less complex forms of life. Those species that adapted to survival reproduced their kind, while others died away. The idea of species evolution shocked people with conventional religious views. Heated arguments arose among scientists and clergymen. Some of the faithful rejected Darwin's doctrine, while others found their faith severely shaken. Most of the faithful, however, eventually came to reconcile science and religion, viewing evolution as a natural process designed by God.

The pervasive effect of Darwinism in late nineteenth-century American intellectual circles was comparable to the effect of romanticism in the first part of the century. Like the earlier reaction against the Enlightenment's praise of reason, the trend in social thought now was turned against abstract logic and toward concrete reality.

Though Darwin's theory actually applied only to biological phenomena, the temptation to apply evolutionary theory to the social world proved irresistible. Darwin's fellow Englishman Herbert Spencer became the first major prophet of what came to be called Social Darwinism, and he exerted an important influence on American thought. Spencer argued that human society and institutions, like plant and animal species, passed through the process of natural selection, which resulted in what he called the "survival of the fittest."

If, as Spencer believed, human society naturally evolved for the better, then individual freedom was inviolable, and any governmental interference with the process of social evolution was a serious mistake. Social Darwinism thus endorsed a hands-off governmental policy, then known as laissez-faire; it decried the regulation of business, the proposals for a graduated income tax, sanitation and housing regulations, and even protection against medical quacks. Such initiatives, no matter how well intended, would only help the "unfit" survive and thereby impede progress. The only acceptable charity was voluntary, and even that was of dubious value. For Spencer and his many supporters, successful businessmen and corporations were the engines of social progress. If small businesses were crowded out by trusts and monopolies, that too was part of the evolutionary process.

Reform Darwinism

The influence of Darwin and Spencer on American intellectuals did not go without challenge. Reform found its major philosopher in an obscure civil servant, Lester Frank Ward, who had fought his way up from poverty and never lost his empathy for the underdog. Ward's book *Dynamic Sociology* (1883) singled out one product of evolution that Spencer and others had neglected, the human brain. Humans, unlike animals, had a mind that could plan for and shape the future. Far from being the helpless pawn of powerful evolutionary forces, Ward argued, humanity could actively shape the process of evolution.

Ward's Reform Darwinism insisted that cooperation, not competition, would better promote social progress. Government could become the agency of progress by striving to ameliorate poverty and promote the education of the masses. Intellect, rightly informed by science, could plan successfully. In the benevolent "sociocracy" of the future, Ward argued, legislatures would function mainly to sanction decisions worked out in the sociological laboratory.

Pragmatism

Around the turn of the century, the evolutionary idea found expression in a philosophical principle set forth in mature form by William James in his book *Pragmatism: A New Name for Some Old Ways of Thinking.* James, a professor of philosophy and psychology at Harvard, shared Lester Frank Ward's concern with the role of ideas in the process of evolution. Truth, to James, arose from the testing of new ideas, the value of which lay in their practical consequences. Pragmatism thus reflected a quality often looked upon as genuinely American: the inventive, experimental spirit focusing on tangible results.

John Dewey, who would become the chief philosopher of pragmatism after James, preferred the term "instrumentalism," by which he meant that ideas were instruments of practical use, especially for promoting social reform. Dewey, unlike James, threw himself into movements for the rights of labor and women, the promotion of peace, and the reform of education. Like Lester Frank Ward, he believed that education was the process through which society would gradually progress toward greater social equality and harmony. Dewey became the prophet of what was later labeled "progressive education," which emphasized the teaching of history, geography, and science in order to enlarge the child's personal experience. Dewey also pointed out that social conditions had so changed that schools now had to find ways to inculcate values once derived from participation in family and community activities.

Clemens, Howells, and James

After the Civil War, fiction reflected the impact of the "rise of realism." Three writers dominated the literary scene: Mark Twain, William Dean Howells, and Henry James. A native of Missouri, Twain (Samuel Clemens) was forced to work at age twelve, becoming first a printer and then a Mississippi riverboat pilot. When the Civil War shut down the river traffic, he briefly joined a Confederate militia company, then left with his brother for Nevada, where he wrote for a local newspaper. He moved on to California in 1864 and first gained widespread notice with his tall tale of the gold country, "The Celebrated Jumping Frog of Calaveras County" (1865). With the success of *Roughing It* (1871), an account of his western years, he moved to Hartford, Connecticut, and was able to set up as a full-time author and lecturer.

Clemens was the first significant American writer born and raised west of the Appalachians. His early writings accentuated his western background, but for his greatest books he drew heavily upon his boyhood in the border state of Missouri and the tall-tale tradition of southwestern humor. In *The Adventures of Tom Sawyer* (1876) he evoked the prewar Hannibal, Missouri. Its story of childhood adventures is firmly etched on the American memory. *Life on the Mississippi* (1882) drew upon what Clemens remembered as his happiest days as a young riverboat pilot before the war. His pseudonym, "Mark Twain," was in fact derived from a phrase that referred to the depth of the river.

Clemens's masterpiece was *The Adventures of Huckleberry Finn* (1884). Huck Finn embodied the instinct of every red-blooded American boy to "light out for the territory" whenever polite society set out to civilize him. Huck's effort to help the runaway slave Jim escape bondage expressed well the moral dilemmas imposed by slavery. One of Clemens's foremost supporters was his close friend William Dean Howells, who wrote "Clemens was sole, incomparable, the Lincoln of our literature."

During the half century after the Civil War, Howells dominated the American literary scene. As editor of the influential *Atlantic Monthly* and later a columnist and critic for *Harper's Monthly,* Howells preached the new doctrine of realism, a literary rebellion against romantic idealism that "was nothing more or less than the truthful treatment of . . . the motives, the impulses, the principles that shape the life of actual men and women."

To this end, Howells wrote novels, plays, travel books, criticism, essays, biography, and autobiography. Amid the varied output of a long and productive life, *The Rise of Silas Lapham* (1885) stands out as his best novel. In it Howells presented a sympa-

Samuel Langhorne Clemens (Mark Twain), whose literary works became American classics.

thetic portrayal of a newly rich manufacturer from the West, and one of the earliest fictional treatments of an American businessman.

The third major literary figure of the times, Henry James, moved in a world far different from that of Clemens or Howells. Brother of the pragmatist philosopher William James and son of wealthy parents, Henry spent most of his adult life as an expatriate in London, where he produced elegant novels that for the first time explored the international society of Americans in Europe. In works such as *Portrait of a Lady* (1881), *The Ambassadors* (1903), and *The Golden Bowl* (1904), James explored the tensions that developed between direct, innocent, and idealistic Americans (most often young women) and sophisticated, devious Europeans. His intense exploration of the inner selves of his characters brought him the title of "father of the psychological novel."

Literary Naturalism

Realism grew into a powerful literary movement during the 1880s, but during the 1890s it took on a new character in the writings of the so-called naturalists. This group of younger writers sought to integrate scientific determinism into literature. Having grown up in the era of Darwin and Spencer, they viewed humankind as prey to environmental forces and internal drives beyond control or full understanding. Frank Norris thus pictured in *McTeague* (1899) the descent of a San Francisco dentist and his wife into madness, driven by greed and lust. Stephen Crane in *Maggie: A Girl of the Streets* (1893) depicted a tenement girl driven to prostitution and death amid scenes so grim and sordid that Crane had to finance publication himself. *The Red Badge of Courage* (1895), Crane's masterpiece, told the story of a young man going through his baptism of fire in the Civil War, and it evoked fear, nobility, and courage amid the carnage of war.

Two of the naturalists, Jack London and Theodore Dreiser, achieved popular success. London was both a professed socialist and a believer in the German philosopher Friedrich Nietzsche's doctrine of the superman. In adventure stories such as *The Call of the Wild* (1903) and *The Sea Wolf* (1904), he celebrated the triumph of brute force and the will to survive.

Theodore Dreiser did not celebrate the overwhelming power of social and biological forces; he dissected them for the reader. The result was powerfully disturbing to readers accustomed to more genteel fare. Dreiser shocked the public with protagonists who sinned without remorse and without punishment. *Sister Carrie* (1900), for example, showed Carrie Meeber surviving illicit loves and going on to success on the stage.

Social Criticism

Behind their dogma of determinism, several of the naturalists harbored intense outrage at human misery. Their indignation was shared by an increasing number of journalists and social critics who addressed themselves more directly to protest and reform. One of the most influential of these reformers was Henry George, a journalist who vowed to seek out the cause of poverty in the midst of the industrial progress he saw around him. The basic social problem, George reasoned in his best-selling *Progress and Poverty* (1879), was the unearned increment in wealth that came to those who owned the land.

George held that everyone had a basic right to the use of the land, since it was provided by nature to all. Nobody had a right to the increasing value of the land, since that was created by the community, not by its owner. He proposed simply to tax the unearned increment in the value of the land, or the rent. George intended his "single-tax" idea to free capital and labor from paying tribute for land, and to put to use lands previously held out of production by specula-

tors. George's idea provoked much discussion and actually affected local tax policy here and there, but his greater influence came from the paradox he posed in his title *Progress and Poverty,* and his plea for social cooperation and equality.

The journalist and freelance writer Henry Demarest Lloyd, son of a minister, addressed himself to what many found a more vital issue than Henry George's, not the monopoly in land but in industry. His best-known book, *Wealth Against Commonwealth* (1894), revealed Rockefeller's chicanery in turning the Standard Oil Company into a monopoly. Lloyd, like George and Lester Frank Ward, saw the key to social progress in cooperation rather than competition. Where monopolies had developed, they should be transferred to public operation in the public interest.

Thorstein Veblen brought to his social criticism a background of formal training in economics. In his best-known work, *The Theory of the Leisure Class* (1899), he examined the values of the affluent and introduced phrases that have since become commonplace: "conspicuous consumption" and "conspicuous leisure." With the advent of industrial society, Veblen argued, the showy display of money and property became the conventional basis of status.

The Social Gospel

While novelists, journalists, and commentators were writing about the rising social tensions and injustices of late-nineteenth-century America, others confronted such problems through direct social action. Some reformers focused on legislative remedies; others stressed philanthropy or organized charity. Fewer promoted socialism or anarchism. Whatever the method or approach, however, social reformers flourished at the turn of the century, and their activities gave to American life a new urgency and energy.

Rise of the Institutional Church

The churches responded slowly to the mounting social ills. Over the years, American Protestantism had become one of the main props of the established order. The Reverend Henry Ward Beecher, for instance, pastor of the fashionable Plymouth Congregational Church in Brooklyn, preached material success, Social Darwinism, and the unworthiness of the poor. Not surprisingly, more and more working-class people felt out of place in churches where affluence was both worshipped and flaunted.

But gradually some religious leaders realized that Protestantism was in danger of losing its working-class constituency unless it reached out to the urban poor. Two organizations were created expressly for that purpose. The Young Men's Christian Association (YMCA) had entered the United States from England in the 1850s and grew rapidly after 1870; the Salvation Army, founded in London in 1876, entered the United States four years later. Individual urban churches also began to develop institutional features that were more social than strictly religious in function. Churches acquired gymnasiums, libraries, lecture rooms, and other facilities in an effort to attract working-class people back to organized religion.

Religious Reformers

Some church reformers who feared that Christianity was becoming irrelevant to the needs and aspirations of the working poor began preaching what came to be called the social gospel. One of the earliest activists, Washington Gladden of Columbus, Ohio, maintained that true Christianity resided not in rituals, dogmas, or even in the mystical experience of God, but in the principle that "Thou shalt love thy neighbor as thyself." The "law of greed and strife," he insisted, "is not a natural law; it is unnatural; it is a crime against nature; the law of brotherhood is the only natural law." He thus argued for labor's right to organize unions, supported maximum-hours laws and factory inspections, and endorsed antitrust legislation.

The Catholic Church

In the post–Civil War years Catholic social thought was initially quite conservative. Papal decrees warned American Catholics against supporting the new social reform movements. But the Vatican's outlook altered drastically in 1891, when Pope Leo XIII issued his encyclical, *Rerum novarum* ("Of modern things"). This new expression of Catholic social doctrine upheld private property as a natural right but condemned capitalism where it had imposed poverty and degradation on workers. It also affirmed the right of Catholics to join labor unions and socialist movements insofar as these were not antireligious. But American Catholics for the most part remained isolated from organized reform movements until the twentieth century, though they themselves were among the most abused victims of urban slums.

Early Efforts at Urban Reform

The Settlement House Movement

At the end of the century, dedicated reformers attacked the problems of the slums by establishing community centers called settlement houses. By 1900 perhaps a hundred settlement houses existed in America, some of the best known being Jane Addams and Ellen Starr's Hull House in Chicago and Lillian Wald's Henry Street Settlement in New York.

Jane Addams.

The settlement houses were staffed by idealistic middle-class young people, a majority of them college-trained women. Settlement workers sought to broaden the horizons and improve the lives of slum dwellers in diverse ways. At Hull House, for instance, workers enrolled neighborhood children in clubs, kindergartens, and a nursery, which served the infant children of working mothers. Settlement houses also provided workingmen an alternative to the saloon as a place of recreation and an alternative to the political boss as a source of social services. Their programs gradually expanded to include health clinics, lectures, music and art studios, employment bureaus, men's clubs, gymnasiums, training in skills such as bookbinding, and savings banks.

Addams and other settlement house leaders realized, however, that the slums were spreading faster than charitable services. Activists therefore organized political support for housing laws, public playgrounds, juvenile courts, mothers' pensions, workers' compensation laws, and legislation against child labor. Julia Lathrop, another Hull House staffer, was appointed in 1912 the first head of the federal Children's Bureau, an agency designed to scrutinize the use and abuse of child labor.

Women's Employment and Suffrage

With rapid population growth in the late nineteenth century the number of employed women steadily increased, as did their percentage of the labor force. The number of employed women doubled from 1880 to 1900 and then doubled again by 1910. Through all those years, domestic work remained the largest category of employment for women; teaching and nursing also remained among the leading fields. The main change was that clerical work (bookkeeping, stenographic work, and the like) and sales jobs became increasingly available to women.

These changes in occupational status had little connection with the women's rights movement, which increasingly focused on

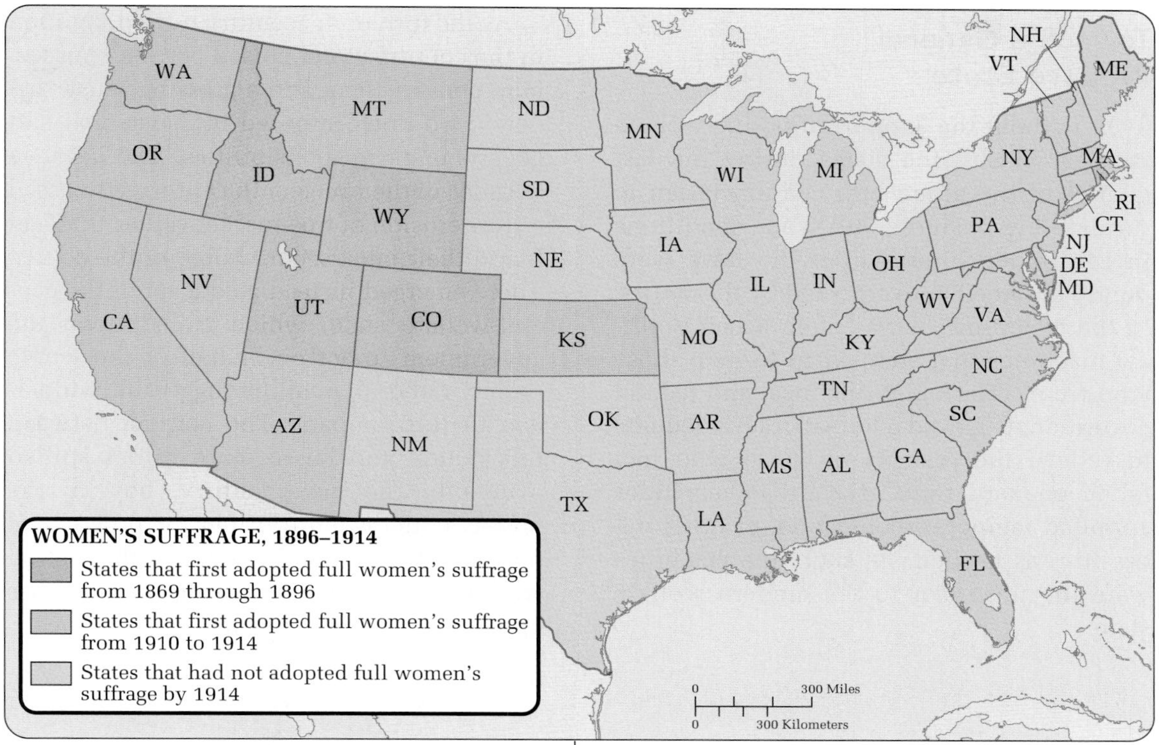

the issue of suffrage. Immediately after the Civil War, Susan B. Anthony, a seasoned veteran of the movement, demanded that the Fourteenth Amendment guarantee the vote for women as well as black males. She made little headway against the defenders of masculine prerogative, however.

In 1869 Anthony and Elizabeth Cady Stanton founded the National Woman Suffrage Association to promote an amendment to the Constitution allowing women to vote, but they looked upon suffrage as but one among many feminist causes to be promoted. Later that same year, Lucy Stone, Julia Ward Howe, and other leaders formed the American Woman Suffrage Association, which focused single-mindedly on the vote as the first and basic reform.

In 1890, after three years of negotiation, the rival groups united as the National American Woman Suffrage Association, with Stanton as president for two years, followed by Anthony until 1900. The work thereafter was carried on by a new generation led by Anna Howard Shaw and Carrie Chapman Catt. Over the years, the movement achieved some victories, as a few states granted woman suffrage in school board or municipal elections. In 1869 the Territory of Wyoming provided full suffrage to women and after 1890 retained women's suffrage when it became a new state. Three other western states soon followed suit, but not until New York acted in 1917 did a state east of the Mississippi adopt universal suffrage.

Despite the focus on the vote, women did not confine their public work to that issue. In 1866 a Young Women's Christian Association, a parallel to the YMCA, appeared in Boston and spread elsewhere. The New England Women's Club, started in 1868 by Julia Ward Howe and others, was an early example of the women's clubs that then proliferated. Many women's clubs confined themselves to "literary" and social activities, but others became deeply involved in charities and reform.

Toward a General Welfare State

Even without the support of voting women in most places, the states during the last quarter of the nineteenth century began to regulate big business and labor conditions in the public interest, but the laws were poorly enforced or overturned by the courts. In the meantime, it was often urban political machines that stepped in to help those who were suffering. While local and federal governments lacked a bureaucracy adequate to relieve the distress of those who had fallen on hard times, the urban machines supplied temporary jobs, food, or other necessities as needed. As such, the machines were the precursor to the modern welfare state.

As the turn of the century neared, opinion in the country stood poised between laissez-faire conservatism and a growing sense that new conditions imposed new personal and governmental responsibilities. The last two decades of the nineteenth century witnessed a slow erosion of free-market values that had found their most secure home in the courts. There emerged instead a concept of the general-welfare state, which called upon the government to act on be-half of the whole society rather than allow rugged individualism to run rampant. The conflict between this notion and laissez-faire values spilled over into the new century, but by the mid–twentieth century, after the progressive movement and the New Deal, the nation would be firmly committed to the premises of the general-welfare state.

CHAPTER

21

Gilded-Age Politics and Agrarian Revolt

This chapter focuses on

- Political developments in the Gilded Age.
- Problems, both real and perceived, affecting American farmers.
- The causes of the agrarian revolt and the rise of the Populists.
- The significant election of 1896.

THE *ESSENTIAL AMERICA* ON-LINE TUTOR

www.wwnorton.com/eamerica/ch21

- **Topic: The populist movement**
  www.wwnorton.com/eamerica/ch21/topic.htm

  Agrarian unrest in nineteenth-century America culminated with the populist movement of the 1890s. Using speeches, party platforms, photographs, cartoons, and historical analyses, consider the significance of the populist movement. What causes did the populists champion?

- **Chapter review: On-line quiz and chapter summary**
  www.wwnorton.com/eamerica/ch21/review.htm

- **Chapter resources: Multimedia index**
  www.wwnorton.com/eamerica/ch21/media.htm

In 1873 writers Mark Twain and Charles Dudley Warner created an enduring label for the post–Civil War era when they collaborated on a novel entitled *The Gilded Age.* The book depicted an era of widespread political corruption, personal greed, and social vulgarity. Perspectives on the times would eventually change, but generations of political scientists and historians have since used the label "Gilded Age" to characterize the last third of the nineteenth century.

Paradoxical Politics

After Reconstruction ended in 1877, political inertia reigned on the national level. A fairly even division between Republicans and Democrats created a sense of stalemate. Neither party was willing to take bold initiatives because its relative strength was so precarious. Many observers then and since considered this a time of political mediocrity in which the major parties refused to confront "real issues" such as the runaway growth of an unregulated economy and its attendant social injustices.

Voters of the time nonetheless thought politics was very important. Turnout during the Gilded Age was commonly about 70 to 80 percent, even in the South, where the disenfranchisement of blacks was not yet complete. (By contrast, the turnout for the 1996 presidential election was barely 50 percent.) The paradox of such high voter participation in the face of the inertia at the national political level raises an obvious question: How was it that leaders who failed to address the "real issues" of the day presided over the most highly organized and politically active electorate in American history?

The answer is partly that the politicians and the voters believed that they *were* dealing with crucial issues: the tariff, monopolies, pensions for veterans, the currency, civil service reform, and immigration. But the answer also reflects the extreme partisanship of the times and the essentially local nature of political culture during the Gilded Age. While people expected little from their national government, they demanded much from their local and state officials.

Partisan Politics

Most Americans after the Civil War were intensely loyal to one of the two major parties, Democratic or Republican. The political parties gave people a focal point of activity and loyalty in an unstable world. Local party officials took care of those who voted their way, and they distributed appointive public offices and other favors to party loyalists. These "city machines" used patronage and favoritism to get and keep the loyalty of business supporters, while providing jobs, food, or fuel to working-class voters who had fallen on hard times.

The political parties were also a key source of recreation and entertainment for voters. The party faithful eagerly took part in rallies and picnics. In a time before movies and television, election campaigns gave citizens a chance to share rituals, express their loyalties, and carouse. In urban neighborhoods throughout the country, saloons served more than alcohol; they also provided gathering places for local Democratic groups.

Party loyalties and voter turnout in the late nineteenth century reflected religious and ethnic divisions as well as geographic differences. The Republican party attracted mainly Protestants of British descent. Their native seat was New England, and their other strongholds were New York and the upper Middle West. Heirs to the abolitionist tradition, Republicans drew to their ranks a host of reformers and moralists, spiritual descendants of the perfectionists who championed the revivals and the reform movements of the antebellum years. The party's heritage of anti-Catholic nativism would also make a comeback in the 1880s. And the

Republicans, the party of Lincoln, could also rely on the votes of blacks and Union veterans of the Civil War.

The Democrats, by contrast, tended to be a more diverse, often unruly coalition embracing southern whites, immigrants and Catholics of any origin, Jews, freethinkers, skeptics, and all those repelled by the "party of morality." As one Chicago Democrat explained, "A Republican is a man who wants you t' go t' church every Sunday. A Democrat says if a man wants to have a glass of beer on Sunday he can have it."

In the Midwest, especially, tensions over religious and social issues, such as Sunday closing laws and liquor prohibition, created intense political allegiances. Republicans pressed nativist causes, calling for restrictions on immigration and on the employment of foreigners, and greater emphasis on the teaching of the "American" language in the schools. Prohibitionism revived along with nativism in the 1880s.

Political Stalemate at the National Level

Between 1869 and 1913, from the presidencies of Ulysses S. Grant to William Howard Taft, Republicans monopolized the White House except during the two nonconsecutive terms of Grover Cleveland. Republican domination, however, was more apparent than real. Between 1872 and 1896, no president won a majority of the popular vote. In each of those presidential elections, sixteen states invariably voted Republican and fourteen voted Democratic, leaving a pivotal six states whose results usually determined the victor. The important swing-vote role that New York and Ohio played helps explain the election of seven presidents from these states from 1870 to 1912.

Deferential presidents also contributed to the political stalemate. No chief executive between Lincoln and Theodore Roosevelt could be described as a "strong" president. None seriously challenged the prevailing view that Congress, not the White House, should formulate policy. Senator John Sherman of Ohio expressed the widely held notion that the legislative branch should take initiative in a republic: "The President should merely obey and enforce the law."

While Congress was evenly divided between representatives and senators from the two parties, Republicans controlled the Senate and Democrats controlled the House during most of the Gilded Age. Political stalemate thus led Congress to postpone making major decisions or launching new programs and to concentrate instead on partisan maneuvering over procedural issues. Only the tariff provoked clear-cut divisions between protectionist Republicans and low-tariff Democrats, but there were individual exceptions even on that. On the important questions of the currency, regulation of big business, farm problems, civil service reform, and immigration, the parties differed very little. As a result, they primarily became vehicles for seeking office and dispensing patronage in the form of government jobs and contracts.

State and Local Initiatives

Most of the significant political activity during the Gilded Age occurred at the state and local levels. Over 60 percent of the nation's spending and taxing were exercised by state and local authorities. Then, unlike today, three-fourths of all public employees worked for state and local governments.

It was state and local governments rather than the national government that first sought to curb the power of corporate interests. By the turn of the century, nearly every state had provided for the regulation of railroads, if not always effectively, and had moved to supervise banks and insurance companies. Between 1887 and 1897, the states and territories passed over 1,600 laws relating to conditions of work, which limited the hours of labor, provided special protection for women, limited or forbade child labor, required regular wage payments in cash, and called for factory inspections.

Initially, the courts upheld state and local laws regulating corporations, although conservative judges often limited the practical impact of such laws. In *Munn* v. *Illinois* (1877), the Supreme Court confirmed the right of state and local governments to regulate industry essential to the public welfare. In the 1880s, however, while the Court continued to oppose monopolies, it protected interstate corporations from local regulation that might interfere with the conduct of business. Thus in *Stone* v. *Farmers Loan and Trust Company* (1886) the Court recognized the authority of Mississippi to regulate railroad rates, but it also declared that there might be cases in which the Court could review the rates: "Under pretense of regulating fares and freights, the State cannot require a railroad corporation to carry persons or property without reward." And in *Wabash* v. *Illinois* (1886), the Court ruled that a state could not regulate the rates of railroads engaged in interstate commerce.

In 1890, in *Chicago, Milwaukee and St. Paul Railway Company* v. *Minnesota,* the justices declared unconstitutional a state law that forbade judicial review of rates set by a railroad commission. This was a direct reversal of the ruling in *Munn* v. *Illinois* that regulation was a legislative prerogative. Now fears that regulation might deprive a company of its property took precedence over protection of the public welfare. It remained only for the Court to overturn rates set directly by a state legislature. That it did when it struck down a Nebraska law in *Smyth* v. *Ames* in 1898, on the grounds that the state had set the rates so low as to be unreasonable.

In thwarting new attempts by states to regulate corporations, the Supreme Court used a revised interpretation of the Fourteenth Amendment clauses forbidding the states to "deprive any person of life, liberty or property without due process of law" or to deny any person the "equal protection of the law." The justices reasoned that corporations could be considered "artificial persons" with the right to own property, buy and sell, sue and be sued like natural persons. The Court also moved away from the old view that "due process" referred only to correct procedures and turned toward a doctrine of "substantive due process," which meant that the courts could review the substance of a law and decide if the law was so extreme that it deprived the person (here, the corporation) of property to an unreasonable degree.

States attempted to regulate how corporations treated their workers, but their efforts were also overturned by the courts. The Supreme Court said that in going to work for a corporation, an employee contracted to work even under the most oppressive conditions without interference from the state. Using this reasoning, the Pennsylvania Supreme Court in 1886 overturned a state law protecting workers against payment in commodities instead of in cash.

Corruption and Reform

While the courts were overturning state regulation of corporations, business and political leaders were forging a close alliance. Congressman James G. Blaine of Maine, for example, and many of his supporters, saw nothing wrong in his accepting stock certificates from an Arkansas railroad after helping it win a land grant from Congress. Railroad passes, free entertainment, and a host of other favors were freely provided politicians, editors, and other leaders in positions to influence public opinion or affect legislation.

On the local level, the exchange of favors for votes was not perceived as improper. People voted for their party because of their intense partisan loyalty. Although they looked to their parties to supply them with favors, entertainment, and even jobs, they did not see themselves as "selling their

The Bosses of the Senate. This 1889 cartoon bitingly portrays the alliance between big business and politics in this period.

votes." This was simply the practice of patronage democracy, in which local party officials awarded party loyalists with contracts and public jobs such as heads of the customs houses and post offices.

Both Republican and Democratic leaders squabbled over the "spoils" of office. These were the appointive offices that were available on both the local and national levels. After each election, it was expected that the victorious party would throw out the appointees from the defeated party and appoint their own supporters in their stead. Each party had its share of corrupt officials willing to buy and sell government appointments or congressional votes, yet each also witnessed the emergence of factions promoting honesty in government. This struggle for clean government soon became one of the foremost issues of the day.

Hayes and Civil Service Reform

Republican Rutherford B. Hayes brought to the White House in 1877 a sharp contrast to the graft and corruption of the Grant administration. The son of an Ohio farmer, Hayes was wounded four times in the Civil War and was promoted to major-general. Elected governor of Ohio in 1867, he served three terms. Honest and respectable, competent and dignified, he lived in a modest style with his wife, who was nicknamed "Lemonade Lucy" because of her refusal to serve alcohol at White House functions.

Yet Hayes's tenure as president suffered from continuing suspicions about his disputed victory in the 1876–1877 election. Snide references to him as "His Fraudulence" denied him any chance at a second term, which he renounced from the beginning. Hayes's own party was split between so-called Stalwarts and Half-Breeds, led respectively by Senators Roscoe Conkling of New York and James G. Blaine of Maine. The difference between these Republican factions was murkier than that between the parties. The Stalwarts generally supported Grant, a Radical southern policy, and the spoils system. The Half-Breeds took a contrary view on the first two and even vaguely supported civil service reform.

For the most part, the Stalwart and Half-Breed factions were loose alliances designed to advance the careers of Conkling and Blaine. For his part, Hayes aligned himself with the growing public discontent over the corruption that had prevailed under Grant. In promoting the cause of civil service reform, he issued an Executive Order in 1877 declaring that those already in office would be dismissed only for the good of the government and not for political reasons. His cabinet tried to carry out the new policy. Secretary of the Treasury John Sherman revealed that both customs collector Chester A. Arthur and naval officer Alonzo Cornell were guilty of "laxity" and of using the New York Customs House for political management on behalf of Conkling's organization. Hayes removed Arthur and Cornell, thereby winning Conkling's lasting hatred.

For all his efforts to clean house, Hayes retained a limited vision of government's role. On the economic issues of the day he held to a conservative line that would guide his successors for the rest of the century. His solution to labor troubles, demonstrated during the Great Railroad Strike of 1877, was to send in troops and break the strike. A financial conservative, he denied the demands of farmers and debtors for an expansion of the currency by vetoing the Bland-Allison Act, which would have expanded silver currency. The bill was passed when Congress overrode Hayes's veto.

Garfield and Arthur

With Hayes unavailable for a second term, the Republicans were forced to look elsewhere in 1880. The Stalwarts, led by Conkling, brought Grant forward for a third time. For two days the Republican convention in Chicago was deadlocked, with Grant holding a slight lead over Blaine and John Sherman. On the thirty-fifth ballot, Wisconsin suddenly switched sixteen votes to former House Speaker (now Senator-elect) James A. Garfield, Sherman's campaign manager. Garfield rose to protest but was ruled out of order, and on the next ballot the convention stampeded to the dark-horse candidate. As a sop to the Stalwarts, the convention tapped Chester A. Arthur for vice-president.

The Democrats named Winfield Scott Hancock, a Union commander at Gettysburg, to counterbalance the Republicans' Brigadier-General Garfield. The election turned out to be the closest of the century. Garfield eked out a plurality of only 39,000 votes with 48.5 percent of the vote, but with a comfortable margin of 214 to 155 in the electoral college.

On July 2, 1881, President Garfield was leaving on a vacation when, as he walked through the Washington, D.C., rail station, a deranged office seeker named Charles Guiteau shot him in the back. "I am a Stalwart," Guiteau shouted to the arresting officers. "Arthur is now President of the United States." Guiteau's announcement would prove crippling to the Stalwarts and his attack fatal to Garfield, who died after a two-month struggle. Garfield had been president for a little over six months.

Chester Arthur, one of the chief henchmen of Stalwart leader Roscoe Conkling, was now president. Little in Arthur's past suggested that he would rise above spoils politics. But Arthur demonstrated surprising leadership qualities as president. He distanced himself from Conkling and the Stalwarts. As Arthur noted, "For the vice-presidency I was indebted to Mr. Conkling, but for the presidency of the United States my debt is to the Almighty."

Most startling of all was Arthur's emergence as something of a civil service and tariff reformer. He supported the reform efforts of "Gentleman George" Pendleton, Democratic senator from Ohio, whose Pendleton Civil Service Act, finally passed in 1883, set up a three-member Civil Service Commission independent from the regular cabinet departments, the first such federal agency established on a permanent basis. Under the act, about 14 percent of all government jobs would be filled on the basis of competitive examinations rather than political connections.

Meanwhile the tariff continued to be the most controversial national political issue. The high protective tariff, a heritage of the Civil War, had by the early 1880s raised federal revenues to the point that the government actually enjoyed a surplus that drew money into the Treasury and out of circulation, thus impeding economic growth. Some argued that lower tariff rates would reduce prices and the cost of living, and at the same time leave more money in circulation. In 1882 Arthur named a special commission to study the problem. The Tariff Commission recommended a 20 to 25 percent rate reduction, which gained Arthur's support, but Congress's effort to enact the proposal produced a raft of special-interest changes. The result was the "Mongrel Tariff" of 1883, so called because of its diverse percentages for different commodities. Overall the tariff provided for a slight rate reduction, but it actually raised the duty on some articles.

Scurrilous Campaign

As the 1884 election neared, Arthur's record might have commended him to the voters, but it did not please the leaders of his party. The Republicans dumped Arthur and turned to the majestic Senator James G. Blaine of Maine, leader of the Half-Breeds.

During the campaign, letters surfaced with disclosures of corrupt dealings embarrassing to Blaine. For the reform element of the Republican party, this was too much, and many bolted the ticket. Party regulars scorned the idealists, and one editor jokingly tagged them Mugwumps, after an Algonquian word meaning a great chieftain.

The rise of the Mugwumps influenced the Democrats to nominate Stephen Grover Cleveland as a reform candidate. Elected mayor of Buffalo in 1881, Cleveland first attracted national attention for effectively battling graft and corruption in that city. In 1882 the Democrats elected him as governor of New York, and he continued to build a reform record by fighting New York's corrupt Tammany Hall organization. A stocky 250-pound man with a droopy mustache, Cleveland possessed little charisma, but he impressed the public with his stubborn integrity. One supporter said: "We love him for the enemies he has made."

Then a scandal erupted when the *Buffalo Evening Telegraph* revealed that bachelor Cleveland had had an affair during the early 1870s with an attractive Buffalo widow, Maria Halpin. Mrs. Halpin had named Cleveland as the father of a son born to her in 1874. Cleveland took responsibility and provided financial help when the child was placed in an orphanage. When supporters asked Cleveland what to say about the affair, he answered with typical candor: "Tell the truth."

Another Voice for Cleveland. Cleveland's acknowledgment of an illegitimate child was one of many personal issues brought to light in the 1884 campaign.

The respective personal escapades of Blaine and Cleveland provided the 1884 campaign with some of the most colorful battle cries in American political history. "Blaine, Blaine, James G. Blaine, the continental liar from the state of Maine," Democrats chanted. Republicans countered with "Ma, ma, where's my pa? Gone to the White House, ha, ha, ha!"

Near the end of the campaign, Blaine and his supporters committed two fateful blunders. The first occurred when Blaine attended a lavish fund-raising dinner with a clutch of millionaire bigwigs. Cartoons and accounts of this "Belshazzar's Feast" festooned the opposition press for days. The second fiasco cost Blaine much of the Irish vote when a Protestant minister visiting Republican headquarters in New York insolently referred to the Democrats as the party of "rum, Romanism, and rebellion." Democrats spread word that he had let the insult pass, even that he had made it himself.

The two incidents may have tipped the election. The electoral vote in Cleveland's favor stood at 219 to 182, although the popular vote ran far closer; Cleveland's plurality was fewer than 30,000 votes.

Cleveland and the Special Interests

For all of Cleveland's hostility to the spoils system and politics as usual, he represented no sharp break with the conservative policies of his Republican predecessors, except in opposing governmental favors to business. He held to a strictly limited view of government's role in both economic and social matters.

Despite his strong convictions, Cleveland had a mixed record on the civil service. Before his inauguration he had repeated his support for the Pendleton Act, and he pledged not to remove able government workers on partisan grounds. But party pressures gradually forced Cleveland's hand. When he left office about two-thirds of the federal officeholders were Democrats, but at the same time Cleveland had almost doubled the number of jobs subject to civil service regulation. He thereby satisfied neither Mugwumps nor spoilsmen; indeed, he managed to antagonize both.

Cleveland incurred the wrath of many Union military veterans by his firm stand against expanded pensions. Congress had passed the first Civil War pension law in 1862 to provide for Union veterans disabled in service and for the widows, orphans, and dependents of veterans. By 1882 veterans were trying to get pensions paid for any disability, no matter how it was incurred. Insofar as time permitted, Cleveland examined such bills and vetoed the dubious ones. Although he signed more than any of his predecessors, he also vetoed more. The issue climaxed in 1887 when Cleveland vetoed a new Dependent Pension bill containing more liberal benefits and qualifications. Cleveland argued that it would become a refuge for frauds rather than a "roll of honor."

About the middle of his term, Cleveland advocated federal railroad regulation. Reacting to *Wabash Railroad* v. *Illinois* (1886), in which the Court had ruled that a state could not regulate rates on interstate traffic, Cleveland urged that since this "important field of control and regulation [has] thus been left entirely unoccupied," Congress should act.

It did, and in 1887 Cleveland signed into law an act creating the Interstate Commerce Commission (ICC), the first such independent federal regulatory commission. The law required that all freight and passenger railroad rates be "reasonable and just," and it empowered the ICC to prosecute violators. Railroads were also forbidden to grant secret rebates to preferred shippers, discriminate against persons, places, and commodities, or enter into pools (agreements to fix rates).

The Tariff Issue

Cleveland's most dramatic challenge to special interests focused on tariff reform. Why was the tariff such an important and controversial issue? By the late nineteenth century, many people charged that government policies had fostered big business at the expense of small producers and retailers. Among those policies was an excessively high tariff. "The mother of all trusts is the tariff bill," proclaimed one business executive. By shielding American manufacturers from foreign competition, the tariff, critics argued, made it easier for them to combine into ever-larger entities. High tariff rates also enabled big corporations to restrict production and fix prices.

Cleveland agreed. Having decided that the tariff rates were too high and included many inequities, he devoted his entire annual message in 1887 to the subject. Cleveland noted that tariff revenues had bolstered the federal surplus, making the Treasury "a hoarding place for money needlessly withdrawn from trade and the people's use." The high tariff pushed up prices for everybody and benefited only a few politically powerful manufacturing interests.

The House soon passed a bill calling for modest tariff reductions from an average level of about 47 percent of the value of imported goods to about 40 percent. But the bill stalled in the Republican Senate and finally died a lingering death in committee. If Cleveland's tariff proposal accomplished his purpose of drawing party lines more firmly, it also confirmed the fears of his advisers. The election of 1888 for the first time in years highlighted a sharp difference between the major parties on an issue of substance.

The Election of 1888

Cleveland was the nominee of his party, whose platform endorsed "the views expressed by the President in his last message to Congress." The Republicans turned to the obscure Benjamin Harrison. Grandson of a former president, Harrison was a flourishing lawyer in Indiana, which was a pivotal state. He also boasted a good war record, and there was little in his political record to offend any voter. The Republican platform accepted Cleveland's challenge to make the protective tariff the chief issue, as well as promising generous pensions to veterans.

Grover Cleveland made the issue of tariff reform central to the politics of the late 1880s.

On the eve of the election, Cleveland suffered a devastating blow from a dirty campaign trick. Posing as an English immigrant and using the false name Charles F. Murchison, a California Republican had written British minister Sir Lionel Sackville-West and asked his advice on how to vote. Sackville-West hinted in reply that he should vote for Cleveland. Published two weeks before the election, the "Murchison letter" aroused a storm of protest against foreign intervention and further linked Cleveland to British free-traders.

Still, the outcome in 1888 was very close. Cleveland won the popular vote by 5,538,000 to 5,447,000, but Harrison, with the key states of Indiana and New York on his side, carried the electoral college 233 to 168. For the first time since John Quincy Adams's election in 1824, the country had not only a minority president, but one who lacked even a plurality in the popular vote.

Republican Reform under Harrison

As president, Benjamin Harrison became a competent and earnest figurehead, overshadowed by his secretary of state, James G. Blaine. His first step was to reward those responsible for his victory. He owed a heavy debt to the old-soldier vote, which he discharged by naming the head of the veterans' group to the office of pension commissioner. The new commissioner proceeded to approve pensions with such abandon that the secretary of the interior removed him six months and several million dollars later. In 1890 Congress passed, and Harrison signed, the Dependent Pension Act, substantially the same measure that Cleveland had vetoed three years earlier. Any veteran unable to make a living by manual labor for whatever reason was granted a monthly pension. The pension rolls almost doubled by 1893.

During the first two years of Harrison's term, the Republicans controlled the presidency and both houses of Congress for the only time in the twenty years between 1875 and 1895. They made the most of their clout. In 1890, several significant pieces of legislation made their way to the White House for Harrison's signature. In addition to the Dependent Pension Act, Congress and the president approved the Sherman Anti-Trust Act, the Sherman Silver Purchase Act, the McKinley Tariff, and the admission of Idaho and Wyoming as new states, following admission of the Dakotas, Montana, and Washington in 1889.

Both parties had pledged themselves to address the growing power of trusts and monopolies. The Sherman Anti-Trust Act, named for Senator John Sherman, chairman of the committee that drafted it, forbade contracts, combinations, or conspiracies in restraint of trade or in the effort to establish monopolies in interstate or foreign commerce. Yet during the next decade, successive administrations expended little effort on the act's enforcement. From 1890 to 1901, the Justice Department instituted only eighteen antitrust suits, and four of those were against labor unions.

Congress meanwhile debated currency legislation against the backdrop of growing distress in the farm regions of the West and South. Hard-pressed farmers were agitating for an increased coinage of silver to inflate the currency supply, which would raise commodity prices, making it easier for farmers to earn the money with which to pay their debts. The pro-silver forces were also strengthened, especially in the Senate, by members from those new western states that had silver-mining interests. Congress thus passed the Sherman Silver Purchase Act of 1890, replacing the Bland-Allison Act of 1878. It required the Treasury to purchase 4.5 million ounces of silver each month and to issue in payment Treasury notes redeemable in either gold or silver. But the act failed to satisfy the demands of the silverites. Although it doubled the amount of silver purchased, that was still too little to have much inflationary impact on the economy. The stage was thus set for the currency issue to eclipse all others during the financial panic that swept the country three years later.

Republicans took their victory over Cleveland as a mandate not just to maintain the protective tariff but to raise it. Piloted through by the prominent Ohio senator William McKinley, the McKinley Tariff of 1890 raised duties on manufactured goods to an average of about 49.5 percent, the highest to that time.

The absence of a public consensus for higher tariffs became clearly visible in the 1890 midterm elections. The voters repudiated the Republican-sponsored McKinley Tariff with a landslide of Democratic votes. In the new House, Democrats outnumbered Republicans almost three to one; in the Senate, the Republican majority was reduced to eight. One of the election casualties was McKinley himself. But there was more to the election than the tariff. Voters also reacted against the baldly partisan measures of the Harrison administration and against its extravagant expenditures on military pensions and other programs.

The large Democratic vote in 1890 may have also been a reaction to Republican efforts on a local level to legislate against alcohol and government-supported Catholic (parochial) schools. In many districts with a high percentage of Catholic constituents, local Democratic legislators had defied the principle of separation of church and state by allocating tax revenues to help support parochial schools. In 1889 Wisconsin Republicans pushed through a law that struck at parochial schools, and turned large numbers of outraged Catholic immigrants into Democratic activists. Between 1880 and 1890, sixteen out of twenty-one states outside the South held referenda on constitutional prohibition of alcoholic beverages (although only six states actually voted for prohibition). With this assault on drinking, Republicans were playing a losing game, arousing wets (anti-prohibitionists) on the Democratic side. In 1890 the Democrats swept state after state.

The Farm Problem and Agrarian Protest Movements

The 1890 election returns reflected more than a reaction against the Republican tariff, patronage politics, extravagant spending, and attempts to impose moral regulations. The returns revealed a deep-seated unrest in the farming communities of the South and West. As the Democrats took power, the beginnings of an economic crisis appeared on the horizon. Farmers' debts mounted as crop prices plummeted.

Disgruntled farmers began to organize for political action, but they faced many obstacles. The deeply ingrained agrarian tradition of rugged individualism and physical isolation impeded communication and organization. American farmers had long prided themselves on their self-reliance, and many balked at sacrificing their independence for collective action. Another hurdle was the fact that after the Civil War agricultural interests had diverged and in some cases conflicted with one another. In the Great Plains, for example, the railroads were the largest landowners. In addition, there were large absentee landowners, some foreign, who leased out vast tracts of land. There were also huge "bonanza" farms that employed hundreds of seasonal workers. Yet the majority of farmers were moderate-size landowners, small land speculators, small landowners, tenant farmers, and hourly wage workers. It was the middle-size landowners who experienced rapidly rising land values and rising indebtedness. Such farmers were concerned with land values and crop prices, while tenants or sharecroppers or farm hands supported land distribution schemes that would give them access to their own land.

Given such a diversity of interests, farm activists discovered that it was often difficult to develop and maintain a cohesive organization. Yet, for all the difficulties, they persevered, and the results were dramatic, if not completely successful. Thus, for example, the deep-seated unrest in the farming communities of the South and West began to find voice in the Granger movement, the Alliance movement, and in the new People's party—agrarian movements of considerable political and social significance.

Economic Conditions

Farmers in the South and Midwest had suffered from a long-term decline in commodity prices from 1870 to 1898, caused by increases in production and growing international competition for world markets. Considerations of such abstract economic forces, however, puzzled many farmers. How could one speak of overproduction when so many remained in need? Instead, many assumed, there must be a screw loose somewhere in the system.

The railroads and the processors and bankers who handled the farmers' products were seen as the villains. Farmers resented the high railroad rates that prevailed in farm regions with no alternative forms of transportation. Individual farmers could not get the rebates the industrial shippers could extract from railroads, nor could they exert the political influence wielded by the railroad lobbies. In other ways farmers found themselves with little bargaining power either as buyers or sellers. When they went to sell wheat or cotton, the buyer set the price; when they went to buy a plow, the seller set the price.

High tariffs operated to the farmers' disadvantage because they protected manufacturers against foreign competition, allowing them to raise the prices of factory goods on which farmers depended. Farmers, however, had to sell their wheat, cotton, and other staples in foreign markets, where competition lowered prices. Tariffs inflicted a double blow on farmers because insofar as they hampered imports, they indirectly hampered exports by making it harder for foreign buyers to get the necessary American currency or exchange to purchase American crops.

Debt, too, had been a perennial agricultural problem. After the Civil War, farmers grew ever more enmeshed in debt: western farmers incurred mortgages to cover the costs of land and machinery, while southern farmers were forced to use their crops as collateral to gain credit from local merchants. As commodity prices dropped, the debt burden grew because farmers had to cultivate more wheat or cotton to raise the same amount of money. By growing more, they furthered the vicious cycle of surpluses and price declines.

The Granger Movement

When the Department of Agriculture sent Oliver H. Kelley, a former Minnesota farmer and post office clerk, on a tour of the South in 1866, it was the farmers' isolation that most impressed him. Resolving to do something about it, Kelley in 1867 founded the Patrons of Husbandry, better known as the Grange (an old word for granary). In the next few years, the Grange mushroomed, reaching a membership as high as 1.5 million by 1874. While the Grange started out as a social and educational response to the isolation of farm folk, as it grew it began to promote farmer-owned cooperatives for the buying and selling of goods. Their ideal was to free farmers from their dependence on the conventional marketplace.

The Grange soon became indirectly involved in politics through independent third parties, especially in the Midwest during the early 1870s. The Grangers' chief political goal was state regulation of the rates charged by railroads and crop warehouses. In five states they brought about the passage of "Granger Laws." In a key case involving warehouse regulation, *Munn* v. *Illinois* (1877), the Supreme Court affirmed that the state under its "police powers" had the right to regulate property that had a direct public interest.

The Granger cooperatives gradually declined (but never vanished) as members' energies were drawn off into political action. In 1875, activists formed the Greenback party, which favored expansion of the currency with more paper money. In the 1878 midterm elections, it polled over 1 million voters and elected fifteen congressmen. But in 1880 the party's fortunes declined, and it disintegrated after 1884.

Farmers' Alliances

As the Grange lost energy, other farm organizations grew in size and significance: the Farmers' Alliances. Like the Grange, Alliances offered social and recreational opportunities, but they also emphasized political action. Farmers throughout the South and Midwest, where tenancy rates were highest, rushed to join the Alliance movement to seek relief from the hardships created by chronic indebtedness, declining prices, and devastating droughts. Unlike the Grange, which was a national organization and tended to attract larger and more prosperous farmers, the Alliance was a grassroots local organization representing marginal farmers.

The Alliance movement swept the cotton belt and established strong positions in Kansas and the Dakotas. In 1886, the Texas Alliance responded to the appeals of black farmers and organized the Colored Alliance. The white leadership endorsed this development because the Colored Alliance stressed that its objective was economic justice, not social equality. By 1890, the Alliance movement had members from New York to California numbering about 1.5 million, and the Colored Farmers' Alliance claimed over 1 million members.

The sense of community provided by the Alliance was a powerful attraction for many isolated, struggling farmers and their families. It welcomed rural women and men over sixteen years old who displayed a "good moral character," believed in God, and demonstrated "industrious habits." One North Carolina woman expressed her appreciation for the "grand opportunities" the Alliance provided women to emerge from traditional domesticity. "Drudgery, fashion, and gossip," she declared, "are no longer the bounds of woman's sphere." The number of women in the Alliance movement grew rapidly, and many assumed key leadership roles.

"I Feed you All," a poster showing the farmer at the center of society, first published in *Prairie Farmer* in 1869.

Farm Politics

In Texas, in 1886, a devastating drought brought matters to a head. When President Grover Cleveland vetoed a bill to aid drought-stricken Texas farmers, Alliance leaders resolved to challenge the Democratic party at the polls. Although conservative members whose primary allegiance was to the Democratic party left the movement, many were ready to carry out the fight both locally and nationally.

In 1887 Charles W. Macune, the new Alliance president, resolved to exert pressure on Congress to assist southern farmers. In addition, he proposed that Texas farmers create their own Alliance Exchange in an effort to free themselves from their dependence on processors and banks. Members of the Exchange would sign joint notes, borrow money from banks, and purchase their goods and supplies from a new corporation created by the Alliance in Dallas. The Exchange would also build its own warehouses to store and market the crops of members. While their crops were being stored, member farmers could obtain credit from the warehouse cooperative so they could buy goods and supplies.

This grand "cooperative" scheme collapsed when the Texas banks refused to accept the joint notes from Alliance members.

This led Macune and others to focus their energies on what Macune called a "subtreasury plan." Under this plan, farmers would be able to store their crops in new government warehouses and obtain government loans for up to 80 percent of their crops' value at 1 percent interest. Besides providing immediate credit, the plan would allow the farmer the leeway to hold a crop for a better price later, since he would not have to sell it immediately at harvest time to pay off debts. The plan would also promote inflation because these loans to farmers would be made in new legal-tender notes.

The subtreasury plan went before Congress in 1890 but was never adopted. Its defeat convinced many farm leaders that they needed political power to secure railroad regulation, currency inflation, state departments of agriculture, antitrust laws, and farm credit.

In the West, where hard times had descended after the blizzards of 1887, farmers were ready for third-party action. In the South, however, white Alliance members hesitated to bolt the Democratic party, seeking instead to control it. Both approaches gained startling success. Independent parties under various names upset the political balance in western states, almost electing a governor under the banner of the People's party (also known as the Populist party) in Kansas (a Populist was elected governor in 1892) and taking control of one house of the legislature there and both houses in Nebraska. In South Dakota and Minnesota, Populists gained a balance of power in the legislatures, while Kansas and South Dakota sent Populists to the Senate.

Mary Elizabeth Lease, 1890.

The farm movement produced colorful leaders, especially in Kansas, where Mary Elizabeth Lease advised farmers "to raise less corn and more hell." Born in Pennsylvania to parents who were political exiles from Ireland, she eventually migrated to Kansas, taught school, raised a family, and finally failed at farming in the mid-1880s. She then studied law for a time, "pinning sheets of notes above her wash tub," and through strenous effort became one of the state's first female lawyers. She also spoke out on behalf of various causes ranging from Irish nationalism to temperance to women's suffrage. By the end of the 1880s, Lease had joined the Alliance as well as the Knights of Labor, and she soon applied her gifts as a fiery speaker to the cause of free silver.

In the South the Alliance won equal if not greater success by forcing the Democrats to nominate candidates pledged to their program. In 1890 the southern states elected four pro-Alliance governors, seven pro-Alliance legislatures, forty-four pro-Alliance congressmen, and several senators. Among the most respected of the southern Alliance leaders was Tom Watson of Georgia. The son of prosperous slaveholders who lost everything during the Civil War, he became a successful lawyer and charismatic orator on behalf of the Alliance cause. He took the lead in appealing to black tenants and sharecroppers to join with their white counterparts in ousting the Bourbon white political elite. "You are kept apart," he told black and white farmers, "that you may be separately fleeced of your earnings."

The Populist Party and the Election of 1892

As economic conditions worsened, many insurgents began promoting the formation of a new national political party. In 1891 delegates from farm, labor, and reform organizations met in Cincinnati to discuss the creation of a People's party. In 1892 a larger meeting at St. Louis proposed a national convention of the People's party at Omaha to adopt a platform and choose national candidates.

The platform demanded the subtreasury plan, free and unlimited coinage of silver, an increase in the amount of money in circulation, and graduated income tax rates. The government should nationalize the railroads, and the telephone and telegraph systems as well. It should also reclaim from railroads and other corporations lands "in excess of their actual needs," and forbid land ownership by illegal aliens. Finally, the platform endorsed the eight-hour work-day and immigration restriction laws, taking these positions to win support from the urban workers, whom Populists looked upon as fellow "producers."

The party's platform turned out to be more exciting than its candidate, Iowa's James B. Weaver. Though an able, prudent man, Weaver carried the stigma of his defeat on the Greenback ticket twelve years before. To balance Weaver, a former Union general, the party named a former Confederate general for vice-president.

The Populist party was the startling new feature of the 1892 campaign. The major parties renominated Grover Cleveland and Benjamin Harrison. The tariff remained the chief issue between them. The outcome, however, was different. Both major candidates polled over 5 million votes, but Cleveland carried a plurality of the popular votes and a majority of the electoral college. Weaver gained over 1 million votes, which was 10 percent of the total vote, and carried Colorado, Kansas, Nevada, and Idaho, for a total of twenty-two electoral votes.

The Economy and the Silver Solution

While the farmers were funneling their discontent into politics and businessmen were consolidating their holdings, a fundamental weakness in the economy prompted a major economic collapse.

An Inadequate Currency

The nation's money supply in the late nineteenth century lacked the flexibility to grow along with America's expanding economy. From 1865 to 1890, the amount of currency in circulation per capita decreased about 10 percent. Such currency deflation increased the cost of borrowing money, as a tight money supply caused bankers to hike interest rates on loans.

Metallic currency dated from the Mint Act of 1792, which authorized free and unlimited coinage of silver and gold at a ratio of 15 to 1. The ratio meant that the amount of precious metal in a silver dollar weighed fifteen times as much as that in a gold dollar. This reflected the relative values of gold and silver at the time. The phrase "free and unlimited coinage" simply meant that owners of precious metals could have any quantity of their gold or silver coined free, except for a nominal fee to cover costs.

A fixed ratio of values, however, could not reflect fluctuations in the relative market value of the metals. When gold rose to a market value higher than that reflected in the official ratio, owners ceased to present it for coinage. The country was actually on a silver standard until 1837, when Congress changed the ratio to 16 to 1, which soon reversed the situation. Silver became more valuable in the open market than in coinage, and the country drifted to a gold standard. This state of affairs prevailed until 1873, when Congress passed a general revision of the coinage laws and dropped the then-unused provision for the coinage of silver.

This occurred, however, just when silver production began to increase, reducing its market value through the growth in supply. Under the old laws, this would have induced owners of silver to present it at the mint for coinage. Soon advocates of currency inflation began to denounce the "crime of '73," the removal of silver coinage, which they had scarcely noticed at the time. Gradually suspicion grew that bankers and merchants had conspired in 1873 to ensure a scarcity of money. But the silverites had little more legislative success than the advocates of greenback inflation. The Bland-Allison Act of 1878 and the Sherman Silver Purchase Act of 1890 provided for some silver coinage, but too little in each case to offset the overall contraction of the currency.

The Depression of 1893

Just before Cleveland started his second term, one of the most devastating business panics in history erupted when the Philadelphia and Reading Railroad declared bankruptcy and set off a panic on Wall Street. By the fall of 1893 over six hundred banks had closed. By 1894 the economy had reached bottom. That year some 750,000 workers went out on strike; millions found themselves unemployed; railroad construction workers, laid off in the West, began tramping east and talked of marching on Washington.

Few of them made it to the capital. One group that did was "Coxey's Army," led by Jacob S. Coxey, a wealthy Ohio quarry owner turned Populist who demanded that the federal government provide unemployed people with meaningful work. Coxey, his wife, and their son, Legal Tender Coxey, rode in a carriage ahead of some 400 hardy protesters who finally straggled into Washington. There Coxey was arrested for walking on the grass. Although his ragtag army dispersed without any violent incidents, its march on Washington as well as the growing political strength of populism struck fear into the hearts of many Americans. Critics portrayed Populists as "hayseed socialists" whose election would endanger property rights.

The 1894 congressional elections took place amid this climate of anxiety. The elections were a severe setback for the Democrats, who paid politically for the economic downturn, and the Republicans were the chief beneficiaries. The Populists emerged with six senators and seven representatives. They had polled 1.5 million votes for their congressional candidates and expected the festering discontent to carry them to national power in 1896.

Silverites versus Goldbugs

The course of events, however, would dash that hope. One of the causes of the 1893 depression had been the failure of a major British bank, which led many British investors to unload their American holdings in return for gold. Soon after Cleveland's inauguration, the gold reserve fell below $100 million. To plug this drain on the Treasury, the president sought repeal of the Sherman Silver Purchase Act to stop the issuance of silver notes redeemable in gold. Cleveland won the act's repeal in 1893, but at the cost of irreparable division in his own party.

Western silver interests now escalated their demands for silver coinage, which presented a strategic dilemma for Populists: Should the party promote the long list of varied reforms it had originally advocated, or should it try to ride the silver issue into power? The latter seemed the practical choice. As a consequence, the Populist leaders decided, over the protest of more radical members, to hold their 1896 convention last, confident that the two major parties would at best straddle the silver issue and that the Populists would then reap a harvest of bolting silverite Republicans and Democrats.

The Election of 1896

Contrary to these expectations, the major parties took clear and opposing positions on the currency issue. The Republicans, as expected, chose William McKinley on a gold-standard platform. On the Democratic side, the pro-silver forces gathered to wrest control of the party from Cleveland and the fiscal conservatives.

In William Jennings Bryan, the silver Democrats found a crusading, charismatic leader. A fervent Baptist and advocate of the free coinage of silver, Bryan was a two-term congressman from Nebraska who had been defeated in the senatorial race in 1894. At the 1896 convention, Bryan delivered a galvanizing speech that had most of the 20,000 delegates on their feet and many in tears. Bryan spoke for free silver and the new West, for the "hardy pioneers" and against the "financial magnates" of the urban East. "Burn down your cities and leave our farms [untouched]," he predicted, "and your cities will spring up again as if by magic; but destroy our farms and the grass will grow in the streets of every city in the country." He then directly challenged Republicans as well as Cleveland and the gold Democrats with a compelling metaphor: "You shall not press down upon the brow of labor this crown of thorns. You shall not crucify mankind upon a cross of gold!"

The next day the heroic Bryan was nominated on the fifth ballot, and in the process the Democratic party was fractured beyond repair. Disappointed pro-gold Democrats walked out of the convention and nominated their own candidate, Alton Parker, who then announced: "Fellow Democrats, I will not consider it any great fault if you decide to cast your vote for William McKinley."

When the Populists met in St. Louis two weeks later, they faced an impossible choice. "If we fuse [with the Democrats]," one Populist admitted, "all the silver men we have will leave us for the more powerful Democrats." But if they named their own candidate, they would divide the silver vote with Bryan and give the election to McKinley. In the end the delegates backed Bryan but chose their own vice-presidential candidate, Georgia's Tom Watson, and invited the Democrats to drop their vice-presidential nominee—an action that Bryan refused to countenance.

The thirty-six-year-old Bryan launched a whirlwind campaign. He crisscrossed the country, exploiting his spellbinding eloquence and radiating honesty, sincerity, and energy. McKinley, meanwhile, conducted a "front-porch campaign," receiving selected delegations of supporters at his home in Canton, Ohio, and giving only prepared re-

Blowing Himself around the Country. An anti-Populist cartoon of 1896 depicting Bryan blowing hot air at his supporters.

sponses. His campaign manager, Mark Hanna, shrewdly portrayed Bryan as a radical whose "communistic spirit" would ruin the capitalist system.

By preying upon such fears, Hanna raised a huge campaign chest and financed an army of Republican speakers who stumped the country in support of McKinley. In the end, the Democratic-Populist-Silverite candidates were overwhelmed. McKinley won the popular vote by 7.1 million to 6.5 million and the electoral college vote by 271 to 176.

Bryan carried most of the West and the South below the border states but garnered little support in the cities east of the Mississippi and north of the Ohio and Potomac Rivers. Urban workers found it easier to identify with McKinley's program of economic development than with Bryan's free silver. Moreover, in the critical midwestern battleground, from Minnesota and Iowa eastward to Ohio, Bryan carried not a single state. Many ethnic voters, normally drawn to the Democrats, were repelled by Bryan's Baptist evangelical style. Farmers in the East and Midwest, moreover, were hurting less than those in the wheat and cotton belts. There was less tenancy and a greater diversity of crops in those farm regions, and the more successful farmers saw little attraction in agrarian radicalism.

A New Era

The election of 1896 was a climactic political struggle between rural and metropolitan America, and metropolitan America won. The values of urban-industrial America had taken firm hold of the political system. As its first important act the McKinley administration called a special session of Congress to raise the tariff again. The Dingley Tariff of 1897 became the highest to that time. By 1897, prosperity was returning, helped along by inflation of the currency, which bore out the arguments of greenbackers and silverites. But the inflation came, in one of history's many ironies, not from silver but from a new flood of gold onto the market and into the mints. During the 1880s and 1890s, new discoveries of gold in South Africa, Canada, and the Yukon led to spectacular new gold rushes, a return to the gold standard, and an end to the free silver movement. To compound the irony, most of the Populist platform, which seemed so radical in 1892, would nevertheless take effect within two decades.

Amid the new prosperity, the old issues of tariffs and currency policy would soon give way to international concerns. "The Spanish War finished us," said Populist Tom Watson. "The blare of the bugle drowned the voice of the Reformer."

PART 6

Modern America

The United States entered the twentieth century in a state of flux. Since the election of Thomas Jefferson in 1800, the country had seen itself relentlessly transformed. A rural, agrarian society largely detached from the concerns of international affairs had turned into a highly industrialized, urban culture with a growing involvement in world politics and commerce. In other words, the United States in 1900 was on the threshold of modernity.

The prospect of modernity both excited and scared Americans. Old truths and beliefs clashed with unsettling new scientific discoveries and social practices. People debated the legitimacy of Darwinism, the existence of God, the dangers of jazz, and the federal effort to prohibit alcoholic beverages. The automobile, airplane, and radio helped shrink the distances of time and space and accelerate a national consciousness. In the process, the United States began to emerge from its isolationist shell.

Noninvolvement in foreign wars and nonintervention in the internal affairs of foreign governments formed the pillars of American foreign policy until the end of the century. In the 1890s, however, expanding commercial interests around the world and imperialism among the great European powers, led a growing number of American expansionists to demand that the United States also adopt a global ambition and join in the hunt for new territories and markets. Such motives helped spark the Spanish-American War of 1898 and justify the resulting acquisition of American colonies outside the continental United States. Entangling alliances with European powers soon followed.

The outbreak of the Great War in Europe in 1914 posed an even greater challenge to American isolationism. The prospect of a German victory over the French and British threatened the European balance of power, which had long ensured U.S. security. By 1917, it appeared that Germany might emerge triumphant and begin to menace the Western Hemisphere. Woodrow Wilson's crusade to use American intervention in World War I to transform the world order in accordance with his idealistic principles severed American foreign policy from its isolationist moorings. It also spawned a prolonged debate about the role of the United States in world affairs, a debate that World War II would resolve on the side of internationalism.

At the same time that the United States was entering the world stage as a great military power, it was also becoming a great industrial power. Cities and factories sprouted across the landscape. An abundance of new jobs served as a magnet attracting millions of immigrants from every corner of the globe. The newcomers were not always welcomed, nor were they readily assimilated. Ethnic and racial strife, as well as labor agitation, increased at the turn of the century. In the midst of such social turmoil and unparalleled economic development, American reformers made their first sustained attempt to adapt their political and social institutions to the realities of the industrial age. The worst excesses and injustices of urban-industrial development—corporate monopolies, child labor, political corruption, hazardous working conditions, urban ghettos—were finally addressed in a comprehensive way. During the Progressive Era (1900–1917), local, state, and federal governments sought to rein in the excesses of industrial capitalism and develop a more rational and efficient public policy.

A conservative resurgence challenged the notion of the new regulatory state in the 1920s. Free enterprise and corporate capitalism witnessed a dramatic revival. But the stock market crash of 1929 helped propel the United States and many other nations into the worst economic downturn in history. The unprecedented severity of the Great Depression renewed public demands for federal government programs to protect the general welfare. "This nation asks for action," declared President Franklin D. Roosevelt in his 1933 inaugural address. The many New Deal initiatives instituted by Roosevelt and his administration created the framework for a welfare state that has since served as the basis for American public policy.

The New Deal helped put people back to work, but it did not end the Great Depression. It took a world war to restore full employment. Mobilizing the nation in support of World War II also accelerated the growth of the federal government. And the incredible scope of the war helped catapult the United States into a leadership role in world politics. The creation of a nuclear bomb to help end the war ushered in a new era of atomic diplomacy that held the fate of the world in the balance. For all of the new creature comforts associated with modern life, Americans in 1945 found themselves living amid an array of new anxieties.

ESSENTIAL THEMES

CRITICAL QUESTIONS

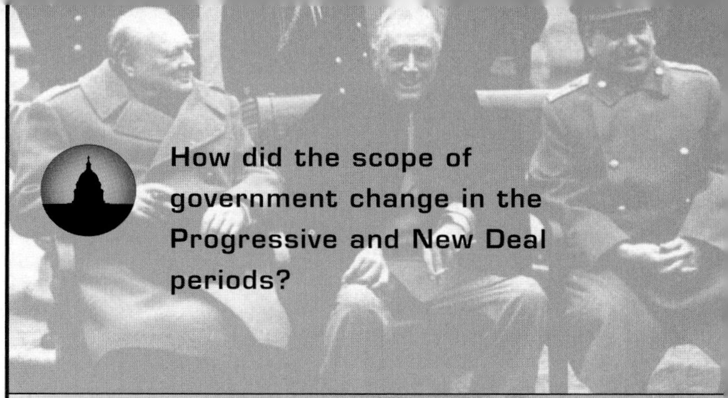

How did the scope of government change in the Progressive and New Deal periods?

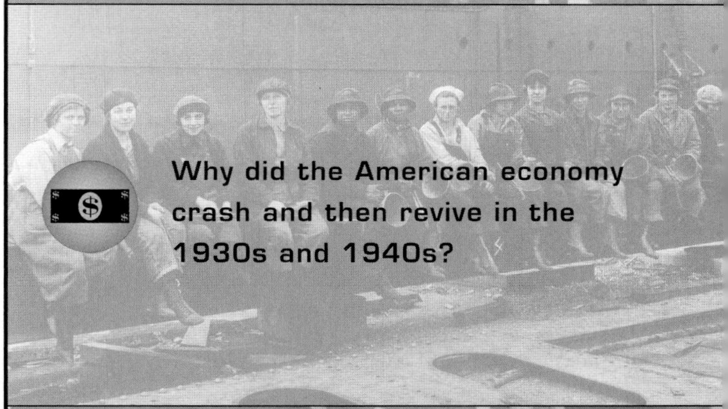

Why did the American economy crash and then revive in the 1930s and 1940s?

What were the effects of the two world wars on American society?

How did modernism find expression in American culture?

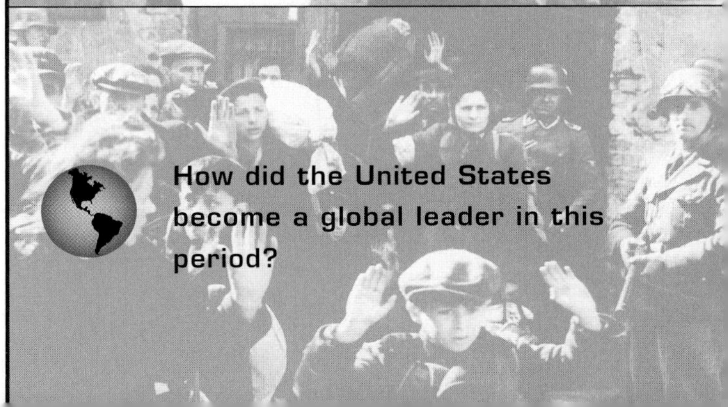

How did the United States become a global leader in this period?

How did the scope of government change in the Progressive and New Deal periods?

CHAPTER 22

An American Empire

- American imperialism
  - **U.S. imperialism and party politics**
  - **Annexing Hawaii (1898)**
  - **Political divisions and the Spanish-American War**
  - **Domestic politics and foreign policy under Roosevelt**

CHAPTER 23

The Progressive Era

- The main features of progressivism
  - **More direct democracy**
  - **Efficient government**
  - **Regulation of business**
  - **Social justice**
- Roosevelt's progressivism
  - **Trust-busting and regulation**
  - **Conservation**
- From Roosevelt to Wilson
  - **Taft**
  - **The election of 1912**
  - **Wilsonian reform: the New Freedom**
  - **The limits of progressive reform**

CHAPTER 24

America and the Great War

- War in Europe and the American response
  - **The debates over neutrality and preparedness**
  - **America's entry into the war**
  - Mobilizing the nation
  - Civil liberties in wartime
- The transition to peace
  - **Wilson and the League of Nations ratification fight**
  - **The Red Scare**

CHAPTER 25

The Modern Temper

- Reaction in the 1920s
  - **Nativist sentiment**
  - Revival of the Ku Klux Klan
  - **Protestant fundamentalism**
  - **Prohibition amendment ratified (1919)**
- Extending the franchise
  - **Resurgence of the women's suffrage movement**
  - Nineteenth Amendment (1920)
  - ERA introduced in Congress (1923)
  - **NAACP founded (1910)**
  - **Marcus Garvey and black nationalism**

CHAPTER 26

Republican Resurgence and Decline

- Presidential politics
  - **Harding's "return to normalcy"**
  - Dismantling progressivism
  - The Teapot Dome scandal (1923)
  - **"Silent Cal" Coolidge**
  - **Hoover, the engineer**
  - Hoover's economic policies

CHAPTER 27

New Deal America

- FDR and the New Deal
  - **FDR's election (1932)**
  - **Shaping the New Deal**
  - The major legislation
  - Power and reform
  - **The Second New Deal**
  - The influence of Eleanor Roosevelt
  - Huey Long and Father Coughlin
  - Opposition from the Supreme Court
  - *Roosevelt's court-packing plan*
  - Legislative achievements of the Second New Deal
  - **Economic policy and later reforms**
- Legacy of the New Deal

CHAPTER 28

From Isolation to Global War

- The Second World War and America's response
  - **"Internationalists" versus isolationists**
  - **United States drawn into war**
  - United States recognizes Russia (1933)
  - Neutrality Act of 1935 forbidding arms sales to belligerents
  - First peacetime conscription enacted by Congress (1940)
  - Lend-Lease Bill (1941)
  - Pearl Harbor and U.S. entry into the war

CHAPTER 29

The Second World War

- United States enters the war
  - **Mobilizing for war**
  - **Setting war aims and strategy**
  - **Fighting the war**
  - The atomic bomb
  - **Shaping the postwar world**

CHAPTER 22
An American Empire

- Economic growth and imperialist expansion
  - **Need for raw materials**
  - Annexation of Hawaii
  - **Search for new markets**
  - The Open Door policy in China
  - Panama Canal completed (1914)

CHAPTER 23
The Progressive Era

- Progressivism
  - **Economic legislation**
  - Theodore Roosevelt and the trusts
- Wilson and the economy
  - **Federal Reserve Act (1913)**
  - **Sixteenth Amendment and the federal income tax (1913)**
  - **Underwood-Simmons Tariff (1913)**
  - **Clayton Antitrust Act (1914)**
  - **Federal Farm Loan Act (1916)**

CHAPTER 24
America and the Great War

- Economic effects of war on the U.S.
  - **The Allied demand for supplies**
  - **American investors advance $2 billion to Allies**
  - **The debate over preparedness**
  - Naval Construction Act (1916)
  - Revenue Act (1916)
  - **Economic mobilization for war**
- The economic transition to peace
  - **Steep price rises**
  - **Labor unrest**

CHAPTER 25
The Modern Temper

- Immigration restriction and the economy
- Prohibition and the economy
  - **Organized crime**

CHAPTER 26
Republican Resurgence and Decline

- Economic policy
  - **Harding: A pro-business administration**
  - Tax cuts for the rich
  - High tariffs
  - Easing of corporate regulation
  - **Hoover tries to manage industry**
- Industry and agriculture
  - **Growing productivity in consumer-goods industries**
  - **Setbacks for unions**
  - **The business of farming in the 1920s**
  - Collapse of commodity prices
  - Pro-farm legislation
- The crash (October 1929)
  - **Hidden weaknesses of the "New Era"**
  - **Hoover's efforts at recovery**

CHAPTER 27
New Deal America

- New Deal economics
  - **Shoring up the financial system**
  - **Relief measures**
  - **Recovery measures**
  - Agricultural Adjustment Act (AAA)
  - National Industrial Recovery Act (NIRA)
  - **Regional planning: the TVA**
  - **The Second New Deal**
  - The Wagner Act (1935)
  - The Social Security Act (1935)
  - The Revenue Act (1935)
  - **The labor movement revives**
  - **The sluggish economy**

CHAPTER 28
From Isolation to Global War

- Economic interests and foreign policy
  - **War debts and reparations**
  - **The "great arsenal of democracy"**

CHAPTER 29
The Second World War

- The economy and the war effort
  - **Converting to a wartime economy**
  - War Productions Board (1942)
  - **Financing the war**
  - Taxes and war bonds
  - **Controls on wages and prices**
  - **Full employment and the end of the Depression**
  - Roles of women, blacks, Hispanics in the labor force
  - Economic development of the West

What were the effects of the two world wars on American society?

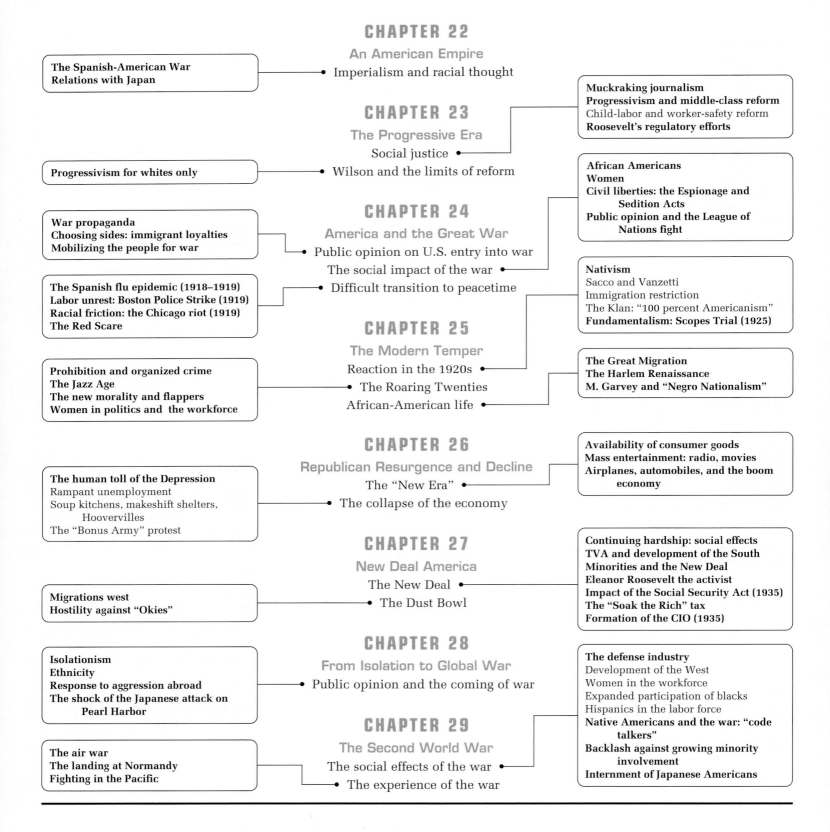

CHAPTER 22
An American Empire

- **Imperialism and racial thought**
  - The Spanish-American War
  - Relations with Japan

CHAPTER 23
The Progressive Era

- **Social justice**
  - Muckraking journalism
  - Progressivism and middle-class reform
  - Child-labor and worker-safety reform
  - Roosevelt's regulatory efforts
- **Wilson and the limits of reform**
  - Progressivism for whites only

CHAPTER 24
America and the Great War

- **Public opinion on U.S. entry into war**
  - War propaganda
  - Choosing sides: immigrant loyalties
  - Mobilizing the people for war
- **The social impact of the war**
  - African Americans
  - Women
  - Civil liberties: the Espionage and Sedition Acts
  - Public opinion and the League of Nations fight
- **Difficult transition to peacetime**
  - The Spanish flu epidemic (1918–1919)
  - Labor unrest: Boston Police Strike (1919)
  - Racial friction: the Chicago riot (1919)
  - The Red Scare

CHAPTER 25
The Modern Temper

- **Reaction in the 1920s**
  - Nativism
  - Sacco and Vanzetti
  - Immigration restriction
  - The Klan: "100 percent Americanism"
  - Fundamentalism: Scopes Trial (1925)
- **The Roaring Twenties**
  - Prohibition and organized crime
  - The Jazz Age
  - The new morality and flappers
  - Women in politics and the workforce
- **African-American life**
  - The Great Migration
  - The Harlem Renaissance
  - M. Garvey and "Negro Nationalism"

CHAPTER 26
Republican Resurgence and Decline

- **The "New Era"**
  - Availability of consumer goods
  - Mass entertainment: radio, movies
  - Airplanes, automobiles, and the boom economy
- **The collapse of the economy**
  - The human toll of the Depression
  - Rampant unemployment
  - Soup kitchens, makeshift shelters, Hoovervilles
  - The "Bonus Army" protest

CHAPTER 27
New Deal America

- **The New Deal**
  - Continuing hardship: social effects
  - TVA and development of the South
  - Minorities and the New Deal
  - Eleanor Roosevelt the activist
  - Impact of the Social Security Act (1935)
  - The "Soak the Rich" tax
  - Formation of the CIO (1935)
- **The Dust Bowl**
  - Migrations west
  - Hostility against "Okies"

CHAPTER 28
From Isolation to Global War

- **Public opinion and the coming of war**
  - Isolationism
  - Ethnicity
  - Response to aggression abroad
  - The shock of the Japanese attack on Pearl Harbor

CHAPTER 29
The Second World War

- **The social effects of the war**
  - The defense industry
  - Development of the West
  - Women in the workforce
  - Expanded participation of blacks
  - Hispanics in the labor force
  - Native Americans and the war: "code talkers"
  - Backlash against growing minority involvement
  - Internment of Japanese Americans
- **The experience of the war**
  - The air war
  - The landing at Normandy
  - Fighting in the Pacific

How did modernism find expression in American culture?

CHAPTER 22

An American Empire

- Imperialist impulses
  - **Social Darwinism**
  - **Mahan's *Influence of Sea Power upon History* (1890)**
  - **Racial thought**
  - **Missionary activities**

CHAPTER 23

The Progressive Era

- Social thought in the Progressive Era
  - **Muckraking journalism**
  - Riis, *How the Other Half Lives* (1890)
  - **Social Reform**
  - Sinclair, *The Jungle* (1906)

CHAPTER 24

America and the Great War

- Morality and idealism in foreign policy: Wilson
- A culture at war
  - **Propaganda**
  - "Americanism"
  - A. Mitchell Palmer

CHAPTER 25

The Modern Temper

- Reaction in the 1920s
  - **Nativism**
  - **Fundamentalism**
- The Roaring Twenties
  - **The Jazz Age**
  - **The Harlem Renaissance**
- Modernism
  - **Science and social thought**
- Literature
  - **Eliot, Stein, Fitzgerald, and Hemingway**
  - **The Southern Renaissance: Faulkner, Wolfe**

CHAPTER 26

Republican Resurgence and Decline

- A material culture
  - **Consumption and leisure**
  - Advertising: Lewis, *Babbit*
  - Movies and radio
  - The automobile

CHAPTER 27

New Deal America

- Culture in the 1930s
  - **Art, literature, and the depression**
  - Steinbeck's *The Grapes of Wrath* (1939)
  - Federal theater, art, and writers' projects
  - *Wright's* Native Son *(1940)*
  - **Popular culture during the Depression**
  - Radio: soap operas, *Amos 'n Andy, The Lone Ranger,* "big band" music
  - Movies: "screwball" comedies, gangster films, musicals

CHAPTER 28

From Isolation to Global War

- The culture of isolationism
- The impulse of idealism

CHAPTER 29

The Second World War

- The cultural tools of mobilization
  - **Uncle Sam**
  - **Rosie the Riveter**
- Civil liberties
  - **Racial thought**

How did the United States become a global leader in this period?

European imperialism in Africa and Asia
American imperialism in the Caribbean and the Pacific
China and the Open Door Policy (1899)
The Spanish-American War (1898)
Monroe Doctrine: the Roosevelt Corollary
Building the Panama Canal (1904–1914)
U. S. intervention in the Americas

CHAPTER 22
An American Empire
- Toward the new imperialism
- The Russo-Japanese War (1904)

The deterioration of U.S. relations with Japan

CHAPTER 23
The Progressive Era
- Domestic influences on foreign policy

Roosevelt, Taft, and Wilson

Intervention in Mexico (1914)
Problems in the Caribbean

CHAPTER 24
America and the Great War
- Wilson and foreign affairs
- World War I
- Wilson and the League of Nations

European alliances and U.S. neutrality
Sinking of the *Lusitania* (May 7, 1915)
The debate over preparedness
America's entry into the war
The decisive power
American forces on the Western Front

Wilson's Fourteen Points
Territory and reparations
Treaty of Versailles
The League of Nations battle

CHAPTER 25
The Modern Temper
- Immigration and nativism
- Science in Europe and America

Immigration restriction
Latin American immigration

The impact of German physics
Einstein, Planck, and Heisenberg
The impact of Freud

High U.S. tariffs and European war debt (1920s)
U.S. loans and investments abroad (1920s)
Farm prices and world markets
A worldwide depression

CHAPTER 26
Republican Resurgence and Decline
- The global depression

The Kellogg-Briand Pact (1928)
The "Good Neighbor" Policy and Latin America

CHAPTER 27
New Deal America
- The New Deal and the world's economy

American neutrality
***Blitzkrieg* and America's growing support of Britain**
Lend-lease and the arsenal of democracy
U.S. naval warfare against Germany
Tragedy at Pearl Harbor

The Spanish Civil War (1936)
Japanese incursions in China
Fascism in Italy and Germany
Axis aggression in Asia and Europe

CHAPTER 28
From Isolation to Global War
- U.S. isolationism after World War I
- Debts, reparations, and disarmament
- Antecedents to World War II
- Erosion of isolationism

Setbacks in the Pacific
Coral Sea and Midway battles (1942)
Leapfrogging to Tokyo
MacArthur and Nimitz
Grinding war against Japan
The atomic bomb: Hiroshima and Nagasaki
Japan surrenders: September 2, 1945

CHAPTER 29
The Second World War
- The war in the Pacific
- The war in Europe

The North Africa campaign (1942–1943)
The Battle of the Atlantic (1943)
Strategic bombing of Germany
D-Day: June 6, 1944
Soviet offensive reaches Germany (1945)
Yalta and the postwar world
V-E Day: May 8, 1945

CHAPTER

22

An American Empire

This chapter focuses on

- The circumstances that led to America's "new imperialism."
- The causes of the Spanish-American War.
- Theodore Roosevelt's foreign policy in Asia and Latin America.

THE *ESSENTIAL AMERICA* ON-LINE TUTOR

www.wwnorton.com/eamerica/ch22

- **Topic: The Spanish-American War**
  www.wwnorton.com/eamerica/ch22/topic.htm

  In 1898 the United States and Spain fought a decisive war that made America an imperial power. Using government records, photographs, maps, and historical analyses, consider the domestic and diplomatic significance of the Spanish-American War. How did the Spanish-American War affect the United States's role in international affairs?

- **Chapter review: On-line quiz and chapter summary**
  www.wwnorton.com/eamerica/ch22/review.htm

- **Chapter resources: Multimedia index**
  www.wwnorton.com/eamerica/ch22/media.htm

Throughout the nineteenth century, most Americans displayed what one senator called "only a languid interest" in foreign affairs. The overriding concerns of the time were industrial development, western settlement, and domestic politics. After the Civil War, an isolationist mood swept across the United States as the country basked in its geographic advantages: wide oceans as buffers on either side, the British navy situated between America and the powers of Europe, and militarily weak neighbors in the Western Hemisphere.

Yet the notion of America having a "Manifest Destiny" ordained by God to expand its territory and influence remained alive in the decades after the end of the Civil War. Several prominent political and business leaders argued that the rapid industrial development of the United States required the acquisition of foreign territories to gain easier access to vital raw materials. In addition, as their exports grew, American companies and farmers became increasingly intertwined in the world economy. This, in turn, required an expanded naval presence to protect the shipping lanes. And a modern steam-powered navy needed bases to replenish the coal and water required for its ships. For these reasons and others, the United States during the last quarter of the nineteenth century began to expand its presence beyond the Western Hemisphere.

Toward the New Imperialism

European powers had already unleashed a new surge of imperialism in Africa and Asia, where they had seized territory, established colonies, and had begun a systematic program of economic exploitation and Christian evangelism. Writing in 1902, the British economist J. A. Hobson declared that imperialism was "the most powerful factor in the current politics of the Western World."

Imperialism in a Global Context

Western imperialism was above all a quest for new markets and raw materials. The industrial revolution generated such dramatic increases in production that business leaders felt compelled to find new markets for their burgeoning supply of goods and new sources of investment for their growing supply of capital. Manufacturers were eager to find new sources of raw materials to supply their expanding needs. At the same time, the aggressive nationalism (called "jingoism" at the time) and bitter rivalries of the European powers made all of them compete with the others as they expanded their empires.

The result was a widespread process of imperial expansion into Africa and Asia, often with brutal consequences for the indigenous peoples. Beginning in the 1880s, the British, French, Belgians, Italians, Dutch, Spanish, and Germans used military force and political guile to conquer and subjugate regions of Africa and Asia. This imperial competition also set in motion clashes among the Western powers that would lead to unprecedented conflict in the twentieth century.

American Imperialism

As the European nations expanded their control over much of the rest of the world, America also began to acquire territories outside the continental United States. Americans became increasingly aware of world markets as developments in transportation and communication quickened the pace of commerce and diplomacy. Americans disagreed whether the expansion of markets should lead to territorial expansion or to intervention in the internal affairs of other countries, but a small yet vocal and influential group of public officials embraced the idea of overseas possessions, regardless of the implications. These expansionists included senators Albert J. Beveridge of Indiana and Henry Cabot Lodge of Massachusetts, Theodore Roosevelt, and not least of all, naval captain Alfred Thayer Mahan.

During the 1880s, Captain Mahan became a leading advocate of sea power and Western imperialism. In 1890 he published *The Influence of Sea Power upon History, 1660–1783,* in which he argued that national greatness and prosperity flowed from a powerful navy, a strong merchant marine, foreign commerce, colonies, and naval bases. Mahan championed America's "destiny" to control the Western Hemisphere, build a canal connecting the Caribbean Sea with the Pacific, and spread Western civilization to Asia. His ideas were widely circulated in popular journals and within the American government.

Imperialist Theory

Certain intellectual concepts bolstered the new imperialist spirit and buttressed claims of racial superiority. Spokesmen in each country, including the United States, used the arguments of Social Darwinism to justify economic exploitation. Among nations as among individuals, expansionists claimed, the fittest survive and prevail.

Josiah Strong, a Congregationalist minister, added the sanction of religion to theories of racial and national superiority. In his book *Our Country: Its Possible Future and Its Present Crisis* (1885), Strong asserted that the Anglo-Saxon was "divinely commissioned to be, in a peculiar sense, his brother's keeper." Moreover, each of the imperial nations, including the United States, dispatched Christian missionaries to convert the subject peoples. By 1900, some 18,000 Christian missionaries were scattered around the world.

Expansion in the Pacific

For expansionists, Asia was an especially tempting target. President Andrew Johnson's secretary of state, William H. Seward, believed that the United States must inevitably exercise commercial domination "on the Pacific Ocean, and its islands and continents." Eager for American manufacturers to exploit Asian markets, Seward believed the United States first had to remove all foreign interests from the northern Pacific coast and gain access to that region's valuable ports. To that end, Seward cast covetous eyes on the British crown colony of British Columbia, sandwiched between Russia's possessions in Alaska and Washington Territory.

Late in 1866, while encouraging annexation sentiment among the British Columbians, Seward learned of Russia's desire to sell Alaska. He leaped at the opportunity, and in 1867 the United States bought Alaska for $7.2 million, less than 2 cents an acre. "Seward's folly" of buying the Alaskan "icebox" proved in time to be the biggest bargain for the United States, economically and strategically, since the Louisiana Purchase.

Samoa and Hawaii

Seward's successors at the State Department sustained his expansionist vision, and the Pacific Ocean remained the major field of overseas activity. During the post–Civil War years, the United States sought coaling stations and trading posts in this area, and it laid claim to various small islands and coral atolls of the mid-Pacific. Two of these islands were especially strategic: Samoa and Hawaii (also known as the Sandwich Islands).

American interest in these islands gradually deepened as commercial activity in the Pacific increased, and in 1878 the Samoans signed a treaty with the United States that granted a naval base at Pago Pago. The following year the German and British governments worked out similar arrangements on other islands of the Samoan group.

In Hawaii, the Americans had a clearer field. The islands, a united kingdom since 1795, hosted a sizable settlement of American missionaries and planters and had long been a popular way station for whalers and traders. They were also strategically more important than Samoa to the United States, since their occupation by another major power might have posed a threat to American sugar interests and even to defense of the continent.

In 1875 the Hawaiians signed a reciprocal trade agreement under which their sugar entered the United States duty free. Twelve years later, the treaty was amended to grant the United States exclusive right to a fortified naval base at Pearl Harbor, near Honolulu. These agreements prompted a boom in sugar growing, and American settlers in Hawaii came to dominate the economy. In 1887 the Americans forced Hawaii's king to grant a constitutional government, which they controlled.

Hawaii's political climate changed sharply when the king's sister, Queen Liliuokalani, ascended the throne in 1891 and began efforts to reclaim power. Shortly before that, the McKinley Tariff had destroyed Hawaii's favored position in the sugar trade by putting the sugar of all countries on the duty-free list and granting growers in the United States a two-cent subsidy per pound of sugar. The resultant economic crisis and discontent in Hawaii led the white population to revolt early in 1893 and to seize power. The American minister brought in marines to support the coup. Within a month, a committee of the new American-dominated government visited Washington, D.C., and, in 1893, signed an annexation treaty.

This occurred just weeks before President Benjamin Harrison left office, however, and Democratic senators blocked ratification. President Cleveland withdrew the treaty and sent a special commissioner to investigate. He recalled the American marines and reported that Americans on the islands had acted improperly. Most Hawaiians opposed annexation, said the commissioner, who thought the revolution had been engineered mainly by sugar planters hoping for annexation in order to get the new domestic sugar subsidy for sugar grown in the United States. Cleveland therefore proposed to restore the queen in return for amnesty to the revolutionists. The provisional government refused and on July 4, 1894, proclaimed the Republic of Hawaii, which had in its constitution a standing provision for American annexation.

When William McKinley became president in 1897, he found an excuse to annex the Hawaiian Islands when the Japanese, also hoping to take over the islands, sent warships to Hawaii. McKinley responded by sending American warships and asked the Senate to approve a treaty to annex Hawaii. When the Senate could not muster the two-thirds majority needed to approve the treaty, McKinley used a joint resolution of the House and Senate to achieve his aims. This resolution passed by simple majorities in both houses, and the United States annexed Hawaii in the summer of 1898.

The Spanish-American War

Until the 1890s, a certain ambivalence about overseas possessions had checked America's drive to expand. Suddenly, in 1898 and 1899, the inhibitions collapsed, but not in a quest for bases and trade. Rather, the chief motive was a sense of outrage at another country's imperialism.

"Cuba Libre"

Throughout the second half of the nineteenth century, Cubans had repeatedly revolted against Spanish rule, only to be ruthlessly put down. At the same time, American investments in Cuba, mainly in sugar and mining, were steadily rising. The United States in fact traded more with Cuba than Spain did. The growing economic interest in their island neighbor made Americans sympathetic to the idea of Cuban independence. When another Cuban insurrection broke out on February 24, 1895, public feeling in the United States sided with the rebels.

In 1896 Spanish general Valeriano Weyler adopted a policy of gathering Cubans behind Spanish lines, often in detention (*reconcentrado*) centers so that no one could join the insurrections by night and appear peaceful by day. In some of these centers, poor food and unsanitary conditions soon brought a heavy toll of disease and death. The American press promptly christened the Spanish commander "Butcher" Weyler.

Events in Cuba supplied exciting copy for the popular press. William Randolph Hearst's *New York Journal* and Joseph Pulitzer's *New York World* were at the time locked in a monumental competition for readers. The sensationalism practiced by both papers came to be called "yellow journalism," and Hearst emerged as the undisputed champion.

Pressure for War

American neutrality toward events in Cuba changed sharply when McKinley entered office. His platform had endorsed Cuban independence, as well as American control of Hawaii and the construction of an isthmian canal. Spain offered Cuba autonomy (self-government without formal independence) in return for peace. What the Cubans might once have welcomed, however, they now rejected as they sensed their growing power. Spain was impaled on the horns of a dilemma, unable to end the war and unready to give up Cuba.

Early in 1898 events moved rapidly to arouse opinion against Spain. On February 9, Hearst's *New York Journal* released the text of a stolen letter from Spanish minister Depuy de Lôme to a friend in Havana in which de Lôme called President McKinley "weak and a bidder for the admiration of the crowd." De Lôme resigned to prevent further embarrassment to his government.

Six days later, during the night of February 15, 1898, the American battleship *Maine* exploded in Havana Harbor and sank with a loss of 266 men. Those eager for a war with Spain demanded an immediate declaration. McKinley's assistant secretary of the navy, Theodore Roosevelt, called the sinking "an act of dirty treachery on the part of the Spaniards."

A naval court of inquiry reported that an external mine had sunk the ship. Lacking hard evidence, the court made no effort to fix the blame, but the yellow press had no need of evidence. The *New York Journal* gleefully reported: "The Whole Country Thrills with War Fever." The jingoistic outcry against Spain rose in a crescendo with the words "Remember the *Maine!* To Hell with Spain!" Few of those promoting war wrestled with the obvious fact that the Spanish government was determined to *avoid* a confrontation with the United States and therefore had nothing to gain from attacking the *Maine*. A comprehensive study in 1976 concluded that the sinking of the *Maine* was an accident, the result of an internal explosion triggered by a fire in its coal bunker.

Under the mounting pressure of public excitement, McKinley, on March 9, 1898, pushed through Congress a $50 million defense appropriation. Still, he sought to avoid war, as did most business spokesmen. Such caution infuriated Roosevelt. "We will have this war for the freedom of Cuba," he fumed on March 26, "in spite of the timidity of the commercial interests."

The Spanish government, sensing the growing militancy in the United States, announced a unilateral cease-fire in early April 1898. On April 10, the Spanish minister gave the State Department a message that amounted to a surrender. But the message came too late. The following day McKinley sent Congress his war message. He asked for the power to use armed forces in Cuba to protect American property and trade. On April 20 a joint resolution of Congress went

An American cartoon depicts the sinking of the *Maine* in Havana Harbor. The uproar created by the incident and its coverage in the "yellow press" edged McKinley toward war.

beyond endorsing the use of the armed forces: it declared Cuba independent and demanded withdrawal of Spanish forces. The Teller Amendment, added on the Senate floor, disclaimed any American designs on Cuban territory. McKinley signed the resolution and sent a copy to the Spanish government. On April 22 the president announced a blockade of Cuba, under international law an act of war. Rather than give in to an ultimatum, the Spanish government declared war on April 24. Congress then, determined to be first, declared war the next day but made it retroactive to April 21, 1898.

Why such a rush into war after the message from Spain indicated that it was ready for an armistice? No one knows for sure, but it seems apparent that too much momentum and popular pressure had already built up for a confidential message to change the course of events. Still, it is fair to ask why McKinley did not take a stand for peace, knowing what he did. He might have defied Congress and public opinion, but in the end he deemed the political risk to high.

Dewey Takes Manila

The war itself lasted only four months. The American victory marked the end of Spain's once-great New World empire, which had begun with Christopher Columbus, and the emergence of the United States as a world power. But if American participation saved many lives by ending the insurrection in Cuba, it also led to American involvement in another insurrection, in the Philippines, and it created a host of commitments in the Caribbean and the Pacific that would haunt American policy makers during the twentieth century.

The war was barely under way before the navy produced a spectacular victory across the Pacific at Manila Bay in the Spanish-controlled Philippines. While public attention centered on Cuba, Roosevelt focused on the Philippines. He ordered Commodore George Dewey, commander of the small American squadron in Asia, to engage Spain's ships in the Philippines. Arriving late on April 30, 1898, Dewey's squadron destroyed or captured all the Spanish warships in Manila Bay. With the help of Filipino insurrectionists under Emilio Aguinaldo, Dewey's forces liberated Manila from Spanish control on August 13.

The Cuban Campaign

While these events transpired halfway around the world, the war reached a surprisingly quick climax closer to home. An invasion force of some 17,000 American troops was hastily assembled at Tampa, Florida. One significant element of that force was the so-called Rough Riders, best remembered because Lieutenant-Colonel Theodore Roosevelt was second in command. Eager to get "in on the fun," and "to act up to my preachings," Roosevelt had quit the Navy Department, ordered a custom-fitted uniform with yellow trim, grabbed a dozen pairs of spectacles, and rushed to help organize a volunteer regiment of Ivy League athletes, leathery ex-convicts, Indians, and southwestern sharpshooters.

Lieutenant-Colonel Theodore Roosevelt posing with his Rough Riders after the Battle of San Juan, 1898.

The major land action of the Cuban campaign occurred on July 1. While a much larger American force attacked Spanish positions at San Juan Hill, a smaller unit, including the dismounted Rough Riders—most of whose horses were still in Florida—and two crack black regiments, seized the enemy position atop nearby Kettle Hill.

The two battles put American forces atop heights from which they could bring Santiago and the Spanish fleet under siege. On July 3 the Spanish ships made a gallant run for it, but the aging vessels were little match for the newer American fleet. The casualties were one-sided: 474 Spanish were killed or wounded and 1,750 were taken prisoner, while only one American was killed and one wounded. Santiago surrendered with a garrison of 24,000 on July 17. On July 25, an American force also moved into the Spanish-held island of Puerto Rico.

The next day the Spanish government sued for peace. After discussions lasting two weeks, negotiators signed an armistice on August 12, 1898, less than four months after the war's start and the day before Americans entered Manila. The peace protocol specified that Spain should give up Cuba, and that the United States should annex Puerto Rico and should occupy the city, bay, and harbor of Manila pending disposition of the Philippines.

And so the "splendid little war," as the future secretary of state, John Hay, called it in a letter to his friend Roosevelt, officially ended. It was splendid only in the sense that its cost was relatively slight. Among more than 274,000 Americans who served during the war and the ensuing demobilization, 5,462 died, but only 379 in battle. Most succumbed to malaria, typhoid, dysentery, or yellow fever. At such a cost the United States was launched onto the world stage as a great power, with all the benefits—and burdens—of that new status.

The Debate over Annexation

The United States and Spain signed the Treaty of Paris on December 10, 1898. Disposition of the Philippines posed the key question, indeed one of the biggest decisions to face United States foreign policy to that time. McKinley, who claimed that at first he himself could not locate the Philippines on a map, gave ambiguous signals to the peace commission, which itself was divided.

There had been no demand for annexation of the Philippines or other Spanish possessions before the war, but Dewey's victory quickly kindled expansionist fever. Business leaders began thinking of the commercial possibilities in the nearby continent of Asia, such as oil for the lamps of China and textiles for its millions of people. Christian missionary societies yearned to save the "little brown brother." Spanish negotiators raised the delicate point that American forces had no claim by right by conquest, and had even taken Manila after the armistice. American negotiators finally offered the Spanish $20 million as compensation for possession of the Philippines as well as Puerto Rico in the Caribbean and Guam in the Pacific.

Meanwhile, Americans had taken other giant steps in the Pacific. Hawaii had been annexed in the midst of the war. The United States also claimed Wake Island (1898), which would be a vital link in a future trans-Pacific cable line. And in 1899, after another outbreak of fighting over the royal succession in Samoa, Germany and the United States agreed to partition the Samoan Islands. The United States annexed the easternmost islands; Germany took the rest, including the largest island.

The Treaty of Paris was opposed by most Democrats and Populists, and some Republicans. Anti-imperialists appealed to traditional isolationism, principles of self-government, the inconsistency of liberating Cuba and annexing the Philippines, the involvement in foreign entanglements that would undermine the logic of the Monroe Doctrine, and the danger that the Philippines would be expensive if not impossible to defend.

The opposition may have been strong enough to kill the treaty had not the populist Democrat William Jennings Bryan influenced the vote for approval. A formal end to the war, he argued, would open the way for the future independence of Cuba and the Philippines. Ratification finally came on February 6, 1899.

By this time Americans had already clashed with Filipino insurrectionists near Manila. The rebel leader, Emilio Aguin-

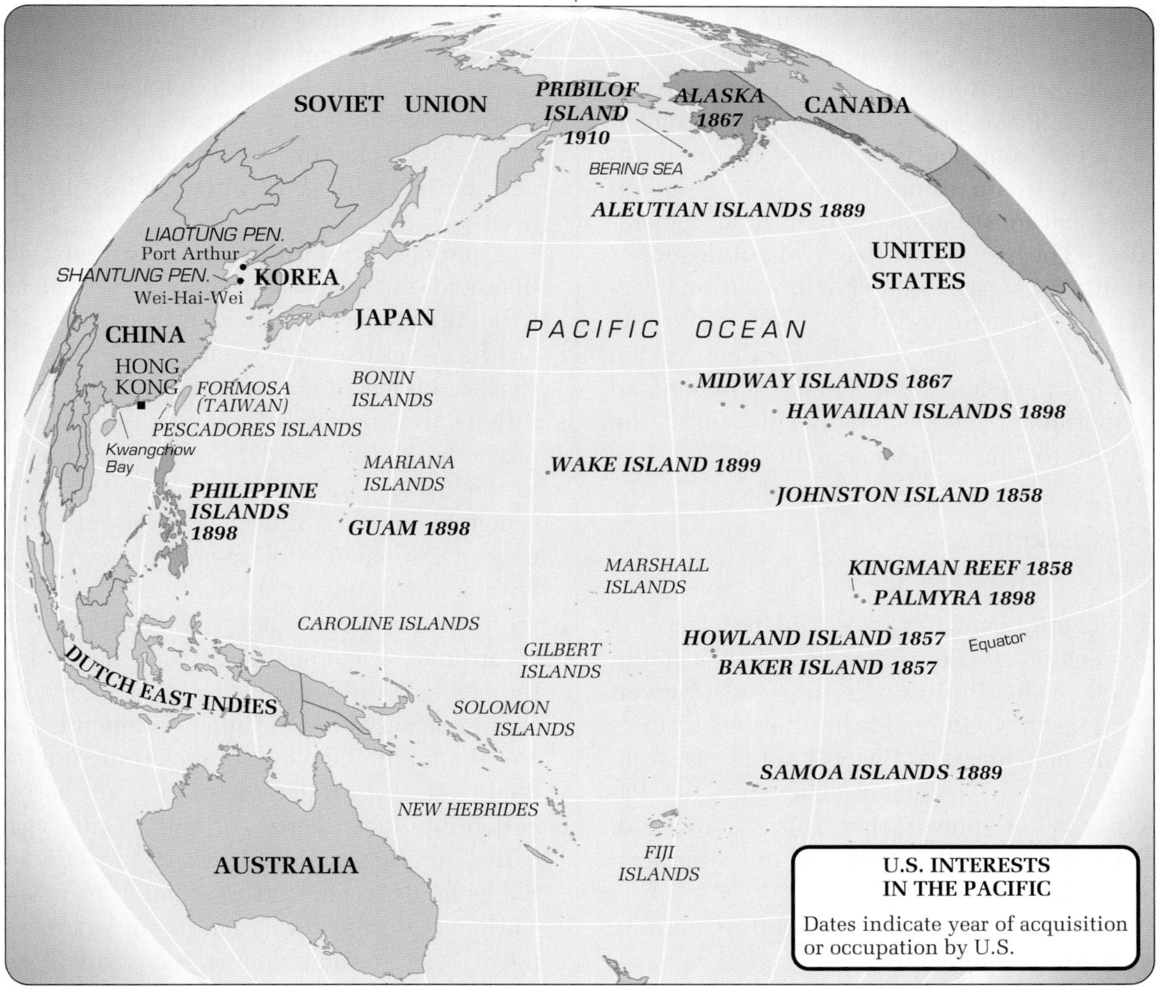

"Well, I Hardly Know Which to Take First." At the end of the nineteenth century it seemed that Uncle Sam had developed a considerable appetite for foreign territory.

aldo, had been in exile until Commodore Dewey brought him back to make trouble for the Spanish. Since Aguinaldo's forces were more or less in control of the islands outside Manila, what followed over the next two years was largely an American war of conquest. Organized Filipino resistance collapsed by the end of 1899, but even after the capture of Aguinaldo in 1901, sporadic guerrilla action lasted until mid-1902.

Against the backdrop of this nasty guerrilla war the great debate over annexation continued. The treaty debates inspired a number of anti-imperialist groups, which united in 1899 as the American Anti-Imperialist League. The league attracted members representing many shades of opinion; the main thing they had in common was that most belonged to an older generation. The usually soft-spoken philosopher William James exploded in opposition to acquiring foreign territory: "God damn the United States for its vile conduct in the Philippine Isles!" The selfish proponents of imperialism, he declared, had caused the nation to "puke up its ancient soul."

Organizing the New Acquisitions

Such criticism, however, did not faze the expansionists. Senator Beveridge boasted in 1900: "The Philippines are ours forever. And just beyond the Philippines are China's illimitable markets. We will not retreat from either. . . . The power that rules the Pacific is the power that rules the world. That power will forever be the American Republic."

In the Philippines, McKinley quickly moved toward setting up a civil government. On July 4, 1901, military government ended, and under an act of Congress, Judge William Howard Taft became the civil governor. The Philippine Government Act, passed by Congress on July 1, 1902, made the Philippine Islands an "unorganized territory" of the United States and made the inhabitants citizens of the Philippines. In 1934 the Tydings-McDuffie Act offered independence, which finally took effect on July 4, 1946.

Puerto Rico had been acquired in part to serve as an American outpost guarding the approaches to the Caribbean and any future isthmian canal. In 1900 the Foraker Act established a civil government on the island. Residents of the island were citizens of Puerto Rico but not of the United States until 1917, when they were granted United States citizenship. In 1952 Puerto Rico became a commonwealth with its own constitution and elected officials, a unique status. Like a state, Puerto Rico is free to change its constitution insofar as it does not conflict with the United States Constitution.

American authorities soon learned that liberated Cuba posed problems at least as irksome as those in the new possessions. After the American forces had restored order, started schools, and improved sanitary conditions, they began turning over the reins of power to the Cubans. The Platt Amendment to the Army Appropriations Bill passed by Congress in 1901, however, required Cuba never to impair its independence by treaty with a third power, to maintain its debt within the government's power to repay out of ordinary revenues, and to acknowledge the right of the United States to intervene for the preservation of Cuban independence and the maintenance of "a government adequate for the protection of life, property, and individual liberty." Finally, Cuba was called upon to sell or lease to the United States lands to be used for coaling or naval stations—a proviso that led to an American naval base at Guantanamo Bay, which remains in existence.

Imperial Rivalries in East Asia

China and the "Open Door"

During the 1890s, not only the United States but also Japan emerged as a world power. Commodore Matthew Perry's voyage of 1853–1854 had opened Japan to Western ways, and the island nation began modernization in earnest after the 1860s. Flexing its new muscles, Japan defeated China's stagnant empire in the Sino-Japanese War (1894–1895) and, as a result, acquired the island of Taiwan (renamed Formosa). China's weakness, demonstrated in the war, led Russia, England, France, and Germany to renew their scramble for "spheres of influence" on that remaining frontier of imperialist expansion.

The possibility that these competing powers would carve up China and erect tariff barriers in their own spheres of influence dimmed the bright prospect of American trade with China. The British had much to lose in a tariff war though, for they already enjoyed substantial trade with China. Fearful of such a development, the British suggested in 1899 that the United States join them in preserving China's commercial and territorial integrity. The State Department agreed that something must be done, but Secretary of State John Hay preferred to act alone rather than in concert with the British.

In its origins and content, what came to be known as the Open Door Policy resembled the Monroe Doctrine. In both cases the United States proclaimed unilaterally a hands-off policy that the British had earlier proposed as a joint statement. The policy outlined in Hay's Open Door Note, dispatched in 1899 to London, Berlin, and St. Petersburg, and a little later to Tokyo, Rome, and Paris, proposed to keep China open to trade with all countries on an equal basis. None except Britain accepted Hay's principles, but none rejected them either, so Hay presumptuously announced that all powers had accepted the policy.

The Open Door Policy was rooted in the self-interest of American businessmen eager to exploit the markets of China. Yet it also tapped the deep-seated sympathies of those who opposed imperialism, especially as it endorsed China's territorial integrity. But it had little more legal standing than a pious affirmation. When the Japanese, concerned about Russian pressure in Chinese Manchuria, asked how the United States intended to enforce the Open Door Policy, Hay replied that the United States was "not prepared" to do so. So it would remain for forty years, a hollow but dangerous commitment, until continued Japanese expansion would bring war with America in 1941.

The Boxer Rebellion

A new crisis arose in 1900, when a group of Chinese nationalists known to the Western world as Boxers rebelled against foreign involvement in China. The Boxers surrounded the foreign embassies in Peking (Beijing). The British, Germans, Russians, Japanese, and Americans quickly mounted a military expedition to relieve the embassy compound. Hay, fearful that the intervention might become an excuse to dismember China, seized the chance to further refine his Open Door Policy. The United States, he declared in a letter of July 3, 1900, sought a solution that would "preserve Chinese territorial and administrative integrity" as well as "equal and impartial trade with all parts of the Chinese Empire." Six weeks later, the multinational expedition reached Peking and put down the Boxer Rebellion.

Roosevelt's Big Stick Diplomacy

More than any other American political leader of his time, Theodore Roosevelt helped transform the role of the United

States in world affairs. The nation had emerged from the Spanish-American War a world power, and he insisted that this entailed major new responsibilities. To ensure that the country accepted such international obligations, Roosevelt stretched both the Constitution and executive power to the limit. In the process, he pushed a reluctant nation onto the center stage of world affairs.

Roosevelt's Rise

In the presidential election of 1900, the Democrats turned once again to William Jennings Bryan, who sought to make imperialism the "paramount issue" of the campaign. The Democratic platform condemned the Philippine conflict as "an unnecessary war." The Republicans in response renominated McKinley and named as his running mate Theodore Roosevelt, who had been elected governor of New York after his role in the Spanish-American War.

The trouble with Bryan's idea of a solemn referendum on imperialism was the impossibility of making any presidential contest so simple. Bryan himself complicated his message by insisting once again on the free coinage of silver, and the tariff became an issue again too. The Republicans' biggest advantage was probably the return to prosperity, for which they took credit. So those who opposed imperialism but also opposed free silver or tariff reduction faced a bewildering choice.

The outcome was a victory for McKinley greater than his last, 7.2 million to 6.4 million in the popular vote and 292 to 155 in the electoral vote. There had been no clearcut referendum on foreign annexation, but the question was settled nonetheless, although it would take yet another year and a half to subdue the Filipino rebels. The job would be finished, however, under the direction of another president.

On September 6, 1901, while McKinley attended a reception at the Pan American Exposition in Buffalo, a fanatical anarchist named Leon Czolgosz approached him with a gun and fired at point-blank range. McKinley died six days later, suddenly elevating Theodore Roosevelt to the White House. "Now look," Republican leader Mark Hanna erupted. "That damned cowboy is President of the United States!"

Six weeks short of his forty-third birthday, Roosevelt was the youngest man ever to take charge of the White House, but he brought to it more experience in public affairs than most and more vitality than any. Born in 1858, the son of a wealthy New York merchant and a Georgia belle, Roosevelt grew up in Manhattan in cultured comfort, visited Europe as a child, and graduated Phi Beta Kappa from Harvard in 1880. Boxer, wrestler, and outdoorsman, he was also a renowned historian and essayist and an outspoken moralist.

After Harvard, Roosevelt won election to the New York State legislature. He later served six years as civil service commissioner in Washington, D.C., and two years as New York City's police commissioner.

As a public servant Roosevelt developed a reputation as a prodigious worker renowned for his integrity and sense of humor. He combined his boundless energy with an unshakable righteousness and a tendency to cast every issue in moral and patriotic terms. He saw the presidency as his "bully pulpit," and he was eager to preach fist-smacking sermons on the virtues of honesty, civic duty, and the strenuous life. But appearances were deceiving. His nervous energy left a false impression of impulsiveness, and the talk of morality actually cloaked a cautious pragmatism. Roosevelt could get carried away on occasion, but as he said of his foreign policy initiatives, this was likely to happen only when "I am assured that I shall be able eventually to carry out my will by force."

Building the Panama Canal

After the Spanish-American War the United States became more deeply involved than ever in the Caribbean area, where one issue overshadowed every other: the Panama

Canal. The narrow isthmus of Panama had excited dreams of an interoceanic canal ever since Vasco Nunez de Balboa's overland crossing in 1513. After America's victory over Spain, Secretary of State John Hay sought Britain's consent to an American plan to build a canal. These negotiations led to the Hay-Pauncefote Treaty of 1901, in which Britain gave its consent to the American plan.

Other obstacles remained, however. From 1881 to 1887, a French company had spent nearly $300 million and sacrificed some 20,000 lives to dig less than a third of a canal through Panama. The company now offered to sell its holding to the United States. Meanwhile, Secretary Hay had opened negotiations with Ambassador Thomas Herrán of Colombia to build a canal across Panama, which was then a reluctant province of Colombia. In return for a Canal Zone six miles wide, the United States agreed to pay $10 million in cash and a rental fee of $250,000 a year. The United States Senate ratified the Hay-Herrán Treaty in 1903, but the Colombian Senate held out for $25 million in cash.

Colombia's rejection of the treaty heightened the desire of Panamanian rebels for independence. Recognizing this development, an employee of the French canal company hatched a plot in collusion with the company's representative, Philippe Bunau-Varilla. He visited Roosevelt and Hay and, apparently with inside information, informed the Panamanian rebels that the U.S.S. *Nashville* would call at Colón in Panama on November 2, 1903.

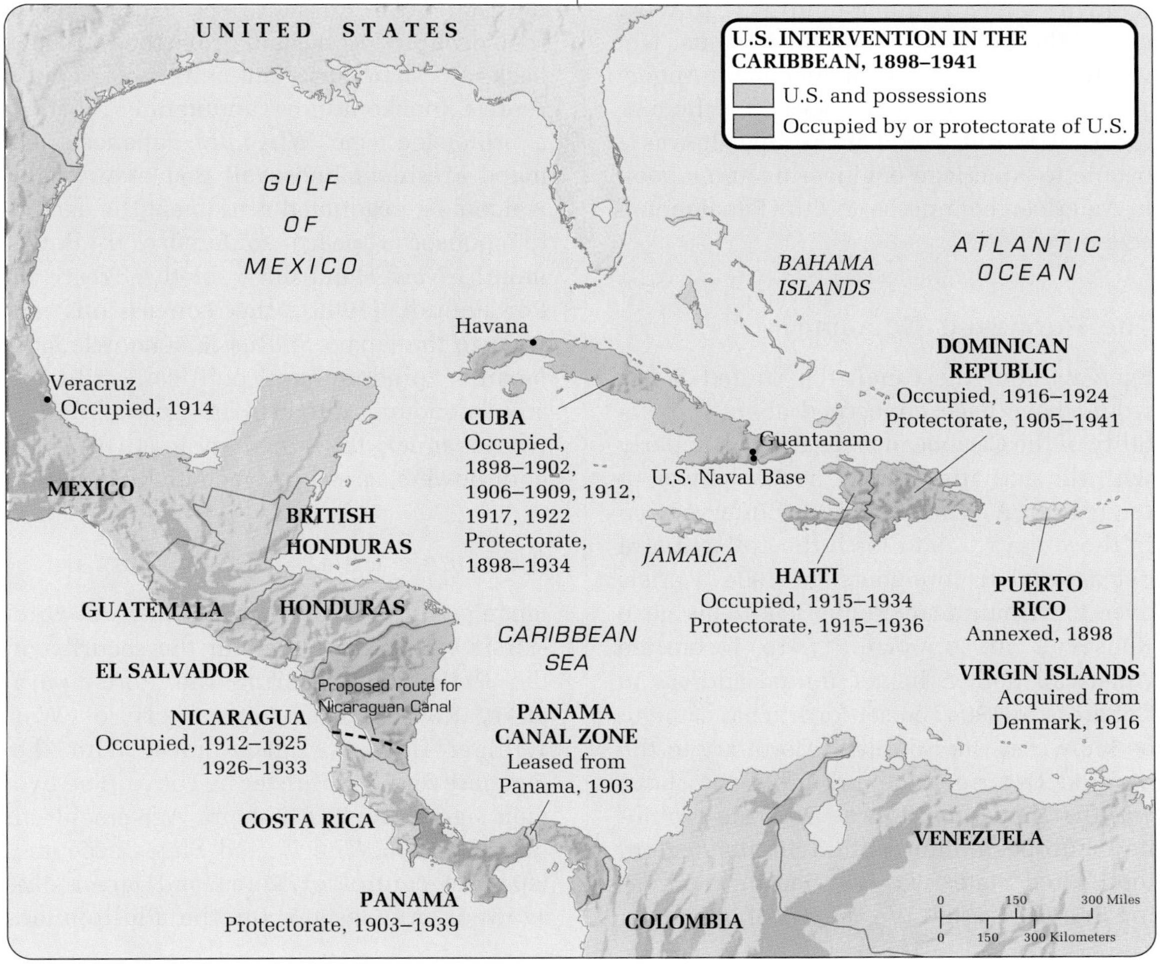

An army of some 500 Panamanians revolted against Colombian rule the next day. Colombian troops, who could not penetrate the overland jungle, found American ships blocking the sea lanes. A few days later the Roosevelt administration made good on its collusion with the revolutionaries by recognizing Panama's independence and by signing a treaty extending the Canal Zone from six to ten miles in width. For $10 million down and $250,000 a year the United States received "in perpetuity the use, occupation and control" of the canal zone. "I took Panama," Roosevelt would later boast.

In essence he had. Colombia eventually got its $25 million from the Harding administration in 1921, but only after America's interest in Colombian oil had lubricated the wheels of diplomacy. There was no apology, but the payment was made to remove "all misunderstandings growing out of the political events in Panama, November, 1903." The canal opened on August 15, 1914, less than two weeks after the outbreak of World War I in Europe. It was a tribute to American engineering and a boon to American commerce and the Panamanian economy.

The Roosevelt Corollary

Even without the canal, the United States would have been concerned about the stability of the Caribbean area, and particularly with the activities of any hostile power in the region. A prime excuse for intervention in those days was to force the collection of debts owed to foreigners. In 1904 a crisis over the Dominican Republic's debts gave Roosevelt an opportunity to formulate American policy. In his annual address to Congress in 1904, he set forth what came to be known as the Roosevelt Corollary to the Monroe Doctrine: the principle, in short, was that since the Monroe Doctrine prohibited European intervention in the region, the United States was justified in intervening first to forestall the actions of outsiders. Roosevelt suggested that the United States could exercise an "international police power" in its own sphere of influence. As put into practice by mutual agreement with the Dominican Republic in 1905, the Roosevelt Corollary called for the United States to appoint a collector of customs, who would apply a portion of the revenues to debt payments. The principle, applied peaceably in 1905, became the basis for military interventions later.

The Russo-Japanese War

In East Asia, meanwhile, the Open Door policy received a serious challenge when tensions between Russia and Japan flared into a fight over China and Korea. On February 8, 1904, war broke out when the Japanese launched a surprise attack that devastated the Russian fleet. The Japanese then occupied Korea and drove the Russians back into Manchuria. But neither side could score a knockout blow, and neither relished a prolonged war. When the Japanese signaled President Roosevelt that they would welcome a negotiated settlement, he agreed to sponsor a peace conference in Portsmouth, New Hampshire. In the Treaty of Portsmouth (1905), the concessions all went to the Japanese. Russia acknowledged Japan's "predominant political, military, and economic interests in Korea" (Japan would annex the kingdom in 1910), and both powers agreed to evacuate Manchuria.

America's Relations with Japan

Japan's show of strength in the war with Russia raised doubts about the security of the Philippines. During the Portsmouth talks, Roosevelt sent Secretary of War William Howard Taft to meet with the Japanese foreign minister in Tokyo. The two men signed the Taft-Katsura Agreement on July 29, 1905. The United States accepted Japanese control of Korea and Japan disavowed any designs on the Philippines.

Three years later, the Root-Takahira Agreement, negotiated by Secretary of State Elihu Root and the Japanese ambassador, endorsed the status quo, promised to respect each nation's possessions, and reinforced the Open Door Policy by supporting "the independence and integrity of China" and "the principle of equal opportunity for commerce and industry in China."

Behind the diplomatic facade of goodwill, however, lay simmering distrust. For many Americans, the Russian threat in east Asia now gave way to fear of Japan's "yellow peril" (a term coined by Germany's Kaiser Wilhelm II). Racial animosities on the West Coast helped sour relations with Japan. In 1906 the San Francisco school board ordered students of Chinese, Japanese, and Korean descent to attend a separate public school. The Japanese government sharply protested such prejudice, and President Roosevelt managed to talk the school board into changing its mind. Japan then agreed to limit sharply its issuance of passports to the United States. This "Gentleman's Agreement" of 1907, the precise terms of which have never been revealed, halted the influx of Japanese immigrants and brought some respite to racial agitations in California.

The United States and Europe

During these years of expansionism abroad, the United States cast its gaze mainly westward and southward. But events in Europe also required attention. While Roosevelt was mediating the Russo-Japanese War in 1905, another dangerous crisis erupted in Morocco, where the Germans and French fought for control. Roosevelt felt that the United States had something at stake in preventing the outbreak of a major war. At the kaiser's behest, he talked the French and British into attending an international conference at Algeciras, Spain, with American delegates present. Roosevelt then maneuvered the Germans into accepting his lead. The Act of Algeciras, signed in 1906, affirmed the independence of Morocco and guaranteed an open door for trade there. Roosevelt received the Nobel Peace Prize in 1906 for his work at Portsmouth and Algeciras.

Before Roosevelt left the White House in March 1909, he celebrated America's rise to world power with one great flourish. In late 1907 he sent the entire United States Navy, by then second in strength only to the British fleet, on a grand tour around the world. The triumphal procession visited Japan and continued home by way of the Mediterranean and steamed back into American waters in 1909, just in time to close out Roosevelt's presidency on a note of success.

But that note would not resonate for long. In time, the mixed consequences of Roosevelt's policies in Latin America and Asia would produce ill will toward the United States that continues to this day.

The World's Constable. Theodore Roosevelt, shown here as the world's policeman, wields the "big stick" symbolizing his approach to diplomacy.

CHAPTER

23

The Progressive Era

This chapter focuses on

- The social roots of progressivism.
- The basic elements of progressive reform.
- The presidencies of Theodore Roosevelt, William H. Taft, and Woodrow Wilson.
- The significance of the election of 1912.

THE *ESSENTIAL AMERICA* ON-LINE TUTOR

www.wwnorton.com/eamerica/ch23

- **Topic: Theodore Roosevelt**
  www.wwnorton.com/eamerica/ch23/topic.htm

  When an assassin killed President William McKinley in 1901, Theodore Roosevelt became the youngest president in U.S. history, and the Progressive Era in American politics was launched. Using audio and video clips, paintings, photographs, historical analyses, and his own writings, explore the significance of Theodore Roosevelt and his presidency. Was Roosevelt more effective as a legislator or as a diplomat?

- **Chapter review: On-line quiz and chapter summary**
  www.wwnorton.com/eamerica/ch23/review.htm

- **Chapter resources: Multimedia index**
  www.wwnorton.com/eamerica/ch23/media.htm

Theodore Roosevelt's emergence as a national leader coincided with the onset of what historians have labeled the Progressive Era (1900–1917). The progressive movement arose in response to many causes, the most powerful of which was the devastating depression of the 1890s and its attendant social unrest. The depression brought hard times to the cities and provoked both the fears and consciences of the rapidly growing middle and upper-middle classes. By the turn of the century, so many outraged activists were at work seeking to improve social conditions and political abuses that people began to speak of a "Progressive Era," a time of fermenting idealism, moral fervor, and constructive social, economic, and political change.

Elements of Reform

Progressivism was a diverse reform movement, quite comprehensive in its goals and motives. Progressives crusaded against the abuses of urban political bosses and corporate robber barons. Their goals were greater democracy, honest and efficient government, more effective regulation of big business and "special interests," and greater social justice for working people. One paradox in the movement was that the regulation of business was often proposed by business leaders. They preferred the stability afforded by a regulated market to the chaos and uncertainty of unrestrained competition.

The progressive movement represented the idealistic spirit of an age rather than a single organized group or party. What reformers shared was a common assumption that the complex social ills and tensions generated by the urban-industrial revolution required expanding the scope of government authority so as to elevate the public interest over private greed.

Governments were now called upon to extend a broad range of direct services: schools, good roads (a movement propelled first by cyclists and then by automobilists), conservation of natural resources, public health and welfare, care of the disabled, farm loans and demonstration agents, among other things. Such initiatives represented the first tentative steps toward the welfare state.

Antecedents to Progressivism

The progressive impulse began at the local level in the 1880s and only gradually emerged on the national level. Beginning in the large cities of the East and Midwest, private citizens promoted reform as an expression of charity. Reformers worked to improve basic public services that had been implemented quickly and often shoddily. Crusaders wanted to reorder government itself through budgets, audits, and a more rationalized structure of government offices. Early efforts to improve public health, education, and factory conditions grew out of a desire to improve the administration and enforcement of local and state laws.

The Mugwumps, those reformers who had fought the spoils system and promoted a civil service based on merit, supplied the progressive movement with an important element of its thinking, the "good-government" ideal. Over the years, their ranks had been supplemented and the good-government outlook broadened by leaders who confronted such old and new urban problems as crime, vice, and the efficient provision of gas, electricity, water, sewers, mass transit, and garbage collection.

Another significant force in fostering the spirit of progressivism was the growing prominence of socialist critiques of living and working conditions. The Socialist party of the time, small but earnest and vocal, served as the left wing of progressivism. Most progressives found socialist remedies unacceptable, and the main progressive reform impulse grew in part from a desire to counter the growing appeal of socialist doctrines.

The Muckrakers

Poverty, unsafe working conditions, epidemics, and child labor in unhealthy factories were complex social issues; remedying them would take more than idealistic desire. Public consciousness needed to be raised. A group of journalists dubbed "muckrakers" rose to the challenge. These writers who thrived on exposing scandal got their name when Theodore Roosevelt compared them to a character in John Bunyan's *Pilgrim's Progress:* "A man that could look no way but downwards with a muckrake in his hands."

Henry Demarest Lloyd is sometimes cited as the first of the muckrakers for his critical examination of the Standard Oil Company and other monopolies in *Wealth Against Commonwealth* (1894). Lincoln Steffens likewise revealed the prevalence of municipal corruption in a series of articles later collected into *The Shame of the Cities* (1904). Another early muckraker was Jacob Riis, a Danish immigrant who, as an influential New York journalist, exposed slum conditions in *How the Other Half Lives* (1890).

In feeding a growing public appetite for facts about the new urban-industrial society, the muckrakers demonstrated one of the salient features of the progressive movement, and one of its central failures. The progressives were stronger on indignant diagnosis than on practical remedy. They harbored a naive faith in the power of democracy. Show the people the facts, expose corruption, and bring government closer to the people, they assumed, and the correction of evils would follow automatically.

The Main Features of Progressivism

Democracy

The most important reform intended to democratize government was the direct primary, in which candidates would be nominated by the vote of all party members rather than by a few political bosses. After South Carolina adopted the first statewide primary in 1896, the concept spread within two decades to nearly every other state.

The primary was but one expression of a broad movement for greater public participation in the political process. In 1898 South Dakota became the first state to adopt the initiative and referendum, procedures that allowed voters to enact laws directly. If a designated number of voters petitioned to have a measure put on the ballot (the initiative), the electorate could then vote it up or down (the referendum). Oregon also adopted a whole spectrum of reform measures, including a voter registration law (1899), the initiative and referendum (1902), the direct primary (1904), a sweeping corrupt-practices act (1908), and the recall (1910), whereby public officials could be removed by petition and vote. By 1920, nearly twenty states had adopted the initiative and referendum and nearly a dozen the recall. The direct election of senators by the people, rather than by the state legislatures, was another progressive political reform. The popular election of senators required a constitutional amendment, and by 1912 the Senate finally agreed to the Seventeenth Amendment, which was ratified by the states in 1913.

Efficiency

A second major theme of progressivism was the "gospel of efficiency." In the business world at the turn of the century and after, Frederick W. Taylor, the original "efficiency expert," developed an array of scientific management techniques designed to cut costs and enhance productivity. "Taylorism," as scientific management came to be known, promised to reduce waste through the careful analysis of labor processes.

In government, the efficiency movement called for "experts" to replace bureaucrats and political appointees. Two new ideas for making municipal government more efficient gained headway in the first decade of the new century. The commission system was first adopted by Galveston, Texas, in 1901, when local government there collapsed in the aftermath of a devastating hurricane that killed 6,000 people and destroyed half the town. It placed ultimate authority for the city in a board composed of elected administrative heads of city departments—commissioners of sanitation, police, utilities, and so on. By 1914 more than 400 towns and small cities across the country had adopted the commission system.

The more durable idea, however, was the city-manager plan, under which a professional administrator ran the government in accordance with policies set by the elected council and mayor. By 1914 the National Association of City Managers heralded the arrival of a new profession.

By the early twentieth century, it was apparent that many functions of government and business now required greater expertise than in pre-industrial America. Wisconsin governor Robert M. ("Fighting Bob") La Follette led the crusade for more efficient government. He established a Legislative Reference Bureau staffed by professors and specialists to provide research, advice, and help in the drafting of legislation designed to curb the power of special interests and promote social justice. This "Wisconsin Idea" of efficient government was widely copied by other states.

Regulation

Of all the problems facing American society at the turn of the century, one engaged a greater diversity of reformers and elicited more controversial solutions than any other: the regulation of giant corporations. Beginning in the 1870s, states had tried to regulate the rates of railroads and the working conditions in other businesses, only to be thwarted by Supreme Court rulings. The judges declared that only the federal government could regulate companies involved in interstate commerce. By the 1890s, the growth of monopolistic corporations spurred reformers to promote trust-busting in the belief that restoring old-fashioned competition would best prevent economic abuses. (The Sherman Anti-Trust Act of 1890 had turned out to be a paper tiger.)

Efforts to restore the competitiveness of small firms proved unworkable in part because breaking up large corporations was more complicated than reformers presumed. Consequently, the main thrust of progressive reform over the years was toward regulation, rather than dissolution, of big businesses. As time passed, however, regulatory agencies often came under the influence or control of those they were supposed to regulate. Railroad executives, for instance, generally had more intimate knowledge of the intricate details involved in their business, giving them the advantage over the outsiders who might be appointed to the Interstate Commerce Commission.

Social Justice

A fourth important feature of the progressive spirit was the impulse toward social justice, which motivated diverse actions from private charity drives to campaigns against child labor and liquor. The settlement house movement of the late nineteenth century had spawned a corps of social workers and genteel reformers devoted to the uplift of slum dwellers. But with time it became apparent that social evils extended beyond the reach of private charities and demanded governmental intervention.

Labor legislation was perhaps the most significant reform to emerge from the drive for social justice. The National Child Labor Committee, organized in 1904, demanded state laws banning the still widespread employment of young children. Within ten years, the committee helped craft new laws in most states banning the labor of underage children (the minimum age varied from

Child worker climbs on a spinning frame. By 1914, states banned the employment of young children and set limits on the working hours of older children.

twelve to sixteen) and limiting the working hours of older children.

Closely linked with the child-labor reform movement was a concerted effort to regulate the hours of work for women. Spearheaded by Florence Kelley, the head of the National Consumers League, this progressive crusade promoted the passage of state laws addressing the distinctive hardships that long working hours imposed on women who were wives and mothers.

The Supreme Court pursued a curiously erratic course in ruling on such state labor laws. In *Lochner* v. *New York* (1905), the Court voided a ten-hour-day law because it violated workers' "liberty of contract" to accept any terms they chose. Then in *Muller* v. *Oregon* (1908), the high court upheld a ten-hour law for women largely on the basis of sociological data that attorney Louis D. Brandeis presented regarding the adverse effects of long hours on the health and morals of women. In *Bunting* v. *Oregon* (1917), the Court accepted a ten-hour workday for both men and women, but held out for twenty more years against state minimum-wage laws.

Legislation to protect workers against avoidable accidents gained momentum from disasters such as the 1911 fire at the Triangle Shirtwaist Company in New York City in which 146 people, mostly young women, died because exits had been locked. The victims were either trapped on the three upper floors of a ten-story building, or they plunged to the street below. Stricter building codes and factory inspection acts followed.

Prohibition

For many progressive activists, the cause of liquor prohibition was the foremost concern. The Women's Christian Temperance Union had been battling the sale of alcoholic beverages since 1874, but the most successful political action followed the formation in 1893 of the Anti-Saloon League, an organization that pioneered the strategy of the single-issue pressure group. In 1913 the league endorsed an amendment to the Constitution prohibiting all alcoholic beverages, which was adopted by Congress that year. By the time it was ratified six years later, state and local action already had dried up areas occupied by nearly three-fourths of the nation's population.

Roosevelt's Progressivism

While most progressive initiatives were started at the state and local levels, calls for national efforts began to appear around 1900. Theodore Roosevelt brought to the White House in 1901 an expansive vision of the presidency that was admirably suited to the cause of progressive reform. More than any other president since Lincoln, Roosevelt possessed an activist bent. Still, his initial approach to reform was cautious. He sought to avoid the extremes of socialism on the one hand and laissez-faire individualism on the other. For him, politics was the art of the possible. Unlike the more radical progressives and the doctrinaire "lunatic fringe," as he called them, he would take half a loaf rather than none at all.

The Trusts

On the issue of huge business trusts, Roosevelt in 1902 proposed a "square deal" for all, calling for enforcement of existing antitrust laws and stricter controls on big business. Effective regulation, he insisted, was better than a futile effort to restore small business, which might be achieved only at a cost to the efficiencies of scale gained in larger operations.

Because Congress balked at regulatory legislation, Roosevelt sought to force the issue by a more vigorous federal prosecution of the Sherman Anti-Trust Act. He chose his target carefully. In the case against the Sugar Trust (*United States* v. *E. C. Knight and Company,* 1895), the Supreme Court had declared manufacturing a strictly *intrastate* activity. Most railroads, however, were beyond question engaged in *interstate* commerce and thus subject to federal authority. Consequently, in 1902 Roosevelt moved against the Northern Securities Company, a holding company controlling the Great Northern and Northern Pacific Railroads. In 1904 the Supreme Court ordered the combination dissolved in *U.S.* v. *Northern Securities Company.*

This 1909 cartoon takes a satirical view of Roosevelt's antitrust and conservation reforms, showing him slaying those trusts he considered "bad" for the public interest and restraining those he considered "good."

The most notable victory against a trust came in *Swift and Company* v. *United States* (1905), a decision against the "beef trust" through which most of the meat packers had avoided competitive bidding in the purchase of livestock. In this decision, the Supreme Court put forth the "stream-of-commerce" doctrine, which overturned its previous holding that manufacturing was strictly intrastate. Since both livestock and the meat products of the meat packers moved in the stream of interstate commerce, the Court reasoned, they were subject to federal regulation. This interpretation of the interstate commerce power would be broadened in later years until few enterprises would remain beyond the reach of federal regulation.

The 1902 Coal Strike

Support for Roosevelt's use of the "big stick" against corporations was strengthened by the stubbornness of mine owners in the anthracite coal strike of 1902. On May 12 the United Mine Workers (UMW) walked off the job in West Virginia and Pennsylvania. They demanded a 20 percent wage increase, a reduction in daily working hours from ten to nine, and formal management recognition of their union. The operators dug in their heels and shut down the mines in an effort to starve out the miners.

To avoid a national coal shortage, Roosevelt called both sides to a conference at the White House. The mine owners attended but refused even to speak to the UMW leaders. The "extraordinary stupidity and temper" of the "wooden-headed" owners outraged Roosevelt. After the conference ended in an impasse, he threatened to take over the mines and run them with the army. When a congressman questioned the constitutionality of such a move, an exasperated Roosevelt roared: "To hell with the Constitution when the people want coal!" Militarizing the mines would have been an act of dubious legality, but the owners feared that Roosevelt might actually do it and that public opinion would support him.

The coal strike ended in October 1902 with an agreement to submit the issues to an arbitration commission named by the president. The agreement enhanced the prestige of both Roosevelt and the union's leaders, although it produced only a partial victory for the miners. By the arbitrators' decision in 1903, the miners won a nine-hour workday but only a 10 percent wage increase and no union recognition.

An Expanding Government

In 1903 Congress strengthened both antitrust enforcement and governmental regulation by creating the Department of Commerce and Labor and by passing the Elkins Act, which made it illegal for corporations to take as well as to give secret rebates to their preferred customers. The Bureau of Corporations, a new federal agency within the new department, had no direct regulatory powers, but it did have a mandate to study and report on the activities of interstate corporations. Its findings could lead to antitrust suits, but its purpose was rather to help corporations correct malpractices and avoid the need for lawsuits. Many companies cooperated, but others held back. When Standard Oil refused to turn over records, the government brought an antitrust suit that resulted in its dissolution in 1911. The Supreme Court ordered the American Tobacco Company broken up at the same time.

Roosevelt's Second Term

Roosevelt's policies built a coalition of progressive- and conservative-minded voters that assured his election in his own right in 1904. An invincible popularity and the sheer force of his personality swept Roosevelt to an impressive victory over the Democratic nominee, Alton B. Parker. Parker carried only the Solid South of the former Confederacy and two border states, Kentucky and Maryland. On election night, Roosevelt announced that he would not run again, a statement he later would regret.

Theodore Roosevelt was an energetic, effusive political personality.

Legislative Leadership

Roosevelt approached his second term with heightened confidence and a stronger commitment to progressive reform. In late 1905 he devoted most of his annual message to the need for greater regulation and control of business. This irked the corporate leaders who had contributed to his campaign. Said steel baron Henry Frick, "We bought the son of a bitch and then he did not stay put." The independent Roosevelt took aim at the railroads first.

Roosevelt asked Congress to extend the authority of the Interstate Commerce Commission (ICC) and to give it effective control over railroad rates. He had to mobilize all the pressure and influence at his disposal to push through the bill introduced by Representative Peter Hepburn of Iowa. Enacted in 1906, the Hepburn Act gave the ICC power to set maximum freight rates. The commission no longer had to go to court to enforce its decisions. The Hepburn Act also extended the ICC's regulatory reach beyond railroads to pipelines, freight companies, sleeping-car companies, bridges, and ferries.

On the very day after passage of the Hepburn Act, a growing movement for the regulation of meat packers, food processors, and makers of drugs and patent medicines reached fruition. Discontent with abuses in these fields had grown rapidly as a result of the muckrakers' disclosures of harmful additives used in the preparation of "embalmed meat" and other food products and dangerous ingredients in some patent medicines.

Perhaps the most telling blow against such abuses was struck by Upton Sinclair's novel *The Jungle* (1906), which graphically portrayed the filthy conditions in Chicago's meat-packing industry. Roosevelt read *The Jungle*—and reacted quickly. He sent two federal agents to Chicago to investigate, and their report confirmed all that Sinclair had said. Soon he and the Congress were hammering out a bill to address the problem.

The Meat Inspection Act of 1906 required federal inspection of meats destined for interstate commerce and empowered officials in the Agriculture Department to impose sanitary standards. The Pure Food and Drug Act, enacted the same day, placed restrictions on the makers of prepared foods and patent medicines and forbade the manufacture, sale, or transportation of adulterated, misbranded, or harmful foods, drugs, and liquors.

Conservation

In addition to regulatory legislation, one of the most enduring legacies of the Roosevelt years was the president's energetic support for the budding conservation movement. Concern for protecting the environment grew with the rising awareness that exploitation of natural resources was despoiling the frontier. As early as 1872, Yellowstone National Park had been set aside as a public reserve, and in 1881, Congress had created a Division of Forestry in the Department of Agriculture. Roosevelt, an ardent hiker, camper, hunter, and bird watcher, strove to halt the unchecked destruction of the nation's natural resources and wonders by providing a barrier of federal regulation and protection. His appointment of Gifford Pinchot as chief forester resulted in vigorous new scientific management of public lands. Roosevelt added fifty federal wildlife refuges, approved five new national parks, and initiated the system of designating national monuments, such as the Grand Canyon. He also used the Forest Reserve Act (1891) to exclude from settlement or harvest some 172 million acres of timberland.

From Roosevelt to Taft

As he neared the end of his second term, Roosevelt reaffirmed his 1904 decision not to run again. Instead he sought to have his secretary of war, William Howard Taft, replace him, and the Republican convention ratified the choice on its first ballot in 1908. The Democrats decided to give William Jennings Bryan one more chance. Still vigorous at forty-eight, Bryan retained a faithful following, but the voters opted for Roosevelt's chosen successor, leaving Bryan only the southern states plus Nebraska, Colorado, and Nevada. The real surprise of the election was the strong showing of the Socialist party candidate, labor hero Eugene V. Debs. He attracted over 400,000 votes, illustrating the mounting intensity of working-class unrest.

Born to a prominent Cincinnati family, Taft boasted more experience in public service than any other president since Martin Van Buren. After graduating second in his class at Yale, he progressed through appointive offices, from assistant prosecutor in Ohio, to governor-general in the Philippines, and secretary of war. The presidency was the only elective office he ever held. Later he would be appointed Chief Justice of the Supreme Court (1921–1930), a job more suited to his temperament.

Taft never felt comfortable in the White House. The political dynamo in the family was his wife, Nellie. One of the major tragedies of Taft's presidency was that Helen "Nellie" Taft suffered a debilitating stroke soon after they entered the White House, and for most of his term, she remained unable to serve as his political adviser.

Tariff Reform

Against Roosevelt's advice, Taft had promised a tariff reduction during the campaign. True to his word, he called a special session of Congress eleven days after his inauguration. A reduced tariff passed the House with surprising ease. But before the Senate passed the bill, it made more than 800 changes, most of which raised rates. Outraged by such obvious catering to special interests, a group of ten progressive Republicans joined the Democrats in an unsuccessful effort to defeat the bill. Taft at first agreed with them, but then, fearful of a party split, he backed the majority and agreed to an imperfect bill. He only made matters worse by calling the tariff the best "that the Republican party ever passed." Taft thereafter drifted into the orbit of the Republican Old Guard and quickly alienated the progressive wing of his party, whom he tagged "assistant Democrats."

Ballinger and Pinchot

In 1910 Taft's policies drove the wedge deeper between the Republican factions. What came to be known as the Ballinger-Pinchot controversy made Taft appear to be a less reliable custodian of Roosevelt's conservation policies than he actually was. The controversy arose after Taft's secretary of the interior, Richard A. Ballinger, turned over coal-rich government lands in Alaska to a group of investor friends who sold part of the lands to a mining syndicate. When Chief of Forestry Gifford Pinchot revealed the scam, Taft fired Pinchot for insubordination. A joint congressional investigation later exonerated Ballinger from all charges of fraud or corruption, but conservationist suspicions created such pressures that he resigned in 1911.

The incident tarnished Taft's public image. He had been elected to carry out the Roosevelt policies, his Republican opponents said, and he *was* carrying them out—"on a stretcher." Events had conspired to cast Taft in a conservative role at a time when progressive sentiment was riding high. The result was a sharp setback for the president in the congressional elections of 1910, first by the widespread defeat of pro-Taft candidates in the Republican primaries, then by the election of a Democratic majority in the House and of enough Democrats in the Senate that progressive Republicans could wield the balance of power.

Baby, Kiss Papa Good-by. This 1909 cartoon shows Theodore Roosevelt departing the White House confident that his chosen successor, William Howard Taft, will carry out his policies.

Taft and Roosevelt

In 1910 Roosevelt had returned from his travels abroad. As news accounts highlighted the Taft "betrayal" of Roosevelt's programs, his followers urged him to take action. After hesitating for several months, Roosevelt again entered the political arena, having concluded that Taft had "sold the Square Deal down the river." At a speech in Kansas in 1910, he gave a catchy name to his latest principles, the "New Nationalism," declaring that he intended to put the national interest above any "sectional or personal advantage." Roosevelt then issued a stirring call for an array of new federal regulatory laws, a social-welfare program, and new measures of direct democracy, including the old populist demands for the initiative, recall, and referendum. His purpose was not to revolutionize American life but to save it from "wild radicalism."

Thereafter, Roosevelt intensified his criticism of the administration. Equally critical of Taft was Senator Robert La Follette of

Wisconsin, who in 1911 helped organize the National Progressive Republican League and soon became its leading candidate for the Republican party nomination. A militant reformer fiercely committed to greater government regulation of business and civil rights for *all* Americans, La Follette was more of a crusader than a politician. Sensing Taft's weakness, Roosevelt also threw his hat in the ring in 1912. But even though many of La Follette's supporters rushed to embrace the ex-president, the Wisconsin idealist stubbornly refused to give way to Roosevelt. He felt that Roosevelt was not genuinely committed to the sweeping reforms necessary for a truly progressive America.

The rebuke implicit in Roosevelt's decision to run against Taft, his chosen successor, was in many ways undeserved. Taft had at least attempted tariff reform, which Roosevelt had never dared. And in the end his administration set aside more public lands for conservation in four years than Roosevelt's had in nearly eight and brought more antitrust suits, by a score of eighty to twenty-five. Taft also established the Bureau of Mines and the Federal Children's Bureau (1912). He supported both the Sixteenth Amendment (1913), which authorized a federal income tax, and the Seventeenth Amendment (1913), which provided for the popular election of senators.

Despite Taft's "progressive" record, Roosevelt now hastened Taft's demise. Brusquely pushing aside La Follette's claim to the "progressive" Republican mantle, Roosevelt won most of the Republican primaries in 1912, even in Taft's Ohio. But such popular support was no match for Taft's advantages as president and party leader. The Taft forces nominated their man by the same "steamroller" tactics that had nominated Roosevelt in 1904. Outraged at such "naked theft," the Roosevelt delegates issued a call for a Progressive party convention, which assembled in Chicago on August 5. The new third-party supporters were a curious mixture of clergymen and laymen, college presidents, professors, journalists, liberal businessmen, and social workers. Roosevelt told the group he felt "fit as a bull moose" in accepting their nomination. Now it was the Democrats' turn.

Wilson's Progressivism

Wilson's Rise

Meanwhile, the emergence of Thomas Woodrow Wilson as the Democratic nominee in 1912 climaxed a political rise even more rapid than that of Grover Cleveland. In 1910, before his election as governor of New Jersey, Wilson had been president of Princeton University, but had never run for public office. Born in Staunton, Virginia, in 1856, the son of a "noble-saintly mother" and a stern Presbyterian minister, he had grown up in Georgia and the Carolinas during the Civil War and Reconstruction.

Driven by a sense of destiny and duty, Wilson was elected governor of New Jersey in 1910. After his election, he promoted progressive measures and pushed them through the legislature. He pressured New Jersey lawmakers to enact a workers' compensation law, a corrupt-practices law, measures to regulate public utilities, and ballot reforms. Such strong leadership in a state known as the "home of the trusts" for its lenient corporation laws brought Wilson to national attention.

In the spring of 1911 a group of southern Democrats in New York opened a Wilson presidential campaign headquarters, and Wilson set forth on strenuous tours into all regions of the country, denouncing special privilege and political bossism. Wilson believed that the president of the country should be as active in directing legislation as in the administration and enforcement of laws. In calling for a strong presidency,

Wilson expressed views closer to those of Roosevelt than to those of Taft. He likewise shared Roosevelt's belief that politicians should promote the general welfare rather than narrow special interests. And, like Roosevelt, he was critical of big business, organized labor, socialism, and agrarian radicalism. Wilson captured the Democratic nomination on the fourteenth ballot.

The Election of 1912

The 1912 presidential election involved four candidates: Wilson and Taft represented the two major parties, while Eugene Debs ran as a Socialist, and Roosevelt headed the Progressive party ticket. After an initial bout of name-calling, the campaign settled down to a debate over the competing ideologies of the two front-runners: Roosevelt's "New Nationalism" and Wilson's "New Freedom." The fuzzy ideas that Roosevelt fashioned into his New Nationalism had first been presented systematically in *The Promise of American Life* (1909), a widely influential book by Herbert Croly, a New York journalist. Its central point was that progressives must give up traditional prejudices against big government and use the power of government to achieve democratic ends in the public interest.

Roosevelt claimed that his New Nationalism would enable government to promote social justice and enact reforms such as graduated income and inheritance taxes, workers' compensation for disabling injuries or illnesses, regulation of the labor of women and children, and a stronger Bureau of Corporations. These and more went into the platform of his Progressive party, which called for a federal trade commission with sweeping authority over business and a tariff commission to set rates on a "scientific basis."

Before the end of his administration, Wilson would embrace such new nationalism too, but initially he adhered to the decentralizing antitrust traditions of his party. Before the start of the campaign, Wilson conferred with Louis D. Brandeis, a progressive lawyer from Boston who focused Wilson's thought much as Croly had focused Roosevelt's. Brandeis's design for the New Freedom differed from Roosevelt's New Nationalism in its belief that the federal government should restore competition rather than regulate monopolies. This required eliminating *all* trusts, lowering tariffs, and breaking up the concentration of financial power on Wall Street. Brandeis and Wilson also dreamed of turning over most social programs to the states and cities. In this sense, they saw the vigorous expansion of federal power as only a temporary necessity, not a permanent condition. Having restored competition and the diffusion of power and programs, the national government would revert to its aloof heritage.

Republican William Howard Taft, Democrat Woodrow Wilson, and Progressive or "Bull Moose" candidate Theodore Roosevelt start on the three-way race for the White House in this 1912 cartoon.

The Republican schism between Taft and Roosevelt opened the way for Woodrow Wilson to win by 435 electoral votes to 88 for Roosevelt and 8 for Taft. The Republican Taft and the former Republican Roosevelt were now private citizens. During the 1920s, Taft was appointed Chief Justice of the Supreme Court and served for nine years with distinction. Even his liberal jurist associates afforded him the highest respect.

The 1912 election was significant in a number of respects. First, it was a high-water mark for progressivism. The candidates debated the basic issues in a campaign unique for its focus on vital alternatives and for its high philosophical tone. And the Socialist party, the left wing of progressivism, polled over 900,000 votes for Eugene V. Debs, about 6 percent of the total vote, its highest proportion ever.

Second, the election brought the Democrats back into effective national power for the first time since the Civil War. For two years during the second Cleveland administration, 1893–1895, they had held the White House and majorities in both houses of Congress, but they had quickly fallen out of power during the most severe depression in American history to that time. Now, under Wilson, the Democrats again held the presidency and enjoyed majorities in the House and Senate.

Third, Wilson's election brought southerners back into the orbit of national and international affairs in a significant way for the first time since the Civil War. Five of Wilson's ten cabinet members were born in the South, and William Jennings Bryan, the secretary of state, was an idol of the southern masses. At the president's right hand, and one of the most influential members of the Wilson circle, was Colonel Edward M. House of Texas. Southern legislators, by virtue of their seniority, held most committee chairmanships. As a result, much of the progressive legislation of the Wilson era would bear the names of the southerners who guided the bills through Congress.

Wilsonian Reform

Whereas Roosevelt had been a strong president by force of personality, Wilson became a strong president by force of conviction. The president, he argued, must become the dynamic voice in national affairs. Wilson courted popular support, but he also courted members of Congress through personal contacts, invitations to the White House, and visits to the Capitol. He used patronage power to reward friends and punish enemies. Though he might have acted through a bipartisan progressive coalition, he chose instead to rely on party loyalty.

The Tariff

The new president's leadership met its first test on the issue of tariff reform. Wilson summoned Congress into special session and addressed it in person—the first president to do so since John Adams. In response to Wilson's request for lower tariff duties to promote competition, Congress passed the Underwood-Simmons Tariff of 1913. It reduced the overall average duty from about 37 percent to about 29 percent. The act lowered tariffs but raised internal revenues with the first federal income tax levied under the newly ratified Sixteenth Amendment.

The Federal Reserve Act

Before the new tariff had cleared the Senate, the administration proposed the first major banking and currency reform since the Civil War. The Glass-Owen Federal Reserve Act of 1913 created a new banking system with twelve regional Federal Reserve Banks, each owned by member banks in its district. All national banks became members of the new Federal Reserve system; state banks could join if they wished. Each member bank had to subscribe 6 percent of its capital to the Federal Reserve Bank and deposit a portion of its reserve there, the amount depending on the size of the community.

These "bankers' banks" dealt chiefly with their members, not with individuals. Along with other banking functions, the chief service to member banks was to take over their outstanding loans in exchange for Federal Reserve Notes (paper currency), which member banks might then use to make further loans. This arrangement made it possible to expand both the money supply and bank credit in times of high business activity, or as the level of borrowing increased. A Federal Reserve Board exercised general supervision over the activities of the member banks and adjusted interest rates to fight inflation or stimulate business. It is hard to exaggerate the significance of the passage of the Federal Reserve Act. Through Wilson's skillful leadership, the Congress took a major step in providing the nation with a sound yet flexible currency system and at the same time helped decentralize the money supply.

Antitrust Laws

Wilson had made trust-busting the central focus of the New Freedom. During the summer of 1914, he decided to make a strong Federal Trade Commission the cornerstone of his antitrust program. Created in 1914, the five-member commission replaced Roosevelt's Bureau of Corporations and assumed new powers to define "unfair trade practices" and to issue "cease and desist" orders when it found evidence of unfair competition.

The Clayton Antitrust Act, passed in 1914, outlawed such practices as price discrimination (charging different customers different prices for the same goods), "tying" agreements that limited the right of dealers to handle the products of competing manufacturers, and corporations' acquisition of stock in competing corporations. In every case, however, conservative forces in the Senate qualified these provisions by tacking on the weakening phrase "where the effect may be to substantially lessen competition" or words of similar effect. And conservative southern Democrats and northern Republicans amended the act to allow for broad judicial review of the Federal Trade Commission's decisions, thus further weakening its freedom of action.

Agrarian reformers, allied with organized labor, won a stipulation in the Clayton Act that declared farm and labor organizations not to be, per se, unlawful combinations in restraint of trade. Injunctions in labor disputes, moreover, were not to be handed down by federal courts unless "necessary to prevent irreparable injury to property." Though hailed by Samuel Gompers as organized labor's "Magna Carta," these provisions were actually little more than pious affirmations, as later court decisions would demonstrate.

Administration of the antitrust laws generally proved disappointing to the more vehement progressives under Wilson. The Justice Department offered advice to business owners interested in arranging matters so as to avoid antitrust prosecutions. The appointment of conservatives to the Interstate Commerce Commission and the Federal Reserve Board won plaudits from the business world and profoundly disappointed progressives.

Social Justice

Wilson had in fact never been committed to social-justice issues. He had carried out his promises to lower the tariff, reorganize the banking system, and strengthen the antitrust laws, but he was not inclined to go much further. Although he endorsed state action for women's suffrage, he declined to support a suffrage amendment because his party platform had not. He withheld support from federal child-labor legislation because he regarded it as a state matter, and he opposed a bill providing federal loans for strapped farmers on the grounds that it was "unwise and unjustifiable to extend the credit of the government to a single class of the community."

Progressivism for Whites Only

Like many other progressives, Woodrow Wilson showed little interest in the plight of African Americans. In fact, he shared many of the racist attitudes prevalent at the time. Although Wilson denounced the Ku Klux Klan's "reign of terror," he sympathized with its motives to restore white rule in the postwar South and to relieve whites of the "ignorant and hostile" power of the black vote during Reconstruction. He also opposed giving the vote to uneducated whites, and he detested the enfranchisement of blacks, arguing that Americans of Anglo-

Saxon origin would always resist domination by "an ignorant and inferior race." He believed that white resistance to black rule was "unalterable."

Later, as a politician, Wilson courted black voters, but he rarely consulted African-American leaders and repeatedly avoided opportunities to associate with them in public. Many of the southerners he appointed to his cabinet were uncompromising racists who systematically began segregating the employees in their agencies, even though the agencies had been integrated for over fifty years. Workplaces were segregated by race, as were toilets and drinking fountains. When black leaders protested these actions, Wilson replied that such racial segregation was intended to eliminate "the possibility of friction" in the federal workplace.

Progressive Resurgence

The need to weld a winning coalition in 1916 pushed Wilson back on the road of reform. Progressive Democrats were restless, and after war broke out in Europe in 1914, further divisions in the party arose over defense and foreign policy. At the same time, the Republicans were repairing their own rift. The Progressive party showed little staying power in the 1914 midterm election, and Roosevelt showed little will to preserve it. Most observers recognized that Wilson could shape a majority only by courting progressives of all parties. In 1916 Wilson scored points with them when he nominated Louis D. Brandeis to the Supreme Court. Conservatives waged a vigorous battle against Brandeis, but Senate progressives rallied to win confirmation of the social-justice champion as the first Jewish member of the Supreme Court.

Wilson meanwhile began to embrace the broad program of farm and labor reforms he had earlier spurned. On the issue of federal farm credit, he reversed himself abruptly, supporting a proposal to set up land banks to sponsor farm loans. With this boost, the Federal Farm Loan Act became law in 1916. It created twelve Federal Land Banks that paralleled the Federal Reserve Banks and offered low-interest loans to farmers.

The dream of cheap rural credit, sponsored by a generation of populists, had come to fruition. Democrats never embraced the populist subtreasury plan, but they made a small step in that direction with the Warehouse Act of 1916. This measure authorized federal licensing of private warehouses, and federal backing made their receipts for stored produce more acceptable to local bankers as collateral for short-term loans to farmers. Other concessions to farm demands included the Smith-Lever Act of 1914 and the Smith-Hughes Act of 1917, both of which passed with little controversy. The first provided federal grants-in-aid for farm demonstration agents to show farmers new planting techniques, fertilizers, and equipment. The second measure funded agricultural and mechanical education in the high schools. Farmers with automobiles had more than a passing interest as well in the Federal Highways Act of 1916, which provided dollar-matching contributions to states with highway departments that met certain federal standards.

The progressive resurgence of 1916 broke the logjam on labor reforms as well. Advocates of child-labor legislation persuaded Wilson to overcome doubts of its constitutionality and sign the Keating-Owen Child Labor Act, which excluded from interstate commerce goods manufactured by children under fourteen. But the Supreme Court soon ruled it unconstitutional on the grounds that regulation of interstate commerce could not extend to the conditions of labor. On the other hand, the Supreme Court upheld the Adamson Act of 1916, which mandated the eight-hour workday for railroad workers.

In Wilson's first term, progressive government reached its zenith. It set a framework within which American politics and society would still function, by and large, near the end of the century. Progressivism had conquered the old premise that the government is best which governs least, whatever political rhetoric might be heard to the contrary. Progressivism, an amalgam of agrarian, business, governmental, and social reform, amounted in the end to a movement for active government on behalf of the public interest.

The Limits of Progressivism

Like all great historic movements, progressivism contained elements of paradox and irony. Despite all the talk of greater democracy at the turn of the century, it was also the age of disenfranchisement for southern blacks and ugly prejudice against "new" immigrants. The initiative and referendum, supposedly democratic reforms, proved subject to manipulation by well-financed publicity campaigns. And much of the public policy of the time came to be formulated by experts and members of appointed boards, not by broad segments of the population.

Progressivism was largely a middle-class movement in which the poor and unorganized had little influence. It is surprising that a movement so dedicated to democratic rhetoric should experience so steady a decline in voter participation. In 1912, the year of the Bull Moose campaign, voting dropped off by almost 7 percent. The new politics of issues and charismatic leaders proved to be less effective in turning out voters than party organizations and bosses had been. And by 1916 the optimism of an age that looked to infinite progress was already confronted by a vast slaughter. Europe had stumbled into war, and America would soon be drawn in. The twentieth century, which had dawned with such bright hopes, held in store episodes of unparalleled horror.

CHAPTER 24

America and the Great War

This chapter focuses on

- Wilson's foreign policy toward Mexico.
- The causes and early years of the Great War in Europe.
- America's entry into and role in the Great War.
- Wilson's efforts to promote his peace plan.
- The aftermath of the war.

Food is
Ammunition -
Don't waste it.

THE *ESSENTIAL AMERICA* ON-LINE TUTOR

www.wwnorton.com/eamerica/ch24

- **Topic: Mobilizing public opinion during World War I**
  www.wwnorton.com/eamerica/ch24/topic.htm

  President Woodrow Wilson decided to generate popular support for World War I by using an unprecedented governmental propaganda campaign. Relying on posters and historical analyses, examine how the Wilson administration created popular support and brought the American people out of their isolationist shell. Why did Wilson opt for a propaganda campaign in lieu of press censorship in order to generate popular support?

- **Chapter review: On-line quiz and chapter summary**
  www.wwnorton.com/eamerica/ch24/review.htm

- **Chapter resources: Multimedia index**
  www.wwnorton.com/eamerica/ch24/media.htm

Throughout the nineteenth century, the United States reaped the benefits of its geographic distance from the wars that plagued Britain and Europe. The Atlantic Ocean provided a welcome buffer. During the early twentieth century, however, events combined to end the nation's comfortable isolation. Ever-expanding world trade entwined American interests with the fate of Europe. In addition, the development of steam-powered ships and submarines meant that foreign navies could threaten American security. At the same time, the election of Woodrow Wilson brought to the White House a stern moralist determined to impose his standards for right conduct on renegade nations. This combination of circumstances turned the outbreak of war in Europe in 1914 into a profound crisis for Americans, a crisis that in the end would transform the nation's role in international affairs.

Wilson and Foreign Affairs

Woodrow Wilson brought to the presidency no background in the conduct of foreign relations. But from 1914 on, foreign relations increasingly preoccupied Wilson's attention. Although lacking in international experience, Wilson did not lack ideas or convictions in this area. He wanted to help create a new world order governed by morality and idealism rather than by greed and crass national interests. Both he and his pious secretary of state, William Jennings Bryan, believed that America had been called to promote democracy and moral progress in the world. How to promote such democratic idealism and self-determination abroad, however, remained a thorny issue, as Wilson soon discovered in responding to rapidly changing events in Mexico.

Woodrow Wilson, the School Teacher. A comment on the reform efforts by the United States in the affairs of Latin American countries.

Intervention in Mexico

In 1910 resentment in Mexico against years of dictatorship boiled over in revolt. A year later, revolutionary armies had occupied Mexico City. The leader of the rebellion, Francisco I. Madero, a charismatic dreamer, proved unable to manage the tough customers attracted to the revolt by the scramble for power. In 1913 General Victoriano Huerta assumed power, and Madero was murdered soon afterward. Wilson challenged the legitimacy of Huerta's violent coup. "I will not recognize a government of butchers," he insisted privately. At the same time, he expressed sympathy with a new revolutionary movement led by Venustiano Carranza and began to put diplomatic pressure on Huerta.

Early in 1914 Wilson removed an embargo on arms to Mexico in order to help Carranza's forces, and he stationed warships off Veracruz to halt foreign arms shipments to Huerta. On April 9, 1914, several American sailors, gathering supplies ashore at Tampico, strayed into a restricted area and were arrested. The Mexican officials quickly released them and sent an apology to the American naval commander. There the incident might have ended, but the naval officer demanded that the Mexicans salute the American flag. Wilson backed him up and won from Congress authority to use force to bring Huerta to terms. Before the Tampico incident could be resolved, Wilson sent a naval force to Veracruz. American marines and sailors went ashore on April 21, 1914, and they forcibly occupied the town at a cost of nineteen killed. At least 200 Mexicans were killed.

In Mexico the American occupation aroused the opposition of all factions, and Huerta tried to rally support against foreign invasion. At this juncture, Wilson accepted a mediation offer by the ABC powers (Argentina, Brazil, and Chile). In 1914 they proposed withdrawal of United States forces, the removal of Huerta, and installation of a provisional government. Huerta refused, but the moral effect of the proposal, his isolation abroad, and the growing strength of his foes forced him to leave office. The Carranzistas entered Mexico City, and the Americans left Veracruz. Wilson's "missionary diplomacy" seemed to have worked.

But no sooner had the Carranzistas taken power than they began to squabble among themselves for the spoils of office. The most incendiary confrontation occurred between Carranza and his foremost general, the charismatic Pancho Villa, a former bandit who claimed to represent "the people" behind the revolution. Such a public stance attracted Wilson's sympathy, and he initially supported Villa. This turned out to be a colossal blunder. As fighting erupted in 1915, the Villistas suffered serious defeats. The Wilson administration, confused and frantic, shifted its stance to that of neutrality, with the president announcing that the Mexicans should be allowed to determine their own fate without outside interference.

Critics, however, charged that Wilson was a bungler and a coward. The always militant Theodore Roosevelt, for example, attacked the president's earlier support of the revolution and called for American military intervention to restore order. Responding to such domestic pressure, Wilson warned the two Mexican factions to stop fighting or risk facing American troops. Villa then requested an armistice, but Carranza, sensing his military dominance, rejected Wilson's right to intrude in Mexico's affairs.

By the fall of 1915, however, relations between Carranza and Wilson improved, as the United States formally recognized his claim as the *de facto* leader of the Mexican nation. This enraged Villa. In early 1916 Villa's men stopped a train and murdered sixteen American mining engineers. They wanted to provoke American intervention, discredit Carranza, and build Villa up as an opponent of the "Gringos." Two months later, Villa's band of renegades entered Columbus, New Mexico, burned the town, and killed seventeen Americans.

Mexican revolutionary Pancho Villa and his followers antagonized the United States with violent attacks.

An outraged Wilson sent General John J. Pershing and a force of some 11,000 men deep inside Mexico to pursue Villa and his men. For nearly a year, Pershing's troops chased Villa through northern Mexico. But Villa eluded the Americans, and they returned home in 1917. Carranza then pressed his own war against the bandits and put through a new liberal constitution in 1917. Mexico was by then well on the way to a more orderly government, almost in spite of Wilson's actions rather than because of them.

Problems in the Caribbean

In the Caribbean, Wilson found it as hard to implement his ideals as in Mexico. During President Taft's term (1909–1913), refinements of Roosevelt's interventionist policy had earned from its opponents the less exalted—if fairly accurate—title of "dollar diplomacy." The policy so tagged had its origin in China in 1909, when President Taft personally cabled the Chinese government on behalf of American investors interested in an international consortium to finance railroad lines in China. In Latin America "dollar diplomacy" worked differently and with somewhat more success. The idea was to encourage American bankers to help prop up the finances of shaky Caribbean governments in which American investors had a stake.

One of the first applications of Wilsonian idealism to foreign policy came when the president renounced so-called dollar diplomacy. The government, he declared, was not supporting any "special groups or interests." Despite Wilson's public stand against using military force to back up American investments, however, he kept the marines in Nicaragua, where they had been sent by Taft in 1912, to prevent renewed civil war. There they would stay almost continuously through 1933. Then in 1915 Wilson dispatched more marines to Haiti after two successive revolutions and subsequent disorders. The American forces stayed until 1934. Turmoil in the Dominican Republic brought American marines to that country in 1916, where they remained until 1924. The presence of American military force in the region only worsened the already prevalent irritation at "Yankee imperialism."

An Uneasy Neutrality

Problems in Mexico and Central America loomed larger in Wilson's thinking than the gathering storm in Europe. The thunderbolt of war in the summer of 1914 struck most Americans, one North Carolinian wrote, "as lightning out of a clear sky." It seemed unreal that civilized Europe could descend into such an orgy of destruction. But the assassination of Austrian archduke Franz Ferdinand by a Serbian nationalist, Austria-Hungary's determination to punish Serbia, and Russia's military mobilization in sympathy with its Slavic brothers in Serbia suddenly triggered a conflict between a European system of alliances: the Triple Alliance or Central Powers (Germany, Austria-Hungary, and Italy) and the Triple Entente or Allied Powers (France, Great Britain, and Russia).

The sequence of decisions leading to World War I unfolded with little thought of their consequences. When Russia refused to stop its mobilization, Germany, which backed Austria-Hungary, declared war on Russia on August 1, 1914, and on Russia's ally France two days later. Germany then invaded Belgium to get at France, which brought Great Britain into the war on August 4. Japan, eager to seize German holdings in the Pacific, declared war on August 23, and Turkey entered on the side of the Central Powers a week later. Although allied with the Central Powers, Italy initially stayed out of the war and struck a bargain under which it joined the Allied Powers in 1915.

The First World War was unlike any previous conflict in its scope and horrors. Over 61 million troops served in the armed forces on both sides, and millions lost their lives. New and enhanced military technologies produced unprecedented carnage. Machine guns, high-velocity rifles, aerial bombing, poison gas, flame throwers, land mines, long-range artillery, and armored tanks changed the nature of warfare and produced massive casualties and widespread destruction. Over 9 million combatants were killed in action; another 19 million were wounded.

The battlefields of World War I were surrealistic in their horrors. Most of the great battles involved hundreds of thousands of men crawling out of their trenches and then crossing "no-man's-land" to attack enemy positions, only to be pushed back themselves a day or a week later. Life in the trenches was miserable. In addition to the dangers of enemy fire, soldiers on both sides were forced to deal with flooding and diseases such as trench foot, which could lead to amputation. Lice and rats were constant companions. The stench was unbearable. Soldiers on both sides ate, slept, and fought amid the reek of death.

America's Initial Reactions

As the trench war along the Western Front in Belgium and in France stalemated, the casualties mounted and pressure for American intervention increased. On the first day of the Battle of the Somme, July 1, 1916, 20,000 British soldiers were killed and 40,000 others were wounded—all in less than twenty-four hours. Shock in the United States gave way to gratitude that an ocean stood between America and the killing fields. President Wilson repeatedly urged Americans to be "neutral in thought as well as in action."

That was more easily said than done. In the 1910 U.S. population of 92 million, more than 32 million were first- or second-generation immigrants who retained close ties to their old countries. Among the more than 13 million from the countries at war, the 8 million German Americans were by far the largest group, and the 4 million Irish Americans harbored a deep-rooted enmity to Britain. These groups instinctively leaned toward the Central Powers.

Other Americans, largely of British origin, supported the Allied Powers. Britain and France, if not their ally Russia, seemed the custodians of democracy, while Germany seemed the embodiment of autocracy and militarism. If not a direct threat to the United States, Germany would pose at least a potential threat if it destroyed the balance of power in Europe.

What effect the propaganda of the warring powers had on American opinion is unclear. The Germans and the British were most active, but German propaganda, which played on American dislike of Russian autocracy and anti-Semitism, fell mainly upon barren ground. Only German Americans and Irish Americans responded to a "hate England" theme. From the outset, the British had one supreme advantage in this area. Once they had cut the direct telegraph cable from Germany early in the war, nearly all news from the battlefronts had to clear through London.

A Strained Neutrality

At first the war brought a slump in American exports and the threat of a depression, but by the spring of 1915 the Allies' demand for supplies generated a wartime boom. France and Britain bought so much that they soon needed loans to continue their purchases. Early in the war, Secretary of State Bryan argued that loans to any warring nation were "inconsistent with the true spirit of neutrality," but Wilson, for all his public professions of neutrality, was determined to aid Great Britain. He quietly began approving credits to sustain trade with the Allies. American investors would advance over $2 billion to the Allies before the United States entered the war, and only $27 million to Germany.

The administration nevertheless clung to its official stance of neutrality through two and a half years of warfare in Europe and tried to uphold the traditions of "freedom of the sea," which had guided American policy since the Napoleonic Wars. Trade on the high seas assumed a new importance as the German drive through Belgium and toward Paris finally ground down into the stalemate of trench warfare. In a war of attrition, survival depended on access to supplies, and in such a war British naval power counted for a great deal. With the German fleet outnumbered and bottled up almost from the outset, the war in many ways assumed the pattern that in 1812 had led America into war with Britain.

In November 1914 the British declared the whole North Sea a war zone and sowed it with mines. Four months later, they announced that they would seize ships carrying goods of presumed enemy destination, ownership, or origin. British policies of search and seizure caused extended delays in shipping, sometimes running into months. Britain also ordered its ships to stop vessels carrying German goods via neutral ports. The State Department protested, but to no avail.

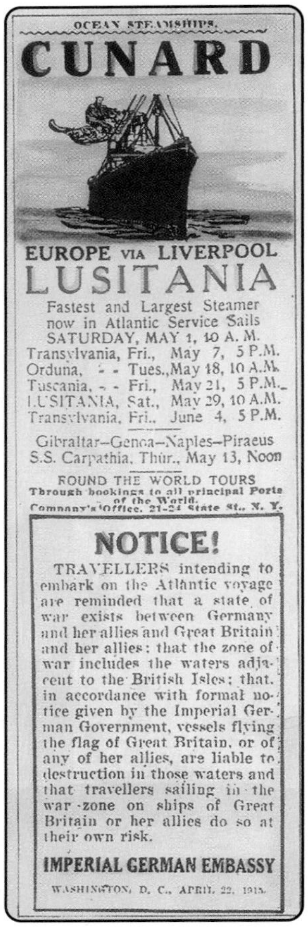

Advertisement from the *New York Herald* announcing the sailing of the British liner *Lusitania* from New York to Liverpool, England. Americans were outraged when a German torpedo sank the ship on May 7, 1915.

Neutral Rights and Submarines

British actions, which included blacklisting companies that traded with the enemy and censoring the mails, raised some old issues of neutral rights, but the German reaction introduced an entirely new question. In the face of the British blockade, only German submarines could venture out to harass the enemy. On February 4, 1915, in response to the "illegal" British blockade, the German government proclaimed a war zone around the British Isles. Enemy merchant ships in those waters were liable to sinking by submarines, the Germans declared. As the chief advantage of U-boat (*Unterseeboot*) warfare was in surprise, it violated the established international procedure of stopping enemy vessels on the high seas and providing for the safety of passengers and crews before sinking the vessel. Since the British sometimes flew neutral flags as a ruse, neutral ships in the zone would also be in danger.

The United States pronounced the German policy "an indefensible violation of neutral rights" and warned that Germany would be held to "strict accountability" for any destruction of American lives and property. On March 28, 1915, one American drowned when the Germans sank a British steamer in the Irish Sea. The following May an American tanker went down with a loss of two lives. The administration was divided on the proper course of action. Secretary of State Bryan wanted to warn American citizens that they entered the war zone at their own risk; other advisers wanted to threaten to break diplomatic relations with Germany.

As Wilson pondered the alternatives, the sinking of the majestic British liner *Lusitania* provoked a crisis. On May 7, 1915, a German U-boat torpedoed the *Lusitania,* which exploded and sank within eighteen minutes. Among the 1,198 persons lost were 128 Americans.

The sinking of the ship was an act of piracy, Theodore Roosevelt declared. Americans were outraged. To quiet the uproar, Wilson urged patience: "There is such a thing as a man being too proud to fight. There is such a thing as a nation being so right that it does not need to convince others by force that it is right." But his previous demand for "strict accountability" forced him to make a strong response. On May 13 Secretary of State Bryan reluctantly signed a note demanding that the Germans abandon unrestricted submarine warfare, disavow the sinking, and pay reparations. The Germans responded that the passenger ship had been armed (which it had not) and had carried a secret cargo of small arms and ammunition (which it had). A second note on June 9 repeated American demands in stronger terms. Bryan, unwilling to risk war over the issue, resigned in protest and joined the peace movement as a private citizen. His successor, Robert Lansing, signed the note.

In response to the uproar over the *Lusitania,* the German government had secretly ordered U-boat captains to avoid sinking large passenger vessels. When, despite the order, two American lives were lost in the sinking of the British liner *Arabic,* bound for New York, the German ambassador demanded and got from Berlin a public assurance, which he delivered on September 1, 1915: "Liners will not be sunk by our submarines without warning and without safety of the lives of non-combatants, provided that the liners do not try to escape or offer resistance." With this *Arabic* pledge, Wilson's resolute stand seemed to have won a victory for his policy.

The Debate over Preparedness

The *Lusitania* incident, and more generally the quarrels over neutral commerce, contributed to a growing demand for a stronger American army and navy. In his annual message in 1915, Wilson alerted Congress to his plans for war preparedness. The response was far from unanimous. Progressives and pacifists, especially in the rural South and West, opposed military expansion. Jane Addams and suffragist Carrie Chapman Catt organized a Women's Peace party. Bryan, La Follette, and other leaders also lent their voices to the peace movement.

Wilson eventually accepted a compromise between advocates of an expanded force under federal control and advocates of a traditional citizen army. The National Defense Act of 1916 expanded the regular army from 90,000 to 175,000 and permitted a gradual enlargement to 223,000. It also authorized a National Guard of 440,000. The Naval Construction Act of 1916 authorized a three-year shipbuilding program.

Progressive opponents of the military buildup determined that the financial burden should rest on the wealthy. The income tax became their weapon. Supported by a groundswell of popular support, they wrote into the Revenue Act of 1916 changes that doubled the basic income tax from 1 to 2 percent, raised the surtax on incomes over $2 million to 13 percent, added an estate tax graduated up to a maximum of 10 percent, levied a 12.5 percent tax on gross receipts of munitions makers, and added a new tax on corporations. The new taxes amounted to the most clear-cut victory of radical progressives in the entire Wilson period, a victory that Wilson supported in preparation for the election of 1916.

The Election of 1916

As the 1916 election approached, the Republican regulars turned to Justice Charles Evans Hughes, a progressive governor of New York from 1907 to 1910. On the Supreme Court since then, he had neither endorsed a candidate in 1912 nor spoken out on foreign policy. The Democrats, as expected, chose Wilson once again. In their platform they endorsed a program of social legislation, neutrality, and reasonable preparedness. The party further commended women's suffrage to the states, denounced groups that placed the interests of other countries above those of the United States, and pledged support for a postwar League of Nations to enforce peace with collective security measures against aggressors. The Democrats found their most popular issue, however, in Wilson's commitment to neutrality. The peace theme, refined into the slogan "He kept us out of war," became the rallying cry of the campaign, one that had the merit of taking credit without making any promises for the future.

In the end, Wilson's twin pledges of peace and progressivism brought victory. The final vote showed a Democratic sweep of the Far West and South, enough for victory in the electoral college by 277 to 254, and in the popular vote by 9 million to 8.5 million. Wilson also carried many social-justice progressives who in 1912 had supported Theodore Roosevelt's Bull Moose campaign.

Last Efforts for Peace

Immediately after the election, the German government announced its readiness to discuss peace terms. Wilson sent identical notes to all the belligerent powers, asking each to state its war aims. When it became apparent that both sides had demands so high as to preclude negotiations, Wilson decided to make one more appeal, in the hope that public opinion would force the hands of the warring governments. Speaking before the Senate, he asserted the right of the United States to share in laying the foundations for a lasting peace. This would have to be a "peace without victory," for only a "peace among equals" could endure.

Although Wilson did not know it, he was already too late. Exactly two weeks before he spoke, German military leaders had decided to wage unrestricted submarine warfare. Faced with weakening resources in a war of attrition, the Germans took the calculated risk of provoking American anger in the hope of scoring a quick knockout.

On February 3, 1917, Wilson informed a joint session of Congress that the United States had broken diplomatic relations with the German government. Then, on March 1, news of the so-called Zimmermann Telegram broke in the American press. The British had intercepted and decoded an important message from German foreign secretary Arthur Zimmermann to his minister in Mexico. The note instructed the envoy to offer an alliance and financial aid to Mexico in case of war between the United States and Germany. In return for diversionary action against the United States, Mexico would recover "the lost territory in Texas, New Mexico, and Arizona." All this was contingent on war with the United States, but an electrified public read in it an aggressive intent.

Later in March another bombshell burst when a revolution overthrew Russia's czarist government and established the provisional government of a Russian Republic. The fall of the czarist autocracy led Americans to believe that all the major Allied Powers were now fighting for constitutional democracy.

The Liberty Loan Act added $5 billion in "Liberty Bonds" to the national debt to help finance the war effort.

America's Entry into the War

In March 1917, German submarines sank five American merchant vessels. On March 20, Wilson's cabinet unanimously endorsed a declaration of war, and the following day the president called for a special session of Congress on April 2. Wilson asked Congress to recognize the war that imperial Germany was already waging against the United States, then turned to a discussion of the issues. The German government had revealed itself as a natural foe of liberty, and, Wilson argued in the rhetoric of progressivism, "The world must be made safe for democracy." The war resolution passed the Senate by a vote of 82 to 6 on April 4. The House concurred, 373 to 50, and Wilson signed the measure on April 6.

How had it come to this, less than three years after Wilson's proclamation of neutrality? Prominent among the various explanations of America's entrance into the war were the effects of British propaganda and America's deep involvement in trade with the Allies, which some observers then and later credited to the intrigues of war profiteers and munitions makers. Some Americans thought German domination of Europe would be a threat to American security, especially if it meant the destruction or capture of the British navy. Whatever the influence of such factors, they likely would not have been decisive without the issue of submarine warfare. Once Wilson had taken a stand for the traditional rights of neutrals and noncombatants, he was to some extent at the mercy of decisions by the German high command. Wilson was then led step by step into a war over what to a later generation would seem a rather quaint, if noble, set of principles.

America's Early Role

Within a month of America's declaration of war, the British and French requested money for military supplies, a request Congress had already anticipated in the Liberty Loan Act, which added $5 billion to the national debt in "Liberty Bonds." Of this amount, $3 billion could be loaned to the Allied Powers. The United States was also willing to furnish naval support, credits, supplies, and munitions.

The United States agreed to send a token army force to bolster Anglo-French morale, and on June 26, 1917, the first American contingent, about 14,500 men commanded by General John J. Pershing, began to disembark on the French coast. After reaching Paris, Pershing decided that the war-weary Allies would be unable to mount an offensive by themselves. He therefore requested that Wilson send a million American troops by the following spring, and the president obliged.

The need for such large numbers of troops converted Wilson to the idea of conscription. Under the Selective Service Act of May 18, 1917, all men aged twenty-one to thirty (later, from eighteen to forty-five) had to register for military service. By July 1917, when the first lottery was held to determine who would actually be drafted to fight in the war, almost 24 million men were registered. In the course of the war, about 2 million Americans crossed the Atlantic and about 1.4 million of them saw some combat.

Mobilizing a Nation

Complete economic mobilization on the home front was also necessary to conduct the war efficiently. In 1916 Congress had created a Council of National Defense, which in turn set up other wartime agencies. The United States Shipping Board, organized in 1917, within two years was constructing more than forty steel and ninety wooden ships monthly. In 1917 Congress created both a Food Administration, headed by Herbert Hoover, and a Fuel Administration. Hoover, a mining engineer and former head of the Commission for Relief in Belgium, had the responsibility of raising crop production while reducing civilian use of foodstuffs. "Food will win the war" was the slogan. Hoover directed a propaganda campaign that "Hooverized" the country with "Meatless Tuesdays," "Wheatless Wednesdays," "Porkless Saturdays," the planting of victory gardens, and the use of leftovers. The Fuel Administration introduced the country to Daylight Saving Time and "heatless Mondays" to save fuel.

The War Industries Board (WIB) was established in 1917, and it soon became the most important of all the mobilization agencies. Wilson summoned Bernard Baruch, a brilliant Wall Street investor, to head the board, giving him a virtual dictatorship over the economy. The WIB could allocate raw materials, tell manufactur-ers what to produce, order construction of new plants, and, with presidential approval, fix prices.

Food is
Ammunition -
Don't waste it

The Food Administration stressed conservation through its slogan, "Food will win the war."

A New Labor Force

The closing off of foreign immigration and the movement of almost 4 million men into the armed services created a labor shortage. To meet it, women, blacks, and other ethnic minorities were encouraged to enter industries and agricultural activities heretofore dominated by white males. Over 400,000 southern blacks began the "Great Migration" northward during the war years, a mass movement that continued unabated through the 1920s. Mexican Americans followed the same migratory pattern. By 1930, the number of African Americans living in the North had tripled from 1910 levels.

But the newcomers were not always welcomed above the Mason-Dixon line. Many white workers resented the new arrivals, and racial tensions sparked riots in cities across the country. Whites would seize upon an incident to rampage through black neighborhoods, killing, burning, and looting, while white policemen looked the other way or encouraged the mobs.

American intervention in World War I also had a significant impact on women. Ini-

With 4 million men in the armed forces and a hiatus in immigration, African Americans and women played key roles in the work force.

tially, females supported the war effort in traditional ways. They helped organize war-bond and war-relief drives, conserved foodstuffs and war-related materials, supported the Red Cross, and joined the Army nurse corps. But as the scope of the war widened, both government and industry sought to mobilize women workers for service on farms, loading docks, and railway crews, as well as in armaments industries, machine shops, steel and lumber mills, and chemical plants.

In fact, however, war-generated changes in female employment were limited and brief. About a million women participated in "war work," but most of them were young, single, and already working outside the home. Most returned to their previous jobs and domestic roles once the war ended. By 1920 the 8.5 million working women made up a smaller percentage of the labor force than they had in 1910. Still, one tangible result of women's contributions to the war effort was Woodrow Wilson's decision to endorse female suffrage. In the fall of 1918, he told the Senate that giving women the vote was "vital to the winning of the war."

The wartime emergency placed organized labor in a position to make solid advances in employment and wages, despite the rise in consumer prices. A newly created United States Employment Service placed some 4 million workers in war-related jobs. Labor unions benefited from expanded employment, the increased demand for labor, and government policies favorable to collective bargaining. From 1913 to 1918, American Federation of Labor membership increased by 37 percent.

War Propaganda and Civil Liberties

The exigencies of winning the war led the government to mobilize more than economic life: the progressive gospel of efficiency suggested mobilizing public opinion as well. On April 14, 1917, eight days after the declaration of war, Wilson established the Committee on Public Information. Its executive director, George Creel, a Denver journalist, sold Wilson on the idea that the best approach to influencing public opinion was "expression, not repression"—propaganda instead of censorship. Creel organized a propaganda machine to convey the Allies' war aims to the people, and above all to the enemy, where it might encourage the forces of moderation.

By arousing public opinion to a frenzy, however, the war effort channeled the zeal of progressivism into grotesque campaigns of "Americanism" and witch-hunting. Popular prejudice equated anything German with disloyalty. Schools even dropped German language courses. The Espionage and Sedition Acts of 1917 and 1918 effectively outlawed criticism of government leaders and war policies. These laws led to more than 1,500 prosecutions and 1,000 convictions.

The impact of these acts fell with most severity upon radicals. In Chicago over 100 leaders of the Industrial Workers of the World went on trial for opposing the war effort. All were found guilty, and the IWW never recovered from the blow. The same fate befell members of the Socialist party. Eugene V. Debs, who had polled over 900,000 votes as the Socialist candidate for president in 1912, ardently opposed American intervention. Debs was arrested and eventually sentenced to twenty years in prison for encouraging draft resistance. In 1920, still in jail, he polled nearly 1 million votes for president.

In an important decision just after the war, the Supreme Court upheld the Espionage and Sedition Acts. *Schenck* v. *United States* (1919) sustained the conviction of a man for circulating antidraft leaflets among members of the armed forces. In this case Justice Oliver Wendell Holmes observed: "Free speech would not protect a man in falsely shouting fire in a theater, and causing a panic." The act applied where there was "a clear and present danger" that free speech in wartime might create evils Congress had a right to prevent.

"The Decisive Power"

American troops played little more than a token role in the European fighting until the end of 1917, when the Allied position turned desperate. In October the Italian lines collapsed in the face of the Austrian offensive. In November, having suffered some 5.5 million casualties and widespread food and ammunition shortages, the Russian provisional republican government succumbed to a revolution led by Vladimir Lenin and his Bolshevik party, which promised the Russian people "Peace, Land, and Bread." With German troops then deep in Russian territory, and with armies of "White" Russians organizing to resist the Bolsheviks, Lenin concluded a separate peace with the Germans in the Treaty of Brest-Litovsk (March 3, 1918). The Central Powers were now free to concentrate their forces on the Western Front, and the American war effort became a "race for France" to restore the balance of strength in that arena.

The Western Front

On March 21, 1918, the Germans began the first of several offensives intended to end the war before the Americans arrived in force. On the Somme River they broke through at the juncture of British and French sectors and penetrated thirty-five miles, nearly to Amiens. Farther north, the Germans struck in Flanders, where the Allies still held a corner of Belgium. At this critical point, on April 14 the Allies made French general Ferdinand Foch the supreme commander of all Allied forces.

By May 1918 there were a million fresh American troops in Europe, and for the first time they made a difference. In early June, an American marine brigade blocked the Germans at Belleau Wood. American army troops took Vaux and opposed the Germans at Château-Thierry. Though these actions had limited military significance, their effect on Allied morale was immense. Each

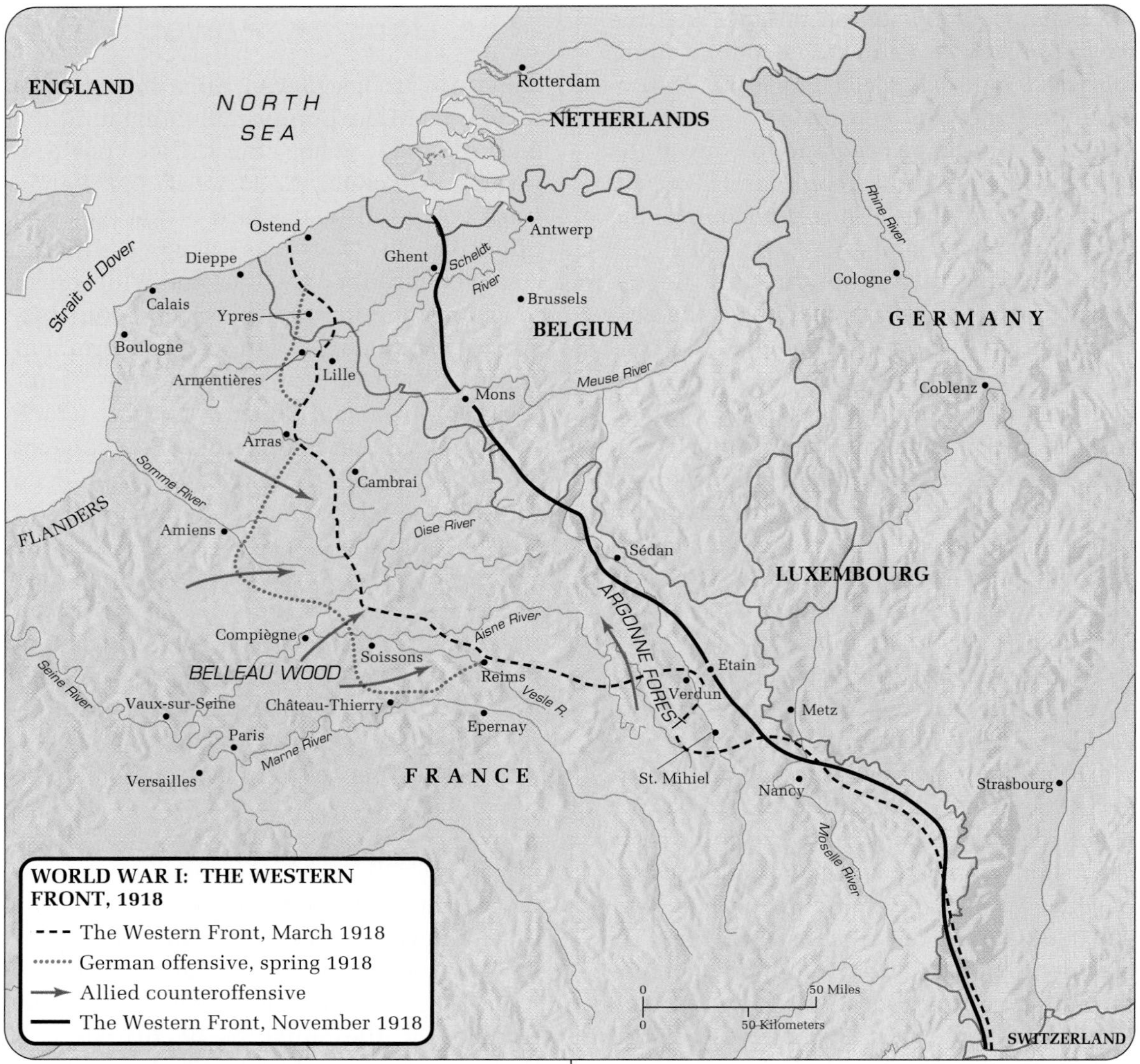

was a solid American success, and together they reinforced Pershing's demand for a separate American army.

Before that could come to pass, the Second Battle of the Marne (July 15, 1918) erupted, and it proved to be the turning point in the western campaign. On both sides of Reims, the Germans commenced their push against the French lines. Within three days, however, they had stalled, and the allies, mainly with American troops, went on the offensive.

Soon the British, French, and American forces began to roll the German front back into Belgium. On September 12, an army of more than 500,000 staged the first strictly American offensive of the war, aimed at German forces at St. Mihiel. Within three days the Germans had pulled back. Two weeks later, the massive Meuse-Argonne offensive employed American divisions in a drive toward the rail center at Sédan, which supplied the entire German front. All along the front from Sédan to Flanders the Germans were in retreat. "America," wrote a German commander, "thus became the decisive power in the war."

Meanwhile, in an effort to prevent stockpiled Allied supplies from falling into German hands, and to encourage the counter-revolutionary Russian "Whites" in their civil war against the "Reds," fourteen Allied nations sent troops into eastern Russia. On August 2, 1918, some 8,000 Americans joined the expedition and remained on Russian soil until April 1920. But the Allied intervention in Russia was a colossal failure. The Bolsheviks were able to consolidate their power, defeat the "Whites," and withdraw from World War I. The Russians therefore did not participate in the peace settlement. Even more importantly, Lenin and the Soviets never forgave the West for attempting to thwart their revolution.

The Fourteen Points

As the conflict was ending, the question of war aims arose again. Neither the Allies nor the Central Powers, despite Wilson's prodding, had stated openly what they hoped to gain through the bloodletting. When a conference in Paris late in 1917 failed to agree on a statement of aims, Wilson formulated his own.

With advice from a panel of experts, Wilson drew up a plan that would be labeled the Fourteen Points. This he presented to a joint session of Congress on January 8, 1918, "as the only possible program" for peace. The first five points of the plan called for open diplomacy, freedom of the seas, removal of trade barriers, armaments reduction, and an impartial adjustment of colonial claims based on the interests of the populations involved. Most of the remainder called on the Central Powers to evacuate occupied lands and to allow self-determination for various nationalities, a crucial principle for Wilson. Point 14, the capstone in Wilson's thinking, called for the formulation of a "league of nations" to guarantee the independence and territorial integrity of all countries, great and small.

Wilson sincerely believed in the Fourteen Points, but they also served important political purposes. One of their aims was to keep Russia in the war by a more liberal statement of purposes—a vain hope, as it turned out. Another was to reassure the Allied peoples that they were involved in a noble cause. A third was to drive a wedge between the governments of the Central Powers and their peoples by the offer of a reasonable peace. But the chaos into which central Europe descended in 1918, as both Germany and Austria-Hungary verged on starvation and experienced socialist uprisings, took matters out of Wilson's hands.

The End of the War

On September 29, 1918, German general Erich Ludendorff advised his government to seek the best peace terms possible. On October 3, a new chancellor made the first German overtures for peace on the basis of the Fourteen Points. The Allies accepted the Fourteen Points as a basis of peace but with two significant reservations: they reserved the right to discuss freedom of the seas further, and they demanded reparations (financial compensation to the victors) for war damages.

Meanwhile, German morale plummeted, culminating in a naval mutiny. Germany's allies, Bulgaria, Turkey, and Austria-Hungary, dropped out of the war during the early fall of 1918. On November 9, the kaiser, head of the German Empire, abdicated, and a German Republic was proclaimed. Two days later, on November 11, 1918, an armistice was signed, ceasing the hostilities. Under the Armistice, the Germans agreed to evacuate occupied territories, pull back behind the Rhine River, and surrender their navy, railroad equipment, and other materials. The Germans were assured that the Fourteen Points would be the basis for the peace conference.

During its nineteen months of participation in the war, the United States saw 114,000 of its troops killed. Germany's war dead totaled over 2 million; France and Russia lost over 1.7 million each. The United States, for good or ill, would be sucked into the vacuum of power created by the destructiveness of the Great War.

The Fight for Peace at Home and Abroad

Domestic Unrest

Wilson made a fateful decision to attend in person the Paris Peace Conference, which convened on January 18, 1919, and would last almost six months. A president had never left the country for so long. From one viewpoint it was a shrewd move, for his prestige and determination made a difference in Paris. But he lost touch with developments at home, where his political coalition was already unraveling under the pressures of wartime discontent. Western farmers complained about the government's control of wheat prices, while Eastern business leaders chafed at revenue policies designed, according to the *New York Sun,* "to pay for the war out of taxes raised north of the Mason and Dixon Line." Organized labor, despite real gains, groused about inflation and the problems of reconversion to a peacetime economy.

In the midterm elections of 1918, Wilson made matters worse with a partisan appeal for a Democratic Congress to ensure support of his foreign policies. Republicans, who for the most part had supported his war measures, took affront. So too did many voters. In elections held a week before the Armistice, the Democrats lost control of both houses of Congress. Now, with an opposition majority in the new Congress, Wilson further weakened his standing by failing to include a single prominent Republican in the American delegation headed for Paris and the treaty negotiations. Former President Taft suggested that Wilson's real intention in going to Paris was "to hog the whole show."

The Paris conference included delegates from all countries that had declared war or broken diplomatic relations with Germany. But it was dominated by the Big Four: the prime ministers of Britain, France, and Italy, and the president of the United States. David Lloyd George of England was a gifted politician fresh from electoral victory on the slogan "Hang the Kaiser." Italy's Vittorio Orlando was there to pick up the spoils promised his country in the secret Treaty of London (1915). French premier Georges Clemenceau, a stern realist, insisted on severe measures to weaken Germany and guarantee French security. He scorned Wilson's idealism. "God gave us the Ten Commandments and we broke them," he sneered. "Wilson gave us the Fourteen Points—we shall see."

The League of Nations

Wilson insisted that his cherished League of Nations must come first in the conference and in the treaty. Whatever compromises he might have to make, whatever mistakes might result, Wilson believed that such a permanent peace agency would maintain international stability.

Wilson presided over the commission to draft a charter for the League. Article X of the charter, which he called "the heart of the League," pledged members to consult on military and economic sanctions against aggressors. The use of arms would be a last resort. On February 14, 1919, Wilson delivered the finished draft of the League charter and departed the next day for a month-long visit home. Already he faced rumblings of opposition. Republican Henry Cabot Lodge, chairman of the Senate Foreign Relations Committee, claimed that the League was unacceptable "in the form now proposed." His statement of March 4 bore the signatures of thirty-nine Republican senators or senators-elect, more than enough to block ratification.

Territory and Reparations

Back in Paris, Wilson grudgingly conceded to French demands for territorial concessions and reparations from Germany. He clashed sharply with Clemenceau, but they agreed that the Allies would occupy a demilitarized German Rhineland for fifteen years, and that the League of Nations would administer Germany's coal-rich Saar Basin. France could use Saar mines for fifteen years, after which the region's voters would determine their status.

In other territorial matters Wilson had to compromise his principle of national self-determination. There was in fact no way to make boundaries correspond to ethnic divisions, because the folk wanderings of centuries had left mixed populations scattered through central Europe. In some areas, moreover, national self-determination yielded to other interests such as trade and defense. The result was a reorganized map of central Europe in which portions of the former Austro-Hungarian Empire became independent, most notably Czechoslovakia and Yugoslavia, and portions became attached to Poland, Romania, and Italy. Ethnic and nationalist tensions continued, and they would contribute to the crisis that culminated in World War II.

The discussion of reparations was among the longest and most bitter at the conference. Despite a pre-Armistice agreement that Germany would be financially liable only for civilian damages, Clemenceau and Lloyd George proposed reparations for the entire cost of the war. On this point Wilson made perhaps his most fateful concessions. He agreed to a clause in the treaty by which Germany accepted responsibility for starting the war and for its entire costs. The "war guilt" clause offended all Germans and provided a source of persistent bitterness.

On May 7, 1919, the victorious powers presented the treaty to the German delegates, who returned three weeks later with 443 pages of criticism protesting that the terms violated the Fourteen Points. A few small changes were made, but when the Germans still refused to sign, Marshal Ferdinand Foch prepared to move his French army across the Rhine River. Finally, on June 28, 1919, the Germans signed the treaty at Versailles.

Wilson's Loss at Home

Wilson returned home with the Versailles Treaty on July 8, 1919. Two days later he called on the Senate to accept "this great duty." The force of Wilson's idealism struck deep, and he returned amid a great clamor of popular support. A third of the state legislatures had endorsed the proposed League of Nations, as had thirty-three of forty-eight governors.

This cartoon portrays Wilson's commitment to the League of Nations. U.S. entry into the League was blocked by thirty-nine Republican senators.

Senator Henry Cabot Lodge, however, harbored serious reservations. A powerful Republican who hated Wilson, Lodge relished a fight. He knew the undercurrents already stirring up opposition to the treaty: the resentment felt by German, Italian, and Irish groups, the disappointment of liberals at Wilson's compromises on reparations and boundaries, the distractions of demobilization and resulting domestic problems, and the revival of isolationism. Theodore Roosevelt, still a popular figure, lambasted the League, noting that he keenly distrusted a "man who cares for other nations as much as his own."

Others agreed. In the Senate a group of "irreconcilables," fourteen Republicans and two Democrats, opposed American participation in the League on any terms. They were mainly western or midwestern progressives who feared that new foreign commitments would threaten domestic programs and reforms. Lodge belonged to a larger group of "reservationists." They were ready to compromise with Wilson but insisted on limiting American involvement in the League and its actions. Wilson said that he had already amended the covenant to these ends, pointing out that with a veto in the League Council the United States could not be obligated to do anything against its will.

Lodge, who set more store by the old balance of power than by the new idea of collective security, offered a set of amendments, or reservations. Wilson agreed to interpretive reservations, but to nothing that would reopen the negotiations with Germany and the Allies. He especially opposed the amendments weakening Article X, which provided for collective action by the signatory governments against aggression.

By September, with momentum for the treaty slackening, Wilson decided to go directly to the people. Against the advice of doctors and friends he set forth on a tour through the Midwest to the West Coast. In all he traveled 6,000 miles in twenty-two days, gave thirty-two major addresses, refuted his opponents, and voiced dire warnings. For a while Wilson seemed to be regaining the initiative, but then his body rebelled. On October 2, 1919, he suffered a severe stroke and paralysis on his left side, leaving him an invalid for the rest of his life.

Lodge was determined to amend the treaty before it was ratified. Between November 7 and 19, the Senate adopted fourteen of Lodge's reservations to the Versailles Treaty, most having to do with the League. Wilson, his illness intensifying his stubbornness, refused to make any compromises or concessions. As a result, the Wilsonians found themselves thrown into an unlikely combination with irreconcilables who opposed the treaty under any circumstances. The Senate vote on the treaty with Lodge's reservations was 39 for and 55 against. On the question of taking the treaty without reservations, irreconcilables and reservationists combined to defeat ratification again, with 38 for and 53 against.

In the face of strong public criticism, however, the Senate voted to reconsider. But the stricken Wilson remained adamant: "Either we should enter the League fearlessly . . . or we should retire as gracefully as possible from the great concert of powers by which the world was saved." On March 19, 1920, twenty-one Democrats deserted Wilson and joined the reservationists, but the treaty once again fell short of a two-thirds majority by a vote of 49 yeas and 35 nays. The real winners were the smallest of the three groups in the Senate, neither the Wilsonians nor the reservationists but the irreconcilables.

When Congress declared the war at an end by joint resolution on May 20, 1920, Wilson vetoed the action; it was not until after he left office, on July 2, 1921, that a joint resolution officially ended the state of war with Germany and Austria-Hungary. Peace treaties with Germany, Austria, and Hungary were ratified on October 18, 1921, but by then Warren Gamaliel Harding was president of the United States.

Lurching from War to Peace

The Versailles Treaty, for all the time it took in the Senate, was but one issue clamoring for public attention in the turbulent period after the war. Demobilization of the armed forces and the government's war effort proceeded without plan, indeed without much sense that a plan was needed once the war ended. The War Industries Board closed shop on January 1, 1919, and the sudden cancellation of war contracts left workers and business leaders to cope with reconversion on their own. Wilson's leadership was missing. He had been preoccupied by the war and the League, and once broken by his illness, he became strangely grim and peevish. His rudderless administration floundered through rough waters during its last two years.

The Spanish Flu

Amid the initial confusion of postwar life, many Americans confronted a virulent menace that produced far more casualties than the war itself. It became known as the Spanish flu, and its contagion spread around the globe. Erupting in the spring of 1918 and lasting a year, the pandemic killed more than 22 million people throughout the world, twice as many as the number who had died in World War I. In the United States alone, the flu accounted for over 500,000 deaths, five times the number of combat deaths in France.

American servicemen returning from France brought the flu with them, and it raced through the congested army camps and naval bases. Some 43,000 American servicemen died of influenza in 1918.

By September 1918 the disease had spread to the civilian population. In that month alone 10,000 Americans died from the disease. Phone booths were locked up, as were other public facilities such as dance halls, poolrooms, and theaters. Even churches and saloons in many communities were declared off limits. Still the death toll rose. From September 1918 to June 1919, a quarter of the population had contracted the illness.

Yet by the spring of 1919 the pandemic had run its course. It ended as suddenly—and as inexplicably—as it had begun. Although another outbreak occurred in the winter of 1920, the population had grown more resistant to its assaults. No disease, plague, war, famine, or natural catastrophe in world history had killed so many people in such a short time.

The Economic Transition

The problems of postwar readjustment were worsened by widespread labor unrest. Prices continued to rise steeply after the war, and discontented workers, released from wartime constraints, were more willing to strike for their demands. In 1919, more than 4 million workers walked out in thousands of disputes. After a general strike in Seattle, public opinion began to turn hostile toward militant workers.

The most celebrated postwar labor confrontation was the Boston Police Strike which inadvertently launched a presidential career. On September 9, 1919, most of Boston's police force went out on strike, demanding recognition of their union. Massachusetts governor Calvin Coolidge mobilized the National Guard to arrest looters and restore order. After four days the strikers were ready to return, but the police commissioner fired them all. When labor leader Samuel Gompers appealed for their reinstatement, Coolidge responded in words that suddenly turned him into a national figure: "There is no right to strike against the public safety by anybody, anywhere, anytime."

Racial Friction

The summer of 1919 also brought violent race riots, both in the North and South. Whites invaded the black section of Longview, Texas, in search of a teacher who had allegedly accused a white woman of a liaison with a black man. They burned shops and houses and ran several blacks out of town. A week later, in Washington, D.C., reports of attacks on white women aroused white mobs, and for four days gangs of white and black rioters waged race war in the streets until soldiers and driving rains ended the fighting.

These were but preliminaries to the Chicago riot of late July, in which 38 people were killed, 537 injured, and a thousand left homeless. It started when a black youth's raft drifted into the white beach area, and whites started stoning him. Another race riot occurred in the rural area around Elaine, Arkansas, where black tenant farmers tried to organize a union. According to official reports, 5 whites and 25 blacks were killed in the violence, but whites told one reporter in the area that in fact more than 100 blacks died. Altogether twenty-five race riots took place in 1919, and more threatened.

The Red Scare

Public reaction to the wave of labor strikes and race riots reflected the impact of Russia's Bolshevik Revolution. A minority of radicals thought America's domestic turbulence, like that in Russia, was the first scene in a drama of revolution. A much larger public was persuaded that they might be right. After all, Lenin's tiny faction in Russia had exploited confusion to impose its will on the entire nation. Wartime hysteria against all things German was thus readily transformed into a postwar Red Scare.

Fears of revolution might have remained latent except for the actions of a lunatic fringe. In April 1919 the postal services intercepted nearly forty bombs addressed to prominent citizens. One slipped through and blew off the hands of a Georgia senator's maid. In June another destroyed the front of Attorney-General A. Mitchell Palmer's house in Washington. Such random violence led many Americans to see Red on all sides and to condone attacks on all minorities in retaliation.

Soon the government itself was promoting witch-hunts. Attorney-General Palmer harbored a bitter distrust of aliens and a strong desire for the presidency. In June 1919 the Justice Department decided to deport radical aliens. On January 2, 1920, police raids in dozens of cities swept up some 5,000 suspects, many taken from their homes without search warrants. About half of those seized were kept in custody. That same month the New York legislature expelled five duly elected Socialist members.

Basking in popular approval, Palmer continued to warn of the Red menace, but like other fads and alarms, the ugly mood of intolerance passed. By the summer of 1920, the Red Scare had begun to evaporate. Communist revolutions in Europe died out, leaving Bolshevism isolated in Russia; bombings tapered off; the wave of strikes and race riots receded. The reactionary attorney-general began to seem more threatening to civil liberties than a handful of radicals were to the social order.

The Red Scare nevertheless left a lasting mark on American life. Part of its legacy was the continuing crusade for "100 percent Americanism" and restrictions on immigration. It also left a stigma on labor unions (already weakened by their own internal ethnic and racial tensions) and contributed to the anti-union open-shop campaign—the "American Plan," its sponsors called it. But for many thoughtful Americans the chief residue of the Great War and its chaotic aftermath was a profound disillusionment with idealistic crusades and grand political promises.

CHAPTER 25

The Modern Temper

This chapter focuses on

- The reactionary strains of the 1920s.
- The social ferment of the Jazz Age.
- The influence of modernism in American culture.

THE *ESSENTIAL AMERICA* ON-LINE TUTOR

www.wwnorton.com/eamerica/ch25

- **Topic: The Jazz Age**
  www.wwnorton.com/eamerica/ch25/topic.htm

  In the early decades of the twentieth century, musicians including Joe Oliver, Charlie Parker, Louis Armstrong, Duke Ellington, and many others traveled a circuit that began in New Orleans and included Kansas City, Chicago, and New York. These great early musicians fused musical motifs into one uniquely American style—jazz. Using recordings, photographs, historical analyses, and personal writings, explore the evolution of jazz from its humble beginnings to its most recent expressions.

- **Chapter review: On-line quiz and chapter summary**
  www.wwnorton.com/eamerica/ch25/review.htm

- **Chapter resources: Multimedia index**
  www.wwnorton.com/eamerica/ch25/media.htm

The horrors of World War I shattered the traditional belief that Western civilization was steadily progressing. The war's unimaginable carnage disillusioned young intellectuals. A new "modernist" sensibility emerged among artists, writers, and journalists. At once a mood and a movement, modernism appeared first in Europe at the end of the nineteenth century and became a pervasive international force by 1920. It arose out of a widespread recognition that Western civilization had entered an era of bewildering change. New technologies, new modes of transportation and communication, and new scientific discoveries such as quantum mechanics and relativity theory ruptured conventional perceptions of reality and generated new forms of artistic expression. "One must never forget," declared Gertrude Stein, the experimentalist writer, "that the reality of the twentieth century is not the reality of the nineteenth century, not at all." Modernism introduced a whole series of intellectual and artistic movements: impressionism, futurism, dadaism, surrealism, Freudianism.

At the same time that the war provided an accelerant for modernism, it also stimulated social tensions and political radicalism. The postwar wave of strikes, bombings, anti-Communist hysteria, and race riots convinced many that America had entered a frightening new era of diversity and conflict. Defenders of tradition located the germs of radicalism in the cities teeming with immigrants and foreign ideas. The defensive mood of the 1920s fed on a growing tendency to connect American nationalism with nativism, Anglo-Saxon racism, and militant Protestantism.

Reaction in the Twenties

Nativism

The foreign connections of so many political radicals strengthened the suspicion that the seeds of sedition were foreign born. In the early 1920s, over half the white men and a third of the white women working in manufacturing and mechanical industries were immigrants, most of them from central or eastern Europe. That socialism and anarchism were prevalent in those regions made such workers especially suspicious in the eyes of "old stock" Americans.

The most celebrated case of nativist prejudice involved two Italian-born anarchists, Nicola Sacco and Bartolomeo Vanzetti. Arrested in 1920 for a robbery and murder in South Braintree, Massachusetts, they were tried by a judge who privately referred to the defendants as "anarchist bastards." Supporters then and since have insisted that Sacco and Vanzetti were sentenced more for their political beliefs and their ethnic origins than for any crime they had committed. The case became a great radical and liberal cause of the 1920s, but despite pleas for mercy and worldwide demonstrations on behalf of the two men, Sacco and Vanzetti were sent to the electric chair in 1927.

The surging postwar nativism fueled new efforts to restrict immigration. Congress, alarmed at the influx of new foreigners after 1919, passed the Emergency Immigration Act of 1921, which restricted new arrivals each year to 3 percent of the foreign-born of each nationality as shown in the 1910 census. A new quota law in 1924 reduced the number to 2 percent based on the 1890 census, which included fewer of the "new" immigrants from southern and eastern Europe. This law set a permanent limitation, which became effective in 1929, of slightly over 150,000 immigrants per year based on the "national origins" of the American people as of 1920. In signing the law, President Coolidge pledged: "America must be kept American."

The purpose of the new quotas was clear: to tilt the balance in favor of the old immigration from northern and western Europe, which was assigned about 85 percent of the total of annual admittees. The law completely excluded people from East Asia. Yet it left the gate open to new arrivals from Western Hemisphere countries, so that an ironic consequence was a great increase in the Hispanic Catholic population. People of Latin American descent (chiefly Mexicans, Puerto Ricans, and Cubans) became the fastest growing ethnic minority in the country.

The Klan

During the postwar years, the nativist atmosphere helped spawn a revived Ku Klux Klan modeled on the group founded during Reconstruction. The new Klan, however, was devoted to "100 percent Americanism" rather than to the old Confederacy, and it restricted its membership to native-born white Protestants. The new Klan was determined to protect its warped notion of the American way of life not only from blacks, but also from Roman Catholics, Jews, and immigrants. America was no melting pot, its founder, the failed Methodist minister William J. Simmons, warned: "It is a garbage can! . . . When the hordes of aliens walk to the ballot box and their votes outnumber yours, then that alien horde has got you by the throat." In going nativist, the new Klan spread far outside the South. It thrived in small towns and cities in the North, and especially in the Midwest.

The Klan represented a vicious reflex against the modern and alien, against shifting moral standards, the declining influence of churches, and the social permissiveness of cities and colleges. Estimates of its peak membership, probably inflated, range from 3 million to 8 million, but the Klan's influence diminished as quickly as its numbers grew. For one thing, the Klan suffered from a decline in nativist excitement after passage of the 1924 immigration law. For another, it suffered recurrent factional quarrels and schisms. And its willing use of violence tarnished its moral pretensions.

In 1925 the Ku Klux Klan staged a 40,000-man parade down Pennsylvania Avenue in Washington, D.C.

Fundamentalism

While the Klan saw a threat mainly in the "alien menace," many adherents of old-time Protestantism saw threats from modernism in the churches: ideas that the Bible should be studied in the light of new scholarship (the "higher criticism"), or that it must be reconciled with scientific theories of evolution. Fearing that such "modernist" notions had infected schools and even pulpits, fundamentalism, grounded in a literal interpretation of the Bible, took on a new defensive militancy.

Among the rural fundamentalist leaders only Democrat William Jennings Bryan had the following, prestige, and eloquence to make the movement a popular crusade. By 1920, Bryan had lost his commanding physical presence, but he remained as silver-tongued as ever. In 1921 he sought to prohibit the teaching of Darwinian evolution in the public schools. Anti-evolution bills began to appear in legislatures, but the only victories came in the South—and there were few of those. Some officials took direct action without legislation. Governor Miriam "Ma" Ferguson of Texas outlawed textbooks upholding Darwinism. "I am a Christian mother . . ." she declared, "and I am not going to let that kind of rot go into Texas schoolbooks."

The climax came in Tennessee, where in 1925 the legislature outlawed the teaching of evolution in public schools and colleges. A young teacher at a high school in Dayton, Tennessee, John T. Scopes, accepted an offer from the American Civil Liberties Union to defend him. It soon was a case heard round the world.

The two stars of the show were Bryan, who led the prosecution of Scopes for teaching evolution in violation of Tennessee law, and Clarence Darrow, renowned Chicago trial lawyer and confessed agnostic, who defended Scopes by challenging the anti-evolution law. The trial quickly became a debate between fundamentalism and modernism. When the judge (a practicing evangelist) damaged Darrow's case by ruling out scientific testimony on evolution, most observers assumed the trial was over.

But the defense rebounded by calling Bryan as an expert witness on biblical interpretation. Darrow, who had once supported Bryan, entrapped the elderly statesman in literal-minded interpretations and exposed Bryan's ignorance of biblical history and scholarship. Bryan insisted that a "great fish" actually swallowed Jonah, that Joshua literally made the sun stand still, that the world was created in 4004 B.C.—all, according to Darrow, "fool ideas that no intelligent Christian on earth believes."

Yet the only issue before the court, the judge ruled, was whether Scopes had in fact taught evolution. He was found guilty, but the Tennessee Supreme Court, while upholding the law, overruled the $100 fine on a legal technicality. Bryan had described the trial as a "duel to the death." A few days after it closed, he died suddenly of a heart condition aggravated by heat and fatigue.

Classroom in Proposed Bryan University of Tennessee. This anti-Bryan cartoon shows a professor, bound and gagged by the ruling in the Scopes trial, teaching that the earth is flat, as Bryan (in portrait) looks on.

Prohibition

Prohibition offered another example during the 1920s of reactionary zeal promoting moral righteousness and conformity. American moralists had been campaigning against excessive drink since the eighteenth century. Around 1900, however, the leading temperance organizations, the Women's Christian Temperance Union and the Anti-Saloon League, shifted their efforts from reforming individuals to campaigning for legal prohibition. The Anti-Saloon League became one of the most effective pressure groups in American history, mobilizing Protestant churches behind its single-minded battle to elect "dry" candidates.

The 1916 elections finally produced two-thirds majorities in both houses of Congress for a prohibition amendment to the Constitution. Soon the wartime spirit of sacrifice, the need to use grain for food, and wartime hostility to German-American brewers transformed the cause virtually into a test of patriotism. On December 18, 1917, Congress sent to the states the Eighteenth Amendment, which, one year after ratification on January 16, 1919, banned nationwide the manufacture, sale, or transport of intoxicating liquors.

But determined Americans kept drinking in defiance of the new law. Enforcement was impossible given the public thirst, the spotty support of local officials, and the profits to be made in bootlegging. It would be too much to say that prohibition gave rise to organized crime, for organized vice, gambling, and extortion had long been practiced, and often tied in with the saloons. But prohibition supplied ruthless criminals, such as "Scarface" Al Capone, with a new source of enormous income, while the automobile and the sub-machine gun provided greater mobility and firepower. Gangland leaders showed remarkable gifts for exploiting loopholes in the law, when they did not simply bribe policemen and politicians.

Capone was by far the most celebrated criminal of the 1920s. In 1927 he pocketed $60 million from his bootlegging, prostitution, and gambling empire. He flaunted his wealth as well as his disregard for legal authorities. He rode in a bulletproof Cadillac, lavishly supported city charities, and insisted that he was merely providing the public with the goods and services it demanded. He neglected to say that he had also bludgeoned to death several conspiring police lieutenants and ordered the execution of dozens of his criminal competitors. Law-enforcement officials began to smash his bootlegging operations in 1929, but they were unable to pin anything on Capone until a Treasury agent infiltrated his gang and uncovered evidence that convicted him later that year for tax evasion. He was sentenced to eleven years in prison.

In the light of the illegal activities of Capone and other organized crime members, it came as no great surprise in 1931 when a commission reported that enforcement of prohibition had broken down. Still, the commission voted to extend prohibition, and President Herbert Hoover chose to stand by what he called the "experiment, noble in motive and far-reaching in purpose."

The Jazz Singers (1937). In this painting, Archibald J. Motley, Jr., an artist of the Harlem Renaissance, merges the cultures of his native New Orleans with the burgeoning energy of 1920s Harlem.

The Roaring Twenties

In many ways the reactionary temper of the 1920s and the repressive movements to which it gave rise seemed the dominant trends of the decade. But they arose in part as responses to disruptive social and intellectual currents. During those years, a new cosmopolitan, urban America confronted provincial, small-town and rural America, and cultural conflict reached new levels of tension.

Self-styled modernists disdained the old-fashioned values of the hinterlands. Sinclair Lewis's novel *Main Street* (1920) caricatured the stifling life of the midwestern town, depicting a "savorless people, gulping tasteless food, and sitting afterward, coatless and thoughtless, in rocking chairs prickly with inane decorations, listening to mechanical music, saying mechanical things about the excellence of Ford automobiles, and viewing themselves as the greatest race in the world." The supposed banality of small-town life became a pervasive theme in much of the literature of the time, and the heartland responded with counterimages of alien cities infested with vice, crime, corruption, and foreigners.

The Jazz Age

Writer F. Scott Fitzgerald dubbed the postwar era the "Jazz Age" because the sensual rhythms of jazz music were immensely popular among rebellious young adults. When people were not listening to "ragtime" or "jazz" music or to the family radio shows that became the rage in the 1920s, they were frequenting movie theaters. By 1930 there were more than 23,000 of them around the country, and they drew almost 100 million customers each week. Movies were by far the most popular form of mass culture in the twenties, and films became even more favored after the introduction of sound in 1927.

The New Morality

Much of the shock to traditionalists during the Jazz Age came from the changes in manners and morals evidenced first among young people, and especially on college campuses. In *This Side of Paradise* (1920), a novel of student life at Princeton, F. Scott Fitzgerald revealed that Victorian mothers had no "idea how casually their daughters were accustomed to be kissed." From such novels, and also from magazines and movies, many Americans learned about the cities' wild parties, bathtub gin, sexual promiscuity, and speakeasies.

Writers also informed the nation about the "new woman" eager to exercise new freedoms. These independent-thinking females discarded corsets and sported bobbed hair, heavy makeup, and shorter skirts; they smoked cigarettes and drank beer, drove automobiles, and in general, defied conventional expectations for womanly behavior.

Sex came to be discussed with surprising frankness during the 1920s. Much of the talk derived from a spreading awareness of Dr. Sigmund Freud, the Viennese father of psychoanalysis who stressed the psychological impact of complex sexual urges. Based on a casual awareness of his theories, people began to discuss libido, inhibitions, Oedipus complexes, sublimation, and repression. Explicitly sexual themes also penetrated popular culture. Radio singers during the 1920s belted out songs with titles such as "Hot Lips," "I Need Lovin'," and "Burning Kisses." Movie ads promised kisses on screen "where heart, and soul, and sense in concert move, and the blood is lava, and the pulse is ablaze."

Fashion also reflected the rebellion against prudishness and a loosening of inhibitions. In 1919 women's skirts were typically six inches above the ground; by 1927 they were at the knees, and the "flapper," with her bobbed hair, rolled stockings, cigarettes, lipstick, and sensuous dancing, was providing a shocking model of the new feminism. The name "flapper" derived from the way female rebels allowed their galoshes to "flap" about their ankles. Conservative moralists saw the flappers as just another sign of a degenerating society. Others saw in the "new woman" an expression of rugged American individualism. "By sheer force of violence," explained the *New York Times* in 1929, the flapper has "established the feminine right to equal representation in such hitherto masculine fields of endeavor as smoking and drinking, swearing, petting, and upsetting the community peace."

Teaching Old Dogs New Tricks. Cartoonist John Held's depiction of the modern woman, from the cover of *Life* magazine, 1926.

By 1930, however, the thrill of rebellion was waning; the revolution against Victorian morality had run its course. Its extreme expressions in time aroused doubts that the indulgence of lust equaled genuine liberation. And the much-discussed revolution in morals was also greatly exaggerated. The twenties "roared" for only a small proportion of the population. F. Scott Fitzgerald reminded Americans in 1931 that the "jazz age" was jazzy only for the "upper tenth of [the] nation."

The Women's Movement

At the same time that many women were embracing new sexual mores, all women were being liberated politically. The suffrage movement, which had been in the doldrums since 1896, sprang back to life in the second decade of the new century. In 1912 Alice Paul, a Quaker social worker, became chair of the National American Woman Suffrage Association's Congressional Committee. She encouraged female activists to picket state legislatures, "punish" politicians who failed to endorse suffrage, chain themselves to public buildings, provoke police into arresting them, and undertake hunger strikes.

In 1915 Carrie Chapman Catt had once again become head of the National Suffrage Association, and she spurred the final campaigns for voting rights. For several years President Wilson had evaded the issue of a suffrage amendment, but he supported a plank in the 1916 Democratic platform endorsing state action for woman suffrage. On June 4, 1919, the Senate finally adopted the Nineteenth Amendment by a bare two-thirds majority, and after an agonizing fourteen months, the states finally ratified the women's suffrage amendment on August 21, 1920, the climactic achievement of the Progressive Era.

Women thereafter entered politics in growing numbers, but this did not suddenly release them from deeply embedded social customs and legal discrimination. The new women voters tended to vote like men on most issues. One group, however, wanted something more. Alice Paul set a new goal, first introduced in Congress in 1923: an Equal Rights Amendment that would eliminate any remaining legal distinctions between the sexes. It would be another fifty years before Alice Paul would see Congress adopt her amendment in 1972; she did not live, however, to see it fall short of ratification.

The sharp increase in the number of women in the workforce during World War I proved short-lived. In the longer view, however, a steady increase in the numbers of employed women occurred in the 1920s and continued through the depression decade of the 1930s. Still, these women remained concentrated in traditional occupations: they were mostly domestics, office workers, teachers, clerks, salespeople, dressmakers, milliners, and seamstresses. On the eve of World War II, women's work was little more diversified than it had been at the turn of the century, but by 1940 it would be on the verge of a great transformation.

The women's suffrage movement was revived in 1912 by activists including Alice Paul and Carrie Chapman Catt. Their efforts eventually led to the Nineteenth Amendment, granting voting rights to women.

Official
Program
WOMAN
SUFFRAGE
Procession
VOTES for WOMEN
Washington
D.C.
March 3, 1913

The "New Negro"

The most significant development in African-American life during the war and after was the Great Migration northward. The movement of blacks from the South to the North began in 1915–1916, when rapidly expanding war industries were experiencing a labor shortage, leaving openings for blacks in the North. Altogether, between 1910 and 1920, the Southeast lost some 323,000 blacks, or 5 percent of the 1920 native black population, and by 1930 it had lost another 615,000 or 8 percent of the native black population. With the migration north, a slow but steady growth in black political influence set in.

Along with political activity came a bristling spirit of protest among northern blacks, a spirit that received cultural expression in a literary and artistic movement labeled the Harlem Renaissance. Claude McKay, a Jamaican immigrant, was the first significant writer of the movement, which sought to rediscover black folk culture.

Other emergent black writers included Langston Hughes, Zora Neale Hurston, Countée Cullen, Jean Toomer, and James Weldon Johnson.

The spirit of the "New Negro" also found an outlet in what came to be called "Negro nationalism," which exalted blackness, black cultural expression, and, at its most extreme, black exclusiveness. The leading spokesman for such views was the flamboyant Marcus Garvey. Racial bias, Garvey said, was so ingrained in whites that it was futile to appeal to their sense of justice. Garvey told American blacks to liberate themselves from the surrounding white culture.

Garvey saw every white person as a "potential Klansman," and he therefore endorsed the "social and political separation of all peoples to the extent that they promote their own ideals and civilization." Such a separatist message appalled other black leaders. W. E. B. Du Bois, for example, labeled Garvey "the most dangerous enemy of the Negro race." Garvey and his aides created their own black version of Christianity, organized their own fraternal lodges and community cultural centers, started their own businesses, and published their own newspaper. Garvey's message of racial pride and self-reliance appealed to many blacks who had grown frustrated and embittered during the postwar economic slump.

In 1916 Garvey brought to New York the United Negro Improvement Association (UNIA), which he had started in his native Jamaica two years before. He quickly enlisted half a million members and claimed as many as 6 million by 1923. At the peak of his popularity, however, Garvey was convicted of mail fraud. He was imprisoned in 1925 and remained so until President Calvin Coolidge pardoned him and deported him to Jamaica in 1927. Garvey died in obscurity in London in 1940, but the memory of his movement kept alive an undercurrent of racial pride that would reemerge later under the slogan of "black power."

Even more influential in promoting black rights was the National Association for the Advancement of Colored People (NAACP). Founded in 1910, it was led by northern white liberals and black leaders such as Du Bois. Its main strategy focused on enforcing the Fourteenth and Fifteenth Amendments. One early victory came with *Guinn* v. *United States* (1915), in which the Supreme Court struck down Oklahoma's grandfather clause, which had been part of the state's attempt to disenfranchise blacks.

In 1919 the NAACP launched a campaign against lynching, still a common atrocity in many parts of the country. An anti-lynching bill making mob murder a federal offense passed the House in 1922, but in the Senate it lost to a filibuster by southern senators. Nonetheless, the bill stayed before the House until 1925, and the continued agitation of the issue helped to reduce lynchings, which declined to a third of what they had been the previous decade.

Marcus Garvey, founder of the United Negro Improvement Association and a leading spokesman for "Negro nationalism" in the 1920s.

The Culture of Modernism

Changes in the realms of science and social thought were even more dramatic than those affecting women and blacks in the interwar years. As the twentieth century advanced, the easy faith in progress and reform expressed by progressives fell victim to a series of frustrations and disasters, including the Great War, Woodrow Wilson's physical and political collapse, and the failure of prohibition. Startling new findings in physics further shook prevailing assumptions of order and certainty.

Science and Social Thought

Physicists of the early twentieth century altered the image of the cosmos in ways that seemed almost a conspiracy against common sense. Conventional wisdom had held the universe to be governed by laws that the scientific method could ultimately uncover. A world of such certain order had bolstered hopes of infinite progress in human knowledge.

This world of order and certainty disintegrated at the turn of the century when Albert Einstein, a young German physicist, announced his theory of relativity. Einstein maintained that space, time, and mass were not absolutes but relative to the location and motion of the observer. Isaac Newton's eighteenth-century laws of mechanics, according to Einstein's relativity theories, worked well enough at relatively slow speeds, but the more nearly one approached the velocity of light (about 186,000 miles per second) the more all measuring devices would change accordingly, so that yardsticks would become shorter, clocks and heartbeats would slow down, even the aging process would ebb.

Certainty dissolved the farther one reached out into the universe and the farther one reached down into the minute world of the atom. The discovery of radioactivity in the 1890s showed that atoms were not irreducible units of matter; some of them emitted particles of energy. This meant, Einstein noted, that mass and energy were not separate phenomena but interchangeable.

Meanwhile, the German physicist Max Planck had discovered that electromagnetic emissions of energy, whether as electricity or light, came in little bundles that he called quanta. The development of quantum theory suggested that atoms were far more complex than once believed. Another pioneering German physicist, Werner Heisenberg, stated in his uncertainty principle in 1927 that atoms were ultimately indescribable. One could never know both the position and the velocity of an electron, Heisenberg concluded, because the very process of observation would inevitably affect the behavior of the particle, altering its position or velocity. Heisenberg's thesis meant that human knowledge had limits. As a Harvard mathematician wrote in 1929, the modern scientist had to "give up his most cherished convictions and faith. The world is not a world of reason, understandable by the intellect of man. . . ." Just as Enlightenment thinkers drew on Isaac Newton's laws of gravitation two centuries before to formulate their views on the laws governing society, the ideas of relativity and uncertainty in the twentieth century provoked people to deny the relevance of absolute values in any sphere of society, which undermined the concepts of personal responsibility and absolute standards.

Modernist Art and Literature

The cluster of scientific ideas associated with Darwin and Einstein helped inspire a "modernist" revolution in the minds of many intellectuals and creative artists during the early twentieth century. Whereas nineteenth-century writers and artists took for granted an accessible world that could be readily observed and accurately represented, self-willed modernists viewed the "real" as something to be created rather than copied, expressed rather than reproduced. As a consequence, they concluded that the subconscious regions of the psyche were more interesting and potent than reason, common sense, and logic.

In the various arts, such concerns resulted in abstract painting, atonal music, free verse poetry, stream-of-consciousness narrative, and interior monologues in stories and novels. Writers showed an intense concern with new forms in language in an effort to violate expectations and shock their audiences.

The chief American prophets of modernism were living in Europe: Ezra Pound and T. S. Eliot in London and Ernest Hemingway and Gertrude Stein in Paris. All were deeply concerned with creating new and often difficult styles of modernist expression. Pound, as foreign editor for *Poetry,* served as the conduit through which many American poets achieved publication in America and Britain. At the same time he became the leader of the imagist movement, a revolt against the ornamental verbosity of Victorian poetry in favor of the concrete image.

Pound's brilliant protégé was the St. Louis–born Harvard graduate, T. S. Eliot, who went to Oxford in 1913 and soon decided to make England his home and poetry his career. Skeptical of the Western notion of social progress through scientific advance and horrified by the slaughter of the Great War, he rejected the nineteenth century's "cheerfulness, optimism, and hopefulness." The modern poet, he insisted, must "be able to see beneath both beauty and ugliness; to see the boredom, and the horror and the glory."

Gertrude Stein, another voluntary exile, settled in Paris in 1903 and became an early champion and collector of modern art. Long regarded as no more than the literary eccentric who wrote "A rose is a rose is a rose is a rose," she would later be recognized as one of the originators of the modernist prose style. At the time she was known chiefly through her influence on such 1920s expatriates as Sherwood Anderson and Ernest Hemingway, whom she told: "All of you young people who served in the war, you are the lost generation."

The earliest chronicler of that "lost" generation, F. Scott Fitzgerald, blazed up brilliantly and then quickly flickered out, like all the carefree, sad young people of his novels. Successful and famous at age twenty-four with the publication of *This Side of Paradise* (1920), he, along with his wife, Zelda, experienced and depicted the "greatest, gaudiest spree in history," and then both had their crack-ups during the Great Depression.

The Southern Renaissance

As modernist literature arose as a response to the changes taking place in Western civilization, so did American southern literature of the twenties reflect a world in the midst of rebirth. A southern renaissance in writing emerged from the conflict between the dying world of tradition and the modern, commercial world struggling to be born in the aftermath of the Great War. While in the South the conflict of values aroused the Ku Klux Klan and fundamentalist furies that tried desperately to bring back the world of tradition, it also inspired the vitality and creativity of the South's young writers.

William Faulkner's achievement was rooted in the coarsely textured social world that produced him. Born near Oxford, Mississippi, he converted his hometown into the fictional Jefferson, Yoknapatawpha County. After a brief stint with the Royal Canadian Air Force, he passed the postwar decade in what seemed to fellow townspeople an aimless drifting, until he finally returned to Oxford. There, in writing *Sartoris* (1929), he began to discover that his "own little postage stamp of native soil was worth writing about" and that he "would never live long enough to exhaust it." Next, as he put it, he wrote his gut into *The Sound and the Fury* (1929). It was one of the triumphs of the modernist style, but most early readers, taking their cue from the title instead of the critics, found it signified nothing.

Modernism and the southern literary renaissance, both of which emerged from the crucible of the Great War and its aftermath, were products of the twenties. But the studied alienation of the artists of the 1920s did not survive the decade. The onset of the Great Depression in 1929 sparked a renewed sense of commitment and affirmation in the arts, as if people could no longer afford the art-for-art's-sake affectations of the 1920s. Alienation would give way to social activism in the decade to come.

CHAPTER

26

Republican Resurgence and Decline

This chapter focuses on

- The conservatism in the presidencies of Harding, Coolidge, and Hoover.
- Growth in the American economy in the 1920s.
- The causes of the Great Depression.

THE *ESSENTIAL AMERICA* ON-LINE TUTOR

www.wwnorton.com/eamerica/ch26

- **Topic: The stock market crash**
  www.wwnorton.com/eamerica/ch26/topic.htm

  In October of 1929 the United States experienced its most devastating financial crisis when stocks on the New York Stock Exchange fell by an average of 37 percent, 13 percent in one day. Using historical analyses, photographs, and biographical data on key participants, examine the causes of the crash and its significance for the United States in the 1920s and 1930s. Did one particular economic philosophy contribute to the market crisis?

- **Chapter review: On-line quiz and chapter summary**
  www.wwnorton.com/eamerica/ch26/review.htm

- **Chapter resources: Multimedia index**
  www.wwnorton.com/eamerica/ch26/media.htm

By 1920, the progressive political coalition that reelected Woodrow Wilson in 1916 had fragmented. It began to show signs of fissure during the war when radicals and other reformers grew disaffected with America's involvement. After the war, Wilson's support continued to erode. Organized labor resented his unsympathetic attitude toward the strikes of 1919–1920, and farmers complained that wartime price controls had discriminated against them. While prominent intellectuals grew disillusioned with the popular support for prohibition and religious fundamentalism, many among the middle class lost interest in political activism. They instead channeled their energies into building a new business-oriented civilization based upon mass production and mass consumption, greater leisure, and the introduction of labor-saving electrical appliances in the home. Moreover, progressivism's final triumphs at the national level were already foregone conclusions before the war's end: the Eighteenth Amendment, which outlawed alcoholic beverages, was ratified in 1919, and the Nineteenth Amendment, which extended women's suffrage to the entire country, became law a year later.

Progressivism, however, did not completely disappear in the 1920s. The progressive impulse for "good government" and extended public services still remained strong, especially at the state and local levels, where movements for good roads, education, public health, and social welfare all gained momentum during the decade. At the same time, however, the reactionary temper of the times gave rise to the drive for moral righteousness and conformity animating the Ku Klux Klan and the fundamentalist and prohibitionist movements.

"Normalcy"

Harding's Election

After World War I, most Americans had grown weary of idealistic crusades and suspicious of leaders promoting reform. When the Republicans met in Chicago in 1920, the Old Guard party regulars found their man in Ohio senator Warren Gamaliel Harding. He set the tone of his campaign when he told a Boston audience: "America's present need is not heroics, but healing; not nostrums, but normalcy; not revolution, but restoration; not agitation, but adjustment. . . ." His prose was clumsy, but Harding caught the mood of the times—a longing for "normalcy" and contentment with the status quo.

Harding's promise of a "return to normalcy" reflected his own conservative values and folksy personality. The son of an Ohio farmer, he described himself as not an intellectual or a crusader but "just a plain fellow" who was "old-fashioned and even reactionary in matters of faith and morals." But far from being an old-fashioned moralist in his personal life, he drank bootleg liquor in the midst of prohibition, smoked and chewed tobacco, relished weekly poker games, and cheated on his austere wife. The general public, however, remained unaware of Harding's self-indulgence and weak character. Instead the voters saw him as a handsome, charming, gregarious, and lovable politician.

The Democrats put their hopes behind James Cox, former newsman and former governor of Ohio. He won the nomination of an increasingly fragmented party on the forty-fourth ballot. For vice-president the convention named Franklin D. Roosevelt, who as assistant secretary of the navy occupied the same position his Republican cousin Theodore Roosevelt had held before him.

The Democrats suffered from the breakup of the Wilsonian coalition and the conservative postwar mood. In the words of progressive journalist William Allen White, Americans in 1920 were "tired of issues, sick at heart of ideals, and weary of being noble." The country voted overwhelmingly for Harding, who got 16 million votes to 9 million for Cox, who carried no state outside the Solid South.

Early Appointments and Policies

Harding in office had much in common with Ulysses Grant. His cabinet, like Grant's, mixed some of the best men in the party with some of the worst. Charles Evans Hughes became a distinguished secretary of state. Herbert Hoover in the Commerce Department, Andrew W. Mellon in Treasury, and Henry A. Wallace in Agriculture were also efficient and forceful figures. Of the others, Secretary of the Interior Albert B. Fall landed in prison and Attorney-General Harry M. Daugherty only narrowly escaped prosecution. Many lesser offices went to members of the notorious "Ohio Gang," headed by Daugherty, a group of Harding's old Ohio friends with whom the president met regularly for poker games lubricated with illegal liquor.

Harding and his friends set about dismantling or neutralizing as many of the social and economic components of progressivism as they could. Harding's four appointments to the Supreme Court were all conservatives, including Chief Justice William Howard Taft, who announced that he had been "appointed to reverse a few decisions." During the 1920s, the Taft Court struck down a federal child-labor law and a minimum wage law for women, issued numerous injunctions against striking unions, and issued rulings limiting the powers of federal regulatory agencies.

The Harding administration established a pro-business tone reminiscent of the McKinley White House. To sustain economic growth, Secretary of the Treasury Mellon promoted government spending cuts and federal tax reduction. Mellon insisted that tax cuts should go mainly to the rich, on the assumption that wealth in the hands of the few would promote the general welfare through increased capital investment.

In Congress a group of western Republicans and southern Democrats fought a dogged battle to preserve the graduated scale built into wartime taxes, but Mellon eventually won out. At his behest, Congress first repealed the wartime excess-profits tax and lowered the maximum rate on personal income from 65 to 50 percent. Subsequent revenue acts eventually lowered the maximum rate to 20 percent. The Revenue Act of 1926 extended further benefits to high-income groups by lowering estate taxes and repealing the gift tax. Much of the tax money released to wealthy people by these acts seems to have fueled the speculative excess of the late 1920s as much as it boosted consumer spending and entrepreneurial activity. Mellon, however, did balance the federal budget for a time. Governmental expenditures fell, as did the national debt.

In addition to tax cuts, Mellon favored the time-honored Republican policy of high tariffs. Wartime innovations in chemical and metal processing revived the argument for protection of infant industries from foreign competition. The Fordney-McCumber Tariff of 1922 dramatically increased rates on chemical and metal products as a safeguard against the revival of German industries that had previously commanded the field. To please the farmers, the new act further extended the duties on imported farm products.

Higher tariffs, however, had unexpected consequences. During the war, the United States had been transformed from a debtor to a creditor nation. In former years foreign capital had flowed into the United States, playing an important role in fueling economic expansion. But the private and public credits given the Allies during the war had reversed the pattern. Mellon now insisted that the European powers must repay all that they had borrowed during the war. The tariff walls erected against imports, however, made it all the harder for other nations to sell in the United States and thereby acquire the dollars with which to repay their war debts. For nearly a decade, further extensions of American loans and investments sent more dollars abroad, postponing the reckoning.

Rounding out the Republican economic program was a more lenient attitude toward government regulation of corporations. Neither Harding nor his successor, Coolidge, could dissolve the regulatory agencies created by progressivism, but they named commissioners who sought to make them more effective for a business constituency that now saw advantages in "friendly" government regulation. Harding appointed advocates of big business to the Interstate Commerce Commission, the Federal Reserve Board, and the Federal Trade Commission.

A Corrupt Administration

The crass members of Harding's "Ohio Gang" used White House connections to line their own pockets. In 1923 Harding learned that the head of the Veterans Bureau was systematically looting the government's medical and hospital supplies. The corrupt administrator resigned and fled to Europe. Harding's general counsel then committed suicide.

Not long afterward, Attorney-General Daugherty himself was implicated in the fraudulent handling of German assets seized after the war. He refused to testify on the grounds that he might incriminate himself. These were but the most visible among many scandals that touched the Justice Department, the Prohibition Bureau, and other agencies under Harding.

Juggernaut. This 1924 cartoon shows the dimensions of the Teapot Dome scandal.

But one major scandal rose above all others. Teapot Dome, like the Watergate break-in fifty years later, became the catchword for an era of government corruption. An oil deposit on federal land in Wyoming, Teapot Dome had been set aside to be administered by the Interior Department under Albert B. Fall. He let private companies exploit the deposits, arguing that such contracts were in the government's interest. Yet Fall acted in secret, without allowing competitive bids.

Suspicion grew when it was revealed that Fall had taken "loans" of about $400,000 from oil executives. For the rest of his life, Fall insisted that the loans were unrelated to the oil leases, and that he had contrived a good deal for the government, but at best the questionable circumstances revealed his fatal blindness to impropriety.

Harding himself avoided public disgrace. How much he knew of the scandals swirling around him remains unclear, but he knew enough to become visibly troubled. "My God, this is a hell of a job!" he confided to a journalist. "I have no trouble with my enemies, I can take care of my enemies all right. But my damn friends, my God-damn friends . . . they're the ones that keep me walking the floor nights!" In 1923 Harding left on what would be his last journey, a western speaking tour and a trip to the Alaska territory. In Seattle he suffered an attack of food poisoning, recovered briefly, then died in a San Francisco hotel.

Not since the death of Lincoln had there been such an outpouring of grief. Harding was a "beloved President," a kindly, ordinary man who found it in his heart (as Woodrow Wilson had not) to pardon the former Socialist candidate Eugene Debs, who had been jailed for opposing U.S. intervention in World War I. As the funeral train moved toward Washington, then back to Ohio, millions stood by the tracks to honor their lost leader.

Eventually, however, grief yielded to scorn and contempt. For nearly a decade after Harding's death, scandalous revelations about his White House associates were paraded before congressional committees and then courts. Harding's extramarital affairs also came to light. As a result of such amorous detours and corrupt associates, Harding's foreshortened administration came to be widely viewed as one of the worst in American history.

More recently, however, scholars have suggested that the scandals obscured several real accomplishments. Some historians credit Harding with leading the nation out of the turmoil of the postwar years and creating the foundation for the decade's remarkable economic boom. They also stress that he was a hardworking president who played a far more forceful role in shaping administrative economic and foreign policies than was previously believed.

"Silent Cal"

The news of Harding's death caught Vice-President Calvin Coolidge visiting his father in the mountain village of Plymouth, Vermont, his birthplace. There at 2:47 on the morning of August 3, 1923, Colonel John Coolidge administered the oath of office to his son. The rustic simplicity of Plymouth evoked just the image of traditional roots and solid integrity that the country would long for amid the wake of the slimy Harding scandals.

Coolidge brought to the White House a clear conviction that the presidency should revert to its passive stance of the Gilded Age and defer to the leadership of Congress. One editor observed that Coolidge "aspired to become the least President the country ever had; he attained his desire." Coolidge insisted on twelve hours of sleep and an afternoon nap.

Americans took to their hearts the unflappability of "Silent Cal" and the pictures of him fishing or pitching hay. As Herbert Hoover once stressed, Coolidge was a "real conservative, probably the equal of Benjamin Harrison. He was a fundamentalist in religion, in the economic and social order, and in fishing, too." (He used live worms for bait.) Even more than Harding, Coolidge embraced the orthodox creed of business. "The chief business of the American people is business," he intoned. "The man who works there worships there." Whereas Harding had sought to balance the interests of labor, agriculture, and industry, Coolidge focused on industrial development at the expense of the other two areas. He sought to unleash the free enterprise system, and, even more than Harding, he tried to end effective government regulation. Business mergers skyrocketed during the 1920s. Coolidge's pro-business stance led the *Wall Street Journal* to exult: "Never before, here or anywhere else, has a government been so completely fused with business."

The Whirlwind Campaign. A comment on Coolidge's characteristic inactivity during the 1924 election.

The 1924 Election

Coolidge successfully distanced himself from the Harding scandals and put two lawyers of undoubted integrity in charge of the prosecutions. He also quietly took control of the Republican party machinery and seized the initiative in the campaign for the 1924 nomination, which he won with only token opposition.

The Coolidge luck held as the Democrats fell victim to continuing internal dissensions, which were enough to prompt humorist Will Rogers's classic statement: "I am a member of no organized political party. I am a Democrat." The party's divisions reflected the deep alienation growing up between the new urban culture and the more traditional hinterland, a gap that the Democratic party could not bridge. It took 103 ballots to bestow the party's tarnished nomination on John W. Davis, a Wall Street lawyer from West Virginia who could hardly outdo Coolidge in conservatism.

While the Democrats fumbled, a new farm-labor coalition mobilized a third-party effort. Meeting in Cleveland on July 4, 1924, farm and labor groups reorganized the Progressive party and nominated Wisconsin senator Robert M. La Follette for president. La Follette also won the support of the Socialist party and the American Federation of Labor.

In the campaign, Coolidge chose to focus on La Follette, whom he called a dangerous radical who would turn America into a "communistic and socialistic state." The country preferred to "keep cool with Coolidge," who swept both the popular and electoral votes by decisive majorities. Davis took only the Democratic "Solid South," and La Follette carried only his native Wisconsin.

The New Era

Business executives interpreted the Republican victory as a vindication of their leadership, and Coolidge saw in surging prosperity a confirmation of his pro-business philosophy. The United States seemed to be entering a "new era" of advanced capitalism in which the majority of people were becoming middle class.

Radio gained such popularity that within a decade millions would tune in to newscasts, soap operas, sporting events, and church services.

A Growing Consumer Culture

The American economy was changing markedly during the 1920s. Dramatic increases in productive efficiency flooded the marketplace with new consumer delights. Goods once available only to the wealthy were now made accessible to the general public: cameras, wristwatches, cigarette lighters, vacuum cleaners, washing machines. But overproduction of such goods threatened to produce economic havoc unless people abandoned traditional notions of frugality and went on a buying spree. Hence, business leaders, salespersons, and public relations experts began a concerted effort to eradicate what was left of the original Protestant ethic's emphasis on plain living. A newspaper editorial insisted that the American's "first importance to his country is no longer that of citizen but that of consumer. Consumption is a new necessity."

By portraying impulse buying as a therapeutic measure to help self-esteem, advertisers shrewdly helped undermine notions of simple living. In his popular novel *Babbitt*, Sinclair Lewis recognized advertising's impact upon middle-class life: "These standard advertised wares—toothpastes, socks, tires, cameras, instantaneous hot water heaters—were the symbols and proofs of excellence."

Inventions in communications, such as motion pictures, radio, and telephones, were also transforming social life and creating a more homogeneous national culture. By 1905 the first movie house opened in Philadelphia, and within three years there were nearly 10,000 nationwide. During the next decade, Hollywood became the center of movie production, spinning out Westerns and the slapstick comedies of Mack Sennett's Keystone Studios, where Charlie Chaplin and others perfected their art into a powerful form of social criticism. In the mid-1920s, motion pictures were attracting 50 million people weekly, equal to half the national population.

Radio broadcasting had an even more spectacular growth. By 1923, there were over 500 stations and some 3 million receivers in action. In 1927 Congress established a Federal Radio Commission to regulate the industry; in 1934 it became the Federal Communications Commission, with authority over other forms of communication as well.

A nationwide mass culture now started to replace the local and regional economies of the nineteenth century. The leading advertising agency explained in 1926 that the advent of nationally circulated magazines, chain stores, syndicated news features, motion pictures, national brand names, and radio programs was creating "a nation which lives to [the same] pattern everywhere." Nonetheless, even though working-class folk could buy brand goods, phonographs, and radios, as well as movie tickets, the new consumer culture did not erase social distinctions. "Participating in mass culture," as one historian stressed, "made them feel no more mainstream or middle class, no less ethnic, religious, or working class than they already felt." And poor rural folk were the least involved with the new consumer culture. As late as 1930, some 45 million farm dwellers had no indoor plumbing and almost no electricity.

Airplanes, Automobiles, and the Economy

Startling advances in transportation were also laying the basis for a transformation of the economy and a narrowing of the distances that separated people. Wilbur and Orville Wright of Dayton, Ohio, owners of a bicycle shop, built and flew the first airplane at Kitty Hawk, North Carolina, in 1903, but the use of planes advanced slowly until the outbreak of war in Europe in 1914. An American aircraft industry developed during the war but foundered in the postwar demobilization. In 1925 the government began to subsidize the industry through airmail contracts, and, the following year, it started a program of federal aid to air transport and navigation, including funds for constructing airports.

Aviation received a psychological boost in 1927 when Charles A. Lindbergh, Jr., flew the first transatlantic solo flight from New York to Paris in thirty-three hours and thirty minutes. The scope of the New York City parade honoring Lindbergh surpassed even the celebration of the Armistice. Four years later New York City honored another pioneering American aviator—Amelia Earhart. In 1931 she became the first woman to fly solo across the Atlantic Ocean. The fifteen-hour feat led Congress to award her the Distinguished Flying Cross, and she was named Outstanding American Woman of the Year. The accomplishments of Earhart and Lindbergh helped catapult the aviation industry into prominence. By 1930 there were forty-three American airline companies in operation.

Ford Motor Company's Highland Park plant, 1913. Gravity slides and chain conveyors aided the mass production of automobiles.

By far the most significant transportation development of the time was the automobile. The first motor car had been manufactured for sale in 1895, but the founding of the Ford Motor Company in 1903 revolutionized the industry. Ford's reliable Model T (the celebrated "tin lizzie") appeared in 1908 at a price of $850 (in 1924 it would sell for $290). Ford aimed "to democratize the automobile. When I'm through everybody will be able to afford one, and about everyone will have one." He was right. In 1916 the number of cars manufactured passed 1 million; by 1920 more than 8 million were registered, and in 1929 more than 23 million. The production of automobiles stimulated the whole economy by consuming large portions of steel, rub-

By 1929 more than 23 million cars were registered in the United States. The automotive revolution enlarged the markets of other industries, including those of oil and real estate.

ber, glass, and textiles. It gave rise to a gigantic market for oil products just as the Spindletop gusher (1901) in Texas heralded the opening of vast southwestern oilfields. The automotive revolution also quickened the movement for good roads, introduced efficient mass-production assembly-line techniques to other industries, speeded transportation and tourism, encouraged the sprawl of suburbs, and sparked real-estate booms in California and Florida.

Stabilizing the Economy

During the 1920s, the efficiency craze, which had been a prominent feature of the progressive impulse, powered the wheels of mass production and consumption and became a cardinal belief of Republican leaders. Herbert Hoover, who served as secretary of commerce through the Harding-Coolidge years, promoted economic expansion and efficiency. He sought out new markets for business and sponsored more than a thousand conferences on product design, production, and distribution. He also continued the wartime emphasis on standardization of everything from automobile tires and paving bricks to bedsprings and toilet paper.

Most of all Hoover endorsed the burgeoning trade-association movement. Through such associations, competing executives in a given field would gather and disseminate information on sales, purchases, shipments, production, and prices. This information allowed them to plan with more confidence, the advantages of which included predictable costs, prices, and markets, as well as more stable employment and wages. Sometimes abuses crept in as trade associations engaged in price-fixing and other monopolistic practices, but the Supreme Court in 1925 held the practice of sharing information as such to be within the law.

The Business of Farming

During the Harding and Coolidge administrations, agriculture remained the weakest sector in the economy. For a brief time after the war, the farmers' hopes had soared on wings of prosperity. The wartime boom lasted into 1920, but then commodity prices collapsed as European farmers began to resume high levels of production.

In some ways farmers shared the business outlook of the so-called New Era. Many farms, like corporations, were getting larger, more efficient, and more mechanized. By 1930 about 13 percent of all farmers had tractors, and the proportion rose even higher on the western plains. Better plows and other new machines were part of the mechanization process that accompanied improved crop yields, fertilizers, and animal breeding.

Farm organizations of the 1920s moved away from the proposed alliance with urban labor that had marked the Populist Era and toward a new view of farmers as profit-conscious business owners. During the postwar farm depression, the idea of marketing cooperatives emerged as the farmer's equivalent to the businessman's trade-association movement. Farm interest groups formed regional commodity-marketing associations that enabled them to negotiate ironclad contracts with producers for the delivery of their crops over a period of years. These associations also brought order to the marketing of farm products, requiring uniform standards and grades, efficient handling and advertising, and a businesslike organization with professional technicians and executives.

The most effective political response to the collapse of farm prices of the early 1920s was the formation of the farm bloc, a congressional coalition of western Republicans and southern Democrats that put through an impressive legislative program from 1921 to 1923. The farm bloc passed bills exempting farm cooperatives from antitrust laws and creating new credit banks that could lend to cooperative producing and marketing associations.

In the spring of 1924 Senator Charles L. McNary of Oregon and Representative Gilbert N. Haugen of Iowa introduced a bill to secure "equality for agriculture in the benefits of the protective tariff." Their plan sought to dump American farm surpluses on the world market in order to raise commodity prices in the home market. The goal was to achieve "parity"—that is, to raise domestic farm prices to a point where farmers would have the same purchasing power relative to other consumer prices that they had enjoyed between 1909 and 1914, a time viewed in retrospect as a golden age of American agriculture. A McNary-Haugen bill finally passed both houses of Congress in 1927 and again a year later, only to be vetoed both times by President Coolidge. He criticized the measure as an unsound effort at pricefixing, and as un-American and unconstitutional to boot. Nonetheless, the bill catapulted the farm problem into the arena of national debate and revived the political alliance between the South and West.

Setbacks for Unions

Urban workers shared more than farmers in the affluence of the times. Non-farm workers gained about 20 percent in real wages between 1921 and 1928, while farm income rose only 10 percent. The benefits of this rise, however, were distributed unevenly. Miners and textile workers suffered a decline in real wages. In these and other trades, technological unemployment followed the introduction of new methods and machines, as technology eliminated as well as created jobs.

Organized labor, however, did no better than organized agriculture in the 1920s. In fact, unions suffered a setback after the growth years of the war as the Red Scare and strikes of 1919 left the uneasy impression that unions practiced political subversion. To suppress unions, employers used intimidation and repression. They often required "yellow-dog" contracts that forced workers to agree to stay out of unions. They also used labor spies, exchanged blacklists, and resorted to other forms of coercion. Some employers tried to kill the unions with kindness. They introduced programs of "industrial democracy" guided by company unions or various schemes of "welfare capitalism" such a profit-sharing, bonuses, pensions, health programs, recreational activities, and the like. Prosperity, propaganda, welfare capitalism, and active hostility combined to cause union membership to drop from about 5 million in 1920 to 3.5 million in 1929.

President Hoover, the Engineer

Hoover versus Smith

Calvin Coolidge's decision not to seek election in 1928 cleared the way for Herbert Hoover to gain the Republican nomination. The party platform took credit for postwar prosperity, debt and tax reduction, and the protective tariff that had been in operation since 1922 ("as vital to American agriculture as it is to manufacturing"). It rejected the McNary-Haugen agricultural program but promised a farm board to manage crop surpluses more efficiently.

The Democratic nomination went to Governor Alfred E. Smith of New York. But when he revealed in his acceptance speech a desire to liberalize prohibition, Smith alienated many Democrats in the southern

Bible Belt. Hoover by contrast called for improved enforcement.

The two candidates projected sharply different images. Hoover was the Quaker son of middle America, the successful engineer and businessman from rural Iowa, the architect of Republican prosperity, a simple man who dressed plainly, spoke tersely, and followed his strong conscience. Smith was the prototype of those things that rural and small-town America distrusted: the son of Irish immigrants, Catholic, and a critic of prohibition. Outside the large cities such qualities were handicaps he could scarcely surmount, for all his affability and wit.

In the election Hoover won in the third consecutive Republican landslide, with 21 million popular votes to Smith's 15 million, and an even more top-heavy electoral majority of 444 to 87. Hoover even cracked the Solid South, leaving Smith only a hard core of six Deep South states plus Massachusetts and Rhode Island. The election was above all a vindication of Republican prosperity, but the shattering defeat of the Democrats concealed a major realignment in the making. Smith had nearly doubled the vote for the Democratic candidate of four years before. Smith's image, though a handicap in the hinterlands, swung big cities back into the Democratic column. And in the farm states of the West there were signs that some disgruntled farmers had switched over to the Democrats. A coalition of urban workers and unhappy farmers was in the making.

Hoover in Control

The milestone year of 1929 dawned with high hopes. The economy seemed robust, incomes were rising, and the pro-business Hoover was about to enter the White House. "I have no fears for the future of our country," Hoover told his inauguration audience. "It is bright with hope."

Forgotten in the rush of later events would be Hoover's credentials as a progressive and humanitarian president. Over the objection of Treasury Secretary Mellon, he announced a plan for tax reductions in the low-income brackets. He shunned corrupt patronage practices, and he refused to countenance "Red hunts" or interference with peaceful picketing of the White House. He also defended his wife's right to invite prominent blacks to the White House, and he sought more money for all-black Howard University.

Hoover showed greater sympathy than Coolidge for the struggling agricultural sector. In 1929 he pushed through a special session of Congress the Agricultural Marketing Act, which established both a Federal Farm Board with a revolving loan fund of $500 million to help farm cooperatives market major commodities and a program in which the Farm Board could set up "stabilization corporations" empowered to buy surpluses off the market.

To open glutted markets, Taft supported the Hawley-Smoot Tariff of 1930, which carried duties on imported manufactures and farm crops to a new high. Average rates went from about 32 to 40 percent. More than 1,000 economists petitioned Hoover to veto the bill because, they predicted, it would raise prices to consumers, damage the export trade and thus hurt farmers, promote inefficiency, and provoke foreign reprisals. Events proved them right, but Hoover felt that he had to go along with his party in an election year. This proved to be a disastrous mistake, for it only exacerbated the growing economic depression.

The Economy Out of Control

Depression? Most Americans had come to assume during the 1920s that there would never be another depression. This misguided optimism proved to be an important factor in generating the economic free-fall after 1929. Throughout the 1920s, the idea grew that American business had entered a "New Era" of *permanent* growth. Such naive talk helped promote an array of get-rich-quick schemes. Speculative mania fueled the Florida real-estate boom, which got under way when the combination of Coolidge prosperity and automobiles made Florida an accessible playground.

The Florida real-estate mania collapsed in 1926, but the stock market took up the slack. Until 1927 stock values had risen with profits, but then they began to soar on wings of fanciful speculation. Gamblers in the market ignored warning signs. By 1927 residential construction and automobile sales were catching up to demand, business inventories rose, and the rate of consumer spending slowed. By mid-1929, production, employment, and other gauges of economic activity were declining. Still the stock market rose, driven by excessive confidence and perennial greed.

By 1929 the stock market had become a fantasy world. Conservative financiers and brokers who counseled caution went unheeded. Hoover worried too, and he sought to discourage speculation, but to no avail. On September 4, stock prices wavered, and the next day they dropped. The Great Bull Market staggered on into October, trending downward but with enough good days to keep hope alive. On October 22 a leading bank president told reporters that there was "nothing fundamentally wrong with the stock market or with the underlying business and credit structure."

The Crash and Its Causes

The next day prices tumbled, and the day after that a wild scramble to unload stocks lasted until word arrived that leading bankers had formed a pool to stabilize prices. For the rest of the week, stock prices steadied, but after a weekend to think the situation over, stockholders began to unload their portfolios. On Tuesday, October 29, the most devastating single day in the market's history to that point, the index dropped almost 13 percent. During October, the value of stocks fell by an average of 37 percent.

Caution was now the watchword for consumers and business leaders. Buyers held out for lower prices, orders fell off, wages fell or ceased altogether, and the decline in purchasing power brought further cutbacks in business activity. From 1929 to 1932, Americans' personal incomes declined by more than half. Unemployment continued to rise exponentially to 25 percent of the labor force by 1933. Farmers, already in trouble, faced catastrophe as commodity prices fell by half. More than 9,000 banks closed during the period, hundreds of factories and mines shut down, entire towns were abandoned, and thousands of farms were sold to pay debts.

The crash had revealed the economy's structural problems. Too many businesses during the boom years had maintained prices and taken profits while holding down wages. By plowing profits back into expansion, business brought on a growing imbalance between rising productivity and declining purchasing power. As the demand for goods declined, the rate of investment in new plants and equipment also began to decline. For a time the softness of purchasing power was concealed by greater use of installment buying, and the deflationary effects of high tariffs were concealed by the volume of loans and investments abroad, which supported foreign demand for American goods. But the flow of American capital abroad began to dry up when the stock market became a more attractive investment. Swollen profits and dividends enticed the rich into market speculation. When trouble came, the bloated corporate structure collapsed.

Governmental policies also contributed to the debacle. Treasury Secretary Mellon's tax reductions brought oversaving, as citizens put their discretionary income in the stock market, which helped diminish demand for consumer goods. The growing money supply fed the fever of speculation by lowering interest rates. Hostility toward unions discouraged collective bargaining and may have worsened the prevalent imbalances in income. High tariffs hindered foreign trade. Lax enforcement of antitrust laws encouraged concentration, monopoly, and high prices.

Another culprit was the gold standard. The world monetary system remained fragile throughout the 1920s. When economic output, prices, and savings began dropping in 1929, policy makers—certain that they had to keep their currencies tied to gold at all costs—either did nothing or tightened money supplies, thus exacerbating the downward spiral. The only way to restore economic stability within the constraints of the gold standard was to let prices and wages continue to fall. The best policy, Andrew Mellon advised, would be to "liquidate labor, liquidate stocks, liquidate the farmers, liquidate real estate," allowing the downturn to "purge the rottenness out of the system." Such passivity helped turn a recession into the world's worst depression.

Homeless camps, labeled "Hoovervilles," in Seattle, Washington.

The Human Toll of Depression

The devastating collapse of the economy caused immense social hardships. By 1933, there were over 13 million people out of work and many more found themselves working fewer hours. Blacks and Mexicans were usually the first laid off. As factories shut down, banks closed, and farms went bankrupt, millions of people found themselves not only jobless, but also homeless and penniless. Hungry people lined up at churches and soup kitchens; others rummaged through trash cans behind restaurants. Many of the destitute slept on park benches or in back alleys. Others congregated in makeshift shelters in vacant lots. Thousands of men in search of jobs sneaked onto empty railway cars and rode from town to town looking for work. During the winter, homeless people wrapped themselves in newspapers to keep warm, referring to them sarcastically as "Hoover blankets." Some grew weary of their grim fate and ended their lives. Suicide rates soared during the 1930s.

Hoover's Efforts at Recovery

Not only did the policies of public officials help bring on economic collapse, but few political or economic leaders acknowledged the severity of the crisis. Those who held to the theory of laissez-faire thought the economy would cure itself. Hoover, however, was unwilling to sit by and let events take their course. In fact, he did more than any previous president in such dire economic circumstances. Still, his own philosophy, now hardened into dogma, set strict limits to action by the federal government, and he refused to set it aside even to meet an emergency.

Hoover believed that the country's main need was confidence. On May 1, 1930, he told the U.S. Chamber of Commerce that "we have passed the worst and with continued effort we shall rapidly recover." To that end, he asked business and labor leaders to keep the mills and shops open, maintain wage levels, and spread the work to avoid layoffs—in short, to let the shock fall on corporate profits rather than on purchasing power. In return, union leaders, who had little choice, agreed to refrain from wage demands and strikes.

While reassuring the American public, Hoover also accelerated the construction of public projects in order to provide jobs, but state and local cutbacks more than offset new federal spending. At Hoover's demand the Federal Reserve returned to an easier credit policy, and Congress passed a modest tax reduction to put more purchasing power in people's pockets. At the same time, the high Hawley-Smoot Tariff, proposed at first to help farmers, brought reprisals abroad, devastating foreign trade.

Despite Hoover's efforts, depression hurt the political party in power, and the floundering president was easy game. In 1930 the Democrats gained their first national victory since 1916, winning a majority in the House and enough gains in the Senate to control it in coalition with western agrarians.

In the first half of 1931 economic indicators rose, renewing hope for an upswing. Then, as recovery beckoned, another shock jolted public confidence. In 1931 the failure of Austria's largest bank triggered a financial panic in central Europe. To halt the domino effect of spreading defaults, President Hoover proposed a one-year moratorium on both reparations and war-debt payments. The major European nations accepted the moratorium and later also a temporary "standstill" on settlement of private obligations between banks. The general shortage of monetary exchange drove Europeans to withdraw their gold from American banks and dump their American securities. One European nation after another abandoned the gold standard and devalued its currency. All these foreign developments worsened the collapse of the American economy, which slid into the third bitter winter of depression.

Congressional Initiatives

With a new Congress in session, demands for federal action impelled Hoover to use governmental resources at least to shore up the financial institutions. In early 1932 the new Congress set up the Reconstruction Finance Corporation (RFC) with $500 million (and authority to borrow $1.5 billion more) for emergency loans to banks, life insurance companies, farm mortgage associations, and railroads. The RFC staved off some bankruptcies, but Hoover's critics charged that it favored business at the expense of workers. The RFC nevertheless remained a key agency through the decade and during World War II.

Further help to the financial structure came with the Glass-Steagall Act of 1932, which eased the availability of commercial loans. It also released about $750 million in gold formerly used to back Federal Reserve notes, countering the effect of foreign withdrawals and domestic hoarding of gold at the same time that it enlarged the supply of credit. For homeowners the Federal Home Loan Bank Act of 1932 created a series of discount banks for home mortgages. They provided savings and loan associations a service much like that which the Federal Reserve System provided to commercial banks.

Hoover's critics argued that all these measures reflected a dubious "trickle-down" theory. If government could help banks and railroads, asked New York senator Robert G. Wagner, "is there any reason why we should not likewise extend a helping hand to that forlorn American, in every village and every city of the United States, who has been without wages since 1929?" The contraction of credit had devastated debtors such as farmers and those who made purchases on the "installment plan" or who held "balloon" mortgages whose monthly payments increased over time.

By 1932 members of Congress were filling the hoppers with bills to provide federal relief for distressed individuals. At that point, Hoover might have pleaded "dire necessity," taken the leadership of the relief movement, and salvaged his political fortunes. Instead he held back and only grudgingly edged toward federal relief. On July 21, 1932, Hoover signed the Emergency Relief and Construction Act, which avoided a direct federal dole (cash payments to individuals) but gave the RFC $300 million for relief loans to the states, authorized loans of up to $1.5 billion for state and local government construction projects, and appropriated $322 million for federal public works.

Government relief for farmers had long since been abandoned. In mid-1931 the government quit buying crop surpluses and helplessly watched prices slide. In 1919 wheat had fetched $2.16 a bushel; by 1932 it had sunk to 38¢. Cotton had reached a high of 41.75¢ a pound in 1919; before the 1932 harvest it went to 4.6¢. Other farm prices declined comparably. Between 1930 and 1934, the titles of nearly a million farms passed from their owners to the mortgage holders.

Farmers and Veterans in Protest

Faced with total loss, some desperate farmers began to defy the law. Angry mobs stopped foreclosures and threatened to lynch bankers and judges. Fears of organized disorder arose when unemployed World War I veterans converged on Washington in the spring of 1932. The "Bonus Expeditionary Force" grew quickly to more than 15,000. Their purpose was to get immediate payment of the cash bonus to war veterans that Congress had voted in 1924. The House approved a bonus bill, but when the Senate voted it down, most of the veterans went home. The rest, having no place to go, camped in vacant government buildings and in a shantytown within sight of the Capitol.

Eager to disperse the destitute veterans, Hoover convinced Congress to vote funds to buy their tickets home. More left, but others stayed even after Congress adjourned, hoping at least to meet with the embattled president. Late in July the administration ordered the shantytown razed. In the ensuing melee, one policeman panicked, fired into the crowd, and killed two veterans. The secretary of war then dispatched about 700 soldiers under General Douglas MacArthur, aided by junior officers Dwight D. Eisenhower and George S. Patton, Jr. The soldiers easily drove out the unarmed veterans and their families, then burned the shacks. The one fatality—from tear gas—was an eleven-week-old boy, born in one of the shanties.

The Hoover administration insisted that the Bonus Army consisted mainly of Communists and criminals, but neither a grand jury nor the Veterans Administration could find evidence to support the charge. The spectacle of army troops using tanks to dislodge unarmed veterans did not help Hoover's eroding image. To most Americans, the Bonus Army was more pathetic than threatening.

As the Depression deepened, Hoover grew frustrated and distressed at his inability to reverse the downturn. His gloom and growing sense of futility were apparent to the country. In a mood more despairing than rebellious, people waited to see what another presidential campaign would bring forth.

CHAPTER 27

New Deal America

This chapter focuses on

- The social effects of the Great Depression and Franklin Roosevelt's efforts at relief, recovery, and reform.
- Criticism of the New Deal, from both the right and the left.
- How the New Deal greatly expanded the federal government's authority and responsibilities.
- The change in cultural life during the 1930s.

THE *ESSENTIAL AMERICA* ON-LINE TUTOR

www.wwnorton.com/eamerica/ch27

- **Topic: The TVA and the New Deal**
  www.wwnorton.com/eamerica/ch27/topic.htm

  Since its inception as part of FDR's New Deal, the Tennessee Valley Authority (TVA) has been one of the nation's largest providers of electrical power while simultaneously creating jobs and providing other necessities—drinking water, for example—for millions of people. Study the significance of the TVA using photographs, TVA archival materials, historical analyses, and Roosevelt's comments. Did the TVA fulfill Roosevelt's expectations of relieving human suffering and economic distress?

- **Chapter review: On-line quiz and chapter summary**
  www.wwnorton.com/eamerica/ch27/review.htm

- **Chapter resources: Multimedia index**
  www.wwnorton.com/eamerica/ch27/media.htm

On June 14, 1932, while the ragtag Bonus Army was still encamped in Washington, glum Republicans gathered in Chicago to renominate Hoover. The Democrats, in contrast, converged on Chicago late in June confident that they would nominate the next president. New York governor Franklin D. Roosevelt already had lined up most of the delegates, and he won the nomination on the fourth ballot.

In a bold gesture, Roosevelt appeared before the convention in person to accept the nomination instead of awaiting formal notification. He told the expectant delegates: "I pledge myself to a new deal for the American people." Roosevelt had little idea as yet what the New Deal would be in practice, but he was much more flexible and willing to experiment than Hoover. What was more, his upbeat personality communicated joy and hope—as did his campaign song, "Happy Days Are Here Again."

From Hooverism to the New Deal

FDR's Election

Born in 1882 into a wealthy New York family, young Franklin Roosevelt earned degrees from Harvard and Columbia University Law School. While a law student, he married Anna Eleanor Roosevelt, his own distant cousin and the niece of President Theodore Roosevelt.

Franklin Roosevelt began work with a prominent Wall Street law firm, but he soon lost interest in legal affairs and decided to enter politics. In 1910 he won a Democratic seat in the New York State Senate. As a freshman legislator he displayed the contradictory qualities that would characterize his political career: an aristocrat with a sincere affinity for common folk; a traditionalist with a penchant for experiment; an affable charmer who was also a skilled political tactician with a shrewd sense of timing and a distinctive willingness to listen to and learn from others.

In 1912 Roosevelt backed Woodrow Wilson for president and served as his assistant secretary of the navy. Then, in 1920, largely on the strength of his name, he gained the vice-presidential nomination. Political defeat in the election was followed by personal crisis. In 1921, at the age of thirty-nine, Roosevelt contracted polio, which left him permanently crippled, unable to stand or walk without braces. A friend recalled that Roosevelt emerged from his struggle with polio "completely warm-hearted, with a new humility of spirit" that led him to identify with the poor and suffering.

For seven years, Roosevelt strengthened his body to compensate for his disability, and in 1928, he was elected governor of New York. Reelected by a large majority in 1930, he became the Democratic front-runner for the presidency in 1932. Roosevelt was obsessed with gaining the highest office in the land; he was willing to sacrifice everything—marriage, health, staff, friends—to that end.

The 1932 Campaign

Partly to dispel doubts about his health, Roosevelt set forth on a grueling campaign tour in 1932. He blamed the depression on Hoover and the Republicans, and he began to define what he meant by his New Deal. Like Hoover, Roosevelt made the requisite pledge to balance the budget, but he left open the loophole that he would incur short-term deficits to prevent starvation. He was evasive on the tariff, and on farm policy he offered several options pleasing to farmers but ambiguous enough not to alarm city dwellers. He did come out unequivocally for strict regulation of utilities, and he consistently stood by his party's pledge to repeal the amendment outlawing alcoholic beverages. Perhaps most important, he recognized that a mature economy would require imaginative national planning. "The country

Democratic party campaign advertisement from the 1932 presidential race.

needs, and, unless I mistake its temper, the country demands bold, persistent experimentation." What came across to voters, however, was less the content of his speeches than his irrepressible confidence. Mired in the persistent depression, the country wanted a new course, a new leadership, a new deal, and the voters in 1932 swept Roosevelt into office by a whopping margin.

The Inauguration

For the last time, the country waited four months, until March 4, for a new president and Congress to take office. The Twentieth Amendment, ratified on February 6, 1933, provided that the president would thereafter take office on January 20 and the newly elected Congress on January 3.

Amid spreading destitution and misery, unemployment continued to rise during the bleak winter of 1932–1933, and panic struck the banking system. As bank after bank failed, people rushed to remove their deposits. The "run" on the banks exacerbated the crisis and paralyzed the economy. When the Hoover administration left office, four-fifths of the nation's banks were closed, and the country teetered on the brink of economic paralysis.

The profound crisis of confidence that prevailed when Roosevelt took office on March 4, 1933, gave way to a mood of expectancy. The new president asserted "that the only thing we have to fear is fear itself." He would not merely exhort, he promised: "This nation asks for action, and action now!" It was exactly what a distraught nation wanted to hear.

Competing Solutions

When Roosevelt and the New Dealers arrived in Washington, they were confronted by three major challenges: reviving the devastated economy, relieving the human misery brought on by the depression, and alleviating the desperate plight of farmers and their families. Roosevelt's "brain trust" of advisers developed conflicting responses. Some promoted vigorous enforcement of the antitrust laws as a means of restoring competition; others argued just the opposite, saying that antitrust laws should be suspended so as to enable large corporations to collaborate with the federal government in "managing" the economy. Still others called for a massive expansion of welfare programs and a prolonged infusion of government spending to revive the economy and aid the suffering.

For his part, Roosevelt vacillated among these three schools of thought. He was willing to try elements of each without embracing one approach completely. In part, this reflected the political reality that conservative southern Democrats controlled most of the major congressional committees. They were committed to states' rights and balanced budgets. Roosevelt was a pragmatist rather than an ideologue. As he once explained, "Take a method and try it. If it fails admit it frankly and try another." Roosevelt's New Deal, therefore, would take the form of a series of trial-and-error actions.

Roosevelt and his lieutenants initially settled on a three-pronged strategy as their first attempt at addressing the problems facing the nation. First, they sought to remedy the financial crisis and to provide emergency relief for the jobless. Second, they tried to promote industrial recovery through increased federal spending and cooperative agreements between management and organized labor. Third, they attempted to raise commodity prices (and thereby farm income) by paying farmers to reduce crops and herds. None of these initiatives worked perfectly, but their combined effect was to restore hope and energy to a nation paralyzed by fear and uncertainty.

Strengthening the Monetary System

The first order of business for the new administration was to free up the channels of finance. On his second day in office, Roosevelt called a special session of Congress and declared a four-day banking holiday. It took Congress only seven hours to pass the Emergency Banking Relief Act, which permitted sound banks to reopen and provided managers for those still in trouble. On March 12, 1933, in the first of his radio "fireside chats," the president insisted that it was safer to "keep your money in a reopened bank than under the mattress." The following day, deposits in reopened banks exceeded withdrawals, and by March 15, banks controlling nine-tenths of the nation's banking resources were open once again.

Having decisively ended the bank panic, Roosevelt next slashed military pensions and government payrolls and then urged Congress to pass the Twenty-first Amendment, which ended prohibition.

These measures were but the beginning of an avalanche of executive and legislative action. Between March 9 and June 16, the so-called Hundred Days, Congress passed more than a dozen of Roosevelt's major proposals, legislation whose scope was unprecedented in American history.

With the banking crisis over, there still remained an acute debt problem for farmers and homeowners. By early 1933, banks were foreclosing on farm mortgages at the rate of 20,000 per month. By executive decree, Roosevelt reorganized all farm credit agencies into the Farm Credit Administration (FCA). Congress authorized the extensive refinancing of farm mortgages at lower interest rates. The Home Owner's Loan Act provided a similar service to city dwellers through the new Home Owner's Loan Corporation (HOLC), which refinanced mortgage loans at lower monthly payments. This helped slow the rate of foreclosures. The Glass-Steagall Banking Act further shored up confidence in the banking system by creating the Federal Deposit Insurance Corporation (FDIC) to insure personal bank deposits up to $5,000. It also required commercial banks to separate themselves from investment brokerages.

Roosevelt and Congress also tightened the regulation of Wall Street. The Federal Securities Act required that new stock and bond issues register with the Federal Trade Commission and later with the Securities and Exchange Commission (SEC), a new agency created to regulate the stock and bond markets.

Throughout 1933 Roosevelt tinkered with devaluation of the currency as a way to raise stock and commodity prices and ease the debt burden on strapped investors and farmers. On April 19 the government officially abandoned the gold standard, which infuriated fiscal conservatives.

Relief Measures

Another urgent priority in 1933 was relieving widespread unemployment and personal distress. Hoover had steadfastly resisted using the federal government to provide direct relief for the unemployed. Roosevelt had fewer qualms. At his behest, Congress created the Civilian Conservation Corps (CCC), which was designed to provide useful jobs for young working-class men aged eighteen to twenty-five with little educational or vocational background.

Nearly 3 million CCC workers took to the woods to perform a variety of jobs in forests, parks, recreational areas, and soil conservation projects. They built roads, bridges, camping facilities, and fish hatcheries, planted trees, taught farmers how to control soil erosion, and fought fires.

The Federal Emergency Relief Administration (FERA) addressed the broader problems of human distress. Designed as a shared undertaking between the federal government and the state and city governments, it was in fact directed by the Roosevelt administration. Harry L. Hopkins, a tireless social worker from Iowa, headed the new effort and became the second most powerful figure in the administration. FERA funds supported state construction of over 5,000 public buildings and 7,000 bridges, organized adult literacy programs, financed college education for poor students, and set up day-care centers for low-income families. The agency also helped local agencies dispense food and clothing for the needy.

The first large-scale experiment with *federal* work relief came with the formation of the Civil Works Administration (CWA). Created in 1933, when it had become apparent that the state-sponsored programs under the FERA were inadequate, the CWA provided federal jobs at competitive wages to those unable to find work that winter. The CWA was hastily conceived and implemented, but during its four-month existence it put to work over 4 million people. The agency spent over $900 million (mostly in wages) for a variety of useful projects, from construction to providing 50,000 teaching jobs that helped keep rural schools open.

As the number of people employed by the CWA soared, the program's costs skyrocketed to over a billion dollars. Roosevelt balked at such high expenditures, and he worried that people would become dependent on federal jobs. He ordered the CWA dissolved in the spring of 1934. By April some 4 million workers were again unemployed.

In 1935 Roosevelt asked Congress for an array of new federal job programs. It responded by passing a $4.8 billion bill providing work relief for the jobless. To manage these programs, Roosevelt created the Works Progress Administration (WPA), headed by Harry Hopkins, to replace the FERA. Some of the new jobs appeared to be make-work or mere "leaning on shovels," but before the WPA died during World War II, it left permanent monuments on the landscape in the form of buildings, bridges, hard-surfaced roads, airports, and schools. The WPA also employed a wide range of talents in the Federal Theatre Project, the Federal Art Project, and the Federal Writers' Project. The National Youth Administration, under the WPA, provided part-time employment to students, set up technical training programs, and aided jobless youth. Although the WPA took care of only 3 million out of some 10 million jobless at any one time, in all it helped some 9 million clients weather desperate times before it expired in 1943.

Recovery through Regulation

In addition to rescuing the banks and providing relief for the unemployed, the New Deal promoted the recovery of the agricultural and industrial sectors. Roosevelt's "brain trust" of university-trained experts, lawyers, and professors initially felt that the trend toward big business was inevitable. They also believed that the mistakes of the 1920s showed that the only way to operate an integrated economy at full capacity and in the public interest was through stringent regulation and centralized planning in cooperation with big business, not through trust-busting. New farm and industrial recovery programs sprang from such beliefs and experiences.

City Life (1933) by Victor Arnautoff. The murals in San Francisco's Coit Tower were commissioned as part of the WPA's Public Works of Art Program, which employed professional artists during the economic recovery of the 1930s.

Agricultural Recovery: The AAA

The sharp decline in crop prices after 1929 meant that many farmers could not afford to plant or harvest their crops. The Agricultural Adjustment Act (AAA) of 1933 sought to help raise commodity prices by paying farmers to cut back production. The money for the benefit payments made to farmers would be raised from a "processing tax" levied on the businesses (such as cotton gins, flour mills, and meat-packing plants) that processed farm products for sale.

As a complement to the AAA, Roosevelt created the Commodity Credit Corporation (another CCC!), which extended loans to farmers above the market price of their crops. But by the time Congress acted, the growing season was already advanced, and the prospect of another bumper cotton crop created an urgent problem. The AAA reluctantly sponsored a plow-under program and encouraged farmers to destroy young livestock as a means of raising prices.

For a while these controversial farm measures worked. By the end of 1934 there were significant declines in wheat, cotton, and corn production and a simultaneous increase in commodity prices. Farm income increased by 58 percent between 1932 and 1935.

The AAA, however, was only partially responsible for such gains. A devastating drought that settled over the Great Plains between 1932 and 1935 played a major role in reducing production and creating the epic "dust bowl" migrations so poignantly evoked in John Steinbeck's novel *The Grapes of Wrath*. Many migrant families had actually been driven off the land by AAA benefit programs that encouraged large farmers to take the lands worked by tenants and sharecroppers out of cultivation first.

Although it created unexpected problems, the AAA achieved real successes in boosting the overall farm economy. Then the Supreme Court in *United States* v. *Butler* (1936) ruled the AAA's processing tax unconstitutional because farm production was intrastate and thus beyond the reach of federal power. The administration hastily devised a new plan to achieve crop reduction indirectly in the Soil Conservation and Domestic Allotment Act (1936). The new act omitted processing taxes and acreage quotas, but it provided benefit payments to farmers who engaged in soil conservation practices and cut back on soil-depleting staple crops. Since the money to pay for these measures came out of general funds and not from taxes, this approach was not vulnerable to lawsuits.

Dust storm approaching, 1930s. When a dust storm blew in, it would bring complete darkness as well as sand and grit that would soon cover every surface, both inside and out.

The act was an almost unqualified success as an engineering and educational project because it went far to heal the scars of erosion and the plague of dust storms. But soil conservation nevertheless failed as a device for limiting production. With their worst lands taken out of production, farmers cultivated their fertile acres more intensively. In response, Congress passed the second Agricultural Adjustment Act (1938), which reestablished the earlier programs but left out the processing taxes. Benefit payments would come from general funds. Increasingly, federal farm programs came to dominate the nation's agricultural economy.

Industrial Recovery: The NRA

The industrial counterpart to the AAA was the National Industrial Recovery Act (NIRA), passed in 1933. The NIRA had two major components. One part created the Public Works Administration (PWA) with $3.3 billion to construct public buildings, highways, bridges, tunnels, and aircraft carriers. Under the direction of Interior Secretary Harold L. Ickes, PWA workers built Virginia's Skyline Drive, New York's Triborough Bridge, the Overseas Highway from Miami to Key West, and Chicago's subway system.

The more controversial and ambitious part of the NIRA created the National Recovery Administration (NRA), headed by the former army general Hugh S. Johnson. Modeled after the War Industries Board of 1917–1918, its purposes were essentially twofold: first, to stabilize the business sector by reducing competition through the implementation of industrywide codes that set wages and prices, and second, to generate more purchasing power by providing jobs and raising wages. The NRA increased trade union hopes for protection of basic hour and wage standards and raised liberal hopes for comprehensive government planning for the economy.

The NRA Eagle was the symbol of compliance with the National Recovery Administration.

In each industry, committees representing management, labor, and government drew up the fair practice codes. The labor standards were quite progressive. Every code set a forty-hour workweek and minimum weekly wages of $13 ($12 in the South, where living costs were lower), which more than doubled earnings in some cases. Child labor under the age of sixteen was prohibited.

Labor unions, already hard pressed by the economic downturn and the loss of members, however, were understandably concerned about the NRA's efforts to reduce competition by allowing businesses to cooperate in fixing wages and prices as well as production levels. To gain their support, the NRA included a provision (Section 7a) that guaranteed the right of workers to organize unions. But while prohibiting employers from interfering with labor organizing efforts, the NRA did not create adequate enforcement measures, nor did it require employers to bargain in good faith with labor representatives.

For a time the NRA stabilized wages and prices, but as soon as economic recovery began, the honeymoon ended. The larger companies dominated the code negotiations and used the codes to stifle competition by dividing up markets and entrenching their own positions. They also engaged in price-fixing that robbed small producers of the chance to compete. The NRA wage codes also excluded agricultural and domestic workers—three out of every four employed blacks. The effort to develop codes for every industry in the nation proved an administrative nightmare, and the daily annoyances of code enforcement inspired growing hostility among business executives.

By 1935 the NRA had developed more critics than friends. In 1935, when the Supreme Court declared the NRA unconstitutional, few mourned. Yet the NRA experiment left an enduring mark. With dramatic suddenness, the codes had set new standards, such as the forty-hour workweek and the end of child labor, from which it proved hard for management to retreat. The NRA's endorsement of collective bargaining also spurred union growth.

Regional Planning: The TVA

The creation of the Tennessee Valley Authority (TVA) was the New Deal's boldest experiment, though it resulted from an old idea. In 1916 the government had started electric power and nitrate (for dynamite) plants at Muscle Shoals, Alabama, to strengthen national defense, promote general industrial development, and provide cheap public power. Water-power development led in turn to improved flood control, and to conservation of soil and forests to prevent silting.

Through the 1920s, Nebraska senator George W. Norris had defeated efforts to sell the Alabama project to private developers, but he failed in his effort to create a federal project to provide electricity for the public. In 1932, however, Norris won Roosevelt's support for a vast enlargement of the Muscle Shoals project.

On May 18, 1933, Congress created the TVA as a multipurpose public corporation. By 1936, the TVA had six dams completed or under way and had developed a master plan to build nine dams on the Tennessee River. The agency, moreover, opened the rivers for navigation, fostered soil conservation and forestry, experimented with fertilizers, drew new industry to the region, and sent cheap electricity pulsating through the valley.

The TVA's success at generating greater power consumption and lower rates awakened private utilities to the mass consumer markets. It also transported farmers from the age of kerosene to the age of electricity. Through loans of more than $321 million to rural cooperatives, the Rural Electrification Administration (REA) paved the way for the electrification of the nation's farms.

The Human Cost of the Depression

Although New Deal programs helped ease the devastation wrought by the depression, they did not restore prosperity or end the widespread human suffering. The depression continued to take a toll on ordinary Americans—factory workers, farmers, bankers, professionals, and others remained in the throes of a shattered economy that only slowly was working its way back to health.

White Angel Bread Line. Dorthea Lange's photographs are moving documents of the hardships of the Great Depression.

Continuing Hardships

As late as 1939, some 9.5 million workers (17 percent of the labor force) remained unemployed. Prolonged poverty led to desperate actions. Petty theft soared during the 1930s, as did street-corner begging and prostitution. Although the divorce rate dropped during the decade, in part because couples could not afford to live separately or pay the legal fees to obtain divorces, all too often husbands down on their luck simply deserted their wives. In 1940 a survey revealed that 1.5 million husbands had left home.

Many couples decided to postpone marriage because of hard times. During the 1930s, the total number of marriages declined by one-fourth compared to the previous decade. With their own future uncertain, married couples often decided not to have children; the birthrate plummeted during the depression. Those with children sometimes could not support them. In 1933 the Children's Bureau reported that one out of every five children was not getting enough to eat. Often, struggling parents sent their children to live with relatives or friends. Some 900,000 other children simply left home and joined the army of homeless "tramps."

Dust Bowl Migrants

During the 1930s, uprooted farmers and their families formed a migratory stream rushing from the South and Midwest toward California, buoyed by currents of hope and desperation. Although frequently lumped together as "Okies," most of the dust bowl refugees were actually from cotton-belt communities in Arkansas, Texas, and Missouri, as well as Oklahoma. During the 1930s and 1940s, some 800,000 people left those four states and headed to the Far West. Not all were farmers; many were professionals, white-collar workers, retailers, and farm implement salesmen whose jobs had been tied to the health of the agricultural sector. Most of the dust bowl migrants were white, and most were young adults in their twenties and thirties who relocated with spouses and children.

Most of the dust bowl migrants who had come from cities gravitated to California's urban areas—Los Angeles, San Diego, or San Francisco. Half of the newcomers, however, moved into the San Joaquin Valley, the agricultural heartland of the state. There they discovered that California was no paradise. Only a few of the migrants could afford to buy land. Most (men and women) found themselves competing with local Hispanics and Asians for seasonal work as pickers in the cotton fields or orchards of large corporate farms.

The "Okies" felt the sting of social prejudice. John Steinbeck explained that "Okie us'ta mean you was from Oklahoma. Now it means you're a dirty son-of-a-bitch." Such hostility drove a third of the "Okies" to return to their home states. Most of the farm workers who stayed tended to fall back upon their old folkways rather than assimilate themselves into their new surroundings.

Minorities and the New Deal

The depression was especially traumatic for the most disadvantaged groups in American society. However progressive Roosevelt was on social issues, he failed to assault longstanding patterns of racism and segregation for fear of alienating southern Democrats. As a result, many of the New Deal programs were for whites only. The Federal Housing Administration (FHA), for example, refused to guarantee mortgages on houses purchased by blacks in white neighborhoods. The Civilian Conservation Corps and the Tennessee Valley Authority both practiced racial segregation.

The efforts of the Roosevelt administration to raise crop prices by reducing production proved especially devastating for blacks and Chicanos. To earn the federal payments for reducing crops as provided by the AAA and other New Deal agricultural programs, many farm owners would first take out of cultivation the marginal lands worked by tenants and sharecroppers. This would drive the landless off farms and cost the jobs of many migrant workers. Over 200,000 black tenant farmers were displaced by the AAA.

Mexican Americans suffered even more. Thousands of Mexicans had migrated to the United States during the 1920s, most of them settling in California, New Mexico, Arizona, Colorado, Texas, and the midwestern states. But because many Mexican Americans were unable to prove their citizenship, either out of ignorance of the regulations or because their migratory work hampered their ability to meet residency requirements, they were denied access to the new federal relief programs under the New Deal. As economic conditions worsened, government officials called for the deportation of Mexican-born Americans to avoid the costs of providing them with public services and relief. By 1935, over 500,000 Mexican Americans and their American-born children had been returned to Mexico. The state of Texas alone deported over 250,000 people.

Native Americans were especially devastated by the Great Depression. They initially were encouraged by Roosevelt's appointment of John Collier as the commissioner of the Bureau of Indian Affairs (BIA). Collier steadily increased the number of Native Americans employed by the BIA and lobbied strenuously with the heads of New Deal agencies to ensure that Indians gained access to the various relief programs. Collier's primary objective, however, was passage of the Indian Reorganization Act. He hoped to reinvigorate traditional Indian cultural traditions by restoring land to tribes, granting Indians the right to charter business enterprises and establish self-governing constitutions, and providing federal funds for vocational training and economic development. The act that Congress finally passed, however, was a much diluted version of Collier's original proposal, and the "Indian New Deal" brought only a partial improvement in the lives of Native Americans.

Culture in the Thirties

The onset of the Great Depression brought a renewed sense of social activism among writers, artists, and intellectuals. In the early 1930s this activism sometimes took the form of allegiance to communist revolution. But few remained Communists for long. Being a notoriously independent lot, most writers and artists rebelled at demands to hew to a shifting party line. And many abandoned communism upon learning that Soviet leader Joseph Stalin practiced a tyranny more horrible than anything under the czars.

Literature and the Depression

Among the writers who addressed themes of immediate social significance during the 1930s, two novelists deserve special notice: John Steinbeck and Richard Wright. The single piece of fiction that best captured the ordeal of the depression, Steinbeck's *The Grapes of Wrath* (1939), avoided political formula to treat workers as people. Steinbeck had taken the trouble to travel with displaced "Okies" driven from the Oklahoma dust bowl in pursuit of jobs in California. The story focused on the Joad family as they made their painful journey west. Met chiefly with contempt and rejection, Ma Joad strove to keep hope alive. At the end, even as the family was breaking up under the pressure, she grasped at a broader loyalty: "Use 'ta be the fambly was fust. It ain't so now. It's anybody. Worse off we get, the more we got to do."

Among the most talented new young novelists emerging in the thirties was Richard Wright, a black writer from Mississippi. He ended his formal schooling with the ninth grade (as valedictorian of his class), worked in Memphis, and greedily devoured books he borrowed on a white friend's library card, all the while saving up to go North to escape the racism of the segregated South. In Chicago, where he arrived on the eve of the depression, the Federal Writers' Project gave him a chance to perfect his talent, and the Communist party excited his idealism.

Native Son (1940), Wright's masterpiece, was set in Chicago. It tells the story of Bigger Thomas, a product of the black ghetto, a man hemmed in and finally impelled to murder by the pervasive racism of American life. "They wouldn't let me live and I killed," he says unrepentently at the end.

Popular Culture during the Depression

While many of America's most talented writers and artists dealt directly with the human suffering and social tensions provoked by the Great Depression, radio programs and movies provided patrons with a welcome "escape" from the decade's grim realities.

By the 1930s, radio had become a major source of family entertainment. More than 10 million families owned a radio, and by the end of the decade the number had tripled. Millions listened to radio "soap operas" during the day. The shows lasted fifteen minutes and derived their name from their sponsors, soap manufacturers. The soap operas provided struggling people with distractions as well as a sense of comparative well-being. As one female listener explained,"I can get through the day better when I hear they have sorrows, too. "

In the evening after supper, families would gather around the radio to listen to newscasts, comedies, adventure dramas such as *The Lone Ranger*, and "big band" musical programs, all interspersed with commercials. On Sundays, most radio stations broadcast church services. Fans could also listen to baseball and football games or boxing matches. Franklin Roosevelt was the first president to take full advantage of the popularity of radio broadcasting. He hosted sixteen "fireside chats" to generate public support for his New Deal initiatives.

In the late 1920s, sound was introduced into what had been "silent" films. The "talkies" made the movie industry by far the most popular form of entertainment during the 1930s—much more popular than today. The introduction of double features in 1931 and the construction of drive-ins in 1933 also boosted interest and attendance. More than 60 percent of the population—70 million people—saw at least one movie each week.

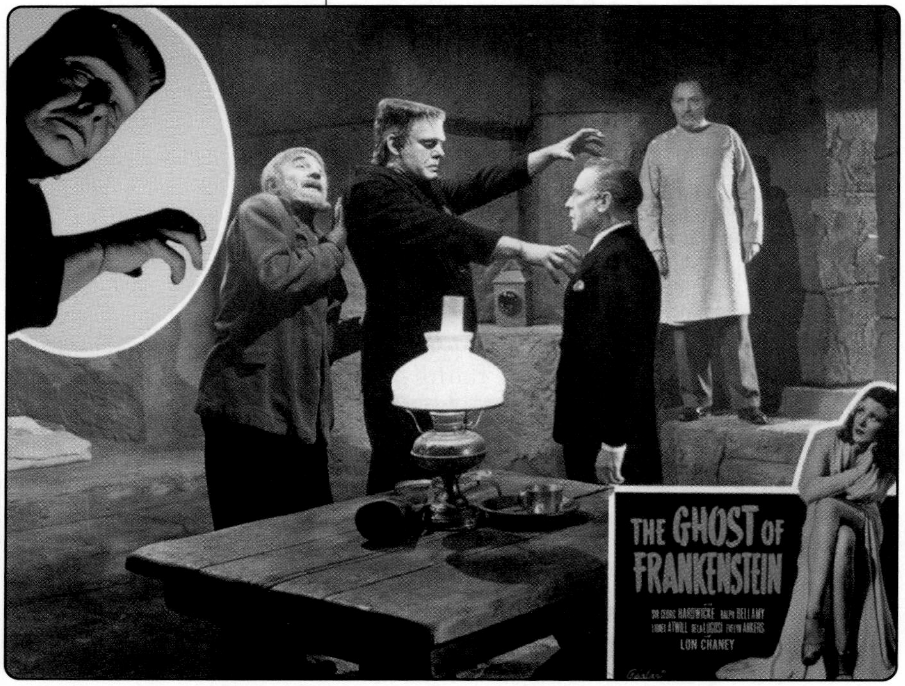

Frankenstein. Popular 1930s movies included gangster, horror, and comedy films, which provided viewers with pure entertainment and distracted them from the burdens of the depression.

Films of the 1930s rarely dealt directly with hard times. Most movies were intended for pure entertainment; they featured adventure, spectacle, and fantasy. People relished "shoot 'em up" gangster films, Walt Disney's animated cartoons, spectacular musicals, Marx Brothers comedies, and classic horror films such as *Frankenstein* (1931) and *The Mummy* (1932).

The Second New Deal

During Roosevelt's first year in office his programs and his personal charms aroused massive support. In the congressional elections of 1934, the Democrats actually increased their strength in both the House and the Senate, an almost unprecedented midterm victory for the party in power. When it was over, only seven Republican governors remained in office throughout the country.

Eleanor Roosevelt

One of the reasons for Roosevelt's unprecedented popularity was his wife, Eleanor, who had increasingly become an enormous political asset and would prove to be one of the most influential and revered leaders of her time. From an early age, Eleanor had channeled her energies into social service, helping the poor and suffering and promoting rights for women and blacks.

After FDR's election, Eleanor redefined the role of presidential spouse. She was the first woman to address a national political convention, to write a nationally syndicated column, and to hold regular press conferences. One of her key functions was to keep the president from being isolated from the public. She served, he said, as his "eyes and ears," as well as his conscience.

A tireless advocate and agitator, Eleanor crisscrossed the nation, defying local segregation ordinances to meet with black leaders, supporting women's causes, highlighting the plight of unemployed youth, and imploring Americans to live up to their humanitarian ideals. She was especially forceful in prodding officials to ease racial discrimination in federal programs and housing. Eleanor Roosevelt deflected criticism from the president by taking progressive stands and running political risks he himself dared not. He was the politician, she once remarked, she was the agitator.

First Lady Eleanor Roosevelt became a political figure in her own right. Here she visits with soldiers at a U.S. Army camp in Australia.

Criticism of the New Deal

Public criticism of the New Deal during 1933 was muted or reduced to helpless carping. But as the sense of crisis passed, the spirit of unity relaxed. The depression's downward slide had been halted, but unemployment remained high (10 million in 1935, more than 20 percent of the workforce) and prosperity remained elusive. Even more unsettling to some was the dramatic growth of executive power and the emergence of welfare capitalism, whereby workers developed a sense of entitlement to federal support programs. In 1934 a group of conservative businessmen and politicians, including Al Smith and John W. Davis, two previous Democratic presidential candidates, formed the American Liberty League to oppose New Deal measures as violations of personal and property rights.

More potent threats to Roosevelt came from the hucksters of social panaceas, old and new. The most flamboyant of the group was Louisiana's "Kingfish," Senator Huey P. Long, Jr. A short, strutting man, Long seemed like a clown to some observers, and he loved to make people think he was a country bumpkin. But underneath all the carefully designed hoopla was a shrewd lawyer and consummate politician. In 1933 Long joined Roosevelt in Washington as a Democratic senator. He initially supported the New Deal but quickly grew suspicious of the NRA's collusion with big business. Promoting himself as a radical egalitarian, a true friend of the people, Long unveiled his own plan for dealing with the Great Depression.

Long's "Share Our Wealth" program was tantalizingly generous and simple. In one version he proposed to confiscate large personal fortunes, guarantee every family a cash grant of $5,000, every worker an annual income of $2,500, provide pensions to the aged, reduce working hours, pay veterans' bonuses, and assure a college education for every qualified student. It did not matter to him that his figures failed to add up or that his program offered little to promote an economic recovery. As he told a group of distressed Iowa farmers, "Maybe somebody says I don't understand it. Well, you don't have to. Just shut your damn eyes and believe it. That's all." Whether he had a workable plan or not, by early 1935 the charismatic Long was claiming 7.5 million supporters.

Another popular social scheme was hatched by a California doctor, Francis E. Townsend. He proposed government pensions for the aged. In 1934 he began promoting the "Townsend Plan." It called for the federal government to pay a pension of $200 a month to every retired citizen over sixty who promised to spend the money within the month and thereby help stimulate the economy. Critics noted that the cost of his program for 9 percent of the population would be more than half the national income. Yet Townsend was indifferent to such factors. "I'm not in the least interested in the cost of the plan," he blandly told a House committee.

A third huckster of panaceas, Father Charles E. Coughlin, the Roman Catholic "radio priest," founded the National Union for Social Justice in 1934. In broadcasts over the CBS network, he promoted schemes for the coinage of silver and made attacks on bankers that carried growing overtones of anti-Semitism.

Coughlin, Townsend, and Long drew support largely from desperate lower-middle-class Americans. Of the three, Long had the widest following. A 1935 survey showed that he could draw 5 to 6 million votes as a third-party candidate for president in 1936, perhaps enough to undermine Roosevelt's chances of reelection. Beset by pressures from both ends of the political spectrum, Roosevelt hesitated for months before deciding to "steal the thunder" from the political left wing by instituting new programs of reform and social security. "I'm fighting Communism, Huey Longism, Coughlinism, Townsendism," Roosevelt told a reporter in early 1935. He resolved "to save our system, the capitalist system," from such "crackpot ideas."

Opposition from the Court

A series of Supreme Court decisions also helped galvanize the president into action. On May 27, 1935, the Court killed the National Industrial Recovery Act by unanimous vote. In *Schechter Poultry Corporation* v. *United States*, quickly tagged the "sick chicken" case, the defendants had been convicted of selling an "unfit chicken" and violating other NRA code provisions. The high court ruled that Congress had delegated too much power to the executive branch when it granted the code-making authority to the NRA, and Congress had exceeded its power under the commerce clause by regulating *intrastate* commerce. The poultry in question, the Court decided, had "come to permanent rest within the state," although it earlier had been moved across state lines. In a press conference soon afterward, Roosevelt fumed: "We have been relegated to the horse-and-buggy definition of interstate commerce." The same line of reasoning, he warned, might endanger other New Deal programs.

Legislative Achievements of the Second New Deal

To rescue his legislative program from such judicial and political challenges, Roosevelt in 1935 launched the so-called Second New Deal. During the next two months, Congress passed another set of significant—and quite controversial—legislation.

The National Labor Relations Act, often called the Wagner Act for its sponsor, New York senator Robert Wagner, gave workers the right to bargain through unions of their own choice and prohibited employers from interfering with union activities. A National Labor Relations Board of five members could supervise plant elections and certify unions as bargaining agents when a majority of the workers approved. The board could also investigate the actions of employers and issue "cease and desist" orders against specified unfair practices.

The Social Security Act of 1935, Roosevelt announced, was the New Deal's "cornerstone" and "supreme achievement." Indeed, it has proven to be the most significant and far-reaching of all the New Deal initiatives. Its centerpiece was a pension fund for retired people over the age of sixty-five and their survivors. Beginning in 1937, workers and employers contributed payroll taxes to establish the pension fund. Benefit payments started in 1940 and averaged $22 per month, a quite modest sum even for those depressed times. Roosevelt knew this, and he stressed that the pension program was not intended to guarantee a comfortable retirement; it was designed to supplement other sources of income and protect the elderly from some of the "hazards and vicissitudes of life."

The Social Security Act also set up a shared federal-state unemployment insurance program, financed by a payroll tax on employers. In addition, the new legislation committed the national government to a broad range of social welfare activities based on the assumption that "unemployables"—people who were unable to work—would remain a state responsibility, while the national government would provide work relief for the able-bodied. To that end, the law inaugurated federal grants-in-aid for three state-administered public assistance programs—old age assistance, aid for dependent children, aid for the blind—and further aid for maternal, child welfare, and public health services.

Relatively speaking, the new federal program was quite conservative. It was the only government pension program in the world financed by taxes on the earnings of current workers. Most other countries funded such programs out of general revenues. The Social Security payroll tax was also a regressive tax in that it entailed a single fixed rate for all, regardless of income level. It thus hurt the poor more than the rich, and it also hurt Roosevelt's efforts to revive the economy because it removed from circulation a significant amount of money in order to establish the pension fund. By taking discretionary income away from workers, the government blunted the sharp increase in public consumption needed to restore the health of the economy. In addition, the Social Security system initially excluded 9.5 million workers who needed it the most: farm laborers, domestic servants, and the self-employed, a disproportionate percentage of whom were black.

Roosevelt regretted such limitations, but he knew that they were necessary compromises in order to see the Social Security Act through Congress and to enable it to withstand court challenges. As he replied to an aide who criticized funding the pension program through employee contributions, "We put those payroll contributions there so as to give the contributors a moral, legal, and political right to collect their pensions and their unemployment benefits. With those taxes in there, no damn politician can ever scrap my Social Security program."

The last of the major bills making up the "Second New Deal" was the Revenue Act of 1935, sometimes called the Wealth Tax Act, but popularly known as the "Soak-the-Rich" tax. The Revenue Act raised tax rates on incomes above $50,000. Estate and gift taxes also rose, as did the corporate tax on all but small corporations (those with less than $50,000 annual income). The new "soak the rich" tax failed to increase federal revenue significantly, nor did it result in a significant redistribution of income. Still, the prevailing view was that Roosevelt had moved in a radical direction. Newspaper editor William Randolph Hearst growled that the Wealth Tax was "essentially communism."

The extent of the new departure taken by the Second New Deal is easy to exaggerate. Such measures as Social Security and higher taxes on the wealthy had long been in the works in Congress and had already been adopted by most other industrial nations. Roosevelt himself stressed his own basic conservatism and asserted that he had no love for socialism. "I am fighting communism. . . . I want to save our system, the capitalistic system." Yet he added that to save it from revolutionary turmoil required a more equal "distribution of wealth."

Roosevelt's Second Term

The 1936 Election

The popularity of Roosevelt and the New Deal impelled the Republican convention in 1936 to avoid candidates too closely identified with the "hate-Roosevelt" contingent. The party chose Governor Alfred M. Landon of Kansas, a former Bull Moose Progressive. A fiscal conservative, Landon had nevertheless endorsed many New Deal programs.

The Republicans hoped that the followers of Long, Coughlin, Townsend, and other dissidents would combine to draw enough votes away from Roosevelt to throw the election to them. But that possibility faded when an assassin gunned down the "Kingfish" in 1935. Coughlin, Townsend, and a remnant of the Long movement supported Representative William Lemke of North Dakota on a Union party ticket, but it was a forlorn effort that polled only 882,000 votes.

In 1936 Roosevelt forged a new electoral coalition that would affect national politics for years to come. While holding the support of most traditional Democrats, FDR made strong gains among beneficiaries of the AAA farm program in the West. In the northern cities, he held on to the ethnic groups helped by New Deal welfare measures. Middle-class voters, whose property had been saved by New Deal measures, flocked to Roosevelt's support, along with intellectuals stirred by the ferment of new governmental ideas. The revived labor movement threw its support to Roosevelt. In the most profound new departure of all, black voters for the first time cast the majority of their ballots for a Democratic president. Roosevelt carried every state except Maine and Vermont, with a popular vote of 27.7 million to Landon's 16.7 million. Democrats would also dominate Republicans in the new Congress, by 77 to 19 in the Senate and 328 to 107 in the House.

The Court-Packing Plan

Roosevelt saw the election of 1936 as a mandate for even more extensive governmental action, but one major roadblock stood in the way: the Supreme Court. By the end of the 1936 term, the Court had ruled against New Deal laws in seven of the nine major cases it reviewed. Suits against the Social Security and Wagner Labor Relations Acts were also pending. The Second New Deal seemed in danger of being nullified like the first.

Roosevelt resolved to change the Court's philosophy by enlarging it, a move for which there was ample precedent and power. Congress, not the Constitution, determines the size of the Court, which at different times had numbered six, seven, nine, and ten justices, and in 1937 numbered nine. On February 5 Roosevelt sent his plan to expand the Supreme Court to Congress, without having consulted congressional leaders. He wanted to create up to fifty new federal judges, including six new Supreme Court justices, and to diminish the power of the judges who had served ten or more years or reached the age of seventy.

But the "court-packing" maneuver, as opponents quickly tagged it, backfired on Roosevelt. It was too contrived, much too brazen, and far too political. By implying that some judges were impaired by senility, Roosevelt affronted the elder statesmen of Congress and the Court, especially Justice Louis D. Brandeis, who was both the oldest and the most liberal of the Supreme Court Judges. The plan also ran headlong into a deep-rooted public veneration of the courts and aroused fears that another president might use the precedent for quite different purposes.

As it turned out, unforeseen events blunted Roosevelt's drive to change the Court. A sequence of Court decisions during the spring of 1937 reversed previous judgments in order to uphold the Wagner Act and the Social Security Act. In addition, a conservative justice resigned, and Roosevelt named to the vacancy one of the most consistent New Dealers, Senator Hugo Black of Alabama.

Roosevelt later claimed he had lost the battle but won the war. The Court had reversed itself on important New Deal legislation, and Roosevelt was able to appoint justices in harmony with the New Deal. But the episode created dissension in his party and blighted Roosevelt's prestige. For the first time, Democrats in large numbers deserted the "champ," and the Republican opposition found a powerful issue to exploit. During the first eight months of 1937, the momentum of Roosevelt's great 1936 victory was lost. As Henry Wallace later remarked. "The whole New Deal really went up in smoke as a result of the Supreme Court fight."

A New Direction for Labor

Rebellions meanwhile erupted on other fronts. Under the impetus of the New Deal, the labor movement stirred anew. John L. Lewis rebuilt the United Mine Workers from 150,000 members to 500,000 within a year. Spurred by the mine workers' example, Sidney Hillman of the Amalgamated Clothing Workers and David Dubinsky of the International Ladies Garment Workers joined Lewis in promoting a campaign to organize workers in the mass-production industries. As leaders of some of the few industrial unions (made up of all workers) in the American Federation of Labor (AFL), they found the smaller, more restrictive, craft unions (made up of male workers, with each limited to a single skilled trade) to be obstacles to organizing the basic industries.

In 1934 these leaders persuaded the AFL and its president William Green to charter "industrial unions" in the unorganized industries. In 1935, with passage of the Wagner Act, action began in earnest. The industrial unionists formed a Committee for Industrial Organization (CIO), and craft unionists began to fear submergence by the mass unions. Jurisdictional disputes spread among the unions, and in 1936 the AFL expelled the CIO unions, which then formed a permanent structure called after 1938 the Congress of Industrial Organizations. The rivalry spurred both groups to greater unionizing efforts.

The CIO's major organizing drives in the automobile and steel industries began in 1936, but they were thwarted by management's use of blacklisting, private detectives, labor spies, vigilante groups, and intimidation. Early in 1937 automobile workers spontaneously adopted a new technique, the "sit-down strike," in which workers refused to leave the shop until employers granted collective bargaining rights.

Led by the fiery young autoworker and union organizer Walter Reuther, thousands of employees at General Motors' assembly plants in Flint, Michigan, occupied the factories and stopped all production. Company officials called in police to harass the strikers, sent spies to union meetings, and threatened to fire the workers. The standoff lasted over a month. Then, on February 11, the company relented and signed a contract recognizing the United Auto Workers (UAW). Other automotive companies soon followed suit. And the following month, United States Steel capitulated to the Steel Workers Organizing Committee (later the United Steelworkers of America), granting it official recognition, a 10 percent wage hike, and a forty-hour workweek.

Having captured two giants of heavy industry, the CIO went on in the next few years to organize much of industrial America: rubber, oil, electronics, and a good part of the textile industry, in which unionists had to fight protracted struggles to organize scattered plants. The slow pace of labor organizing in textiles denied the CIO a major victory in the South comparable to its swift conquest of autos and steel in the North, but union membership in the United States grew from under 3 million in 1933 to 8.5 million in 1940.

A Slumping Economy

The years 1935 and 1936 had seen steady economic improvement, achieved largely through government spending. On top of relief and public-works outlays, Congress in 1936 provided cash payments of veterans' bonuses upon demand. By the spring of 1937, economic output had moved above the 1929 level. But Roosevelt, worried about federal budget deficits and rising inflation, ordered sharp cuts in government spending. At the same time, the Treasury began to reduce disposable income by collecting $2 billion in Social Security from employee paychecks. The result was the slump of 1937. By the end of the year, an additional 4 million people had been thrown out of work.

Economic Policy and Late Reforms

In the spring of 1938, Roosevelt asked Congress to adopt a large-scale spending program to increase mass purchasing power. Congress voted almost $3.3 billion, mainly for public works. In a short time, the increase in spending reversed the economy's decline, but the recession and Roosevelt's reluctance to adopt massive, sustained government spending forestalled the achievement of full economic recovery. Only the massive crisis of World War II would return the American economy to full production and full employment.

The 1937 recession helped further erode Roosevelt's prestige. Only a few major new reforms were enacted for the benefit of the "ill-housed, ill-fed, and ill-clad." They included the Wagner-Steagall National Housing Act, the Bankhead-Jones Farm Tenant Act, and the Fair Labor Standards Act.

The Housing Act set up the United States Housing Authority (USHA) in the Department of the Interior, which extended long-term loans to local agencies willing to assume part of the cost for slum clearance and public housing. The agency also subsidized rents for low-income residents.

Congress in 1937 also passed the Farm Tenant Act, administered by a new agency, the Farm Security Administration (FSA). The program made available loans to prevent marginal farmers from sinking into tenancy. It also offered loans to tenants to help them purchase their own farms.

The Fair Labor Standards Act of 1938 applied to employees in enterprises that operated in or affected interstate commerce. It set a minimum wage of 40¢ an hour and a maximum workweek of forty hours, to be put into effect over several years. The act also prohibited child labor under the age of sixteen, and in hazardous occupations under eighteen. Southern congressmen howled in opposition to the bill because it would increase employers' expenses.

The Legacy of the New Deal

Setbacks for the President

Although critics were unable to defeat the Fair Labor Standards Act, their stiff resistance revealed that an effective opposition to the New Deal was emerging within the president's own party, especially in the southern wing. Southern Democrats were at best uneasy bedfellows with organized labor and blacks, and more and more of them drifted toward closer cooperation with conservative Republicans. By the end of 1937, a formidable anti–New Deal bloc had developed.

In 1938 the bipartisan conservative opposition stymied a bill granting Roosevelt authority to reorganize the executive branch, crying that it would lead to dictatorship. The House of Representatives also set up a Committee on Un-American Activities chaired by Martin Dies of Texas. Dies launched a crusade against Communists, and soon he began to brand New Dealers as Red dupes.

The elections of November 1938 handed the administration another setback, as Republicans made sharp gains in both the House and Senate. The Democrats still enjoyed majorities, but the president headed an increasingly divided party. In his State of the Union message in 1939, Roosevelt for the first time proposed no new reforms, but he spoke of the need "to *preserve* our reforms." Roosevelt did manage, however, to put through his plan to reorganize the executive branch. Under the Administrative Reorganization Act of 1939, the president could "reduce, coordinate, consolidate, and reorganize" the agencies of government. With that, Roosevelt's domestic innovations feebly ended.

A Halfway Revolution

By the end of the 1930s, the New Deal had lost momentum, but it had wrought several enduring changes. The power of the national government was vastly enlarged over what it had been in 1932, and hope had been restored to people who had grown despondent. But the New Deal entailed more than just bigger government and revived public confidence. It also constituted a significant change from the progressivism of Theodore Roosevelt and Woodrow Wilson. Those earlier reformers, despite their sharp differences, had assumed that the function of progressive government was to ensure through aggressive regulation that the people had equal opportunity to pursue their notions of happiness.

Franklin Roosevelt and the New Dealers went beyond this regulatory-state concept by insisting that the government should not simply *respond* to social crises but take positive steps to *avoid* them. To this end, the New Deal's various welfare and benefit programs conferred on government the responsibility to ensure a minimum level of well-being for all Americans. The New Deal established minimum qualitative standards for labor conditions and public welfare and helped middle-class Americans hold on to their savings, their homes, and their farms. The protection afforded by bank deposit insurance, unemployment pay, and Social Security pensions has provided a safeguard against future depressions.

In implementing his domestic program, Roosevelt steered a zigzag course between the extremes of laissez-faire capitalism and socialism. The first New Deal had experimented for a time with a managed economy under the NRA, but it had abandoned that experiment for a turn toward enforcing competition and priming the economy with increased government spending. This finally produced full employment during World War II.

Roosevelt was a pragmatist in developing policy: he kept what worked and discarded what did not. The result was, paradoxically, both profoundly revolutionary and profoundly conservative. Roosevelt sharply increased the regulatory functions of the federal government and laid the foundation for what would become an expanding welfare state. But despite what his critics charged, his initiatives fell far short of socialism; they left the basic capitalistic structure in place. In the process of such bold experimentation and dynamic preservation, the New Deal represented a "halfway revolution" that permanently altered the social and political agenda.

CHAPTER 28

From Isolation to Global War

This chapter focuses on

- Isolationism and peace movements between the two World Wars.
- America's response to Nazi aggression in Europe.
- How events in Asia led to Japan's attack on Pearl Harbor and America's entry into the global war.

THE *ESSENTIAL AMERICA* ON-LINE TUTOR

www.wwnorton.com/eamerica/ch28

- **Topic: Pearl Harbor**
  www.wwnorton.com/eamerica/ch28/topic.htm

  On December 7, 1941, the Japanese military launched a surprise attack on the U.S. naval base at Pearl Harbor, killing more than two thousand people and drawing the United States into the Second World War. Relying on FDR's own notes, photographs taken by Japanese and American soldiers, historical analyses, an audio recording, and captured Japanese military documents, examine the attack on Pearl Harbor. Did the Japanese achieve their military objectives? What was the attack's overall significance?

- **Chapter review: On-line quiz and chapter summary**
  www.wwnorton.com/eamerica/ch28/review.htm

- **Chapter resources: Multimedia index**
  www.wwnorton.com/eamerica/ch28/media.htm

In the late 1930s the winds of war swept across Asia and Europe, abruptly shifting the focus of American politics from domestic to foreign affairs. Roosevelt had to turn his attention from social and economic reform to military preparedness and war. And the public again had to wrestle with the painful choice between involving the country in volatile world affairs or remaining aloof and officially neutral.

Postwar Isolationism

The League and the United States

Between Woodrow Wilson and Franklin Roosevelt lay two decades of relative isolation from foreign entanglements. The postwar mood of 1920 set the pattern. The voters expressed their resistance to international commitments, and President-elect Harding lost little time in disposing of American membership in the League of Nations. The spirit of isolation found other expressions as well: the higher tariff walls, the Red Scare, the rage for "100 percent Americanism," and restrictive immigration laws by which the nation all but shut the door to any more newcomers.

Average citizens may have felt the urge to insulate themselves from a wicked world, but American agriculture and business now had worldwide connections. America's overseas possessions, moreover, directly involved the country in world affairs, especially in the Pacific. Even the League of Nations was too great an organization to ignore entirely. After 1924 the United States gradually entered into joint efforts with the League on such matters as policing the international trade in drugs and arms, and on a variety of economic, cultural, and technical conferences.

Attempts at Disarmament

Yet for all the isolationist sentiment of the time, a lingering doubt, tinged with guilt, haunted many Americans about their rejection of the League of Nations. Before long the Harding administration hit upon a happy substitute—disarmament. The conviction had grown after World War I that the armaments race had caused the war, and that arms limitation would therefore bring lasting peace. The United States had no intention of maintaining a large army, but under the naval building program begun in 1916, it had constructed a fleet second only to that of Britain.

Neither the British nor the Americans relished a naval armaments race, but both shared a common concern about the alarming growth of Japanese military power. During World War I, Japan had taken China's Shantung Peninsula and the islands of Micronesia from its enemy, Germany. In 1917, after the United States entered the war, Viscount Kikujiro Ishii visited Washington to secure American recognition of Japan's expanded position in Asia. To forestall the loss of an ally, Secretary of State Robert Lansing signed an ambiguous agreement saying that "Japan has special interests in China." Americans were unhappy with the Lansing-Ishii Agreement, but it was viewed as the only way to keep Japan in the war.

After the war ended, Japanese-American relations grew more tense. To address the problem, President Harding invited countries to an armaments conference at which Pacific and East Asian affairs would also be discussed. The Washington Armaments Conference of 1921 opened with a surprise announcement by the American secretary of state, Charles Evans Hughes, who told the delegates that "the way to disarm is to disarm." It was one of the most dramatic moments in American diplomatic history. In less than fifteen minutes, one reporter said, Hughes had destroyed more tonnage "than all the admirals of the world have sunk in a cycle of centuries."

Delegates from the United States, Britain, Japan, France, and Italy signed a Five-Power Naval Treaty (1922) incorporating Hughes's plan for tonnage limits and a moratorium of ten years during which no battleships would be built. These powers also agreed to refrain from further fortification of their Pacific possessions. The agreement in effect partitioned the world: United States naval power became supreme in the Western Hemisphere, Japanese power in the western Pacific, British power from the North Sea to Singapore.

Two other major agreements emerged from the Washington Conference. With the Four-Power Treaty, the United States, Britain, Japan, and France agreed to respect each other's possessions in the Pacific and to refer any disputes or any outside threat to consultation. The Nine-Power Treaty for the first time formally pledged the signers to support the principle of the Open Door enunciated by Secretary of State John Hay at the turn of the century. The Open Door enabled all nations to compete for trade and investment opportunities in China on an equal footing rather than allow individual nations to create economic monopolies in particular regions of that country. The signers of the Nine-Power Treaty also promised to respect the territorial integrity of China. The powers, in addition to those signing the Five-Power Treaty, were China, Belgium, Portugal, and the Netherlands.

With these agreements in hand, President Harding's supporters could boast of a brilliant diplomatic stroke. Yet the agreements were uniformly without obligation and without teeth. The naval disarmament treaty set limits only on battleships; the race to build other warships continued.

The Kellogg-Briand Pact

During and after World War I, the ideal of simply abolishing war altogether seized the American imagination. Peace societies thrived, and the glorious vision of ending war by the stroke of a pen culminated in the Kellogg-Briand Pact of 1928. This unique treaty originated when French foreign minister Aristide Briand proposed to President Coolidge's secretary of state, Frank B. Kellogg, that the two countries promise never to go to war with each other. Kellogg countered with a scheme to have all nations sign the pact.

The Pact of Paris (its official name) solemnly declared that the signatories "condemn recourse to war . . . and renounce it as an instrument of national policy." Eventually sixty-two powers joined the pact, but all explicitly or tacitly reserved "self-defense" as an escape hatch. The United States Senate included a reservation declaring the Monroe Doctrine necessary to America's self-defense, and then ratified the agreement by a vote of 85 to 1. A Virginia senator who voted for "this worthless, but perfectly harmless peace treaty" wrote a friend that he feared it would "confuse the minds of many good people who think that peace may be secured by polite professions of neighborly and brotherly love."

The "Good Neighbor" Policy

In Latin America the spirit of peace and noninvolvement helped allay resentments against the United States, which had freely intervened in the Caribbean during the first two decades of the century. In 1924 American marines left the Dominican Republic after an eight-year occupation. American troops left Nicaragua a year later, but returned in 1926 with the outbreak of disorder and civil war.

In 1928 President-elect Hoover improved America's image in Latin America by permitting publication of a memorandum that denied that the Monroe Doctrine justified American intervention in Latin America. It stopped short of repudiating intervention on any grounds, but that fine point hardly blunted the celebration in Latin America. Although Hoover never endorsed this so-called Clark Memorandum, he never ordered American military intervention in the region. Before he left office, steps had already been taken to withdraw American forces from Nicaragua and Haiti.

Franklin D. Roosevelt likewise embraced "the policy of the good neighbor" and promised not to intervene in the region. Under Roosevelt the marines completed their withdrawals from Nicaragua and Haiti, and in 1934 the president negotiated with Cuba a treaty that abrogated the Platt Amendment (1901), which had given America a formal right to intervene in Cuba.

War Clouds

Japanese Incursions in China

The lessening of irritants in the Western Hemisphere during the 1930s proved an exception in an otherwise dismal world scene, as war clouds darkened over Europe and Asia. Actual conflict erupted first in Asia, where unsettled social and political conditions in China had attracted foreign encroachments since before the turn of the century. In 1929 Chinese nationalist aspirations and China's subsequent clashes with Russia convinced the Japanese that their own extensive rights in Manchuria, including the South Manchurian Railway, were in danger.

Japanese military occupation of Manchuria began with the Mukden Incident of 1931, when an explosion destroyed a section of railway track near that city. The Japanese "Kwantung Army," based in Manchuria to guard the railway, blamed the incident on the Chinese and used it as a pretext to begin its occupation, which it extended during the winter of 1931–1932 to all of Manchuria. In 1932 the Japanese converted Manchuria into the puppet empire of "Manchukuo."

Mussolini and Hitler in Munich, Germany, June 1940.

The Manchuria Incident, as the Japanese called their undeclared war, flagrantly violated the Nine-Power Treaty, the Kellogg-Briand Pact, and Japan's pledges as a member of the League of Nations. But when China asked the League and the United States for help, neither obliged. President Herbert Hoover refused to invoke either military or economic sanctions.

In early 1932, Japan's indiscriminate bombing of civilians in Shanghai, China's great port city, aroused Western indignation but provoked no action. When the League of Nations condemned Japanese aggression in 1933, Japan withdrew from the League. Thereafter, hostilities in Manchuria gradually subsided and ended with a truce. An uneasy peace settled upon East Asia for four years, during which time Japan's military leaders further extended their political sway at home.

Italy and Germany

The rise of the Japanese militarists paralleled the rise of dictators in Italy and Germany. In 1922 Benito Mussolini had seized power in Italy after organizing the fascist movement, which was based on a composite of superheated nationalism and socialism. The party's program, and above all Mussolini's promise to restore order and pride in a country fragmented by dissension and self-doubts, enjoyed a wide appeal. Once in power, Mussolini largely abandoned the socialist part of his platform and gradually suppressed all opposition. By 1925 he wielded dictatorial power as Il Duce (the leader).

There was always something ludicrous about the strutting Mussolini. Italy, after all, was a minor European power. But Germany was another matter, and most Americans were alarmed by Il Duce's German counterpart, Adolf Hitler. Hitler's National Socialist (Nazi) party duplicated the major features of Italian fascism, including the ancient Roman salute. Hitler capitalized both on the weakness of Germany's postwar government, especially in the face of world depression, and on festering German resentment toward the Versailles Treaty. Most Germans never accepted their nation's "guilt" for starting World War I. They also believed the postwar sanctions against them were punitive.

Named chancellor on January 30, 1933, Hitler swiftly intimidated the opposition, won dictatorial powers, and in 1934 assumed the title of Reichsführer (national leader). The Nazi police state cranked up the engines of tyranny, persecuting Jews, whom Hitler blamed for all Germany's troubles, and rearming in defiance of the Versailles Treaty. Hitler flouted international agreements, pulled Germany out of the League of Nations in 1933, and proclaimed his intention to extend control over all German-speaking peoples. Despite one provocation after another, the European democracies lacked the will to resist Hitler.

Russian Recognition

Isolationist sentiment in the United States grew even more potent during the early 1930s, but one significant exception to American insularity was Roosevelt's decision to favor official recognition of Soviet Russia. By 1933 the reasons for American refusal to recognize the Bolshevik regime had grown stale. Seen as an expansive market for American goods, Russia stirred fantasies of an American trade boom, much as China had at the turn of the century. Japanese expansionism in Asia, moreover, gave the Soviet Union and the United States a common foreign policy concern. Roosevelt invited the Soviet commissar for foreign affairs to visit Washington. After nine days of talks, a formal exchange of notes on November 16, 1933, signaled the renewal of diplomatic relations. The commissar promised that his country would abstain from propaganda in the United States, extend religious freedom to Americans in the Soviet Union, and reopen the question of prerevolutionary Russian debts to the United States.

Polish Jews evicted from the Warsaw Ghetto. In the years leading up to World War II, Jews were increasingly harassed and persecuted while their political and legal options rapidly diminished.

The March of Aggression

During the early 1930s, a catastrophic chain of events in Asia and Europe sent the world hurtling toward disaster. In 1934 Japan renounced the Five-Power Naval Treaty. The next year Mussolini commenced Italy's conquest of Ethiopia. That same year a referendum in Germany's Saar Basin, held in accordance with the Versailles Treaty, delivered that coal-rich region into the hands of Hitler. In 1936 Hitler reoccupied the Rhineland with armed forces, in violation of the Versailles Treaty but without any forceful response from the French.

The year 1936 also brought the Spanish Civil War, which began with an uprising of the Spanish armed forces in Morocco, led by General Francisco Franco, against the democratically elected Spanish Republic. Over the next three years, Franco established a fascist dictatorship with help from Hitler and Mussolini while the Western democracies left the Spanish Republic to its fate.

On July 7, 1937, Japanese and Chinese troops clashed at the Marco Polo Bridge near Peking (Beijing), and the incident quickly developed into a full-scale war. It was the beginning of World War II in Asia, two years before fighting erupted in Europe. That same year Japan joined Germany and Italy in establishing an alliance known as the Rome-Berlin-Tokyo "Axis."

By 1938 the peace of Europe trembled in the balance. Having rebuilt German military force, Hitler forced the *Anschluss* (union) of Austria with Germany in March 1938. Six months later Germany took the mountainous Sudetenland, largely German in population, which had been given to Czechoslovakia at the Versailles Peace Conference in 1919 because of its strategic importance to that new nation's defense. Germany's latest aggression came shortly after a conference at Munich at which British and French leaders sought to appease Hitler by agreeing to abandon Czechoslovakia, a country that had probably the second strongest army in central Europe.

After promising that the Sudetenland would be his last territorial demand, Hitler in 1939 brazenly broke his pledge. He occupied the remainder of Czechoslovakia and seized former German territory from Lithuania. In quick succession the Spanish Republic finally collapsed on March 28, and Mussolini seized the kingdom of Albania on April 7. Finally, on September 1, 1939, Hitler launched his conquest of Poland. A few days before, he had signed a nonaggression pact with Soviet Russia. Having deserted Czechoslovakia, Britain and France now honored their commitment to go to war if Poland were invaded.

Degrees of Neutrality

During these years of deepening crisis, the Western democracies seemed paralyzed, hoping in vain that each concession would appease the appetites of fascist dictators. Americans retreated more deeply into isolationism.

A lengthy Senate inquiry into the origins of American involvement in World War I reinforced the desire to stay out of Europe's conflicts. Under Senator Gerald P. Nye of North Dakota, a progressive Republican, the committee sat from 1934 to 1937 and concluded that bankers and munitions makers had made scandalous profits from the war. Although Nye never proved that greed for profit had actually impelled President Woodrow Wilson into war, he did insist that the administration had been duped by the "merchants of death." If the United States wanted to remain neutral in the current world crisis, therefore, it would have to keep Americans out of war zones, keep belligerents' vessels out of American ports, embargo arms shipments, and set quotas on the export of contraband. Such ideas became official policy as war enveloped Asia and Europe.

Like generals who are said to be always preparing for the last war, Congress occupied itself with keeping out of World War I. Neutrality laws of the 1930s moved the United States toward complete isolation from the quarrels of Europe. But while Americans wanted to keep out of war, their sympathies were more strongly than ever with the Western democracies, and the triumph of fascist aggression aroused growing fears for national security.

The Neutrality Act of 1935 forbade the sale of arms and munitions to all belligerents whenever the president proclaimed that a state of war existed. Roosevelt would have preferred discretionary authority to levy an embargo only against aggressors, but he reluctantly accepted the act because it was to be effective for only six months, and for the time being it met "the need of the existing situation." That is, it would likely be enforced against Italy, which was then threatening war with Ethiopia.

On October 3, 1935, Italy invaded Ethiopia and Roosevelt invoked the Neutrality Act. When Congress reconvened in 1936, it extended the arms embargo and added a provision forbidding loans to belligerents. Then in July 1936 the Spanish Civil War broke out. Roosevelt now became more isolationist than some of the isolationists. Although the Spanish Civil War involved a fascist uprising against a recognized, democratic government, Roosevelt accepted the French and British position that only nonintervention would localize the fight and keep it from spreading to the rest of Europe.

Roosevelt asked for a "moral embargo" on the arms trade, and he encouraged Congress to extend the neutrality laws to cover civil wars. Congress did so in 1937 with only one dissenting vote. The Western democracies then stood witness while German and Italian soldiers, planes, and armaments supported Franco's overthrow of Spanish democracy.

In the spring of 1937 isolationist sentiment in the United States peaked. A Gallup poll found that 94 percent of its respondents preferred efforts to keep out of war over efforts to prevent war. That same spring Congress passed yet another neutrality law, which continued restraints on arms sales and loans, forbade Americans to travel on belligerents' ships, and prohibited the arming of American merchant ships trading with belligerents. The new law also empowered the president to require that goods other than arms or munitions exported to belligerents be placed on a cash-and-carry basis (that is, the nation purchasing the goods would have to pay in cash and then deliver the cargo in its own ships). This was an ingenious scheme to preserve a profitable trade without running the risk of war.

The new law had its first test in July 1937, when Japanese and Chinese forces clashed at the Marco Polo Bridge. Since neither side declared war, Roosevelt was able to avoid invoking the neutrality law, which would have favored the Japanese, since China had greater need of American arms but few means to get supplies past the Japanese navy. A flourishing trade in munitions to China flowed around the world as ships carried American military equipment across the Atlantic to England, where it was reloaded onto British ships bound for Hong Kong. Roosevelt, by inaction, had challenged strict isolationism.

Roosevelt soon ventured a step further. In Chicago on October 5, 1937, he denounced the "reign of terror and international lawlessness" in which 10 percent of the world's population threatened the peace of the other 90 percent. He called for a "quarantine" against those nations "creating a state of international anarchy and instability from which there is no escape through mere isolation or neutrality." On the whole, public reaction to the speech was mixed, but the president nevertheless quickly backed off from its implications and refused to spell out any specific program for dealing with aggression.

The continuing Japanese war against China brought public outrage and protests from Secretary of State Cordell Hull. In 1938, after nearly a year of war in China, the State Department notified domestic aircraft manufacturers and exporters that it opposed sales to those guilty of attacks on civilian populations. To have imposed an outright embargo would have violated a commercial treaty of 1911 with Japan, but after another year, on July 26, 1939, the United States gave six months' notice of the termination of the treaty—thus clearing the way for an embargo on all war materials to Japan.

Meanwhile, after the German occupation of Czechoslovakia, Roosevelt no longer pretended impartiality in the impending European struggle. He urged Congress to repeal the embargo and permit the United States to sell arms on a cash-and-carry basis to Britain and France, but to no avail. When the Germans attacked Poland on September 1, 1939, Roosevelt proclaimed official neutrality, but in a radio talk he stressed that he did not, like Woodrow Wilson, ask Americans to remain neutral in thought because "even a neutral has a right to take account of the facts."

Roosevelt summoned Congress into special session and asked it again to amend the Neutrality Act. "I regret the Congress passed the Act," he confessed. "I regret equally that I signed the Act." Under the Neutrality Act of 1939, the Allies could buy supplies with cash and take away in their own ships arms or anything else they wanted. American ships, on the other hand, were excluded from belligerent ports and from specified war zones.

American attitudes toward the European conflict continued to vacillate. Once the great democracies of western Europe faced war, American public opinion, appalled at Hitler's tyranny, came to support measures short of war to help their cause, and for a time it seemed that the Western Hemisphere could remain insulated from the war. After Hitler overran Poland in less than a month, the war settled into an uneasy stalemate that began to be called the "phony war." What lay ahead, it seemed, was a long war of attrition—much like World War I—in which Britain and France would have the resources to outlast Hitler. This illusion lasted from October 1939 through the winter of 1940.

The Storm in Europe

Blitzkrieg

In the spring of 1940 the long winter lull in the fighting suddenly erupted into *Blitzkrieg*—lightning war. At dawn on April 9, without warning, Nazi troops entered Denmark and disembarked along the Norwegian coast. Denmark fell in a day, Norway within a few weeks. On May 10 Hitler unleashed his dive bombers and tank divisions on neutral Belgium and the Netherlands. On May 21 German troops reached the English Channel, cutting off a British force sent to help the Belgians and French. A desperate evacuation from the beaches at Dunkirk enlisted every available boat, from warship to tug. Some 338,000 men, about a third of them French, escaped to England.

The German forces rushed ahead, cutting the French armies to pieces and spreading panic. On June 10 Italy entered the war as Germany's ally. Four days later, the Nazi swastika flew over Paris.

Nazi troops occupied Paris in the spring of 1940.

America's Growing Involvement

Britain now stood alone, but its new prime minister, Winston Churchill, breathed defiance. "We shall go on to the end," he pledged; "we shall never surrender."

Despite such grim resolution, America itself suddenly seemed vulnerable as Hitler unleashed his air force against Britain. In response to Churchill's appeal for American military supplies, the War and Navy Departments began releasing stocks of arms, planes, and munitions to the British.

The summer of 1940 brought the desperate Battle of Britain, in which the Royal Air Force finally forced the Germans to give up plans to invade the British Isles. Submarine warfare meanwhile strained the resources of the battered Royal Navy. To relieve the pressure, Churchill urgently requested the transfer of American destroyers. Secret negotiations led to an executive agreement under which fifty "overaged" destroyers went to the British in return for ninety-nine-year leases on naval and air bases in Newfoundland, Bermuda, and islands in the Caribbean. Two weeks later, on September 16, 1940, Congress adopted the first peacetime conscription in American history. All men aged twenty-one to thirty-five were required to register for a year's military service within the United States.

The new state of affairs prompted vigorous debate between "internationalists," who believed national security demanded aid to Britain, and isolationists, who charged that Roosevelt was drawing the United States into a needless war. In 1940 the nonpartisan Committee to Defend America by Aiding the Allies was organized, drawing its strongest support from the East and West Coasts and the South. Two months later, isolationists formed the America First Committee. Before the end of 1941, the committee had about 450 chapters around the country, but probably two-thirds of its members lived within a 300-mile radius of Chicago. The isolationists argued that a Nazi victory, while distasteful, would pose no threat to American national security.

A Third Term for FDR

In the midst of these profound developments, the quadrennial presidential campaign came due. Isolationist sentiment was strongest in the Republican party, yet their nominee took a different stance. Wendell L. Willkie was a former Democrat who had voted for Roosevelt in 1932 and openly supported aid to the Allies.

The Nazi victory over France ensured another nomination for Roosevelt. For his new running mate, Roosevelt tapped his secretary of agriculture, Henry Wallace, a devoted supporter who would appeal to farm voters.

Willkie attacked New Deal spending, but as his campaign languished, he began criticizing Roosevelt's conduct of foreign policy: "If you re-elect him you may expect war in April, 1941." To this Roosevelt responded, "I have said this before, but I shall say it again and again and again: Your boys are not going to be sent into any foreign wars."

Roosevelt won the election by a comfortable margin of 27 million votes to Willkie's 22 million, and a wider margin of 449 to 82 in the electoral college.

The Arsenal of Democracy

Bolstered by the mandate for an unprecedented third term, Roosevelt moved quickly to provide greater aid to Britain. Since direct government loans would arouse memories of earlier war-debt defaults—the Johnson Act of 1934 forbade such loans anyway—the president created an ingenious device to bypass that issue and yet supply British needs: the "lend-lease" program. The Lend-Lease Bill, introduced in Congress on January 10, authorized the president to sell, transfer, exchange, lend, lease, or otherwise dispose of arms and other equipment and supplies to "any country whose defense the President deems vital to the defense of the United States."

For two months a bitter debate over the lend-lease bill raged in Congress and around the country. Isolationists saw it as the point of no return. Lend-lease became law in early 1941, and Britain and China were the first beneficiaries.

While the nation debated, the war intensified, and by early 1941 Hitler controlled nearly all of Europe. Then, on June 22, 1941, he suddenly ordered an invasion of the Soviet Union, his ally, hoping to eliminate the potential threat on his rear with another lightning stroke. The Nazis moved with seeming invincibility until, after four months, the Russian soldiers and civilians rallied. During the winter of 1941–1942, Hitler began to learn the bitter lesson the Russians had taught Napoleon and his French invaders in 1812.

Winston Churchill had already decided to provide British support to the Soviet Union in case of such an attack. Roosevelt adopted the same policy, offering American aid two days after the German invasion. Stalinist Russia, so long as it held out, ensured Britain's survival. American aid was now indispensable to Europe's defense, and the logic of lend-lease led to deeper American involvement. To deliver aid to Britain, American goods had to be maneuvered through the German U-boat "wolf packs" in the North Atlantic. So on April 11, 1941, Roosevelt informed Churchill that the United States Navy would extend its patrol areas in the North Atlantic nearly all the way to Iceland.

In August 1941 Roosevelt and Churchill held a secret naval rendezvous off Newfoundland and drew up a statement of principles known as the Atlantic Charter. In effect it amounted to a joint declaration of war aims. It called for the self-determination of all peoples, economic cooperation, freedom of the seas, and a new international system of collective security. The Soviet Union later endorsed the statement.

Having entered into a joint statement of war aims with the anti-Axis powers, the United States soon became involved in shooting incidents in the North Atlantic. The first attack on an American warship occurred on September 4, when a German submarine fired two torpedoes at a destroyer. A week later the president ordered American ships to "shoot on sight" any German or Italian raiders ("rattlesnakes of the Atlantic") that ventured into American defensive waters. Five days later the United States Navy announced it would convoy merchant ships all the way to Iceland.

Further attacks hastened Congress into making changes in the Neutrality Act already requested by the president. On November 17 Congress removed the bans on arming merchant vessels and allowed them to enter combat zones and belligerent ports. Step by step the United States was giving up neutrality and embarking on naval warfare against Germany. Still, the American people hoped to avoid taking the final step into all-out war. The decision for war would come in an unexpected quarter—the Pacific.

The Storm in the Pacific

Japanese Aggression

After the Nazi victories in the spring of 1940, America's relations with Japan also took a turn for the worse. On September 27, 1940, the Tokyo government signed a Tripartite Pact with Germany and Italy, by which each pledged to declare war on any nation that attacked any of them. The Germans hoped to persuade Japan to enter Siberia when Nazi forces entered the Soviet Union from the west, but Japan signed a nonaggression pact with the Soviet Union on April 13, 1941.

In July 1941 Japan announced that it was assuming a protectorate over all of French Indochina. Responding to this latest act of aggression, Roosevelt froze all Japanese assets in the United States and restricted exports of oil to Japan. Forced to secure oil supplies elsewhere, the Japanese army and navy began to plan attacks on the Dutch and British colonies in Southeast Asia.

Actions by both sides put the United States and Japan on the path to a war neither wanted. In his regular talks with the Japanese ambassador, Secretary of State Cordell Hull insisted that Japanese withdrawal from Indochina and China was the price of renewed trade with the United States. A more flexible position might have strengthened the moderates in Japan. Premier Fumimaro Konoye, however, caved in to pressures from the militants.

The Japanese military leaders, for their part, seriously misjudged the United States. The desperate wish of Americans to stay out of war might still have enabled the Japanese to conquer the British and Dutch colonies before an American decision to act. But the Japanese decided that they dared not leave the American navy intact and the Philippines untouched on the flank of their new lifeline to the south.

Tragedy at Pearl Harbor

Thus a tragedy began to unfold with a fatal certainty mostly out of sight of the American people, whose attention was focused on the war in the Atlantic. Late in August 1941 Premier Konoye proposed a personal meeting with President Roosevelt. Hull advised Roosevelt not to meet unless agreement on fundamentals could be reached in advance. On September 6, a Japanese imperial conference approved preparations for a surprise attack on Hawaii and gave Premier Konoye six more weeks to reach a settlement.

The Japanese emperor's clear displeasure with the risk of an attack afforded the premier one last chance to pursue a compromise, but the presence of Japanese troops in China remained a stumbling block to any American agreement. In October Konoye urged War Minister Hideki Tojo to consider withdrawal while saving face by keeping some troops in North China. Tojo responded with his "maximum concession" that Japanese troops would stay in China no longer than twenty-five years if the United States stopped aiding the Chinese. Faced with this rebuff and with Tojo's threat to resign and bring down the cabinet, Konoye himself resigned on October 15. Tojo became premier the next day. The war party was now in complete control of the government.

On the very day that Tojo became premier, a special Japanese envoy conferred with Hull and Roosevelt in Washington. His arrival was largely a cover for Japan's war plans, although neither he nor Japan's ambassador to the United States knew that. On November 20 they presented Tojo's final proposal to Hull: Japan would occupy no more territory if the United States would cut off aid to China, restore trade with Japan, and help the Japanese get supplies from the Dutch Indies. In that case Japan would pull out of southern Indochina immediately and abandon the remainder once peace had been established with China—presumably on Japanese terms. Tojo expected the United States to refuse such demands. On November 26 Hull repeated that Japan must withdraw altogether from China. That same day a Japanese naval force began heading across the North Pacific toward Pearl Harbor, Hawaii.

Washington officials already knew that an attack was imminent. Reports of Japanese troop transports moving south from Formosa prompted Washington to send warnings to Pearl Harbor and Manila, and to the British government. The massive Japanese movements southward clearly signaled attacks on the British and the Dutch. American leaders had every reason to expect war in the southwest Pacific, but none expected that Japan would commit most of its aircraft carriers to another attack 5,000 miles away at Pearl Harbor.

On the morning of December 7, 1941, Americans decoded the last part of a secret Japanese message breaking off the negotiations in Washington. The War Department sent out an alert at noon that something was about to happen, but the message, which went by commercial wire because radio contacts were broken, arrived in Hawaii eight and a half hours later.

It was still a sleepy Sunday morning when the first Japanese planes began their assault on Hawaii. At 7:53 A.M. the flight commander sounded the cry "Tora! Tora! Tora!" (Tiger! Tiger! Tiger!), the signal that the attackers had taken the American navy by surprise. For nearly two hours the Japanese planes kept up their fierce attack. Of the eight U.S. battleships in Pearl Harbor, three were sunk and the others were badly battered. Before it was over the raid had killed more than 2,400 American servicemen and civilians.

The attack on Pearl Harbor, December 7, 1941. The attack brought on destruction and confusion, as well as a U.S. declaration of war.

The surprise attack fulfilled the dreams of its planners, but it fell short of total success in two ways. The Japanese ignored oil storage tanks, without which the surviving ships might have been forced back to the West Coast, and they missed the American aircraft carriers that had fortuitously left port a few days earlier. In the naval war to come, these carriers would be decisive.

Later the same day (December 8 in the western Pacific), Japanese forces began assaults on the Philippines, Guam, and Midway. With one stroke, the Japanese had silenced America's debate on neutrality, and a suddenly unified and vengeful nation resolutely prepared for the struggle.

The day after the attack President Roosevelt told Congress that December 7 was "a date which will live in infamy," and he asked for a declaration of war. It was approved unanimously, with the sole exception of Representative Jeanette Rankin, a pacifist who was unable in good conscience to vote for war in 1917 or 1941. On December 11, Germany and Italy declared war on the United States. The separate wars in Asia and Europe had become one global conflict—and American isolationism was cast aside.

CHAPTER

29

The Second World War

This chapter focuses on

- The social and economic effects of World War II, especially in the West.
- How the Allied forces won the war.
- The efforts of the Allies to shape the postwar world.

THE *ESSENTIAL AMERICA* ON-LINE TUTOR

www.wwnorton.com/eamerica/ch29

- **Topic: The internment of Japanese Americans during World War II**
  www.wwnorton.com/eamerica/ch29/topic.htm

  On February 19, 1942, President Franklin Roosevelt issued Executive Order 9066, forcibly removing more than 100,000 Japanese Americans from their homes and relocating them in government-controlled "War Relocation Camps." Use the text of the order, minutes from meetings where government officials planned the relocation and then evaluated it, maps, photographs, propaganda posters, and historical analyses to examine the significance of the relocation. Why did American officials decide to imprison these people when more than 60 percent were American citizens?

- **Chapter review: On-line quiz and chapter summary**
  www.wwnorton.com/eamerica/ch29/review.htm

- **Chapter resources: Multimedia index**
  www.wwnorton.com/eamerica/ch29/media.htm

The Japanese attack on Pearl Harbor launched America into a world war that would transform the nation's social and economic life as well as its position in international affairs. The Second World War would become the most destructive and far-reaching conflict in history. Devilish new instruments of destruction were invented—plastic explosives, flame throwers, rockets, jet airplanes, and atomic weapons—and systematic genocide emerged as an explicit war aim of the Nazis. Racist propaganda flourished on both sides, and intense hatred of the enemy caused many military and civilian prisoners to be executed. Over 50 million deaths were attributed to the war, and the physical destruction was incalculable. Whole cities were leveled, nations dismembered, and societies transformed. The world is still struggling to cope with the consequences of the Second World War.

America's Early Battles

Setbacks in the Pacific

In early December 1941, American military leaders focused on halting the Japanese advance and mobilizing the whole nation for war. In the Philippines, where General Douglas MacArthur, commander of U.S. forces in the Far East, abandoned Manila on December 27, the main American forces, outmanned and outgunned, held out tenaciously on Bataan Peninsula until April 9, and then again on the fortified island of Corregidor. By May 6, when American forces surrendered Corregidor, Japan controlled a new empire that stretched from Burma eastward through the Dutch Indies and extended to Wake Island and the Gilbert Islands.

Coral Sea and Midway

American forces finally halted the Japanese advances in two decisive naval clashes. The Battle of the Coral Sea (May 7–8, 1942) stopped a fleet convoying Japanese troop transports toward New Guinea. There were heavy American losses, but Japanese designs on Australia were thwarted.

Less than a month after the Coral Sea engagement, Admiral Isoruku Yamamoto, the Japanese naval commander, forced a showdown in the central Pacific. With nearly every ship under his command, he headed for Midway Island, from which he hoped to render Pearl Harbor helpless. This time it was the Japanese who were the victims of surprise. American cryptanalysts had by then broken the Japanese naval code, and Admiral Chester Nimitz, commander of the central Pacific, knew their plan of attack.

The first Japanese foray against Midway, on June 4, 1942, severely damaged the American installation on the island. But before another attack could be mounted, American torpedo planes and dive bombers caught three of the four Japanese aircraft carriers in the process of servicing their planes. Dive bombers sank three of them during the first assault. The Japanese defeat at Midway was the turning point of the Pacific war.

Mobilization at Home

The Pearl Harbor attack ended not only the long debate between isolation and intervention but also the long economic depression that had ravaged the country in the 1930s. The war effort required all of America's huge productive capacity and full employment of the workforce. Men between eighteen and forty-five became subject to military service. Altogether more than 15 million American men and women would serve in the armed forces during the war.

Economic Conversion

The economy, too, was mobilized. Congress authorized the president to reshuffle government agencies and to allot materials and facilities as needed for defense. The War Production Board (WPB), created in 1942, directed the conversion of private industries to war production. The Office of Scientific Research and Development mobilized thousands of scientists to develop new military weapons and technology.

The pressure of wartime needs and the stimulus of government spending doubled the gross national product between 1940 and 1945. Government expenditures during the war years soared. Massive federal spending also encouraged greater centralization and consolidation in private industry. The larger companies tended to win the most government contracts, and the more they won the larger they became. Conversely, those without government contracts withered and died. In 1942 alone 300,000 businesses shut down.

Financing the War

To cover the war's huge cost, the president preferred taxes to borrowing. But Congress, dominated by fiscal conservatives, feared taxes more than deficits. As a result, the government covered about 45 percent of its 1939–1946 costs with tax revenues; the rest was borrowed by issuing war bonds. In all, the national debt grew by the end of the war to $260 billion, about six times its size at the time of the attack on Pearl Harbor.

America's basic economic problem during the war years was no longer creating jobs but finding workers for the booming shipyards, aircraft factories, and munitions plants. Millions of people, especially women, were now brought into the workforce. Labor unions benefited directly from the dramatic growth of the civilian workforce. Union membership increased significantly during the war years, from about 11 million to 15 million.

Economic Controls

Increased incomes and spending during the war sparked inflation, as military priorities created shortages of civilian goods. Consumer durables such as cars, washing machines, and housing ceased to be produced at all. Only strict restraints would keep prices of scarce goods from soaring out of sight. In 1941 Roosevelt created the Office of Price Administration (OPA), and the following year Congress authorized it to set price ceilings. With prices frozen, scarce goods such as tires and gasoline had to be allocated through rationing.

At first, war prosperity offered farmers a chance to recover from two decades of distress, and farm-state legislators raised both floors and ceilings on farm prices. However, higher food prices reinforced worker demands for higher wages. To relieve this inflationary pressure, the president won new authority to control wages and farm prices. Both business and workers chafed at the new controls, and on occasion the government was forced to seize industries threatened by strike. The coal mines and railroads were both nationalized for a short time in 1943. Despite these problems, the government's program to stabilize the war economy succeeded. By the end of the war, consumer prices had risen about 31 percent, a far better record than the World War I rise of 62 percent.

To make the economic controls work, the government launched a program to encourage conservation of resources. As one popular slogan had it, "Use it up, wear it out, make it do or do without." The public collected scrap metal and grew their own food in backyard "victory gardens."

Domestic Conservatism

As the war dragged on, public discontent with price controls, labor shortages, and rationing spread. In 1942 the congressional elections registered a national swing against FDR and the New Deal. Republicans gained forty-six seats in the House and nine in the Senate, chiefly in the farm areas of the midwestern states. Democratic losses outside the South strengthened the southern delegation's position within the party, and the delegation itself reflected conservative victories in southern primaries. A coalition of Democratic and Republican conservatives proceeded to cut back "nonessential" New Deal agencies. In 1943 Congress abolished the Works Progress Administration, the National Youth Adminstration, and the Civilian Conservation Corps.

Organized labor, despite substantial gains during the war, felt the impact of the conservative trend. In the spring of 1943, when John L. Lewis led the coal miners out on strike, widespread public resentment prompted Congress to pass the Smith-Connally War Labor Disputes Act, which authorized the government to seize plants useful to the war effort. In 1943 a dozen states adopted laws restricting picketing and other union activities, and in 1944 Arkansas and Florida set in motion a wave of "right-to-work" legislation that outlawed the closed shop (which required that all employees be union members).

Social Effects of the War

Mobilization and the Development of the West

The dramatic expansion of defense production after 1940 accelerated economic development and the population boom in the western states. Nearly 8 million people moved into the states west of the Mississippi River between 1940 and 1950. Most of this expansion occurred in metropolitan centers. Indeed, the Far West experienced the fastest rate of urban growth in the country. Small cities such as Phoenix and Albuquerque mushroomed, while Seattle, San Francisco, Los Angeles, and San Diego witnessed dizzying growth.

Defense-related jobs at high wages enticed people to the western states, as California alone garnered 10 percent of all the defense contracts during the war years. City services could not keep up with the influx of workers and military personnel. Employees at Seattle's shipyards and the huge Boeing airplane plant lived in tents because of a housing shortage. To address the problem, Congress passed the Lanham Act, which authorized the federal government to finance over a million new temporary housing units across the country. Yet this federal housing program did not meet the demand.

The migration of workers to new defense jobs in the West had significant demographic effects. Communities with few African Americans witnessed an influx of blacks. Lured by news of job openings and higher wages, African Americans from Texas, Oklahoma, Arkansas, and Louisiana headed west. During the war years, Seattle's black population jumped from 4,000 to 40,000; Portland's, from 2,000 to 15,000.

Changing Roles for Women

The war marked an important watershed in the changing status of women. With millions of men going into military service, the demand for labor challenged old prejudices about sex roles in the workplace—and in the military. Nearly 200,000 women went into the Women's Army Corps (WAC) and the navy's equivalent, Women Accepted for Volunteer Emergency Service (WAVES). Lesser numbers joined the Marine Corps, the Coast Guard, and the Army Air Force.

Even more significant were the 6 million women who entered the workforce during the war. By 1944 over a third of all women were in the labor force. To draw women into traditional male jobs, the government launched an intense publicity campaign featuring "Rosie the Riveter," a strong, beautiful woman dressed in overalls.

Expanded Participation of Blacks

The most incendiary domestic issue ignited by the war was that of black participation in

As "Uncle Sam" enjoined American men to enlist in military service, "Rosie the Riveter" recruited women to join the labor force.

Tuskeegee airmen, 1942. One of the last segregated military training schools, the flight school at Tuskeegee trained African-American men for combat during World War II.

the defense effort. From the start, black leaders demanded full civil rights in the armed forces and defense industries. Eventually about a million African Americans served in the armed forces. But most served in segregated units. Every army camp had its separate facilities and its periodic racial "incidents." The most important departure from this pattern came in a 1940 decision to give up segregation in officer candidate schools. A separate military flight school at Tuskegee, Alabama, trained about 600 black pilots, many of whom later distinguished themselves in combat.

War industries were even less accessible to black influence and pressure. In 1941 A. Philip Randolph, the head of the Brotherhood of Sleeping Car Porters, organized a March on Washington Movement to protest racial discrimination in defense industries. Alarmed at the prospect of a mass march on Washington, the administration struck a bargain. The Randolph group called off its demonstration in return for an executive order prohibiting discrimination in defense work and training programs.

Blacks quickly broadened their drive for wartime participation into a challenge to all kinds of discrimination, including racial segregation itself. Membership in the NAACP soared during the war from 50,000 to 450,000. Blacks could look forward to greater political participation after the Supreme Court, in *Smith* v. *Allwright* (1944), struck down Texas's whites-only primary on the grounds that Democratic primaries were part of the election process and thus subject to the Fifteenth Amendment.

Growing black activism aroused antagonism from some whites. The level of racial violence did not approach that of World War I, but rising tensions on a hot summer afternoon in Detroit sparked two days of fighting in 1943. Twenty-five blacks and nine whites were killed.

Hispanics in the Labor Force

As rural folk moved to the western cities, the farm counties experienced a labor shortage. In an ironic about-face, local and federal government authorities who before the war strove to force Mexican alien laborers back across the border now recruited them to harvest crops. The Mexican government, however, first insisted that the United States ensure certain minimum work and living conditions before it would assist in providing the needed workers. The result was the creation of the *bracero* program in 1942. Mexico agreed to provide seasonal farm workers in exchange for a promise by the American government not to draft them into military service. The workers were hired on year-long contracts that offered wages at the prevailing rate, and American officials provided transportation from the border to their job sites.

The rising tide of Mexican Americans in Los Angeles provoked a growing stream of anti-Hispanic editorials and incidents. Even though Mexican Americans fought in the war with great valor, earning seventeen Congressional Medals of Honor, there was tension between servicemen and Mexican-American gang members and teenage "zoot-suiters" in southern California. "Zoot suits" were the flamboyant clothes worn by some young Chicano men. In 1943, several thousand off-duty sailors and soldiers, joined by hundreds of local white civilians, rampaged through downtown Los Angeles streets, assaulting Hispanics, blacks, and Filipinos. The violence lasted a week and came to be labeled the "zoot suit" riots.

Native Americans and the War Effort

Indians may have supported the war effort more fully than any other group in American society. Almost a third of eligible Native American men, over 25,000 in all, served in the armed forces. Another one-fourth worked in defense-related industries. Thousands of Indian women volunteered as nurses or joined the Women's Voluntary Service. As was the case with African Americans, Indians benefited from the broadening experiences afforded by the war. Those who left reservations to work in defense plants or to join the military gained new vocational skills as well as a greater awareness of opportunities available in the larger American society.

Why did Native Americans so eagerly fight for a nation that had stripped them of their lands and decimated their heritage? Some felt that they had no choice. Mobilization for the war effort ended many New Deal programs that had provided Indians with jobs. Reservation Indians thus faced the necessity of finding new jobs elsewhere. Many viewed the Nazis and Japanese as threats to their own homeland. The most common sentiment animating Indian involvement in the war effort, however, seems to have been a genuine sense of patriotism.

Whatever the reasons, Indians distinguished themselves in the military during the war. Unlike their African-American counterparts, Indian servicemen were integrated within the regular units. Perhaps the most distinctive activity performed by Indians was their service as "code talkers." Every military branch used Indians—Oneidas, Chippewas, Sauks, Foxes, Comanches, and Navajos—to "encode" and decipher messages in Indian languages so as to prevent enemy discovery.

Internment of Japanese Americans

The record on civil liberties during World War II was on the whole better than that during World War I, if only because there was virtually no opposition to the war effort. Neither German Americans nor Italian Americans faced the harassments meted out to their counterparts in the previous war; few had much sympathy for Hitler or Mussolini. The shameful exception to an otherwise improved record was the treatment given to Americans of Japanese descent.

In the months following the attack on Pearl Harbor, fear and racial prejudice abounded in the West. Idaho's governor declared: "A good solution to the Jap problem would be to send them all back to Japan, then sink the island. They live like rats, breed like rats, and act like rats." Such attitudes were widespread, and the government finally succumbed to demands that it force all Japanese, citizens or not, into "War Relocation Camps" in the interior.

Caught up in the war hysteria and racial prejudice, President Roosevelt triggered the removal of Japanese Americans when he issued Executive Order 9066 on February 19, 1942. More than 60 percent of the internees were U.S. citizens; a third were under the age of nineteen. Forced to sell their farms and businesses at great losses, the internees lost not only their liberty but also their property and livelihoods. More than 100,000 were eventually removed from their homes and businesses in this sorry episode. Not until 1983 did the government finally acknowledge the injustice of the internment policy. Five years later, Congress voted to give $20,000 and an apology to each of the 60,000 former internees who were still living.

More than 100,000 Japanese Americans were forced to sell their property and enter "War Relocation Camps."

The Allied Drive toward Berlin

In mid-1942 the "home front" began to learn from the war fronts that some of the Allied lines were holding at last. By midyear a fleet of American air and sea sub-chasers was ending six months of happy hunting for German U-boats off the Atlantic coast. This was promising because Allied war plans called for the defeat of Germany first.

War Aims and Strategy

There were many reasons for giving top priority to defeating Hitler: Nazi forces in western Europe and the Atlantic posed a more direct threat to North America; German war potential exceeded Japan's; and German science was more likely to come up with some devastating new weapon. Yet Japanese attacks involved Americans directly in the Pacific war from the start, and as a consequence, during the first year of fighting more Americans went to the Pacific than across the Atlantic.

No sooner had the United States entered the war than it began joint military planning with Great Britain, one of the few times in history when allies truly cooperated in achieving military objectives. To be sure, it was a wartime alliance marked as much by disagreement and suspicion as by common purposes. Although Winston Churchill and Franklin Roosevelt admired each other, they disagreed about military strategy and the likely makeup of the postwar world. They often pursued the interests of their own country at the expense of the military alliance; they occasionally deceived each other; in a few cases, they lied to each other. Roosevelt worried about Churchill's excessive drinking, and Churchill worried about Roosevelt's "naive" understanding of Soviet behavior and his innocent faith in Stalin's integrity.

The two Allied leaders did agree on the priority of first winning the war against Germany, but they differed on strategy. American officials wanted to strike German-held France directly across the English Channel before the end of 1942. With vivid memories of the last war, the British feared a mass bloodletting in trench warfare if they struck prematurely. The Soviets, bearing the brunt of the German attack in the east, insisted that the Western Allies must do something to relieve the pressure along the Russian front. Finally, the Americans accepted Churchill's proposal to invade French North Africa.

The North Africa Campaign

On November 8, 1942, Anglo-American forces under the command of General Dwight D. Eisenhower landed in Morocco and Algeria. Completely surprised, French forces under the Vichy government (which collaborated with the Germans) had little will to resist. Farther east, British forces were pushing German armies back across Libya. Before spring, the Germans were caught in a gigantic pincers. Hammered from all sides, unable to retreat across the Mediterranean, an army of 275,000 Germans surrendered on May 13, 1943, leaving all of North Africa in Allied hands.

While this North African campaign was still unfolding, Roosevelt, Churchill, and the Combined Chiefs of Staff met at Casablanca, Morocco. Stalin declined to leave Russia for the meeting but continued to press for the opening of a second front in Europe to relieve the beleaguered Russians. The Anglo-American planners, however, decided to postpone the cross-Channel invasion and to carry out Churchill's scheme to attack Sicily and then Italy.

Before leaving Casablanca, Roosevelt announced, with Churchill's endorsement, that the war would end only with the "unconditional surrender" of all enemies. This demand was designed to reassure Stalin that the Western Allies would not negotiate separately with the Germans. The West desperately needed Soviet cooperation in defeating Germany, and Roosevelt and Churchill were eager to reassure Stalin of their good intentions.

The announcement also reflected Roosevelt's determination to see that "every person in Germany should realize that this time Germany is a defeated nation." This dictum was later criticized for having stiffened enemy resistance, but it probably had little effect; in fact neither the Italian nor Japanese surrender would be totally unconditional. But the decision virtually assured eventual Soviet control of eastern Europe because it required Stalin's armies to pursue Hitler's forces all the way to Germany. And as they liberated the countries of eastern Europe, the Soviets created puppet governments they could easily control.

The Battle of the Atlantic

While fighting raged in North Africa, the more crucial Battle of the Atlantic reached its climax on the high seas. Several factors brought success to the Allied effort. Scientists perfected a variety of new detection devices: radar, sonar, and advanced magnetic equipment that enabled aircraft to detect objects under water. New escort aircraft carriers ("baby flat-tops") and improvements in depth charges added to the effectiveness of convoys.

The German U-boats kept up the Battle of the Atlantic until the war's end, but their commander later admitted that the battle was lost by the end of May 1943. He credited the difference largely to radar. What he did not know then was that the Allies had a secret weapon. By early 1943 their cryptanalysts were routinely decoding secret messages and telling their sub-hunters where to look for U-boats.

Sicily and Italy

After the Allied victory in the North African campaign, on July 10, 1943, about 250,000 British and American troops landed on Sicily, scoring a complete surprise. The German-Italian collapse in Sicily ended Mussolini's twenty years of fascist rule. On July 25, 1943, Italy's king notified the dictator of his dismissal as premier. A new Italian regime startled the Allies when it offered not only to surrender but to switch sides in the war. Unfortunately, mutual suspicions prolonged talks until September 3, while the Germans poured reinforcements into Italy and seized key points. In the confusion the Italian army disintegrated, although most of the navy escaped to Allied ports. A few army units later joined the Allied effort, and many of the Italian soldiers joined bands of partisans who fought behind the German lines. Mussolini, plucked from imprisonment by a daring German airborne raid, became head of a puppet government in northern Italy.

The Allied assault on the Italian mainland therefore did not turn into an easy victory. Heavy German resistance and mountainous terrain caused the fighting to stall through the winter of 1943–1944 in some of the most miserable, muddy, and frigid conditions of the war. After a five-month siege, the Americans finally took Rome on June 4, 1944. Yet they enjoyed only a brief moment

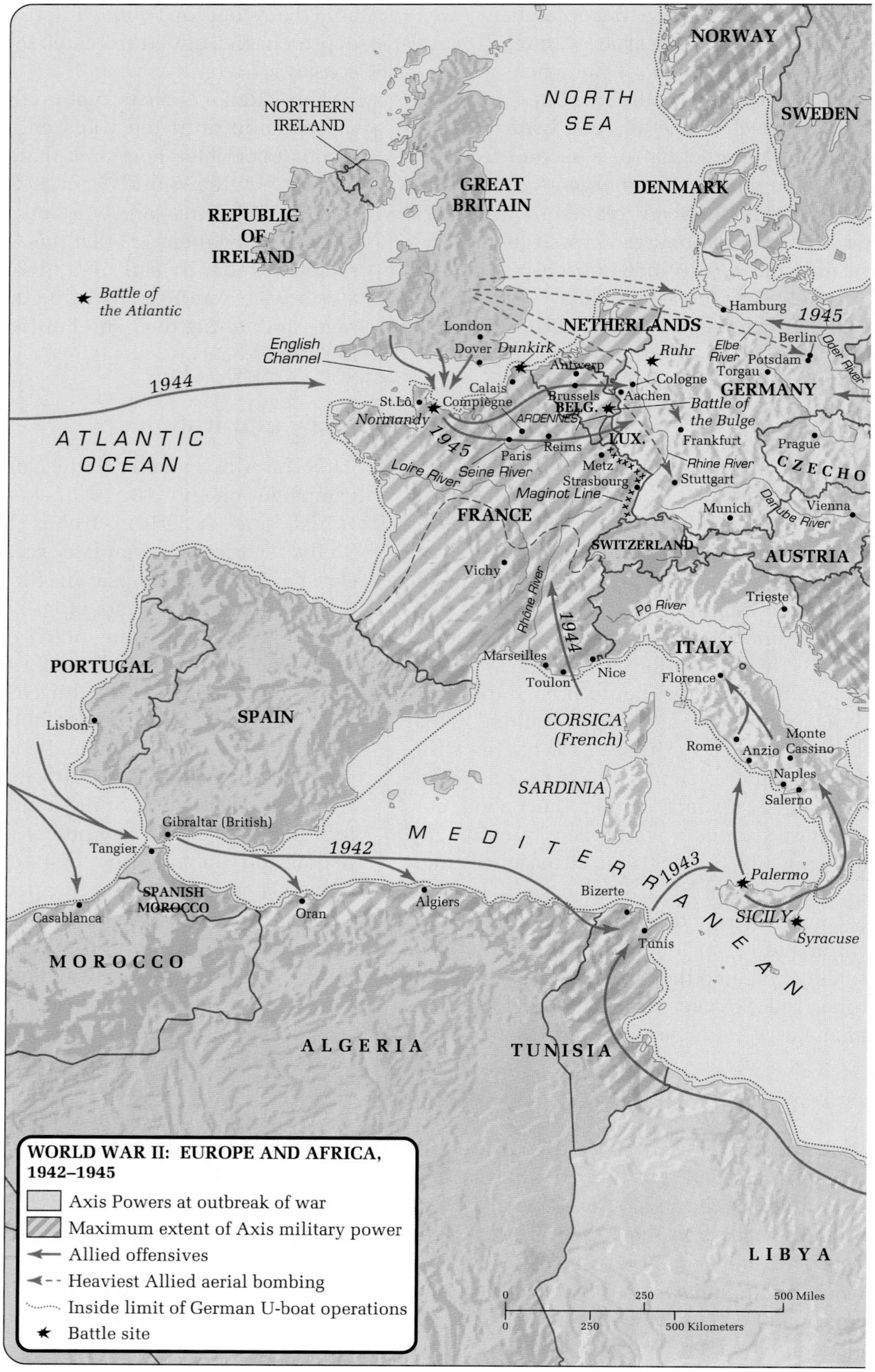
NORWAY
SWEDEN
NORTH SEA
NORTHERN IRELAND
GREAT BRITAIN
DENMARK
REPUBLIC OF IRELAND
Battle of the Atlantic
London
Dover
Dunkirk
English Channel
NETHERLANDS
Hamburg
1945
Berlin
Elbe River
Potsdam
Oder River
Torgau
Ruhr
Antwerp
Cologne
Calais
Aachen
GERMANY
1944
St.Lô
Compiègne
Brussels
BELG.
Battle of the Bulge
Normandy
ARDENNES
Frankfurt
Prague
ATLANTIC OCEAN
1945
Reims
LUX.
Paris
Metz
Rhine River
CZECHO
Loire River
Seine River
Strasbourg
Stuttgart
Maginot Line
Munich
Danube River
Vienna
FRANCE
SWITZERLAND
AUSTRIA
Vichy
Rhône River
Trieste
Po River
1944
ITALY
PORTUGAL
Marseilles
Nice
Toulon
Florence
Lisbon
SPAIN
CORSICA (French)
Rome
Anzio
Monte Cassino
Naples
SARDINIA
Salerno
Gibraltar (British)
MEDITERRANEAN
Tangier
1942
1943
Palermo
SPANISH MOROCCO
Bizerte
Casablanca
Oran
Algiers
SICILY
Tunis
Syracuse
MOROCCO
ALGERIA
TUNISIA
WORLD WAR II: EUROPE AND AFRICA, 1942–1945
Axis Powers at outbreak of war
Maximum extent of Axis military power
Allied offensives
Heaviest Allied aerial bombing
Inside limit of German U-boat operations
Battle site
LIBYA
0 250 500 Miles
0 250 500 Kilometers

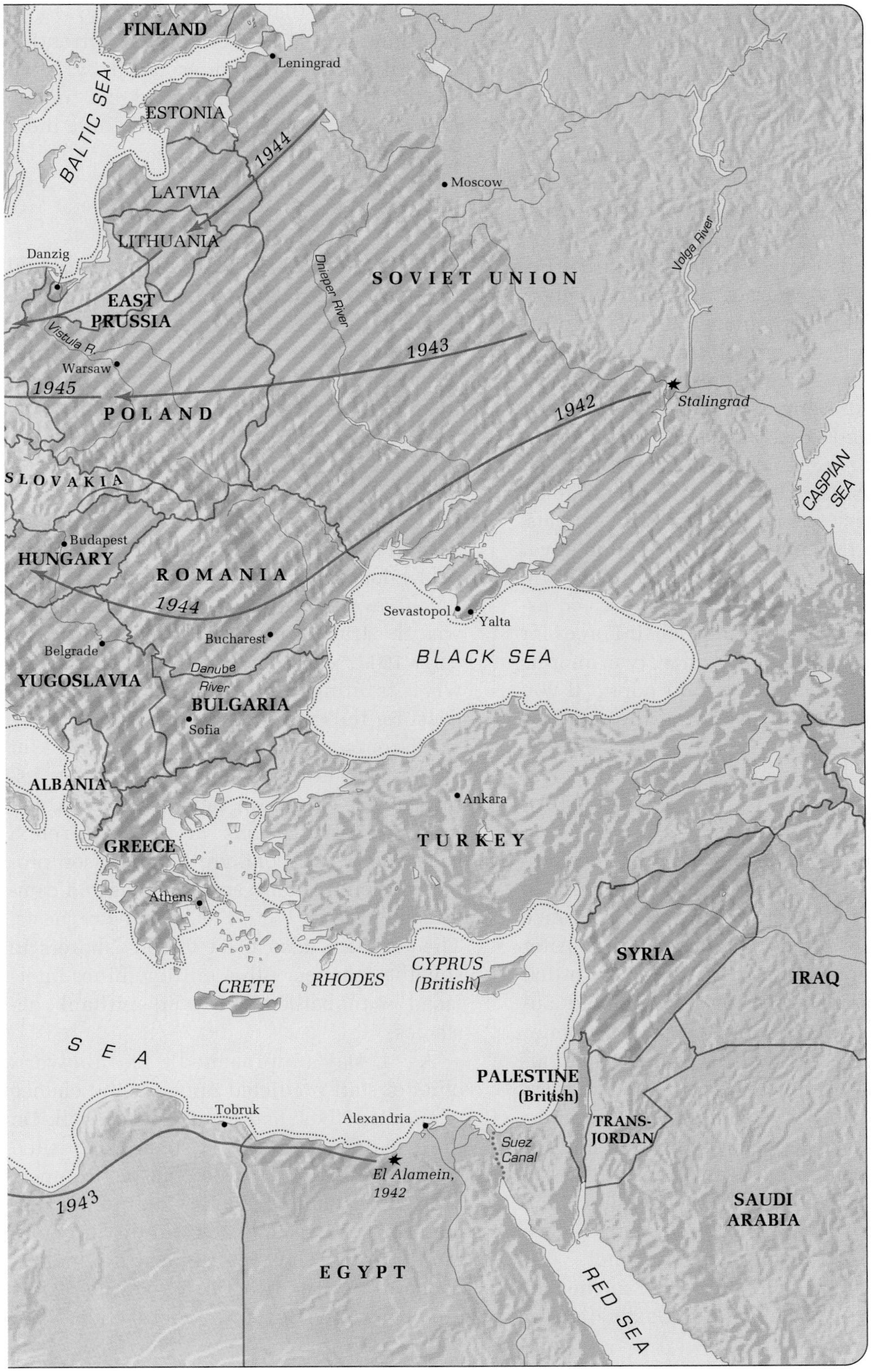
FINLAND
Leningrad
BALTIC SEA
ESTONIA
1944
LATVIA
Moscow
LITHUANIA
Danzig
Dnieper River
SOVIET UNION
Volga River
EAST PRUSSIA
Vistula R.
1943
Warsaw
1945
Stalingrad
POLAND
1942
SLOVAKIA
CASPIAN SEA
Budapest
HUNGARY
ROMANIA
1944
Sevastopol
Yalta
Bucharest
Belgrade
BLACK SEA
Danube River
YUGOSLAVIA
BULGARIA
Sofia
ALBANIA
Ankara
TURKEY
GREECE
Athens
SYRIA
CYPRUS (British)
CRETE
RHODES
IRAQ
SEA
PALESTINE (British)
Tobruk
Alexandria
TRANS-JORDAN
Suez Canal
El Alamein, 1942
1943
SAUDI ARABIA
EGYPT
RED SEA

of glory, for the long-awaited cross-Channel landing in France began two days later.

The Air War in Europe

Behind the long-postponed landings on the Normandy beaches lay months of preparation. While waiting, the United States Army Air Force and the Royal Air Force (RAF) carried the battle into Hitler's "Fortress Europe." By 1943 American strategic bombers were full-fledged partners of the RAF in the effort to pound Germany into submission. Yet the strategic air offensive failed to cut severely into German production or, as later studies found, to break civilian morale.

With air supremacy assured by the end of 1943, the Allies were free to concentrate on their primary urban and industrial targets, and, when the time came, to provide cover for the Normandy landings. On April 14, 1944, General Dwight D. Eisenhower assumed control of the Strategic Air Forces for use in the landings, less than two months away. On D-Day he told the troops: "If you see fighting aircraft over you, they will be ours."

The Teheran Meeting

Late in November 1943, Churchill and Roosevelt met with Stalin in Teheran, Iran, to coordinate plans for the invasion of France and a Soviet offensive from the east. After Churchill and Roosevelt assured Stalin that a cross-Channel invasion of Nazi-held Europe was finally coming, the Soviet premier promised to enter the war against Japan after Germany's defeat. The Allied leaders also agreed to begin plans for a new international peacekeeping organization and for the occupation of postwar Germany.

Earlier, in November 1943, while on the way to the Teheran meeting with Stalin, Churchill and Roosevelt had met with China's Generalissimo Chiang Kai-shek in Cairo, Egypt. The resulting Declaration of Cairo affirmed that war against Japan would continue until its unconditional surrender, that all Chinese territories taken by Japan would be restored to China, and that "in due course Korea shall become free and independent."

D-Day and After

In early 1944 General Eisenhower arrived in London to take command at Supreme Headquarters, Allied Expeditionary Forces (SHAEF). Already battle-tested in North Africa and the Mediterranean, he now faced the ultimate test of planning and conducting Operation "Overlord," the cross-Channel assault on Hitler's "Atlantic Wall." This required him to manage the Allied generals, as egotistical a group as any war had ever seen. It also required him to keep the political leaders at arm's length. In some respects, Eisenhower's role as supreme commander was the true turning point of the war. By early 1944, over a million American soldiers were training along England's southern coast for the cross-Channel invasion.

Of course, Hitler had been preparing for such an assault as well. German forces using captive European laborers had created massive fortifications along the French coastline. Huge concrete blockhouses protected their artillery, and trenches and camouflage shielded their machine-gun nests. The Germans also used forced laborers to sow the beaches with 4 million mines interlaced with barbed wire and antitank obstacles.

As D-Day approached, Eisenhower's chief of staff predicted only a 50-50 chance of success. "Ike" had his doubts as well. On the evening of June 5, Eisenhower visited some of the 16,000 American paratroopers preparing to land in France behind the German lines to create chaos and disrupt communications. The men noticed his look of concern and tried to lift his spirits. "Now quit worrying, General," one of them said, "we'll take care of this thing for you." After the planes took off, Eisenhower returned to his car with tears in his eyes. "Well," he said quietly to his driver, "it's on."

Operation Overlord surprised the Germans. Eisenhower fooled them into believing that the invasion would come at Pas de Calais, on the French-Belgian border. Instead, the landings occurred in Normandy, about 200 miles south. Airborne forces dropped behind the beaches during the night while planes and battleships pounded the coastal defenses.

At dawn on June 6, 1944, D-Day, the invasion fleet of some 4,000 ships and 150,000 men (57,000 Americans) filled the horizon off the Normandy coast. Overhead, thousands of Allied planes supported the invasion force. Sleepy German soldiers awoke to see the vast armada arrayed before them.

For several hours, the local German commanders misread the Normandy landings as merely a diversion for the "real" attack at Pas de Calais. When Hitler learned of the Allied landings, he boasted that "the news couldn't be better. As long as they were in Britain, we couldn't get at them. Now we have them where we can destroy them."

Despite Eisenhower's meticulous planning and the imposing array of Allied troops and firepower, the D-Day invasion almost failed. Cloud cover and German antiaircraft fire caused many of the paratroopers and glider pilots to miss their landing zones. Some oceangoing landing craft delivered their troops to the wrong locations. Low clouds also led the Allied planes assigned to soften up the seaside defenses to drop their bombs too far inland. The naval bombardment was equally ineffective. Moreover, rough seas caused many of the soldiers to become seasick and dozens of landing craft to capsize. Over a thousand men drowned. Waterlogged radios failed to work, and the deafening noise of the artillery and gunfire made oral communication impossible.

American soldiers land on the beach at Normandy, June 6, 1944.

By nightfall there were some 5,000 killed or wounded Allied soldiers strewn across Normandy beaches, but the Allies had breached Hitler's supposedly impregnable "Atlantic Wall." Operation Overlord was the greatest military invasion in the annals of warfare and the climactic battle of World War II. With the beachhead secured, the Allied leaders knew that victory was now in their grasp. Stalin, who had been clamoring for the cross-Channel invasion for years, applauded the Normandy operation and heaped praise on the Allies as their armies fanned out across France.

Leapfrogging to Tokyo

In the Pacific, Allied forces by 1944 had brought the war within reach of the Japanese homeland. The first American offensive in fact had been in the southwest Pacific.

There in 1942 the Japanese were building an airstrip on Guadalcanal from which they could attack Allied transportation routes to Australia. On August 7, the American First Marine Division landed on Guadalcanal. The Americans suffered heavy losses, but they finally cleared Guadalcanal of Japanese soldiers six months later.

MacArthur in New Guinea

Meanwhile, American and Australian forces under General Douglas MacArthur had begun to push the Japanese out of their positions on New Guinea's northern coast. These costly battles, fought through some of the hottest, most humid and mosquito-infested swamps in the world, secured the eastern tip of New Guinea by the end of January 1943.

At this stage, American war planners made a critical decision. MacArthur proposed to move his forces westward along the northern coast of New Guinea toward the Philippines and ultimately to Tokyo. Admiral Chester Nimitz argued for a sweep through the islands of the central Pacific toward Formosa and China. The Combined Chiefs of Staff agreed to MacArthur's plan, but they also ordered Nimitz to undertake his sweep in order to protect MacArthur's northern flank. Another consideration in this decision was pitifully political: to keep both leaders satisfied, as well as the two rival armed services they represented.

A new tactic expedited the movement. During the air Battle of the Bismarck Sea (March 2–3, 1943), American bombers sank eight Japanese troopships and ten warships bringing reinforcements. Thereafter the Japanese dared not risk sending transports to points under siege, making it possible to use the tactic of neutralizing Japanese strongholds with air and sea power, then moving on, leaving them to die on the vine. Some called it "leapfrogging," and it was a major cause of Allied victory. By the end of 1943, MacArthur's forces controlled the northern coast of New Guinea.

Nimitz in the Central Pacific

Admiral Nimitz's advance through the central Pacific had as its first target Tarawa in the Gilbert Islands. It was one of the most heavily protected islands in the Pacific. There nearly 1,000 American soldiers, sailors, and marines lost their lives rooting out 4,000 Japanese who refused to surrender. The Gilberts provided airfields from which the Seventh Air Force began softening up strong points in the Marshall Islands to the northwest.

The Battle of the Philippine Sea, fought mostly in the air on June 19 and 20, 1944, secured the Marianas for the Allies, and soon large B-29 bombers were attacking the Japanese homeland. Defeat in the Marianas finally convinced General Tojo that the war was lost. On July 18, 1944, he and his entire cabinet resigned.

The Battle of Leyte Gulf

With New Guinea and the Marianas all but conquered, President Roosevelt met with General MacArthur and Admiral Nimitz in Honolulu to decide the next major step. Previous plans had marked China as the essential springboard for invading Japan, but a Japanese offensive in April 1944 had taken most of the South China airfields from which American air power had operated. This strengthened MacArthur's opinion that the Philippines would provide a safer staging area. He also had a personal desire to recapture the islands he and his American troops had earlier defended. MacArthur made his move into the Philippines on October 20, 1944, landing first on the island of Leyte.

The Japanese, knowing that loss of the Philippines would cut them off from the essential resources of the East Indies, brought in fleets from three directions. The three encounters that resulted on October 25 came to be known collectively as the Battle of Leyte Gulf, the largest naval engagement in history. The Japanese lost most of their remaining sea power and the ability to defend the Philippines. The battle included the first use of suicide attacks by Japanese pilots, who crash-dived into American carriers, thereby killing themselves but also damaging the Allied ships.

A New Age Is Born

Roosevelt's Fourth Term

In 1944, war or no war, the calendar dictated another presidential election. This time the Republicans turned to the former crime-fighter and New York governor, Thomas E. Dewey, as their candidate. Once again no Democratic challenger rose high enough to contest Roosevelt, who chose as his running mate the relatively unknown Missouri senator Harry S. Truman.

Dewey did not propose to dismantle Roosevelt's programs, rather he argued that it was time for younger men to replace the tired old leaders of the New Deal. The problem was that, even though considerably younger than Roosevelt, Dewey showed few signs of vitality. Roosevelt betrayed distinct signs of illness and exhaustion, but nevertheless, on November 7, 1945, he was elected for the fourth time.

Converging Fronts

The war in Europe had bogged down; final victory remained elusive. After the quick sweep across France, the Allies lost momentum in the fall of 1944 and settled down to slugging it out on the frontiers of Germany. The Germans sprang a surprise on December 16, 1944. The Nazis advanced along a fifty-mile bulge in the Allied lines in Belgium and Luxembourg (hence the name the Battle of the Bulge) before they stalled at Bastogne. Reinforced by the Allies just before it was surrounded, Bastogne held out for six days against all the Germans could bring against it. On December 26, the besieged American army was relieved, but Germany's sudden thrust upset Eisenhower's timetable and made continued coordination with the Soviet army even more crucial.

The Nazi counterattack in the west had weakened their defense of the eastern front, and in January 1945 the Soviets began their final offensive. The destruction of Hitler's last reserve units at the Battle of the Bulge also left open the door to Germany's heartland. The western offensives started in February, and by early March Allied forces were pouring across the Rhine River. By this time the Soviet offensive had also reached Germany itself.

With the British and American armies racing across western Germany and the Soviets moving in from the east, the attention of the war planners turned to Berlin. Churchill had grown suspicious of the Soviets and worried that if they arrived in Berlin first, they would gain dangerous leverage in deciding the postwar map of Europe. He told Eisenhower of his concerns and urged him to get to Berlin first. Eisenhower, however, refused to mix politics with military strategy. Berlin, he said, no longer was of military significance. His purpose remained the destruction of the enemy's ground forces. Churchill disagreed and appealed to Roosevelt, but the American leader, now seriously ill, left the decision to the Supreme Commander. Eisenhower left Berlin for the Soviets to conquer.

Yalta and the Postwar World

As the final offensives got under way, the Big Three Allied leaders met again in early February 1945 at Yalta, a resort in southern Russia. While the focus at the Teheran conference in 1943 had been on wartime strategy, it was now on the shape of the postwar world. Two aims loomed large in Roosevelt's thinking. One was the need to ensure that the Soviet Union join the war against

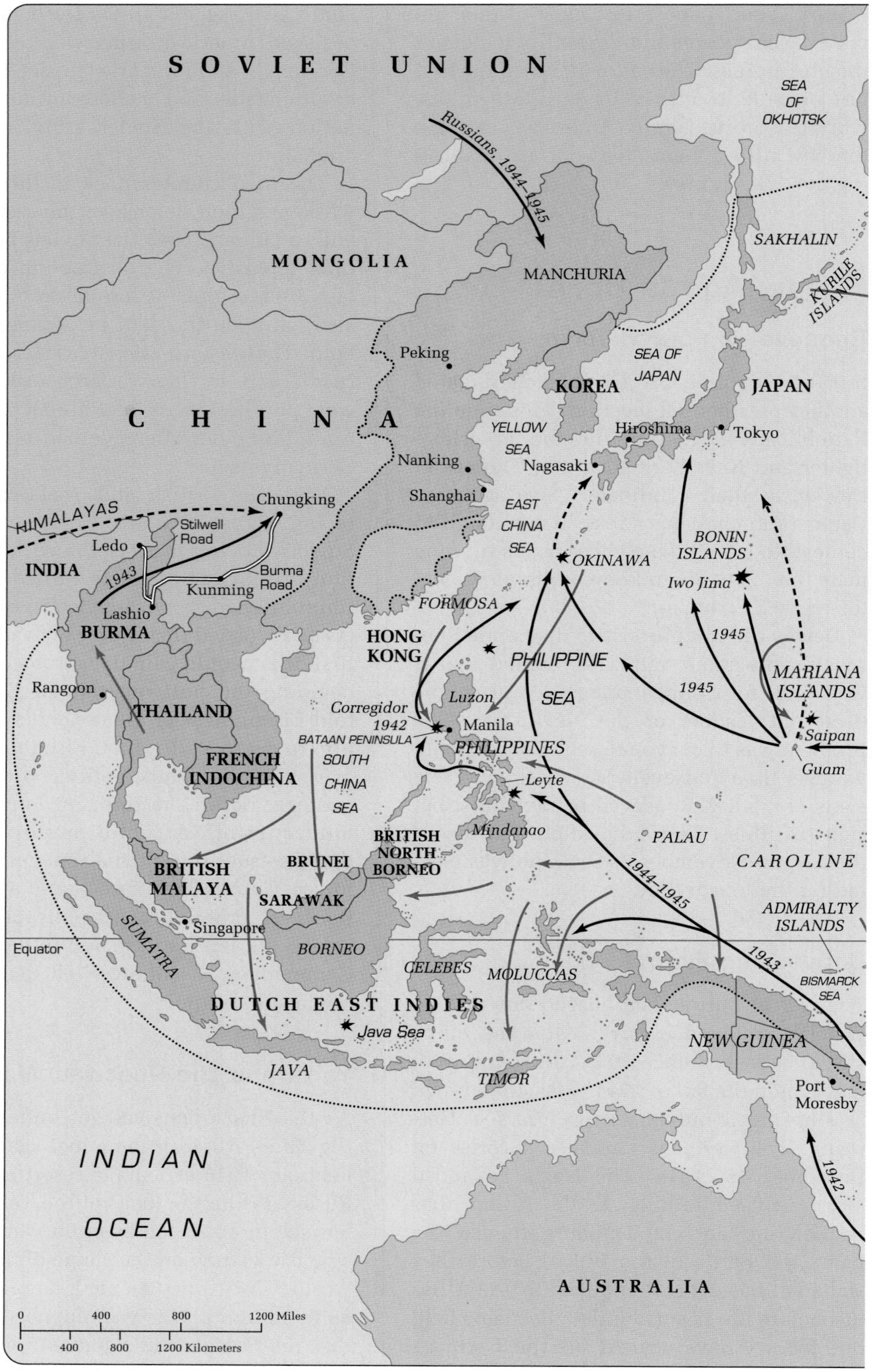
SOVIET UNION
SEA OF OKHOTSK
Russians, 1944–1945
MONGOLIA
MANCHURIA
SAKHALIN
KURILE ISLANDS
Peking
SEA OF JAPAN
KOREA
JAPAN
CHINA
YELLOW SEA
Hiroshima
Tokyo
Nanking
Nagasaki
Shanghai
EAST CHINA SEA
HIMALAYAS
Chungking
Stilwell Road
Ledo
1943
Burma Road
Kunming
INDIA
Lashio
BURMA
OKINAWA
BONIN ISLANDS
Iwo Jima
FORMOSA
HONG KONG
1945
PHILIPPINE SEA
MARIANA ISLANDS
Rangoon
THAILAND
Luzon
Corregidor 1942
Manila
BATAAN PENINSULA
PHILIPPINES
Saipan
Guam
FRENCH INDOCHINA
SOUTH CHINA SEA
Leyte
Mindanao
PALAU
CAROLINE
BRITISH NORTH BORNEO
BRUNEI
BRITISH MALAYA
SARAWAK
1944–1945
ADMIRALTY ISLANDS
Singapore
SUMATRA
Equator
BORNEO
CELEBES
MOLUCCAS
1943
BISMARCK SEA
DUTCH EAST INDIES
Java Sea
NEW GUINEA
JAVA
TIMOR
Port Moresby
INDIAN OCEAN
1942
AUSTRALIA
0 400 800 1200 Miles
0 400 800 1200 Kilometers

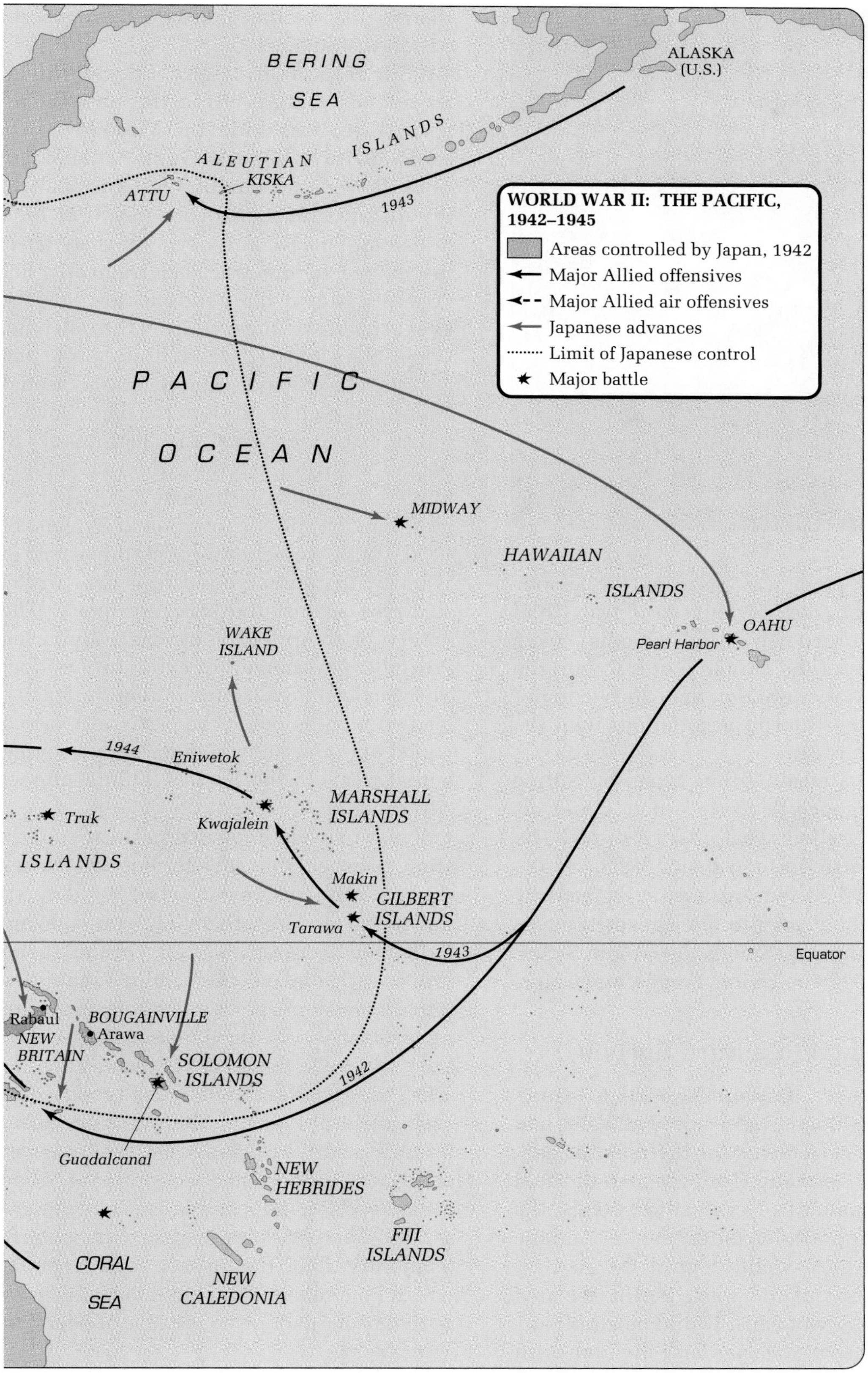
WORLD WAR II: THE PACIFIC, 1942–1945
Areas controlled by Japan, 1942
Major Allied offensives
Major Allied air offensives
Japanese advances
Limit of Japanese control
Major battle
BERING SEA
ALASKA (U.S.)
ALEUTIAN ISLANDS
KISKA
ATTU
1943
PACIFIC OCEAN
MIDWAY
HAWAIIAN ISLANDS
OAHU
Pearl Harbor
WAKE ISLAND
1944
Eniwetok
Kwajalein
MARSHALL ISLANDS
Truk
ISLANDS
Makin
GILBERT ISLANDS
Tarawa
1943
Equator
Rabaul
NEW BRITAIN
BOUGAINVILLE
Arawa
SOLOMON ISLANDS
1942
Guadalcanal
NEW HEBRIDES
FIJI ISLANDS
CORAL SEA
NEW CALEDONIA

The Yalta Conference, February 1945. Stalin (right), FDR (center), and Churchill (left) confer on the shape of the postwar world.

Japan. The other was based on the lessons he drew from the previous world war. Chief among the mistakes to be remedied were the failures of the United States to join the League of Nations and of the Allies to maintain a united front in negotiations with the German aggressors.

The Yalta meeting thus began by calling for a conference to create a new world organization called the United Nations. The conferees also decided that substantive decisions in the new organization's Security Council would require the agreement of its five permanent members: the United States, Britain, the Soviet Union, France, and China.

Germany and Eastern Europe

With Hitler's "Thousand-Year Reich" stumbling to its doom, the leaders at Yalta had to make arrangements for the postwar governance of Germany. The war map dictated the basic pattern of occupation zones: the Soviet Union would control the east and the Western Allies would control the rich industrial areas of the west. Berlin, isolated within the Soviet zone, would be jointly occupied. Austria was similarly divided, with Vienna, like Berlin, under joint occupation within the Soviet zone.

With respect to eastern Europe, where Soviet forces were advancing on a broad front, there was little the Western Allies could do to influence events. Poland became the main focus of Western concern. Britain and France had gone to war in 1939 to defend Poland, and now, six years later, the course of the war had ironically left Poland's fate in the hands of the Soviets. Events had long foreshadowed the outcome. When they entered Poland in 1944, the Soviets placed civil administration under a puppet regime in Lublin. The Soviets refused to recognize the legitimacy of Poland's government-in-exile in London, formed by officials who had fled the country following Hitler's invasion in September 1939. With Soviet troops at the gates of Warsaw, the underground resistance in the city rose against the Nazi occupiers. The Polish underground, however, supported Poland's government-in-exile in London. The Soviets then stopped their offensive for two months while the Nazis in Warsaw wiped out thousands of Poles who were potential rivals to the Soviets' Lublin puppet government.

It was naive to hope that postwar cooperation between the Soviets and Americans could survive such events. The Western Allies found at Yalta that they could do no more than acquiesce or stall. On the Soviet proposal to expand the Lublin Committee into a provisional government together with representatives of the London Poles, they acquiesced. On the issue of Poland's boundaries, they stalled. The Soviets proposed to keep eastern Poland, offering land taken from Germany as compensation. Roosevelt and Churchill accepted the proposal. They considered Poland's new western boundary at the Oder–Western Neisse Rivers only temporary, but the peace conference at which Poland's western boundary was to be settled never took place because of later disagreements.

The Big Three also promised to sponsor free elections, democratic governments, and constitutional safeguards of political freedom throughout the rest of Europe. The Yalta Declaration of Liberated Europe reaffirmed faith in the principles of the Atlantic Charter and the United Nations, but in the end it made little difference. It may have postponed Communist takeovers in eastern Europe for a few years, but before long Communist members of coalition governments had their hands on the levers of power and purged the opposition. Russia, twice invaded by Germany in the twentieth century, was determined to create buffer states between it and the Germans.

Yalta's Legacy

Critics later attacked the Yalta agreements for "giving" eastern Europe over to Soviet domination. Some argued that Roosevelt's declining health caused him to buckle under Stalin's insistent demands. But the course of the war shaped the actions at Yalta, not personal diplomacy. The Red Army had the upper hand in eastern Europe.

Perhaps the most bitterly criticized of the Yalta understandings was a secret agreement on the Far East, not made public until after the war. The Joint Chiefs of Staff still estimated that Japan could hold out for eighteen months after the defeat of Germany. Costly campaigns thus lay ahead, and the atomic bomb was still an expensive and untested gamble. Roosevelt felt that he had no choice but to accept Stalin's demands on postwar arrangements in the Far East: continued Soviet control of Outer Mongolia, acquisition of the Kurile Islands from Japan, and recovery of rights and territory lost after the Russo-Japanese War of 1905. Stalin in return promised to enter the war against Japan two or three months after the German defeat, to recognize Chinese sovereignty over Manchuria, and to conclude a treaty of friendship and alliance with the Chinese Nationalists. Roosevelt's concessions would later appear in a different light, but given their geographical advantages in Asia as in eastern Europe, the Soviets were in a position to get what they wanted in any case.

The Third Reich Collapses

The collapse of Nazi resistance was imminent by early 1945, but President Roosevelt did not live to join the celebrations. All through 1944 his health had been declining, and on April 12, 1945, while he was drafting a speech, he suffered a cerebral hemorrhage, which brought sudden death.

Hitler's Germany collapsed less than a month later. The Allied armies rolled up almost unopposed to the Elbe River, where they met advance detachments of Soviets on April 25. Three days later, Italian partisans captured and killed Mussolini and his mistress. In Berlin, which was under siege by the Soviets, Hitler married his mistress, Eva Braun, on the last day of April, just before killing her and himself. On

U. S. troops encounter surviving inmates at the Nazi concentration camp at Wobbelin, Germany, May 1945.

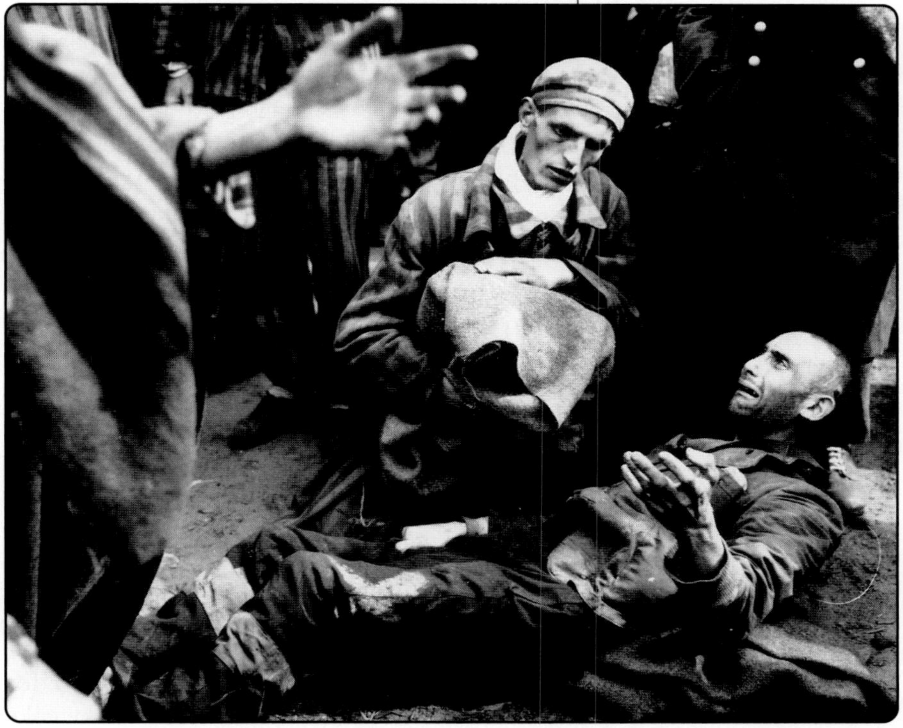

May 2 Berlin fell to the Soviets. That same day German forces in Italy surrendered. On May 7 the Germans signed an unconditional surrender in Allied headquarters at Reims.

Massive American victory celebrations on V-E Day, May 8, 1945, were tempered by the tragedies that had engulfed the world: mourning for the lost president and the death and mutilation of untold millions. Most shocking was the revelation of the Nazi Holocaust: the wholesale extermination of some 6 million Jews along with more than 1 million others from occupied countries.

During the war, reports from Red Cross and underground sources had amassed growing evidence of Germany's systematic genocide against European Jews. Stories appeared in major American newspapers as early as 1942, but they were nearly always buried on inside pages. And reports of such horror seemed beyond belief. American government officials, even some Jewish leaders, dragged their feet on the question for fear that relief efforts for Jewish refugees might stir latent anti-Semitism at home. Finally, Roosevelt set up a War Refugees Board in 1944, but with few resources at its disposal. It nevertheless managed to rescue about 200,000 European Jews and some 20,000 others. But more might have been done. The Allied handling of the Holocaust was inept at best and disgraceful at worst.

A Grinding War against Japan

The sobering thought that Japan must still be defeated cast a further pall over the victory celebrations. American forces continued to penetrate and disrupt the Japanese Empire in the early months of 1945, but at heavy cost. On February 19, 1945, American marines invaded Iwo Jima, a volcanic island 750 miles from Tokyo. The island was needed to provide fighter escort for bombers over Japan and as a landing strip for disabled B-29s. It took nearly six weeks to secure Iwo Jima from defenders hiding in an underground labyrinth, and the cost was high.

The fight for Okinawa, beginning on Easter Sunday, April 1, was even bloodier. The island was large enough to afford a staging area for the invasion of the Japanese islands, and its capture required the largest amphibious operation of the Pacific war, involving some 300,000 troops. Desperate Japanese counterattacks inflicted heavy losses. Kamikaze (suicide) pilots attacked by the hundreds. The battle for Okinawa raged until late June. When resistance on Okinawa collapsed, the Japanese emperor instructed his new premier to seek peace terms. Washington decoded Japanese messages that suggested either an effort to avoid unconditional surrender or perhaps just a stall.

The Atomic Bomb

During the summer of 1945, President Truman learned of the first successful test of an atomic bomb. In 1939, Albert Einstein had alerted President Roosevelt to German research on nuclear fission. In 1940 the president diverted army and navy funds into research that grew ultimately into the $2 billion top-secret Manhattan Project.

A group of physicists directed by Dr. J. Robert Oppenheimer worked out the scientific and technical problems of bomb construction in a laboratory at Los Alamos, New Mexico. On July 16, 1945, the first atomic fireball rose from the desert. The test explosion broke windows 125 miles away, and a blind woman saw the flash. After learning of the successful test, President Truman wrote in his diary: "We have discovered the most terrible bomb in the history of the world."

How to use this new weapon posed unique problems. Some scientists favored a demonstration explosion for the Japanese in a remote area, but this was vetoed because only two bombs were available, and even those might misfire. The choice of targets received more consideration. After deciding against Kyoto, Japan's ancient capital and repository of many national and religious treasures, priority went to Hiroshima, a port city of 400,000 people in southern Japan, which was a center of war industries, headquarters of the Second General Army, and command center for the homeland's defenses.

On July 25, 1945, President Truman ordered the bomb dropped if Japan did not surrender before August 3. The ferocious Japanese defense of Okinawa had convinced American military planners that the alternative to the bomb, an amphibious invasion of Japan itself, scheduled to begin on November 1, 1945, could cost as many as 250,000 Allied casualties and even more Japanese losses. Moreover, some 100,000 Allied prisoners of war being held in Japan were to be executed whenever an invasion began. It is important to remember as well that the bombing of cities and the consequent killing of civilians had become accepted military practice during 1945. The firebomb raids on Tokyo on a single night in March 1945 killed 100,000 civilians and left over a million people homeless. By July more than sixty of Japan's largest cities had been firebombed, resulting in 500,000 deaths and 13 million civilians left homeless. The use of atomic bombs on Japanese cities was thus seen as a logical next step in an effort to end the war without an invasion of Japan. As it turned out, American scientists greatly underestimated the physical effects of the atomic bomb.

On July 26 the heads of the American, British, and Chinese governments issued the Potsdam Declaration demanding that Japan surrender or face "prompt and utter destruction." The deadline passed, and on August 6, 1945, at 8:15 in the morning, flying at 31,600 feet over Hiroshima, the *Enola Gay* released the five-ton uranium bomb nicknamed "Little Boy." Forty-three seconds later, having tumbled to an altitude of 1,900 feet, it exploded as planned with the force of 15,000 tons of TNT. A blinding flash of light prefaced a fireball towering to 40,000 feet.

The shock wave, firestorm, cyclonic winds, and radioactive rain killed some 80,000 people, including thousands of Japanese soldiers assigned to the Second General Army headquarters and 23 American prisoners of war housed in the city. By the end of the year, the death toll had reached 140,000 as the effects of radiation burns and infection took their toll. In addition, 70,000 buildings were destroyed, and four square miles of the city were turned to rubble.

In the United States, Americans greeted the news of the bomb with elation: it promised a quick end to the long nightmare of war. "No tears of sympathy will be shed in America for the Japanese people," the *Omaha World Herald* predicted. "Had they possessed a comparable weapon at Pearl Harbor, would they have hesitated to use it?" Others were more circumspect. "Yesterday," journalist Hanson Baldwin wrote in the *New York Times,* "we clinched victory in the Pacific, but we sowed the whirlwind." Only later would people realize that it marked the start of a more enduring nightmare, the nuclear arms race.

Rubble is all that remained following the detonation of an atomic bomb over Hiroshima, Japan, on August 6, 1945.

Two days after the Hiroshima bombing, an opportunistic Soviet Union hastened to enter the war in east Asia. The next day, on August 9, an American plane dropped a second atomic bomb over the port city of Nagasaki, killing 36,000 more people. That night the emperor urged his cabinet to accept the inevitable and surrender on the sole condition that he remain as sovereign. On September 2, 1945, General MacArthur and other Allied representatives accepted Japan's formal surrender on board the battleship *Missouri.*

The Final Ledger

Thus ended the most deadly conflict in human history. One estimate has it that 70 million in all fought in the war, at a cost of some 50 million military and civilian dead. Material costs were also enormous, perhaps $1 trillion in military expenditures and twice that in property losses. The Soviet Union suffered the greatest losses of all, over 13 million military deaths, more than 7 million civilians dead, and at least 25 million left homeless. World War II was more costly for the United States than any other of the country's foreign wars: 292,000 battle deaths and 114,000 other deaths. But in proportion to population, the United States suffered less than any of the major Allies or enemies, and American territory escaped the devastation inflicted on so many other parts of the world.

World War II had profound effects on American life and society. Mobilization for war stimulated a phenomenal increase in American productivity and brought full employment, thus ending the Great Depression and laying the foundation for a new era of unprecedented prosperity. New technologies and products developed for military purposes—radar, computers, electronics, plastics and synthetics, jet engines, rockets, atomic energy—soon began to transform the private sector as well. And new opportunities for women as well as for blacks and other minorities set in motion changes that would culminate in the civil rights movement of the 1960s and the feminist movement of the 1970s.

The Democratic party benefited from the war effort by solidifying its control of both the White House and Congress. The dramatic expansion of the federal government occasioned by the war continued after 1945. Presidential authority and prestige increased enormously at the expense of congressional and state power. The isolationist sentiment in foreign relations that had been so powerful in the 1920s and 1930s disintegrated as the United States emerged from the war with global responsibilities and interests. Thus the war's end opened a new era for the United States in the world arena. It accelerated the growth of American power while devastating all other world powers, leaving the United States economically and militarily the strongest nation on earth.

PART 7

The American Age

The United States emerged from World War II the preeminent military and economic power in the world. Americans had a monopoly over the atomic bomb and enjoyed a commanding position in international trade. While much of Europe and Asia struggled to recover from the physical devastation of the war, the United States was virtually unscathed, its economic infrastructure intact and operating at peak efficiency. By 1955 the United States, with only 6 percent of the world's population, was producing well over half of the world's goods.

Yet the specter of a "cold war" cast a pall over the buoyant revival of the American economy after World War II. The ideological contest with the Soviet Union and Communist China produced numerous foreign crises and sparked a domestic witch-hunt for Communists that far surpassed earlier episodes of political and social repression in the nation's history. Both Republican and Democratic presidents affirmed the need to "contain" the spread of Communist influence around the world.

This bedrock assumption eventually embroiled the United States in a tragic war in Southeast Asia that destroyed Lyndon Johnson's presidency and revived neoisolationist sentiments. The Vietnam War also was the catalyst for a countercultural movement in which young idealists of the "baby-boom" generation rebelled against a government that in their eyes had become oppressive and corrupt. The youth revolt provided energy for many overdue social reforms, including the civil rights, women's, and environmental movements, but it also contributed to an array of social ills, such as drug abuse and sexual promiscuity. The social upheavals of the 1960s and early 1970s provoked a conservative backlash that overreached itself as well. In their efforts to restore "law and order," mayors violated civil liberties in their cities. Richard Nixon's paranoid reaction to his critics led to the destruction of his presidency as a result of the Watergate investigations.

Through all of this turmoil, however, the basic premises of welfare state capitalism that Franklin Roosevelt had instituted with his New Deal programs remained essentially intact. With only a few exceptions, both Republicans and Democrats after 1945 came to accept the notion that the federal government must assume greater responsibility for the welfare of individuals. Even Ronald Reagan, a sharp critic of social-welfare programs, recognized the need for the federal government to provide a "safety net" for those who could not help themselves.

Yet this fragile consensus about public policy began to disintegrate in the late 1980s amid stunning international events and less visible domestic developments. The internal collapse of the Soviet Union and the disintegration of European communism surprised observers and forced policy makers to adapt to a post–cold war world in which the United States remained the only legitimate superpower. After forty-five years, American foreign policy was no longer centered on a single adversary, and world politics lost its bipolar quality. During the early 1990s, the European Community coalesced, the two Germanys reunited, apartheid in South Africa finally ended, and Israel and the Palestinians signed a heretofore unimaginable peace treaty.

At the same time, American foreign policy began to focus less on military power and more on economic competition and technological development. In those arenas, Japan and a reunited Germany challenged the United States for preeminence. By reducing the public's fear of nuclear annihilation, the ending of the cold war also reduced public interest in foreign affairs. The presidential elections of 1992 and 1996 were the first since 1936 in which foreign policy issues played virtually no role. This was an unfortunate development, for post–cold war world affairs remained volatile and dangerous. The implosion of Soviet communism unleashed a series of ethnic, nationalist, and separatist conflicts throughout Eurasia. In the face of inertia among other governments and pleas for assistance, the United States found itself being drawn into crises in faraway locations such as Iraq, Bosnia, Rwanda, Somalia, Chechnya, and Kosovo.

As the new multipolar world emerged, fault lines began to appear in the American social and economic landscape. Economic inequality widened, and a gargantuan federal debt and rising annual deficits threatened to bankrupt a nation that was becoming top-heavy with retirees. Yet by the start of the twenty-first century, a prolonged period of economic growth, low inflation, budget surpluses, dazzling new computer technology enterprises, and a record-setting stock market revived the myth of perennial prosperity.

ESSENTIAL THEMES

CRITICAL QUESTIONS

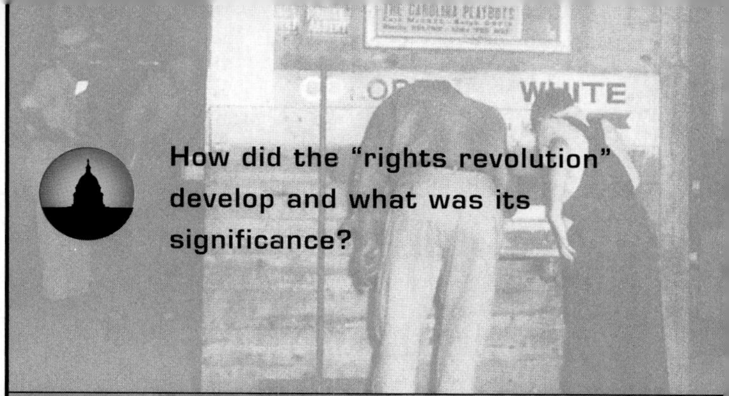

How did the "rights revolution" develop and what was its significance?

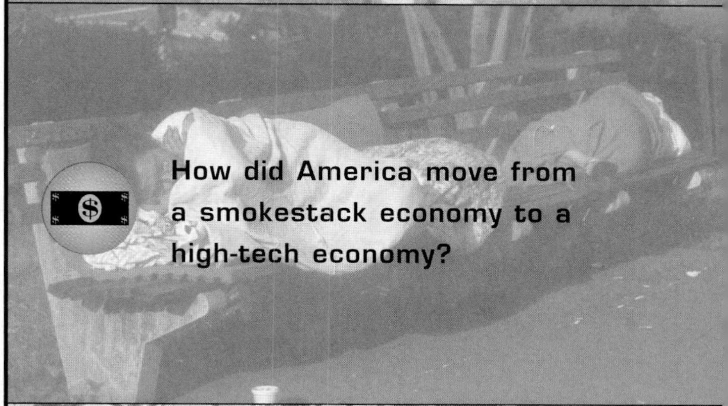

How did America move from a smokestack economy to a high-tech economy?

What effects did the baby-boom generation have on society after 1950?

How did the counterculture emerge through the 1960s and 1970s?

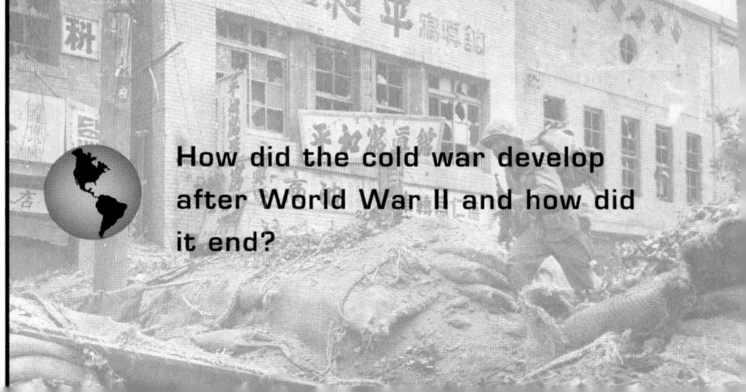

How did the cold war develop after World War II and how did it end?

How did the "rights revolution" develop and what was its significance?

CHAPTER 30
The Fair Deal and Containment

- The Fair Deal
  - **Truman and the Republican Congress, civil rights**
  - **The Fair Deal and liberal policy**
- The cold war
  - **Containment**
  - The Truman Doctrine
  - The Marshall Plan in Europe
  - Building NATO
  - National Security Act (1947)
  - McCarran Internal Security Act (1950)
  - Development of hydrogen bomb (1950)
  - War in Korea

CHAPTER 31
Through the Picture Window

- The postwar role of government
  - **Politics and community in the 1950s**

CHAPTER 32
Conflict and Deadlock

- Eisenhower's "hidden-hand" presidency
- The cold war
  - **Armistice in Korea**
  - **The decline of McCarthyism**
  - **Internal security stiffened**
  - **Dulles's "brinksmanship"**
  - **The beginnings of U.S. involvement in Vietnam**
  - **Crises in Middle East, Eastern Europe**
  - **Eisenhower warns of dangers of the "military-industrial complex"**
- The rise of the civil rights movement
  - **The Brown decision (1954)**
  - **Desegregation crisis at Little Rock**

CHAPTER 33
New Frontiers

- Civil rights
  - **Sit-ins and freedom riders**
  - **The March on Washington (1963)**
  - **The Warren Court and civil liberties**
  - *Gideon v. Wainwright* (1963)
  - *Miranda v. Arizona* (1966)
- The Kennedy Era
  - **Kennedy and Cuba**
  - The Bay of Pigs
  - The Cuban missile crisis
  - **Kennedy and Vietnam**
  - **Kennedy's assasination**
- Lyndon Johnson and the Great Society
  - **Johnson as politician**
  - **The "war on poverty"**
  - **Great Society legislation**
  - **The Civil Rights Act of 1964**
  - **The Immigration Act of 1965**
  - **The Voting Rights Act of 1965**
- Johnson and Vietnam
  - **Escalation and opposition**
  - **Chicago and Miami conventions**

CHAPTER 34
Rebellion and Reaction in the 1960s and 1970s

- The New Left
  - **The Free Speech Movement**
  - **Students for a Democratic Society**
  - **The 1968 Democratic Convention**
- Extension of civil rights
  - **Feminism and the ERA**
  - **César Chavez and the UFW union**
  - **The American Indian Movement (AIM)**
  - **Gay activism**
- The Nixon and Ford years
  - **Nixon and Vietnam**
  - Gradual withdrawal
  - Bombing and negotiations
  - The evacuation of Saigon
  - **Nixon's social policies**
  - EPA established (1970)
  - *Roe* v. *Wade* (1973)
  - **Relations with China, the Soviet Union**
  - **Watergate**
  - Break-in and cover-up (1972–1974)
  - Nixon's resignation (1974)
- The Carter interregnum
  - **Energy and the economy**
  - **Camp David Accords**
  - **The crisis in Iran**

CHAPTER 35
Conservative Insurgency

- The Reagan revolution
  - **Reagan's election, Reaganomics**
  - **The environment, labor, civil rights**
  - **The defense buildup**
  - **Anti-Communist foreign policy**
  - **Arms reduction deals with Soviets**
  - **The Iran-Contra Affair (1986)**
- The Bush years
  - **Domestic initiatives**
  - Antidrug legislation
  - **End of the cold war**
  - **The Gulf War**

CHAPTER 36
Cultural Politics

- Republican turmoil
  - **Gingrich and the Contract with America**
- Democratic resurgence: Clinton
  - **Economic legislation**
  - **Derailing of health care reform**
  - **The scandal machine: Whitewater, the Starr Report, the Lewinsky scandal**
  - Impeachment and trial of Clinton
  - **Election of 2000**

CHAPTER 30
The Fair Deal and Containment

- Demobilization and return to peacetime economy
  - **Postwar inflation**
  - **Labor unrest and Truman's response**
  - **GI Bill of Rights**
  - **Tax reduction vs. debt reduction (1948)**
  - **The anti-union Taft-Hartley Act (1947)**

CHAPTER 31
Through the Picture Window

- Postwar economic expansion
  - **Government spending**
  - **Industrial expansion**
  - **Growth of consumer demand**
  - Federal Housing Administration: middle-class housing loans
  - Credit soars 800 percent (1945–57)

CHAPTER 32
Conflict and Deadlock

- The cold war economy
  - **Foreign aid**
  - **Defense expenditures**
- Eisenhower's economic policies

CHAPTER 33
New Frontiers

- The economy under Kennedy
- Johnson's "war on poverty"
  - **Medicare and Medicaid (1965)**
  - **Billions of federal dollars for education (1965)**
  - **Housing and Urban Development Act (1965)**
  - **"Guns and butter"**

CHAPTER 34
Rebellion and Reaction in the 1960s and 1970s

- Nixon's economic policies
  - **A floundering economy**
  - Inflation and unemployment: stagflation
  - Wage and price controls
- Ford's approach
  - **The rise of OPEC**
- Carter's struggles
  - **Inflation and recession**
  - Interest rates of 20 percent (1980)

CHAPTER 35
Conservative Insurgency

- The economy under Reagan
  - **Reaganomics**
  - Tax cuts, especially at high income levels
  - Increased defense spending
  - Unbalanced budgets
  - Massive cuts in social spending
  - National debt reaches $2.6 trillion
  - **Black Monday (October 19, 1987)**
  - **Recession of early 1990s**

CHAPTER 36
Cultural Politics

- Economic impact of the baby boom
- The computer revolution
- The economy under Bush
  - **Recession and downsizing**
- The economy under Clinton
  - **Deficit reduction**
  - Tax hikes and spending cuts (1992)
  - **NAFTA and economic globalization**
  - **The "new economy"**
  - The surging stock market
  - First federal surplus in 30 years (1999)
  - The Internet and market globalization

What effects did the baby-boom generation have on society after 1950?

CHAPTER 30
The Fair Deal and Containment

- Civil rights during the 1940s
  - **Committee on Civil Rights (1946)**
  - **Desegregation of federal workforce, military (1948)**
  - **Truman versus the Dixiecrats (1948)**
- Taft-Hartley Act of 1947
  - **Weakening of organized labor**

CHAPTER 31
Through the Picture Window

- Postwar prosperity
  - **GI Bill of Rights**
  - **Corporate America**
  - **The postwar "baby boom"**
  - **The "ideal" middle-class woman**
  - **Spread of the suburbs**
  - **Critics of conformity and materialism**
  - **Religion and community**
  - **Migration of blacks to the North**
- Youth culture
  - **Rock 'n' roll**
  - **Alienation in the arts**
  - The Beats

CHAPTER 32
Conflict and Deadlock

- Eisenhower and the cold war
  - **Anti-Communist ethos**
  - Public response to Sputnik
- The civil rights movement
  - ***Brown* v. *Board of Education* (1954)**
  - **The Montgomery bus boycott**
  - **Martin Luther King and the SCLC**
  - **Desegregation in Little Rock (1958)**

CHAPTER 33
New Frontiers

- The growth of the civil rights movement
  - **Martin Luther King's "militant nonviolence"**
  - "Letter from a Birmingham Jail"
  - **Sit-ins and freedom rides**
  - **Federal intervention in Mississippi and Alabama**
  - **March on Washington (Aug. 28, 1963)**
- From civil rights to black power
  - **Effects of the Civil Rights Act (1964) and the Voting Rights Act (1965)**
  - Stokely Carmichael
  - Malcolm X
  - **Race riots (1965–1969)**
- LBJ's "war on poverty"
- Social effects of the Great Society
- Immigration Act of 1965
- The traumatic year of 1968
  - **Assassination of Martin Luther King**
  - **Assassination of Robert F. Kennedy**

CHAPTER 34
Rebellion and Reaction in the 1960s and 1970s

- The roots of rebellion
  - **Protests and the baby boomers**
  - **The counterculture and social strains**
  - **Feminism**
  - National Organization for Women (NOW)
  - **Hispanic Rights**
  - César Chavez founds the UFW (1962)
  - **Native American Rights**
  - American Indian Movement (AIM)
  - **Gay Rights**
  - Stonewall rebellion (1969)
- Backlash by the "silent" majority
  - **Social divisions in the early 1970s**
  - **Nixon fights school busing and affirmative action**
  - **The public response to Watergate**
- Carter and America's "crisis of confidence"

CHAPTER 35
Conservative Insurgency

- The Reagan revolution
  - **Conservative Sunbelt America**
  - **Jerry Falwell's Moral Majority**
  - **Opulence and poverty in the 1980s**
  - **AIDS**

CHAPTER 36
Cultural Politics

- America's changing face
  - **The new immigration**
  - **Demographic shifts**
  - **Access to the information revolution**
- Globalization and American labor
  - **Downsizing and the workforce**
- Dismantling affirmative action
  - ***Adarand Constructors* v. *Peña* (1995)**
  - ***Hopwood* v. *Texas* (1996)**
  - **Proposition 209 passes in California (1996)**

CHAPTER 30
The Fair Deal and Containment

- Racial integration — **Jackie Robinson and Major League Baseball (1947)**
- Anticommunist witch-hunts — **House Un-American Activities Committee (HUAC) (1947)**

CHAPTER 31
Through the Picture Window

- Consumer culture — **Television**, Advertising
- Culture of conformity — **Cult of feminine domesticity**, **Revival of religion in the 1950s**
- Alienation from the norm —
  - **Rock 'n' Roll**: Chuck Berry, Ray Charles, Ritchie Valens, Elvis Presley
  - **Theater**: Arthur Miller, Edward Albee, Tennessee Williams
  - **Literature**: J. D. Salinger, Norman Mailer, Joyce Carol Oates, John Updike
  - **Painting**: Jackson Pollock, Robert Motherwell, Willem de Kooning, Mark Rothko
  - **The Beats**: Jack Kerouac, Allen Ginsberg, William Burroughs, Gregory Corso

CHAPTER 32
Conflict and Deadlock

- The effects of the cold war — **Culture of suspicion: the Army-McCarthy hearings (June 1954)**; **The shock of Sputnik (1957)**

CHAPTER 33
New Frontiers

- The Kennedy style
- Sixties rebellion — **The impact of Kennedy's assassination**; **The culture of black power**; **Antiwar culture**

CHAPTER 34
Rebellion and Reaction in the 1960s and 1970s

- The New Left —
  - **Feminism**: Friedan, *The Feminine Mystique* (1963)
  - **The counterculture**: Timothy Leary; Woodstock (1969); The Pentagon Papers (1971)
- Impact of Watergate

CHAPTER 35
Conservative Insurgency

- The Reagan revolution — **Sunbelt America**; **Rise of the religious right**

CHAPTER 36
Cultural Politics

- Clinton's baby-boom administration — **The new immigration and multicultural America**; **The rise of computer culture**; Culture of the Internet

How did the cold war develop after World War II and how did it end?

CHAPTER 30
The Fair Deal and Containment
The cold war

- **Building the United Nations**
- **Conflict with Soviets: legacy of Yalta**
- **George F. Kennan: containment**
- **Truman Doctrine and Marshall Plan**
- **German division and the Berlin crisis**
- **Building NATO**
- **Communist triumph in China (1949)**
- **Soviet atomic bomb test; beginning of arms race (1949)**
- **Early U.S. involvement in Vietnam**
  - U.S. supports French against Vietnamese (1950)
- **War in Korea**
  - U.S. responds to N. Korean invasion of S. Korea
- McCarthyism

CHAPTER 31
Through the Picture Window
American abundance

- **Devastation of other industrial nations strengthens U.S. manufactures**
- **U.S. standard of living exceeds the rest of the world's**
  - With 6 percent of world's population, U.S. produces and consumes two-thirds of world's goods (1970)

CHAPTER 32
Conflict and Deadlock
The continuing cold war

- **Armistice in Korea**
- **Eisenhower and U.S. internal security**
- **John Foster Dulles's diplomacy of "brinksmanship"**
- **Arming for "massive retaliation"**
- **CIA interventions: Iran (1953), Guatemala (1954)**
- **Indochina**
  - The Geneva Accords (1954)
  - U.S. involvement in Vietnam (1950s)
- **Crisis in the Middle East**
- **Soviet repression in Hungary (1956)**
- **Sputnik: the first satellite in space (1957)**
- **Castro and the Cuban revolution (1959)**

CHAPTER 33
New Frontiers
Cuba and the United States

- **The Bay of Pigs (1961)**
- **The Cuban missile crisis (1962)**

Vietnam

- **Kennedy: an uncertain policy**
- **The Gulf of Tonkin incident (Aug. 1964)**
- **Johnson's policies in Vietnam**
- **The Tet offensive (1968): a turning point**

CHAPTER 34
Rebellion and Reaction in the 1960s and 1970s
Nixon, Kissinger, and Vietnam

- **Negotiation**
- **"Vietnamizing" the war**
- **The air war**
- **Peace treaty ends war between United States, North Vietnam (1973)**
- **North Vietnam overthrows government of South Vietnam (1975)**

Foreign policies of Nixon and Kissinger

- **Breakthrough with China**
- **Détente with the Soviet Union**
- **Diplomacy in the Middle East**

Ford, OPEC, and the Energy Crisis

Carter's policies abroad

- **Panama Canal Treaties**
- **Camp David Accords (1978)**
- **The SALT II treaty (1979)**
- **Soviets invade Afghanistan (1979)**
- **The Iran crisis (1979–1981)**

CHAPTER 35
Conservative Insurgency
Reagan's defense policies

- **Defense buildup: SDI**
- **U.S. support for the Nicaraguan Contras**
- **U.S. involvement in Lebanon**
- **Invasion of Grenada**
- **Arms control negotiations**
- **Iran-Contra Affair**
- **Treaty to eliminate intermediate-range missiles (1987)**

Democracy movements abroad

- **Protests and violence in Beijing's Tiananmen Square (1989)**
- **Collapse of Soviet Bloc in Eastern Europe (1989)**
- **Berlin Wall torn down (1989)**
- **The Gulf War (1990): U.S. response to Iraqi aggression**
- **The breakup of the Soviet Union (1991)**

CHAPTER 36
Cultural Politics
The post–cold war world

- **The Middle East peace process**
  - Assassination of Yitzhak Rabin (1995)
  - The Wye River Accord (1998)
- **The Balkans: "ethnic cleansing"**
- **Globalizing the economy**

CHAPTER

30

The Fair Deal and Containment

This chapter focuses on

- The economic, social, and political aftermath of World War II.
- The origins and early development of the cold war.
- Truman's Fair Deal program.
- U.S. involvement in the Korean War.
- The sources of McCarthyism.

THE *ESSENTIAL AMERICA* ON-LINE TUTOR

www.wwnorton.com/eamerica/ch30

- **Topic: The House Un-American Activities Committee**
  www.wwnorton.com/eamerica/ch30/topic.htm

  Beginning in 1939 and continuing through the early 1950s, Americans experienced the second Red Scare as the House Un-American Activities Committee (HUAC) worked to root out Communists in government and entertainment. Using testimony given before the committee, photographs, a sound recording, and historical analyses, study the significance of the HUAC. Why did a single congressional committee achieve such considerable influence in government and society?

- **Chapter review: On-line quiz and chapter summary**
  www.wwnorton.com/eamerica/ch30/review.htm

- **Chapter resources: Multimedia index**
  www.wwnorton.com/eamerica/ch30/media.htm

No sooner did the Second World War end than a cold war began. The uneasy wartime alliance between the United States and the Soviet Union disintegrated by the fall of 1945. The two strongest nations to emerge from the carnage of World War II could not bridge their ideological differences over human rights, individual liberties, and religious beliefs. Mutual suspicion and competitive efforts to gain influence over the so-called Third World countries further polarized the two nations. The defeat of Japan and Germany created power vacuums that sucked America and the Soviet Union into an unrelenting war of words fed by clashing strategic interests. At the same time, the destruction of western Europe and the exhaustion of its peoples led to anticolonial uprisings in Asia and Africa that threatened to strip Britain and France of their empires. The postwar world was thus an unstable one in which international tensions shaped the contours of domestic politics and culture as well as foreign adventures.

Demobilization under Truman

Truman's Uneasy Start

"Who the hell is Harry Truman?" Roosevelt's chief of staff asked the president in the summer of 1944. The question was on more lips when, after less than twelve weeks as vice-president, Harry Truman took the presidential oath on April 12, 1945.

Born in 1884 in western Missouri, Truman grew up in Independence, outside of Kansas City. During World War I, he served in France as captain of an artillery battery. Afterward, he started a clothing business, but it failed during the recession of 1922, and Truman then entered politics. In 1934 Missouri sent him to the United States Senate.

Something about Harry Truman evoked the spirit of Andrew Jackson: his decisiveness, feisty character, and family loyalty. On September 6, 1945, Truman sent Congress a comprehensive peacetime program that in effect proposed to continue and enlarge the New Deal. Its twenty-one points included expansion of unemployment insurance, a higher minimum wage, a permanent Fair Employment Practices Commission, slum clearance and low-rent housing projects, and a public works program. "Not even President Roosevelt asked for so much at one sitting," charged the House Republican leader. "It's just a plain case of out-dealing the New Deal." Truman, however, soon saw his new domestic proposals mired down in disputes over the transition to a peacetime economy.

Converting to Peace

After Japan's surrender, the public demanded that the president and Congress "bring the boys home" as soon as possible. By 1947 the total armed forces were down to 1.5 million from a wartime high of almost 12 million. By early 1950 the army had shrunk to 600,000.

The World War II veterans returned to schools, new jobs, wives, and babies. Population growth, which had dropped off sharply in the depression decade, now soared. Americans born during this postwar period comprised what came to be known as the baby-boom generation, an oversized population cohort that continues to exercise a disproportionate influence on American life.

The end of the war, with its sudden demobilization and reconversion to a peacetime economy, generated a wave of labor unrest and strikes but not the postwar depression that many feared. Several shock absorbers cushioned the economic impact of demobilization: unemployment pay and other Social Security benefits; the Servicemen's Readjustment Act of 1944, known as the "GI Bill of Rights," under which $13 billion was spent for veterans on education, vocational training, medical treatment, unemployment insurance, and loans for building houses or going into business; and, most important, the pent-up demand for consumer goods that was fueled by wartime shortages. Instead of sinking into depression after the war, the economy enjoyed a spurt of private investment in new industrial plants and equipment.

Controlling Inflation

The most acute economic problem was not depression but inflation. Released from wartime restraints, the demands of businesses for higher prices and of workers for higher wages frustrated Truman's efforts to stabilize the economy. He endorsed "reasonable" wage increases, which he thought businesses could absorb without raising prices, and which he considered necessary to sustain consumer purchasing power. Management, however, did not agree. Within six weeks of the war's end, corporations refused union demands for higher wages and better benefits, and a series of strikes followed in the automotive, steel, mining, petroleum, and railroad industries.

Truman resented what he considered to be excessive union demands, including a 30 percent wage boost. He used powers granted the chief executive during wartime to seize the mines and threatened to draft striking railroad workers into the armed forces. A strike in the steel industry finally gave rise to a formula for settling most of the disputes. President Truman suggested a pay raise of 18½¢ per hour, which the Steel Workers accepted but management refused. To break the logjam, the administration in 1946 agreed to let the steel companies increase their prices. That pattern then became the basis for settlements in other industries, setting a dangerous precedent of price-wage spirals that would plague consumers in the postwar world.

The wartime Office of Price Administration maintained some restraint on price increases while gradually ending the rationing of most goods, and Truman asked for a one-year renewal of its powers. But during the late winter and spring of 1946, business lobbyists mounted a massive campaign against price controls, and Truman allowed them to end. After the 1946 congressional elections, Truman gave up the battle against inflationary prices, ending all price controls except those on rents, sugar, and rice.

Partisan Conflict

As congressional elections approached in the fall of 1946, public discontent ran high, most of it directed against the administration. Truman caught the blame for labor problems from both sides. Union supporters tagged him "the No. 1 strikebreaker," while much of the public, angry at the striking unions, blamed the White House for the strikes. In 1946 Truman fired Henry A. Wallace as secretary of commerce in a disagreement over foreign policy, thus offending the Democratic left. At the same time, Republicans charged that Communists had infiltrated the government. In the midterm elections of 1946, Republicans won majorities in both houses of Congress for the first time since 1928.

With momentum building up against organized labor, the new Republican Congress quickly passed the Taft-Hartley Act of 1947 to curb the power of unions. It banned the closed shop (in which nonunion workers could not be hired) but permitted a union shop (in which workers newly hired were required to join the union), except where banned by state law. The anti-union legislation outlawed "featherbedding" (pay for work not done), established procedures to punish unions that refused to bargain in good faith, and restricted unions from contributing to political campaigns. Unions' political action committees were allowed to function only on a voluntary basis, and union leaders had to take oaths that they were not members of the Communist party. The act forbade strikes by federal employees, and it imposed a "cooling-off" period of eighty days on any strike that the president found to be dangerous to the national health or safety.

Truman vetoed the Taft-Hartley bill, which unions called the "slave-labor act." This restored his credit with labor and brought many unionists who had voted Republican in 1946 back to the Democratic fold. But Congress passed the controversial bill over Truman's veto. Its most severe impact probably was on "Operation Dixie," a drive for a more secure union foothold in the South. By 1954 fifteen states, mainly in the South, had used the Taft-Hartley Act's authority to pass "right-to-work" laws forbidding the union shop. These laws also eroded union strength in the North as many firms began to migrate to "right-to-work" states.

Truman clashed with the Republicans on other domestic issues, including a tax reduction. He vetoed a tax cut, arguing that in times of high production and employment the federal debt should be reduced. In 1948, however, Congress overrode his veto of a $5 billion tax cut at a time when government debt still ran high.

These conflicts between Truman and Congress obscured the high degree of bipartisan cooperation marking matters of governmental reorganization and foreign policy. In 1947 a bipartisan majority in Congress passed the National Security Act. It created a national military establishment, headed by a secretary of defense with subcabinet departments of army, navy, and air force, and a new National Security Council (NSC), which included the president, heads of the defense departments, and the secretary of state, among others. The act made permanent the Joint Chiefs of Staff, which had been a wartime innovation, and established the Central Intelligence Agency (CIA), to coordinate intelligence-gathering abroad.

The Cold War

Building the U.N.

On April 25, 1945, two weeks after Roosevelt's death and two weeks before the German surrender, delegates from fifty nations at war with the Axis met in San Francisco to draw up the charter of the United Nations (U.N.). Additional members could be admitted by a two-thirds vote of the General Assembly. This body, one of the two major agencies set up by the charter, included delegates from all member nations and was to meet annually in regular session to approve the budget, receive annual reports from U.N. agencies, and choose members of the Security Council and other bodies.

The Security Council, the other major charter agency, would remain in permanent session and would have "primary responsibility for the maintenance of international peace and security." Its eleven (after 1965, fifteen) members included six (later ten) members elected for two-year terms and five permanent members: the United States, the Soviet Union, Britain, France, and China. Each permanent member could veto any question of substance. The Security Council might investigate any dispute, recommend settlement or reference to another U.N. body—the International Court of Justice at the Hague, in the Netherlands—and take measures, including a resort to military force. The United States Senate, in sharp contrast to the reception it gave the League of Nations, ratified the U.N. charter by a vote of 89 to 2.

Differences with the Soviets

Since the end of World War II, historians have debated which side was more responsible for the onset of the cold war. The conventional or "orthodox" view declares that the Soviets, led by Joseph Stalin, a paranoid dictator, tried to dominate the globe, and the United States had no choice but to stand firm in defense of democratic capitalist values.

By contrast, those scholars known as "revisionists" argue that Truman and American economic imperialists were the culprits. Instead of maintaining Roosevelt's efforts to collaborate with Stalin and ensure the survival of the alliance after the war, these scholars assert, Truman adopted an unnecessarily belligerent stance and expansionist foreign policy that itself sought to create American spheres of influence around the world. He and his military advisers exaggerated the Soviet threat, in part to justify an American military buildup. Their provocative policies thus crystallized the tensions between the two countries. Yet such an interpretation fails to recognize that Truman inherited a deteriorating relationship with the Soviets. Events of 1945 made compromise and conciliation more and more difficult.

There were signs of trouble in the grand alliance as early as the spring of 1945, as the Soviet Union moved to set up compliant governments in eastern Europe, violating the Yalta Conference promises of democratic elections. On February 1 the Polish Committee of National Liberation, a puppet Soviet government, moved from Lublin to Warsaw. In March the Soviets installed a puppet premier in Romania. Protests against such actions led to Soviet counterprotests that the British and Americans were negotiating German surrender in Italy "behind the back of the Soviet Union."

Such was the atmosphere when Truman entered the White House. On May 12, 1945, four days after victory in Europe, Winston Churchill sent him a telegram: "What is to happen about Europe? An iron curtain is drawn down upon [the Russian] front. We do not know what is going on behind [it]." Nevertheless, as a gesture of goodwill, and over Churchill's protest, the American forces withdrew from the occupation zone in Germany assigned to the Soviet Union at Yalta. Americans still hoped that the Yalta agreements would be carried out, and they were even more eager to have Soviet help against Japan.

Although the Soviets admitted British and American observers to their sectors of eastern Europe, there was little the Western powers could have done to prevent Soviet control of the region even if they had kept up their military strength. The presence of Soviet armed forces frustrated the efforts of non-Communists in the eastern European countries to gain political influence. Opposition leaders were either exiled, silenced, executed, or imprisoned.

Secretary of State James F. Byrnes, who took office in 1945, adopted a confrontational stance with the Soviets. As early as April 1945, he had suggested to Truman that possession of the atomic bomb "might well put us in a position to dictate our own terms at the end of the war." After becoming secretary of state, he tried on several occasions to threaten Soviet diplomats with America's growing arsenal of nuclear weapons. But they paid little notice, and such attempts at intimidation were soon dropped.

The United States, Britain, and Canada (partners in developing the atomic bomb), proposed in 1946 to internationalize the control of atomic energy. Under the plan presented to the U.N. Atomic Energy Commission, an International Atomic Development Authority would have a monopoly of atomic explosives and atomic energy. The Soviets, fearing Western domination of the agency, proposed instead simply to outlaw the manufacture and use of atomic bombs, with enforcement vested in the Security Council and thus subject to a veto. Later they conceded the right of international inspection, but they still refused to give up the veto. The American government rejected the arrangement, which it considered a compromise of international control.

Containment

By the beginning of 1947, relations with the Soviet Union had become even more troubled. The year before, Stalin had already pronounced international peace impossible "under the present capitalistic development of the world economy." George F. Kennan, counselor of the American Embassy in Moscow, predicted that the Soviets would try to fill "every nook and cranny available . . . in the basin of world power." Therefore, he insisted, the United States must pursue "a long-term, patient but firm and vigilant *containment* of Russian expansive tendencies."

Kennan's "containment" concept lay behind the new departure in foreign policy that America's political leaders had already decided to take. The containment strategy reflected a growing fear that Soviet aims reached beyond eastern Europe, posing dangers in the eastern Mediterranean, the Middle East, and western Europe itself. After the war, the Soviet Union began to press Turkey for territorial concessions and the right to build naval bases on the Bosporus, an important gateway between the Black Sea and the Mediterranean. In 1946 civil war broke out in neighboring Greece between a British-backed government and a Communist-led faction that held the northern part of Greece. In 1947 the British ambassador informed the American government that the British could no longer bear the economic and military burden of aiding Greece and suggested that the United States assume the responsibility.

The Truman Doctrine and the Marshall Plan

On March 12, 1947, Truman asked Congress for $400 million in economic and military aid to Greece and Turkey. In his speech to

Congress, the president announced what quickly became known as the Truman Doctrine. Although intended as a response to a specific crisis, its rhetoric was dangerously universal. "I believe," Truman declared, "that it must be the policy of the United States to support free peoples who are resisting attempted subjugation by armed minorities or by outside pressures." In 1947 Congress passed the Greek-Turkish aid bill, and by 1950 had spent $659 million on the program. Turkey achieved economic stability, and Greece defeated the Communist insurrection in 1949.

But such immediate gains created long-term problems. For the Truman Doctrine marked the beginning of a contest that soon was labeled "a cold war." Greece and Turkey were but the front lines of an ideological struggle for world power and influence between East and West. That struggle quickly focused on western Europe, where wartime damage had devastated factory production, and a severe drought in 1947, followed by a harsh winter, had destroyed crops. In Berlin, people were freezing or starving to death. The transportation system in Europe was in shambles. Bridges were out, canals clogged, and rail networks destroyed. Amid the chaos, the Communist parties of France and Italy were flourishing.

In the spring of 1947, George C. Marshall, who had replaced James Byrnes as secretary of state, called for a program of massive aid to rescue western Europe from disaster and possible Communist subversion. "Our policy," he pledged, "is directed not against country or doctrine, but against hunger, poverty, desperation, and chaos." Marshall offered aid to all European countries, including the Soviet Union, but Moscow refused to participate in the "imperialist" scheme.

Soon after the war ended, the former leaders of Hitler's Third Reich were put on trial in Nuremberg, Germany, for war crimes. The Nuremberg trial was conducted by a joint United States-British-French-Soviet military tribunal.

In late 1947 Truman submitted his proposal for the European Recovery Program to Congress. Two months later, a Communist coup d'état in Czechoslovakia ended the last remaining coalition government in eastern Europe. The Communist seizure of power in Prague assured congressional passage of the Marshall Plan, which from 1948 until 1951 provided $13 billion to promote European recovery.

Dividing Germany

The breakdown of the wartime alliance left the problem of postwar Germany unsettled, and tensions between the Soviets and Americans over how best to reconstruct and administer Germany fed much of the suspicions animating the cold war. The German economy had stagnated, requiring the American army to carry a staggering burden of relief. Slowly, occupation zones evolved into functioning governments. In 1948 the British, French, and Americans merged their zones, and the West Germans then elected delegates to a federal constitutional convention.

The Soviets opposed the Marshall Plan and the unification of West Germany. The dispute with the Western Allies over the fate of Germany soon focused on Berlin, situated deep in the Soviet occupation zone. The city was divided in half, with the western side administered by the United States, France, and Great Britain. In April 1948 the Soviets began to restrict the flow of traffic into West Berlin; on June 23 they stopped all traffic. The Soviets hoped the blockade would force the Allies to give up either Berlin or the plan to unify West Germany. But the American commander in Germany proposed to stand firm. "If we mean . . . to hold Europe against communism," he told his superiors at the Pentagon, "we must not budge."

Truman agreed. After considering the use of armed convoys to supply West Berlin, he opted for a massive airlift. The Allied air forces brought in planes from around the world, and soon they were flying in nearly 5,000 tons of food and coal a day. Altogether, from June 1948 to mid-May 1949, the Berlin Airlift provided more than 1.5 million tons of supplies, or well over a half ton for each of the 2.2 million West Berliners.

Finally, on May 12, 1949, after extended talks, the Soviets lifted the blockade. Before the end of the year, the German Federal Republic in West Germany had a functioning government. At the end of May 1949, a German "Democratic" Republic arose in the Soviet-dominated eastern zone, dividing Germany into two independent states.

Building NATO

As relations between the Soviets and western Europe chilled, transatlantic unity ripened into an outright military alliance. At the end of 1947, Ernest Bevin, the British foreign secretary, told U.S. secretary of state George Marshall that the Soviet Union "will not deal with the West on any reasonable terms in the foreseeable future." Bevin therefore proposed that the United States and the European democracies form a defensive military alliance.

On April 4, 1949, diplomats signed the North Atlantic Treaty in Washington. Twelve nations were represented: the United States, Britain, France, Belgium, the Netherlands, Luxembourg, Canada, Denmark, Iceland, Italy, Norway, and Portugal. Greece and Turkey joined the alliance in 1952, West Germany in 1955, and Spain in 1982. The treaty pledged that an attack against any one of the signers would be considered an attack against all, and it provided for a council of the North Atlantic Treaty Organization (NATO), which could establish other necessary agencies.

The eventful year 1948 produced one other foreign policy decision with long-term consequences. Late in 1947 the U.N. General Assembly voted to partition Palestine into Jewish and Arab states. Despite fierce Arab opposition, Jewish leaders proclaimed the independence of the new state of Israel on May 14, 1948.

The Berlin Airlift. An American airplane arrives in West Berlin with much-needed supplies, 1948.

The neighboring Arab states thereupon went to war against Israel. The outnumbered Israelis held their own, with steadfast American support. U.N. mediators gradually worked out truce agreements with Israel's Arab neighbors that restored an uneasy peace by May 11, 1949, when Israel was admitted as a member of the United Nations. But the mutual hatred and intermittent warfare between Israel and the Arab states have festered ever since, complicating American foreign policy, which has tried to maintain friendship with both sides while insisting on the legitimacy of the Israeli nation.

Harry Gives 'Em Hell

Civil Rights during the 1940s

The social tremors triggered by World War II and the onset of the cold war transformed America's racial landscape. The vicious racism of the German Nazis, Italian fascists, and Japanese imperialists focused attention on the need for the United States to improve its own race relations and to provide for equal rights under the law.

For most of his political career, Harry Truman had shown little concern about the plight of African Americans. He had grown up assuming that both blacks and whites preferred to be segregated from one another. As president, however, he began to reassess his beliefs.

In the fall of 1946, Truman hosted a delegation of civil rights activists who graphically described incidents of torture and intimidation against blacks in the South. Truman was aghast. Two months later, he appointed a Committee on Civil Rights to investigate violence against African Americans and to recommend preventive measures. The committee recommended the renewal of the Fair Employment Practices Committee (FEPC) and the creation of a permanent civil rights commission to investigate abuses. It also argued that federal aid be denied to any state that mandated segregated schools and public facilities.

On July 26, 1948, Truman banned racial discrimination in the hiring of federal employees. Four days later, he issued an Executive Order ending racial segregation in the armed forces. Desegregating the military was, Truman claimed, "the greatest thing that ever happened to America."

Jackie Robinson, 1949. In 1947 Jackie Robinson of the Brooklyn Dodgers became the first African American to play major league baseball.

Meanwhile, racial segregation was being confronted in a much more public field of endeavor—professional baseball. In April 1947, as the baseball season opened, the National League's Brooklyn Dodgers included on their roster the first black player to cross the color line in major league baseball: Jackie Robinson. Robinson was an army veteran and baseball player in the Negro leagues. Branch Rickey, president of the Dodgers, selected Robinson to integrate professional baseball not only for his athletic potential but because of his willingness to control his temper in the face of virulent racism. Teammates and opposing players viciously baited Robinson, and spectators booed and taunted him in every city. Hotels refused him rooms, and restaurants denied him service. On the other hand, black spectators were electrified by Robinson's courageous example. They turned out in droves at baseball games to see him play.

Robinson was named Rookie of the Year in 1947, and as time passed, he won over many fans and opposing players through his quiet courage, self-deprecating wit, and determined performance. Soon, other teams began to sign black players. Jackie Robinson vividly demonstrated that racism, not inferiority, impeded African-American advancement in the postwar era and that segregation need not be a permanent condition of American life.

Truman's Agenda

Just as some of the owners of professional sports teams were slowly desegregating their teams, so Truman was also making efforts to desegregate the federal workforce. But while some people found his civil rights initiatives laudatory, others were appalled.

Liberals felt his solutions were too conservative. Southern Democrats resented his attempts to shake up the status quo.

After three years in the White House, Truman had yet to overcome the impression that he was not up to the job of leading the country. But he had a game plan for the 1948 campaign. His advisers knew that to win another presidential term he needed the support of the midwestern and western farm belts. In metropolitan areas he needed to carry the labor and the black vote, which Truman wooed by working closely with unions and pressing the cause of civil rights. Truman's advisers counted on the Solid South to stay in the Democratic column. With the South and West supporting him, Truman could afford to lose some Democratic liberals alienated by what they deemed Truman's social conservatism and still win. This strategy erred chiefly in underrating the rebellion that would take four Deep South states out of Truman's camp because of his support for civil rights.

The 1948 Election

Scenting victory in November, Republican delegates again nominated Thomas Dewey, former New York governor. The platform endorsed most of the New Deal reforms as an accomplished fact and approved the administration's bipartisan foreign policy, but as Alf Landon had in 1936, Dewey promised to run things more efficiently.

In July a glum Democratic convention gathered in Philadelphia, expecting to do little more than go through the motions, only to find itself doubly surprised: first by the battle over the civil rights plank, and then by Truman's acceptance speech. To keep from stirring southern hostility, the administration sought a platform plank that opposed racial discrimination only in general terms. Activists, however, sponsored a plank that called on Congress for specific action and commended Truman "for his courageous stand on the issue of civil rights." After the convention nominated Truman, the president delivered a rousing, combative address, unlike most of his earlier speeches, which he usually read in a flat drone. Near the end he dropped a bombshell. He would call Congress back into session "to get the laws the people need."

Truman's support of civil rights for African Americans had its political costs, as this 1948 cartoon suggests.

A group of rebellious southern Democrats, miffed by Truman's civil rights plank, met in Birmingham, Alabama, and nominated South Carolina governor J. Strom Thurmond on a States' Rights Democratic ticket, quickly dubbed the "Dixiecrat" party. The Dixiecrats sought to draw enough electoral votes to preclude a majority for either major party, throwing the election into the House, where they might strike a sectional bargain. A few days later, the left wing of the Democratic party gathered in Philadelphia to name Henry A. Wallace on a Progressive party ticket. These splits in the Democratic ranks seemed to spell the final blow to Truman. The special session of Congress petered out in futility.

But Truman, undaunted, set out on a 31,000-mile "whistle-stop" train tour during which he castigated the "do-nothing" Eightieth Congress, provoking cries from his audiences: "Give 'em hell, Harry." Truman responded: "I don't give 'em hell. I just tell the truth and they think it's hell." Dewey, in contrast, ran a restrained campaign designed to avoid controversy. By so doing, he may have snatched defeat from the jaws of victory.

To the end, the polls and the pundits predicted a sure win for Dewey. But on election day Truman chalked up the biggest upset in

American history, taking 24 million votes (49.5 percent) to Dewey's 22 million (45.1 percent) and winning a thumping 303 to 189 margin in the electoral college. Thurmond and Wallace each got more than a million votes, but the revolt of right and left worked to Truman's advantage. The Dixiecrat rebellion reassured black voters who had questioned the Democrats' commitment to civil rights, while the Progressive movement, which had received support from the Communist party, made it hard to tag Truman as "soft on communism." Strom Thurmond, the Dixiecrat candidate, carried four Deep South states, and his success started a momentous disruption of the Democratic party's hold over the Solid South. But Truman's victory also carried Democratic majorities into Congress.

Truman viewed his upset victory as a vindication for the New Deal and a mandate for liberalism. His State of the Union message repeated the agenda he had set forth a year previously. "Every segment of our population and every individual," he stressed, "has a right to expect from his government a fair deal." Whether deliberately or not, he had invented a tag, the "Fair Deal," to distinguish his program from the New Deal.

Congress passed some of Truman's Fair Deal proposals, but they were mainly extensions or enlargements of New Deal programs already in place: a higher minimum wage, a broadening of Social Security recipients, extension of rent controls, farm price supports, a sizable slum-clearance and public housing program, and more money for the TVA, rural electrification, and farm housing. Despite Democratic majorities in Congress, however, the conservative coalition disdained any drastic new departures in domestic policy. Congress balked at civil rights bills, national health insurance, federal aid to education, and a plan to provide subsidies that would hold up farm incomes rather than farm prices. Congress also turned down Truman's demand for repeal of the anti-union Taft-Hartley Act.

The Cold War Heats Up

Global concerns, never far from center stage in the postwar world, plagued Truman's second term, as they had his first. People began to live in real fear that the Communists were infiltrating American society and were intent upon world domination. In his inaugural address, Truman called for an anti-Communist foreign policy resting on four pillars: the United Nations, the Marshall Plan, NATO, and a "bold new plan" for technical assistance to underdeveloped parts of the world, a sort of global Marshall Plan that came to be known simply as "Point Four." This program to aid the postwar world never accomplished its goals, in part because other international problems soon diverted Truman's attention.

"Losing" China and the Bomb

One of the most intractable problems, the China tangle, was fast coming unraveled in 1949. The Chinese Nationalists (Kuomintang) of Chiang Kai-shek had been fighting Mao Tse-tung* and the Communists since the 1920s. The outbreak of war with Japan in 1937 halted the civil war, and both Roosevelt and Stalin believed that the Nationalists would organize China after the war.

The commanders of American forces in China during World War II, however, concluded that Chiang's government had become hopelessly corrupt, tyrannical, and inefficient. U.S. policy during and immediately after the war was to promote peace between the factions in China. But when the civil war resumed in 1945, American forces ferried nationalist armies back into the eastern and northern provinces as the Japanese withdrew.

*The traditional (Wade-Giles) spellings are used in this text. After Mao's death, the Chinese government adopted the "Pinyin" transliterations that are widely used today: Mao Tse-tung became Mao Zedong; and Peking became Beijing.

It soon became a losing fight for the Nationalists, as the Communists radicalized the land-hungry peasantry. By late 1948, Mao's forces were in Peking and heading southward. A year later they had taken the port city of Canton, and the Nationalist government had fled to the island of Formosa, which it renamed Taiwan.

From 1945 through 1949, the United States funneled some $2 billion in aid to the Nationalists, to no avail. Administration critics asked bitterly: "Who lost China?" and a State Department report blamed Chiang for his failure to hold the support of the Chinese people. In fact it is hard to imagine how the United States government could have prevented the outcome short of military intervention, which would have been very risky, quite costly, and exceedingly unpopular. The United States continued to recognize the Nationalist government on Taiwan as the rightful government of China, delaying formal relations with "Red" China for thirty years.

As the Communists secured control in China, American analysts in 1949 found evidence that the Soviets had set off an atomic explosion. The discovery led Truman in 1950 to order the construction of a hydrogen bomb, a weapon far more powerful than the Hiroshima bomb. The National Security Council recommended rebuilding conventional military forces to provide options other than nuclear war. This represented a major departure from America's time-honored aversion to keeping large standing armies in peacetime, and it was an expensive proposition. But the American public was growing more receptive to the nation's role as world leader, and an invasion of South Korea by Communist forces from the North clinched the issue for most.

War in Korea

The Japanese had occupied Korea during World War II, and after their defeat and withdrawal, the victorious Allies faced the difficult task of creating a new nation. Complicating that task was the fact that Soviet troops had advanced into northern Korea and had accepted the surrender of Japanese forces above the 38th parallel, while American forces did the same south of the line. The Soviets quickly organized a Korean government along Stalinist lines, while the Americans set up a Western-style regime in the South.

By the end of 1948, separate regimes had appeared in the two sectors and occupation forces had withdrawn. The weakened state of the demobilizing U.S. military helped convince the Communists that South Korea was vulnerable. Believing that the United States would not intervene, Stalin encouraged the North Koreans to use force to unify their country.

North Korean forces crossed the 38th parallel on June 25, 1950, and swept down the peninsula. President Truman told Congress that the North Korean attack was directed by Moscow and was brazen evidence "that communism has passed beyond the use of subversion to conquer independent nations and will now use armed invasion and war."

An emergency meeting of the U.N. Security Council quickly censured the North Korean "breach of peace." The Soviet delegate, who held a veto power, was at the time boycotting the council because it would not seat Communist China in place of Nationalist China. On June 27, the Security Council called on U.N. members to "repel the armed attack" against South Korea and "restore international peace and security in the area."

Truman ordered American air, naval, and ground forces into action. Even-

A mushroom cloud rises into the sky following the test detonation by the United States of an 11-megaton nuclear device over Bikini Atoll.

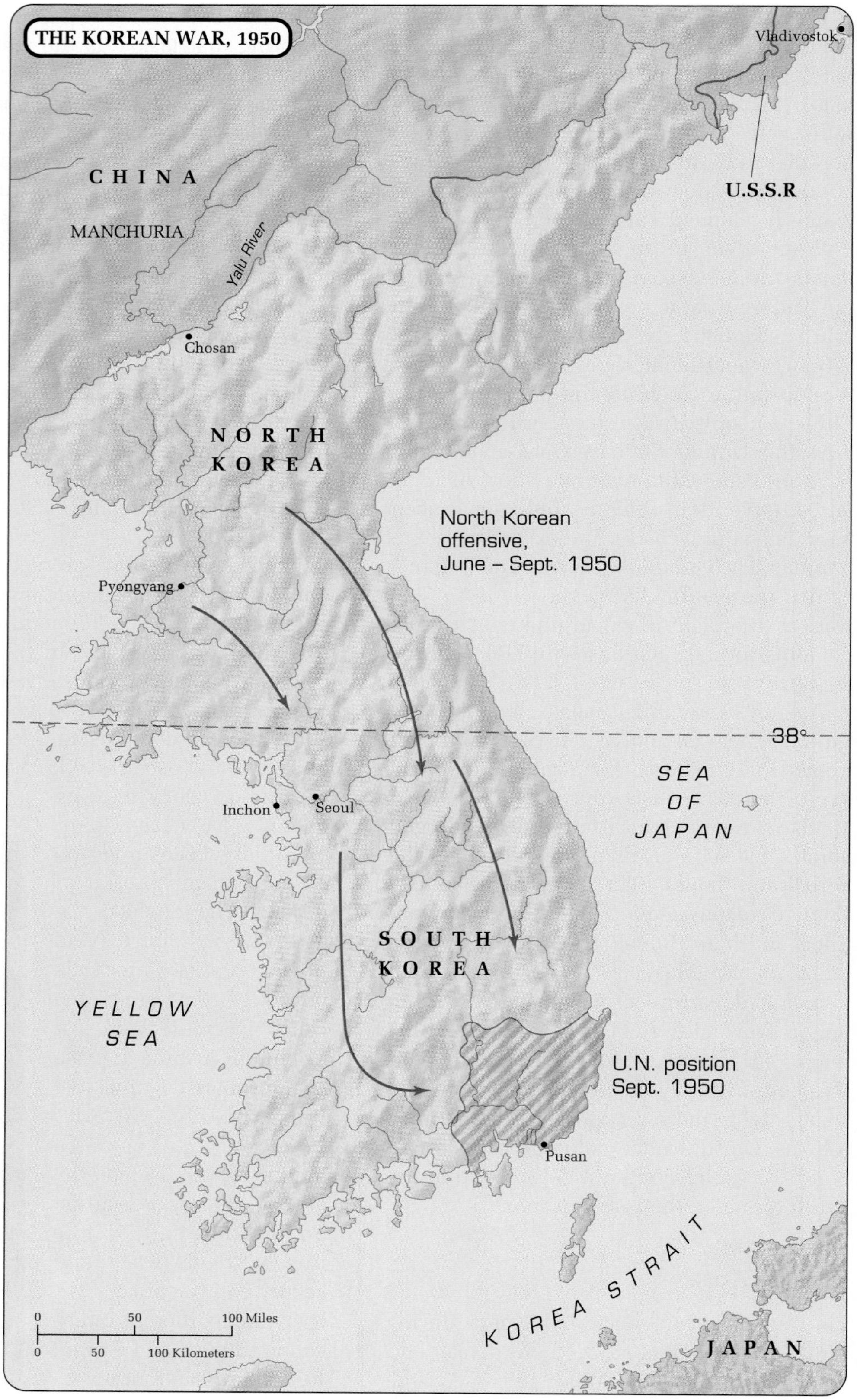
THE KOREAN WAR, 1950
Vladivostok
CHINA
MANCHURIA
Yalu River
U.S.S.R
Chosan
NORTH KOREA
North Korean offensive, June – Sept. 1950
Pyongyang
38°
SEA OF JAPAN
Inchon
Seoul
SOUTH KOREA
YELLOW SEA
U.N. position Sept. 1950
Pusan
KOREA STRAIT
JAPAN
0 50 100 Miles
0 50 100 Kilometers

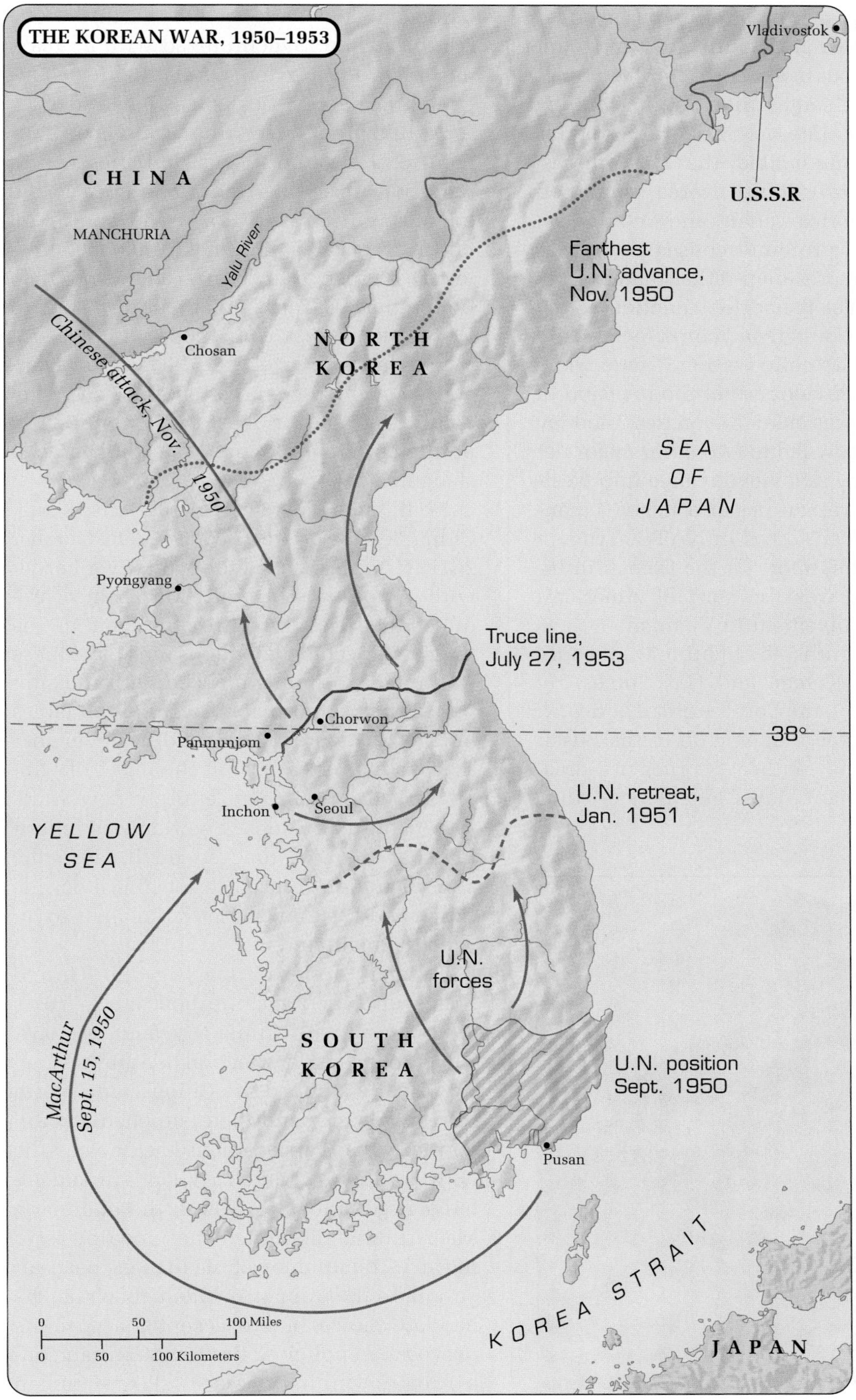
THE KOREAN WAR, 1950–1953
Vladivostok
CHINA
MANCHURIA
Yalu River
U.S.S.R
Farthest U.N. advance, Nov. 1950
Chosan
Chinese attack, Nov. 1950
NORTH KOREA
SEA OF JAPAN
Pyongyang
Truce line, July 27, 1953
Chorwon
Panmunjom
38°
U.N. retreat, Jan. 1951
Inchon
Seoul
YELLOW SEA
U.N. forces
MacArthur Sept. 15, 1950
SOUTH KOREA
U.N. position Sept. 1950
Pusan
KOREA STRAIT
JAPAN
0 50 100 Miles
0 50 100 Kilometers

tually American forces numbered over 350,000, while the South Koreans contributed 400,000. In all, some fourteen other U.N. members sent military units totaling about 50,000 people. General Douglas MacArthur commanded the U.N. forces. The defense of South Korea remained chiefly an American affair, and one that set a precedent of profound consequence: war by order of the president rather than by vote of Congress. Yet it had the sanction of the U.N. Security Council and could technically be considered a "police action," not a war.

Truman's conviction that the invasion of South Korea was actually orchestrated by Stalin in Moscow led to two other major decisions. Fearing a Soviet advance into western Europe, Truman began a major expansion of American forces in NATO. Truman also increased support for the French in Indochina. This was the start of America's deepening involvement in Vietnam.

For three months, the fighting went badly for the South Korean and U.N. forces. By September 1950, the South Korean and U.N. forces were barely hanging on to the Pusan perimeter in the southeast corner of Korea. Then, in a brilliant ploy, General MacArthur landed a new force to the North Korean rear at Inchon. Synchronized with a breakout from Pusan, the sudden blow stampeded the enemy back across the border.

At this point, MacArthur convinced Truman to allow him to push on and seek to reunify Korea. American forces crossed the boundary into North Korea and continued northward against minimal resistance. President Truman, concerned about possible Communist Chinese intervention, flew to Wake Island for a conference with General MacArthur on October 15. There the general discounted chances that the Red Army would act, but if it did, he confidently predicted, "there would be the greatest slaughter."

That same day Peking announced that China "cannot stand idly by." On October 26, U.N. units reached the Yalu River border with Communist China. MacArthur predicted total victory by Christmas, but on the night of November 25, thousands of Chinese "volunteers" counterattacked with the support of tanks and planes, turning the tables on the U.N. forces and sending them into a desperate retreat just at the onset of winter. It had become "an entirely new war," MacArthur concluded. Soon he was reporting that the war dragged on because the administration refused to let him blockade China and use Taiwanese Nationalists to invade the mainland.

Truman opposed leading the United States into the "gigantic booby trap" of a ground war with China. By January 1951, U.N. troops under General Matthew Ridgway finally stopped the Chinese and North Korean advance and then launched a counterattack that carried them back across the 38th parallel in March. When Truman offered negotiations to restore the boundary, MacArthur undermined the move by issuing an ultimatum for China to make peace or be attacked. Truman decided then that he had no choice but to accept MacArthur's provocative policy or fire him. Civilian control of the military was at stake, Truman

U. N. forces recapture Seoul from the North Koreans, September 1950.

later asserted. On April 11, 1951, with the backing of the Joint Chiefs of Staff, the president removed MacArthur from all his commands and replaced him with Matthew Ridgway.

Truman's action set off an uproar across the country, and a tumultuous reception greeted MacArthur upon his return home for the first time since 1937. His dramatic speech to a joint session of Congress provided the climactic event. "Once war is forced upon us," he maintained, "there is no alternative than to apply every available means to bring it to a swift end." A Senate investigation brought out the administration's arguments, best summarized by General Omar Bradley, chairman of the Joint Chiefs of Staff. The MacArthur strategy "would involve us in the wrong war at the wrong place at the wrong time and with the wrong enemy."

On June 24, 1951, the Soviet representative at the United Nations proposed a cease-fire and armistice along the 38th parallel, and a few days later Secretary of State Dean Acheson accepted. China and North Korea responded favorably—at the time General Ridgway's "meat-grinder" offensive was inflicting severe losses. Truce talks started in July, only to drag out for another two years while the fighting continued. The chief snags were prisoner exchanges and the insistence of South Korea's president on unification.

By the time a truce was finally reached on July 27, 1953, Truman had relinquished the White House to Dwight D. Eisenhower. No final peace conference ever took place, and Korea, like Germany, remained divided. The war had cost the United States more than 33,000 deaths and 103,000 wounded or missing. South Korean casualties, all told, were about 1 million, and North Korean and Chinese casualties totaled an estimated 1.5 million.

The Korean War was the first military clash of the cold war and the first limited war of the nuclear age. It was the first time that the United States fought against Communist China, and the first war conducted by the United Nations. The Korean War caused the United States to bolster its military strength. During the early 1950s, the defense budget quadrupled. The war also accelerated the racial integration of the armed forces and in the process helped set the stage for the civil rights movement.

Another Red Scare

In calculating the costs of the Korean War, one must add in the far-reaching consequences of the second Red Scare. Fear of Communist subversion had become the domestic counterpart to the fear of aggression abroad, and it reached a crescendo during the Korean conflict. Since 1938, the House Un-American Activities Committee (HUAC) had kept up a barrage of accusations about pro-Communist subversives in government.

The case most embarrassing to the administration involved Alger Hiss, president of the Carnegie Endowment for International Peace, who had served in several government departments, including the State Department. Whittaker Chambers, a former Soviet agent and later an editor of *Time* magazine, told the House Un-American Activities Committee in 1948 that Hiss had given him secret documents ten years earlier, when Chambers worked as an agent for the Soviets. Hiss sued for libel, and Chambers produced microfilms of the State Department documents he claimed Hiss had passed on to him. Hiss denied the accusation, whereupon he was indicted for perjury and, after one mistrial, convicted in 1950. The charge was perjury, but he was convicted of lying about espionage—for which he could not be tried because the statute of limitations on the crime had expired.

Most damaging to the administration was the fact that President Truman, taking at face value the many testimonials to Hiss's integrity, called the charges against him a "red herring." Secretary of State Dean Acheson compounded the damage when, meaning to express compassion, he pledged not "to turn my back on Alger Hiss." The Hiss affair had another political consequence: it raised to national prominence a young California congressman, Richard M. Nixon, who doggedly insisted on pursuing the case and then exploited an anti-Communist stance to win election to the Senate in 1950.

More cases of Communist infiltration surfaced. In 1950 the government disclosed the existence of a British-American spy network that had fed information about the development of the atomic bomb to the Soviet Union. These disclosures led to the arrest of, among others, Julius and Ethel Rosenberg, who were convicted of espionage in wartime and executed in 1953.

McCarthy's Witch-hunt

Such revelations encouraged politicians in both parties to exploit public fears of communist subversion. And recent discoveries document that Soviet agents had indeed penetrated deeply into American life, government, science, and industry.

Early in 1950 a hitherto obscure Republican senator from Wisconsin, Joseph R. McCarthy, suddenly surfaced as the shrewdest and most ruthless exploiter of anti-Communist anxieties. He began with a speech in which he claimed that the State Department was infested with Communists and that he held in his hand a list of their names.

Challenged to provide the names, McCarthy finally pointed to Owen Lattimore of the Johns Hopkins University, an Asia expert, as head of "the espionage ring in the State Department." A special Senate committee looked into the matter and pronounced McCarthy's charges "a fraud and a hoax." But Republicans encouraged him to keep up the game. By 1951 he was riding so high as to list Generals George C. Marshall and Dwight D. Eisenhower among the disloyal. McCarthy kept up his campaign until the end of the Korean War, but he never uncovered a single Communist agent in government.

Under the influence of the anti-Communist hysteria, the Congress in 1950 passed the McCarran Internal Security Act over President Truman's veto. The act required Communist and Communist-front organizations to register with the attorney-general. Aliens who had belonged to totalitarian parties were barred from admission to the United States.

Assessing the Cold War

In retrospect, the onset of the cold war takes on an appearance of terrible inevitability. America's preference for international principles such as free elections conflicted with Stalin's preference for controlling his neighbors. Russia, after all, had suffered two massive German invasions in the first half of the twentieth century, and Soviet leaders wanted compliant buffer states on their borders for protection. The people of eastern Europe, as usual, were caught in the middle. But the Communists themselves held to a universal principle: world revolution.

To create a defensive shield against the spread of communism, the United States signed mutual defense treaties. Under the Treaty of Rio de Janeiro, the nations of the Western Hemisphere agreed to aid any country in the region that was attacked. In 1951, the United States and Japan signed a treaty that permitted the United States to maintain military forces in Japan. That same year, American negotiators signed other mutual defense treaties with the Philippines, Australia, and New Zealand.

If international conditions set the stage for the cold war, the actions of political leaders and thinkers set events in motion. President Truman may have erred in suggesting that the United States must intervene anywhere in the world to stop the tide of Communist aggression. His failure to challenge McCarthy, and his own efforts to uncover Communists through a "loyalty program," may have heightened the anti-Communist hysteria of the times.

The policy initiatives of the Truman years had led the country to abandon its long-standing aversion to peacetime alliances and committed it to a major and permanent national military establishment. By 1952 this newly entrenched sector of the government included the National Security Council, the Central Intelligence Agency, and the enormous National Security Agency, entrusted with the monitoring of foreign media and communications. It was a far cry from the world of 1796, when George Washington in his farewell address warned against "those overgrown military establishments which . . . are inauspicious to liberty" and advised his country "to steer clear of permanent alliances with any portion of the foreign world." But, then, Washington had warned only against participation in the "ordinary" combinations and collisions of Europe, and surely the postwar years had seen extraordinary events and unprecedented combinations.

CHAPTER

31

Through the Picture Window: Society and Culture, 1945–1960

Refrigerator-Freezers!
THE FINAL FROST BARRIER
IT'S HERE!
A FROST-PROOF
FOOD FREEZER!
NO FROST!
NO FROST-LOCK
FOODS!
NO DEFROSTING

This chapter focuses on

- American prosperity in the postwar period.
- Social life of the 1950s, with its strains of conformity and innovation.
- America's burgeoning consumer culture.

THE *ESSENTIAL AMERICA* ON-LINE TUTOR

www.wwnorton.com/eamerica/ch31

- **Topic: Conformity in the 1950s**
  www.wwnorton.com/eamerica/ch31/topic.htm

  The postwar years ushered in an era of conformity in lifestyles, social habits, customs, and housing as the nation moved from 1940s originality to 1950s convention. Using speeches by prominent politicians, photographs, documents regarding housing, and historical analyses, explore the significance of the postwar years. How did the transition from the ideal of Rosie the Riveter to that of the perfect homemaker affect Americans?

- **Chapter review: On-line quiz and chapter summary**
  www.wwnorton.com/eamerica/ch31/review.htm

- **Chapter resources: Multimedia index**
  www.wwnorton.com/eamerica/ch31/media.htm

Americans emerged from World War II elated, proud of their military strength and industrial might. As the editors of *Fortune* magazine proclaimed in 1946, "This is a dream era, this is what everyone was waiting through the blackouts for. The Great American Boom is on." So it was that people who had known deprivation and sacrifice for the past decade and a half began to enjoy unprecedented prosperity.

Yet in the midst of such rising affluence and optimism, many social critics, writers, and artists expressed a growing sense of unease. Was postwar American society becoming too complacent, too conformist, too materialistic? These questions reflected the perennial tension in American life between idealism and materialism, a tension that arrived with the first settlers and remains with us today. Americans have always struggled to accumulate goods on the one hand and cultivate goodness on the other. During the postwar era, the nation tried to do both. For a while, at least, it appeared to succeed.

People of Plenty

The dominant feature of post–World War II American society was its remarkable prosperity. After a surprisingly brief postwar recession, the economy soared to record heights. By 1970, the gap between living standards in the United States and the rest of the world had become a chasm: with 6 percent of the world's population, Americans produced and consumed nearly two-thirds of the world's goods. Such abundance generated a mood of giddy optimism. The expectation of unending plenty became the reigning assumption of social thought in the two decades after 1945.

Several factors contributed to this sustained economic surge. The massive federal expenditures for military needs during World War II had catapulted the economy out of the depression. High government spending continued to drive the postwar economy, thanks to the tensions generated by the cold war and the increase in defense spending provoked by the Korean conflict. Military-related research also helped spawn the new glamour industries of the postwar era: chemicals, electronics, plastics, and aviation.

The other major industrial nations of the world—England, France, Germany, Japan, the Soviet Union—had been physically devastated during the war, which meant that American manufacturers enjoyed a virtual monopoly over international trade. In addition, the widespread use of more efficient machinery and computers led to a 35 percent jump in the productivity of American workers between 1945 and 1955.

The major catalyst in promoting economic expansion after 1945, however, was the unleashing of pent-up consumer demand. During the war, Americans had postponed purchases of major items such as cars and houses and in the process had saved over $150 billion. Now they were eager to buy. The United States after World War II thus experienced a buying frenzy.

The GI Bill of Rights

Part of the surge in consumption was financed by the federal government. People feared that a sharp drop in military spending and the sudden influx of veterans back into the civilian workforce would send the economy into a downward spiral and produce widespread unemployment. Such concerns led Congress to pass the Servicemen's Readjustment Act of 1944. Popularly known as the GI Bill of Rights (GI meant "government issue," a phrase stamped on military uniforms and also slang for a serviceman), it led to the creation of a new government agency, the Veterans Administration. The GI Bill also included provisions for mustering-out pay, unemployment pay for one year, preference for veterans seeking civil service jobs, loans for home construction, access to government hospitals, and generous subsidies for college or professional training.

The infusion of funds into the economy provided by the GI Bill helped fuel the postwar prosperity. Almost 8 million veterans took advantage of $14.5 billion in subsidies to attend college or to enroll in job training programs. Some 5 million people used additional monies from the GI Bill to buy new homes. These two programs combined to produce a social revolution.

The GI Bill democratized higher education. It provided a generation of working-class Americans with an opportunity to earn a college degree for the first time. In turn, a college education served as a lever into the middle class and economic security. But while the GI Bill helped erode class barriers, it was less successful in dismantling racial barriers. Many black veterans could not take equal advantage of the education benefits. Most colleges and universities after the war remained racially segregated, either by regulation or by practice.

The historically black colleges, most of which were in the South, could not expand quickly enough to meet the demand. In 1940 black colleges enrolled 43,000 students; in 1950 the number had soared to 77,000. Yet over 20,000 were denied admission because of overcrowded facilities. As a result, most black veterans did not get into a college. In 1946 only one-fifth of the 100,000 who had applied for educational benefits had enrolled. In other cases, black veterans were inadequately prepared for college-level work. As late as 1950, some 70 percent of black adults in the southern states had only a seventh-grade education or less.

The return of some 12 million veterans to private life also helped generate the postwar "baby boom," which peaked in 1957. Between 1946 and 1964, America's total population grew by almost 40 million, a 30 percent increase. Such a dramatic growth rate had a host of reverberating effects. Initially the postwar baby boom created a massive demand for diapers, baby food, toys, medicines, schools, books, teachers, furniture, and housing. It also spurred the growth of new suburban communities as the burgeoning population moved from the cities into the countryside.

An Expanding Consumer Culture

Postwar America soon became a beehive of construction activity and prolific factory output of the tools and materials to build and furnish the new homes. The proportion of homeowners in the population increased by 50 percent between 1945 and 1960. And those new homes were increasingly filled with the latest electrical appliances—refrigerators, washers, sewing machines, vacuum cleaners, freezers, and mixers.

What differentiated the affluence of the post–World War II era from earlier periods of prosperity was its ever-widening dispersion. Although pockets of rural and urban poverty persisted, few noticed such exceptions to the prevailing prosperity. After being sworn in as head of the AFL-CIO in 1955, George Meany proclaimed that "American labor never had it so good."

On the surface, many blacks were also beneficiaries of the wave of prosperity that swept over postwar American society. By 1950, African Americans were earning on average more than four times their 1940 wages. One black journalist declared in 1951 that "the progressive improvement of race relations and the economic rise of the Negro in the United States is a flattering example of democracy in action." While gains had been made, however, blacks and other minority groups lagged behind whites in their rate of improvement. Indeed, the gap between the average yearly income of whites and blacks widened during the decade of the 1950s. Yet the need to present a united front against communism led commentators to ignore or gloss over issues of racial and economic injustice. Such corrosive neglect would fester and explode during the 1960s, but for now the emphasis was on consensus, conformity, and economic growth.

To perpetuate the postwar prosperity, economists repeated the basic marketing strategy of the 1920s: the public must be taught to consume more. Advertising became a more crucial component of the consumer culture than ever before, and its primary medium was television. In 1946 there were only 7,000 TV sets in the country; by 1960 there were 50 million. Nine out of ten homes had one, and by 1970, 38 percent owned new color sets. Time previously devoted to reading, visiting, playing, listening to the radio, or movie-going was now spent in front of the "electronic hearth." TV advertising expenditures increased 1,000 percent during the 1950s. The president of the National Broadcasting Company (NBC) claimed in 1956 that the primary reason for the postwar economic boom was that "advertising has created an American frame of mind that makes people want more things, better things and newer things." Paying for such "things" was no problem; the age of the credit card had arrived. Between 1945 and 1957, consumer credit soared 800 percent.

Shopping became a major recreational activity. In 1945 there were only eight shopping centers in the entire country; by 1960 there were almost 4,000. Much as life in a medieval town revolved around the cathedral, life in postwar suburban America seemed to center on the new giant shopping centers and malls. Young Americans especially participated in this shopping culture. Teens in the postwar era were immersed in abundance from an early age and took the notion of carefree consumption for granted.

The Suburban Frontier

The population increase of the 1950s and 1960s was an urban as well as a suburban phenomenon. Dramatic new technological advances in agricultural production reduced the need for manual laborers and thereby led 20 million Americans to leave the land for the city between 1940 and 1970. Much of the urban population growth occurred in the South, the Southwest, and the West, in an arc that stretched from the Carolinas down through Texas and into California, diverse states that by the 1970s were being lumped together into the "Sunbelt." But the Northeast remained the most densely populated area; by the early 1960s, 20 percent of the national population lived in the corridor that stretched from Boston to Norfolk, Virginia.

While more concentrated in cities, Americans after World War II were simultaneously spreading out within metropolitan areas. In 1950 the Census Bureau redefined the term "urban" to include suburbs as well as central cities. During the 1950s, suburbs grew six times faster than cities. By 1970, more Americans lived in suburbs (76 million) than in central cities (64 million). "Suburbia," proclaimed the *Christian Century* in 1955, "is now a dominant social group in American life."

William Levitt, a brassy New York developer, led the suburban revolution. In 1947, on 1,200 acres of Long Island farmland, he built 10,600 houses that were immediately sold and inhabited by more than 40,000 people—mostly adults under thirty-five and their children.

Within a few years, there were similar Levittowns in Pennsylvania and New Jersey, and other developers soon followed suit around the country. The federal government aggressively subsidized this suburban revolution. By insuring loans for up to 95 percent of the value of a house, the Federal Housing Administration made it easy for a builder to borrow money. Military veterans were given added benefits. A veteran could buy a Levitt house with no down payment and monthly installments of $56.

Expanded automobile production and highway construction also facilitated the rush to the suburbs, as more and more people were able to commute longer distances to work. Car production soared from 2 million in 1946 to 8 million in 1955, and a "car culture" soon emerged. As one commentator observed, the proliferation of automobiles "changed our dress, manners, social customs, vacation habits, the shape of our cities, consumer purchasing patterns, and common tastes." In 1947 Congress authorized the construction of 37,000 miles of highways, and nine years later it funded 42,000 additional miles of interstate expressways.

Such new roads provided access to the suburbs, and Americans—mostly young middle-class whites—rushed to take advantage of the new living spaces. Motives for moving to the suburbs were numerous. The availability of more spacious homes as well as greater security and better educational opportunities for children all played a role. Racial considerations were also a factor. Those engaged in "white flight" from increasingly multiracial cities were often eager to maintain segregation in their new suburban communities. Contracts for homes in Levittown, Long Island, for example, specifically excluded "members of other than the Caucasian race." Such discrimination, whether explicit or implicit, was widespread; the nation's suburban population in 1970 was 95 percent white.

The Great Black Migration

World War II, like World War I, helped spur a mass migration of rural southern blacks to the cities of other regions. This second great migration was much larger in scope than the first, and its social consequences were much more dramatic. After 1945, more than 5 million southern blacks, mostly farm folk, left their native region in search of better jobs, decent housing, and greater social equality. During the 1950s, for example, the black population of Chicago more than doubled. The South Side of Chicago soon became known as the capital of black America. It remains the largest concentration of African Americans in the country. In its scope and effects, this internal migration of blacks from South to North was every bit as significant as the post–Civil War settlement of the West.

In northern cities such as Chicago, Philadelphia, Newark, Detroit, New York, Boston, and Washington, D.C., blacks from the rural South confronted harsh new realities. Slumlords often gouged them for rent, employers refused to hire them, and some union bosses denied them membership. City governments sought to deal with the migrants and alleviate racial stress by constructing massive, all-black public housing projects to accommodate the newcomers. These overcrowded racial enclaves, however, were essentially segregated prisons. Soon the promised land had become for many an ugly nightmare of joblessness, illiteracy, dysfunctional families, welfare dependency, street gangs, pervasive crime, and racism.

Levittown, Pennsylvania. A rapidly growing population of young Americans moved to the suburbs in the postwar years.

A Conforming Culture

Much of white middle-class social life during the two decades after the end of World War II exhibited an increasingly homogenized character. While fears generated by the cold war initially played a key role in encouraging orthodoxy, corporations and advertisers also came to play an increasingly important role in promoting homogeneity. Suburban life itself encouraged uniformity, as people felt a need for companionship and a sense of belonging as they moved into new communities of strangers. "Conformity," predicted an editor in 1954, "may very well become the central social problem of this age."

Women's "Place"

Increasing conformity in middle-class business and corporate life was mirrored in the middle-class home. A special issue of *Life* magazine in 1956 featured the "ideal" middle-class woman, a thirty-two-year-old

A 1956 *Life* magazine cover story pronounced the ideal woman a "pretty and popular" suburban housewife who "attends club or charity meetings, drives the children to school, does the weekly grocery shopping, makes ceramics, and is planning to study French."

"pretty and popular" suburban housewife, mother of four, who had married at age sixteen. Described as an excellent wife, mother, hostess, volunteer, and "home manager" who made her own clothes, she hosted dozens of dinner parties each year, sang in the church choir, worked with the PTA and Campfire Girls, and was devoted to her husband.

Life's ideal of the middle-class woman reflected a veritable cult of feminine domesticity in the postwar era. The soaring birthrate reinforced the deeply embedded notion that a woman's place was in the home. "Of all the accomplishments of the American woman," the *Life* cover story proclaimed, "the one she brings off with the most spectacular success is having babies."

Even though millions of women had responded to wartime appeals and joined the traditionally male workforce, afterward they were encouraged—and even forced to turn their jobs over to the returning veterans and assume a full-time commitment to home and family. "Back to the kitchen" was the repeated refrain after 1945. Nonetheless, despite the ideal of women remaining in the home and the stigma associated with violating this norm, overall the percentage of women working outside the home increased during the 1950s.

Search for Community

Another illustration of the conformist pressures of middle-class life during the 1950s was the spiraling growth of membership in social institutions and organizations. This was in part because of the great mobility of Americans after World War II. Some 20 percent of the population changed their place of residence each year. As they moved from central cities to suburbs, from suburb to suburb, from farm to city, from state to state, newcomers looked for a way to connect with strangers. They joined civic clubs, garden clubs, car pools, and babysitting groups.

Americans also joined churches and synagogues in record numbers. The postwar era witnessed a massive renewal of religious participation. In 1940 less than half of the adult population belonged to churches; by 1960 over 65 percent were official communicants. Bible sales soared, and books, movies, and songs with religious themes were stunning commercial successes.

The prevailing tone of the popular religious revival during the 1950s was upbeat and soothing. People did not want their consciences overly burdened with a sense of personal sin or social guilt over issues such as segregation or inner-city poverty. Instead they wanted to be reassured that their own comfortable way of life was indeed God's will.

By far the best salesman of this gospel of reassuring "good news" was the Reverend Norman Vincent Peale, the pastoral promoter of feel-good theology. No speaker was more in demand during the 1950s, and no writer was more widely read. Peale's book *The Power of Positive Thinking* (1952) was a phenomenal best-seller throughout the decade—and for good reason. It offered a simple "how-to" course in personal happiness. "Flush out all depressing, negative, and tired thoughts," Peale advised. "Start thinking faith, enthusiasm, and joy." By following this simple formula for success, he pledged, the reader could become "a more popular, esteemed, and well-liked individual."

Cracks in the Picture Window

Although Peale's positive message appealed to many Americans, others found it shallow and misleading, lacking in genuine conviction and commitment. Reinhold Niebuhr, a brilliant preacher-professor at New York's Union Theological Seminary, led the "neo-orthodox" movement that lambasted the "undue complacency and conformity" settling over American life in the postwar era. He deemed the popular religion of self-assurance and material success promoted by Peale and his followers woefully inadequate prescriptions for the ills of modern society.

One of the most striking aspects of postwar American life was the sharp contrast between Peale's message that everything was fine and for the best as long as people believed in God, the American Way, and themselves, and the increasingly bitter criticism of American life coming from the intellectual classes. As the philosopher and editor Joseph Wood Krutch recognized in 1960, "the gap between those who find the spirit of the age congenial and those who do not seems to have grown wider and wider."

The Lonely Crowd

The criticism of postwar American life and values began in the early 1950s and quickly gathered momentum among intellectuals, theologians, writers, and artists. Social scientists, too, attacked the prevailing optimism of the time. In *The Affluent Society* (1958), for example, economist John Kenneth Galbraith warned that sustained economic growth would not necessarily solve chronic social problems. He reminded readers that the nation had yet to confront the chronic poverty plaguing the nation's inner cities and rural hamlets.

Postwar cultural critics also questioned the supposed bliss offered by middle-class suburban life. John Keats, in *The Crack in the Picture Window* (1956), launched a savage assault on life in the huge new suburban developments. In these rows of "identical boxes spreading like gangrene," commuter fathers were always at work and "mothers were always delivering children, obstetrically once and by car forever after." Locked into a deadly routine, hounded by financial insecurity, and engulfed by mass mediocrity, suburbanites were living in a "homogeneous, postwar Hell."

Social critics repeatedly cited the huge modern corporation as an equally important source of regimentation in American life. The most comprehensive analysis of the docile new corporate character was David Riesman's *The Lonely Crowd* (1950). Riesman, a social psychologist, detected a fundamental shift in the dominant American personality from what he called the "inner-directed" to the "other-directed" type. Inner-directed people, Riesman argued, possessed a deeply internalized set of basic values implanted by strong-minded parents or other elders.

Such an assured, self-reliant personality, Riesman claimed, had been dominant in American life throughout the nineteenth century. But during the mid–twentieth century a new, other-directed personality had displaced it. In the huge, hierarchical corporations that abounded in postwar America, employees who could win friends and influence people thrived; rugged individualists indifferent to personal popularity did not. The other-directed people who adapted to this corporate culture had few internal convictions and standards; they did not follow their conscience so much as adapt to the prevailing standards of the moment.

Riesman amassed considerable evidence to show that the other-directed personality was widely dispersed throughout middle-class life. One source, he suggested, was Dr. Benjamin Spock's influential advice on raising children, *The Common Sense Book of Baby and Child Care,* which sold an average of 1 million copies a year between its first appearance in 1946 and 1960. Spock stressed that parents should foster in their children qualities and skills that would enhance their chances in what Riesman called the "popularity market." Riesman charged that this made the middle-class mother a "chauffeur and booking agent," determined to "cultivate all the currently essential talents, especially the gregarious ones. It is inconceivable to some that a child might prefer his own company or that of just another child."

Youth Culture and Delinquency

Heeding Dr. Spock's advice, most parents of the 1950s tended to be permissive with their children, who occupied a distinctive place in postwar life. One commentator described the family in 1957 as a "child-centered anarchy."

The children of the postwar baby boom were becoming adolescents during the 1950s, and in the process, a distinctive "teen" subculture began to emerge. Living in such a prosperous era, teenagers had more money and free time than any previous generation. This "silent generation" was generally content to cavort at proms or fraternity parties or "sock hops" before landing a job with a large corporation, marrying, and settling down into the routine of middle-class suburban life.

A drive-in movie, 1951. Accessibility to cars gave teenagers in the 1950s mobility and freedom from adult supervision.

Yet such conformity and striving for popularity masked a great deal of turbulence. During the 1950s, a wave of juvenile delinquency swept across middle-class society. By 1956, over a million teens a year were being arrested. Car theft was the leading offense, but larceny, rape, and murder were not uncommon.

What was causing such delinquency? J. Edgar Hoover, the head of the FBI, insisted that the root of the problem was a lack of religious training in more and more households. Others pointed to the growing number of urban slums, whose "bad" and "brutish" environments could lead to criminality. Yet such factors failed to explain why so many middle-class kids from "good" families were becoming delinquents. One explanation may have been the unprecedented mobility of young people. Access to automobiles enabled teens to escape parental control.

Rock 'n' Roll

Many concerned observers blamed the delinquency problem on a new form of music that emerged during the postwar era—rock 'n' roll. Rock music combined a strong beat with off-beat accents and repeated harmonic patterns to produce its distinctive sound, and the electric guitar was the basic instrument. By the mid-1950s it had captured the imagination of young Americans.

Alan Freed, a Cleveland disc jockey, had coined the term "rock 'n' roll" in 1951. While visiting a record store, he had noticed an interesting new musical trend: white teenagers were buying rhythm and blues (R & B) records that had heretofore been purchased only by African Americans and Chicanos. Freed wanted to take advantage of the new trend, but he realized that few white households would listen to a radio program featuring what was then called "race music." So he began playing R & B records but labeled the music rock 'n' roll (a phrase used in black communities to refer to dancing and sex) to surmount the racial barrier.

Freed's radio program was an immediate success, and its popularity helped bridge the gap between "white" and "black" music. African-American singers such as Chuck Berry, Little Richard, and Ray Charles, and Chicano performers such as Ritchie Valens (Richard Valenzuela) suddenly were the rage among young, white middle-class audiences eager to claim their own cultural style and message. At the same time, Elvis Presley, a young white truck driver and aspiring singer raised in Memphis, Tennessee, began experimenting with "rockabilly" music, his own unique blend of gospel, country-and-western, and R & B rhythms and lyrics.

Presley appeared on numerous television variety shows, starred in movies, and by the end of the decade had captured the attention of the world. His long hair and sideburns, his grins and sneers, his leather jacket and tight blue jeans—all shouted defiance against adult conventions. His sexually suggestive stage performances featuring twisting hips and a gyrating pelvis drove teenagers, especially girls, wild.

Such hysterics prompted cultural conservatives to urge parents to confiscate and destroy Presley's records because they promoted "a pagan concept of life." A Catholic cardinal denounced Presley as a vile symptom of a new teen "creed of dishonesty, violence, lust and degeneration." Patriotic groups claimed that rock music was a tool of Communist insurgents designed to corrupt American youth.

Rock 'n' roll not only survived such assaults, it flourished as a musical idiom directed at young people experiencing the turbulence of puberty. It gave adolescents a self-conscious sense of being a unique social group with distinctive characteristics. And it represented an unprecedented intermingling of racial, ethnic, and class identities. As such, rock music would become one of the major vehicles of the youth revolt of the 1960s.

Alienation in the Arts

Dissatisfaction with the conventions and conformity of American society not only surfaced in rock 'n' roll; it was also manifested in literature in the 1950s as well as in some of the paintings of the times.

Many of the best novels and plays of the postwar period reinforced David Riesman's image of modern society as a "lonely crowd" of individuals, hollow at the core, groping for a sense of belonging and affection. Arthur Miller's much-celebrated play *Death of a Salesman* (1949) powerfully explored this theme. Willy Loman, an aging traveling salesman in decline, centers his life and that of his family on the notion of material success through personal popularity. After he is fired and his eldest son rebels against him, he commits suicide.

Death of a Salesman and many other postwar plays written by Arthur Miller, Edward Albee, and Tennessee Williams portray a central theme of American literature and art during the postwar era: the sense of alienation experienced by sensitive individuals in the face of an oppressive mass culture. In the aftermath of the horrors of World War II and the Holocaust, and in the midst of the cold war nuclear terror, many of the country's foremost writers, painters, and poets refused to embrace the prevailing celebration of modern American life and values.

While millions were reading heartwarming religious epics, literary critics were praising the more disturbing and sobering novels of James Baldwin, Saul Bellow, John Cheever, Ralph Ellison, Joseph Heller, James Jones, Norman Mailer, Joyce Carol Oates, J. D. Salinger, William Styron, John Updike, and Eudora Welty. There were few happy endings here—and even fewer celebrations of contemporary American life. J. D. Salinger's *The Catcher in the Rye* (1951), for example, was an unsettling exploration of a young man's search for meaning and self in a smothering society.

This brooding sense of alienation dominated the best literature in the two decades

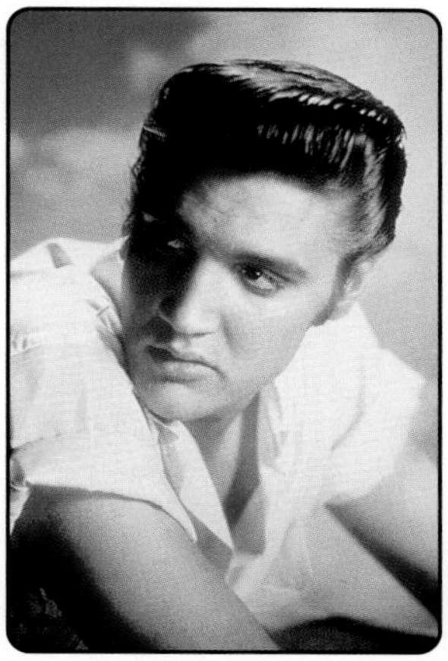

Elvis Presley, 1958. In the 1950s middle-class America made rock 'n' roll a thriving industry and Elvis its first star.

after 1945. The characters in novels such as Ralph Ellison's *Invisible Man* and John Updike's *Rabbit, Run,* among many others, tended to be like Willy Loman—tormented, impotent individuals who can find neither contentment nor respect in an impersonal world.

Many artists also explored the theme of desolate loneliness in urban-industrial American life. For example, virtually all of Edward Hopper's paintings depict isolated, anonymous individuals: a woman undressing for bed, a diner seated at a counter in an all-night restaurant, a housewife in a doorway, a businessman at his desk, a lone passerby in the street. The silence of his scenes is deafening, the monotony striking, the alienation absorbing.

A younger group of painters in New York City felt that postwar society was so chaotic that it denied any attempt at literal representation. Led by Jackson Pollock, the abstract expressionists during the 1950s dominated the American art scene. The abstract artists included Robert Motherwell, Willem de Kooning, Arshile Gorky, Clyfford Still, and Mark Rothko. They believed that the *act* of painting was as important as the final result, and that art no longer had to represent one's visual surroundings. Instead it could unapologetically represent the painter's personal thoughts and actions. Wyoming-born Pollock, for example, placed his huge canvases flat on the floor and then walked around each side, pouring and dripping his paints, all in an effort to "literally be *in* the painting." Such action paintings, with their commanding size, bold form, powerful color contrasts, and rough texture, conveyed the whole spectrum of aesthetic qualities: they were vibrant, frenzied, meditative, disorienting, provocative. Many among the general public found them simply provoking. One wit observed that "I suspect any picture I think I could have made myself."

Watery Paths (1947). Jackson Pollock poured, dripped, and splattered paint across the canvas to create his "action paintings."

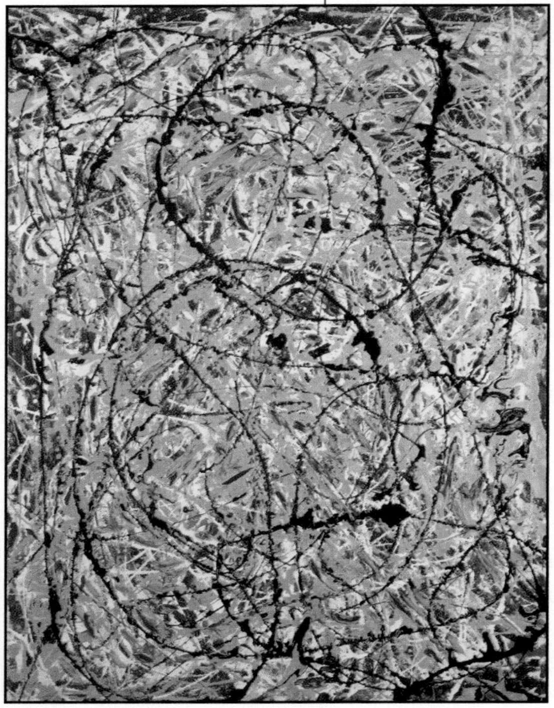

The Beats

The desire to liberate self-expression and reject middle-class conventions also animated a small but highly visible and controversial group of young writers, poets, painters, and musicians known as the Beats. The Beats grew out of the bohemian underground in New York's Greenwich Village. These angry young men—Jack Kerouac, Allen Ginsberg, Gary Snyder, William Burroughs, and Gregory Corso, among others—rebelled against the mundane horrors of middle-class life. The Beats were not lost in despair, however; they strenuously embraced life. But it was life on their own terms, and their terms were shocking to most observers.

The Beats sought personal rather than social solutions to their hopes and anxieties. As Kerouac insisted, his friends were not beat in the sense of beaten; they were "mad to live, mad to talk, mad to be saved." Their road to salvation lay in hallucinogenic drugs and alcohol, sex, a penchant for jazz and the street life of urban ghettos, an affinity for Buddhism, and a restless, vagabond spirit that took them speeding back and forth across the country between San Francisco and New York.

This existential mania for intense experience and frantic motion provided the subject matter for the Beats' writing. Ginsberg's long prose-poem *Howl* (1956) featured an explicit sensuality as well as an impressionistic attempt to catch the color, movement, and dynamism of modern life. Ginsberg howled at the "Robot apartments! invincible suburbs! skeleton treasuries! blind capitals! demonic industries!" Kerouac published his autobiographical novel *On the Road* a year later. In frenzied prose it portrayed the Beats' life of "bursting ecstasies" and maniacal traveling.

Howl and *On the Road* provoked angry sarcasm from many reviewers, but the books enjoyed brisk sales, especially among young people. *On the Road* made the best-seller list, and soon the term "Beat Generation" or "beatnik" referred to almost any young rebel who openly dissented from the comfortable ethos of middle-class life. Defiant young actors such as James Dean and Marlon Brando were added to the pantheon of Beat "antiheroes." In *The Wild One* (1954) a waitress asks Brando what he is rebelling against. He replies: "Whattaya got?" A young folksinger from Minnesota named Bob Dylan was directly inspired by *Howl* and *On the Road.* In this sense the anarchic gaiety of the Beats played an important role in preparing the way for the more widespread youth revolt of the 1960s.

A Paradoxical Era

For all their eccentricities and vitality, the Beats had little impact on the prevailing patterns of postwar social and cultural life. The same held for most of the other critics who attacked the smug conformity and excessive materialism they saw pervading their society. The public had become weary of larger social or political concerns in the aftermath of the depression and the war. Instead, Americans eagerly focused their efforts on personal and family goals and material achievements.

Yet those achievements, considerable as they were, eventually created a new set of problems. The benefits of abundance were by no means equally distributed, and millions of Americans still lived in poverty. For those more fortunate, unprecedented affluence and security fostered greater leisure and independence, which in turn provided opportunities for pursuing more diverse notions of what the good life entailed. Yet the conformist mentality of the cold war era discouraged experimentation. By the mid-1960s, tensions between innovation and convention would erupt into open conflict. Many members of the baby-boom generation would become the leaders of the 1960s rebellion against the corporate and consumer cultures. Ironically, the person who would warn Americans of the 1960s about the mounting dangers of the burgeoning "military-industrial complex" was the president who had long symbolized its growth—Dwight D. Eisenhower.

CHAPTER

32

Conflict and Deadlock: The Eisenhower Years

This chapter focuses on

- Eisenhower's "dynamic conservatism."
- American foreign policy in the 1950s.
- The civil rights movement in the 1950s.
- The origins of the Vietnam War.

THE *ESSENTIAL AMERICA* ON-LINE TUTOR

www.wwnorton.com/eamerica/ch32

- **Topic: Martin Luther King and the March on Washington**
  www.wwnorton.com/eamerica/ch32/topic.htm

  In August 1963 Dr. Martin Luther King Jr. began a new phase of activism in American history when he led 250,000 people in a March on Washington. Since then, various groups have followed Dr. King's example by marching on the nation's capitol to make a point to the entire nation. Using speeches, photographs, and historical analyses, consider how marching on Washington has become part of our national identity. What is the historical significance of Dr. King's March on Washington? What do his actions and his vision teach us about our nation?

- **Chapter review: On-line quiz and chapter summary**
  www.wwnorton.com/eamerica/ch32/review.htm

- **Chapter resources: Multimedia index**
  www.wwnorton.com/eamerica/ch32/media.htm

The New Deal political coalition established by Franklin Roosevelt and sustained by Harry Truman posed a formidable challenge to Republicans after World War II. To counter the unlikely but potent combination of "Solid South" white Democrats, blacks and ethnics, and organized labor, the Grand Old Party in 1952 turned to General Dwight David Eisenhower, a military hero capable of attracting independent voters as well as tenuous Democrats. His commitment to a "moderate Republicanism" promised to slow the rate of federal government expansion while at the same time retaining many of the coveted social programs established by Roosevelt and Truman. His two terms as president are often characterized as representing a lull between two eras of Democratic activism. But Eisenhower wanted to restore the authority of state and local governments and restrain the executive branch from political and social "engineering." In the process, he sought to reinforce traditional virtues and inspire people with a vision of a brighter future.

"Time for a Change"

By 1952 the Truman administration had piled up a heavy burden of political liabilities. Its bold stand in Korea had brought a bloody stalemate abroad, renewed wage and price controls at home, reckless charges of subversion and disloyalty, and exposure of corrupt lobbyists and influence peddlers who rigged favors in Washington. The disclosure of government corruption led Truman to fire nearly 250 employees of the Bureau of Internal Revenue. But doubts lingered that he would ever finish the housecleaning.

Eisenhower's Political Rise

It was, in a slogan of the day, "time for a change," and Republicans saw public sentiment turning their way as the 1952 election approached. The Republican field quickly narrowed to two men, Ohio senator Robert A. Taft and General Dwight D. Eisenhower. Bumper stickers across the land announced simply, "I like Ike," and the immensely popular Eisenhower won the nomination on the first ballot. He then balanced the ticket with a youthful Californian, the thirty-nine-year-old Senator Richard M. Nixon, who had built a career on strenuous opposition to domestic "subversives."

The 1952 Election

The Twenty-second Amendment, ratified in 1951, forbade any president to seek a third term. The amendment exempted the incumbent, but weary of the war in Korea, harassed by charges of subversion and corruption in his administration, and with his popularity declining, Truman decided to withdraw. In a wide-open Democratic race, he supported Illinois governor Adlai E. Stevenson, who won the nomination.

The campaign was uneven from the start. Eisenhower, though a political novice, was a world hero who had been in the public eye for a decade. Stevenson was hardly known outside Illinois. The genial Eisenhower, who disliked politics and politicians, pledged to clean up "the mess in Washington." To this he added a promise, late in the campaign, that as president-elect he would go to Korea to secure "an early and honorable" peace. Stevenson offered a keen intellect spiced with a quick wit, but the Republicans labeled him an "egg-head," in contrast to Eisenhower, the folksy man of the people, the man of decisive action.

In the end, the war hero triumphed in a landslide of 33.9 million votes to 27.3 million. The election marked a turning point in Republican fortunes in the South: for the first time since the 1850s the solidly Democratic South was moving toward a two-party system. Stevenson carried only eight southern states plus West Virginia; Eisenhower picked up five states on the periphery of the Deep South: Florida, Oklahoma, Tennessee, Texas, and Virginia. The "nonpolitical" Eisenhower had made it respectable, even fashionable, to vote Republican in the South. Elsewhere, too, the general made inroads into the Democrats' New Deal coalition, attracting supporters among the ethnic and religious minorities in the major cities.

The voters, it turned out, liked Ike better than they liked his party. In the 1952 elections, Democrats retained most of the governorships, lost control of the House by only eight votes, and broke even in the Senate. The congressional elections two years later would weaken the Republican grip on Congress, and Eisenhower would have to work with a Democratic Congress until he left office.

Eisenhower's "Hidden-Hand" Presidency

Ike

Born in Denison, Texas, in 1890, Dwight David Eisenhower grew up in Abilene, Kansas. After finishing West Point, he spent nearly his entire adult life in military service. After World War II, he became chief of staff and supreme commander of NATO forces, with a brief interlude in between as president of Columbia University.

Far from being a "do-nothing" president, as some have charged, Eisenhower was in fact an effective leader. While Ike talked with genuine feeling about traditional virtues such as duty, honesty, and thrift, he was not above a calculated dissimulation. One student of Eisenhower's techniques has spoken of a "hidden-hand" presidency in which Ike deliberately cultivated a public image of passivity to hide his active involvement in policy decisions.

"Dynamic Conservatism" at Home

Like Ulysses Grant, Eisenhower betrayed a weakness for hobnobbing with rich men. His cabinet, a journalist quipped, consisted of "eight millionaires and a plumber." The plumber, Secretary of Labor Martin Durkin, was gone in eight months, charging that the administration had reneged on a promise to change the Taft-Hartley Act. The president of General Motors became secretary of defense, and two auto distributors were appointed secretary of the interior and postmaster-general. The New Dealers, Adlai Stevenson wryly remarked, "have all left Washington to make way for the car dealers."

Eisenhower called his domestic program "dynamic conservatism," which meant being "conservative when it comes to money and liberal when it comes to human beings." Eisenhower warned repeatedly against the dangers of "creeping socialism," huge bureaucracies, and budget deficits. His administration ended wage and price controls and reduced some farm subsidies.

But though Eisenhower chipped away at New Deal programs, his presidency in the end served rather to solidify the New Deal by keeping its basic structure and premises intact during an era of prosperity. In some ways, moreover, the administration not only maintained the New Deal but extended its reach, especially after 1954, when it had the help of Democratic Congresses. Amendments to the Social Security Act in 1954 and 1956 brought coverage to millions in categories formerly excluded: professional people, domestic and clerical workers, farm workers, and members of the armed forces. The federal minimum wage rose in 1955 from 75¢ to $1 an hour. Federal expenditures for public health rose steadily in the Eisenhower years, and low-income housing continued to be built, although on a much reduced scale. Some farm-related aid programs were actually expanded during the Eisenhower years.

Despite Eisenhower's general disapproval of federal electric power programs, he continued to support public works for which he saw a legitimate need. Indeed, two such programs left major monuments to his presidency: the St. Lawrence Seaway and the interstate highways. The St. Lawrence Seaway, opened in 1959 as a joint venture with Canada, made it possible for oceangoing ships to reach the Great Lakes. The Federal Highway Act of 1956 authorized the federal government to put up 90 percent of the cost of building 42,500 miles of limited-access interstate highways to serve the needs of commerce and defense, as well as private convenience. The states provided the remaining 10 percent. It was only afterward that people realized that the huge national commitment to the automobile might have come at the expense of America's railroad system, already in a state of advanced decay.

Concluding an Armistice

America's new global responsibilities in the postwar world continued to absorb Eisenhower's attention. The most pressing problem when he entered office was the continuing deadlock in the Korean peace talks. Many prisoners of war from North Korea wished to remain in South Korea. U.N. negotiators refused to return prisoners of war who did not want to go back to the North. The North Koreans and Red Chinese insisted that all prisoners be returned regardless of their wishes.

To break the stalemate, Eisenhower took a bold stand. In mid-May 1953 he stepped up aerial bombardment of North Korea, then had Secretary of State John Foster Dulles warn the Chinese of his willingness to use atomic bombs. Whether for that reason or others, negotiations then moved quickly toward an armistice along the established border just above the 38th parallel, and toward a complicated arrangement for prisoner exchange that allowed captives to decide whether to accept or refuse repatriation.

On July 26, 1953, Eisenhower announced the conclusion of the Korean armistice agreement. No one knows if he actually would have forced the issue with atomic weapons. Perhaps the more decisive factors in bringing about a settlement were the size of Chinese Communist losses, which they increasingly found unacceptable, and the new spirit of uncertainty and caution felt by Russian Communists after the death of Joseph Stalin on March 5, 1953—six weeks after Ike's inauguration.

The Army-McCarthy Hearings, June 1954. Joseph Welch (hand on head) listens dejectedly after McCarthy's attempt to smear one of Welch's associates.

Concluding a Witch-hunt

The Korean armistice helped to end the meteoric career of Senator Joseph R. McCarthy, which had flourished amid the anxieties of wartime. Convinced that the government was thoroughly infested with Communists and spies, the Wisconsin senator launched a one-man crusade to root them out. In the process, he and his aides lied, falsified evidence, and bullied or blackmailed witnesses.

McCarthy finally overreached himself in 1954 when, as chairman of the Senate's Government Operations Committee, he made the absurd charge that the United States Army itself was "soft" on communism. The televised Army-McCarthy hearings displayed McCarthy at his worst, as he descended into new depths of mean-spirited desperation, now directing charges at his own colleagues in the Senate. On December 2, 1954, the Senate voted 67 to 22 to "condemn" McCarthy for contempt of that body. McCarthy was finished and increasingly took to alcohol. Three years later, at the age of forty-eight, he was dead.

McCarthyism, Ike joked, had become McCarthywasm, though not for those whose reputations had been wrecked. To the end, Eisenhower kept his resolve not to "get down in the gutter with that guy" and sully the dignity of the presidency. He did work resolutely against McCarthy behind the scenes, but some scholars consider his "hidden hand" approach to have been ineffective at best and cowardly at worst. Eisenhower shared, nevertheless, the widely held conviction that espionage posed a real danger to national security.

Internal Security

The anti-Communist crusade survived McCarthy's downfall. Even before 1954, Eisenhower stiffened the government security program that Truman had set up six years before. In 1953 he issued an executive order broadening the basis for firing government workers. Under the new edict, federal workers could lose their jobs because of dubious associations or personal habits that might make them careless or vulnerable to blackmail.

The Supreme Court, however, modified some of the more extreme expressions of this new Red Scare. In 1953 Eisenhower appointed as chief justice former governor Earl Warren of California, a decision the president later pronounced the "biggest damnfool mistake I ever made." Warren, who had seemed safely conservative while in electoral politics, led an active Court on issues of civil rights and civil liberties. The Warren Court (1953–1969), under the chief justice's influence, became an important agency of social and political change through the 1960s.

Foreign Intervention

Dulles and Foreign Policy

The Eisenhower administration promised new foreign policy departures under the direction of Secretary of State John Foster Dulles. Grandson of one secretary of state and nephew of another, Dulles pursued a lifetime career as an international lawyer and sometime diplomat. Tall, spare, and stooped, he was a man of immense energy, intelligence, and experience.

The foreign policy planks of the 1952 Republican platform, which Dulles wrote, showed both the moralist and the tactician at work. Truman's policy of containment was needlessly defensive, Dulles thought. Containment implied contentment with the status quo. He saw no need for the United States to accept a permanent Soviet presence in eastern Europe. Americans instead should promote the "liberation" of sovereign nations from Soviet domination. This conviction meshed nicely with the conventional wisdom of the right wing that the Yalta Conference agreements were perhaps a betrayal, at best a blunder. The 1952 Republican platform, therefore, promised to "repudiate all commitments . . . such as those of Yalta which aid Communist enslavement" and to end "the negative, futile and immoral policy of 'containment' which abandons countless human beings to a despotism and godless terrorism." A new policy of liberation, the platform promised, would help trigger independence movements within the Communist bloc.

The policy verged perilously close to proclaiming a holy war, but Dulles stressed that he did not intend forcible liberation. Soon it became apparent that it was less a policy than a web of rhetoric to catch ethnic voters whose homelands had fallen captive to the Soviets. The hollowness of the policy became evident when the administration did nothing but deplore a Soviet crackdown on rebellious East German workers in 1953. For three more years Dulles assumed that his rhetoric was undermining the Communist hold on Eastern Europe—until ruthless Soviet suppression of the 1956 uprising in Hungary underscored the danger of stirring futile hopes among captive peoples.

Insofar as American interventions occurred abroad, they were covert operations by the Central Intelligence Agency (CIA) in countries outside the Soviet sphere. In two cases early in the Eisenhower years the CIA was used to overthrow governments believed hostile to American interests: in Iran (1953) and in Guatemala (1954).

Brinksmanship

For all his talk of liberating eastern Europe, Dulles made no significant departure from the containment strategy created under Acheson and Truman. Dulles betrayed a fatal affinity for colorful phrases. In addition to "liberation" and "roll back," he added two major new contributions while in office: "massive retaliation" and "going to the brink."

"Massive retaliation" was an effort to get, in the slogan soon current, "more bang for the buck." Budgetary considerations lay at the root of the administration's military plans, for Eisenhower and his cabinet feared that in the effort to build up superior nuclear firepower the country could spend itself into bankruptcy. During 1953 the Joint Chiefs of Staff designed a new military posture. The heart of their so-called New Look was the assumption that nuclear weapons could be used in limited-war situations, which would allow reductions in conventional forces and thus budgetary savings.

Dulles's policy of "brinksmanship" depended for its strategic effect on those fears of nuclear disaster brought about by the New Look strategy. He argued in 1956 that in following a tough policy of confrontation with communism, a nation sometimes had to "go to the brink" of war. Such a firm stand had supposedly halted further aggression in Korea when Ike had threatened to use atomic weapons. Dulles also employed brinksmanship in Indochina in 1954, when American aircraft carriers moved into the South China Sea "both to deter any Red Chinese attack against [French] Indochina and to provide weapons for instant retaliation."

Indochina: The Background to War

Like the rest of the old colonial world of Asia and Africa, Indochina experienced a wave of nationalism in the years after World War II. By the early 1950s, most of British Asia was independent or on the way: India, Pakistan, Ceylon (now Sri Lanka), Burma (now Myanmar), and the Malay States (now Malaysia). The Dutch and French, however, were less willing to give up their colonies. Americans sympathized with colonial nationalists who sometimes invoked the example of 1776, but Americans also wanted Dutch and French help against the spread of communism. The Truman administration felt obliged to comply with the Dutch and French pleas for aid in reconquering areas that had passed from Japanese occupation into the hands of local patriots.

French Indochina, created in the nineteenth century out of the old kingdoms of Cambodia, Laos, and Vietnam, offered a variation on Third World nationalism. During World War II, opposition to the Japanese occupation of Indochina was led by the Viet Minh (Vietnamese League for Independence). They were nationalists who fell under the influence of Communists, most notably the magnetic rebel Ho Chi Minh. At the end of the war, the Viet Minh controlled part of northern Vietnam, and on September 2, 1945, Ho Chi Minh proclaimed a Democratic Republic of Vietnam, with its capital in Hanoi. Ho had received secret American help against the Japanese during the war, but his bids for further aid after the war went unanswered. Vietnam took low priority in American diplomatic concerns, which at the time were focused on restoring western Europe and containing the spread of communism there.

In 1946 the French government recognized Ho's new government as a "free state" within the French colonial union. Before the year was out, however, Ho opposed French efforts to establish another regime in the southern provinces, and this clash soon expanded into the First Indochina War.

This was a troubling development for the American government. On the one hand, the United States resented France's determination to restore colonial rule. Yet Truman was even more determined to see France become a bulwark against communism in Europe. As a result, the American government acquiesced in France's efforts to crush Vietnamese nationalism.

The Viet Minh movement thereafter became more completely dominated by Ho Chi Minh and his Communist associates, and more dependent on the Soviet Union and China for help. When the Korean War ended, American aid to the French in Vietnam, begun by the Truman administration, escalated dramatically. By the end of 1953, the Eisenhower administration was paying about two-thirds of the cost of the French war effort.

But even with lavish American aid the French were unable to suppress the well-organized and tenacious Viet Minh. In 1954 a major French force had been sent to Dien Bien Phu in the northwest corner of Vietnam. The French soon found themselves surrounded.

The French government requested an American air strike to relieve the pressure on Dien Bien Phu. Eisenhower, however, opposed direct military action unless the British lent support. When they refused, Eisenhower backed away from unilateral action, explaining that it would be a "tragic error to go in alone as a partner of France."

America's decision not to intervene sealed the fate of the besieged French garrison at Dien Bien Phu. On May 7, 1954, the Viet Minh overwhelmed the French forces. It was the very eve of the day an international conference at Geneva took up the question of Indochina. Six weeks later, as French forces continued to suffer defeats in Vietnam, a new French government promised an early settlement. On July 20 representatives of France, Britain, the Soviet Union, the People's Republic of China, and the Viet Minh reached agreement on the Geneva Accords. The agreement made Laos and Cambodia neutral and divided Vietnam at the 17th parallel. The Viet Minh would take power in the North, and the French would remain south of the line until elections in 1956 should reunify Vietnam. American and anti-Communist Vietnamese representatives refused to join in the accord.

Dulles responded to the growing Communist influence in Vietnam by organizing mutual defense arrangements for Southeast Asia. On September 8, 1954, at a meeting in Manila, the United States joined seven other countries in forming Southeast Asia Treaty Organization (SEATO). The impression that it paralleled NATO was false, for the Manila Defense Accord was neither a common defense organization like NATO nor was it primarily Asian. The signers agreed that in case of an attack on one, the others would act according to their "constitutional practices," and in case of threats or subversion they would "consult immediately."

The members of SEATO included only three Asian countries—the Philippines, Thailand, and Pakistan—together with Britain, France, Australia, New Zealand, and the United States. India and Indonesia, the two most populous countries in the region, refused to join. A special protocol added to the treaty extended coverage to Indochina. The treaty reflected what Dulles's critics called "pactomania," which by the end of the Eisenhower administration had contracted the United States to defend forty-three other countries.

After the Geneva Conference, Ho Chi Minh and his government in Hanoi quickly sought to consolidate control throughout the North. In the hinterlands, local Communists held kangaroo courts that tried and executed landowners and confiscated their lands. Residents of the North who wished to leave for southern Vietnam did so with

Ho Chi Minh, leader of the Viet Minh nationalist movement.

American aid. Over 900,000 refugees, most of them Catholics, relocated to the South.

Power in the South gravitated to a new premier: Ngo Dinh Diem, a Catholic nationalist who had opposed both the French and the Viet Minh. In 1954 Eisenhower offered to assist Diem in return for his carrying out "needed reforms." Instead of instituting comprehensive reforms, however, Diem tightened his grip on the country, suppressing opposition on both right and left, offering little or no land distribution, and permitting widespread corruption. In 1956 he refused to join in the elections to reunify Vietnam, and the United States endorsed his decision. But Diem's efforts to eliminate all opposition only played into the hands of the Communists, who found more and more recruits among the discontented. By 1957 guerrilla forces in the South, known as the Viet Cong, had begun attacks on the Diem government, and in 1960 the resistance formed its own political arm, the National Liberation Front. As guerrilla warfare gradually disrupted South Vietnam, Eisenhower was helpless to do anything but "sink or swim with Ngo Dinh Diem."

Reelection and Foreign Crises

As the United States continued to forge postwar alliances and to bring pressure to bear on foreign governments by practicing brinksmanship, a new presidential campaign unfolded. Despite having suffered a coronary seizure in the fall of 1955, Eisenhower decided to run for reelection. He retained the support and confidence of the public, although the Democrats controlled Congress. Meanwhile, new crises in foreign and domestic affairs required him to take decisive action.

A Landslide for Ike

In 1956 the Republican convention renominated Eisenhower and again named Richard Nixon as the vice-presidential candidate. The Democrats turned again to Adlai Stevenson, with a platform that revived party issues: less "favoritism" to big business, repeal of the anti-union Taft-Hartley Act, increased aid to farmers, and tax relief for those in low-income brackets.

Voters handed Eisenhower a landslide victory. He lost one border state, Missouri, but in carrying Louisiana became the first Republican to win a Deep South state since Reconstruction; nationally, he carried all but seven states.

Crisis in the Middle East

To forestall Soviet penetration into the Middle East, the Eisenhower-Dulles foreign policy sought to cultivate Arab friendships. In 1955 Dulles had completed his line of alliances across the "northern tier" of the Middle East. Under American sponsorship, Britain had joined Turkey, Iraq, Iran, and Pakistan in the Middle East Treaty Organization (METO), or Baghdad Pact, as the treaty was commonly called. By linking the easternmost NATO state (Turkey) to the westernmost SEATO state (Pakistan), METO had a certain superficial logic. But after Iraq, the only Arab member, withdrew in 1959, METO collapsed. Below the northern tier, moreover, the Arab states remained aloof from the organization. These were the states of the Arab League (Egypt, Jordan, Syria, Lebanon, and Saudi Arabia), which had warred on Israel in 1948–1949 and remained committed to its destruction.

The most fateful developments in the region turned on the rise of Egyptian general Gamal Abdel Nasser, who overthrew King Farouk in 1952. Nasser's nationalist regime soon pressed for the withdrawal of British forces guarding the Suez Canal, the crucial link between the Mediterranean Sea and the Indian Ocean. Eisenhower and Dulles supported Nasser's demand, and in 1954 an Anglo-Egyptian treaty provided for British withdrawal within twenty months.

Nasser, like other leaders of the Third World, remained unaligned in the cold war and sought to play both sides off each other. The United States in turn courted Egyptian support by offering a loan to build a great hydroelectric plant at Aswan on the Nile River. From the outset, the administration's proposal was opposed by Jewish constituencies concerned with Egyptian threats to Israel, and by southern congressmen who feared the competition from Egyptian cotton. When Nasser increased trade with the Soviet bloc and recognized Red China, Dulles abruptly canceled the loan offer in 1956.

Unable to retaliate against the United States, Nasser nationalized the Anglo-French Suez Canal Company and earmarked its revenues for the Aswan Dam project, thereby enhancing his prestige in the Arab world. The British and French reacted strongly. While negotiations dragged out, Israeli forces invaded the Gaza Strip and Sinai peninsula. Ostensibly their aim was to root out Arab guerrillas, but actually it was to synchronize with the British and French, who jointly began bombing Egyptian air bases and occupied Port Said. The British and French claimed that their actions were meant to protect the canal against the opposing belligerents.

The Suez War put the United States in a quandary. Either the administration could support its Western allies and see the troublesome Nasser crushed, or it could stand on the United Nations Charter and champion Arab nationalism against imperialistic aggression. Eisenhower opted for the latter course, with the unusual result that the Soviet Union sided with the United States. The threat of American embargoes forced Anglo-French-Israeli capitulation, and the Soviets capitalized on the situation by threatening to use missiles against the Western aggressors. This belated bravado won for the Soviet Union some of the credit in the Arab world for what the United States had actually accomplished.

Repression in Hungary

In the Soviet Union, Nikita Khrushchev had come out on top in the post-Stalinist power struggles. Khrushchev had delivered a "secret speech" on the crimes of the Stalin era in 1956 before the Communist Party Congress and hinted at relaxed policies and suggestions that different countries might take "different roads to socialism." This new policy of "de-Stalinization" put Stalinist leaders in the satellite countries of eastern Europe on the defensive and emboldened the more independent leaders to take action. Riots in the Polish city of Poznan led to the rise of Wladyslaw Gomulka, a Polish nationalist, to leadership of the Polish Communist party. Gomulka managed to win a greater degree of independence by avoiding an open break with the Soviets.

In Hungary, however, a similar movement got out of hand. On October 23, 1956, fighting broke out in Budapest, followed by the installation of Imre Nagy, a moderate Communist, as head of the government. Again the Soviets seemed content to let "de-Stalinization" follow its course, and on October 28 they withdrew their forces from Budapest. But Nagy's announcement three days later that Hungary would withdraw from the Warsaw Pact brought Soviet tanks back into Budapest. Although Khrushchev was willing to relax relations with the eastern European satellites, he refused to allow them to break with the Soviet Union or abandon their mutual defense obligations. The Soviets installed a more compliant leader, Janos Kadar, and hauled Nagy off to Moscow, where a firing squad executed him in 1958.

Sputnik

On October 4, 1957, the Soviets launched the first satellite, called Sputnik, an acronym for the Russian phrase "fellow traveler of earth."

Soviet success with Sputnik frightened the United States and led to efforts to enlarge defense spending, to offer NATO allies intermediate-range ballistic missiles (IRBMs) pending development of long-range intercontinental ballistic missiles (ICBMs), to set up a new agency to coordinate space efforts, and to establish a crash program in science education. The "Sputnik syndrome," compounded by a sharp recession through the winter of 1957–1958, loosened the purse strings of frugal legislators, who added to the new budget more than Eisenhower wanted for both defense and domestic programs. In 1958 Congress created the National Aeronautics and Space Agency (NASA) to coordinate research and development in the space program. Before the end of the year, NASA had a program to put a manned craft in orbit, but the first manned flight by an American, Commander Alan B. Shepard, Jr., did not take place until May 5, 1961.

Festering Problems Abroad

Once the Suez and Hungary crises faded from the front pages, Eisenhower enjoyed eighteen months of smooth sailing in foreign affairs. Nonetheless, a brief flurry occurred in 1958 over hostile demonstrations in Peru and Venezuela against Vice-President Nixon, who was on a goodwill tour of eight Latin American countries. Meanwhile, problems in the Middle East and Europe continued to fester, only to reemerge again with new force in 1958. The cold war would again be played out in the Middle East and in eastern Europe, as well as at America's back door, in Cuba.

The Middle East

In 1958 the Middle East flared up again. By this time the president had secured from Congress authority for what came to be called the Eisenhower Doctrine, which promised to extend economic and military aid to Middle East nations, and to use armed forces if necessary to assist any such nation against military aggression from any Communist country.

Egypt's President Nasser meanwhile had emerged from the Suez crisis with heightened prestige, and in 1958 he created the United Arab Republic (UAR) by merger (a short-lived one) with Syria. Then a leftist coup in Iraq, supposedly inspired by Nasser and the Soviets, threw out the pro-Western government. Lebanon, already unsettled by internal conflict, appealed to the United States for support against a similar fate. Eisenhower immediately ordered 5,000 marines into Lebanon. Once the situation stabilized, and all the Lebanese factions reached a compromise, American forces withdrew.

Berlin

The problem of Berlin being situated in East Germany continued to create a flashpoint for Cold War tensions. Premier Khrushchev called it a "bone in his throat." West Berlin provided a "showplace" of Western democracy and prosperity in the middle of Communist East Germany, a listening post for Western intelligence, and a funnel through which news and propaganda from the West penetrated what Winston Churchill had called "the iron curtain." Although East Germany had sealed its western frontiers, refugees could still pass from East to West Berlin. On November 10, 1958, Khrushchev threatened to give East Germany control of East Berlin and the air lanes into West Berlin. After the deadline he set, May 27, 1959, the Western occupation authorities would have to deal with the East German government, in effect recognizing it, or face the possibility of another blockade.

But Eisenhower refused to budge from his position on Berlin. And Khrushchev, it turned out, was no more eager for confrontation than Eisenhower. Khrushchev's deadline passed almost unnoticed. In 1959,

Premier Khrushchev visited the United States, where he endorsed "peaceful coexistence." He and Eisenhower agreed to hold a summit meeting in the spring.

The U-2 Summit

The summit meeting, however, blew up in Eisenhower's face. On May 1, 1960, a Soviet rocket brought down an American U-2 spy plane on a mission over the Soviet Union. After a period of international jousting with Khrushchev, Eisenhower finally took personal responsibility for the incident—an unprecedented action for a head of state—and justified the action on grounds of national security. At a summit meeting in Paris five days later, Khrushchev called on the president to repudiate the U-2 flights, which had been going on for more than three years. When Eisenhower refused, Khrushchev left the meeting.

Castro's Cuba

The greatest thorn in Eisenhower's side was the Cuban regime of Fidel Castro, which took power on January 1, 1959, after three years of guerrilla warfare against a right-wing dictator. In their struggle, Castro's forces had the support of many Americans who hoped for a new day of democratic government in Cuba. But these hopes were dashed when American television reported trials and executions conducted by the victorious Castro. Staged before crowds of howling spectators, the trials offered little in the way of legal procedure or proof. Castro, moreover, began programs of land reform and nationalization of foreign-owned property that further eroded relations with the United States. Some observers believed, however, that by rejecting Castro's requests for loans and other help, the American government lost a chance to influence the direction of the revolution.

The Soviets, on the other hand, were eager to help the new government, and in 1960 Castro entered a trade agreement to swap Cuban sugar for Soviet oil and machinery. One of Eisenhower's last acts as president was to suspend diplomatic relations with Cuba. The president also secretly authorized the CIA to begin training a force of Cuban refugees (some of them former Castro stalwarts) for a new revolution. But the final decision on its use would rest with the next president, John F. Kennedy.

Fidel Castro became Cuba's premier in 1959 after three years of guerilla warfare against the Batista regime.

The Early Civil Rights Movement

While the cold war produced an uneasy stalemate by the mid-1950s, race relations in the United States threatened to destroy the domestic tranquility masking years of injustice. Eisenhower entered office committed to civil rights in principle, and he pushed the issue in areas of federal authority. During his first three years, public services in Washington, D.C., were desegregated, as were navy yards and veterans' hospitals. Beyond that, however, two aspects of the president's philosophy inhibited vigorous action in enforcing the principle of civil rights: his preference for state or local action over federal involvement, and his doubt that laws could change racial attitudes. For the time, then, leadership in the civil rights field came from the judiciary more than from the executive or legislative branches of the government.

In the 1930s, the National Association for the Advancement of Colored People (NAACP) had resolved to test the "separate but equal" doctrine that had upheld racial segregation since the *Plessy* court decision in 1896. In *Sweatt* v. *Painter* (1950), the Supreme Court ruled that a separate black law school in Texas failed to measure up because of intangible factors, such as its isolation from most of the future lawyers with whom its graduates would interact.

The *Brown* Decision

By the early 1950s, challenges to state laws mandating segregation in the public schools were rising through the appellate courts. Five such cases, from Kansas, Delaware, South Carolina, Virgina, and the District of Columbia—usually cited by reference to the first, *Brown* v. *Board of Education of Topeka, Kansas*—came to the Supreme Court for joint argument by NAACP attorneys in 1952. Chief Justice Earl Warren wrote the opinion, handed down on May 17, 1954, in which a unanimous Court declared that "in the field of public education the doctrine of 'separate but equal' has no place." A year later, after further argument, the Court directed "a prompt and reasonable start toward full compliance" with desegregation, ordering that the process should move "with all deliberate speed."

Eisenhower refused to take any part in leading white southerners toward compliance. While token integration began as early as 1954 in the border states, hostility mounted in the Deep South and Virginia, led by the newly formed Citizens' Councils. The Citizens' Councils were middle- and upper-class versions of the Ku Klux Klan that spread quickly across the region and eventually included 250,000 members. Instead of physical violence and intimidation, the Councils used economic coercion to discipline blacks who crossed racial boundaries. African Americans who defied white supremacy would lose their jobs, have their insurance policies canceled, or be denied personal loans or home mortgages. The Citizens' Councils grew so powerful that membership in them became almost a prerequisite for an aspiring white politician.

Racial segregation continued in the South during the 1950s.

Before the end of 1955, moderate sentiment in the South gave way to surly reaction against desegregation of the schools. Virginia senator Harry F. Byrd supplied a rallying cry: "Massive Resistance." State legislatures sought futilely to interpose their power between the courts and the schools. In 1956, 101 southern members of Congress signed a "Southern Manifesto," which denounced the Court's decision in the *Brown* case as "a clear abuse of judicial power." At the end of 1956, in six southern states, not a single black child attended school with whites.

The Montgomery Bus Boycott

The essential role played by the NAACP and the courts in providing a legal lever for the civil rights movement often overshadows the courageous contributions of individual African Americans who took great personal risks to challenge segregation. For example, in Montgomery, Alabama, on December 1, 1955, Rosa Parks, a black seamstress and local activist, was arrested for refusing to give up her seat on a segregated city bus to a white man. The next night black community leaders met in the Dexter Avenue Baptist Church to organize a massive bus boycott under the aegis of the Montgomery Improvement Association.

In Dexter Avenue's twenty-six-year-old pastor, Martin Luther King, Jr., the movement found a charismatic leader. Born in Atlanta, the grandson of a slave and the son of a minister, King was endowed with exceptional intelligence, courage, and eloquence. After attending Morehouse College in Atlanta and then receiving a seminary degree, he earned a Ph.D. in philosophy from

Boston University before accepting a call to preach in Montgomery. He brought the movement a message of nonviolent disobedience based on the Gospels, the writings of Henry David Thoreau, and the example of Mahatma Gandhi in India. "We must use the weapon of love," he told his people.

The bus boycott achieved a remarkable solidarity. For over a year, blacks in Montgomery formed carpools, hitchhiked, or simply walked rather than use city buses. The boycotters finally won a federal case they had initiated against bus segregation, and in 1956 the Supreme Court let stand without review an opinion of a lower court that "the separate but equal doctrine can no longer be safely followed as a correct statement of the law." The next day King and other blacks boarded the buses. To keep alive the spirit of the bus boycott, King and a group of associates in 1957 organized the Southern Christian Leadership Conference (SCLC).

The Civil Rights Act

Despite Eisenhower's reluctance to take the lead in desegregating schools, he supported the right of blacks to vote. In 1956, hoping to exploit divisions between northern and southern Democrats and to reclaim some of the black vote for Republicans, Eisenhower proposed legislation that became the Civil Rights Act of 1957, the first civil rights law passed since Reconstruction. It established the Civil Rights Commission and a new Civil Rights Division in the Justice Department, which could seek injunctions to prevent interference with the right to vote. Yet, by 1959 the Civil Rights Act had not added a single southern black to the voting rolls. Neither did the Civil Rights Act of 1960, which provided for federal court referees to register blacks where a court found a "pattern and practice" of discrimination, and also made it a federal crime to interfere with any court order or to cross state lines to destroy any building. This bill, too, lacked teeth and depended upon vigorous presidential enforcement to achieve any real results.

Desegregation in Little Rock

A few weeks after the Civil Rights Act of 1957 passed, Arkansas governor Orval Faubus called out the National Guard to prevent nine black students from entering Little Rock's Central High School under federal court order. A conference between the president and the governor proved fruitless, but on court order Faubus withdrew the National Guard. When the students tried to enter the school, an hysterical white mob forced their removal for their own safety. At that point, Eisenhower ordered a thousand paratroopers to Little Rock to protect the students.

The following year Faubus closed the high schools of Little Rock rather than allow integration, and court proceedings dragged on into 1959 before the schools could be reopened. In that year, massive resistance to integration in Virginia collapsed when both state and federal courts struck down state laws that had cut off funds from integrated schools. Thereafter, massive resistance for the most part was confined to the Deep South where five states, from South Carolina west through Louisiana, still opposed even token integration.

Assessing the Eisenhower Years

Eisenhower entered office in 1953 after being elected in a landslide and held high approval ratings for ending the Korean War and his strong handling of foreign crises. He won a second landslide election in 1956. Yet support for the president did not translate into support for his party. Eisenhower's decisive win failed to swing a congressional majority for Republicans in either house, leaving the country in the hands of a Republican president and a Democratic Congress. Eisenhower was thus the first president to face three successive Congresses controlled by the opposition party. This meant that he could manage few new initiatives in domestic policy, although he did oversee the admission of the first states not contiguous to the continental forty-eight: Alaska became the forty-ninth state on January 3, 1959, and Hawaii became the fiftieth on August 21, 1959.

During Eisenhower's second term, the country experienced an economic slump, a drop in tax revenues, and a large federal deficit. The country also suffered the embarrassment of the U-2 incident and of Cuba's falling into the Communist orbit. Emotional issues such as civil rights and defense policy and corrupt aides also compounded Eisenhower's troubles. As a result of domestic and foreign problems during his presidency, the Eisenhower administration did not draw much acclaim.

Yet opinion about Eisenhower's presidency has improved with time. Even critics now grant that Eisenhower succeeded in ending the war in Korea and settling the dust raised by McCarthy. If Eisenhower failed to end the cold war and in fact institutionalized global confrontation, he did sense the limits of American power and kept its application to low-risk situations. He also tried to restrain the arms race. If he took few initiatives in addressing social and racial problems that would erupt in the 1960s, he did sustain the major innovations of the New Deal. If he tolerated unemployment of as much as 7 percent at times, inflation remained minimal during his two terms.

Eisenhower's farewell address to the American people showed his remarkable foresight in his own area of special expertise, the military. Like George Washington, Eisenhower couched his wisdom largely in the form of warnings: that America's "leadership and prestige depend, not merely upon our unmatched material strength, but on how we use our power in the interests of world peace and human betterment"; that the temptation to find easy answers should take into account "the need to maintain balance in and among national problems"; and above all that Americans "must avoid the impulse to live only for today, plundering, for our own ease and convenience, the precious resources of tomorrow."

As a soldier, Eisenhower highlighted, perhaps better than anyone else could have, the dangers of a "military-industrial complex." He confessed that his great disappointment was his inability to affirm "that a lasting peace is in sight," only that "war has been avoided."

CHAPTER

33

New Frontiers: Politics and Social Change in the 1960s

This chapter focuses on

- Kennedy's New Frontier and Johnson's Great Society.
- The achievements of the civil rights movement and ensuing splinter movements.
- America's growing involvement in Vietnam and the rising opposition to it.
- Kennedy's efforts to combat communism in Cuba.

THE *ESSENTIAL AMERICA* ON-LINE TUTOR

www.wwnorton.com/eamerica/ch33

- **Topic: The Cuban missile crisis**
  www.wwnorton.com/eamerica/ch33/topic.htm

  In October 1962 the United States discovered that Soviet missile sites were under construction in Cuba, triggering a thirteen-day stand-off that brought the world closer than it had ever been to the brink of nuclear destruction. Relying on a sound recording, personal correspondence, photographs, maps, and historical analyses, examine the meaning and context of the Cuban missile crisis. What options did Kennedy have, and why did he opt for a "quarantine" of Cuba to resolve the standoff with the USSR?

- **Chapter review: On-line quiz and chapter summary**
  www.wwnorton.com/eamerica/ch33/review.htm

- **Chapter resources: Multimedia index**
  www.wwnorton.com/eamerica/ch33/media.htm

For those pundits who considered the social and political climate of the 1950s dull, the following decade would provide a striking contrast. The 1960s were years of extraordinary turbulence and innovation in public affairs—as well as tragedy and trauma. Many social ills that had been simmering for decades suddenly forced their way onto the national agenda during the 1960s. At the same time, the deeply entrenched assumptions of cold war ideology led the nation into its longest, most controversial, and least successful war.

The New Frontier

Kennedy versus Nixon

The 1960 presidential election featured two candidates—Vice-President Richard M. Nixon and Senator John F. Kennedy of Massachusetts—who seemed to symbolize the becalmed politics of the 1950s. Though better known than Kennedy because of his eight years as Eisenhower's vice-president, Nixon had developed the reputation of a cunning chameleon, the "Tricky Dick" who concealed his duplicity behind a series of masks. But Nixon possessed great ability, tenacious energy, and a compulsive love for politics, the more combative the better.

Kennedy lacked Nixon's experience and name recognition. But he did have an abundance of assets, including a widely publicized record of heroism in World War II, a glamorous young wife, a Harvard education, and a wealthy family. During his campaign for the Democratic nomination, Kennedy had shown that he had the energy to match his grace and ambition. As the first Catholic to run for the presidency since Al Smith, he strove to dispel the impression that his religion was a major political liability. By the time of the Democratic convention in 1960, he had traveled over 65,000 miles and made over 350 speeches. In his acceptance speech Kennedy found the stirring rhetoric that would stamp the rest of his campaign and his presidency: "We stand today on the edge of a New Frontier—the frontier of unknown opportunities and perils—a frontier of unfulfilled hopes and threats."

The turning point in the presidential campaign came when Nixon agreed to debate his less prominent opponent on television. During the first of four debates, some 70 million viewers saw Nixon, still weak from a recent illness, perspiring heavily and sporting a five-o'clock shadow. He looked haggard, uneasy, and even sinister before the camera. Kennedy, on the other hand, projected a cool poise that made him seem equal, if not superior, in his fitness for the office. Kennedy's popularity immediately shot up in the polls.

When the votes were counted, Kennedy and his running-mate, Lyndon B. Johnson of Texas, had won the closest presidential election since 1888. The winning margin was only 118,574 votes out of the 68 million cast. Kennedy's wide lead in the electoral vote, 303 to 219, belied the paper-thin margin in several key states, especially Illinois, where Chicago mayor Richard Daley's Democratic machine appeared to have lived up to its legendary campaign motto: "In Chicago we tell our people to vote early and to vote often."

The New Administration

At 43, Kennedy was the youngest person ever elected president, and his cabinet appointments put an accent on youth and "Eastern Establishment" figures. He asked Robert McNamara, one of the "whiz kids" who had reorganized the Ford Motor Company, to bring his managerial magic to bear on the Department of Defense. Then Kennedy appointed Harvard professor McGeorge Bundy as special assistant for national security affairs, and chose as secretary of state Dean Rusk, a career diplomat and former Rhodes Scholar. When critics attacked the appointment of Kennedy's thirty-

President John F. Kennedy sets the tone for his New Frontier at his inauguration, January 20, 1961.

five-year-old brother Robert as attorney-general, the president quipped, "I don't see what's wrong with giving Bobby a little experience before he goes into law practice."

The inaugural ceremonies set the tone of elegance and youthful vigor that would come to be called the "Kennedy style." The new president dazzled listeners with his uplifting rhetoric. "Let every nation know," he proclaimed, "that we shall pay any price, bear any burden, meet any hardship, support any friend, oppose any foe, to assure the survival and success of liberty. And so, my fellow Americans: ask not what your country can do for you—ask what you can do for your country."

The Kennedy Record

For all of his idealistic rhetoric, however, Kennedy had a difficult time launching his New Frontier domestic program. Elected by a razor-thin margin, he did not have a popular mandate. Nor did he show much skill in dealing with a Democratic majority in Congress that remained in the grip of a conservative southern coalition. It blocked his efforts to increase federal aid to education, provide health insurance for the aged, and create a new Department of Urban Affairs.

Administration proposals, nevertheless, did win some notable victories in Congress. They included a new Housing Act that appropriated nearly $5 billion for urban renewal over four years, a raised minimum wage, and increased Social Security benefits. Just two months into his administration Kennedy launched the celebrated Peace Corps to supply young volunteers for educational and technical service in underdeveloped countries. Kennedy also won support for an accelerated program to land astronauts on the moon before the end of the decade. Congress readily approved a series of broad foreign aid programs to help Latin American nations, dubbed the "Alliance for Progress." Another important Kennedy initiative was a bold tax-reduction bill intended to accelerate economic growth. Although it was not passed until 1964, after Kennedy's death, it provided a potent boost to the economy. Perhaps Kennedy's most significant legislative accomplishment was the Trade Expansion Act of 1962, which eventually led to tariff cuts averaging 35 percent between the United States and the European Common Market.

The Warren Court

Under Chief Justice Earl Warren, the Supreme Court continued to be a decisive influence on American domestic life during the 1960s. The Court's decisions on civil liberties proved as controversial as its earlier decisions on civil rights. In 1962 the Court ruled that a school prayer adopted by the New York State Board of Regents violated the constitutional prohibition against an established religion. In *Gideon* v. *Wainwright* (1963), the Court required that every felony defendant be provided a lawyer regardless of the defendant's ability to pay. In 1964 the Court ruled in *Escobedo* v. *Illinois* that a person accused of a crime must also be allowed to consult a lawyer before being interrogated by police. Two years later, in *Miranda* v. *Arizona,* the Court issued perhaps its most bitterly criticized ruling when it ordered that an accused person in police custody must be informed of certain basic rights: the right to remain silent; the right to know that anything said can be used against the individual in court; and the right to have a defense attorney present during interrogation. In addition, the Court established rules for police to follow in informing suspects of their legal rights before questioning could begin.

Expansion of the Civil Rights Movement

Sit-ins and Freedom Riders

The most important development in American domestic life during the 1960s occurred in civil rights. After the Montgomery bus boycott of 1955, Martin Luther King's philosophy of "militant nonviolence" inspired thousands to challenge Jim Crow practices with direct action. At the same time, lawsuits to desegregate the schools activated thousands of parents and young people. The momentum generated the first genuine mass movement in the history of African Americans when four black college students sat down and demanded service at a "whites only" Woolworth's lunch counter in Greensboro, North Carolina, on February 1, 1960. Within a week, the "sit-in" movement had spread to six more towns in the state, and within two months, demonstrations had occurred in fifty-four cities in nine states.

In 1960 the student participants, black and white, formed the Student Nonviolent Coordinating Committee (SNCC), which worked with King's Southern Christian Leadership Conference (SCLC) to spread the movement. The sit-ins at restaurants became "kneel-ins" at churches and "wade-ins" at segregated public pools. During the year after the Greensboro sit-ins, over 3,600 black and white activists spent some time in jail. In many communities they were assaulted with clubs, cattle prods, rocks, and fire hoses, and subjected to unending verbal abuse. Nonetheless, the protesters refused to retaliate.

In 1961 the Congress of Racial Equality (CORE) sent a group of black and white "freedom riders" on buses to test a federal ruling that had banned segregation on buses and trains, and in their depots. In Alabama, mobs attacked the young travelers with fists and pipes, burned one of the buses, and assaulted Justice Department observers, but the demonstrators persisted, drawing national attention and generating new support for their cause.

Federal Intervention in 1962

During the early 1960s, southern state governments defied the civil rights rulings of federal courts. When Governor Ross Barnett of Mississippi ignored a court order and refused to allow African American James H. Meredith to enroll at the University of Mississippi, Attorney-General Robert Kennedy dispatched federal marshals to enforce the law, but they were thwarted by a violent white mob. Federal troops had to intervene, and Meredith was finally registered at "Ole Miss," but only after two deaths and many injuries.

Everywhere, it seemed, black activists and white supporters were challenging deeply entrenched patterns of segregation and prejudice. In 1963 Martin Luther King

Eugene "Bull" Connor's police unleash attack dogs on civil rights demonstrators in Birmingham, Alabama, May 1963.

With his "I Have a Dream" speech, the Rev. Martin Luther King, Jr., focused and united the 1963 March on Washington.

launched a series of demonstrations in Birmingham, Alabama, where Police Commissioner Eugene "Bull" Connor proved the perfect foil for King's tactic of nonviolent civil disobedience. Connor's policemen used dogs, tear gas, electric cattle prods, and fire hoses on the protesters while millions of outraged Americans watched the confrontations on television.

King, who was arrested and jailed during the demonstrations, then wrote his "Letter from a Birmingham Jail," a stirring defense of his nonviolent strategy that became a classic of the civil rights movement. He also signaled a shift in his strategy for social change. Heretofore King had emphasized the need to educate southern whites about the injustice of segregation and discrimination. Now he focused more on gaining federal enforcement and new legislation by provoking racists to display their violent hatreds in public. As King admitted in his "Letter," he sought through organized nonviolent protest to "create such a crisis and foster such a tension that a community which has constantly refused to negotiate is forced to confront the issue." This concept of civil disobedience angered J. Edgar Hoover, the powerful head of the FBI, who labeled King "the most dangerous Negro of the future in this nation." He ordered agents to follow King and authorized the use of wiretaps on his telephones and in his motel rooms.

Southern traditionalists remained steadfast in opposing racial integration. In 1963, Governor George Wallace stood in the doorway of a building at the University of Alabama to block the enrollment of several black students, but he stepped aside in the face of insistent federal marshals. Later the same night NAACP official Medgar Evers was shot to death as he returned home in Jackson, Mississippi.

The high point of the integrationist phase of the civil rights movement occurred on August 28, 1963, when over 200,000 blacks and whites marched down the Mall in Washington, D.C. The March on Washington for Jobs and Freedom was the largest civil rights demonstration in American history. Standing in front of Lincoln's statue, King delivered one of the memorable public speeches of the century: "Even though we face the difficulties of today and tomorrow, I still have a dream. It is a dream chiefly rooted in the American dream . . . one day . . . the sons of former slaves and the sons of former slave-owners will be able to sit together at the table of brotherhood." That the time for such racial harmony had not yet arrived, however, became clear a little over two weeks later when a bomb exploded in a Birmingham church, killing four black girls who had arrived early for Sunday school.

Yet King's dream—shared and promoted by thousands of other activists—survived. The intransigence and violence that civil rights workers encountered won converts to their cause across the country. Persuaded by his brother Robert, a man of greater passion, compassion, and vision, and by the pressure of events, President Kennedy finally decided that enforcement of existing statutes was not enough; new legislation was needed to deal with the race question. In 1963 he told the nation that racial discrimination "has no place in American life or law." He then endorsed an ambitious civil rights bill intended to end discrimination in public facilities, desegregate the public schools, and protect black voters. But southern conservatives quickly blocked the bill in Congress.

Foreign Frontiers

Early Setbacks

Kennedy's record in foreign affairs was mixed, more so than his domestic record. Upon taking office, he learned of a CIA operation designed to prepare 1,500 anti-Castro Cubans for an invasion of their homeland. The Joint Chiefs of Staff endorsed the plan; analysts reported that the invasion would inspire Cubans on the island to rebel against Castro. Yet the scheme, poorly conceived and executed, had little chance of succeeding. When the invasion force landed at Cuba's Bay of Pigs on April 17, 1961, it was brutally subdued in two days, and over a thousand men were captured. A *New York Times* columnist lamented that the United States "looked like fools to our friends, rascals to our enemies, and incompetents to the rest."

Two months after the Bay of Pigs disaster, Kennedy met the Soviet premier, Nikita Khrushchev, in Vienna, Austria. Khrushchev tried to bully the young and inexperienced Kennedy and threatened to limit Western access to Berlin, the divided city located deep within Communist East Germany. Kennedy was shaken by the aggressive Soviet stand. Upon his return home, he demonstrated his resolve by mobilizing Army Reserve and National Guard units. The Soviets responded by erecting the Berlin Wall, which cut off movement between East and West Berlin and became a symbol of the eroding relations between the Soviet Union and the United States.

The Cuban Missile Crisis

A year later, Khrushchev posed another serious challenge, this time just ninety miles south of Florida. Khrushchev granted Fidel Castro's request for nuclear missiles in Cuba to protect the island from future American-sponsored invasions, as well as to redress the strategic imbalance caused by the presence of American missiles in Turkey aimed at the Soviet Union. While such missiles would hardly alter the military balance, they would be placed in areas not covered by American radar systems and, if launched, would arrive too quickly for warning. More important to Kennedy was the psychological effect of American acquiescence to a Soviet military presence on its doorstep.

On October 14, 1962, American intelligence flights discovered that Soviet missile sites were under construction in Cuba. The administration immediately decided that they had to be removed. In a series of secret meetings, the Executive Committee of the National Security Council debated between a "surgical" air strike and a naval blockade of Cuba. They opted for a blockade, but since this would technically represent an act of war, they called it a "quarantine." It offered the advantage of forcing the Soviets to shoot first, if it came to that, and it left open further options of stronger action. Monday, October 22, began one of the most anxious weeks in world history. On that day, the president announced the discovery of the missile sites in Cuba; he also announced the naval quarantine.

Tensions grew as Khrushchev blustered that Kennedy had pushed humankind "to the abyss of a world nuclear-missile war." Soviet ships, he declared, would ignore the quarantine. But on Wednesday, October 24, five Soviet supply ships stopped short of the American warships. Two days later an agent of the Soviet embassy proposed that the Soviet Union would withdraw the missiles in return for a public pledge by the United States not to invade Cuba. On Sunday, October 28, Khrushchev agreed to remove the missiles, and the United States promised not to invade Cuba.

In the aftermath of the crisis, the United States took several symbolic steps to relax tensions: an agreement to sell surplus wheat to the Soviets, the installation of a "hot line" telephone between Washington and Moscow to provide instant contact between the heads of government, and the removal of obsolete American missiles from Turkey, Italy, and Britain. The United States also negotiated a treaty with Soviet and British representatives to stop nuclear testing in the atmosphere.

Kennedy and Vietnam

As tensions with the Soviet Union were easing, a crisis was growing in Southeast Asia that would become the greatest American foreign policy debacle of the century. During John Kennedy's "thousand days" in office, the turmoil of Indochina never preoccupied public attention for any extended period, but it dominated international diplomatic debates.

The Geneva Accords of 1954 had declared the landlocked kingdom of Laos a neutral country, but thereafter a complex power struggle erupted between the Communist Pathet Lao insurgents and the Royal Laotian Army. There matters stood when Eisenhower left office. After a lengthy consideration of alternatives, the Kennedy administration decided to back the formation of a neutralist coalition government including Pathet Lao representatives. This would preclude American military involvement in Laos, yet prevent a Pathet Lao victory. The Soviets, who were extending aid to the Pathet Lao, indicated a readiness to negotiate, and in May 1961 talks began in Geneva. After more than a year of tangled negotiations, the three factions in Laos agreed to a neutral coalition government.

Meanwhile, North Vietnam kept open the Ho Chi Minh Trail through eastern Laos, over which it supplied its Viet Cong allies fighting in South Vietnam. There the situation worsened under the leadership of the Catholic premier Ngo Dinh Diem, whose repressive tactics, directed not only against Communists but also against the Buddhist majority and other critics, played into the hands of his enemies.

In 1961 White House assistant Walt Rostow and General Maxwell Taylor became the first in a long line of presidential emissaries to South Vietnam's capital, Saigon. They proposed a major increase in the American military presence, but Kennedy refused, and instead continued to dispatch more military "advisers." When he took office, there had been 2,000 American troops in South Vietnam; by the end of 1963, there were 16,000, none of whom had been officially committed to battle. But the Diem regime continued to be its own worst enemy. By mid-1963, growing Buddhist demonstrations made the public discontent in South Vietnam more visible. The spectacle of Buddhist monks setting themselves on fire on Saigon streets in protest of Diem's iron-fisted rule shocked Americans.

By the fall of 1963, the Kennedy administration had decided that Diem was a lost cause. When dissident Vietnamese generals proposed a coup d'état, American ambassador Henry Cabot Lodge assured them that Washington would not stand in the way. On November 1 the insurgent military leaders seized the government and murdered Diem. Yet the generals provided no more stability than earlier regimes, as successive coups set South Vietnam spinning from one military leader to the other.

Kennedy's Assassination

Some of Kennedy's aides later argued that he would never have allowed a dramatic escalation of American military involvement in Vietnam. Others strongly disagreed. The answer of course will never be known, for on November 22, 1963, while on a campaign swing through downtown Dallas, Kennedy was shot twice and died almost immediately. A few hours later Dallas police arrested Lee Harvey Oswald, a twenty-four-year-old ex-Marine drifter who had worked in the building from which the shots were fired. Investigators had several reasons to suspect Oswald: he had recently returned from a prolonged stay in the Soviet Union, in recent years he had also visited Cuba, and his family had ties to a Mafia member who had made threats to kill Kennedy. Yet before Oswald could be thoroughly interrogated, he too was killed. Two days after Oswald's arrest, as television cameras covered his transfer to another jail, Jack Ruby, a Dallas nightclub owner, stepped from the crowd of onlookers and fatally shot Oswald.

Oswald's death ignited a controversy over the assassination that still simmers today. In December 1963 President Johnson appointed a commission to investigate Kennedy's murder. Headed by Chief Justice Earl Warren, it concluded that Oswald had acted alone. Yet many people were (and are) not convinced, and since 1963 dozens of alternate theories have been proposed. Some blame the CIA or the Mafia, others point to Fidel Castro, whom the CIA had once tried to assassinate. Still others insist that Cuban exiles in Miami, angered by Kennedy's failure to rescue their comrades during the Bay of Pigs fiasco, were behind the assassination. Whatever the actual story of the assassination, Kennedy's tragic death enshrined him in the public imagination as a martyred leader cut down in the prime of his career.

Lyndon Johnson and the Great Society

Texan Lyndon Johnson took the oath as president of the United States on board the plane that took John Kennedy's body back to Washington from Dallas. At age fifty-five, Johnson had spent twenty-six years on the Washington scene and had served nearly a decade as Senate Democratic leader, where he had displayed the greatest gift for compromise since Henry Clay.

Johnson brought to the White House a marked change of style from his predecessor. A self-made man, he had used gritty determination and shrewd manipulation to work his way out of a hardscrabble rural Texas background to become one of Washington's most powerful figures. He had none of the Kennedy elegance or charisma.

Yet those who viewed Johnson as a stereotypical southern conservative ignored the depth of his concern for poor people and his heartfelt commitment to the cause of civil rights. The day after the assassination he told an aide: "I am a Roosevelt New Dealer. As a matter of fact . . . Kennedy was a little too conservative to suit my taste." In foreign affairs Johnson was a novice. But in the domestic arena during the 1950s he was unsurpassed in his ability to shepherd legislation through the gauntlet of special-interest lobbyists and Congress.

The Johnson Mystique

Lyndon Johnson was a baffling paradox, capable of altering himself to fit any occasion. On the one hand, he was a compulsive worker and achiever, animated by greed and ambition, an overbearing man capable of ruthlessness and deceit and driven by egotism. On the other hand, he could be warm, caring, and gracious. He made friends easily and displayed genuine concern for the welfare of the disadvantaged.

Politics and Poverty

President Johnson established domestic politics as his first priority. He exploited the nation's grief after the assassination by declaring that Kennedy's legislative program, stymied in several congressional committees, would now be passed. The logjam in the Congress that had blocked Kennedy's program broke under Johnson's force-

The Johnson Treatment. Johnson used powerful body language and facial expressions to intimidate anyone who disagreed with him.

ful leadership, and a torrent of legislation poured through.

At the top of Johnson's agenda were the stalled measures for tax reduction and civil rights. He then added to his "must" list a bold new commitment of his own: Johnson declared "unconditional war on poverty in America." The particulars of this "war on poverty" were to come later, the product of a task force already at work before Johnson took office.

Americans had suddenly rediscovered poverty in the early 1960s when the social critic Michael Harrington published a powerful exposé titled *The Other America* (1962). Harrington argued that while most Americans had been celebrating their rising affluence during the postwar era, some 40 to 50 million people were mired in a "culture of poverty," hidden from view and passed on from one generation to the other. Unlike the upwardly mobile immigrant poor at the turn of the century, most of these modern poor had lost hope.

President Kennedy read a review of *The Other America* in 1963 and asked his advisers to investigate the problem and suggest a plan of attack. Upon taking office, Johnson announced that he wanted an anti-poverty package that was "big and bold, that would hit the nation with real impact." Money for the program would come from the economic growth generated by the tax reduction of more than $10 billion passed in 1964.

The administration's "war on poverty" was embodied in an Economic Opportunity Bill that incorporated a wide range of programs: a Job Corps for inner-city youths, a Head Start program for disadvantaged preschoolers, work-study jobs for college students, grants to farmers and rural businesses, loans to those willing to hire the chronic unemployed, the Volunteers in Service to America (VISTA, a "domestic Peace Corps"), and the Community Action Program, which would provide "maximum feasible participation" of the poor in directing neighborhood programs designed for their benefit. Johnson committed his administration to creating a "Great Society" resting on "abundance and liberty for all." The Great Society, he explained, "demands an end to poverty and racial injustice." In theory it was liberalism triumphant; in practice its considerable achievements were accompanied by administrative bungling, corruption, and misguided idealism.

The 1964 Election

As the 1964 election approached, Johnson was conceded the Democratic nomination from the start. He chose as his running mate Hubert H. Humphrey of Minnesota, the popular liberal senator.

In the Republican party, conservatives charged that the party had given in to the same internationalism and big-government policies as liberal Democrats. Ever since 1940, so the theory went, the party had nominated "me-too" candidates who differed little from their Democratic opponents. Now it must nominate a true conservative. Offer the voters "a choice, not an echo," they reasoned, and a truly conservative majority would assert itself.

In 1964 Arizona senator Barry Goldwater emerged as the leader of the Republican right. "I would remind you," Goldwater told the convention delegates who nominated him, "that extremism in the defense of liberty is no vice."

Goldwater displayed an unusual gift for frightening voters. Accusing the administration of waging a "no-win" war in Vietnam, he urged wholesale bombing of North Vietnam and left the impression of being trigger-happy. He also savaged Johnson's war on poverty and the New Deal tradition. Republican campaign buttons claimed: "In your heart, you know he's right." Democrats responded: "In your guts, you know he's nuts."

Johnson, on the other hand, appealed to the middle of the political spectrum. In contrast to Goldwater's bellicose rhetoric on

Vietnam, he pledged not "to send American boys nine or ten thousand miles from home to do what Asian boys ought to be doing for themselves." The election was a landslide. Johnson polled 61 percent of the total vote; Goldwater carried only Arizona and five states in the Deep South. Johnson won the electoral vote by an incredible 486 to 52.

Landmark Legislation

Johnson took advantage of his new mandate to launch his Great Society program. It would, he promised, end poverty, renovate the decaying central cities, provide every young American with the chance to attend college, protect the health of the elderly, enhance cultural life, clean up the air and water, and make the highways safer and more attractive.

To accomplish such goals, the Johnson administration pushed an array of new legislation through the Congress at a pace unseen since Roosevelt's Hundred Days. Priority went to health insurance and aid to education, proposals that had languished since President Truman advanced them in 1945. A federal medical insurance act not only created the Medicare program for the aged, but it added another program, Medicaid, that provided states with federal grants to help cover medical payments for the indigent.

Johnson next sent to Congress a proposal for $1.5 billion in federal aid to elementary and secondary education. Such proposals had been ignored since the 1940s, blocked alternately by issues of segregation or separation of church and state. Now Johnson and congressional leaders devised a means of extending aid to "poverty-impacted" school districts, regardless of their public or parochial character.

The momentum generated by the passage of these measures continued through the following year. Altogether the tide of Great Society legislation carried 435 bills through the Congress. Among them was the Appalachian Regional Development Act of 1966, which allocated $1.1 billion for programs to enhance the standard of living of those in remote mountain coves. The Housing and Urban Development Act of 1965 provided for construction of 240,000 housing units and $2.9 billion for urban renewal. Rent supplements for low-income families followed in 1966, and in that year there began a new Department of Housing and Urban Development, headed by Robert C. Weaver, the first black cabinet member.

The Immigration Act

Little noticed among the legislation flowing from the Congress was a major new immigration bill that passed the Congress in the fall of 1965. Johnson stressed that the new law would redress the wrong done to those "from southern and eastern Europe" and the "developing continents" of Asia, Africa, and Latin America. It did so by abolishing the discriminatory quotas based on national origins that had governed immigration policy since the 1920s.

The Immigration Act of 1965 treated all nationalities and races equally. In place of national quotas it created hemispheric ceilings on visas issued: 170,000 for persons from outside the Western Hemisphere, 120,000 for persons from within. It also stipulated that no more than 20,000 people could come from any one country each year. The new act allowed the entry of immediate family members of American residents without limit.

During the prosperous 1960s, few western Europeans sought to emigrate to the United States; those living in Communist-controlled eastern Europe could not leave. But Asians and Latin Americans flocked to American consulates in search of visas. And within a few years, the new arrivals in turn used the family-preference system to bring their family members as well. This so-called chain immigration quickly filled the annual quotas for nations such as the Philippines,

Mexico, Korea, and the Dominican Republic, and Hispanics and Asians became the largest contingents of new Americans.

The Great Society: Successes and Failures

The Great Society programs included several genuine success stories. The Highway Safety Act and the Traffic Safety Act established safety standards for automobile manufacturers and highway design, and the scholarships provided for college students under the Higher Education Act were quite popular. Many Great Society initiatives aimed at improving the health, nutrition, and education of poor Americans, young and old, made headway against these intractable problems. So, too, did efforts to clean up air and water pollution. But several ambitious programs were hastily designed and ill conceived, others were vastly underfunded, and many were mismanaged. Medicare, for example, removed any incentives for hospitals to control costs, and medical bills skyrocketed. Often funds appropriated for various programs never made it through the tangled bureaucracy to the needy. Widely publicized cases of welfare fraud placed a powerful weapon in the hands of those opposed to liberal social programs. By 1966 middle-class resentment over the cost and waste of the Great Society programs helped generate a strong conservative backlash.

From Civil Rights to Black Power

Civil Rights Legislation

Among the successes of the Great Society were several key pieces of civil rights legislation. After Kennedy's death, President Johnson called for passage of the long-stalled civil rights bill as a memorial to the fallen leader. The Civil Rights Act of 1964 outlawed racial discrimination in hotels, restaurants, and other public accommodations. In addition, the attorney-general could now initiate suits for school desegregation, relieving parents of a painful necessity. Federally assisted programs and private employers alike were required to eliminate discrimination. An Equal Employment Opportunity Commission administered a ban on job discrimination by race, religion, national origin, or sex.

Perhaps equally important, the Civil Rights Act gave new momentum to activists. Early in 1965 Martin Luther King, the recipient of the Nobel Peace Prize the year before, announced a voter-registration drive aimed at the 3 million unregistered blacks in the South. On March 7 civil rights protesters began a march for voting rights from Selma, Alabama, to Montgomery, only to be violently dispersed by state troopers and a mounted posse. A federal judge then agreed to allow the march, and President Johnson provided federal protection. By March 25, when the demonstrators reached Montgomery, they numbered 35,000, and King delivered a rousing address from the steps of the state capitol.

Several days before the march, President Johnson went before Congress with a moving plea for voting rights legislation. The resulting Voting Rights Act of 1965 ensured all citizens the right to vote. It authorized the attorney-general to dispatch federal examiners to register voters. In states or counties where fewer than half the adults had voted in 1964, the act suspended literacy tests and other devices commonly used to defraud citizens of the vote. By the end of the year, some 250,000 blacks were newly registered.

"Black Power"

In the midst of success, however, the civil rights movement began to fragment. On August 11, 1965, less than a week after the passage of the Voting Rights Act, the predominantly black Watts area of Los Angeles exploded in a frenzy of riots and looting. When the uprising ended, there were thirty-four dead, almost 4,000 rioters in jail, and massive property damage. The Watts upheaval marked the beginning of four "long hot summers" of racial conflagration. Riots in the summer of 1966 erupted in Chicago and Cleveland, along with forty other American cities. The following summer Newark and Detroit burst into flames. Detroit provided the most graphic example of urban violence, as tanks rolled through the streets.

In retrospect, it was understandable that the civil rights movement would begin to focus on the plight of urban blacks. By the middle 1960s, about 70 percent of America's black population lived in metropolitan areas, most of them in central-city ghettos that had been bypassed by the postwar prosperity. It seems clear, also in retrospect, that the nonviolent tactics that had worked in the rural South would not work in the northern cities. In the North, racial problems resulted from segregated residential patterns not amenable to changes in law. A special Commission on Civil Disorders noted that, unlike earlier race riots that had been started by whites, the urban upheavals of the middle 1960s were initiated by blacks themselves in an effort to destroy what they could not stomach and what civil rights legislation seemed unable to change.

In the midst of such upheaval, a new philosophy of racial separatism began to emerge. Radical members of SNCC had become estranged from Martin Luther King's theories of nonviolence. When Stokely Carmichael, a twenty-five-year-old graduate of Howard University, became head of SNCC in 1966, he adopted a separatist philosophy of "black power" and ousted whites from the organization. Carmichael joined the Black Panther party, a self-professed group of urban revolutionaries founded in Oakland, California, in 1966. Headed by Huey P. Newton and Eldridge Cleaver, the Black Panthers terrified the public by wearing bandoleras and carrying rifles. Eventually the Panthers fragmented in spasms of violence, much of which the FBI and local police officials helped to provoke.

The most articulate spokesman for black power was one of the earliest, Malcolm X (formerly Malcolm Little, with the "X" denoting his lost African surname). Malcolm had risen from a ghetto childhood involving narcotics and crime to become the chief disciple of Elijah Muhammad, the Black Muslim leader who encouraged black culture and black pride. By 1964 Malcolm had broken with Elijah Muhammad and founded his own organization, which was committed to the establishment of alliances between American blacks and the nonwhite peoples of the world. He also had begun to abandon his earlier separatist agenda and violent tactics. But just after the publication of his *Autobiography* in 1965, Malcolm was gunned down in Harlem by Black Muslim assassins.

Although widely publicized and highly visible, the "black power" movement never attracted more than a small minority of African Americans. Only about 15 percent of blacks labeled themselves separatists. The preponderant majority continued to identify with the philosophy of nonviolent integration promoted by Martin Luther King, Jr., and organizations such as the NAACP. King dismissed black separatism and reminded his followers that "we can't win violently."

Yet the black power philosophy, despite its hyperbole and violence, had positive effects upon the civil rights movement. First, it helped African Americans take greater pride in their African roots and their American

Civil rights leader Martin Luther King, Jr., with "black power" advocate Malcolm X.

accomplishments. Second, the black power phenomenon forced King and other mainstream black leaders to launch a new stage in the civil rights movement focused on the plight of poor inner-city blacks. Legal access to restaurants, schools, and other public accommodations, King pointed out, meant little to people mired in a culture of urban poverty. They needed jobs and decent housing as much as they needed legal rights. The time had come for radical measures "to provide jobs and income for the poor." Yet as King and others sought to escalate the war on poverty at home, the war in Vietnam was taking more and more of America's resources and energies.

The Tragedy of Vietnam

At the time of President Kennedy's death, there were 16,000 American military "advisers" in Vietnam. Lyndon Johnson inherited a commitment to prevent a Communist takeover in South Vietnam along with a reluctance to assume the military burden for fighting the war. One president after another had done just enough to avoid being charged with having "lost" Vietnam. Johnson did the same, fearing that any other course would undermine his influence and endanger his Great Society programs in Congress. But this path took him and the United States inexorably deeper into an Asian war.

Escalation

The official sanction for America's "escalation"—a Defense Department term coined in the Vietnam era—was the Tonkin Gulf Resolution, voted by Congress on August 7, 1964. Johnson reported in a national television address that two American destroyers had been attacked by North Vietnamese vessels on August 2 and 4 in the Gulf of Tonkin off the coast of North Vietnam. Although he described the attacks as unprovoked, in truth the destroyers had been monitoring South Vietnamese raids against two North Vietnamese islands—raids planned by American advisers. Even though there was no tangible evidence that the American ships had been attacked, the Tonkin Gulf Resolution authorized the president to "take all necessary measures to repel any armed attack against the forces of the United States and to prevent further aggression."

Three months after his landslide victory over Goldwater, Johnson made the crucial decisions that shaped American policy in Vietnam for the next four years. On February 5, 1965, Viet Cong guerrillas killed 8 Americans at Pleiku. More attacks on Americans later that week led Johnson to order operation "Rolling Thunder," the first sustained American bombings of North Vietnam, which were intended to stop the flow of soldiers and supplies into the South.

In March 1965 the new American army commander in Vietnam, General William C. Westmoreland, requested and got the first installment of combat troops, ostensibly to defend American airfields. By the end of 1965, there were 184,000 American troops in Vietnam; in 1966 the troop level reached 385,000. As combat operations increased throughout South Vietnam, so did American casualties, announced each week on the nightly news.

The Context for Policy

Johnson's decision to "Americanize" the Vietnam War, so ill-starred in retrospect, was entirely consistent with the foreign policy principles pursued by all American presidents after World War II. The version of the containment theory articulated in the Truman Doctrine, endorsed by Eisenhower and Dulles throughout the 1950s, and reaffirmed by Kennedy, pledged United States opposition to the advance of communism anywhere in the world. "Why are we in Vietnam?" Johnson asked rhetorically at Johns Hopkins University in 1965. "We are there because we have a promise to keep." Secretary of State Dean Rusk repeated this rationale be-

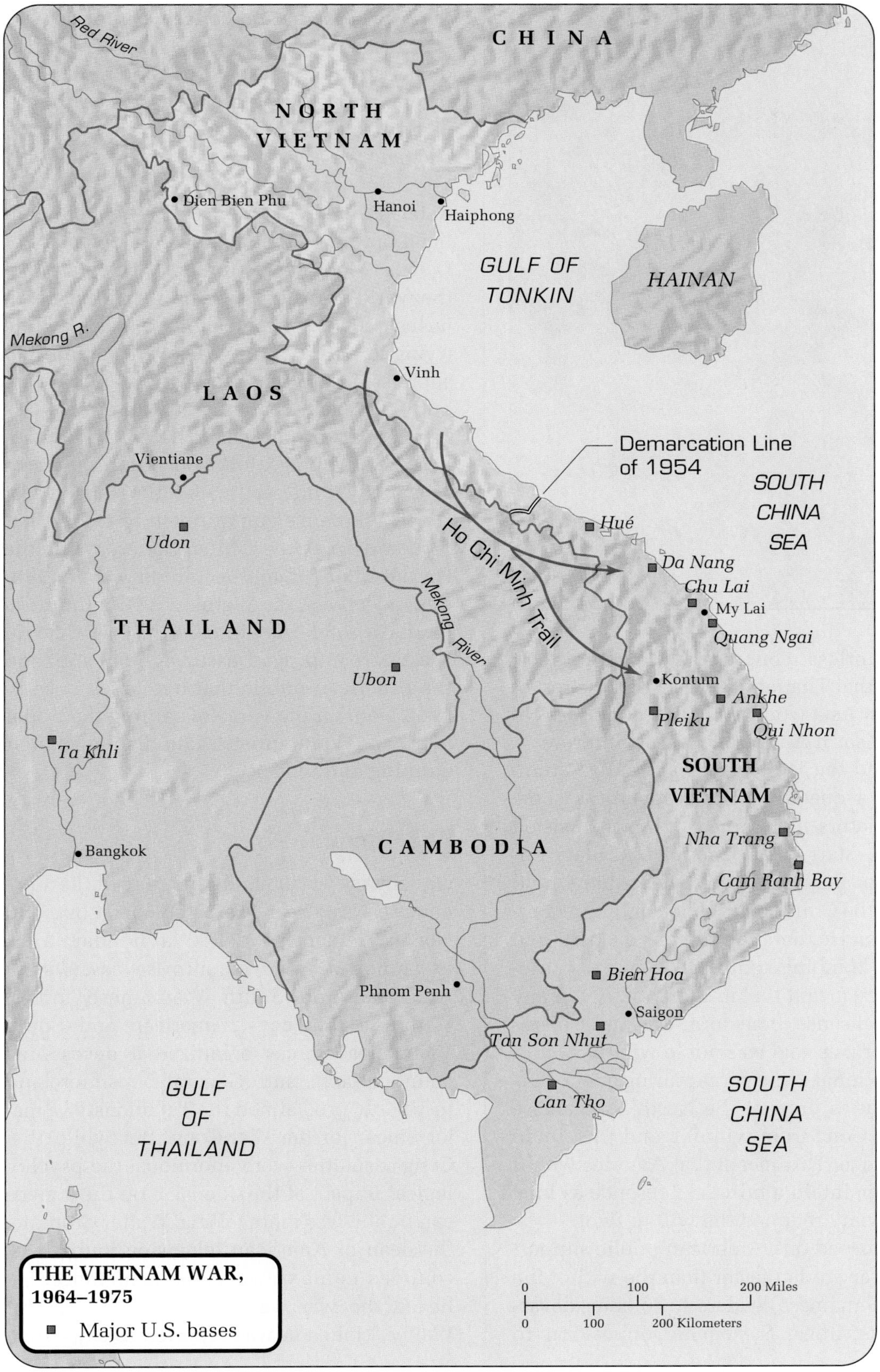
CHINA
Red River
NORTH VIETNAM
Dien Bien Phu
Hanoi
Haiphong
GULF OF TONKIN
HAINAN
Mekong R.
Vinh
LAOS
Demarcation Line of 1954
Vientiane
SOUTH CHINA SEA
Udon
Hué
Ho Chi Minh Trail
Da Nang
Chu Lai
My Lai
Quang Ngai
THAILAND
Mekong River
Ubon
Kontum
Ankhe
Pleiku
Qui Nhon
Ta Khli
SOUTH VIETNAM
Nha Trang
Bangkok
CAMBODIA
Cam Ranh Bay
Bien Hoa
Phnom Penh
Saigon
Tan Son Nhut
GULF OF THAILAND
Can Tho
SOUTH CHINA SEA
THE VIETNAM WAR, 1964–1975
Major U.S. bases
0
100
200 Miles
0
100
200 Kilometers

U.S. troops wade through marshland during a joint operation on South Vietnam's Mekong Delta, April 1967.

fore countless congressional committees, warning that Thailand, Burma, and the rest of Southeast Asia would fall "like dominoes" to communism if American forces withdrew.

Nor did the United States blindly "stumble into a quagmire" in Vietnam, as some commentators maintained. Johnson insisted from the start that American military involvement must not reach levels that would provoke the Chinese or Soviets into direct intervention. He therefore exercised a tight rein over the bombing campaign. Such a restrictive policy meant that military victory in any traditional sense of the term was never possible. America's goal was not to win the war in a conventional sense by capturing enemy territory, but to prevent the North Vietnamese and Viet Cong from winning and thereby to force a truce. This meant that America would have to maintain a military presence as long as the enemy retained the will to fight.

As it turned out, American public support for the war eroded faster than the will of the North Vietnamese leaders to tolerate devastating casualties. Systematic opposition to the war broke out on college campuses with the escalation of 1965. By 1967 antiwar demonstrations in New York and at the Pentagon were attracting massive support. Nightly television accounts of the fighting—Vietnam was the first war to receive extended television coverage, and hence has been dubbed the "living room war"—made the official optimism look fatuous. As Secretary of Defense McNamara admitted, "The picture of the world's greatest superpower killing or injuring 1,000 noncombatants a week, while trying to pound a tiny backward nation into submission on an issue whose merits are hotly disputed, is not a pretty one."

In a war of political will, North Vietnam had the advantage. Johnson and his advisers grievously underestimated the tenacity of North Vietnam's commitment to unify Vietnam and expel the United States. While the United States fought a limited war for limited objectives, the Vietnamese Communists fought a total war. Indeed, just as General Westmoreland was assuring Johnson and the American public that his forces in early 1968 were on the verge of gaining the upper hand, the Communists again displayed their cunning and tenacity.

The Turning Point

On January 31, 1968, the first day of the Vietnamese New Year (Tet), the Viet Cong and North Vietnamese defied a holiday truce to launch a wave of surprise assaults on American and South Vietnamese forces. Within a few days, American and South Vietnamese forces organized a devastating counterattack, and General Westmoreland justifiably proclaimed the Tet offensive a major defeat for the Viet Cong. But while Viet Cong casualties were enormous, the psychological impact of the offensive on the American public was more telling. Walter Cronkite, the dean of American television journalists, confided to his viewers that he no longer believed the war was winnable. "If I've lost Walter," Johnson was reported to say, "then it's over. I've lost Mr. Average Citizen." Polls showed that Johnson's popularity had declined to 35 percent, lower than any president since Truman in his darkest days.

During 1968 Johnson grew increasingly isolated from the public and the media. The secretary of defense reported that a task force of prominent soldiers and civilians saw no prospect for a military victory; the war was hopelessly stalemated. Robert Kennedy was considering a run for the presidency in order to challenge Johnson's Vietnam policy, and Senator Eugene McCarthy of Minnesota decided to oppose Johnson in the Democratic primaries. With antiwar activists rallying to his candidacy, McCarthy polled 42 percent of the vote to Johnson's 48 percent in New Hampshire's March primary. It was a remarkable showing for a little-known senator. Each presidential primary now promised to become a referendum on Johnson's Vietnam policy.

On March 31 Johnson announced a limited halt to the bombing of North Vietnam and fresh initiatives for a negotiated ceasefire. Then he added a dramatic postscript: he would not seek reelection. Although American combat troops would remain in Vietnam for seven more years and the casualties would mount, the quest for military victory had ended. Now the question was how the most powerful nation in the world could extricate itself from Vietnam with a minimum of damage to its prestige. It would not be easy. When direct negotiations with the North Vietnamese finally began in Paris in May 1968, they immediately bogged down over North Vietnam's demand for an American bombing halt as a precondition for further discussion.

Sixties Crescendo

A Traumatic Year

History seemed to move at a fearful pace throughout the 1960s, but 1968 was a year of extreme turbulence even for that volatile decade. On April 4, only four days after Johnson's withdrawal from the presidential race, Martin Luther King, Jr., was gunned down while standing on the balcony of a motel in Memphis, Tennessee. Debate still continues over whether the assassin acted alone or was a pawn in an organized conspiracy. King's death set off an outpouring of grief among whites and blacks. It also set off riots in over sixty American cities, with the most serious in Chicago and Washington, D.C.

Two months later, on June 6, Robert Kennedy was shot by a young Palestinian who resented Kennedy's strong support of Israel. Kennedy died at the end of the day on which he had convincingly defeated Eugene McCarthy in the California Democratic primary, thereby assuming leadership of the antiwar forces in the race for the nomination for president.

Chicago and Miami

In August 1968 Democratic delegates gathered inside the convention hall at Chicago to nominate Vice-President Hubert Humphrey. Outside the convention hall, 24,000 police and National Guardsmen and a small army of television reporters stood watch over several thousand diverse protesters herded together miles away in a public park. Chicago mayor Richard Daley warned that he would not tolerate disruptions. Nonetheless, riots broke out in front of the Hilton Hotel and were televised nationwide. As police tear gas and billy clubs struck demonstra-

Anti–Vietnam War protesters march down Pennsylvania Avenue. Many considered the war to be immoral, and thousands of young men evaded the draft.

tors, others chanted, "The whole world is watching."

The Democratic party's liberal tradition was clearly in disarray, a fact that gave heart to the Republicans who gathered in Miami to nominate Richard Nixon. Nixon's nomination represented a remarkable political comeback. He offered a vision of stability and order that a majority of Americans—soon to be called "the silent majority"—wanted desperately.

But others were ready as well to challenge the Democratic party regulars. George Wallace, the Democratic governor of Alabama, ran as a third candidate in the campaign on the American Independent party ticket. Wallace had made his political reputation as a brazen defender of segregation, but in his campaign for national office in 1968 he moderated his position on the race issue. And he appealed even more candidly than Nixon to the fears generated by antiwar protesters, the expanding welfare system, and the growth of the federal government. Wallace's platform was compelling in its simplicity: rioters would be shot, the war in Vietnam won, states' rights and law and order restored, open-housing laws repealed, and welfare cheats jailed.

Wallace's candidacy generated considerable appeal outside his native South, especially in white working-class communities where resentment against Johnson's Great Society liberalism seethed. Although never a possible winner, Wallace had to be taken seriously: he could deny Humphrey or Nixon an electoral majority and thereby throw the choice into the House of Representatives.

Nixon Again

It did not happen that way. Nixon enjoyed an enormous early lead in the polls, which narrowed as the election approached. Wallace's campaign was hurt by his outspoken running mate, retired Air Force general Curtis LeMay, who suggested using nuclear weapons in Vietnam. In October 1968, Humphrey, tainted by his ties to LBJ and the Democratic party bosses, announced that, if elected, he would stop bombing North Vietnam "as an acceptable risk for peace."

In the end, Nixon and his running mate, Governor Spiro Agnew of Maryland, eked out a narrow victory by roughly 500,000 votes, a margin of about 1 percentage point. The electoral vote was more decisive, 301 to 191. Wallace won 10 million votes, 13.5 percent of the total, the best showing by a third-party candidate since Robert La Follette in 1924. All but one of Wallace's 46 electoral votes were from the Deep South. Nixon swept all but four of the states west of the Mississippi, while Humphrey's support came almost exclusively from the Northeast.

So at the end of a turbulent year, near the end of a traumatic decade, power passed peacefully to a president who was associated with the superficial stability of the 1950s. A nation that had seemed on the verge of self-destructing in spasms of violence looked to Richard Nixon to provide what he had promised in the campaign: "peace with honor" in Vietnam and a middle ground on which a majority of Americans, silent or otherwise, could come together.

CHAPTER

34

Rebellion and Reaction in the 1960s and 1970s

This chapter focuses on

- Social rebellion and struggles for minority rights in the 1970s.
- Ending the war in Vietnam.
- Watergate and Nixon's resignation.
- The Ford and Carter administrations.

THE *ESSENTIAL AMERICA* ON-LINE TUTOR

www.wwnorton.com/eamerica/ch34

- **Topic: Student protest and lethal response in the Vietnam War era**
  www.wwnorton.com/eamerica/ch34/topic.htm

  In May 1970 National Guard troops opened fire on demonstrators at Ohio's Kent State University, killing four student bystanders and sparking months of intense protest. Only eleven days later, local police and highway patrolmen, responding to reports of a riot, opened fire on students at Jackson State College, killing two. Using photographs from Kent State and Jackson State, as well as an audio recording, first-person accounts of both incidents, and historical analyses, examine student activism toward the end of the Vietnam War era. What triggered the confrontations at Kent State and Jackson State, and why did officials respond with lethal force?

- **Chapter review: On-line quiz and chapter summary**
  www.wwnorton.com/eamerica/ch34/review.htm

- **Chapter resources: Multimedia index**
  www.wwnorton.com/eamerica/ch34/media.htm

The turbulent events of 1968 revealed how deeply divided American society had become and how difficult a task President Nixon faced in carrying out his pledge to restore social harmony. Yet his policies and his combative temperament served to heighten rather than reduce the tensions wracking the nation. What had caused such a seismic breakdown in social harmony? Ironically, many of the same forces that had promoted the flush times of the Eisenhower years helped generate the social upheavals of the 1960s and 1970s.

The Roots of Rebellion

Youth Revolt

By the 1960s, the postwar "baby-boomers" were maturing. Record numbers of these young people were attending American colleges and universities during the 1960s: college enrollment quadrupled between 1945 and 1970. At the same time, many universities had become increasingly dependent upon research contracts from giant corporations and the federal government. As these "multiversities" grew more bureaucratic and hierarchical, they unknowingly invited resistance from students wary of involvement in what Eisenhower had called the "military-industrial complex."

The Greensboro student sit-ins in 1960 not only precipitated a decade of civil rights activism; they also signaled an end to the supposed apathy that had enveloped college campuses and social life during the 1950s. Although primarily concerned with the rights and status of black people, the sit-ins, marches, protests, principles, and sacrifices associated with the civil rights movement provided inspiring models and uplifting rhetoric for other groups demanding justice, freedom, and equality.

During 1960–1961, a small but significant number of white students joined the sit-in movement. They and many others were also inspired by President Kennedy's direct appeals to their youthful idealism. Thousands enrolled in the Peace Corps and VISTA. Later, as criticism of escalating American involvement in Vietnam mounted, more and more young people grew disillusioned with the government and other institutional bastions of the status quo. By the mid-1960s, a full-fledged youth revolt erupted on many campuses, and rebellious students began to flow into two distinct movements: the New Left and the counterculture.

The New Left

The explicitly political strain of the youth revolt coalesced when Tom Hayden and Al Haber, two student radicals at the University of Michigan, formed the Students for a Democratic Society (SDS) in 1960. Two years later, Hayden drafted what became known as the Port Huron Statement. The manifesto focused on the absence of individual freedom in modern American life. The country, Hayden insisted, was dominated by huge organizational structures—governments, corporations, universities—all of which conspired to oppress and alienate the individual. Hayden declared that students had the power to restore "participatory democracy" to American life by wresting "control of the educational process from the administrative bureaucracy" and then forging links with other dissident movements. He and others soon adopted the term "New Left" to distinguish their efforts at grassroots democracy from the Old Left of the 1930s, which had espoused an orthodox Marxism.

In the fall of 1964, students at the University of California at Berkeley took Hayden's program to heart. When Clark Kerr, the university chancellor, announced that sidewalk solicitations for political causes would no longer be allowed, several thousand students staged a sit-in. After a tense standoff the administration relented. Student groups then formed the Free Speech

Movement (FSM). Led by Mario Savio, a philosophy major and compelling public speaker, the FSM in 1964 marched into the administration building and organized a sit-in. In the early morning hours, 600 police officers moved in and arrested the protesters.

The program and tactics of the FSM and SDS soon spread to universities throughout the country, but their focus changed as escalating American involvement in Vietnam brought a dramatic expansion of the military draft, and millions of young men faced the grim prospect of participating in an increasingly unpopular war. Several thousand male collegians would flee to Canada or Sweden to escape the draft, while hundreds of thousands engaged in various protests against a war they considered to be immoral.

In the spring of 1967, 500,000 marchers of all ages converged on New York's Central Park. Dozens of young men ceremoniously burned their draft cards, and the so-called Resistance phase of the antiwar movement was born. Thereafter a coalition of protest groups around the country sponsored draft-card burning rallies and sit-ins that led to numerous arrests.

During the spring of 1968, spreading campus unrest reached a climax with the disruption of Columbia University. Mark Rudd, leader of the campus SDS chapter, and a small group of radicals occupied some campus buildings, and the protest quickly spread. During the following week, more buildings were occupied, faculty and administrative offices were ransacked, and classes were cancelled. University officials finally called in New York City police. That same spring, similar clashes between students, administrators, and eventually police occurred at Harvard, Cornell, and San Francisco State.

At the 1968 Democratic convention in Chicago, the polarization of American society reached a tragic and bizarre climax. Inside the tightly guarded convention hall, Democrats were nominating Lyndon Johnson's faithful vice-president, Hubert Humphrey. At the same time, Chicago's streets were filled with the whole spectrum of antiwar dissenters, from the earnest supporters of Eugene McCarthy, through the Resistance and SDS, to the nihilistic Yippies (the Youth International Party).

The outlandish behavior of the protesters did not justify the unrestrained response of Chicago's arch-conservative Mayor Richard Daley and the thousands of police and National Guard troops mobilized to ensure "law and order." As a national television audience watched, many of the police went berserk, clubbing and gassing demonstrators as well as bystanders caught up in the chaotic scene. The spectacle lasted three days and generated a wave of anger among many middle-class Americans, anger that Richard Nixon and the Republicans shrewdly exploited at their convention in Miami. At the same time, the Chicago riots helped to fragment the antiwar movement.

By 1971 the New Left was dead as a political movement. In large measure it had committed suicide by abandoning the democratic and pacifist principles that had originally inspired participants and given the movement its moral legitimacy. The larger antiwar movement also began to fade as American troops returned home from Vietnam and the draft ended. A *New York Times* survey of college campuses in 1969 revealed that many students were transferring their attention to the environment. This ecological conscience would blossom in the 1970s into one of the most compelling items on the nation's social agenda.

The Counterculture

The numbing events of 1968 led other disaffected activists away from radical politics altogether and toward another manifestation of the sixties youth revolt: the "counterculture." Long hair, tie-dyed shirts, recreational drugs, rock music, and group living arrangements were more important than revolutionary ideology or mass protest to the "hippies," the direct descendants of the Beats of the 1950s. These advocates of the counterculture were primarily well-educated young whites alienated by the Vietnam War, racism, political corruption and parental demands, runaway technology, and a crass corporate mentality that equated the good life with material goods. They eagerly embraced the tantalizing credo announced by the zany Harvard professor Timothy Leary, "Turn on to the scene, tune in to what's happening, and drop out."

Huge outdoor rock music concerts were a popular source of community for hippies. The largest of these was the Woodstock Music Festival, held in 1969 on a 600-acre farm near the tiny rural town of Bethel, New York. For three days some 500,000 young people reveled in good music and cheap marijuana. But the Woodstock karma was short-lived. When promoters tried to repeat the scene four months later, this time at a Rolling Stones concert in Altamont, California, members of the Hell's Angels motorcycle gang beat to death a man wielding a knife in front of the stage.

Just as the 1968 Democratic convention in Chicago marked the end of the New Left as a vital political force, the violence at Altamont sharply diminished the appeal of the counterculture. Moreover, many of the flower children themselves grew tired of their riches-to-rags existence and returned to school. The search on the part of alienated youth for a better society and a good life was strewn with both comic and tragic aspects, and it reflected the deep social ills that had been allowed to fester throughout the post–World War II period.

Feminism

The logic and lure of liberation that spanned the sixties helped accelerate a powerful women's rights crusade. Like the New Left, the new feminism drew much of its inspiration and initial tactics from the civil rights movement. Its aim was to challenge the cult of domesticity that had been touted as the ideal for women during the 1950s.

The mainstream of the women's movement was led by Betty Friedan. Her influential book, *The Feminine Mystique* (1963), launched a new phase of female protest on a national level. Women, Friedan wrote, had actually lost ground during the years after World War II, when many left wartime

The Woodstock festival drew nearly half a million people to a New York farm in August 1969. The concert was billed as three days of "peace, love, and music."

assembly lines and settled down in suburbia to care for the kids. Advertisers and women's magazines promoted the "feminine mystique" of blissful domesticity, while in Friedan's view, the American middle-class home had become "a comfortable concentration camp" where women saw their individual potential suffocated in an atmosphere of mindless materialism, daytime TV, and neighborhood gossip.

The Feminine Mystique raised the consciousness of many women who had long suffered from a feeling of being trapped in a rut. In 1966 Friedan and a small group of activists founded the National Organization for Women (NOW), whose membership grew rapidly. NOW spearheaded efforts to end job discrimination on the basis of sex, to legalize abortion, and to obtain federal and state support for child-care centers.

Pressured by NOW, Congress and the Supreme Court in the early 1970s advanced the cause of sexual equality. Under Title IX of the Educational Amendments Act of 1972, colleges were required to institute "affirmative action" programs to ensure equal opportunity for women in such areas as admissions, faculty and staff hiring, and athletics. In the same year, Congress overwhelmingly approved the Equal Rights Amendment (ERA) to the Constitution. In 1973 the Supreme Court, in *Roe* v. *Wade,* struck down state laws forbidding abortions during the first three months of pregnancy on the grounds of a constitutional right of privacy. Meanwhile, many bastions of male education, including Yale and Princeton, led a new movement for coeducation that swept the nation.

In 1967 Syracuse University student Kathy Switzer challenged the Boston Marathon's men-only tradition. Officials tried to pull her from the course, but with the aid of fellow runners she completed the race. Women became official entrants in 1971.

By the end of the 1970s, however, sharp divisions between moderate and radical feminists, as well as the failure of the movement to broaden its appeal much beyond the white middle class, caused reform efforts to stagnate. In 1982 the Equal Rights Amendment died, several states short of ratification. And the very success of NOW's efforts to liberalize state abortion laws helped generate a powerful backlash, especially among Catholics and fundamentalist Protestants, who mounted a potent "right to life" crusade.

Yet the women's movement endured despite setbacks. The growing political power of women and their expanding presence in the workforce combined to become one of the most dramatic developments of the era. By 1976 over half the married women in America and nine of ten women college graduates were employed outside the home. Women were changing traditional sex roles and childbearing practices to accommodate the two-career family, which had replaced the established pattern of male breadwinner and female housekeeper as the new American norm.

Hispanic Rights

The activism that animated the student revolt, the civil rights movement, and the crusade for women's rights soon spread to various ethnic minority groups. Hispanic-American activists during the 1950s and 1960s mirrored the efforts of black civil rights leaders. They too denounced widespread discrimination in hiring and housing, promoted efforts to improve the quality of public education, and struggled to increase Hispanic-American political influence and overcome widespread poverty. Like their black peers, Hispanic college students during the 1960s seized upon ways to heighten their sense of ethnic pride and distinctiveness and to bolster their solidarity.

In southern California, students formed Young Chicanos for Community Action, a social service group designed to promote greater self-reliance and local involvement within Chicano neighborhoods. Wearing brown berets, the members protested the disproportionate number of Hispanics being killed in the Vietnam War and demanded improvements in their neighborhood schools. Unlike their black counterparts, however, Chicano leaders faced an awkward dilemma: what should they do about the continuing stream of illegal Mexican aliens flowing across the border? Many Mexican-Americans argued that their own hopes for economic advancement and social equality were put at risk by the influx of Mexican laborers willing to accept low-paying jobs. Mexican-American leaders thus helped to end the *bracero* program (which trucked in *braceros,* Mexican contract day laborers, at harvest time) in 1964 and to form the United Farm Workers (UFW) in 1962 (originally the National Farm Workers Association) to represent Mexican-American migrant workers.

The founder of the UFW was César Chavez. Born in Yuma, Arizona, in 1927 to Mexican immigrant parents, Chavez moved with his parents and four siblings to California in 1939. In 1952 Chavez joined the Community Service Organization (CSO), a social service group that sought to educate and organize the migrant poor so that they could become more self-reliant. He founded new CSO chapters and was named general director in 1958.

Chavez left the organization in 1962 when it refused to back his proposal to establish a union for farm workers. Other CSO leaders believed that it was impossible to organize migrant workers into an effective union. They thought the farm workers were too mobile, too poor, too illiterate, too ethnically diverse, and too easily replaced by *braceros.* Moreover, farm workers did not enjoy protected status under the National Labor Relations Act of 1935 (the Wagner Act). Unlike industrial laborers, they were not guaranteed the right to organize or to receive a minimum wage. Nor did federal regulations govern the safety of their workplaces.

Despite such obstacles, Chavez resolved to organize the migrant farm workers. His fledgling Farm Workers Association gained national attention in 1965 when it joined a strike by Filipino farm workers against the corporate grape farmers in California's San Joaquin Valley. Soon the UFW began organizing migrant workers in the lettuce fields of the Salinas Valley.

Still, the grape strike itself brought no tangible gains. So Chavez called for a nationwide consumer boycott of grapes. In 1970, the grape strike and consumer boycott finally succeeded in bringing twenty-six grape growers to the bargaining table. They signed formal contracts recognizing the UFW, and wages increased and working conditions improved. In 1975 the California state legislature passed a bill that required growers to bargain collectively with the elected representatives of the farm workers.

But the chief strength of the Hispanic movement lay less in the duplication of the civil rights strategies than in the sheer growth of the Hispanic population. In 1960 Hispanics had numbered slightly more than 3 million; by 1970 they had increased to 9 million, and by 1990 they numbered over 22 million, making them the largest minority in America after African Americans.

Native Americans

American Indians—many of whom now called themselves Native Americans—also emerged as a new political force in the late 1960s. Two conditions combined to make Indian rights a priority: first, white Americans felt a persistent sense of guilt for the destructive policies of their ancestors toward the people they had displaced; second, the plight of the Native American mi-

Members of AIM marched on Wounded Knee, South Dakota, to bring attention to dependence on welfare, poor living conditions, and rampant alcoholism that plagued Native Americans on reservations nationwide.

nority was more desperate than that of any other group in the country. Indian unemployment was ten times the national rate, their life expectancy was twenty years lower than the national average, and the suicide rate was one hundred times higher than that for whites.

At first, Indian activists copied the tactics of civil rights reformers. In 1968 two Chippewas living in Minneapolis, George Mitchell and Dennis Banks, founded the American Indian Movement (AIM) to promote "red power." The leaders of AIM occupied Alcatraz Island in San Francisco Bay in 1969. And in 1972, a sit-in at the Department of the Interior's inept Bureau of Indian Affairs (BIA) in Washington attracted national attention to their cause. Indian protesters, however, soon discovered a more effective tactic than direct action and sit-ins. They went into federal courts armed with copies of old treaties and demanded that these become the basis for restitution. In Alaska, Maine, and Massachusetts, they won significant settlements that provided legal recognition of their tribal rights and financial compensation at levels that upgraded the standard of living on several reservations.

Gay Rights

The liberationist impulses of the 1960s also encouraged homosexuals to organize and assert their own right to equal treatment and basic dignity. On June 17, 1969, New York City police raided the Stonewall Inn, a transvestite bar in the heart of Greenwich Village. The patrons fought back and the struggle spilled into the streets. Rioting lasted throughout the weekend. When it ended, gays had forged a new sense of solidarity and a new organization called the Gay Liberation Front.

As news of the Stonewall riots spread across the country, the gay rights movement assumed national proportions. One of its main tactics was to encourage people to "come out" and make public their homosexuality. By 1973 almost 800 gay and lesbian organizations had been formed across the country, and every major city had a visible gay community and cultural life.

Like the civil rights crusade and the women's movement, however, the campaign for gay rights soon suffered from internal divisions and aroused a conservative backlash. Gay activists engaged in fractious disputes over tactics and objectives, and conservative moralists and Christian fundamentalists launched a nationwide counterattack. They successfully repealed new local laws banning discrimination against homosexuals. By the end of the 1970s, the gay rights movement had lost its initial momentum and was struggling to salvage many of its hard-won gains.

Nixon and Vietnam

The numerous liberation movements of the 1960s fundamentally changed the tone and texture of American social life. By the early 1970s, however, the pendulum of national mood was swinging back toward conservatism. But large as the gap was between the conservative majority and the varied forces of dissent, they agreed on one thing: that the Vietnam War remained the dominant event of the time. Until the war was ended and all American troops were returned home, the nation would find it difficult to achieve the equilibrium that the new president had promised.

Gradual Withdrawal

The Nixon administration promised a new course in Vietnam. Nixon and his special assistant for national security affairs, Henry Kissinger, claimed to have a secret plan to achieve "peace with honor." But peace was long in coming and not very honorable when it came. By the time a settlement was finally reached in 1973, another 20,000 Americans had died, the morale of the American army had been shattered, millions of Asians had been killed or wounded, and fighting in fact continued in Southeast Asia. In the end, Nixon's policy gained little that he could not have accomplished in 1969.

The administration's new strategy in Vietnam moved along three separate fronts. The first front was at the deadlocked Paris peace talks, where American negotiators demanded the withdrawal of North Vietnamese forces from South Vietnam and the preservation of the American-supported regime of President Nguyen Van Thieu. The North Vietnamese and Viet Cong negotiators, however, insisted on retaining a military presence in the South and reunifying the Vietnamese people under a government dominated by the Communists.

Second, Nixon tried to defuse domestic unrest generated by the war. To this end, he sought to "Vietnamize" the conflict by turning over most of the combat missions to Vietnamese units and sharply reducing the number of American ground forces. To assuage the South Vietnamese, he provided more equipment and training for their troops. From a peak of 540,000 personnel in 1969, American combat units were withdrawn gradually, so that by 1973 only 50,000 American troops remained in Vietnam.

Third, while reducing the number of American combat troops in Vietnam, Nixon and Kissinger secretly expanded the air war in an effort to persuade the enemy to come to terms. On March 18, 1969, American planes began "Operation Menu," a fourteen-month-long bombing of Communist sanctuaries in Cambodia. Over 100,000 tons of bombs were dropped, four times the tonnage dropped on Japan during World War II. Congress did not learn of these raids until 1970, when Nixon announced what he called an "incursion" by United States troops into supposedly "neutral" Cambodia to "clean out" North Vietnamese staging areas.

Divisions at Home

News of the Cambodia "incursion" came on the heels of another incident that rekindled public indignation against the war. Late in 1969 the story of the My Lai massacre broke. During the next two years, the public learned the gruesome tale of Army Lieutenant William Calley, who ordered the murder of over 200 Vietnamese civilians in My Lai village in 1968. Twenty-five officers were charged with complicity in the massacre and subsequent cover-up, but only Calley was convicted of murder. Nixon shortly thereafter granted him parole.

The loudest public outcry against Nixon's Indochina policy occurred in the wake of the Cambodian "incursion." Campuses across the country witnessed a new wave of protests in 1970. At Kent State University, the Ohio National Guard arrived to quell rioting, during which the campus Reserve Officer Training Corps (ROTC) building was burned down by antiwar protesters. Pelted by rocks and verbal taunts, the poorly trained guardsmen panicked and opened fire on the demonstrators, killing four bystanders. Eleven days later, on May 15, Mississippi highway patrolmen riddled a dormitory at Jackson State College with bullets, killing two black students. Although an official investigation of the Kent State episode condemned the "casual and indiscriminate shooting," polls indicated that the American public supported the National Guard; students had "got what they were asking for."

The following year, in 1971, the *New York Times* began publishing

National Guardsmen shot and killed four student bystanders during antiwar demonstrations on the campus of Kent State University.

excerpts from a secret Defense Department study on the Vietnam War. The so-called Pentagon Papers, leaked to the press by a former Pentagon official, Daniel Ellsberg, confirmed what many critics of the war had long suspected: Congress and the public had not received the full story on the Gulf of Tonkin incident of 1964. Contingency plans for American entry into the war were being drawn up even while Johnson was promising the American people that combat troops would never be sent to Vietnam. The Nixon administration attempted to block publication of the Pentagon Papers, arguing that publication would endanger national security and prolong the war. By a vote of six to three, the Supreme Court ruled against the government. Newspapers throughout the country began publication the next day.

War without End

Although Nixon's decision in the spring of 1970 to use American forces to root out Communist bases in Cambodia brought a tactical victory, it also served to widen a war he had promised to end. Moreover, his hopes that the South Vietnamese units replacing American forces could hold their own against the North Vietnamese were dashed when they suffered repeated defeats in 1971 and 1972. Disorganized, poorly led, and lacking tenacity, the South Vietnamese soldiers had to call upon American air power to fend off North Vietnamese offensives.

The deteriorating ground war along with mounting social divisions at home and the approach of the 1972 presidential elections combined to produce a shift in the American negotiating position in Paris. In the summer of 1972, Henry Kissinger dropped his insistence on the removal of all North Vietnamese troops from the South before the withdrawal of American troops. On October 26, only a week before the American presidential election, he announced: "Peace is at hand." But the Thieu regime in South Vietnam objected to the plan, fearful that the continued presence of North Vietnamese troops in the South virtually guaranteed an eventual Communist victory. Hanoi then stiffened its position by demanding that Thieu resign.

The talks broke off on December 16, and Nixon told his military advisers that only a massive show of American air power would make the North Vietnamese more cooperative at the negotiating table. Two days later, the United States unleashed furious B-52 raids on Hanoi and Haiphong. The so-called "Christmas bombings" aroused worldwide protest, but Kissinger claimed Nixon's "jugular diplomacy" worked, for the talks in Paris soon resumed.

On January 27, 1973, the United States, North and South Vietnam, and the Viet Cong signed an "agreement on ending the war and restoring peace in Vietnam." The North Vietnamese were allowed to keep troops in the South and remained committed to the reunification of Vietnam under one government. The South Vietnamese accepted these terms, albeit reluctantly, on the basis of Nixon's promise that the United States would respond "with full force" to any violation of the peace. On March 29, 1973, the last American combat troops left Vietnam.

In 1975 the North Vietnamese launched a full-scale armored invasion against the South. President Thieu appealed to Washington for assistance, but the Democratic majority in Congress refused, and on April 30, 1975, Americans watched on television as North Vietnamese tanks rolled into Saigon, soon to be renamed Ho Chi Minh City.

The longest war in American history was finally over, leaving in its wake a bitter legacy. The war suggested that democracy was not easily transferable to Third World regions. It also eroded respect for the military so thoroughly that many young Americans came to regard military service as inherently ignoble. Fought to show the world that the United States was united in its convictions, the Vietnam War instead divided Americans more drastically than any event since the Civil War and cost the nation some 58,000 deaths and $150 billion. Little wonder that the dominant public reaction to the war's end was the urge to "put Vietnam behind us" and revert to a noninterventionist foreign policy.

Nixon and Middle America

Richard Nixon had been elected in 1968 as the representative of "Middle America," those citizens fed up with the liberal politics and social radicalism of the 1960s. The Nixon cabinet and White House staff reflected the values of this "silent majority." The chief figures were John Mitchell, the gruff attorney-general who had made his fortune as a lawyer in Nixon's old firm, and H. R. Haldeman and John Ehrlichman, advisers on domestic policy whose major experience before their association with the Nixon campaign had been in advertising. The cabinet was all white, all male, all Republican.

Domestic Affairs

Confronting a Congress controlled by Democrats, Richard Nixon focused his energies on foreign policy, where presidential initiatives were less restricted and where he, in tandem with Henry Kissinger, achieved several stunning breakthroughs. He also continued to support the American space program and the efforts to beat the Soviets to the moon. In July 1969 American astronaut Neil Armstrong became the first person to walk on the moon. Back on earth, however, Nixon sought to stop social-welfare programs in their tracks. Yet, like Eisenhower before him, he found it difficult to dismantle liberal programs.

Despite the efforts of the Nixon administration, the civil rights legislation enacted during the Johnson years continued to take effect. Congress extended the Voting Rights Act over Nixon's veto. The Supreme Court, in the first decision made under the new Chief Justice Warren Burger—a Nixon appointee—ordered the integration of the Mississippi public schools. During Nixon's first term, and despite his wishes, affirmative action made major inroads and more schools were desegregated than in all the Kennedy-Johnson years combined.

Nixon's attempts to block desegregation efforts in urban areas also failed. The Burger Court ruled unanimously in *Swann* v. *Charlotte-Mecklenburg Board of Education* (1971) that school systems must bus students out of their neighborhoods if necessary to achieve racial integration. Yet protest over desegregation now began to manifest itself more in the North than in the South, as white families in Boston, Denver, and other cities denounced the destruction of "the neighborhood school." Busing opponents won a limited victory when the Supreme Court ruled in 1974 that requiring the transfer of students from the inner city to the suburbs was unconstitutional. This ruling, along with the *Bakke* v. *Board of Regents of California* (1978) decision, which restricted the use of quotas to achieve racial balance in university classrooms, marked the transition of desegregation from an issue of simple justice to a more

In July 1969, a program begun by President Kennedy reached its goal: putting a person on the moon.

tangled thicket of conflicting group and individual rights.

It also reflected the growing conservatism of the Supreme Court, a trend encouraged by Nixon. Circumstance and the aging of the justices on the Warren Court gave Nixon the opportunity to make four new appointments. Only one, William Rehnquist, would consistently support Nixon's conservative interpretation of the Constitution, but overall the tenor of the Court did shift toward a more moderate stance.

Meanwhile, the Democratic Congress moved forward with new legislation: the right of eighteen-year-olds to vote in national elections (1970) and, under the Twenty-sixth Amendment (1971), in state and local elections as well; increases in Social Security benefits tied to the inflation rate; a rise in food-stamp funding; the Occupational Safety and Health Act (1970), and the Federal Election Campaign Act (1972).

During Nixon's first term, Americans in large numbers began to lobby for government action to improve and protect the natural environment. In 1970 hundreds of thousands of activists rallied across the country in support of the first "Earth Day." In response, Congress established new programs to control water pollution and passed the Clean Air Act (1970) over Nixon's veto. Congress also created the Environmental Protection Agency (EPA) to oversee federal guidelines for air pollution, toxic wastes, and water quality. The EPA began requiring developers to perform environmental impact studies before new construction could begin. The agency also set fuel efficiency standards for automobiles and required manufacturers to reduce the level of carbon monoxide emissions from car engines.

Economic Malaise

The major domestic development during the Nixon years was a floundering economy. Exacerbated by the expense of the Vietnam War, inflation reached 12 percent by 1974, and it remained in double digits for most of the 1970s. Unemployment climbed to 6 percent by the end of 1970 and threatened to keep rising. Somehow the American economy was undergoing a recession and inflation at the same time. Economists coined the term "stagflation" to describe the syndrome that defied the orthodox laws of economics.

The economic malaise had at least three deep-rooted causes. First, the Johnson administration had attempted to pay for both the Great Society's social-welfare programs and the war in Vietnam without a major tax increase, thus generating larger federal deficits, a major expansion of the money supply, and rapid price inflation. Second, and more important, by the late 1960s, American productivity growth had begun to slow. The country also began to experience a growing trade deficit. Third, the American economy had grown heavily dependent on cheap sources of energy.

Just as domestic petroleum reserves began to dwindle and dependence on foreign sources increased, the nations in the Organization of Petroleum Exporting Countries (OPEC), centered in the Middle East, combined to use their oil as a political and economic weapon. In 1973, when the United States sent massive aid to Israel during the Yom Kippur War against Egypt and Syria, OPEC announced that it would not sell oil to nations supporting Israel and that it was raising its prices by 400 percent. American motorists thereafter faced long lines at gas stations, schools and offices closed down, factories cut production, and the inflation rate soared.

Another condition leading to stagflation was the flood of new workers—mainly baby-boomers and women—entering the labor market. From 1965 to 1980, the workforce grew by 40 percent, or almost 30 million workers, a figure greater than the total labor force of France or West Germany. The number of new jobs created could not keep up, leaving many unemployed. At the same time, worker productivity declined, pushing up prices in the face of rising demand.

Stagflation posed a new set of economic problems, but the Nixon administration responded erratically and ineffectively with old remedies. First, it tried to reduce the federal deficit by raising taxes and cutting the budget. When the Democratic Congress refused to cooperate with this approach, the White House encouraged the Federal Reserve Board to reduce the money supply by raising interest rates. But the move backfired as the stock market immediately collapsed, plunging the economy into the "Nixon recession."

A sense of desperation then seized the White House. On August 15, 1971, Nixon froze all wages and prices for ninety days, yet the economy still floundered. By 1973 the wage and price guidelines were made voluntary, and therefore almost entirely ineffective. Stagflation continued, and it would plague the economy for the rest of the decade.

Nixon Triumphant

China

If the economy's ailments proved more than Nixon could remedy, in foreign policy his administration managed to improve American relations with the major powers of the Communist world—China and the Soviet Union—and to shift fundamentally the pattern of the cold war. In 1971, Henry Kissinger secretly visited Beijing (Peking) to explore the possibility of American recognition of China. In 1972, Nixon himself arrived in Beijing and made recognition an official and public fact. The irony of the event was overwhelming. Richard Nixon, the former anti-Communist crusader who had condemned the State Department for "losing" China in 1949, had accomplished a diplomatic feat that his Democratic predecessors could not.

Détente

China sought the breakthrough in relations with the United States because its rivalry with the Soviet Union, with which it shares a long border, had become increasingly bitter. Soviet leaders, troubled by the Sino-American agreements, were also anxious for an easing of tensions with the United States now that they had, as the result of a huge arms buildup following the Cuban missile crisis, achieved virtual parity with the United States in nuclear weapons. Once again Nixon surprised the world, by announcing that he would visit Moscow in 1972 for discussions with Leonid Brezhnev, the Soviet premier.

What became known as "détente" with the Soviets offered the promise of a more orderly and restrained competition between the two superpowers. Nixon and Brezhnev signed the Strategic Arms Limitation Talks (SALT) agreement, which in effect allowed the Soviets to retain a greater number of missiles with greater destructive power while the United States retained a lead in the total number of warheads. No limitations were placed on new weapons systems, though each side agreed to work toward a permanent freeze on all nuclear weapons.

Shuttle Diplomacy

The Nixon-Kissinger initiatives in the Middle East were less dramatic and less conclusive than the agreements with China and the Soviet Union, but they did show that America recognized Arab power in the region and its own dependence on the oil from Islamic states fundamentally opposed to Israel. After Israel recovered from the initial shock of the Arab attacks that triggered the Yom Kippur War of 1973, it recaptured the Golan Heights and seized additional Syrian territory. Kissinger initiated the negotiations leading to a cease-fire and exerted pressure to prevent Israel from taking more Arab territory. American reliance on Arab oil led to closer ties with Egypt and its president, Anwar el-Sadat, and more restrained support for Israel.

The 1972 Election

Nixon's foreign policy achievements allowed him to stage the campaign of 1972 as a triumphal procession. The first threat to his reelection came from Democratic Alabama governor George Wallace, who had the potential to deprive the Republicans of conservative votes. But on May 15, 1972, Wallace was shot and paralyzed below the waist by a deranged man, and he was forced to withdraw from the campaign.

Meanwhile, the Democrats were further ensuring Nixon's victory by nominating Senator George S. McGovern of South Dakota, a former college history professor and crusading liberal whose antiwar and social-welfare positions were associated with the turbulence of the 1960s.

Nixon won the greatest victory of any Republican presidential candidate in history, capturing 520 electoral votes to only 17 for McGovern. During the course of the campaign, McGovern complained about the "dirty tricks" of the Nixon administration, most especially the curious incident during the summer of 1972 in which burglars were caught breaking into the Democratic National Committee headquarters in the Watergate apartment complex in Washington, D.C. McGovern's accusations seemed shrill and biased at the time. Nixon and his staff made plans for "four more years" as the investigation of the fateful Watergate break-in unfolded.

Watergate

During the trial of the accused Watergate burglars, the relentless prodding of Judge John J. Sirica led one of the accused to tell the full story of the Nixon administration's complicity in the episode. James W. McCord, a former CIA agent and security chief for the Committee to Re-elect the President (CREEP), was the first of many informers in a melodrama that unfolded over the next two years. It ended in the first resignation of a president in American history, the conviction and imprisonment of twenty-five officials of the Nixon administration, including four cabinet members, and the most serious constitutional crisis since the impeachment trial of President Andrew Johnson.

Uncovering the Cover-up

No evidence surfaced that Nixon had ordered the break-in or that he had been aware of plans to burglarize the Democratic National Committee. From the start, however, Nixon participated in the cover-up, using his presidential powers to discredit and block the investigation. Perhaps most alarming was that the Watergate burglary proved to be one small part of a larger pattern of corruption and criminality sanctioned by the Nixon White House. Since 1970, Nixon had ordered intelligence agencies to spy on his opponents, open their mail, and even burglarize their homes in an effort to uncover compromising information.

The cover-up began to unravel when the acting director of the FBI resigned in 1973 after confessing that he had destroyed several incriminating documents. On April 30 presidential assistants Ehrlichman and Haldeman resigned, together with Attorney-General Richard Kleindienst. A few days later Nixon nervously assured the public in a television address, "I'm not a crook." New evidence suggested otherwise. White House legal counsel John Dean, whom Nixon had dismissed, testified before a Senate committee that Nixon had approved the cover-up. In another "bombshell" disclosure, a White House aide told the committee that Nixon had installed a secret taping system in the White House and that many of the conversations about Watergate had been recorded.

A year-long battle for the "Nixon tapes" then began. Harvard law professor Archibald Cox, whom Nixon had appointed as a special prosecutor to handle the Watergate case, took the president to court in 1973 to obtain the tapes. Nixon, pleading "executive privilege," refused to release them and ordered Cox fired. In what became known as the "Saturday Night Massacre," the new attorney-general and his deputy resigned rather than execute the president's order. Cox's replacement as special prosecutor also took the president to court. In March 1974 a Watergate grand jury indicted Ehrlichman, Haldeman, and Mitchell for obstruction of justice, and it named Nixon as an "unindicted coconspirator."

On July 24, 1974, the Supreme Court ruled unanimously that the president must surrender the tapes. A few days later the House Judiciary Committee voted to recommend three articles of impeachment: obstruction of justice through the payment of "hush money" to witnesses and the withholding of evidence; abuse of power through using federal agencies to deprive citizens of their constitutional rights; and defiance of Congress by withholding the tapes. Before the House of Representatives could meet to vote on impeachment, however, Nixon handed over the complete set of White House tapes. On August 9, 1974, fully aware that the evidence on the tapes implicated him in the cover-up, Richard Nixon resigned from office.

Effects of Watergate

Vice-President Spiro Agnew did not succeed Nixon, because Agnew himself had been forced to resign in 1973 when it became known that he had accepted bribes from contractors before and during his term as vice-president. The vice-president at the time of Nixon's resignation was Gerald Ford, the former minority leader in the House from Michigan, whom Nixon had appointed with congressional approval, under the provisions of the Twenty-fifth Amendment (1967). Ford insisted that he had no intention of pardoning Nixon, who was still liable for criminal prosecution. But a month after Nixon's resignation, the new president issued the pardon, explaining that it was necessary to end the national obsession with the Watergate scandals. Many suspected that Nixon and Ford had secretly agreed that Nixon would be pardoned.

If there was a silver lining in Watergate's dark cloud, it was the vigor and resiliency of the institutions that had brought a president down—the press, Congress, the courts, and an aroused public opinion. The Watergate revelations provoked Congress to pass several pieces of legislation designed to curb executive power in the future. The War Powers Act (1973) required presidents to inform Congress within forty-eight hours if U.S. troops were being deployed in combat abroad and to withdraw troops after sixty days unless Congress specifically approved

Having resigned his office, Richard Nixon waves farewell outside the White House, August 9, 1974.

their stay. In an effort to correct abuses of campaign funds, Congress enacted legislation in 1974 that set new ceilings on political contributions and expenditures. In reaction to the Nixon claim of "executive privilege" as a means of withholding evidence, Congress strengthened the 1966 Freedom of Information Act to require prompt responses to requests for information from government files and to place on government agencies the burden of proof for classifying information as secret.

With Nixon's resignation, the nation had weathered a profound constitutional crisis, but the aftershock of the Watergate episode produced a deep sense of disillusionment with the "imperial presidency." It also heightened public cynicism toward a government that had systematically lied to the people and violated their civil liberties. Restoring credibility and respect became the primary challenge facing Nixon's successors. Unfortunately, an array of new economic and foreign crises would make that task doubly difficult.

An Unelected President

While the Watergate crisis dominated the Washington scene, major domestic and foreign problems received little executive attention. The perplexing combination of inflation and recession worsened, as did the oil crisis. At the same time, Henry Kissinger, who assumed control over the management of foreign policy, watched helplessly as the South Vietnamese forces began to crumble before North Vietnamese attacks, attempted with limited success to establish a framework for peace in the Middle East, and supported a CIA role in overthrowing the popularly elected Marxist president of Chile.

The Ford Years

Gerald Ford inherited these simmering problems, as well as the burden of being an unelected president. An amiable, honest man, Ford enjoyed widespread popular support for only a short time. His pardon of Nixon generated a storm of criticism. The *New York Times* called it "an unconscionable act."

Ford believed that the federal government exercised too much power over domestic affairs. In his fifteen months as president, he vetoed thirty-nine bills, thereby outstripping Herbert Hoover's veto record in less than half the time. By resisting congressional pressure to reduce taxes and increase federal spending, he plummeted the economy into the deepest recession since the Great Depression. Unemployment jumped to 9 percent in 1975, and the federal deficit hit a record the next year.

In foreign policy, Ford retained Henry Kissinger as secretary of state and attempted to pursue Nixon's goals of stability in the Middle East, rapprochement with China, and détente with the Soviet Union. Late in 1974, Ford met with Soviet leader Leonid Brezhnev and accepted the framework for another arms-control agreement that was to serve as the basis for SALT II. Meanwhile Kissinger's tireless shuttling between Cairo and Tel Aviv produced an agreement: Israel promised to return to Egypt most of the Sinai territory captured in the 1967 war, and the two nations agreed to rely on negotiations rather than force to settle future disagreements.

These limited but significant achievements should have enhanced Ford's image, but they were drowned in the sea of criticism that followed the loss of South Vietnam to North Vietnam in 1975. Not only had a decade of American effort in Vietnam proven futile, but the Khmer Rouge, the Cambodian Communist movement, had also won a resounding victory, plunging that country into a fanatical bloodbath. And the OPEC oil cartel was threatening another worldwide boycott, while other Third World nations denounced the United States as a depraved imperialistic power.

The 1976 Election

In the midst of such turmoil, the Democrats could hardly wait for the 1976 election. At the Republican convention, Ford managed to thwart a powerful challenge for the nomination from former California governor and Hollywood actor Ronald Reagan. The Democrats chose an obscure former naval officer and engineer turned peanut farmer who had served one term as governor of Georgia. Jimmy Carter capitalized on the post-Watergate cynicism by promising never to "tell a lie to the American people" and by citing his independence from traditional Washington power politics.

To the surprise of many pundits, the little known Carter revived the New Deal coalition of southern whites, blacks, urban labor, and ethnic groups to win the election, 41 million votes to Ford's 39 million. The real story of the election, however, was the low voter turnout. Almost half of America's eligible voters, apparently alienated by Watergate and the lackluster candidates, chose to sit out the election.

The Carter Interregnum

Early Successes

During the first two years of his term, Carter enjoyed several successes. His administration appointed more blacks, Hispanics, and women than any before. He also offered amnesty to the thousands of young men who had fled the country rather than serve in Vietnam, closing one of the remaining open wounds of that traumatic event. He reformed the civil service to provide rewards for meritorious performance, and he created new cabinet-level Departments of Energy and Education. Carter also pushed significant environmental legislation through Congress, including a bill to regulate strip mining, and a "superfund" to clean up chemical waste sites.

His success was short-lived, however. Carter's political predicament emerged during the debate over energy policy. His proposed energy bill called for tax incentives and penalties to encourage conservation and new oil and gas production as well as solar power and synthetic fuels, and the increased development of nuclear power as a "last resort." Yet the energy bill passed in 1978 was a gutted version of Carter's original proposal. It focused primarily on new oil and gas production rather than conservation. Carter and his aides lacked the experience and the flexibility to maneuver his proposals around congressional obstacles.

In the summer of 1979, when renewed violence in the Middle East produced a second fuel shortage, motorists were forced to wait in long lines again for limited supplies of gasoline that they regarded as excessively expensive. Soon they directed their frustration at the White House. Opinion polls showed Carter with an approval rating of only 26 percent, lower than Nixon during the worst moments of the Watergate crisis.

Several of Carter's early foreign policy initiatives got caught in political crossfires. Soon after his inauguration, Carter vowed that "the soul of our foreign policy" should be the defense of human rights abroad. But the human rights campaign provoked attack from two sides: those who feared that it sacrificed a detached appraisal of national interest for high-level moralizing, and those who believed that human rights were important but that the administration was applying the standard inconsistently.

Carter's successful negotiation of treaties to turn over control of the Panama Canal to the Panamanian government in twenty years also generated intense criticism. The administration reminded Americans that Theodore Roosevelt himself had admitted "stealing" the Canal Zone for American use, but Republican Ronald Reagan falsely declared that the Canal Zone was sovereign American soil purchased "fair and square." Carter argued that the limitations on American influence in Latin America and the deep resentment toward American colonialism in Panama left the United States with no choice. The Senate ratified the treaties by a paper-thin margin (68 to 32, one vote more than the required two-thirds). The Canal Zone would revert in stages to Panama by 1999.

The Camp David Accords

Carter's crowning diplomatic achievement was the arrangement of a peace agreement between Israel and Egypt. In 1978 Carter invited Egypt's President Anwar el-Sadat and Israel's Prime Minister Menachem Begin to Camp David for two weeks of difficult negotiations. The first part of the eventual agreement required Israel to return all land in the Sinai in exchange for Egyptian recognition of Israel's sovereignty. This agreement was successfully implemented in 1982 when the last Israeli settler vacated the Sinai. But the second part of the agreement, calling for Israel to negotiate with Sadat a resolution to the Palestinian refugee dilemma, began to unravel soon after the Camp David summit. Still, Carter and Secretary of State Cyrus Vance had orchestrated a dramatic display of high-level diplomacy that, whatever its limitations, made an all-out war between Israel and the Arab world less likely. It also represented a significant first step toward a comprehensive settlement of the region's volatile tensions.

Mounting Troubles

Like Ford, Carter inherited a bad economy and left it worse. Carter tried to fight unemployment with a tax cut and increased public spending, but while unemployment declined slightly, from 8 to 7 percent in 1977, inflation soared; it reached 10 percent in 1978 and kept rising. By midterm, to fight inflation, Carter was delaying tax reductions and vetoing government spending programs that he had proposed in his first year. Yet the recession deepened, with unemployment at 7.5 percent in 1980, mortgage rates at 15 percent, interest rates at an all-time high of 20 percent, and a runaway inflation averaging between 12 and 13 percent.

The signing of a controversial SALT II treaty with the Soviets in 1979 put Carter's leadership to the test just as the mounting economic problems made him the subject of biting editorial cartoons. To pacify his conservative critics, who charged that SALT II would give the Soviets a decided advantage in the number and destructive power of land-based missiles, Carter announced that the United States would build the new MX missile system.

But the SALT II treaty became moot in 1979 when the Soviet army invaded Afghanistan in order to extend "fraternal assistance" to the faltering Communist government there, which was being challenged by Muslim rebels. While continuing the MX missile program, Carter immediately shelved SALT II, suspended grain shipments to the Soviet Union, and began a campaign for an international boycott of the 1980 Olympics, which were to be held that summer in Moscow.

Iran

Next, the Iranian crisis exploded in a yearlong barrage of unwelcome events that epitomized the inability of the United States to control world affairs. The crisis began in 1979 with the overthrow of the shah of Iran, a right-wing dictator brought to power by a CIA-sponsored coup in 1953. The revolutionaries who toppled the shah rallied around Ayatollah Ruhollah Khomeini, a fundamentalist Muslim leader who symbolized the Islamic values the shah had tried to replace with Western ways.

Late in 1979, Carter allowed the exiled shah to enter the United States in order to undergo treatment for cancer. A few days later, on November 4, a frenzied mob stormed the American Embassy in Teheran and seized the staff. Khomeini applauded the mob action and demanded the shah's return along with all his wealth in exchange for the release of the fifty-three American hostages. In the meantime, the Iranian militants staged daily demonstrations, burning the American flag and effigies of Carter for the benefit of worldwide news and television coverage.

Carter appealed to the United Nations, protesting what was a clear violation of diplomatic immunity and international law. But Khomeini scoffed at U.N. requests for the release of the hostages. Carter then froze all Iranian assets in the United States and appealed to American allies for a trade embargo of Iran. The trade restrictions were only partially effective—even America's most loyal European allies did not want to lose access to Iranian oil.

So a frustrated Carter, hounded by a public and press demanding "action," authorized a risky rescue attempt by American commandos in April 1980. The raid, however, was aborted in the Iranian desert because of helicopter malfunctions, and it ended with eight fatalities when another American helicopter collided with a transport plane. Carter's presidency died with them. Secretary of State Cyrus Vance resigned in protest against the ill-fated rescue mission. Meanwhile, nightly television coverage of the taunting Iranian rebels generated a near obsession with the seeming impotence of the United States and the fate of the hostages. The crisis ended after 444 days of captivity when Carter released several billion dollars of Iranian assets to ransom the kidnapped hostages.

The turbulent events of the 1970s—the conquest of South Vietnam, the Watergate scandal and Nixon's resignation, the energy shortage and stagflation, the Iranian hostage episode—provoked among Americans what Carter labeled a "crisis of confidence." By 1980, American power and prestige seemed to be on the decline, the economy remained in a shambles, and the rights revolution launched in the 1960s had sparked a backlash of resentment among "Middle America." With theatrical timing, Ronald Reagan emerged to tap the growing reservoir of public frustration and transform his political career into a crusade to make "America stand tall again."

CHAPTER

35

Conservative Insurgency

This chapter focuses on

- The demographic, social, and economic reasons for the rise of Ronald Reagan and Republican conservatism.
- Changing relations with the Soviet Union, including the end of the cold war.
- The economic and social aspects of the 1980s.
- The causes and aftermath of the Gulf War.

THE *ESSENTIAL AMERICA* ON-LINE TUTOR

www.wwnorton.com/eamerica/ch35

- **Topic: The collapse of Communism**
  www.wwnorton.com/eamerica/ch35/topic.htm

  In the fall of 1989 the Warsaw Pact collapsed, Communist East Germany dismantled its government, and the Berlin Wall—the symbol of Communist repression for three decades—was torn down. Using photographs, speeches delivered at the wall by U.S. presidents, an audio recoding, and historical analyses, consider the significance of the Berlin Wall. How can one object become a universally recognized symbol of conflicting political ideals?

- **Chapter review: On-line quiz and chapter summary**
  www.wwnorton.com/eamerica/ch35/review.htm

- **Chapter resources: Multimedia index**
  www.wwnorton.com/eamerica/ch35/media.htm

President Jimmy Carter and his embattled Democratic administration hobbled through 1979. The economy remained sluggish, double-digit inflation continued unabated, and failed efforts to free the American hostages in Iran made the administration appear indecisive. Carter's inability to mobilize the nation behind his energy program revealed basic flaws in his reading of the public mood and his understanding of legislative politics. Carter's claim that a "crisis of confidence" was paralyzing the nation and his insistence that the days of dramatic economic growth were over fell on deaf or indignant ears.

While the Carter administration was foundering, Republican conservatives were forging a plan to win the White House in 1980. Those plans centered on the popularity and charisma of Ronald Reagan, the Hollywood actor turned California governor and prominent political commentator.

Reagan was not a deep thinker, but he was a superb analyst of the public mood and a committed advocate of conservative principles. He was also charming and cheerful, a likable politician renowned for his folksy anecdotes. Whereas the dour Carter denounced the evils of free enterprise capitalism and tried to scold Americans into reviving long-forgotten virtues of frugality, a sunny Reagan promised a "revolution of ideas" designed to unleash the capitalist spirit, restore national pride, and regain international respect. More specifically, Reagan wanted to increase military spending, dismantle the "bloated" federal bureaucracy, reduce taxes and regulations, and in general, undo the welfare state. To please the religious right, he also wanted to outlaw abortions and reinstitute school prayer. Reagan's appeal derived from his remarkable skills as a public speaker and his dogmatic commitment to a few overarching ideas and simple themes. As a true believer and an able compromiser, he combined the fervor of a revolutionary with the pragmatism of a diplomat.

Such attributes won Reagan two presidential terms in 1980 and 1984 and ensured the election of his successor, George Bush, in 1988. Just how revolutionary the Reagan era was remains a subject of intense partisan debate. What cannot be denied, however, is that Reagan's actions and beliefs set the tone for the decade.

The Reagan Revolution

The Move to Reagan

By the eve of the 1980 election, three developments had made Reagan's conservative vision of America very appealing to a majority of voters. First, the 1980 census revealed that the American population (226.5 million) was aging, and that it was moving in large numbers from the liberal Northeast to the conservative "Sunbelt" states of the South and West. This dual development meant that demographic forces were carrying the electorate toward Reagan's conservative position.

Second, in the 1970s the country experienced a major revival of evangelical religion comparable to the Great Awakenings of the eighteenth and early nineteenth centuries. The Reverend Jerry Falwell's "Moral Majority" organization expressed the political sentiments of the religious right wing: the business sector should be freed from government regulation, big government should be shrunk, abortion should be outlawed, prayer in school should be reinstated, evolution should be replaced in schoolbooks by the biblical story of creation, women should remain in the home, and Soviet expansion should be opposed as a form of pagan totalitarianism. The moralistic zeal and financial resources of the religious right made them effective backers of Reagan.

A third factor contributing to the conservative resurgence was a well-organized and well-financed backlash against the feminist movement. During the 1970s, women who opposed the social goals of feminism formed counter-organizations with names such as "Women Who Want to Be Women" and "Females Opposed to Equality." Spearheading such efforts was Phyllis Schlafly, a right-wing Republican activist from Illinois. She orchestrated the campaign to defeat the Equal Rights Amendment (ERA) and thereafter served as the galvanizing force behind a growing antifeminist movement.

Many of Schlafly's supporters in the anti-ERA campaign also participated in a mushrooming anti-abortion or "pro-life" movement. By 1980 the National Right to Life committee, created by the National Conference of Catholic Bishops, boasted 11 million members representing all religious denominations. The intensity of their commitment made them a powerful political force in their own right, and the Reagan campaign was quick to highlight its own support for conservative values. Such a stance helped convince many northern working-class Democrats to support Reagan. Whites alienated by the increasingly liberal social agenda of the Democratic party became a crucial element in Reagan's electoral strategy.

On election day Reagan swept to a decisive victory, with 489 electoral votes to 49 for Carter, who carried only six states. The popular vote proved equally lopsided: 44 million (51 percent) to 35 million (41 percent), with 7 percent going to John Anderson, a moderate Republican who had bolted the party after Reagan's nomination and had run on an independent ticket.

In addition to affirming Reagan's conservative agenda, the election reflected the triumph of what one political scientist called the "largest mass movement of our time"—nonvoting. Almost as striking as Reagan's one-sided victory was the fact that his vote total represented only 28 percent of the potential electorate. Only 53 percent of eligible voters cast ballots in the 1980 election.

Where had all the voters gone? Analysts noted that most of the nonvoters were working-class Democrats in the major urban centers. Voter turnout was lowest in poor inner-city neighborhoods such as New York's Bedford-Stuyvesant district, which had a 19 percent voter participation rate. Turnout was highest, by contrast, in the affluent suburbs of large cities, areas where the Republican party was experiencing a dramatic surge in popularity. Such trends meant that American office-holders were being selected during the 1970s by an electorate increasingly dominated by middle- and upper-class white voters.

There were varied explanations for the high levels of voter apathy among working-class Americans. Some stressed the continuing sense of disillusionment with government growing out of the Watergate affair. Others believed that the Democratic party had alienated its traditional blocs of support among common folk. Democratic leaders no longer spoke eloquently on behalf of those at the bottom of America's social scale. By embracing a fiscal conservatism indistinguishable from that of the Republicans, "new" Democrats had lost their appeal among blue-collar workers and ghetto dwellers. When viewed in this light, Ronald Reagan's victory represented less a resounding victory for conservative Republicans than a self-inflicted defeat by a fractured Democratic party. For the moment, however, such results were masked by the Republicans' euphoric victory celebrations. Flush with a sense of power and destiny, Ronald Reagan headed toward Washington with a blueprint for dismantling the welfare state.

Reagan's First Term

Reaganomics

Ronald Reagan brought to Washington a simple conservative philosophy. "Government is not the solution to our problem," Reagan insisted; "Government is the problem." Reagan credited Calvin Coolidge and his treasury secretary, Andrew Mellon, with demonstrating that by reducing taxes and easing government regulation of business, free-market capitalism would revive the economy. Like his Republican predecessors of the 1920s, he wanted to unleash entrepreneurial energy as never before. By cutting taxes and nonmilitary federal spending, he claimed, a surging economy would produce greater government revenues that would help reduce the budget deficit.

Among his first decisions, Reagan abandoned price controls on oil and ended the wheat embargo on the Soviet Union. He then focused on dramatically increasing defense spending, sharply reducing social spending, and passing a sweeping tax reform proposal. On August 1, 1981, Reagan signed the Economic Recovery Tax Act, which cut personal income taxes by 25 percent, lowered the maximum rate from 70 to 50 percent for 1982, cut the capital gains tax on investment income by a third, and offered a broad array of other tax concessions.

The new legislation embodied an idea that went back to Alexander Hamilton, George Washington's treasury secretary: more money in the hands of the affluent would benefit society at large, since the wealthy would engage in productive investment. A closer parallel was Treasury Secretary Andrew Mellon's tax reduction program of the 1920s. The difference was that the Reagan tax cuts were accompanied by massive increases in defense spending that generated ever-mounting federal budget deficits. Reagan's advisers insisted that such unbalanced budgets were only temporary; once the new tax plan began to take effect, the sluggish economy would take off and government tax revenues would soar as personal incomes and corporate profits skyrocketed. But it did not work out that way. By the summer of 1983, a major economic recovery was underway, but the federal deficits grew ever larger, so much so that the president, who in 1980 had pledged to have a balanced federal budget by 1983, had in fact run up debts larger than those of all his predecessors combined.

Budget Cuts

In trying to slash expenditures, David Stockman, Reagan's budget director, pushed through $35 billion in budget cuts in educational and cultural programs, housing, food stamps, and school lunches in 1981. But Stockman realized that the cuts in domestic spending were far short of what would be needed to balance the budget in four years as Reagan had promised. The result was the worst economic recession since the 1930s, which continued through most of 1982. That same year the federal deficit doubled. Aides finally convinced Reagan that to reassure the public about deficits and the threat of inflation the government needed "revenue enhancements," a euphemism for tax increases. With Reagan's support, Congress passed a new tax bill in 1982 that would raise almost $100 billion.

Conflicts of Interest

Like Harding and Coolidge in the 1920s, Reagan named people to government positions who frequently were unsympathetic to the regulatory functions for which they were responsible. The most visible early example was Interior Secretary James Watt, who castigated environmentalists for hindering the commercial use of timber and mineral resources. The Reagan administration also paralleled the Harding administration by finding itself embroiled in charges of conflict of interest, ethical misconduct, and actual criminal behavior. Public outcry forced the administrator of the Environmental Protection Agency to resign for granting favors to industrial polluters.

Although some 200 Reagan appointees were accused of unethical or illegal activities, the president himself remained untouched by any hint of impropriety. His personal charisma and aloof managerial style helped shield him from the political fallout associated with the growing scandals and conflicts of interest among his aides and cronies. Public affection for him as a person led one member of Congress to label the Reagan White House the "Teflon Presidency," where the buck never stopped because the blame never stuck.

Organized labor suffered severe setbacks during the Reagan years. Presidential appointments to the National Labor Relations Board tended to favor management, and in 1981 Reagan fired members of the Professional Air Traffic Controllers (PATCO) who had participated in an illegal strike. Even more important, Reagan's smashing electoral victories in 1980 and 1984 broke the political power of the AFL-CIO. His criticism of unions seemed to reflect a general trend in public opinion. By 1987 unions represented only 17 percent of the nation's full-time workers, down from 24 percent in 1979.

Reagan also went on the offensive against feminism. He ardently opposed the Equal Rights Amendment, abortion on demand, and the legal guarantee of equal pay for jobs of comparable worth. He did name Sandra Day O'Connor as the first woman justice to the Supreme Court, but critics labeled it a token gesture rather than a reflection of any genuine commitment to gender equality.

Blacks and other minorities shared a similar aggravation at the administration's limited support for affirmative action programs in employment. Reagan cut funds for civil rights enforcement and the Equal Employment Opportunity Commission, and he initially opposed renewal of the Voting Rights Act of 1965, but he was overruled by Congress.

The Defense Buildup

Reagan's conduct of foreign policy reflected his belief that trouble in the world stemmed mainly from Soviet efforts to promote global communism. He and Secretary of Defense Caspar Weinberger embarked on a major buildup of nuclear and conventional weapons to close the gap that they claimed had developed between Soviet and American military forces.

In 1983 Reagan escalated the nuclear arms race by authorizing the Defense Department to develop a Strategic Defense Initiative (SDI). It involved a complex antimissile defense system using super-secret laser and high-energy particles weapons to destroy enemy missiles in outer space well before they reached their targets. Journalists quickly dubbed the program "Star Wars" in reference to the popular science fiction film. Despite skepticism among the media and many scientists that such a "foolproof" celestial defense system could be built, it forced the Soviets to launch an expensive research and development program of their own to keep pace.

Reagan vowed to challenge "Communist aggression anywhere in the world." Soviet-American relations deteriorated even further when the Soviets imposed martial law in Poland during the winter of 1981. The crackdown came after Polish workers, united under the banner of an independent union called Solidarity, challenged the Communist monopoly of power. As with Hungary in 1956 and Czechoslovakia in 1968, there was little the United States could do except register protest and impose economic sanctions against Poland's Communist government.

The Americas

Reagan's foremost international concern, however, was in Central America, where he detected the most serious Communist threat. The tiny nation of El Salvador, caught up since 1980 in a brutal struggle between Communist-supported revolutionaries and right-wing extremists, received American commitments of economic and military assistance. Reagan stopped short of sending American troops, but he did increase the number of military advisers and the amount of financial aid to the Salvadoran government. He also abandoned Carter's strident criticism of right-wing Salvadoran militants whose "death squads" engaged in systematic terror and murder.

By 1984, however, the American-backed government of President José Napoleón Duarte brought a modicum of stability to El Salvador.

Even more troubling was the situation in Nicaragua. The Reagan State Department claimed that the Cuban-sponsored Sandinista government in Nicaragua, which had only recently taken control of the country after ousting a corrupt dictator, was funneling Soviet and Cuban arms to leftist Salvadoran rebels. In response, the administration ordered the CIA to train and supply guerrilla bands of disgruntled Nicaraguans, tagged "Contras," who staged attacks on Sandinista bases and officials from sanctuaries in Honduras. In supporting these "freedom fighters," Reagan sought not only to impede the traffic in arms to Salvadoran rebels but also to overthrow the Communist Sandinistas.

Critics of Reagan's anti-Sandinista policy accused the Contras of being right-wing fanatics who indiscriminately killed civilians as well as Sandinista soldiers. They also feared that the United States might eventually commit its own combat forces, thus threatening another Vietnam-like intervention. Reagan warned that if the Communists prevailed in Central America, "our credibility would collapse, our alliances would crumble, and the safety of our homeland would be jeopardized."

The Middle East

The Middle East remained a tinderbox of geopolitical conflict throughout the Reagan years. No peaceable end seemed possible to the bloody Iran-Iraq war, which had erupted in 1980, entangled as it was with the passions and politics of Islamic fundamentalism. In 1984 both sides began to attack tankers in the Persian Gulf, a major source of the world's oil. Although the Reagan administration harbored no affection for either nation, it viewed Iranian fundamentalism as the greater threat and funneled aid to Iraq, a policy that produced unforeseen consequences.

American diplomats continued to see Israel as the strongest ally in the region, all the while seeking to encourage moderate Arab groups. Israel's aim in the area was to secure peaceful borders, America's goal was to prevent Soviet involvement through its ally Syria. But both objectives ran up against the continuing chaos in Lebanon, where ethnic and religious tensions erupted into an anarchy of warring groups. The capital, Beirut, became a battleground for rival Muslim and Christian factions, the Palestine Liberation Organization (PLO) army, Syrian invaders cast as peacekeepers, and Israeli forces.

French, Italian, and American forces thereupon moved into Beirut as "peacekeepers," but in such small numbers as to become targets themselves. On October 23, 1983, an Islamic suicide bomber drove a truck laden with explosives into the U.S. Marine quarters at the Beirut airport. The bombing left 241 Americans dead. Reagan declared that a continued American presence in the city was essential, but he soon began preparations for the withdrawal of American troops. On February 7, 1984, he announced that the Marines would be redeployed on warships offshore. The Israelis pulled back to southern Lebanon, while the Syrians remained in eastern Lebanon and imposed a tenuous peace upon the faction-ridden country.

Grenada

In a fortunate turn for the Reagan administration, an easy military triumph closer to home eclipsed news of the debacle in Lebanon. On the tiny Caribbean island of Grenada, the smallest independent nation in the Western Hemisphere, a leftist government had admitted Cuban workers to build a new airfield and had signed military agreements with several Communist-bloc countries.

Appeals from the governments of neighboring islands led Reagan in 1983 to order 1,900 paratroopers and marines to invade the island, depose the leftist regime, and evacuate a group of American students at Grenada's medical school. The U.N. General Assembly condemned the action, and many Latin Americans saw it as a revival of American interventionism, but most Grenadans and their neighbors acclaimed the action, and it was immensely popular in the United States. Although it was a lopsided affair, the attack on the island made Reagan look decisive, and it served notice on Latin American left-wing revolutionaries that the president might use force elsewhere in the region.

Reagan's Second Term

By 1983 prosperity had returned, and the Reagan economic program seemed to be working as touted. Countervailing policies of fiscal stimulus (tax cuts and heavy defense spending) and monetary restraint (high interest rates) brought at least in the short run an economic recovery with little inflation. But critics argued that the return of prosperity was more the result of the cyclical swings inherent in the economy and the dramatic fall in energy costs following the collapse of the OPEC cartel.

The Election of 1984

As the presidential election approached, however, Reagan and the Republicans were able to take credit for the economic recovery. The Democratic nominee, the former Minnesota senator and vice-president, Walter Mondale, faced an uphill struggle. But he quickly won the endorsement of several major organizations—the AFL-CIO, National Organization for Women, and the NAACP. He also received a lot of media attention by choosing as his running mate a woman, New York representative Geraldine Ferraro. This attention soon focused, however, on her husband's dubious business finances.

Mondale further complicated his campaign by a fit of frankness in his acceptance speech. "Mr. Reagan will raise taxes, and so will I," he told the convention. "He won't tell you. I just did." Reagan in turn vowed never to approve a tax increase, and he chided his opponent's candid stand. Thereafter, Mondale never caught up. In the end, Reagan won almost 59 percent of the popular vote and lost only Minnesota and the District of Columbia. His coattails, however, were not as long as in 1980. Republicans had a net gain of only fifteen seats in the House, leaving them still greatly outnumbered by Democrats, 253 to 182. They also lost two Senate seats, leaving their majority margin only 53 to 47.

Domestic Challenges

After Reagan's reelection, domestic problems that he had tried to ignore demanded his attention and shook his complacency. The ethical and criminal violations of his subordinates continued to make headlines, and strains began to appear between the political conservatives in the party and the social conservatives who dominated evangelical religious groups.

Still, for a while, the Reagan luck held out. OPEC continued to lower oil prices, sending inflation down and the stock market up. In his 1985 State of the Union message, the president clarified what had come to be called the Reagan Doctrine in foreign affairs. America, he proclaimed, would support anti-Communist forces around the world seeking to "defy Soviet-supported aggression." In effect, he was challenging the isolationism provoked by the nation's humbling experience in Vietnam. America, he promised, would not hesitate to intervene in world hot spots. Turning to domestic policy, the president dared Congress to raise taxes. His veto pen was ready, as was his commitment to cut current taxes.

Soviet premier Mikhail Gorbachev (left) and Ronald Reagan (right) at the Geneva summit, November 1985.

Arms Control

Meanwhile, Reagan, for all his stern talk about the Soviet Union being "an evil empire," strove to reach an arms control agreement with the Soviets. In Geneva in 1985 he met with Mikhail Gorbachev, the innovative new leader of the Soviet Union. The two signed several cultural and scientific agreements and issued a statement on arms limitations talks, but no treaty was in the offing. A major stumbling block was Reagan's refusal to consider any restrictions on his pursuit of the Strategic Defense Initiative.

Nearly a year after the Geneva summit, Gorbachev and Reagan met in Iceland to discuss arms reduction. Early reports predicted a major breakthrough, as the two leaders discussed the possibility of a total ban on nuclear weapons, but the talks collapsed over disagreement about SDI. After the Iceland meeting, the two nations reduced the scope of their discussions in order to break the impasse. Talks now focused on eliminating short-range nuclear weapons from Europe.

The Iran-Contra Affair

During the fall of 1986, the Reagan administration suffered a double blow. In the midterm elections the Democrats regained control of the Senate by 55 to 45. For his final two years in office, Reagan would face an opposition Congress. What was worse, on election day, reports surfaced that the United States, with Israeli assistance, had been secretly selling arms to Iran in hope of securing the release of American hostages held in Lebanon by extremist Islamic groups with close ties to Iran. Such action contradicted Reagan's repeated public insistence that his administration would never negotiate with terrorists. It angered America's allies and many Americans who vividly remembered the 1979 Iranian takeover of the American Embassy.

There was more to the story. Over the next several months, a series of revelations disclosed a more complicated series of covert activities carried out by administration officials. At the center of what came to be dubbed "Irangate" was the much-decorated Marine Lieutenant-Colonel Oliver North. An aide to the National Security Council who specialized in counterterrorism, North had been running secret operations from the basement of the White House involving numerous governmental, private, and foreign individuals. His most far-fetched scheme sought to use the profits gained from the secret sale of arms to Iran to subsidize the Contra rebels fighting in Nicaragua, at a time when Congress had voted to ban such aid.

North's activities, it turned out, had been approved by National Security Adviser Robert McFarlane, his successor Admiral John Poindexter, and CIA Director William Casey. Secretary of State George Shultz and Secretary of Defense Caspar Weinberger both had criticized the sale of arms to Iran, but their objections were ignored. Later, on three occasions, Shultz threatened to resign because no one was trying to stop the "pathetic" scheme. As information about the illegal dealings surfaced in the press, McFarlane attempted suicide, Poindexter resigned, and North was fired. Casey, who denied any connection, left the CIA for health reasons.

The White House, meanwhile, assumed a siege mentality as the president's popularity plummeted. Under increasing criticism and amid growing doubts of his own credibility and ability, Reagan appointed both an independent counsel and a three-man commission, led by former Republican senator John Tower, to investigate the spreading scandal.

The Tower Commission issued a devastating report early in 1987 that placed much of the responsibility for the bungled Iran-Contra Affair on Reagan's loose management style. The report portrayed Reagan as uninformed and forgetful, a leader detached from the inner workings of his own administration.

The Iran-Contra Affair eroded support for the Nicaraguan Contras in the Congress, and it undermined much of Reagan's popularity. The investigations of the independent counsel led to six indictments in 1988. A Washington jury found Oliver North guilty of three relatively minor charges but innocent of nine more serious counts, apparently reflecting the jury's reasoning that he had acted as an agent of higher-ups. His conviction was later overturned on appeal. Of those involved in the affair, only John Poindexter got a jail sentence—six months for his conviction on five felony counts of obstructing justice and lying to Congress.

An Economy Driven by Debt

During the 1980s, all kinds of debt—personal, corporate, and governmental—increased dramatically. Whereas in the 1960s, Americans on average saved 10 percent of their income, in 1987 they saved less than 4 percent. Commentators talked of a compulsive materialism energizing the young, upwardly mobile urban professionals dubbed "Yuppies." Caught up in the race for money, goods, and status, these post–World War II baby-boomers in the fast lane captured the tone and mood of affluent life in the 1980s.

Then, on October 19, 1987, the bill collector suddenly arrived at the nation's doorstep. On that "Black Monday," the stock market plummeted an astounding 22.6 percent, nearly doubling the record 12.8 percent fall of October 28, 1929. With cyclonic suddenness, the nation's financial mood went from boom to gloom during the fall of 1987. Most analysts agreed that the fundamental problem was the nation's spiraling indebtedness and chronically high trade deficits. Americans were consuming more than they were producing, importing the difference, and paying for it with borrowed money and a dollar sharply declining in value. Foreign investors had lost confidence in Reaganomics and were no longer willing to finance America's spending binge.

In the aftermath of the calamitous selling spree on Black Monday, Reagan agreed to work with Congress in developing a deficit reduction package, and for the first time indicated that he was willing to include increased taxes in such a package. Yet the eventual compromise plan was so modest that it did little to restore investor confidence.

The Poor, the Homeless, and AIDS Victims

The 1980s were years of vivid contrasts in America's social and economic landscape. Despite unprecedented affluence, there were also uncounted beggars in the streets and homeless people sleeping in doorways, in cardboard boxes, and on heat grates. A variety of causes created the shortage of low-cost housing: reduced government funding; urban renewal, which demolished blighted areas but provided no housing for the displaced; and the upscaling of neighborhoods, called "gentrification."

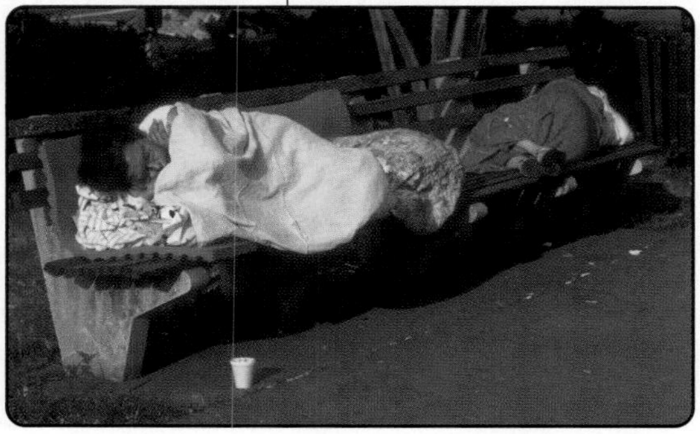

Despite the nation's prosperity and efforts to build low-cost housing, the number of homeless people continued to increase during the 1980s.

Other causes of homelessness included family disorganization, as well as the deinstitutionalization of the mentally ill based on the promise of community mental health services that failed to materialize—a program started under President Kennedy but never adequately funded.

Still another group cast aside were those suffering from a new malady known as AIDS (acquired immune deficiency syndrome). At the beginning of the decade, public health officials had begun to report that gay men and intravenous drug users were especially at risk for this syndrome. Those infected with AIDS showed signs of fatigue, developed combinations of infections, and eventually died. Researchers struggled to discern the origins of the new malady. Eventually they linked it to a virus (HIV) originating in Africa and spread from there to Europe and America. People contracted it by coming into contact with the blood or body fluids of an infected person.

By 2001, AIDS had claimed over 300,000 American lives. Over a million people were estimated to be carrying the deadly HIV virus, and AIDS had become the leading cause of death among men aged twenty-five to forty-four. With no prospect of a cure and with skyrocketing treatment costs, AIDS had become one of the nation's, and the world's, most horrifying and intractable problems.

An Historic Treaty

In the midst of a weakening economic situation, the main prospect for positive achievement before the end of Reagan's second term seemed to lie in arms reduction agreements with the Soviet government. Under Mikhail Gorbachev the Soviets promoted renewed détente in order to free their energies and financial resources to address pressing domestic problems. Reagan and Gorbachev met amid much fanfare in Washington on December 9, 1987, and signed a treaty to eliminate intermediate-range (300–3,000 miles) nuclear forces (INF).

It was an epochal event, not only because it marked the first time that the two nations had agreed to destroy a whole class of weapons systems but because it represented a key first step toward the eventual end of the arms race altogether. Under the terms of the treaty, the United States would destroy 859 missiles and the Soviets would eliminate 1,752. Provision was also made for on-site inspections by each side to verify compliance. Still, this winnowing of weapons would represent only 4 percent of the total number of nuclear missiles on both sides. Arms-control advocates thus looked toward a second and more comprehensive treaty eliminating long-range strategic missiles.

The Reagan Legacy

Historians are just beginning to assess the legacy of the nation's fortieth president. Although Reagan had declared in 1981 his intention to "curb the size and influence of the federal establishment," the welfare state remained intact when Reagan left office. Neither the Social Security system nor

The AIDS Quilt. Started in 1985, the quilt is a memorial for those who have died of AIDS and an attempt to spread awareness of the disease's devastating impact. To date it stretches 16 football fields and contains 43,000 panels.

Medicare nor other major welfare programs had been dismantled or overhauled. And the federal agencies that Reagan had threatened to abolish, such as the Department of Education, not only remained in place in 1989, their budgets grew. The federal budget as a percentage of the gross domestic product (GDP) was actually higher when Reagan left office than when he had entered. Moreover, he did not try to push through Congress the incendiary social issues championed by the religious right such as school prayer and a ban on abortions.

Yet Ronald Reagan nonetheless succeeded in redefining the national political agenda and accelerated the conservative insurgency that had been developing for over twenty years. His greatest successes were in renewing America's confidence, bringing inflation under control, negotiating the nuclear disarmament treaty, and helping to light the fuse of democratic freedom in eastern Europe. By redirecting the thrust of both domestic and foreign policy, he put the Democratic party on the defensive and forced conventional New Deal "liberalism" into a panicked retreat. The fact that Reagan's tax policies widened the gap between the rich and poor and created huge budget deficits for future presidents to confront did not diminish the popularity of the "Great Communicator."

The 1988 Election

As a new presidential election unfolded, the Democratic primary became a two-man race between Massachusetts governor Michael Dukakis and Jesse Jackson, the black civil rights activist who had been one of Martin Luther King, Jr.'s chief lieutenants. Dukakis eventually won out, and he managed a difficult reconciliation with the Jackson forces that left the Democrats unified and confident as the fall campaign began. As in 1960, they envisioned a popular president and his tired presidency giving way to a cool, poised politician from Massachusetts.

The Republicans nominated Reagan's two-term vice-president, George Bush, who after a bumpy start had easily cast aside his rivals in the primaries. As Reagan's handpicked heir, Bush claimed credit for the administration's successes, but like all dutiful vice-presidents, he also faced the challenge of defining and asserting his own political identity. Although he was a veteran government official, having served as a Texas congressman and as head of the CIA, Bush projected none of Reagan's charisma or rhetorical skills. Early polls showed Dukakis with a surprisingly wide lead.

Yet at the Republican convention Bush delivered a forceful address that sharply enhanced his stature. He promised to use the White House to fight bigotry, illiteracy, and homelessness. The most memorable line was "read my lips: *no new taxes.*"

Bush attacked Dukakis as a camouflaged liberal who would increase federal spending, raise taxes, gut the defense program, refuse to intervene against Communist aggression abroad, and oppose the pledge of allegiance to the flag. The Republican onslaught took its toll against the more high-toned but less organized Dukakis campaign. Moreover, the Republicans benefited from the population growth in the Sunbelt states, the shift of population from the Democratic cities to the Republican suburbs, and from the votes of many moderate and conservative Democrats and Independents. In the election, Dukakis took ten states plus the District of Columbia, with clusters in the Northeast, Midwest, and Northwest. Bush carried the rest, with a margin of about 54 percent to 46 percent in the popular vote and 426 to 111 in the electoral college.

The Bush Years

George Bush viewed himself as a guardian president rather than an activist. Lacking Reagan's visionary outlook and his skill as a speaker, Bush was a pragmatic caretaker eager to avoid "stupid mistakes" and to find a way to get along with the Democratic majority in Congress.

Domestic Initiatives

The Reagan administration left some issues that demanded immediate attention from the Bush White House. In 1989 Bush tackled the most pressing of these, the savings and loan crisis. Savings and loan institutions (also called S & L's or "thrifts") had been set up to help people buy homes. To enable S & L's to compete with commercial banks, Reagan had pushed through Congress a bill that had allowed S & L's to invest depositors' funds in commercial real estate and junk bonds (risky investments with the possibility of very high returns) as well as in the traditional single-family housing market.

The result was catastrophic. Incompetent or corrupt lenders engaged in a frenzy of speculative high-risk investments and freewheeling personal expenditures. By 1989 hundreds of S & L's had failed, and Bush responded with a rescue plan to close or sell ailing S & L's and bail out the depositors. At the time, the cost to taxpayers of the bailout was put at $300 billion over thirty years, although in 1990 the General Accounting Office estimated the cost at $500 billion.

The biggest hangover from the 1980s was the national debt, which stood at $2.6 trillion by the time Bush was elected, nearly three times its 1980 level. By early 1990, according to one political writer, the country faced "a horrendous fiscal mess." Congress finally approved a budget settlement with the Bush administration in October, although most Republicans still opposed it. Through a combination of tax hikes and spending cuts, the measure promised to reduce the budget deficit by $43.1 billion in 1991 and by $331.4 billion in 1991–1995.

The War on Drugs

As with Bush's "no new taxes" pledge, there was more symbolism than substance in the administration's plans to deal with the deadly matter of drug abuse. During the 1980s, cocaine addiction had spread through sizable segments of American society. Bush vowed to make drug abuse his number-one domestic priority.

Bush's war on drugs was planned along three fronts: more stringent law enforcement, drug testing in the workplace, and heightened efforts to cut off the supply of drugs coming from Colombia and Peru. Although drug-related arrests increased 20 percent from 1988 to 1989, cocaine in its smokable form, known as "crack," remained readily available and immensely popular. In 1989 some 375,000 American babies were born addicted to cocaine or heroin. Equally sobering was the connection between the drug subculture and the street gangs terrorizing inner cities across the country. Like Reagan before him, Bush chose to focus on arrests and interdiction, which led to a prison-building boom and a prison population nearing 2 million by 2000. This focus failed to address the basic question: Why were so many young people attracted by drugs? The answer involved many factors, but the disproportionate incidence of drug and alcohol abuse among poor people pointed to the culture of poverty as a primary culprit.

The Democracy Movement Abroad

Bush entered the White House with more foreign policy experience than most presidents, and he found the spotlight of the world stage more congenial than wrestling with the budget deficit. Within two years of his inauguration, George Bush would lead the United States into two wars, a record unequaled by any of his predecessors. Throughout most of 1989, however, he merely had to sit back and observe the dissolution of one totalitarian or authoritarian regime after another. For the first time in years, democracy was suddenly on the march in a sequence of mostly bloodless revolutions that took the world by surprise.

Although in China a suddenly risen democracy movement came to a tragic end in 1989, when government forces mounted a deadly assault on demonstrators in Beijing's (Peking's) Tiananmen Square, eastern Europe had an entirely different experience. Mikhail Gorbachev set events in motion by responding to Soviet economic problems with policies of *perestroika* (restructuring) and *glasnost* (openness), a loosening of central economic planning and censorship. His foreign policy sought rapprochement and trade with the West, to relieve the Soviet economy of burdensome military costs.

Gorbachev backed off from Soviet imperial ambitions. Early in 1989, Soviet troops left Afghanistan, where they had been bogged down in a civil war. Then in July, in Paris, Gorbachev repudiated the "Brezhnev Doctrine," which had asserted the right of the Soviet Union to intervene in the internal affairs of Communist countries. The days when Soviet tanks would roll through Warsaw and Prague were over, and hard-line leaders in the East-bloc countries found themselves beset by demands for democratic reform. With opposition strength building, the old Stalinist regimes fell in rapid order, and with surprisingly little bloodshed. Communist party rule ended first in Poland and Hungary, then in hard-line Czechoslovakia, Bulgaria, and Romania.

The most spectacular event in the collapse of the Soviet empire in eastern Europe came on November 9, 1989, when the chief symbol of the cold war—the Berlin Wall—was torn down by Germans, and the East German government succumbed to popular pressures for change. With the borders to the West fully open, the Communist government of East Germany collapsed, a freely elected government followed, and on October 3, 1990, the five states of East Germany were united with West Germany. The reunified German nation remained in NATO, and the Warsaw Pact alliance was dissolved.

The democratic movement also reached other parts of the world. In Chile, Augusto Pinochet, who had become military dictator in a bloody coup in 1973, was defeated in presidential elections in 1989. In South Africa, against which Congress had applied trade sanctions in protest of its apartheid (racial segregation) policies since 1986, a new prime minister, Frederik W. DeKlerk, came to office in 1989. In early 1990 he freed black nationalist Nelson Mandela, who had served twenty-seven years in prison, and he announced plans to abandon apartheid gradually. By early 1992 DeKlerk had pushed through a constitution ending apartheid and setting up procedures for the full integration of blacks into government and society.

But the reform impulse that Gorbachev helped unleash in the East-bloc countries began to generate opposition within the Soviet Union itself. On August 18, 1991, a cabal of Communist hardliners and military leaders accosted Gorbachev at his vacation retreat in the Crimea and demanded that he sign a decree proclaiming a state of emergency and transferring his powers to them. He replied: "Go to hell," whereupon he was placed under house arrest.

As the drama unfolded in the Soviet Union, a crescendo of indignation welled up from foreign leaders around the world. On August 20 President Bush convinced world leaders to join him in refusing to recognize the legitimacy of the new Soviet government. Siberian coal miners went on strike to oppose the coup. The next day word began to seep out that the plotters had given up and were fleeing. Several committed suicide, and a newly released Gorbachev ordered the others arrested. But his freedom did not bring a restoration of his power. Boris Yeltsin, the president of the Russian republic, emerged as the most popular political figure in the country. Gorbachev reclaimed the title of president, but he was

Berliners celebrate atop the Berlin Wall on November 10, 1989, one day after all crossings between East and West Germany were opened.

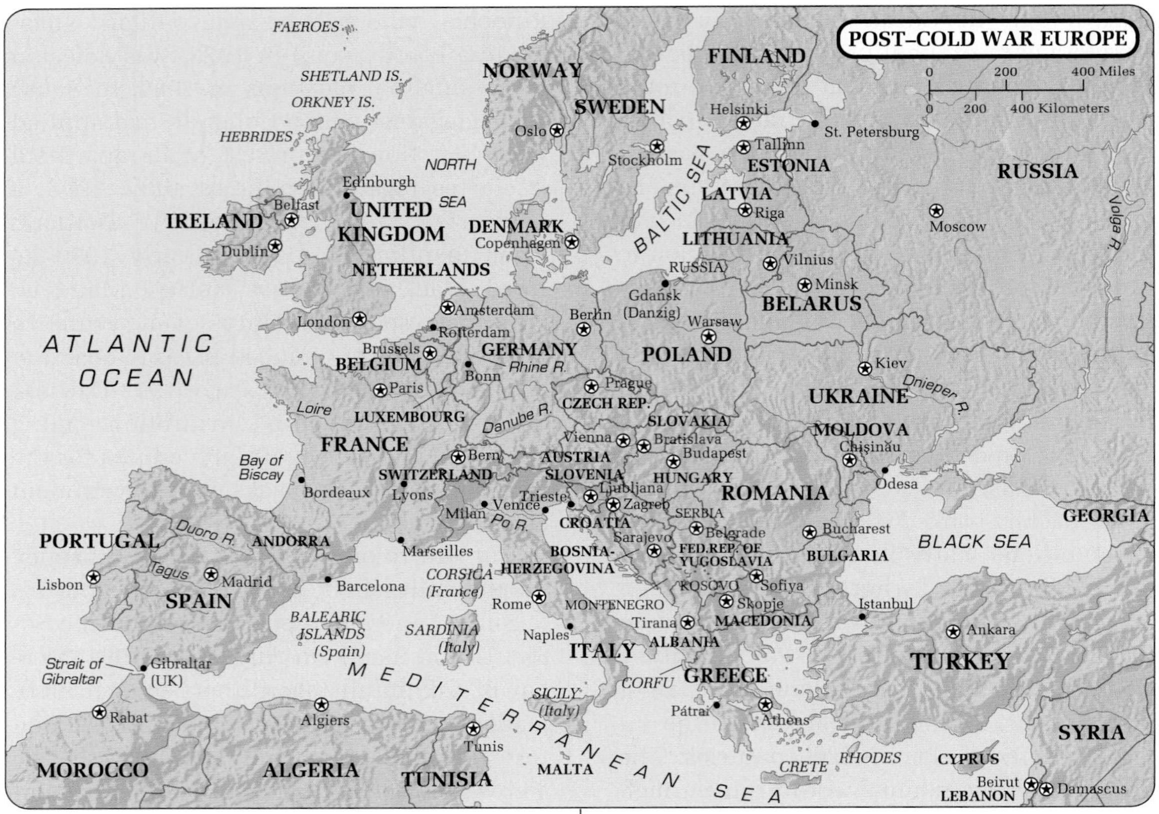

forced to resign as head of the Communist party and admit that he had made a grave mistake in appointing the men who had turned against him.

What began as a reactionary coup turned into a powerful accelerant for stunning new changes in the Soviet Union. No sooner had the plotters been arrested than most of the fifteen Soviet republics proclaimed their independence, with the Baltic republics of Latvia, Lithuania, and Estonia regaining the status of independent nations. The Communist party apparatus was dismantled.

By the end of 1991, the Soviet Union had dissolved into a new—and fragile—Commonwealth of Independent States made up of twelve autonomous republics. Held together by little other than historic ties and contiguous borders, the federated republics soon suffered outbreaks of ethnic tensions and separatist movements.

The aborted coup accelerated Soviet and American efforts to reduce the stockpiles of nuclear weapons. In 1991 President Bush stunned the world by announcing that the United States would destroy all its tactical nuclear weapons on land and at sea in Europe and Asia, take its long-range bombers off twenty-four-hour alert status, and initiate discussions with the Soviet Union for the purpose of instituting sharp cuts in ICBMs with multiple warheads. The Soviets responded by announcing reciprocal cutbacks. As Joint Chiefs of Staff Chairman Colin Powell remarked, the cold war "has vaporized before our eyes."

The dilution of the Soviet military threat led the Defense Department in 1992 to withdraw large numbers of military personnel from bases in Asia and Europe. The Pentagon also announced a plan to shrink the armed forces by 500,000 troops over the next five years. In 1992 Bush and the new

Soviet president Yeltsin announced their intention to reduce their combined arsenals of nuclear weapons from about 22,500 to no more than 7,000 by the year 2003. All land-based multiple-warhead missiles would be destroyed.

Panama

The end of the cold war did not, however, spell the end of international tensions and conflicts. Indeed, in some respects the world was more unstable. A tense situation in Panama flared into conflict in December 1989 when President Bush ordered an invasion of Panama to capture the head of state, General Manuel Noriega for trial on American indictments of drug smuggling and money laundering.

The 12,000 American military personnel in Panama were quickly joined by 12,000 more, and in the early morning of December 20, they disabled and seized the headquarters of the Panamanian Defense Forces. Noriega surrendered to American forces a week later. Twenty-three American servicemen were killed in the action; estimates of Panamanians killed and wounded ranged up to 4,000, including many civilians caught in the crossfire.

The Gulf War

Months after Panama had moved to the background of public attention, Saddam Hussein, dictator of Iraq, focused attention on the Middle East when his army suddenly fell upon his tiny, wealthy neighbor Kuwait on August 2, 1990. Kuwait had raised its production of oil contrary to agreements with the Organization of Petroleum Exporting Countries (OPEC). The resulting drop in oil prices hurt Iraq, deep in debt and heavily dependent on oil revenues. Complaining of "economic aggression" against Iraq, he demanded that Kuwait reduce its oil production and, with Saudi Arabia, cancel Iraqi debts of $30 million.

The U.N. Security Council quickly voted 14–0 to condemn the invasion and demand withdrawal. On August 6–7, the United States dispatched planes and troops to Saudi Arabia on a "wholly defensive" mission—to protect Saudi Arabia. British forces soon joined in, as did Arab troops from a half dozen nations. On August 22, President Bush ordered the mobilization of American reserve forces for the operation dubbed "Desert Shield."

On November 8, Bush announced that he was doubling American forces in the Middle East from about 200,000 to 400,000, to build up "an adequate offensive military capability." Bush asserted that he had authority to take such action under the Security Council resolutions. Bush's position was strengthened on November 29 by U.N. Resolution 678, which authorized the use of force to dislodge Iraq from Kuwait and set a deadline for Iraqi withdrawal of January 15, 1991.

Saddam refused to yield. On January 10, Congress began to debate authorizing the use of U.S. armed forces. The outcome was uncertain to the end, but on January 12 a resolution for the use of force passed the

Three Kuwaiti refugees head toward Kuwait City soon after a cease-fire ends the Gulf War, March 1991.

House by 250 to 183, and the Senate by 52 to 47.

By January 1991, a twenty-eight-nation allied force launched Operation Desert Storm. Missiles and planes began to hit Iraq at about 2:30 A.M., January 17, Baghdad time. With the allies in control of the air from the beginning, Saddam's only recourse was to fire off lumbering Soviet-made SCUD missiles, which he aimed from the first day into Israel with the hope of provoking Israeli retaliation and undermining the coalition against him. But the damage and casualties were light, and the Israelis showed remarkable restraint in the face of the continuing attacks.

The allied ground assault began on February 24 and lasted only four days. Thousands of Iraqi soldiers surrendered, and there was a quick breakthrough into Kuwait. On February 28, six weeks after the fighting began, President Bush called for a cease-fire, the Iraqis accepted, and the shooting ended. American fatalities numbered 137. The lowest estimate of Iraqi fatalities, civilian and military, was around 100,000, and the destruction of infrastructure in Iraq would lead to thousands of deaths in the following decade. The Persian Gulf War, the "mother of all battles," in Saddam Hussein's words, had been intense and had left consequences to be played out far into the future. Yet, despite all the destruction, Saddam Hussein remained in power.

CHAPTER

36

Cultural Politics

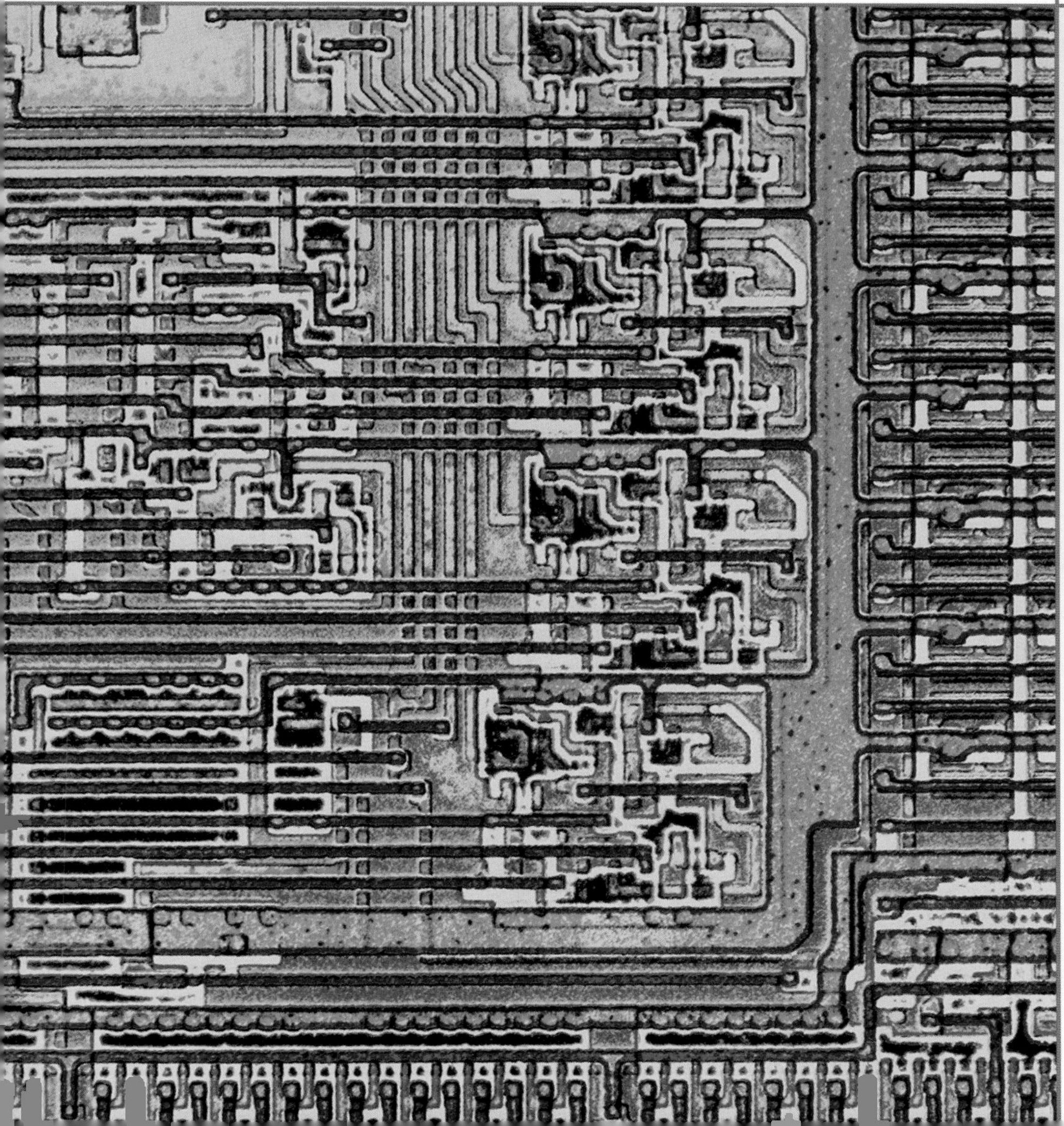

This chapter focuses on

- Demographic patterns from the 1990 census and the "new immigrants" of the 1980s and 1990s.
- The Democratic resurgence of the early 1990s and the Republican landslide of 1994.
- The "new economy" and the digital revolution.
- The record of the Clinton White House.

THE *ESSENTIAL AMERICA* ON-LINE TUTOR

www.wwnorton.com/eamerica/ch36

- **Topic: The Internet**
  www.wwnorton.com/eamerica/ch36/topic.htm

  The technological revolution of the 1980s and 1990s brought us the personal computer and the Internet, the two bases of our new economy. Using archival materials from various companies, U.S. military materials, a map, photographs, and historical analyses, examine the significance of the technology revolution. How did the computer evolve from the 3,000-cubic-foot ENIAC to the tabletop appliance in millions of homes in America and elsewhere?

- **Chapter review: On-line quiz and chapter summary**
  www.wwnorton.com/eamerica/ch36/review.htm

- **Chapter resources: Multimedia index**
  www.wwnorton.com/eamerica/ch36/media.htm

During the 1980s and 1990s, various cultural and political developments combined to transform American society and institutions. The makeup of the population shifted as the baby-boomers reached middle age. Immigrants to America now arrived primarily from Asia and Latin America rather than from Europe. The political landscape also began to shift, as many conservatives won election to local, state, and federal government offices, and many conservative judges were appointed or elected to the courts. In response to the resurgence of conservatism, the Democratic party began to moderate its liberal activism and promote a "moderate" or "centrist" stance. In an effort to become more productive and competitive, American businesses embraced new technology and engaged in "reengineering" efforts that often brought widespread job cuts. As corporations began to downsize, people began to lose faith in company loyalty and job security. At the same time, a backlash against racial preferences created new social tensions. Whites in large numbers and several prominent black conservatives argued that affirmative action was unjust and no longer necessary. This conservative trend promoted a balanced budget, an end to corruption in government, and a revival of "traditional" moral values.

America's Changing Face

Demographic Shifts

During the 1980s and 1990s, the nation's population grew by 20 percent, or some 50 million people, boosting the total to almost 275 million. The much-discussed baby-boom generation—the 43 million people born between 1946 and 1964—entered middle age. This generation's maturation and its preoccupation with practical concerns such as raising families, paying for college, and buying houses helped explain the surge of political conservatism during the 1980s. Surveys revealed that baby-boomers wanted stronger family and religious ties and a greater respect for authority. Yet having come to maturity during the turbulent sixties and early seventies, the baby-boomers also displayed more tolerance of social and cultural diversity than their parents.

During the last quarter of the twentieth century, the "Sunbelt" states of the South and West continued to lure residents from the Midwest and Northeast. Fully 90 percent of the nation's total population growth during the 1980s occurred in southern or western states. These population shifts forced a massive redistricting of the House of Representatives, with Florida and California gaining three more seats each and Texas two, while states such as New York lost seats.

Americans at the end of the century tended to settle in large communities. This continuing move to the cities largely reflected trends in the job market, as the "postindustrial" economy continued to shift from manufacturing to professional service industries, particularly those specializing in telecommunications and information processing. By 2000 fewer than 2 million people out of a total population of 275 million worked on farms.

Women continued to enter the workforce in large numbers. In 1970, 38 percent of the workforce was female; in 2000 the figure was almost 50 percent. Women made up over a third of the new medical doctors (4 percent in 1970); 40 percent of new lawyers (8 percent in 1970); and 23 percent of new dentists (less than 1 percent in 1970).

The decline of the traditional family unit—two parents with children—continued. In 2000 only 65 percent of children lived with two parents, down from 85 percent in 1970. And more people were living alone than ever before, largely as a result of high divorce rates or a growing practice of delaying marriage until well into the twenties. The number of single mothers increased 35 percent during the decade. The rate was much higher for African Americans: in 2000 less than 32 percent of black children lived with both parents, down from 67 percent in 1960.

Young blacks burdened by the absence of one or both parents faced shrinking economic opportunities at the start of the twenty-first century. The urban poor were particularly victimized by high rates of crime and violence, with young black males suffering the most. In 2000 the leading cause of death among black males between the ages of fifteen and twenty-four was homicide. Over twenty-five percent of black males aged twenty to twenty-nine were in prison, on parole, or on probation, while only 4 percent were enrolled in college. Forty percent of black adult males were functionally illiterate.

The New Immigrants

The racial and ethnic composition of the country also changed rapidly at the turn of the century. Almost 30 percent of Americans claimed African, Asian, Hispanic, or American Indian ancestry. Blacks represented 13 percent of the total population, Hispanics 11 percent, Asians about 4 percent, and American Indians almost 1 percent. The rate of increase among those four groups was twice as fast as it had been during the 1970s.

The primary cause of this dramatic change in the nation's ethnic mix was a surge of immigration. During the 1990s, legal immigration into the United States totaled over 10 million people, 40 percent higher than the previous decade and more than in any other decade. These figures do not include the hundreds of thousands of illegal aliens, mostly Mexicans and Haitians. In 2000 the United States welcomed more than twice as many immigrants as all other countries in the world combined.

For the first time in the nation's history, the majority of immigrants came not from Europe but from other parts of the world—Asia, Latin America, and Africa. Among the legal immigrants, Mexicans made up the largest share, averaging over 100,000 a year.

The wave of new immigration brought rising conflict between old and new ethnicities. Critics charged that America was being "overrun" with foreigners; they questioned whether Hispanics and Asians could be "assimilated" into American culture. In 1994 a large majority of California voters approved Proposition 187, a controversial initiative that denied the state's estimated 4 million illegal immigrants access to public schools, nonemergency health care, and other social services. It also required teachers, doctors, and government officials to report anyone suspected of being an undocumented immigrant. In 1998 California voters passed a referendum ending bilingual education.

The bitter irony of this new nativism was that it targeted recent immigrants for bringing with them to the United States virtues long prized by Americans—hope, energy, persistence, and an aggressive work ethic. Like most of their predecessors who had braved tremendous hardships to make their way to America, the new immigrants toiled long and hard for a share of the American dream, and most economic studies concluded that their presence was beneficial to the nation. They created more wealth than they consumed, and many of them compiled an astonishing record of achievement. The median household income of Asian Americans, for example, exceeded every other group, including native whites, and Asian Americans were disproportionately represented in the nation's most prestigious colleges and universities. Yet the very success of the new immigrants contributed to the resentment they encountered from other groups.

The Computer Revolution

Not only demographic shifts and immigration but technological changes were transforming the nation. A surge in productivity and prosperity during the 1980s and 1990s resulted from a dramatic revolution in information technology. Cellular phones, laser printers, VCRs, fax machines, and personal computers became commonplace at work and in homes. The computer age had arrived.

The idea of a programmable machine that would rapidly perform mental tasks had been around since the eighteenth century, but it took the crisis atmosphere of World War II to gather the intellectual and financial resources needed to create such a "computer." A team of engineers at the University of Pennsylvania created ENIAC (Electronic Numerical Integrator and Computer), the first all-purpose, all-electronic digital computer. Unveiled in 1944, it could perform 5,000 operations per second. ENIAC took up 3,000 cubic feet of space and included 18,000 vacuum tubes (glass canisters designed to amplify electrical current), 70,000 resistors, 10,000 capacitors, and 6,000 switches.

During the 1950s and 1960s, corporations (such as International Business Machines—IBM) and government agencies transformed computers from mathematical calculators to electronic data-processing machines. The key development in facilitating such a transformation occurred in 1947 when three physicists at Bell Laboratories in central New Jersey invented the transistor (so named because it *trans*fers electric current across a re*sistor,* which is a conductor used to control voltage in an electrical circuit). Tiny transistors took the place of the glass vacuum tubes. The availability of transistors led to the development of hearing aids and portable radios.

The next major breakthrough was the invention in 1971 of the microprocessor—literally a computer on a silicon chip. The functions that had once been performed by computers taking up an entire room could now be performed by a microchip circuit the size of a postage stamp. Engineers soon incorporated microchips into television sets, wristwatches, automobiles, kitchen appliances, and spacecraft.

The Electronic Numerical Integrator and Computer (ENIAC), 1946. Developed for the army, the ENIAC was cumbersome but could perform complex calculations in minutes.

The invention of the microchip made possible the idea of a personal computer. In 1975, an engineer named Ed Roberts developed the first prototype of a "personal computer." The Altair 8800 was imperfect and cumbersome, with no display, no keyboard, and not enough memory to do anything useful. But its potential excited a young Harvard sophomore named Bill Gates. He offered his software programming services for the Altair 8800 and formed a new company called Microsoft. By 1977, Gates and others had helped to transform the personal computer from a hobby machine to a mass consumer product. In 1986 Gates became a billionaire at the age of thirty-one.

By the end of the 1980s, there were 60 million personal computers in the United States, and people began to talk about an "information superhighway," a worldwide network of linked computers and databases connected by fiber-optic lines that facilitated high-speed transmission.

During the 1990s, the development of the Internet and electronic mail enabled anyone with a personal computer and modem the opportunity to travel on the information superhighway. Such advances helped to facilitate almost instantaneous communication across the continents. Yet those too poor to

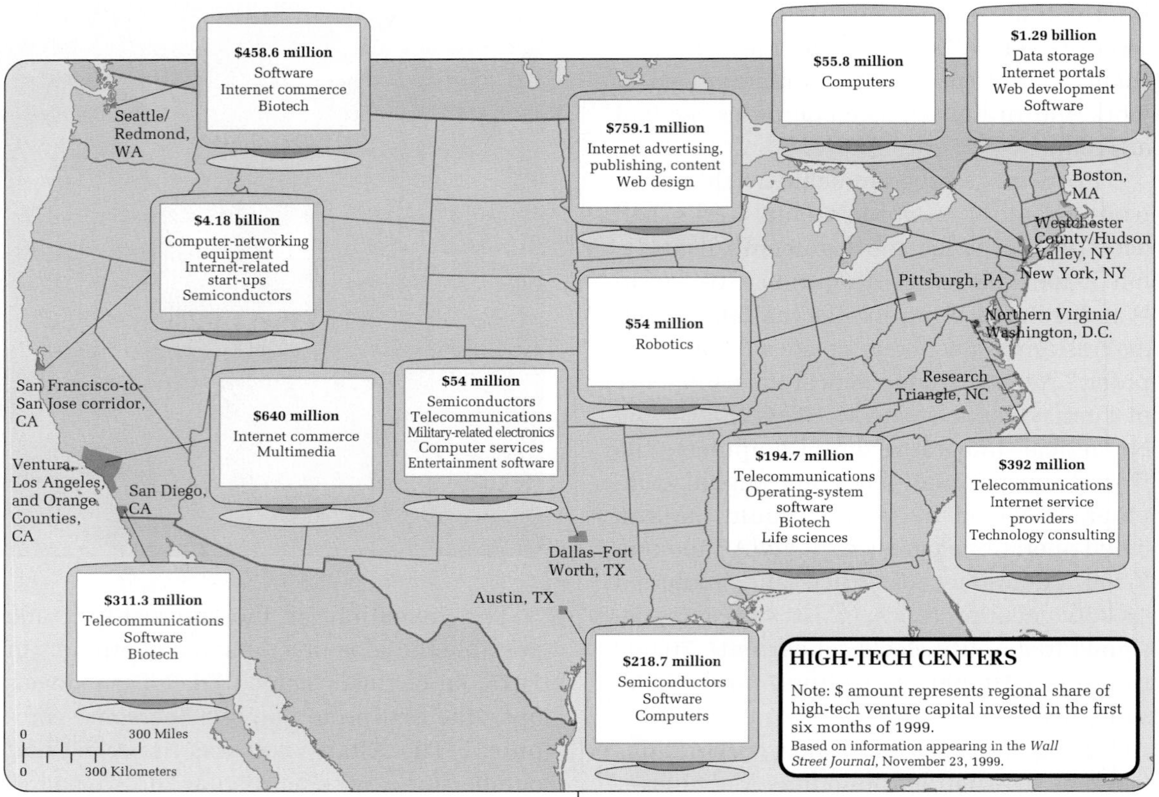

gain easy access to the information revolution faced a bleak future. To the extent that computers had become essential tools for educational and economic success, they threatened to widen the gap between rich and poor. As always, it seems, technological progress has provided uneven benefits.

Cultural Conservatism

Dogmatic cultural conservatives helped elect Ronald Reagan and George Bush in the 1980s, but they were disappointed in the results. Once in office, neither president had, in their eyes, adequately addressed their moral agenda, including a complete ban on abortions and the restoration of prayer in public schools. By the 1990s, a new generation of young conservative activists, mostly political independents or Republicans, emerged as a force to be reckoned with in national affairs. They were more ideological, more libertarian, more partisan, and more impatient than their predecessors.

Attacks on Liberalism

The new breed of conservatives abhorred the "excesses" of cultural and political liberalism: "political correctness," unrestrained individualism, and lack of respect for religion. They especially attacked affirmative action programs designed to redress historic injustices against women and minorities. During the 1990s, powerful groups inside and outside the Republican party mobilized to roll back government programs giving preferences to specified social groups. Prominent black conservatives supported such efforts, arguing that racially based preferences were condescending remedies.

The Religious Right

Although quite diverse, cultural conservatives tended to be evangelical Christians or orthodox Catholics who joined together to exert increasing pressure on the political process. In 1989 the television evangelist Pat Robertson organized the Christian Coalition to replace Jerry Falwell's Moral Majority as the flagship organization of the resurgent religious right.

With a well-organized grassroots movement in every state, the Christian Coalition chose the Republican party as the best vehicle for transforming its campaign into new public policies. It encouraged its supporters to withhold political support from any candidate who did not provide an ironclad promise to support the Coalition's school prayer, anti-abortion, anti–gay rights positions. In addition to promoting "traditional family values," it urged politicians to "radically downsize and delimit government."

As a centrist professional politician, George Bush initially tried to keep the cultural conservatives at arm's length, only to find himself the target of their attacks. His Democratic successor, Bill Clinton, also underestimated the growing strength of organized groups such as the Christian Coalition. In many respects, they took control of the political and social agendas in the nineties.

Bush to Clinton

For months after the Gulf War, President George Bush seemed unbeatable. In the polls his approval rating rose to 91 percent. But the aftermath of Desert Storm was mixed, with Saddam Hussein's grip on Iraq still intact. Despite his image of strength abroad, at home the president began to look weak even on foreign policy. The Soviet Union meanwhile stumbled on to its surprising end. On December 25, 1991, the Soviet flag over the Kremlin was replaced by the flag of the Russian Federation. The cold war had ended with not just the collapse but the dismemberment of the Soviet Union into its fifteen constituent republics. As a result, the United States was now the world's only superpower.

"Containment" of the Soviet Union, the bedrock of American foreign policy for more than four decades, had lost its reason for being. Bush struggled to interpret the fluid new international scene. He spoke of a "New World Order" but never defined it. By his own admission he had trouble with the "vision thing."

Recession and Downsizing

In 1988, a few days after George Bush was elected president, a journalist observed that the nation's deepening financial debt "is the issue that probably will determine the fate of the President. Indeed, it could also be his ultimate undoing." It was an accurate prediction. For the Bush administration and for the nation, the most devastating development in the early nineties was a prolonged economic recession that began in 1990. By early 1992, over 2 million jobs had dried up. During 1991, 25 million workers—about 20 percent of the labor force—were unemployed at some time.

What made this recession unusual was that its victims included large numbers of white-collar workers. In the corporate world, terms such as "restructuring" and "downsizing" ruled the day. Companies began reducing personnel, switching employees to part-time status to reduce their benefits, and finding other ways to cut labor costs.

Some critics compared Bush to Hoover: both presidents and their aides initially denied that there was a problem with the economy and then assured the nation that the recession would be short and self-correcting. The euphoria over the allied victory in the Gulf War quickly gave way to anxiety and resentment generated by the depressed economy. With his domestic policies in disarray and his foreign policy abandoned, George Bush tried a clumsy balancing act in addressing the recession, on the one hand acknowledging that "people are hurting" while on the other urging Americans that "this is a good time to buy a car."

Thomas Hearings and the Women's Movement

Other developments affected the president's popularity, among them the retirement in 1991 of the first black Supreme Court justice, Thurgood Marshall, after twenty-four years on the bench. To succeed him Bush named Clarence Thomas, a black federal judge whose views delighted conservative senators. He questioned the wisdom of the minimum wage, school busing for desegregation, and affirmative action hiring programs, and he preached "black self-help."

Such opinions promised trouble in the Democratic Senate, but the real explosion occurred when Anita Hill, a soft-spoken law professor at the University of Oklahoma, charged that Thomas had sexually harassed her when she worked for him at the Equal Employment Opportunity Commission in the 1980s. An indignant Thomas denied her charges and called the Senate confirmation hearings a "high-tech lynching for uppity blacks." The televised hearings revealed that either Hill or Thomas had lied, and the committee's tie vote reflected the doubt: seven to recommend confirmation and seven against. The full Senate then narrowly confirmed Thomas by a 52 to 48 margin.

The Thomas hearings sparked a new surge in the women's movement. Anita Hill's rough treatment at the hands of male senators revitalized feminism as an organized political movement. An unprecedented number of women ran for national and local offices in 1992. The Thomas confirmation struggle thus widened the gender gap for a Republican party already less popular with women than with men.

Republican Turmoil

President Bush had already set a political trap for himself when he declared in his 1988 convention address: "Read my lips. No new taxes!" Fourteen months into his term, he decided that the deficit was a greater risk than violating his "no tax" pledge. After intense negotiations with congressional Democrats, Bush announced that reducing the federal deficit required "tax revenue increases." Bush's backsliding set off a revolt among House Republicans, but a bipartisan majority (most Republicans opposing) finally approved a tax measure raising the top personal rate from 28 to 31 percent. Conservative Republicans would not let George Bush forget his abandoned pledge.

Social issues had been one of the adhesives in the Reagan coalition, keeping the focus away from divisive economic issues, but as hardships crowded in on the attention of blue-collar workers, the economy surged to the fore. Moreover, social issues strengthened the force of the new "Christian Right" and grated on traditional Republicans. Reagan had been adept at exploiting moral issues, especially abortion, while doing little or nothing about them in practice. Bush's efforts to talk up such issues eventually ran out of control when right-wing militants seized the podium and the attention of the TV cameras at the 1992 Republican convention.

Democratic Resurgence

In contrast to such disarray, the Democrats presented an image of moderate forces in control. For several years, the Democratic Leadership Council (DLC), in which Arkansas governor William Jefferson Clinton figured prominently, had pushed the party toward a more centrist outlook. A graduate of Georgetown University, Clinton had won a Rhodes scholarship to Oxford and then earned a law degree from Yale, where he met and married Hillary Rodham. By 1979, at age thirty-two, he was back in his native Arkansas as the youngest governor in the country. He served three more terms as governor and in the process emerged as a dynamic young leader within the national Democratic party.

A self-described moderate, Clinton promised to cut the defense budget, provide tax relief for the middle class, and create a massive economic aid package for the former republics of the Soviet Union. Clinton, however, often seemed so determined to become president that he was willing to sacrifice consistency and principle. He made extensive use of polls to shape his stance on issues, pandered to special-interest groups, and flip-flopped on controversial issues, leading critics to label him "Slick Willie." Even more enticing to the media and more embarrassing to Clinton were salacious reports that he was a chronic adulterer and that he had manipulated the ROTC program during the Vietnam War to avoid the draft. Clinton's denials of both allegations could not dispel a lingering distrust of his personal character.

After a series of bruising party primaries, Clinton emerged as the front-runner by the time of the Democratic nominating convention in the summer of 1992. The Clinton forces dominated the convention, where Clinton chose Albert Gore, Jr., of Tennessee as his running mate.

Flushed with their convention victory, sporting a ten-point lead in the polls, the Clinton-Gore team stressed economic issues to win over working-class white and black voters. This strategy worked. Exit polls on election day showed that the most important issue had been the economy. Clinton won with 370 electoral votes and about 43 percent of the popular vote; Bush had 168 electoral votes and 39 percent of the popular vote; and off-and-on Reform party candidate H. Ross Perot of Texas garnered 18 percent of the popular vote but no electoral votes.

Domestic Issues

During the campaign, Clinton had promised to submit to Congress within 100 days a comprehensive economic program and a health care reform plan. In both cases, he failed to muster the necessary support of Congress and the public.

The Economy

Clinton entered office determined to reduce the federal deficit without damaging the economy. To this end, he laid out a program of tax hikes and spending cuts. He proposed higher taxes for corporations and for individuals in higher tax brackets and called for an economic stimulus package for "investment" in public works (transportation, utilities, and the like) and in "human capital" (education, skills, health, and welfare). Clinton's deficit reduction package provoked opposition from both Republicans and conservative Democrats, but the bill finally passed in the House and Senate by the narrowest of margins.

Equally contested was approval of the North American Free Trade Agreement

President Bill Clinton and Vice-President Al Gore at the Old State House in Little Rock, Arkansas, following the 1996 presidential election.

(NAFTA), which the Bush administration had negotiated with Canada and Mexico. The debate revived old arguments on the tariff, pro and con. Clinton stuck with his party's tradition of low tariffs and urged approval of NAFTA, which would make North America the largest free trade area in the world. He and his supporters argued that tariff reductions would open up foreign markets to American industries. Opponents of the bill, such as organized labor, favored barriers against cheaper foreign products and believed that with NAFTA, thousands of American jobs would be lost to Mexico. Environmentalists complained of the lack of environmental protection guidelines in the agreement. Nonetheless, NAFTA was approved with solid Republican support but the loss of a sizable minority of Democrats, mostly from the South.

Health Care Reform

Clinton's major public policy initiative was a new health care plan. Government-subsidized health insurance was not a new idea. Other industrial countries had long since started national health insurance programs, Germany as early as 1883, Britain in 1911. Off and on the idea had been a subject of political discussion in the United States throughout the twentieth century. Medicare, initiated in 1965, provided insurance for people sixty-five and older, and Medicaid supported state medical assistance for the indigent. These programs had grown enormously in the years since, as had business spending on private health insurance.

Sentiment for health care reform spread as annual medical costs approached the trillion-dollar mark, and some 39 million Americans had no insurance. Universal medical coverage as proposed by Clinton would have entitled every American and legal immigrant to health insurance. But the bill aroused opposition from vested interests, especially the pharmaceutical and insurance industries. By midsummer 1994, the health insurance plan was doomed. The Democrats acknowledged defeat and gave up the fight for universal medical coverage.

Mistrust of Government and the Militia Movement

While Clinton sparred with Republicans in Washington, a burgeoning "militia" or "patriot" movement spread across the country in the 1990s. Convinced that the federal government was conspiring against individual liberties (especially the right to bear arms), thousands of mostly working-class folk joined well-armed militia organizations. Some militias harkened back to the origins of the Ku Klux Klan and fomented racial and ethnic hatred. Others aligned themselves with right-wing Christian groups, particularly the militant faction of the anti-abortion movement. In the Far West, several of the militias challenged the federal control of public lands, refused to pay taxes, and threatened to arrest and execute local government officials and judges.

In Waco, Texas, a siege resulted in catastrophic consequences. The Branch Davidians, an apocalyptic sect, were discovered to be stockpiling weapons and violating immigration and other federal laws. Agents from the Treasury Department's Bureau of Alcohol, Tobacco, and Firearms (BATF) tried to serve a warrant on the sect on February 28, 1993. When the agents entered the sect's compound, they were met with gunfire. Four agents and two Branch Davidians were killed, and twenty or so people were injured. The next day, the FBI took over the siege of the compound. After fifty days of fruitless psychological warfare against the Branch Davidians, the FBI attacked the compound with armored vehicles and tear gas. Amid the commotion, the compound caught fire and quickly burned to the ground. At least seventy-seven people died in the inferno.

On the second anniversary of the Waco incident, April 19, 1995, a massive truck bomb exploded in front of the federal office building in Oklahoma City, Oklahoma. The entire front portion of the nine-story building collapsed, killing 168 people, 19 of them children in a day-care center that was in the building. Six hundred others were injured. Within days, the FBI charged three men with the bombing. All three were militia members who hated the federal government and who had been incensed by the way the BATF and FBI had dealt with the Branch Davidians at Waco. The Oklahoma City bombing shocked and saddened the nation. It brought to public attention the rise of right-wing militia groups and revealed the depth of their anti-government sentiment.

Republican Insurgency

During 1994, Clinton began to see his presidency unravel. After failing to get either health care reform or welfare reform bills through the Democratic Congress or to carry out his campaign pledge for middle-class tax relief, Clinton and his party found themselves on the defensive.

In the midterm elections of 1994, the Democrats suffered a humbling defeat. For the first time since 1952, Republicans captured both houses of Congress at the same time. Republicans also won a net gain of eleven governorships and fifteen state legislatures. The election signaled a repudiation of Clinton and the Democratic Congress. Squabbling between the president and congressional Democrats did not help matters. Nor did Clinton's response to the Republican takeover of Congress in 1994 endear him to party loyalists. Initially, he and his aides decided to adopt a passive role, letting the Republicans initiate policies and programs and then hoping that they would be decimated by the affected interest groups. He offered no deficit reduction plan, no welfare reform proposal, no new health reform initiative.

Clinton's waffling on major issues began to convince many in his own party that he was a politician rather than a leader, someone who thrived as a campaigner but was bereft of genuine convictions. When Clinton joined conservatives calling for a scaling back of affirmative action plans designed to remedy historic patterns of racial discrimination in hiring and the awarding of government contracts, liberals felt betrayed.

Contract with America

A Georgian named Newton Leroy Gingrich led the Republican insurgency in Congress. In early 1995 he became the first Republican Speaker of the House in forty-two years. In the late 1980s "Newt" Gingrich had launched a series of attacks on the ethics of the Democratic leadership in the House, ultimately leading to the resignation of the Democratic Speaker. Gingrich had also helped mobilize religious and social conservatives associated with the Christian Coalition.

In 1995 Gingrich assaulted the "welfare state" and galvanized support for conservative values and principles. He mobilized freshman Republicans behind what Gingrich called the "Contract with America." The ten-point contract outlined an anti-big-government program with less regulation, less conservation, term limits for members of Congress, a line-item veto for the president, welfare reform, and a balanced-budget amendment.

By April 13, exactly 100 days after taking office, the Republicans had passed twenty-six bills growing out of the Contract with America. Nonetheless, twenty-two of these bills did not become law. Among the bills that did were: a bill by which Congress agreed to stop imposing mandated programs on local and state governments without footing the cost; a large defense spending bill, which Clinton reluctantly accepted, lest Republicans rebel on foreign policy; and a new crime bill providing for stiff penalties for child abuse and pornography.

Thereafter, the much ballyhooed GOP revolution and the Contract with America fizzled out. The revolution that Gingrich touted was far too ambitious to enact in so limited a time, with so slim a majority, and with so little sense of crisis. What is more, many of the Republican freshmen in the house disdained compromise, and they limited the Speaker's room for maneuver. The Senate rejected many of the bills that had been passed in the House. Finally, President Clinton shrewdly moved to the political center and co-opted much of the Republican agenda.

Legislative Breakthrough

In the late summer of 1996, as lawmakers were preparing to adjourn and participate in the presidential nominating conventions, the 104th Congress broke through its partisan gridlock and passed a flurry of important legislation that President Clinton quickly signed, including bills increasing the minimum wage and broadening access to health insurance.

Even more significant was the passage of a comprehensive welfare reform measure that ended the federal government's open-ended guarantee of aid to the poor, a guarantee that had been in place since 1935. The Personal Responsibility and Work Opportunity Act of 1996 turned over the major federal welfare programs to the states. In exchange, the states would receive federal grants to fund the programs. The bill also limited the time a person could receive welfare benefits funded by federal money and required that at least half of a state's welfare recipients have jobs or be enrolled in job training programs by the year 2002. Those states failing to meet the deadline would have their federal funds cut.

After Clinton signed the Republican-sponsored welfare reform legislation, Senator Patrick Moynihan, a leading New York Democrat, charged that the president was abdicating Democratic social principles in order to gain reelection amid the conservative climate of the times. Clinton and his centrist advisers, however, dismissed such criticisms. With his reelection bid at stake, he was determined to live up to his 1992 campaign pledge to "end welfare as we know it." Clinton also knew that most voters in both parties were eager to see major cuts in federal entitlement programs.

The 1996 Campaign

After clinching the Republican presidential nomination in 1996, Majority Leader Bob Dole resigned his Senate seat in order to devote his attention to defeating Bill Clinton. As the 1996 presidential campaign unfolded, Clinton maintained a large lead in the polls. With a generally healthy economy and with no major foreign policy crises to confront, cultural and personal issues surged into prominence. Concern about Dole's age (seventy-three) and his acerbic manner, as well as rifts in the Republican party between economic and social conservatives over issues such as abortion and gun control, hampered Dole's efforts to generate widespread support.

Late in the campaign, Dole charged that the Democrats had raised unprecedented sums of money by dubious means. There were even suspicions that money from abroad had found its way into Democratic accounts. Yet while Clinton excited extreme animosity in his enemies, he was also like Reagan, the "Teflon president," to whom none of their charges stuck. The polls favored Clinton so heavily that a pall of depression seemed to fall over the Dole campaign.

On November 5 Clinton won again with an electoral vote of 379 to 159 and 49 percent of the popular vote. Dole received 41 percent and Ross Perot, in his repeat bid, got 8 percent of the popular vote. Clinton remained a minority president, and once again the Republicans kept their control of Congress. The resulting deadlock reflected the conservative mood of the times.

Economic and Social Trends

After his reelection, Clinton reshuffled his cabinet and other governmental posts. Madeleine Albright, ambassador to the United Nations, became the first woman to head the State Department, and Senator William Cohen, a Republican from Maine, took over at the Defense Department. The overall direction of Clinton's changes was a move to the right.

The "New Economy"

As the twentieth century came to a close, the United States benefited from a prolonged period of unprecedented prosperity. Buoyed by low inflation, high employment, declining federal budget deficits, dramatic improvements in productivity, the rapid "globalization" of economic life, and the astute leadership of Federal Reserve Board Chairman Alan Greenspan, American business and industry witnessed record profits.

The stock market soared during the 1990s. In 1993 the Dow Jones industrial average hit 3,500. By 1996 it had topped 6,000. During 1999, it went past 11,000, defying the predictions of experts that the economy could not sustain such performance. In 2000 unemployment was barely 4 percent, the lowest since 1970. Inflation was modest. Greenspan and others began to talk of a "new economy" that defied the boom-and-bust cycles of the previous hundred years. By 1999 swelling tax revenues generated a federal budget surplus, the first in over thirty years.

Before President Clinton took office, he was persuaded to support Greenspan's monetarist policies and was convinced that a balanced budget was necessary to keep government borrowing from putting inflationary pressure on interest rates. Clinton chose to reduce deficits in part by cutting spending, in part by raising taxes on upper income brackets. At the same time, he abandoned promised tax cuts for middle income brackets.

In the 1990s, many in the Clinton administration believed that the surging economy resulted in large measure from "globalization." Greenspan favored free markets on a world scale—markets without tariffs and other barriers. Gigantic corporations such as International Business Machines and General Electric had become international in scope. They encouraged free trade agreements such as NAFTA or most-favored-nation treatment for China and other countries. Globalization enabled many American companies to "outsource" much of their production to plants in countries with lower labor costs. This led to a decline of the labor union movement in the United States as blue-collar labor lost ground to cheap labor in assembly plants or "sweatshops" elsewhere in the world.

Race Initiative

Since the triumphs of the civil rights movement in the 1960s, the momentum for minority advancement had run out. In the 1980s and 1990s, the federal courts began to shift to the right. One consequence was a challenge to the legality of gerrymandering (redrawing) congressional and legislative districts to create black or Hispanic majorities. Minorities had favored gerrymandering to increase minority officeholding, and Republicans had favored it because such districts would draw minority votes from other districts. But in *Thaw* v. *Reno* (1993), the Court ruled that such districts in North Carolina violated equal protection of the law.

In 1995, a conservative Supreme Court again ruled against election districts redrawn to create black or Hispanic majorities, narrowed federal affirmative action programs, and limited the legal remedies for segregated public schools. All were decided by the same 5 to 4 vote (Chief Justice Rehnquist, and Justices Kennedy, O'Connor, Scalia, and Thomas deciding against Justices Breyer, Ginsburg, Souter, and Stevens).

In one of the cases, *Adarand Constructors v. Peña* (1995), the Court assessed a program that gave advantages to businesses owned by "disadvantaged" minorities. An Hispanic-owned firm had won a highway guard rail contract over a lower bid by a white-owned company. The white-owned company sued on the ground of "reverse discrimination." For the majority, Justice Sandra Day O'Connor said that such programs had to be "narrowly tailored" to serve a "compelling national interest." O'Connor did not define what the Court meant by a "compelling national interest," but the implication of her language was clear: the Court had come to embrace the growing public suspicion of the value and legality of such race-based programs.

In 1996 two major steps were taken against affirmative action in college admissions. In *Hopwood* v. *Texas*, the Fifth Circuit Court ruled that considering race to achieve a diverse student body at the University of Texas was "not a compelling interest under the Fourteenth Amendment." In November, the state of California, while voting for Clinton, also passed Proposition 209, an initiative that ruled out race, sex, ethnicity, or national origin as criteria for preferring any group.

As the century came to a close, programs of affirmative action remained under siege. And affirmative action still did not address intractable problems that lay beyond civil rights, that is, problems of illiteracy, poverty, unemployment, urban decay, and slums.

The Scandal Machine

Just as the administration of Warren G. Harding was rocked by revelations of personal corruption and moral scandal, the Clinton White House also became the focus of incessant investigations and gossip. During his first term, Clinton was dogged by allegations of improper involvement in the Whitewater Development Company. In 1978, as governor of Arkansas, he had invested in a resort project on the White River in northern Arkansas. The project turned out to be a fraud and a failure, and the Clintons took a loss on their investment. Reports surfaced that an Arkansas savings and loan association that had put money into the foundering Whitewater project had also misused funds in the Clinton campaign. An independent counsel was named in 1993 to investigate the allegations of improper Clinton involvement in Whitewater. While revealing that Hillary Clinton had handled some legal work for the Whitewater Development Company, evidence was not uncovered that the Clintons were involved in the fraud.

In 1994, the Justice Department appointed Republican Kenneth Starr as an independent federal counsel to investigate the Whitewater case. After nearly four years of expensive investigation, Starr found no criminal involvement by the Clintons, although a number of their close associates were convicted of various charges.

Besides the Whitewater case, investigators looked into allegations by Paula Jones that Clinton had sexually harassed her while he was governor and she was a state employee in Arkansas. In the course of the investigation, it surfaced that the president might have had a sexual affair with a former White House intern, Monica Lewinsky, and might have pressed her to lie about it under oath. In August 1998, President Clinton agreed to testify before a grand jury. He was the first president in history to do so. During his six hours of testimony, the president recanted his earlier denials and acknowledged having had "inappropriate intimate physical contact" with White House intern Monica Lewinsky, but he insisted he had done nothing illegal. He then went on to attack the "politically inspired" investigation.

Public reaction to Clinton's remarkable about-face was mixed. A majority of Americans expressed sympathy for the president because of his public humiliation and wanted the entire matter dropped. But polls also showed that Clinton's credibility had suffered a serious blow.

Meanwhile, Kenneth Starr continued his tenacious investigation. On September 9, 1998, he submitted to Congress a 445-page report and eighteen boxes of supporting material. The Starr Report found "substantial and creditable" evidence of presidential wrongdoing. Drawing upon such evidence, the Republican-controlled House Judiciary Committee voted 21–16 to recommend a full impeachment inquiry into perjury and obstruction of justice allegations against Clinton. On October 8, the House of Representatives voted 258 to 176 to begin a wide-ranging impeachment inquiry of President Clinton. Thirty-one Democrats joined Republicans in supporting the investigation.

On December 19, 1998, William Jefferson Clinton became the second president to be impeached by the House of Representatives. The House officially approved two articles of impeachment, charging Clinton with lying under oath to a federal grand jury and obstructing justice.

The Senate trial of President Clinton began on January 7, 1999, with the swearing in of Chief Justice William Rehnquist to preside and the senators as jurors. Five weeks later, on February 12, the Senate acquitted Clinton. Rejecting the first charge of perjury, 10 Republicans and all 45 Democrats voted "not guilty." On the charge of obstruction of justice, the Senate split 50-50 (which meant acquittal, since 67 votes would have been needed to convict Clinton). In both instances, senators had a hard time interpreting Clinton's sexual adventures as "high crimes and misdemeanors," the constitutional requirement for removal of a president. Clinton's supporters portrayed him as the victim of a puritanical special prosecutor and partisan conspiracy run amok. His critics lambasted him as a lecherous man without honor or integrity.

Both characterizations were accurate, yet incomplete. Politically astute, charismatic, and well-informed, Clinton had as much ability and potential as any president. Yet he was also shamelessly self-indulgent. The result was a scandalous presidency punctuated by dramatic achievements in welfare reform, economic growth, as well as foreign policy.

Foreign Policy Challenges

Like Woodrow Wilson, Lyndon Johnson, and Jimmy Carter before him, Clinton was a Democratic president who came into office determined to focus on the nation's domestic problems, only to find himself mired in foreign entanglements that had no easy resolution.

Clinton continued the Bush administration's intervention in Somalia, on the northeastern horn of Africa, where collapse of the government early in 1991 had left the coun-

House Judiciary Committee Representative Edward Pease puts his hands on his head during the vote to approve the third of four articles on the impeachment of President Clinton, December 1998.

try in anarchy, prey to tribal marauders. President Bush in 1992 had gained U.N. sanction for a military force led by American troops to relieve hunger and restore peace. In early 1993, U.S. troop levels peaked and began to shrink with the arrival of international forces. The Somalia operation proved successful at its primary mission, but it never solved the political problems that lay at the root of the starvation.

Haiti

The most successful departure in foreign policy for the Clinton administration during its first term came in Haiti. The island nation had emerged suddenly from a cycle of coups with a rebellion in the army rank and file and a democratic election in 1990, which brought to the top a popular priest, Jean-Bertrand Aristide. When a Haitian army general ousted Aristide, the United States immediately announced its intention to bring him back and welcomed the U.N. to the process.

With drawn-out negotiations leading nowhere, Clinton eventually moved in July 1994 to get a U.N. resolution authorizing force as a last resort. At this juncture, former president Jimmy Carter asked permission to negotiate. He went to Port-au-Prince and convinced the military leaders to quit by October 15. The first American forces were already in the air and landed September 19, without opposition and to a cordial welcome from the people. Aristide returned to Haiti and on March 31, 1995, the occupation was turned over to a U.N. force commanded by an American general.

President Clinton presides over the signing of the peace accord between Israel and the Palestinians with Israeli prime minister Yitzhak Rabin (left) and PLO leader Yasir Arafat (right), September 1993.

The Middle East

Clinton also continued the Bush policy of sponsoring patient negotiations between Arabs and Israelis. A new development was the inclusion of the Palestine Liberation Organization (PLO) in the negotiations. In 1993 a draft agreement between Israel and the PLO resulted from secret talks between Israeli and Palestinian representatives in Oslo, Norway. It provided for the restoration of Palestinian self-rule in the occupied Gaza Strip and in Jericho on the West Bank, in an exchange of land for peace as provided in U.N. Security Council resolutions. A formal signing occurred at the White House on September 13, 1993. With President Clinton presiding, Israeli prime minister Yitzhak Rabin and PLO leader Yasir Arafat exchanged handshakes, and their foreign ministers signed the agreement.

In the aftermath of this dramatic agreement, talks continued by fits and starts, interrupted by violent incidents provoked by extremist Jewish settlers and Palestinian factions. In October 1994 Israel and the kingdom of Jordan signed an agreement at ceremonies on their border, which were attended by President Clinton. But the Middle East peace process suffered a terrible blow in early November 1995 when Israeli prime minister Yitzhak Rabin was assassinated at a peace rally in Tel Aviv by an Israeli Jewish zealot who resented Rabin's efforts to negotiate with the Palestinians.

Some observers feared that the assassin had killed the peace process as well when seven months later conservative hard-liner Benjamin Netanyahu narrowly defeated the U.S.-backed Shimon Peres in the election for a new prime minister. Arab leaders responded to Netanyahu's election by threatening to reconsider the concessions they had made over the previous five years. Yet in October 1998, Clinton brought Arafat and Netanyahu together at a conference center in Wye Mills, Maryland, and with the ailing King Hussein of Jordan brokered an agreement, the Wye River Accord, whereby Israel would surrender land in return for security guarantees by the Palestinians. As hardliners attempted to derail the tenuous peace process, Netanyahu decided to call elections early. An Israeli public weary of war swept into power former general Ehud Barak in May 1999. Barak promised to jump-start the peace process.

The Balkans

Clinton's foreign policy also addressed the transition in eastern Europe. With the collapse of Communist power, old ethnic and religious enmities quickly resurfaced, often leading to violent clashes that were difficult to resolve quickly. This was especially true in the former Yugoslavia, a volatile, fractious scene of warring ethnic groups, chiefly Eastern Orthodox Serbs, Catholic Croats, and Bosnian or Albanian Muslims. When Yugoslavia imploded in 1991, fanatics and tyrants provoked ethnic conflict as four of its six republics seceded. Serb minorities, backed by Serbia itself, stirred up civil wars in Croatia and Bosnia. In Bosnia especially, the war involved "ethnic cleansing"—driving Muslims from their homes and towns. The United States faced sobering options: to ignore the butchery, to accept the refugees, to use American airpower, or to risk introducing ground troops. Clinton settled for dropping food and medical supplies to besieged Bosnians and sending planes to retaliate for attacks on places designated "safe havens" by the United Nations.

In 1995 American negotiators finally convinced the foreign ministers of Croatia, Bosnia, and Yugoslavia to agree to a comprehensive peace plan. Bosnia would remain a single nation but would be divided into two states: a Muslim-Croat federation controlling 51 percent of the territory and a Bosnian-Serb republic controlling the remaining 49 percent. Basic human rights would be restored and free elections held to appoint a parliament and joint presidency. To enforce the agreement, 20,000 American troops would be dispatched to Bosnia as part of a 60,000-person NATO peacekeeping operation. A cease-fire went into effect in October 1995.

In 1998 the Balkan tinderbox flared up again, this time in the Yugoslav province of Kosovo. A rugged rural region the size of Connecticut, Kosovo has long been considered sacred ground to Christian Serbs. By 1989, however, over 90 percent of the 2 million Kosovars were ethnic Albanian Muslims. In that year, Yugoslav president Slobodon Milosevic decided to reassert Serbian control over the province. He stripped Kosovo of its autonomy and established de facto martial law. When the Albanian Kosovars resisted and large numbers of Muslim men began to join the Kosovo Liberation Army, Serbian soldiers and state police ruthlessly suppressed them and launched another program of ethnic cleansing, burning Albanian villages, murdering males, raping females, and displacing hundreds of thousands of Muslim Albanian Kosovars.

On March 24, 1999, NATO, relying heavily upon American military resources and leadership, launched air strikes against Yugoslavia. "Ending this tragedy is a moral imperative," explained President Clinton. After 72 days of unrelenting bombardment, Slobodon Milosevic sued for peace on NATO's terms. An agreement was reached on June 3, 1999. It was an unprecedented victory for air power and for NATO, which was celebrating its fiftieth birthday. Not a single allied pilot was killed in combat.

The Democratic ticket in 2000: Al Gore (right) and Joseph Lieberman, senator from Connecticut.

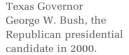

As the Albanian Kosovars started to return to Kosovo, however, large numbers of Serbs began to leave the province in fear of Muslim retribution, and some of them were killed. Members of the Kosovo Liberation Army stepped into the vacuum left by the departing Serbs and began to take control of the province.

Fin-de-Siècle America

The approach of the year 2001 prompted contradictory reflections upon American life at the start of the twenty-first century. As at the close of the 1800s, referred to as the *fin-de-siècle* (a French term for "end of the century"), many people celebrated the unprecedented prosperity and amazing technological breakthroughs of the times, while other observers were more gloomy. Skeptical of material notions of perpetual progress and worried about the cohesion of an increasingly diverse population as well as the growing political power of multinational corporations, they expressed an anxious foreboding about societal dissolution and decay.

Texas Governor George W. Bush, the Republican presidential candidate in 2000.

As the twentieth century drew to a close, the United States seemed to be experiencing the best and worst of times. The economy remained on the crest of a wave of record-setting productivity and profits, inflation was dormant, and the federal government was enjoying balanced budgets for the first time in over a generation. The cold war was over, the nuclear arms race had ended, and the digital revolution was in full swing. Americans were enjoying their personal freedoms, their cornucopia of consumer goods, and their sophisticated technologies. They were also living longer than ever.

Yet a *Times Mirror* survey portrayed a prosperous nation awash in anxiety and self-doubt, with some 73 percent of Americans expressing dissatisfaction with "the way things are going." New technologies were improving productivity and efficiency, but many people were working harder and longer than ever before to keep up with the "wired" workplace and a culture of rising expectations.

The most acute concern today, however, remains the ability of our multicultural society to get along in the midst of our seductive freedoms. Seemingly intractable issues threaten to unravel the social fabric. Religious, racial, and ethnic tensions are growing, and the gap between rich and poor is widening. Divisive issues such as abortion, gun control, doctor-assisted suicide, affirmative action, prayer in schools, "political correctness," and gay rights, to name a few, have fostered a special-interest sectarianism that has disrupted and divided communities, political parties, and churches.

"Our greatest responsibility," said President Clinton in his second inaugural address, "is to embrace a new spirit of community for a new century." It is an old ideal. In 1630 Governor John Winthrop told the Puritan colonists settling near Boston that "We must delight in each other, make others' conditions our own, rejoice together, mourn together, labor and suffer together, having always before our eyes our community as members of the same body." *E pluribus unum*—one out of many. At the start of a new century, it remains the best definition of what the unique American experiment in self-government means. It also remains America's greatest hope—and its greatest challenge.

The Election of 2000

The election of 2000 revealed that the voters in this pluralistic republic were split just about evenly along partisan lines. The two major party candidates for president, Democratic vice president Al Gore and Texas's Republican governor George W. Bush, the son of the former president, presented sharply contrasting views on the role of the federal government, the feasibility of tax cuts, and the best way to preserve Social Security and Medicare. Gore favored an active federal government and reaffirmed support for controversial agencies such as the Environmental Protection Agency and the Interior Department. Bush sought to place more power in the hands of the individual states, particularly on environmental and educational issues. In international affairs, Bush advocated a relatively isolationist stance, questioning the need to maintain peacekeeping forces in Bosnia or allocate funds overseas to address global concerns. By contrast, Gore promised to sustain America's fiscal and military involvement around the world, favoring U.S. support for humanitarian and environmental concerns abroad.

In the end, it was one of the closest presidential races in American history. On an election night filled with high drama and confused counts, Gore held a slight lead in the popular vote, by some 200,000 out of 101 million votes cast. The television networks initially reported that Gore had taken the state of Florida and its 25 electoral votes. Later in the evening, however, the networks confessed that they had erred. Florida was too close to call. In the early morning hours, the networks declared Bush the winner. An hour later, Gore called Bush to concede, only to issue a retraction a short time later when the networks again declared Florida too close to call. The final tally in Florida showed Bush with a razor-thin lead, but state law required a recount.

As a painstaking hand count of presidential ballots began, disputes erupted over misleading ballot designs and indeterminate punch-card votes. "Pregnant chads" became the subject of national debate. Both sides pursued victory through legal maneuvers in the Florida courts and the U.S. Supreme Court. The electoral drama continued for more than a month beyond election day. Americans were by turn transfixed, appalled, and exhausted by the political wrangling between the courts, the county electoral boards, and the partisans of both sides. But the general willingness to seek a solution within the political system rather than outside it provided a valuable demonstration of the continuing vitality of the republic, regardless of the outcome of the presidential contest.

Further Reading

Chapter 1

A fascinating study of Pre-Columbian migration is Brian M. Fagan's *The Great Journey: The Peopling of Ancient America* (1987). Alice B. Kehoe's *North American Indians: A Comprehensive Account* (1992) provides an encyclopedic treatment of Native Americans. An evocative portrait of the Aztecs can be found in Michael E. Smith's *The Aztecs* (1997). An excellent introduction to the prehistory of the American Southwest, its people, and archaeology is Stephen Plog's *Ancient Peoples of the American Southwest* (1997).

The most comprehensive overviews of European exploration are two volumes by Samuel E. Morison, *The European Discovery of America: The Northern Voyages, A.D. 500–1600* (1971), and *The Southern Voyages, 1492–1616* (1974). David B. Quinn's *North America from Earliest Discovery to First Settlements* (1977) is also useful. A good outline of the forces of exploration is John H. Parry's *The Age of Renaissance* (1963).

The voyages of Columbus are surveyed in William D. Phillips, Jr., and Carla Rahn Phillips's *The Worlds of Christopher Columbus* (1992). David J. Weber examines Spanish colonization in *The Spanish Frontier in North America* (1993). For the French experience, see William J. Eccles's *France in America* (1972).

Bernard Bailyn's multivolume work *The Peopling of British North America,* the first two volumes of which have appeared (*The Peopling of British North America: An Introduction,* 1986, and *Voyagers to the West: A Passage in the Peopling of America on the Eve of the Revolution,* 1986), provides a comprehensive view of European migration. Carl Bridenbaugh's *Vexed and Troubled Englishmen, 1590–1642* (1968) helps explain why so many sought a new home in a strange land. English constitutional traditions and their effect on the colonists are examined in Edmund S. Morgan's *Inventing the People: The Rise of Popular Sovereignty in England and America* (1988). Jack P. Greene provides a brilliant synthesis of British colonization in *Pursuits of Happiness: The Social Development of Early Modern British Colonies and the Formation of American Culture* (1988). Carl Bridenbaugh's *Jamestown, 1544–1699* (1980) traces the English experience on the Chesapeake. Alfred W. Crosby's *Ecological Imperialism: The Biological Expansion of Europe, 900–1900* (1986) explores the ecological effects of European settlement.

Daniel K. Richter's *The Ordeal of the Longhouse: The Peoples of the Iroquois League in The Era of European Colonization* (1992) provides a history of the northeastern Iroquois Nation. The conflict between Native Americans and Europeans is treated well in James Axtell's *The Invasion Within: The Contest of Cultures in Colonial North America* (1986) and *Beyond 1492: Encounters in Colonial North America* (1992). Karen O. Kupperman's *Settling with the Indians: The Meeting of English and Indian Cultures in America, 1580–1640* (1980) stresses the racist nature of the conflict. Alfred A. Cave's *The Pequot War* (1996) and Jill Lepore's *The Name of War: King Philip's War and the Origins of American Identity* describe the conditions leading to war between settlers and Indians. An excellent description of the go-betweens who for a time helped to maintain peace between settlers and Indians along the Pennsylvania frontier is provided by James Merrell's *Into the American Woods: Negotiators on the Pennsylvania Frontier* (1999).

A succinct overview on Puritanism can be found in Alan Simpson's *Puritanism in Old and New England* (1955). Andrew Delbanco's *The Puritan Ordeal* (1989) is a powerful study of the tensions inherent in the Puritan outlook. Useful works on the problem of dissent in a theocracy include Edmund S. Morgan's *Roger Williams, the Church, and the State* (1967) and Emery Battis's *Saints and Sectaries: Anne Hutchinson and the Antinomian Controversy in Massachusetts Bay Colony* (1962).

The pattern of settlement in the middle colonies is illuminated in Barry Levy's *Quakers and the American Family: British Settlement in the Delaware Valley* (1988). Randall Balmer's *A Perfect Babel of Confusion: Dutch Religion and English Culture in the Middle Colonies* (1989) describes how the English conquest of New Netherlands intensified the cultural complexity of the middle colonies. The influence of Quakers can be studied through Gary B. Nash's *Quakers and Politics: Pennsylvania, 1681–1726* (1968).

Settlement of the areas along the South Atlantic is traced in Wesley F. Craven's *The Southern Colonies in the Seventeenth Century, 1607–1689* (1949) and Clarence L. Ver Steeg's *Origins of a Southern Mosaic* (1975). Robert M. Weir's *Colonial South Carolina* (1983) covers the activities of the Lords Proprietors. For a study of race and the settlement of South Carolina, see Peter Wood's *Black Majority: Negroes in Colonial South Carolina from 1670 through the Stono Rebellion* (1975). Those interested in the colonization of Georgia should consult *Oglethorpe in Perspective: Georgia's Founder after Two Hundred Years* (1989), edited by Phinizy Spalding and Harvey H. Jackson. A brilliant book on relations between the Catawba Indians and their black and white neighbors is James H. Merrell's *The Indians' New World: Catawbas and Their Neighbors from European Contact through the Era of Removal* (1989).

Chapter 2

The diversity of colonial societies may be seen in David Hackett Fischer's *Albion's Seed: Four British Folkways in America* (1989). Timothy H. Breen's *Puritans and Adventurers: Change and Persistence in Early America* (1980) describes early settlement patterns, especially in Virginia and Massachusetts. Gary B. Nash examines early race relations in *Red, White, and Black* (2nd ed., 1982) and the growth of seaports in *The Urban Crucible* (1979). David Hall's *Worlds of Wonder, Days of Judgment* (1979) describes New Englanders' religious experiences and beliefs. Other useful works include Richard F. Hofstadter's *America at 1750: A Social Portrait* (1971), and James A. Henretta's *The Evolution of American Society, 1700–1815* (1973). Also see Jack P. Greene's *Imperatives, Behaviors, and Identities: Essays in Early American Cultural History* (1992).

Until recently, Puritan communities received the bulk of scholarly attention. Studies of the New England town include Darrett B. Rutman's *Winthrop's Boston: Portrait of a Puritan Town, 1630–1649* (1965) and Kenneth A. Lockridge's *A New England Town: The First One Hundred Years* (2nd ed., 1985). John Frederick Martin's *Profits in the Wilderness: Entrepreneurship and the Founding of New England Towns in the Seventeenth Century* (1991) indicates that economic concerns rather than spiritual motives were driving forces in many New England towns.

Paul S. Boyer and Stephen Nissenbaum's *Salem Possessed* (1974) connects the notorious witch trials to changes in community structure. For an interdisciplinary approach, see John Demos's *Entertaining Satan: Witchcraft and the Culture of Early New England* (1982). Bernard Rosenthal challenges many myths concerning the Salem witch trials in *Salem Story: Reading the Witch Trials of 1692* (1993).

Of the more recent works dealing with New England society, see Janice Knight's *Orthodoxies in Massachusetts: Rereading American Puritanism* (1994), and Stephen Innes's *Creating the Commonwealth: The Economic Culture of Puritan New England* (1995).

Discussions of women in the New England colonies can be found in Laurel Ulrich's *Good Wives: Image and Reality in the Lives of Women in Northern New England, 1650–1750* (1982), Joy Buel and Richard Buel, Jr.'s *The Way of Duty* (1984), and Carol Karlsen's *The Devil in the Shape of a Woman: Witchcraft in Colonial New England* (1987). John Demos describes family life in *A Little Commonwealth: Family Life in Plymouth Colony* (1970).

For the social history of the southern colonies, see Allan Kulikoff's *Tobacco and Slaves: The Development of Southern Cultures in the Chesapeake, 1680–1800* (1986) and *Colonial Chesapeake Society* (1988), edited by Lois Green Carr. Family life along the Chesapeake is described in Gloria L. Main's *Tobacco Colony* (1982) and Daniel B. Smith's *Inside the Great House: Planter Family Life in Eighteenth-Century Chesapeake Society* (1980).

Edmund S. Morgan's *American Slavery, American Freedom: The Ordeal of Colonial Virginia* (1975) examines Virginia's social structure, environment, and labor patterns in a biracial context. More specific on the racial nature of the origins of slavery are Winthrop D. Jordan's *White over Black: American Attitudes toward the Negro* (1968) and David B. Davis's *The Problem of Slavery in Western Culture* (1986). Philip D. Curtin's *The Atlantic Slave Trade* (1969) is a valuable quantitative study. On the interaction of the cultures of blacks and whites, see Mechal Sobel's *The World They Made Together: Black and White Values in Eighteenth Century Virginia* (1987). Black viewpoints are presented in Timothy H. Breen and Stephen Innes's *"Myne Owne Ground": Race and Freedom on Virginia's Eastern Shore, 1640–1676* (1980). David W. Galenson's *White Servitude in Colonial America* (1981) looks at the indentured labor force.

Henry F. May's *The Enlightenment in America* (1976) examines intellectual trends in eighteenth-century America. Lawrence A. Cremin's *American Education: The Colonial Experience, 1607–1783* (1970) surveys educational developments.

On the Great Awakening, see Edwin S. Gaustad's *The Great Awakening in New England* (1957), Patricia U. Bonomi's *Under the Cope of Heaven: Religion, Society, and Politics in Colonial America* (1986), and Timothy D. Hall's *Contested Boundaries: Itinerancy and the Reshaping of the Colonial Religious World* (1994). The political impact of the new religious enthusiasm is shown in Rhys Issac's *The Transformation of Virginia, 1740–1790* (1982). Patricia J. Tracy's *Jonathan Edwards, Pastor* (1980) stresses the Northampton minister's relations to his community.

Chapter 3

The economics motivating colonial policies are covered in John J. McCusker and Russell R. Menard's *The Economy of British America, 1607–1789* (rev. ed., 1991). The problems of colonial customs administration are explored in Micheal Kammen's *Empire and Interest: The American Colonies and the Politics of Mercantilism* (1970).

Jack P. Greene's *The Quest for Power: The Lower Houses of Assembly in the Southern Royal Colonies, 1689–1776* (1963) describes the politics of the southern colonies, and Richard P. Johnson's *Adjustment to Empire* (1981) examines New England. The Andros crisis and related topics are treated in Jack M. Sosin's *English America and the Revolution of 1688* (1982). Stephen S. Webb's *The Governors-General: The English Army and the Definition of Empire, 1569–1681* (1979) argues that the crown was more concerned with military administration than with commercial regulation, and Webb's *1676: The End of American Independence* (1984) shows how the Indian wars undermined the autonomy of colonial governments.

The early Indian wars are treated in Jill Lepore's *The Name of War: King Philip's War and the Origins of American Identity* (1998) and Francis Jennings's *The Invasion of America* (1975). See also Jennings's *The Ambiguous Iroquois Empire* (1984) and *Empire of Fortune: Crowns, Colonies, and Tribes in the Seven Years War in America* (1988) and Richard Aquila's *The Iroquois Restoration: Iroquois Diplomacy on the Colonial Frontier, 1701–1754* (1983).

A good introduction to the imperial phase of the colonial conflicts is Howard H. Peckham's *The Colonial Wars, 1689–1762* (1964). More analytical is Douglas Leach's *Arms for Empire: A Military History of the British Colonies in North America* (1973). Fred Anderson's *A People's Army* (1984) is a social history of the Seven Years' War.

Chapter 4

For a narrative survey of the events leading to the Revolution, see Edward Countryman's *The American Revolution* (1985). For the perspective of Great Britain on the imperial conflict, see Sir Lewis Namier's *England in the Age of the American Revolution* (2nd ed., 1961) and Ian Christie, *Crisis of Empire* (1966).

The intellectual foundations of revolt are traced in Bernard Bailyn's *The Ideological Origins of the American*

Revolution (1967) and in John Phillip Reid's *Constitutional History of the American Revolution: The Authority of Rights* (1987). To understand how these views were connected to organized protest, see Pauline Maier's *From Resistance to Revolution: Colonial Radicals and the Development of American Opposition to Britain, 1765–1776* (1972). The transfer of allegiance from king to Congress is examined in Jerrilyn Marston's *King and Congress: The Transfer of Political Legitimacy, 1774–1776* (1987).

Profiles of the Revolutionary generation of leaders can be found in Bernard Bailyn's *Faces of Revolution: Personalities and Themes in the Struggle for American Independence* (1990), in Pauline Maier's *The Old Revolutionaries: Political Lives in the Age of Samuel Adams* (1980), and in A.J. Langguth's *Patriots: The Men Who Started the American Revolution* (1988).

A number of books deal with specific events in the chain of crisis. Oliver M. Dickerson's *The Navigation Acts and the American Revolution* (1951) stresses the change from trade regulation to taxation in 1764. Edmund S. Morgan and Helen M. Morgan's *The Stamp Act Crisis* (rev. ed., 1962) gives the colonial perspective on that crucial event. Also valuable are Hiller B. Zobel's *The Boston Massacre* (1970), Benjamin W. Labaree's *The Boston Tea Party* (1964), and David Ammerman's *In the Common Cause: American Response to the Coercive Acts of 1774* (1974). Thomas Doerflinger's *A Vigorous Spirit of Enterprise: Merchants and Economic Development in Revolutionary Philadelphia* (1986) describes the role of that influential group in the imperial crisis.

Pauline Maier's *American Scripture: Making the Declaration of Independence* (1997) is the best analysis of the framing of that document. For accounts of the imperial controversy at the colony level, see Edward Countryman's *A People in Revolution* (1981), on New York; Richard L. Bushman's *King and People in Provincial Massachusetts* (1985); James H. Hutson's *Pennsylvania Politics, 1746–1770* (1972); Rhys Isaac's *The Transformation of Virginia, 1740–1790* (1982), and A. Roger Ekirch's *"Poor Carolina": Politics and Society in Colonial North Carolina, 1729–1776* (1981).

Events west of the Appalachians are chronicled concisely by Jack M. Sosin in *The Revolutionary Frontier, 1763–1783* (1967). Military affairs in the early phases of the war are handled in John W. Shy's *Toward Lexington: The Role of the British Army in the Coming of the American Revolution* (1965) and in other works listed in Chapter 5.

Chapter 5

The Revolutionary War is the subject of Colin Bonwick's *The American Revolution* (1991), Theodore Draper's *A Struggle for Power: The American Revolution* (1996), Gordon S. Wood's *The Radicalism of the American Revolution* (1991), and Benson Bobrick's *Angel in the Whirlwind: The Triumph of the American Revolution* (1997). David Hackett Fischer's *Paul Revere's Ride* (1994) details the events surrounding the immediate outbreak of fighting, while Jeremy Black's *War for America: The Fight for Independence, 1775–1783* (1991) focuses on the war itself.

On the social history of the Revolutionary War, see John W. Shy's *A People Numerous and Armed* (1976), Charles Royster's *A Revolutionary People at War* (1979), Lawrence D. Cress's *Citizens in Arms* (1982), and E. Wayne Carp's *To Starve the Army at Pleasure: Continental Army Administration and American Political Culture, 1775–1783* (1984). Colin G. Calloway tells the neglected story of the Indian experiences in the Revolution in *The American Revolution in Indian Country: Crisis and Diversity in Native American Communities* (1995).

Why some Americans remained loyal to the crown is the subject of Bernard Bailyn's *The Ordeal of Thomas Hutchinson* (1974), Robert M. Calhoon's *The Loyalists in Revolutionary America, 1760–1781* (1973), and Mary Beth Norton's *The British-Americans* (1972).

A superb community-level study of Revolutionary change is Robert A. Gross's *The Minutemen and Their World* (1976). The definitive study of African Americans during the Revolutionary era remains Benjamin Quarles's *The Negro in the American Revolution* (1961). Mary Beth Norton's *Liberty's Daughters* (1980) and Linda K. Kerber's *Women of the Republic* (1980) document the role women played in securing independence. Joy D. Buel and Richard Buel, Jr.'s *The Way of Duty* (1984) shows the impact of the Revoluton on one New England family.

The standard introduction to the diplomacy of the Revolutionary era is Jonathan R. Dull's *A Diplomatic History of the American Revolution* (1985). Richard B. Morris's *The Peacemakers* (1965) examines more closely the negotiations for the Peace of Paris.

Chapter 6

A good overview of the Confederation period is Richard B. Morris's *The Forging of the Union, 1781–1789* (1987).

Another useful analysis of this period is Richard Buel, Jr.'s *Securing the Revolution: Ideology in American Politics, 1789–1814* (1974). Relevant chapters of Gordon S. Wood's *The Creation of the American Republic, 1776–1787* (1969) trace the changing contours of political philosophy during these years.

David P. Szatmary's *Shays' Rebellion: The Making of an Agrarian Insurrection* (1980) covers that fateful incident. For a fine account of cultural change during the period, see Joseph J. Ellis's *After the Revolution: Profiles of American Culture* (1979) and Oscar Handlin and Lillian Handlin's *A Restless People: America in Rebellion, 1770–1787* (1982).

Excellent treatments of the post-Revolutionary era include Edmund S. Morgan's *Inventing the People* (1988), Michael Kammen's *Sovereignty and Liberty* (1988), and Forrest McDonald's *Novus Ordo Seclorum: The Intellectual Origins of the Constitution* (1985). Among the better collections of essays on the Constitution are *Toward a More Perfect Union* (1988), edited by Neil L. York, and *The Framing and Ratification of the Constitution* (1987), edited by Leonard W. Levy and Dennis J. Mahoney.

Bruce Ackerman's *We the People: Foundations* (1990) examines Federalist political principles. For the Bill of Rights that emerged from the ratification struggles, see Robert A. Rutland's *The Birth of the Bill of Rights, 1776–1791* (1955).

Michael Kammen's *A Machine That Would Go of Itself: The Constitution in American Culture* (1986) is a comprehensive cultural history of the Constitution that shows how it has become revered by the American public.

Chapter 7

The best introduction to the early Federalists remains John C. Miller's *The Federalist Era, 1789–1800* (1960). Other works analyze the ideological debates among the nation's first leaders. Richard Buel, Jr.'s *Securing the Revolution: Ideology in American Politics, 1789–1815* (1974), Joyce Appleby's *Capitalism and a New Social Order* (1984), Drew McCoy's *The Elusive Republic: Political Economy in Jeffersonian America* (1982) and *The Last of the Fathers: James Madison and the Republican Legacy* (1989), and Stanley Elkins and Eric McKitrick's *The Age of Federalism* (1993) trace the persistence and transformation of ideas first fostered during the Revolutionary crisis. John F. Hoadley's *Origins of American Political Parties, 1789–1803* (1986) is superb.

The 1790s may also be understood through the views and behavior of national leaders. See the following biographies: Forrest McDonald's *Alexander Hamilton: A Biography* (1979), Richard Brookhiser's *Founding Father: Rediscovering George Washington* (1996), E. Harrison Clark's *All Cloudless Glory: The Life of George Washington* (1996), Joseph J. Ellis's *Passionate Sage: The Character and Legacy of John Adams* (1993), and John Ferling's *John Adams: A Life* (1996). For a female perspective, see Phyllis Lee Levin's *Abigail Adams* (1991) and Edith B. Gelles's *Portia: The World of Abigail Adams* (1992). The opposition viewpoint is the subject of Lance Banning's *The Jeffersonian Persuasion: Evolution of a Party Ideology* (1978).

Federalist foreign policy is explored in Jerald A. Comb's *The Jay Treaty* (1970), William C. Stinchcombe's *The XYZ Affair* (1980), and Felix Gilbert's *To the Farewell Address: Ideas of Early American Foreign Policy* (1961).

For specific domestic issues, see Thomas Slaughter's *The Whiskey Rebellion: Frontier Epilogue to the American Revolution* (1986) and Harry Ammon's *The Genêt Mission* (1973). Patricia Watlington's *The Partisan Spirit: Kentucky Politics, 1779–1792* (1972) examines the Kentucky Resolutions. The treatment of Indians in the Old Northwest is explored in Richard H. Kohn's *Eagle and Sword: The Federalists and the Creation of the Military Establishment in America, 1783–1802* (1975). For the Alien and Sedition Acts, consult James Morton Smith's *Freedom's Fetters: The Alien and Sedition Laws and American Civil Liberties* (1956). Daniel Sisson's *The American Revolution of 1800* (1974) is useful for its treatment of that important election.

Several books focus on social issues of the post-Revolutionary period, including *Keepers of the Revolution: New Yorkers at Work in the Early Republic* (1992), edited by Paul A. Gilje and Howard B. Rock, Ronald Schultz's *The Republic of Labor: Philadelphia Artisans and the Politics of Class, 1720–1830* (1993), and Peter Way's *Common Labour: Workers and the Digging of North American Canals, 1780–1860* (1993).

The African-American experience in the Revolutionary era is detailed in Mechal Sobel's *The World They Made Together: Black and White Values in Eighteenth-Century Virginia* (1988) and Gary B. Nash's *Forging Freedom: The Formation of Philadelphia's Black Community, 1720–1840* (1988).

Chapter 8

Marshall Smelser's *The Democratic Republic, 1801–1815* (1968) presents an overview of the Republican administrations. The standard biography of Jefferson is Joseph J. Ellis's *American Sphinx: The Character of Thomas Jefferson* (1997). On the life of Jefferson's friend and successor, see Drew R. McCoy's *The Last of the Fathers: James Madison and the Republican Legacy* (1989). McCoy's *The Elusive Republic* (1982) discusses the political economy of these years in the context of republicanism; Joyce Appleby's *Capitalism and a New Social Order* (1984) minimizes the impact of republican ideology.

Linda K. Kerber's *Federalists in Dissent: Imagery and Ideology in Jeffersonian America* (1970) explores the Federalists while out of power. The concept of judicial review and the courts can be studied in Richard E. Ellis's *The Jeffersonian Crisis* (1971). On John Marshall, see G. Edward White's *The Marshall Court and Cultural Change, 1815–1835* (1991). Milton Lomask's two-volume *Aaron Burr: The Years from Princeton to Vice President, 1756–1805* (1979) and *The Conspiracy and the Years of Exile, 1805–1836* (1982) trace the career of that remarkable American.

For the Louisiana Purchase, consult Alexander De Conde's *This Affair of Louisiana* (1976). For a captivating account of the Lewis and Clark expedition, see Stephen Ambrose's *Undaunted Courage: Meriwether Lewis, Thomas Jefferson and the Opening of the American West* (1996). Bernard W. Sheehan's *Seeds of Extinction* (1973) is more analytical about the Jeffersonians' Indian policy and opening of the West.

Burton Spivak's *Jefferson's English Crisis: Commerce, the Embargo, and the Republican Revolution* (1979) discusses Anglo-American relations during Jefferson's administration; Clifford L. Egan's *Neither Peace nor War* (1983) covers Franco-American relations. An excellent revisionist treatment of the events that brought on war in 1812 is J. C. A. Stagg's *Mr. Madison's War* (1983). The war itself is the focus of Donald R. Hickey's *The War of 1812: A Forgotten Conflict* (1989). See also David Curtis Skaggs and Gerard T. Altoff's *A Signal Victory: The Lake Erie Campaign, 1812–1813* (1997).

Chapter 9

The standard overview of the Era of Good Feelings remains George Dangerfield's *The Awakening of American Nationalism, 1815–1828* (1965). The gathering sense of a national spirit, hindered by an equally growing sectionalism, can be traced in Daniel J. Boorstin's *The Americans: The Nationalist Experience* (1965).

For discussions of the American System, see Bray Hammond's *Banks and Politics in America from the Revolution to the Civil War* (1957) and George R. Taylor's *The Transportation Revolution, 1815–1860* (1951). A classic overview of the economic trends of the period is Douglas C. North's *The Economic Growth of the United States, 1790–1860* (1961).

The political temper of the times is treated in biographical studies of principal figures: Irving Bartlett's *Daniel Webster* (1981) and *John C. Calhoun: A Biography* (1993), Noble Cunningham's *The Presidency of James Monroe* (1996), Clement Eaton's *Henry Clay and the Art of American Politics* (1957), Paul C. Nagel's *John Quincy Adams: A Public Life, A Private Life* (1997), and Jean Edward Smith's *John Marshall: Definer of a Nation* (1997).

A stimulating synthesis of economic, social, and political developments is Sean Wilentz's *Chants Democratic: New York City and the Rise of the American Working Class, 1788–1850* (1983). The emergence of slavery as the most divisive sectional issue is treated in Donald L. Robinson's *Slavery in the Structure of American Politics, 1765–1820* (1971).

On diplomatic relations during James Monroe's presidency, see William Earl Weeks's *John Quincy Adams and American Global Empire* (1992). For relations after 1812, see Ernest R. May's *The Making of the Monroe Doctrine* (1975) and Dexter Perkin's *A History of the Monroe Doctrine* (1955).

Background on Andrew Jackson can be obtained from works cited in Chapter 11. The campaign that brought Jackson to the White House is analyzed in Robert V. Remini's *The Election of Andrew Jackson* (1963).

Chapter 10

A survey of events covered in the chapter is Daniel Feller's *The Jacksonian Promise: America, 1815–1840* (1995). A more political focus can be found in Harry L. Watson's *Liberty and Power: The Politics of Jacksonian America* (1990). Lee Benson's *The Concept of Jacksonian Democracy* (1961) remains an important revisionist interpretation. Edward Pessen's *Jacksonian America: Society,*

Personality, and Politics (rev. ed., 1979) stresses the lack of genuine democracy in society and politics.

A still valuable standard introduction to the development of political parties of the 1830s is Richard P. McCormick's *The Second Party System* (1966). For an outstanding analysis of women in New York City during the Jacksonian period, see Christine Stansell's *City of Women: Sex and Class in New York, 1789–1860* (1986). In *Chants Democratic: New York City and the Rise of the American Working Class, 1788–1850* (1984), Sean Wilentz analyzes the social basis of working-class politics. John Marszalek's *The Petticoat Affair: Manners, Mutiny, and Sex in Andrew Jackson's White House* (1997) assesses the Peggy Eaton controversy.

The best biography of Jackson remains Robert V. Remini's three volume work: *Andrew Jackson: The Course of American Empire, 1767–1821* (1977), *Andrew Jackson: The Course of American Freedom, 1822–1832* (1981), and *Andrew Jackson: The Course of American Democracy, 1833–1845* (1984). On Jackson's successor, consult John Niven's *Martin Van Buren: The Romantic Age of American Politics* (1983). Studies of other major figures of the period include John Niven's *John C. Calhoun and the Price of Union* (1988), Merrill Peterson's *The Great Triumvirate: Webster, Clay, and Calhoun* (1987), and Robert Remini's *Henry Clay: Statesman for the Union* (1992) and *Daniel Webster: The Man and His Time* (1997).

The political philosophies of Jackson's opponents are treated in Daniel W. Howe's *The Political Culture of the American Whigs* (1979) and William P. Vaughn's *The Antimasonic Party in the United States, 1826–1843* (1983).

Two studies of the impact of the Bank controversy are William G. Shade's *Banks or No Banks: The Money Question in the Western States, 1832–1865* (1972) and James R. Sharp's *The Jacksonians versus the Banks: Politics in the States after the Panic of 1837* (1970). Daniel Feller's *The Public Lands in Jacksonian Politics* (1984) is a good introduction to that important topic.

The outstanding book on the nullification issue remains William W. Freehling's *Prelude to Civil War: The Nullification Controversy in South Carolina, 1816–1836* (1966). John M. Belohlavek's *"Let the Eagle Soar!": The Foreign Policy of Andrew Jackson* (1985) is a thorough study of Jacksonian diplomacy. Ronald N. Satz's *American Indian Policy in the Jacksonian Era* (1974) surveys that tragedy; Michael P. Rogin's *Fathers and Children: Andrew Jackson and the Subjugation of the American Indian* (1975) is a psychological interpretation of Jackson's Indian policy.

Chapter 11

On economic development in the nation's early decades, see Stuart W. Bruchey's *Enterprise: The Dynamic Economy of a Free People* (1990). The classic study of transportation and economic growth is George R. Taylor's *The Transportation Revolution, 1815–1860* (1951). A fresh view is provided in Sarah H. Gordon's *Passage to Union: How the Railroads Transformed American Life, 1829–1929* (1997).

The impact of technology is traced in David J. Jeremy's *Transatlantic Industrial Revolution: The Diffusion of Textile Technologies between Britain and America, 1790–1830s* (1981) and Merritt R. Smith's *Harper's Ferry Armory and the New Technology: The Challenge of Change* (1977). The evolution of the nation's postal system is ably recounted in Richard R. John's *Spreading the News: The American Postal System from Franklin to Morse* (1996).

Paul Johnson's *A Shopkeeper's Millennium: Society and Revivals in Rochester, New York, 1815–1837* (1978) studies the role religion played in the emerging industrial order. The attitude of the worker during this time of transition is surveyed in Edward E. Pessen's *Most Uncommon Jacksonians: The Radical Leaders of the Early Labor Movement* (1967). Detailed case studies of working communities include Anthony F. C. Wallace's *Rockdale: The Growth of an American Village in the Early Industrial Revolution* (1978); Thomas Dublin's *Women at Work: The Transformation of Work and Community in Lowell, Massachusetts, 1826–1860* (1979); Stephan Thernstrom's *Poverty and Progress: Social Mobility in a Nineteenth-Century City* (1964), on Newburyport, Massachusetts; and Sean Wilentz's *Chants Democratic* (1984), on New York City. Walter Licht's *Working for the Railroad: The Organization of Work in the Nineteenth Century* (1983) is rich in detail.

For a fine treatment of urbanization, see Charles N. Glaab and A. Theodore Brown's *A History of Urban America* (1976). A valuable case study is Edward K. Spann's *The New Metropolis: New York City, 1840–1857* (1981). Another excellent study of New York City is Edwin G. Burrows and Mike Wallace's *Gotham: A History of New York City to 1898* (1998). On immigration, see Michael Coffey and Terry Golway, *The Irish in America* (1997). The rise of an indigenous American musical tradition is detailed in Ken Emerson's *Doo-Dah! Stephen Foster and the Rise of American Popular Culture* (1997).

Chapter 12

Russel B. Nye's *Society and Culture in America, 1830–1860* (1974) provides a wide-ranging survey. On the reform impulse, consult Ronald G. Walter's *American Reformers, 1815–1860* (1978). Revivalist religion is treated in Nathan O. Hatch's *The Democratization of American Christianity* (1989), and Christine Heyrman's *Southern Cross: The Beginnings of the Bible Belt* (1997). On the Mormons, see Leonard J. Arrington's *Brigham Young: American Moses* (1985).

The best introduction to transcendentalist thought is Paul Boller's *American Transcendentalism, 1830–1860* (1974). A more recent treatment is Carlos Baker's *Emerson Among the Eccentrics: A Group Portrait* (1997). Several good works describe various aspects of the antebellum reform movement. For temperance, see W. J. Rorabaugh's *The Alcoholic Republic: An American Tradition* (1979) and Barbara Leslie Epstein's *The Politics of Domesticity: Women, Evangelism, and Temperance in Nineteenth-Century America* (1981). Stephen Nissenbaum's *Sex, Diet, and Debility in Jacksonian America* (1980) looks at health reform. On prison reform and other humanitarian projects, see David J. Rothman's *The Discovery of the Asylum* (1971), Gerald N. Grob's *Mental Institutions in America* (1973), Charles Rosenberg's *The Care of Strangers: The Rise of America's Hospital System* (1987), and Thomas J. Brown's biography, *Dorothea Dix: New England Reformer* (1998).

Lawrence A. Cremin's *American Education: The National Experience, 1783–1876* (1980) traces early school reform. For other views, see Stanley K. Schultz's *The Culture Factory: Boston Public Schools, 1789–1860* (1973) and Carl F. Kaestle and Eric Foner's *Pillars of the Republic* (1983).

On women during the antebellum period, see Nancy F. Cott's *The Bonds of Womanhood: "Woman's Sphere" in New England, 1780–1835* (1977) and Ellen C. DuBois's *Feminism and Suffrage: The Emergence of an Independent Women's Movement in America, 1848–1869* (1978). Also valuable are Shirley Samuels's *The Culture of Sentiment: Race, Gender, and Sentimentality in Nineteenth-Century America* (1992), Jeanne Boydston's *The Limits of Sisterhood: The Beecher Sisters on Women's Rights and Woman's Sphere* (1988), and Mary P. Ryan's *Women in Public: Between Banners and Ballots, 1825–1880* (1990).

A small but growing literature on ideals of masculinity and changing roles of men in the nineteenth century includes David Leverenz's *Manhood and the American Renaissance* (1989), Mark C. Carnes's *Secret Ritual and Manhood in Victorian America* (1989), Mary Ann Clawson's *Constructing Brotherhood: Class, Gender, and Fraternalism* (1989), and E. Anthony Rotundo's *American Manhood: Transformations in Masculinity from the Revolution to the Modern Era* (1993). Changing ideals of the family in the nineteenth century are described in Steven Mintz and Susan Kellogg's *Domestic Revolutions: A Social History of American Family Life* (1988).

Michael Fellman's *The Unbounded Frame: Freedom and Community in Nineteenth-Century American Utopianism* (1973) surveys the utopian movements. Specific experiments are treated in Robert D. Thomas's *The Man Who Would Be Perfect* (1977), on John Humphrey Noyes; J. F. C. Harrison's *Robert Owen and the Owenites in Britain and America: The Quest for the New Moral World* (1969), Maren L. Carden's *Oneida* (1969); and Henri Desroche's *The American Shakers: From Neo-Christianity to Pre-Socialism* (1971). Lawrence Foster's *Religion and Sexuality* (1981) discusses the Oneida, Shaker, and Mormon communities.

Chapter 13

For background on Whig programs and ideas, see Richard P. McCormick's *The Second American Party System: Party Formation in the Jacksonian Era* (1966). Several works help interpret the expansionist impulse. Frederick Merk's *Manifest Destiny and Mission in American History* (1963) remains a classic. Another treatment of expansionist ideology is Thomas R. Hietala's *Manifest Design: Anxious Aggrandizement in Late Jacksonian America* (1985).

The best survey of western expansion is Richard White's *"It's Your Misfortune and None of My Own": A New History of the American West* (1991). Robert M. Utley's *A Life Wild and Perilous: Mountain Men and the Paths to the Pacific* (1997) tells the dramatic story of the rugged pathfinders who found corridors over the Rocky Mountains. The movement of settlers to the West is ably documented in John Mack Faragher's *Women and Men on the Overland Trail* (1979). The best account of the California gold rush is Malcolm J. Rohrbough's *Days of Gold: The California Gold Rush and the American Nation* (1997).

Gene M. Brack's *Mexico Views Manifest Destiny, 1821–1846* (1975) takes Mexico's viewpoint on American designs on the West. On James K. Polk, see John H. Schroeder's *Mr. Polk's War* (1973). The best survey of the military conflict is John S. D. Eisenhower's *So Far from*

God: The U.S. War with Mexico, 1846–1848 (1989). For a textured account of the soldier's life in the war, see Richard Bruce Winders's *Mr. Polk's Army: The American Military Experience in the Mexican War* (1997). John S. D. Eisenhower's *Agent of Destiny: The Life and Times of General Winfield Scott* (1997) illuminates the greatest American soldier between George Washington and Ulysses S. Grant.

An excellent analysis of the diplomatic aspects of Mexican-American relations is David M. Pletcher's *The Diplomacy of Annexation: Texas, Oregon, and the Mexican War* (1973). On California, see Kevin Starr's *Americans and the California Dream, 1850–1915* (1973). On Oregon, see Earl Pomeroy's *The Pacific Slope: A History of California, Oregon, Washington, Idaho, Utah, and Nevada* (1965).

Chapter 14

Those interested in the problem of discerning myth and reality in the southern experience should consult William R. Taylor's *Cavalier and Yankee: The Old South and American National Character* (1961) and W. J. Cash's *The Mind of the South* (1941). Two efforts to understand the mind of the Old South and its defense of slavery are Eugene D. Genovese's *The Slaveholders' Dilemma: Freedom and Progress in Southern Conservative Thought, 1820–1860* (1992) and Eric H. Walther's *The Fire-Eaters* (1992).

Contrasting analyses of the plantation system are Eugene D. Genovese's *The World the Slaveholders Made* (1969) and Gavin Wright's *The Political Economy of the Cotton South* (1978). Stephanie McCurry's *Masters of Small Worlds: Yeoman Households, Gender Relations, and the Political Culture of the Antebellum South Carolina Low Country* (1995) greatly enriches our understanding of households, religion, and political culture.

Other essential works on southern culture and society include Bertram Wyatt-Brown's *Honor and Violence in the Old South* (1986), Elizabeth Fox-Genovese's *Within the Plantation Household: Black and White Women of the Old South* (1988), Suzanne Lebsock's *The Free Women of Petersburg* (1984), Catherine Clinton's *The Plantation Mistress: Woman's World in the Old South* (1982), Joan Cashin's *A Family Venture: Men and Women on the Southern Frontier* (1991), and Theodore Rosengarten's *Tombee: Portrait of a Cotton Planter* (1987).

William J. Cooper, Jr.'s *Liberty and Slavery: Southern Politics to 1860* (1983) and Robert F. Durden's *The Self-Inflicted Wound* (1985) cover southern politics of the era. For a look at the role of religion in southern political life, see Mitchell Snay's *Gospel of Disunion: Religion and Separatism in the Antebellum South* (1993).

A provocative discussion of the psychology of black slavery can be found in Stanley M. Elkins's *Slavery: A Problem in American Institutional and Intellectual Life* (3rd ed., 1976). John W. Blassingame's *The Slave Community: Plantation Life in the Antebellum South* (2nd ed., 1979); Eugene D. Genovese's *Roll, Jordan, Roll: The World the Slaves Made* (1974), and Herbert G. Gutman's *The Black Family in Slavery and Freedom, 1750–1925* (1976) all stress the theme of a persisting and identifiable slave culture. Discussions of the diversity of the experience of slavery in particular places can be found in John C. Inscoe's *Mountain Masters: Slavery and the Sectional Crisis in Western North Carolina* (1989) and Randolph B. Campbell's *An Empire for Slavery: The Peculiar Institution in Texas, 1821–1865* (1989).

On the question of slavery's profitability, see Robert W. Fogel and Stanley L. Engerman's *Time on the Cross: The Economics of Negro Slavery* (2 vols., 1974), which argues that not only did planters benefit financially from bondage, but the slaves themselves incorporated a Victorian work ethic based on incentives. Herbert G. Gutman reviewed this controversy in *Slavery and the Numbers Game* (1975). See also Robert Fogel's reflections on the subject in *Without Consent or Contract* (1992).

Other works on slavery include Lawrence W. Levine's *Black Culture and Black Consciousness: Afro-American Folk Thought from Slavery to Freedom* (1977), Albert J. Raboteau's *Slave Religion: The "Invisible Institution" in the Antebellum South* (1978), Dorothy Sterling's *We Are Your Sisters* (1984), Deborah Gray White's *Ar'n't I a Woman? Female Slaves in the Plantation South* (1985), and Joel Williamson's *The Crucible of Race* (1985). Charles Joyner's *Down by the Riverside* (1984) offers a vivid reconstruction of one slave community. Editors Alonzo Johnson and Paul Jersild have compiled insightful essays dealing with slave culture in *"Ain't Gonna Lay My 'Ligion Down": African American Religion in the South* (1996).

Useful surveys of abolitionism include Ronald G. Walters's *The Antislavery Appeal: American Abolitionism after 1830* (1976) and James B. Stewart's *Holy Warriors: The Abolitionists and American Slavery* (1976). William S. McFeely's *Frederick Douglass* (1990) portrays the most eminent black male abolitionist while Nell Painter's *Sojourner Truth: A Life, A Symbol* (1996) profiles the leading female activist. For the proslavery argument as it developed in the South, see Larry Tise's *Proslavery: A History of the Defense of Slavery in America, 1701–1840* (1988), and James Oakes's *The Ruling Race: A History of American Slaveholders* (1982). The problems southerners had in justifying slavery are explored in Drew G. Faust's *A Sacred Circle: The Dilemma of the Intellectual in the Old South, 1840–1860* (1977), Kenneth S. Greenberg's *Masters and Statesmen: The Political Culture of American Slavery* (1985), and Carl N. Degler's *The Other South: Southern Dissenters in the Nineteenth Century* (1974)

Chapter 15

The best surveys of the forces and events leading to the Civil War include James M. McPherson's *Battle Cry of Freedom: The Civil War Era* (1988), Stephen B. Oates and Buz Wyeth's *The Approaching Fury: Voices of the Storm, 1820–1861* (1997), and Bruce Levine's *Half Slave and Half Free: The Roots of the Civil War* (1992). The most recent narrative of the political debate leading to secession is Michael A. Morrison's *Slavery and the American West: The Eclipse of Manifest Destiny and the Coming of the Civil War* (1997). Interpretive analyses can be found in Eric Foner's *Politics and Ideology in the Age of the Civil War* (1980) and Joel H. Silbey's *The Partisan Imperative: The Dynamics of American Politics before the Civil War* (1985).

Mark Stegmaier's *Texas, New Mexico, and the Compromise of 1850: Boundary Dispute and Sectional Crisis* (1996) probes that crucial dispute while Michael F. Holt's *The Political Crisis of the 1850s* (1978) traces the demise of the Whigs. Eric Foner shows how events and ideas combined in the formation of a new political party in *Free Soil, Free Labor, Free Men: The Ideology of the Republican Party before the Civil War* (1970). A more straightforward study of the rise of the Republicans is William E. Gienapp's *The Origins of the Republican Party, 1852–1856* (1987). The economic, social, and political crises of 1857 are examined in Kenneth Stampp's *America in 1857: A Nation on the Brink* (1990).

Robert W. Johannsen's *Stephen A. Douglas* (1973) analyzes the issue of popular sovereignty. A more national perspective is provided in James A. Rawley's *Race and Politics: "Bleeding Kansas" and the Coming of the Civil War* (1969). On the role of John Brown in the sectional crisis, see Stephen B. Oates's *To Purge This Land with Blood: A Biography of John Brown* (2nd ed., 1984). Two other issues that divided the nation can be studied in Stanley W. Campbell's *The Slave Catchers* (1970), on attempts to enforce the Fugitive Slave Act, and in Don E. Fehrenbacher's *Slavery, Law, and Politics* (1981), on the Dred Scott case.

An excellent study on the South's journey to secession is William Freehling's *The Road to Disunion* (1990). Studies of southern states include J. Mills Thornton's *Politics and Power in a Slave Society: Alabama, 1800–1860* (1978), Michael P. Johnson's *Toward a Patriarchal Republic: The Secession of Georgia* (1977), and Steven A. Channing's *Crisis of Fear: Secession in South Carolina* (1970). For developments in the border states, see Daniel W. Croft's *Reluctant Confederates: Upper South Unionists in the Secession Crisis* (1989).

On Lincoln's role in the coming crisis of war, see Don E. Fehrenbacher's *Prelude to Greatness* (1962). Harry V. Jaffa's *Crisis of the House Divided* (1959) details the Lincoln-Douglas debates, and Maury Klein's *Days of Defiance: Sumter, Secession, and the Coming of the Civil War* (1997) treats the Fort Sumter controversy.

Chapter 16

The best one-volume overview of the Civil War period is James M. McPherson's *Battle Cry of Freedom: The Civil War Era* (1988). A good introduction to the military events is Herman Hattaway's *Shades of Blue and Gray: An Introductory Military History of the Civil War* (1997). The outlook and experiences of the common soldier are explored in James M. McPherson's *For Cause and Comrades: Why Men Fought in the Civil War* (1997) and Earl J. Hess's *The Union Soldier in Battle: Enduring the Ordeal of Combat* (1997).

For emphasis on the South, turn first to Gary W. Gallagher's *The Confederate War* (1997). For a sparkling account of the birth of the Rebel nation, see William C. Davis's *"A Government of Our Own": The Making of the Confederacy* (1994). The same author provides a fine biography of the Confederate president in *Jefferson Davis: The Man and His Hour* (1992). The best study of Confederate political culture is George C. Rable's *The Confederate Republic: A Revolution Against Politics* (1994).

Insightful biographies of southern military leaders are Emory Thomas's *Robert E. Lee* (1995), Jeffrey D. West's *General James Longstreet: the Confederacy's Most Controversial Soldier* (1992), and James I. Robertson, Jr.'s *Stonewall Jackson: The Man, the Soldier, the Legend* (1997).

Analytical scholarship on the military conflict includes Joseph L. Harsh's *Confederate Tide Rising: Robert E. Lee and the Making of Southern Strategy, 1861–1862* (1998), Steven E. Wordworth's *Jefferson Davis and His Generals: The Failure of Confederate Command in the West* (1990), and Paul D. Casdorph's *Lee and Jackson: Confederate Chieftains* (1992). A cultural interpretation of Confederate military behavior is Grady McWhiney and Perry D. Jamieson's *Attack and Die: Civil War Military Tactics and the Southern Heritage* (1982). Lonnie R. Speer's *Portals to Hell: The Military Prisons of the Civil War* (1997) details the ghastly experience of prisoners of war.

The history of the North during the war is surveyed in Philip S. Paludan's *"A People's Contest": The Union and Civil War, 1861–1865* (1988) and J. Matthew Gallman, *The North Fights the Civil War: The Home Front* (1994). Treatments of northern politics during the war include Harold M. Hyman's *A More Perfect Union: The Impact of the Civil War and Reconstruction on the Constitution* (1973), and Allan G. Bogue's *The Earnest Men: Republicans of the Civil War Senate* (1981).

The central northern political figure, Abraham Lincoln, is the subject of many books. Two good biographies are David H. Donald's *Lincoln* (1995) and Stephen B. Oates's *With Malice toward None* (1977). The election of 1864 is treated in John C. Waugh's *Reelecting Lincoln: The Battle for the 1864 Presidency* (1998). On Lincoln's assassination, see William Hanchett's *The Lincoln Murder Conspiracies* (1983). For a fine biography of Lincoln's wife, see Jean H. Baker's *Mary Todd Lincoln: A Biography* (1987).

Concerning specific military campaigns, see Larry J. Daniel's *Shiloh: The Battle That Changed the Civil War* (1997), Thomas Goodrich's *Black Flag: Guerrilla Warfare on the Western Border, 1861–1865* (1995), Stephen W. Sears's *Landscape Turned Red: The Battle of Antietam* (1983) and *To the Gates of Richmond: The Peninsula Campaign* (1993), James Lee McDonough and James Pickett Jones's *War So Terrible: Sherman and Atlanta* (1992), Robert Garth Scott's *Into the Wilderness with the Army of the Potomac* (1985), and Albert Castel and Laura K. Poracsky's *Decision in the West: The Atlanta Campaign of 1864* (1992).

Biographical studies of the northern military leaders include Michael Fellman's *Citizen Sherman: A Life of William Tecumseh Sherman* (1995), Brooks D. Simpson's *Let Us Have Peace: Ulysses S. Grant and the Politics of War and Reconstruction, 1861–1868* (1991), John F. Marszalek's *Sherman: A Soldier's Passion for Order* (1992), Charles Royster's *The Destructive War: William Tecumseh Sherman, Stonewall Jackson, and the Americans* (1991), and William S. McFeely's *Grant: A Biography* (1981).

The experience of the black soldier is surveyed in Joseph T. Glatthaar's *Forged in Battle: The Civil War Alliance of Black Soldiers and White Officers* (1989); Ira Berlin, Joseph P. Reidy, and Leslie S. Rowland's *Freedom's Soldiers: The Black Military Experience in the Civil War* (1998); and *On the Altar of Freedom: A Black Soldier's Civil War Letters from the Front* (1991), edited by James H. Gooding, James M. McPherson, and Virginia M. Adams. Louis S. Gerteis's *From Contraband to Freedman: Federal Policy toward Southern Blacks, 1861–1865* (1973) traces the federal government's policies dealing with freed slaves during the war. For the black woman's experience, see Susie King Taylor and Patricia W. Romero's *A Black Woman's Civil War Memoirs: Reminiscences of My Life in Camp with the 33rd U.S. Colored Troops* (1988) and Jacqueline Jones's *Labor of Love, Labor of Sorrow: Black Women, Work and the Family from Slavery to the Present* (1985).

Recent gender and ethnic studies include *Divided Houses: Gender and the Civil War,* edited by Catherine Clinton and Nina Silber (1992), Drew Gilpin Faust's *Mothers of Invention: Women of the Slaveholding South in the American Civil War* (1997), Shirley Samuels's *The Culture of Sentiment: Race, Gender, and Sentimentality in Nineteenth-Century America* (1992), George C. Rable's *Civil Wars: Women and the Crisis of Southern Nationalism* (1989), and William L. Burton's *Melting Pot Soldiers: The Union's Ethnic Regiments* (2nd ed., 1998). For a fine biography of the North's most famous nurse, see Stephen B. Oates's *A Woman of Valor: Clara Barton and the Civil War* (1994).

Chapter 17

Reconstruction has long been "a dark and bloody ground" of conflicting interpretations. The most comprehensive treatment is Eric Foner's *Reconstruction: America's Unfinished Revolution, 1863–1877* (1988). More specialized works give closer scrutiny to the aims of the principal political figures. For a study of Andrew Johnson, see Hans L. Trefousse's *Andrew Johnson: A Biography* (1989).

Scholars have been fairly sympathetic to the aims and motives of the Radical Republicans. See, for instance,

Herman Belz's *Reconstructing the Union* (1969) and Richard Nelson Current's *Those Terrible Carpet-baggers: A Reinterpretation* (1988). The ideology of these Radicals is explored in Michael Les Benedict's *A Compromise of Principle: Congressional Republicans and Reconstruction, 1863–1869* (1974).

The intransigence of southern white attitudes is examined in Michael Perman's *Reunion without Compromise* (1973), Dan T. Carter's *When the War Was Over: The Failure of Self-Reconstruction in the South, 1865–1867* (1985), and Richard Zuczek's *State of Rebellion: Reconstruction in South Carolina* (1996). Allen W. Trelease's *White Terror* (1971) covers the various organizations that practiced vigilante tactics, chiefly the Ku Klux Klan. The difficulties former laborers had in adjusting to the new labor system are documented in James L. Roark's *Masters without Slaves* (1977). Books on southern politics during Reconstruction include Michael Perman's *The Road to Redemption* (1984), Terry L. Seip's *The South Returns to Congress* (1983), and Mark W. Summer's *Railroads, Reconstruction, and the Gospel of Prosperity* (1984).

Numerous works have appeared on the freed blacks' experience in the South. Start with Leon F. Litwack's *Been in the Storm So Long* (1979),which covers the transition from slavery to freedom. Willie Lee Rose's *Rehearsal for Reconstruction* (1964) examines Union efforts to define the social role of former slaves during wartime emancipation. Joel Williamson's *After Slavery* (1965) argues that South Carolina blacks took an active role in pursuing their political and economic rights. For discussions of the political activity of freed slaves in other areas of the South, see Howard N. Rabinowitz's *Southern Black Leaders of the Reconstruction Era* (1982) and Edmund L. Drago's *Black Politicians and Reconstruction in Georgia: A Splendid Failure* (1982). Peter Kolchin's *First Freedom* (1972), a study of freed slaves in Alabama, is also useful. The role of the Freedmen's Bureau is explored in William S. McFeely's *Yankee Stepfather: General O.O. Howard and the Freedmen* (1968). The situation of freed slave women, which was often quite different from that of freed slave men, is discussed in Jacqueline Jones's *Labor of Love, Labor of Sorrow: Black Women, Work, and the Family from Slavery to Present* (1985).

The land confiscation issue is discussed in Eric Foner's *Politics and Ideology in the Age of the Civil War* (1980); Beth Bethel's *Promiseland* (1981), on a South Carolina black community; and Janet S. Hermann's *The Pursuit of a Dream* (1981), on the Davis Bend experiment in Mississippi.

The politics of corruption outside the South is depicted in William S. McFeely's *Grant: A Biography* (1981). The political maneuvers of the election of 1876 and the resultant crisis and compromise are explained in C. Vann Woodward's *Reunion and Reaction* (1951) and William Gillette's *Retreat from Reconstruction, 1869–1879* (1979).

For an examination of the lives of southern men and women who moved North between 1865 and 1880, see Daniel E. Sutherland's *The Confederate Carpetbaggers* (1992).

Chapter 18

The classic study of the emergence of the New South remains C. Vann Woodward's *Origins of the New South, 1877–1913* (1951). A more recent treatment of southern society after the end of Reconstruction is Edward L. Ayers's *Southern Crossing: A History of the American South, 1877–1906* (1995).

For Bourbon politics, see Jack P. Maddex's *The Virginia Conservatives, 1867–1879* (1970) and William J. Cooper's *The Conservative Regime: South Carolina, 1877–1890* (1968). On the development of southern politics since Reconstruction, see Dewey W. Grantham's *The Life and Death of the Solid South: A Political History* (1988).

A good survey of industrialization in the South is James C. Cobb's *Industrialization and Southern Society, 1877–1984* (1984). Scholarship on the textile industry, which formed the heart of the New South's aspirations, includes Patrick J. Hearden's *Independence and Empire: The New South's Cotton Mill Campaigns, 1865–1901* (1982), David L. Carlton's *Mill and Town in South Carolina, 1880–1920* (1982), and Jacqueline D. Hall et al.'s *Like a Family: The Making of a Southern Cotton Mill World* (1987). For developments in the tobacco industry, consult Robert F. Durden's *The Dukes of Durham, 1865–1929* (1975). A fine study of convict leasing is Alex Lichtenstein's *Twice the Work of Free Labor: The Political Economy of Convict Labor in the New South* (1996).

C. Vann Woodward's *The Strange Career of Jim Crow* (3rd ed., 1974) remains the standard on southern race relations. Some of Woodward's points are challenged in Howard N. Rabinowitz's *Race Relations in the Urban South, 1865–1890* (1978), Joel Williamson's *The Crucible of Race*

(1984), and John W. Cell's *The Highest Stage of White Supremacy* (1982).

Leon Litwack's *Trouble in Mind: Black Southerners in the Age of Jim Crow* (1998) treats the rise of legal segregation. David M. Oshinsky focuses on race relations and convict leasing in Mississippi in *"Worse Than Slavery": Parchman Farm and the Ordeal of Jim Crow Justice* (1996). J. Morgan Kousser's *The Shaping of Southern Politics: Suffrage Restriction and Establishment of the One-Party South, 1880–1910* (1974) handles disenfranchisement. An award-winning study of white women and the race issue is Glenda Gilmore's *Gender and Jim Crow: Women and the Politics of White Supremacy in North Carolina, 1896–1920* (1996).

Several good books discuss developments in southern agriculture. Roger L. Ransom and Richard Sutch's *One Kind of Freedom: The Economic Consequences of Emancipation* (1977) examines the origins of sharecropping. A more recent sociological analysis is Edward Royce's *The Origins of Southern Sharecropping* (1993).

Good overviews of the transformation of the West are Rodman W. Paul's *The Far West and the Great Plains in Transition, 1859–1908* (rev. ed., 1998) and Geoffrey Ward, David Duncan, and Ken Burns's *The West: An Illustrated History* (1996). The Turner thesis is best presented by Frederick Jackson Turner himself in *The Frontier in American History* (1920).

For powerful and provocative reinterpretations of the frontier and the development of the West, see William Cronon's *Nature's Metropolis: Chicago and the Great West* (1991), Patricia Nelson Limerick's *The Legacy of Conquest: The Unbroken Past of the American West* (1987), Richard White's *"It's Your Misfortune and None of My Own": A New History of the American West* (1991), Donald Worster's *Under Western Skies: Nature and History in the American West* (1992), and *Under an Open Sky: Rethinking America's Western Past* (1992), edited by William Cronon, George Miles, and Jay Gitlin.

The role of blacks in western settlement is the focus of William L. Katz's *The Black West* (1996) and Nell Painter's *Exodusters: Black Migration to Kansas after Reconstruction* (1992). The best account of the conflicts between Indians and whites is Robert Utley's *The Indian Frontier of the American West, 1846–1890* (1984). For a presentation of the Native American side of the story, see Peter Nabokov and Vine Deloria's *Native American Testimony: A Chronicle of Indian-White Relations from Prophecy to the Present, 1492–1992* (1992).

Federal government efforts to facilitate western agriculture are detailed in William D. Rowley's *Reclaiming the Arid West: The Career of Francis G. Newlands* (1996).

Chapter 19

For a masterly synthesis of post–Civil War industrial development, see Walter Licht's *Industrializing America: The Nineteenth Century* (1995). Of more specialized interest are Alfred D. Chandler's *The Visible Hand: The Managerial Revolution in American Business* (1977), and Maury Klein's *The Flowering of the Third America: The Making of an Organizational Society, 1850–1920* (1992).

On the growth of railroads see Albro Martin's *Railroads Triumphant: The Growth, Rejection, and Rebirth of a Vital American Force* (1992) and Sarah Gordon's *Passage to Union: How the Railroads Transformed America, 1829–1929* (1997). Walter Licht's *Working for the Railroad: The Organization of Work in the Nineteenth Century* (1983) treats the life of the railroad workers. Gabriel Kolko's *Railroads and Regulation, 1877–1916* (1965) argues that the entrepreneurs themselves sought government regulation.

On entrepreneurship in the iron and steel sector, see Thomas J. Misa's *A Nation of Steel: The Making of Modern America, 1865–1925* (1995). The best biography of the leading business tycoon is Ron Chernow's *Titan: The Life of John D. Rockefeller, Sr.* (1998). A new book on J. Pierpont Morgan is Jean Strouse's *J. P. Morgan: American Financier* (1999).

Nathan Rosenberg's *Technology and American Economic Growth* (1972) documents the growth of invention during the period. For an absorbing biography of the foremost inventor of the era, see Neil Baldwin's *Edison: Inventing the Century* (1995).

Much of the scholarship on labor stresses the traditional values and the culture of work that people brought to the factory. Herbert G. Gutman's *Work, Culture, and Society in Industrializing America* (1976) best introduces these themes. The best survey remains David Montgomery's *The Fall of the House of Labor: The Workplace, the State and American Labor Activism, 1865–1925* (1987).

For the role of women in the changing workplace, see Alice Kessler-Harris's *Out to Work* (1983), Susan E. Kennedy's *If All We Did Was to Weep at Home: A History of White Working-Class Women in America* (1979), and

S. J. Kleinberg's *The Shadow of the Mills: Working-Class Families in Pittsburgh, 1870–1907* (1989).

As for the labor groups, Gerald N. Grob's *Workers and Utopias* (1961) examines the difference in outlook between the Knights of Labor and the American Federation of Labor. For the Knights, see Leon Fink's *Workingmen's Democracy* (1983). Also useful is Susan Levine's *Labor's True Woman* (1984), on the role of women in the Knights. To trace the rise of socialism among organized workers, see Nick Salvatore's *Eugene V. Debs: Citizen and Socialist* (1982) and Robert J. Constantine's *Letters of Eugene V. Debs* (1990). Strikes are discussed in Kevin Kenny's *Making Sense of the Molly Maguires* (1998), Paul Avrich's *The Haymarket Tragedy* (1984), and Paul Krause's *The Battle for Homestead, 1880–1892: Politics, Culture, and Steel* (1992).

Chapter 20

The best survey of urbanization remains Charles N. Glaab and A. Theodore Brown's *A History of Urban America* (3rd ed., 1983). Gunther P. Barth discusses the emergence of a new urban culture in *City People: The Rise of Modern City Culture in Nineteenth Century America* (1980). Urban politics is surveyed in Jon C. Teaford's *The Unheralded Triumph: City Government in America, 1870–1900* (1994). Oliver E. Allen's *The Tiger: The Rise and Fall of Tammany Hall* (1994) assesses the significance of New York's famous political machine.

John Bodnar provides a synthesis of the urban immigrant experience in *The Transplanted: A History of Immigrants in Urban America* (1985). Walter Nugent's *Crossings: The Great Transatlantic Migrations, 1870–1914* (1992) provides a wealth of demographic information and insight. John Higham's *Strangers in the Land: Patterns of American Nativism, 1860–1925* (2nd ed., 1988) examines how old-stock residents reacted to the influx of newcomers.

For the growth of urban leisure and sports, see Roy Rosenzweig's *Eight Hours for What We Will: Workers and Leisure in an Industrial City, 1870–1920* (1983) and Steven A. Riess's *City Games: The Evolution of American Urban Society and the Rise of Sports* (1989). Steven A. Riess's *Touching Base: Professional Baseball and American Culture in the Progressive Era* (1980) and Dominick Cavallo's *Muscles and Morals: Organized Playgrounds and Urban Reform, 1880–1920* (1981) link athletics to new forms of organization and socialization.

Richard Hofstadter's *Social Darwinism in American Thought* (rev. ed., 1992) and Cynthia E. Russett's *Darwin in America* (1976) examine the impact of the theory of evolution. On the rise of realism in thought and the arts during the second half of the nineteenth century, see David Shi's *Facing Facts: Realism in American Thought and Culture, 1850–1920* (1995).

William L. O'Neill's *Everyone Was Brave: The Rise and Fall of Feminism in America* (1969) and Eleanor Flexner's *Century of Struggle: The Woman's Rights Movement in the United States* (rev. ed., 1975) survey the condition of women in the late nineteenth century.

Chapter 21

For overviews of the Gilded Age see Robert H. Wiebe's *The Search for Order, 1877–1920* (1967), John A. Garraty's *The New Commonwealth, 1877–1890* (1968), and Vincent P. DeSantis's *The Shaping of Modern America, 1877–1920* (2nd ed., 1989). Nell Painter's *Standing at Armageddon: The United States, 1877–1919* (1987) focuses on the experience of the working classes.

Party politics is the emphasis of H. Wayne Morgan's *From Hayes to McKinley: National Party Politics, 1877–1896* (1969) and Richard J. Jensen's *The Winning of the Midwest: Social and Political Conflict, 1888–1896* (1971). Public participation in politics is explained in Paul Kleppner's *Who Voted? The Dynamics of Electoral Turnout, 1870–1980* (1982).

On the Gilded-Age presidents, see William S. McFeely's *Grant: A Biography* (1981), Allan Peskin's *Garfield: A Biography* (1978), Thomas C. Reeves's *Gentleman Boss: The Life of Chester Alan Arthur* (rev. ed., 1991), and Lewis L. Gould's *The Presidency of William McKinley* (1980).

Scholars have also examined various Gilded-Age issues and interest groups. John G. Sproat's *The Best Men: Liberal Reformers in the Gilded Age* (1968) and Gerald W. McFarland's *Mugwumps, Morals, and Politics, 1884–1920* (1975) examine the issue of reforming government service. Tom E. Terrill's *The Tariff, Politics, and American Foreign Policy, 1874–1901* (1973) lends clarity to that complex issue. The finances of the Gilded Age are covered in Irwin Unger's *The Greenback Era: A Social and Political History of American Finance, 1865–1879* (1964) and Walter T. K. Nugent's *Money and American Society, 1865–1880* (1968).

One of the most controversial works on populism is Lawrence Goodwyn's *The Populist Movement: A Short*

History of the Agrarian Revolt in America (1978). Goodwyn's emphasis on the cooperative nature of agrarian protest and his criticism of the western branch as a sham movement contradicted the prevailing interpretations. A more judicious account is Robert C. McMath, Jr.'s *American Populism: A Social History, 1877–1898* (1993). Jeffrey Ostler's *Prairie Populism: The Fate of Agrarian Radicalism in Kansas, Nebraska, and Iowa, 1880–1892* (1993) minimizes the role of the financial panic in stimulating the grassroots movement.

Chapter 22

An excellent survey of the diplomacy of the era is Charles Campbell's *The Transformation of American Foreign Relations, 1865–1900* (1976). For background to the events of the 1890s, see Walter LeFeber's *The American Search for Opportunity, 1865–1913* (1993) and David Healy's *U. S. Expansionism: The Imperialist Urge in the 1890s* (1970). The dispute over American policy concerning Hawaii is covered in Thomas J. Osborne's *"Empire Can Wait": American Opposition to Hawaiian Annexation, 1893–1898* (1981).

Ivan Musicant's *Empire by Default: The Spanish-American War and the Dawn of the American Century* (1998) is the most comprehensive volume on the conflict. Frank Freidel's *The Splendid Little War* (1958) shows what the war was like for those who fought it. Gerald F. Linderman's *The Mirror of War: American Society and the Spanish-American War* (1974) discusses the war at home. For the war's aftermath in the Philippines, see Stuart C. Miller's *"Benevolent Assimilation": American Conquest of the Philippines, 1899–1903* (1982). Robert L. Beisner's *Twelve Against Empire: The Anti-Imperialists, 1898–1900* (1985) handles the debate over annexation.

A good introduction to American interest in China is Michael H. Hunt's *The Making of a Special Relationship: The United States and China to 1914* (1983). Also useful is Marilyn B. Young's *The Rhetoric of Empire: America's China Policy, 1893–1901* (1968). Kenton J. Clymer's *John Hay: The Gentleman as Diplomat* (1975) examines the role of this key secretary of state in forming policy.

For American policy in the Caribbean and Central America, see Walter LeFeber's *Inevitable Revolutions: The United States in Central America* (1983) and Bruce J. Calder's *The Impact of Intervention: The Dominican Republic During the U.S. Occupation of 1916–1924* (1984). David McCullough's *The Path between the Seas: The Creation of the Panama Canal, 1870–1914* (1977) presents the fullest account of how the United States secured the Panama Canal.

Chapter 23

A splendid introduction to the topic of progressivism can be found in Arthur S. Link and Richard L. McCormick's *Progressivism* (1983). Progressivism has been interpreted in many ways. Robert H. Wiebe's *The Search for Order, 1877–1920* (1967) presents the organizational model for reform. Richard Hofstadter's *The Age of Reform: From Bryan to F.D.R.* (1955) examines an emerging middle-class consensus as the basis of reform. Gabriel Kolko sees the reform movement as a means of social control in *The Triumph of Conservatism* (1963). Dewey W. Grantham's *Southern Progressivism: The Reconciliation of Progress and Tradition* (1983) shows the distinctiveness of reform in that region. See also Alan Dawley's *Struggles for Justice: Social Responsibility and the Liberal State* (1991).

Biographers of the three progressive presidents, Roosevelt, Taft, and Wilson, elaborate on the complexity of reform. Edmund Morris's *The Rise of Theodore Roosevelt* (1979) and H. W. Brands's *T.R.: The Last Romantic* (1997) offer compelling portraits. For the Taft years, see Paolo E. Coletta's *The Presidency of William Howard Taft* (1973). Arthur S. Link's multivolume biography *Wilson (1947–1965)*—particularly *The New Freedom* (1956)—is the place to start on that president. John Milton Cooper, Jr., compares Roosevelt and Wilson in *The Warrior and the Priest* (1983).

The evolution of government policy toward business is examined in Martin J. Sklar's *The Corporate Reconstruction of American Capitalism, 1890–1916: The Market, the Law, and Politics* (1988). Roy Lubove's *The Progressives and the Slums* (1962), Mina Carson's *Settlement Folk: Social Thought and the American Settlement Movement, 1885–1930* (1990), and Jack M. Holl's *Juvenile Reform in the Progressive Era* (1971) examine the problem of urban decay.

Robert Kanigel's *The One Best Way: Frederick Winslow Taylor and the Enigma of Efficiency* (1997) highlights the role of efficiency in the Progressive Era. Samuel P. Hays's *Conservation and the Gospel of Efficiency: The Progressive Conservation Movement, 1890–1920* (rev. ed., 1969) and Harold T. Pinkett's *Gifford Pinchot: Private and Public*

Forester (1970) cover conservation and the Ballinger-Pinchot controversy.

An excellent study of the role of women in progressivism's emphasis on social justice is Kathryn Kish Sklar's *Florence Kelley and the Nation's Work: The Rise of Women's Political Culture, 1830–1900* (1995).

Chapter 24

Frederick S. Calhoun's *Power and Principle: Armed Intervention in Wilsonian Foreign Policy* (1986) surveys one aspect of Wilsonian diplomacy. For the Mexican intervention, consult John S. D. Eisenhower's *Intervention!: The United States and the Mexican Revolution, 1913–1917* (1993). A lucid and thoughtful overview of events covered in this chapter is Daniel M. Smith's *The Great Departure: The United States and World War I, 1914–1920* (1965).

A number of scholars have concentrated on the neutrality issue. Arthur S. Link, Wilson's greatest biographer, is sympathetic to the ideals of the president in *Woodrow Wilson: Revolution, War, and Peace* (1979). For a more critical view, see Ross Gregory's *The Origins of American Intervention in the First World War* (1971). A notable biography is August Heckscher's *Woodrow Wilson: A Biography* (1991).

Edward M. Coffman's *The War to End All Wars: The American Military Experience in World War I* (1968) is a detailed presentation of America's military involvement. The best survey of the war from the European perspective is John Keegan's *The First World War* (1999). David M. Kennedy's *Over Here: The First World War and American Society* (1980) surveys the impact of the war on the home front. Maurine Weiner Greenwald's *Women, War, and Work: The Impact of World War I on Women Workers in the United States* (1980) discusses the role of women. Ronald Schaffer's *America in the Great War: The Rise of the War Welfare State* (1991) shows the effect of war mobilization on business organization. Richard Polenberg's *Fighting Faiths: The Abrams Case, the Supreme Court, and Free Speech* (1987) examines prosecutions under the 1918 Sedition Act.

How American diplomacy fared in the making of peace has received considerable attention. In addition to the Link book on Wilson, the role of the president is treated in Robert H. Ferrell's *Woodrow Wilson and World War I, 1917–1921* (1985), Arno J. Mayer's *Politics and Diplomacy in Peacemaking: Containment and Counterrevolution at Versailles, 1918–1919* (1967), and N. Gordon Levin, Jr.'s *Woodrow Wilson and World Politics: America's Response to War and Revolution* (1968). Thomas J. Knock interrelates domestic affairs and foreign relations in his explanation of Wilson's peacemaking in *To End All Wars: Woodrow Wilson and the Quest for a New World Order* (1992).

The problems of the immediate postwar years are chronicled by a number of historians. On the Spanish flu, see Alfred W. Crosby's *America's Forgotten Pandemic: The Influenza of 1918* (1990). Labor tensions are examined in David E. Brody's *Labor in Crisis: The Steel Strike of 1919* (1965) and Francis Russell's *A City in Terror: 1919, the Boston Police Strike* (1975). On racial strife, see William Tuttle, Jr.'s *Race Riot: Chicago in the Red Summer of 1919* (1970). The fear of Communists is analyzed in Robert K. Murray's *Red Scare: A Study in National Hysteria, 1919–1920* (rev. ed., 1980).

Chapter 25

For a standard survey of the interwar period, start with William E. Leuchtenburg's *The Perils of Prosperity, 1914–1932* (rev. ed., 1993). The best introduction to the culture of the 1920s remains Loren Baritz's *The Culture of the Twenties* (1970). See also Lynn Dumenil's *The Modern Temper: American Culture and Society in the 1920s* (1995). Paula S. Fass's *The Damned and the Beautiful: American Youth in the 1920s* (1977) describes the social attitudes of youth.

John Higham's *Strangers in the Land: Patterns of American Nativism, 1860–1925* (rev. ed., 1988) details the story of immigration restriction. Paul Avrich's *Sacco and Vanzetti: The Anarchist Background* (1991) treats the famous case. For analysis of the revival of Klan activity, see Nancy MacLean's *Behind the Mask of Chivalry: The Making of the Second Ku Klux Klan* (1994). Two contrasting views of prohibition are Andrew Sinclair's *Prohibition: The Era of Excess* (1962) and Norman H. Clark's *Deliver Us from Evil: An Interpretation of American Prohibition* (1976).

Women's suffrage is treated extensively in Eleanor Flexner's *Century of Struggle: The Women's Rights Movement in the United States* (rev. ed., 1975). See Charles F. Kellogg's *NAACP: A History of the National Association for the Advancement of Colored People* (1967) for his analysis of the pioneering court cases against racial discrimination. Nathan I. Huggins's *Harlem Renaissance* (1971) assesses the cultural impact of the Great Migration in New York. On the migration to Chicago, see James R. Grossman's *Land of Hope: Chicago, Black Southerners, and the Great Migration* (1989). Nicholas Lemann's *The Promised Land* (1991) is a fine exposition of the changes brought about by the Great Migration in both the South and North.

Much of our treatment of "modernism" comes from Daniel J. Singal's *The War Within: From Victorian to Modernist Thought in the South, 1919–1945* (1982). Stanley Coben's *Rebellion Against Victorianism: The Impetus for Cultural Change in 1920s America* (1991) surveys the appeal of "modernism" among writers, artists, and intellectuals. On developments in physics, see Stanley Goldberg's *Understanding Relativity: Origin and Impact of a Scientific Revolution* (1984). Nathan G. Hale, Jr.'s *Freud and the Americans* (1971) examines the impact of psychoanalysis.

Chapter 26

A fine synthesis of events immediately following the First World War is Ellis W. Hawley's *The Great War and the Search for a Modern Order: A History of the American People and Their Institutions, 1917–1933* (1979).

For an introduction to Harding, see Francis Russell's *The Shadow of Blooming Grove: Warren G. Harding in His Times* (1968). Robert K. Murray's *The Harding Era: Warren G. Harding and His Administration* (1969) is more favorable to Harding. On Coolidge, see Donald R. McCoy's *Calvin Coolidge: The Silent President* (1967). Studies on Hoover include Joan Hoff Wilson's *Herbert Hoover: Forgotten Progressive* (1975) and George Nash's multivolume work, *The Life of Herbert Hoover* (1983–1987). Other works on politics include Burl Noggle's *Teapot Dome: Oil and Politics in the 1920s* (1962) and David Burner's *The Politics of Provincialism: The Democratic Party in Transition, 1918–1932* (1968).

The impact of transportation is gauged in Reynold M. Wik's *Henry Ford and Grassroots America* (1972). Roland Marchand's *Advertising the American Dream: Making Way for Modernity, 1920–1940* (1985) covers the development of national advertising in the 1920s. Susan J. Douglas's *Inventing American Broadcasting, 1899–1922* (1989) is a cultural history of the formative years of radio. Motion pictures are the subject of Robert Sklar's *Movie-Made America: A Cultural History of American Movies* (1975) and Lary May's *Screening out the Past: The Birth of Mass Culture and the Motion Picture Industry* (1980).

Overviews of the depressed economy are found in Charles P. Kindleberger's *The World in Depression, 1929–1939* (rev. ed., 1986) and Peter Fearon's *War, Prosperity and Depression: The U.S. Economy, 1917–1945* (1987). John Kenneth Galbraith details the fall of the stock market in *The Great Crash, 1929* (1955). A different interpretation is given in Peter Temin's *Did Monetary Forces Cause the Great Depression?* (1976).

John A. Garraty's *The Great Depression: An Inquiry into the Causes, Course, and Consequences of the Worldwide Depression of the Nineteen Thirties* (1986) describes how people survived the depression. Firsthand accounts of the Great Depression can be found in Tom E. Terrill and Jerrold Hirsch's *Such As Us: Southern Voices of the Thirties* (1978), Studs Terkel's *Hard Times* (1970), Robert S. McElvaine's *Down and Out in the Great Depression: Letters from the Forgotten Man* (1983), and *"Slaves of the Depression": Workers' Letters about Life on the Job* (1989), edited by Gerald Markowitz and David Rosner.

Chapter 27

The best recent interpretive survey of the 1930s is David M. Kennedy's *Freedom from Fear: The American People in Depression and War, 1929–1945* (1999). An engaging introduction to the decade of the New Deal is Anthony J. Badger's *The New Deal: The Depression Years, 1933–1940* (1989). Van L. Perkins's *Crisis in Agriculture* (1969) and Sidney Baldwin's *Poverty and Politics: The Rise and Decline of the Farm Security Administration* (1969) look at agricultural reforms. Michael E. Parrish's *Securities Regulation and the New Deal* (1970) and Ellis W. Hawley's *The New Deal and the Problem of Monopoly: A Study in Economic Ambivalence* (1966) analyze government attempts to forestall another market crash.

Alan Brinkley's *The End of Reform: New Deal Liberalism in Recession and War* (1995) suggests that the New Deal reformers did not go far enough in their efforts to curb big business. Bernard Bellush's *The Failure of the NRA* (1977) studies government relations with business. William R. Brock's *Welfare, Democracy, and the New Deal* (1988) describes the development of welfare policy.

For scholarship about the various groups involved in the New Deal, consult Lois Scharf's *To Work and to Wed:*

Female Employment, Feminism, and the Great Depression (1980), on women; Nancy J. Weiss's *Farewell to the Party of Lincoln: Black Politics in the Age of FDR* (1983) and Harvard Sitkoff's *A New Deal for Blacks* (1978), on blacks; and John M. Allswang's *A House of All Peoples: Ethnic Politics in Chicago, 1890–1936* (1971), on immigrants. On Roosevelt's prominent wife, see Blanche Wiesen Cook's *Eleanor Roosevelt* (2 vols.; 1998–1999).

Works on the critics of the New Deal include T. Harry Williams's *Huey Long* (1969) and Alan Brinkley's *Voices of Protest: Huey Long, Father Coughlin, and the Great Depression* (1982). For leftist reactions to reform, see Harvey Klehr's *The Heyday of American Communism: The Depression Decade* (1984) and David Shannon's *The Socialist Party of America* (1955).

One interest group that both supported and criticized New Deal policies was organized labor. See Sidney Fine's *Sit-down: The General Motors Strike of 1936–1937* (1969) and Lizabeth Cohen's *Making a New Deal: Industrial Workers in Chicago, 1919–1939* (1990).

The most complete introduction to the New Deal in the South remains the relevant chapters in George B. Tindall's *The Emergence of the New South, 1913–1945* (1967). How southern farmers fared is examined in David E. Conrad's *The Forgotten Farmers: The Story of the Sharecroppers in the New Deal* (1965). Dan T. Carter provides an insightful analysis of the influence of reform on race relations in the 1930s in his *Scottsboro: A Tragedy of the American South* (1969).

James M. Gregory's *American Exodus: The Dust Bowl Migration and Okie Culture in California* (1989) describes the migratory movement's effect on American culture. For the cultural impact of the New Deal, consult Richard H. Pells's *Radical Visions and American Dreams: Cultural and Social Thought in the Depression Years* (1973) and Richard D. McKinzie's *The New Deal for Artists* (1973). The best analysis of the end of the New Deal is Alan Brinkley's *The End of Reform: New Deal Liberalism in Recession and War* (1995).

Chapter 28

The best overview of interwar diplomacy remains Selig Adler's *The Uncertain Giant: American Foreign Policy between the Wars* (1965). Joan Hoff Wilson's *American Business and Foreign Policy, 1920–1933* (1971) highlights the efforts of Republican administrations during the 1920s to promote international commerce. Robert Dallek's *Franklin D. Roosevelt and American Foreign Policy, 1932–1945* (1979) provides a judicious assessment of Roosevelt's foreign policies during the 1930s.

Other scholars have concentrated on particular diplomatic issues of the 1920s. Thomas H. Buckley's *The United States and the Washington Conference, 1921–1922* (1970) examines disarmament. For a study of the Kellogg-Briand Pact, see Robert H. Ferrell's *Peace in Their Time: The Origins of the Kellogg-Briand Pact* (1968). Relations between the United States and Europe are covered in Frank Costigliola's *Awkward Dominion: American Political, Economic, and Cultural Relations with Europe, 1919–1933* (1984). A comprehensive analysis of American responses to Nazi aggression is Arnold Offner's *American Appeasement: United States Foreign Policy and Germany, 1933–1938* (1969).

For American relations in East Asia during the period, see Akira Iriye's *After Imperialism: The Search for a New Order in the Far East, 1921–1931* (1965) and the relevant chapters in Walter LaFeber's work *The Clash: A History of U.S.-Japan Relations* (1997). More specific studies are Warren I. Cohen's *America's Response to China: An Interpretive History of Sino-American Relations* (2nd ed., 1981) and Jonathan G. Utley's *Going to War with Japan, 1937–1941* (1985). For relations with Latin America, see Irwin F. Gellman's *Good Neighbor Diplomacy: United States Policies in Latin America, 1933–1945* (1979).

The best general account of the onset of World War II is Donald Watt's *How War Came: The Immediate Origins of the Second World War, 1938–1939* (1990). A noteworthy study of America's entry into World War II is Waldo Heinrichs's *Threshold of War: Franklin D. Roosevelt and American Entry into World War II* (1988). Other interpretations include Robert A. Divine's *The Reluctant Belligerent* (2nd ed., 1979) and Patrick Hearden's *Roosevelt Confronts Hitler: America's Entry into World War II* (1986). Bruce M. Russett's *No Clear and Present Danger* (1972) provides a critical account of American actions. American relations with Great Britain are detailed in David Reynolds's *The Creation of the Anglo-American Alliance, 1937–1941* (1981).

On Pearl Harbor, see Gordon W. Prange's *Pearl Harbor: The Verdict of History* (1986). The Japanese perspective is given in Robert J. C. Butow's *Tojo and the Coming of War* (1961).

Chapter 29

John Keegan's *The Second World War* (1990) surveys the European conflict in its entirety, while Charles B. MacDonald's *The Mighty Endeavor: The American War in Europe* (rev. ed., 1992) concentrates on American involvement. Roosevelt's wartime leadership is analyzed in Eric Larrabee's *Commander in Chief: Franklin Delano Roosevelt, His Lieutenants and Their War* (1987).

Books on specific campaigns in Europe include Stephen E. Ambrose's *D Day, June 6, 1944: The Climactic Battle of World War II* (1994) and Charles B. MacDonald's *A Time for Trumpets: The Untold Story of the Battle of the Bulge* (rev. ed., 1997).

For the war in the Far East, see John Costello's *The Pacific War, 1941–1945* (1983), Ronald H. Spector's *Eagle against the Sun: The American War with Japan* (1984), John Dower's award-winning *War Without Mercy: Race and Power in the Pacific War* (1986), and Dan van der Vat's *The Pacific Campaign: The U.S.–Japanese Naval War, 1941–1945* (1992).

An excellent overview of the war's effects on the home front is Michael C. C. Adams's *The Best War Ever: America and World War II* (1993). The government's effort to use movies to influence public opinion is described in Clayton R. Koppes and Gregory D. Black's *Hollywood Goes to War: How Politics, Profits and Propaganda Shaped World War II Movies* (1987).

Susan M. Hartmann's *The Home Front and Beyond: American Women in the 1940s* (1982) and Karen Anderson's *Wartime Women: Sex Roles, Family Relations, and the Status of Women during World War II* (1981) treat the new working environment for women. Neil Wynn looks at the participation of blacks in *The Afro-American and the Second World War* (rev. ed., 1993). The story of the oppression of Japanese Americans is told in Peter Irons's *Justice at War* (1983) and David J. O'Brien and Stephen S. Fugita's *The Japanese American Experience* (1993).

A sound introduction to American diplomacy during the conflict can be found in Gaddis Smith's *American Diplomacy during the Second World War, 1941–1945* (2nd ed., 1985). To understand the role that Roosevelt played in policy making, consult Warren F. Kimball's *The Juggler: Franklin Roosevelt as Wartime Statesman* (1991). Diane Shaver Clemens is critical of Roosevelt in *Yalta* (1970).

The issues and events that led to the deployment of atomic weapons are addressed in Gregg Herken's *The Winning Weapon: The Atomic Bomb in the Cold War, 1945–1950* (1980) and Martin J. Sherwin's *A World Destroyed: The Atomic Bomb and the Grand Alliance* (1975). Gar Alperovitz's *Atomic Diplomacy: Hiroshima and Potsdam* (2nd ed., 1995) details how the bomb helped shape American postwar policy.

Chapter 30

The cold war remains a hotly debated topic. The traditional interpretation is best reflected in John L. Gaddis's *The United States and the Origins of the Cold War, 1941–1947* (1972). Both superpowers, Gaddis argues, were responsible for causing the cold war, but the Soviet Union was more culpable. The revisionist perspective is represented by Gar Alperovitz's *Atomic Diplomacy* (rev. ed., 1994). He places primary responsibility for the conflict on the United States. Also see H. W. Brands's *The Devil We Knew: Americans and the Cold War* (1993), Michael J. Hogan's *The End of the Cold War: Its Meaning and Implications* (1992), Melvyn P. Leffler's *A Preponderance of Power: National Security, the Truman Administration, and the Cold War* (1992), John Lewis Gaddis's *The Long Peace: Inquiries Into the History of the Cold War* (rev. ed., 1993), and Wilson D. Miscamble's *George F. Kennan and the Making of American Foreign Policy, 1947–1950* (1992).

Other scholars concentrate on more specific events in the buildup of international tensions. Lynn Etheridge Davis's *The Cold War Begins: Soviet-American Conflict over Eastern Europe* (1974) and Bruce Kuklick's *American Policy and the Division of Germany* (1972) deal with initial tensions at the close of the war. For the Truman administration's reliance on the atomic bomb monopoly, see Michael Mandelbaum's *The Nuclear Question: The United States and Nuclear Weapons, 1946–1976* (1979) and Daniel Yergin's *Shattered Peace: The Origins of the Cold War and the National Security State* (1977).

For a positive assessment of Truman's leadership, see Alonzo Hamby's *Beyond the New Deal: Harry S. Truman and American Liberalism* (1973). The domestic policies of the Fair Deal are treated in William C. Berman's *The Politics of Civil Rights in the Truman Administration* (1970), Richard M. Dalfiumes's *Desegregation of the United States Armed Forces* (1969), and Maeva Marcus's *Truman and the Steel Seizure Case: The Limits of Presidential Power* (rev. ed., 1994). The most comprehensive biography of Truman is David McCullough's *Truman* (1992).

For an introduction to the tensions in Asia, see Akira Iriye's *The Cold War in Asia* (1974). For the Korean conflict, see Callum A. MacDonald's *Korea: The War before Vietnam* (1986) and Max Hasting's *The Korean War* (rev. ed., 1993). The high-command perspective is revealed in Michael Schaller's *Douglas MacArthur: The Far Eastern General* (1989).

The anti-Communist syndrome is surveyed in David Caute's *The Great Fear: The Anti-Communist Purge under Truman and Eisenhower* (1978). Thomas C. Reeves's *The Life and Times of Joe McCarthy* (1982) covers McCarthy himself. For a well-documented account of how the cold war was sustained by superpatriotism, intolerance, and suspicion, see Stephen J. Whitfield's *The Culture of the Cold War* (1990). See also Richard Fried's *Nightmare in Red: The McCarthy Era in Perspective* (1990).

Chapter 31

Two excellent overviews of social and cultural trends in the postwar era are William H. Chafe's *The Unfinished Journey: America Since World War II* (rev. ed., 1995) and William E. Leuchtenburg's *A Troubled Feast: America Since 1945* (rev. ed., 1983). For fascinating insights into the cultural life of the 1950s, see Douglas T. Miller and Marion Nowak's *The Fifties: The Way We Really Were* (1977), Jeffrey Hart's *When the Going Was Good: American Life in the Fifties* (1982), and David Halberstam's *The Fifties* (1993).

The baby-boom generation and its impact are vividly described in Paul C. Light's *Baby Boomers* (1988). Readers interested in economic trends should consult David P. Calleo's *The Imperious Economy* (1981). A comprehensive history of the advertising industry and its cultural implications can be found in Jackson Lears's *Fables of Abundance: A Cultural History of Advertising in America* (1994). The emergence and impact of the television industry are discussed in Erik Barnouw's *Tube of Plenty: The Evolution of American Television* (1982) and Ella Taylor's *Prime-Time Families: Television Culture in Postwar America* (1989).

A comprehensive account of the process of suburban development is Kenneth Jackson's award-winning study *Crabgrass Frontier: The Suburbanization of the United States* (1985). Michael Danielson examines racial discrimination in the suburbs in *The Politics of Exclusion* (1976). For an analysis of the development of western cities in this century, see Carl Abbott's *The Metropolitan Frontier: Cities in the Modern American West* (1993).

The middle-class ideal of family life in the 1950s is examined in Elaine Tyler May's *Homeward Bound: American Families in the Cold War Era* (1988). Thorough accounts of women's issues in the twentieth century are found in William Chafe's *The American Woman: Her Changing Social, Economic, and Political Roles: 1920–1970* (rev. ed., 1988) and Wini Breines Young's *Young, White and Miserable: Growing up Female in the 1950s* (1992).

For an overview of the resurgence of religion in the 1950s, see George Marsden's *Religion and American Culture* (1990). For a treatment of one of the leading religious leaders, see Carol V. R. George's *God's Salesman: Norman Vincent Peale and the Power of Positive Thinking* (1992).

The origins and growth of rock 'n' roll music are surveyed in Carl Belz's *The Story of Rock* (1972). Thoughtful interpretive surveys of postwar American literature include Josephine Hendin's *Vulnerable People: A View of American Fiction Since 1945* (1978) and Malcolm Bradbury's *The Modern American Novel* (1984). The colorful Beats are brought to life in Steven Watson's *The Birth of the Beat Generation: Visionaries, Rebels, and Hipsters, 1944–1960* (rev. ed., 1998).

Chapter 32

Scholarship on the Eisenhower years is extensive. A carefully balanced overview of the period is Chester Pach, Jr., and Elmo Richardson's *The Presidency of Dwight D. Eisenhower* (1991). For the manner in which Eisenhower conducted foreign policy, see Robert A. Divine's *Eisenhower and the Cold War* (1981).

The conservatism of the 1950s is documented in George H. Nash's *The Conservative Intellectual Movement in America* (1976) and Richard M. Fried's *Nightmare in Red: The McCarthy Era in Perspective* (1990). On links between business and government, see Louis Galambos and Joseph Pratt's *The Rise of the Corporate Commonwealth: United States Business and Public Policy in the Twentieth Century* (1988).

Several specialized studies are illuminating. See Robert A. Divine's work *The Sputnik Challenge: Eisenhower's Response to the Soviet Satellite* (1993) and Tom Lewis's

Divided Highways: Building the Interstate Highways, Transforming American Life (1997).

For the buildup of American involvement in Indochina, consult Lloyd C. Gardner's *Approaching Vietnam: From World War II through Dien Bien Phu, 1941–1954* (1988), and David L. Anderson's *Trapped by Success: The Eisenhower Administration and Vietnam, 1953–1961* (1991). For more on foreign policy, see Stephen Ambrose and Douglas Brinkley's *Rise to Globalism: American Foreign Policy Since 1938* (rev. ed., 1997), James A. Bill's *The Eagle and the Lion: The Tragedy of American-Iranian Relations* (1988), and Stephen G. Rabe's *Eisenhower and Latin America: The Foreign Policy of Anticommunism* (1988).

Two introductions to the impact wrought by the Warren Supreme Court during the 1950s are Alexander Bickel's *The Supreme Court and the Idea of Progress* (1970) and Paul Murphy's *The Constitution in Crisis Times, 1918–1969* (1972). Also helpful is Archibald Cox's *The Warren Court: Constitutional Decision as an Instrument of Reform* (1968). A masterful study of the important Warren Court decision on school desegregation is Richard Kluger's *Simple Justice: The History of Brown v. Board of Education and Black America's Struggle for Equality* (1975).

For the story of the early civil rights movement, see Taylor Branch's *Parting the Waters: America in the King Years, 1954–1963* (1988), and Robert Weisbrot's *Freedom Bound: A History of America's Civil Rights Movement* (1990).

Chapter 33

Herbert Parmet traces the influence of John F. Kennedy in two volumes, *Jack: The Struggle of John Fitzgerald Kennedy* (1980) and *JFK: The Presidency of John Fitzgerald Kennedy* (1983). Critical assessments can be found in Thomas C. Reeves's *A Question of Character: The Life of John F. Kennedy* (rev. ed., 1998) and Bruce Miroff's *Pragmatic Illusions: The Presidential Politics of John F. Kennedy* (1976). The best study of the Kennedy administration's domestic policies is Irving Bernstein's *Promises Kept: John F. Kennedy's New Frontier* (1991). For details on the assassination, see David W. Belin's *Final Disclosure: The Full Truth about the Assassination of President Kennedy* (1988). A more recent critique of the conspiracy theories is Gerald L. Posner's *Case Closed: Lee Harvey Oswald and the Assassination of John F. Kennedy* (1993).

The most comprehensive biography of LBJ is Robert Dallek's two-volume work, *Lone Star Rising; Lyndon Johnson and His Times, 1908–1960* (1991) and *Flawed Giant: Lyndon B. Johnson, 1960–1973* (1998). An intriguing analysis of the tense relationship between Johnson and Robert Kennedy is Jeff Shesol's *Mutual Contempt: Lyndon Johnson, Robert Kennedy, and the Feud That Defined a Decade* (1997).

Among the works that interpret liberal social policy during the 1960s, John Schwarz's *America's Hidden Success: A Reassessment of Twenty Years of Public Policy* (1983) offers a glowing endorsement of Democratic programs. For a contrasting perspective, see Charles Murray's *Losing Ground: American Social Policy, 1950–1980* (rev. ed., 1995).

On foreign policy, see *Kennedy's Quest for Victory: American Foreign Policy, 1961–1963* (1989), edited by Thomas G. Paterson. To learn more about Kennedy's problems in Cuba, see Mark White's *Missiles in Cuba: Kennedy, Khrushchev, Castro and the 1962 Crisis* (1997). For an understanding of the Alliance for Progress, see Jerome Levinson and Juan de Onis's *The Alliance That Lost Its Way* (1970). On the Peace Corps, see Elizabeth Hoffman's *All You Need Is Love: The Peace Corps and the Spirit of the 1960s* (1998).

American involvement in Vietnam has received voluminous treatment from all political perspectives. For an overview, see Larry Berman's *Planning a Tragedy: The Americanization of the War in Vietnam* (1982) and *Lyndon Johnson's War: The Road to Stalemate in Vietnam* (1989), as well as Stanley Karnow's *Vietnam: A History* (rev. ed., 1991). Tensions between the secretary of defense and the military leadership are detailed in H. R. McMaster's *Dereliction of Duty: Johnson, McNamara, the Joint Chiefs of Staff and the Lies That Led to Vietnam* (1997). Works that portray American policy in a favorable light include Norman Podhoretz's *Why We Were in Vietnam* (1982), Guenter Lewy's *America in Vietnam: Illusion, Myth and Reality* (1978), and Leslie Gelb and Richard Bett's *The Irony of Vietnam: The System Worked* (1979). An excellent analysis of policy making concerning the Vietnam War is David M. Barrett's *Uncertain Warriors: Lyndon Johnson and His Vietnam Advisors* (1994). Former secretary of defense Robert McNamara confesses his mistakes in *In Retrospect: The Tragedy and Lessons of Vietnam* (1995).

Many scholars have dealt with various aspects of the civil rights movement and race relations of the 1960s. See especially Carl Brauer's *John F. Kennedy and the Second Reconstruction* (1977), David Garrow's *Bearing the Cross: Martin Luther King, Jr., and the Southern Christian*

Leadership Conference (1986), Adam Fairclough's *To Redeem the Soul of America: The Southern Christian Leadership Conference and Martin Luther King, Jr.* (1987), and David Lewis's *King: A Biography* (2nd ed., 1978). For the legal turns the civil rights movement took during the 1960s, see J. Harvey Wilkinson's *From Brown to Bakke: The Supreme Court and School Integration, 1954–1978* (1978). William Chafe's *From Civilities to Civil Rights: Greensboro, North Carolina and the Black Struggle for Freedom* (1980) details the original sit-ins. An award-winning study of racial and economic inequality in a representative American city is Thomas J. Sugrue's *The Origins of the Urban Crisis: Race and Inequality in Postwar Detroit* (1996).

Chapter 34

Engaging overviews of the cultural trends of the 1960s include William L. O'Neill's *Coming Apart: An Informal History of America in the 1960s* (1972) and Godfrey Hodgson's *America in Our Time* (1976). The scholarly literature on the New Left includes Irwin Unger's *The Movement: A History of the American New Left, 1959–1972* (1974). On the Students for a Democratic Society, see Kirkpatrick Sale's *SDS* (1973) and Allen J. Matusow's *The Unraveling of America: A History of Liberalism in the 1960s* (1984). Also useful is Todd Gitlin's *The Sixties: Years of Hope, Days of Rage* (rev. ed., 1993).

Two influential asessments of the counterculture by sympathetic commentators are Theodore Roszak's *The Making of a Counterculture: Reflections on the Technocratic Society and Its Youthful Opposition* (1969) and Charles Reich's *The Greening of America* (1970). A good scholarly analysis of the hippies that takes them seriously is Timothy Miller's *The Hippies and American Values* (1991). On the communal movement, see Keith Melville's *Communes in the Counter Culture* (1972).

There is a wealth of good books dealing with the women's liberation movement. Among the most powerful accounts are those by participants. See Shulamith Firestone's *The Dialectic of Sex* (1972), Betty Friedan's *It Changed My Life: Writings on the Women's Movement* (1976), Kate Millett's *Sexual Politics* (1971), and *Sisterhood Is Powerful* (1970), edited by Robin Morgan. Sara Evans explains the ambivalent relationship of feminism with the civil rights movement in *Personal Politics: The Roots of Women's Liberation in the Civil Rights Movement and the New Left* (1980).

The organizing efforts of César Chavez are detailed in Ronald Taylor's *Chavez and the Farm Workers* (1975). The struggles of Native Americans for recognition and power are sympathetically described in Stan Steiner's *The New Indians* (1968). On the shifting cultural mood of the 1970s, see Christopher Lasch's influential critique, *The Culture of Narcissism* (1978). Peter Clecak convincingly questions the stereotypic notion of the seventies as an age of apathy and narcissism in *America's Quest for the Ideal Self* (1983).

On Nixon see Stephen Ambrose's *Nixon: The Triumph of a Politician, 1962–1972* (1989) and *Nixon: Ruin and Recovery, 1973–1990* (1991). Equally valuable is Herbert S. Parmet's *Richard Nixon and His America* (1990). For a solid overview of the Watergate scandal, see Stanley Kutler's *The Wars of Watergate: The Last Crisis of Richard Nixon* (1990).

For the way the Rupublicans handled affairs abroad, consult Tad Szulc's *The Illusion of Peace: Foreign Policy in the Nixon Years* (1978). Secretary of State Henry Kissinger recounts his role in policy formation in *The White House Years* (1978). A less favorable report of the Kissinger role appears in Seymour M. Hersh's *The Price of Power: Kissinger in the Nixon White House* (1983).

The loss of Vietnam and the end of American involvement are traced in Allan E. Goodman's *The Lost Peace: America's Search for a Negotiated Settlement of the Vietnam War* (1978), Frank Snepp's *Decent Interval: An Insider's Account of Saigon's Indecent End Told by the CIA's Chief Strategy Analyst in Vietnam* (1977), and Gareth Porter's *A Peace Denied: The United States, Vietnam and the Paris Agreement* (1975). William Shawcross's *Sideshow: Kissinger, Nixon, and the Destruction of Cambodia* (1978) deals with the broadening of the war, while Larry Berman's *Planning a Tragedy: The Americanization of the War in Vietnam* (1982) assesses the final impact of American involvement. The most comprehensive treatment of the antiwar movement in the United States is Tom Wells's *The War Within: America's Battle over Vietnam* (1994). A recent effort to reflect upon the lingering impact of the Vietnam War is Arnold R. Isaacs's *Vietnam Shadows: The War, Its Ghosts, and Its Legacy* (1997).

To examine the rise of Jimmy Carter, consult Betty Glad's *Jimmy Carter: In Search of the Great White House* (1980). The best overview of the Carter administration is Burton I. Kaufman's *The Presidency of James Earl Carter, Jr.* (1993). A work more sympathetic to the Carter administration is John Dumbrell's *The Carter Presidency: A Re-Evaluation* (1993). Also useful is Kenneth E. Morris's

Jimmy Carter: American Moralist (1997). Gaddis Smith's *Morality, Reason, and Power* (1986) provides an overview of American diplomacy in the Carter years. Zbigniew Brzezinski's *Power and Principle: Memories of the National Security Advisor, 1977–1981* (1983) and Cyrus Vance's *Hard Choices: Critical Years in America's Foreign Policy* (1983) lend insight into the Carter approach to foreign policy. Background on how the Middle East came to dominate much of American policy is found in William B. Quandt's *Decade of Decisions: American Policy toward the Arab-Israeli Conflict, 1967–1976* (1977).

Chapter 35

Two brief accounts of the Reagan administration, are David Mervin's *Ronald Reagan and the American Presidency* (1990) and Michael Schaller's *Reckoning with Reagan: America and Its President in the 1980s* (1992).

On Reaganomics, see David Stockman's *The Triumph of Politics: How the Reagan Revolution Failed* (1986) and Robert Lekachman's *Greed Is Not Enough: Reaganomics* (1982). On the issue of arms control, see Strobe Talbott's *Deadly Gambits: The Reagan Administration and the Stalemate in Nuclear Arms Control* (1984).

For Reagan's foreign policy in Central America, see James Chace's *Endless War: How We Got Involved in Central America and What Can Be Done* (1984) and Walter LaFeber's *Inevitable Revolutions. The United States in Central America* (2nd ed., 1993). Insider views of Reagan's foreign policy are offered in Alexander M. Haig, Jr.'s *Caveat: Realism, Reagan, and Foreign Policy* (1984) and Caspar W. Weinberger's *Fighting for Peace: Seven Critical Years in the Pentagon* (1990).

On Reagan's second term, see Jane Mayer and Doyle McManus's *Landslide: The Unmaking of the President, 1984–1988* (1988). For a masterful work on the Iran-Contra Affair, see Theodore Draper's *A Very Thin Line: The Iran Contra Affair* (1991). Several collections of essays include varying assessments of the Reagan years. Among these are *The Reagan Revolution* (1988), edited by B. B. Kymlicka and Jean V. Matthews; *The Reagan Presidency: An Incomplete Revolution* (1990), edited by Dilys M. Hill, et al.; and *Looking Back on the Reagan Presidency* (1990), edited by Larry Berman.

On the 1988 campaign see Jack Germond and Jules Witcover's *Whose Broad Stripes and Bright Stars? The Trivial Pursuit of the Presidency, 1988* (1989) and Sidney Blumenthal's *Pledging Allegiance: The Last Campaign of the Cold War* (1990). Major issues in economic and social policy are addressed in Robert Reich's *The Work of Nations: Preparing Ourselves for Twenty-first Century Capitalism* (1991) and William Julius Wilson's *The Truly Disadvantaged: The Inner City, the Underclass, and Public Policy* (1987).

On the banking and other scandals, see L. William Seidman's *Full Faith and Credit: The Great S & L Debacle and Other Washington Sagas* (1993). The onset and growth of the AIDS epidemic are traced in *And the Band Played On: Politics, People, and the AIDS Epidemic* (1987) by Randy Shilts, a journalist who reported much of the story, and in essays edited by historians Elizabeth Fee and Daniel M. Fox, *AIDS: The Burdens of History* (1988) and *AIDS: The Making of a Chronic Disease* (1992).

For further treatment of the end of the cold war, see Michael K. Beschloss's *At the Highest Levels: The Inside Story of the End of the Cold War* (1993), Thomas J. McCormick's *America's Half Century: United States Foreign Policy in the Cold War and After* (2nd ed., 1995), Richard Crockatt's *The Fifty Years War: The United States and the Soviet Union in World Politics, 1941–1991* (1995), and Zbigniew Brzezinski's *Out of Control: Global Turmoil on the Eve of the Twenty-first Century* (1994).

On the Panama and Persian Gulf conflicts, see Edward W. Flanagan's *Battle for Panama: Inside Operation Just Cause* (1993), Bruce W. Jentleson's *With Friends Like These: Reagan, Bush, and Saddam, 1982–1990* (1994), and Lester H. Brune's *America and the Iraqi Crisis, 1990–1992: Origins and Aftermath* (1993).

Chapter 36

On the Bush presidency, see Ryan J. Barilleaux and Mary E. Stuckey's *Leadership and the Bush Presidency: Prudence or Drift in an Era of Change* (1992), Charles Tiefer's *The Semi-Sovereign Presidency: The Bush Administration's Strategy for Governing without Congress* (1994). Among the journalistic accounts of the presidential election of 1992, the best narrative is Jack Germond and Jules Witcover's *Mad as Hell: Revolt at the Ballot Box, 1992* (1993). The best scholarly study is Theodore J. Lowi and Benjamin Ginsberg's *Democrats Return to Power: Politics and Policy in the Clinton Era* (1994).

On Bill Clinton, up to his presidency, the best treatment is David Maraniss's *First in His Class: A Biography of Bill*

Clinton (1995). The early months of the Clinton presidency are most thoroughly covered in Elizabeth Drew's *On the Edge: The Clinton Presidency* (1994). Bob Woodward's *The Agenda: Inside the Clinton White House* (1994) focuses on financial policies and the economy. For a psychoanalytic assessment of Clinton, see Stanley A. Renshon's *High Hopes: The Clinton Presidency and the Politics of Ambition* (1996). Further analysis of the Clinton years can be found in *The Clinton Presidency: First Appraisals* (1995), edited by Colin Campbell and Bert A. Rockman, and *Back to Gridlock?: Governance in the Clinton Years* (1996), edited by James L. Sundquist. For a Republican perspective, see Haley Barbour's *Agenda for America: A Republican Direction for the Future* (1996).

On social and cultural problems and issues of the times, a good account is Haynes Johnson's *Divided We Fall: Gambling with History in the Nineties* (1994), based on street interviews. Collections of magazine and newspaper articles are in John Leo's *Two Steps Ahead of the Thought Police* (1994), Molly Ivins's *Nothin' But Good Times Ahead* (1993), and George F. Will's *The Leveling Wind: Politics, the Culture, and Other News, 1990–1994* (1994).

Aspects of fundamentalist and apocalyptic movements are the subject of Paul L. Boyer's *When Time Shall Be No More: Prophecy and Belief in Modern American Culture* (1992), George M. Marsden's *Understanding Fundamentalism and Evangelicalism* (1991), and Ralph Reed's *Politically Incorrect: The Emerging Faith Factor in American Politics* (1994).

Discussion of recent cultural debates can be found in *Culture Wars: Documents from the Recent Controversies in the Arts* (1992), edited by Richard Bolton; Gerald Graff's *Beyond the Culture Wars: How Teaching the Conflicts Can Revitalize American Education* (1992); and *The Politics of Liberal Education* (1992), edited by Darryl Gless and Barbara Herrnstein Smith.

Corporate restructuring and downsizing are the subject of Bennett Harrison's *Lean and Mean: The Changing Landscape of Corporate Power in the Age of Flexibility* (1994). The story of the Whitewater affair is the subject of Martin L. Gross's *The Great Whitewater Fiasco: An American Tale of Money, Power, and Politics* (1994).

The Declaration of Independence

WHEN IN THE COURSE OF HUMAN EVENTS, it becomes necessary for one people to dissolve the political bands which have connected them with another, and to assume among the Powers of the earth, the separate and equal station to which the Laws of Nature and of Nature's God entitle them, a decent respect to the opinions of mankind requires that they should declare the causes which impel them to the separation.

We hold these truths to be self-evident, that all men are created equal, that they are endowed by their Creator with certain unalienable rights, that among these are Life, Liberty, and the pursuit of Happiness. That to secure these rights, Governments are instituted among Men, deriving their just powers from the consent of the governed. That whenever any Form of Government becomes destructive of these ends, it is the Right of the People to alter or to abolish it, and to institute new Government, laying its foundation on such principles and organizing its powers in such form, as to them shall seem most likely to effect their Safety and Happiness. Prudence, indeed, will dictate that Governments long established should not be changed for light and transient causes; and accordingly all experience hath shown, that mankind are more disposed to suffer, while evils are sufferable, than to right themselves by abolishing the forms to which they are accustomed. But when a long train of abuses and usurpations, pursuing invariably the same Object evinces a design to reduce them under absolute Despotism, it is their right, it is their duty, to throw off such Government, and to provide new Guards for their future security.—Such has been the patient sufferance of these Colonies; and such is now the necessity which constrains them to alter their former Systems of Government. The history of the present King of Great Britain is a history of repeated injuries and usurpations, all having in direct object the establishment of an absolute Tyranny over these States. To prove this, let Facts be submitted to a candid world.

He has refused his Assent to Laws, the most wholesome and necessary for the public good.

He has forbidden his Governors to pass Laws of immediate and pressing importance, unless sus-pended in their operation till his Assent should be obtained; and when so suspended, he has utterly neglected to attend to them.

He has refused to pass other Laws for the accommodation of large districts of people, unless those people would relinquish the right of Representation in the Legislature, a right inestimable to them and formidable to tyrants only.

He has called together legislative bodies at places unusual, uncomfortable, and distant from the depository of their public Records, for the sole purpose of fatiguing them into compliance with his measures.

He has dissolved Representative Houses repeatedly, for opposing with manly firmness his invasions on the rights of the people.

He has refused for a long time, after such dissolutions, to cause others to be elected; whereby the Legislative powers, incapable of Annihilation, have returned to the People at large for their exercise; the State remaining in the mean time exposed to all dangers of invasion from without, and convulsions within.

He has endeavoured to prevent the population of these States; for that purpose obstructing the Laws of Naturalization of Foreigners; refusing to pass others to encourage their migrations hither, and raising the conditions of new Appropriations of Lands.

He has obstructed the Administration of Justice, by refusing his Assent to Laws for establishing Judiciary powers.

He has made Judges dependent on his Will alone, for the tenure of their offices, and the amount and payment of their salaries.

He has erected a multitude of New Offices, and sent hither swarms of Officers to harass our People, and eat out their substance.

He has kept among us, in times of peace, Standing Armies without the Consent of our legislature.

He has affected to render the Military independent of and superior to the Civil Power.

He has combined with others to subject us to a jurisdiction foreign to our constitution, and unacknowledged by our laws; giving his Assent to their Acts of pretended Legislation:

For quartering large bodies of armed troops among us:

For protecting them, by a mock Trial, from Punishment for any Murders which they should commit on the Inhabitants of these States:

For cutting off our Trade with all parts of the world:

For imposing taxes on us without our Consent:

For depriving us of many cases, of the benefits of Trial by jury:

For transporting us beyond Seas to be tried for pretended offences:

For abolishing the free System of English Laws in a neighbouring Province, establishing therein an Arbitrary government, and enlarging its Boundaries so as to render it at once an example and fit instrument for introducing the same absolute rule into these Colonies:

For taking away our Charters, abolishing our most valuable Laws, and altering fundamentally the Forms of our Governments:

For suspending our own Legislatures, and declaring themselves in vested with Power to legislate for us in all cases whatsoever.

He has abdicated Government here, by declaring us out of his Protection and waging War against us.

He has plundered our seas, ravaged our Coasts, burnt our towns, and destroyed the lives of our people.

He is at this time transporting large armies of foreign mercenaries to compleat the works of death, desolation, and tyranny, already begun with circumstances of Cruelty & perfidy scarcely paralleled in the most barbarous ages, and totally unworthy the Head of a civilized nation.

He has constrained our fellow Citizens taken Captive on the high Seas to bear Arms against their Country, to become the executioners of their friends and Brethren, or to fall themselves by their Hands.

He has excited domestic insurrections amongst us, and has endeavoured to bring on the inhabitants of our frontiers, the merciless Indian Savages, whose known rule of warfare, is an undistinguished destruction of all ages, sexes, and conditions.

In every stage of these Oppressions We have Petitioned for Redress in the most humble terms: Our repeated Petitions have been answered only by repeated injury. A Prince, whose character is thus marked by every act which may define a Tyrant, is unfit to be the ruler of a free people.

Nor have We been wanting in attention to our British brethren. We have warned them from time to time of attempts by their legislature to extend an unwarrantable jurisdiction over us. We have re-minded them of the circumstances of our emigration and settlement here. We have appealed to their native justice and magnanimity, and we have conjured them by the ties of our common kindred to disavow these usurpations, which, would inevitably interrupt our connections and correspondence. They too must have been deaf to the voice of justice and of consanguinity. We must, therefore, acquiesce in the necessity, which denounces our Separation, and hold them, as we hold the rest of mankind, Enemies in War, in Peace Friends.

WE, THEREFORE, the Representatives of the UNITED STATES OF AMERICA, in General Congress, Assembled, appealing to the Supreme Judge of the world for the rectitude of our intentions, do, in the Name, and by Authority of the good People of these Colonies, solemnly publish and declare, That these United Colonies are, and of Right ought to be FREE AND INDEPENDENT STATES; that they are Absolved from all Allegiance to the British Crown, and that all political connection between them and the State of Great Britain, is and ought to be totally dissolved; and that as Free and Independent States, they have full Power to levy War, conclude Peace, contract Alliances, establish Commerce, and to do all other Acts and Things which Independent States may of right do. And for the support of this Declaration, with a firm reliance on the Protection of Divine Providence, we mutually pledge to each other our Lives, our Fortunes, and our sacred Honor.

The foregoing Declaration was, by order of Congress, engrossed, and signed by the following members:

John Hancock

NEW HAMPSHIRE
Josiah Bartlett
William Whipple
Matthew Thornton

MASSACHUSETTS BAY
Samuel Adams
John Adams
Robert Treat Paine
Elbridge Gerry

RHODE ISLAND
Stephen Hopkins
William Ellery

CONNECTICUT
Roger Sherman
Samuel Huntington
William Williams
Oliver Wolcott

NEW YORK
William Floyd
Philip Livingston
Francis Lewis
Lewis Morris

NEW JERSEY
Richard Stockton
John Witherspoon
Francis Hopkinson
John Hart
Abraham Clark

PENNSYLVANIA
Robert Morris
Benjamin Rush
Benjamin Franklin
John Morton
George Clymer
James Smith
George Taylor
James Wilson
George Ross

DELAWARE
Caesar Rodney
George Read
Thomas M'Kean

MARYLAND
Samuel Chase
William Paca
Thomas Stone
Charles Carroll, of Carrollton

VIRGINIA
George Wythe
Richard Henry Lee
Thomas Jefferson
Benjamin Harrison
Thomas Nelson, Jr.
Francis Lightfoot Lee
Carter Braxton

NORTH CAROLINA
William Hooper
Joseph Hewes
John Penn

SOUTH CAROLINA
Edward Rutledge
Thomas Heyward, Jr.
Thomas Lynch, Jr.
Arthur Middleton

GEORGIA
Button Gwinnett
Lyman Hall
George Walton

Resolved, That copies of the Declaration be sent to the several assemblies, conventions, and committees, or councils of safety, and to the several commanding officers of the continental troops; that it be proclaimed in each of the United States, at the head of the army.

Articles of Confederation

To all to whom these Presents shall come, we the undersigned Delegates of the States affixed to our Names send greeting.

Whereas the Delegates of the United States of America in Congress assembled did on the fifteenth day of November in the Year of our Lord One Thousand Seven Hundred and Seventy-seven, and in the Second Year of the Independence of America agree to certain articles of Confederation and perpetual Union between the States of Newhampshire, Massachusetts-bay, Rhodeisland and Providence Plantations, Connecticut, New York, New Jersey, Pennsylvania, Delaware, Maryland, Virginia, North-Carolina, South-Carolina and Georgia in the Words following, viz.

Articles of Confederation and perpetual Union between the States of Newhampshire, Massachusetts-bay, Rhodeisland and Providence Plantations, Connecticut, New-York, New-Jersey, Pennsylvania, Delaware, Maryland, Virginia, North-Carolina, South-Carolina and Georgia.

Article I. The stile of this confederacy shall be "The United States of America."

Article II. Each State retains its sovereignty, freedom and independence, and every power, jurisdiction and right, which is not by this confederation expressly delegated to the United States, in Congress assembled.

Article III. The said States hereby severally enter into a firm league of friendship with each other, for their common defence, the security of their liberties, and their mutual and general welfare, binding themselves to assist each other, against all force offered to, or attacks made upon them, or any of them, on account of religion, sovereignty, trade or any other pretence whatever.

Article IV. The better to secure and perpetuate mutual friendship and intercourse among the people of the different States in this Union, the free inhabitants of each of these States, paupers, vagabonds and fugitives from justice excepted, shall be entitled to all privileges and immunities of free citizens in the several States; and the people of each State shall have free ingress and regress to and from any other State, and shall enjoy therein all the privileges of trade and commerce, subject to the same duties, impositions and restrictions as the inhabitants there of respectively, provided that such restrictions shall not extend so far as to prevent the removal of property imported into any State, to any other State of which the owner is an inhabitant; provided also that no imposition, duties or restriction shall be laid by any State, on the property of the United States, or either of them.

If any person guilty of, or charged with treason, felony, or other high misdemeanor in any State, shall flee from justice, and be found in any of the United States, he shall upon demand of the Governor or Executive power, of the State from which he fled, be delivered up and removed to the State having jurisdiction of his offence.

Full faith and credit shall be given in each of these States to the records, acts and judicial proceedings of the courts and magistrates of every other State.

ARTICLE V. For the more convenient management of the general interests of the United States, delegates shall be annually appointed in such manner as the legislature of each State shall direct, to meet in Congress on the first Monday in November, in every year, with a power reserved to each State, to recall its delegates, or any of them, at any time within the year, and to send others in their stead, for the remainder of the year.

No State shall be represented in Congress by less than two, nor by more than seven members; and no person shall be capable of being a delegate for more than three years in any term of six years; nor shall any person, being a delegate, be capable of holding any office under the United States, for which he, or another for his benefit receives any salary, fees or emolument of any kind.

Each State shall maintain its own delegates in a meeting of the States, and while they act as members of the committee of the States.

In determining questions in the United States, in Congress assembled, each State shall have one vote.

Freedom of speech and debate in Congress shall not be impeached or questioned in any court, or place out of Congress, and the members of Congress shall be protected in their persons from arrests and imprisonments, during the time of their going to and from, and attendance on Congress, except for treason, felony, or breach of the peace.

ARTICLE VI. No State without the consent of the United States in Congress assembled, shall send any embassy to, or receive any embassy from, or enter into any conference, agreement, alliance or treaty with any king, prince or state; nor shall any person holding any office of profit or trust under the United States, or any of them, accept of any present, emolument, office or title of any kind whatever from any king, prince or foreign state; nor shall the United States in Congress assembled, or any of them, grant any title of nobility.

No two or more States shall enter into any treaty, confederation or alliance whatever between them, without the consent of the United States in Congress assembled, specifying accurately the purposes for which the same is to be entered into, and how long it shall continue.

No State shall lay any imposts or duties, which may interfere with any stipulations in treaties, entered into by the United States in Congress assembled, with any king, prince or state, in pursuance of any treaties already proposed by Congress, to the courts of France and Spain.

No vessels of war shall be kept up in time of peace by any State, except such number only, as shall be deemed necessary by the United States in Congress assembled, for the defence of such State, or its trade; nor shall any body of forces be kept up by any State, in time of peace, except such number only, as in the judgment of the United States, in Congress assembled, shall be deemed requisite to garrison the forts necessary for the defence of such State; but every State shall always keep up a well regulated and disciplined militia, sufficiently armed and accoutred, and shall provide and constantly have ready for use, in public stores, a due number of field pieces and tents, and a proper quantity of arms, ammunition and camp equipage.

No State shall engage in any war without the consent of the United States in Congress assembled, unless such State be actually invaded by enemies, or shall have received certain advice of a resolution being formed by some nation of Indians to invade such State, and the danger is so imminent as not to admit of a delay, till the United States in Congress assembled can be consulted: nor shall any State grant commissions to any ships or vessels of war, nor letters of marque or reprisal, except it be after a declaration of war by the United States in Congress assembled, and then only against the kingdom or state and the subjects thereof, against which war has been so declared, and under such regulations as shall be established by the United States in Congress assembled, unless such State be infested by pirates, in which case vessels of war may be fitted out for that occasion, and kept so long as the danger shall continue, or until the United States in Congress assembled shall determine otherwise.

ARTICLE VII. When land-forces are raised by any State of the common defence, all officers of or under the rank of colonel, shall be appointed by the Legislature of each State respectively by whom such forces shall be raised, or in such manner as such State shall direct, and all vacancies shall be filled up by the State which first made the appointment.

ARTICLE VIII. All charges of war, and all other expenses that shall be incurred for the common defence or general welfare, and allowed by the United States in Congress assembled, shall be defrayed out of a common treasury, which shall be supplied by the several States, in proportion to the value of all land within each State, granted to or surveyed for any person, as such land and the buildings and improvements thereon shall be estimated according to such mode as the United States in Congress assembled, shall from time to time direct and appoint.

The taxes for paying that proportion shall be laid and levied by the authority and direction of the Legislatures of the several States within the time agreed upon by the United States in Congress assembled.

ARTICLE IX. The United States in Congress assembled, shall have the sole and exclusive right and power of determining on peace and war, except in the cases mentioned in the sixth article—of sending and receiving ambassadors—entering into treaties and alliances, provided that no treaty of commerce shall be made whereby the legislative power of the respective States shall be restrained from imposing such imposts and duties on foreigners, as their own people are subjected to, or from prohibiting the exportation or importation of and species of goods or commodities whatsoever—of establishing rules for deciding in all cases, what captures on land or water shall be legal, and in what manner prizes taken by land or naval forces in the service of the United States shall be divided or appropriated—of granting letters of marque and reprisal in times of peace—appointing courts for the trial of piracies and felonies committed on the high seas and establishing courts for receiving and determining finally appeals in all cases of captures, provided that no member of Congress shall be appointed a judge of any of the said courts.

The United States in Congress assembled shall also be the last resort on appeal in all disputes and differences now subsisting or that hereafter may arise between two or more States concerning boundary, jurisdiction or any other cause whatever; which authority shall always be exercised in the manner following. Whenever the legislative or executive authority or lawful agent of any State in controversy with another shall present a petition to Congress, stating the matter in question and praying for a hearing, notice thereof shall be given by order of Congress to the legislative or executive authority of the other State in controversy, and a day assigned for the appearance of the parties by their lawful agents, who shall then be directed to appoint by joint consent, commissioners or judges to constitute a court for hearing and determining the matter in question: but if they cannot agree, Congress shall name three persons out of each of the United States, and from the list of such persons each party shall alternately strike out one, the petitioners beginning, until the number shall be reduced to thirteen; and from that number not less than seven, nor more than nine names as Congress shall direct, shall in the presence of Congress be drawn out by lot, and the persons whose names shall be so drawn or any five of them, shall be commissioners or judges, to hear and finally determine the controversy, so always as a major part of the judges who shall hear the cause shall agree in the determination: and if either party shall neglect to attend at the day appointed, without reasons, which Congress shall judge sufficient, or being present shall refuse to strike, the Congress shall proceed to nominate three persons out of each State, and the Secretary of Congress shall strike in behalf of such party absent or refusing; and the judgment and sentence of the court to be appointed, in the manner before prescribed, shall be final and conclusive; and if any of the parties shall refuse to submit to the authority of such court, or to appear or defend their claim or cause, the court shall nevertheless proceed to pronounce sentence, or judgment, which shall in like manner be final and decisive, the judgment or sentence and other proceedings being in either case transmitted to Congress, and lodged among the acts of Congress for the security of the parties concerned: provided that every commissioner, before he sits in judgment, shall take an oath to be administered by one of the judges of the supreme or superior court of the State where the case shall be tried, "well and truly to hear and determine the matter in question, according to the best of his judgment, without favour, affection or hope of reward:" provided also that no State shall be deprived of territory for the benefit of the United States.

All controversies concerning the private right of soil claimed under different grants of two or more States, whose jurisdiction as they may respect such lands, and the states which passed such grants are adjusted, the said grants or either of them being at the same time claimed to have originated antecedent to such settlement of jurisdiction, shall on the petition of either party to the Congress of the United States, be finally determined as near as may be in the same manner as is before prescribed for deciding disputes respecting territorial jurisdiction between different States.

The United States in Congress assembled shall also have the sole and exclusive right and power of regulating the alloy and value of coin struck by their own authority, or by that of the respective States—fixing the standard of weights and measures throughout the United States—regulating the trade and managing all affairs with the Indians, not members of any of the States, provided that the legislative right of any State within its own limits be not infringed or violated—establishing and regulating post-offices from one State to another, throughout all of the United States, and exacting such postage on the papers passing thro' the same as may be requisite to defray the expenses of the said office—appointing all officers of the land forces, in the service of the United States, excepting regimental officers—appointing all the officers of the naval forces, and commissioning all officers whatever in the service of the United States—making rules for the government and regulation of the said land and naval forces, and directing their operations.

The United States in Congress assembled shall have authority to appoint a committee, to sit in the recess of Congress, to be denominated "a Committee of the States," and to consist of one delegate from each State; and to appoint such other committees and civil officers as may be necessary for managing the general affairs of the United States under their direction—to appoint one of their number to preside, provided that no person be allowed to serve in the office of president more than one year in any term of three years; to ascertain the necessary sums of money to be raised for the service of the United States, and to appropriate and apply the same for defraying the public expenses—to borrow money, or emit bills on the credit of the United States, transmitting every half year to the respective States an account of the sums of money so borrowed or emitted,—to build and equip a navy—to agree upon the number of land forces, and to make requisitions from each State for its quota, in proportion to the number of white inhabitants in such State; which requisition shall be binding, and thereupon the Legislature of each State shall appoint the regimental officers, raise the men and cloath, arm and equip them in a soldier like manner, at the expense of the United States; and the officers and men so cloathed, armed and equipped shall march to the place appointed, and within the time agreed on by the United States in Congress assembled: but if the United States in Congress assembled shall, on consideration of circumstances judge proper that any State should not raise men, or should raise a smaller number of men than the quota thereof, such extra number shall be raised, officered, cloathed, armed and equipped in the same manner as the quota of such State, unless the legislature of such State shall judge that such extra number cannot be safely spared out of the same, in which case they shall raise officer, cloath, arm and equip as many of such extra number as they judge can be safely spared. And the officers and men so cloathed, armed and equipped, shall march to the place appointed, and within the time agreed on by the United States in Congress assembled.

The United States in Congress assembled shall never engage in a war, nor grant letters of marque and reprisal in time of peace, nor enter into any treaties or alliances, nor coin money, nor regulate the value thereof, nor ascertain the sums and expenses necessary for the defence and welfare of the United States, or any of them, nor emit bills, nor borrow money on the credit of the United States, nor appropriate money, nor agree upon the number of vessels to be built or purchased, or the number of land or sea forces to be raised, nor appoint a commander in chief of the army or navy, unless nine States assent to the same: nor shall a question on any other point, except for adjourning from day to day be determined, unless by the votes of a majority of the United States in Congress assembled.

The Congress of the United States shall have power to adjourn to any time within the year, and to any place within the United States, so that no period of adjournment be for a longer duration than the space of six months, and shall publish the journal of their proceedings monthly, except such parts thereof relating to treaties, alliances or military operations, as in their judgment require secresy; and the yeas and nays of the delegates of each State on any question shall be entered on the Journal, when it is desired by any delegate; and the delegates of a State, or any of them, at his or their request shall be furnished with a transcript of the said journal, except such parts as are above excepted, to lay before the Legislatures of the several States.

ARTICLE X. The committee of the States, or any nine of them, shall be authorized to execute, in the recess of Congress, such of the powers of Congress as the United States in Congress assembled, by the consent of nine States, shall from time to time think expedient to vest them with; provided that no power be delegated to the said committee, for the exercise of which, by the articles of confederation, the voice of nine States in the Congress of the United States assembled is requisite.

ARTICLE XI. Canada acceding to this confederation, and joining in the measures of the United States, shall be admitted into, and entitled to all the advantages of this Union: but no other colony shall be admitted into the same, unless such admission be agreed to by nine States.

ARTICLE XII. All bills of credit emitted, monies borrowed and debts contracted by, or under the authority of Congress, before the assembling of the United States, in pursuance of the present confederation, shall be deemed and considered as a charge against the United States, for payment and satisfaction whereof the said United States, and the public faith are hereby solemnly pledged.

ARTICLE XIII. Every State shall abide by the determinations of the United States in Congress assembled, on all questions which by this confederation are submitted to them. And the articles of this confederation shall be inviolably observed by every State, and the Union shall be perpetual; nor shall any alteration at any time hereafter be made in any of them; unless such alteration be agreed to in a Congress of the United States, and be afterwards confirmed by the Legislatures of every State.

And whereas it has pleased the Great Governor of the world to incline the hearts of the Legislatures we respectively represent in Congress, to approve of, and to authorize us to ratify the said articles of confederation and perpetual union. Know ye that we the undersigned delegates, by virtue of the power and authority to us given for that purpose, do by these presents, in the name and in behalf of our respective constituents, fully and entirely ratify and confirm each and every of the said articles of confederation and perpetual union, and all and singular the matters and things therein contained: and we do further solemnly plight and engage the faith of our respective constituents, that they shall abide by the determinations of the United States in Congress assembled, on all questions, which by the said confederation are submitted to them. And that the articles thereof shall be inviolably observed by the States we respectively represent, and that the Union shall be perpetual.

In witness thereof we have hereunto set our hands in Congress. Done at Philadelphia in the State of Pennsylvania the ninth day of July in the year of our Lord one thousand seven hundred and seventy-eight, and in the third year of the independence of America.

The Constitution of the United States

We the People of the United States, in order to form a more perfect Union, establish Justice, insure domestic Tranquility, provide for the common defence, promote the general Welfare, and secure the Blessings of Liberty to ourselves and our Posterity, do ordain and establish this Constitution for the United States of America.

Article. I.

Section. 1. All legislative Powers herein granted shall be vested in a Congress of the United States, which shall consist of a Senate and House of Representatives.

Section. 2. The House of Representatives shall be composed of Members chosen every second Year by the People of the several States, and the Electors in each State shall have the Qualifications requisite for Electors of the most numerous Branch of the State Legislature.

No Person shall be a Representative who shall not have attained to the Age of twenty five Years, and been seven Years a Citizen of the United States, and who shall not, when elected, be an Inhabitant of that State in which he shall be chosen.

Representatives and direct Taxes shall be apportioned among the several States which may be included within this Union, according to their respective Numbers, which shall be determined by adding to the whole Number of free Persons, including those bound to Service for a Term of Years, and excluding Indians not taxed, three fifths of all other Persons. The actual Enumeration shall be made within three Years after the first Meeting of the Congress of the United States, and within every subsequent Term of ten Years, in such Manner as they shall by Law direct. The Number of Representatives shall not exceed one for every thirty Thousand, but each State shall have at Least one Representative; and until such enumeration shall be made, the

State of New Hampshire shall be entitled to chuse three, Massachusetts eight, Rhode-Island and Providence Plantations one, Connecticut five, New-York six, New Jersey four, Pennsylvania eight, Delaware one, Maryland six, Virginia ten, North Carolina five, South Carolina five, and Georgia three.

When vacancies happen in the Representation from any state, the Executive Authority thereof shall issue Writs of Election to fill such Vacancies.

The House of Representatives shall chuse their Speaker and other Officers; and shall have the sole Power of Impeachment.

Section. 3. The Senate of the United States shall be composed of two Senators from each State, chosen by the legislature thereof, for six Years; and each Senator shall have one Vote.

Immediately after they shall be assembled in Consequence of the first Election, they shall be divided as equally as may be into three Classes. The Seats of the Senators of the first Class shall be vacated at the Expiration of the second Year, of the second Class at the Expiration of the fourth Year, and of the third Class at the Expiration of the sixth Year, so that one third maybe chosen every second Year; and if Vacancies happen by Resignation, or otherwise, during the Recess of the Legislature of any State, the Executive thereof may make temporary Appoint-ments until the next Meeting of the Legislature, which shall then fill such Vacancies.

No Person shall be a Senator who shall not have attained to the Age of thirty Years, and been nine Years a Citizen of the United States, and who shall not, when elected, be an Inhabitant of that State for which he shall be chosen.

The Vice President of the United States shall be President of the Senate, but shall have no Vote, unless they be equally divided.

The Senate shall chuse their other Officers, and also a President pro tempore, in the Absence of the Vice President, or when he shall exercise the Office of President of the United States.

The Senate shall have the sole Power to try all Impeachments. When sitting for that Purpose, they shall be on Oath or Affirmation. When the President of the United States is tried, the Chief Justice shall preside: And no Person shall be convicted without the Concurrence of two thirds of the Members present.

Judgment in Cases of Impeachment shall not extend further than to removal from Office, and disqualification to hold and enjoy any Office of honor, Trust or Profit under the United States: but the Party convicted shall nevertheless be liable and subject to Indictment, Trial, Judgment and Punishment, according to Law.

Section. 4. The Times, Places and Manner of holding Elections for Senators and Representatives, shall be prescribed in each State by the Legislature thereof; but the Congress may at any time by Law make or alter such Regulations, except as to the Places of chusing Senators.

The Congress shall assemble at least once in every Year, and such Meeting shall be on the first Monday in December, unless they shall by Law appoint a different Day.

Section. 5. Each House shall be the Judge of the Elections, Returns and Qualifications of its own Members, and a Majority of each shall constitute a Quorum to do Business; but a smaller Number may adjourn from day to day, and may be authorized to compel the Attendance of absent Members, in such Manner, and under such Penalties as each House may provide.

Each House may determine the Rules of its Proceedings, punish its Members for disorderly Behaviour, and, with the Concurrence of two thirds, expel a Member.

Each House shall keep a Journal of its Proceedings, and from time to time publish the same, excepting such Parts as may in their Judgment require Secrecy; and the Yeas and Nays of the Members of either House on any question shall, at the Desire of one fifth of those Present, be entered on the Journal.

Neither House, during the Session of Congress, shall, without the Consent of the other, adjourn for more than three days, not to any other Place than that in which the two Houses shall be sitting.

Section. 6. The Senators and Representatives shall receive a Compensation for their Services, to be ascertained by Law, and paid out of the Treasury of the United States. They shall in all Cases, except Treason, Felony and Breach of the Peace, be privileged from Arrest during their Attendance at the Session of their respective Houses, and in going to and returning from the same; and for any Speech or Debate in either House, they shall not be questioned in any other Place.

No Senator or Representative shall, during the Time for which he was elected, be appointed to any civil Office under the Authority of the United States, which shall have been created, or the Emoluments whereof shall have been encreased during such time; and no Person holding any Office under the United States, shall be a Member of either House during his Continuance in Office.

Section. 7. All Bills for raising Revenue shall originate in the House of Representatives; but the Senate may propose or concur with Amendments as on other Bills.

Every Bill which shall have passed the House of Representatives and the Senate shall, before it become a Law, be presented to the President of the United States; If he approve he shall sign it, but if not he shall return it, with his Objections to that House in which it shall have originated, who shall enter the Objections at large on their Journal, and proceed to reconsider it. If after such Reconsideration two thirds of that House shall agree to pass the Bill, it shall be sent, together with the Objections, to the other House, by which it shall likewise be reconsidered, and if approved by two thirds of that House, it shall become a Law. But in all such Cases the Votes of both Houses shall be determined by yeas and Nays, and the Names of the Persons voting for and against the Bill shall be entered on the Journal of each House respectively. If any Bill shall not be returned by the President within ten Days (Sundays excepted) after it shall have been presented to him, the Same shall be a Law, in like Manner as if he had signed it, unless the Congress by their Adjournment prevent its Return, in which Case it shall not be a Law.

Every Order, Resolution, or Vote to which the Concurrence of the Senate and House of Representatives may be necessary (except on a question of Adjournment) shall be presented to the President of the United States; and before the Same shall take Effect, shall be approved by him, or being disapproved by him, shall be repassed by two thirds of the Senate and House of Representatives, according to the Rules and Limitations prescribed in the Case of a Bill.

Section. 8. The Congress shall have Power To lay and collect Taxes, Duties, Imposts and Excises, to pay the Debts and provide for the common Defence and general Welfare of the United States; but all Duties, Imposts and Excises shall be uniform throughout the United States;

To borrow Money on the credit of the United States;

To regulate Commerce with foreign Nations, and among the several States, and with the Indian Tribes;

To establish an uniform Rule of Naturalization, and uniform Laws on the subject of Bankruptcies throughout the United States;

To coin Money, regulate the Value thereof, and of foreign Coin, and fix the Standard of Weights and Measures;

To provide for the Punishment of counterfeiting the Securities and current Coin of the United States;

To establish Post Offices and Post Roads;

To promote the Progress of Science and useful Arts, by securing for limited Times to Authors and Inventors the exclusive Right to their respective Writings and Discoveries;

To constitute Tribunals inferior to the supreme Court;

To define and punish Piracies and Felonies committed on the high Seas, and Offences against the Law of Nations;

To declare War, grant Letters of Marque and Reprisal, and make Rules concerning Captures on land and Water;

To raise and support Armies, but no Appropriation of Money to that Use shall be for a longer Term than two Years;

To provide and maintain a Navy;

To make Rules for the Government and Regulation of the land and naval Forces;

To provide for calling forth the Militia to execute the Laws of the Union, suppress Insurrections and repel Invasions;

To provide for organizing, arming, and disciplining, the Militia, and for governing such Part of them as may be employed in the Service of the United States, reserving to the States respectively, the Appointment of the Officers, and the Authority of training the Militia according to the discipline prescribed by Congress.

To exercise exclusive Legislation in all Cases whatsoever, over such District (not exceeding ten Miles square) as may, by Cession of Particular States, and the Acceptance of Congress, become the Seat of the Government of the United States, and to exercise like Authority over all Places purchased by the Consent of the Legislature of the State in which the Same shall be, for the Erection of Forts, Magazines, Arsenals, dock-Yards, and other needful Buildings;—And

To make all Laws which shall be necessary and proper for carrying into Execution the foregoing Powers, and all other Powers vested by this Constitution in the Government of the United States, or in any Department or Officer thereof.

Section. 9. The Migration or Importation of such Persons as any of the States now existing shall think proper to admit, shall not be prohibited by the Congress prior to the Year one thousand eight hundred and eight, but a Tax or duty may be imposed on such Importation, not exceeding ten dollars for each Person.

The Privilege of the Writ of Habeas Corpus shall not be suspended, unless when in Cases of Rebellion or Invasion the public Safety may require it.

No Bill of Attainder or ex post facto Law shall be passed.

No Capitation, or other direct, Tax shall be laid, unless in Proportion to the Census or Enumeration herein before directed to be taken.

No Tax or Duty shall be laid on Articles exported from any State.

No Preference shall be given by any Regulation of Commerce or Revenue to the Ports of one State over those of another: nor shall Vessels bound to, or from, one State, be obliged to enter, clear, or pay Duties in another.

No Money shall be drawn from the Treasury, but in Consequence of Appropriations made by Law; and a regular Statement and Account of the Receipts and Expenditures of all public Money shall be published from time to time.

No Title of Nobility shall be granted by the United States: And no Person holding any Office of Profit or trust under them, shall, without the Consent of the Congress, accept of any present, Emolument, Office, or Title, of any kind whatever, from any King, Prince, or foreign State.

Section 10. No State shall enter into any Treaty, Alliance, or Confederation; grant Letters of Marque and Reprisal; coin Money; emit Bills of Credit; make any Thing but gold and silver Coin a Tender in Payment of Debts; pass any Bill of Attainder, ex post facto Law, or Law impairing the Obligation of Contracts, or grant any Title of Nobility.

No State shall, without the Consent of the Congress, lay any Imposts or Duties on Imports or Exports, except what may be absolutely necessary for executing its inspection Laws: and the net Produce of all Duties and Imposts, laid by any State on Imports or Exports, shall be for the Use of the Treasury of the United States; and all such Laws shall be subject to the Revision and Controul of the Congress.

No State shall, without the Consent of Congress, lay any Duty of Tonnage, keep Troops, or Ships of War in time of Peace, enter into any Agreement or Compact with another State, or with a foreign Power, or engage in War, unless actually invaded, or in such imminent Danger as will not admit of delay.

Article. II.

Section. 1. The executive Power shall be vested in a President of the United States of America. He shall hold his Office during the term of four Years, and, together with the Vice President, chosen for the same Term, be elected, as follows:

Each State shall appoint, in such Manner as the Legislature thereof may direct, a Number of Electors, equal to the whole Number of Senators and Representatives to which the State may be entitled in the Congress: but no Senator or Representative, or Person holding an Office of Trust or Profit under the United States, shall be appointed an Elector.

The Electors shall meet in their respective States, and vote by Ballot for two Persons, of whom one at least shall not be an Inhabitant of the same State with themselves. And they shall make a List of all the Persons voted for, and of the Number of Votes for each; which List they shall sign and certify, and transmit sealed to the Seat of the Government of the United States, directed to the President of the Senate. The President of the Senate shall, in the Presence of the Senate and House of Representatives, open all the Certificates, and the Votes shall then be counted. The Person having the greatest Number of Votes shall be the President, if such Number be a Majority of the whole Number of Electors appointed; and if there be more than one who have such Majority, and have an equal Number of Votes, then the House of Representatives shall immediately chuse by Ballot one of them for President; and if no Person have a Majority, then from the five highest on the List the said House shall in like Manner chuse the President. But in chusing the President, the Votes shall be taken by States, the Representation from each State having one Vote; A quorum for this Purpose shall consist of a Member or Members from two thirds of the States, and a Majority of all the States shall be necessary to a Choice. In every Case, after the Choice of the President, the Person having the greatest Number of Votes of the Electors shall be the Vice President. But if there should remain two or more who have equal Votes, the Senate shall chuse from them by Ballot the Vice President.

The Congress may determine the Time of chusing the Electors, and the Day on which they shall give their Votes; which Day shall be the same throughout the United States.

No Person except a natural born Citizen, or a Citizen of the United States, at the time of the Adoption of this Constitution, shall be eligible to the Office of President; neither shall any Person be eligible to that Office who shall not have attained to the Age of thirty five Years, and been fourteen Years a Resident within the United States.

In Case of the Removal of the President from Office, or of his Death, Resignation, or Inability to discharge the Powers and Duties of the said Office, the Same shall devolve on the Vice President, and the Congress may by Law provide for the Case of Removal, Death, Resignation or Inability, both of the President and Vice President, declaring what Officer shall then act as President, and such Officer shall act accordingly, until the Disability be removed, or a President shall be elected.

The President shall, at stated Times, receive for his Services, a Compensation, which shall neither be encreased or diminished during the Period for which he shall have been elected, and he shall not receive within that Period any other Emolument from the United States, or any of them.

Before he enters on the Execution of his Office, he shall take the following Oath or Affirmation:—"I do solemnly swear (or affirm) that I will faithfully execute the Office of President of the United States, and will to the best of my Ability, preserve, protect and defend the Constitution of the United States."

Section. 2. The President shall be Commander in Chief of the Army and Navy of the United States, and of the Militia of the several States, when called into the actual Service of the United States; he may require the Opinion, in writing, of the principal Officer in each of the executive Departments, upon any Subject relating to the Duties of their respective Offices, and he shall have Power to grant Reprieves and Pardons for Offences against the United States, except in Cases of Impeachment.

He shall have Power, by and with the Advice and Consent of the Senate, to make Treaties, provided two thirds of the Senators present concur; and he shall nominate, and by and with the Advice and Consent of the Senate, shall appoint Ambassadors, other public Ministers and Consuls, Judges of the supreme Court, and all other Officers of the United States, whose Appointments are not herein otherwise provided for, and which shall be established by Law; but the Congress may by Law vest the Appointment of such inferior Officers, as they think proper, in the President alone, in the Courts of Law, or in the Heads of Departments.

The President shall have Power to fill up all Vacancies that may happen during the Recess of the Senate, by granting Commissions which shall expire at the End of their next Session.

Section. 3. He shall from time to time give to the Congress Information of the State of the Union, and recommend to their Consideration such Measures as he shall judge necessary and expedient; he may, on extraordinary Occasions, convene both Houses, or either of them, and in Case of Disagreement between them, with Respect to the Time of Adjournment, he may adjourn them to such Time as he shall think proper; he shall receive Ambassadors and other public Ministers; he shall take Care that the Laws be faithfully executed, and shall Commission all the Officers of the United States.

Section. 4. The President, Vice President and all civil Officers of the United States, shall be removed from Office on Impeachment for, and Conviction of, Treason, Bribery, or other high Crimes and Misdemeanors.

Article. III.

Section. 1. The judicial Power of the United States, shall be vested in one supreme Court, and in such inferior Courts as the Congress may from time to time ordain and establish. The Judges, both of the supreme and inferior Courts, shall hold their Offices during good Behavior, and shall, at stated Times, receive for their Services, a Compensation, which shall not be diminished during their Continuance in Office.

Section. 2. The judicial Power shall extend to all Cases, in Law and Equity, arising under this Constitution, the Laws of the United States, and Treaties made, or which shall be made, under their Authority;—to all Cases affecting Ambassadors, other public Ministers and Consuls;—to all Cases of admiralty and maritime Jurisdiction;—the Controversies to which the United States shall be a Party;—to Controversies between two or more States;—between a State and Citizens of another State;—between Citizens of different States;—between Citizens of the same State claiming Lands under Grants of different States, and between a State, or the Citizens thereof, and foreign States, Citizens or Subjects.

In all cases affecting Ambassadors, other public Ministers and Consuls, and those in which a State shall be Party, the supreme Court shall have original Jurisdiction. In all the other Cases before mentioned, the supreme Court shall have appellate Jurisdiction, both as to Law and Fact, with such Exceptions, and under such Regulations as the Congress shall make.

The Trial of all Crimes, except in Cases of Impeachment, shall be by Jury; and such Trial shall be held in the State where the said Crimes shall have been committed; but when not committed within any State, the Trial shall be at such Place or Places as the Congress may by Law have directed.

Section. 3. Treason against the United States, shall consist only in levying War against them, or in adhering to their Enemies, giving them Aid and Comfort. No Person shall be convicted of Treason unless on the Testimony of two Witnesses to the same overt Act, or on Confession in open Court.

The Congress shall have Power to declare the Punishment of Treason, but no Attainder of Treason shall work Corruption of Blood, or Forfeiture except during the Life of the Person attainted.

ARTICLE. IV.

Section. 1. Full Faith and Credit shall be given in each State to the public Acts, Records, and judicial Proceedings of every other State. And the Congress may by general Laws prescribe the Manner in which such Acts, Records and Proceedings shall be proved, and the Effect thereof.

Section. 2. The Citizens of each State shall be entitled to all Privileges and Immunities of Citizens in the several States.

A Person charged in any State with Treason, Felony, or other Crime, who shall flee from Justice, and be found in another State, shall on Demand of the executive Authority of the State from which he fled, be delivered up, to be removed to the State having Jurisdiction of the Crime.

No Person held to Service or Labour in one State, under the Laws thereof, escaping into another, shall, in Consequence of any Law or Regulation therein, be discharged from such Service or Labour, but shall be delivered up on Claim of the Party to whom such Service or Labour may be due.

Section. 3. New States may be admitted by the Congress into this Union; but no new State shall be formed or erected within the Jurisdiction of any other State; nor any State be formed by the Junction of two or more States, or Parts of States, without the consent of the Legislatures of the States concerned as well as of the Congress.

The Congress shall have Power to dispose of and make all needful Rules and Regulations respecting the Territory or other Property belonging to the United States; and nothing in this Constitution shall be so construed as to Prejudice any Claims of the United States, or of any particular States.

Section. 4. The United States shall guarantee to every State in this Union a Republican Form of Government, and shall protect each of them against Invasion; and on Application of the Legislature, or of the Executive (when the Legislature cannot be convened) against domestic Violence.

ARTICLE. V.

The Congress, whenever two thirds of both Houses shall deem it necessary, shall propose Amendments to this Constitution, or, on the Application of the Legislatures of two thirds of the several States, shall call a Convention for proposing Amendments, which, in either Case, shall be valid to all Intents and Purposes, as Part of this Constitution, when ratified by the Legislatures of three fourths of the several States, or by Conventions in three fourths thereof, as the one or the other Mode of Ratification may be proposed by the Congress; Provided that no Amendment which may be made prior to the Year One thousand eight hundred and eight shall in any Manner affect the first and fourth Clauses in the Ninth Section of the first Article; and that no State, without its Consent, shall be deprived of its equal Suffrage in the Senate.

ARTICLE. VI.

All Debts contracted and Engagements entered into, before the Adoption of this Constitution, shall be as valid against the United States under this Constitution, as under the Confederation.

This Constitution, and the Laws of the United States which shall be made in Pursuance thereof; and all Treaties made, or which shall be made, under the Authority of the United States, shall be the supreme Law of the Land; and the Judges in every State shall be bound thereby, any Thing in the Constitution or Laws of any State to the Contrary notwithstanding.

The Senators and Representatives before mentioned, and the Members of the several State Legislatures, and all executive and judicial Officers, both of the United States and of the several States, shall be bound by Oath or Affirmation, to support this Constitution; but no religious Test shall ever be required as a Qualification to any Office or public Trust under the United States.

ARTICLE. VII.

The Ratification of the Conventions of nine States, shall be sufficient for the Establishment of this Constitution between the States so ratifying the Same.

Done in Convention by the Unanimous Consent of the States present the Seventeenth Day of September in the Year of our Lord one thousand seven hundred and Eighty seven and of the Independence of the United States of America the Twelfth. In witness thereof We have hereunto subscribed our Names,

G^{o}. WASHINGTON—Presd^{t}.
and deputy from Virginia.

New Hampshire	John Langdon Nicholas Gilman
Massachusetts	Nathaniel Gorham Rufus King
Connecticut	Wm Saml Johnson Roger Sherman
New York: . . .	Alexander Hamilton
New Jersey	Wil: Livingston David A. Brearley. Wm Paterson. Jona: Dayton
Pennsylvania	B Franklin Thomas Mifflin Robt Morris Geo. Clymer Thos FitzSimons Jared Ingersoll James Wilson Gouv Morris
Delaware	Geo: Read Gunning Bedford jun John Dickinson Richard Bassett Jaco: Broom
Maryland	James McHenry Dan of St Thos Jenifer Danl Carroll
Virginia	John Blair— James Madison Jr.
North Carolina	Wm Blount Richd Dobbs Spaight. Hu Williamson
South Carolina	J. Rutledge Charles Cotesworth Pinckney Charles Pinckney Pierce Butler.
Georgia	William Few Abr Baldwin

AMENDMENTS TO THE CONSTITUTION

ARTICLES IN ADDITION TO, and Amendment of the Constitution of the United States of America, proposed by Congress, and ratified by the Legislatures of the several States, pursuant to the fifth Article of the original Constitution.

AMENDMENT I.

Congress shall make no law respecting an establishment of religion, or prohibiting the free exercise thereof; or abridging the freedom of speech, or of the press; or the right of the people peaceably to assemble, and to petition the Government for a redress of grievances.

AMENDMENT II.

A well regulated Militia, being necessary to the security of a free State, the right of the people to keep and bear Arms, shall not be infringed.

AMENDMENT III.

No Soldier shall, in time of peace be quartered in any house, without the consent of the Owner, nor in time of war, but in a manner to be prescribed by law.

AMENDMENT IV.

The right of the people to be secure in their persons, houses, papers, and effects, against unreasonable searches and seizures, shall not be violated, and no Warrants shall issue, but upon probable cause, supported by Oath or affirmation, and particularly describing the place to be searched, and the persons or things to be seized.

AMENDMENT V.

No person shall be held to answer for a capital, or otherwise infamous crime, unless on a presentment or indictment of a Grand Jury, except in cases arising in the land or naval forces, or in the Militia, when in actual service in time of War or public danger; nor shall any person be subject for the same offence to be twice put in jeopardy of life or limb; nor shall be compelled in any criminal case to be a witness against himself, nor be deprived of life, liberty, or property, without due process of law; nor shall private property be taken for public use, without just compensation.

AMENDMENT VI.

In all criminal prosecutions, the accused shall enjoy the right to a speedy and public trial, by an impartial jury of the State and district wherein the crime shall have been committed, which district shall have been previously ascertained by law, and to be informed of the nature and cause of the accusation; to be confronted with the witnesses against him; to have compulsory process for obtaining witnesses in his favor, and to have the Assistance of Counsel for his defence.

AMENDMENT VII.

In Suits at common law, where the value in controversy shall exceed twenty dollars, the right of trial by jury shall be preserved, and no fact tried by a jury, shall be otherwise re-examined in any Court of the United States, than according to the rules of the common law.

AMENDMENT VIII.

Excessive bail shall not be required, nor excessive fines imposed, nor cruel and unusual punishments inflicted.

AMENDMENT IX.

The enumeration in the Constitution, of certain rights, shall not be construed to deny or disparage others retained by the people.

AMENDMENT X.

The powers not delegated to the United States by the Constitution, nor prohibited by it to the States, are reserved to the States respectively, or to the people. [The first ten amendments went into effect December 15, 1791.]

AMENDMENT XI.

The Judicial power of the United States shall not be construed to extend to any suit in law or equity, commenced or prosecuted against one of the United States by Citizens of another State, or by Citizens or Subjects of any Foreign State. [January 8, 1798.]

AMENDMENT XII.

The Electors shall meet in their respective states, and vote by ballot for President and Vice-President, one of whom, at least, shall not be an inhabitant of the same state with themselves; they shall name in their ballots the person voted for as President, and in distinct ballots the person voted for as Vice-President, and they shall make distinct lists of all persons voted for as President, and of all persons voted for as Vice President, and of the number of votes for each, which lists they shall sign and certify, and transmit sealed to the seat of the government of the United States, directed to the President of the Senate;—The President of the Senate shall, in the presence of the Senate and House of Representatives, open all the certificates and the votes shall then be counted;—The person having the greatest number of votes for President, shall be the President, if such number be a majority of the whole number of Electors appointed; and if no person have such majority, then from the persons having the highest numbers not exceeding three on the list of those voted for as President, the House of Representatives shall choose immediately, by ballot, the President. But in choosing the President, the votes shall be taken by states, the representation from each state having one vote; a quorum for this purpose shall consist of a member or members from two-thirds of the states, and a majority of all the states shall be necessary to a choice. And if the House of Representatives shall not choose a President whenever the right of choice shall devolve upon them, before the fourth day of March next following, then the Vice-President shall act as President, as in the case of the death or other constitutional disability of the President.—The person having the greatest number of votes as Vice-President, shall be the Vice-President, if such number be a majority of the whole number of Electors appointed, and if no person have a majority, then from the two highest numbers on the list, the Senate shall choose the Vice-President; a quorum for the purpose shall consist of two-thirds of the whole number of Senators, and a majority of the whole number shall be necessary to a choice. But no person constitutionally ineligible to the office of President shall be eligible to that of Vice-President of the United States. [September 25, 1804.]

AMENDMENT XIII.

Section 1. Neither slavery nor involuntary servitude, except as a punishment for crime whereof the party shall have been duly convicted, shall exist within the United States, or any place subject to their jurisdiction.

Section 2. Congress shall have power to enforce this article by appropriate legislation. [December 18, 1865.]

AMENDMENT XIV.

Section 1. All persons born or naturalized in the United States, and subject to the jurisdiction thereof, are citizens of the United States and of the State wherein they reside. No State shall make or enforce any law which shall abridge the privileges or immunities of citizens of the United States; nor shall any State deprive any person of life, liberty, or property, without due process of law; nor deny to any person within its jurisdiction the equal protection of the laws.

Section 2. Representatives shall be apportioned among the several States according to their respective numbers, counting the whole number of persons in each State, excluding Indians not taxed. But when the right to vote at any election for the choice of electors for President and Vice President of the United States, Representatives in Congress, the Executive and Judicial officers of a State, or the members of the Legislature thereof, is denied to any of the male inhabitants of such State, being twenty-one years of age, and citizens of the United States, or in any way abridged, except for participation in rebellion, or other crime, the basis of representation therein shall be reduced in the proportion which the number of such male citizens shall bear to the whole number of male citizens twenty-one years of age in such State.

Section 3. No person shall be a Senator or Representative in Congress, or elector of President and Vice President, or hold any office, civil or military, under the United States, or under any State, who, having previously taken an oath, as a member of Congress, or as an officer of the United States, or as a member of any State legislature, or as an executive or judicial officer of any State, to support the Constitution of the United States, shall have engaged in insurrection or rebellion against the same, or given aid or comfort to the enemies thereof. But Congress may by a vote of two-thirds of each House, remove such disability.

Section 4. The validity of the public debt of the United States, authorized by law, including debts incurred for payment of pensions and bounties for services in suppressing insurrection or rebellion, shall not be questioned. But neither the United States nor any State shall assume or pay any debt or obligation incurred in aid of insurrection or rebellion against the United States, or any claim for the loss or emancipation of any slave; but all such debts, obligations and claims shall be held illegal and void.

Section 5. The Congress shall have power to enforce, by appropriate legislation, the provisions of this article. [July 28, 1868.]

Amendment XV.

Section 1. The right of citizens of the United States to vote shall not be denied or abridged by the United States or by any State on account of race, color, or previous condition of servitude—

Section 2. The Congress shall have power to enforce this article by appropriate legislation.—[March 30, 1870.]

Amendment XVI.

The Congress shall have power to lay and collect taxes on incomes, from whatever source derived, without apportionment among the several States, and without regard to any census or enumeration. [February 25, 1913.]

Amendment XVII.

The Senate of the United States shall be composed of two senators from each State, elected by the people thereof, for six years; and each Senator shall have one vote. The electors in each State shall have the qualifications requisite for electors of the most numerous branch of the State legislature.

When vacancies happen in the representation of any State in the Senate, the executive authority of such State shall issue writs of election to fill such vacancies: *Provided,* That the legislature of any State may empower the executive thereof to make temporary appointments until the people fill the vacancies by election as the legislature may direct.

This amendment shall not be so construed as to affect the election or term of any senator chosen before it becomes valid as part of the Constitution. [May 31, 1913.]

Amendment XVIII.

After one year from the ratification of this article, the manufacture, sale, or transportation of intoxicating liquors within, the importation thereof into, or the exportation thereof from the United States and all territory subject to the jurisdiction thereof for beverage purposes is hereby prohibited.

The Congress and the several States shall have concurrent power to enforce this article by appropriate legislation.

This article shall be inoperative unless it shall have been ratified as an amendment to the Constitution by the legislatures of the several States, as provided in the Constitution, within seven years from the date of the submission thereof to the States by Congress. [January 29, 1919.]

Amendment XIX.

The right of citizens of the United States to vote shall not be denied or abridged by the United States or by any State on account of sex.

The Congress shall have power by appropriate legislation to enforce the provisions of this article. [August 26, 1920.]

AMENDMENT XX.

Section 1. The terms of the President and Vice-President shall end at noon on the twentieth day of January, and the terms of Senators and Representatives at noon on the third day of January, of the years in which such terms would have ended if this article had not been ratified; and the terms of their successors shall then begin.

Section 2. The Congress shall assemble at least once in every year, and such meeting shall begin at noon on the third day of January, unless they shall by law appoint a different day.

Section 3. If, at the time fixed for the beginning of the term of the President, the President-elect shall have died, the Vice-President-elect shall become President. If a President shall not have been chosen before the time fixed for the beginning of his term, or if the President-elect shall have failed to qualify, then the Vice-President-elect shall act as President until a President shall have qualified; and the Congress may by law provide for the case wherein neither a President-elect nor a Vice-President-elect shall have qualified, declaring who shall then act as President, or the manner in which one who is to act shall be selected, and such person shall act accordingly until a President or Vice-President shall have qualified.

Section 4. The Congress may by law provide for the case of the death of any of the persons from whom the House of Representatives may choose a President whenever the right of choice shall have devolved upon them, and for the case of the death of any of the persons from whom the Senate may choose a Vice-President whenever the right of choice shall have devolved upon them.

Section 5. Sections 1 and 2 shall take effect on the 15th day of October following the ratification of this article.

Section 6. This article shall be inoperative unless it shall have been ratified as an amendment to the Constitution by the legislatures of three-fourths of the several States within seven years from the date of its submission. [February 6, 1933.]

AMENDMENT XXI.

Section 1. The eighteenth article of amendment to the Constitution of the United States is hereby repealed.

Section 2. The transportation or importation into any State, Territory or possession of the United States for delivery or use therein of intoxicating liquors, in violation of the laws thereof, is hereby prohibited.

Section 3. This article shall be inoperative unless it shall have been ratified as an amendment to the Constitution by convention in the several States, as provided in the Constitution, within seven years from the date of the submission thereof to the States by the Congress. [December 5, 1933.]

AMENDMENT XXII.

Section 1. No person shall be elected to the office of the President more than twice, and no person who has held the office of President, or acted as President, for more than two years of a term to which some other person was elected President shall be elected to the office of the President more than once. But this Article shall not apply to any person holding the office of President when this Article was proposed by the Congress, and shall not prevent any person who may be holding the office of President, or acting as President, during the term within which this Article becomes operative from holding the office of President or acting as President during the remainder of such term.

Section 2. This article shall be inoperative unless it shall have been ratified as an amendment to the Constitution by the legislatures of three-fourths of the several states within seven years from the date of its submission to the States by the Congress. [February 27, 1951.]

AMENDMENT XXIII.

Section 1. The District constituting the seat of government of the United States shall appoint in such manner as the Congress may direct:

A number of electors of President and Vice-President equal to the whole number of Senators and Representatives in Congress to which the District would be entitled if it were a State, but in no event more than the least populous State; they shall be in addition to those appointed by the States, but they shall be considered, for the purposes of the election of President and Vice-President, to be electors appointed by a State; and they shall meet in the District and perform such duties as provided by the twelfth article of amendment.

Section 2. The Congress shall have the power to enforce this article by appropriate legislation. [March 29, 1961.]

AMENDMENT XXIV.

Section 1. The right of citizens of the United States to vote in any primary or other election for President or Vice President, for electors for President or Vice President, or for Senator or Representative in Congress, shall not be denied or abridged by the United States or any State by reason of failure to pay any poll tax or other tax.

Section 2. The Congress shall have power to enforce this article by appropriate legislation. [January 23, 1964.]

AMENDMENT XXV.

Section 1. In case of the removal of the President from office or of his death or resignation, the Vice President shall become President.

Section 2. Whenever there is a vacancy in the office of Vice President, the President shall nominate a Vice President who shall take office upon confirmation by a majority vote of both Houses of Congress.

Section 3. Whenever the President transmits to the President pro tempore of the Senate and the Speaker of the House of Representatives his written declaration that he is unable to discharge the powers and duties of his office, and until he transmits to them a written declaration to the contrary, such powers and duties shall be discharged by the Vice President as Acting President.

Section 4. Whenever the Vice President and a majority of either the principal officers of the executive departments or of such other body as Congress may by law provide, transmit to the President pro tempore of the Senate and the Speaker of the House of Representatives their written declaration that the President is unable to discharge the powers and duties of his office, the Vice President shall immediately assume the powers and duties of the office as Acting President.

Thereafter, when the President transmits to the President pro tempore of the Senate and the Speaker of the House of Representatives his written declaration that no inability exists, he shall resume the powers and duties of his office unless the Vice President and a majority of either the principal officers of the executive departments or of such other body as Congress may by law provide, transmit within four days to the President pro tempore of the Senate and the Speaker of the House of Representatives their written declaration that the President is unable to discharge the powers and duties of his office. Thereupon Congress shall decide the issue, assembling within forty-eight hours for that purpose if not in session. If the Congress, within twenty-one days after receipt of the latter written declaration, or, if Congress is not in session, within twenty-one days after Congress is required to assemble, determines by two-thirds vote of both Houses that the President is unable to discharge the powers and duties of his office, the Vice President shall continue to discharge the same as Acting President; otherwise, the President shall resume the powers and duties of his office. [February 10, 1967.]

AMENDMENT XXVI.

Section 1. The right of citizens of the United States, who are eighteen years of age or older, to vote shall not be denied or abridged by the United States or by any State on account of age.

Section 2. The Congress shall have power to enforce this article by appropriate legislation. [June 30, 1971.]

AMENDMENT XXVII.

No law, varying the compensation for the services of the Senators and Representatives shall take effect, until an election of Representatives shall have intervened. [May 8, 1992.]

Presidential Elections

Year	Number of States	Candidates	Parties	Popular Vote	% of Popular Vote	Electoral Vote	% Voter Partici-pation
1789	11	**GEORGE WASHINGTON**	No party designations			69	
		John Adams				34	
		Other candidates				35	
1792	15	**GEORGE WASHINGTON**	No party designations			132	
		John Adams				77	
		George Clinton				50	
		Other candidates				5	
1796	16	**JOHN ADAMS**	Federalist			71	
		Thomas Jefferson	Democratic-Republican			68	
		Thomas Pinckney	Federalist			59	
		Aaron Burr	Democratic-Republican			30	
		Other candidates				48	
1800	16	**THOMAS JEFFERSON**	Democratic-Republican			73	
		Aaron Burr	Democratic-Republican			73	
		John Adams	Federalist			65	
		Charles C. Pinckney	Federalist			64	
		John Jay	Federalist			1	
1804	17	**THOMAS JEFFERSON**	Democratic-Republican			162	
		Charles C. Pinckney	Federalist			14	
1808	17	**JAMES MADISON**	Democratic-Republican			122	
		Charles C. Pinckney	Federalist			47	
		George Clinton	Democratic-Republican			6	
1812	18	**JAMES MADISON**	Democratic-Republican			128	
		DeWitt Clinton	Federalist			89	
1816	19	**JAMES MONROE**	Democratic-Republican			183	
		Rufus King	Federalist			34	
1820	24	**JAMES MONROE**	Democratic-Republican			231	
		John Quincy Adams	Independent			1	
1824	24	**JOHN QUINCY ADAMS**	Democratic-Republican	108,740	30.5	84	26.9
		Andrew Jackson	Democratic-Republican	153,544	43.1	99	
		Henry Clay	Democratic-Republican	47,136	13.2	37	
		William H. Crawford	Democratic-Republican	46,618	13.1	41	
1828	24	**ANDREW JACKSON**	Democratic	647,286	56.0	178	57.6
		John Quincy Adams	National-Republican	508,064	44.0	83	

Year	Number of States	Candidates	Parties	Popular Vote	% of Popular Vote	Electoral Vote	% Voter Partici-pation
1832	24	**ANDREW JACKSON**	Democratic	688,242	54.5	219	55.4
		Henry Clay	National-Republican	473,462	37.5	49	
		William Wirt	Anti-Masonic	101,051	8.0	7	
		John Floyd	Democratic			11	
1836	26	**MARTIN VAN BUREN**	Democratic	765,483	50.9	170	57.8
		William H. Harrison	Whig	739,795	49.1	73	
		Hugh L. White	Whig			26	
		Daniel Webster	Whig			14	
		W. P. Mangum	Whig			11	
1840	26	**WILLIAM H. HARRISON**	Whig	1,274,624	53.1	234	80.2
		Martin Van Buren	Democratic	1,127,781	46.9	60	
1844	26	**JAMES K. POLK**	Democratic	1,338,464	49.6	170	78.9
		Henry Clay	Whig	1,300,097	48.1	105	
		James G. Birney	Liberty	62,300	2.3		
1848	30	**ZACHARY TAYLOR**	Whig	1,360,967	47.4	163	72.7
		Lewis Cass	Democratic	1,222,342	42.5	127	
		Martin Van Buren	Free Soil	291,263	10.1		
1852	31	**FRANKLIN PIERCE**	Democratic	1,601,117	50.9	254	69.6
		Winfield Scott	Whig	1,385,453	44.1	42	
		John P. Hale	Free Soil	155,825	5.0		
1856	31	**JAMES BUCHANAN**	Democratic	1,832,955	45.3	174	78.9
		John C. Frémont	Republican	1,339,932	33.1	114	
		Millard Fillmore	American	871,731	21.6	8	
1860	33	**ABRAHAM LINCOLN**	Republican	1,865,593	39.8	180	81.2
		Stephen A. Douglas	Democratic	1,382,713	29.5	12	
		John C. Breckinridge	Democratic	848,356	18.1	72	
		John Bell	Constitutional Union	592,906	12.6	39	
1864	36	**ABRAHAM LINCOLN**	Republican	2,206,938	55.0	212	73.8
		George B. McClellan	Democratic	1,803,787	45.0	21	
1868	37	**ULYSSES S. GRANT**	Republican	3,013,421	52.7	214	78.1
		Horatio Seymour	Democratic	2,706,829	47.3	80	
1872	37	**ULYSSES S. GRANT**	Republican	3,596,745	55.6	286	71.3
		Horace Greeley	Democratic	2,843,446	43.9	66	
1876	38	**RUTHERFORD B. HAYES**	Republican	4,036,572	48.0	185	81.8
		Samuel J. Tilden	Democratic	4,284,020	51.0	184	
1880	38	**JAMES A. GARFIELD**	Republican	4,453,295	48.5	214	79.4
		Winfield S. Hancock	Democratic	4,414,082	48.1	155	
		James B. Weaver	Greenback-Labor	308,578	3.4		
1884	38	**GROVER CLEVELAND**	Democratic	4,879,507	48.5	219	77.5
		James G. Blaine	Republican	4,850,293	48.2	182	
		Benjamin F. Butler	Greenback-Labor	175,370	1.8		
		John P. St. John	Prohibition	150,369	1.5		

Year	Number of States	Candidates	Parties	Popular Vote	% of Popular Vote	Electoral Vote	% Voter Partici-pation
1888	38	**BENJAMIN HARRISON**	Republican	5,477,129	47.9	233	79.3
		Grover Cleveland	Democratic	5,537,857	48.6	168	
		Clinton B. Fisk	Prohibition	249,506	2.2		
		Anson J. Streeter	Union Labor	146,935	1.3		
1892	44	**GROVER CLEVELAND**	Democratic	5,555,426	46.1	277	74.7
		Benjamin Harrison	Republican	5,182,690	43.0	145	
		James B. Weaver	People's	1,029,846	8.5	22	
		John Bidwell	Prohibition	264,133	2.2		
1896	45	**WILLIAM McKINLEY**	Republican	7,102,246	51.1	271	79.3
		William J. Bryan	Democratic	6,492,559	47.7	176	
1900	45	**WILLIAM McKINLEY**	Republican	7,218,491	51.7	292	73.2
		William J. Bryan	Democratic; Populist	6,356,734	45.5	155	
		John C. Wooley	Prohibition	208,914	1.5		
1904	45	**THEODORE ROOSEVELT**	Republican	7,628,461	57.4	336	65.2
		Alton B. Parker	Democratic	5,084,223	37.6	140	
		Eugene V. Debs	Socialist	402,283	3.0		
		Silas C. Swallow	Prohibition	258,536	1.9		
1908	46	**WILLIAM H. TAFT**	Republican	7,675,320	51.6	321	65.4
		William J. Bryan	Democratic	6,412,294	43.1	162	
		Eugene V. Debs	Socialist	420,793	2.8		
		Eugene W. Chafin	Prohibition	253,840	1.7		
1912	48	**WOODROW WILSON**	Democratic	6,296,547	41.9	435	58.8
		Theodore Roosevelt	Progressive	4,118,571	27.4	88	
		William H. Taft	Republican	3,486,720	23.2	8	
		Eugene V. Debs	Socialist	900,672	6.0		
		Eugene W. Chafin	Prohibition	206,275	1.4		
1916	48	**WOODROW WILSON**	Democratic	9,127,695	49.4	277	61.6
		Charles E. Hughes	Republican	8,533,507	46.2	254	
		A. L. Benson	Socialist	585,113	3.2		
		J. Frank Hanly	Prohibition	220,506	1.2		
1920	48	**WARREN G. HARDING**	Republican	16,143,407	60.4	404	49.2
		James M. Cox	Democratic	9,130,328	34.2	127	
		Eugene V. Debs	Socialist	919,799	3.4		
		P. P. Christensen	Farmer-Labor	265,411	1.0		
1924	48	**CALVIN COOLIDGE**	Republican	15,718,211	54.0	382	48.9
		John W. Davis	Democratic	8,385,283	28.8	136	
		Robert M. La Follette	Progressive	4,831,289	16.6	13	
1928	48	**HERBERT C. HOOVER**	Republican	21,391,993	58.2	444	56.9
		Alfred E. Smith	Democratic	15,016,169	40.9	87	
1932	48	**FRANKLIN D. ROOSEVELT**	Democratic	22,809,638	57.4	472	56.9
		Herbert C. Hoover	Republican	15,758,901	39.7	59	
		Norman Thomas	Socialist	881,951	2.2		
1936	48	**FRANKLIN D. ROOSEVELT**	Democratic	27,752,869	60.8	523	61.0
		Alfred M. Landon	Republican	16,674,665	36.5	8	
		William Lemke	Union	882,479	1.9		

Year	Number of States	Candidates	Parties	Popular Vote	% of Popular Vote	Electoral Vote	% Voter Partici-pation
1940	48	**FRANKLIN D. ROOSEVELT**	Democratic	27,307,819	54.8	449	62.5
		Wendell L. Willkie	Republican	22,321,018	44.8	82	
1944	48	**FRANKLIN D. ROOSEVELT**	Democratic	25,606,585	53.5	432	55.9
		Thomas E. Dewey	Republican	22,014,745	46.0	99	
1948	48	**HARRY S. TRUMAN**	Democratic	24,179,345	49.6	303	53.0
		Thomas E. Dewey	Republican	21,991,291	45.1	189	
		J. Strom Thurmond	States' Rights	1,176,125	2.4	39	
		Henry A. Wallace	Progressive	1,157,326	2.4		
1952	48	**DWIGHT D. EISENHOWER**	Republican	33,936,234	55.1	442	63.3
		Adlai E. Stevenson	Democratic	27,314,992	44.4	89	
1956	48	**DWIGHT D. EISENHOWER**	Republican	35,590,472	57.6	457	60.6
		Adlai E. Stevenson	Democratic	26,022,752	42.1	73	
1960	50	**JOHN F. KENNEDY**	Democratic	34,226,731	49.7	303	62.8
		Richard M. Nixon	Republican	34,108,157	49.5	219	
1964	50	**LYNDON B. JOHNSON**	Democratic	43,129,566	61.1	486	61.9
		Barry M. Goldwater	Republican	27,178,188	38.5	52	
1968	50	**RICHARD M. NIXON**	Republican	31,785,480	43.4	301	60.9
		Hubert H. Humphrey	Democratic	31,275,166	42.7	191	
		George C. Wallace	American Independent	9,906,473	13.5	46	
1972	50	**RICHARD M. NIXON**	Republican	47,169,911	60.7	520	55.2
		George S. McGovern	Democratic	29,170,383	37.5	17	
		John G. Schmitz	American	1,099,482	1.4		
1976	50	**JIMMY CARTER**	Democratic	40,830,763	50.1	297	53.5
		Gerald R. Ford	Republican	39,147,793	48.0	240	
1980	50	**RONALD REAGAN**	Republican	43,901,812	50.7	489	52.6
		Jimmy Carter	Democratic	35,483,820	41.0	49	
		John B. Anderson	Independent	5,719,437	6.6		
		Ed Clark	Libertarian	921,188	1.1		
1984	50	**RONALD REAGAN**	Republican	54,451,521	58.8	525	53.1
		Walter F. Mondale	Democratic	37,565,334	40.6	13	
1988	50	**GEORGE H. BUSH**	Republican	47,917,341	53.4	426	50.1
		Michael Dukakis	Democratic	41,013,030	45.6	111	
1992	50	**BILL CLINTON**	Democratic	44,908,254	43.0	370	55.0
		George H. Bush	Republican	39,102,343	37.4	168	
		H. Ross Perot	Independent	19,741,065	18.9	0	
1996	50	**BILL CLINTON**	Democratic	47,401,185	49.0	379	49.0
		Bob Dole	Republican	39,197,469	41.0	159	
		H. Ross Perot	Independent	8,085,295	8.0	0	

Candidates receiving less than 1 percent of the popular vote have been omitted. Thus the percentage of popular vote given for any election year may not total 100 percent.
Before the passage of the Twelfth Amendment in 1804, the Electoral College voted for two presidential candidates; the runner-up became vice-president.

Admission Of States

Order of Admission	State	Date of Admission	Order of Admission	State	Date of Admission
1	Delaware	December 7, 1787	26	Michigan	January 26, 1837
2	Pennsylvania	December 12, 1787	27	Florida	March 3, 1845
3	New Jersey	December 18, 1787	28	Texas	December 29, 1845
4	Georgia	January 2, 1788	29	Iowa	December 28, 1846
5	Connecticut	January 9, 1788	30	Wisconsin	May 29, 1848
6	Massachusetts	February 7, 1788	31	California	September 9, 1850
7	Maryland	April 28, 1788	32	Minnesota	May 11, 1858
8	South Carolina	May 23, 1788	33	Oregon	February 14, 1859
9	New Hampshire	June 21, 1788	34	Kansas	January 29, 1861
10	Virginia	June 25, 1788	35	West Virginia	June 30, 1863
11	New York	July 26, 1788	36	Nevada	October 31, 1864
12	North Carolina	November 21, 1789	37	Nebraska	March 1, 1867
13	Rhode Island	May 29, 1790	38	Colorado	August 1, 1876
14	Vermont	March 4, 1791	39	North Dakota	November 2, 1889
15	Kentucky	June 1, 1792	40	South Dakota	November 2, 1889
16	Tennessee	June 1, 1796	41	Montana	November 8, 1889
17	Ohio	March 1, 1803	42	Washington	November 11, 1889
18	Louisiana	April 30, 1812	43	Idaho	July 3, 1890
19	Indiana	December 11, 1816	44	Wyoming	July 10, 1890
20	Mississippi	December 10, 1817	45	Utah	January 4, 1896
21	Illinois	December 3, 1818	46	Oklahoma	November 16, 1907
22	Alabama	December 14, 1819	47	New Mexico	January 6, 1912
23	Maine	March 15, 1820	48	Arizona	February 14, 1912
24	Missouri	August 10, 1821	49	Alaska	January 3, 1959
25	Arkansas	June 15, 1836	50	Hawaii	August 21, 1959

Population of the United States

Year	Number of States	Population	% Increase	Population per Square Mile
1790	13	3,929,214		4.5
1800	16	5,308,483	35.1	6.1
1810	17	7,239,881	36.4	4.3
1820	23	9,638,453	33.1	5.5
1830	24	12,866,020	33.5	7.4
1840	26	17,069,453	32.7	9.8
1850	31	23,191,876	35.9	7.9
1860	33	31,443,321	35.6	10.6
1870	37	39,818,449	26.6	13.4
1880	38	50,155,783	26.0	16.9
1890	44	62,947,714	25.5	21.1
1900	45	75,994,575	20.7	25.6
1910	46	91,972,266	21.0	31.0
1920	48	105,710,620	14.9	35.6
1930	48	122,775,046	16.1	41.2
1940	48	131,669,275	7.2	44.2
1950	48	150,697,361	14.5	50.7
1960	50	179,323,175	19.0	50.6
1970	50	203,235,298	13.3	57.5
1980	50	226,504,825	11.4	64.0
1985	50	237,839,000	5.0	67.2
1990	50	250,122,000	5.2	70.6
1995	50	263,411,707	5.3	74.4

Source: U.S. Census Bureau.

Immigration to the United States, fiscal years 1820–1998

Year	Number
1820–1989	**55,457,531**
1820	8,385
1821–30	143,439
1821	9,127
1822	6,911
1823	6,354
1824	7,912
1825	10,199
1826	10,837
1827	18,875
1828	27,382
1829	22,520
1830	23,322
1831–40	**599,125**
1831	22,633
1832	60,482
1833	58,640
1834	65,365
1835	45,374
1836	76,242
1837	79,340
1838	38,914
1839	68,069
1840	84,066
1841–50	**1,713,251**
1841	80,289
1842	104,565
1843	52,496
1844	78,615
1845	114,371
1846	154,416
1847	234,968
1848	226,527
1849	297,024
1850	369,980
1851–60	**2,598,214**
1851	379,466
1852	371,603
1853	368,645
1854	427,833
1855	200,877
1856	200,436
1857	251,306
1858	123,126
1859	121,282
1860	153,640
1861–70	**2,314,824**
1861	91,918
1862	91,985
1863	176,282
1864	193,418
1865	248,120
1866	318,568
1867	315,722
1868	138,840
1869	352,768
1870	387,203
1871–80	**2,812,191**
1871	321,350
1872	404,806
1873	459,803
1874	313,339
1875	227,498
1876	169,986
1877	141,857
1878	138,469
1879	177,826
1880	457,257
1881–90	**5,246,613**
1881	669,431
1882	788,992
1883	603,322
1884	518,592
1885	395,346
1886	334,203
1887	490,109
1888	546,889
1889	444,427
1890	455,302
1891–1900	**3,687,564**
1891	560,319
1892	579,663
1893	439,730
1894	285,631
1895	258,536
1896	343,267
1897	230,832
1898	229,299
1899	311,715
1900	448,572
1901–10	**8,795,386**
1901	487,918
1902	648,743
1903	857,046
1904	812,870
1905	1,026,499
1906	1,100,735
1907	1,285,349
1908	782,870
1909	751,786
1910	1,041,570
1911–20	**5,735,811**
1911	878,587
1912	838,172
1913	1,197,892
1914	1,218,480
1915	326,700
1916	298,826
1917	295,403
1918	110,618
1919	141,132
1920	430,001
1921–30	**4,107,209**
1921	805,228
1922	309,556
1923	522,919
1924	706,896
1925	294,314
1926	304,488
1927	335,175
1928	307,255
1929	279,678
1930	241,700
1931–40	**528,431**
1931	97,139
1932	35,576
1933	23,068
1934	29,470
1935	34,956
1936	36,329
1937	50,244
1938	67,895
1939	82,998
1940	70,756
1941–50	**1,035,039**
1941	51,776
1942	28,781
1943	23,725
1944	28,551
1945	38,119
1946	108,721
1947	147,292
1948	170,570
1949	188,317
1950	249,187
1951–60	**2,515,479**
1951	205,717
1952	265,520
1953	170,434
1954	208,177
1955	237,790
1956	321,625
1957	326,867
1958	253,265
1959	260,686
1960	265,398
1961–70	**3,321,677**
1961	271,344
1962	283,763
1963	306,260
1964	292,248
1965	296,697
1966	323,040
1967	361,972
1968	454,448
1969	358,579
1970	373,326
1971–80	**4,493,314**
1971	370,478
1972	384,685
1973	400,063
1974	394,861
1975	386,914
1976	398,613
1976	103,676
1977	462,315
1978	601,442
1979	460,348
1980	530,639
1981–90	**7,338,062**
1981	596,600
1982	594,131
1983	559,763
1984	543,903
1985	570,009
1986	601,708
1987	601,516
1988	643,025
1989	1,090,924
1990	1,536,483
1991–98	**7,605,068**
1991	1,827,167
1992	973,977
1993	904,292
1994	804,416
1995	720,461
1996	915,900
1997	798,378
1998	660,477

Source: U.S. Immigration and Naturalization Service, 1999.

Immigration By Region And Selected Country Of Last Residence, Fiscal Years 1820-1998

Region and Country of Last Residence[1]	1820	1821–30	1831–40	1841–50	1851–60	1861–70	1871–80	1881–90
All countries	8,385	143,439	599,125	1,713,251	2,598,214	2,314,824	2,812,191	5,246,613
Europe	7,690	98,797	495,681	1,597,442	2,452,577	2,065,141	2,271,925	4,735,484
Austria-Hungary	—[2]	—[2]	—[2]	—[2]	—[2]	7,800	72,969	353,719
Austria	—[2]	—[2]	—[2]	—[2]	—[2]	484[3]	63,009	226,038
Hungary	—[2]	—[2]	—[2]	—[2]	—[2]	7,124[3]	9,960	127,681
Belgium	1	27	22	5,074	4,738	6,734	7,221	20,177
Czechoslovakia	—[4]	—[4]	—[4]	—[4]	—[4]	—[4]	—[4]	—[4]
Denmark	20	169	1,063	539	3,749	17,094	31,771	88,132
France	371	8,497	45,575	77,262	76,358	35,986	72,206	50,464
Germany	968	6,761	152,454	434,626	951,667	787,468	718,182	1,452,970
Greece	—	20	49	16	31	72	210	2,308
Ireland[5]	3,614	50,724	207,381	780,719	914,119	435,778	436,871	655,482
Italy	30	409	2,253	1,870	9,231	11,725	55,759	307,309
Netherlands	49	1,078	1,412	8,251	10,789	9,102	16,541	53,701
Norway-Sweden	3	91	1,201	13,903	20,931	109,298	211,245	568,362
Norway	—[6]	—[6]	—[6]	—[6]	—[6]	—[6]	95,323	176,586
Sweden	—[6]	—[6]	—[6]	—[6]	—[6]	—[6]	115,922	391,776
Poland	5	16	369	105	1,164	2,027	12,970	51,806
Portugal	35	145	829	550	1,055	2,658	14,082	16,978
Romania	—[7]	—[7]	—[7]	—[7]	—[7]	—[7]	11	6,348
Soviet Union	14	75	277	551	457	2,512	39,284	213,282
Spain	139	2,477	2,125	2,209	9,298	6,697	5,266	4,419
Switzerland	31	3,226	4,821	4,644	25,011	23,286	28,293	81,988
United Kingdom[5,8]	2,410	25,079	75,810	267,044	423,974	606,896	548,043	807,357
Yugoslavia	—[9]	—[9]	—[9]	—[9]	—[9]	—[9]	—[9]	—[9]
Other Europe	—	3	40	79	5	8	1,001	682
Asia	6	30	55	141	41,538	64,759	124,160	69,942
China[10]	1	2	8	35	41,397	64,301	123,201	61,711
Hong Kong	—[11]	—[11]	—[11]	—[11]	—[11]	—[11]	—[11]	—[11]
India	1	8	39	36	43	69	163	269
Iran	—[12]	—[12]	—[12]	—[12]	—[12]	—[12]	—[12]	—[12]
Israel	—[13]	—[13]	—[13]	—[13]	—[13]	—[13]	—[13]	—[13]
Japan	—[14]	—[14]	—[14]	—[14]	—[14]	186	149	2,270
Korea	—[15]	—[15]	—[15]	—[15]	—[15]	—[15]	—[15]	—[15]
Philippines	—[16]	—[16]	—[16]	—[16]	—[16]	—[16]	—[16]	—[16]
Turkey	1	20	7	59	83	131	404	3,782
Vietnam	—[11]	—[11]	—[11]	—[11]	—[11]	—[11]	—[11]	—[11]
Other Asia	3	—	1	11	15	72	243	1,910
America	387	11,564	33,424	62,469	74,720	166,607	404,044	426,967
Canada & Newfoundland[17,18]	209	2,277	13,624	41,723	59,309	153,878	383,640	393,304
Mexico[18]	1	4,817	6,599	3,271	3,078	2,191	5,162	191,319
Caribbean	164	3,834	12,301	13,528	10,660	9,046	13,957	29,042
Cuba	—[12]	—[12]	—[12]	—[12]	—[12]	—[12]	—[12]	—[12]
Dominican Republic	—[20]	—[20]	—[20]	—[20]	—[20]	—[20]	—[20]	—[20]
Haiti	—[20]	—[20]	—[20]	—[20]	—[20]	—[20]	—[20]	—[20]
Jamaica	—[21]	—[21]	—[21]	—[21]	—[21]	—[21]	—[21]	—[21]
Other Caribbean	164	3,834	12,301	13,528	10,660	9,046	13,957	29,042
Central America	2	105	44	368	449	95	157	404
El Salvador	—[20]	—[20]	—[20]	—[20]	—[20]	—[20]	—[20]	—[20]
Other Central America	2	105	44	368	449	95	157	404
South America	11	531	856	3,579	1,224	1,397	1,128	2,304
Argentina	—[20]	—[20]	—[20]	—[20]	—[20]	—[20]	—[20]	—[20]
Colombia	—[20]	—[20]	—[20]	—[20]	—[20]	—[20]	—[20]	—[20]
Ecuador	—[20]	—[20]	—[20]	—[20]	—[20]	—[20]	—[20]	—[20]
Other South America	11	531	856	3,579	1,224	1,397	1,128	2,304
Other America	—[22]	—[22]	—[22]	—[22]	—[22]	—[22]	—[22]	—[22]
Africa	1	16	54	55	210	312	358	857
Oceania	1	2	9	29	158	214	10,914	12,574
Not specified[22]	300	33,030	69,902	53,115	29,011	17,791	790	789

See footnotes at end of table.
— represents zero.

Region and Country of Last Residence[1]	1891–1900	1901–10	1911–20	1921–30	1931–40	1941–50	1951–60	1961–70
All countries	3,687,564	8,795,386	5,735,811	4,107,209	528,431	1,035,039	2,515,479	3,321,677
Europe	3,555,352	8,056,040	4,321,887	2,463,194	347,566	621,147	1,325,727	1,123,492
Austria-Hungary	592,707[23]	2,145,266[23]	896,342[23]	63,548	11,424	28,329	103,743	26,022
Austria	234,081[3]	668,209[3]	453,649	32,868	3,563[24]	24,860[24]	67,106	20,621
Hungary	181,288[3]	808,511[3]	442,693	30,680	7,861	3,469	36,637	5,401
Belgium	18,167	41,635	33,746	15,846	4,817	12,189	18,575	9,192
Czechoslovakia	—[4]	—[4]	3,426[4]	102,194	14,393	8,347	918	3,273
Denmark	50,231	65,285	41,983	32,430	2,559	5,393	10,984	9,201
France	30,770	73,379	61,897	49,610	12,623	38,809	51,121	45,237
Germany	505,152[23]	341,498[23]	143,945[23]	412,202	114,058[24]	226,578[24]	477,765	190,796
Greece	15,979	167,519	184,201	51,084	9,119	8,973	47,608	85,969
Ireland[5]	388,416	339,065	146,181	211,234	10,973	19,789	48,362	32,966
Italy	651,893	2,045,877	1,109,524	455,315	68,028	57,661	185,491	214,111
Netherlands	26,758	48,262	43,718	26,948	7,150	14,860	52,277	30,606
Norway-Sweden	321,281	440,039	161,469	165,780	8,700	20,765	44,632	32,600
Norway	95,015	190,505	66,395	68,531	4,740	10,100	22,935	15,484
Sweden	226,266	249,534	95,074	97,249	3,960	10,665	21,697	17,116
Poland	96,720[23]	—[23]	4,813[23]	227,734	17,026	7,571	9,985	53,539
Portugal	27,508	69,149	89,732	29,994	3,329	7,423	19,588	76,065
Romania	12,750	53,008	13,311	67,646	3,871	1,076	1,039	2,531
Soviet Union	505,290[23]	1,597,306[23]	921,201[23]	61,742	1,370	571	671	2,465
Spain	8,731	27,935	68,611	28,958	3,258	2,898	7,894	44,659
Switzerland	31,179	34,922	23,091	29,676	5,512	10,547	17,675	18,453
United Kingdom[5,8]	271,538	525,950	341,408	339,570	31,572	139,306	202,824	213,822
Yugoslavia	—[9]	—[9]	1,888[9]	49,064	5,835	1,576	8,225	20,381
Other Europe	282	39,945	31,400	42,619	11,949	8,486	16,350	11,604
Asia	74,862	323,543	247,236	112,059	16,595	37,028	153,249	427,642
China[10]	14,799	20,605	21,278	29,907	4,928	16,709	9,657	34,764
Hong Kong	—[11]	—[11]	—[11]	—[11]	—[11]	—[11]	15,541[11]	75,007
India	68	4,713	2,082	1,886	496	1,761	1,973	27,189
Iran	—[12]	—[12]	—[12]	241[12]	195	1,380	3,388	10,339
Israel	—[13]	—[13]	—[13]	—[13]	—[13]	476[13]	25,476	29,602
Japan	25,942	129,797	83,837	33,462	1,948	1,555	46,250	39,988
Korea	—[15]	—[15]	—[15]	—[15]	—[15]	107[15]	6,231	34,526
Philippines	—[16]	—[16]	—[16]	—[16]	528[16]	4,691	19,307	98,376
Turkey	30,425	157,369	134,066	33,824	1,065	798	3,519	10,142
Vietnam	—[11]	—[11]	—[11]	—[11]	—[11]	—[11]	335[11]	4,340
Other Asia	3,628	11,059	5,973	12,739	7,435	9,551	21,572	63,369
America	38,972	361,888	1,143,671	1,516,716	160,037	354,804	996,944	1,716,374
Canada & Newfoundland[17,18]	3,311	179,226	742,185	924,515	108,527	171,718	377,952	413,310
Mexico[18]	971[19]	49,642	219,004	459,287	22,319	60,589	299,811	453,937
Caribbean	33,066	107,548	123,424	74,899	15,502	49,725	123,091	470,213
Cuba	—[12]	—[12]	—[12]	15,901[12]	9,571	26,313	78,948	208,536
Dominican Republic	—[20]	—[20]	—[20]	—[20]	1,150[20]	5,627	9,897	93,292
Haiti	—[20]	—[20]	—[20]	—[20]	191[20]	911	4,442	34,499
Jamaica	—[21]	—[21]	—[21]	—[21]	—[21]	—[21]	8,869[21]	74,906
Other Caribbean	33,066	107,548	123,424	58,998	4,590	16,874	20,935[21]	58,980
Central America	549	8,192	17,159	15,769	5,861	21,665	44,751	101,330
El Salvador	—[20]	—[20]	—[20]	—[20]	673[20]	5,132	5,895	14,992
Other Central America	549	8,192	17,159	15,769	5,188	16,533	38,856	86,338
South America	1,075	17,280	41,899	42,215	7,803	21,831	91,628	257,954
Argentina	—[20]	—[20]	—[20]	—[20]	1,349[20]	3,338	19,486	49,721
Colombia	—[20]	—[20]	—[20]	—[20]	1,223[20]	3,858	18,048	72,028
Ecuador	—[20]	—[20]	—[20]	—[20]	337[20]	2,417	9,841	36,780
Other South America	1,075	17,280	41,899	42,215	4,894	12,218	44,253	99,425
Other America	—[22]	—[22]	—[22]	31[22]	25	29,276	59,711	19,630
Africa	350	7,368	8,443	6,286	1,750	7,367	14,092	28,954
Oceania	3,965	13,024	13,427	8,726	2,483	14,551	12,976	25,122
Not specified[22]	14,063	33,523[25]	1,147	228	—	142	12,491	93

See footnotes at end of table.

— represents zero.

A54 Immigration by Region and Country

Region and Country of Last Residence[1]	1971–80	1981–90	1991-94	1995	1996	1997	1998	Total 179 Years 1820–1998
All countries	4,493,314	7,338,062	4,509,852	720,461	915,900	798,378	660,477	64,599,082
Europe	800,368	761,550	631,921	132,914	151,898	122,358	92,911	38,233,062
Austria-Hungary	16,028	24,885	13,426	2,190	2,325	1,964	1,435	4,364,122
Austria	9,478	18,340	9,600	1,340	1,182	1,044	610	1,842,722[3]
Hungary	6,550	6,545	3,826	850	1,143	920	825	1,675,324[3]
Belgium	5,329	7,066	3,055	694	802	633	557	216,297
Czechoslovakia	6,023	7,227	3,050	1,057	1,299	1,169	931	153,307
Denmark	4,439	5,370	2,799	588	795	507	447	375,548
France	25,069	32,353	16,021	3,178	3,896	3,007	2,961	816,650
Germany	74,414	91,961	42,667	7,896	8,365	6,941	6,923	7,156,257
Greece	92,369	38,377	10,096	2,404	2,394	1,483	1,183	721,464
Ireland[5]	11,490	31,969	46,564	4,851	1,611	932	907	4,779,998
Italy	129,368	67,254	48,841	2,594	2,755	2,190	1,966	5,431,454
Netherlands	10,492	12,238	5,891	1,284	1,553	1,197	1,036	385,193
Norway-Sweden	10,472	15,182	8,149	1,607	2,015	1,517	1,344	2,160,586
Norway	3,941	4,164	2,572	465	552	391	327	758,026[6]
Sweden	6,531	11,018	5,577	1,142	1,463	1,126	1,017	1,257,133[6]
Poland	37,234	83,252	96,482	13,570	15,504	11,729	8,202	751,823
Portugal	101,710	40,431	11,588	2,611	3,024	1,690	1,523	521,697
Romania	12,393	30,857	19,142	4,565	5,449	5,276	4,833	244,106
Soviet Union	38,961	57,677	193,077	54,133	61,895	48,238	28,984	3,830,033
Spain	39,141	20,433	8,251	1,664	1,970	1,607	1,185	299,825
Switzerland	8,235	8,849	4,752	1,119	1,344	1,302	1,090	369,046
United Kingdom[5,8]	137,374	159,173	76,780	14,207	15,564	11,950	10,170	5,247,821
Yugoslavia	30,540	18,762	11,507	7,828	10,755	9,913	7,264	183,538
Other Europe	9,287	8,234	9,783	4,874	8,583	9,113	9,970	224,297
Asia	1,588,178	2,738,157	1,314,833	259,984	300,574	258,561	212,799	8,365,931
China[10]	124,326	346,747	170,191	41,112	50,981	44,356	41,034	1,262,050
Hong Kong	113,467	98,215	58,676	10,699	11,319	7,974	7,379	398,277[11]
India	164,134	250,786	149,374	33,060	42,819	36,092	34,288	751,349
Iran	45,136	116,172	32,828	5,646	7,299	6,291	4,945	233,860[12]
Israel	37,713	44,273	20,252	3,188	4,029	2,951	2,546	170,506[13]
Japan	49,775	47,085	31,982	5,556	6,617	5,640	5,647	517,686[14]
Korea	267,638	333,746	76,901	15,053	17,380	13,626	13,691	778,899[15]
Philippines	354,987	548,764	248,466	49,696	54,588	47,842	33,176	1,460,421[16]
Turkey	13,399	23,233	14,036	4,806	5,573	4,596	4,016	445,354
Vietnam	172,820	280,782	110,300	37,764	39,922	37,121	16,534	699,918[11]
Other Asia	244,783	648,354	401,827	53,404	60,047	52,072	49,543	1,647,611
America	1,982,735	3,615,225	2,429,423	282,270	407,813	359,619	298,156	16,844,829
Canada & Newfoundland[17,18]	169,939	156,938	87,613	18,117	21,751	15,788	14,295	4,453,149
Mexico[18]	640,294	1,655,843	1,400,108	90,045	163,743	146,680	130,661	5,819,966
Caribbean	741,126	872,051	436,471	96,021	115,991	101,095	72,948	3,525,703
Cuba	264,863	144,578	47,556	17,661	26,166	29,913	15,415	885,421[12]
Dominican Republic	148,135	252,035	180,055	38,493	36,284	24,966	20,267	810,201[20]
Haiti	56,335	138,379	80,867	13,872	18,185	14,941	13,316	375,938[20]
Jamaica	137,577	208,148	71,927	16,061	18,732	17,585	14,819	568,624[21]
Other Caribbean	134,216	128,911	56,066	9,934	16,624	13,690	9,131	885,519
Central America	134,640	468,088	267,591	32,020	44,336	43,451	35,368	1,242,394
El Salvador	34,436	213,539	117,463	11,670	17,847	17,741	14,329	453,717[20]
Other Central America	100,204	254,549	150,128	20,350	26,489	25,710	21,039	788,677
South America	295,741	461,847	237,615	46,063	61,990	52,600	44,884	1,693,441
Argentina	29,897	27,327	13,760	2,239	2,878	2,055	1,649	153,699[20]
Colombia	77,347	122,849	55,407	10,641	14,078	12,795	11,618	399,892[20]
Ecuador	50,077	56,315	30,627	6,453	8,348	7,763	6,840	215,798[20]
Other South America	138,420	255,356	137,821	26,730	36,686	29,987	24,777	924,052
Other America	995	458	25	4	2	5	–	110,176
Africa	80,779	176,893	108,645	39,818	49,605	44,668	37,494	614,375
Oceania	41,242	45,205	24,846	5,472	6,008	4,855	4,403	250,206
Not specified[22]	12	1,032	184	3	2	8,317	14,714	290,679

Source: U.S. Immigration and Naturalization Service, 1999.
See footnotes next page.

[1] Data for years prior to 1906 relate to country whence alien came; data from 1906–79 and 1984–1998 are for country of last permanent residence; and data for 1980–83 refer to country of birth. Because of changes in boundaries, changes in lists of countries, and lack of data for specified countries for various periods, data for certain countries, especially for the total period 1820–1998, are not comparable throughout. Data for specified countries are included with countries to which they belonged prior to World War I.
[2] Data for Austria and Hungary not reported until 1861.
[3] Data for Austria and Hungary not reported separately for all years during the period.
[4] No data available for Czechoslovakia until 1920.
[5] Prior to 1926, data for Northern Ireland included in Ireland.
[6] Data for Norway and Sweden not reported separately until 1871.
[7] No data available for Romania until 1880.
[8] Since 1925, data for United Kingdom refer to England, Scotland, Wales, and Northern Ireland.
[9] In 1920, a separate enumeration was made for the Kingdom of Serbs, Croats, and Slovenes. Since 1922, the Serb, Croat, and Slovene Kingdom recorded as Yugoslavia.
[10] Beginning in 1957, China includes Taiwan.
[11] Data not reported separately until 1952.
[12] Data not reported separately until 1925.
[13] Data not reported separately until 1949.
[14] No data available for Japan until 1861.
[15] Data not reported separately until 1948.
[16] Prior to 1934, Philippines recorded as insular travel.
[17] Prior to 1920, Canada and Newfoundland recorded as British North America. From 1820 to 1898, figures include all British North America possessions.
[18] Land arrivals not completely enumerated until 1908.
[19] No data available for Mexico from 1886 to 1893.
[20] Data not reported separately until 1932.
[21] Data for Jamaica not collected until 1953. In prior years, consolidated under British West Indies, which is included in "Other Caribbean."
[22] Included in countries "Not specified" until 1925.
[23] From 1899 to 1919, data for Poland included in Austria-Hungary, Germany, and the Soviet Union.
[24] From 1938 to 1945, data for Austria included in Germany.
[25] Includes 32,897 persons returning in 1906 to their homes in the United States.
—represents zero.

NOTE: From 1820 to 1867, figures represent alien passengers arrived at seaports; from 1868 to 1891 and 1895 to 1897, immigrant aliens arrived; from 1892 to 1894 and 1898 to 1998, immigrant aliens admitted for permanent residence. From 1892 to 1903, aliens entering by cabin class were not counted as immigrants. Land arrivals were not completely enumerated until 1908. For this table, fiscal year 1843 covers 9 months ending September 1843; fiscal years 1832 and 1850 cover 15 months ending December 31 of the respective years; and fiscal year 1868 covers 6 months ending June 30, 1868.

Presidents, Vice-Presidents, and Secretaries of State

	President	Vice-President	Secretary of State
1.	George Washington, Federalist 1789	John Adams, Federalist 1789	Thomas Jefferson 1789 Edmund Randolph 1794 Timothy Pickering 1795
2.	John Adams, Federalist 1797	Thomas Jefferson, Dem.-Rep. 1797	Timothy Pickering 1797 John Marshall 1800
3.	Thomas Jefferson, Dem.-Rep. 1801	Aaron Burr, Dem.-Rep. 1801 George Clinton, Dem.-Rep. 1805	James Madison 1801
4.	James Madison, Dem.-Rep. 1809	George Clinton, Dem.-Rep. 1809 Elbridge Gerry, Dem.-Rep. 1813	Robert Smith 1809 James Monroe 1811
5.	James Monroe, Dem.-Rep. 1817	Daniel D. Tompkins, Dem.-Rep. 1817	John Q. Adams 1817
6.	John Quincy Adams, Dem.-Rep. 1825	John C. Calhoun, Dem.-Rep. 1825	Henry Clay 1825
7.	Andrew Jackson, Democratic 1829	John C. Calhoun, Democratic 1829 Martin Van Buren, Democratic 1833	Martin Van Buren 1829 Edward Livingston 1831 Louis McLane 1833 John Forsyth 1834
8.	Martin Van Buren, Democratic 1837	Richard M. Johnson, Democratic 1837	John Forsyth 1837
9.	William H. Harrison, Whig 1841	John Tyler, Whig 1841	Daniel Webster 1841

	President	Vice-President	Secretary of State
10.	John Tyler, Whig and Democratic 1841	None	Daniel Webster 1841 Hugh S. Legaré 1843 Abel P. Upshur 1843 John C. Calhoun 1844
11.	James K. Polk, Democratic 1845	George M. Dallas, Democratic 1845	James Buchanan 1845
12.	Zachary Taylor, Whig 1849	Millard Fillmore, Whig 1849	John M. Clayton 1849
13.	Millard Fillmore, Whig 1850	None	Daniel Webster 1850 Edward Everett 1852
14.	Franklin Pierce, Democratic 1853	William R. King, Democratic 1853	William L. Marcy 1853
15.	James Buchanan, Democratic 1857	John C. Breckinridge, Democratic 1857	Lewis Cass 1857 Jeremiah S. Black 1860
16.	Abraham Lincoln, Republican 1861	Hannibal Hamlin, Republican 1861 Andrew Johnson, Unionist 1865	William H. Seward 1861
17.	Andrew Johnson, Unionist 1865	None	William H. Seward 1865
18.	Ulysses S. Grant, Republican 1869	Schuyler Colfax, Republican 1869 Henry Wilson, Republican 1873	Elihu B. Washburne 1869 Hamilton Fish 1869
19.	Rutherford B. Hayes, Republican 1877	William A. Wheeler, Republican 1877	William M. Evarts 1877

	President	Vice-President	Secretary of State
20.	James A. Garfield, Republican 1881	Chester A. Arthur, Republican 1881	James G. Blaine 1881
21.	Chester A. Arthur, Republican 1881	None	Frederick T. Frelinghuysen 1881
22.	Grover Cleveland, Democratic 1885	Thomas A. Hendricks, Democratic 1885	Thomas F. Bayard 1885
23.	Benjamin Harrison, Republican 1889	Levi P. Morton, Republican 1889	James G. Blaine 1889 John W. Foster 1892
24.	Grover Cleveland, Democratic 1893	Adlai E. Stevenson, Democratic 1893	Walter Q. Gresham 1893 Richard Olney 1895
25.	William McKinley, Republican 1897	Garret A. Hobart, Republican 1897 Theodore Roosevelt, Republican 1901	John Sherman 1897 William R. Day 1898 John Hay 1898
26.	Theodore Roosevelt, Republican 1901	Charles Fairbanks, Republican 1905	John Hay 1901 Elihu Root 1905 Robert Bacon 1909
27.	William H. Taft, Republican 1909	James S. Sherman, Republican 1909	Philander C. Knox 1909
28.	Woodrow Wilson, Democratic 1913	Thomas R. Marshall, Democratic 1913	William J. Bryan 1913 Robert Lansing 1915 Bainbridge Colby 1920
29.	Warren G. Harding, Republican 1921	Calvin Coolidge, Republican 1921	Charles E. Hughes 1921
30.	Calvin Coolidge, Republican 1923	Charles G. Dawes, Republican 1925	Charles E. Hughes 1923 Frank B. Kellogg 1925

	President	Vice-President	Secretary of State
31.	Herbert Hoover, Republican 1929	Charles Curtis, Republican 1929	Henry L. Stimson 1929
32.	Franklin D. Roosevelt, Democratic 1933	John Nance Garner, Democratic 1933 Henry A. Wallace, Democratic 1941 Harry S. Truman, Democratic 1945	Cordell Hull 1933 Edward R. Stettinius, Jr. 1944
33.	Harry S. Truman, Democratic 1945	Alben W. Barkley, Democratic 1949	Edward R. Stettinius, Jr. 1945 James F. Byrnes 1945 George C. Marshall 1947 Dean G. Acheson 1949
34.	Dwight D. Eisenhower, Republican 1953	Richard M. Nixon, Republican 1953	John F. Dulles 1953 Christian A. Herter 1959
35.	John F. Kennedy, Democratic 1961	Lyndon B. Johnson, Democratic 1961	Dean Rusk 1961
36.	Lyndon B. Johnson, Democratic 1963	Hubert H. Humphrey, Democratic 1965	Dean Rusk 1963
37.	Richard M. Nixon, Republican 1969	Spiro T. Agnew, Republican 1969 Gerald R. Ford, Republican 1973	William P. Rogers 1969 Henry Kissinger 1973
38.	Gerald R. Ford, Republican 1974	Nelson Rockefeller, Republican 1974	Henry Kissinger 1974
39.	Jimmy Carter, Democratic 1977	Walter Mondale, Democratic 1977	Cyrus Vance 1977 Edmund Muskie 1980

	President	Vice-President	Secretary of State
40.	Ronald Reagan, Republican 1981	George Bush, Republican 1981	Alexander Haig 1981 George Schultz 1982
41.	George Bush, Republican 1989	J. Danforth Quayle, Republican 1989	James A. Baker 1989 Lawrence Eagleburger 1992
42.	William J. Clinton, Democratic 1993	Albert Gore, Jr., Democratic 1993	Warren Christopher 1993 Madeleine Albright 1997

Credits

Part 1-3: Courtesy, American Antiquarian Society; **Part 1-3:** Courtesy of the Massachusetts Historical Society: **Part 1-3:** *The Cheney Family,* Gift of Edgar William and Bernice Chrysler Garbisch. Photograph © 2000 Board of Trustees, National Gallery of Art, Washington; **Part 1-3:** *Quaker Meeting,* Unidentified Artist, British. Bequest of Maxim Karolik, 64.456. Courtesy, Museum of Fine Arts, Boston. Reproduced with permission. © 2000 Museum of Fine Arts, Boston. All rights reserved.; **Part 1-3:** Courtesy, Winterthur Museum; **p. 1:** © Copyright The British Museum; **p. 3:** © Bodleian Library, University of Oxford 2001 MS Arch. Selden. A. 1, fol. 67r; **p. 8:** Biblioteca Nacional, Madrid; **p. 17:** Courtesy, American Antiquarian Society.; **p. 22:** © Copyright The British Museum; **p. 22:** © Copyright The British Museum; **p. 24:** *Quaker Meeting,* Unidentified Artist, British. Bequest of Maxim Karolik, 64.456. Courtesy, Museum of Fine Arts, Boston. Reproduced with permission. © 2000 Museum of Fine Arts, Boston. All rights reserved.; **p. 28:** *The Cheney Family,* Gift of Edgar William and Bernice Chrysler Garbisch. Photograph © 2000 Board of Trustees, National Gallery of Art, Washington; **p. 31:** *The Cheney Family,* Gift of Edgar William and Bernice Chrysler Garbisch Photograph. © 2000 Board of Trustees, National Gallery of Art, Washington; **p. 33:** The Metropolitan Museum of Art, Gift of Edgar William and Bernice Chrysler Garbisch, 1963 (63.201.3). Photograph © 1984 The Metropolitan Museum of Art; **p. 35:** Abby Aldrich Rockefeller Folk Art Museum, Williamsburg, VA; **p. 44:** The Metropolitan Museum of Art, The Friedsam Collection, Bequest of Michael Friedsam, 1931. (32.100.132). Photograph © 1981 The Metropolitan Museum of Art; **p. 47:** Courtesy of the Massachusetts Historical Society.; **p. 50:** Courtesy, Winterthur Museum; **p. 55:** © Gianni Dagli Orti/CORBIS; **p. 56:** The Historical Society of Pennsylvania (HSP) "Join, or Die," Pennsylvania Gazette 1754; **p. 61:** Courtesy of the Library of Congress (LC-USZC4-538); **p. 65:** Courtesy, American Antiquarian Society; **p. 68:** © Burstein Collection/CORBIS; **p. 70:** Courtesy of the Library of Congress (LC-USZC4-538); **p. 71:** © The British Museum; **p. 72:** The John Carter Brown Library at Brown University; **p. 75:** Courtesy, American Antiquarian Society; **Part 2-3:** Independence National Historic Park; **Part 2-3:** The Beinecke Rare Book and Manuscript Library; **Part 2-3:** Print Collection, Miriam and Ira D. Wallach Division of Art, Prints and Photographs, The New York Public Library, Astor, Lenox and Tilden Foundations; **Part 2-3:** Tray, 39.002. Museum of Art, Rhode Island School of Design, gift of Miss Lucy T. Aldrich; **Part 2-3:** Collection of Davenport West, Jr.; **p. 77:** Anne S. K. Brown Military Collection, Brown University Library; **p. 79:** Courtesy of the Pennsylvania Academy of the Fine Arts, Philadelphia. Gift of Maria McKean Allen and Phebe Warren Downes through the bequest of their mother, Elizabeth Wharton McKean; **p. 81:** Anne S. K. Brown Military Collection, Brown University Library; **p. 88:** John Trumbull, *The Surrender of Lord Cornwallis at Yorktown, 19 October 1781,* Yale University Art Gallery, Trumbull Collection; **p. 94:** Tray, 39.002. Museum of Art, Rhode Island School of Design, gift of Miss Lucy T. Aldrich; **p. 96:** Independence National Historic Park; **p. 99:** Independence National Historic Park; **p. 102:** The Library Company of Philadelphia; **p. 106:** Courtesy of the Library of Congress (LC-USZC4-4097); **p. 108:** Independence National Historic Park; **p. 111:** George Caleb Bingham, *Daniel Boone Escorting Settlers Through the Cumberland Gap,* 1851–1852. Oil on canvas, 36 1/2 × 50 1/4″. Washington University Gallery of Art, St. Louis. Gift of Nathaniel Phillips, 1890.; **p. 115:** © Francis G. Mayer/CORBIS; **p. 118:** © Bettmann/CORBIS; **p. 122:** George Caleb Bingham, *Daniel Boone Escorting Settlers Through the Cumberland Gap,* 1851–1852. Oil on canvas, 36 1/2 × 50 1/4″. Washington University Gallery of Art, St. Louis. Gift of Nathaniel Phillips, 1890.; **p. 123:** Boston Athenaeum; **p. 124:** The Huntington Library, Art Collections, and Botanical Gardens, San Marino, California/SuperStock; **p. 126:** © Bettmann/CORBIS; **p. 127:** Joseph Bailey/NGS Image Collection.; **p. 130:** The Warder Collection, New York; **p. 133:** Lewis and Clark Codex J, 93: Eulachon (candlefish). American Philosophical Society.; **p. 136:** Print Collection, Miriam and Ira D. Wallach Division of Art, Prints and Photographs, The New York Public Library, Astor, Lenox and Tilden Foundations; **p. 138:** © Bettmann/CORBIS; **p. 142:** New Orleans Museum of Art: Gift of Edgar William and Bernice Chrysler Garbisch; **p. 143:** Collection of Davenport West, Jr.; **p. 145:** Maryland Historical Society, Baltimore, Maryland; **p. 149:** Maryland Historical Society, Baltimore, Maryland; **p. 153:** © Bettmann/CORBIS; **p. 155:** Collection of Ashland, The Henry Clay Estate, Lexington, Kentucky; **p. 156:** © The Corcoran Gallery of Art/CORBIS; **p. 157:** Collection of the New-York Historical Society, neg. 8838; **p. 159:** Courtesy of the Library of Congress (LC-USZC4-970); **Part 3-3:** © Bettmann/CORBIS; **Part 3-3:** Courtesy of the Library of Congress (LC-USZC4-970); **Part 3-3:** Courtesy of the Library of Congress (LC-USZ62-32284); **Part 3-3:** Hancock Shaker Village, Pittsfield, Massachusetts; **Part 3-3:** Courtesy of the Library of Congress (LC-USZ62-31580); **p. 162:** From the Art Collection of Bank of America; **p. 164:** National Portrait Gallery, Smithsonian Institution; **p. 168:** National Museum of American Art, Washington D.C./Art Resource, NY; **p. 170:** Collection of the New-York Historical Society, neg. 42459; **p. 173:** Courtesy of the Library of Congress (LC-USZ62-1562); **p. 173:** Courtesy of the Library of Congress (LC-D416-409); **p. 176:** American Textile History Museum, Lowell, Mass.; **p. 180:** © Bettmann/CORBIS; **p. 184:** The Granger Collection, New York; **p. 186:** George A. Hayes, *Bare Knuckles,* Gift of Edgar William and Bernice Chrysler Garbisch, Photograph © 2000 Board of Trustees, National Gallery of Art, Washington; **p. 188:** Courtesy of the Library of Congress (LC-USZ62-32284); **p. 194:** The Granger Collection, New York; **p. 197:** The Granger Collection, New York; **p. 200:** The Metropolitan Museum of Art, Bequest of Mrs. David Dows, 1909. (09.95) Photograph © 1979 The Metropolitan Museum of Art; **p. 201:** *New England* Magazine; **p. 201:** Concord Free Public Library; **p. 203:** Richard Caton Woodville, *War News from Mexico,* Private Collection on loan to the National Gallery of Art, Photograph © Board of Trustees, National Gallery of Art, Washington; **p. 204:** The Metropolitan Museum of Art, Gift of I. N. Phelps Stokes, Edward S. Hawes, Alice Mary Hawes, and Marion Augusta Hawes, 1937 (37.14.22); **p. 206:** Courtesy of the Library of Congress (LC-USZ61-791); **p. 207:** Hancock Shaker Village, Pittsfield, Massachusetts; **p. 209:** Courtesy, American Antiquarian Society; **p. 213:** George Catlin, *Buffalo Lancing in the Snow Drifts—Sioux,* Paul Mellon Collection, Photograph © 2000 Board of Trustees, National Gallery of Art, Washington; **p. 214:** Courtesy, American Antiquarian Society; **p. 217:** William Tylee Ranney, *Old Scout's Tale* (1853) 0126.2261, from the Collection of Gilcrease Museum, Tulsa; **p. 219:** National Archives (NWDNS-111-B-4614A); **p. 219:** Courtesy of the Library of Congress (LC-USZ62-31580); **p. 225:** 1972.186.3. Adolphe-Jean-Baptiste Bayot after Carl Nebel. *Battle of Buena Vista,* 1851. Toned lithograph. Amon Carter Museum, Fort Worth, Texas; **Part 4-3:** Courtesy of the Library of Congress (LC-USZ62-2069); **Part 4-3:** From the South Carolina Historical Society Collections.; **Part 4-3:** Courtesy of the Library of Congress; **Part 4-3:** Courtesy of the Library of Congress; **Part 4-3:** Abby Aldrich Rockefeller Folk Art Museum, Williamsburg, VA; **p. 227:** P&S-1957.0027 Chicago Historical Society; **p. 230:** Collection of the New-York Historical Society, neg. 37628; **p. 233:** Collection of the New-York Historical Society, neg. 47843; **p. 236:** Abby Aldrich Rockefeller Folk Art Museum, Williamsburg, VA; **p. 237:** From the South Carolina Historical Society Collections; **p. 238:** The Metropolitan Museum of Art, Gift of I. N. Phelps Stokes, Edward S. Hawes, Alice Mary Hawes, Marion Augusta Hawes, 1937 (37.14.37); **p. 239:** Collection of the New-York Historical Society, neg. 16989; **p. 239:** National Portrait Gallery, Smithsonian Institution; **p. 241:** P&S-1954.0015 Chicago Historical Society; **p. 245:** P1988.10. Gold Miners, ca. 1850, daguerreotype. Amon Carter Museum, Fort Worth, Texas; **p. 247:** Hood Museum of Art, Dartmouth College, Hanover, New Hampshire; Gift of Dr. George C. Shattuck, Class of 1803; **p. 249:** The Granger Collection, New York; **p. 251:** National Portrait Gallery, Smithsonian Institution; **p. 253:** Kansas State Historical Society; **p. 257:** Denver Public Library, Western History Collection; **p. 258:** Boston Athenaeum; **p. 263:** Courtesy of the Library of Congress; **p. 270:** Courtesy of the Library of Congress; **p. 275:** Courtesy of the Library of Congress (LC-USZ62-2069); **p. 275:** Courtesy of the Library of Congress; **p. 276:** Courtesy of the Library of Congress; **p. 277:** Courtesy of the Library of Congress; **p. 279:** National Archives; **p. 282:** Courtesy of the Library of Congress (Illus. in E468.7.G19 copy 2); **p. 283:** © CORBIS; **p. 283:** Massachusetts Commandery Military Order of the Loyal Legion and the U.S. Army Military History Institute; **p. 284:** Courtesy of the Library of Congress (LC-B811-3623); **p. 285:** © CORBIS; **p. 287:** The Granger Collection, New York; **p. 290:** Courtesy of the Library of Congress; **p. 291:** Courtesy of the Library of Congress; **p. 292:** National Portrait Gallery, Smithsonian Institution; **p. 297:** Library of Congress; **p. 299:** The Granger Collection, New York; **p. 300:** Courtesy of the Library of Congress; **p. 300:** Rutherford B. Hayes Presidential Center; **p. 303:** Courtesy of the Library of Congress. **Part 5-3:** National Archives (111-SC-82522); **Part 5-3:** Union Pacific Museum Collection; **Part 5-3:** Brown Brothers; **Part 5-3:** Brown Brothers; **Part 5-3:** Courtesy of the Library of Congress; **p. 307:** Courtesy University of Nebraska Press; **p. 313:** National Archives; **p. 314:** Courtesy of the Library of Congress; **p. 314:** The Warder Collection, New York; **p. 316:** The Denver Public Library, Western History Collection; **p. 317:** *California Crossing, South Platte River,* by William Henry Jackson, from the Collection of Gilcrease Museum, Tulsa; **p. 319:** Courtesy University of Nebraska Press; **p. 320:** National Archives (111-SC-82522);

p. 322: Nebraska State Historical Society, Solomon D. Butcher Collection; **p. 324:** Steel Industry Heritage Task Force; **p. 327:** Union Pacific Museum Collection; **p. 330:** © Bettmann/CORBIS; **p. 331:** © Hulton-Deutsch Collection/CORBIS; **p. 331:** Steel Industry Heritage Task Force; **p. 332:** Reprinted with permission of Joanna T. Steichen; **p. 332:** © Bettmann/CORBIS; **p. 337:** Photoworld; **p. 339:** Brown Brothers; **p. 340:** The Granger Collection, New York; **p. 343:** New York Transit Museum Archives, Brooklyn; **p. 346:** Courtesy of the Library of Congress; **p. 346:** Courtesy of the Library of Congress; **p. 348:** Courtesy of the Library of Congress LC-USZC6-57 or LC-USZC4-1479; **p. 349:** Andrew Ritchie, *Major Taylor, the Extraordinary Career of a Champion Bicycle Racer* (Johns Hopkins University Press, Baltimore, 1996); **p. 350:** Brown Brothers; **p. 352:** © Christie's Images/CORBIS; **p. 355:** © Bettmann/CORBIS; **p. 358:** Culver Pictures; **p. 361:** © Bettmann/CORBIS; **p. 366:** Courtesy of the Library of Congress; **p. 368:** The Granger Collection, New York; **p. 369:** © Bettmann/CORBIS; **p. 373:** © Bettmann/CORBIS; **p. 374:** Kansas State Historical Society; **p. 377:** The Granger Collection, New York; **p. 379:** The Granger Collection, New York; **Part 6-3:** National Archives (War and Conflict #750); **Part 6-3:** National Archives; **Part 6-3:** Courtesy of the Library of Congress; **Part 6-3:** © Bettmann/CORBIS; **Part 6-3:** The Warder Collection, New York; **p. 385:** Chicago Historical Society ICHi-08428, creator: Kurz & Allison; **p. 386:** National Archives (War and Conflict #299); **p. 388:** Courtesy of the Library of Congress; **p. 393:** The Granger Collection, New York; **p. 394:** The Granger Collection, New York; **p. 399:** Courtesy of the Library of Congress; **p. 400:** The Granger Collection, New York; **p. 401:** © CORBIS; **p. 403:** The Granger Collection, New York; **p. 405:** The Granger Collection, New York; **p. 410:** Slide US2886, Hoover Institution Archives, Stanford University; **p. 412:** The Granger Collection, New York; **p. 413:** Courtesy of the Library of Congress; **p. 416:** The Granger Collection, New York; **p. 418:** © CORBIS; **p. 419:** Slide US2886, Hoover Institution Archives, Stanford University; **p. 420:** National Archives; **p. 425:** The Granger Collection, New York; **p. 429:** Archibald J. Motley, Jr. "The Jazz Singers," c. 1937; WPA. Courtesy Western Illinois University Art Gallery, Macomb, Illinois; **p. 432:** © Bettmann/CORBIS; **p. 433:** The Granger Collection, New York; **p. 434:** Archibald J. Motley, Jr. "The Jazz Singers," c. 1937; WPA. Courtesy Western Illinois University Art Gallery, Macomb, Illinois; **p. 435:** The Granger Collection, New York; **p. 436:** Courtesy of the Library of Congress; **p. 437:** Moorland-Spingarn Research Center, Howard University; **p. 440:** The Granger Collection, New York; **p. 444:** Courtesy of the Library of Congress; **p. 445:** The Granger Collection, New York; **p. 446:** The Granger Collection, New York; **p. 447:** From the Collections of Henry Ford Museum & Greenfield Village; **p. 448:** © Bettmann/CORBIS; **p. 452:** MSCUA, University of Washington Libraries, Neg #LU20102; **p. 455:** © Robert Holmes/CORBIS; **p. 460:** © Robert Holmes/CORBIS; **p. 461:** Courtesy of the Library of Congress; **p. 462:** © Bettmann/CORBIS; **p. 463:** © The Dorothea Lange Collection, Oakland Museum of California, City of Oakland. Gift of Paul S. Taylor; **p. 466:** © Bettmann/CORBIS; **p. 467:** © Bettmann/CORBIS; **p. 474:** The Granger Collection, New York; **p. 478:** National Archives (War and Conflict #746); **p. 479:** The Warder Collection, New York; **p. 482:** Roger-Viollet; **p. 485:** National Archives (War and Conflict #1134); **p. 487:** National Archives; **p. 491:** National Archives; **p. 491:** National Archives; **p. 492:** AP/Wide World Photos; **p. 494:** © CORBIS; **p. 499:** AP/Wide World Photos; **p. 504:** National Archives (War and Conflict #750); **p. 505:** National Archives; **p. 507:** AP/Wide World Photos; **Part 7-3:** AP/Wide World Photos; **Part 7-3:** © Joseph Sohm; ChromoSohm Inc./CORBIS; **Part 7-3:** Standard Oil (New Jersey) Collection; Special Collections: Photographic Archives, University of Louisville; **Part 7-3:** © Cornell Capa/Magnum Photos; **Part 7-3:** AP/Wide World Photos; **p. 509:** © Bettmann/CORBIS; **p. 516:** © Bettmann/CORBIS; **p. 517:** U.S. Information Agency; **p. 518:** AP/Wide World Photos; **p. 519:** C. K. Berryman, *The Washington Star,* 1948; **p. 521:** © CORBIS; **p. 524:** AP/Wide World Photos; **p. 528:** The Granger Collection, New York; **p. 533:** © Cornell Capa/Magnum Photos; **p. 534:** Joe Steinmetz Studio; **p. 536:** © Bettmann/CORBIS; **p. 537:** © Bettmann/CORBIS; **p. 538:** © Archivo Iconografico, S.A./Corbis; **p. 540:** © David J. & Janice L. Frent Collection/CORBIS; **p. 544:** © Bettmann/CORBIS; **p. 547:** © Bettmann/CORBIS; **p. 551:** © Bettmann/CORBIS; **p. 552:** Standard Oil (New Jersey) Collection; Special Collections: Photographic Archives, University of Louisville; **p. 555:** © Wally McNamee/CORBIS; **p. 558:** John F. Kennedy Library, Boston, MA; **p. 560:** AP/Wide World Photos; **p. 563:** Yoichi R. Yokomoto, Lyndon B. Johnson Library, Austin, Texas; **p. 567:** Courtesy of the Library of Congress; **p. 570:** AP/Wide World Photos; **p. 571:** © Wally McNamee/CORBIS; **p. 573:** © Bettmann/CORBIS **p. 577:** John Dominis/LIFE Magazine © Time Inc.; **p. 578:** © Bettmann/CORBIS; **p. 580:** © Bettmann/ CORBIS; **p. 581:** *Valley News Dispatch,* John Filo; **p. 583:** © CORBIS; **p. 587:** AP/Wide World Photos; **p. 592:** © Alexandra Avakian/Woodfin Camp; **p. 600:** © CORBIS; **p. 601:** © Joseph Sohm; ChromoSohm Inc./CORBIS; **p. 602:** © Lee Snider/CORBIS; **p. 605:** AP/Wide World Photos; **p. 607:** AP/Wide World Photos; **p. 609:** © William James Warren/CORBIS; **p. 613:** Courtesy of the Library of Congress; **p. 617:** AP/Wide World Photos; **p. 623:** AP/Wide World Photos; **p. 624:** AP/Wide World Photos; **p. 626:** AP/Wide World Photos; **p. 626:** © Reuters NewMedia Inc./CORBIS

INDEX

2-d
3-b
4-c
5-d
6-d
7-c
8-a
9-d
10-d
11-d
12-c
13-a
14-a
15-a
16-a
17-b
18-a